COMMUNISM
IN KOREA

PART I: THE MOVEMENT

Published under the auspices of
The Center for Japanese and Korean Studies
University of California, Berkeley

COMMUNISM

ROBERT A. SCALAPINO &

PART I:

 University of California Press

IN KOREA

CHONG-SIK LEE

THE MOVEMENT

Berkeley, Los Angeles, and London

UNIVERSITY OF CALIFORNIA PRESS
BERKELEY AND LOS ANGELES, CALIFORNIA
UNIVERSITY OF CALIFORNIA PRESS, LTD.
LONDON, ENGLAND
COPYRIGHT © 1972, BY
THE REGENTS OF THE UNIVERSITY OF CALIFORNIA
ISBN: 0-520-02080-4
LIBRARY OF CONGRESS CATALOG CARD NUMBER: 79-165236
PRINTED IN THE UNITED STATES OF AMERICA
DESIGNED BY DAVE COMSTOCK

Chong-Sik Lee wishes to dedicate this work
to the memory of his father
and to his mother

Robert A. Scalapino to his daughters,
Diane, Leslie, and Lynne,
and to
John, Wesley, and Allen

PREFACE

The purpose of this study is to trace the development of Communism in Korea from its inception to the present, and to analyze the contemporary North Korean Communist system, using selected social science methods and various comparative data. Thus, this work is divided into two parts of approximately equal length. While each part has its own integrity, we regard it as important that both parts of the work be read, since one of our efforts is to wed history and the social sciences.

The source materials used in this study are diverse and complex. Therefore, a brief explanation concerning sources and research techniques is essential. This study has been under way for more than a decade. Initially, we made an effort to collect those materials that shed light upon the pre-1945 origins and subsequent evolution of the Korean Communist movement. Here, several types of sources proved extremely valuable. Most extensive—and in general, most reliable—were official Japanese documents, especially those from the *tokkō keisatsu* (secret police), Justice Ministry, Home Ministry, and Government-General of Korea files as well as the archives of the Foreign and the Army ministries. These contained daily intelligence reports; verbatim police and prosecutors' interrogations; court trial documents; large quantities of confiscated primary source materials produced by the Communists; police reports written on the basis of the above; and "confessions" or interpretive essays written by political prisoners at the command of the authorities. Most of these materials were marked "Top Secret" or "Secret" and became available only because of Japanese defeat in World War II.

In using such materials, one must be cognizant of distortion, exaggeration, and concealment. The tendency of Japanese officials was to inflate the charges and portray the movement in its worst light. The arrested, of course, often did everything possible to camouflage their role and that of others. On occasion, the Japanese actually manufactured incidents, such as the so-called attempt to assassinate Governor-General Terauchi in 1911. But this was rare; and in the case of the Communist trials, the testimony is buttressed by confiscated documents available to us.

When possible, of course, such materials were checked against other types of sources. Despite the massive destruction of Communist materials and the fugitive character of most, some journals, leaflets, and newspapers —even a few mimeographed items—survived, usually in private hands, and to the extent that these were available they provided valuable corroborative evidence. The North Koreans have made selective documents of the prewar era available since 1945, notably those that advance the prestige of Kim Il-sŏng. Some important materials are also to be found in Chinese and Soviet sources, as our footnotes and bibliography will indicate. From Japanese Communist records, additional items of considerable importance were discovered, especially materials pertaining to Korean Communist activities in Japan.

A few memoirs or biographies of key participants have been written, several of them exceedingly valuable. These have been supplemented when possible by in-depth interviews with veterans of that era. We were especially fortunate to have had the opportunity to interview Chang Kŏn-sang, Chŏng Hwa-am, Ra Yong-gyun, Yi Hong-gŭn, Yi Tong-hwa, and Yu Sŏk-hyŏn, as well as the late Cho Pong-am, Kim Chun-yŏn, and Kim Sŏng-suk. Each of these individuals had either had personal experience with the prewar Korean Communist movement or intimate knowledge concerning some aspect of it.

Finally, we should not omit the importance of Comintern documents pertaining to Korean Communism. Naturally, such materials must be used with care, but they are invaluable in presenting the prevailing Kremlin/ ECCI position on major issues and current trends.

With the advent of the Communists to power, the character of the materials available changes dramatically. Of crucial importance, of course, are those materials put out by the Communists themselves. We have made extensive use of *Nodong Sinmun, Kŭlloja,* and a wide range of other Party organs or official publications. Many hard-to-get or unavailable Korean language materials of an official nature have been translated by the Joint Publications Research Service, either in their earlier series, *Political Translations on North Korea* (later, *Translations of Political and Sociological Information on North Korea*) and *Economic Report on North Korea,* or in the later, composite *Translations on North Korea,* currently being published. Naturally, if the original Korean source is available, and one can read Korean, it is better to use it, since errors not infrequently creep into JPRS translations. The JPRS service, nevertheless, is extremely valuable to every scholar concerned with North Korea.

The Foreign Languages Press in P'yŏngyang has published a fair number of pamphlets, journals, and monographic materials in English and other foreign languages. In the main, these are reproductions of official speeches and reports. A similar function is played by the official organ of the General Federation of Koreans Resident in Japan, *The People's Korea,* and by the *P'yŏngyang Times* and *Korea Today,* both published in North Korea. Needless to say, the English language materials are dwarfed by the Korean language sources.

Obviously, official Communist materials must be used with a full realization of the ideological perspectives, the political biases, and the various taboos that accompany them. None of these elements, however, make them unimportant. On the contrary, the discerning user can often read between the lines, especially when aided by other sources, and construct a close approximation of certain internal trends and immediate issues. From radio broadcasts also, a wealth of data is available.

This study, representing a private research project, is based upon open, nonclassified sources, except for the permission granted us to use archival materials of the American Occupation Forces in Korea (1945–1948). Our notes from those materials were declassified and permission to make use of them in this publication was granted. When used, they are cited in the footnotes. These materials proved to be very useful, especially with respect to Communist activities in South Korea before 1948, and in providing early data on North Korea, generally in the 1945–1946 period.

We are also grateful to those South Korean and American pioneers who have ventured into the field of North Korean studies. Benefiting from their work, we have sought to acknowledge their contributions to this study at the appropriate places.

The above sources constitute the central body of materials upon which this work is based. However, we are also deeply indebted to thirty-four ex-North Koreans with whom we conducted in-depth interviews in the 1967–1970 period, and whose information in many cases was unique. As the reader will note, we have made substantial use of the materials given us by these informants, particularly in the later chapters of the work. Their names deserve mention: Chang Tae-hyŏng, Cho Sŏng-jik, Ch'oe Kwang-sŏk, Ch'oe Sŏng-sik, Mrs. Ch'oe Sŏng-sik, Chŏn Chun, Chŏng Tong-jun, Han Chae-dŏk, Han Hong-sik, Hong Chŏn-jong, Kang Ko-muk, Kim Chŏng-gi, Kim Hyŏk, Kim Nam-sik, Kim Sŏk-yong, Kim Sŏng-ch'il, Kim Yŏn-gil, Kim Yong-jun, Ko Tŏng-un, O Ki-wan, O Yŏng-jin, Pak Am, Pak Wan-ho, U Kil-myŏng, Yang Ho-min, Yi Hang-gu, Yi Ki-gŏn, Yi Kwan-un, Yi Pil-ŭn, Yi Pyŏng-ch'ŏl, Yi Tae-won, Yi Tong-hwa, Yi Yŏng-myŏng, and Yu Wan-sik. (In a number of cases, these individuals are using names different from their original names, to protect various persons in the north, and themselves.)

The importance—and the validity—of such data has rightfully been debated by scholars involved in research on Communism. Let us state our opinion at the outset: when interviews are carefully integrated with other types of data; when they are properly timed, coming after the bulk of the research on primary and secondary written materials has been concluded; and when the information given is thoroughly checked against other sources, interviews can be of major significance. Certain additional caveats are clearly in order. With a few exceptions, these respondents were either defectors or captured enemy agents who had decided to abandon the Communist cause. We interviewed most of them in South Korea—and it is probable that in a number of cases they were not prepared to tell "all," particularly concerning their own lives and some of their more complicated emotional-political reactions. Moreover, some of the interviews conducted by the senior author were conducted with a government-connected interpreter present (in other cases, former students were used as interpreters). The junior author did not require interpreter services.

It should be noted, however, that these interviews came toward the conclusion of our research, when a huge mass of written materials had already been canvassed. We knew—or thought we knew—the basic facts, and we had various hypotheses to test. Each interview was conducted in private and, with only a few exceptions, with a single respondent present. The interviews were lengthy and frequently stretched into several sessions or more. We were able to cross-check most critical information, asking a large number of people identical or similar questions. All interviews either were tape-recorded, or extensive notes were taken during the interview itself.

We are convinced that, for the most part, the information given us was genuine (although not necessarily complete), and in general it matched the written materials available to us, as well as being consistent within our total interview schedule. The exceptions—where differences were sharp or the information given seemed dubious—are noted in the text or footnotes if it seems important.

Perhaps our confidence is enhanced by a particular episode which occurred toward the end of 1968. One of those interviewed by the senior author was Yi Su-gun, the highest ranking defector in recent years, formerly vice director of the North Korean News Agency. Yi had made his escape from the north in dramatic fashion. At Panmunjŏm, he had signaled to American officials present that he wished to defect; at the appropriate moment, he dived into the back seat of a waiting car, which then sped off amid a hail of North Korean bullets. Yi had been treated royally in the south, given a substantial sum of money and a house. He had also remarried. He was used throughout the country as an anti-Communist lecturer.

The first interview with Yi, conducted on November 29, 1968, was highly unsatisfactory. His answers were either simplistic or totally lacking in substance. Against the background of earlier interviews, Yi appeared to be singularly different. A second interview was requested, and it was conducted on December 2, 1968. It was equally disappointing. At that point, we decided that, for whatever reasons, Yi either did not wish to cooperate or was far less well informed than his former position might indicate. We did not then know the facts, namely, that he was a North Korean agent sent to the south personally by Kim Il-sŏng. This he confessed some eight weeks later, after being seized in Saigon while engaged in an effort to reach Cambodia and the North Korean Embassy there. However, the fact that we were able to detect quickly the dubious quality of this informant's information in contrast to that of all others served to strengthen our confidence in the interview method, properly utilized.

It should also be noted that we conducted a number of interviews with specialists on North Korean affairs within the governments of the United States, the Republic of Korea, and Japan. In addition, discussions were held with various other people who had had experiences in North Korea, including certain Japanese journalists. These sessions were also very useful.

No project as extended as this and as complex could possibly have been conducted without substantial financial support. First, Robert A. Scalapino would like to acknowledge the major financial and intellectual support that he has received from the Institute of International Studies of the University of California, Berkeley, and to express his deep appreciation to its director, Professor Ernst Haas. Without financial aid extending over three years, the fulfillment of this work would not have been possible, and he is extremely grateful. He is also indebted to the Center of Japanese and Korean Studies, University of California, for sustained research support. Chong-Sik Lee would like to acknowledge the support of the Social Science Research Council and the Ford Foundation, both generous in their financial assistance, and the University of Pennsylvania, which was willing to grant him three leaves of absence so that the work could be vigorously pursued. Both authors wish to thank the Rockefeller Foundation for financial aid in 1965–66.

We are also deeply indebted to various research institutes and libraries whose personnel were extraordinarily generous in their expenditure of time and in their painstaking efforts on our behalf. We would like to salute in particular the Asiatic Research Center, Korea University, and its directors, Professors Sang Eun Lee and Kim Jun-yop (this Center was truly our headquarters when we were in Korea); the Library of Congress, and particularly Mr. Key P. Yang, who provided invaluable assistance in our quest for materials; the National Assembly Library, Seoul, and its director, Kang Choo-jin, who opened up his facilities for us and provided us with introductions to other sources. The staff of the East Asiatic Library of the University of California, Berkeley, and especially Mr. Eiji Yutani and Mr. Yong Kyu Choo, aided us on numerous occasions, and long hours were spent in the Newspaper Room of the UC library, and with the staff of the interlibrary loan service—the personnel of which were invariably cooperative; the Hoover Institution and Harvard-Yenching facilities were also of major significance for us, and we are indebted to their staffs for their aid. The Institute of Asiatic Peoples in Moscow, and its library director, kindly enabled us to obtain microfilmed issues of *Nodong Sinmun* for the early 1950s, available nowhere else; the Diet Library in Tokyo and several Japanese university libraries provided other materials; the Center for International Studies in Seoul, and particularly Kang In-dok, were most cooperative, as was the Korean Research Center, Seoul, and its directors, Dong Chon and Ch'on Mun-am, who were generous in sharing their collections and providing leads for us.

We also benefited greatly from the private collections of numerous individuals, or their willingness to give us access to such collections. Professors Sun Kun Lee, Yong Hee Lee, and I-sup Hong all aided us in finding and microfilming rare documents, and Seoul National University extended its facilities in this respect to us. Messrs. Paek Sun-jae and O Han-gŭn opened their private collection for our use, and Professor Sohn Paw-key provided us with the invaluable *Shisō ihō* collection.

We are equally indebted to those who helped us arrange interviews. In this connection, we should like to pay special tribute to two men whose aid was indispensable: Kim Nam-sik and the late Han Chae-dŏk. Both of these men were extraordinarily generous, giving us countless hours of their time, and without them the project would not have been possible in its present form. Kim Nam-sik arranged many of the interviews personally and commented upon much of the final draft of the manuscript. We are also indebted to O Ki-wan and Yang Ho-min for similar services. And we repeat our thanks to all of the other respondents whose names were mentioned above. With the exception of Yi Su-gun, all were cooperative, valuable informants.

Our debt is also extensive to our colleagues, students, and friends in the United States, Korea, and Japan. In the course of this lengthy project, Ki-shik Han, Pyoung Hoon (Michael) Kim, Sung Joo Han, and Dae-kwon Choi served as research assistants to Scalapino, with Monica Brown and Masaaki Takane also providing special services. Myong Soo Ha, Hyong Soo Lee, Won Bo Lee and Chong Bum Lee aided Lee.

We are indebted to Professor Glenn D. Paige for his translation from the Russian of the important Kuusinen essay. To several Soviet specialists we also owe a special debt of gratitude. Professor George Ginsburgs not only read and commented upon several draft chapters, but also went through a number of Russian materials for us, and provided the Russian section of the bibliography. Professor Gregory Grossman read and commented upon the economic sections of this work, saving us from various errors; and Mr. Andris Trapans spent time surveying Russian sources for additional statistical data on North Korean economic production. Bernard Krisher of *Newsweek* shared with us his interviews with several North Korean defectors, thereby augmenting our own materials.

It should be noted that the first chapter is a revision of a two-part article by the authors which appeared under the title "Origins of the Korean

Communist Movement," in *Journal of Asian Studies,* XX, No. 1 (November 1960), pp. 9–31, and XX, No. 2 (February 1961), pp. 149–167.

Ours is the sole responsibility for the contents of this study, but we owe all of the above individuals and a sizable number of others a very substantial debt—as well as those institutions rendering financial assistance.

At various stages, we have had to call upon secretaries for work both complex and voluminous. All have performed with skill and willingness, but we must single out Miss Louise Lindquist for a special word of thanks. And as every author knows, a project of this type requires the patience, endurance, and cooperation of wives. In this case, we had this in abundance, together with concrete assistance in the project itself, especially the interviews. Thus, our thanks to Dee and Myung Sook.

We would express our sincere appreciation to a number of colleagues and students who read portions of the manuscript in connection with symposia and colloquia, providing us with suggestions for revision. Many of their suggestions were accepted, and we believe that they resulted in improvements.

Finally, our editors, Mr. Michael Edwards and Mr. Jerome Fried, had a truly mammoth task. It was performed with extraordinary skill. And to old friends—known to us and to them—at the University of California Press—we offer a special thank-you.

Robert A. Scalapino
Chong-Sik Lee

January 1972
Berkeley, California
Havertown, Pennsylvania

CONTENTS OF PART I:
THE MOVEMENT

MAPS

CONTENTS OF PART II: THE SOCIETY

NUMBERED TABLES TO PART I

UNNUMBERED TABLES TO PART I

INTRODUCTION

In this work, we seek to combine two basic approaches. The first eight chapters represent a historical, developmental, analytical treatment. Drawing upon the widest range of sources available to us, we have sought to provide hypotheses and interpretations relating to the origins and evolution of the Korean Communist movement. In this manner, we hope to shed light upon such questions as the wellsprings of Korean Communism and its relation to other Asian Communist movements at various points in its development; the socioeconomic character of early Communist leadership, and the subsequent changes that took place; the capacities of a police-state, Japanese style, to handle extreme dissidence; the additional problems bequeathed to an underground movement, and one largely in exile; the role of Soviet leaders and the Comintern in the movement; and the basic causes for failure before 1945.

It is in this part also that we explore the manner in which factionalism was met after 1945; the rise of Kim Il-sŏng to a position of absolute power; the evolution of economic policies—both industrial and agricultural; the emergence of chuch'e as a dominant theme; and the extraordinarily important, complex, and changing relations with the Soviet Union and China.

In the second and final seven chapters, we turn to topical social science-oriented analysis, seeking to probe the key facets of the North Korean system and its basic style of operation. It is in this part that we attempt to deal with the evolving character of the political elite in its broadest dimensions; the special characteristics of Communist organization; the role of ideology at this point in time; the status and functions of special groups within the society, notably the Party cadres, the military, and the intellectuals; the essential nature of the economic structure and its performance to date; and the actual life-style of the worker and peasant in the Kim era.

This is not the place to prejudge the evidence or to produce our conclusions. It is appropriate here, however, to suggest the reasons for the particular treatment of the data outlined above. Some aspects of Korean

Communism can be understood only in historical perspective. Had we concentrated solely upon the Democratic People's Republic of Korea in its contemporary setting, it would have been impossible to have probed deeply into such questions as the reasons for monocracy, the sociopolitical character of the elite today, the pervasiveness of nationalism, and the intriguing relations between the DPRK and its two giant Communist neighbors.

At the same time, a historical, developmental treatment alone is not sufficient. It does not permit the isolation of certain elements of the political system and an intensive treatment of these via the use of selective methods from a modern social science perspective. It does not encourage the reexamination of certain widely used terms and concepts—ideology, organization, authority, and many others—so as to determine their operational as apart from their formal meanings. And it does not permit us to explore the actual life-style of both the system and the individual in a Communist setting.

It is also by way of the second approach that one can more easily undertake a comparative treatment. As will become clear, we are dealing throughout this work with three overarching variables; Communism, emergence, and tradition. North Korea, as we shall learn, is a Communist state, sharing the broad attributes of other contemporary Communist societies: a strong commitment to Marxist-Leninist ideology; an organizational system characterized by a unique form of political linkage and a combination-separation of mass and elite functions; a political environment that centers upon the nation-state; a changing but formidable coercion-persuasion structure; a command, planned economy; and the commitment to the creation of a New Socialist Man.

These are the qualities—with all of the unique Korean variations to be noted—that make the Democratic People's Republic of Korea a Communist state. We have sought in this study to explore rather intensively how that state in its essentials relates to other Communist systems, particularly to those of Russia and China with which it has been so closely associated. As we shall note, the study of comparative Communism, now in its pioneer days, offers great possibilities in helping us to establish a more accurate typology of Communist systems—including a delineation of their common and particular features.

As we shall emphasize, however, North Korea is also an "emerging" state, with its recent background that of a colony. It has therefore shared the twin objectives of nation-building and economic development with non-Communist emerging states, differing with them on means but not upon fundamental goals. It thus becomes imperative to keep this second comparison in mind. Korean "Communism" is molded by the stage of development of (North) Korean society. Much that has happened to make Communism anti-Marxist relates to the requirements of a late-developing society.

The third element—that of tradition—is perhaps more elusive, less easily isolated and defined. At first glance, the rolling revolution of the last twenty-five years appears to have swept all before it, obliterating the cultural and political landmarks of the past. Yet, upon closer examination, this clearly is not true. Suddenly one discovers that even in such a crucial element as leadership style, the past is present in considerable degree. It is not merely that "feudal remnants" remain rooted in Korean peasant psychology, but that they remain also attached to Kim Il-sŏng! Nor are Communist organizational techniques exempt. It will be one of the main themes of this study that the primordial group—sometimes altered in its precise form— has been of critical importance to the Communist organizational structure.

As we have said, we are dealing with three crucial elements in seeking to discern this system and compare it with others: Communism, emergence, and tradition. Our effort to wed the historical and the social-science approaches is in part an effort to encompass each of these variables as thoroughly as possible. This is not a rigorously quantitative study. Neither the available data nor the broader subject matter under discussion make that possible. We have sought to quantify what can be quantified—and to use in limited fashion such techniques as content analysis when these seemed appropriate and possible. Beyond that, it is difficult to go at present, and our approach has been more in the political-sociological vein.

To the larger issues raised in this study, there are no fixed and final answers. Our conceptual formulations and hypotheses will need to be reexamined in the light of additional data from this and other systems, this and other eras—just as we have reexamined conclusions and hypotheses put forward earlier by our colleagues. Fortunately, the future is promising in this respect, with many studies of Communist systems under way.

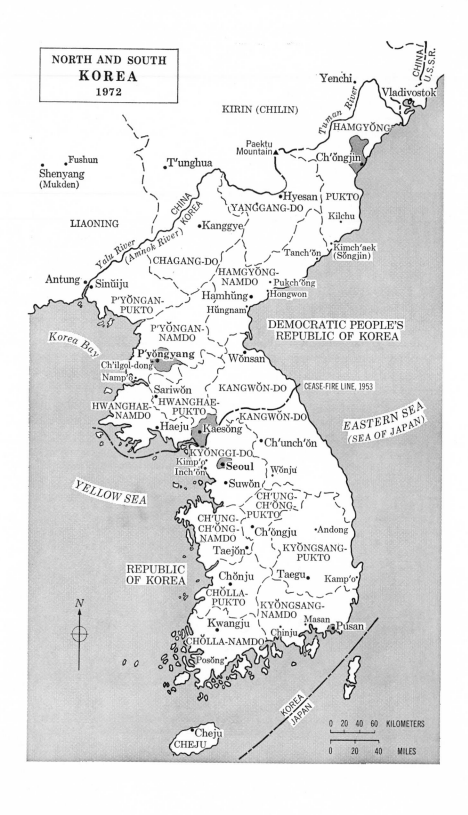

KIRIN (CHILIN)

Yenchi

Vladivostok

CHINA
U.S.S.R.

Tuman River

HAMGYŎNG-

Paektu
Mountain

Ch'ŏngjin

Fushun

Shenyang
(Mukden)

T'unghua

Hyesan PUKTO

YANGGANG-DO

Kilchu

LIAONING

Kanggye

CHINA

KOREA

Tanch'ŏn

Kimch'aek
(Sŏngjin)

Yalu River
(Amnok River)

CHAGANG-DO

HAMGYŎNG-
NAMDO

Pukch'ŏng

Antung

Sinŭiju

Hamhŭng

Hongwon

P'YŎNGAN-
PUKTO

Hŭngnam

P'YŎNGAN-
NAMDO

DEMOCRATIC PEOPLE'S
REPUBLIC OF KOREA

Korea Bay

P'yŏngyang

Wŏnsan

Ch'ilgol-dong

Namp'o

Sariwŏn

KANGWŎN-DO

CEASE-FIRE LINE, 1953

HWANGHAE-
PUKTO

HWANGHAE-
NAMDO

Haeju

Kaesŏng

KANGWŎN-DO

EASTERN SEA
(SEA OF JAPAN)

Ch'unch'ŏn

KYŎNGGI-DO

Kimp'o

Inch'ŏn

Seoul

Wŏnju

YELLOW SEA

Suwŏn

CH'UNG-
CH'ŎNG-
PUKTO

CH'UNG-
CH'ŎNG-
NAMDO

Ch'ŏngju

Andong

Taejŏn

KYŎNGSANG-
PUKTO

REPUBLIC
OF KOREA

N

Chŏnju

Taegu

Kamp'o

CHŎLLA-
PUKTO

KYŎNGSANG-
NAMDO

Kwangju

Chinju

Masan

Pusan

CHŎLLA-NAMDO

Posŏng

KOREA
JAPAN

0 20 40 60   KILOMETERS

0   20   40   MILES

Cheju
CHEJU

PART I

THE MOVEMENT

CHAPTER I

THE ORIGINS OF KOREAN COMMUNISM

When the Bolsheviks came to power in October 1917, Korea had been under complete Japanese rule for only seven years, but these had been years of momentous political change. After the annexation of 1910, the Japanese successfully eliminated the bands of patriots who resisted them. They then placed Korea under the strictest control: arms were confiscated, political assembly prohibited, and the press tightly regulated. Resentment against the new colonial rulers continued to run high, as did the desire to regain independence. But the Koreans had no public means of expressing these sentiments.

Under such conditions, the Bolshevik Revolution could have little impact upon Koreans at home. There were, however, a large number of Korean expatriates in eastern Siberia and Manchuria who were quickly engulfed in the turmoil created by the Revolution. Not all of them by any means were prepared to play the role of political activists, but the more ardent nationalists among them were eager to do so. And these Koreans had a clear utility to the new Soviet leaders, who desperately needed allies in their struggle for Siberia. Japan represented an immediate threat, and who could counter that threat at less cost to the Russians than mobilized Koreans, bitter at the recent seizure of their country? Soviet exploitation of Korean nationalism, together with Soviet mobilization of Siberia-based Koreans, thus produced the first Korean political movement to operate under Red banners.

These early Korean "Communists" had at best a precarious hold upon Marxist doctrine. Their primary interest, as would be expected, lay in the reestablishment of Korean independence. In most cases, their interest in ideology was minimal. One must never forget, moreover, that in this era the concept of communism was very obscure to most people. Imprecision and confusion dominated the ideological scene; to each recruit, the idea of communism held a different meaning and appeal. Hence, as we shall see, it was easy in a later period to denounce the first Korean Communists as "petty bourgeois" nationalists, hopelessly inadequate in their understanding of Marxism-Leninism.[1]

Korean Radicalism in Siberia

Our story thus begins in Siberia. Since the late nineteenth century Koreans had been moving there in substantial numbers. Approximately 200,000 lived there by 1919. Ample inducements were present. Siberia not only provided lebensraum; along with Manchuria, it served as a political sanctuary for Korean nationalists after Japanese pressure upon Korea became intense.

By the end of World War I, the political caldron was boiling furiously.[2] Cities like Vladivostok, Irkutsk, Chita, and Khabarovsk all had large Korean populations, and Korean farms dotted the Siberian hinterland.

1. For two examples of the brief, unfavorable attention given the early Korean Communist movement by Communist publications, see *Democratic People's Republic of Korea* (in English), P'yŏngyang, 1958, pp. 57 ff.; and Yi Na-yŏng, *Chosŏn minjok haebang t'ujaengsa* (*History of the Korean People's Struggle for Emancipation*), P'yŏngyang, 1958.

2. One prior event might be mentioned. According to an official Japanese source, Shin Kyu-sik, a Korean nationalist, organized the Chosŏn Sahoe-dang (Korean Socialist Party) in Shanghai as early as August 1917. We have doubts that this "party" was socialist or in any sense connected with subsequent radical movements. Its raison d'etre seems to have been to present a demand for Korean independence to the Stockholm International Socialist Conference. In any case, it soon disappeared. See *Shōwa jūshichinen chū ni okeru shakai undō no jōkyō* (*Conditions of Social Movements in 1942*), Tokyo, 1943, pp. 971–972.

Shin Kyu-sik himself, however, is of some interest because in many ways he was typical of the ardent Korean nationalists of his era, some of whom did get involved in the early Communist movement. Born in 1879, son of a yangban (gentry) family of North Ch'ungch'ŏng Province, he received a traditional education and then proceeded to the Military Academy in Seoul, graduating in 1900. In 1905, when the Protectorate Treaty was signed, he attempted to foment a military uprising which failed. Distraught by events, Shin then tried to commit suicide, taking poison. An early discovery of this effort by his family prevented death, but the poison permanently affected his right eye. After the Japanese annexation, Shin sought to keep the nationalist movement alive by engaging in educational work, but in 1911 he went into exile in China. There he joined Sun Yat-sen's T'ung Mêng Hui, and worked closely with such men as Hu Han-min, Sung Chiao-jen, and Ch'en Ch'i-mei. He put his available funds into a nationalist newspaper, *Min-ch'uan-pao* (*The People's Rights News*), and served in the Korean Shanghai Provisional Government as minister of Justice. For these and other details, see Min Sŏk-rin (ed.), *Hanguk ui ŏl* (*The Spirit of Korea*), Seoul, 1955.

Manchuria had an even larger Korean population: some 430,000 in 1919, most of whom lived in the southeast (Chientao). These included a number of militant activists who were anxious to challenge Japan. About 1912, when the Korean "Righteous Army" had finally been defeated in its last-ditch struggle against the Japanese, a number of these activists had re-treated to Manchuria, mingling with the thousands of Koreans already farming there. Military centers were established, and from them Korean guerrilla forces continued to conduct forays into Korea proper on a small scale. Chinese authorities were sympathetic enough to interpose few ob-stacles.

This was the general situation at the time of the Russian Revolution. With it, new opportunities were presented to Korean patriots. For several years, however, the situation was extremely confusing from both the politi-cal and the military standpoints. Czarist, Czech, and Allied forces peri-odically controlled various major centers in eastern Siberia. As is well known, Japanese troops formed an especially large contingent of the ex-peditionary armies, and Japanese motives were a matter of grave concern to friend and foe alike.

To some Korean nationalists the only correct policy at this point was full-scale war against Japan—a war they hoped and expected would be supported by the Lenin government. The chances of Western assistance were scant. Indeed, disillusionment with the West among Koreans became increasingly widespread, especially after Versailles. And the Washington Conference of 1921–22 certainly added nothing to Western prestige in the eyes of Korean nationalists generally. On the other hand, they were im-pressed by the Bolsheviks, especially when Bolshevik leaders spoke with fervor about liberating the oppressed peoples of the Far East. There was no doubt that the Bolsheviks were strongly anti-imperialist and, more im-portantly, strongly anti-Japanese, since Japanese armies were on Russian soil. The Bolsheviks needed allies; desperate and alone, they found it easy to turn to men who could mount a second front against the Japanese ex-pedition. It was thus natural that between 1918 and 1920 a Russian-Korean alliance should develop, the first Soviet alliance with an Asian people.

It is essential to distinguish between the two principal types of Koreans living in Russian territory, namely, those who were long-time residents and therefore Russianized to a considerable degree, and those who were bas-ically newcomers and refugees, thoroughly Korean in outlook and al-legiance. It was not easy for these two groups to work together, despite Soviet encouragement; differences, both of culture and commitment, could not be denied. Indeed, this fragmentation of the overseas Koreans, some of whom were acquiring new loyalties and modes of life, created a complex problem for modern Korea, especially when superimposed upon tra-ditional patterns of internal factionalism and provincialism. Even today, no aspect of Korean politics can be fully understood without giving this factor careful attention.[3]

Both the Russianized and the "pure" Koreans were solicited by Soviet representatives in the critical period after the Czarist overthrow. The first overtures came in mid-1917, in the opening stages of the struggle for Siberia. The Bolsheviks, of course, were vitally interested in enlisting the support of all ethnic minorities living beyond the Urals. One early leader in this movement to rally Koreans was Alexandra Petrovna Kim, a woman born on February 22, 1885, in one of the Korean villages of the Primorsk region near Nikol'sk-Ussuriisk.[4] She had joined the Bolshevik party in 1917, and in the summer of that year had been sent to Siberia to undertake party work among the local Koreans. In October 1917, in Vladivostok, she took part in the Second Territorial Conference of Bolsheviks. At the Third Far Eastern Congress of Soviets, which took place in Khabarovsk in December, she was elected a member of the territorial Soviet executive committee. The extent of participation by other Russian-Koreans in these meetings is unclear, but in February 1918 a Soviet-sponsored conference of Korean "revolutionaries" was held in Khabarovsk.[5] Among them were Kim Rip, Pak Ae, and probably Yi Tong-hwi who, as we shall see, was soon to become the foremost leader of the Korean militants.[6]

Either at this point, or shortly after, the Hanin Sahoe-dang (Korean People's Socialist Party) was organized. Yi, famed military leader and Korean patriot, became chairman.[7] He symbolized the die-hard resistance

3. On this point, and on many other aspects of the Korean political culture of critical importance, see the excellent study of Gregory Henderson, *Korea: The Politics of the Vortex*, Cambridge, Mass., 1968.

4. Information on Kim and other valuable material on the early Korean Communist movement can be found in Kim Syn Khva (Kim Sŭng-hwa), *Ocherki po istorii Sovetskikh Koreitsev (Essays on the History of Soviet Koreans)*, Alma Ata, USSR, 1965 (esp. pp. 90–103). We are greatly indebted to Professor George Ginsburgs of the Graduate Faculty of The New School, New York, for bringing this work and other Russian materials to our attention, and assisting us in translation.

5. Kim Sŭng-hwa, giving the Soviet perspective, criticizes many of the conference participants as retaining a "bourgeois-nationalist viewpoint," and for wishing to separate the Korean "liberation" movement from the Soviet cause. Quoting from a Korean Communist publication in 1927, however, he asserts that "the left wing" understood that the only path to Korean independence lay in the victory of the socialist revolution and fraternal friendship with Soviet Russia. *Ibid.*, pp. 90–91.

6. Kim Sŭng-hwa lists among the participants, "Kim Don Khi," but frequently the common surnames Kim and Yi are mistakenly transposed, and since there is no further record of a Kim Tong-hwi, we suspect that the individual was in fact Yi Tong-hwi.

7. For additional materials on Yi and his career, see Chong-Sik Lee, *The Politics of Korean Nationalism*, Berkeley and Los Angeles, 1963; for an appraisal by a Korean Communist, see Kim San and Nym Wales, *Song of Ariran*, New York, 1941, esp. pp. 51–59. The latter must be used with great caution as it contains many inaccuracies.

Yi Tong-hwi, a native of South Hamgyŏng Province, had been a major in the

to Japan that had managed to survive years of defeat and disillusion. Matvei Pak (Pak Ae?) served as vice-chairman, Chŏn Il as chief of the Propaganda Bureau, Pak Chin-sun (Yi's secretary) as head of the Secretariat, Yi Han-ŏp as Political Bureau chief, and Kim Rip as head of the Communications Bureau. As can be seen, the party was structured completely after the contemporary Soviet model, with three primary functions: propaganda, political organization, and military activities.

Under Soviet guidance, the newly organized party sought to mobilize support among Korean and Chinese communities throughout the Siberian

---

Korean Army at the time of its dissolution in 1907, and was one of the founders of the Taehan Shinmin-hoe (Korean New People's Association), in 1908, a secret organization founded to counter Japanese influence and promote Korean industrial and educational development. Yi continued to be prominent in nationalist activities, organizing schools, delivering speeches, and propagating Christianity—both within Korea and among the Korean communities in Chientao, Manchuria.

In early 1915, he and Pak Ŭn-sik organized the Koryŏ Hyŏngmyŏng-dan (the Korean Revolutionary Corps), to conduct military operations against the Japanese. Their hope was that Germany would win the war, enabling Koreans to reestablish their independence. It is interesting to note that hopes were pinned on Germany before being directed toward Russia (or the United States). All Korean nationalists recognized the absolute necessity of external assistance.

The name and date of founding of this first party, together with the events surrounding it, are in some dispute. A near contemporary source on the events of this period is a secret memorandum prepared by the Japanese Ministry of Foreign Affairs: *An Outline of the Kōrai Communist Party and the All-Russian Communist Party of Koreans Living in Russia,* an investigation of November 1922, in Kōtō Keisatsu (Higher Police) (hereafter cited as Kōkei), Document Number (hereafter cited as DN) 4105, 1–15–1923, Archives of the Japanese Army, Navy, and Other Agencies, microfilmed for the Library of Congress (hereafter cited as *AJAN*), Reel 128 (hereafter R), Frame 44177 (hereafter F). According to this source, the party labeled Hanin Sahoe-dang was founded in Khabarovsk on June 28, 1918, with the guidance of various Russians, including Kurekornov, who was later appointed the first Comintern Propaganda Commissar in the Far East.

Kim Chun-yŏp and Kim Ch'ang-sun, *Hanguk kongsan chuŭi undongsa,* Vol. I, Seoul, 1967, p. 120, say that the date of the foundation was June 26, 1918. This major work, incidentally, is a landmark in Korean scholarship and deserves high praise.

Kim Sŭng-hwa, cited above, indicates that a party of similar name, which he refers to as the Union of Korean Socialists, was founded in February or March; it does appear that some permanent organization came out of the February conference. Other accounts of the period used include Bureau of Justice, Korean Government-General, *Chōsen dokuritsu shisō undō no hensen* (*Changes in the Korean Independence Thought Movement*), Seoul, 1931, p. 43; Thought Section, Prosecutor's Bureau, Keijō District Court, *Chōsen kyōsantō jiken* (*The Korean Communist Party Incident*), Seoul, no date, p. 9; Ch'oe Ch'ang-ik, "The Korean Proletarian Movement," in *Chōsen minzoku kaihō tōsō shi* (*A History of the Korean People's Struggle for Emancipation*), Japanese translation of the Korean (P'yŏngyang) 1949 original edition, Kyoto, 1952, p. 257; and Kim Tu-jŏng, "A Short History of the Korean Communist Party," in *Hankyō sōsho* (*Anti-Communist Series*), No. 8, Tokyo, Oct. 30, 1939, pp. 101–123.

region. Its activities, particularly in the Maritime Province, were extensive, but it was handicapped by a relative lack of ties with the peasantry; the most prominent leaders appear to have been largely émigré in character. To aid in recruitment, a journal, *The Bell,* was published. The Bolshevik-affiliated Left, however, was not the only Korean group engaged in organizational activities. A more broadly based group was the Korean National Council, which had been founded before the Bolshevik Revolution. Later Communist sources describe the leadership of this group variously as "wealthy Koreans" or "those under the influence of the Mensheviks." [8] In any case, the Council convened a Second Congress in May 1918, in Nikol'sk-Ussuriisk, with some 130 delegates present, including representatives of the Left. According to Kim Sŭng-hwa, the Left proposal to elect a new central committee was defeated, after which most leftists walked out of the congress. This is but one indication among many of the numerous fissures plaguing Korean political activities during this period.[9] Organizational efforts, nevertheless, continued, with the Left especially active. By the end of July 1918, the first Korean Red Guard Detachment had reportedly been formed, comprising approximately a hundred men.

One Bolshevik leader (Krasnoshchekov?) evidently made a strong appeal at this congress for support, stressing the theme that to join the Communist movement was the most effective method of supporting the liberation of Korea, promising that a Korean representative would be placed on the Commissariat of Foreign Affairs in Moscow, and renewing Soviet pledges of autonomy and equality for all ethnic minorities within the Union. During this period, the political-military situation in Siberia was chaotic, with the tides of battle constantly changing.[10] Bolsheviks vied with Social Democrats and Czarists for the control of key cities. Areas were won and lost by Whites, Czechs, Japanese, and others. Naturally, this had an important effect both on the continuity of the first Korean political activities within the Siberian area and on relations among the various groups involved. An orderly, coordinated movement would not have been possible even if personal rivalries could have been completely eliminated.

Thus, in late August 1918, after a series of military defeats, Korean

8. For details, see S. A. Khan, "Unchastie Koreiskikh trudyashchikhsya v grazhdanskoi voine na Russkom Dalnem Vostoke (1919–1922)" ("Participation of Korean Workers in the Civil War in the Russian Far East, 1919–1922"), in *Koreya, istoriya i ekonomika* (*Korea, History and Economics*), Moscow, 1958, pp. 54–55.

9. Another interesting account of this meeting is to be found in Kido Katsumi, *Zai Ro-ryō hainichi Chōsenjin torishmari ni kansuru shiken* (*Private Views Concerning the Control of Anti-Japanese Koreans in Russia*), manuscript dated October 3, 1918, written by an interpreter with the Korean Government-General (original in Hoover Library), no pagination.

10. For an excellent account of developments, see James W. Morley, *The Japanese Thrust into Siberia, 1918*, New York, 1957.

Red Guard commanders in the Trans-Baikal region, meeting in Urulga, agreed to disband their units and turn to partisan warfare. At the same time, all Soviet Party organs, including those of the Koreans, were ordered to move from Khabarovsk to the Amur region. However, when the White forces seized Khabarovsk with Japanese aid on September 4, a number of Communists and their supporters were discovered and shot. Among them was Alexandra Petrovna Kim, who at the time of her death appears to have been not only secretary of the Khabarovsk Bolshevik organization but also a commissar on the Far Eastern Council of the Commissariat of Foreign Affairs.

The military defeats inflicted on the Communists in Siberia during this period caused a number of defections. For a time, the only Korean organization of any significance was the aforementioned Korean National Council, and many of its members reportedly welcomed the arrival of the White armies.

As Bolshevik authority began to reassert itself, however, two Siberian areas became important centers of Korean radical politics: the Maritime Province, particularly the Vladivostok area, and the Omsk-Irkutsk region. On January 22, 1919, a group of Koreans in Irkutsk met to establish a Korean Section of the Irkutsk Communist Party.[11] In the succeeding weeks, party regulations and rules were enacted, and several elections for officers were held. The leaders of this group included Nam Man-ch'ong, Kim Ch'ŏl-hun, O Ha-muk, Pak Sŭng-man, Yun Hyŏp, and Cho Hun. Party units were also set up in many other cities of this area.

Several months later, on April 25, 1919, a conference of various pro-Bolshevik Korean elements, led by Yi Tong-hwi's group, opened in the so-called New Korean Village on the outskirts of Vladivostok.[12] The March Uprising in Korea had taken place only a few weeks before; in Moscow, the Comintern had just been launched. At the conference, it was decided to set up a coordinated committee for Korean Socialist organizations, with Vladivostok as headquarters; to form a single command for all Korean partisan units operating in the Russian Far East; to establish contacts with Korean guerrilla units operating in Manchuria and Korea; to step up agitation and propaganda among Koreans throughout the area by means of newspapers, journals, and leaflets; to boycott the Korean National Council; and to send representatives to Moscow to meet for the first time with the central Soviet government and the Third International.

11. *Chŏkki* (*Red Flag*), April 7, 1920, published by the Irkutsk Communist Party, Korean Section, and translated, Kōkei, DN 5283, 2–16–1921, *AJAN*, R 123, F 37308–14.

12. "The Development of the Communist Movement in Manchuria and Recent Conditions," in Kōtō Hōin, Kenjikyoku (High Court, Prosecutor's Bureau), *Shisō Ihō* (*Ideological Series*), No. 14, March 1938, pp. 7 ff.

Kim Sŭng-hwa indicates that this conference took place in May 1918, but that date is almost certainly incorrect.

In accordance with the latter decision, Pak Chin-sun, Pak Ae, and Yi Han-ŏp, key officials of the Korean People's Socialist Party, were dispatched to Moscow. In addition, Kurekornov, a Comintern official, also certified two other party members, Yun Hae and Ko Ch'ang-il, to serve as delegates to the Korean National Council in Moscow and to attend the Paris Peace Conference. Thus, a five-man delegation set out for the Soviet capital in the late spring of 1919.

When Pak Chin-sun and his comrades arrived in Moscow in mid-1919, they were warmly received. Some funds were provided from Comintern sources to finance the movement. In return, the Korean representatives signed an agreement with the new Soviet government pledging their party to work for the liberation of Korea and the espousal of the Communist cause.[13] On August 5, the Pak delegation left Moscow for the Far East. Their mission must have seemed wholly successful. Later that month, however, an event occurred that was to lead to major problems.

Throughout this period, as we have noted, the Allied Expeditionary Forces and the Japanese and the White Russian armies had been operating extensively in the Siberian hinterland. Many Bolshevik positions were overrun, or had to be evacuated in a hurry. Some regions changed hands repeatedly. Casualties on all sides were high, and Communist propaganda activities suffered a general decline. No quarter was asked or given, especially where key political and military figures were concerned. On August 28, Kurekornov fell into the hands of a Czarist unit and was summarily executed. This was a serious loss to the Yi Tong-hwi group, with whom he had established a close working relationship. More surprises were to follow. In late August, Yi himself left for Shanghai. Shortly thereafter, he assumed the office of premier in the Korean Provisional Government that had been set up in Shanghai. Consequently, his party headquarters was moved to that city.

Thus, when Pak and the others arrived in Irkutsk on September 10, they discovered a new and complex political situation. Kurekornov had been replaced by Boris Shumiatsky as head of the Comintern's Far Eastern Bureau. After his appointment, Shumiatsky had immediately been contacted by Korean leaders in Irkutsk, who had established a Communist Party unit earlier, in January. With his encouragement, on September 5 they created the "Communist Party of All Koreans in Russia." Based on Irkutsk, it was essentially a continuation of earlier activities.[14] The Irkutsk

13. "An Outline of the Kōrai Communist Party . . ." *op. cit.*, F 44180.
14. See Kim Hong-il, "Before and After the Free City Incident," *Sasanggye (The World of Thought)*, February 1965, p. 221. According to Kim, the key Irkutsk figures were Ch'oe Ko-ryŏ, Han Myŏng-se, Kim Ha-sŏk, and O Ha-muk—all second-generation Koreans, thoroughly Russianized. Chang Kŏn-sang, interviewed by Pang In-hu in 1966, provided some interesting recollections of these men which help us to understand what kind of people were participating in the movement at this early time. Ch'oe, according to Chang, was "a completely Russianized man," a second-

group, supported by Shumiatsky, forced Pak to turn over the Comintern funds to them, arguing that, with Kurekornov dead, they had inherited the authority of the Korean People's Socialist Party.[15]

The rivalry between the Irkutsk and Shanghai factions of the Korean Communist movement really began at that point. Already, the main differences between them can be discerned. A very considerable gap separated those Russianized Koreans who, for all practical purposes, were prepared to become an integral part of the Communist movement *within the Soviet Union,* from those Korean nationalists who wanted Soviet help in securing the independence of Korea. To this problem must be added the hardships involved in developing a coordinated movement under prevailing political and military conditions, and the personal factionalism that inevitably existed in Korean circles. Cleavages among the Soviet spokesmen provided an additional complexity. For example, several sources speak of the differences that developed between Shumiatsky and Shtikov, premier of the short-lived Far Eastern Republic. These differences had immediate repercussions within the contending Korean factions, the Yi Tong-hwi group siding with Shtikov and the Irkutsk group with Shumiatsky.

Korean Communism in China and Manchuria

Let us now shift our attention to Shanghai. Following the March First Uprising in Korea, an event involving hundreds of thousands of Koreans in a nationalist outburst against Japanese rule, the leading nationalists pooled their efforts to establish a provisional government in Shanghai. In some respects, Korean politics during this period foreshadowed the Chinese politics of a few years later: a broadly based popular front govern-

---

generation Korean whose parents had come from Hamgyŏng Province. He was regarded as a man of "good quality," thoroughly indoctrinated with Bolshevik concepts. Han also was a second-generation Korean, about forty years of age, well educated, and with "the manner of an aristocrat." Despite his Russian education, he valued Korean customs, according to Chang, and thus respected age and protected the "face" of those with whom he dealt; he proved to be an excellent organization man. Kim Ha-sŏk was described by Chang as "a very flexible man with considerable ability." He remained in the Soviet Union throughout his life, taking an active role in the Korean movement. O Ha-muk, also a second-generation Korean, had graduated from a military academy during the Czarist era, and slightly later, in 1920, organized a partisan group of some 1,000 men which joined forces with the Red Army in the struggle against the Semenov Army.

It will thus be noted that most if not all of the principal leaders of the Irkutsk party were thoroughly Russianized Koreans, considerably different from Yi Tong-hwi and his followers.

Chang also asserted that Shumiatsky had great power. "He interfered in everything and we had to receive his permission for any action. We did not do anything without consulting him."

15. See *ibid.,* and *Chōsen dokuritsu shisō undō no hensen, op. cit.,* p. 44. See also "The Development of the Communist Movement in Manchuria and Recent Conditions," *op. cit.,* p. 10.

ment lasted a brief time, and then split under multiple pressures, with the Communists setting up a rival organization. Initially, every political hue was represented in the Shanghai Provisional Government. Nationalism was the only common bond among men who professed political beliefs from conservatism to communism (or should we make anarchism the end of the spectrum?). Like the later Kuomintang-Communist alliance, however, the Korean nationalist-Communist coalition could not be maintained. The first Provisional Government was composed of men affected by different ideologies, supporting different tactics, and looking toward different sources of support. Under these circumstances, factionalism was certain to get worse. Perhaps the main substantive issue to emerge was that of immediate action against Japan versus a consolidation of strength. But there were innumerable other conflicts, and the coalition lasted less than two years. Nevertheless, these were important years for the Korean Communist movement.

As noted earlier, Yi Tong-hwi was elected premier of the Provisional Government in September 1919, having arrived in Shanghai on September 18 of that year. By December, he and his supporters held many of the important posts in the government. We are told that the Pak delegation informed Yi of the Irkutsk Incident in Shanghai at the beginning of November. Yi was furious, and later supervised the drafting of a petition that equated the Provisional Government with the Korean Communist Party, and promised to assume the responsibility of spreading communism among the Koreans.[16]

Soon Pak was en route to Moscow with the petition and a letter. Reports indicate that Pak's new negotiations were largely successful. Supposedly, Comintern authorities agreed that the funds should have gone to the Yi group, and that henceforth the Irkutsk Party would get its funds directly from Shumiatsky and confine its activities to propagating communism among the Koreans inside Siberia. The Korean People's Socialist Party, on the other hand, was to have the responsibility for engaging in propaganda and organizational activities among all Koreans outside Siberia. The agreement embodying this division of labor was sent to Shumiatsky by Comintern authorities. Simultaneously, the Shanghai Provisional Government was accepted as a vehicle of the Korean People's Socialist Party.

Long before this agreement, however, the Bolsheviks had encouraged and given material support to a variety of military activities by Korean nationalists. In the Maritime Province and in Manchuria in the 1918–19 period, Korean units were being formed and weapons obtained via Vladivostok with the assistance of Soviet officials. A Japanese report of

16. See "An Outline of the Kōrai Communist Party . . ." *op. cit.,* F 44181. According to this account, the petition was sent in the name of the Provisional Government, an obvious attempt to obtain full recognition from Soviet and Comintern authorities.

June 14, 1919, listed Yi Tong-hwi, Mun Ch'ang-bŏm, and Hwang Pyŏng-gil as prominent military leaders with substantial forces at their command.[17] The report asserted that Yi, having been in Nikol'sk, had recently gone to the Manchurian town of Mishan, where he had proceeded to establish a Korean Military Academy. As academy director, he had gathered together ex-officers of the old Korean Army and was using them as instructors for the young recruits. The report also claimed that Yi had issued draft orders for all twenty-year-old Koreans throughout the Siberian-China area who were not naturalized. (Another source gives the age of those being drafted as eighteen years.) A twenty-yuan tax (or tax in kind) was also being assessed upon every Korean household in this region. Recruiting stations had been established at Chita (Yi Kang), Nikol'sk (Mun Ch'ang-bŏm and An Myŏng-gŭn), Vladivostok (Ŏm In-sŏp), and Ssuch'êng in Manchuria (Yi Tong-hwi). "According to rumor," some four thousand Koreans had already gathered to form an army of independence.[18]

In the Omsk-Irkutsk region, there were also substantial military activities. In Omsk, a Korean Officer Training School had been organized by Tamul Yi and An Kyŏng-ŏk with the assistance of Piyotol Kim.[19] Yi was listed as head of the school as well as president of the Korean Communist Party in Omsk. An was president of the academy student body, and Kim was president of the Korean Youth Association in Novo Nikolaesk. According to this account, some eighty students had been collected for a four-month program. In Krasnoyarsk, young Koreans had been given military drill at night. In Irkutsk, hundreds of Koreans had joined the Red Army or formed units of their own; by June 1921, according to one Japanese report, there was a Korean Battalion in the Irkutsk city International Unit.[20] Thus, both major factions of the Korean Communist movement were receiving Bolshevik support in their military activities, whether as independent guerrillas or as elements of the Red Army.

An expansion of Comintern activities in the Far East, particularly the establishment of a bureau in Shanghai, greatly facilitated Soviet ties with the Korean Provisional Government. The spring of 1920 was of special

17. "Report Concerning the Korean Uprising Incident," No. 22, Japanese Korean Army Headquarters, 6–14–1919, *AJAN*, R 122, F 35646–55.

18. It would appear that the Korean partisans in Siberia were at least nominally under Soviet command in this period. According to Kim Sŭng-hwa, some thirty-six Korean partisan units, numbering 3,700 men, were fighting the Japanese by 1921 as units within the People's Revolutionary Army of the Far Eastern Republic. An additional 250 Koreans were reportedly serving in Russian partisan units. Kim also writes that there were fifty Korean Communist cells in the Soviet Far East in 1921, each attached to the Communist Party of the Soviet Union. These cells contained 578 party members and more than 1,000 candidate members, with an additional 800 Korean youth in the Komsomol. Kim Sŭng-hwa, *op. cit.*, pp. 100 and 103.

19. *Red Flag*, April 7, 1920, *op. cit.*

20. Bureau of Police Affairs, Korean Government-General, "Relations between Dissident Koreans and the Russian Extremists," 6–8–1921, *AJAN*, R 122, F 36366.

importance in this respect. In March, a Russian Bolshevik representative
reportedly came to Shanghai with Han Hyŏng-gwŏn, Nikolai Yi, and Hsia
Ch'i-fêng to conduct detailed negotiations with officials of the Provisional
Government. We do not know the identity of the Russian, although one
source, as we shall soon note, refers to contacts with a "General Podapov."
The three Asians had been participants in the Second All-Russian Congress
of Communist Organizations of Peoples of the East that took place in
December 1919. Han, concerning whom we shall have much more to say
later, was classified as a "representative of Korean workers," Yi as a
"naturalized Russian of Korean descent," and Hsia as a "Chinese labor
representative." This delegation was followed shortly by another: young
Grigorii Voitinsky, who was to organize the Far Eastern Bureau, arrived
in Shanghai with Yang Ming-chai, a Russianized Chinese from Vladivostok.
The date of their arrival is uncertain, but it may have been May.[21]

No detailed records of conversations between Comintern representa-

21. Most sources state that Voitinsky arrived in China in the spring of 1920:
Robert C. North, *Moscow and Chinese Communists,* Stanford, 1953, p. 54; Conrad
Brandt, *Stalin's Failure in China, 1924–1927,* Cambridge, Mass., 1958, p. 20; C.
Martin Wilbur and Julie Lien-ying How, eds., *Documents on Communism, Nationalism and Soviet Advisors in China—1918–1927,* New York, 1956, p. 79. Schwartz
gives the date June 1920: Benjamin Schwartz, *Chinese Communism and the Rise
of Mao,* Cambridge, 1958 edition, p. 32. One Chinese intellectual who participated
in the socialist movement of this period has written that Voitinsky and Yang arrived
in Shanghai in May 1920: see Liang Ping-hsien (using the pen-name Hai-yü Ku-k'ê),
"Chieh-fang pieh-lu" (Records of the Emancipation"), *Chih-yu jên (The Free Man),*
Hong Kong (Nos. 73–86, Nov. 14–Dec. 29, 1951, 14 installments), No. 76, p. 4.
According to Liang, the Chinese had already had contact with a Russian Bolshevik
named "Puluwei," who lived in Tientsin and had earlier formed a loosely knit group
of anarchists, socialists, and others into a Socialist Alliance led by Ch'en Tu-hsiu in
Peking.

Who was "Puluwei"? Chang Hsi-man, another participant in the events of this
period, has written that "Peliehwei," a self-styled specialist in Chinese classics who
had come to China to learn the vernacular language, had managed to get himself
appointed Cultural Representative of the Third International in Tientsin, and was providing secret entry papers to those Chinese going to Russia around 1921. Chang
claimed that "Peliehwei" was corrupt and pocketed funds intended for others; when
this issue was raised, he was ordered back to Russia, but he refused to return and ultimately took American citizenship. See Chang Hsi-man, *Li-shih hui-i (Historical
Reflections),* Shanghai, 1949, p. 5. Tse-tsung Chow in his *The May Fourth Movement,* Cambridge, 1960, has written that Sergei A. Polevoy was professor of Russian
language at Peking University, and that he put Voitinsky in touch with Chinese radicals he had earlier contacted (p. 244).

It seems clear that when Voitinsky arrived in Shanghai, Ch'en was already living
in the French Concession there. Ch'en immediately called a meeting at his home to
have Alliance members and others meet Voitinsky; Liang mentions only one Korean
name among those present, namely, the nationalist Kim Ku. According to Liang,
Voitinsky gave 2,000 yuan to aid in the establishment of a printing plant that could
be used by all socialist parties and groups, and a few days later the Yu Hsin Printing
Plant was in operation.

tives and the Provisional Government leaders have been found. Fortunately, we have a number of letters intercepted by Japanese agents during this period. Two of them are especially revealing; they were sent from Shanghai to Ku Ch'un-sŏn, president of the Korea National Association in Chientao. The first, dated May 11, 1920, was signed by three leading officials of the Provisional Government, Premier Yi, Kim Rip (chief secretary of the cabinet, a Yi man), and Ke Pong-u (member of the Provisional Legislative Assembly from Chientao).[22] The letter begins by lamenting the fact that although "our people have declared independence and advocated a climactic war," little has actually been accomplished to date except for the development of some military power in Chientao, and even this is not well coordinated. The writers admit that Japanese pressure has become intense, but declare that counteraction must be taken. They then note that the Chientao Korea National Association has established a budget of 40,000 yuan for military training, besides sending Chu Chin-sul and others to Russia. Because the writers clearly want such activities to come under their control, they reveal their own negotiations with Soviet representatives:

> The Lenin government is working very closely with our efforts for independence. Mr. Pak Chin-sun who was sent to Russia has already joined the foreign affairs department of the Soviet government, and Mr. Han Hyŏng-gwŏn will soon arrive in Moscow. Also, we have concluded firm secret agreements with major figures in Shanghai and Tientsin, that is to say, diplomatic agents of Russia.[23]

The letter goes on to suggest that when the provisional government representative, Yi Yong, arrives, the National Association should accept from him government bonds in the value of 100,000 yuan, and hand him the 40,000 yuan assigned for military training. Yi will give them detailed information, "but we have an agreement with the delegates from the Lenin government to begin the training of officers north of Irkutsk, and at the same time, airplanes and cannons will be made available. We will cooperate with the Bolsheviks in carrying out the final operations." [24]

A second letter, dated May 14, 1920, was sent from Ke Pong-u to Ku. It states that two special delegates of the Lenin government came to the Provisional Government with Kim Man-gyŏm[25] and delivered an official communication from their government. The letter said that "brothers of

---

22. Bureau of Police Affairs, Korean Government-General, *Rokoku kagekiha to Kantō futei senjindan to no kankei* (*Relations Between Russian Extremists and Dissident Koreans in Chientao*), Archives of the Japanese Ministry of Foreign Affairs microfilmed for the Library of Congress (hereafter cited as AJMFA, July 1920, R Sp. 44, Special Studies No. 134, pp. 11–13.

23. *Ibid.*, p. 12.

24. *Ibid.*, p. 12.

25. Kim Man-gyŏm was identified by Chang Kŏn-sang as another second-generation Korean "who spoke Russian better than Korean." He was associated with the Irkutsk faction.

your government must also come to Moscow and join others in carrying out a great revenge in the Far East." [26] We are told from other sources that Kim, who had been a vice-president of the Korean National Council, had come to Shanghai from Vladivostok both as a member of the Korean Communist Party and as Comintern propaganda agent.[27] Reportedly, he brought 40,000 yuan for organizational and propaganda purposes. His traveling companion was Kang Han-t'aek, a fifty-year-old Korean who was also thoroughly Russianized.

The situation among Korean émigrés in Shanghai at this point was particularly complex. As noted above, in August 1919 a strenuous and partly successful effort to establish a united front of all Korean nationalists had been undertaken. In September, a reorganized Provisional Government of Korea had been inaugurated, with its headquarters in Shanghai. After complex and delicate negotiations, Syngman Rhee (then in the United States) had been acknowledged as president and Yi Tong-hwi as premier. At the same time, Yi remained head of the pro-Bolshevik Korean People's Socialist Party. Perhaps the most concrete issue separating the various nationalist groups of this period, however, was not socialism but the question of military action. Yi and his supporters, as can be seen from the letters cited above, favored immediate military action against the Japanese. Indeed, this was the reason for their close ties with the new Bolshevik government, from which alone they could expect significant military aid. Other elements of the so-called Provisional Government, notably Syngman Rhee, Kim Kyu-sik, and Philip Jaisohn, regarded immediate military action as unrealistic and unduly costly. Their ties were with the West, especially the United States, and they favored diplomatic efforts and propaganda. Others took an intermediate position.

Negotiations with the Soviets

As noted in the first of the two letters cited above, Pak Chin-sun had been sent back to Moscow, where the Russian leaders, in accordance with their promises, had appointed him an official adviser on Korean affairs in the Commissariat of Foreign Affairs. The records of the Second Comintern Congress (July 19–August 7, 1920) note the presence of Pak Chin-sun as a delegate of the Korean Communist Party. Indeed, Pak participated in the section on "national and colonial questions," and delivered an extremely interesting speech. He started by condemning the First and Second Internationals for having ignored or minimized the Eastern question, and then proceeded to set forth the Leninist strategy for Asia in succinct and

26. *Ibid.*, p. 16.
27. Asia Bureau, Japanese Ministry of Foreign Affairs, *Chōsen dokuritsu undō mondai* (*Problems of the Korean Independence Movement*), "Historical Reference Materials," No. 24, AJMFA, R Sp. 4, p. 148.

sophisticated terms. His speech reveals with startling clarity the source-springs of Maoism:

> Admitting that the first stage of the revolution in the East will be the victory of the liberal bourgeoisie and the nationalistic intelligentsia, we should nevertheless now prepare our forces for the next stage, drawing from the depths of the peasant masses enslaved by the feudal regime organized forces for an agrarian-social revolution in Asia as soon as possible. The industrial proletariat, if Japan is not taken into consideration, is too weak in Asia for us to cherish serious hopes of an early Communist revolution; but there is no doubt of the success of an agrarian revolution if we are able to grasp the immediate problems of the great bloody struggle.
>
> The Russian proletariat, standing as the vanguard of the world social revolution, could withstand a desperate three-year onslaught of the bourgeoisie of the whole world only because it knew how to attract the poorest and middle classes of peasantry to its side.[28]

By June 1920, Pak had been joined in Moscow by Han Hyŏng-gwŏn, who was soon to conduct vitally important negotiations with the top Soviet leaders, including Lenin himself. A memoir has recently been uncovered that sets forth the details of his role during this period.[29] Han was Russian-educated and had lived in Vladivostok. Earlier, he had been active in radical nationalist circles. When the Japanese occupied eastern Siberia, he had moved with others to Harbin and thence to Shanghai, where he was associated with a Korean-language newspaper, *Shin-Taehan Ilbo* (*New Great Korean Daily News*). In late 1919, or early 1920, Han wrote several letters and subsequently got in touch with the mysterious "General Podapov," who supposedly had come to Shanghai from Japan. Han argued that, from both an ideological and a strategic viewpoint, it was essential for the Soviet government to destroy Japanese imperialism. The first step had to be the liberation of the Korean people—a task that the Korean nationalists could undertake if they were given sufficient funds.

According to Han, Podapov finally agreed and recommended that the Provisional Government send some official representatives to Moscow.

---

28. Pak Dinshun, "The Revolutionary East and the Immediate Problems of the Communist International," Petrograd *Pravda,* July 27, 1920, in *The Second Congress of the Communist International as Reported and Interpreted by the Official Newspapers of Soviet Russia,* Washington, 1920, p. 135. We have no way of knowing, of course, what kind of assistance Pak may have had in preparing this speech.

29. An article entitled "Hyŏngmyŏng-ga ui hoesangrok" ("Recollections of a Revolutionary"), appears under the name of Han Hyŏng-gwŏn in the October 1, 1948, issue of *Samch'ŏlli* (*Three Thousand Ri*), a Seoul journal. From the article, however, it is clear that the actual writing was done by a journalist on the basis of Han's statements to him. We are greatly indebted to Mr. Paek Sun-jae of Seoul for making this article available to us.

Han then contacted Premier Yi Tong-hwi. After a cabinet meeting, according to Han, it was decided to dispatch Yŏ Un-hyŏng, An Kong-gŭn, and Han as special envoys. An, however, was in Siberia and it proved impossible to contact him—or so we are told. Yŏ reportedly did not want to go through the Gobi desert, and decided he would wait until the European route to Moscow opened. In any case, Han departed for Moscow alone, with various letters of accreditation and state papers.[30] On his journey, he was given extraordinary attention by the Soviets. At Verkhneudinsk (now Ulan Ude), some 200 Korean soldiers were mustered before him, with Korean flags waving, in a full ceremony. From Irkutsk onward an official railway car was put at his disposal, with two Red Army soldiers as guards. At each stop, local officials came to the station to greet him, and when he arrived in Moscow top Soviet officials, including Leo Karakhan, were waiting at the railway station.

Han subsequently had a number of meetings with Karakhan, Foreign Minister Georgi Chicherin, and finally Lenin himself. According to his account, he advanced four proposals: (1) that Soviet Russia should recognize the Korean Provisional Government; (2) that the Soviet Government should furnish the Korean Independence Army with sufficient arms and facilities to equal the strength of the Red Army; (3) that a Korean Military Academy should be established in some designated location in Siberia for the training of military officers; (4) that the Provisional Government

30. Yŏ Un-hyŏng, as we shall see, was to achieve fame as a long-time leader of the left-nationalist cause, and frequently to be associated with the Communists. An Kong-gŭn, younger brother of An Chung-gŭn, the assassin of Itō Hirobumi, was later to be connected with the Chinese Nationalist Government in the period after the Manchurian Incident, as a part of the moderate wing of the Korean nationalist movement.

Han's version of the Provisional Government's (Yi's) decision may not be entirely accurate. According to Kim Chun-yŏp and Kim Ch'ang-sun, Han Hyŏnggwŏn was sent to Moscow primarily to protect the Yi Tong-hwi group and their representations about the Shanghai Government. Earlier, Pak Chin-sun had supposedly carried two letters to Moscow, one containing charges that the Irkutsk faction had illegally seized the funds intended for the Shanghai group, and another portraying the Shanghai Provisional Government as the government of the Korean Socialist Party. Since Yŏ and An were not affiliated at this point with the Yi group, Han alone could maintain that latter position on behalf of the Yi faction. Kim and Kim, op. cit., Vol. 1, pp. 197–198; see also pp. 198–208 for detailed accounts of the mission.

This interpretation is supported by Yŏ Un-hyŏng's later statement to the Japanese police that Yi had kept Han's trip secret from him and all others in the Provisional Government—thus contradicting Han's story. See "Ro Un-kyō jimmon chōsasho" (Interrogation of Yŏ Un-hyŏng), in Thought Section, Prosecutor's Bureau, High Court (Kōtō Hōin, Kenji-kyoku, Shisōbu), Chōsen shisō undō chōsa shiryō (Research Materials on the Korean Thought Movement), No. 2, Seoul, 1933 (hereafter cited as Yŏ Interrogation).

should be given funds to be used by it for the independence movement.[31]

Lenin responded favorably from the beginning. Han's recollection of his remarks was as follows:

> I know full well that without destroying Japanese imperialism and militarism the freedom and happiness of the Asian peoples cannot be attained. In Korea, a proletarian social revolution is not necessary at this time. It is the time only for a national revolution, an independence movement. We will therefore support the Korean independence movement with all of our strength.[32]

Lenin authorized a payment of 2 million rubles as an initial grant to the Korean cause. The difficulty was how to transport the funds in usable form, since the paper ruble at that time was not acceptable in international transactions. Thus, the first payment was given in gold rubles, the gold divided into seven boxes, each containing twenty sacks of gold coins. Han recalled the weight of each box as having been in the neighborhood of 700 pounds! Even this amount represented only 400,000 rubles, but Karakhan told him to get it to Shanghai first and pick up the rest later.[33]

When Han arrived in Omsk, he was met by Kim Rip, then serving as secretary-general of the Provisional Government state council. Kim gave Han the discouraging news that the Shanghai headquarters was racked with dissent. Nevertheless, Han decided to persevere. Entrusting both gold and reports to Kim Rip, he turned round and headed back to Moscow to get the remaining 1.6 million rubles. But when he got there, he found the situation even more depressing. Korean nationalists of various persuasions were busily attacking each other, and even within the Korean Communist movement the Shanghai and Irkutsk factions were in violent conflict. Han himself, in a message sent to Lenin and the Comintern, was charged with being of noble lineage and a "feudalist." That attack was part of a larger assault directed primarily at the Shanghai Provisional Government as "a combination of imperialist groups without mass support." It presumably came from Irkutsk supporters.

31. It is interesting to note that these four proposals coincide with those reported by the press at the time. For example, the *Ōsaka Asahi* on December 10, 1920, published an account of a six-point "treaty" that had been concluded between the Lenin Government and the Korean Provisional Government, and the six points are virtually identical with the four proposals noted above. See Kōkei DN 41, 493, 1–10–1921, *AJAN*, R 123, F 36987.

32. Han Hyŏng-gwŏn, *op. cit.*, p. 10.

33. Han recalled that various government officials came to the station to see him off, including Karakhan. The latter's final words were: "Sleep on top of those golden nuggets!" Han indicated that he followed that advice quite literally. According to Ra Yong-gyun, a gold ruble at that time was worth 1 Japanese yen, or 50 American cents, Chong-Sik Lee interview with Ra Yong-gyun, August 26, 1966, Seoul.

Han says he admitted to Lenin that there were serious splits in the Shanghai government, but assured him that such difficulties were inevitable in the course of a political movement and that they could be overcome. Lenin was sympathetic, and once again reiterated his belief that the movement should concentrate upon nationalist, not communist, goals. He promised that the pledge of assistance to the Shanghai government would be kept, complained that the Third International often created problems by "meddling" in his government's decisions, and authorized Han to settle the details with Foreign Minister Chicherin.

However, after some four months of so-called negotiations, Han was told by Chicherin that "because the situation with respect to the Provisional Government is unsettled, we cannot give you the entire 1.6 million rubles." Chicherin continued, "I would like to give you the entire amount, but the Comintern has interfered in this matter and made it impossible." Han was then given 200,000 rubles, which he converted into US dollars in Berlin. He returned to Shanghai via the European route, accompanied by Ko Ch'ang-il.

Han reports that he was deeply saddened by the fact that the Provisional Government had lost the confidence of most foreigners with whom he had contact during this period. A brief résumé of developments in Shanghai will indicate some of the reasons. The turmoil had been going on for months. Syngman Rhee, who bore the title of president, had arrived in Shanghai from Washington on December 8, 1920. In the weeks that followed, bitter quarreling among the Korean leaders took place, with arguments over tactics, principles, and personalities. The fortunes of the movement were at a low ebb—always a signal for trouble. Efforts to obtain support for Korean independence at Versailles had failed, as had all other approaches to the Western powers. Increasing Japanese pressure in Siberia and Manchuria had rendered military operations costly in terms of manpower and ever more difficult to mount. Finances, too, were a constant problem. And major differences over tactics interacted with personal rivalries to deepen the cleavages stemming from differences in ideology and foreign associations.[34]

The Era of Rising Dissidence and Comintern Intervention

On January 26, 1921, the Provisional Government suffered an open split, with a number of cabinet members resigning. The dissidents, who included Premier Yi Tong-hwi, sharply criticized Rhee's policies and denounced him and his supporters. The united front had collapsed.

It is quite possible that the funds obtained by Han Hyŏng-gwŏn in Moscow contributed to this event. To understand how, we must return to certain events that took place in 1920. After Han turned over the first funds to Kim Rip in Siberia, Kim, together with Pak Chin-sun (who had

34. For details, see Chong-Sik Lee, *op. cit.*, pp. 148–153.

accompanied Han), returned to China by a circuitous route so as to avoid the Irkutsk group. Pak deposited some funds in Peking, in care of his Russian wife. Kim proceeded to Shanghai, arriving there in December 1920.

There had been previous difficulties over money. When Kim Man-gyŏm had brought some 40,000 yuan to Shanghai earlier from Comintern sources, he had at first worked with Yi and Kim Rip in sponsoring various Communist activities and publications. Personal rivalries and differences over policy soon led to a rupture.[35] By the end of 1920, when Kim Rip returned to Shanghai with sizable new funds, Kim Man-gyŏm's money was exhausted. However, both the Kim Man-gyŏm group and the non-Communist elements of the Provisional Government were studiously ignored in connection with the new Soviet grant. Indeed, every effort was made initially to conceal the fact that such funds had come. As might have been expected, when word leaked out there was a tremendous furor.

All of Yi's opponents now charged that the Yi–Kim Rip clique was attempting to keep the Moscow funds a secret in order to have exclusive use of them. They asserted that they had discovered the existence of such funds only when word of their arrival was received directly from Moscow. More serious charges were leveled. It was claimed that Kim Rip had engaged in outright embezzlement, using some of the funds to buy himself a farm in Chientao and to establish luxurious quarters in Shanghai, replete with a Chinese concubine.[36] An accounting of the funds was demanded, but Yi stood by his associate. By the spring of 1921, not only the Provisional Government but also the Korean Communists were split wide open, with the leading personalities scattered in many directions.[37]

35. According to one source, Ch'oe Ch'ang-sik, a friend of Kim Man-gyŏm, had promoted a cleavage between Kim and the Yi–Kim Rip team because Kim Rip had taken the post of Cabinet Chief Secretary from him: *Chōsen dokuritsu undō mondai, op. cit.,* p. 148. In any case, the struggle soon came to a head over the expenditure of funds for publications. The Yi group had published three issues of *Shin Taehan Tongnippo (New Korea Independence News)*, using some 8,000 yuan given by Kim Man-gyŏm. Because of Ch'oe's objections, the funds were then shut off and publication ceased. Meanwhile, Ch'oe and Kim Man-gyŏm had started their own publication, *Kongsan (The Communist)*: ibid., pp. 148–149.

36. See Kim Ku, *Paek Pŏm ilji, Kim Ku chasŏjŏn (The autobiography of Kim Ku, Memoirs of Paekbŏm)*, Seoul, 1947, p. 283. Many sources tend to identify Kim Rip as the villain. Chang Kŏn-sang, for example, asserted: "Everyone knew about Kim Rip. Were it not for him, Yi Tong-hwi would have been a very good man and received the highest plaudits from all of us. But Kim Rip was his ruin. He was a man capable of any deceit, and he was quite properly assassinated."

37. The activities and movements of Yi and other leading Communist personalities at this time are not completely clear. According to the Japanese Foreign Office source cited above, Yi went to Weihaiwei at one point, intending to go north and join with comrades in Siberia, but on this occasion he was persuaded to return to Shanghai. There is also a report that at one point in this period Yi spent some time in Canton with the Chinese Communist leader Ch'en Tu-hsiu. We know from Liang

At some point in this period, the group associated with Yi Tong-hwi reorganized their party. It will be recalled that Yi had led the "Communist party" established in early 1918 in Khabarovsk as the Korean People's Socialist Party. After he moved to Shanghai, a new Korean Communist Party was organized under his leadership. Accounts vary concerning its name and date of establishment. In his interrogation at the hands of Japanese police, Yŏ Un-hyŏng indicated that the party was reconstructed as the Koryŏ Kongsan-dang (Koryŏ Communist Party) in May 1920.[38] Other sources place the date in 1921, after the split in the Provisional Government.[39] There is also some controversy over the first name of the new party.[40]

According to Yŏ Un-hyŏng, the declaration and regulations of the party were written by Kang Han-t'aek, with combined nationalist and socialist appeals being featured. A demand for the immediate liberation of the Korean people was coupled with a call for the abolition of capitalism in Korea, and the creation of a Korean soviet government. Yŏ admitted to Japanese interrogators that he served as head of the party's translation service. He himself translated *The Communist Manifesto* into Korean during this period, after which it was distributed in the Chientao area and in other regions where there were Korean communities. Additional works on socialism and communism, some of them from British Labour Party sources, were also translated and distributed.

---

that Voitinsky and a group of Chinese radicals had visited Ch'en Ch'iung-ming, the reform-minded military leader, in Fukien Province in the late spring or summer of 1920. Russian economic and technical assistance had been pledged to Ch'en by Voitinsky. Later, as is well known, General Ch'en moved into Kwantung Province and for a time supported Sun Yat-sen, who had returned to Canton. In this period (late 1920 or early 1921), Ch'en Tu-hsiu came south and, after a discussion with Ch'en Ch'iung-ming, agreed to direct an educational program for the region under the General's control. See Liang, *op. cit.,* Nos. 80–84. Thus, Yi may well have joined Ch'en Tu-hsiu in Canton for a brief time, as the Japanese Foreign Office reported. As we shall shortly note, however, by early 1921 Yi and his main supporters were back in Siberia.

38. Yŏ Interrogation, *op. cit.,* p. 41.

39. Dae-Sook Suh, in his work *The Korean Communist Movement, 1918–1948,* Princeton, 1967, citing another source, asserts that the Koryŏ Kongsan-dang was officially created in Shanghai on January 10, 1921, after Kim Rip brought in the new funds. Suh's work contains many details on the early Korean Communist movement, varying to some extent from our account, but with no major difference.

Still another account states that the Koryŏ Communist Party was established in October 1921, when Communist representatives meeting in Shanghai voted to change their official name.

40. Chang Kŏn-sang, in his interview with Pang In-hu, insists that the party organized under Yi in Shanghai was called the Chosŏn Kongsan-dang, Korean Communist Party, because the Irkutsk element had already organized a Koryŏ Communist Party there, and the same title could not be used. Koryŏ, incidentally, was the name of the dynasty (935–1392) in Korea that preceded the Yi dynasty.

In the spring of 1921, dissidence within the Korean Communist movement reached a new peak, and Comintern intervention became unavoidable. In the aftermath of the split in the Provisional Government and the charges against Kim Rip, nearly one-half of the members of Yi Tonghwi's Shanghai Communist Party withdrew. The air was thick with charges and countercharges. Meanwhile, the Irkutsk Party renewed its old attacks upon the Shanghai Party as mere nationalists and opportunists. Finally, the Far Eastern Secretariat of the Comintern decreed that a meeting of representatives from Siberia, Manchuria, and China should be held in March 1921 to iron out the major problems and produce a unified party.

Despite the difficulties in Shanghai, Yi and his followers appear to have been the strongest group initially. They had wanted the meeting held in Chita or at least some place near Vladivostok, their center of strength. The meeting, however, was postponed until May, and meanwhile men from the Irkutsk faction were busily recruiting delegates.[41] At last the conference opened—in Irkutsk. By this time the Irkutsk faction, with the approval of Shumiatsky and the Far Eastern Secretariat, had obtained the right to pass upon the credentials of the various delegates. As a result, even Yi Tong-hwi was denied permission to attend, and a number of his supporters, including Pak Ae and Chang To-jŏng, were actually sentenced to prison on the charge that they were "antiparty." Completely triumphant at this point, the Irkutsk faction appropriated the name Koryŏ Communist Party. In an effort to secure full Soviet support, Han Myŏng-se, Nam Man-ch'un, and Chang Kŏn-sang were selected to go to Moscow as the Party's representatives. It was also decided that O Ha-muk and Yu Tong-yŏl should command the Party's armed forces. They were dispatched to Alekseyevsk, with a Russian adviser.[42]

Despite the severe setback at Irkutsk, Yi and his followers did not abandon the fight. There are varying accounts of their activities during the period immediately before and after the Irkutsk Conference. According to one official Japanese source, they reorganized their party in Khabarovsk

41. For example, Chang Kŏn-sang, who was in Peking at the time, was recruited by Cho Hun, who also made contact with many others in the Peking area who seemed likely prospects. Cho instructed Chang to contact Kim Man-gyŏm in Shanghai for travel instructions and funds. Chang subsequently attended the Irkutsk meeting.

42. For details, see Kim Hong-il, op. cit., p. 211. Also see Kōkei DN 18,636, 6–7–1921, AJAN, R 122, F 36331.

According to a Korean author, some forty-five Korean leaders were in Irkutsk in May 1921 (when the Koryŏ Communist Party was organized there), including Mun Ch'ang-bŏm, Han Hyŏng-gwŏn, and Kim Kyu-sik. The Political Bureau of the reorganized Party reportedly consisted of seven members, including Mun, Han, Kim, Yu Ye-gyun, Nam Man-ŏn, and Chang Kŏn-sang. The Military Bureau of the Party had five members, including Yi Ch'ŏng-ch'ŏn, Kim Tong-sam, Yu Tong-yŏl, and Ch'oe Sang-jin: Yu Sŏk-in, Aeguk ui pyŏl dŭl (The Patriotic Stars), Seoul, 1965, pp. 201–202.

on February 22, 1921, calling it the Hanjok Kongsan-dang (Korean People's Communist Party). On April 25, just before the Irkutsk meeting, Party headquarters were reportedly moved to Chita, capital of the Far Eastern Republic. This same account asserts that the Party officials were not formally installed until July 3, after the Irkutsk Conference (it lists them as Yi, Kim Rip, Shin Ch'ae-ho, and Pak Yong-man).[43]

Whether or not the reorganization took place precisely in this manner, the Yi faction continued to assert its claim to legitimacy. Indeed, it clearly wished to be considered *the* Korean government-in-exile, the only legitimate successor to the Shanghai Provisional Government. Thus, the terms it used for various Party offices in the fall of 1921 were identical to those in use by the Shanghai government from which it had separated itself. Yi was called president; Shin, director of internal affairs; Pak, director of foreign affairs. This organizational structure reveals quite clearly the basic difference between the Yi group and their Irkutsk rivals, who were content for the moment with being simply the Korean Communist Party.

Whatever designation was being used by the Yi faction at this point, their 1921 program—sometimes called the Chita Communist Program—has been preserved in several similar versions. One lists the following basic points:

> 1. While territorial boundaries exist, there is no boundary in con-nection with beliefs: persons of any nationality can be our comrades if they agree with communism.
> 2. We must reconstruct our past political and social system, organiz-ing a new society in which all may live in perfect happiness.
> 3. Clothing, food, and housing must be distributed equally to all, regardless of sex, age, wealth, or social origin. We must save the countless people who have suffered under class systems based upon bureaucratism and capitalism.
> 4. Those who oppose the principles of our party shall be regarded as enemies, and military force may be used against them.
> 5. We shall propagandize communism for Korea by means of our

---

43. See Thought Section, Prosecutor's Office, *Chōsen shisō undō chōsa shiryō*, No. 1, *op. cit.*, pp. 18–19. This report, incidentally, states that Yi went to Siberia im-mediately after his resignation as premier in January 1921. It does not mention the Weihaiwei or Canton trips noted earlier.

However, Kim Chun-yŏp and Kim Ch'ang-sun argue that this account is in error. They assert that Yi Tong-hwi was still in Shanghai in this period, too preoccupied with other matters to engage in party reorganization. (Some Japanese accounts, in-deed, do indicate that Yi himself did not leave Shanghi until July 1921, *after* the Irkutsk Conference.) Moreover, citing other Japanese sources, they state that Yi's main followers—Pak Ae, Kim Chin, and Ke Pong-u—were all arrested in late April 1921 in Chita, and sent to Shumiatsky in Irkutsk. Kim and Kim, *op. cit.*, Vol. 1, pp. 222–226.

According to Yu Sŏk-in, the Shanghai group did not move to Chita until the fall of 1921. Yu, *op. cit.*, p. 200.

headquarters, main branches, secondary branches, sub-units, village cells, and liaison offices.

6. The receipt and redistribution of such items as clothing, food, and housing shall be determined by established regulations.[44]

As will be noted, the above program paid the necessary homage to communism, albeit in extremely vague language, without any show of Marxist dialectics. Party objectives, however, were revealed just as well by the plans for an extensive organizational network. From the outset, the Korean People's Communist Party envisaged operations among all major Korean communities, wherever they existed. Main party branches were scheduled for Nikol'sk, Harbin, Kirin (Chilin), Shanghai, Seoul, and San Francisco, with secondary branches in Vladivostok, Chientao, Py'ŏngyang, Taegu, and Hamhŭng, and subunits in a number of towns including Khabarovsk, Muling, Mukden, and Hunch'un. Moreover, four "special liaison points" were to be established at Moscow, Peking, Antung, and Tokyo.

Thus, by mid-1921, the Irkutsk and Shanghai factions, to call them by their popular designations, were locked in a desperate struggle to obtain the support of Moscow and the Comintern, and also to secure as many party members and military recruits as possible. Because the Yi faction had its main source of strength within China in Shanghai, the Irkutsk faction decided to make Peking its main Chinese headquarters. Chang Kŏn-sang, An Pyŏng-ch'an, Yi Chae-bok (alias Yi Chŏng), and Kim Ch'ŏl-hun, among others, came to Peking for organizational activities. Yi Chae-bok and Kim Ch'ŏl-hun were the principal leaders, since the Irkutsk Party had equipped them with funds. Pamphlets were issued and members recruited.

Meanwhile, in Shanghai, there was open competition between the two factions. An Pyŏng-ch'an came down from Peking to recruit supporters. Naturally, that old enemy of the Yi group, Kim Man-gyŏm, played an important role; indeed, the new Shanghai-based unit of the Irkutsk faction was often called the Kim faction. Among its members were Yŏ Un-hyŏng, Ch'oe Ch'ang-sik, Pak Hŏn-yŏng, Cho Tong-ho, and Kim T'ae-yŏn (Tan-ya).[45]

44. Kōkei DN 24,562, 8-6-1921, *AJAN,* R 122, F 36545.

45. Ch'oe Ch'ang-sik had participated in nationalist causes having a variety of ideological connotations. Together with Kim Ku and others, he had helped to organize the Ro Pyŏng-hoe ("Worker-Soldier Society"), which set out to raise one million yen in a ten-year period for military and political activities. He had also been involved in the establishment of the Korean United Independence Party (Yu-il Tongnipdang). In April 1930, he was arrested by the Japanese police in the Shanghai French concession and, in November of that year, was sentenced to a three-year prison term. See *Tong Kwang (Eastern Light),* No. 21, May 1931, p. 47.

According to some sources, anticommunists in the Provisional Government, angered by Ch'oe's gravitation to the left, secretly informed the police of his whereabouts, causing his arrest. Whether or not the story is true, similar acts were not

According to Japanese reports, a number of Irkutsk Party and Korean Communist Youth League workers drew regular salaries, possibly from the Shanghai bureau of the Comintern. The Kim faction, however, had serious financial problems, since the Yi faction had retained the Moscow funds. Yŏ later complained that their group suffered from acute poverty, and that this was one reason why they had so few members and such limited activities. One account states that Yŏ himself obtained 100 yuan a month for propaganda work from a Russian source.[46] Yŏ did not mention this in his interrogation by Japanese authorities, but he did say that Kim Man-gyŏm had probably received assistance from Voitinsky, since the two had become close friends. Another account mentions a Comintern donation of from 20,000 to 30,000 yuan to the Kim faction.[47] And various sources indicate that by the summer of 1921 the Yi faction had already lost favor with the Comintern as a result of the embezzlement charges and other tales carried by the enemies of Yi and Kim Rip.[48]

Nevertheless, in the initial period at least, the Yi faction enjoyed some signal advantages over its opponents. Indeed, it was operating on a very wide front. Thanks to Moscow, it was plentifully supplied with funds, and it had Yi, the most important single leader. As a result, it retained a majority of the Shanghai Communist Party members (partly for this reason, it continued to be called the Shanghai faction). One account states

---

uncommon, given the bitter factionalism of the period. The practice was employed by all elements.

Pak Hŏn-yŏng, as is well known, was, after 1945, to become one of the key leaders of the Korean Communist Party. During his early life, Pak became secretary of the Kim faction's Korean Communist Youth League in Shanghai, with Ch'oe serving as chairman of the Executive Committee. (For the constitution and bylaws of the Youth League, see *Kōkei* DN 23552, 7–20–1921, *AJAN*, R 122, F 36501–2. Cho Tong-ho had studied at Chinlung University in Nanking, majoring in the Chinese language. (Yŏ Un-hyŏng had studied theology at the same institution as a fellow student.) Cho subsequently worked as a journalist. Kim Tan-ya, as we shall see, was also to have an active career in the Communist movement.

46. Song Sang-do, *Kiro sup'il* (*Random Notes on Donkey Back*), Korean Historical Materials Series, No. 2, edited by the National History Editorial Committee, Seoul, 1955, p. 246. According to Song, a library to propagandize communism was set up, and some books in Korean were sent to Yi Shi-hyŏn.

47. *Kōkei* DN 28562, 10–27–1921, *AJAN*, R 123, F 36837–8. The Kim faction also seems to have had a "funds incident." Ch'oe Ch'ang-sik, who first served as treasurer, resigned on Oct. 3, 1921, over an issue of fund disbursement, and was replaced by Yŏ Un-hyŏng.

48. See, for example, *Chōsen dokuritsu undō mondai, op. cit.*, p. 150. According to this source, when a Soviet delegation came to China while investigating the condition of various Communist parties in the Far East, Kim Man-gyŏm and Ch'oe Ch'ang-sik arranged an early meeting with a Soviet agent in Soochow and there elaborated upon the faults of Kim and Yi. Shortly thereafter, three of the Yi group were reportedly arrested in Russia.

that the Yi faction had fifty members at the outset and the Kim faction thirty or forty.[49]

Communist printing presses now began to turn out an amazing quantity of literature addressed to Koreans and other Far Eastern peoples. Much of it, of course, was in the form of straight translations of foreign material, most of it Russian.[50] By the fall of 1921, Japanese authorities estimated that 150,000 Koreans in Manchuria and Siberia had been influenced by "Bolshevik propaganda" (as compared with only 20,000 similarly tainted Chinese, they said).[51] It is clear that the Yi group—the so-called Shanghai faction—played the major role in propaganda and recruitment throughout the China-Manchuria-Eastern Siberia area, with forays into Japan and Korea proper.

The Seeding of Asian Communist Movements

The largest amount of Soviet money was used to finance the Shanghai-Chita operations. Once again, a major effort was made to unify the various warring Korean elements, nationalist and Communist, in order to create another popular front. There were innumerable discussions among the various factions, both those supporting and those opposing the Provisional Government. Representatives from Korean groups in Shanghai, Peking, Tientsin, Manchuria, Siberia, Tokyo, and Korea itself participated. The leading role was not generally taken by the Communists, but the funds and energy expended by them were not insignificant. Kim Rip, for example, poured a substantial amount of money into publishing activities in both Peking (which now had a sizable Korean Communist group) and Shanghai. Kim's activities, of course, were directed toward influencing all Koreans on such issues as the unification of the nationalist movement and other questions affecting "national liberation."

In the years between 1921 and 1923, the renewed attempt to achieve a united front progressed slowly and painfully. Its climax was the opening of a National Representatives Conference on January 3, 1923, in Shanghai. But new issues combined with old ones to prevent unification.[52] Thus, in

49. Kōkei DN 18936, 6–10–1921, *AJAN*, R 122, F 36337–8.

50. Japanese translations of the following four pamphlets are available: *Selling Water*, *AJAN*, R 122, F 36397–408; *Direction for Our Proletariat Class*, *AJAN*, R 122, F 36533–4; *The Communist Manifesto*, *AJAN*, R 122, F 36647–92; *Political Platforms of the Russian Communist Party*, *AJAN*, R 123, F 36783–819. For lists of other publications circulated by the Hanjok Communist Party and other Korean Communist groups, see *AJAN*, R 122, F 36508 and F 36729–30.

51. See Kōkei DN 28072, 10–5–1921, *AJAN*, R 122, F 36729–30. These same figures are given in a speech made by Yi Tong-yŏl, May 11, 1920, in Chientao. See *Rokoku kagekiha to Kantō futei senjindan to no kankei, op. cit.,* p. 10.

52. For details, see Chong-Sik Lee, *op. cit.,* pp. 175–179. At the National Representatives Conference, some 61 groups and 113 delegates were present. A leader from Chientao, Kim Tong-sam, was elected president of the conference, and An Ch'ang-ho,

the very period when, in China, an alliance was being forged between the Kuomintang and Chinese Communist elements, Korean efforts in the same direction came to nothing, and the Korean Communists themselves remained a divided, quarreling group.

Some of the Shanghai faction's funds were also directed toward Korea itself. There exist several accounts of the first Communist probes into Korea proper. In one Japanese source, we are informed that Kim Ch'ŏl-su, one of the Irkutsk group, went into Korea from Shanghai with propaganda funds in July 1921, and that this represented "the first extension of Russian hands into Korea." [53] Another account has stated that Kim Rip gave a substantial sum of money (a total of some 80,000 yen, or yuan, according to Yŏ Un-hyŏng) to Yi Pong-su, a Meiji University graduate, who took it into Korea. Supposedly, most of it went to Chang Tŏk-su, chief editor of the *Tong-A Ilbo* (*East Asia Daily News*) and a vigorous nationalist leader.[54]

One of the many complaints of the Kim faction was that the funds sent into Korea had been wasted on a few nationalists who were neither Communists nor interested in movements other than their own. The Kim group, it should be noted, was attempting to establish its own beachhead in Korea, especially through its Youth League. Plans were made to entrust Ch'oe P'al-yong, an editor of the Keijō (or Kyŏngsŏng) Book Company, with the creation of a Seoul unit. Chŏng Kyu-jŏng came to Shanghai from Seoul shortly after the league was established, and helped to open up liaison channels. The year 1921 thus marked the beginnings of the Communist movement inside Korea. Already sharp doctrinal rivalry existed between the various Communist factions. This was in addition to their differences over the broader issue of nationalist-Communist relations. But in truth, the two sets of issues were inseparable. Thus from the outset the Korean Communist movement was plagued with factional divisions at home as well as abroad.

The Yi group also contributed money to the Chinese Communist movement. Reportedly, a sum of 20,000 yuan was given to a Chinese named Huang to aid in the establishment of a Chinese Communist Party. The full facts of this episode are not yet known. Yŏ says that the Huang

---

vice-president. Neither man belonged to the Communist wing of the nationalist movement. The conference extended over three months and 92 meetings, with issues like the Free City Incident (to be noted later) and factionalism among the Manchurian guerrilla groups prominent in the discussions. In the end, conciliation proved impossible.

Han Hyŏng-gwŏn, incidentally, expended a sizable amount of the Moscow money entrusted to him on this conference.

53. *Chōsen dokuritsu shisō undō no hensen, op. cit.,* p. 45.

54. For the reference to Yi Pong-su, see Kōkei DN 21272, 7–7–1921, *AJAN,* R 122, F 36459. For the funds to Chang, see Thought Section, Prosecutor's Bureau, *Chōsen kyōsantō jiken, op. cit.,* p. 10.

party was different from the one then being established by Ch'en Tu-hsiu, and that it soon disappeared.[55]

Finally, the Yi group financed the attempted launching of a Communist movement in Japan. According to one Japanese source, the first contact with Japan was made in June 1920, when Yi's follower, Yi Ch'un-suk, a graduate of Chūō University and previously vice-minister of military affairs in the Provisional Government, returned to Tokyo from Shanghai with the intention of spreading communism.[56] Yi Ch'un-suk, according to this account, held frequent meetings with a Meiji University student, Yi Chŭng-rim, and the two discussed the possibility of establishing a propaganda organ in collaboration with Ōsugi Sakae, the noted Japanese anarchist leader.

Yi Ch'un-suk returned to Shanghai in August 1920. Somewhat later (the dates vary, both October and December being mentioned), Ōsugi himself went to Shanghai. According to his own heavily censored account, he met with a number of Communists, including Ch'en, a Russian he calls T—— (Voitinsky), and various Koreans.[57] Ōsugi later maintained that he was not happy with T——'s detailed instructions, and at first refused funds. But he finally accepted some money, and used it to revive his defunct anarchist journal, *Rōdō Undō* (*The Labor Movement*).[58]

55. Yŏ says, "Of course, the Chinese Communist Party assisted by Yi Tong-hwi soon dissolved. It was a separate one from that organized by Ch'en Tu-hsiu." Yŏ Interrogation, *op. cit.*, p. 56.

Kim Chun-yŏp and Kim Ch'ang-sun assert that the Chinese involved was Huang Chiao, a close friend of Yŏ Un-hyŏng in Shanghai and publisher of *Chiu-Kuo Jih-pao*. According to their findings, Huang Chiao was an active Communist who hired Cho Tong-ho as a reporter on his newspaper, encouraged the anti-Japanese movement among Koreans in the Shanghai area, and introduced some Koreans into Chinese military academies: Kim and Kim, *Hanguk kongsan chuŭi undongsa*, Vol. 1, *op. cit.*, pp. 244–245.

Earlier, we had surmised that the Chinese involved might be Huang Ch'ao-hai, a Peking University professor extremely active in the Socialist Alliance and close to Li Ta-chao and the early North China Communist movement. Liang Ping-hsien, in his article previously cited, indicates that members of the Northern section of the Socialist Alliance proposed to expand the organization and call it the Chinese Communist Party, but that the project failed.

56. Higher Police Section, Police Department, Heian Nandō (P'yŏngan Namdo), *Zai Tōkyō Chōsenjin no genkyō* (*The Present Condition of the Koreans in Tokyo*), 1922, mimeographed, no pagination (Hoover Library). For general details, see Robert A. Scalapino, *The Japanese Communist Movement, 1920–1966*, Berkeley, 1967, pp. 12 ff., and the fine study by George M. Beckmann and Okubo Genji, *The Japanese Communist Party, 1922–1945*, Stanford, 1969.

57. Ōsugi Sakae, *Nihon datshutsu ki* (*Memoirs of Escape from Japan*), Tokyo 1923, pp. 22–32. The Koreans included Yi Tong-hwi and Yŏ Un-hyŏng, and at least one meeting took place at Ch'en Tu-hsiu's residence.

58. The first issue of *Rōdō Undō* had been published on October 6, 1919, but the newspaper had ceased publication on June 1, 1920. Publication was again begun on Jan. 29, 1921, with two Communists, Kondō Eizō and Takatsu Seidō added to the anarchist staff.

Ōsugi, however, remained an anarchist, and the Comintern therefore turned its attention elsewhere. Yi Chŭng-rim, who had been furnished several thousand yen by Yi Tong-hwi and Yi Ch'un-suk in 1920, seems to have served as its Tokyo agent. In early 1921, he contacted Ōsugi again, but then shifted his attention to Yamakawa Hitoshi and Sakai Toshihiko, two veteran Japanese socialists who were moving into the Communist camp. Neither man, however, was prepared to make the trip to Shanghai. He therefore selected Kondō Eizō, a student recently returned from the United States who had come to Communism in New York.

Kondō went to Shanghai in April 1921. He has described the whole episode in some detail.[59] He met with a group of thirteen men; most were Koreans but at least one—Huang Chiao—was Chinese. The leader of the group seemed to be Pak Chin-sun, "a Comintern representative dispatched from Moscow." Kondō describes Pak as a stately figure, but goes on to remark that later, when he was in Moscow, he found Pak in "pathetic decline. . . . Some problem had emerged and he had been excluded from the Party, and was having difficulty in finding enough to eat." [60] Kondō's testimony thus corroborates in very convincing fashion the other evidence that relations between Moscow and the Yi faction deteriorated badly in this period.

It is interesting that Kondō considered the leader of the meeting to be Pak, because Yi Tong-hwi was present. Kondō called him "the most dramatic figure of the Shanghai meeting," a man in his mid-fifties who "grasped me with a hearty embrace." Concerning Yi's ideological purity and depth, however, Kondō had substantial reservations, echoing those of many others. Presumably the Comintern had purchased his experience, his fervor, and his character, wrote Kondō, but he doubted that such a man was capable of ideological thoroughness.[61]

59. Kondō Eizō, *Cominterun no misshi* (*Secret Messenger of the Comintern*), Tokyo, 1949, pp. 94 ff.

60. *Ibid.,* pp. 128–129.

61. *Ibid.,* p. 129. Yŏ Un-hyŏng, unquestionably one of the most brilliant and educated of the Korean leftists, agreed with Kondō. When asked about Yi and Kim Man-gyŏm, he asserted that neither of them knew the essentials of communism or Marxian theory. Yi is the kind of man, said Yŏ, who would not understand what is meant by communism. Yŏ Interrogation, *op. cit.,* p. 41.

For another account of Yi's views, which places stronger emphasis upon his communism but appears to make him a "deviationist" from the two-stage revolutionary theory, see Kim Ku, *op. cit.,* pp. 280–281. According to Kim, one day while he was still premier, Yi asked Kim to take a walk with him. They discussed the Communist movement, with Yi requesting Kim's assistance. Yi said that revolution was necessarily a bloody business. At present, the Korean movement merely aimed at bourgeois revolution, and thus, if it succeeded, a second Communist revolution would be required. The Korean people would be forced to undergo bloodshed twice, a most undesirable thing; hence Kim should join in promoting a Communist revolution now. Kim reported that he then asked Yi whether a Communist revolution could be car-

The first meeting closed with a party, and the following day a more formal committee session was held. Kondō states that the beautiful Mrs. Pak, a Russian, took notes after being given the essentials by Pak in fluent Russian. Kondō produced the documents he was carrying from the Japanese Communists' self-styled preparatory committee, and requested recognition and aid. Many details concerning the Japanese movement and Comintern policy were then discussed. According to Kondō, Pak had a good knowledge of Japanese radical activities. Pak saw no possibility of a tie between the Comintern and Ōsugi, because the latter had not only retained his anarchist views but had even asserted that, if there were outside interference in Japanese affairs, he would not accept aid. Thus Pak designated Kondō as the "number one person."

A discussion of Japanese delegates to the Third Comintern Congress was also conducted. Pak raised the name of Yamakawa. But Kondō indicated that Yamakawa was too ill even to come to Shanghai, so Kondō's name was substituted once again. One of the last items discussed was money. Kondō wrote that he submitted a monthly budget of 20,000 yen, which the group agreed to take up with Moscow. He added that the immediate funds obtained amounted to 6,500 yen (5,000 yen in American currency, the remainder in Japanese). This sum was to be divided into 5,000 yen for expenses in connection with the Communist movement, 1,000 yen for Kondō's personal expenses, and 500 yen as a gift for Ōsugi and for medical expenses (presumably to keep relations between Ōsugi and Kondō smooth, and to phase out relations between Ōsugi and the Comintern).[62]

Kondō's subsequent activities can be dealt with in brief.[63] Through a series of misadventures, he missed the train from Shimonoseki to Tokyo on the eve of his return from Shanghai. He got drunk, ended up in a house of prostitution, became rowdy, and was arrested. The police quickly discovered the money, and after a while learned a considerable part of Kondō's story. However, he was not kept in jail long, and for some unaccountable reason was allowed to take the funds with him upon release. His story was that this was because he promised to spend the money for

---

ried out without taking orders from the Third International. Yi shook his head and said, "No." Kim stated that he then admonished Yi for violating the Constitution of the Provisional Government by being subject to the control of others and asserted that he was no longer willing to receive guidance from Yi as premier.

It is interesting to note that recent Soviet sources, including the work by Kim Sŭng-hwa, totally ignore Yi Tong-hwi, never mentioning his name.

62. Kondō, *op. cit.,* pp. 132–133.

63. For details concerning the early Japanese Communist movement, see the excellent pioneer study by A. Rodger Swearingen and Paul F. Langer, *Red Flag in Japan: International Communism in Action, 1919–1951,* Cambridge, 1952; Scalapino, *The Japanese Communist Movement, op. cit.,* Chapter I; and Beckmann and Okubo, *op. cit.*

personal uses. However this may be, some of the money was later used
for propaganda activities, albeit rather minor ones. In August 1921, Kondō
fostered the creation of a secret group, the Gyōmin Kyōsantō (Enlightened
People's Communist Party) in Tokyo. Its nucleus was composed of the
radical Waseda student group, Gyōminkai (Enlightened Men's Society).
The Gyōmin Kyōsantō printed various posters and handbills. During the
fall military exercises in the Tokyo area, a special attempt was made to
distribute antimilitary leaflets to the soldiers. A number of arrests were
made in November. But after the Shimonoseki mishap, Kondō was not
fully trusted either by the Japanese Communists or by Comintern representatives, and gradually became separated from the movement.

The Clash at Alekseyevsk and Its Repercussions

We have seen that the Shanghai faction played a central role in seeding early Communist movements throughout northeast Asia, although the
effectiveness of most of its initial efforts is open to serious question. Before seeking to analyze the opening stage of Communism in Korea, however, let us describe another aspect of the struggle between rival Korean
factions. By the end of 1920, Japanese forces in Manchuria had launched
a punishing offensive against Korean military units in the Chientao area,
forcing them to retreat into Siberia. In the spring of 1921, these units were
reorganized and amalgamated. On April 12, the Taehan Tongnip-dan
(Greater Korea Independence Corps) was established, with some thirty-
six different organizations participating.[64] One unit was stationed at Iman,
and another at Ningan, in Kirin Province. Meanwhile, negotiations were
being carried out at Chita between the representatives of the Chientao
Korean forces and the Bolsheviks. An agreement was reached whereby
the Koreans would assist the Soviets against their enemies in exchange for
Soviet aid.[65] Korean troops from the east then began to move into the
Chita area. A military academy in Irkutsk was activated for their benefit
and, as we have recounted, Yi and his followers, who were allied with these
troops, appear to have moved their Communist Party headquarters to
Chita on April 25.[66]

At this point, the conflict between the Irkutsk faction and the Chita-

64. Police Affairs Bureau, Korean Government-General, *Taishō jūnen gogatsu
chū Kantō chihō jōkyō no gaiyō* (*Summary of Conditions in the Chientao Area in
May 1921*), June 1921, *AJAN*, R 122, F 36418–37 (at 36436).

Chang Tso-lin, under heavy Japanese pressure at the time, allegedly offered the
Korean guerrillas 15,000 silver yuan (Mexican dollars?) if they would leave Manchurian soil. See Chi Hŏn-mo, *Ch'ŏngch'ŏn Changgun hyŏkmyŏng t'ujaeng-sa,* Seoul,
1949, p. 55.

65. Kōkei DN 29238, 12–5–1921, *AJAN,* R 123, F 36938 ff. See also Ch'ae
Kŭn-sik, *Mujang tongnip undong pisa* (*Secret History of the Armed Independence
Movement*), Seoul, 1947?, pp. 100–102.

66. From Kim Hong-il, who had some involvement in the so-called "Free City

based Korean People's Communist Party (Shanghai faction) mounted on both the political and military fronts. In June 1921, O Ha-muk, Ch'oe Ko-ryŏ, and Kim Ha-sŏk of the Irkutsk faction, supported by the Far Eastern Secretariat of the Comintern in Irkutsk (where Boris Shumiatsky was still in charge), organized the Koryŏ Hyŏngmyŏng Kunjŏng Ŭi-hoe (Korean Revolutionary Military Congress), which insisted that all Korean troops in Siberia were to be united under its command.[67] Naturally, this position was rejected by the Greater Korea Independence Corps on the grounds that the Irkutsk faction, instead of struggling for independence, was scheming to gain control over Korean military forces, and then integrate them with the Bolshevik army.[68] The Irkutsk group, on the other hand, charged the Independence Corps with being an antirevolutionary group adhering solely to nationalism. It was, as we have seen, an old and irreconcilable issue.

On June 27, troops of the Irkutsk faction and their Russian allies surrounded forces of the Independence Corps at Alekseyevsk, some eighty miles north of Blagoveshchensk, and demanded that they lay down their arms immediately. Fighting broke out, and hundreds of Koreans were killed or wounded. Nearly a thousand Independence Corps soldiers were

---

Incident," we have the most detailed account available of developments leading up to the crisis.

Kim, a graduate of a Kweichow military academy, had arrived in Shanghai on Dec. 20, 1920, to find the Provisional Government in deep trouble. He recalls that the Communist faction under Yi was quite strong and even No Paek-rin, the government's minister of defense, was "leaning toward the Communist position." No advised Kim to proceed to Siberia, telling him that Lenin was planning to establish an international army, composed of Korean, Chinese, and Mongolian forces, which could counter the Japanese. He further stated that these forces were to be concentrated in Siberia, and that both he and Yi Tong-hwi would shortly be enroute there.

On his way, Kim persuaded a number of scattered Korean bands in Manchuria to head for Iman (in Siberia). When he reached Iman, he and others sought transportation to Alekseyevsk (now Svobodny), where the new forces were supposedly being gathered. But problems emerged, and the group decided to send Kim on alone so that he could find out about the situation. Kim arrived in Alekseyevsk on June 2, and conferred with Yu Tong-yŏl, one of the key Korean military leaders. Despite the fact that Kim told Yu of No's suggestion to him, Yu told Kim that his troops should wait in Iman, since internal unity among the various groups congregated in Alekseyevsk had not been attained. Yu, O Ha-muk, and a Soviet general were serving as a committee of three to establish the International Army. Kim Hong-il, *op. cit.*

Kim, op was thus waiting at Iman when the fighting commenced.

67. One proclamation of the Korean Revolutionary Military Congress, dated Sept. 30, 1921, is available in full on *AJAN,* R 123, F 36965–67.

68. A statement issued by eleven Korean military groups in Manchuria in September 1921 regarding the Free City Incident sets forth these and other charges. See *AJAN,* R 123, F 36959–64.

captured and taken to Irkutsk, where some of their leaders were imprisoned and a number of the enlisted men mustered into the Red Army. This was the celebrated Free City Incident.[69]

The repercussions were far-reaching. Both factions immediately sought to get representatives to Moscow to present their respective versions of what had happened.[70] The Comintern made its own independent investiga-

69. According to Kim Hong-il, the immediate cause of the bloodshed lay in a conflict between the "Sakhalin Unit" and the "Free Battalion." The former was a partisan group led by Iliya Pak containing many tribal youths. Pak, having been influenced by Yi Tong-hwi earlier, was staunchly nationalist. The "Free Battalion," led by O Ha-muk, one of the Irkutsk leaders, was composed primarily of Russianized Koreans and Mongols, and O himself was thoroughly integrated into the Soviet system.

Kim asserts that some 7,000 troops had been gathered in the area, approximately 1,000 each in the two units noted above, assorted second-generation Korean units from such areas as Iman, and nearly 4,000 Koreans from Manchuria. The sociopolitical makeup of these groups made a unified command structure impossible. Hence, the three military commissars (Yu, O, and the Russian General) made a decision to reorganize the forces totally, mixing the men and assigning each new unit to the command of an officer who had had professional military training, intensive training then being provided either at Irkutsk or Omsk. Those current commanders who did not fit into such a structure would be assigned to party branches. Naturally, such a plan threatened the authority of men like Iliya Pak and most other pure nationalists. Only the Irkutsk leaders would be placed in authority.

Immediately, the Sakhalin Unit leader and others, including Yi Yong, general commander of the non-Irkutsk forces, began to look for means of escape from the area. The Irkutsk group, in turn, set up an intensive surveillance system, determined to prevent the escape of these forces to the east. At this point, it should be noted that as a result of the Nikolaesk Incident in the winter of 1920, when Korean partisans had sacked the city, slaughtering hundreds of people, the Japanese had demanded that all Korean armed groups in Siberia be disarmed by the Soviets as a precondition for any settlement. The Soviet representative had denied that any Korean groups were operating in their territory. For this reason the Soviets wanted to organize an "International Army" to cover up the Korean units. Naturally, if such units escaped and marched east, engaging the Japanese there, it would place the Soviets in a very awkward position.

These were the circumstances, according to Kim, under which the leaders at Alekseyevsk demanded the immediate disarming of the dissident units and their removal to Irkutsk. In the resistance to this order, the Sakhalin Unit was the first to explode: intense fighting occurred. Kim records that some 700–800 men were killed, more than 1,000 were wounded, and a large number were sent to prison or placed in lumbering camps at forced labor. A sizable number, however, did manage to escape, fleeing to the Maritime Province, where they were brought under the command of Yi Yong, Kim Ŭng-ch'ŏn, or Yim Pyŏng-guk.

See also Yŏ Un-hyŏng's *Memoirs, op. cit.,* for another account of the incident.

70. According to Japanese authorities, Yi, greatly disturbed by the Free City Incident, decided to go to Moscow himself to demand that the Comintern take severe disciplinary action against the Irkutsk faction and support him in his efforts to produce a unified Korean Communist Party. It was agreed that the Siberian route was too dangerous, so Yi made plans to leave from Shanghai by sea for western Europe, thence overland to the Soviet Union. To obtain the necessary documents, he persuaded a French Catholic priest who was scheduled to return to France to accept

tion, and a three-man committee composed of Bela Kun, Otto V. Kuusinen, and G. I. Safarov issued a statement on November 15, 1921.[71] The report placed some blame on both sides, and recommended that an equal number of officers from both factions be selected to form a temporary Party Central Committee until further instructions could be given.

Unquestionably, the serious friction within Korean ranks worried and perplexed Russian authorities. They did not know how to deal with it. Meanwhile, disillusionment grew rapidly among those Koreans who had seen Communism primarily as a vehicle to achieve Korean independence. The ranks of the Shanghai faction were particularly affected by the events at Alekseyevsk, and Yi saw many of his followers fade away. The Korean National Council was also racked by dissension.

From two non-Korean sources, further evidence is available. A Japanese specialist on the Korean Communist movement of this period, Hoshino Keigo, emphasizes the strongly Russianized character of the Irkutsk leaders, and their commitment to the Soviet cause. He contrasts them with the Koreans who came from China and Manchuria, who besides being primarily nationalist had a quite different approach to organizational matters. Thus the Manchurian Korean forces adhered to strict military discipline, in the fashion of the Japanese army, but the Irkutsk forces called each other *tovarich,* and made "no distinction between superior and subordinate." [72]

The second source is even more revealing. Only a few months after the Free City Incident, an anonymous Chinese Socialist had a conversation with a man he describes as the head of the Korean National Council in Russia.[73] The conversation took place in Chita in October 1921, while

---

him as "an employee." Complications in obtaining a passport and visa delayed matters. Finally they sailed on July 20, with Pak Chin-sun accompanying Yi as a Russian interpreter. The trip proved to be a fiasco: en route, the French priest died; Yi attempted to return to Shanghai but, because of passport problems, became stranded in some British port. Yi waited there for five months until finally he and Pak received permission to proceed to Paris, on January 10, 1922. As a result, they did not arrive in Moscow in time for the "First Congress of the Toilers of the Far East," as we shall later note.

See Kōkei DN 4105, 15–1–1923, *op. cit.*

71. We are indebted to Dae-Sook Suh's research on this point. He uncovered two important sources relating to the Comintern report: Yamauchi Shirō, "Kyōsantō ni kansuru yakushutsu bunsho sōfu no ken" ("Concerning the Sending of Translated Materials of the Communist Party") *AJAN,* R S721 (S.9.4.5.2–30), and *Taishō jūichinen Chōsen chian jōkyō sono: ni kokugai* (*The State of Public Peace and Order in Korea in 1922*), Section 2 Abroad, *AJMFA,* R SP 46, pp. 430–9.

72. Hoshino Keigo, *Zaiman senjin ni tsuite* (*Concerning the Koreans in Manchuria*), No. 1, April 1928, pp. 5–7.

73. "Yu-chê Kuan-ch'a" ("Observations of a Traveler"), *Hsin O Hui-hsiang-lu* (*Recollections of the New Russia*) (hereafter cited as Observations of a Traveler), no publication place or date (possibly published in 1924), original in Hoover Library, pp. 11–13.

the author was en route to Moscow. We must treat his report with care since he was strongly anti-Communist when he wrote the book from which it is taken. But much of what he tells us is confirmed from other sources. His Korean informant, he says, was an unhappy and rather bitter man. Dissension had long existed between the National Council and the Irkutsk group, but the former had been promised Russian aid if they would unite. However, negotiations for a united front had broken down over the question of who would control the military forces. Earlier, when Japanese pressure had grown heavy in Manchuria, the Bolsheviks had given arms to Korean miners and farmers. Together with certain National Council troops, they had withdrawn into Siberia. But the Irkutsk group had sought to assert their authority with Russian assistance, and a bloody battle had resulted. The Korean leader supposedly concluded his conversation by asserting that, among Koreans, only "shallow youth" really espoused the Communist cause; most others merely paid lip service to it, and were primarily interested in Korean independence.

From these sources and many others, we can appreciate the crisis that had engulfed the Korean Communist movement by mid-1921. The Shanghai faction, now under a cloud as far as many Russian leaders were concerned, still had control over various military and political organizations in Manchuria and the Siberian Maritime Province. Membership in the Korean People's Communist Party (Yi Tong-hwi's faction) was estimated at about 6,000, whereas the Irkutsk Party reportedly had about 4,500 members.[74] The Shanghai faction was itself the complex product of numerous alliances. Its leadership was professedly Communist but its immediate objectives were strongly nationalist, and, as we have noted, there was ample reason to suspect both the depth and the orthodoxy of its leaders' Marxist-Leninist convictions. It wanted an alliance with the new Soviet government in order to support its struggle for independence; some of its spokesmen even saw the Soviet state as a possible model for a new Korea. But nationalist strains clearly predominated over those of international Communism. Indeed, many members of the Yi faction found it difficult if not impossible to accept the status of being a branch of an international movement controlled by Moscow. They did not want to be absorbed in any fashion by the Russians. And since they were separated from the Irkutsk faction by violent personal cleavages as well as by matters of policy and orientation, they also had no intention of being controlled either politically or militarily by these "Russianized Koreans."

The Irkutsk faction was a heterogeneous group too. Although it was dominated by Russianized Koreans it included a number of Shanghai op-

74. *Ibid.* When auxiliary organizations and military forces available to the two factions, particularly the Red Army, were added, however, the Irkutsk faction was undoubtedly stronger in contests involving sheer power.

ponents of the Yi–Kim Rip forces who could not be so classified. More-over, because it was more fully integrated with the Siberian Bolshevik movement, it obtained increasing support from Soviet and Comintern authorities in the field. Nevertheless, the more purely nationalist elements within the Irkutsk faction cannot be overlooked, as we shall note later. Many individuals had joined this group for personal not policy reasons, because they were anti-Yi.

At this point, relations between the two factions were so bad that friendly contact of any type was out of the question. Travelers carrying letters of introduction from one faction were in mortal peril if they were intercepted by associates of the other. Members of the Shanghai faction en route to Russia had to choose very circuitous routes in order to avoid Irkutsk territory. A pattern of assassinations began to emerge, with vio-lence on both sides.

This situation was of course enormously troublesome to the new Soviet government, dedicated as it was to the concept of an alliance with key Asian nationalist movements. Moreover, it was a government that wanted maximum pressure exerted against Japan. In theory, at least, it did not demand that all recipients of its aid be Communists. Indeed, as will be recalled, when Lenin first authorized assistance to the Koreans, he thought the funds were going to the Provisional Government, and he con-tinued to urge the creation of unified nationalist movements composed of Communists and non-Communists. But to apply this principle successfully was very difficult, as the situation with respect to Koreans now indicated. Of course, the Korean problem had its special complexities: many Koreans were Russian citizens, and it was natural to seek their further integration into Soviet politics and the Soviet armed forces. But it was also natural that some of these Russianized Koreans, with local Bolshevik support, should attempt to take over the direction of the entire Korean nationalist-Communist movement, much of which was now based in Soviet territory.

The Moscow Congress of Asian "Toilers"

This was the situation in the summer of 1921, when the Soviet leaders were preparing for the first major conference of Far Eastern peoples. The conference was originally scheduled for Irkutsk in the late summer or early fall, and was intended as a sequel to the Baku Conference of Sep-tember 1920, which had been attended mainly by delegates from the Mid-dle East. But it was also planned as the Soviet answer to the Washington Conference. Competition between the Soviet Union and the United States for the support of Asian peoples can be dated from this time, although initially Moscow was much more aware of this fact than Washington.

For various reasons, the conference site and time were changed. The recruitment and transportation of delegates were more difficult and took more time than had been envisaged, and a number of mishaps occurred.[75] Finally, on January 21, 1922, the so-called First Congress of the Toilers of the Far East opened in Moscow.[76] The sessions ran until February 2, the final meeting being held in Petrograd.

Koreans took a prominent part in this conference. Of the 144 accredited delegates, more than one-third, or 52, were Koreans. The next largest delegation, from China, numbered 37. The English-language edition of the conference proceedings contains a statistical analysis of 48 members of the Korean group with respect to age, occupation, and party affiliation.[77] In age they ranged from twenty to fifty-five, with the largest number being under thirty-five. In occupation, 25 were classified as "peasants," 18 as "intellectuals," only 3 as "workers," and 2 as "other." Ten members of the delegation had had higher education and an additional 29 had had intermediate schooling. Like most of the delegations, the Korean group was dominated by young intellectuals—or more accurately, "petty intellectuals."

According to the Soviet account, 37 of the 48 delegates polled pronounced themselves members of the Communist Party, with an additional 5 stipulating that they were Communist Youth League members. Thus the delegation was heavily "Communist," and from the various sources available it would appear that the Irkutsk faction had the larger representation. Only a few of the Korean delegates can be identified. They included Kim Shi-hyŏn, Chang Kŏn-sang, Yŏ Un-hyŏng, Kim Kyu-sik, Ra (Na) Yong-gyun, Kim Wŏn-gyŏng, Kim Tan-ya, Pak Hŏn-yŏng, and, of course, Yi Tong-hwi, who arrived late with Pak Chin-sun. Most of these delegates came via Siberia. Yŏ has related that he left Shanghai in late November 1921; traveling with Kim Kyu-sik and Ra Yong-gyun he crossed the Gobi desert, proceeded to Moscow via the Trans-Siberian Railway, and arrived

75. For example, Kim Ch'an told the Japanese police that Shumiatsky and Voitinsky had requested Shigeki Kyūhei and himself to bring thirty Japanese delegates from Harbin to Irkutsk but, according to Kim, Shigeki misspent the money and hence the delegates could not come. "Preliminary Trial of Kim Ch'an (alias Kim Nak-jun)" (hereafter cited as Kim Ch'an Trial), Kōtō Hōin, Kenjikyoku, Prosecutor's Bureau, High Court, *Shisō geppō* (*Thought Monthly*), Vol. 2, No. 2, May 1932, *AJMFA*, R S357, pp. 1882–3.

76. Various private accounts of this Congress from Asian participants are available. The following were very useful: Observations of a Traveler, *op. cit.;* Arahata Kanson, *Roshiya ni hairu* (*Entering Russia*), Tokyo, 1924; Kondō Eizō, *op. cit.;* Yŏ Interrogation, *op. cit.;* Suzuki Mosaburō, *Aru shakaishugisha no hansei* (*Half the Life of a Certain Socialist*), Tokyo, 1958; Watanabe Tomoo, *Katayama Sen to tomo ni* (*Together with Katayama Sen*), Tokyo, 1955. Robert A. Scalapino also conducted interviews with Chang Kŏn-sang, Seoul, Sept. 28, 1957, and Chang Kuo-t'ao, Hong Kong, Nov. 27, 1957. Chong-Sik Lee has interviewed Ra Yong-gyun, Seoul, Aug. 26, 1969. The official English-language record is *The First Congress of the Toilers of the Far East,* published by The Communist International, Petrograd, 1922.

77. *Ibid.,* p. 238.

there in mid-January.[78] Of course, a large delegation went from Irkutsk itself. A few Koreans approached Moscow from the West. Yi Tong-hwi and Pak Chin-sun, as we noted earlier, were delayed by a series of accidents. One account suggests that they were accompanied by a Chinese

78. Yŏ Interrogation, *op. cit.,* p. 34.

Fortunately, we have also located a portion of a six-part memoir written by Yŏ Un-hyŏng about his trip to Moscow in 1921, published in the magazine *Chung-ang* (*The Center*) in 1936. After a miserable trip across the Gobi Desert and Outer Mongolia, Yŏ arrived at the Soviet border and spent a few days in Safarov's house before pushing on to Irkutsk where the conference was originally scheduled to be held. En route, he spent three days at Verkhneudinsk. On the last day, they were taken to an old train to wait departure. "In the evening, a Russian came in with a dark log and proceeded to split it with an ax. We thought he was going to kindle the stove. But, in fact, it was dark bread. It contained not merely flour, but straw as well. Old and solidly frozen. It could only be cut with an ax. This bread plus some fish eggs and salted fish was all we had for dinner . . . We had one sugar cube each. . . . There was no heat in the train, and the temperature was 30 degrees below zero."

When the train arrived from Moscow enroute to Chita, conditions improved somewhat. They had heat and the black bread did not have to be cut with an ax. There were even candies and meat. But "signs of famine and war were everywhere. . . . We saw Korean women in Korean dresses carrying water on top of their heads. They lived in Siberian style farm houses that were about to fall down. We wanted to jump out and talk to them."

After recounting their arrival in Irkutsk, Yŏ relates how he was drafted to serve as a juror in the trial of "the reactionaries" involved in the Black River (Alekseyevsk) Incident. His account of the incident is essentially the same as we have reported, although much briefer, and biased against the Yi faction. He reports that "several tens" were being tried and minimizes the punishments meted out, but admits that "this trial oppressed us causing great anxiety and depression."

In December, suddenly "a surprising order" was received directing the "delegates" to proceed to Moscow. Yŏ explains that the conference had originally been planned for November to counter the Washington Conference, but since it was already too late for this the decision had been made to bring the delegates to Moscow so they could observe the New Russia in its construction phase from the capital.

Yŏ traveled to Moscow in a first-class compartment, with Shumiatsky and his officers. When they reached Moscow, moreover, he was chosen to give words of greeting to the Russian crowd that had been assembled at the station to meet them. "Although the temperature was 30 degrees below zero, I was sweating when I finished my speech in English."

We have one additional account, that of Ra Yong-gyun, interviewed on Aug. 26, 1969, by Chong-Sik Lee. Ra had traveled with Kim Kyu-sik and Yŏ Un-hyŏng. According to him, the three had received funds from Yi Tong-hwi to make the trip. They were aided by the son of a Peking American professor, one Coleman, who was a leather-and-skin dealer in Changchiak'ou.

Ra also comments on the extreme cold and the bad food. "The bread in Russia at that time was a mixture of mud and wheat stalks. Only about 25% of it was wheat flour. As soon as you ate it, you got diarrhea. . . . Even though the Russians there [in the hostel where he stayed] were allegedly Communists, a ten cent tip went a long way in getting better service."

Because Ra had become friendly with Mun Shi-hwan, who was Yi Tong-hwi's

Communist, Yao Tso-pin, and that, when they finally reached Germany, Wilhelm Pieck, the well-known German Communist leader, joined them in the pilgrimage to Moscow.[79]

When a delegate reached the Soviet border, he no longer needed to worry about expenses, since he became a guest of the Soviet government. Ordinarily he received very good treatment, often the very best that could be provided. This was a difficult period in the Soviet Union, however. Inflation was extremely serious. There were major food shortages, and prices were fantastically high. Accommodations were often very meager. While the most important leaders were housed at the Lux Hotel (for example, Yi Tong-hwi and Katayama Sen), lesser figures usually had very austere quarters. Our Chinese author grumbles that some of the lodgings resembled "third-class hospital rooms."[80] Yŏ stayed in the same Greek Orthodox church where the conference meetings were held after the opening session.

Thus, many of the Asian visitors were disappointed in the "workers' paradise." As we have noted, some had serious complaints about food, transport, and general living conditions. Others were shocked by the privation they saw among the Russian people. But there were also points upon which a number of them were prepared to comment favorably: the stress on education, the seeming absence of racial discrimination, and the heightened interest shown toward Asia and the Asian.

The conference opened within the Kremlin, in the theater, on the evening of January 21. A huge picture of Marx hung as a stage backdrop to chairs for some specially invited workers' representatives, a table, and additional chairs for the conference chairman and seven or eight committeemen. Everywhere were hung banners with Chinese, Japanese, and

---

secretary at the time, he was watched closely by the dominant Irkutsk group. Moreover, his problems deepened. He refused to sign a lengthy declaration prepared by Kim Kyu-sik, Yŏ Un-hyŏng, Ch'oe Ch'ang-sik, and others highly laudatory of Communism. According to Ra, he stated that his group had not authorized him to sign such a statement, despite the fact that everyone else had joined either the Communist Party or the Communist Youth League—at least nominally, for many were not Communists. In the ensuing argument, Ra threw an ashtray at Ch'oe Ch'ang-sik. Some time later, a Russian soldier came to his room and took him to an execution stand. Twelve soldiers aimed their guns at him, and then put the guns down; this performance was repeated a second time. According to Ra, a second Korean, Paek Nam-jun, who had refused to affix his seal to the document, was similarly treated.

Moreover, after he returned to Shanghai, Ra asserted, he was shot at by men of the Irkutsk faction, the bullet grazing his clothing and hitting a companion, Yun Hae, who was hospitalized for five months.

To add to his disasters, Ra then learned that his father, who had also contributed funds for their trip, had been sentenced to six months in the Hamhŭng prison in Korea.

79. Yi Kŭk-no, *Kot'u sasim-nyŏn (Forty Years of Struggle)*, Seoul, 1947, pp. 28–31.

80. Observations of a Traveler, *op. cit.*, pp. 146–147.

Korean characters. The first ten rows of seats were reserved for the delegates, some 150 in all, with nonvoting delegates and spectators sitting in the rear. The business sessions really began the next day; according to one source, they were not well attended.[81]

81. "A Chinese Traveler" wrote that, after the opening session, only 10 to 20 percent of the delegates attended the meetings. *Ibid.*, p. 154.

Based upon a 1921 trip to Moscow, "Ernestine Evans" (a pseudonym) wrote a fascinating article, including first-hand observations of "The University of the Toiling Masses of the Eastern Autonomous and Associated Republics," to which a number of Asians were being sent, and on the Moscow Conference, which she (he?) observed. The article is entitled "Looking East from Moscow," *Asia*, XXII, No. 12, Dec. 1922, pp. 972–976, 1011–1012.

Evans' comments are worthy of extensive quotation. Describing the arrival of "four car-loads" of Asians on the Trans-Siberian Railway, "she" related: "European hangers-on at the Hotel Lux were turned out to make room for them. The Third Soviet House, a former seminary for Russian Orthodox priests, put clean sheets on its beds and arranged wards for Koreans, for Mongolians, for Japanese, for Siberians, for Chinese. 'Welcome' and 'Workers of the World Unite,' painted in ideographs, hung on scarlet pennants over the seminary door. Stacked pine-trees scented the seminary dooryard. A sledge-load of black bread and kegs of herrings arrived at the seminary kitchen."

Of the opening night of the Conference in Sverdlov Hall, Evans, after commenting on the dubious credentials of many of the delegates, wrote: "The usual chalky, bewhiskered bust of Karl Marx, draped in streamers with Chinese and Japanese characters, towered over the platform. Across the aisle from me sat a Mongolian prince in salmon-pink robe; beside me a Chinese student read *The New Republic*. Making far too much noise in the row behind was an ugly little Mongolian 'Peck's Bad Boy' who had got himself adopted by the delegation and thought the whole show an adventure in getting free victuals."

The author then described the progression of the Conference, from Shumiatsky's opening speech of welcome through the endless speeches that followed. In a priceless aside, Evans related for posterity this item:

"Bucharin, editor of *Pravda*, sat on the platform, mocking the endless addresses of welcome and scribbling the following parody, which he passed on to a visiting Englishman (the author?)—but never printed in his paper:

People, O People!
East, O East!
(I beg pardon) Far East, O Far East!
Anyway, People, O People!
I have to apologize to you that you should have today to endure four and twenty addresses of welcome.
But remember that the sacred cause of the World Revolution calls for sacrifice.
Remember, too, that your trials are as nothing to ours,
who had, during five long years, sword in hand, to read Stekloff's daily editorials in *Izvestia*.
On the Workers' and Peasants' Republic the sun never sets. (That is why we have a famine.)
The day you arrived in Moscow the snow was falling.

The main themes of the Moscow congress were set forth by chairman
Grigorii Zinoviev in his opening remarks of January 21 and in a second

Pay no heed to that. It was a white plot.
Und so weiter."

Perhaps it is small wonder that Bukharin, given that sense of humor—and
realism—could not survive the Stalin era.

Evans' comments about the Koreans are of particular interest here. "There
were fifty-two Koreans," he noted, "representing various organizations and classes.
They came from Vladivostok, from Manchuria, from Shanghai. Fifteen, with prices
on their heads, had slipped out of Korea. They had boarded boats on the Yalu River
and landed on the Manchurian side. A good number of the delegates were belted and
spurred, men of the 'Korean army'—that is, members of the irregular Partisan troops
in Siberia. Kim See [Kim Kyu-sik], chairman of the delegation, estimated the
number of Korean soldiers and officers in Siberia as several thousand. 'If there is
ever an American-Japanese war,' he said, 'our irregulars are not ignoble allies for
the Americans.' These Koreans had fought steadily with the Russians against Japanese intervention, thus, according to some nationalist views, gaining valuable experience and, according to others, dissipating their national strength on Russia's
behalf.

"Kim See [See in Korean means 'Mister'] was a young man, a graduate of
Roanoke College in Virginia. The Provisional Korean government at Shanghai, of
which he was a Cabinet member, had sent him as a delegate to Versailles. Thence,
because some of the leaders in Shanghai clung to hope in Wilson, he had advanced
to Washington as head of the Korean mission there. His experience had made him
cynical. He might have been spared his cynicism if he had only not entertained the
hope that the United States would go the limit on behalf of Korea—the limit being
war with Tokyo.

"Now he was a professing communist, for two reasons. He had seen the communist analysis of the world situation and he had no more faith than the Russian
Communists in reformist tactics in the East. Moreover, if there was no spiritual
or material hope for Korea in Moscow, there was none anywhere. He had come
to the last resort: I thought he had come a little sadly, as we sat there in the Korean
dormitory, talking over his country's chances.

"Beside him sat a jovial soul, named Hyung, I believe, who told me that he
was a 'parson,' a divine ordained in the Methodist Episcopal Church by Bishop
Harris himself. He had taken the first Korean emigrants, seeking freedom, to
Hawaii. He had found Christian Hawaii discouraging to any and all revolutionary
projects that did not bear directly on sugar profits. He said he had seen his colony
grow to eight thousand and dwindle to four thousand. He had two thousand members in his native church. But he had it in mind to have a much larger congregation
and he was going to preach communism to Korean Christians.

"Beside him sat another Korean, a sober business man connected with a mission
book company in Shanghai (Yŏ Un-hyŏng). He had taken three months off to come
to Moscow in order to be able to advise his associates on what would be wise Korean
policy in dealing with the Russians. He agreed with a well-known American observer
of the Far East, who had said to me: 'The Russians are the greatest political dreamers
and theoreticians in the world. They are always weaving a perfect and fantastic
political pattern, filmy spider-webs. They seem to spin them out of their own bodies.
They are at the same time very practical politicians. My advice to the Koreans is to
beware of sitting spellbound while the Russians spin schemes. At the practical moment the Russians will be thinking of Russia, and neither of the Dream without End,
nor of the Korean Republic. Naturally.' "

speech of January 23.[82] First, complete Communist victory would come only through *world revolution*. The Third International, recognizing that fact, was the first revolutionary organization to seek the membership and support of the world proletariat. Zinoviev was contemptuous of the provincial, Europe-centered attitude of rival Western reformers and Socialists. Only when areas like Asia were totally free of Western domination, he assured his audience, would the world Communist movement have achieved its primary goals. Hence, the Communists were especially interested in the "toiling, oppressed masses of the East." Accordingly, a leading theme of the conference was "Asia first."

Second, the competition offered by the West, and particularly by the United States, to Communist (Russian) influence in Asia was clearly recognized. Moscow had organized this conference as an answer to Washington, and the central target was never forgotten. Zinoviev described the Four-Power Treaty achieved a few weeks earlier as an "Alliance of the Four Bloodsuckers." He denounced in the strongest possible language Western actions at Versailles ("the Wilson betrayal") and the subsequent refusal of the Western powers to acknowledge "the legitimate aspirations of the Asian people for independence." Here, attention could be focused directly on the Korean group. Certain elements were therefore chided for having put their faith in America, and were admonished against continuing this folly. Again and again, the theme was reiterated: Washington stands only for the status quo. Korean nationalism could not be advanced except by reliance upon Soviet Russia and the world proletariat. "The word 'Korea,' " Zinoviev charged, "was not even mentioned at the Washington Conference, as though Korea did not exist upon the globe, as though at Washington were assembled such powers that never heard of the existence of Korea. . . . If the Korean people needed any other lessons then I think that they can get no more convincing lesson than the one furnished by the silence in Washington." [83]

The third broad theme pertained to nationalist-Communist interaction, the vital center of Leninism, and of current Soviet tactics. Zinoviev and other Russian speakers gave full support to the decisions of the Second Comintern Congress. All possible assistance was to be given the great nationalist uprisings against Western (and Japanese) imperialism and capitalism. This was to be the main line of Communist policy. At the same time, however, the limitations of nationalism, its dangers, and its essentially transient character had to be fully appreciated. For example, there could be no legitimate national antagonism among the toilers of Japan, China, Korea, and Mongolia. And at no point should nationalism itself become a primary goal, when only proletarian brotherhood and alliance with the Soviet Union could forward the legitimate aspirations of the workers of

82. *The First Congress of the Toilers of the Far East, op. cit.*, pp. 3–6, 21–39.
83. Speech of Zinoviev, 2nd Session, Jan. 23, 1922, *ibid.*, p. 25.

the world. In short, the ingenious Leninist doctrine of simultaneous support for and opposition to nationalism was powerfully set forth by the Soviet speakers.[84]

Safarov, sitting as a member of the presidium of the congress, in his speech of January 26 elaborated upon these themes and their relevance for the Korean situation.

> The problems confronting the toiling masses of Korea are more simple. There as well as in China we shall support any national revolutionary movement which stands against any compromises with imperialism and is ready to go persistently to the goal of national emancipation. We shall not become confused and hesitate over the fact that some of these organizations are peasant societies, and others are religious sects, etc.
>
> While fully realizing that this movement is a bourgeois democratic movement, we are nevertheless supporting it, as we support every nationalist movement for emancipation, because it is directed against imperialism and because it is in harmony with the interests of the international proletariat. And we demand this also from the Korean workers. There, it is Japanese imperialism which is the imperialist power which has destroyed the Korean aristocracy. Therefore, it is right to speak there of the united national front, but, at the same time, one must expose, in the most determined fashion, every attempt to achieve the emancipation of the country by compromise and pacifism.[85]

The speeches of Zinoviev and Safarov made abundantly clear the policy to be followed by the Korean Communists. It was the Leninist policy of a broad nationalist coalition, that is, an alliance of Communist and nationalist forces. It seems unlikely that the Russians could have approved the departure of Yi and his followers from the Provisional Government, although they probably had no opportunity to affect Yi's decision. For the Korean Communists, as for the Chinese, the first task was to concentrate upon consummating the bourgeois-democratic nationalist revolution. At the same time, however, none of the internal integrity of the Communist movement was to be sacrificed. Those elements of the nationalist movement who persisted in looking to the West, advocating "compromise and pacifism" and other "reactionary" policies, were to be rigorously attacked and undermined. Yŏ later confirmed this general policy by saying that at the Far Eastern peoples' conference, it was decided that the Korean revolutionary movement should be conducted by supporting the Provisional Government, encouraging and *modifying* it; and that since Korea was an agrarian

84. As we have noted from certain remarks directed to "Ernestine Evans," and the later recollections of Ra Yong-gyun and others, however, this tactic was far from uniformly successful in wooing Asian nationalists to the Communist cause.

85. Speech of Safarov, Jan. 26, 1922, *ibid.*, pp. 167–168.

country without knowledge of communism, the emphasis should be upon nationalism, with the peasants as primary targets.[86]

It was easy for Korean speakers of varying political persuasion to give verbal support to this policy, with its various provisos and caveats. One Communist speaker, "Kor-Khan," put it this way:

> We shall unreservedly support all nationalist revolutionary and bourgeois organizations, but only insofar as these organizations will not follow the imperialists, will have no connection with the imperialists, with these world plunderers, and will not extend them even a finger. I declare that with the element which will carry out a conciliatory policy, we the Korean Communists, will never unite. Our Communist Party which has for a long time had under its influence 7,126,000 farm labourers, 300,000 industrial workers and 292,127 fishermen aims at the union of all the proletarian elements of Korea and all possible cooperation with revolutionary and bourgeois organizations, but not with those which stand for a reconciliatory policy.[87]

Setting aside the fantastic exaggerations about Korean Communist Party influence, these remarks give a very good indication of how Leninist doctrines on the united front were intended to be interpreted.

At an earlier point the speaker had laid bare certain internal problems within the Korean Communist movement itself. Speaking of those who wanted to go to Washington, but not to Irkutsk, he said:

> Among us, there are such "Communists" who act like bats. It was these very persons, among whom there are some who call themselves members of some Party Central Committee, that supported the sending of a representative of the Shanghai Government to the Washington Conference.
>
> They emphasized the necessity of it and even put some obstacles in the way of our delegates who were leaving for the Congress of the Toilers of the Far East. They said: "If the Washington imperialists find out that our representatives are going to Irkutsk in order to participate in the Congress of the Toilers of the East, they will, perhaps, refuse to admit our representatives. Do not go to Irkutsk. Washington will solve our destinies." [88]

No one could deny that anyone taking this position would have to be accounted a bad Communist. But the statement sounds suspiciously like an embroidering of the facts so as to score against the Shanghai faction. There can be no doubt that non-Communist nationalists talked in this fashion, and it is probably also true that some Communists favored approaches to the West as well as to the Soviet Union. There is no evidence, however,

86. Yŏ Interrogation, *op. cit.*, p. 34.
87. Speech of "Kor-Khan," 9th Session, Jan. 27, 1922, *The First Congress of the Toilers of the Far East*, p. 178.
88. *Ibid.*, p. 177,

that any important element within the Yi faction favored shunning Moscow, nor does it seem logical.

Every Korean speaker paid his respects to the three major themes outlined by Zinoviev and Safarov. The idea of Asians participating as equals in the world revolutionary movement, the concept of partnership with the West, was particularly appealing. Despite Kipling, said "Pak-Kieng" (Pak Chin-sun?), East and West were meeting in Moscow.[89] And the attack upon Washington struck home especially to the Koreans. "Pak-Kieng" began his speech by asserting that Moscow, the past symbol of imperial despotism and expansion, was now the center of the world revolutionary movement, welcoming the oppressed peoples of the Far East, whereas Washington, once a symbol of liberty, now stood at the "center of the world's capitalist exploitation and imperialist expansion." [90] The Soviet attack on Washington had indeed struck home!

In certain respects, then, the Lenin government scored a signal success with the Moscow congress of 1922. Moscow had offered support and guidance at a time when most Asian nationalist movements were weak, malleable, and in desperate need of external aid. Many Asian nationalists were disillusioned with the West and ready for a change. Here was their chance—and the strings were not always visible. Not only their policies, but also their egos were catered for. Compared to the treatment of Korean delegations at Versailles and Washington, the reception given to the Koreans at the Moscow congress amounted to lionization. The Soviet leaders played upon their pride and sense of importance, while the West gave them an inferiority complex. Perhaps the most surprising thing is that more Koreans did not shift their attention—and their ideology—to the East.

There was, however, another side to this picture. This was a time of transition toward the New Economic Policy, and conditions in Russia were bad. As has been mentioned, delegates could not close their eyes completely to this fact. Moreover, even in the formal conference, "pure" nationalism caused some trouble, particularly since few of the delegates were truly Communists.

The Intensification of Factional Struggles

It is difficult to gather details about political activities taking place behind the scenes. Unfortunately, in the Korean case these were of supreme importance. As has been noted, Yi was long delayed in reaching the Soviet capital. When he arrived, the Irkutsk faction had been present in force for a considerable time, and its claims had been widely circulated among Moscow officials. Indeed, at an earlier point the Irkutsk faction had gone to some pains to seek out Comintern officials traveling in Asia so that their

89. Speech of "Pak-Kieng," 1st Session, Jan. 21, 1922, *ibid.*, p. 13.
90. *Ibid.*, p. 12. See also Pak-Kieng's second, more lengthy speech, "The Korean Revolutionary Movement," 2nd Session, Jan. 23, 1922, *ibid.*, pp. 74–98.

case could be presented at the first opportunity. Yŏ later credited their strong position to the fact that they had gotten to the Russians first.[91]

This is not the whole story. After all, the Shanghai faction had had representatives like Han Hyŏng-gwŏn in Moscow continuously, and contact could certainly be made with Voitinsky in Shanghai. There is some reason to believe that the Irkutsk faction had had the edge from the very beginning. We have already noted that Shumiatsky gave his support to it when it was first organized in 1919. Probably the embezzlement charge against Kim Rip further compromised Yi and his followers in the eyes of the Comintern. At any rate, Voitinsky appears to have been close to Kim Man-gyŏm after Kim's break with the Yi–Kim Rip team.

Once again, our anonymous Chinese author has written a revealing account of Korean Communist factionalism as he observed it in Moscow.[92] We cannot check everything he says but, according to him, the Korean Communists were divided into two groups. The first comprised the "old revolutionaries," men like "Yi" (Yi Tong-hwi?), "Han" (Hyŏng-gwŏn?), and "Kim" (Kim Rip?). This group had contacts with the Shanghai Provisional Government and the Korean National Council in Russia. They were also "old friends of Lenin and Trotsky." [93] The other faction was composed of younger men. It had been organized following the Russian Revolution, in close cooperation with the Far Eastern Bureau of the Comintern, set up in Irkutsk by Shumiatsky. Voitinsky had followed him there, and later centered operations in Shanghai. Both the new Korean group and "that certain Chinese group" (Ch'en Tu-hsiu's "Chinese Communist Party"?) were the work of these two, and they had the support of the head of the Far Eastern Department of the Third International.

The author described these men as "ruthless," and said that the old Korean revolutionaries distrusted them, but could do nothing about the situation. According to him, an attempt was actually made by the Irkutsk faction and their Russian allies to exclude the Yi group from participation in the congress. Some of the author's details here are in error, but the general story appears to be true. He noted that Yi and Shumiatsky were bitter opponents, especially after the Free City Incident. Prior to Yi's arrival in Moscow, Shumiatsky reportedly sought to prevent Yi's delegate (Han Hyŏng-gwŏn?) from participating in the activities. The author as-

91. Yŏ Interrogation, op. cit., p. 53.
92. Observations of a Traveler, op. cit., pp. 111–113.
93. Ra Yong-gyun partially confirmed this remark in the following manner: "Shumiatsky was the head of the Irkutsk group, but he was a terrible man. Krasnoshchekov was in Chita, seat of the Far Eastern Republic. The difficulty was that the Irkutsk faction were the running dogs of Shumiatsky and the Chita faction were the running dogs of Krasnoshchekov. They constantly engaged in factional struggles. When I went to Moscow, moreover, I found that the Irkutsk faction were aligned with the Zinoviev faction, and the Chita faction were with the Trotsky faction." Chong-Sik Lee interview with Ra Yong-gyun.

serted that Yi actually did not arrive in Moscow until after the congress was over, which checks out. He adds that Yi's name was omitted from the list of signatures appended to the congress resolutions, and that when Lenin noticed this he insisted Yi be asked to sign, since he was a famous revolutionary whose name would carry weight throughout East Asia. According to our author, however, Yi declined when approached by one of the functionaries and, when told that it was his duty as a Communist Party member, replied that he would do so only if he were presented with a written order from the Communist Party.

We have confirmation of the enmity between Yi and Shumiatsky from another Chinese source. Chiang K'ang-hu, a well-known non-Communist Socialist, was in Russia at this time.[94] Chiang wrote that Yi and his group blamed Shumiatsky personally for the Free City Incident. They regarded him as the real boss of the Irkutsk movement, and charged that, even before the bloody conflict at Alekseyevsk, he had jailed those Korean revolutionaries who opposed him. He had even executed such staunch radicals as Ke Pong-u, Kim Chin, and Chang To-jŏng. Thus Yi, Pak, and others were coming to Moscow to bring charges against Shumiatsky before the Comintern. According to Chiang, the reason Yi and his companions had traveled by way of Europe rather than Siberia was their fear of being "taken care of" by Shumiatsky.

Some type of hearing or debate was held on this matter. The Yi group sought Shumiatsky's dismissal, return of the Koreans imprisoned by him and the Irkutsk group—at least those of them who were still living —and payment of proper compensation. Chiang wrote, however, that Shumiatsky had strong support at this time, both from Russian circles in the Comintern and from the Irkutsk group itself. (Our anonymous source tells us he soon quarreled with his superior and lost his position.) In any case, Yi was defeated in his campaign against his rivals.

The Yi group had some assets that saved them from being liquidated. As has been noted, they had long had contacts with the top Soviet leadership, and Lenin in particular seems to have wanted Yi in the fold. Perhaps this was largely because Yi did have great personal prestige among Koreans of diverse political views—or so Lenin and some others thought. Thus, the Yi group were able to save Yao Tso-pin when he came under heavy attack by Chinese opponents as a "false Communist" (he was, however, forced to leave Russia).[95] And Yŏ told Japanese interrogators that the Russian government did consider arresting Yi for having aided in the embezzlement of Comintern funds. But the idea was abandoned because it was feared that if Yi, the most famous Communist Party leader of Korea, were ar-

94. Kiang Kang-hu (Chiang K'ang-hu), *Kiang Kang-hu hsin-O yu-chi* (*The Record of Kiang Kang-hu's Travels in the New Russia*) (English title: *One Year in Soviet Russia*), Shanghai, 1923, pp. 61 ff.
95. Observations of a Traveler, *op. cit.*, p. 110.

rested, many Koreans would resent the Comintern and the entire movement might be jeopardized.[96] Yŏ also confessed that, in the course of the Moscow congress, M. I. Yurin told him the Soviet government had no intention of paying the additional 1.4 million rubles remaining from the grant made by Lenin to the Yi group, because they were disappointed in the actions of the Koreans.[97] Behind the scenes, there must have been much tough talk of this nature, especially to the Shanghai faction.

Reconciliation by Fiat

When spring arrived, the two major Korean Communist factions were still at odds. Intense reconciliation efforts had already been conducted in Moscow, Chita, Shanghai and elsewhere. On April 22, 1922, in the aftermath of yet another abortive unification effort, the Comintern finally issued a six-point directive. Those who had been punished and deprived of Party membership by the Irkutsk Party as a result of the Free City Incident were to be restored to full status; four individuals, Pak Chin-sun, Pak Ae, Ch'oe Ko-ryŏ, and Kim Kyu-guk, were to be prohibited from Party activities until unity had been achieved; unification was to be accomplished within three months; until it was accomplished, no further financial assistance would be given to the Korean Communist Party by the Comintern, and the remainder of the Comintern's earlier grant would have to be returned; the Korean Communist Party was to establish its headquarters at Chita, with both Irkutsk and Shanghai headquarters to be closed, and the Party was to concentrate henceforth on establishing itself inside Korea; finally, efforts were to be made to convert Koreans resident in China and Siberia to the Communist movement.[98]

In the main, this directive represented a defeat for Yi and his followers. But they had little choice except to make an effort at compliance. At this point, it should be noted, the Irkutsk or "Pan-Russian" faction— whose leader was now considered generally to be Mun Ch'ang-bŏm—had been greatly strengthened not merely by events connected with the Moscow congress but also by the Red Army victories throughout Siberia. With the ascendancy of the Bolsheviks in Soviet Asia, the position of the Russianized Koreans became stronger and that of Yi's nationalist Koreans weaker.

Another reconciliation conference was held at Verkhneudinsk on October 20, 1922, after elaborate preparations. By mid-July, each party had selected twelve representatives. These were then dispatched to all major Korean communities with letters of authorization from Yi Tong-hwi

96. Yŏ Interrogation, *op. cit.*, p. 52.

97. *Ibid.*, p. 48. According to Yŏ, the 200,000 yen (rubles) left by Han in Moscow from the initial payment was eventually brought to Shanghai by Ko Ch'ang-il and Yun Hae.

98. See Dae-Sook Suh, *op. cit.*, pp. 42–43, quoting from *Public Peace and Order of 1922*, pp. 428–430.

and Shumiatsky calling for delegates to be sent to the conference. According to one account, some 70 Koreans and 20 Russians attended; another source states that there were nearly 200 participants in all.[99] In any case, almost all of the important figures in the Korean Communist movement were present. The leaders of the Irkutsk faction were Mun Ch'ang-bŏm and Han Myŏng-se, with Kim Man-gyŏm also in attendance. The Shanghai faction was led by Yi Tong-hwi; it included Yun Cha-yŏng, another important faction leader. Despite all the Comintern's efforts, the conference failed. Chŏng Chae-dal blamed it on the fact that the Shanghai faction managed to dominate the proceedings and refused to compromise.

The failure was naturally reported, in various versions, to Comintern headquarters, which reacted with a flood of telegrams. Yi Tong-hwi and Yun Cha-yŏng of the Shanghai faction, Han Myŏng-se and Kim Man-gyŏm of the Irkutsk faction, and Chŏng Chae-dal and Chŏng T'ae-sin, who were classified as independents, were all instructed to come to Moscow.[100] They seem to have arrived in mid-December 1922. One informant says that representatives of each group rushed to Bukharin, insisting that they were the proper group to lead the Korean Communist movement, and reciting the sins of the other side. "You are both the same!" responded Bukharin. "None of you know the real facts about Socialism or Communism. You're actually engaged only in an independence movement, so make up your personal differences and unify yourselves." [101]

The two warring factions were ordered dissolved, to be replaced by a Far East Area Committee, Korea Bureau (Korburo). The Commissars appointed to this bureau included Yi Tong-hwi and Yun Cha-yŏng of the old Shanghai faction, and Han Myŏng-se, Kim Man-gyŏm, and Chang Kŏn-sang of the old Irkutsk faction, with Voitinsky as chairman.[102] Chŏng

99. One first-hand account of the Verkhneudinsk conference is contained in the statement of Chŏng Chae-dal before the preliminary trial judge in *Chōsen dokuritsu shisō undō no hensen, op. cit.,* pp. 46–47. (This source gives the figure of nearly 200 participants.) For the former figures, see "An Outline of the Korean Communist Party . . ." *op. cit.,* which also contains an interesting account of this conference. In addition, Robert A. Scalapino interviewed Cho Pong-am, a participant in the Verkhneudinsk conference, on Sept. 27, 1957.

100. Chŏng Chae-dal statement, *op. cit.,* p. 47. According to the author of "An Outline of the Korean Communist Party . . ." at the close of the Verkhneudinsk conference, there had been an agreement to have a committee representing the two major factions and including such men as Yi Tong-hwi, Pak Chin-sun, Kim Ch'ŏl-hun, and O Ha-muk, with Shumiatsky serving as adviser "to solve the basic problems" relating to the movement and, thereby, to be in a condition to receive Comintern funds on the occasion of the Fourth Comintern Congress, scheduled for November, 1922.

101. Robert A. Scalapino interview with Cho Pong-am.

102. Katayama Sen was also appointed commissar, representing Comintern headquarters, but he withdrew from this operation at an early point. Voitinsky also left rather quickly, returning to Shanghai. See Kim Ch'an Trial, *op. cit.,* pp. 1885–6.

Chae-dal was given the job of managing bureau affairs since he was accounted an independent and also knew the Korean situation well. With this reorganization set forth, the disputants all returned to Vladivostok, the new bureau headquarters, at the end of January 1923.

Even before this, Korean Communist activities in Shanghai had almost ceased. After Yi's departure for Moscow, Kim Rip had been put in charge of the Shanghai faction, but its strength began to wane. Soon Kim himself was assassinated because of the embezzlement charge.[103] Meanwhile, many of the Irkutsk faction had gone to Moscow or moved to Siberia, so activities in Shanghai were reduced to a minimum.

Communism in the Homeland

One development of this period deserves special emphasis. From the end of 1922, the Comintern dedicated itself to transferring the bulk of Korean Communist and nationalist activities to Korea proper. It was natural, of course, to want a Korean Communist Party to have its roots in Korea. Even earlier, Lenin had told Yun Cha-yŏng that the Korean Communist Party could not be established as a recognized branch of the International as long as it was confined to foreign bases. It would first have to be established in the homeland.[104] By 1922, however, the Bolsheviks had much more reason to stress this point. In that year, Japan decided to withdraw its troops from Vladivostok and agreed to negotiations with the Soviet government. For the first time since the October Revolution, the immediate threat to Soviet Siberia was removed.

Once the Japanese menace had declined, Soviet officials became much less enthusiastic about sustaining both a Korean Independence Army and a full-fledged Korean Communist Party on Siberian soil. Now these would be provocative forces, giving Japan ample reason to disregard Chinese and Russian boundaries. The Soviet government, beset on all sides by internal problems, did not want to court international trouble so openly. Thus a damper was put upon Korean military and political activities in Siberia. Occasion was found to disband Korean troops (unless they were part of the Red Army), and the Russians became more insistent that the Korean Communist Party operate from Korea. Since an alliance with Korean nationalism was now less important to the national interests of the Soviet Union, a go-slow policy was initiated—much to the dismay of those Koreans who had anticipated a quick victory over Japan with Bolshevik assistance. Later, this new policy was confirmed by the Soviet-Japanese

103. According to Chŏng Hwa-am, Kim Rip was assassinated by O Myŏn-jik and Kim Tong-u at the instruction of Kim Ku. Chong-Sik Lee interview with Chŏng Hwa-am, Seoul, Jan. 25, 1967. (Chŏng Hwa-am was formerly an anarchist leader in China who had worked closely with Kim Ku in the 1930s and 1940s.)

104. Yŏ Interrogation, p. 55.

treaty of January 1925, which established official relations between the two powers. Korean hopes and aspirations went for nothing.[105]

Meanwhile, serious difficulties had arisen in the attempt to establish Communist roots inside Korea with Vladivostok as a base. The old factional rivalries continued, both in Siberia and in Korea. Once again, Korean representatives of various factions and regions went to Moscow. It was decided to reorganize the Vladivostok operation. According to Kim Ch'an, a new Orgburo or supervisory committee was created, with Yi Tong-hwi, Chŏng Chae-dal, Nam Man-ch'un, Yi Chae-bok, and four or five others taking the leading roles.[106]

A 1924 report of the Executive Committee of the Communist International admitted that Korea represented a real problem. It pointed out that the nationalist movement was torn by internal conflicts, and that the National Representatives Conference had ended in failure.[107] Nevertheless, the report argued, class differentiation was developing in Korea, as the peasants and workers disassociated themselves more and more from the purely nationalist movement.

> The scattered and weak Labour organisations are rallying, and the question of an organisation on a national scale which is to establish close contact with the Japanese Labour movement is one of the moment. Differences of opinion exist in the young Communist Party of Korea over this new situation.
>
> The Executive has thoroughly investigated this situation and drawn up instructions for the Communist Party of Korea. Besides strengthening the Communist Party, the chief task of our comrades in Korea should consist in furthering the formation and unification of the pure Labour

105. After the Karakhan-Yoshizawa Agreement of 1925, the Soviets expelled all Korean nationalists who were not considered Russian citizens. Among those forced to leave Vladivostok on the S.S. *Lenin* were Cho Wan-gu and Won Se-hun, both of whom had been pressured to become candidate members of the Communist Party and were thus eligible for a Japanese jail when they arrived in Korea. Such actions caused men like Won to become vigorous anticommunists. Chong-Sik Lee interview with Song Nam-hŏn, Seoul, Dec. 17, 1966. (Song Nam-hŏn had been a political secretary to Kim Kyu-sik between 1946 and 1950.)

106. Kim Ch'an Trial, *op. cit.*, pp. 1891–2. Kim Chun-yŏp and Kim Ch'ang-sun, however, raise doubts about this data. They assert that Yi Tong-hwi, Han Myong-sŏ, Kim Man-gyŏm, and Chŏng Chae-dal were excluded from the Orgburo at this point. Instead, they list as members a foreigner whose transliterated name was "Indersen," Chang To-jŏng, Chang Kŏn-sang, Yi Hyŏng-gŏn, Pak Ŭng-ch'il, Nam Man-ch'un, and Kim Ch'ŏl-hun, deriving these names from statements of Chŏng Chae-dal and Yi Chae-bok. See Kim and Kim, *Hanguk Kongsan chuŭi undongsa*, Vol. 1, *op. cit.*, pp. 429–433.

107. *From the Fourth to the Fifth World Congress, Report of the Executive Committee of the Communist International*, London, 1924, p. 76. In another section, the report stated: "In Korea the attempts of the Eastern Department to unite all the groups have thus far been fruitless. At present, fresh attempts are being made to build a unified Communist Party": p. 103.

organisations, and in substituting revolutionary-minded comrades for the Right Wing elements in the organisations. In the purely Nationalist movement, the Communists should work for the establishment of a united front of the National-revolutionary struggle.

The necessary clarity on these questions has not yet been arrived at among the Korean Communists; the immediate task of the Party is to bring this about.[108]

Noteworthy here is the attempt to distinguish between a "purely nationalist movement" and one that would come under a "revolutionary" (that is, Communist) aegis. This, together with the insistence upon united front tactics, was of course standard Comintern policy at this point, not only for Korea but for China and other regions as well. In terms of Comintern objectives, however, progress in Korea was extremely slow. Factionalism within the Korean Communist movement was only one of the problems. The efficiency of the Japanese police and military was such as to produce a staggering casualty rate among organizers. Indeed, few Communist agents entering Korea managed to stay out of police hands for longer than several months. Many were picked up as they crossed the Yalu River, after Japanese authorities had obtained detailed information on their plans and route of travel. For example, Pak Hŏn-yŏng, Yim Won-gŭn, and Kim Tan-ya, men of the Irkutsk faction in Shanghai, were arrested by Japanese police while attempting to enter Korea from Antung in April 1921. (They returned to the movement after their release—Pak Hŏn-yŏng as early as August 1924—to play a conspicuous role, as we shall see.) Even the Comintern was forced to pay homage to the remarkable effectiveness of the Japanese security apparatus.[109]

As we noted earlier, Communist penetration of Korea proper began as early as 1921. We must now explore in somewhat greater detail internal developments from that point. It should be indicated at the outset that the March Uprisings of 1919 produced a change in Japan's Korea policy. Rigid militarism gave way to the so-called cultural policy of the Saito administration. The new policy was based upon increased fraternization between Japanese and Koreans, more attention to social policies, and greater freedom. It was an attempt to win support by persuasion rather than by mere coercion, and as such it had considerable effect. But it also enabled a number of liberal, nationalist, and "progressive" (in the Asian usage, generally meaning leftist) Korean organizations to emerge between 1920 and 1925. Perhaps these can be divided into three broad categories: press and publication groups; labor, farmer, and social service associations; and finally, intellectual "study groups."

The Korean press was given new life by the policies of the Saito ad-

108. *Ibid.*, p. 76.
109. See The Communist International, *Between the Fifth and the Sixth World Congress, 1924–28*, London, 1928, pp. 458–463.

ministration. *Tong-A Ilbo* (*East Asia Daily News*), *Chosŏn Ilbo* (*Korea Daily*), *Shisa Sinbo* (*Current Affairs News*), and *Onmun Sinmun* (*Vernacular News*) were all established in 1920, and several of these figured prominently in the nationalist movement of this period. By 1923, a number of independent magazines had also commenced publication. These included *Shin-saeng-hwal* (*New Life*), *Shin-ch'ŏnji* (*New Universe*), *Chosŏn ji kwang* (*Light of Korea*), and *Kaebyŏk* (*Creation*). Korean journalists formed a substantial part of the intellectual class. They were also among the most politically active elements in that class; a number were ardent nationalists, and some quickly became involved in the Communist movement. Thus funds from the Yi faction went in 1921 to Chang Tŏk-su, editor of *Tong-A Ilbo,* a newspaper that enjoyed great respect from the nationalists and indeed served as their unofficial organ. Chang was also a leader in the youth movement and had a number of young associates grouped around him. Some of the Moscow money went to these men.[110] And yet Chang was not a Communist. He merely stood on the periphery of the movement and lent a bit of support. The world of Korean journalism was an excellent place from which to observe the complex interrelations between nationalism and Communism during this period.

The second category of "progressive" Korean organizations was to be found in the labor and youth movements. In April 1920, the first Korean labor organization was set up by Ch'a Kŭm-bong: the Chosŏn Nodong Kongje-hoe (Korean Labor Fraternal Association). Initially, this organization was based upon Christian socialist principles. Its slogan was: Solve labor problems in accordance with God's will. A leftward movement soon got under way, however, and by 1922 an internal split occurred.[111] The radical faction created the Nam Chosŏn Nonong Ch'ongdongmaeng (South Korean Labor-Farmer Federation). Beginning in September 1923, efforts were made to consolidate various unions, and in April 1924, the

110. For details, see *Chōsen Kyōsantō jiken, op. cit.,* pp. 8 ff. Reportedly, 80,000 yen went to Chang, Kim Myŏng-sik (*Tong-A* reporter), O Sang-gŭn (chairman of the Korean Youth Federation), and Ch'oe P'al-yong (manager of the Korea Student Union).

111. Kim Tu-jŏng, "A Short History of the Korean Communist Party," *op. cit.,* p. 107. For a contemporary Communist account, see Ch'oe Ch'ang-ik, "The Korean Proletarian Movement," *op. cit.,* pp. 259 ff.

The April 1922 issue of *Shin-saeng-hwal* contains a report of the 4th General Conference of the Chosŏn Nodong Kongje-hoe, held on April 1 and 2, 1922—just before the split. It reports that two branches, those in Ch'ŏngjin and Kamp'o, were developing into "pure labor unions," and that two week-long strikes conducted by the Kamp'o branch members were the longest strikes in the history of Korea. Among the topics discussed during the two-day session were the tailor-shop workers' strike in Seoul and the transport workers' strike in Pusan, the organization of consumer unions, the development of workers' night schools, and tenant farm problems. Shin Pin-bŏl, "The Fourth General Conference of the Chosŏn Nodong Kongje-hoe," April 1922, pp. 30–34.

Chosŏn Nonong Ch'ongdongmaeng (Korean Labor-Farmer Federation) was launched. Youth organizations followed a similar pattern and time-table. In November 1920, the Ch'ŏngnyŏn Yŏnhap-hoe (Youth Federa-tion) was formed, and soon scores of other youth groups had sprung up. Internal friction was rife in this field also; for instance, Chang Tŏk-su was accused of using the Moscow funds to promote his own interests. Chang's Korean Youth League Federation, organized in April 1924, was even-tually split by the secession of the important Seoul Youth League.[112] The latter group, led by Kim Sa-guk, Kim Han, and Pak Il-byŏng, became the nucleus of the so-called Seoul faction of the Korean Communist move-ment.[113]

The first serious efforts to establish a Communist Party within Korea began in 1923, after the establishment of the Korburo in Vladivostok. Chŏng Chae-dal left Vladivostok for Seoul in early May. Traveling via Shanghai and Japan, he reached his destination in late June or early July. A month or so earlier, a certain Kim Ch'an (an alias of Kim Nak-jun) had also come to Seoul, and had discussed with a few labor and youth leaders the possibility of organizing a Communist Party group.[114] The men involved in the initial discussions in May 1923, included Kim Chae-bong and Shin Yong-gi; during June, others were brought into the dis-

112. *Chōsen kyōsantō jiken, op. cit.,* p. 10.
113. *Ibid.,* p. 11. Kim Han of the Proletarian League, Kim Sa-guk of the Seoul Youth League, and Shin Paek-u of the Labor Mutual Assistance Society formed a triangular alliance against the Chang Tŏk-su group, accusing Chang of using the name of the proletarian movement to promote his private interests.

For a censored version of Kim Sa-guk's lecture, "The Defects of Modern Economic Organization," delivered in Seoul Nov. 17, 1921, see *Kaebyŏk,* No. 18, Dec. 1921, pp. 58–59. Even in censored form, this article gives a flavor of the radical thought of the time. Defining the capitalist system as a "people eat people system," Kim urged disobedience to an order based upon struggle and competition, and an insistence upon the type of system that would guarantee "the right to live," couching his appeal in terms of humanitarianism and mutual aid. At no point in the printed version, of course, is there any reference to Marxism. Hence the flavor is liberal rather than radical, but revealing at the same time of the role that traditional communalist sentiments could play in forwarding opposition to the highly individual-ist, competitive doctrines of modern Western culture.

114. Kim Ch'an was typical of one type of youthful Korean dissident of this era—the rebellious child of a conservative family. His father, a leader of the Ilchin-hoe, a society favoring Japanese annexation in 1910, had been made prefectural governor, and Kim Ch'an was therefore in an extremely favored position. However, for reasons unclear, he broke with his father, and by 1919 he was working as a factory laborer in Japan, secretly planning to gather a hundred or so men who would set fire to major Japanese cities so as "to put the nation out of commission." This dream did not materialize. Shortly afterward he went to Vladivostok in hopes of obtaining military training. Disappointed by the absence of a program he could enter, he returned to Japan and continued his studies, and then engaged in an abortive attempt to set up a guerrilla band in Manchuria. Kim Ch'an was one of the key figures in the Tuesday Society and, as we shall note, in the 1st KCP.

cussion. The hope was to unify labor and youth in the Seoul area at least, but the Seoul Youth Association would not cooperate. However, with men from the Korean Labor-Farmer Federation as its nucleus, a Korburo unit was established in Seoul at this time. Its officers included Kim Chae-bong, Won U-gwan, Shin Paek-u, Kim Tu-jŏn (better known by his alias, Kim Yak-su), and Yi Pong-su. In July, Shin Yong-gi went to Vladivostok to report the establishment of this organization and also of a Youth Bureau.[115] Chŏng Chae-dal, however, was to tell Japanese authorities that "due to the malicious propaganda of the Shanghai faction," he was treated in an unfriendly fashion by Ch'a Kŭm-bong and several others of the Korean Labor Fraternal Association, and even beaten by them.[116]

As a front organization of young intellectuals, the Shin Sasang Yŏngu-hoe (New Thought Study Society) was set up on July 4, 1923. The following year, on Marx's birthday, November 19, it was renamed the Hwayo-hoe (Tuesday Society), because the day happened to be Tuesday. The Society became a major vehicle of the Communist movement, and included among its members such young radicals as Kim Ch'an, Kim Chae-bong, Cho Pong-am, Kim Tan-ya, Pak Hŏn-yŏng, Yim Wŏn-gŭn, and Hong Chŭng-sik. Meanwhile, in January 1923, Korean students in the Tokyo area led by Kim Yak-su had organized the Puksŏng-hoe (North Star Society) as another group dedicated to socialism.[117] The North Star Society later merged with a group organized in Korea, the Kŏnsŏlsa Tong-maeng (Construction League), to form the Pukp'ung-hoe (North Wind Society), which became another vital element in Communist activities.

115. Kim Ch'an Trial, *op. cit.,* pp. 1887–8.

116. Chŏng Chae-dal statement, *op. cit.,* p. 47. The Korburo unit was organized by Ku Yŏn-hŭm, Hong Chŭng-sik, Hong Myŏng-hui, and Pak Il-byŏng, with others joining, including Kim Chae-bong, Hong Tŏk-yŭ, Yi Chae-sŏng, Yun Tŏk-byŏng, Won U-gwan, and Yi Chae-bok.

117. The role of Kim Yak-su looms large in the annals of early Korean student radicalism in Japan, and a brief description of his activities is warranted. He first went to Tokyo in the spring of 1915, seeking to enter a military academy. He later wrote that he felt that Korean students were weak because so frequently they devoted themselves to subjects like literature. However, the principal of the military academy, possibly sensing a rebel, urged him to devote his attention to agriculture or commerce rather than soldiering. He and his group thereupon took off for China, where he entered the Peking Military Academy. His finances, however, did not permit lengthy study, and just before the March Incident of 1919 he was embarked upon a new venture: trying to organize Korean farmers in Manchuria as both workers and fighters. This effort, and the plans of Kim Ch'an for a Korean guerrilla army in Manchuria, noted earlier, are evidence of how widespread such notions were before the advent of Kim Il-sŏng.

After the March 1919 Incident, Kim Yak-su returned to Japan with Yi Yŏ-sŏng with the deliberate aim of shifting from "military" to "political" operations. Immediately, he began the publication of a political journal, *Taejung Shidae (Mass Era)*, and proceeded to become deeply involved in student radicalism. See Kim Yak-su, "Killim kwa Namgyŏng esŏ" ("At Kirin and Nanking"), *Samch'ŏlli,* January 1932, Vol. 4, No. 1, pp. 33–34.

The influence of Japanese radicalism was of course very strong upon the young Koreans. This was a period of great intellectual ferment in Japan, and the tide of Marxism was running high. Societies like the Shinjinkai (Society of New Men) and Reimeikai (Dawn Society) came into existence together with many other "progressive" student associations. Such professors as Yoshino Sakuzō, Abe Isoo, and Sano Manabu—the first two Social Democrats, the last a Communist—were having a major impact upon Korean students in Tokyo and elsewhere. The Japanese university was almost the only place where Koreans could feel bonds of sympathy, equality, and comradeship. Naturally, they moved to the left at the same pace as many of their Japanese comrades—in some cases, more rapidly. During this period, more Korean Marxists were being made in Japan than in Russia.[118]

Gradually, Communist cells were planted in various Korean cities. The main targets were labor and study groups and newspaper plants. Kim Ch'an reported that about 130 members were obtained in the initial period.[119] Biweekly cell meetings were held to discuss Korburo directives and policies. In Seoul, such meetings were conducted in the homes of Kim Ch'an, Pak Hŏn-yŏng, and (later) Hong Chŭng-sik. Various youth front organizations were formed, with a magazine, Shinhŭng Ch'ŏngnyŏn (New Rising Youth), serving as their organ. As yet, however, an official Korean Communist Party had not been organized. These activities were all regarded as preliminary steps. Moreover, they were not taken without trouble. It was not only the Japanese authorities; internal quarreling took a heavy toll. Before the first year had passed, a number of figures had dropped out, or had been ousted on charges of "sabotage." The latter group included Yi Pong-su and Shin Yong-gi. The Shanghai and Irkutsk factions continued to battle inside as well as outside Korea, and a new "Seoul faction" was emerging to further complicate matters.

Despite the problems, the first Korean Communist Party to be established on Korean soil was shortly to emerge. The Vladivostok Bureau had been reorganized in the spring of 1924. In the early summer, Chŏng Chae-

---

118. In January 1920, some 300 Korean students in Tokyo, led by Kim Ch'an, Kim Yak-su, Pak Yŏl, and Song Tŏk-man (Song Pong-u), established the Tongkyŏng Chosŏn Kohaksaeng Tongu-hoe (Comradely Association of Korean Students in Tokyo). Nearly two years later, in November 1921, some twenty activists grouped around Kim Yak-su set up the first truly radical group, calling themselves the Huk-to-hoe (Black Current Society). Actually Iwasa Sakutaro, a well-known Japanese anarchist, helped in the formation of this group, and both his presence and the name of the society suggest that the strong anarchist currents that were running in Japan at that point had had a major influence on the young Korean radicals. Men like Ōsugi Sakae were the heroes of the day.

By the 1923–24 period, however, the anarchist star was waning, and its place was being taken by the communist movement. This shift was duly reflected in the North Star Society and its successors.

119. Kim Ch'an Trial, op. cit., pp. 1888–9.

dal was sent back to Korea. He was soon joined by Yi Chae-bok, who had also been in Vladivostok receiving instructions. Chŏng and Yi conferred with Kim Ch'an and many others with a view to enlarging the movement and getting the Party formally launched. Before any action could be taken, however, they were arrested by Japanese police and sentenced to three years in prison.[120]

At this point, the new Orgburo in Vladivostok was being supported by both the Irkutsk and the Shanghai factions. The former was dominant in the Tuesday Society; the latter drew its strength from the Korean Youth League Federation and the Korean "Labor-Farmer Party" group. For the moment, these various groups were cooperative. Only the new Seoul faction, with its center in the Seoul Youth Association, insisted upon taking a separate course. It was still in opposition when the first official Korean Communist Party was formed in Seoul on April 17, 1925. The lead in the formation of the Party was taken by Tuesday Society members, and indeed it has often been called the Hwayo-hoe Communist Party. This group decided to take advantage of an All-Korea Press Reporters' Conference, scheduled for mid-April, to convene party supporters. At 1:00 P.M. on April 17, while the attention of the police was focused on a journalists' party being held elsewhere, some fifteen men gathered at the Ya Shue Yuen (in Korean, Asowon), a Chinese restaurant in downtown Seoul, and formally organized the Korean Communist Party.[121]

Kim Yak-su presided and Kim Chae-bong gave the opening talk, stressing the immediate need for a formal party organization. It was in this same period, it should be noted, that Comintern authorities were chastising the Japanese Communists for having disbanded the first Japanese Communist Party. The Comintern had ordered that the Party be reestablished, but a strong majority of the Japanese Communists thought that, in the absence of effective mass organizations among the workers and peasants, a formal party was premature and even a liability, since it exposed members to the likelihood of imprisonment. This position, however, was sharply condemned by Voitinsky and his superiors as "capitulationism." Thus, the Korean comrades were pursuing the approved course of action.

Kim Chae-bong, Cho Pong-am, and Kim Ch'an served as a nominating committee, selecting seven members of a Central Executive Committee

120. *Chōsen kyōsantō jiken, op. cit.,* p. 11.

121. Those present were Kim Yak-su, Kim Chae-bong, Cho Pong-am, Kim Ch'an, Yu Chin-hi, Kim Sang-ju, Chu Chong-gŏn, Song Tŏk-man, Cho Tong-ho, Tokko Chŏn, Chin Pyŏng-gi, Chŏng Un-hae, Ch'oe Won-t'aek, Yun Tŏk-byŏng, and Hong Tŏk-yu: *ibid.,* pp. 12–13. This source gives a very detailed account of the first meeting, and all events of this period. The Kim Ch'an Trial statement is also excellent. For another account, see the article by Hong Tŏk-yu, one of the participants, in the April 17, 1946, issue of *Chosŏn Inminbo (Korean People's News),* written for the twenty-first anniversary of the party founding.

and three members of a Central Inspection Committee. The Executive Committee members included three Tuesday Society men, two North Wind Society men, and two members of other groups. The Inspection Committee was composed of one Tuesday Society man, one North Wind man, and Cho Pong-am who had connections with both the Tuesday Society and the Irkutsk faction. From the outset, the Korean Communists had to think in factional terms and seek the kind of representational balance that would preserve maximum unity. Under such circumstances, however, no tightly knit, highly structured organization was possible.

At the initial meeting of the Party, little was done beyond establishing the formal organization. The following evening, at the home of Kim Ch'an, the Executive Committee held its first meeting. The Committee was divided into sections, and various assignments were made. Kim Chae-bong was put in charge of the Secretariat, Organization was assigned to Cho Tong-ho, Propaganda to Kim Ch'an, Personnel to Kim Yak-su, Labor and Agriculture to Chŏng Un-hae, Politics and Economics to Yu Chin-hi, and Security to Chu Chong-gŏn.[122] These were impressive titles to be bandied about by such a minuscule group.

Preparations had also been made in advance for the restructuring of the old Youth Bureau into an official Communist Youth League. On April 18, the day after the establishment of the KCP, the League was formally created.[123] Once again, the nominating committee was composed of Cho Pong-am, Pak Hŏn-yŏng, and Kim Tan-ya. They established a Central Executive Committee. That same evening, this committee made Pak Hŏn-yŏng head of the Secretariat, and gave Organization to Kwon O-sŏl, Propaganda to Shin Ch'ŏl-su, Education and Training to Kim Tan-ya, Security to Hong Chŭng-sik, and Liaison to Cho Pong-am.

Both the KCP and the Communist Youth League held several executive committee meetings prior to November 1925. The Party held its second such meeting in May at the home of Kim Ch'an to discuss the Party constitution and bylaws that had been drafted by Cho Tong-ho. It was decided at that time to send Cho as an official delegate to Moscow to request Comintern recognition for the new Party, with Cho Pong-am going

122. Kim Ch'an Trial, *op. cit.,* p. 1893. *Chōsen kyōsantō jiken, op. cit.,* reverses the assignments to Cho Tong-ho and Kim Ch'an (pp. 12–13).

123. The meeting was held at the home of Pak Hŏn-yŏng, with the following present: Kim Ch'an, representing the KCP, Pak Hŏn-yŏng, Kwŏn O-sŏl, Hong Chŭng-sik, Yim Wŏn-gŭn, Kim Sang-ju, Shin Ch'ŏl-su, Chang Sun-myŏng, Chin Pyŏng-gi, Cho Ri-hwan, Pak Kil-yang, Kim Tan-ya, Cho Pong-am, Chŏng Kyŏng-ch'ang, and Kim Tong-myŏng: Kim Ch'an Trial, *op. cit.,* p. 1899. It is to be noted that there was some overlap between the membership of the KCP and the YCL.

Also, when interrogated by the Japanese police, the participants of the meeting gave different accounts of the composition of the nominating committee, some listing three, others naming five. See Kim and Kim, *Hanguk kongsan chuŭi undongsa,* Vol. 2, *op. cit.,* pp. 314–315.

as deputy delegate and representative of the League. Cho Pong-am left Seoul almost immediately, and Cho Tong-ho followed in early June. Unofficial approval for the two Korean organizations was quickly granted in Moscow; official recognition came in May 1926. The Comintern must have been enormously pleased that the two major factions, so long at odds, were now seemingly reconciled and working together.

Cho Pong-am had also been charged with the responsibility of working out arrangements for a Korean student training program in Moscow. From the early days of the Bolshevik era, Korean students had attended such schools as the so-called Communist University of the Toilers of the East, but there had been no systematic recruitment program from Korea proper. Now, the Communist Youth International instructed Cho Pong-am to arrange for twenty students to be sent at once. At its fifth meeting on October 10, 1925, the Executive Committee of the Communist Youth League in Seoul selected a group of students, and these were dispatched to the Soviet Union by the middle of November.[124] Meanwhile, the KCP had begun to make policy decisions: its first efforts were to struggle for control of the Korean Labor-Farmer Federation, to establish a publication organ, and to create a KCP bureau in Manchuria.

Before the KCP was well established, however, the so-called Sinŭiju Incident occurred in November 1925, and most Party members were soon under arrest.[125] The Shinman Ch'ŏngnyŏn-hoe (Shinman Youth Society) had sponsored a party at a Sinŭiju restaurant on November 15 to celebrate the wedding of one of the society members. Among those attending were Tokko Chŏn and Kim Kyŏng-sŏ, both affiliated with the secret Communist movement. After imbibing freely, a few of this group, including the two just mentioned, wandered downstairs and became involved in a brawl with another partying group that included a Korean lawyer and a Japanese policeman. In the course of the fight the young radicals gave voice to their political sentiments.

Shortly afterward, quite possibly at the instigation of Japanese authorities, the lawyer filed charges against Tokko and Kim, charging them with bodily injury. They were arrested and their houses were searched. At Tokko Chŏn's home, a number of Communist documents and materials were discovered. These included a business report of the Communist Youth League Central Executive Committee, and a list of the students being sent to the Soviet Union. It was also discovered that these documents had been entrusted by Pak Hŏn-yŏng to others for delivery in Shanghai. Among the documents found when Pak and six associates were arrested in Seoul were

124. Kim Ch'an Trial, op. cit., p. 1901. The names of the students are given in this source.

125. For a very detailed account of this incident, see Chōsen kyōsantō jiken, op. cit., pp. 5–6; Kim and Kim, Hanguk kongsan chuŭi undongsa, op. cit., Vol. 2, pp. 350–362.

the Soviet constitution (in Russian) and a program for the establishment of Communist training schools. By analyzing these various documents and by subjecting the prisoners to intensive questioning (which no doubt included strong-arm methods), the Japanese police succeeded in finding out almost every detail concerning the KCP. Ultimately, about a hundred persons were arrested and some eighty-three were convicted. The first Korean Communist Party came to grief almost as soon as it was launched.

The Initial Phase: A Summary

At this point, it might be well to reflect upon the broader implications of this first phase of the Korean Communist movement. First, it would be a major error to assume too great a sense of order, power, and control on the part of the new Soviet leaders in the Asian Communist movements of this period. Things were considerably more chaotic than has generally been acknowledged. Moreover, despite the very real strength of Leninism, it had no magical qualities. When juxtaposed with Western policies toward Asia during this period, Leninism can easily seem impressive. But viewed in a strictly Asian context, Leninism reveals certain weaknesses quite apart from the question of its basic values. In the interests of a balanced appraisal of the initial Leninist impact upon the Far East, these weaknesses should be further explored. Perhaps there are two key and interrelated problems involving both theory and practice. One is the relationship between nationalism and Communism, the other the question of revolutionary stages.

As is well known, the Marxism-Leninism of the period held that Communism in Asia must support nationalist movements, encourage bourgeois-democratic revolutions, and exploit the growing cleavage between Asia and the West as the first stage of a "democratic revolution." At the same time, however, internal Communist movements were to be seeded and nurtured, their purity and integrity were to be protected at all costs, and they were to be groomed for leadership in the critical second stage. Leninism was based upon the premise that for certain purposes and periods it was essential that nationalism and Communism work together. But Lenin was totally opposed to any homogenization of the two. At all times, the Communist movement had to be the supreme object of loyalty, an entity unto itself, disciplined, pure, and firmly internationalist. In these respects, as we have seen, the early Korean Communists were a great disappointment to the Lenin government. The Korean Communist movement was a homogenized movement, and the purely nationalist element in it could never be satisfactorily strained out.

The events of this period afford a fascinating insight into the curious relationship between Communist theory and practice. Marx and Lenin proved to be "wrong" in some of their most basic theoretical assumptions both about Communism and about Asia, but ironically, they proved to be "right" in certain equally basic tactical decisions based on those assumptions. Without a grasp of this paradox it is impossible to understand the Communist role in the Far East. Both Marx and Lenin were wrong in assuming that nationalism and Communism could not, or should not, be homogenized. But Lenin was right to suppose that the Communist movement could profit greatly by using nationalism, working with and through it. Communism in Asia has in fact been most successful where it has been able to integrate and interact with nationalism on a continuing basis. If this has been contrary to one fundamental tenet of Marxism-Leninism, so much the worse for that tenet, for it has satisfied another, more important one: Marxism is the science of *successful* revolution.

In a general sense then, and in the long run, Lenin's tactical sense was technically correct, whereas his theoretical stance was demonstrably faulty. But precisely because there was conflict between tactical sense and theoretical stance, actual policy directives were often ambiguous and impossible to follow. It is obvious that the elements of strain and contradiction within Marxism-Leninism created harsh difficulties for the early Asian Communists. Perhaps the Korean Communists were its first victims. It was all right, of course, to be both Communist and nationalist in and toward the Soviet Union, for that was to protect "the fatherland of socialism and the proletariat." Otherwise, it was dangerous. To those Asian Communists whose nationalist quotient was high, Soviet leaders frequently applied such epithets as "petty bourgeois" and "right-wing opportunist." Almost the entire Korean Communist movement of this era ultimately incurred these labels, as we shall see. But to those whose militancy and aggressiveness on behalf of Communism led to hostility on the part of non-Communists, a collapse of the popular front, isolation, and impotence, another label could be applied, that of "left-wing extremist." In the course of Asian Communism's first decade, many a Japanese, Chinese, and Korean Communist fell under this axe also.

To steer between the Scylla of right-wing opportunism and the Charybdis of left-wing extremism was tremendously difficult for sincere Asian Communists because Leninism was itself fundamentally ambiguous on the issue of nationalist-Communist relationships. Indeed, it was capable of defining "the correct position" only after the event. And if it was difficult to follow the Comintern line in the early period, when the Communist movement was still relatively fluid and free, it became much more difficult as discipline became more rigorously enforced by a Soviet Union that was steadily growing in power and in a sense of its own national interest. Concerning this point, we shall have much more to say later.

There is a second, closely related concept concerning which Lenin's tactical judgments were sound although his theoretical premises were faulty. This is the concept of the two-stage revolution. Marxism-Leninism has proven basically incorrect in its thesis that all societies must undergo the same general economic and political stages of evolution, and that a given economic stage produces a given political form. Indeed, it has itself helped mightily to disprove this thesis by its own impact upon such societies as Russia, China, and North Korea. Thus, the thesis that Asia would first pass through a "bourgeois-democratic" revolution cast in the Western mold, a thesis much emphasized in the early 1920s, was faulty. But the tactic derived from this thesis was politically sound. In this fashion, Marxism-Leninism could align itself with currently popular ideas, values, and institutions, seeking to appropriate them while at the same time attacking their shortcomings. Lenin's tactic of the use and abuse of democracy was a brilliant tactical maneuver in Asia, where the practice of Western-style democracy has always been difficult at best, but where its appeal to the intelligentsia has been great. It was a maneuver that did not have to stand upon the soundness of the theoretical premise that supposedly underlay it. Paradoxically, indeed, it was perhaps better served as a tactic by the inadequacy of that premise.

Thus far, we have explored only the first few years of the Korean Communist movement. But this is sufficient to reveal some of the incipient strengths and weaknesses of Asian Communism in general. The strengths were considerable, as we have suggested. Communism had come to the Far East as a movement promising the liberation of colonial peoples, and this alone could arouse many a patriot. But the Russian Communists did not stop with promises; they rendered material aid in the form of money, weapons, and technical assistance. They entered into an alliance with people whose identity had been taken from them, men who were outcasts before the world as a result of Japanese imperialism. Communism, moreover, promised something beyond the liberation of colonies, namely, the liberation of man. It catered to men desirous of drastic change, and a number of Koreans, especially from the petty intellectual class, were in that category.

As we have noted, some of the weaknesses implicit in the Korean Communist movement had already revealed themselves. To a great extent, of course, they derived from the nature of Korean society and Korea's status as a colony. Korea was a deeply conservative society, with a hierarchical social structure and Confucian social values, especially in the rural areas. It was also a society basically antiforeign in many respects and hence less easily attuned to any Western ideology. Some 75 percent of the people were peasants, the urban working class was of negligible size, and the middle class very small. In its initial stages, therefore, the Communist movement was inevitably one composed primarily of students and intellectuals, many of whom had difficulty in communicating with the common man.

Intellectually led movements are guided by visions, beliefs, and values —in short, by ideologies. But it is possible to give this factor too much weight. Most persons classifiable as intellectuals have well-developed egos, are hypersensitive, and exhibit certain other qualities strongly conducive to factionalism. In the Korean Communist movement, of course, the prevalence of factionalism was not due merely to the extensive role played by the intellectuals and petty intellectuals. The problems of any exile or predominantly exile movement, operating from scattered bases and in the face of seemingly hopeless odds, are always formidable. How many European movements-in-exile have survived more than a few years? People with little to do except worry about the future soon begin to quarrel. Just as important, however, was the factionalism embedded in Korean life. This factionalism was, in one sense, impersonal, because it stemmed from the familial, small-group character of all human relations in that society. This was to be a major problem for Marxism-Leninism even after a Communist society had been established in North Korea.

One must also pay homage to the efficiency of the modern state and its capacity to cope effectively with a subversive movement. From the very beginning, the Korean Communist Party had exceedingly limited opportunities to organize, to keep any continuity of leadership, or to reach the masses within Korea. The Japanese authorities, through their agents and informers, obtained an extraordinary amount of detailed information about the Korean Communist movement on an almost current basis. It is intriguing to read the Japanese official files, and one wonders how so many top-secret documents and so much information fell into Japanese hands. The Japanese police knew more about the Korean Communist movement than did any individual Korean Communist!

To be sure, such affairs as the Sinŭiju Incident do not indicate much sophistication on the part of the young Korean Communists. It must also be borne in mind, however, that Japanese authoritarianism, while often cruel, was neither as complete nor as thorough in this era as the totalitarian societies spawned by the modern West. Nevertheless, it was fully capable of controlling both nationalism and Communism in Korea. Moreover, as we shall see, at no point was its power seriously threatened by an internal movement there. Perhaps one lesson to be drawn from the early Korean Communist movement is that only relatively inefficient states—or relatively democratic ones—are likely to fall to an internal foe in our times. Consciously or unconsciously, Korean nationalists recognized that fact as early as 1918. That is why so many colored their nationalism in accordance with their judgment of which foreign power was most likely to challenge Japan, since they generally despaired of their own capacity to do so unaided.

In this connection, it is interesting to note the parallels and contrasts between the events immediately after 1917 and those during and immediately after World War II. In both instances, Koreans dedicated to the struggle for independence were confronted by the realities of Japanese power, and in both cases a portion of them turned to Russia, hoping for

Russian support against Japanese imperialism. In the first instance, Soviet leaders reached an accommodation with Japan, and largely abandoned their Korean allies. Thus, those Koreans who had gambled on Soviet support for Korean nationalist aspirations were as badly disillusioned as those who had counted upon American aid. In the second instance, however, the gamble of those who had attached themselves to the Russians paid off, at least in North Korea. Having participated (at the last possible moment) in the overthrow of Japanese rule, the Russians quickly installed their own protégés in power. For many, however, this represented merely the exchange of one type of foreign domination by another—and ultimately, as we shall see, even the Soviet "protégés" acknowledged that fact. Thus, the demands presented by nationalism upon Communism by no means ceased with "liberation."

CHAPTER II

THE YEARS OF TRIAL

The period immediately after 1925 was one of unending frustration and failure for the Korean Communists. Within three years, there were no less than four attempts to establish a Korean Communist Party. Each rapidly ended in failure. The Communists, to be sure, were not alone in their troubles: the whole Korean nationalist movement, beset by divisions and defeatism, was in the doldrums. Japanese rule of Korea now seemed solidly established and the overwhelming majority of Koreans had apparently reconciled themselves to this fact. Japanese influence, indeed, now extended beyond Korea into Manchuria. This involvement in Manchurian politics, together with the increasingly important role of the Japanese Kwantung Army, signaled to the shrewd observer the events that were to unfold after 1930.

Nevertheless, it was an era of paradox. In Japan proper, political liberalism was close to its prewar zenith. Parliamentary politics were the order of the day, and the political parties, whatever their weaknesses, had managed to wrest a considerable measure of power within the political system. More importantly, a remarkable measure of freedom to speak and publish prevailed in Japan during the 1920s and early 1930s. Japanese authorities tended to make a distinction between the right to engage in radical political action and the right to speak or write in a radical style. This distinction, incidentally, reflected both traditional and modern concepts of the legitimate role of the intellectual in Japanese society.

Thus, a flood of Marxist and pseudo-Marxist literature was published and avidly read by various students and intellectuals. Inevitably, this stimulated radical thought among Koreans as among Japanese, especially since a growing number of the former were seeking higher education in Japan. Even in Korea, however, such literature was available. Accordingly, there emerged a "proletarian culture movement" that, as a political phenomenon, was quite distinct from a formal Communist Party. At a time when Communist political action was rigorously controlled, this latter movement abetted the radicalization of a small but potentially important number of Korean students and intellectuals. Some of these individuals, as we shall see, were to associate themselves with the Korean Communist movement both in the pre-1945 and in the post-1945 periods.

The Persistence of Factionalism

In this period, factionalism remained the central problem of the Korean Communists, as it did for all other groups on the Korean political scene. At the outset, therefore, it is essential to set forth the major factional divisions. The two basic competitors of the earlier period, as will be remembered, were commonly known as the Shanghai and Irkutsk factions. Their differences, stemming as they did from varying degrees of identification with the Soviet cause, extended into the realm of ideology and policy. But personal factors were always present. Over time, as a result of a series of abrasive confrontations, they loomed ever larger. Under heavy Comintern pressure, a superficial unity had been attained long enough to launch the first Korean Communist Party in April 1925. That unity, however, did not last long and, in fact, had never existed in any politically meaningful sense.

With the onset of official Communist activities inside Korea, new factions developed alongside of—and in most cases, intertwined with— the old ones. These new factions increasingly moved toward the center of the Communist stage. The two most important groups, the Tuesday Society and the North Wind Society, have already been mentioned briefly. For some eighteen months after its establishment, until it was destroyed by the successive arrests of almost all of its members, the Tuesday Society was the central organ of Korean radicalism. At its zenith, the Society had some ninety members, one-third of whom were active members of the Communist Party.[1] And this one-third were among the leaders; they in-

1. For highly interesting details on the Tuesday Society and other factions within the KCP movement of this period, see a report dated March 17, 1926, prepared by the 2d Central Executive Committee of the KCP: "A Report Concerning the Present Condition of the KCP," contained in Kōtō Hōin, Kenjikyoku (High Court, Prosecutor's Bureau), *Chōsen shisō undō chōsa shiryō* (*Research Materials on the Korean Thought Movement*), Seoul, 1932, No. 1, Part 2, pp. 29–32 (henceforth cited as KCP, 2d CEC, March 17, 1926, Report).

According to this report, the KCP had fashioned a "Committee of the Union of Four Organizations," with its nucleus in the Tuesday Society, a group having ninety members, thirty-two of whom were KCP members and ten more candidate members. The other factions in the committee were the North Wind Society, the Proletarian League, and the Labor Party, each to be discussed shortly.

cluded a number of the most intelligent and committed Party officials. The nucleus of the Tuesday Society was a group of young intellectuals, a high percentage of whom made their living as journalists.[2] As we shall see, there were good reasons why the journalists' role in the early Korean Communist movement was a significant one.

The primary competitor of the Tuesday Society was the North Wind Society, which had about forty members in early 1926 at about the time it was suppressed. The North Wind Society traced its roots to Japan; in essence, it was a group of returned students heavily imbued with the prevailing currents of Japanese radicalism. Its origins were as follows. In November 1921, Korean students in Japan had organized the Hŭk-to-hoe (Black Current Society) in Tokyo. This society reflected the period when anarcho-syndicalist tendencies were still strong, and the battles between the Japanese Anarchists and Communists were just beginning. When that struggle reached its peak, in 1923, the Black Current Society split, with the anarchist wing calling itself P'ung-ryoe-hoe (Wind and Thunder Society), led by Pak Chun-sik (alias Pak Yŏl), and the Marxist wing Puk-sŏng-hoe (North Star Society), led by Kim Yak-su (alias Kim Tu-jŏn).[3]

Most of the North Star Society members soon returned to Korea where they found their way into political activities very easily. Some of them joined the New Thought Study Society. But most retained their old ties, and in December 1924, thirteen of the key activists designated themselves the North Wind Society.[4] A month later, their compatriots in Japan dropped the title North Star Society and renamed themselves the January Society (Ilwŏl-hoe), commemorating the first anniversary of Lenin's death. The January Society remained active in Tokyo, where it published several jour-

---

2. As we shall note, those associated with *Chosŏn Ilbo* (*Korea Daily*) were particularly active in the Communist movement of this period; journalists of *Shidae Ilbo* (*The Times*) were also deeply involved.

3. See Yoshiura Daizō (a judge in certain political criminal proceedings of this period), *Chōsenjin no kyōsanshugi undō* (*Communist Movements Involving Koreans*), Bureau of Criminal Affairs, Ministry of Justice (Shihō-shō), Thought Study Materials, No. 71, 1940, p. 60. Other members of the North Star Society were An Kwang-ch'ŏn, Yi Yŏ-sŏng, Kim Chong-bŏm, Song Pong-u, Paek Mu, and Pyŏn Hi-yong.

According to the Preliminary Trial statement of Kim Ch'an, the original members of the Black Current Society included Chŏng Chae-dal, Cho Pong-am, and Kim Ch'an himself. See Kōtō Hōin, Kenjikyoku, *Shisō geppō* (*Thought Monthly*), Vol. 2, No. 2, Archives of the Japanese Ministry of Foreign Affairs (hereafter abbreviated AJMFA), Reel (hereafter abbreviated R) S357, Frame (hereafter abbreviated F) 1883.

4. The name North Wind Society was reportedly adopted in the hope that as the cold wind from the north sweeps away all bedbugs, so this society would eliminate factional bickerings.

According to the March 17, 1926, Report, the North Wind Society had forty members, including five KCP members. The initial "thirteen" were Kim Yak-su, Kim Chong-bŏm, Ma Myŏng, Chŏng U-hong, Chŏng U-ho, Chŏng Un-hae, Nam Chŏng-ch'ŏl, Sŏ Chŏng-hi, Pak Ch'ang-han, Pak Se-hi, Shin Yong-gi, Song Pong-u, and Yi Ho.

nals, held monthly study meetings, and participated in various demonstrations organized by the Japanese Left, such as the May Day parades.[5]

Three other groups formed a part of the spectrum of this embryonic Korean left. We have already noted the emergence of the Seoul faction, with its nucleus in the Seoul Youth Association. The fact that this group stood aloof from initial Party activities in Korea enabled it to assume a more significant role later, as we shall see. In addition, there was the Musanja Tongmaeng-hoe (Proletarian League Society), with some thirty-three members, twenty-three of whom were listed at one point as official members of the Korean Communist Party. Finally, a small group of about thirty, including Kim Tŏk-han, Yi Chŏng-su, Yi Ch'ung-mo, and Kim Yŏn-ui, had set up the Chosŏn Nodong-dang (Korean Labor Party), although this so-called party had little influence.

The critical issue for all of these groups, of course, in addition to the problem of internal unity, was the degree of success they could have in interacting with and gaining control of such mass organizations as existed or could be created. Intellectually, this point was well understood. The influence of men like Yamakawa Hitoshi, leading spokesman for the Japanese Communists in the period of their emergence, had been substantial. Yamakawa's famous article, "To the Masses!" was published in 1923; it spelled out in forceful terms the Leninist doctrine of elitist-directed, mass-based organizational power and had been read by almost all of the young Korean radicals. And in Korea as in Japan three general areas appeared to be available for exploitation: labor-farmer unions, student organizations, and the community of outcasts.

At the outset, there seemed reason for optimism. The Korean Labor-Farmer Federation had emerged in April 1924 as the primary vehicle of the Marxist-oriented labor movement, and Communist Party influence within it was very substantial. By 1926, moreover, it could claim a membership of 110,000, divided into 194 subunits (79 labor, 78 farmer, and 37 mixed).[6] An additional 30 labor and 50 farmer unions totaling 21,000 members existed separately; many of them were reportedly under the influence of the Seoul faction. These figures may well be inflated, but in any case Korean Marxists had reason to compare their position in the labor-peasant movement favorably with that of their Japanese comrades.[7]

5. For one informative source on Korean Communist activities in Japan during this period, see the article by Ko Kyŏng-hŭm, "How Did the Korean Communist Movement in Tokyo Develop?" reproduced in *Shisō geppō*, No. 8, November 1931, *AJMFA*, R S356, pp. 872–84. This article was written for Japanese authorities while Ko was in prison, but its basic accuracy has been established by comparing it with other sources, including Japanese police records.

6. KCP, 2d CEC, March 17, 1926, Report, *op. cit.*, pp. 32–33.

7. For the labor situation in Japan, see Arahata Kanson, *Nihon shakaishugi undō shi* (*A History of the Japanese Socialist Movement*), Tokyo, 1948; Ayusawa, Iwao, *A History of Labor in Modern Japan,* Honolulu, 1966; Naimushō (Home Min-

On the youth front, too, the situation facing the Korean Communists was not an unpromising one. By the end of 1926, the Korean youth movement encompassed some 1,092 organizations.[8] Eighteen youth federations had been established to cover the whole of Korea. The Korean Youth League Federation had been established as a national organization, but it drew many local youth groups into its fold. The youth movement, like the labor movement, had been strongly infiltrated by adherents of Marxism— Communists and proto-Communists. The Seoul faction in particular played a dominant role through the Seoul Youth Association, and this, of course, caused serious factional problems. If Communist unity could be attained, however, the Korean youth movement presented an ideal area for mass organization.

The party was also hopeful of expanding its influence among the *paek-jŏng* (slaughterers) outcasts. Like their counterpart, the *eta* in Japan, the paek-jŏng had long belonged to a class of despised people along with sorcerers and slaves, distinguished by such occupations as butchering and leather work, occupations considered lowly in the Buddhist society in which they lived. Traditionally, they had not been allowed to reside within the city walls. The paek-jŏng population in this period was more than 400,000, and around 1923 a movement was begun to better their status. Soon some 170,000 paek-jŏng were organized in 247 branches. Communist leaders quickly established communications with the leaders and sought to affect political trends within the movement.[9]

---

istry of the Japanese Government), *Shōwa sannen ni okeru shakai undō no jōkyō* (*Conditions of the Social Movements in 1928*) (and succeeding years), issued annually, 1928–1942; and Ōkōchi Kazuo, *Labor in Modern Japan,* Tokyo, 1958.

8. Note the following figures on youth organizations provided by Japanese authorities:

1920	1921	1922	1923	1924	1925	1926
251	446	488	584	742	847	1,092

1927	1928	1929	1930	1931	1932	1933
1,127	1,320	1,433	1,509	1,402	863	1,004

Chōsen Sōtokufu, Keimukyoku (Government-General of Korea, Police Affairs Bureau), *Saikin ni okeru Chōsen chian jōkyō* (*Recent Conditions of Public Security in Korea*), May 1934, pp. 168–169.

At the end of 1932, there were some 53,708 youth organization members; this figure dropped to 40,950 at the end of 1933. The average membership of a group was from 40 to 50 members.

9. The March 17, 1926, Report asserts: "The people of this class do not have much class consciousness, and even their leaders, Chang Chi-p'il and O Sŏng-hwan, do not have a thorough, class-conscious understanding of social revolution. Therefore, a healthy movement here is yet to be constructed. However, since the leaders of the movement have friendly individual connections with the members of 'Y' (the KCP), they are receiving a certain degree of guidance from 'Y.' It is planned to assign appropriate 'Y' members to this aspect of the movement, so that it can be consolidated and the sphere of 'Y' expanded": p. 33.

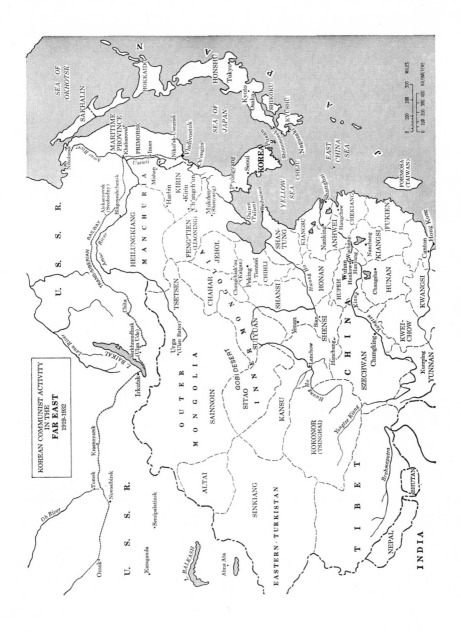

KOREAN COMMUNIST ACTIVITY
IN THE
FAR EAST
1919-1932

The potentialities latent in the labor, peasant, student, and outcast movements had to be weighed against the obstacles represented by a society that in many respects was the most conservative, the most tradition-bound in East Asia, and that was, moreover, thoroughly controlled at this point by a foreign power. Could the Korean Communists break out of their narrow intellectual circles and find ways of smashing through the social barriers of Korean society to mobilize the masses and articulate for them their interests and desires? Could faction-ridden intellectual study groups be transformed into a unified political movement?

Most Communist leaders were in jail after the mass arrests of November 1925. By chance, however, Party Secretary Kim Chae-bong initially escaped detection. As the days passed, he realized that the police would sooner or later learn of his role in the Party. He therefore undertook a hasty search for someone to take his place so that the Party could be reorganized while he and the others were in prison. After conferring with Hong Tŏk-yu, head of the local news section of *Chosŏn Ilbo,* it was agreed that Kang Tal-yŏng, chief of the Chinju branch of the newspaper, would be an appropriate successor. On December 13, 1925, Kang was summoned to Seoul and the affairs of the Party were transferred to him.[10] Six days after, Kim Chae-bong was arrested; he was later sentenced to six years in prison. Kang made a second trip to Seoul in late January 1926, and reached some initial decisions about the Party with Yi Chun-t'ae, leader in the Korean Labor-Farmer Federation. In the middle of February, Kang moved to Seoul so as to devote full time to Party matters.

During the early months of 1926, Party leaders sought to tackle four basic tasks: a Party reconstruction campaign based upon such elements of the first KCP as were available and such new members as could be re-

10. Many details concerning the Communist movement within Korea at this point are to be found in the *Chōsen kyōsantō jiken* (*The Korean Communist Party Incident*), prepared by the Police Affairs Bureau, Korean Government-General, and transmitted by the Chief of Staff of the Japanese Garrison Army in Korea, Hayashi Senji, to the Vice Minister of the Army, Hata Eitarō, on Sept. 25, 1926, in the Archives of the Japanese Army, Navy and Other Agencies (hereafter abbreviated *AJAN*), Reel (hereafter abbreviated R) 102, Frame (hereafter abbreviated F) 08744 ff.

See also the Preliminary Trial statement of Kim Ch'an, *Shisō geppō, op. cit.,* Vol. 2, No. 2, May 1932, *AJMFA,* R S356, p. 1895. According to Kim Ch'an, Kim Chae-bong after conferring with Chu Chong-gŏn and him decided to entrust the affairs of the Party to Kang Tal-yŏng, Yi Chun-t'ae, Hong Nam-p'yo, Yi Pong-su, and Kim Ch'ŏl-su. It was also agreed that the Communist Youth League would be put in the hands of Kwŏn O-sŏl, Chŏn Hae, and Chŏn Tŏk.

A five-man Central Executive Committee was formed at Ku Yŏn-hŭm's home in mid-February, composed of Kang, Yi Chun-t'ae, Yi Pong-su, Kim Ch'ŏl-su, and Hong Nam-p'yo. Two more members were added later: Kwŏn O-sŏl and Chŏn Tŏk. See Kim Chun-yŏp and Kim Ch'ang-sun, *Hanguk Kongsan chuŭi undongsa* (*History of the Korean Communist Movement*), Seoul, 1967, Vol. I, p. 371.

cruited; preparation of a Party constitution and bylaws; establishment of Party branches abroad and renewal of contacts with the Comintern; and formation of a united front with non-Communist nationalists. Each of these tasks posed serious problems.

The Second Korean Communist Party and Its Demise

After the arrests of November 1925, the Korean Communist Party could never again operate under the cloak of total secrecy. Party members or sympathizers, once identified, were kept under more or less permanent surveillance even after they had served their prison terms. Thus, contact with old Party members had to be made with extreme care, and recruitment of new members could be undertaken only after elaborate soundings and precautions. Security requirements, indeed, are a considerable part of the reason why KCP cells were often composed of intimate friends, who could trust each other. In this respect, the police system acted to bolster the traditional Korean organizational structure.

By March 1926, after three months of strenuous effort, the new Executive Committee was able to report to the Comintern that the reconstructed Party had 130 full members and 104 candidate members within Korea, with more than one-third of that membership coming from Seoul.[11] New Party officials had already been selected. Kang became Party secretary, with Yi Chun-t'ae serving as second in command. After some shifts, other top Party posts, now reduced to three in number, were assigned as follows: Organization, Kim Ch'ŏl-su; Propaganda, Yi Pong-su; Inspection, Hong Tŏk-yu. Once again, the top leadership of the Party came from the Tuesday Society, as did a substantial number of Party members.

The first Korean Communist Party had never adopted a constitution despite the preparation of a draft document. In March 1926, the new Executive Committee appointed Kwŏn O-sŏl and Yi Pong-su to undertake the task of writing a constitution, and on March 26 the document was approved. The constitution, together with the Party bylaws, drafted by Kang Tal-yŏng and Hong Tŏk-yu, give us an interesting picture of Party organizational aims and problems, although it must be remembered that the regulations could never be completely applied. Before being accepted as a regular Party member, each individual had to serve a certain period

11. KCP, 2d CEC, March 17, 1926, Report, *op. cit.,* pp. 36–37.
Of the 130 full members within Korea, 46 came from Seoul and 9 from In'chŏn, making a total of 51 from Kyŏnggi Province; the next highest number, 29, came from South Kyŏngsang Province, followed by South Chŏlla (14), South Hamgyŏng (9), Hwanghae (6), North P'yŏngan (5), South P'yŏngan (5), North Kyŏngsang (4), North Ch'ungch'ŏng (2), North Chŏlla (2), Kangwŏn (2), and South Ch'ung-ch'ŏng (1). The Party also listed 16 members outside of Korea: Manchuria, 7; Tokyo 4; Shanghai, 4; Vladivostok, 1.
From these figures, two facts quickly emerge: the Party was minuscule in size, and its membership came primarily from southern Korea, especially the Seoul area.

as a candidate member, the period varying with his class status.[12] Cells, the basic Party units, were to be organized within factories, schools, military units, farm groups, and government offices, and each cell was to have between three and seven members. KCP cells in the Soviet Union, it was stipulated, could have up to twenty members, and in Japan, up to ten; but because of the extremely difficult security problem in Korea proper, cell membership there was to be limited to seven. It was the responsibility of cell heads to hold weekly meetings for purposes of ideological discussion and policy development. The Party was also to have an organization at the prefectural level for each prefecture and one for the whole metropolitan area of Seoul. Similarly, each province was to have a province-level organization. The various Party branches were to elect delegates to a national Party congress. This, in orthodox Communist fashion, would constitute "the supreme Party authority," with the power to elect the Central Executive Committee and other national Party organs.

In the main, this organizational structure was very much after the approved Soviet pattern. There was, however, the issue of overseas branches —strictly speaking, a violation of the Comintern injunction, "One country, one party." The new Executive Committee argued that because various overseas Korean groups had already established several Communist parties, and "education and unity among them are lacking," it was essential to coordinate the Korean Communist movement under the aegis of the KCP (Seoul) by establishing branches of the KCP in or near the main overseas Korean settlements. In this fashion, all Koreans could get to know Party regulations and policy decisions, thereby eliminating the international factionalism of the past. Perhaps the Comintern's earlier division of authority between the Shanghai and Irkutsk factions was kept in mind: after various changes, the Irkutsk Party (the Communist Party of All Koreans in Russia) had been given responsibility for central and west Siberia, while the Shanghai Party had been allowed to operate in east Siberia as well as elsewhere overseas. Presumably the function allotted to the Irkutsk Party had been to integrate Koreans into the Soviet system. In any case, KCP officials in Seoul now proposed to set up branches or liaison offices in Tokyo, Shanghai, Manchuria, and the Maritime Province of Siberia.[13]

12. The varying time lengths specified are curious: three months for workers and farmers; six months for those such as small industrialists who "exploit" the labor of others; and one year for white-collar and professional people. See *Report on the Korea Communist Party Incident, op. cit.,* F 08760.

13. See *ibid.,* F 08764. It appears that the Maritime Province branch was never established because of the well-established status of the Korean Bureau within the Soviet Communist Party in this area, and because the Koreans living in eastern Siberia were too faction-ridden to accept a unified, new organization.

In Tokyo, Kim Chŏng-gyu was aided by Yi Sŏk, Chŏng Un-hae, Yi Sang-ho, and Kim Han-gyŏng in establishing a branch.

The Shanghai branch was set up by certain elements from the 1st KCP: Kim

As noted previously, this second Korean Communist Party was basically under the control of the Tuesday Society, which, incidentally, had legal status as a social organization. (At this time, Japanese authorities allowed certain groups to register as a "social organization," although it would not permit any to identify itself as a political organization.) In some respects, therefore, it was more unified than its predecessor. Even the North Wind faction was largely excluded from the new Party. Given the recent background of factional strife among Korean radicals, however, it was impossible to achieve a broadly based, unified movement at this point. Just before the demise of the first Party, for example, two secret dispatches sent from Seoul to Shanghai revealed the deep troubles that existed. These dispatches, both dated October 20, 1925, were signed by "Comrade P" and sent in the name of the Communist Youth League. They clearly reflected the mainstream view—that is, the view of the Tuesday Society.[14] Kim Yak-su, North Wind leader, was labeled a "fraud" and a "rat" who was plotting against the Party with Han Myŏng-se and Kim Ha-sŏk, old Irkutsk leaders then in Vladivostok. In another dispatch, entitled "Report on Reactionaries," more detailed charges were advanced, with Han again the central villain. According to the report, both the Seoul and the North Wind factions were conspiring with the Vladivostok group to seize the Party for themselves. Kim Yŏng-man and Pak T'ae-sŏn of the Seoul faction, it was said, had "joined hands" with Han Myŏng-se, intending to organize a Communist Party of their own and then solicit the Comintern for support. But the Han faction had even broader ambitions, according to Comrade P. They were seeking to wrest Party control from the present leadership by organizing a united front of leftist factions under their influence. To this end, they had offered funds to Kim Tŏk-han and Yi Chŏng-su of the Korean Labor Party as well as to the Seoul faction itself. In collaboration with the

---

Ch'an, Kim Tan-ya, Cho Pong-am, Yŏ Un-hyŏng, Nam Man-ch'un, and Cho Tong-ho. The branch was first headed by Kim Ch'an, and later by Kim Tan-ya when Kim Ch'an was appointed First Secretary of the Manchurian branch on April 6, 1926. Several of these men conceived of themselves as the key leaders of the 2d KCP, and sought to give orders to Kang Tal-yŏng. This resulted in conflict. The Shanghai branch was closed in July 1926. The timing suggests that the branch was not prepared to carry on alone after the destruction of the 2d KCP in Korea.

The Manchurian branch was organized by Kim Ch'an as noted above, but he dispatched Cho Pong-am and Ch'oe Wŏn-t'aek to the scene to undertake the actual construction of the branch in April–May 1926. After meetings with Kim Ch'ŏl-hun, Kim Ha-gu, and Yun Cha-yŏng, the two men formed the Manchurian General Bureau with three departments: Secretariat, Cho Pong-am; Propaganda, Yun Cha-yŏng; Organization, Ch'oe Wŏn-t'aek. Headquarters was established in Kirin Province; Ningan hsien, Ningkut'a and three districts were organized. This branch was dissolved in May 1930 after the so-called Chientao Incident, which we shall subsequently discuss. For other details on these developments, see Kim Chun-yŏp and Kim Ch'ang-sun, *op. cit.*, Vol. I, pp. 389 ff.

14. See KCP, 2d CEC, March 17, 1926, Reports, *op. cit.*, p. 26.

North Wind faction, moreover, they intended to send agents to Korea who would attempt to dominate the next Party congress. Already, charged the dispatch, money had been paid to thugs to attack Labor Party headquarters, and Kim Ha-sŏk had given Kim Yak-su 5,000 yen for the North Wind group.

The dispatch ended with a sharp criticism of the Soviet Party. The Korburo (Irkutsk) faction was seeking to destroy the KCP, asserted Comrade P. Why was the Soviet Party allowing it? Why were the reactionary activities conducted in Vladivostok through the machinery of the Soviet Party not prevented? When the internationally recognized Korean Communist Party could do nothing because of a lack of funds, why did the reactionaries receive large sums? The report concluded with the demand that these matters be brought before the Comintern.[15]

There is other evidence concerning this period of factional troubles and the fruitless efforts to end them. Before the destruction of the first Korean Communist Party, a united committee of four organizations was established in Seoul. The organizations were the Tuesday Society, the Proletarian League, the North Wind Society, and the Labor Party (the Seoul faction continued to remain aloof). Participants in the union agreed to operate under the discipline of the Communist Party, but soon Party leaders were claiming that such North Wind spokesmen as Kim Yak-su and Chŏng Un-hae were plotting to control both the newly organized union and the Party. An investigation was ordered, and their Party rights were simultaneously suspended. The North Wind faction responded by sending representatives to Vladivostok and Manchuria to garner support from the remnants of the Irkutsk faction. There they found Kim Yŏng-man of the Seoul faction on a similar mission.[16]

To what extent did these rival factions succeed in undermining the KCP leadership on the international scene? Comrade P's reports would indicate that the Tuesday Society leaders were angered by the lack of support they received from Soviet and Comintern sources. And from the Central Executive Committee report of March 1926, we learn that because the

15. *Ibid.,* pp. 28–29. The last paragraph of the report read: "The Korburo faction (Irkutsk faction) is planning to destroy the Korean Communist Party. Why does the Soviet Party allow this? Why do you (living in Siberia) not prevent these reactionary activities from being conducted in the Vladivostok area via the machinery of the Soviet Party? While the officially recognized Party can do nothing because of a lack of funds, the reactionaries receive great sums of money. We are helpless. Unless this is brought to the attention of the Comintern, the situation in Korea will be hopeless. This is very regretable."

16. KCP, 2d CEC, March 17, 1926, Report, *op. cit.,* pp. 29–30. In this report, it was charged that not only did Kim Yak-su "show no inclination for reform," but that he had sent Kim Chong-bŏm and Yi Hŏn, collaborators of Shin Ch'ŏl, to Manchuria and Siberia to contact Han Myŏng-se, Kim Ha-sŏk, and Ch'oe Ko-ryŏ, "remnants of the Irkutsk faction," and there they made common cause with Kim Yŏng-man of the Seoul faction.

Comintern International Peasants Union had sent 20,000 yen for famine relief in 1925 to North Wind Society leaders, the latter had been given the opportunity to claim that they alone had official connections with the international Communist movement.[17]

It was not surprising that Soviet and Comintern authorities were confused, beset as they were with continual charges and countercharges from rival claimants for recognition and support. Thus, when Cho Tong-ho (Tuesday Society) reported in Moscow during the winter of 1925–26 on the reorganization of the KCP, Shin Ch'ŏl (North Wind Society), Kim Yŏng-man (Seoul faction), and a dissident representative from the Korean Labor Party were all in the Soviet capital urging the Comintern to denounce the new Central Executive Committee and demand that a more representative group be formed.[18] According to this account, however, the Comintern did recognize the reorganized KCP and ordered the others to join it.

The second KCP, however, continued to be plagued by the most serious internal disorders. After Kim Yak-su and a number of other North Wind Society leaders had been imprisoned as a result of the Sinŭiju Incident, most remaining Society members decided to join the Party. According to Party leaders, however, these North Wind members continued to engage in factional activities, obeying only the commands of Kim Yak-su. Finally, on April 6, 1926, Kang Tal-yŏng, KCP secretary, wrote to the Central Executive Committee of the Comintern via Kim Ch'an and Kim Tan-ya in Shanghai, informing them that the Party had officially expelled twelve North Wind Society members.[19] The Seoul faction, too, remained a major problem; in fact, it refused to cooperate with the second Party in any manner. All groups at this point were engaged in bitter attacks upon each other, using whatever means were available to undermine their opponents; Tuesday Society leaders openly admitted that the Party had planted one man in the North Wind Society to conduct internal splitting operations. Charges of bribery, beatings, and even of informing on rivals to the police were common during this period and for the next several years.[20]

The first KCP had not been able to establish formal branches or

17. *Ibid.,* p. 30.

18. "Concerning the Return of the Graduates of the International University (in Moscow) to Korea," Chief of the Police Affairs Bureau, Korean Government-General, Dec. 28, 1928, p. 26, *AJMFA,* R S722. (This reel has no numbered frames.)

19. For the full text, see *Shisō geppō, op. cit.,* Vol. 2, No. 8, Nov. 1932, *AJMFA,* R S357, F 2620–2627.

Those expelled were charged with "reactionary activities and the exposure of Party secrets." The purgees were headed by Kim Yak-su, who was accused of having deposited the famine relief fund of 20,000 yen in his own account and using it for North Wind Society propaganda. Numerous other accusations were made in a long, rambling philippic.

20. Some KCP faction leaders actually had bodyguards to protect them against rivals within the movement,

bureaus overseas, although it had established liaison with Yŏ Un-hyŏng in Shanghai, and made use of other men, including Cho Pong-am, Kim Ch'an, and Cho Tong-ho in China and Manchuria. At the outset, as we have noted, the second KCP decided to establish overseas branches. At the third meeting of the new Executive Committee on February 26, 1926, it was voted to open branches in Japan, Shanghai, and the Maritime Province immediately. This did not prove to be a simple task. Kim Chŏng-gyu, scheduled to head the Tokyo office, acquired a letter of introduction from Yŏ Un-hyŏng in Shanghai to Sano Manabu, a Japanese Communist leader. It was regarded as essential to obtain permission from the Japanese Communist Party in view of the one country-one party rule. Subsequently, other Japanese Communists were contacted, and the Tokyo operation finally got under way.

Kim Ch'an, as noted earlier, was designated secretary in charge of the Shanghai liaison office. A proposal to rename this office the Overseas Bureau was sharply debated, and rejected. Decisions with respect to Manchuria and the Maritime Province (Vladivostok) also caused much trouble. Kang complained that he had not been told enough about the agreements reached in the era of the first KCP and that the Executive Committee in Seoul was not only having grave difficulties in exchanging messages with those outside Korea, but also did not have sufficient familiarity with the current situation abroad, including the status of factional divisions. For example, some committee members argued that Cho Pong-am should not be appointed secretary in charge of the Manchurian Bureau because he was strongly disliked by the Shanghai faction. Thus, the appointment of Cho was held up pending an investigation and report by Kim Ch'an in Shanghai. Finally, on May 13, Cho was named to the Manchurian post, and Kim Ch'ŏl-su was dispatched there to confer with him.

Meanwhile, in March, members of the old Shanghai faction currently residing in the Maritime Province, including Yi Tong-hwi, Kim Mikhail, Kim Ch'ang-sun, and Ke Pong-u, sent Pak Ŭng-ch'il to Korea to indicate their desire to cooperate with the KCP. A KCP representative was sent to Chientao and Vladivostok in May. Gradually, the second KCP was establishing its bases abroad. The continued opposition of rival factions overseas, however, particularly the activities of the Irkutsk faction in Vladivostok, hampered the Party. On March 17, 1926, the Executive Committee of the Party in Seoul had passed a resolution, to be submitted to the Comintern, asserting that if the activities in Vladivostok were not restrained, serious problems for the KCP would continue.

The resolution proposed four steps. First, the problem should be solved through the cooperation of the Communist Party of the Soviet Union, the Comintern, and the KCP in accordance with the one country-one party principle. Thus, Koreans in Russia should be prohibited from organizing either secret or public organizations that would interfere with the development of the KCP. Second, in order to train Koreans in Siberia as correct revolutionaries and to remove factional ways of thought, a KCP supporters' association should be organized in the Maritime Province, and the decisions of the KCP on all matters concerning Korea should be binding upon this group. Third, this supporters' association should be organized before May 1926, and two persons should be dispatched by the KCP to the Comintern to formalize arrangements. Finally, to implement this policy and to facilitate better liaison, the head of the Korean section of the CPSU's Maritime Province office should be nominated by the KCP.[21]

This resolution is most interesting because it demonstrates clearly that the Party leaders in Seoul not only regarded the Vladivostok problem as serious, but that in considerable measure they blamed Soviet authorities for it and were now prepared to propose rather drastic remedies. The idea in particular that the KCP should nominate the key Korean official within the Soviet Party's Maritime Province branch must have startled the Russians. In any case, we have no evidence that they gave this resolution serious attention.

No matter how angry the leaders of the KCP might become, they could scarcely afford any sustained posture of defiance before Soviet or Comintern authorities. Neither their power base nor their finances permitted that. A Party registry subsequently seized by Japanese police indicates that, during the whole period that the second KCP was active, it collected only 7,320 yen, and that most of this money was supplied from Shanghai by Kim Tan-ya.[22] This was scarcely enough to conduct major operations, espe-

21. This document is reproduced in KCP, 2d CEC, March 17, 1926, Report, *op. cit.,* pp. 39–40.

22. It is interesting to note the sources of funds, and the uses, when indicated. In mid-1925, the Far Eastern Women's Division of the Comintern sent 150 yen via the Harbin Soviet Consulate, to aid the "Korean Women's Movement." The money was obtained by Pak Kwang-su, who gave it to Pak Hŏn-yŏng, and it was used for the Koryŏ Communist Youth League. In early 1926, Pak Hŏn-yŏng received 1,850 yen from Yŏ Un-hyŏng in Shanghai; 1,500 yen of this money was used to send twenty-one students to the USSR. Slightly earlier, Kim Tan-ya, who had fled to Shanghai at the time of the 1st KCP arrests, obtained 2,000 yen there from the Far Eastern Revolutionary Assistance Association (MOPR), a Comintern front. The money was delivered via Pak Ch'ŏn to Kwŏn O-sŏl in Korea. In mid-January (1926), Kim sent an additional 1,200 yen, supposedly from the savings of some forty Korean students studying in Moscow. The following month, 400 yen was dispatched from Kim, and in March he sent 500 yen with the notation that an additional 500 yen had been applied to the activities of the Manchurian General Bureau. In April, Kim gave Yi Pong-su 220 yen, and he gave Kim Sŏng-sun 1,000 yen to take into Korea.

The KCP books thus indicated that 7,320 yen had been made available in about nine months, beginning in July 1925. However, from other sources it was reported that larger funds were being sent to the KCP. One source claimed that the KCP received 25,000 yen from the Comintern after the 1st KCP collapsed, 5,000 yen being for the expenses involved in sending students to Moscow.

See *Report on the Korean Communist Party Incident, op. cit.,* F 08781–5.

cially since the record reveals that some of the Party leaders had to draw upon these funds for livelihood.

In the budget that they submitted to the Comintern in April 1926, the KCP leaders described how they thought their poverty should be remedied. The document is sufficiently interesting to be worth reproducing in full.

1. Party Conferences			3,600 yen
2. Party Agencies			134,840
a. Central Committee		41,600	
b. Provincial committees		62,920	
c. Manchurian Bureau		10,400	
d. Temporary Japan Bureau		11,000	
e. Temporary Shanghai Office		6,760	
f. Temporary Vladivostok Office		2,160	
3. Party Activities			215,360
a. Propaganda		23,800	
b. Education and training		32,760	
c. Investigation		7,800	
d. Assistance to nationalist movement		30,000	
e. Armed movement		40,000	
f. Others		81,000	
4. Reserve Funds			10,000
TOTAL			363,800 yen

This budget was accompanied by a lengthy statement explaining the expenditures. On the internal condition of the Party, the preface, in particular, was most revealing:

> Normally these funds should be produced by the members of the Korean Communist Party. However, the KCP is in the weakest condition of any Communist Party of the world. Members have abandoned their normal work and are sacrificing themselves either for Party activities or for the mass movement. Even if Party headquarters could provide members with the means for livelihood, they could not possibly produce the funds necessary for Party activities. Therefore, the above sum is requested of you.[23]

Operational funds accounted for slightly more than one-third of the budget, and most of these, as was to be expected, were to be spent in Korea proper. Among the program items, the largest single expenditure was slated for "the armed movement." It was promised that Party members would be provided with thorough military training, and that terrorist groups would be organized to "intimidate capitalists, grey elements and reactionaries." Clearly, the KCP leaders were prepared to use violence as a primary technique.

23. Keijō Chihō Hōin, Kenjikyoku (Seoul District Court, Prosecutor's Bureau), *Chōsen kyōsantō jiken* (*The Korean Communist Party Incident*), Seoul, no date, p. 16.

The sum of 30,000 yen "to assist the nationalist movement" was intended to foster the creation of a Communist-dominated united front. "The purpose," asserted the authors, "is to guide the masses who have previously been succumbing to the manipulations of professional, compromising nationalists toward a [new] nationalist party." An additional 20,000 yen from the activities budget was to be used to sustain and expand front organizations among peasants and workers.

We do not know the precise response to this budget request. One account states that the Comintern decided to allot 100,000 yen to the Korean Communist Party for the year 1926, with one-half of the amount scheduled to be sent in July.[24] At any rate, the money did not arrive in time. As the result of a new incident, the Party was soon to be smashed once again.

On April 25, 1926, King Sunjong, the last monarch of the Yi dynasty, died. Since the March First Movement of 1919 had arisen on the occasion of the funeral of Sunjong's father, King Kojong, it was natural enough for some Korean nationalists to weigh the opportunities presented by this event. However, the nationalist movement in general was at a low ebb, and the groups that had participated in the 1919 uprising contemplated no action. The field was thus left open for the Communists, although it was the Communist leaders in Shanghai, Kim Tan-ya and Kim Ch'an, who initially decided that some program should be undertaken. The funeral was scheduled for June 10. On May 1, Kim Tan-ya met in Antung with Kwŏn O-sŏl, secretary of the Communist Youth League, and outlined to him the idea of making the funeral an occasion for Communist agitation.

Kim argued that, since most Korean socialists were also nationalists, it was entirely proper for Communists to serve as a vanguard for the nationalist movement. This was also wise from a tactical point of view, since nationalism was and would remain a much stronger force in most quarters than Communism. But if the Communists became leaders of a national uprising, they would have an excellent chance of winning over the central figures of the nationalist movement to the Communist cause.[25]

The plan was to distribute large quantities of throw-sheets and leaflets among the crowds along the route of the funeral and elsewhere in Korea. The leaflets would demand Korean independence. Activists would also encourage the people to shout "Manse!" ("Long live!" implying Long live

24. *Ibid.* See also *Report on the Korean Communist Party Incident, op. cit.,* F 08781.

25. For details, see Yoshino Fujizō, "Arrests and the Complete Account of the Second Korean Communist Party Incident," pp. 24–46, in Chi Chung-se (trans. and ed.), *Chosŏn sasangbŏm kŏmgŏ silhwajip (Collected Authentic Stories of the Arrests of Korean Thought Criminals),* Seoul, 1946. This unusual book contains a substantial number of accounts by Japanese and Korean police officials charged with primary responsibility for apprehending "subversives" in the Japanese era. The accuracy of the writings holds up very well when the details are checked against other sources.

Korean independence). Kwŏn was given 1,000 yen by Kim for expenses. He returned to Korea and arranged to have printed some 50,000 leaflets of five different types. Longer declarations were printed in Peking and smuggled into Seoul. A detailed plan was drawn up for the distribution of these materials throughout Korea; the main channels were to be the youth societies. By May 30, all of the materials were ready and had been stored in a Ch'ŏndogyo building.[26] Ch'ŏndogyo (Heavenly Way Religion) authorities were not involved in the plot, but Pak Rae-wŏn, who had taken charge of the printing operation, was a nephew of Pak In-ho, the senior Ch'ŏndogyo official.[27]

None of the leaflets bore the name of the Korean Communist Party nor were the great majority of them overtly Communist in content. The throw-sheets printed in Korea merely set forth anti-Japanese slogans and demanded Korean independence. However, some of the materials from Peking had a stronger ideological tone. One two-page leaflet asserted that the fight for political independence was in truth a battle for economic independence, since all colonial people were a part of the proletariat.[28] Another four-page leaflet printed in China advanced the theme that the sorrow of the Korean people over the death of their emperor was in actuality a mourning over the death of the nation in 1910, and that the only way to overcome this sorrow was to drive the Japanese imperialists out of Korea.

Appended to these leaflets were the names of various fictitious organizations such as the Great Korean Independence Party and the Fire Sparks Group. An exception was one mimeographed leaflet, produced in Korea, that carried the names of Ch'oe Rin, Kim Sŏng-su, and Ch'oe Nam-sŏn, three prominent nationalists of this period. Since these individuals were not on good terms with the Communists, and since they currently favored a moderate approach, there is every reason to suppose that their signatures on this leaflet were put there without their authorization. Indeed, since the Communists regarded them as obstacles to the formation of a united front, it is quite possible that the leaflet was part of a Communist plot to remove them from the political scene.[29]

In any case, before the day of the funeral had arrived, Japanese au-

26. For details, see *ibid.*, pp. 30–33. See also the reminiscences of Hong Tŏk-yu, Pak Rae-wŏn, and others at a 1946 round table published in *Chosŏn Inminbo* (*Korean People's News*), June 9, 1946.

27. *Ibid.*, p. 1.

28. For a reproduction of the leaflets, see KCP, 2d CEC, March 17, 1926, Report, No. 1, Part 3, *op. cit.*, pp. 52–53.

29. This leaflet carried a simple message: "Our eternal enemy is Capitalist-Imperialist Japan. Twenty million compatriots! Let us fight to the death." Unlike the others, it was mimeographed, and since it carried the names of the three moderate nationalists it was probably intended to get them into trouble as well as to enlist more mass support for the radical cause.

thorities knew all about the Communist plans, and had confiscated most of the printed materials. It was a woman's curiosity that triggered the series of events that led to the collapse of the Second Korean Communist Party. A female employee of the Ch'ŏndogyo-operated magazine *Kaebyŏk* heard about the leaflets as a result of gossip among some of the workers in the building. Out of curiosity, she stole two leaflets from the stored cartons, and took them home to her husband. One of them, after passing through various hands, ended up in the home of a man who was suspected by the police of being a counterfeiter. They happened to pick this occasion to invade his home and question him, and in the course of the search they discovered the crumpled leaflet in an ashtray. After prolonged and intensive interrogations (Japanese authorities did not hesitate to use torture in such cases), the leaflet was traced back to the Ch'ŏndogyo building and Pak Rae-wŏn's involvement was made known. Interrogation of Pak led in turn to Kwŏn O-sŏl, mastermind of the operation, on whose person the police found a receipt for a package of 5,000 propaganda sheets from Peking. Eventually, the trail reached Kang Tal-yŏng, secretary of the KCP. He was arrested, and a full set of Party documents, many of them in code, was discovered. At first Kang refused to reveal his system of coding, and even attempted suicide. The police, however, succeeded in breaking part of the code by themselves and so persuaded Kang that further resistance was useless. All the documents were then decoded. Armed with this information, the police began the systematic arrest of all members of the Korean Communist Party and the Communist Youth League, ultimately jailing 176 persons.[30] The second KCP, after less than six months' existence, had been wiped out.

With the plot uncovered, Japanese authorities managed to control the situation on June 10 with very little difficulty. Some leaflets did escape seizure and were distributed. A few students sought to demonstrate, and shouts of "Manse!" echoed in a variety of places. There were even a number of arrests. But the national uprising for which the Communists had hoped was not forthcoming. Instead, the disturbances remained sporadic and small in scale.[31]

These events naturally had a major impact upon the nascent Korean Communist movement. In spite of various weaknesses, the first two Korean Communist Parties and Youth Leagues had encompassed the great bulk of the dedicated, able, and active Marxist intellectuals of the period. Such leadership as was available had now been used up. Most of the self-styled

30. Yoshino Fujizō, *op. cit.*, pp. 34–66.
31. See Yi Ki-baek, *Kuksa sinron* (*A New National History*), Seoul, 1961, p. 37. According to Yi the shouting of "Tongnip Manse!" ("Long Live Independence!") and other incidents led to the arrest of more than 500 persons. Some 4,000 police and soldiers had been mobilized to prevent trouble, according to *Shidae Ilbo* (June 11, 1926), p. 1, with most of those arrested being higher school and college students.

vanguard were either in prison or in exile, unable to play an active role. Even if one escaped arrest, if one remained in Korea it was almost impossible to be active politically, because the police at this point had the most minute information on the past activities of almost everyone who had had previous connections with any part of the Left. Suspects were kept under constant surveillance. Consequently, many of those not arrested chose to depart for Manchuria or Shanghai. The potential leadership for future Communist activities was thus greatly reduced. This affected not only the Party, but also the various legally constituted organizations connected with the peasant, labor, student, and nationalist movements in which Communists had previously been active, and which they had hoped to develop as major fronts.

The Japanese authorities now knew all about the Korean Communist movement. The arrests of 1925 and 1926 had been a product of accident; from now on, however, the Japanese police never had to rely mainly on luck. Seldom if ever in the history of revolutionary movements was so much known by ruling powers about their radical opponents as was known by Japanese authorities about the Korean Communists by mid-1926. This fact deeply affected future developments.

The 1925–26 arrests also had a pronounced effect upon the factional balance of power within Korean radicalism. Although the first KCP had represented a coalition of factions, the Tuesday Society had played the predominant role in it. This was even more true of the second KCP. Indeed, Tuesday Society leadership had been the principal cause of dissension on the part of the other factions. However, the June Tenth Incident, as it came to be called, virtually destroyed the Tuesday Society and with it such stability as the movement possessed. Factional squabbles not only continued to be intense; the lines of authority now became much more obscure.

The Third Korean Communist Party

After the summer of 1926, two main contenders for the shattered remains of the Communist movement emerged, namely, the Seoul Youth Association (Seoul faction) and the January Society. The latter had had its base in Tokyo and was associated historically with the North Wind faction. Many of its members were now back in Korea. Both of these groups thus had new opportunities for leadership. The Seoul faction, having previously refused to participate in the Party, was not implicated in the incidents that had shattered it. Hence, most of its members avoided jail and were still available for political activity. The January Society, with its locus in Tokyo, had also been relatively uninvolved. Now, with the old leaders gone, it was natural for these student radicals, deeply steeped in Marxism-Leninism as a result of their experiences in Japan, to aspire to the leadership of the Korean Communist movement. Almost without exception, they were strongly under the influence of Fukumoto Kazuo, the dynamic young theorist and Japanese Communist leader, who was now at the height of his power.[32]

The first efforts to rebuild the Party were begun in September 1926 by Kim Ch'ŏl-su and a few comrades who remained after the arrests. Kim, a Shanghai faction man, had been a member of the KCP Executive Committee but for some reason had escaped detention.[33] On December 6, a so-called Second Party Congress approved a revised Party leadership, with An Kwang-ch'ŏn, a January Society member recently returned from Tokyo, named Party secretary. Kim Chun-yŏn, then chief editor of *Chosŏn Ilbo,* was induced to join the Party and accept the post of Propaganda Bureau chief.[34] Ha P'il-won, another member of the January Society, headed the Organization Bureau, Han Wi-gŏn, a Shanghai faction man, Yang Myŏng, a Chŏng-u-hoe member, and Kwon T'ae-sŏk, a Seoul faction member, occupied the other three posts on the Central Committee. Thus was launched the Third Korean Communist Party. The Communist Youth League was also restored. Initially, Kim Kwang-su was named League secretary, but he was replaced by Yang Myŏng because of the objections of the Seoul faction. Kim Ch'ŏl-su and Kim Kwang-su were later dispatched to Moscow to report on reestablishing the Party.

Once again, the KCP sought to resume its basic program. A new slate of provincial officers was approved, and the reconstruction of local cells got under way in most areas. Efforts were focused upon students, workers,

32. See Robert A. Scalapino, *The Japanese Communist Movement, 1920–1966,* Berkeley and Los Angeles, 1967, pp. 26–31, and George M. Beckmann and Okubo Genji, *The Japanese Communist Party, 1922–1945,* Stanford, 1969, pp. 105–137.

33. A temporary party organization had been established by October with Kim Ch'ŏl-su as secretary, An Kwang-ch'ŏn as head of the Propaganda Department, and O Ui-sŏn, a Tuesday Society man, head of the Organization Department. Wŏn U-gwan, another Tuesday Society man, and Yang Myŏng, a Chŏng-u-hoe man, served as additional Central Executive Committee members.

From this point, Kim Ch'ŏl-su sought to enlarge factional support for the new venture. He tried to win over elements of both the Seoul and M-L Executive Committee groups and, as a result, a number of men were added to the roster by the time of the "2nd Party Congress." See Pang In-hu, *Puk-Han "Chosŏn Nodong-dang" ui hyŏngsŏng kwa palchŏn (The Formation and Development of the North Korean "Korean Workers' Party"),* Seoul, 1967, pp. 41–42.

34. Kim Chun-yŏn, some of whose background we have already set forth, was considered one of the best educated Koreans of this period. A graduate of Tokyo Imperial University, he had done postgraduate work there and then studied at the University of Berlin. According to Kim, various Party members were particularly impressed with him because he had translated Stalin's *Lenin and Leninism* from German into Korean even before Stalin had become the dominant Soviet figure. While Kim had read Communist literature in Japan and Germany, and considered himself sympathetic to the Communist cause, he did not join the KCP until 1926. Robert A. Scalapino interview with Kim Chun-yŏn, Sept. 26 and 27, 1957, Seoul. See also Chōsen Sōtokufu, Hōmukyoku (Government-General of Korea, Bureau of Justice), *Chōsen dokuritsu shisō undō no hensen (Changes in the Korean Independence Thought Movement),* Seoul, 1931.

and tenant farmers, with special attention being directed toward middle school students. Party and League members encouraged provincial youth societies and left-oriented student organizations to sponsor lectures and seminars with a Marxist flavor. Propaganda material printed in Tokyo was mailed to various student leaders and educational institutions; it featured denunciations of Korean education as a system geared to Japanese imperialism and capitalism, and therefore totally inappropriate for Korea. Students were encouraged to carry out school strikes to protest Japanese policies, and the authorities admitted that a number of strikes did indeed occur in Korean middle schools during 1927. These efforts culminated the next year in a Communist plan to launch a nationwide student demonstration on the occasion of the anniversary of the March First Uprising. But the plan was scrapped when leaders of the Shingan-hoe (New Korea Society), the leading nationalist organization, opposed the idea as premature.[35]

The top strength of the Third Korean Communist Party was probably around 200 members divided into some 30 cells. In addition, branches of both the Party and the Youth League were established in Tokyo in May 1927, with Pak Rak-jong as head of the Party branch and Han Rim of the Youth League. Special emphasis was placed upon activities among manual workers, who constituted the great bulk of the Korean population in Japan.

Once again, however, serious factional problems quickly made their appearance. They centered upon rivalry between the Seoul and January factions. The Seoul faction, angered because they were given no key posts in the reorganized Party, constantly attacked the returned students as snobbish school boys worshiping abstract theory and having no practical knowledge of Korean society. The January faction, in its turn, charged that the Seoul group had no theoretical understanding of Marxism-Leninism, and was therefore totally unsuited for Communist leadership. There can be no doubt that Fukumoto's notions of "separation and unity" had deeply permeated the January Society group. Taking up one element of Leninism, Fukumoto had argued that it was essential to purify the Communist movement by achieving ideological sophistication, even though this would produce certain splits as various deviationist and opportunistic elements left the Party. In the long run, he insisted, a deep and correct ideological understanding was vital to Party unity and growth. In accordance with these teachings, January Society members, together with a few Seoul faction elements whom they had won over, formed a new group dedicated to ideological purity that they called the Marxist-Leninist League. For this reason, the Executive Committee of the Third KCP was later labeled the M-L Group.

35. Kyŏnggi Province (Keikidō) Police Department, "Suppression of Secret Organizations, Including the Korean Communist Party and the Koryŏ Communist Youth League," Oct. 27, 1928, in *AJMFA,* R S722. This mimeographed report of approximately 150 pages presents a detailed account of the so-called "Fourth KCP Incident" (hereafter cited as "The Suppression of Secret Organizations . . .").

As the factional struggle gained momentum, there were a number of shifts in the leadership. At a fairly early point, An Kwang-ch'ŏn was replaced as Party secretary by Kim Chun-yŏn.[36] He in turn was succeeded by Kim Sŏng-hyŏn (alias Kim Se-yŏn), another January Society man. While serving as Party secretary, Kim Chun-yŏn was severely beaten by unknown assailants, possibly at the instigation of the Seoul group (he later stated that those who attacked him wanted to know all about the disposal of Comintern funds sent to the Party). Kim Tu-jŏng has written that the attack was a part of the general struggle for control over the Party.[37]

Finally, on December 21, 1927, Yi Yŏng, leader of the Seoul Youth Association, summoned his provincial representatives to a meeting in Seoul.[38] There it was agreed that a new Korean Communist Party would be established exclusively by the Seoul faction. In subsequent meetings, Yi Yŏng was made Party secretary, and heads of the Political, Organizational, Propaganda, and Inspection Bureaus were selected. A separate Korean Communist Youth League was also organized by this group in January 1928. At last, the Seoul faction had openly established its own separatist movement, as it had long threatened to do. Representatives of the new Party quickly departed for Moscow to seek Comintern recognition.[39]

36. Pang In-hu asserts that An was a very cunning plotter who arranged to have the Central Executive Committee members resign en masse, under the pretext that someone was responsible for the leakage of Party secrets, in order to get rid of one man, Kwon T'ae-sŏk, a leading Seoul faction figure. Then, according to Pang, An arranged to have Kim Chun-yŏn elected. See Pang, *op. cit.,* pp. 43–44.

Another source indicates that An was removed because his membership in a provincial fraternal organization was considered unbecoming a good Communist.

37. Kim's statement was made in the interview with Robert A. Scalapino cited above. For Kim Tu-jŏng's account, see his "A Short History of the KCP," in *Hankyō sōsho* (*Anti-Communist Series*), No. 8 (Tokyo, Oct. 30, 1939), p. 119.

38. For additional details, and the trial of Yi Yŏng and his group, see *Chōsen dokuritsu shisō undō no hensen, op. cit.,* pp. 226–233.

The Seoul meeting was held at a restaurant, with twelve provincial representatives present, and it was agreed to organize the new party exclusively on the basis of the Seoul Youth Association faction. At a subsequent meeting, Yi Yŏng was made Party secretary and other officers were chosen. In January 1928, the group also organized its own Korean Communist Youth League.

One source (*Kōtō keisatsu yōgo jiten—A Dictionary of Terms for the Higher Police,* prepared by the Bureau of Police Affairs of the Korean Government-General, Seoul, 1933), states that the Comintern regarded the 3rd KCP as a party based upon Fukumotoism, and a hindrance to the movement. It therefore presented Kim Yŏng-man with an eleven-point set of instructions to correct the situation when he was in Vladivostok. Kim returned to Korea in September 1927 but found no means whereby he could alter the existing situation. Hence, he helped to create a new party: p. 327.

As late as November 1927, however, a 3rd KCP representative received 3,300 yen from a Comintern agent in Tokyo (*Chōsen dokuritsu shisō undō no hensen, op. cit.,* p. 213). Cho Pong-am told the senior author that the Comintern did denounce the M-L group in this period, without mentioning a precise date: interview with Cho Pong-am, September 27, 1957. In all probability, there was a good deal of confusion in Comintern as well as in KCP quarters.

39. *Kōtō keisatsu yōgo jiten, op. cit.,* p. 327.

The formation of the Seoul-faction Party raised factional struggle to new heights. There is reason to believe that rival Communists in some cases went so far as to inform on each other to the police.[40] Involuntary leakage of secrets also increased as a result of the chaotic situation within the movement. From the beginning of the third KCP, of course, the police had had some information. Within weeks after the event, they knew of the efforts to reestablish the Party Executive Committee, an activity that got under way in September 1926. The low level of activities, however, made speed unnecessary. By February 1928, Japanese authorities finally had decided to move. On February 2, in a series of raids, police seized a large number of third Party members. The arrests continued as interrogations uncovered more facts, and in April most members of the Seoul-faction Party were also rounded up.[41]

The Fourth Korean Communist Party and Final Dissolution

As usual, a few Party members eluded the dragnet. On February 27, three weeks after the third Party leaders had been jailed, twelve Communist delegates met in Seoul. The delegates represented eight Korean provinces, the Japanese and Manchurian bureaus, and Party headquarters. This miniature national conference, originally scheduled for January 5, proceeded to approve Party bylaws, discuss the most recent Comintern resolution on Korea, and decide upon a report on the Korean situation to be submitted to the Comintern. The group also selected a three-member nominating committee, giving it authority to reestablish the Party Executive Committee. On the very next day, two of the three members of the nominating committee were arrested by police. What ensued will seem amazing to those unfamiliar with the curious mix of authoritarianism and tolerance that characterized the pre-1945 Japanese system. The two arrested Communists were able not only to conduct their business in jail but to smuggle out the list of nominees for the fourth Executive Committee simply by giving it to a fellow Communist who was being released. Ch'a Kŭm-bong was named the new Party secretary. An Kwang-ch'ŏn, restored to the hierarchy, was nominated to head the Political Bureau; Kim Han-gyŏng was to serve as Organization Bureau chief; Han Wi-gŏn was made Inspection Bureau head; and Kim Chae-myŏng was appointed head of the Communist Youth League. Other headquarters officials selected included Yang Myŏng, Han

---

40. Kim Chun-yŏn, in his interview with the senior author, asserted that informing the police concerning one's rivals did occur, and that he strongly suspected opponents within the movement of having informed the *kempeitai* about the 3rd KCP.

41. See Migi Konji, "Naichi ni okeru Chōsenjin to sono hanzai ni tsuite" ("Concerning the Koreans in Japan and Their Crimes") in *Shihō kenkyū* (*Studies on the Administration of Justice*), No. 17, published by the Ministry of Justice, Tokyo, March 1933. (Migi was a governmental prosecutor at the time and had handled certain cases involving Korean Communists.)

Myŏng-ch'an, Han Hae, Yi Sŏng-t'ae, and Yun T'aek-kŭn. The fourth Korean Communist Party had been organized—from a Seoul jail.[42]

The new Executive Committee controlled Party affairs, at least nominally, until July 4, 1928. Its members then decided that they should resign en masse. Because of police surveillance, it had been nearly impossible to carry out any functions. Spies and infiltrators had become an increasingly effective police weapon as the Party continued to be rent by internal feuds, and Party leaders suspected the Japanese authorities had a complete membership list. To continue operating as an Executive Committee, therefore, would merely guarantee swift arrest without any conceivable advantage being gained.

The decision to resign was different from the decision to dissolve the Party reached by the Japanese Communists some four years earlier, in March 1924. That decision had been based upon the premise that a formal Communist party was premature in Japan, and that Marxist-Leninists could work more profitably in organizing unions and mass movements among the workers, peasants, and students, thereby preparing the ground more thoroughly for a Communist party. The decision of the Japanese leaders had been bitterly attacked by the Comintern, whose basic position was that a Communist party had to be kept in existence at all costs to serve as vanguard and tutor for the masses. They had thus insisted that the Japanese Communist Party be reestablished, an action undertaken in 1925.[43]

Perhaps the Korean members of the fourth Executive Committee had this background in mind. In any case, they did not call for the dissolution of the Party. Rather, they requested that Party reorganization be entrusted to Yang Myŏng in Shanghai. Once again, the primary responsibility for the Korean Communist movement was to shift to overseas bases. There was no alternative. It had become impossible to sustain a meaningful movement in Korea proper; the Japanese authorities were too efficient, and the Party was too disorganized by factional hatreds.

The decision to resign did not save most of the fourth KCP Executive Committee. It is quite possible that an informer attended the meeting of July 4. In any case, the following day, two prominent committee members, Han Myŏng-ch'an and Yun T'aek-kŭn, were arrested. Other arrests followed in the same month. With information obtained from these first detainees, police conducted a series of nationwide raids on August 20–22; ultimately, some 175 individuals were arrested. The stragglers were picked up during the fall of 1928. By the end of the year, the Korean Communist movement was, for all practical purposes, defunct.[44]

42. Most of the information relating to the "4th KCP" comes from "The Suppression of Secret Organizations . . . ," *op. cit.*

43. See Scalapino, *The Japanese Communist Movement, op. cit.,* pp. 22–26.

44. After the August arrests, Yi Myŏng-su, the head of the Youth League in North Chŏlla, attempted to continue the movement, but he and his followers were

The Comintern as Guide and Reformer

At about the time that the Seoul-faction Party was being organized, the Comintern was preparing new instructions for the Korean Communists. These instructions, brought into Korea via Shanghai in January 1928 by Yi Chŏng-yun, are worthy of some attention.[45] The first sentence gives the main thrust: "The most important and urgent task of the militant Korean proletariat is the realization of a unified Party and the immediate dissolution of all existing factions and groups." There follows a harsh attack on factional struggles as "unprincipled, without any political basis, and against the resolutions of the International." These struggles, assert the Comintern authors, had paralyzed Korean revolutionary development, and resulted in the betrayal of all radical organizations to the police.

The document seemed to make clear Comintern support for the mainstream (M-L Group) leadership and to disavow the Seoul faction. The KCP resolutions of August 18 and November 14 (1926) were declared "absolutely correct," as was the Youth League resolution regarding the Seoul Youth Association. It was further stated that the national officials selected by the "Party Congress" of December 6, 1926, had been recognized by the International and that all external groups and individuals who came under the guidance of the International should join both the Party and the Youth League forthwith. None of this could possibly have pleased the Seoul faction.

The Comintern's instructions on factionalism are among the most revealing examples of Comintern–single Party relations of their kind that the era has provided. The KCP leaders were ordered to give top priority to eliminating factionalism; those who furthered it were to be "unconditionally punished." At the same time, the whole problem was to be ended "peacefully," by "disciplined Party debates accompanied by comradely love." The Executive Committee had to avoid driving the factional struggle outside the Party and so allowing a separatist movement to develop. Given the actual status of the problem at this point and the nature of these instructions, it is little wonder that, at the meeting of late February, Party leaders found that they had little to say on this matter. The Comintern, however, had positioned itself well to be critical in the future no matter what happened. If Party leaders were not guilty of "rightist opportunism" (over-compromise), which was unlikely in this case, they could always be charged with "leftist extremism" (rigidity perpetuating the split). Only success—the most unlikely event of all—could save them.

The Comintern's instructions also contained exhortations that more

---

also arrested shortly thereafter. See the trial statement of Yi Myŏng-su, Yim Chong-hang, and fifteen others, *Shisō geppō, op. cit.*, No. 3, *AJMFA*, R S355, pp. 129–135, and No. 5, pp. 244–256.

45. The full Comintern document is to be found appended to "The Suppression of Secret Organizations . . . ," *op. cit.*, in *AJMFA*, R S722.

workers be brought into the Party. "The Party must infiltrate deeply into all factories; otherwise, it cannot fulfill its historical role." Poor peasants, farm tenants, and other suitable agrarian elements also needed to be mobilized. "In a nationalist revolution," asserted the document, "it is not necessary for the Communists to occupy all the leadership positions in a national revolutionary mass party." However, Communist ideological and organizational influence over the masses was critical. Any nationalist organization had to be molded by the proletariat (Party). Closer relations with the masses had to be established, and the true Leninist spirit had to be grasped. This could happen only as factionalism ceased.

These instructions are interesting among other reasons, because they were drafted only a few months after a major thesis had been issued on the Japanese Communist movement. After lengthy hearings in Moscow, the Comintern, on July 15, 1927, had issued a blistering attack on both Fukumotoism and Yamakawaism. The former was equated with leftist deviationism, the latter with rightist opportunism. Fukumotoism, according to the Comintern, misused Leninism, overpoliticized the union movement, separated the Party from the masses, and placed an excessive value on the intellectuals, thereby abetting sectarianism. A Party based upon people who "think in correct Marxist terms," insisted the Comintern, will essentially be a party of intellectuals. It will not be a mass-struggle organization based upon the proletariat.

Similar concerns about the Korean movement must have been in the mind of the Comintern authorities when they penned the instructions just described. They knew very well that the M-L Group currently in control of the KCP were disciples of Fukumoto. But there was another circumstance that must have weighed even more heavily. This was a time of appalling troubles for the Chinese Communist movement. The alliance with the Kuomintang had been shattered, thousands of Communists had been killed, and the Chinese Communist Party was in desperate straits. The debacle was all the more serious for the Kremlin because Stalin's China policy was one of the significant issues in the internal struggle for power in which Stalin and Trotsky were the chief figures. At all costs, therefore, the failure in China had to be blamed upon indigenous elements. It is this that explains the purge of Ch'en Tu-hsiu on charges of having compromised Party integrity and independence in connection with the alliance with the Kuomintang: he had misunderstood the essential elements of a "correct united front policy." This was soon to be an issue that would weigh heavily upon the Korean Communists.

At the Seoul conference of February 27, 1928, the KCP leaders present took the position that factionalism within the Korean Communist movement had disappeared since early 1927, with "the small factional groups currently existing" being non-Communist in character.[46] To take

46. *Ibid.*

this line, of course, was to define the Seoul faction as non-Communist, because that faction certainly still existed; indeed, it insisted that it and it alone was the true representative of the Korean Communist movement. Nor were the February Theses of the KCP accurate in other respects on the issue of factionalism. Factional divisions were still a critical problem even though many of the old leaders were now in prison.

Most of the February Theses were taken up with a detailed discussion of how to bring the national liberation movement under Communist control and make the KCP a mass party. As was to be expected, the Party leaders identified themselves with the proletariat, although by Marxist standards the overwhelming majority of them were petty-bourgeois intellectuals. They proclaimed that the central problem of the militant proletariat was to transform the Party into a mass party, and that this could be done only as the worker vanguard aroused the broad peasant masses. This vanguard had to become the organizer and leader of the peasants in their struggle for an agrarian revolution. But while the worker-peasant base had to be made secure, the cooperation of the bourgeoisie was no less essential. To be sure, the worker-farmer classes had to be made acutely aware of the danger that the bourgeoisie might betray them. The lesson of the Chinese revolution had to be taken to heart. But bourgeois collaboration was still necessary at the present stage of the Korean liberation movement.

Such an analysis was no more than a straightforward application of Leninist-Stalinist doctrines, and it put the fourth KCP totally in line with prevailing Comintern policies. It would appear, moreover, that for the rest of its existence, the fourth KCP continued to get Comintern support. In March 1928, Yang Myŏng, currently serving as liaison man in Shanghai, forwarded 2,500 yen for publication expenses and other needs; in June, just before the decision of the Executive Committee to dissolve, he sent another 1,000 yen, although only 500 yen is supposed to have reached Korea.[47]

Contacts with Moscow also continued. Han Hae and Kim Kyŏng-sik left Korea for Moscow on February 20, 1928, to attend a Profintern congress. This they did in March, returning to Korea in April. Then Han was

47. Some of these funds were used for Party publications. *Chosŏn ji kwang* (*Light of Korea*) had been designated as the Party organ; a few issues of this magazine have been preserved. The bureaus in Japan and Manchuria also published magazines and newspapers on behalf of the Party. In Japan, the main publications were *Taejung Sinmun* (*Mass Newspaper*), *Hyŏn-dange* (*Present Stage*), and *Ch'ŏngnyŏn Chosŏn* (*Young Korea*). The Manchurian General Bureau published *Hyŏngmyŏng* (*Revolution*) as the Party organ, and *Pulkot* (*Spark*) for the Youth League. The Shanghai branch also published an organ, with An Kwang-ch'ŏn as editor in charge. An had earlier been removed as head of the Party's Political Bureau for making a false report concerning his mistress and restoring her to membership after her expulsion.

dispatched again, with Yang Myŏng; together they attended the June Comintern meetings as KCP delegates. The KCP also sent Kang Chin as Youth League representative to participate in the League's international congress. In this period, there was no indication of major trouble. On the contrary, all Korean delegates were apparently treated well. Kim, for example, when he returned, reported to the Seoul Executive Committee that a French delegate had publicly commented that Kim, a carpenter and official in the Korean Labor Federation, was the first Korean worker to have attended a Profintern congress, and hailed this sign of progress.

Within a few months, however, the Comintern was to launch a broad-scale attack upon the Korean Communist movement, excoriating *all* factions and almost all the movement's past actions, and challenging the class credentials of Party spokesmen. On December 10, 1928, the Polit-Secretariat of the Comintern Executive Committee approved a resolution on the Korean Question (the so-called December Theses) that in effect demanded the abandonment of the old Korean Communist movement, and the creation of a new one, with new leaders, new policies, and new organizational principles.[48] Since the old movement lay in ruins, this was, perhaps, not such a radical step as it might appear. Nevertheless, a careful study of the resolution indicates certain major changes of attitude and policy. To appreciate these, however, it is necessary first to retrace our steps and take up in some detail the evolution of Communist-nationalist relations, especially the central issue of a national revolutionary united front.

Nationalists, Communists, and the United Front

From the very beginning, the Korean Communists were under strong Soviet-Comintern pressure to form a united front with militant nationalists. Such a policy, of course, was one of the most fundamental tenets of Leninism, and was frequently reiterated via Soviet and Comintern channels from 1920 to 1927. It will be remembered that, when Lenin ordered the Soviet treasury to transmit two million rubles to Han Hyŏng-gwŏn, he believed that these funds would be used to strengthen a Provisional Government in Shanghai that represented a broad coalition of Communists and nationalists. Indeed, Lenin like other Soviet leaders sensed that the nationalist quotient within the so-called Communist movement was so strong that, for the moment at least, the most for which one could hope was a powerful national liberation movement in which, at a later point, a stronger Socialist component could be developed. As we have seen, none of the early efforts at

48. For the full thesis of the Executive Committee of the Communist International, see *International Press Correspondence*, Vol. 9, No. 8, Feb. 15, 1929, pp. 130–133: "Resolution of the E. C. C. I. on the Korean Question," adopted by the Polit-Secretariat of the E. C. C. I. on December 10, 1928. See also Dae-Sook Suh, *Documents of Korean Communism—1918–1948*, Princeton, 1970, pp. 243–256.

a united front were successful; indeed, the Communists could not even find a path to unity among themselves. Nevertheless, Comintern authorities continued to urge a broader coalition. Thus, a 1924 report of the Comintern Executive Committee stated that

> besides strengthening the Communist Party, the chief task of our comrades in Korea should consist in furthering the formation and unification of the pure labour organisations, and in substituting revolutionary-minded comrades for the Right Wing elements in the organisations. In the purely Nationalist movement, the Communists should work for the establishment of a united front of the National-revolutionary struggle.[49]

This exhortation, it will be noted, was delivered even before a Communist party had been organized in Korea proper. When word of the formation of the first Korean Communist Party reached Moscow, therefore, it was natural that the very first Comintern resolution concerning the new Party should direct that it ought to "give first priority to the national liberation struggle by uniting with the workers, peasants, and all other working elements: handicraftsmen, the intelligentsia, and the petty and middle bourgeoisie." [50]

According to Otto Kuusinen, joint discussions were conducted at this time (probably with Korean delegates Cho Tong-ho and Cho Pong-am) on the question of forming in Korea a national revolutionary party of the Kuomintang type.[51] This, of course, would have been the most logical step. Soviet and Comintern authorities were elated at this point with developments in China. The Kuomintang-Communist alliance was proceeding very satisfactorily from their point of view. Russian advisers such as Mikhail Borodin as well as Comintern representatives of many nationalities were operating with growing effectiveness on the Chinese scene; top CCP figures were moving into key positions within the Chinese government; the Kuomintang as a whole was moving leftward. Should not the general tactics being employed in China be used elsewhere?

The current line for Korean Communists was succinctly set forth in another Comintern resolution of this period: "The most important task facing the revolutionary movement in Korea at the present time is the task

---

49. The Communist International, *From the Fourth to the Fifth World Congress, Report of the Executive Committee of the Communist International,* London, 1924, p. 76.

50. Resolution of 1925, quoted in Otto Kuusinen, "O koreiskom kommunistcheskom dvizhenii" ("On the Korean Communist Movement"), *Revolyutsionnyi vostok,* Moscow, No. 11–12, 1931, pp. 99–116. We are greatly indebted to Professor Glenn D. Paige for uncovering and translating this source, and we have used his translation dated December 1963, available in mimeographed form. Pagination refers to the Paige translation. For the quotation cited above, see p. 9. Reference should also be made to a translation now available in Dae-Sook Suh, *Documents, op. cit.,* pp. 257–282.

51. *Ibid.,* p. 9.

of creating a broad national revolutionary front that includes handicrafts-men, the intelligentsia, and the petty and middle bourgeoisie along with the workers and peasants." [52] No doubt Cho Tong-ho informed his comrades in Seoul of the Moscow discussions when he returned to Korea shortly after the sessions in the Soviet capital ended. There is no record, however, of any action on the part of the first Korean Communist Party. But immediately after the Party was reconstituted, on February 26, 1926, "the national problem" was carried on the agenda. However, the minutes of the meeting merely record the following: "Make Ch'ŏndogyo group the foundation of Kukmindang [Nationalist Party]. Investigate the Ch'oe Rin and Kwon Tong-jin factions within the [Ch'ŏndogyo] group before initiating action." [53] Two weeks later, on the evening of March 10, the first meeting between Communists and nationalists took place. Kang Tal-yŏng, secretary of the KCP, met secretly with Shin Sŏk-u (publisher of *Chosŏn Ilbo*), An Chae-hong (manager of the same newspaper), Kwon Tong-jin (Ch'ŏndogyo leader), and several others, including Yu Ŏk-gyŏm, Pak Tong-wan, and O Sang-jun. A thorough discussion of the "uncompromising national libera-tion movement" took place, and it was agreed that a united front involving Kwon Tong-jin's faction in Ch'ŏndogyo, "socialists," Christians, and other militant nationalists should be formed.[54]

Shortly thereafter, the KCP submitted a report to the Comintern that included a section on "The Condition of the National Liberation Move-ment and Its Relationship With 'Y' [the Party]." [55] This report indicates, among other things, how grossly Korean Communist leaders often exag-gerated the situation in their favor. The section began with the assertion that, since the March First Movement, most nationalist leaders had moved into the Communist camp, and that the remainder were now in process of joining the Communists as a means of attaining a national revolution. The only organizations, the report admitted, that were directly engaged in na-tional revolutionary front activities were in south and north Manchuria. These were the Uiyŏldan (Righteous Fighters' Corps), which was currently engaged in terrorist activities, the Shinmin-bu (New People's Group), and the T'ongui-bu (United Righteous Group).

There followed an evaluation of various Korean groups as they re-lated to national liberation. Ch'ŏndogyo and Taejonggyo, a splinter faction from Ch'ŏndogyo, were described as favorable to the cause. Moreover, the Ch'ŏndogyo "old faction," under Kwon Tong-jin, had agreed to cooperate with the Party in establishing a national revolutionary organization. The Party had held a few unofficial meetings with the group "with the intent of

---

52. *Ibid.*
53. KCP, 2d CEC, March 17, 1926, Report, No. 1, Part 2, *op. cit.*, pp. 1–2.
54. *Ibid.*, p. 8.
55. A report submitted by the KCP to the Comintern in March 1926, "The Con-dition of the National Liberation Movement and Its Relation to Y" ("Y" stands for the KCP), reproduced in *ibid.*, p. 34.

organizing a powerful revolutionary organization under instructions from the International, and this matter is still under investigation." [56]

Another primary source of information for the period is the diary of Kang Tal-yŏng, Party secretary.[57] On March 18, 1926, he recorded that at a meeting of the Tuesday Society it had been decided that a conference of "uncompromising nationalists" should be convened in Manchuria. After that, a national party should be organized with Communists assuming an active role. Headquarters would have to be maintained abroad because of the extraordinary hazards involved in political activity in Korea, but a branch should be established in Seoul. On April 6, Kang wrote to Kim Ch'an, KCP liaison man in Shanghai: "We are planning to organize a Korean Nationalist Party in cooperation with uncompromising nationalists. We plan to become the core of the party and to maintain a dual organization system. Since the attitude of the Ch'oe Rin group is unclear, we are conducting investigations. When these are finished we shall immediately put the plans into effect." [58]

56. The report continued by saying that, while it was likely that the Party could join with the Kwon Tong-jin faction, since the full facts were not yet known concerning the Ch'oe Rin group, final policies had not yet been established. The report also referred to the problem of finances, indicating that funds were not sufficient for large-scale organizational efforts.

57. Reproduced in *ibid.,* No. 1, Part 2.

58. This letter is reproduced in *Shisō geppō, op. cit.,* Vol. 2, No. 9, Dec. 15, 1932, pp. 2755–66, *AJMFA,* R S357. When read in its entirety, this letter is a fascinating document, revealing all of the difficulties faced by a small, faction-ridden organization operating under very dangerous circumstances and trying to coordinate its far-flung branches. Note, for example, the following passage:

"There were some here who argued that comrade Pak Ch'ŏl-hwan [Cho Pong-am] is strongly disliked by the Shanghai faction, and that therefore it would be a major obstacle to the work in Manchuria if comrade Pak [Cho] were appointed as the secretary in charge. To adjust this matter, comrade Kim Ch'an was requested to make an investigation. The reason why the Shanghai office is called a Temporary Bureau is because Shanghai lacks the permanent value of Manchuria, which will become the center of our movement abroad, at least in the north.

"But the environment in which we work is not very simple. As the adage goes, the child of a widow has many belly buttons. The North Wind faction has been planning a strong attack in recent days, and there are many misunderstandings, even among comrades Yi Pong-su and Kim Ch'ŏl-su. Therefore, it is impossible to appoint comrade Pak Ch'ŏl-hwan [Cho Pong-am] as head of the Manchurian Bureau. . . . You said before, in Shanghai, that the Manchurian Bureau could not be established, but now you say that the Manchurian Bureau has been established, and has even won CI [Communist International] recognition. Why do you contradict yourself, making others suspicious? . . .

"The old officers of the Center [the Seoul underground KCP] have promised the Shanghai faction that 'If you do not oppose us, we shall work together.' They have also given us a signed document promising that they will obey the Party. There are frequent arguments that unless different elements are conciliated and cooperate, nothing can be done. That is the reason that the list of party officials has been constructed as it is. It is also for this reason that the right to control the activities of the members abroad was given to the Manchurian Bureau."

Stimuli in this period came not only from the Soviet Union and China, but also from Japan. After the passage of the Universal Manhood Suffrage Act there in 1925, activities in the direction of forming a legal proletarian party were greatly stepped up. Intensive discussions between various factions and groups continued throughout the spring and summer. Finally, on December 1, 1925, the Nōmin Rōdōtō (Farmer-Labor Party) made its appearance. This party was strongly leftist; almost all the moderates had already withdrawn from it, and it included the Japanese Communist contingent. It was almost immediately suppressed, but on March 5, 1926, the Rōdō Nōmintō (Labor-Farmer Party), representing a much wider spectrum of the Left, made its appearance.[59] These events, of course, were followed closely by the Korean student-intellectual activists, including the small Communist group.[60]

Events in Korea, however, were to take a different course from those in Japan, and for good reasons. In Japan, the effort was toward a unified, left-leaning "proletarian party" that could compete in the electoral arena with the "bourgeois" parties. In Korea, however, it was toward the creation of a broadly gauged nationalist movement spread over a wide political spectrum, with the one essential test being militant nationalism. One short-lived attempt was made to build a specifically leftist union to oppose bourgeois nationalism. On May 16, 1927, the Chŏn-jin-hoe (Advance Society), an intellectual study group consisting mainly of Seoul Youth Association members, inaugurated a body with the high-sounding name of

59. See Robert A. Scalapino, *Democracy and the Party Movement in Prewar Japan,* Berkeley, 1953, pp. 329–340. Also George O. Totten, III, *The Social Democratic Movement in Prewar Japan,* New Haven and London, 1966.

60. Ko Kyŏng-hŭm, *op. cit.* Ko reported that the study of socialism had been very popular among Korean students in the Tokyo area since 1924; we have already outlined the major organizations. In the same period, of course, the labor movement spawned various radical unions, one of which was Zai Tokyo Chōsen Rōdōkai (Chae-Tonggyŏng Chosŏn Nodong-hoe), the All-Tokyo Korean Labor Union. Both this organization and the Proletarian Youth League in Tokyo were essentially ideological associations, not true workingmen's units.

In 1926, however, with the new emphasis upon united front activities, various Japan-based Korean organizations adjusted to the new themes, dissolving and reorganizing in an effort to broaden their bases. In the latter part of 1927, Ko reported, branches of the Shingan-hoe and Kŭnu-hoe (The Korean Women's League) were opened in Tokyo, and mass organizations appeared to flourish. The year 1928, however, proved to be a traumatic one for the Korean Communists in Japan as elsewhere. First, the M-L line of Fukumoto was smashed by the Comintern. Then in the autumn, mass arrests took place, decimating the KCP's Japan Bureau. More than thirty prominent Korean Communists were arrested, and the offices of Shingan-hoe, Kŭnu-hoe, the Communist Youth League, and the Labor Congress were suddenly deserted.

In 1929, activities commenced again. The magazine *Hyŏn-dange (The Present Stage)* was reactivated, and various other operations got under way. However, morale and efficiency were low, and when, in July a second series of arrests occurred, this proved to be too great a blow. Korean Communist activities in Tokyo ceased to exist on any meaningful scale, although the Koreans proved to be an important part of the illegal Zenkyō, All-Japan Labor Council, which was operating in this period.

the Central Council of Korean Thought Organizations. So-called leading Korean socialists from various regions, including Japan and Manchuria, were brought together. One of the items on the agenda was the question of establishing a united proletarian party to counter the bourgeois political movements. However, police prohibited further meetings of the Council after the first day, and with its demise efforts of this sort largely disappeared.

Thus far, we have examined the first moves toward a united front largely from a Communist standpoint. Where did the non-Communist nationalists stand? After the March First Uprising, the broad nationalist movement had entered a period of stagnation. Attempts to win foreign assistance had produced no results. First the West, then the Soviet Union had pursued policies leading to disillusionment and sadness on the part of Korean nationalist leaders. Activities sank to a minimum. In December 1922, a few nationalist leaders had organized a Society for the Promotion of Korean Products under the leadership of Yi Chong-rin. The Society had as its objective the cultivation of nationalism by strengthening the Korean economy—an approach that proved to have its limits. Meanwhile, various nationalist leaders were beginning to move in other directions.

Two main trends predominated. One group of nationalists led by such figures as Kim Sŏng-su, publisher of *Tong-A Ilbo,* and Ch'oe Rin, one of the principal Ch'ŏndogyo leaders, gradually began to lean toward the idea of seeking Korean autonomy within the Japanese empire. More radical elements, of course, rejected this position as one that compromised Korean integrity. The hallmark of the nationalist, they insisted, must be his unflinching opposition to Japanese rule. The term "uncompromising nationalists," as we have seen, was used in Communist literature and elsewhere to symbolize this group. Its main leaders were Shin Sŏk-u, publisher of *Chosŏn Ilbo,* and Kwon Tong-jin, factional opponent of Ch'oe Rin in the Ch'ŏndogyo. Understandably, the Communists turned to this latter group in their initial efforts to build a united nationalist front.

If trends in China affected Communist views in Moscow and Seoul, they also affected the outlook of Korean nationalist leaders. The two leading Korean newspapers, *Tong-A Ilbo* and *Chosŏn Ilbo,* always followed developments in China and India very closely. Indeed, the Society for the Promotion of Korean Products had obviously been founded in emulation of the Gandhian movement's attempt to encourage native industry. Thus it also occurred to certain Korean nationalists that there might be merit in following the example of the Kuomintang, which had successfully established a united front with the Chinese Communists.

One example of the currents flowing in nationalist circles is reflected in a *Tong-A Ilbo* editorial of September 27, 1925, some months in advance of the date on which the KCP actually approached the nationalist leaders. The editorial was entitled "The Direction of Our Movement." Asserting that there were at present two political trends in Korean society, the national movement and the social movement, the author deplored the divisions between them and urged that those involved in the social movement join the national movement, accepting it as necessarily the mainstream. "Everyone would probably agree that trampling on life and property or suppressing human rights and freedom are more likely to result from the abuse of political power than of financial power. Ever since ancient times, political power in an authoritarian regime could destroy life or take away property. In Korea, then, the best way of promoting prosperity or freedom is to control power rather than to reject capitalism." [61]

The thrust of this editorial is unmistakable: a union of the "social" and "national" movements is essential, although a firm priority should be given the latter. While the critical questions of leadership, organization, and policy remain largely unexplored, a receptivity to united front operations is clear (*Tong-A Ilbo,* it should be remembered, generally took a more moderate line on questions of political tactics).

By the summer of 1926, the stage appeared to be set for the launching of a united front. Just at that point, however, the so-called June Tenth Incident occurred, and many members of the second KCP were arrested. Men like Kang Tal-yŏng were no longer in a position to carry out earlier plans. Nevertheless, in July 1926, while the arrests of Communists were still continuing, a number of Communists and militant nationalists joined together to announce that they had selected a preparatory committee to form the Chosŏn Min-hŭng-hoe (Korean People's Prosperity Society). Shin Sŏk-u, publisher of *Chosŏn Ilbo,* strongly supported this action, and since his newspaper currently represented the backbone of the united front movement, an editorial of July 11 in it may be taken as an authoritative expression of "uncompromising" nationalism. The following excerpts have been chosen to illustrate basic themes prevalent at the time.

> The purpose of the Chosŏn Min-hŭng-hoe is to strive for the common interest of the Korean nation [*minjok*] and to establish a single-front organ of the Korean people. It advocates the unity and consolidation of the entire. people—those engaged in industry, religious activities, and the various movements involving women, youth, outcasts, students, and intellectuals.
>
> The purpose of national consolidation ought to be the liberation of the Korean nation. . . . The movement will inevitably be expressed as an anti-imperialist movement . . . in the past, however, it has possessed strong class connotations and the nation was divided. But it is noticeable in the recent period that even among those participating in class movements, there has been a passionate demand for a unified national movement. . . .
>
> Just as the proletarian class joined hands with the capitalists in Europe in order to destroy feudalism and authoritarianism, they [the

61. *Tong-A Ilbo,* Sept. 27, 1925, p. 1.

Korean socialists] have realized the necessity for mobilizing classes that have a common interest in the anti-imperialist movement. . . . Since it is inevitable that class interests will ultimately come into conflict, even in Korea, the solidarity of the Korean nation cannot last forever. In spite of this, however, one cannot avoid recognizing the necessity for the two camps to unite in the solution of the most immediate problems. . . .

We would like such a movement to model its development after that of the Kuomintang in China.[62]

The Chosŏn Min-hŭng-hoe was subsequently organized, but it remained a rather ineffective body. Conditions, however, were becoming more propitious for a broader effort at a united front. A change in Communist policy was clearly signaled by the end of 1926. Organizations such as the Chŏng-u-hoe (True Friends' Society), an alliance of purely Communist or proto-Communist groups such as the Tuesday Society, North Wind Society, Korean Labor Party, and Proletarian League, announced their voluntary dissolution. Similarly, the Labor-Farmer Federation, which was under the control of the Tuesday faction, proclaimed itself ready to turn to the masses, and accepted a division into two federations, one for workers and one for farmers. In both organizational and policy terms, therefore, few obstacles to a nationalist-Communist alliance existed by 1927.

The initiative in connection with a united front now passed to the nationalists. Toward the close of 1926, Kim Sŏng-su, Ch'oe Rin, and Song Chin-u held a meeting with a high Japanese official to discuss the question of autonomy for Korea. The gist of this conversation was later related to Ch'oe Nam-sŏn, the author of the Declaration of Independence of 1919 and a prominent nationalist figure. Ch'oe in turn held a lengthy conversation with his friend, Hong Myŏng-hui, a teacher at Osan School in Chŏngju who later became publisher of *Shidae Ilbo.* Ch'oe and Hong decided that the movement for an autonomous Korea should be halted at all costs since it represented a weak compromise. The best means of accomplishing this would be to establish a united nationalist party. Hong then visited Shin Sŏk-u and An Chae-hong, manager of *Shidae Ilbo,* and the first organizational steps were taken.

Contacts were rapidly made with a number of important nationalists. Among others, Kwŏn Tong-jin, Pak Rae-hong, Pak Tong-wan, Han Yong-un, and Ch'oe Ik-hwan agreed to participate, as did Shin Ch'ae-ho, a nationalist leader in Peking. Meanwhile, Shin Sŏk-u contacted Japanese government officials to secure approval of the organization. After lengthy negotiations, it was granted.[63] Thus, on January 19, 1927, twenty-seven prom-

62. *Chosŏn Ilbo,* July 11, 1926, p. 1.
63. "The Suppression of Secret Organizations . . . ," *op. cit.,* pp. 44–45.
Some Japanese sources have indicated that permission to establish the Shingan-hoe was granted so that authorities could determine the scope and character of the Korean nationalist movement.

inent nationalists announced their intention to establish the Shingan-hoe (New Korea Society). The inauguration date was set for February 15.

From the outset, it was clear that Shingan-hoe was intended as an "uncompromising" nationalist organization that could accommodate all elements of the Left. The published program had to be kept vague in order to avoid suppression. But even here, a militant intent could be discerned:

1. We shall promote political and economic awareness.
2. We shall consolidate unity.
3. We shall deny all opportunism.[64]

Spokesmen for the group, moreover, did not attempt to hide the fact that the Shingan-hoe, having been formed to combat rightist tendencies within the nationalist movement, aimed at the formation of a leftist front. On February 11, just a few days before the new organization was launched, the Min-hǔng-hoe agreed to join it, provided that certain offices went to its leaders. Four days later, the Shingan-hoe initiation ceremonies were held at the YMCA hall in Seoul. Some two hundred persons attended. Shin Sŏk-u served as temporary president, with three secretaries: Kim Chun-yŏn (who had recently been recruited to the KCP), Shin Hyŏn-ik, and Chang Chi-yŏn. The members elected Yi Sang-jae as permanent president, and Hong Myŏng-hui as vice-president.

Shingan-hoe branches expanded very rapidly throughout Korea. Within a year, there were more than 100 branches and over 10,000 members. Nor was the newly restored Executive Committee of the third KCP slow to seek a prominent role in the Shingan-hoe. Local KCP branches were instructed to provide positive support, and all Party members were urged to join. In Seoul, at KCP national headquarters, Kwon T'ae-sŏk, Song Nae-ho, Kim Chun-yŏn, and Han Wi-gŏn served as links between the Party and the Shingan-hoe. Moreover, Shingan-hoe vice-president Hong Myŏng-hui was himself reportedly a secret Party member.[65] The tactics employed were a combination of "united front from above" and "united front from below." In addition to the close liaison attempted with

64. For the full statement which accompanied the first public announcement of Shingan-hoe, see *Tong-A Ilbo,* Jan. 20, 1927, p. 1.

65. Hong was never indicted as a Communist, although Kim Chun-yŏn later (1945) called him "a secret member of the KCP." Irrespective of Hong's precise affiliations, however, there can be no doubt of extensive Communist infiltration into Shingan-hoe from the outset. A police report dated October 7, 1928, includes a list of the names of KCP or CYL (Youth League) members on the Shingan-hoe rolls. Some forty-five Communists occupied official positions in the forty-four branches listed, including four who held the post of branch secretary. For example, the Seoul Shingan-hoe branch had two officers who were KCP members; in Kaesŏng, three officers, including the general secretary, were Communists. These facts, incidentally, were brought to light as a result of the arrests and interrogations connected with the uncovering of the 4th KCP. See "The Suppression of Secret Organizations . . . ," pp. 37–39.

Shingan-hoe leaders, Party officials hastened to form tenant and labor unions as front organizations. They provided the unions with "correct Marxist-Leninist education," and encouraged them to join the Shingan-hoe en masse so as to provide the organization with sturdy "proletarian units." This policy was officially issued to Party branches in April 1927, only a few weeks after the Shingan-hoe was established.[66]

By the time of its first anniversary, the Shingan-hoe could celebrate some notable successes. Its increasing radicalization, however, had now become a problem of both internal and external relations. Indeed, police prohibited the scheduled anniversary meeting because they had decided that many Shingan-hoe branches were Communist controlled or Communist influenced. Shingan-hoe headquarters itself admonished some branches for excessively radical activities and forced a few to replace their officers, partly to forestall government suppression. The increasingly tough attitude of the police was unquestionably connected with the discovery and arrest of the Party Executive Committee in February 1928. Those arrests involved among others, Kim Chun-yŏn, Han Wi-gŏn, and Kwŏn T'ae-sŏk, each of whom held important official positions in the Shingan-hoe.

None of these developments, however, deterred the Communists. The Executive Committee of the hastily created fourth KCP immediately adopted a "Theses on the National Liberation Movement" that reiterated previous policies. These theses are worthy of some attention.[67] They began with an analysis of previous shortcomings: in the past, the Korean Communists had avoided the political struggle, confining themselves mainly to the development of economic consciousness. Not understanding the historical significance of the Korean national liberation movement sufficiently, they had initially refused to participate in it. Since the latter part of 1926, however, this situation had fundamentally changed. The Party, now actively involved in the Shingan-hoe, had helped to bring the liberation movement to its present level of strength. There followed a sketch of the conditions characterizing Korean society: Korea under Japanese imperialism suffered from extreme economic exploitation and political suppression. In socio-economic terms, the society was marked by the presence of feudal remnants; the backwardness of national industry; the weakness of the proletariat; and the still greater weakness of the national bourgeoisie. The proletariat, however, occupied the supreme position in the revolutionary struggle because of "the maturity of its vanguard and the special characteristics of Korean society." Among these special characteristics was the great numerical strength of the poor peasants and tenant farmers who were rapidly being organized under the leadership of the proletariat.

Given the social and historical conditions, continued the theses, the Korean revolution had to be a bourgeois-democratic revolution. It had to

66. *Ibid.,* p. 40.
67. The Theses are reproduced in full in *ibid.,* Appendix.

concentrate upon the struggle against Japanese imperialism and the feudal remnants within Korean society supported by Japan. Hence the importance of the fight against the landlords: the battle for agrarian reform was critical. The Korean national liberation movement could develop successfully only under the leadership of the labor-farmer class. To date, that movement had followed three stages. The first stage, covering the period from the March First Movement of 1919 to the establishment of the Labor-Farmer Federation in 1923, had had as its propelling force the Korean bourgeoisie. Some elements of the aristocracy, the so-called Confucian landlord class, and various "feudalistic" religious groups had also been involved. The peasants and workers had followed the bourgeoisie, and the guiding spirit of the movement had been "pure bourgeois nationalism." Soon, this movement split and became powerless, with the greater part of the feudalistic elements and some of the bourgeoisie dropping out. The Communist movement, which had originated in this period, now began to split the bourgeois movement.

During the second stage, from 1923 to the creation of the Shingan-hoe in 1927, the workers and peasants had emerged as independent forces. "Progressive intellectual elements" rapidly turned to Communism; labor and farm tenant strikes arose in various places; unions and youth groups came under Communist direction. A proletarian vanguard was being formed. Meanwhile, the bourgeois nationalist movement had become impotent. The labor-peasant "vanguard," however, being dominated by erroneous principles, refused to play an active political role and served only as a disruptive force.

With the third stage, which began in early 1927, the Korean proletariat had changed its policies to accept political struggle. Thus it had emerged as a positive force in the national liberation front. This, together with the stimulus of the Chinese revolution and various other developments, had given the remaining classes courage. As a result, the liberation movement was enjoying a resurgence. It was clear that the movement's principal aim had to be the struggle against Japanese imperialism, that it had to be a united struggle. The movement, however, had already reached the stage where it could not be directed by the forces of bourgeois nationalism. The workers and peasants were now required to play the dominant role; only they could direct the revolution; only they could propel it to a successful conclusion. It was therefore essential for the Korean proletariat to establish hegemony over the entire movement.

There were, of course, revolutionary forces other than workers and peasants. As long as these forces engaged in the revolutionary struggle, the worker-peasant classes should be allied with them, utilizing their revolutionary energy. The intelligentsia played an important role in the Korean national liberation movement. Inevitably, however, as the struggle advanced, the bourgeoisie and a portion of the petty bourgeoisie would "lean to the right," drop out, or become counterrevolutionary. The vanguard of the Korean proletariat therefore had to strive constantly to organize left-wing forces based upon the worker-peasant masses within the national liberation front. In this way the rise of bourgeois reactionarism would be delayed as long as possible, and the impact of bourgeois withdrawal would be minimized. In this respect, especially, the Chinese revolution provided the Korean revolution with a salutary lesson.

In order to guide the Korean national liberation movement properly, the Korean proletariat would have to eliminate certain prevailing leftist and rightist errors. The two-party theory of the Yi Hang-bal group was a form of leftist infantilism. This group, failing to appreciate the nature of the present stage of the liberation struggle and being unable to comprehend "the national role" of the proletariat, opposed the organization of a national united front, mechanically adhering to "the independence of the proletarian movement" and so to a separate proletariat party. But the Korean proletariat could not separate its class duties and its national duties at this point, and in the national political struggle it had to have a broad spectrum of allies.

On the other hand, the Chang Il-sŏng–Kwon T'ae-sŏk group were guilty of advocating an abandonment of the class movement. Intoxicated by the idea of unprincipled cooperation, they had denounced the policy of the hegemony of the proletariat over the entire struggle and were prepared to give up the political independence of the proletariat. Their position represented an abandonment of proletarian consciousness. Under no circumstances should the political independence of the proletariat be sacrificed for the sake of national unity. The nature of the alliance should not be confused. The critical struggle against the weakness and treachery of the bourgeoisie and the petty-bourgeois intellectuals should not be neglected. Hegemony should not fall into their hands, nor should they be trusted too much.

The goal of the Korean national liberation movement, asserted the theses, lay in the complete independence of Korea. The movement for Korean autonomy within the Japanese empire—the attempt to strike a bargain among the imperialists, the Korean aristocracy, and the decadent Korean bourgeoisie—had to be resolutely opposed. The future power structure of Korea had to hinge upon "a revolutionary people's republic." To advocate the construction of a soviet republic in Korea was a leftist infantile position; to support the development of a bourgeois republic was a rightist one.

At the present stage of the Korean national liberation movement, the theses concluded, "the Shingan-hoe [was] the most appropriate alliance of revolutionary classes." The broad spectrum of the masses had not yet been involved, however; consequently, the struggle had been weak. The Korean Communists would have to enter the Shinghan-hoe in force, guide its struggles, and strive toward completing its development as a mass party. In operating within the organization, Communists should seek to guide the entire operation. But they should not confuse the Shingan-hoe with a proletarian party (the KCP); the organization should not be taken over mechanically. The Communists needed to concentrate upon bringing workers, peasants, and poor people into the Shingan-hoe, thus establishing a massive left wing. Then, when the right wing developed, as it inevitably would, the Communists could engage in a successful struggle to separate it from the masses.

The February theses of the KCP have been presented here in some detail because nowhere is there a clearer outline of basic Communist policy with respect to the united front. The Communists were not to be deterred by the recent catastrophe in China. The answer to that failure lay in creating a powerful worker-peasant left within the front, a left securely under Communist control and capable of defending itself against the counterrevolutionary thrust from the bourgeoisie that would surely come. The theses were permeated with an immense distrust of the bourgeoisie and petty bourgeoisie. This was partly the result of developments in China. However, one cannot fail to be impressed with the irony of the situation, since the Korean Communist leaders, almost without exception, were themselves petty bourgeois intellectuals by Marxist standards. But in any case, the tone and terminology of the theses did not bode well for an intimate, trusting relationship within the Shingan-hoe. Indeed, the Communists were almost brutally frank in outlining the limits and objectives of cooperation. To be sure, there was to be no mechanistic application of Communist procedures and policies. Communists were to keep in mind the fact that an association like the Shingan-hoe was different from the KCP. Offices had to be shared with elements of the *revolutionary* bourgeoisie, and it was necessary to pursue policies that differed somewhat from the Party's own. Under no conditions, however, should any Communist become confused with respect to his primary loyalties. The basic independence and integrity of the Party could never be compromised, and the Party's immediate objective should be hegemony over the *total* revolutionary movement.

The theses also made it clear that, while the Korean revolution had to be a bourgeois-democratic revolution, it was also to be a *managed* bourgeois revolution. The managers, of course, were to be the vanguard of the proletariat, that is, the KCP. The bourgeoisie themselves were not capable of completing their own revolution, nor were their objectives, such as parliamentarism, at all desirable. The immediate goal for Korea was neither a soviet republic nor a parliamentary-democratic system but a people's revolutionary republic. Only via this route could the managed bourgeois revolution be completed and the transition to socialism be undertaken.

The fact that these themes were spelled out so lucidly in the theses of February 1928 is of major significance for the study of Communist ideology. The themes, so basic to what was later to be called Maoism, could not possibly have been derived from Mao Tse-tung, either directly or indirectly. First formulated in 1927 (the theses did not suddenly emerge in final form), they were centrally derived from Comintern channels at a time when Mao was relatively unknown and of no ideological importance to the international movement. It is equally interesting in this respect to note the substantial emphasis in the theses upon the importance of the peasantry. Leninism, to be sure, had always stressed the vital need for the proletariat to build a mass peasant base in all societies that were still largely precapitalist. Now, however, the peasants were being advanced as a counterweight to bourgeois treachery, with the Chinese experience vividly in mind. By mobilizing the masses (that 80 percent of the society most of whom were in the ranks of the rural proletariat), the bourgeoisie could be effectively blocked, no matter how vicious their counterrevolutionary plots. In order to develop a peasant base, however, it would be necessary *first* to liberate the peasant from the rural authority structure. Centrally, that meant a frontal assault upon the landowning gentry. The first slogan of the revolution, therefore, had to be agrarian reform.

The Hardening International Line and Its Repercussions
We are now in a position to return to the Comintern's resolution of December 1928. As we have noted, relations between the Korean Communists (now dominated by the M-L Group) and the Comintern appeared to be good in the spring and summer of 1928. The Korean Communist movement, however, had come under fierce attack from the Japanese authorities, and it had been decided in mid-1928 to transfer Party organizational activities from Korea proper to Shanghai. By the fall of that year, it was difficult to say whether a Korean Communist party actually existed. Against this background, the Comintern issued the December Theses.

With respect to its analysis of the objective situation prevailing in Korean society and the basic tasks of the Korean Communist Party, the December resolution paralleled the KCP's February theses in almost every detail. Korea was a typical colonial country in the sense outlined by the Sixth Comintern Congress, a base of agricultural and other raw materials for Japanese imperialism. Its industrial development was meager, and even its agriculture was mostly at a precapitalist stage, with a small group of landlords exploiting a vast mass of poor peasants. Thus the urban proletariat, since it remained closely connected with the rural villages, was as weak in class consciousness as in numbers. "The vast majority of the Korean population consists of economically enslaved peasants who are suppressed and downtrodden by the terroristic police regime and who have no prospects of an improvement of their position without a revolution." [68]

With this alleged fact another had to be coupled: the Korean land-owners and urban bourgeoisie—the manufacturers, merchants, and money-lenders—were increasingly connected with and subordinate to Japanese capitalism. These conditions dictated that the Korean revolution had to be directed against two basic enemies, Japanese imperialism and Korean feudalism. The following quotation contains the essence of Comintern thinking on that fundamental question:

> It [the Korean revolution] will be directed towards the abolition of all pre-capitalist remnants and survivals, towards a cardinal change in the agrarian relations, towards a cleansing of the land from pre-capitalist forms of slavery. The revolution in Korea must be an agrarian revolution.
>
> Thus the overthrow of imperialism and the revolutionary solution of the agrarian problem is the main objective historical meaning of the revolution in Korea in the first phases of its development. In this sense the Korean Revolution will be a bourgeois-democratic revolution.[69]

This bourgeois-democratic revolution, however, should in no sense be captured and held by the bourgeoisie. Once again, the recent experiences in China dominated and directed the analysis. The task of the Korean Communists was a dual one: first, to strengthen the proletarian revolutionary movement and guarantee *its complete independence* with respect to the petty-bourgeois national-revolutionary movement; second, to capture that national-revolutionary movement, dissociating it from "compromising national-reformism" by fighting energetically against all bourgeois-nationalists.

If the bourgeois revolution were to be captured and led by the proletariat, as was essential, the agrarian problem had to be harnessed to the national revolution. Once again, the critical importance of the peasant is highlighted:

> There can be no victorious national liberation struggle without an unfoldment of the agrarian revolution. It is precisely the almost complete absence of control [linkage] between the national-liberation struggle and the struggle for land that is responsible for the defeat of the revolutionary movement of recent years (1919–20). A victory over the imperialist yoke presupposes a revolutionary solution of the agrarian problem and the establishment of a democratic dictatorship of the proletariat and the peasants [in the form of Soviets] through which the bourgeois-democratic revolution under the hegemony of the proletariat is transformed into a Socialist Revolution.
>
> Under these conditions, the peasant problem, the problem of the

68. "Resolution of the E. C. C. I. on the Korean Question," *op. cit.*
69. *Ibid.,* p. 131.

agrarian revolution, is of greatest importance for Communist activity in Korea. Only by bringing the peasants under their influence, only by appealing to them by means of intelligible and popular slogans and demands, will the working class and its vanguard be able to accomplish a victorious revolution in Korea.[70]

The Communist injunction was clear: to the masses—and especially to the rural masses! Only if Korean Communists undertook "mass Bolshevik work" in the factories, shops, and fields, only if they built effective labor and peasant organizations, could they fend off the reformist and counter-revolutionary plots of the bourgeoisie. Mass organizations like the Party had to have their integrity protected. This meant that all bourgeois vacillations had to be ruthlessly exposed.

But could the Korean Communist movement, as it previously existed, accomplish these tasks? The Comintern answer was an unequivocal no, and it proceeded to level a slashing attack against the Korean comrades focusing upon the factional problem. Factionalism, according to the December Theses, had made the party vulnerable to spies and agent provocateurs, made impossible the necessary organizational foundations for work among the masses, and violated all Marxist norms. The time had come to conduct an all-out attack upon factionalism; discard the "pseudo-scientific phrases" that had previously dominated the party and develop cadres having genuine Communist conceptions and truly scientific Marxist-Leninist modes of thought; and change the socioeconomic character of the Party. "The ranks of the Communist Party of Korea have in the past consisted almost exclusively of intellectuals and students. A Communist Party built on such foundations cannot be a consistently Bolshevik and organizationally sound Party." [71]

The December Theses ended by outlining in some detail the specific policies that should be advocated by the Party. The slogans of the daily struggle had to be coordinated with those of the struggle against Japanese imperialism. Slogans against imperialist war and for the Soviet Union were naturally to be given top priority. The broad program to be advanced would center upon national independence, a democratic dictatorship of the workers and peasants, and an agrarian revolution, involving the free distribution of estates and government land to the peasants. At the same time, however, the Party should advance as its immediate program a series of social reforms aimed at everyday economic problems: recognition for trade unionism, an eight-hour day, equal pay for men and women, better safeguards against industrial accidents, equality between Japanese and Korean workers, rent control, abolition of price ceilings for farm produce, and social laws protecting the peasant against "feudal" conditions.

70. *Ibid.*
71. *Ibid.,* p. 132.

The December Theses had laid down a general directive to the Korean Communist movement based upon the decisions of the Sixth Comintern Congress. Despite many problems, that directive was to govern the Korean Communists for the next few years. Meanwhile, two other Comintern documents of this general period shed further light upon the evolving situation.

Let us first turn to the remarks of the influential Finn, Otto Kuusinen. As a member of the Comintern Executive Committee, Kuusinen had obviously spent a great deal of time wrestling with the Korean problem. It is not clear when the remarks published in 1931 were first made, but they were definitely made in the presence of Korean representatives, whether at the time the December Theses were unveiled or at some point thereafter. The precise date, however, is not important; it is the central themes, which parallel and amplify the December Theses, that are interesting.

Kuusinen could not have been more caustic or more sweeping in his denunciation of past trends within the Korean Communist movement. Not one faction, he charged, had had a consistently correct line; among the various factions and individual comrades, there had been deviations of every color of the rainbow, so many that it was difficult to determine which predominated. The Party, moreover, had apparently benefited little from the discussions that had followed the Sixth Comintern Congress. Its pettybourgeois weaknesses continued, and "even if you tried to find workers in the factional groups with binoculars you could still not find them." [72] Even if the Comintern had wanted to give the leadership of the Korean Communist Party to one faction or another, the situation had become such after the Sixth Comintern Congress that it would have been impossible "for the simple reason that the police knew the whole factional mess, including the leadership and composition of each group." The Party had become totally bankrupt.

Thus the Comintern had decided to take drastic action. It had adopted "a serious antifactional course," a course designed not "to unite the factions but to destroy them, to liquidate them, and to create a new party, a new nucleus of leaders." Already, claimed Kuusinen, the new Comintern policy had succeeded in paralyzing the factional work of the former groups and factions [or was it the Japanese who had done this!]. He had to admit that "the factional elders" were very cunning, each of them playing the role of "kings in exile, pretenders to the throne of the future Communist Party of Korea." Kuusinen was firm. "Our answer to them is this: They are not needed for the future Communist Party of Korea; they can be only harmful elements in the revolutionary movement." [73]

A genuine Bolshevik Party required "a healthy proletarian composition together with the best, truly Communist forces from the revolutionary

72. Kuusinen, *op. cit.*, p. 18,
73. *Ibid.*, p. 24.

intelligentsia—such forces as have deep roots among the laboring masses."
It also required "iron discipline and indestructible unity" and "a politics of
principle based on Leninism and its correct application."

But at the end Kuusinen softened a bit. Some comrades, he asserted,
were adherents of the Comintern line in the present struggle, and therefore willing to fight against their old factional comrades. These individuals
were necessary and would be welcomed by the movement.

Of equal interest is the fact that the Comintern leader engaged in some
self-criticism. "In several matters," he acknowledged, "we are not without
error and this is especially true of the Korean question." Comintern resolutions from 1925 on had emphasized the importance of forming a national
revolutionary party patterned after the Kuomintang. While the Communist
Party had been given the task of unifying mass national organizations for
this purpose, it had been told that the work was to be done not in the
name of the Party but under the slogan of "a consistent struggle for
Korean independence." And so "in the end, the Communist Party was
thrown in a heap with all the other parties." Kuusinen then became deeply
apologetic. "Comrades, if these errors had not been so grave and if there
had not been a clear deviation I would not have recalled them." The Sixth
Comintern Congress had corrected the errors, but serious harm had been
done the Korean Communist movement. Previously, only *one* of the three
basic tasks of the bourgeois nationalist revolution had been stressed, namely,
that of national liberation. They had ignored the crucial need for agrarian
revolution as well as the vital importance of achieving the hegemony of
the proletariat. The Comintern, in sum, had failed to provide the type of
direction that would have allowed the Party to capture the revolution,
thereby enabling the bourgeoisie to consolidate their power and shift the
revolution to the right.

To be sure, the Korean Communists had often misled the Comintern
by exaggerating their gains or prospects. For example, they had reported
that the Shingan-hoe had more than 10,000 members, but Kuusinen
sharply challenged these figures as inflated, and insisted that the Shingan-
hoe was not a real mass organization at all. In any case, the current task
of the Korean Communists was *not* "to create a common national revolutionary party (à la Kuomintang) on the basis of individual membership,"
but to use joint action committees to create "a real bloc under proletarian
Communist leadership," and show up the petty bourgeois nationalists for
what they were. Kuusinen thus appeared to be calling for a change of
tactics that might include abandonment of the Shingan-hoe, or at least a
basic shift in Communist relations with it.

In any case, there was to be no repetition of the mistakes made in
connection with the Kuomintang. At another point, Kuusinen emphasized
the two basic errors signaled by the Sixth Comintern Congress concerning

the role of the national bourgeoisie in colonial countries. On the one hand, by failing to appreciate the "national reformist line" of this class, the Party could allow the bourgeoisie to gain the initiative. The result of this would be that the sharp distinction between proletariat and bourgeoisie would be blurred, and the most important revolutionary slogans, especially that of agrarian reform, would be stifled. The Chinese Communist Party had made this basic error in 1925–27. On the other hand, to underestimate the special significance of bourgeois reformism as distinct from feudalism and imperialism could lead to the isolation of the Communists from the masses and the rise of leftist sectarianism.[74]

The second Comintern document of interest to appear in this period was a Profintern resolution of September 18, 1930, concerning the tasks of the Korean revolutionary labor movement.[75] For nearly two years at this point, Comintern authorities had been calling upon the Korean Communists to turn to the worker-peasant masses. In this resolution, the same appeal was reiterated strongly in a context of surprising optimism. As the economic crisis involving Japanese capitalism worsened, proclaimed the resolution, the national struggle for emancipation from Japanese imperialism was growing, especially the class struggle of the Korean proletariat. Strikes, demonstrations, and partisan uprisings all signaled the approach of a new, larger mass movement.

Significantly, the resolution cast even graver doubts upon the reliability of the "national-reformist bourgeoisie." This group and their organs, having received bribes from Japanese imperialism and having been frightened by the revolutionary waves in China, India, and Korea, saw Chiang Kai-shek and his counterrevolution as worthy of emulation, were seeking collaboration with Japan, and did not hesitate to vilify the Soviet Union. The Shingan-hoe among others was specifically attacked as "a national reformist organization as [had] been proved by its policy of sabotage during the student and workers' movements." [76]

The tone of the 1930 resolution was unmistakably militant, as indeed the Comintern's whole policy tended to be at this point. In a series of specific recommendations, the Profintern urged Korean revolutionaries to plunge directly into all economic and political struggles, thereby exposing and eliminating petty bourgeois and national-reformist elements. Strikes, demonstrations, and intensive propaganda efforts were urged, with an immediate effort to establish a left faction within the trade union movement.

74. *Ibid.*, pp. 5–6.
75. Under the title "Tasks of the Revolutionary Trade Union Movement in Corea," Resolution adopted by the R.I.L.U., Executive Bureau, Sept. 18, 1930, this document is published in English in Red International of Labour Unions, *Resolutions of the Fifth Congress of the R.I.L.U.*, London, 1931, pp. 152–158.
76. *Ibid.*, p. 153.

The Dissolution of the United Front

Against this background, let us now return to trends in the united front, particularly relations between the Korean Communists and the Shingan-hoe. In the period between 1927 and 1929, the Shingan-hoe rapidly gained in strength and tended to pursue a militant course. By 1930, the organization claimed 386 branches and 76,939 members, although Japanese authorities reported that there were only 260 branches and 37,000 members.[77] No doubt Shingan-hoe membership, like that of most organizations, was very fluid. In most areas, however, the Shingan-hoe became an official or unofficial coordinating center for the local youth league, labor and farmer unions, and other social-nationalist groups. In this fashion, despite its relatively limited membership, it could claim to represent such Korean nationalist voices as existed. The Japanese, who kept careful statistics upon various aspects of "the Korean social movement," were deeply concerned about the way things were going during these years. As can be seen from

TABLE 1
Korean Socio-Political Organizations, 1920–1930

Year	Type of Organization							
	Nationalist	Socialist	Labor	Farmer	Youth[a]	Boys[a]	Outcasts	Total
1920	—	11	33	—	251	1	—	296
1921	—	18	90	3	446	14	—	571
1922	—	19	81	23	488	25	—	636
1923	—	55	111	107	584	43	—	900
1924	1	86	91	112	742	81	83	1,196
1925	1	83	128	126	847	127	99	1,411
1926	2	38	182	119	1,092	203	130	1,766
1927	104	85	352	160	1,127	247	150	2,225
1928	182	75	432	307	1,320	293	153	2,762
1929	214	56	465	564	1,433	366	162	3,260
1930	246	56	561	943	1,509	461	165	3,941

SOURCE: Korean Government-General, Police Affairs Bureau, *Saikin ni okeru Chōsen chian jōkyō* (*Recent Conditions of Public Security in Korea*), Seoul, 1934, pp. 168–169.

[a] It is believed that "youth" refers to individuals over seventeen years of age, "boys" to those less than seventeen years of age, although no explanation has been discovered by the authors.

tables 1 and 2, from 1927 to 1930 the number of meetings prohibited, restrained, or dispersed each year increased rapidly, as did the total number of Korean social and political organizations. At a later point, we

77. High Court, Prosecutor's Bureau, *Chōsen keiji seisaku shiryō* (*Materials on the Criminal Affairs Policies in Korea,* 1930 edition), Seoul, 1931, pp. 23–25, contains the report of the Japanese chief prosecutor on the ties between *Chosŏn Ilbo* and Shingan-hoe, and the Japanese assessment of the latter organization's political activities.

TABLE 2
Meetings in Korea Prohibited, Restrained, or Dispersed, 1927–1930

Year	Prohibited [a]	Restrained [b]	Dispersed [c]	Total
1927	283	398	126	807
1928	371	509	89	969
1929	727	1,288	36	2,050
1930	1,087	1,274	26	2,387

SOURCE: *Ibid.*, pp. 164–167.

[a] "Prohibited" indicates cases where meeting permits were denied.

[b] "Restrained" indicates cases where speakers were halted, or not permitted to address the audience, because their speeches were deemed to be subversive.

[c] "Dispersed" indicates cases where the police ordered the meeting dispersed because of the subversive content of the meeting.

shall discuss trends in the labor and peasant movements. Here, it is sufficient to note the substantial increase in the number of organizations involving such groups. The nationalist organizational figures refer to Shingan-hoe branches; and while the totals are considerably lower than those claimed by the association or cited by other Japanese sources, the increases are still extensive.

How was such rapid organization realized? We have some detailed information on Hongwon Prefecture, South Hamgyŏng Province, that suggests the catalytic role of the Shingan-hoe and its young radical leaders. On September 30, 1927, Ŏm Won-sik and Chŏng Ryŏm-su, two local residents, took the initiative in convening an inaugural meeting of the Hongwon branch of the Shingan-hoe, with the leaders of twenty-four sociopolitical organizations in the prefecture participating. Ŏm was a schoolteacher who had sought higher education in Seoul but had failed and been forced to return home. Chŏng had been to Japan and had attended Japan University in Tokyo for several months. He, too, had been forced to return, because of poor health and lack of money. Both young men had read Marxist literature and had Marxist sympathies, although neither had been a member of any Communist party. Both were ardent nationalists.

Although the data on provincial leaders of the radical nationalist movement is not sufficient to permit firm generalizations, the indications are strong that Ŏm and Chŏng were rather typical examples. Provincial leaders of the Shingan-hoe (and the KCP) came heavily from the ranks of those who had received some higher education but failed to achieve any real success in life. Many of them had sought opportunities in Japan or in Seoul only to be forced to return home because of educational failure, lack of funds, or health or family problems. Deeply frustrated, but with some experience and education, they were natural leaders for any radical movement.

In the case of Hongwon Prefecture, the organization of a new Youth

League followed swiftly upon the establishment of a Shingan-hoe branch. The League was established on November 6, 1927, with some 70 persons participating, including a number active in the Shingan-hoe. The old General Youth Federation provided a base. Eventually, the Hongwon Youth League claimed 800 members and 12 branches. Meanwhile, on December 1, the Hongwon Farmers' Union was organized in similar fashion, with 30 founding members, most of whom had Shingan-hoe connections. Within a few years, it too had a number of branches and sub-branches.[78]

In its opening years, the Shingan-hoe hewed to a strongly leftist course. Communists occupied a number of important posts, and Marxist themes were prominent in both Shingan-hoe tactics and programs. Japanese authorities, of course, were not unaware of these facts. *Chosŏn Ilbo* received more than twenty administrative orders from the government in the 1927–28 period as a result of its news stories or editorials. Some of the editorials, incidentally, were amazingly bold. On one occasion, for example, the newspaper asserted that the only solution to Korean problems lay in replacing political imperialism and economic capitalism, and urged that the Korean movement be harmonized with the "world reform movement of Red Russia."[79]

Certain local branches of the Shingan-hoe were totally under Communist or "uncompromising" nationalist control, and countless meetings were halted by police when speakers uttered "subversive words," or counseled militant action. Among many examples, we may cite two that occurred in 1930. In April, when the Seoul branch of the Shingan-hoe held its annual conference, a local branch sent the following telegram: SMASH THE CHAINS OF REACTIONARY SUPPRESSION AND DASH TOWARD THE REVOLUTIONARY FRONT.[80] A month later, on May 27, a Shingan-hoe official asserted: "Did not the Indian saint, Gandhi, leader of three hundred million Indians, declare independence? How do we Koreans see this? It has been three years since we established our organization, but we have not done any great work. Within a few years, however, we may produce a hero such as he. It is toward this end that everyone should strive."[81]

The Shingan-hoe national conferences scheduled for February 1928 and March 1929 were both prohibited by the Japanese authorities, who were aware of the branches' radical activities and looked askance at the

78. *Shisō geppō, op. cit.*, Vol. 3, No. 12, March 1934, *AJMFA*, R S358, pp. 13–44. The Farmers' Union published the following program: 1. To win economic and political advantages, and consolidate class unity. 2. To seek the immediate interests of the landless farming masses and their "qualitative" (ideological) unity. 3. To cultivate the consciousness of the proletariat, and provide mutual assistance.

79. Cited in *Chōsen keiji seisaku shiryō, op. cit.*, p. 23.

80. *Ibid.*, p. 24.

81. *Ibid.*, p. 24.

proposed conference agenda. Indeed, by 1930 the Japanese were convinced that the Shingan-hoe was really engaged in fostering Communism.[82] Eighty-nine Shingan-hoe members were indicted between January 1927 and June 1930 for "harboring subversive thoughts." Moreover, among the individuals arrested specifically for Communist activities a significant number held Shingan-hoe membership. Thus Japanese suspicions were confirmed.[83]

Throughout this period, both the radical nationalists and the Communists were seeking to create a mass response. It was for this reason that they concentrated upon labor, peasant, and student movements. Only one event, however, the Kwangju Student Incident of 1929, came close to justifying these hopes. On October 30, 1929, a fight occurred between a Korean and a Japanese student on a commuter train near Kwangju. (Korean and Japanese students attended segregated schools, and commuter trains provided one of the few points of intimate contact.) The fight was broken up but it created tensions that erupted next day in a larger fracas at the railway station. By November 3, which was a holiday to commemorate the birthday of the Emperor Meiji, Korean and Japanese students were moving in groups, looking for trouble. Some fights took place. In addition, the Korean students conducted a demonstration and attempted to raid the Japanese school. Some sixty Korean students were arrested, but no Japanese. This discriminating action by the Japanese authorities triggered large-scale demonstrations. Leaflets were passed out that demanded, among other things, "an abolition of the colonial slave educational system." [84] Strict press censorship was imposed, but its main effect was that wild rumors spread throughout Korea.

The Shingan-hoe had been involved in this incident from an early point. As the trouble grew more serious, the Kwangju branch sent a report to headquarters in Seoul. Headquarters immediately dispatched three officials who conferred with local Shingan-hoe officers. On December 10, the society decided to launch a national campaign against the government for its discriminatory policies. Public meetings, street demonstrations, and

82. *Ibid.,* p. 25.

83. *Ibid.,* pp. 24–25. Prosecutor Sakai reported that from its founding to June 16, 1930, eighty-nine persons charged with subversive activities had been Shingan-hoe members. Among the eighty suspects arrested in April 1930 by the Kyŏnggi Province Police Department in connection with the Communist Party Incident, twenty-five were Shingan-hoe members. Among the eighty-six suspects involved in the Communist Party Incident and arrested in May by the North Hamgyŏng Province Police Department, sixty-four were Shingan-hoe members.

84. For a detailed analysis of the background of the Kwangju student incident and its unfolding, see Yang Tong-ju, *Kwangju haksaeng tongnip undongsa (A History of the Independence Movement of the Students in Kwangju),* Kwangju, 1956. See also Prosecutor's Bureau, High Court, *Keijō shi nai jogakusei banzai sōjō jiken (The Disturbance Involving Girl Students in Seoul Shouting 'Manse'),* Seoul, 1930.

the dissemination of literature on a wide scale were planned. Local newspapers and some eighty Shingan-hoe local branches were notified.

Would the March First Incident be repeated on an even more impressive scale? Japanese authorities, deeply concerned, gathered all possible evidence concerning the plans and then moved swiftly. They arrested the Shingan-hoe leaders most deeply involved (Hŏ Hŏn, Yi Kwan-yong, Hong Myŏng-hui, Yi Wan-hyŏk, Cho Pyŏng-ok, and Kim Tong-jun), seized such literature as could be uncovered, and kept close surveillance over all schools. A large-scale outburst was avoided—much to the disappointment of the nationalists. However, there were a number of sympathy strikes, involving some 194 schools and 54,000 students. The strikes continued until March 1930.

The Kwangju Incident had a far-reaching impact upon the Shingan-hoe. A number of its more radical leaders were arrested and thus temporarily removed from the scene. Among those remaining, a reappraisal of past policies and positions gradually got under way, both at headquarters and in certain local branches and affiliated organizations. One group within the Korean Youth Federation, for example, is reported to have argued that because of past Communist leanings the Federation had been rendered impotent by continual suppression. To continue the ultra-militant line would simply lead to self-destruction. Moreover, such a position was not in conformity with the original spirit of the Federation.[85] The moderate faction within the Federation began to meet with new Shingan-hoe headquarters officials and, over time, representatives of this group were sent to various local branches, urging a shift away from extremism.

These trends naturally provoked a reaction from the Left. As noted earlier, since the disaster in China, the international Communist line had been veering left. The idea was to capture organizations like the Shingan-hoe, but under no conditions to be submerged by them. Capture, promising in the early period, seemed increasingly unlikely as time passed. As we have seen, the Korean Communists were subjected to a series of mass arrests throughout the "united front" period, and their capacity to retain positions of influence within the Shingan-hoe hierarchy was correspondingly weakened. The arrests continued during 1928 and 1929, finally leaving the Communist movement a mere shell. Meanwhile, the theses of February and December 1928 both warned in stern terms of the danger of being betrayed by the Korean bourgeoisie.

Perhaps it is not surprising, therefore, that as early as August 1, 1929, only two and one-half years after the organization of the Shingan-hoe, one group of Korean Communists in Manchuria was urging withdrawal from the association. Its resolution on this matter deserves quotation.

85. *Saikin ni okeru Chōsen chian jōkyō, op. cit.,* 1934, p. 32.

The Party has committed a grave error on the question of the nationalist party. The Party has mobilized its entire membership and compelled all Party members to join the nationalist party, and it has also actively solicited members for that party. As a result, the program of our Party has not been achieved whereas the program of the nationalist party has been realized. The Party believed that to expand the activities of the nationalist party was to expand its own program. But it is fundamentally wrong to foster and abet our arch-enemy, the nationalists. Objectively, this is to aid the bourgeoisie, and put ourselves behind. Instead of winning hegemony over the peasants, we have merely handed over the peasants to the bourgeoisie.

This has created a crisis within our own ranks, and produced many obstacles for the Party. The theses on colonialism of the sixth Comintern Congress distinguished sharply between petty bourgeois groups and Communist organizations, and indicated the absolute necessity of maintaining the independence of the revolutionary labor movement. They also indicated that a temporary alliance could be established with the national-revolutionary movement under special circumstances for the convenience of the revolutionary struggle—but only if the movement were revolutionary.

The Party must courageously correct the basic errors of past policies with regard to the nationalist party, and cease advocating a single nationalist party for the nation. We must define our policy toward such a party as follows:

1. Members of the Communist Youth League and all of the masses under Communist Party influence must withdraw from membership in the unified nationalist party.
2. As preparation for withdrawal, the lack of need for such a party should be explained to its officials and rank and file.
3. At the appropriate time, a plenary conference of the Communist Party Executive Committee should be convened to explain the lack of need for a single, united-front nationalist party and to announce our withdrawal from it. However, a joint struggle organization should be created in place of the old unified party structure so that coordinated propaganda can be carried out against the aggression of the Japanese imperialists in Manchuria and Mongolia.[86]

By 1930, there were two Communist groups operating in Korea: a combination of the old Shanghai and Seoul factions, and the M-L Group. However, no organized party existed and there was no official chain of command other than that existing within the Shingan-hoe. Under these circumstances, Communist initiative with respect to policy quite naturally

86. "Resolution of the Central Presidium of the Manchurian General Bureau of the Koryŏ Communist Youth League," reported by the Japanese Consul-General in Kirin to the Foreign Minister, Aug. 27, 1929, and contained on *AJMFA*, R S722 (no pagination). The Koryŏ Communist Youth League was located in Tungchingch'eng, Ningan hsien (Prefecture), and was composed of elements of the Tuesday faction.

tended to come from outside the country—first, Moscow, than Manchuria, Shanghai, or Tokyo. Even in Japan, the current political climate was much freer than in Korea proper.

The movement to separate the Communists from the Shingan-hoe and to work for the dissolution of the latter was finally undertaken by the M-L Group in the person of one of its most articulate leaders, Ko Kyŏng-hŭm, who was then residing in Tokyo. Ko's faction had regrouped in Shanghai after the demise of the fourth Korean Communist Party in 1928, and then gradually filtered back into Korea and Japan in early 1930. Once Ko had reestablished himself in Tokyo, he began writing articles and pamphlets disseminating the new Moscow line. Since the Communists in Korea were both disorganized and isolated, Ko's works quickly assumed importance, especially in the M-L Group. In an article entitled "Tasks for the Bolshevization of the Korean Communist Party," published in April 1930, Ko demanded a drastic and immediate shift in Korean Communist policies.[87] Support for a single nationalist party or a national united-front party, he argued, was in reality support for the theory of dissolution of the Communist party, a theory long condemned by true Communists (and known as Yamakawaism in Japan). In its attitude toward the Shingan-hoe, asserted Ko, the Korean Communists had fallen into this type of error. Unable to become a vanguard party of the masses, the KCP had remained essentially a "thought society," that is, it consisted of people who were busy *thinking* about Communism rather than engaging in the struggle against imperialism and feudalism. Ignoring the need to undertake these tasks in the name of the Party, it had failed in its responsibilities to the international Communist movement.

Again, in an article of August 1930, entitled "Smash the Reactionary Rampages of the National Reformists," Ko echoed the strong left line that was now being promulgated through international Communist channels. Labeling the current Shingan-hoe leaders as "national reformists," he demanded that Korean Communists struggle against them resolutely. This struggle, he announced, was now the Communist movement's primary task. Of course, the struggle had to be waged against left-wing as well as right-wing national reformists. In Korea, the right-wing reformists were grouped around *Tong-A Ilbo,* while the left-wing ones were "that group of upper-class petty-bourgeois types who constitute the leaders of the Shingan-hoe."

There were only two roads, the Communist and the reformist. Those who sought a middle course were merely indulging in the delusion of *inmin chui* (popularism).

Ko Kyŏng-hŭm was completely in tune with the current Soviet line

87. The article is reprinted in *Chōsen zeneitō borushebiki-ka no tame ni (For the Bolshevization of the Korean Vanguard),* Tokyo, July 1931, pp. 47–48. This pamphlet contains three other articles by Ko as well as the two theses issued by the Comintern and the Profintern cited earlier.

as illustrated by the Profintern resolution of September 1930 and a number of other documents of the period. In other countries, too, the united front was being dissolved. A dispute was currently raging among the Japanese far left over whether to dissolve the Nihon Rōnōtō (Japan Labor-Farmer Party), which had been intended as the chief legal vehicle for militants, including Communists. Long-time united front supporters such as Ōyama Ikuo suddenly found themselves under attack by Japanese Communist spokesmen such as Hososako Kanemitsu. The basic reason, of course, was that reestablishment of a legal far-left party violated the current Comintern line. Indeed, objective conditions in Korea and Japan mattered little; policy had been set and had to be followed. The new line, it should be noted, had been set before the moderate line took hold in the Shingan-hoe.

Ultimately, the dissolution controversy spread to radical circles within Korea. Radical journals such as *Haebang* (*Liberation*), *Kun-gi* (*Mass Flag*), *Chosŏn ji kwang* (*Light of Korea*), *He-sŏng* (*Comet*), and others took up the issue. As the arguments progressed, a number of local Shingan-hoe branches under Communist control or influence voted to dissolve. These included the Seoul, Tokyo, Inch'ŏn, T'ongyŏng, and Pusan branches.

On May 15, 1931, a Shingan-hoe national conference was opened. It was the first to be allowed by the police since the founding of the organization.[88] The probabilities are very strong that the conference was permitted specifically to allow the proponents of dissolution to administer the coup de grace to the association, thus saving the police the trouble. Communist and Japanese governmental objectives at this point coincided perfectly. Shingan-hoe headquarters officials fought vigorously to save the organization, even attempting to withhold credentials from some of the delegates who favored dissolution. They failed, however, and on the second day dissolution was approved by a large majority. After the vote, the conference was about to proceed to a discussion of dissolution procedures and other future activities when a police official quickly announced that, since the organization was already defunct, there was no basis for further discussion. Thus ended the Shingan-hoe, and with it the united front era. Henceforth, the Communist goal was to be the establishment of an underground movement based upon workers and peasants.

The Proletarian Culture Movement

There is one aspect of the radical movement of this period that deserves more specialized treatment than we have yet given it, and that is

88. The full proceedings of the conference are covered by Pak Han-sik, "Shingan-hoe ch'oejong chŏnguk taehoe" ("The Last All-Korea Conference of the Shingan-hoe"), *He-sŏng* (*Comet*), June 15, 1931, pp. 38–42. For police reports, see "The Dissolution of the Shingan-hoe," *Shisō geppō, op. cit.,* Vol. 1, No. 3, June 1931, pp. 15–16, *AJMFA*, R S355, and Japan, Ministry of Home Affairs, Bureau of Police and Security (Naimushō, Keihōkyoku), *Shōwa rokunen chū ni okeru shakai undō no jōkyō* (*Conditions of Social Movements in 1931*), pp. 1114–1129.

the so-called Proletarian Culture Movement. A high percentage of the Party members of this era can be described as either intellectuals or petty intellectuals. Let us make clear our usage of these terms. The intellectual has to be defined in terms of educational and occupational criteria; not all intellectuals are intelligent, and not all intelligent people by any means are intellectuals. Accordingly, we shall use the term to denote individuals who have received a higher education (generally, college or university) and who occupy roles as academicians, literary writers, journalists, and similar positions, at a more or less prestigious level. Too often, the term "intellectual" has been used to cover much too broad a range of occupations and individuals. It is essential, therefore, to distinguish a class of petty intellectuals. These are individuals who have had a better than average education (at least middle school and possibly some college), and who serve in such occupations as primary or secondary teaching, library work, or the lower levels of writing and journalism. We should also group the professional students in this category. The Communist movement throughout Asia depended heavily upon both intellectuals and petty intellectuals in its opening stages. Some attention to left-wing intellectual activities in Korea during the 1920s is therefore warranted, particularly since a few of the key actors will reappear in North Korea after 1945.[89]

The New Culture Movement emerged for the first time in Korea at the close of World War I, about the time of the March First Movement. As might have been expected, it was largely a reflection of trends in liberal Japanese circles; indeed, much of its stock in trade was either a direct import, or a Korean translation, of Japanese-language materials. The new cry was for naturalistic literature and the freedom of the individual artist; the most prominent demand was that of "art for art's sake." Initially, the movement was limited almost wholly to literature: leftists, of course, subsequently referred to this era as the assault of the bourgeois liberals against "feudalistic" ideas.

In 1924–25, the new movement had gravitated to the left, spawning its first organizational efforts. One of these was the so-called New Tendency Group, led by such men as Pak Yŏng-hi, Kim Ki-jin, and Yi Sang-ik. Having largely cast off the earlier liberal (and anarchist) influences, these men showed themselves to be strongly influenced by Marxism-Leninism in their efforts at literary criticism, short-story writing, and the creation of "new novels." In highly self-conscious fashion, they proclaimed them-

89. In addition to sources cited earlier that pertain directly to this subject, two essays of particular importance are available, both of them written by participants in the form of accounts submitted to the Japanese police. An P'il-sung (An Mak), "A Brief History of the Korean Proletarian Culture Movement," published in *Shisō geppō, op. cit.,* No. 10, January 1932, pp. 1550–1600, *AJMFA,* R S356; and Kim Ki-jin (pen name, Kim P'al-bong), "The Past and Present of the Proletarian Culture Movement in Korea," *ibid.,* pp. 1510–49 (from a manuscript submitted at Nishi Diamon Prison, Seoul, on October 11, 1931).

selves the possessors of a materialist point of view, as well as of an acute political awareness. Such magazines as *Paekjo* (*White Tide*), *Kaebyŏk,* and *Sasanggye* (*The World of Thought*) served as their vehicles.

In July 1925, these and other writers formed the Chosŏn Proretaria Yesul Tongmaeng (Korean Proletarian Art Federation). Kim Ki-jin, one of the main participants, was later to assert that the League was relatively inactive, and that the movement between 1923 and 1926 was in every sense a primitive one. For the most part, these young "Marxists" contented themselves with novels about poverty, exploitation, and the tragedy of the "little man." One characteristic theme was the badly exploited worker who stored up grievances until he could no longer contain them. Then, in a fiery burst of emotion, he killed his capitalist boss and ended his life in prison, ruining his family. The concept of revenge, always popular in Korean literature, was a central motif in many such works.

Gradually, through such groups as the January Society in Tokyo, and its counterpart in Seoul, theoretical debate became a popular but increasingly time-consuming pastime among the young writers of the Left. The key subjects can be imagined; they must have been those of young leftist writers everywhere. The leaders at this period were Pak Yŏng-hi and Kim Ki-jin, with Cho Chung-gon, Yun Ki-ho, and Han Sŏl-ya (the latter to figure prominently in North Korea later). Among the leading leftist poets were Yim Hwa, Yu Wan-hi, Pak P'al-yang, and Yi Sang-hwa. (Yim Hwa is another about whom we shall hear much more during the Communist era.)

The literary merit of these leftist novels is highly debatable. Ch'oe Sŏ-hae's *Hongyŏn* (*Red Flame*) and Cho P'o-sŏk's *Nakdong-gang* (*Nakdong River*) were generally regarded as the best. Yim Hwa and Yu Wan-hi were considered the leading "proletarian" poets.

In 1927, the Proletarian Culture Movement underwent a further shift to the left. This undoubtedly reflected the rising influence of Fukumotoism upon the young radicals, both Japanese and Korean, of this period. The Korean Proletarian Art Federation was reorganized, with the older members generally being shunted aside in favor of the young firebrands. *Yesul Undong* (*The Art Movement*) became the Federation's organ; later, it became *Musansha* (in Korean *Musanja*) (*The Proletariat*). A vigorous debate covering both tactical and theoretical points broke out among the writers of the Left. If art were to influence the masses, what style was necessary? Moderates such as Kim Ki-jin argued that the writer's work had at least to pass police inspection, otherwise the masses could never be reached at all. Yim Hwa, among others, attacked this position, asserting that Kim's proposals represented a form of ideological disarmament. The militants also strongly attacked those whom they designated exponents of "nationalist literature," that is, the writers who insisted that political appeals should be to Koreans *as Koreans,* not to class differences. The latter, such writers argued, did not constitute a problem in a colonial, backward society like Korea.

Gradually, splits within the Proletarian Culture Movement developed that could not be healed. Like all other aspects of the Left, the movement became deeply factionalized. Meanwhile, however, Marxist-Leninist influences had spread beyond literature into drama, the cinema, and the fine arts. Thanks to the Pulgaemi, or Red Ant Theatre, political plays were written and performed. In the autumn of 1929, the Shinhŭng Yŏnghwa Tongmaeng (New Cinema League) was organized to influence the embryonic motion-picture field.

The attacks and counterattacks between so-called moderates (men like Kim Ki-jin and Ch'oe Sŏ-hae) and militants (Pak Yŏng-hi and Yim Hwa) probably reached their height in the summer of 1929. When to these were added the mass arrests of February 1928 and the rise of the Shingan-hoe, it is not surprising that the Proletarian Culture Movement suddenly declined. The Proletarian Art Federation became largely defunct. In the spring of 1930, however, the young militants in Tokyo argued for its reorganization, with Yim Hwa, Kwŏn Hwan, An Mak (another whom we shall meet again after 1945), and Kim Hyo-sik taking the lead. Thus, in April of that year, at a central committee meeting of the Federation, Kwŏn, An, and Ŏm Hŭng-sŏp were added as alternate members, with the full committee membership including Pak Yŏng-hi, Yim Hwa, Yun Ki-yŏng, Song Yŏng, Kim Ki-jin, Yi Ki-yŏng, and Han Sŏl-ya. The Federation was now restructured very much in the fashion of a Communist party, with various sections and subsections based upon different functional responsibilities and fields of endeavor. However, the arrests continued. An Mak, for example, was arrested in August 1931, and forty days later Kim Ki-jin was detained. From each of these men (and many others), Japanese police obtained a detailed account of the policies, activities, and personnel involved in the Federation and related organizations. Whether arrested or not, all primary figures were put under constant surveillance. Thus, by the time of the Manchurian Incident, the Proletarian Culture Movement had fallen upon exceedingly hard times.

It would be difficult to argue that the Korean intellectual leftists exercised a major influence upon their society in this era. A few novels and poems produced by them were fairly widely read, primarily by middle school and college students. For all of the talk about the importance of addressing art to the masses, the movement's contacts with the common man were extremely slim. Indeed, the petty intellectuals of the Left probably wielded a much greater influence—and on balance, they were probably more important within the Party itself. Nevertheless, the Korean Proletarian Art Federation provided a milieu for the study of Marxism-Leninism in an intellectual atmosphere, and for its application to various cultural fields. In these terms, as we shall see, it was storing up a legacy to bequeath to the period after World War II. A few hard-core leftist intellectuals adhered to their basic position and were thus available to the guerrilla-soldiers who came to power in North Korea after 1945.

Socioeconomic Characteristics and Motives
of First-Generation Korean Communists

Having examined the activities of the Korean leftist intellectuals during this period, let us turn to certain broader questions. What were the predominant socioeconomic characteristics of those who were drawn into the Korean Communist movement during this period? What were the primary motivations for joining the Party? Fortunately, official Japanese records provide extensive data, some of which have been used to compile tables 3–11.

TABLE 3

Occupations of Those Convicted in the First and Second KCP Incidents and Those Arrested in the Fourth KCP Incident

Occupational Category						Percentage of Total
Bourgeois or Petty Bourgeois					95	42.4
Intellectual or Petty Intellectual			76	33.9		
Newspaper and magazine man	53	23.7				
Student	16	7.1				
Other writer	3	1.3				
Teacher	4	1.8				
Merchant			19	8.5		
Unemployed					65	29.0
Peasant					29	13.0
Farmer			27	12.0		
Fisherman			2	1.0		
Worker					26	11.6
Laborer			15	6.7		
White-collar			11	4.9		
Government employee	3	1.3				
Clerk	8	3.6				
Others					9	4.0
TOTAL					224	100.0

SOURCE: Tables 3–11 are taken from "A Report on the Korean Communist Party Incidents," *AJAN*, R 102, and "The Suppression of Secret Organizations . . .," Appendices.

What conclusions can we draw here? Looking first at the occupational divisions, it is clear that those whom Marxists would label "bourgeois" or "petty bourgeois" held a commanding position within the Party, just as the Comintern had so often charged. If we take the breakdown presented in table 3, over 40 percent of all Party members fell into the "bourgeois" or "petty bourgeois" category, and within this group the overwhelming majority were intellectuals or petty intellectuals. Moreover, most of those in these two categories were journalists. Indeed, they accounted for nearly 25 percent of all Party members.

The figures in table 3 understate the proportion of intellectuals, since among the unemployed a significant number could have been assigned to that category. Some were professional political activists without a fixed occupation, others unemployed ex-students or idle members of the literati. At least some of those in the white-collar worker group, especially the government employees, could as easily be listed as intellectuals. Finally, the "other" category included some professionals. It would certainly be no exaggeration to say that well over 50 percent of all Party members came from the ranks of the bourgeoisie, and primarily from intellectual occupations.

Why were so many of them journalists? Several reasons may be advanced. In Korea during this period, recruitment to the professions normally available to intellectuals was in many cases partly or wholly closed, not untypical of a colonial situation. Thus, openings in government and academic life were very limited, and the flow of better educated Koreans into journalism, one of the few unrestricted fields, was natural. Moreover, the world of journalism, as we have noted, became the focal point of the Korean nationalist movement, especially after 1920 when the authority of religious leaders began to decline. Finally, since personal contacts were one very significant factor in Party recruitment, once a nucleus of journalists had made the commitment it was easier to obtain others. Indeed, among those listed in the "worker" category, a not inconsiderable number were printers, delivery men, and others associated with newspaper plants. Thus in some measure, Party membership followed company lines.

The total number of Party members who were workers of any type, however, was extraordinarily small. Kuusinen's remark that even if one searched with binoculars for workers in the Korean Communist Party one would not find them had a strong element of truth in it. The "worker" category involved only 11.6 percent of the total membership—and that included white-collar workers. The manual labor contingent was approximately 60 percent of this, although both the proportion of laborers and the proportion of workers in general would be increased if the figures for the unemployed were redistributed by habitual occupation. As for the peasants, although some 80 percent of the Korean population, including most of the true proletariat of the country, fell into this class, they accounted for a mere 13 percent of total Party membership.

If one were to measure class not in occupational but in property terms, however, the Korean Communist movement could claim a somewhat better proletarian rating. The statistics in tables 4, 5, and 6 indicate that approximately 50 percent of all Party members had properties valued at less than 1,000 yen, and that an additional 33 percent were in the 1,000–

TABLE 4
**Property and Occupation of Those Convicted
in the First and Second KCP Incidents**

Occupation	Property (*Value in Yen*)				
	Below 1,000 yen	*1,000 to 5,000 yen*	*5,000 to 10,000 yen*	*Above 10,000 yen*	*Total*
Newspaper reporter	15	8	2	3	28
Unemployed	11	3	1	1	16
Laborer	8	—	—	—	8
Farmer	3	4	1	—	8
Merchant	5	3	—	—	8
Student	2	—	1	2	5
Writer	2	1	—	—	3
Teacher	3	—	—	—	3
Others	2	2	—	—	4
TOTAL	51	21	5	6	83

SOURCE: *Ibid.*

TABLE 5
Property and Occupation of Those Arrested in the Fourth KCP Incident

Occupation	Property (*Value in Yen*)				
	Below 1,000 yen	*1,000 to 5,000 yen*	*5,000 to 10,000 yen*	*Above 10,000 yen*	*Total*
Newspaper and magazines	8	13	1	3	25
Unemployed	23	19	4	3	49
Laborer[a]	6	1	—	—	7
Farmer	8	7	2	2	19
Merchant[b]	2	5	1	3	11
Fisherman	1	1	—	—	2
Student	3	2	1	5	11
Government employee	2	1	—	—	3
Clerk	4	2	2	—	8
Teacher	1	—	—	—	1
Others	2	2	—	1	5
TOTAL	60	53	11	17	141

SOURCE: *Ibid.*
  [a] Includes 1 printer and 2 carpenters.
  [b] Includes 4 winery operators and liquor salesmen.

TABLE 6
Property of Those Convicted in the First
and Second KCP Incidents and Those Arrested
in the Fourth KCP Incident

	Number	Percentage of Total
Below 1,000 yen (poor)	111	49.6
1,000–5,000 yen (middle class)	74	33.0
5,000–10,000 yen (upper middle class)	16	7.1
Above 10,000 yen (upper class)	23	10.3
TOTAL	224	100.0

SOURCE: *Ibid.*

5,000 yen range—middle class but scarcely affluent. The significance of these figures can of course be challenged. The Korean family system being extremely close knit, many of those in bourgeois occupational categories could presumably count upon aid when in need. Or they might live at a standard not necessarily reflected in their personal property holdings; to deflate the value of one's property for tax purposes was a fine art in Korea as elsewhere. In any case, the educational statistics (tables 7–10) show that under no conditions could the entire 50 percent of Party members with properties valued at less than 1,000 yen (see table 6) be considered truly

TABLE 7
Age and Educational Level of Those Convicted in the First
and Second KCP Incidents

Age	University[a]	College[b]	Middle School	Primary School	Others[c]	Total
Below 20	—	—	—	1	—	1
20–25	2	2	4	11	2	21
26–30	5	2	12	5	3	27
31–35	5	4	5	3	2	19
36–40	—	—	5	1	2	8
Over 40	—	1	2	1	3	7
TOTAL	12	9	28	22	12	83

SOURCE: *Ibid.*

[a] Each category presented here includes those who attended as well as those who graduated.

[b] College refers to *semmon gakkō*, roughly equivalent to junior college level in the United States. One could enroll in *semmon gakkō* after 6 years of primary school and 4 years of middle school (or even less), while the university or *daigaku* required 5 years of middle school and an additional 2 years of high school.

[c] "Others" here probably refers to those who attended rural schools where Chinese classics were taught as well as to those with no education.

proletarian. In this connection, we must remember that the great bulk of Party members were very young.

Nevertheless, it would be unwise to dismiss the data on properties. It was a fact, of course, that the general standard of living in Korea was deplorably low, and that such professions as journalism had a certain prestige, but did not pay particularly well. Thus, we can assume that a substantial number of Party recruits were young "intellectuals" who were profoundly dissatisfied with their economic lot as well as with conditions in general. The statistics on motivation support such a conclusion to some extent (see table 11). The Party, however, was not without its upper middle class and upper class members, some 10 percent of the members falling into the latter category.

Tables 7 and 8 make it abundantly clear that Korean Communist Party members were overwhelmingly young, about 75 percent of the total

TABLE 8
**Age of Those Convicted in the First
and Second KCP Incidents and Those Arrested
in the Fourth KCP Incident**

Age	Number	Percentage
Below 20	1	0.5
20–25	77	33.8
26–30	91	39.9
31–35	32	14.0
36–40	16	7.0
Over 40	11	4.8
TOTAL	228	100.0

SOURCE: *Ibid.*

TABLE 9
**Educational Level of Those Convicted in the First
and Second KCP Incidents and Those Arrested
in the Fourth KCP Incident**

	Number	Percentage
University	29	12.7
College	15	6.6
Middle School	63	27.6
Primary School	95	41.7
Others	26[a]	11.4
TOTAL	228	100.0

SOURCE: *Ibid.*
[a] Includes 13 known to have had no education.

membership being thirty years of age or under, and more than 95 percent of all members being forty or under. This fact is basic to an understanding of property held. With respect to education, however, Party members could not in any sense be considered typical young Koreans. As tables 9 and 10 make clear, Communists were vastly better educated. Nearly 47

TABLE 10

Age and Educational Level of Those Arrested in the Fourth KCP Incident

Age	University Grad.	University With-drew	College (Semmon gakkō) Grad.	College With-drew	Middle School Grad.	Middle School With-drew	Grammar School Grad.	Grammar School With-drew	Country School	None	Total
20–25	1	8	—	2	10	7	23	3	—	2	56
26–30	3	5	1	2	9	6	31	2	1	4	64
31–35	—	—	—	1	1	—	10	—	—	1	13
36–40	—	—	—	—	1	—	4	—	—	3	8
Over 40	—	—	—	—	1	—	—	—	—	3	4
TOTAL	4	13	1	5	22	13	68	5	1	13	145

SOURCE: *Ibid.*

percent of all Party members had attended middle school or beyond, and nearly 20 percent had attended college or university (see table 9). Those with no education represented fewer than 10 percent.

Perhaps the most interesting data are those in table 11, available as a result of intensive Japanese interviews with members arrested in the incident of the Fourth Korean Communist Party. Several facts of major significance emerged from these interviews. First, how heavily did Party members weigh specific sociopolitical issues as the factors that motivated them to join the Party, and what were these issues, in order of significance? Of the reasons given, 22.7 percent stressed nationalism and 15.5 percent socioeconomic reforms. These factors, however, important though they were, accounted for less than 50 percent of the answers, and one factor, "influenced by theoretical studies," was actually cited more frequently than socioeconomic reform. This motivational factor might be labeled "the discovery of truth," that is, the intellectual stimulus derived from schooling—formal or informal—in Marxist-Leninist literature.

Motivation for joining the Party, however, could not be analyzed wholly—or in some cases, at all—in terms of what might be termed substantive or "issue" factors. Over 40 percent of the answers stressed personal or group-contact factors. It must be acknowledged, of course, that no such arbitrary division can be established between "substantive" and "personal" motivation. No doubt when a respondent asserted that he was motivated to join the Party because of his contacts with the peasant movement, for example, a part of his motivation was his familiarity with the issues stressed by the movement. From this point of view, the substantive factors may well be undervalued in this analysis. Nevertheless, if a respondent asserts that his *primary* reason for joining the Party was his contact

TABLE 11
Primary Reasons Given for Joining the Communist Movement
by Those Arrested in the Fourth KCP Incident

Reason		Percentage of Total
Nationalist Factors	44	22.7
Desired national emancipation	42	21.7
Because of the tyranny of Japanese individuals	1	.5
Because of discrimination against Koreans	1	.5
Socioeconomic Reform Factors	30	15.5
Desired social reform	15	7.7
Because of difficulty in livelihood	7	3.6
Because of poverty of farmers	3	1.6
Because of economic crisis in Korea	3	1.6
Because of suppression of press	2	1.0
Personal and Group-Contact Factors	81	41.7
Because of persuasion by friends	37	19.1
Because of familial problems (noneconomic)	4	2.1
Through contact with social movement	21	10.8
Through contact with peasant movement	10	5.0
Through contact with a student strike	1	.5
Through contact with labor movement	1	.5
Through contact with student study group	1	.5
Through contact with Chinese revolution	3	1.6
Seeking fame	3	1.6
Intellectual Factors	37	19.1
Influenced by theoretical studies	37	19.1
Unclear	2	1.0
TOTAL	194	100.0

SOURCE: *Ibid.*
NOTE: There were 145 persons arrested and 194 reasons adduced, since more than one reason could be given by an individual.

with the peasant movement rather than, let us say, his concern over the poverty of farmers, then it would seem valid to assert that, by his own account, he was motivated by "group-contact" rather than by "issue" factors.

Nor should this be regarded as strange. Recent studies of political motivation—and, indeed, of social behavior in general—provide new evidence that group influences can be paramount. The desire to identify with friends and the willingness to be influenced by one's own group without necessarily having a high level of ideological commitment are behavioral traits cutting across all cultures in some degree. And such traits were likely to be pronounced in a society like Korea, where familial and kinship bonds were exceedingly strong, and could be transferred to small-group relations in the setting of school, office, plant, or workshop. If political activism can be and often is a form of therapy for personal strains and problems, it can also be one element in a mosaic of obligations, an act of reciprocity among friends or associates. In fact, our evidence suggests that the "personal problem" element (for example, anger at father) played less of a motivating role for radicalism than "personal obligation" (for example, persuasion of friends).

Indeed, it is basically correct to assert that the Korea of this period was a highly structured society in which the political elite available for any form of political activity was extremely small. It also tended to be drawn from the same general socioeconomic group and to be receptive to essentially the same stimuli. These facts do not of themselves necessarily rule out deep ideological or political commitments. Such commitments can either develop within this framework or, occasionally, outside it. The fact, however, that nearly one-fifth of all Communists arrested in 1928 as members of the fourth KCP listed "persuasion by friends" as a primary factor motivating their membership in the Party challenges any notion of Party membership as the result of a purely individual decision. The factionalism that beset Korean Communism, along with all other aspects of Korean politics, is more understandable when placed within the intricate social setting of group relations and group actions.

Thus, we can draw a reasonably accurate profile of the typical Korean Communist Party member in the initial period of the Communist movement. He was a young man, urbanized, best described as a petty intellectual, with limited means but with sufficient education to set him strongly apart from the average Korean and mark him as a member of the political elite, at least potentially. He had joined the Party because his friends or work associates were joining or already belonged. This did not mean, however, that he was essentially apolitical. On the contrary, he had probably found Marxist theories intellectually stimulating, as well as guideposts for effecting the political change that he regarded as right and necessary. To study Marxism-Leninism was for him a profound intellectual experience that seemed to combine fact and value, science and religion, an explanation of his society that related it to the entire world, both past and present, together with a vigorous defense of such values as "democracy," "social justice," and "progress," and a prescription as to how they could be realized. All of this he related to two concrete issues: the reestablishment of Korean independence and the alleviation of poverty and other prevailing social injustices.

Our young Communist was thus essentially an ideologue. Together with his friends, he talked and thought about communism as a part of an intellectual study group. As long as he contented himself with such activities he had a certain latitude. But when he felt compelled to translate theory into action, and proceeded to attempt demonstrations, broader organizational activities, or "subversion," he was quickly apprehended. After two to six years in prison, he was released and in most cases did not return to active Party service. There were important exceptions, however; a small hard-core group of devoted members returned again and again to the fray, seemingly capable of absorbing endless punishment and frustration. But these were the exceptions, and even they were incapable of exercising sustained leadership. No individual—indeed, no single faction—was able to place an imprimatur firmly upon the KCP because all tenure in office was too brief.

Failure and Its Basic Causes

In contrast to the earlier period, when it had been almost completely an external effort, the Korean Communist movement in this era concentrated upon building an indigenous base. Invoking the one country-one party principle, its leaders sought to make Seoul the operational headquarters and to get all exile groups, including those residing in Siberia, to accept its authority. At the same time, pleading a special history and special needs, the Party leaders in Korea continued to post representatives in such overseas Korean centers as Vladivostok, Shanghai, Tokyo, and Chientao. But their efforts to achieve a unified, coordinated movement were doomed to futility.

Rampant factionalism continued. It was a product of the most fundamental causes: the nature of organization and group relations in Korean culture; the dispersed, self-contained character of overseas radical centers; the diverse influences that could play upon a movement that had extensive contact with Soviet, Chinese, and Japanese radicals; the erosive effects of continuous failure; the very narrow base from which participants could be recruited; and the effectiveness of Japanese tactics in separating "moderates" from "extremists." The Party became a group of tired men who had known each other too long and too well.

As centers of radical activity, the old Shanghai and Irkutsk factions were replaced by new ones: first, the Tuesday and the North Wind societies; then the January Society, which later became the M-L Group, and the Seoul Group. Factional combinations formed and dispersed, rose and fell. But despite pledges at home and dire threats from abroad, the era ended as it began, without even a semblance of internal unity.

Once again, as this period came to a close, an effort was being made to shift the Party's organizational functions overseas. There seemed to be no alternative. Four times within less than four years, the Party organization in Korea proper had been smashed by the Japanese and almost all of its members arrested. No Party in the world had been so penetrated by government agents and had its secrets so fully exposed. Korea was a colony; its security was handled by a highly efficient police organization. The strongly group-oriented character of Korean culture made the task of authorities easier in certain respects. A single arrest, combined with "intensive" interrogation, could unravel a big ball.

What were the alternatives to a flickering underground existence, so precarious and so unrewarding? If at the end of this period the reestablishment of strong overseas bases seemed the only feasible alternative, at an earlier point the emphasis had been upon the creation of a powerful indigenous united front. The Korean Communists always recognized that they could not by themselves hope to compete with various religious and social organizations that had deep roots in Korean society. The Party, indeed, could be significant only as it was able to interact with the broader nationalist movement, and with the various socioeconomic interest groups, some of which were now in their first formative stage of development.

Thus, for the Communists, the united front tactic was eminently logical. Nationalism was the one and only issue that provided any conceivable basis for a radical mass movement in Korea at that time—and even here the chances of success were admittedly slim. Japanese rule was now long established, and quite secure. Most nationalists had reconciled themselves in some measure to its continuance, and moderates talked increasingly of autonomy within the Japanese empire. As was the case almost everywhere in a colonial context, the Korean nationalist movement in all of its forms was a strongly elitist movement; it scarcely touched the rural masses and was capable of extending its influence to the grass roots level only in gross forms, such as sporadic racial incidents. Nevertheless, to capture the nationalist issue offered the best hope for the Korean Communists, now as in the past, not least because most of them continued to be nationalists.

Why, then, did the Communists fail in their efforts to exploit the potential for a united front when for a brief period the prospects seemed so promising? Two factors were of critical importance. First, the Communists were never permitted by Japanese authorities to gain sufficient strength to dominate an organization such as the Shingan-hoe. At the outset, their influence was very extensive, and a number of local Shingan-hoe branches were under their control. Indeed, some of the most important never left the Communist orbit. But the mass arrests of the second, third, and fourth KCP Executive Committees made the full exploitation of united front tactics impossible. No organization forced to operate under the threat of periodic annihilation could develop the type of discipline and authority necessary to control a heterogeneous front group. Increasingly, moreover, the more moderate elements within the front recognized the disadvantages of associating with Communists and following a Communist line. The issue became one of whether reform was not a more feasible goal than revolution. In this regard, moreover, Japanese policy was skillful. While taking an exceedingly tough line against the far Left, the government allowed the moderate nationalists sufficient scope to prevent them from moving further leftward. Under these circumstances, growing fissures within the united front were inevitable.

Of equal importance was the timing of the Korean effort. The Shingan-hoe was born in January 1927 just a few months before the fiery end of the Kuomintang-Communist alliance in China. The disaster that befell the Chinese Communists had immediate repercussions throughout the Communist world. Had it occurred earlier, Stalin himself might have been jeopardized, because he and his closest confidants had clearly dictated the tactics pursued by the Chinese Communists, as the Trotskyites knew well. By mid-1927, Stalin had sufficient control over the Soviet Party and state to survive the debacle, but he still needed to take drastic measures. It was first necessary to find scapegoats in China, and that was quickly done. Ch'en Tu-hsiu's "rightist opportunism" was thoroughly condemned; he was blamed for having misjudged both the character of the national bourgeoisie and the role of the Chinese Communist Party, thus having fallen into a liquidationist policy. Meanwhile, the international Communist line was shifted, with the Sixth Comintern Congress, held in September 1928, being a significant turning point. The emphasis was now upon the untrustworthy nature of most elements of the national bourgeoisie, and the dangers of collaborating with them.

Lip service was still paid to united front tactics, and the Comintern made no public acknowledgment of basic errors with respect to China. With respect to Korea, however, at least one Comintern official, Kuusinen, was more candid. By the end of 1928, new directives had been issued to the Korean Communist movement. They were radically different from those of 1924–27. A united front was still to be an objective—but a united front strictly on Communist terms. The integrity—the independence—of the Communist Party and its so-called mass organizations was to be protected at all costs. The aim had to be to seize the front, not to be absorbed by it. The revolution had to be a bourgeois-democratic revolution because of the nature of Korean society and its stage of development; the need was still to struggle against imperialism and feudalism. But the bourgeoisie were not capable of leading their own revolution. It was therefore essential that this be a *managed* bourgeois-democratic revolution, led by the proletariat. To accomplish this successfully, it was necessary to mobilize the worker-peasant masses, a task that required heavy emphasis upon the peasants who constituted the overwhelming majority of the masses. Thus, the key slogans had to be agrarian reform and the establishment of rural bases. In a very real sense, the failure of the united front in China led the Comintern to substitute the peasant for the bourgeois as the most logical ally of the proletariat. Leninism, as opposed to Marxism, had always had a certain proclivity for this position. The events of the early 1920s had caused the tactical pendulum to swing toward the Asian "bourgeoisie." Now, it was swinging back.

Thus, almost before the Korean united front had gotten under way, the international signals had been changed. Quickly, the notion of a single, unified nationalist party became a form of liquidationism, a variant of

Yamakawaism and Ch'en Tu-hsiu's rightist deviation. United front tactics were now to be pursued in a different way. The single party was to be dissolved; in its place, a joint struggle committee or liaison group was to be established. Meanwhile, the Korean Communist Party was to have established itself at the grass roots level, building a mass worker-peasant organization securely under its discipline and control. It would *share* power with no one; it would not risk the loss of its identity and the dilution of its policies; it would not run the danger of being overthrown from within. By 1930–31, with the blessing of the Comintern, this had become Korean Communist policy. As a policy of "a united front from below" it dictated the Communist sabotage of the Shingan-hoe—a sabotage in which Japanese officials joyfully concurred.

The evolution of united front tactics during this period is only one example of the nature of Comintern-KCP relations. Those relations, in every respect, were dominated by the Comintern. When Kuusinen asserted matter-of-factly that one of the conditions that would make a KCP factional struggle permissible and necessary was agreement and approval by the Comintern, he was simply reiterating what he and other Comintern officials accepted as a basic principle. Note these words of his: "Since 1919 [when the Comintern was founded] no factional struggle is acceptable without the permission of the Comintern. Of course, no such permission has ever been granted to you." [90]

In this period, no Party ever challenged Comintern directives; those individuals who felt compelled to do so either left the movement or were ejected from it. And the Comintern, in turn, was essentially a creature of Soviet policy. The Korean Communist Party, of course, was in a particularly dependent position. As its leaders acknowledged, it was one of the weakest parties in the world, almost wholly dependent upon external sources of financing and external bases of operation. Korea, like Japan, was a small, "well-ordered" society, and there was little opportunity to establish an independent Communist enclave on home soil. Only Siberia or possibly Manchuria could provide a suitable base. Having stressed these points, however, and having observed that this was a period when, for various reasons including internal politics, Soviet-Comintern authorities were taking an intense interest in the Asian Communist movement, it would be wise to note also that, to those committed to radical doctrines of nationalism and social reform, the Comintern offered support when none was forthcoming elsewhere.

It remains to compare the Korean Communist movement at this point with neighboring movements in Japan and China. As we have seen, the Korean movement derived considerable stimulus from both Japanese and Chinese comrades, though in different ways. As the Party of the mother

90. Kuusinen, *op. cit.,* p. 17.

country, the Japanese Party played an intimate role in the molding of Korean comrades. This relationship was the one that developed elsewhere between mother countries and their colonies. Many Koreans came to Communism during their schooling in Japan, and the prominent Japanese Communists of this period all had their devoted Korean disciples. This was especially true of Fukumoto Kazuo, who could claim with considerable justice to be the father of the M-L Group. The Japanese atmosphere—and once again, this was symptomatic of a mother country–colonial situation— was somewhat freer than that of Korea. Radical associations survived more easily (providing they were not overtly Communist, or clearly Communist-controlled), and radical publications circulated more freely. In some respects Tokyo became a haven where controversial articles could be published, discussion groups could meet, and even the Proletarian Culture Movement could flourish unchecked.

Toward the end of this period, however, the situation tightened in Japan and it became almost as difficult as Korea for Communists. By 1928–30, mass arrests, the penetration of all Communist and proto-Communist organizations by government agents, and periodic liquidation of Communist publications were characteristic of the Japanese scene. Thus, the Korean and Japanese Communist movements both had to exist in an efficient authoritarian state where it was impossible to maintain an effective Party organization, develop experienced leadership, or establish mass bases. Up to 1927, the situation with respect to the Chinese Communist Party was of course radically different. Initially, the foreign concession in Shanghai had served as a privileged sanctuary, and after 1923 the Communists could operate freely in those areas under Kuomintang control or influence. By 1926–27, this included almost the whole of China. Then came the coup. Within weeks, thousands of Chinese Communists were killed; violence on a scale never paralleled in Japan or Korea took place. By the end of this era, it was undoubtedly more dangerous to be captured in Nationalist China as a Communist than to suffer the same fate in the Japanese empire. Nevertheless, the roots of an indigenous Communist movement in China were being reestablished in Kiangsi, a development that could not be emulated within Korea or Japan.

By 1930, the Communist movement throughout Northeast Asia was in desperate shape. The gamble to capture the nationalist movement seemed lost. In Japan, of course, the chance had never existed. The Japanese Communists had been forced to fight their nationalist movement from the beginning, and accept anti-imperialism and Soviet-oriented internationalism in its place. For them, Russia was the only true fatherland. The Chinese Communists, on the other hand, had come close to making the united front work on their behalf, close to turning nationalism into *their* weapon. But then they failed, and nationalism became the weapon of the Kuomintang.

In Korea also, the most promising nationalist organ was scuttled by the Communists, who were following the thesis that they too would lose control of the broader nationalist movement if they were integrated with it.

Everywhere in Northeast Asia, the Communist movement had been essentially a petty bourgeois movement of young ideologues, a thought-society movement plunging sporadically into action as it sought to make an impact upon students, workers, or peasants. The last source remained almost completely untapped at the end of this period. The workers had been reached only in a few major industrial centers, and the costs of radicalism for them had been so great that most of them had deserted the movement, wiser and sadder. Only with each successive generation of young students did the message find some echo—thereby perpetuating the petty bourgeois character of the party. Once again, by 1930, China was a partial exception: a new Party was being built in an area remote from students or urban workers. Thus only the Chinese Communists were in a position to execute the new Comintern exhortations of emphasis upon the peasant and agrarian reform.

The Comintern in this era dominated the Communist parties of Korea, Japan, and China, and it would be difficult to distinguish any significant differences in the degree of control. Their basic theses were the Comintern theses, influenced by Soviet leadership and reflective of Soviet interests. Until his purge, Nikolai Bukharin had been a key voice in Asian policy, together with men like Grigorii Voitinsky, Mikhail Borodin, General Galen (Vasily Blücher), and many others, including the Baltic revolutionary Jonson in Japan. The rationalization for Comintern domination, of course, was that this was an international association of comrades, democratically chosen, and wedded to the same goals and purposes. In fact, the Comintern, subservient to Stalin, made a series of tragic errors in this period that deeply hurt the Asian Communists. And none was more serious than the turn to the left after 1927 that each of these three parties attempted so faithfully to follow. It is doubtful, however, whether there could have been a "correct policy" for Communism in Northeast Asia during this era. Certainly, the Korean Communists could not logically have hoped for any quick or easy rise to prominence and power whatever the route chosen. That would have to await events they could not possibly have foreseen, events going far beyond Korea. But these events were already in the offing.

CHAPTER III

WORKERS, PEASANTS, AND PARTISANS

After 1928, the broad guide lines for the Korean Communist movement were set by resolutions of the Sixth Comintern Congress and the December Theses, which applied those resolutions specifically to Korea. A swing to the left had been ordered, largely because of the shocking failure in China. The united front was still a stated objective, but under stipulations that made its attainment virtually impossible. Now, the emphasis was upon a united front from below, that is, the mobilization of workers and peasants under Communist banners as a solid revolutionary phalanx capable of thwarting the "reactionary proclivities" of the bourgeoisie.

The Comintern directed that the Communist Party of Korea be completely rebuilt in accordance with this task. Its petty bourgeois intellectual leadership had to be replaced by "genuine representatives of the proletariat," men armed with "correct Marxist-Leninist principles" and capable of executing them. Its narrow "study-group" organizational structure had to be totally revamped, with the new movement resting its foundations upon revolutionary labor and peasant unions. The Party had to find its soul in the worker-peasant masses and develop its leadership out of "the most advanced proletarian elements" emanating from this source. At all costs, moreover, the Communist movement had to safeguard its independence from the bourgeoisie. To this end, it had to be constantly alert to the crucial distinction between *tactical* and *organic* union with national-reformist groups.

In obedience to these orders, the Korean Communists proceeded to aid in the liquidation of the Shingan-hoe, as we have seen. Meanwhile, they began the enormously difficult task of trying to create a mass-based Communist movement along the lines indicated by Comintern and Profintern directives. To appreciate these efforts and the results, we must retrace our steps slightly, returning to mid-1928. As will be recalled, the Communist Party of Korea had just been wiped out for the fourth time by the mass arrests of its Executive Committee. Moreover, in August, the Sixth Comintern Congress had refused to grant recognition to either of the rival Korean delegations. Instead, a Comintern committee had been appointed to prepare a resolution on the Korean Communist movement. That resolution (the December Theses) had demanded a thorough reorganization of the Party, meanwhile withholding recognition from all contending factions.

As of mid-1928, therefore, no Communist Party of Korea existed. Nor was a Party reestablished officially until after World War II, despite the fact that the Korean Communist movement continued in many forms and in many quarters. A small band of intrepid individuals who remained in Korea sought to keep the movement alive. They paid heavily for their efforts, as we shall see. The major efforts of the Korean Communists, however, were once again initiated from overseas bases, as in the period before 1925. Faced with the impossibility of maintaining a strong indigenous base, the Communists of Korea were again forced to operate primarily from widely scattered centers in Manchuria, Japan, Siberia, and China proper. Relations among these centers were characterized by liaison and alignment on the one hand, and by rivalry and division on the other. New Comintern directives, as well as ethnic divisions within the Asian Communist movement, created further complications.

Korean Communism in Manchuria After 1925

Let us begin with events in Manchuria. From every standpoint, this was a region of critical importance. In Chientao Province alone, there were nearly 400,000 Koreans in 1930, and the total Korean population of Manchuria was over 600,000 at this time.[1] Could a meaningful portion of this

1. By 1910, at the time of Korean annexation, the Korean population in Chientao had already reached 109,500 while the Chinese population was only 33,500, testifying to the close geographic relation between this area and Korea, and the relative availability of land for Chinese in other, more accessible parts of Manchuria. After 1910, another wave of Korean immigrants came into the region, many of them for political reasons. Note the population growth:

Population in Chientao

	Koreans	Chinese
1910	109,500	33,500
1912	163,000	49,000
1916	203,426	60,896
1921	307,806	73,748
1926	356,016	86,347
1931	395,847	120,394

For this table and other details, see Division of Advisers, Department of Defense, ethnic group be mobilized for political purposes, and by whom? The Japanese had long been deeply concerned over Communist activities in the area, complaining that Chinese officials were so lax that adequate security measures were impossible to apply. In 1930, they asserted that one-tenth of the adult Korean population in Manchuria could be accounted "Communist or sympathetic to the Communists." [2]

Manchukuo, *Manshū kyōsanhi no kenkyū* (*A Study of Communist Insurgents in Manchuria*), no place of publication, 1937, pp. 543 ff.

Figures on the total number of Koreans in Manchuria during this period vary considerably. In 1926, for example, when the Japanese Consulate was reporting 542,185 Koreans there, South Manchurian Railroad authorities were reporting 783,-187. Government figures were:

Korean Population in Manchuria

1919	431,198	1927	558,280
1920	459,427	1928	577,052
1921	488,656	1929	597,677
1922	515,865	1930	607,119
1923	528,027	1931	630,982
1924	531,857	1932	672,649
1925	531,973	1933	673,794
1926	542,185	1934	719,988

Drawn from *ibid.*, pp. 513–514. For a discussion of statistical discrepancies on population, see Yi Hun-gu (Hoon Koo Lee), *Manju wa Chosŏnin* (*Manchuria and the Koreans*), P'yŏngyang, 1931, pp. 88–89.

It should be emphasized that the Korean community in Manchuria was overwhelmingly rural. In 1932, when certain Japanese officials were estimating a total Korean population in Manchuria of 800,000 only four cities had a Korean population of over 5,000: Mukden (27,227), Antung (13,677), T'iehling (8,226), and Changchun (5,079). *Manshū kyōsanhi no kenkyū, op. cit.*, pp. 513–514.

2. This statement was made in a report from Chientao Consul-General Okada to Minister of Foreign Affairs Shidehara, *The Recent Condition of Various Factions of the Korean Communist Party in East Manchuria*, March 4, 1930, *Archives of the Japanese Ministry of Foreign Affairs* (hereafter *AJMFA*), microfilmed for the Library of Congress, Washington, D.C., Reel (hereafter R) S102, Frame (hereafter F) 6179–98.

One may get some impression of trends in the mid-1920s by noting the following:

Propaganda Materials Confiscated in the Chientao Region

	1923		1924		1925		1926		1927	
	Kinds	Copies	Kinds	Copies	Kinds	Copies	Kinds	Copies	Kinds	Copies
Communist materials	45	2,078	40	631	101	2,527	136	2,519	239	7,867
Nationalist materials	81	2,130	124	2,819	101	1,881	123	687	91	2,548
TOTAL	126	4,208	164	3,450	202	4,408	259	3,206	330	10,415

"Statistics Concerning the Communist Movement in the Chientao and Hunch'un Areas," *AJMFA*, R S722. Incidentally, Yenchi hsien (Prefecture), Chientao Province, produced the largest number of "subversive" materials, far outdistancing other prefectures in this respect. Yenchi, it is to be noted, was one of the hsien bordering North Hamgyŏng.

There are no reliable surveys setting forth the reasons why Koreans migrated to Manchuria. No doubt the great majority left Korea for economic reasons. Life was always hard in Korea and for some Korean farmers it grew harder after the Japanese occupation. But a substantial number of migrants went to Manchuria for political reasons. Precisely because there were so many militant nationalists among the Korean population there, the region constituted fertile ground for the Communists. Again, it must be reiterated that the distinction between Communism and nationalism was extremely hazy among almost all Koreans at the grass-roots level, especially since anticolonialism was one of the most prominent and persistent of the Communist themes.

Severe economic problems also existed within the Korean community in Manchuria. Foremost were issues of land and land rights. Under the Chientao Treaty of 1909 signed by the Chinese and Japanese governments, Koreans were permitted equal rights with Chinese with respect to land and property in Chientao. In other parts of Manchuria, however, Koreans could not own land unless they were naturalized citizens. Even in Chientao, 56.6 percent of all Koreans in this period were either pure or part tenants, while only 23.7 percent of the Chinese fell into this category.[3] In sum, poverty was widespread among the Koreans living in Manchuria. The Communists did not overlook this opportunity.

The most serious problem for Korean farmers in Manchuria, however, was the severe suppression they suffered at the hands of the Chinese authorities. Before 1925, this situation had not existed. Earlier, indeed, Korean immigrants had been encouraged, since they were opening up the wastelands and converting them into paddy fields. For a time, moreover, Chinese authorities supported Korean nationalists, providing some of them with active assistance. Gradually, this amicable relationship changed, partly because Koreans increasingly became symbols of Japanese power rather than symbols of resistance to that power. While the Japanese were worrying about that "one-tenth" who were "pro-Communist," the Chinese focused upon that "nine-tenths" whom they regarded as either "pro-Japanese" or convenient excuses for Japanese encroachment. To many Chinese, the Manchurian Koreans were "running dogs" of Japanese imperialism. The more the Korean communities developed, the larger became the number of Japanese police and consular officials sent to Manchuria. Sometimes, Japanese troops also came—to protect "loyal" Koreans and to suppress "recalcitrant" ones.[4]

3. In 1930, 31.2 percent of all Korean farmers in Chientao were pure tenants, possessing no land of their own; 13.7 percent of the Chinese farmers there were in that category. See *Manshū kyōsanhi no kenkyū, op. cit.,* p. 554.

4. As the Korean community grew, an increasing number of conflicts developed between Koreans and Chinese. In such cases, the Japanese Consulate often claimed extraterritoriality on behalf of the Koreans, thereby humiliating the Chinese and adding to the bitterness between the two ethnic groups.

In 1925, an agreement between Chang Tso-lin's Mukden government and the Korean governor general was signed, relating to the control of so-called Korean subversives. The agreement provided for the active co-operation of the Mukden government; there was to be a reward in money for each arrest. The Korean nationalist and Communist movements suffered heavily as a result of this agreement, but so did a number of non-political Koreans. In many cases, the order to suppress "recalcitrant Koreans" became a license for local officials to abuse their authority. Under the pretext of suppressing radicals, Chinese officials sometimes killed, molested, or arrested innocent farmers, extracted large sums of money in "fines," and drove them off their land. These and similar outrages were increasingly frequent after 1927.[5]

One survey exists relating specifically to grievances among Korean farmers in Manchuria during this period. Some 201 heads of households in one community were asked in 1930 what were the three most serious problems facing them, in order of priority (see table 12).

TABLE 12
Grievances of the Koreans in Manchuria, 1930[6]

	Problem of					
	1st Importance		*2nd Importance*		*3rd Importance*	
	No.	*Percent*	*No.*	*Percent*	*No.*	*Percent*
Sustaining livelihood[a]	41	20.4	13	6.5	6	3.0
Earning sufficient money[a]	46	23.0	15	7.6	7	3.5
Political insecurity	42	21.0	79	39.4	26	12.8
Personal dangers	24	12.0	37	18.5	86	43.2
Lawlessness, suppression, and the demands of Chinese officials	12	5.8	18	8.9	21	10.4
The bandit problem	3	1.4	10	5.0	12	6.0

SOURCE: Yi Hun-gu, *Manju wa Chosŏnin*, pp. 105–106.

 [a] The first category presumably refers to sustaining life whereas the second refers to acquiring any surplus, especially cash surplus.

While it would be unwise to place too much emphasis upon a survey of one community, the results generally support data derived from other sources. If we group several of the above categories together, we can see that economic and political problems were regarded by the Manchurian

5. For details, see Yi Hun-gu, *op. cit.,* pp. 239–263.

6. Yi, who states that 201 individuals were questioned, does not explain why neither the total number of answers nor the percentages equals 201 (or 100 percent), the range being from 172 to 158 (85.9 to 78.9 percent). Perhaps the remainder refused to answer, gave miscellaneous answers, or responded, "Don't know." We have reproduced the figures given by Yi.

Koreans as of approximately equal importance. The difficulties of obtaining a livelihood or rising above the minimum subsistence level were indeed serious. But so were the problems of living in a region where the government was weak, corrupt, and prejudiced. It is not surprising that the Manchurian Koreans often turned to the Japanese authorities for protection—even in some cases, Koreans who secretly harbored nationalist sentiments. Nor is it startling to learn that various Korean nationalist groups attempted to organize self-protection units on behalf of the Korean community.

This turbulent environment attracted and sustained the Korean Communist movement. Moreover, there was one additional factor of major importance. The very location of Manchuria guaranteed its significance in this era. Bounded on the northeast by the Soviet Union, on the north and west by China, and on the south by Korea, it lay in the vital center of the rising military-political struggle that was first to engulf Northeast Asia and then the world.

The Korean Communists had been active in Manchuria since 1920, and at one time or another nearly every major Manchurian center had served as a base of Korean radical activity. As was noted earlier, even in 1921 a Japanese report estimated that 150,000 Koreans in the Manchurian area had been influenced by Communist propaganda.[7] The activities of the old Shanghai and Irkutsk factions had declined somewhat after 1923. But with the establishment of a Communist Party in Korea proper, a new drive got under way. Within a brief time, all the Korean Communist factions had established a base of operations in the Manchurian area. The first prominent effort was under the aegis of the Tuesday Society which, as we have noted, dominated the first and second Korean Communist Parties. The first Executive Committee had directed that a bureau be established in Manchuria, but it took no further action before being shattered by the arrests of November 1925. In May 1926, however, the Manchurian General Bureau was established, thanks largely to the initiative of Kim Ch'an, one of the few Executive Committee members who had escaped in November.[8] Its headquarters were located at Ningkut'a, Ningan Prefecture, where the Shanghai-Chita faction had previously had its headquarters.

7. See Chapter I, p. 27.
8. Kim, escaping from Seoul, reached Shanghai in January 1926. There, he conferred with such exiles as Nam Man-ch'un, Cho Pong-am, Kim Tan-ya, and Yŏ Un-hyŏng. The decision to establish a headquarters in Shanghai was made and, at the same time, Kim urged Cho to establish the Manchurian General Bureau in accordance with the decision of the executive committee. Cho left Shanghai in mid-April with Kim Ch'i-jŏng (Kim Tong-myŏng) and Ch'oe Won-t'aek, proceeding to Manchuria. (Kim Ch'i-jong, incidentally, was a graduate of the Communist University in Moscow.) The three held discussions with various people, including three veteran Communists who had come from Vladivostok: Yun Cha-yŏng, Kim Ch'ŏl-hun, and Kim Ha-gu. It was agreed to establish the Bureau, and Cho served as the first secretary, with Ch'oe Won-t'aek heading the Organization Department and Yun Cha-yŏng the Propaganda Department. These three, together with Kim Ha-gu, Kim Ch'ŏl-hun,

Communist organizational activities in Manchuria were more or less under the control of the Tuesday Society faction until late 1927. Even during this period, there were serious problems of liaison and coordination between Seoul and Manchuria.[9] But organizational efforts made considerable progress. It is true that neither the Party nor the Communist Youth League reached impressive levels of membership. Moreover, the nationalist quotient within the Communist movement was so high that there was some question whether there were any "pure Communists" in the Party at all.[10] But for that very reason, perhaps, the Party was developing an influence out of all proportion to its size, especially among the educated youth. By the end of 1927, Japanese authorities were deeply concerned.

As an initial action, Manchurian General Bureau officials established three basic branches to cover east, south, and north Manchuria. Our information is most extensive on the activities of the eastern branch, the most important one. Branch officers were instructed to investigate the old Communist cells previously established by the Shanghai and Irkutsk factions, and to recruit "desirable elements" from them into the new organization. In areas where there was a substantial Korean population, "educational institutes" of approximately one month's duration were initiated, to provide "basic political training." A central library and mobile libraries were also developed in an effort to disseminate "progressive" literature. The numerous Korean schools in Manchuria along with the youth move-

---

and Kim Yong-nak, made up the executive committee. For details, see "The Preliminary Trial of Kim Ch'an," in Kōtō Hōin, Kenjikyoku (High Court), Prosecutor's Bureau), *Shisō geppō* (*Thought Monthly*), Vol. 2, No. 2, May 1932, *AJMFA*, R S357, pp. 1896–7.

9. Some of the problems, of course, stemmed from the rapid turnover of Party officials in Korea. Kang Tal-yŏng, as we have noted, complained in his letter to Kim Ch'an dated April 4, 1926, that the previous Party secretary, Kim Chae-bong, had not informed him about the Manchurian General Bureau at all, and, moreover, that some members of the new executive committee in Seoul were suspicious of the motives of the Shanghai comrades. We have also cited the controversy over Cho Pong-am. Indeed, Kang listed Kim Ch'an as secretary in his report to the Comintern of April 6, 1926. This particular problem was eased when Cho returned to China shortly thereafter. Beginning in January 1927, O Ik-sŏn (alias Wu Tan-u) assumed leadership of the Bureau. (For Kang's letters, see *ibid.*, Vol. 2, No. 9, pp. 2757–60; for the shift to O Ik-sŏn, see "A Synopsis of the Interrogation Concerning the System, Organization, and Activities of the Korean Communist Party," *AJMFA*, R S722, no pagination. This is a report on the interrogation of Chŏng Chae-yun, the alias of An Ki-sŏng, secretary of the East Manchurian branch of the Bureau.)

10. An Ki-Sŏng (*ibid.*) told Japanese authorities that he faced a number of difficulties in developing good Communists. The educational and cultural level among the Koreans in Chientao was generally low, he asserted, and nationalist sentiment very strong. Consequently, there were almost no "pure Communists" in the membership, he stated. He also told his interrogators that progress in stabilizing economic conditions had reduced Communist effectiveness among the farmers, and that even among the students few became truly dedicated Communists.

ments that tended to develop around them, became a special target. Teachers in particular were solicited, in the hope that they would become key figures in the movement.[11]

Intensive efforts were also made to interact with the various nationalist groups in the area, and with such labor and farmer associations as existed. This was, of course, the era of the united front, and the Executive Committee of the second KCP, which was in Seoul, had specifically instructed the Manchurian Bureau to build a united front with "all of those elements opposed to imperialism." The Bureau was not, however, to reveal its identity or join the local Shingan-hoe. These instructions were followed, at least by the eastern branch of the Bureau. The contemplated joint action with nationalists, moreover, extended to military as well as political matters. The minutes of a meeting of January 25, 1927, for example, reveal that the Communists voted to promote the organization of a leaders' group that would in turn establish the Chosŏn Tongnip-dan (Korean Independence Corps).[12] The eastern branch compiled a list of all militarily experienced Korean residents as possible candidates for the corps.

These various activities were disrupted in October 1927, when the Manchurian Bureau was almost wiped out by Japanese police action. As the Korean Communists had become stronger, they had become more diversified in their contacts, and more bold. Gradually, Japanese agents penetrated Communist organizations, and acquired vital information. They learned, for example, that the village of Lungching was a center of Communist activity in the east, and that Chŏng Chae-yun (alias An Ki-sŏng) was the secretary of the eastern branch. Finally, through an agent, the Japanese learned that a secret meeting of top Communist leaders was to be held on October 3. While the meeting was in progress, they burst in, arresting such men as Ch'oe Won-t'aek, head of the Bureau's Organization Department, Kim Ch'i-jŏng (alias Kim Tong-myŏng), head of the Bureau's Propaganda Department, and An. These arrests led them to a huge number of documents, including instructions from Seoul and from Bureau headquarters, minutes of various meetings, files of reports submitted, and detailed lists of the various cells and the members of the eastern branch. When these materials had been studied, the Japanese police had almost as much knowledge concerning the Bureau, or at least its eastern branch, as the Communist leaders themselves. Arrests on a major scale followed.

11. Despite these efforts, the Party roster seized at the time of the October 1927 arrests indicates that the Eastern Manchurian branch had only 73 full and 42 candidate members, many of whom had been active in the Communist movement of the previous era.

12. For details, see Japanese Consulate General in Chientao, *Kantō oyobi setsujō chihō kyōsanshugi undō no gaikyō* (*A Resume of the Condition of the Communist Movement in the Chientao and Adjacent Areas*), June 25, 1928, a mimeographed document in *AJMFA*, R S721–722.

More than 200 individuals were picked up, and the 28 whom the Japanese considered top leaders were sent to Korea for trial.[13]

The Manchurian Bureau never really recovered from this blow, although a skeleton organization was quickly put together. In November, the Bureau was relocated in Tungchingch'eng, Ningan Prefecture, with Yi Tong-san as Bureau secretary.[14] The Bureau subsequently helped to organize certain nationalist demonstrations, and sought to rebuild its local units. However, it remained largely dormant until June 1929, when Wu Yŏng-sŏn and Yu Il-gŭn revived it, starting with a group of about thirty individuals. As of March 1930, the Wu-Yu group had five cells, with forty-eight members; seventy-four affiliates from the Minjok Yuil-dang (United National Party); and fifty-seven members in the Party-controlled Youth League.[15]

The Tuesday Society, however, could never recover from the mass arrests of the 1925–1927 period, both in Korea and abroad. Up to October 1927, as we have noted, the Manchurian General Bureau had been dominated by those identified with the Tuesday Society faction, although much of the Bureau's membership had come from those belonging to the old Shanghai or Irkutsk factions. After October, the increasing factionalism within the Korean Communist Party at home was quickly reflected in Manchuria. For this situation, of course, the Japanese could take considerable credit. Having destroyed the dominant Party organization both in Korea and in Manchuria, and having arrested almost all of the key leaders by 1927, they had created the conditions for the emergence of a number of splinter groups.

At this point, it will be recalled, the M-L Group was emerging as the most significant Communist element on the Korean scene. When An Kwang-ch'ŏn, an M-L Group member, became secretary of the third KCP, he appointed Pak Yun-sŏ to reestablish the Manchurian General Bureau. What contact if any Pak had with Yi Tong-san and the old Bureau is unclear. In any case, no merger occurred. Instead Pak set up a new Bureau in January 1928. Headquarters were first opened in Vladivostok, but soon moved to Panshih hsien (Prefecture) Kirin (Chilin) Province. Also at this time, the M-L Group set up its own Youth League; later, it added a Military

13. For details, see *Shisō geppō, op. cit.,* Vol. 3, No. 4, July 1933, p. 55, *AJMFA,* R S358.

14. In addition to Yi Tong-san, other officers of the reorganized Bureau included Kim Paek-p'a (Organization) and Kim Hong-sŏn (Propaganda). In the Youth League, Ch'oe Ch'ung-ho became secretary; other officers were Sŏk Kŭm-san (Organization) and Han Pyŏl (Propaganda). "The Preliminary Trial in Connection with the Chientao May 30 Incident," *ibid.,* Vol. 1, No. 4, July 15, 1931, pp. 173–200 (at 176), *AJMFA,* R S355.

15. "The Recent Condition of the Various Factions of the Korean Communist Party in East Manchuria," *op. cit.,* F 6190–1.

Department to its Bureau in order to provide members with military training.

Thus, by 1928, the M-L Group and the Tuesday Society faction had competitive organizations in Manchuria. And while these formed the most important organized groups of Korean Communists in that region, both the Shanghai and Seoul factions also had organizations there. Seeking to take up where the Tuesday Society had ended, the Shanghai faction had organized the so-called Korean Communist Group in Manchuria in Lungching, Chientao, shortly after October 1927. Leading roles were taken by Chu Kŏn together with several others previously active in the eastern branch of the Bureau. The Seoul faction, using the simple designations "Korean Communist Party" and "Koryŏ Communist Youth League," also opened a drive for provincial and prefectural support.[16]

This was the chaotic situation in Manchuria at the opening of the Sixth Comintern Congress. It will be recalled that the Shanghai and Seoul factions had united against the M-L Group in the struggle to gain Comintern recognition, and they had been represented in Moscow by the veteran Yi Tong-hwi, with Kim Kyu-yŏl. When these men returned to Vladivostok, they naturally gave their colleagues a detailed account of Comintern views. A decision was thereupon reached to form a "faction-free party," and various individuals associated with the Tuesday Society and M-L Group factions were solicited.[17] As usual, the effort for unity met with limited success, partly, no doubt, because it had been undertaken by old factional leaders. An Sang-hun, formerly of the Tuesday Society, and Kim Yŏng-sik, a former member of the M-L group, did join the new organization. But this scarcely made it "faction-free."

It was generally agreed that the Party ought to be established in Korea proper. Unhappily, severe police repression made this impossible. Hence, a site convenient to Korea was selected: Tunhwa, a town in Kirin Province, Manchuria. The Vladivostok group, with the exception of Yi Tong-hwi, who remained as liaison man with the Comintern, thereupon moved to Tunhwa.[18] Beginning in January 1929, they held organizational and

16. In addition to Chu Kŏn, Yi In-yŏng, Pak Ch'ang-ik, Kim Il-su, and Yŏ Nam-su were active in establishing the Shanghai faction association. Top offices were held by Chu, Kim Hi-ch'ang, O Sŏng-se, and Kang Mun-su. The association reportedly recruited about 130 members, and 146 members in its Youth League. The Japanese accorded it top position in 1930 in terms of membership and influence. *Ibid.*, F 6180-3.

The Seoul faction's activities are discussed in "The Preliminary Trial in Connection with the Chientao May 30 Incident," *Shisō geppō, op. cit.,* p. 180.

17. The key figures involved in Vladivostok, in addition to Yi and Kim Kyu-yŏl, were Kim Ch'ŏl-su, Ch'oe Tong-uk, O Sŏng-se, Kim Il-su, and Yun Cha-yŏng of the Shanghai faction, and Kim Yŏng-man, Seoul faction leader.

18. Yi was now in his sixties, and this period represents the last phase of his political activities. On Jan. 31, 1935, he died in Vladivostok of "old age and fatigue." With his passing, one of the last of the old-line fighters for Korean independence

planning meetings in the homes of Chu Kŏn and An Sang-hun, outside the old walled city. It was decided that An Sang-hun should be sent to Korea to reestablish contact with various comrades, relay Comintern instructions, and aid in the reorganization of the Party in accordance with the new program.[19] Armed with a copy of the December Theses and letters of introduction from Kim Ch'ŏl-su and Kim Yŏng-man, An proceeded to Seoul in February 1929. There he ultimately made contact with two old Seoul faction men, Pang Han-min and Yi Chun-yŏl. He later made other contacts in Pusan and in his home town in Andong Prefecture. Actually, Pang and other remnants of the Seoul faction had already begun efforts to rebuild the Party; they had been informed about the December Theses and were anticipating instructions.[20] With An's arrival, activities were stepped up. Within three months, however, the old cycle was repeated. Communist operations were detected by police and, by early June, a total of seventy-five persons had been arrested, including all of the key figures. Pang Han-min, Yi Chun-yŏl, Yi Pin-yong, and Chong Hŏn-t'ae were each sentenced to seven years in prison; surprisingly, An's term was only four. Another round had ended in failure.

The Tunhwa group reconvened in late June to assess the situation. It was decided that, rather than attempting to reestablish the Party in Korea immediately, it would be wiser to continue primary operations in Manchuria. Permanent officers were therefore selected, and the group decided to call itself Chosŏn Kongsan-dang Chae-Kŏnsŏl Chunbi Wiwon-hoe (Pre-

---

was removed from the scene. As noted earlier, Yi was scarcely a "good Communist" from a Comintern standpoint. His concern with, and understanding of, Marxist-Leninist doctrines were minimal. His interest in Communism stemmed primarily from the fact that it promised a militant approach to the struggle for independence and provided Korean fighters with access to the Soviet Union, a necessary refuge and the only conceivable source of substantial material and political assistance. If we may believe "Kim San," however, Yi was unhappy in his final years. Kim San and Nym Wales, *Song of Ariran*, New York, 1941, p. 54. It is most revealing, moreover, that recent Russian works on the Korean Communist movement do not even mention Yi Tong-hwi. To contemporary Soviet historians, he has become a non-person.

19. An was not only a former Tuesday Society member, but he was another one of the twenty-one students who had been sent to Moscow in the fall of 1925 by the KCP executive committee to study in the University of the Toilers of the East.

20. The career of Pang Han-min paralleled that of many other Korean Communists of this period. Pang studied briefly at Nihon Daigaku (Japan University) in Tokyo, and returned to Korea to assume a journalistic career, first with *Tong-A Ilbo,* then with *Chosŏn Ilbo*. Concurrently, he did some teaching. Earlier, Pang had been arrested for Communist activities and served five years of a ten-year sentence in prison; he was released in June 1928. Just before he left for Vladivostok in the summer of 1928, Yi Un-hyŏk, a Seoul faction leader, had instructed Yi Chun-yŏl, a comrade and schoolteacher, to get in touch with Pang as soon as he was released from prison and to revive the Seoul faction KCP. This work was under way when An arrived. See "Concerning the Plan for the Organization of the KCP and the Arrests of Various Persons," a report from Kyŏnggi Province, Aug. 10, 1929, *AJMFA,* R S722.

paratory Society for the Reconstruction of the Korean Communist Party).
Headquarters were temporarily located in Chu Kŏn's home, and Kim
Ch'ŏl-su was chosen as the Society's chairman. (Kim, it will be recalled, had
brought the first Comintern funds to Korea from Shanghai in 1921 and
had later served as a member of the Executive Committee of the second
KCP in December 1925.)

On June 25, in connection with the launching of the Preparatory Society, the group issued a declaration entitled "To All Korean Communist
Comrades." [21] As would be expected this declaration hewed closely to the
line of the December Theses. It asserted that the miserable defeats suffered
by Korean Communism were the result of police suppression, the isolation
of the Party from the masses, and the former intense factionalism within
the Party. It announced that the factional struggles of the past had been
"unprincipled," and that all factional groups must be "bravely dissolved."
This "historic duty" was now being undertaken by the Preparatory Society.

Reading between the lines, however, one could easily discern that
neither factionalism nor genuine disputes over tactics had ended. Essentially, the Society was an organization of the Shanghai-Seoul factions, and
all Korean Communists knew this. Moreover, the declaration made it clear
that a number of "erroneous theories" relating to the Party still existed.
It sharply criticized the "federalist theory," whereby all factions would be
united under a semiautonomous, federated system; such a theory was a
new device to promote factionalism, and the product of "infantile thinking." It also condemned the "natural growth theory" (now known widely
as Yamakawaism), according to which Communists should concentrate at
this point upon building and capturing mass organizations, leaving the
construction of the Party to a more appropriate time. Such a theory, proclaimed the declaration, denied the critical importance of the role of the
Communist Party as the only possible vanguard of the working class. It
was not only erroneous, insisted the declaration, but would inevitably lead
to an exacerbation of factional struggles. At the same time, it was wrong
to demand that only those with complete ideological understanding should
develop the Party; this would lead to exclusivism and isolation from the
masses. In this fashion, the declaration challenged both Fukumotoism and
its exponents, the M-L Group. Finally, there was an allusion to "certain
stubborn leaders in every faction" who held to a "gamble theory," that is,
they were to fight it out, disregarding Comintern decisions and allowing
the outcome of continued factional struggles to determine the Party's future. Such individuals, remarked the declaration, were merely manifesting
a bourgeois fear of self-criticism.

The Preparatory Society undertook its operations with some vigor.
Kim Yŏng-man represented it at the Pan-Pacific Trade Union Conference

21. For the complete text, see *Shisō geppō, op. cit.,* Vol. 1, No. 6, *AJMFA,* R
S355, pp. 299–306.

in Vladivostok in August 1929, and so kept it abreast of Profintern policies. The organizational network was expanded, particularly in Manchuria. Under the Manchurian Department, headed by Chu Kŏn, regional branches covering east, south, and north Manchuria were once again created and, beneath these, many local units. Meanwhile, a number of the Society's agents were sent into Korea. Kim Ch'ŏl-su went back in January 1930 to undertake assignments originally given to An Sang-hun. In May, O Sŏng-se returned to reestablish a Communist Youth League. Some twenty members of the Tunhwa Group had reentered Korea by the end of 1930. One of these, Kim Il-su, had begun a cadre training program: some fifteen young men had been selected from within the country and sent to Chientao for special training. In Manchuria, they underwent two or three weeks' intensive training in Communist doctrine and revolutionary tactics, after which they returned home to enter the struggle.[22]

During this period, the remnants of the M-L Group and the Tuesday Society were generally quiescent. Nevertheless, such organizations as they possessed remained intact. For this reason, individuals who had been connected with these factions generally refrained from joining the Preparatory Society. Thus, despite its intentions, the Society did not represent a break with the factional traditions of the past. This fact soon became known to the Comintern, where it caused profound unhappiness. In late 1929, therefore, a radical new plan for attacking Korean Communist factionalism was devised under Comintern aegis. The Communist Party of China was ordered to assume full responsibility for the Korean Communist movement in Manchuria. All previous Korean Communist organizations were to be disbanded, and all Koreans eligible for Party membership were to join the Chinese Communist Party.

To put this new policy in context, we must recall earlier relations between the Korean and Chinese Communist movements and note briefly key recent developments. From the very beginning of the colonial era, a great variety of Korean radicals had used China as a place of refuge and an operational base. The Communist movement had been nurtured there at least as early as 1920, and Shanghai had involuntarily loaned its name to one of the prominent Korean Communist factions. Peking also had harbored many a Korean Communist. This situation continued even after the

22. The training was provided by Yun Cha-yŏng in Yenchi *hsien,* Chientao Province. Some of the trainees were placed in the Korean Nitrogen Fertilizer Plant in Hŭngnam, one of the areas marked for intensive labor activities by the Communists. See "The Development of the Korean Communist Movement," *Shisō geppō, op. cit.,* Vol. 3, No. 2, May 15, 1933, pp. 19–20, *AJMFA,* R S358.

The attrition rate among the Tunhwa group who returned to Korea continued to be high. Kim Ch'ŏl-su, for example, was arrested in May 1930. For details, see the Criminal Affairs Department, Keijō District Court, *Chōsen kyōsantō saiken undō nado jiken hanketsu utsushi* (*Transcript of the Judicial Decision on the Korean Communist Party Reconstruction Movement, and Other Matters*), Seoul, 1933.

break between the Kuomintang and the Chinese Communist Party, albeit
on a more muted scale. Many leading Korean Communists, including Kim
Ch'an, Kim Tan-ya, and Cho Pong-am, used such areas as the French
concession in Shanghai to great advantage.

The politics of the Korean refugee movement were, of course, enormously complicated. Koreans in China ran the political gamut, with an intense nationalism being the only common political denominator. Anarchists, conservative but militant nationalists, and nationalist-Communists
were all present.[23] Even among the so-called Communists, there were
major differences of style and alliance. Some, as we shall see, maintained
ties with the Kuomintang. Many more, of course, had connections with
the Chinese Communist Party. During this period, Koreans were involved
with the Chinese revolution at almost every level, despite the fact that
their numbers were not large. For example, some attended and even
taught at the Whampoa Military Academy. Others participated jointly with
Chinese in left-wing publishing ventures. Koreans had been participants in
the Far Eastern Bureau of the Comintern in Shanghai since its founding.
Korean radicals were also involved in the labor, cultural, and student movements now burgeoning on the Chinese scene.

The collapse of the Kuomintang-Communist alliance was naturally a
traumatic experience for Korean Communists resident in China. A number
of Koreans were killed in the course of the Canton uprising, including some
of the most experienced revolutionaries.[24] And from this point, of course,

23. For details, see Chong-Sik Lee, *The Politics of Korean Nationalism,* Berkeley, 1963, esp. Chapters 9 and 10.

24. In early December 1927, the Chinese Communists sought to seize the city
of Canton and establish a commune there. For a few days, between Dec. 11 and 14,
the Communists held the city, and then they were defeated and driven out with heavy
losses. There are good reasons to believe that this foolish adventure was not only
sanctioned by the Comintern but demanded by it. Several months earlier, in September, the Comintern has approved a complete break with the Kuomintang and
espoused the establishment of a Soviet regime; after that, they insisted upon militancy.

Kim San, who claims to have been in Canton during the entire period between
1925 and 1927, and who took an active role in the uprising, gives us some information on the role of Koreans in this affair. By 1927, he asserts, over 800 Koreans
were in Canton, almost all of them political revolutionaries, including a number of
Communist Party members from Manchuria. They were all young, average age
about 23, none over 40; they belonged to many groups, with no unified leadership
and—according to Kim—with the Chinese Communist Party believing that it had
the right to give orders to all of them. Kim asserts that some 80 Koreans from
various backgrounds were organized in a secret group known as the KK (Korean
Communists in German!—possible testimony to the influence of the German Communist Heinz Neumann, who was in Canton at this time).

At the time of the KMT-CCP break, in the spring of 1927, a number of Koreans
left Canton, considering the place too dangerous. When the uprising began, there
were approximately 200 Koreans in the city, according to Kim, and a large number
of them participated actively in the struggle. Says Kim: "In all branches of work,

work in the Kuomintang-controlled cities became much more dangerous. Most of those closely associated with the Party migrated. A few Koreans went with the Chinese Communists who later helped to set up Mao's Kiangsi Republic, and one of them, Mu Chŏng (pronounced Wu Ting in Chinese), became chief of staff to General P'eng Teh-huai. Of the Korean Communists who spent the 1927–28 period in China, most went to Manchuria, partly for security reasons and partly because this had become the logical area from which to fight Japanese imperialism.

We do not know precisely when or how the Comintern reached its decision to grant the CCP control over the Korean Communist movement in Manchuria. In one sense, of course, such a decision was completely in line with the Comintern's long-standing one country-one party policy. But with respect to the Korean movement this policy had never been enforced. One thing is clear. The new Comintern policy was not based upon the strength of the Chinese Communist movement in this region. Contact with Manchuria on the part of the Chinese Communists had begun as early as 1923, but progress had been very slow.[25] The first group to bear the name of the Chinese Party officially had been the Dairen Regional Committee of the CCP, organized in July 1926. Not until January 1928, however, was a Manchurian branch of the Party created.[26] Although considerable efforts had been made to organize the workers in such industrial centers as Dairen, Harbin, Mukden, and Fushun, the Party's Manchurian branch was still in its infancy when the Comintern instructions were relayed. Moreover, despite the preponderance of farmers in the area, the Party had almost

---

Koreans were put into responsible positions because they were more experienced and many had had good political and military training in Moscow. They acted as a network of party agents during the Commune, though many Chinese did not know they were Koreans." Kim San and Nym Wales, *op. cit.*, p. 92.

Some allowance should be made for Kim's anti-Chinese and strongly nationalist biases, but this account undoubtedly has a substantial measure of truth in it. And evidently Korean losses in the fighting were very high. Kim asserts flatly, "We lost the flower of the Korean Revolution and the nucleus of our whole party membership in the Commune disaster" (*ibid.*, p. 129).

25. In the latter part of 1923, the Talien Chung-hua Kung-hsüeh-hui (Dairen Chinese Workers Study Association) had been organized among factory workers in the Southern Manchuria Railroad shops. According to Japanese sources, this association had Communist leadership. See Southern Manchuria Railroad Company, *Manshū kyōsantō undō gaikan (A Survey of the Manchurian Communist Party Movement)*, Dairen, 1935, p. 2.

26. For additional details, see Chong-Sik Lee, *Communism and Counter-Insurgency in Manchuria* (to be published), Chapter I.

When the Chinese first set up their Manchuria Committee in 1928, its headquarters was in Mukden, with three branch offices serving the major regions: Mukden itself was used for the south, Harbin for the north, and Yenchi for the east. Under these offices came the city and prefectural committees as well as certain special branches. The Chinese also established a Youth League and a Revolutionary Mutual Assistance Association.

no rural ties. In addition, the general position of the Chinese Communist Party in this period was extremely precarious. Thus, it is likely that the primary motive of the Comintern was to end Korean Communist factionalism at all costs. It is also possible, however, that the Comintern hoped as well to provide the Chinese Communists with additional strength and so help establish the basis for a *Chinese* defense of Manchuria in the critical years that lay ahead.[27]

In any case, two agents were dispatched from Moscow to Shanghai in November 1929, with instructions to serve as advisers to the Communist movement in Manchuria.[28] One of these agents was Han Pin, a Siberian-born Korean and a graduate of the Communist University of the Toilers of the East in Moscow. Han had earlier received a five-year prison sentence in Seoul for Communist activities. The second agent was Li Ch'un-shan, a Chinese graduate of the same university. With their Comintern directive in hand, the two young men conferred with Chinese Communist Party officials and then proceeded to Harbin. In January 1930, accompanied by a high CCP official named Ssu Wên, they convened a conference in Harbin attended by fourteen Chinese officials of the CCP Manchuria Province Executive Committee and about a dozen Korean Communist leaders representing the various factions. The Comintern proposals were presented at this meeting.

A few Korean Communists objected to the idea of being subordinated to the Chinese Communist movement, but most accepted. In early April, therefore, the M-L Group formally dissolved its Manchurian organizations. The Tuesday Society followed suit in June, and in the same month, the Shanghai-Seoul factions disbanded the Preparatory Society. By mid-1930, all Korean Communists in Manchuria were legally under the jurisdiction of the CCP.[29]

27. Later, however, we shall note that similar instructions were given to Koreans in Japan, namely, orders that Korean Communist organizations be dissolved, their members to join the Japanese Communist Party. This strongly suggests that the decision to enforce the "one country, one Party" rule had been made because Korean factionalism was rampant abroad, and to encourage the rebuilding of the Party at home.

28. All details are given in Chientao Consulate General, "The Process of the Amalgamation of the Korean Communist Party in Manchuria into the Chinese Communist Party, and the Present Situation with Respect to Korean and Chinese Communists in the Yenpien Area," Report to the Foreign Minister, Sept. 18, 1930, *AJMFA*, R SP102, F 6537–50.

29. According to the Japanese report, Kim Ch'an, secretary of the Manchurian General Bureau, was one of those objecting to the amalgamation. By June 1930, however, the Comintern was told that although the old Bureau was supported by Kim Ch'an's group, "more than 80 percent of all Korean Communists including those of every faction" had joined the CCP, and the old Bureau existed only in name.

Under the new structure, each prefectural office had a secretary, and divisions on organizations, propaganda, education, guerrilla operations, and mass actions. Each

To appreciate subsequent developments, it is essential to understand the status of the Chinese Communist movement at this particular point. Unfortunately for the Korean comrades, this was an era of the deepest troubles for Chinese Communism. Indeed, the years 1930–31 can legitimately be regarded as the point of lowest ebb in the CCP's fortunes, a period of intense factionalism, repeated failures, successive purges, and the slaughter of countless Communists by the now bitterly anti-Communist Kuomintang (KMT) government.[30]

Trends with respect to Party leadership reflected these problems. Ch'en Tu-hsiu, the scholarly CCP leader who had for so long attempted faithfully to follow Comintern policies in spite of recurring private reservations, had had to pay the price for the collapse of the KMT-CCP alliance and the bloody extermination of Communists that followed. Ch'en's successor, Ch'ü Ch'iu-pai, could not survive the disastrous failure of the Canton Commune. Thus, by the spring of 1928, the chief position had devolved upon Li Li-san, a Shanghai labor leader regarded as the "hero" of the May Thirtieth Movement. Li's tenure extended almost to the end of 1930 when he in turn was succeeded by the so-called returned student group headed by Wang Ming (Ch'en Shao-yü). At this point, however, the Chinese Communist Party lay in ruins, at least outside the Kiangsi Soviet Area. Everywhere, factionalism was rampant.

This period was soon to be denounced by Party ideologues as one of "left extremism," which indeed it was. The policies of Li and his successors, however, were completely in line with Comintern directives. So, too, had been those of his predecessors. There is no possible way in which the Comintern—and more precisely Stalin, then at the summit of power— can be exonerated from responsibility for the failure in China. It is true, of course, that all major Comintern pronouncements tended to be somewhat oracular. Asian leaders frequently found themselves uncertain as to the meaning of the instructions which they received, or unable to follow them due to circumstances beyond their control. The very ambiguity of

---

division, according to the plan, was to have both a Chinese and a Korean head. This cochairman arrangement was intended to facilitate cooperation. In practice, however, as we shall note, most of the officials were Korean, since there were no Chinese to serve.

A temporary Korean Communist League in Manchuria was established to compile lists of the various factional KCP members, to be given a CCP admissions committee which would pass upon the qualifications for transfer. When all KCP members had been thus reviewed, the League would be dissolved. *Ibid.,* pp. 6540–4.

30. For details in English on the Chinese Communist movement during this period, see Conrad Brandt, *Stalin's Failure in China, 1924–1927,* Cambridge, Mass., 1958; Harold R. Isaacs, *The Tragedy of the Chinese Revolution,* Stanford, 1951 edition; Robert C. North, *Moscow and Chinese Communists,* Stanford, 1953; Benjamin Schwartz, *Chinese Communism and the Rise of Mao,* Cambridge, Mass., 1951; and Edgar Snow, *Red Star Over China,* New York, 1938. In Japanese, see Hatano Kanichi, *Chūgoku kyōsantō shi,* Vols. 1–3 (of 7 volumes), Tokyo, 1961 edition.

various Comintern directives, however, enabled the Comintern (and the Kremlin) to emerge ideologically unscathed from a series of failures. The basic tactic of the Soviet leaders, as noted earlier, was always to hold a *centrist* position. Thus "right opportunism" and "left extremism" could be attacked alternately or even simultaneously, depending upon prevailing trends and so-called objective developments. Centrism, to be sure, is not unique to Communism; indeed, it lies at the root of most successful politics. But it was a particularly important factor in relations between the Soviet and Asian Communist movements during this period.

By 1930, Comintern analysis of China was trapped deep in a tortuous labyrinth of its own devising. Inextricably bound up with internal Soviet politics, "the China problem" had used up thousands of Soviet man-hours and millions of Soviet words. At this point, Stalin must have hated the very mention of China. Because he himself had made it a critical issue in his struggle for power with Trotsky and his followers, he was now forced to defend every basic Comintern decision of the past. "We planned it that way" became the Stalinist line; every development in the Chinese scene was fitted into an imaginary blueprint for victory. This required an extraordinary degree of optimism, and the Stalinists were never more optimistic than when viewing developments in China during this period. Some escape hatches, however, were essential, and these had to be provided by indigenous sources. If the blueprint was not followed exactly, it had to be the fault of the Chinese Communists. Thus, Comintern insistence upon a united front with the Kuomintang had *always* been correct; the problem lay in the fact that leaders like Ch'en Tu-hsiu had had an incorrect understanding of the role of the Communist Party in the alliance, and so had not timed their policy changes correctly. But the Stalinist position had to be propped up in yet another way. Stalin and the Comintern having insisted "we planned it that way," and having cast their appraisal of developments in highly optimistic terms, absolutely had to find or produce at least some events to back them up. Thus was born the era of left extremism.

According to the Comintern, the essential elements in the Chinese scene at this point were the following. Leading portions of the bourgeoisie, as expected, had deserted the revolution. The Kuomintang currently represented a coalition of feudalist and bourgeois forces destined to play a counterrevolutionary role. The Communist-Kuomintang alliance, once valid, was thus wholly unthinkable at this stage. The essential tactic was now a united front from below. The working and farming masses had to be wooed, organized, and led by the Party, that vanguard of the proletariat. And with this coalition properly organized and led, the bourgeois-democratic revolution would at last be brought to fruition. That revolution— still the proper objective—could not be consummated by the bourgeoisie; their hour of leadership had passed. It was not even a revolution in their favor. On the contrary, it was to be essentially an agrarian revolution.

The peasantry, whose numbers and strategic economic functions rendered them crucial to revolutionary success, were at this stage destined to replace much of the bourgeoisie in the coalition led by the proletariat. In fact, Comintern sources even went so far as to describe such mobilization of the peasantry as enabling them to play their historic revolutionary role. Gone was almost all of the massive Marxist antagonism to the peasant. Leadership, to be sure, was still vested in "proletarian" hands. But could not anyone proletarianize himself by an act of faith? Finally, despite certain zigzags, China was set on a revolutionary course, and policies appropriate to that course were essential. At all costs, the revolutionary momentum had to be continued. Both in urban centers and in rural areas, *the Party had to turn to the masses and give them their heads.* In certain areas, the establishment of a Soviet regime was undoubtedly appropriate; in others, the wholesale mobilization of labor and the peasantry; in all areas, a vigorous, frontal challenge to the forces of reaction. Naturally, this would involve the formation of a Red Army and, at lower levels, teams of partisan fighters. Only thus could the revolution continue on its course to victory.

To summarize the China policy of the Comintern as of about 1930 in so brief a form is necessarily to slight the latest shifts, the powerful elements of ambiguity and contradiction, and the significant nuances represented in that policy. At the same time, however, to emphasize the policy's dominant themes in stark, unadorned fashion is to dramatize the plight of the Asian Communists who sought to live and work in this period. It is worthy of note in this connection that, except for a few themes specifically involving the Chinese scene, these policies were directed at the Korean and Japanese Communists as much as the Chinese. For example, all of the basic points outlined above were in line with those propounded in the December Theses. And why not? They had a common parent—the Sixth Comintern Congress. This was not an era when the international Communist movement was prepared to develop different basic policies for each Party. Any such attempt would have run the grave risk of overtly challenging the universal "truths" of Marxism-Leninism, especially at a time when they had to be polished to reflect only the national interests of the Soviet Union. Nor was it prepared to allow the indigenous leaders of those parties to undertake this task on their own, in pragmatic fashion. The fact that each Party was *a branch* of the Comintern was ceaselessly reiterated.

Naturally, the ascendancy of the Li Li-san line had a direct effect upon the Communist movement in Manchuria. Hitherto, Communist analysis of Manchuria had tended to treat it as unique, sharing nothing with the rest of China on either a social or an economic level. Manchuria, so it was argued, had been little affected by the ravages of warlordism. It had been ruled by a single warlord, Chang Tso-lin, who had succeeded in maintaining his authority unchallenged. Hence the peasants, unlike those in China proper, had not been impoverished through constant warfare. In addition,

Manchuria had a substantial amount of undeveloped land; tenancy, at least among the Chinese, was therefore a less serious problem than in most parts of China. Moreover, as a result of political tranquility and other factors, the Manchurian urban economy was in better shape. For all of these reasons, the worker and peasant movements were poorly developed in Manchuria, and the political consciousness of the Manchurian "masses" was extremely limited.

Such an analysis accorded with cautious and limited activities. It scarcely met the requirements imposed by the new militant line. So much the worse for the analysis! Since Manchuria now had to be politically integrated into China proper, it had to be seen in a new light. The thesis of the Li Li-san era went as follows: Chang Hsueh-liang's involvement in the politics of China proper had ended the isolation of Manchuria. The Manchurian working and farming masses had been fully exposed to the tragedies of war. Further, the American sale of weapons to Chang Hsueh-liang had created a rivalry between him and the Japanese-supported group that had clustered around Chang Tso-lin—a rivalry that would ultimately lead to a struggle between these two military cliques. Finally, the Manchurian economy was being increasingly affected by the global depression, and there was mounting unrest among the workers and peasants.[31] Conditions were thus ripe for a revolutionary upsurge here as well as elsewhere.

The burden of militancy in Manchuria necessarily fell upon the Korean Communists. It was they who were called upon to translate into action both the Comintern theories and the Li Li-san line. The Koreans constituted the only significant group of Communists in Manchuria at this time, small though their numbers were. The Chinese Communists in the area were limited to a handful of intellectuals and a very small number of workers in a few urban centers.[32]

Thus, even before the annexation of the Korean Communist movement to the Chinese Communist Party had been completed, the Chinese called upon their Korean comrades to launch a major uprising in Chientao. The purpose of this uprising was to be no less than the ouster of both Japanese imperialism and the "reactionary Kuomintang military clique,"

31. About economic conditions, Communist analysis had some merit. The price of soy beans (approximately one-third of the farm produce in Chientao) had declined from a 1924–28 norm of 100, to 88 in 1929, and 64.8 in 1930. In 1932, the decline reached 35. *Manshū kyōsanhi no kenkyū, op. cit.*, p. 74.

For broader aspects of Li Li-san-ism in Manchuria, see North, *op. cit.*, Chapter 9.

32. Some organizational activities had been undertaken by Chinese Communists in Fushun, and plans for a "riot" there in 1930 were disrupted when Party headquarters was raided. There were also small Party groups in Kirin and Mukden. See Central Police Control Committee, Manchukuo, *Manshū ni okeru kyōsan undō no suii gaikyō (A Resume of the Changes in the Communist Movement in Manchuria)*, no place of publication, 1937, p. 22.

and the replacement of them with a soviet republic. Orders were drafted
to this effect in the spring of 1930 by the Manchurian Committee of the
CCP; the date selected for the opening assault was May 30, the fifth an-
niversary of the Shanghai anti-imperialist movement, which had placed
Li Li-san's star in the ascendancy. Pak Yun-sŏ, formerly an official in the
M-L Group's Manchurian General Bureau and currently a member of the
CCP, was sent to Lungching as a special representative of the Committee.
There, he conferred with officials of the eastern branch of the Manchurian
Bureau set up by the M-L Group early in 1928. The Bureau had been
formally dissolved at this point, but its eastern branch had remained in
operation, supposedly to aid in the transfer of members to the CCP. Party
instructions were transmitted, and details were arranged. Kim Kŭn agreed
to accept overall charge of the operation. During the next month, contacts
were made with various comrades, including former members and associates of the Tuesday Society. On the evening of May 29, the action started.

The hard-core leadership of the May 30 riots consisted of no more
than 150–200 individuals, but according to the official Japanese accounts
damage was fairly extensive. The vandalism, moreover, spread throughout
the whole of the Chientao area. Using guns, gasoline-filled bottles, and
ordinary matches, the rioters attacked government offices, power facilities, transport and communication lines, and the homes of certain "police
informers, pro-Japanese individuals, and wealthy bourgeoisie." [33] These
"riots" were only the first in a series of terrorist actions undertaken by
Korean radicals during this period under the orders of the Chinese Communist Party. On August 1 (Red International Day) and again on August
29 (National Humiliation Day, the date of Korea's annexation to Japan),
Koreans in the area along the Kirin-Tunhwa railroad carried out numerous
acts of sabotage and violence. Small-scale "partisan" operations also developed in the fall of 1930; these involved the burning of harvested crops
and the destruction of landlord properties.[34] When orders finally reached
the Manchurian Communists to discard the Li Li-san line in the spring of
1931, and the "riots" came to an end, some 190 persons had been killed
or injured and damage to property—public and private—had been extensive.[35]

It must be remembered that this was a period in which similar events
took place in China proper on a much more massive scale. On July 28,
1930, the Fifth Red Army under P'eng Teh-huai had attacked Changsha,

33. For a very detailed account of the May 30 riots, see "The Preliminary Trial
in Connection with the Chientao May 30th Incident," *Shisō geppō, op. cit.*, pp. 173–
200.

34. See Southern Manchuria Railroad Company, *Manshū kyōsantō undō gaikan,
op. cit.*, p. 4; also Bureau of Police and Security, Ministry of Home Affairs, Japan,
*Chūka minkoku ni okeru kyōsanshugi undō no genkyō (The Present Condition of
the Communist Movement in the Republic of China)*, Tokyo, 1931, p. 30.

35. *Manshū kyōsanhi no kenkyū, op. cit.*, p. 69.

holding this important city for a few days before being driven out with bloody losses. The seizure of Changsha had been hailed by Comintern sources in ecstatic terms—until failure came. That failure sealed the doom of Li Li-san, although he managed to survive for a few months longer. In mid-November, the Comintern issued a letter criticizing Li's "adventurism" and "putschism" in devastating terms. It mattered not that Li had tried to be a faithful translator of Comintern policies. Like Ch'en Tu-hsiu and Ch'ü Ch'iu-pai before him, he had failed, and it continued to be important that failure in China be placed anywhere but at the door of the Kremlin.

New emphases once again appeared in the tactics signaled from Moscow. The old line had strongly underwritten the importance of the peasant, and insisted that agrarian revolution provided the key to the success of the bourgeois-democratic phase of the revolutionary progression. But it had also stressed the need for the Party *and* the Red Army to provide Communism with an urban base as a source of proletarian hegemony over the revolution. Such catastrophic failures as Canton and Changsha, however, finally forced the Comintern to place greater emphasis upon the immediate establishment of defensible soviet areas beyond the reach of Kuomintang power. This meant the development of a Red Army working in concert with these areas, and only these areas. Under force of circumstance, urbanism was slipping away from Communist doctrine for China, as the Communists sought desperately to prevent their total destruction. The Comintern letter of November 16, 1930, was a landmark in this respect, and its major themes were fully supported by the CCP Central Committee at its Fourth Plenum, held on January 7, 1931.[36] At this point, the so-called returned students, aided by Pavel Mif, the key Comintern figure in China at this time, were rapidly moving into power to replace the fallen Li. The Party, however, had never been in such a state of confusion, bitterness, and despair.

Given these developments, it is not surprising that the official Korean Communist histories were later to brand the May 30 riots as "an expression of the adventurist and blind actions initiated by the sectarians of this period in east Manchuria, in accordance with the extremist policies of Li Li-san." [37] More significantly, however, the Korean Communist leaders at the time themselves privately assessed the riots and similar acts of violence

36. For the Comintern letter, see *Ch'ih-fei fan-tung wên-chien hui-pien* (*A Collection of Documents of the Red Bandits*) (Documents of the CCP and its branch organs collected by the Kuomintang) in the Ch'en Cheng Collection, pp. 212–220; for the Fourth Plenum Resolution, see Conrad Brandt, Benjamin Schwartz, and John K. Fairbank, *A Documentary History of Chinese Communism*, Cambridge, Mass., 1952, pp. 209–216.

37. Yim Ch'un-ch'u, *Hangil mujang t'ujaeng sigi rŭl hoesang hayŏ* (*Recalling the Period of the Anti-Japanese Armed Struggle*), P'yŏngyang, 1960, p. 4.

as a failure.[38] The masses had not been aroused to action; indeed, for the most part, they had been alienated. It was rather the Japanese who had responded—with vigor. Up to April 1931, 3,168 individuals had been arrested in east Manchuria for suspected complicity in subversive activities. Never had it been so dangerous to be involved with the Communist movement, even in the slightest degree. This fact seriously hampered Communist efforts to "reach out to the masses" and develop a united front from below. In August 1930, a reorganization of the Communist structure for Chientao had been ordered. The Party began a campaign to create front organizations.[39] Suddenly, such groups as the Peasants' Association, the Anti-Imperialist League, the Mutual Assistance Association, the Women's League, and a variety of other organizations had sprung up. But, given the circumstances, recruitment proved to be extraordinarily difficult.

By the spring of 1931, the new CCP line had been promulgated. In March, Kim Sang-sŏn became head of the Yen-Ho prefectural committee of the Party. The same month, he submitted a highly revealing report to the East Manchurian Special Committee.[40] "The only way of survival for the revolutionary masses in Yen-Ho," he asserted, "is to establish true Soviet

38. A Communist document captured by Japanese authorities and identified as a message from the P'ing-ch'u Communist Committee assessed the riots as a failure, indicating the following reasons: "improper guidance of the Chinese and Korean working masses," with only struggle being emphasized and no understanding of the meaning of that struggle being set forth; an insufficiency of actual strength, with the masses harboring "dependent emotions," expecting that arms would be supplied by the Chinese Communist Party or the Soviet Union and subsequently being disappointed; finally, mass mobilization "through intimidation." *Manshū kyōsanhi no kenkyū, op. cit.*, pp. 69–70.

39. At this time, the old Yenpien Border Party Branch was converted into the East Manchurian Special Committee, and under it was established the Yen-Ho (Yenchi-Holung) prefectural committee and other prefectural committees. See *ibid.*, p. 69.

40. Kim Sang-sŏn had been head of the Organizational Department of the M-L Group's Manchurian General Bureau since May 1929. He served a year's sentence in Korea because of his participation in the March First (1919) demonstrations, and attended various colleges in China, including the Wuhan Central Military and Political Academy in Hankow. He joined the CCP in July 1930 and was assigned to Chientao in December, becoming Yen-Ho prefectural committee head in March 1931. All other officials of this committee and of its front organizations were also Koreans.

For details, see the Chientao Consulate General, Chü-chih-chieh Branch, Police Department, *En-wa-ken nai ni okeru kyōsan undō no jitsujō oyobi tō himitsu bunsho yakubun (The Condition of the Communist Movement in Yenchi-Holung Prefectures and Translations of the Party's Secret Documents)*, May 1931, *AJMFA*, R S373–4, and "The Organization and Activities of the CCP Yen-Ho Central Prefectural Committee Farmers' Association," Report of the Chientao Consul-General to the Foreign Minister, Nov. 7, 1930, *AJMFA*, R SP103, F 6756–61. The March Report is carried in *Manshū kyōsanhi no kenkyū, op. cit.*, pp. 183–190.

regimes through struggle." In the recent period, the report continued, some 1,300 revolutionaries had been arrested, including 200 members of the Party. The revolution, however, was continuing and, indeed, gaining momentum as a result of the steadily worsening economic and political crises. The Yen-Ho masses were struggling for land and liberation. "Thorough execution of land reform is the central task of the moment." And the methods? Guerrilla warfare was under way, asserted the report; eight villages had already become Red Districts, with properties having been confiscated and distributed to indigent Chinese and Koreans. Anti-revolutionary parties had been destroyed, the "running dogs" of the enemy had been openly killed, the communications of the ruling class had been severed, and the meaning of soviets had been propagated to the people. On February 7, for example, several thousand persons had been mobilized in Lao-t'ou-kou to celebrate Workers' Day.

The Yen-Ho committee admitted certain serious weaknesses. Party contacts with both the urban laboring masses and the soldiers had been very slight.[41] Furthermore, there were almost no Chinese participants. The Yen-Ho prefectural Party was wholly Korean. Except for four or five Chinese in the Peasants' Association and the Anti-Imperialist League in the Ping-kang district, no progress in recruiting Chinese had been made. One reason given was that the Kuomintang was "passionately arousing national emotions and pursuing deceitful policies." As we shall soon note, there were other factors of at least equal significance.

The report ended by setting forth the current tasks of the Party: The Korean and Chinese masses had to be mobilized in the struggle for land and power, and a broad united front built from below. Both Japanese imperialism and the Kuomintang ruling class had to be smashed. Soviet districts had to be established, and land distributed to poor peasants. The Soviet Union had to be vigorously supported, and the Korean revolution advanced.

These were the goals toward which the Communists were striving when, in September 1931, the Manchurian Incident began. Naturally, this event had a major impact upon subsequent developments. The Japanese now had additional reasons for suppressing the Manchurian Communists, and additional power to attempt the task. Immediately after the Japanese thrust began, Korean Communists in east Manchuria sought to establish ties with local Chinese patriotic groups. But they failed to create any solid links. In fact, Chinese-Korean relations, now as in the past, tended to be dominated by attitudes of hostility and suspicion. Indeed, the events of this period generally augmented those attitudes. As Japanese pressure increased, a number of Chinese nationalists surrendered and some of them, in an effort to win Japanese favor, agreed to divulge such information concerning the Communist movement as they possessed. With this help, the

41. *Ibid.*, pp. 188–190.

Japanese began a large-scale mopping-up campaign in April 1932. By the end of the year, the Japanese consul-general in Chientao reported that more than 1,200 "Communists and their sympathizers" had been shot, and another 1,500 had been imprisoned.[42]

An active Communist movement in Manchurian urban centers or in rural districts easily accessible to Japanese forces had now become impossible. Thus, the new CCP line emphasizing the importance of creating soviets in areas where they could survive, and developing a Red Army to defend them, now became the only possible strategy. In late 1932, the remnants of the East Manchurian Special Committee took their followers into the hinterlands of Chientao. Between November 1932, and February 1933, five "soviet districts," involving a total of approximately 4,100 persons, were organized in Yenchi, Wangch'ing, and Hunch'un Prefectures. An additional six "revolutionary committees" were established in localities where Communist control was not sufficiently strong to permit the emergence of soviets.

Necessarily, the Communist emphasis was now upon armed power. Each soviet and revolutionary committee had a military unit of thirty to a hundred men.[43] These units, however, were forced to act defensively. At most, the Communist-controlled regions served as refuges from Japanese forces, not bases of attack. As time passed, however, Japanese cordons were thrown around them, isolating them from neighboring areas. The Communists found it impossible to maintain or even create their own food supply. They were therefore forced to raid outside localities. Because of such raids, and the harsh land-confiscation policy pursued by the Com-

42. Report of the Chientao Consul-General to the Foreign Minister, *AJMFA*, R S373, p. 78.

In June 1931, officials of the Manchuria Committee in Mukden were arrested by Chinese authorities. Sweeping raids elsewhere followed, almost ending Party activities in urban centers. Several Chinese leaders, however, escaped the roundup and sought to rebuild a central Party or organization. Meeting in Mukden parks, Li Ch'eng-hsiang and Liu I-ch'eng, together with Chang Meng-kuan who had been sent from CCP headquarters, reconstructed the committee. Chang became chairman, Li head of Organization, Liu head of Propaganda. When the Manchurian Incident began, the Party was able to distribute anti-Japanese handbills and, for a time, it even had a newspaper. Again in September 1931, however, top leaders were captured by Japanese secret police, and the Party organization was wrecked. In January 1932, the Party moved its Manchurian headquarters to Harbin, and other organizational adjustments took place at the same time.

43. *Ibid.*, p. 80. A skeletonal Party organization continued to exist in Manchurian urban centers, the primary focus being on the labor movement. According to one account, the Manchuria Committee was ordered to maintain contact with and receive instructions from the Vladivostok Pan-Pacific Labor Union Secretariat; and it was with the help of this Profintern agency that the General Labor Federation of Manchuria was established in Harbin during this period. Li Yao-kuei was reportedly sent from Vladivostok, after first conferring with Pavel Mif, member of the Far Eastern Bureau of the Comintern, in Moscow in January 1933.

munists in the areas under their control, the "Reds" became practically indistinguishable from bandits in the minds of the ordinary inhabitants of the area. And, indeed, there were many "gray" elements. We are told that even poor peasants became alienated during this period. The Japanese propaganda that continually referred to the Communists as "Red bandits" thus gained credibility.

There were striking parallels with current developments in China proper. Like their counterparts in Manchuria, the Chinese Communists under Mao were at this point attempting to defend their "Kiangsi Soviet Republic" against successive Kuomintang campaigns. Also like them, the Kiangsi Communists were later to admit "left extremist" errors in connection with "land reform." Their internal party conditions were marked by similarly bitter factional struggles. As is well known, the Kiangsi area ultimately became untenable for the Chinese Communists, and in mid-1934 preparations for a movement to the north began. The famous Long March followed.

For the Korean Communists in Manchuria, however, there was no Yenan. After two and one-half years of the most precarious existence, the East Manchurian Committee finally decided to abandon the "soviet districts." This was in early 1935. To what extent this was linked with the decision to abandon the Kiangsi base is not clear, but the timing suggests that there may have been a connection. The small number of farmers who still remained in the soviets were permitted to surrender to the enemy. The guerrilla units organized under the soviets, with the revolutionary committees, became the basis for the Second Army of the Northeastern People's Revolutionary Army. This Second Army had first been authorized in June 1933; by March 1934, it reportedly consisted of 1,000 men.[44]

Japanese statistics on the strength of the Communist movement in east Manchuria for the period 1933–1936 are most instructive. First, despite the heavy punishment dealt the Party and its auxiliaries in the 1930–32 period, it is clear that the Communists in Chientao managed to survive. In the 1933–34 period, Party membership was approximately 500 (see table 13). We must assume, however, that almost all these members lived in the soviet districts, or at least in areas where the revolutionary committees existed, and that the great bulk of them were very young recruits, recently brought in to fill the ranks after most of the veterans had been killed or imprisoned.

44. *Ibid.*, pp. 164–165. It should be noted that one Japanese source asserts that, early in 1932, the Comintern, discussing the situation in Manchuria, came to the conclusion that it was too early to establish Soviet districts in Manchuria. It once again urged an anti-Manchukuo, anti-Japan national movement based upon urban centers. It was supposedly this same Moscow session that ordered the Manchuria Committee to establish close connections with the Profintern branch in Vladivostok. See Kotō Hōin, Kenjikyoku (High Court, Prosecutor's Bureau), "The Sasaki Inspection Tour of Manchuria," *Shisō ihō* (*Thought Series*), No. 3, pp. 130 ff.

TABLE 13
Communist Strength in Chientao

	September 1933	April 1934	December 1934
Communist Party	580	360	465
Communist Youth League	830	418	731
Anti-Japanese Society	11,800	2,960	912
People's Revolutionary Army	560	920	1,096

SOURCE: Based on a report from the Chientao Consul-General, quoted in *Manshū kyōsanhi no kenkyū*, p. 96.

Second, the bulk of Party membership continued to be Korean, although some Chinese were now enrolled. If we take the combined Party-front organization figures, it can be seen that Chinese involvement remained extremely low, less than one-twentieth that of the Koreans (see table 14). The population of this region, to be sure, was predominately

TABLE 14
Chinese and Korean Elements Within the Chientao Communist Movement at the End of 1933

	Korean	Chinese	Total
Communist Party	580	217	797
Communist Youth League	830	19	849
Communist Young Pioneers	1,950	14	1,964
Anti-Japanese Society	11,800	390	12,190
Guerrillas	565	16	581
TOTAL	15,725	656	16,381

SOURCE: Ōsaka *Asahi Shimbun* (Ōsaka *Asahi News*), Jan. 11, 1934, quoted in *Manshū kyōsantō undō gaikan*, p. 45.

Korean. In any case, the Communist movement in east Manchuria was overwhelmingly made up of young Koreans, most of them raw recruits with very brief Party experience, and almost all of them serving as guerrilla fighters. Under the prevailing circumstances, the Communist movement was likely to be dominated by men in their twenties, committed to activism and capable of enduring hardship. This was scarcely a period for the "study group" approach or indeed any type of leadership by intellectuals—a situation that was to have a deep impact upon the Party's later history.

It should also be noted that total Communist strength, as shown in table 13, had declined drastically by early 1934, primarily because of falling off in the membership of the Anti-Japanese Society, a group generally considered available for Communist purposes. The People's Revolutionary Army, on the other hand, was slowly growing in this period. All of these developments will soon be analyzed more closely, when we discuss the emergence of Kim Il-sŏng. Meanwhile, it can be seen that the Communist movement was being progressively isolated in its mountain retreats,

The strength of the Communist guerrillas operating in east Manchuria fluctuated considerably, but in the 1935–36 period it averaged about 1,000 men (see table 15). Of course, the Japanese had to contend with so-called rebel troops and bandits as well as Communists (see table 16). The rebel troops were primarily anti-Manchukuo Chinese forces connected with the Kuomintang. Bandits were endemic to this area; they took advantage of the wild terrain and general political confusion to live off the land and rob the people. Some of them were of the Robin Hood variety; others were

TABLE 15
Monthly Tabulation of Communist Guerrilla Strength in East Manchuria,[a] 1935–1936

1935		1936	
January	1,180	January	780
February	1,500	February	830
March	1,630	March	870
April	1,080	April	970
May	1,410	May	1,460
June	1,950	June	1,260
July	1,380	July	1,510
August	1,180		
September	850		
October	1,000		
November	810		
December	690		

SOURCE: *Manshū kyōsanhi no kenkyū*, pp. 169–170, based on a monthly report of the Second Military District of Manchukuo.

[a] The area covered included the prefectures of Yenchi, Wangch'ing, Hunch'un, Holung, O'mu, Tunhwa, Hwatien, and Ant'u, but not those of Fusung, Ningan, and Tungning, where the Second Army also operated.

TABLE 16
Strength of Various Armed Groups in the Second Military District, Manchukuo

Date	Communist Insurgents	Rebel (Nationalist) Troops	Bandits	Total
January 1935	1,695	1,660	2,241	5,596
July 1935	1,260	960	2,715	4,935
October 1935	1,290	1,680	2,403	5,373
January 1936	780	250	1,750	2,780
April 1936	1,150	110	1,290	2,550
July 1936	950	360	1,305	2,615

SOURCE: *Ibid.*, pp. 184–186.

not. To be sure, Japanese designations of the various groups were not always accurate. Moreover, the groups themselves, as noted earlier, were not always sharply distinct. Nevertheless, all categories of "insurgents" or "subversives" had been substantially reduced in the Second Military District by mid-1936. Rebel troops had been practically eliminated and the Communists had been reduced to less than 1,000, leaving the bandits as the largest single contingent. Taking east Manchuria as a whole (table 15), the Communists were gaining again in early 1936, but by July their guerrillas still numbered only about 1,500. This certainly posed no threat to a Japanese army that now numbered in the hundreds of thousands.

As was noted earlier, the East Manchurian Special Committee of the CCP had ordered the Chientao soviet districts abandoned in early 1935. Communist guerrillas, now the nucleus of the Second Army of the Northeastern People's Revolutionary Army, moved into more remote hinterlands in the west. Here, in the region adjoining the First Army's area of operations, they made a stand. Japanese forces relentlessly pursued them, however, in an intensive "annihilation campaign" conducted in the fall and winter of 1935. By this time, the so-called Second Army was scarcely operating at battalion strength and had virtually no armaments except small arms (see table 17). It was broken into two contingents. One ele-

TABLE 17

Nationalities and Weapons of the Second Army, Northeastern People's Army (as of December 1935)

Manpower	
Korean	517
Chinese	189
TOTAL	706
Weapons	
Mortar	1
Heavy machine gun	1
Light machine guns	4
Rifles	648
Pistols	58
Bombs	232

SOURCE: *Ibid.*, p. 186, based on a report from the Harbin Police Department.

ment, the Second Division, moved north to the Ningan region to join the Fifth Army under Chou Pao-chung. The First Division joined the First Army.[45]

Thus, by 1936, Korean Communist guerrillas had given up their operations in Chientao. The Japanese could proudly proclaim that the Communist movement in east Manchuria had been virtually eliminated

45. For details, see *Manshū kyōsanhi no kenkyū, op. cit.*, pp. 171–182.

There can be no doubt that the application of heavy and continuous Japanese pressure had contributed much to that end. Additional factors, however, were also involved. The fish saw the water in which they were supposed to swim dry up. On every side, the guerrilla forces lost civilian support. Recall, for example, the fact that the membership of the Anti-Japanese Society dropped from nearly 12,000 in the fall of 1933 to less than 1,000 by the end of 1934 (table 13). In fifteen months, the number of civilians whose political commitments were such as to guarantee their sympathy and support dwindled by 93 percent.

Why? Between 1930 and 1934, as we have already suggested, almost every action of the Korean Communists in Chientao had the effect of alienating or angering the general population. Violence, looting, and the general lawlessness—much of it purposeless—that characterized this "adventurist" era won little support from the populace, especially the Chinese. But possibly even more important was the growing ambivalence of the Korean community toward Japanese ascendancy in Manchuria. This area, to be sure, had long been a hotbed of Korean nationalism, and no doubt a large number of Koreans, when they thought of the best of all possible worlds, thought of Korean independence. But in spite of the heroism of individual nationalists, this dream had always been remote. Now it was more remote than ever. A second alternative was Chinese rule, which Manchurian Koreans had experienced up to 1931. The Chang Hsueh-liang regime had not been a benevolent government. After 1925, as we noted earlier, Koreans felt themselves harshly treated, and friction between Chinese and Koreans had steadily risen. Thus, in Manchuria, the Japanese government could cast itself in the role of liberator rather than oppressor of Koreans, and it proceeded to do so. The declining membership of the Anti-Japanese Society is but one example among many of the effectiveness of Japanese propaganda—and actions—among the Korean population during this period. Another indication can be found in the large number of defectors from the Chientao soviet districts. Nearly 5,000 individuals surrendered to the Japanese between the beginning of 1933 and the middle of 1935.[46]

Yet another factor did incalculable damage to the Communists during this period, namely, the intensification of savage infighting within Communist ranks. It was accompanied by bloody purges. Many events of this period are likely to remain undisclosed. A full revelation of the facts would profoundly embarrass the Communists. Among other things, it would bring to light a friction between Chinese and Koreans within the Communist movement that bore all the marks of racial prejudice.

Our data on the purges are far from complete, but the story is nevertheless a fascinating one. One must start with the People's Livelihood Corps issue. In November 1931, a small group of Koreans formed an organiza-

46. *Ibid.*, pp. 110–111, based upon reports from the Chientao Consulate.

tion called the Minsaengdan (Minshêngt'uan in Chinese) or People's Livelihood Corps. The Minsaengdan was first established in Chü-chih-chieh, the commercial center of Chientao. It had Japanese blessing, and its purpose was supposedly the improvement of the living conditions of the Korean population in Chientao. Despite formal approval, however, Japanese officials quickly became suspicious of the organization, detecting certain trends within it toward Korean nationalism. As a result, it expired in July 1932, after scarcely eight months of existence.

If the Japanese had grave doubts about the Minsaengdan, so did the Communists—from a very different perspective. They saw the organization as a weapon of the Japanese to infiltrate Korean Communist cells, and they charged that its leaders were secretly collaborating with the Japanese.[47] The truth is extremely difficult to determine. Undoubtedly, some Minsaengdan members were Japanese agents. After all, the Japanese usually managed to insert some spies into the Communist Party itself. Moreover, it is quite possible that other Minsaengdan members, starting in good faith, later became informers, either because of persuasion or coercion. We can also assume that bona fide Communists strenuously resisted any concept of dual membership, or a united front from above. Such tactics were completely out of vogue at this point.

In any case, Communist leaders, demoralized in this period of grave adversity by the heavy blows being dealt them by the Japanese and by the large number of deserters, suddenly developed true paranoid tendencies. They began to suspect everyone of plotting against the movement, and instituted a series of brutal purges. According to later Communist admissions, many "true revolutionaries" in guerrilla bases were accused of being Minsaengdan members. When such individuals refused to confess, they were killed on the grounds that they were unwilling to recant and divulge the organization's secret plans. Some of the accused confessed falsely in order to escape torture or harassment, and most of them too were shot. People in the soviet districts were mobilized to serve as "people's courts" in order to legitimize the killings.[48]

As is well known, these trends, including the use of "people's courts,"

---

47. The Party line as revealed in captured documents went as follows: "After the Japanese imperialist occupation of Manchuria, some factional leaders on our side openly surrendered to the enemy; others remained in our ranks, and by utilizing their comradely connections established the Minsaengdan within our organization. To promote their own interests and positions, these factional leaders remaining in our ranks did not openly surrender to the enemy, but secretly developed the Minsaengdan organization in alliance with the Japanese imperialists.

"Because of their limited political consciousness, the majority of the masses, including Party and Youth League members, are not aware of the deceptive operations of the Minsaengdan. Therefore, it is easily able to operate among revolutionary units." *Ibid.*, p. 113.

48. Yim Ch'un-ch'u, *op. cit.*, p. 93.

had their parallels during this period in the Chinese Communist movement of Kiangsi. In Manchuria, the Japanese were quick to take advantage of internal party conditions, thereby exacerbating the problem for the Communists. In September 1934, they organized a civilian group called the Hsüeh-chu-hui (Hyŏp-cho-hoe in Korean) or Mutual Assistance Society. The Society was established for the specific purpose of eliminating Communist guerrillas. It was used to gather intelligence, conduct propaganda activities, negotiate surrenders, separate guerrilla leaders from their rank and file, and drive wedges between different guerrilla units. A large proportion of the Society's members were themselves surrendered Communists familiar with guerrilla activities and personalities. Many of them had been deeply alienated by earlier purges and internal struggles.

Between September 6, 1934, when the Society was founded and June 20, 1936, the following results from its activities were claimed:

Induced surrenders	2,255 persons
Communists captured	3,207 persons
Communist cells uncovered	287
Weapons confiscated	237
Ammunition confiscated	4,506 rounds[49]

The Japanese may well have given the Mutual Assistance Society too much credit: the Communists of this period had a remarkable capacity for destroying themselves without outside assistance. Undoubtedly, however, the existence of the Society and its operations added to the paranoiac atmosphere in Communist ranks. Suddenly, Communists of high standing found themselves being investigated by their comrades. Even Chu Chin, commander of the First Division of the Second Army, and Yi Sang-muk, head of the Organization Department of the East Manchurian Special Committee, were suspected of being enemy agents. Fearful of being murdered, Chu Chin surrendered to the Japanese and Yi fled to join a non-Communist guerrilla group.[50]

There is no evidence that either of these men was a Japanese agent at the time of the accusations. But Chu had become embittered by his experiences, and he volunteered his services to the Japanese after his surrender. Such a development merely served to confirm Communist suspicions, and the "purification campaign" rolled on. The Manchurian Committee of the CCP fully supported it, and dispatched an agent, Wei Chêng-min, to head a special "purge committee" in east Manchuria. This ad hoc organization was supervised by the East Manchurian Committee, of which Wei subsequently became secretary.

49. Advisory Section, Military Department, Manchukuo, *Kokunai chian taisaku no kenkyū* (*A Study of Countermeasures with Respect to Domestic Security*), no place of publication, 1937, p. 155.

50. See Yim Ch'un-ch'u, *op. cit.*, pp. 96–97. Yi Sang-muk was eventually captured by the Japanese police in April 1936; *AJMFA*, R SP105, p. 9606.

In addition, a more serious development got under way. The Manchurian Committee now decided that the root of the trouble lay in the fact that the east Manchurian branch of the Party had too many Korean members. Korean Party members were therefore segregated, and the leadership of the Party at various levels was assigned to Chinese. To justify this action, Chinese leaders now claimed that *all* Korean Communists had either joined the Minsaengdan or been influenced by it, even those that were "unconscious" of the fact.[51] Indeed, Chinese thought and action at this point had strong racist overtones. Behind the Minsaengdan, according to the Chinese, were "sectarian Communists," behind whom were Korean nationalists, behind whom were supporters of Japanese imperialism. Thus, once again, the charge was leveled that all Korean Communists were either factionalists or nationalists. Whatever the element of truth in this charge, the fact that it was raised by Chinese, and that they proceeded to remove Koreans from Party offices aroused deep Korean resentment. As we shall note later, it has become a part of the lore of Korean Communist history that Kim Il-sŏng later took the lead in "decisively correcting the leftist errors that had been committed in the course of the anti-Minsaengdan struggle," a struggle that remained unresolved for some years.[52] Will this period be used at some later point as a landmark in establishing the independence of the Korean Communists from their Chinese comrades?

These were the factors chiefly responsible for the erosion of the Korean Communist movement in Manchuria. By 1936, the party and its guerrilla forces had had to abandon Chientao completely. The small number of Korean Communists who remained were now attached to the Northeastern People's Revolutionary Army under Chinese command. This army gener-

51. Yim Ch'un-ch'u, *op. cit.*, pp. 93–95. For a most interesting comment that interacts with the data collected by us, note the comment by Kim San, who also had to meet the accusations of comrades: "After my spy case and discipline as a Li Li-sanist, my mind was confused and disturbed. I could not avoid feeling that part of my trouble came because I was a Korean among Chinese; even the Communists in China had a tendency toward nationalism. The foreigner is always the first to be blamed. It was a time of general demoralization; reprisals against the Li Li-san uprisings were very cruel. Thousands of Communists were arrested and executed or imprisoned. Others were betrayed and turned over to the Kuomintang or became passive. Still others became Trotskyists or Fascists. Party work became weaker and weaker on the outside, and morale within broke down." Kim San and Nym Wales, *op. cit.*, p. 171.

And later: "At the time of the 6th Congress, everyone died bravely, believing the revolution would surely succeed; later on, however, many were confused and didn't really believe in the party line. . . . This doubt existed from Canton to Manchuria. The Manchuria Committee was arrested and nearly all betrayed—and 300 Korean Communists were arrested in Kirin in 1932" (*ibid.*, p. 186).

It should be remembered that Kim San was a proclaimed Communist when these words were uttered; yet, a certain bitterness toward all Chinese, including Chinese Communist comrades, flavors his writing.

52. Among numerous references, see Pak Sang-hyŏk, *Chosŏn minjok ui widaehan yŏngdoja* (*The Great Leader of the Korean People*), Tokyo, 1965, p. 69.

ally operated in the hinterlands of northeast Manchuria along the Russian border and in south Manchuria along the Korean border. As we shall note in some detail later, Kim Il-sŏng's guerrilla band was one of the units involved. However, before the second China Incident opened in 1937, Japan had reduced the Communist threat in Manchuria to a mere shadow, just as the Kuomintang had reduced the Communists in China proper. In both situations, moreover, the policies of the Chinese Communist Party (or rather the Comintern, which bore ultimate responsibility) had contributed mightily to these results.

Korean Communist Activities in China

Within China proper, Shanghai, Peking, and Canton had long served as centers of Korean radicalism. While the number of Korean exiles in these cities was very small in comparison with the total Korean population of Manchuria, the percentage of activist radical leaders was much higher. After 1923, however, disunity was rampant. All efforts to establish a broadly representative Korean government in exile had proven abortive, and even liaison among the various Korean expatriate groups was impossible to maintain. Under the stimulus of Comintern directives, however, the Communists began to work once again in the mid-1920s for a new united front modeled after the Kuomintang-Communist alliance. They finally succeeded when, on March 21, 1927, the Association for the Promotion of the United Korean Independence Party was established in Shanghai.[53]

The timing could scarcely have been less auspicious. Within less than a month, the Kuomintang-Communist alliance cracked wide open, and Shanghai became the scene of bloody attacks upon the Communists. Thus, the Association accomplished almost nothing, and was dissolved in October 1929. In this period, the French concession in Shanghai still provided some security to foreign Communists. Here, in January 1928, a number of Koreans in the city, including Hong Nam-p'yo, Chŏng Paek, Hyŏn Chong-gŏn, and Ko Kyŏng-hŭm, joined the Chinese Communist Party and established a Korean Section of the Party's French Concession (South District) Branch, which in turn was under the jurisdiction of the Kiangsu Province Committee.[54]

53. See *Shina oyobi Manshū ni okeru kyōsan undō gaikyō* (*A Summary of Conditions in the Communist Movement in China and Manchuria*), Tokyo, Sept. 1933, p. 66. This report covers events up to December 1932.

54. *Ibid.* Another source says that the Korean section was established in September 1927. Naimushō, Keiho-kyoku (Ministry of Home Affairs, Police and Security Bureau, Japan), *Shōwa shichinen chū ni okeru shakai undō no jōkyō* (*Conditions of Social Movements in 1932*), Tokyo, p. 1558. This annual report (1927–1942) will be cited henceforth as *Shakai undō no jōkyō,* followed by the year.

The document setting forth this development, along with many others of this period, includes Yŏ Un-hyŏng as a member of the CCP. When Yŏ was arrested and

From this point on, an independent Korean Communist movement in China ceased to exist; the Korean Communists were now harnessed to the Chinese Communist Party. As noted earlier, this same policy was shortly to be enforced in Manchuria, and its significance can scarcely be over-estimated. Unquestionably, the Comintern had played the crucial role in determining the new policy. The basic formula was to encourage loyal Korean comrades to join the CCP as individuals, but also to permit the establishment of what amounted to ethnic branches or sections within the Chinese Communist Party. These branches, composed totally of Koreans, provided opportunities for fraternization and some degree of autonomy or (more accurately, perhaps) specialization. Thus such journals as *App'uro* (*Forward*), published by the Korean branch, emphasized specific Korean issues in addition to carrying the general Party line. However, the chain of command now went from the Comintern and its agents to the Chinese Party and its leaders, and *thence* to the Korean comrades. Thus, the fate of the Korean Communists in China, both as individuals and as a group, had come to hinge upon developments in the Chinese Communist movement.

By 1930, Communist operations in Shanghai had become increasingly difficult. French police had now begun to cooperate with Japanese and Chinese authorities, arresting Korean revolutionaries in the Concession. After the dissolution of the Association for the Promotion of the United Korean Independence Party, the Korean Communists, with CCP approval, had set up their own organization, the League of Korean Independence Movement Workers. However, its leading figure, Ko Kyŏng-hŭm, was picked up by Shanghai police in September 1930, and the organization collapsed.[55] For nearly a year, activities were at a standstill. Then, in

---

interrogated, however, he emphatically denied his membership in any Communist Party. See "Ro Un-kyŏ jimmon chōsasho" ("Interrogation of Yŏ Un-hyŏng"), in Thought Section, Prosecutor's Bureau, High Court, *Chōsen shisō undō chōsa shiryō* (*Research Materials on the Korean Thought Movement*), No. 2, Seoul, March 1933.

55. The court decision on Ko Kyŏng-hŭm is reprinted in *Shisō geppō, op. cit.,* Vol. 1, No. 11, Jan. 1932, pp. 1701–1715, *AJMFA*, R S356. Ko, whose activities have been noted earlier, had a background typical in many ways of the nationalist-communist leaders of the 1920s. Born about 1899, he had a traditional education, studying the Chinese classics and then serving as a page at court during the final days of the Yi dynasty. At about the time of the Japanese annexation, Ko went to Manchuria in protest. Later, in 1919, he became a reporter for a Korean newspaper in Mukden. He returned to Korea in 1921. By 1924, he was the head of the local news department of *Tong-A Ilbo* in Seoul. The following year, he became head of the editorial department of *Shidae Ilbo*, a competitive newspaper. Previously, in July 1923, he had helped to organize the Shin Sasang Yŏngu-hoe (New Thought Study Society), with Hong Tŏk-yu, Kim Chae-bong, Kim Ch'an, and others. He joined the KCP in June 1925 and, under Kang Tal-yŏng, became a CEC member in February 1926. In October of that year he escaped to Shanghai and became absorbed in organizational activities there until his arrest, except for a brief period in March 1927 when he went to Moscow to attend the 2nd Congress of the MOPR.

August 1931, Cho Pong-am became secretary of the Korean Section of the Shanghai CCP, and began strenuous efforts to expand its activities. Korean front organizations were brought within the Party, and a journal, *Hyŏngmyŏng-ji-u* (*The Friend of Revolution*), was issued with the support of the CCP Central Committee. After the outbreak of the Manchurian Incident, moreover, Cho and Hong Nam-p'yo, with between thirty and forty comrades, organized the Shanghai Korean Anti-Imperialist League. This group now served as the focal point for Korean Communist activities in the region. It conducted a vigorous anti-Japanese propaganda campaign while at the same time supporting all the basic policies and slogans of the Chinese Communist Party.[56]

Both Japanese and French police pressure continued to mount. Between September and December 1932, ten influential Korean Communists, including both Cho and Hong, were arrested in Shanghai. Naturally, this had a depressing impact upon Korean Communist activities throughout the region, and after 1932 the Shanghai movement was extremely furtive and conducted its operations on a very small scale. Shanghai now joined Canton as a city of memories for Korean Communists; it was no longer a city of promise. It had become so much easier to contemplate single or group acts of terrorism than to attempt the maintenance of sustained organizational activities.

Nevertheless, some individuals carried on. Kim Tan-ya, who had managed to escape arrest, now became the key figure. Through him, the Comintern and the CCP provided funds and instructions for a few individuals who were ordered to return to Korea for Communist service. One of these was Kim Hyŏng-sŏn; another was Pak Hŏn-yŏng.[57] Like other

56. *Shina oyobi Manshū ni okeru kyōsan undō gaikyō, op. cit.,* pp. 66–67. Through its organ, *Chŏkki* (*Red Flag*), the League condemned the arrest of An Ch'ang-ho and other Korean nationalists by Japanese and French police, supported the strikes of Shanghai workers, publicized the campaign to raise funds for airplanes with which to fend off Japanese attacks, directed polemic letters to Japanese soldiers in Shanghai, and denounced the Kuomintang as a "reactionary, capitulationist force."

57. Kim Hyŏng-sŏn's career as a Communist dated back to 1924. After graduating from a Masan primary school, he attempted to obtain a secondary education but, because of financial difficulties, he was forced to withdraw from a local agricultural school after the first semester. After that, he worked as longshoreman and clerk; by 1926, however, he was a manager of the Masan branch of *Chosŏn Ilbo,* as well as an officer in the Masan Youth League and the Longshoremen's Union.

In the summer of 1924, Kim organized the Masan Young Communist League and also a Masan Communist Party, which became an officially recognized cell in April 1925 when the 1st KCP was established. Kim went to Shanghai in early 1926 after the pressures in Korea became intense. There, in 1928, he joined the Korean section of the CCP and became active in various Korean radical causes. See *Shisō ihō, op. cit.,* No. 2, pp. 12–13.

We have already set forth some aspects of Pak Hŏn-yŏng's career, but a few additional details are warranted here. Pak had been arrested in connection with

underground workers, however, Kim and Pak were soon picked up, and the liaison between Shanghai and Korea was broken. Kim Tan-ya had also been instructed by the CCP to reorganize the Shanghai Korean branch in 1933; he was to concentrate upon the reconstruction of the Korean Anti-Imperialist League and the Mutual Assistance Society, and also assist in the recruitment of men for the Manchurian guerrilla forces. Dogged by intensive Japanese surveillance, he attained rather minor results, and in January 1934, when he mysteriously disappeared, the movement collapsed once again.

Soon, however, there was a new development that offered the Korean Communists some hope. This was the emergence of a left-oriented united front. After three years of preparatory work, including the most intricate negotiations, the Minjok Hyŏngmyŏng-dang (Korean National Revolutionary Party) was established in early July 1935, preliminary meetings having opened in Nanking on June 20.[58] Once again, the timing was significant. The Seventh Comintern Congress was held in Moscow in July–August 1935; subsequently, the foremost objective of the international Communist movement became the creation of an anti-Japanese united front. The new Korean party was predominately leftist, and was strongly influenced by the Uiyŏldan (Righteous Fighters' Corps), headed by Kim Won-bong. Kim himself took the position of secretary-general of the party. To explore Kim and his activities is to add still another facet to the complex story of the Korean nationalist-revolutionary movement.[59]

Kim Won-bong had begun his political career as a terrorist shortly after the March First Movement. He was then in his early twenties. He had gathered a dozen followers in Manchuria; together they had pledged themselves to remain blood brothers, dedicated to the task of killing Japanese and pro-Japanese Koreans. The group took the name Uiyŏldan. Until the end of World War II, this small band remained loyal to that task. Probably the most notable terrorist act for which the group was responsible was the attempted assassination of General Tanaka Giichi in Shanghai on March 28, 1933.

---

the 1st KCP Incident, but he feigned mental disorder and was released in 1928. That August he and his wife broke parole and fled to Vladivostok via Chientao. In June 1929, he enrolled in the preparatory department of the Marx Institute in Moscow, and he attended that Institute until the summer of 1931. He then returned to Vladivostok, taught there in a Korean school for about one year, and, in August 1932, returned to Shanghai to participate in the Communist movement. He located Kim Tan-ya in January 1933 and helped him in sending funds and agents to Korea until his arrest in July. He was then returned to Korea and was sentenced to six years in prison, being released on the eve of World War II.

58. For the details, see Chong-Sik Lee, *The Politics of Korean Nationalism, op. cit.,* pp. 163–164, 194–196, 207–210.

59. The role of Kim Won-bong during this period is set forth in detail in *ibid.,* pp. 189 ff. See also Kim Won-bong's biography by Pak T'ae-won, *Yaksan kwa Uiyŏldan (Yaksan and the Uiyŏldan),* Seoul, 1947. (Yaksan was Kim's pen name.)

Precisely when Kim began to consider himself a Communist is unclear. The first hard evidence pertains to 1928, when he met An Kwang-
ch'ŏn, former M-L Group leader, in Shanghai. Eventually, the Communist
leaders provided Kim with some funds and an assignment. In 1929, he
went to Peking for the purpose of organizing a Korean Communist Party
Reconstruction League, and also of establishing a political-military school
there to train Korean revolutionaries.[60] Between February 1930 and February 1931, some nineteen students graduated from Kim's training program; most of them were sent back to Korea for organizational activities.

The Manchurian Incident and resulting Japanese pressures in north
China caused Kim to move to Nanking. There, in the spring of 1932, he
contacted the highest officials of the Kuomintang government with a plan
for a Sino-Korean alliance against Japanese imperialism. Reportedly,
Chiang Kai-shek himself took a strong personal interest in Kim's work;
at any rate, he assigned Chiang To to serve as Kim's "adviser" and agreed
to furnish 3,000 yuan monthly for expenses. He also provided Kim with a
training center outside Nanking. It is unclear whether the Kuomintang
knew of Kim's Communist connections, or what intimate understandings
may have been reached.

Provided with this assistance, Kim got under way again in the autumn
of 1932. His first class of twenty-six men was graduated in April 1933,
and a second class of thirty-five precisely one year later. Instruction was
divided into political and military parts, and the trainees were supposed to
be sent later to Korea or Manchuria for a variety of anti-Japanese assignments.[61] Originally, the agreement with the Chinese government appears
to have been that these men would be used for military or terrorist activities in Manchuria. But, in fact, most of them were sent into Korea, where
they sought to organize workers, farmers, or students, and to establish
branches of either the Uiyŏldan or the Communist Party.

There can be no doubt that Kim's work contributed substantially to

60. Chōsen Sōtokufu, Keimukyoku (Police Affairs Bureau, Government General of Korea), *Saikin ni okeru Chōsen chian jōkyō* (*Recent Conditions of Public
Security in Korea*), Seoul, May 1934, p. 299. This school was known as the Lenin
Institute, after its Moscow counterpart. Students were provided with six months'
training in Communist doctrine, the history of Korean revolutionary movements, and
military-political tactics and strategy.

It is most interesting to note the varied backgrounds of some of the students of
this Institute. Yi Chin-il, a Seoul high school dropout, went to China to enter the
KMT Nanking Central Military Academy, but he met a friend in Tientsin who
persuaded him to go to the Lenin Institute instead! After four months' training, he
was sent back to Korea an ardent Communist. Chŏng Tong-won, also a Seoul high
school dropout, went to Peking to attend a minor "university" and drifted into
Communist circles, thence to Lenin Institute. O Yun-bong, graduated from Whampoa
Military Academy in March 1929, was assigned to Hopei Province but left his unit,
and ended up as a Lenin Institute student.

61. Chong-Sik Lee, *The Politics of Korean Nationalism, op. cit.,* pp. 190 ff.

the Communist movement of this period—probably more, indeed, than that of any other Korean. At the same time, Kim remained always on the periphery of the Korean Communist movement, primarily because he was never a Comintern Communist. Indeed, some individuals who knew Kim intimately, like Chŏng Hwa-am, do not consider him to have been a bona fide Communist at any point. It would seem appropriate to consider Kim as an almost perfect example of the nationalist-Communist who, from the standpoint of the Communist establishment of this period, exemplified petty bourgeois vices at their worst.

Kim's path was therefore a thorny one. By the middle of 1936, the Korean National Revolutionary Party, with Kim at its head, had established branches in east China (Shanghai), south China (Canton), west China (Nanchang), and north China (Peking), in addition to its Nanking headquarters. Although a number of hard-core nationalists like Kim Ku had refused to join the organization, it could claim to be the strongest Korean nationalist group in existence. Trouble, however, developed from two sources. First, the Chinese government, under great pressure from the Japanese, advised Kim and others that it would no longer be able to provide active assistance. Student training, therefore, had to be discontinued, and the group decided to dispatch all personnel to Korea, Manchuria, and north China for espionage, terrorist, and organizational work. By the spring of 1937, there was another serious problem: because of personal, ideological, and policy differences among its leaders, especially Kim Won-bong and Yi Ch'ŏng-ch'ŏn, the Party split.[62]

Thus, on the eve of the second China Incident, the Korean nationalist movement in China continued to be deeply divided. The non-Communists under Kim Ku and others had been seriously weakened, since the bulk of the nationalists had gravitated to the left. Despite its bitterly anti-Communist domestic policies, the Kuomintang had given substantial support to the leftist Korean National Revolutionary Party until Japanese pressure forced them to stop. The Left itself, however, had split once more, and many elements had ceased to accept the discipline of Kim Won-bong, a national-Communist who had never been acknowledged by the Comintern-aligned movement.

On July 7, 1937, came the struggle at Marco Polo Bridge, nine miles southwest of Peking. There ensued an undeclared war between China and Japan. Once again, the Chinese government became extremely interested in mobilizing Korean support. On July 10, it took the lead and invited various Korean leaders to a joint conference at Lushan, near Nanking. Funds were supplied, and a united front was urged. In September, both Kim Won-bong and Kim Ku were requested to rally their followers for training and action. Young Koreans, most of them leftists connected with

62. *Ibid.,* p. 196,

Kim Won-bong's party, were gathered at Shengtze Military Academy in Nanking during the winter of 1937.

The Chinese nationalists, however, were soon forced to abandon Shanghai and Nanking along with other major coastal cities. The Korean revolutionaries were faced with two choices: they could move into the interior, or go north, joining guerrilla forces. Most of the Shengtze Academy students decided to go to Manchuria in the spring of 1938, either to join the Chinese Northeastern People's Revolutionary Army, or to act in liaison with it. Kim Won-bong opposed the movement to Manchuria; he wanted to confine the activities of the party and its military units to Kuomintang-controlled areas, and thereby strengthen his hand in dealing with the Chinese government. There was another major split over this issue. An anti-Kim group organized itself as the Korean Youth Wartime Service Corps, moved to Hankow, and made contacts with the Chinese Communist Eighth Route Army in north China. Its leader, Ch'oe Ch'ang-sŏk (better known later as Ch'oe Ch'ang-ik), was a fervent Communist who believed that Kim was a poor Marxist-Leninist, incapable of giving the Party or the movement proper guidance. No doubt Ch'oe had the advice of counsel with respect to this charge.

After lengthy negotiations, however, the open breach was healed by a compromise. It was agreed that a Korean volunteer army would be established and that all Koreans, including the Korean Youth Wartime Service Corps, would join it. This army would have its units sent to various war fronts. The Service Corps, in serious financial straits, accepted the plan. After renaming itself the Korean Youth Vanguard League, it re-joined the united front—now called the Korean National Front Federation. Nor was this all. On October 10, 1938, the Chosŏn Ŭiyong-dae (Korean Volunteer Corps) came into existence in Hankow under a guidance committee composed of five members of the Political Department of the Chinese Military Council and four directors of the Korean National Front Federation. They chose Kim Won-bong as Corps commander. Ultimately, the Corps established eighty-three branches in China, with small units in almost every major center. Prescribed activities covered a wide range of functions, from the collection of intelligence materials and the interrogation of captured Japanese soldiers to the propagandization of Korean civilians living in China.

The old issue, however, remained unresolved. Where was the Korean unit to operate? Vanguard League leaders wanted to move north. Kim wanted Corps members to remain in Chungking. Attempts, moreover, to widen the united front by incorporating elements like Kim Ku failed. The Communists, divided among themselves and uncertain of their individual positions, refused to share power with the so-called Right. Then a new development occurred. With Chinese Communist backing, a new Korean leader had been emerging in north China, Mu Chŏng. Mu, who had served as P'eng Teh-huai's chief of staff and made the Long March, had been in eclipse for a time as a result of illness. When he recovered, however, the Chinese Communists permitted him to gather about three hundred young Koreans from such old political centers as Shanghai, Nanking, Peking, and the Wuhan cities, and establish a Korean military unit.

Some of Mu Chŏng's men were graduates of the Anti-Japanese Political and Military "University" (K'ang-Ta in Chinese) in Yenan. Others were graduates of military schools in Moscow. A few had been trained at Whampoa. Some had little or no formal training. By 1939, Mu Chŏng's Korean unit was involved in active military operations, and word of his activities spread quickly among Korean revolutionaries. Now, Kim Won-bong had still another rival—and a significant one. Naturally, Korean Volunteer Corps members who were dissatisfied with Kim rallied around Mu Chŏng. Yenan, too, became significantly involved in internal Korean politics. For example, a leader of the Vanguard League established a preparatory committee for a North China Korean Youth Federation (Hwabuk Chosŏn Yŏnhap-hoe) in 1939 after visiting Yenan. On January 10, 1941, this Federation was formally inaugurated; Mu Chŏng became its president, and various branches were established. In keeping with the united front politics of the period, the Korean Youth Federation did not openly proclaim itself as Communist, but its literature made its identity abundantly clear.[63]

By mid-1941, most of the Korean Volunteer Corps members had been shifted to north China. The Kuomintang and Kim Won-bong had lost

63. According to Japanese sources, the Youth Federation was assigned the following basic activities: promotion of the Korean independence movement; recruitment of Koreans for military and political activities; "destruction" of the Japanese forces in cooperation with the Eighth Route Army; cultivation of "antiwar" movements.

They also reported that a fourteen-point agreement was concluded at this time between Kim Chong-shin, representing the Koreans, and the CCP Central Committee providing for the following understandings: the CCP would help the Korean independence movement: the Korean Youth Party (Chosŏn Ch'ŏng-nyŏn-dang) was to be under the "guidance" of the CCP, but its policies could not be changed without Korean consent except "under special circumstances" involving temporary measures; upon Korean independence, the "views" of the CCP with respect to internal "recovery" policies in Korea would be accepted; Koreans in China would have equal roles with Chinese in the anti-Japanese movement, and close cooperation in the war would be promoted. This all comes from a report written in Peking and introduced by Public Prosecutor Sano Shigeki, *Shisō ihō,* Vol. 26, Oct. 1943 (reprinted from Japan, Ministry of Justice, *Shisō geppō,* No. 99), pp. 85–86.

In this report as in other secret Japanese communications of this period, the assessment of Korean-Chinese Communist relations was candid and revealing. According to Japanese agents, the CCP was utilizing Korean nationalism, while the Koreans were consciously using the CCP for their own purposes: "their ultimate purpose is Korean independence and not in serving the CCP in a simple sense" (*ibid.,* p. 85).

control of the movement. The victors were the Chinese Communists and Mu Chŏng. On paper, Kim Won-bong continued to be corps commander, and the north China unit officially remained a part of the Korean National Front Federation. In reality, however, the units in the north obtained their financial and material support from Yenan and looked to Mu Chŏng for leadership. We know some of the details of Kim's decline as a result of revelations by Ssu Ma-lu, a graduate of the Communist Party school in Yenan who was Chinese private secretary to Kim in Chungking during this period.[64]

According to Ssu, the some three hundred members of the Korean Volunteer Corps attracted the attention of Chou En-lai as early as September 1940, when he was in Chungking. Through Ssu, the Communists acquired detailed information about the corps, including material on its internal rivalries. Later, Ssu was assigned the task of persuading Kim Won-bong to send the corps members to north China where the Communists were in control. Aided by Koreans close to Kim, Ssu was successful. The Chungking government was then tricked. False reports were given it concerning the location of corps units, and some 80 percent of the members were sent out without Kuomintang leaders becoming suspicious. Kim Won-bong fully expected to join the corps in the north, and undoubtedly had accepted the shift only on this basis. Once the corps personnel got to the Communist area, however, Kim was dumped. When he requested transportation north, Chou En-lai informed him that revolutionary activities could be conducted in Chungking as well as in Yenan. Ultimately, he was branded by the CCP as "petty bourgeois," opportunist, and guilty of "individual heroism."

Meanwhile, the Korean Youth Federation was expanding its activities, some of which were recorded in the CCP organ, *Chieh-fang Jih-pao* (*Liberation Daily*), Yenan. At a plenary conference of August 1942, the North China Korean Youth Federation was renamed the Korean Independence League (Chosŏn Tongnip Tongmaeng), and the Korean Volunteer Corps was henceforth referred to as the Korean Volunteer Army. Kim Tu-bong, noted Korean scholar, came to Yenan from Chungking and became chairman of the Korean Independence League's executive committee.[65] Mu

64. Ssu Ma-lu, *Tou-chêng shih-pa-nien* (*Eighteen Years of Struggle*), Hong Kong, 1952, pp. 173–180.

65. Chong-Sik Lee, *The Politics of Korean Nationalism, op. cit.,* p. 221.

For a contemporary account of Kim Tu-bong, see Yi Yun-jae, "A Visit with Mr. Kim Tu-bong, the Great Authority on the Korean Language," *Pyŏlgongŏn* (*Separate World*), Vol. 4, No. 7, Dec. 1929, pp. 12–16. Yi visited Kim on August 8, 1929, in Shanghai where he and his family were then living. This article, admittedly prepared with the knowledge that Japanese censors would omit any offensive material, depicts Kim as an apolitical man, yet one embroiled in a quarrel with the Communists. According to Yi, Kim, then serving as principal of the Insŏng primary school (for Korean children in Shanghai) while also working on his dictionary of

Chŏng replaced Pak Hyo-sam as the commander of the Korean Volunteer Army. In November 1942, the North China Korean Youth Revolutionary School was opened in T'aihang, with Mu Chŏng serving as head of the school.

The Korean contingent which operated from Yenan headquarters was not a large one; full-time activists probably numbered no more than two or three hundred at any point between 1941 and 1945. *Chieh-fang Jih-pao,* indeed, gave much greater attention to the Japanese antiwar group in Yenan headed by Okano Susumu (Nosaka Sanzō). Nevertheless, Koreans fought and died in engagements with the Japanese army.[66] The March First Uprising was duly commemorated each year, as were certain other events connected with Korean history.[67] And the Korean comrades loyally followed their Chinese friends. Thus, when the rectification movement was launched in Yenan by Mao and his close supporters, it was duplicated by the Koreans. The Korean Youth School, moreover, renamed the North China Korean Revolutionary Military-Political School in late 1943, attempted to parallel its Chinese counterpart, the Anti-Japanese Political and Military University.[68]

The Chinese Communists regarded Mu Chŏng as the key figure among Korean revolutionaries. He was the only Korean to be given prominence in the Chinese Communist press of this period, and the title "Revolutionary Leader" by which he was designated made it apparent that the Chinese Communist leaders of Yenan acknowledged him as the central leader of the Korean independence (Communist) movement.

The events just depicted were of critical importance to the future. In the fifteen years preceding Japanese surrender, the Chinese Communists

---

the Korean language, charged that the Communists wanted to use the school as a meeting place and also sought to indoctrinate "the pure and naive children" attending the school.

It would thus appear that Kim Tu-bong moved into the Communist camp via united front activities only some time later.

66. For example, on Sept. 20, 1942, *Chieh-fang Jih-pao* carried a full page listing and eulogizing eleven Koreans who had been killed in action. On the following day, a memorial service was held, with Chu Teh, commander-in-chief of the Chinese Communist military forces, making a brief speech. *Chieh-fang Jih-pao,* Sept. 21, 1942, p. 2.

67. See *ibid.,* March 2, 1942, p. 2. On the occasion of the thirty-third anniversary of the downfall of the old Korean kingdom, Mu Chŏng made a speech equating the earlier Kuomintang "compromises" with the Japanese with the actions of Yi Wan-yong, the last premier of Korea and the man who signed the treaty of annexation. *Ibid.,* Sept. 5, 1943, p. 1.

68. A report from T'aihang indicated that "many Korean youth" from enemy occupied areas had come to the school. Students studied "twenty-two books and documents," simultaneously engaging in labor, including the growing of vegetables, the planting of wheat, and the production of charcoal. With the change in the name of the school, two departments (military and political) were created, providing more "formal" training. *Ibid.,* Feb. 13, 1944, p. 1.

had increasingly taken control of the Korean revolutionary movement in China. They had succeeded in reducing Kuomintang influence, especially over the Korean "Left," to a negligible amount. Moreover, they had created and encouraged their own Korean leaders, typified by men like Mu Chŏng who had clearly won out in the power struggle with Kim Won-bong. As we shall later discover, these developments were to figure prominently in the complex pattern of North Korean politics after August 1945.

The Soviet Role

Meanwhile, was there a Soviet counterpart influence during this period, apart from that exercised by the Comintern directly? The evidence is scanty. It would appear, however, that Vladivostok continued to serve as refuge, training center, and supply depot for Korean revolutionaries. The testimony of Yim Min-ho, a Korean Communist arrested in 1934 in connection with Red farmer unions, probably conveys a typical situation.[69] When the Chientao police began their sweep of Korean Communists in east Manchuria in December 1927, Yim fled to Vladivostok. There, enough Korean Communists had collected to enable the convening of an "exiles' conference." Subsequently, Yim was sent to Moscow to study in a school specializing in labor and commerce. He returned to Vladivostok in 1932, received instructions there from the Profintern East Asian Branch, and reentered Korea in September of the same year. His assignment was that of organizing revolutionary labor unions in Hamhŭng.

A number of Communists arrested in Korea during this period by the Japanese authorities related a story like Yim's. The Vladivostok branch of the Profintern, as noted earlier, had supposedly been given broad jurisdiction over the labor and peasant movements in Manchuria, Japan, and Korea. It is a reasonable supposition that Soviet-Comintern authorities during this period were concentrating upon such labor-peasant organizational activities as trade unionism, political demonstrations, and propaganda distribution, whereas Yenan was involved mainly in the expansion of direct military action. We shall return to this later.

Korean Radicals in Japan

One important overseas center of Korean radicalism remains to be discussed: Japan. From the very beginning of the Korean Communist movement, Japan had been a major source of inspiration. There was a well-traveled path between Tokyo University and other Japanese institutions of higher learning and the Korean Communist Party—ending in a Japanese prison. This was the "study group" route, replete with passionate conviction, intellectual excitement, and a certain remoteness from social realities—and the laboring masses. It was also a route that combined national-

69. See *Shisō ihō, op. cit.,* No. 3, pp. 10–27.

ism and Communism, and established intimate relations between Japanese and Korean radicals. From Japan had come the young intellectuals who comprised the nuclei of such groups as the North Wind Society and the M-L Group. Always, close ties between Japanese and Korean Communists were maintained. Thus, the eclipse of Fukumoto had immediate repercussions among his young supporters in Korea, the leaders of the M-L Group.

The number of Koreans studying in Japan steadily increased after 1919. The only exceptions to this trend were several years immediately after the anti-Korean riots that followed the 1923 Kantō earthquake, and during the depths of the depression.

Korean Students in Japan
(at the secondary level or above)[70]

Dec. 1918	592	Dec. 1928	2,984
Dec. 1919	448	June 1929	4,433
Dec. 1920	980	Oct. 1930	5,285
Dec. 1921	1,516	Oct. 1931	5,062
Dec. 1922	1,912	Dec. 1932	4,977
Dec. 1923	667	Dec. 1933	5,369
Dec. 1924	990	Dec. 1934	6,093
Dec. 1925	1,575	Dec. 1935	7,292
Dec. 1926	2,256	Dec. 1936	7,810
Dec. 1927	2,482	Dec. 1937	9,914

Most of the Korean students were forced by circumstances to be partly or wholly self-sufficient. Many worked during the day and attended school at night. The number actually graduating was small; most were forced to withdraw for economic or scholastic reasons. In general, Korean students in Japan lived together, choosing roommates on the basis of old home-town or school relationships. Almost all belonged to a haku-hoe, that is, a "comradely study association" or alumni group. Economic conditions, patterns of life, and the generally high incidence of personal frustration combined to encourage political radicalism. Japanese prejudice against Koreans was probably more acutely felt at the student level than among the lower economic classes; certainly, nationalist sentiment was higher among the students.

The latter group actually comprised a very small part of the total Korean population in Japan. This population grew astronomically after the mid-1920s. At the end of 1913, there had been only 3,635 Koreans in Japan. The figure reached 22,411 at the end of 1918. Ten years later, it was more than 230,000, and concern over the rapid influx was being expressed. Attempts to restrict or control Korean immigration began in

70. Yoshiura Daizō, *Chōsenjin no kyōsanshugi undō* (*Communist Movements Involving Koreans*), Bureau of Criminal Affairs, Ministry of Justice (Shihō-shō), Thought Study Materials, No. 71, 1940, no place of publication, p. 13.

1925, but strenuous resistance was encountered from a variety of sources.[71]

By the end of 1937, the number of Koreans in Japan had reached 730,000. Naturally, huge social and political problems had developed as a result of this rapid increase. The great bulk of the immigrants were south Koreans from the lower socioeconomic class. Previously, they had been tenant farmers or day laborers, uneducated and unskilled. The stereotyped Japanese impresson of the Korean immigrants was that they were crude, "easily excited and susceptible to outside influences," unsanitary, shiftless, idle, and boorish.[72]

The statistics show clearly that the great bulk of the Koreans living in Japan were forced into the most menial tasks as a result of educational and vocational deficiencies reinforced by prejudice. One source estimated in 1930 that only about 10 percent of the Koreans in Japan could be considered "middle class," and that an additional 15 percent were regularly employed in factories and mines. The remainder worked irregularly as construction laborers, street cleaners, farm workers, and in a variety of odd jobs. The percentage of unemployed was extremely high, and in the great Korean slums of Ōsaka conditions were terrible. The Japanese had organized some relief work, both on an official and on a private basis. But it was scarcely adequate, and some cases of starvation occurred each year. In general, the largest concentrations of Koreans were in Ōsaka, Kyōtō, and the Kantō area.

It is not surprising, therefore, that violence and lawlessness were endemic among the Korean community in Japan, and that various radical movements saw in this community the possibility of massive support. At an earlier point, Japanese anarchists like Ōsugi Sakae had bid for such support, and the anarchist movement in Japan contained a substantial Korean contingent. The Japanese Communist movement also, from its origins, had close ties with Koreans, both at home and abroad. We have previously noted those Koreans who served as Comintern representatives or messengers, as well as the emergence in Japan of the Black Current Society, the North Star Society, the January Society, and similar study groups bent on political action.

After 1925, moreover, Korean radicalism showed itself in unionism as well as in student-intellectual groups. The Chae Ilbon Chosŏn Nodong Ch'ong Tongmaeng (Korean General Labor Federation in Japan) was established in February 1925, and quickly affiliated itself with the left wing of the Japanese labor movement. However, the sustained government attack upon the Communist movement that began in 1928 weakened the Korean Communists in Japan no less than their Japanese comrades. This at any rate is the impression given by table 18, which derives from official Japanese sources. Of course, one must accept the categories provided by

71. *Ibid.*, p. 7.
72. *Ibid.*, pp. 17–18.

TABLE 18

Annual Compilation of Various Korean Groups in Japan by Political Affiliation

	Communist Groups				Total		Anarchists		National Communists		Nationalists	
	Extreme Left		Left									
	Groups	Persons	Groups	Persons	Groups	Persons	Groups	Persons	Groups	Persons	Groups	Persons
Sept. 1929	—	—	—	—	40	25,370	15	335	12	2,455	98	7,162
Oct. 1930	—	—	—	—	38	8,393	13	565	—	—	143	13,182
Oct. 1931	—	—	—	—	50	12,400	12	644	—	—	147	11,887
Dec. 1932	86	10,766	33	3,078	119	13,844	13	1,026	—	—	179	22,133
Dec. 1933	86	8,158	27	2,758	113	10,943	12	662	—	—	182	22,564
Dec. 1934	39	2,604	35	2,657	74	5,261	11	616	—	—	230	18,036
Dec. 1935	33	2,094	31	2,470	61	4,488	10	547	—	—	251	16,135
Dec. 1936	20	1,104	26	2,248	46	3,352	5	430	—	—	301	19,508
Dec. 1937	7	463	34	2,269	41	2,732	5	210	—	—	304	19,540

SOURCE: Yoshiura Daizo, *Chōsenjin no kyōsanshugi undō* (*Communist Movements Involving Koreans*), Bureau of Criminal Affairs, Ministry of Justice (Shihō-shō), Thought Study Materials, No. 71, 1940, n.p., p. 13.

Dash indicates no estimate made.

the Japanese as well as the accuracy of the figures given. From supplementary data, it would appear that "extreme left" referred to Korean Communists who accepted Comintern discipline, and hence the discipline of
the Japanese Communist Party. "Left" and "National Communists" are not
clear, but the latter may refer to groups like the Uiyŏldan. In any case,
there were nearly 30,000 Korean "Communists" in Japan in 1929, but
only about 8,000 in the fall of 1930. The mass arrests of leaders and the
subsequent fear among their followers, especially in the labor movement,
had caused the decline. The Communists also discovered that, when they
sought to move from legal to illegal modes of organization, they could
carry only the smallest segment of the masses with them.

After 1930, the Communists in Japan were never able to regain their
earlier position, despite some gains in the 1930–32 period. From 1933 onward there was such a precipitous decline that by the end of 1937 the
Japanese could claim to have exterminated Korean Communism as a
significant force in Japan proper. At that point, the non-Communist nationalist movement, weak though it was, posed a much more serious problem.

Let us look briefly at some of the details. A Japan Bureau of the
Korean Communist Party had been first established in 1927. Pak Nak-
jong served as secretary, Organization was headed by Ch'oe Ik-han, and
Propaganda by Han Rim. In early 1928, however, the Bureau lost its
cover, and Pak and Ch'oe were arrested. Reconstruction quickly followed,
with Kim Han-gyŏng taking over the top position. A Japanese section of
the Korean Communist Youth League had also been established, and the
two organizations maintained very close relations. On August 29, 1928—
National Humiliation Day—the Communists conducted a Tokyo rally:
some 150 Koreans marched through the streets singing revolutionary songs.
Police made a number of arrests, and once again the existence of Korean
Communist organizations in Japan was exposed. Direct links were also
established between the KCP and such legal bodies as the Korean General
Labor Federation in Japan and the Japan branch of the Shingan-hoe. The
arrests that followed almost obliterated both the Bureau and the Youth
League. For several years after 1928, Korean Communist activities in
Japan were carried on primarily through the labor movement.

It was not until the end of 1931 that the Japan branches of the Korean
Communist Party and the Communist Youth League were formally dissolved and Korean Communists in Japan ordered to join Japanese Communist organizations. The evidence, however, makes it clear that the decision had actually been made in 1928, and that it emanated from Comintern
sources. On December 23, 1931, Sekki (Red Flag), the Japanese Communist organ, published the dissolution declarations of the KCP Japan
Bureau and Youth League Japan branch.[73] The statements made it clear

73. Sekki (Red Flag), No. 61, Dec. 23, 1931, p. 12; republished by Akahata
Hombu, Tokyo, 1954, Vol. I.

that the dissolution orders had come from the Comintern in 1928, but that before action could be taken both the Bureau and the Youth League had been destroyed by "White terrorism." Explaining the need for dissolution, the statements asserted that it was an "irregular phenomenon" to have a foreign Party operating in another country independently, without any functional relationship to the proletariat of that country. Recognizing this, the Korean "masses" had not awaited formal orders. Rather, amalgamation with the Japanese Communist Party had already developed as "a natural demand from the masses themselves" (the usual Comintern formula). This phenomenon, proclaimed the *Sekki* statements, proved that they had transcended narrow national lines and become aware of the common interests of the international working class, finding trustworthy comrades of different nationalities in the process of the actual struggle.

The "left extremism" implicit in the Comintern line of this period was affecting the Japanese Communist movement quite as much as the movement in China.[74] And for Japanese as well as Chinese comrades, it was a period of enormous hardship. The Japanese Communists had come very close to the surface when they campaigned for leftist candidates in the general elections of February 1928. One month later, armed with massive amounts of evidence, Japanese police rounded up some 1,200 individuals, nearly 500 of whom were prosecuted on charges of subversive activities. Only those Communists who had been abroad at the time escaped the dragnet and were available when the Party was reorganized. For the most part, these were young students. Thus Japan, like China, moved into the "returned student" era after 1928.

Few of the students who came back from Moscow survived long after they reached Japan. Generally, they were caught after a few months and given long prison sentences. Party leadership was thus constantly revolving, and Party organization was in a shambles. Faced with this situation, a number of those on the left—even some Communists and Communist sympathizers—believed that their only recourse was to establish a legal leftist party in which they could find a home. A group headed by Ōyama Ikuo and Hososaka Kanemitsu therefore organized the Rōnōtō (Labor-Farmer Party) in the fall of 1929. The Comintern-affiliated Communists, however, violently opposed this action on the grounds that the new party would detract from the Communist Party, and from the importance of illegal action. The international line was left; the Japanese Communist Party had an obligation to see that that line was maintained. Significantly, the Party also counted upon Korean comrades to help in blocking the Labor-Farmer Party. On October 3, 1929, for example, some 150 Koreans from the Korean General Labor Federation and the Shingan-hoe broke up a meeting at which Ōyama and other supporters of the Labor-Farmer Party were presenting their case.

74. Robert A. Scalapino, *The Japanese Communist Movement, 1920–1966,* Berkeley, 1967, pp. 39–44.

After 1929 the Communist Party of Japan steadily increased its emphasis upon the Korean issue, and found an ever larger percentage of its members within the Korean community. To accommodate Korean members, the Party had established the Minzoku-bu (Nationalities Bureau). The Bureau concentrated upon the Korean and Formosan questions, and actively solicited workers and students from these areas. The basic Communist appeal to Koreans, of course, was on two fronts: independence and equal treatment. With respect to the first issue, the Communists had a virtual monopoly within the Japanese political spectrum; the only outlet for unalloyed Korean nationalism in Japanese politics was through the Communist movement. This is a fact that should never be overlooked.

After the outbreak of the Manchurian Incident, moreover, the Japanese Communist Party put an even stronger emphasis upon links with Korean revolutionaries. Its main concern was now to build the anti-imperialist front that the international Communist movement so badly needed. Thus the JCP Theses of 1932, in addition to proclaiming that all colonies should be liberated from the yoke of Japanese imperialism, also asserted that one of the defects of past struggles had been the inadequate support given to the revolutionary activities of Korean workers, farmers, and guerrilla fighters.[75] And *Sekki,* in mid-1932, was to announce that the Korean independence movement was inseparable from the antiwar movement.[76] Korean liberation would constitute a massive blow to Japanese imperialism, it insisted, and thereby prevent Japan from engaging in further war. Hence, the closest integration of the activities of Japanese and Korean comrades was essential. "Top fighters" from Japan should be sent to Korea for Party work, and the highest priority should be given to arousing the Korean masses.

Behind the *Sekki* articles lay some specific underground activities. In September 1929, Korean Communist leaders in Shanghai had held a meeting to discuss the problem of reconstructing the Party within Korea.[77] Most of the current leaders of the Korean branch of the CCP were involved, including Han Wi-gŏn, Yang Myŏng, and Ch'oe Pong-gwan among others. It was decided that the reestablishment of the Korean Communist Party was a matter of the highest priority, and that as a first step some comrades should proceed to Japan and Manchuria to establish bases for liaison with Korea. Five men were ordered to Tokyo with instructions to join leftist labor unions and cultural associations.

75. For the full text of the 1932 Japanese Communist Party Thesis, see *International Press Correspondence,* May 26, 1932. For a detailed discussion of the thesis and its repercussions, see George M. Beckmann and Okubo Genji, *The Japanese Communist Party, 1922–1945,* Stanford, 1969, pp. 229–238.
    76. *Sekki, op. cit.,* No. 91, Aug. 20, 1932, p. 1 (Vol. III of 1954 *Akahata Hombu* edition).
    77. *Shakai undō no jōkyō, op. cit.,* 1932, p. 1504.

When the Shanghai agents, including Ko Kyŏng-hŭm and Kim Ch'i-jŏng, arrived in Tokyo in early 1930, they first grouped themselves around a small publishing house, Musanja-sa (Proletariat Publishing Company). It was decided to use *The Proletariat,* a journal put out by the group, as the new Party reconstruction organ; the editors were to be Ko Kyŏng-hŭm, Kim Sam-gyu, and Kim Ch'i-jŏng. The key writer, however, was Ko, and between April and November 1930 he produced a number of articles and pamphlets dealing with various phases of the Korean Communist movement. Most of them were widely disseminated among Korean radicals in Japan and Korea. As we noted earlier, one of his pamphlets helped to end the Communist–Shingan-hoe alliance, although primary credit for this should undoubtedly go to the Comintern-Profintern directives. In late 1930, Ko returned to China, seeking funds. He received a small sum from Han Wi-gŏn in Peking, and returned to Tokyo in the spring of 1931. In August, however, Japanese authorities smashed the Musanja group, arresting Ko, Kim Sam-gyu, and a number of others.[78]

Responsibility for carrying on the movement now shifted to Kim Ch'i-jŏng, Kim Tu-jŏng, and others who had escaped arrest.[79] They recommenced activities in early 1932, finally calling their front organization Nodong Kegŭpsa (Labor Class Company). The first issue of *Nodong Kegŭp* (*The Labor Class*) was published on June 20, 1932. Meanwhile, connections were established with top JCP circles. Kim Ch'i-jŏng contacted the JCP Nationalities Bureau and joined the Party itself. In July he submitted an action proposal to the JCP Central Committee that argued the case for taking immediate practical measures to reconstruct the Korean Communist Party. The JCP appointed a special committee headed by Konno Yojirō, a key Party figure who had recently returned from Moscow. In September, Konno, speaking on behalf of the committee, accepted the basic outline of Kim's proposal, asserting that the actual struggle in Korea must be a joint effort of Koreans and Japanese, and that able agents should be dispatched at once.[80]

Thus, by 1932, the Japanese Communist Party was seeking to give full support to KCP reconstruction efforts. The Korean Communists,

78. *Ibid.,* p. 1477.
79. *Ibid.,* pp. 1508–1512. Along with Ko Kyŏng-hŭm, Kim Ch'i-jŏng was a key figure in the Korean Communist movement of this period, especially as it related to activities in Japan. Kim, orphaned when he was fourteen and raised in "an unfavorable environment," went to Shanghai early in 1927. He had become a first lieutenant in the Chinese Nationalist Army by January 1929, assigned to a government-operated aircraft workshop in Shanghai. Then he came into contact with Kim Won-bong and others, gradually acquiring a commitment to Communism. Joining the Korean Youth League and the Shanghai City Committee of the CCP, Kim became active in the movement. He arrived in Japan in January 1930.
80. *Shisō ihō, op. cit.,* No. 6, p. 182. See also *ibid.,* No. 3, p. 50, and *Shakai undō no jōkyō, op. cit.,* 1933, p. 1586.

for their part, had given up all independent organizations in Japan and were working solely through the JCP and its various front organizations. Koreans, indeed, were forming an ever larger proportion of JCP membership. Its formal membership never exceeded 1,000 in the period before 1945, although the front organizations were much larger. In 1932, forty-nine Koreans were arrested in Japan charged with being JCP members; in the following year, the corresponding figure was eighty-five, and an additional sixty-four were charged with being members of the Communist Youth League. Despite their numerical position in the Party, however, Koreans were not given top Party posts, although several held offices at the city and prefectural committee levels.

The main influence of Korean Communists during this period was in the Japanese labor movement. The Japanese trade union movement had been split in 1925, with the Communists taking the initiative in the establishment of Nihon Rōdō Hyōgikai (Labor Union Council of Japan). The Council had about 15,000 members and was under very strong Communist influence until its forced dissolution by government edict in mid-1928. A few months later, on December 25, 1928, an underground successor was officially launched. This was Nihon Rōdō Kumiai Zenkoku Kyōgikai (National Council of Japanese Labor Unions), or Zenkyō in abbreviated form. Zenkyō was completely under the control of the Communists; nearly all its leaders were Party members. In December 1929, the Korean General Labor Federation in Japan, which reportedly had 23,530 members and nine branch unions, agreed to dissolve and join Zenkyō. The Federation was then temporarily renamed the Zenkyō Korean Committee, and efforts to transfer members got under way. Kim Tu-jŏng headed the Committee. In April 1930, however, a number of top Korean labor leaders were arrested, and the Zenkyō Korean Committee was almost totally wiped out.

Nevertheless, by the end of 1930, more than 2,600 Korean Federation members had joined Zenkyō. Since that organization had a total of less than 6,000 members, the Korean contingent represented a sizable proportion of the membership. By October 1931, there were reportedly 4,500 Koreans in Zenkyō. According to Japanese security officials, this group had to be considered the hard core of Korean radicalism, both quantitatively and qualitatively. Nearly 2,400 of them came from the Ōsaka area, and about 1,400 from Tokyo. Most were construction workers, but laborers in the chemical, publishing, textile, and metal industries were also represented. By the end of 1933, at a point when total Zenkyō membership had declined, there were still 3,970 Koreans in the organization. By now they constituted a majority. Nine Koreans, moreover, held important positions of leadership. It is not surprising that a Korean edition of the union journal, *Nodong Sinmun* (*The Workers' News*), began on November 30, 1933.

Thus, by the early 1930s, the Korean role in the Japanese Communist movement had become very substantial, especially in numerical terms. Koreans accounted for more than one-half of the membership of the Communist labor movement in Japan, and possibly one-third of the Communist Party membership, although exact statistics on the Party are not available. However, one must also consider the general decline of the Japanese Communist movement during this period. If Koreans were playing a greater role in the Japanese Communist movement, this was primarily because it held less and less attraction for Japanese. Indeed, two leading Japanese Communists, Sano Manabu and Nabeyama Sadachika, charged in 1933 that the international Communist movement was merely a vehicle for Russian national interests. Although they were in prison at the time, they proclaimed themselves still committed to the cause of socialism. But it had to be a distinctively Japanese socialism. The difference between Japanese and Korean nationalism at this point was never so apparent: Sano and Nabeyama influenced a number of Japanese comrades to defect, but not a single Korean.[81] Nevertheless, by the mid-1930s, Communism in Japan had been reduced to a mere shadow. Only the legacy of Koreans as "prone to radicalism and violence" remained against the backdrop of the Japanese militarist era.

Communism in the Korean Homeland After 1928

What of the efforts to rehabilitate the Party and the movement in Korea itself? It will be recalled that the fourth Korean Communist Party had been destroyed in mid-1928, and that the few survivors left in Korea had despaired of any immediate revival efforts. For this reason, Kim Tan-ya in Shanghai had been urged to establish Party headquarters there. The Comintern, moreover, had refused to recognize either of the two competing factions who presented themselves in Moscow at the time of the Sixth Comintern Congress, but instead had ordered a full investigation of the Korean situation. This was the genesis of the Comintern's resolution of December 1928, which, coupled with the Profintern's theses of Septem-

---

81. There were, however, defections among Koreans convicted of violating the public security laws, and the number rapidly increased after 1930. Note the following figures (from *Shisō ihō*, No. 4, p. 181):

1927— 4	1929—50	1931—122	1933—313
1928—15	1930—73	1932—337	1934—473

In 1935, an investigation of the motives of eighty-six defectors was conducted. Fifty stated that they recanted because of "self-awareness" of their errors, sixteen because of the "guidance of officials," eight because of "love of family," five because they had obtained jobs with governmental help, and one for vague reasons. While these categories are highly unsatisfactory, the reasons given appear to have little connection with the factors influencing Sano and other key Japanese leaders. Rather they tend to be personal, emotional, and apolitical. An overarching factor should be emphasized, however: it is easy to leave a political movement in the doldrums, wracked by successive defeats and with no seeming hope for the future.

ber 1930, set forth the basic tasks of the Korean Communist movement.

The most important injunction was that workers and poor peasants had to be attracted into the Party so that its petty bourgeois character could be altered and mass foundations built. Primary attention had to be given the development of Red worker and peasant unions. In regard to this task, the Profintern theses struck a note of optimism. The support given by Korean peasants to recent workers' strikes, it proclaimed, showed that laborers and farmers had an inclination toward joint movements. "A proletariat-peasant alliance under the leadership of the working class" had already begun to blossom in Korea.[82] At this point, asserted the theses, the need was to build "left" unions outside the Korean General Confederation of Labor, a "reformist" body whose 45,000 members were headed by "petty bourgeois and nationalist elements." To win the support of the masses, economic and political issues had to be linked, and organizations like the Confederation and Shingan-hoe had to be ruthlessly exposed. Starting with problems like wages, working conditions, and other immediate economic concerns, vanguard leaders had to guide the working masses toward a struggle for political rights and agrarian revolution and against Japanese imperialism.

Clearly, the emphasis was less upon the immediate reconstruction of the Korean Communist Party, and more upon the development of mass foundations for Communism—the unfolding of a militant, independent struggle for the support of the urban laborer and the rural peasant. This struggle, to be conducted via unionism, would of necessity have to be largely underground, and it would have to be directed against most elements of the Korean bourgeoisie quite as much as against the Japanese.

The opening efforts of the Communists within Korea after 1929 must be viewed in the light of these instructions. Two other basic developments must also be recalled. First, the one country-one party principle was now being rigorously applied by the Comintern. All Korean Communists residing outside Korea had been ordered to join the Communist Party of the country in which they lived. Second, the bulk of Korean Communists currently not in jail were scattered among five or six regions or centers: Manchuria, Shanghai, Peking, Tokyo-Ōsaka, Vladivostok, and Moscow. And all orders to the contrary notwithstanding, liaison among them was far from perfect, factionalism far from dead. It is both interesting and important, therefore, to note the uncoordinated efforts that each group made to penetrate the homeland.

As we have emphasized, the Korean Communist movement abroad was always numerically strongest in Manchuria. When orders reached this area for Korean Communists to disband their own organizations and join the Chinese Communist Party, most obeyed, albeit not without some re-

---

82. "Tasks of the Revolutionary Trade Union Movement in Corea," *Resolutions of the Fifth Congress of the R.I.L.U.*, London, 1931, p. 153.

sentment. This meant dissolving the Preparatory Society for the Reconstruction of the Korean Communist Party that had been initiated mainly by the old Shanghai and Seoul factions after Yi Tong-hwi and Kim Kyu-yŏl returned from the Sixth Comintern Congress. Some leaders of the Society, however, had already returned to Korea or did so shortly after the dissolution order was carried out. In September 1930, a few of them gathered in Hŭngnam and decided to continue with efforts to rebuild the Korean Communist Party.[83] Apparently, they believed that if the Society's headquarters were moved to Korea, no violation of the new Comintern edict would be involved.

To report on their decisions and to receive further instructions from Comintern-Profintern sources, the newly elected secretary of the group, Kim Il-su, was dispatched to Vladivostok in October. There, he was told that all matters relating to the reconstruction of the Party in Korea would henceforth be handled by the Chinese Communist Party. There could no longer be any doubt that Korean Communism had been subordinated to the Chinese Party, whether activities took place in China-Manchuria or in Korea itself. In accordance with Comintern instructions, indeed, the Chinese Communist Party had already made administrative provision for this new responsibility. A Korean Internal Activities Committee had been established under the East Manchurian Special Committee of the CCP, the latter committee being headed by a Chinese named Huang.[84]

All of these facts were explained to the Hŭngnam group at another meeting held on December 25, 1930. This meeting, moreover, was attended by Chu Kŏn, previously head of the Preparatory Society in Manchuria, who now claimed to be an agent of the new Korean Internal Activities Committee. Chu Kŏn announced that he had come to survey conditions in Korea on the Committee's behalf. The Hŭngnam group decided that Kim Il-su should be sent to Chientao to establish personal contact with Huang, and to pledge support for the Comintern-Profintern programs. The trip was made in February 1931. From Huang, Kim got confirmation of the new administrative structure. He was also told that the East Manchurian

83. The meeting, attended by Yun Cha-yŏng, Kim Il-su (Kim Pyŏng-t'aek), O Sŏng-se, and Cho Tŏk-jin, took place at Pak Wŏn-jin's home in Hŭngnam. Kim Il-su was named secretary-in-charge, Yun head of Propaganda, Cho head of Organization, and O head of the Youth League. It was decided that, for organizational purposes, Korea would be divided into five regions, each region to be in charge of one of the small group. See *Chōsen kyōsantō saiken undō nado jiken hanketsu utsushi, op. cit.*, p. 31.

84. *Ibid.* In June 1930, the Comintern had instructed the Chinese Communist Party to restore liaison between the Japanese Communist Party and the Comintern, to reestablish the Formosan Communist Party, *and* to assist in the reconstruction of the Korean Communist Party. It was on the basis of this order that the CCP had instructed its Manchurian Provincial Executive Committee to undertake the reconstruction of the KCP. The Manchurian committee thereupon established the Korean Internal Activities Committee (*ibid.*, p. 30).

Special Committee was prepared to work only with Koreans who had "abandoned their factional way of thinking." Obviously there was to be some screening of participants in the movement.

On March 20, after Kim returned to Korea, another meeting was convened. In the course of lengthy discussions, the group decided to halt all efforts to reestablish the Party at this point, and concentrate instead upon "providing the Korean workers and peasants with Communist education and training." The main thrust was to be toward the creation of revolutionary labor and peasant unions. Clearly, this course of action had been recommended to Kim by Huang, and was regarded as the proper interpretation of Comintern policies. Thus, the group transformed itself into a Preparatory Society for a National Council of Left Trade Unions. The model was clearly Zenkyō in Japan. All of the old officers were retained, with Kim continuing to serve as secretary.

Using past contacts, the Hŭngnam group immediately started to get in touch with former Communists and Communist sympathizers throughout Korea.[85] Once planning began to be translated into action, however, the old problems reemerged. Japanese police discovered a scheme to distribute revolutionary leaflets on May Day, and those involved were quickly rounded up. One arrest led to another, and ultimately 245 persons were seized, of whom 79 were brought to trial. A few leaders remained at large briefly, but by the fall of 1931 the movement had been completely smashed.[86]

The next efforts that emanated from Manchuria bore the direct imprimatur of the Comintern. At its Fifteenth Plenum in May 1931, the Comintern had reportedly discussed the Korean situation yet again. Subsequently, it had ordered the Eastern Bureau in Khabarovsk to send some top Korean agents to Manchuria to stimulate activities in Korea proper. Presumably, these were to be men trained by the Russians to a level at which they would be above factional quarreling. About a dozen Koreans were dispatched from Khabarovsk; the most important was Yun Hae, a veteran who had started out in the Shanghai faction. It was decided that Yun should head a new Korean Liaison Department in Hunch'un, near the Korean border. The Korean Internal Activities Committee was now to come under the Department's direction.[87]

85. See *Shisō geppō, op. cit.*, Vol. 3, No. 1, pp. 19–21.
86. For details, see *Chōsen kyōsantō saiken undō, op. cit.*, which contains the trial statements of fifty-nine individuals (142 pp.). The figures concerning the incident are taken from *Shisō geppō, op. cit.*, Vol. 2, No. 6, Sept. 1932, p. 2373, *AJMFA*, R S357.
87. Consul-General Okada to Foreign Minister Shidehara, "On the Establishment of the KCP Liaison Department in Eastern Manchuria," *AJMFA*, R S374, F S9452, pp. 478–482. The officers of the Liaison Department named were Yun Hae (head), O Sŏng-rin, Pak Yun-sŏ, Ch'oe Il, and five others. Yun Hae was also reported to be the head of the Wangch'ing Prefectural Committee under the Eastern Manchuria Special Committee of the CCP in this report.

At this point, with the external supervisory bureaucracy becoming ever more complex, a new agent, Han Chŏn-jong, was sent into Korea in an effort to revive the movement. Han, whose revolutionary career paralleled that of many other young Communists, entered the country in November 1931, and was followed by a few others dispatched from the same source.[88] After five months' work, the new group had managed to reestablish a small number of Communist cells in Seoul, Hŭngnam, and P'yŏngyang. In April 1932, however, Japanese police uncovered the new movement and picked up the seventy-eight persons centrally involved.[89]

While the Manchuria-based Korean Communists were moving from failure to failure, a separate effort was being mounted from Shanghai. Here, as we noted earlier, operations were under the supervision of the veteran Communist, Kim Tan-ya. With the support of the Chinese Communist Party of his area, he sent a small number of agents into Korea with instructions to reach the workers and peasants with Communist literature. The first to go was Kim Hyŏng-sŏn, who arrived in Seoul in February 1931. An assistant, O Ki-man, was later dispatched, and Kim Hyŏng-sŏn's sister, Kim Myŏng-shi, one of the twenty-one students sent to Moscow in 1925 by the Communist Youth League in Seoul, also joined them with additional funds and instructions. The small unit from Shanghai made efforts to organize a Red union among the steel workers near P'yŏngyang; they also distributed Communist literature in Seoul, Inch'ŏn, and certain other cities. As usual, arrests were swift in coming. Kim Hyŏng-sŏn avoided the first roundup and fled back to Shanghai. After consultations with Kim Tan-ya, he returned to Korea in mid-1932. Following a year of largely fruitless efforts, he was arrested and given a lengthy prison sentence. At about the same time, Japanese police in Shanghai succeeded in smashing the organization there.[90]

If the Manchurian-based Koreans had failed, the Shanghai-based

88. Han became an activist while still a student at the Higher Agricultural and Forestry School in Suwon. Because of political activities, he was suspended from school. His family, rendered destitute because of a flood, later moved to Chientao. Han became a teacher and then managed a newspaper branch office. Afterward, he returned to South Hamgyŏng Province, where he worked as a clerk in a mine. In 1929 he started reading Communist literature and became acquainted with some of the Manchuria-based Korean Communists. In October 1931, he was invited by Chu Kŏn on behalf of the East Manchuria Special Committee of the CCP to undertake the Korean assignment.

89. For the trial statement of Han Chŏn-jong and others, see *Shisō ihō, op. cit.,* No. 1, pp. 19–33. See also Chōsen Sōtokufu, Keimukyoku (Government General of Korea, Police Affairs Bureau), *Manshū jihen ni taisuru hansen undō no gaikyō* (*Condition of the Anti-War Movement Against the Manchurian Incident*), mimeographed, Dec. 1932, in *AJMFA*, R S403, File S9452, F59–270.

This case was also known as the "Posŏng Higher Common School Student Anti-Imperialist Group Incident." Of the seventy-eight arrested, sixteen were convicted and sentenced from six months to four years in prison.

90. *Shina oyobi Manshū ni okeru kyōsan undō gaikyō, op. cit.,* p. 68.

Koreans had left an even slighter monument to their efforts. More success-ful was the Ko Kyŏng-hŭm group, operating from Japan. We have already noted the activities of this group in Tokyo; now let us look briefly at their efforts in Korea. On February 17, 1931, Ko, who had just returned from Peking, conferred briefly with a group of old colleagues from the M-L Group at a secret rendezvous in Kimp'o, near Seoul. The decision was made to establish a Korean Communist Party Reconstruction League, at the same time seeking to carry out current Comintern-Profintern policies. Kwon Tae-hyŏng was elected secretary.[91] Two months later, however, the group decided to disband the formal organization on the score that its existence would merely contribute to factional strife. What external or internal pressures may have led to this decision is unclear. In any case, this group like the others pledged itself to work for the development of revolutionary labor and peasant unions. To this end, a division of labor was established. Two teams were set up: Kwon Tae-hyŏng, Sŏ In-sik, and Ko Kyŏng-hŭm were to be concerned mainly with publications, and Yi Chŏng-rim, Kang Chin, and Kim Ki-sŏn with organizational activities.

This group, in the roughly two years during which it was operative, was able to make connections of a fairly significant nature, particularly with certain student and labor elements. It managed to penetrate Keijō Imperial University, and also to establish cells in several other schools of higher education in the Seoul area.[92] Despite some arrests in early 1932, these efforts continued, with agents going south to Taegu and Kwangju, the latter city the scene of the student demonstrations of 1929. In the same cities, strenuous efforts were made to develop revolutionary labor units, and these efforts bore some fruit.[93] In this connection, fairly sub-

91. Kwon was another typical Communist of the period. Once a student at Waseda University's Technical School, he had withdrawn from school in March 1926 after only one year of work. Subsequently, his background included affiliation with such "thought" and political groups as the January Society, the Shinhŭng Science Research Society, the Korean Youth League in Tokyo, and the Korean Labor Federation in Japan. For details, see "The Trial Statements of the Korean Communist Conference Incident," *Shisō geppō, op. cit.*, Vol. 3, No. 4, July 1933, pp. 11–21.

92. See "The Trial Statements of the Keijō Imperial University Anti-Imperialist League Incident," *ibid.*, Vol. 2, No. 9, Dec. 1932, pp. 2801–2855, *AJMFA*, R S357.

Yi Chŏng-rim managed to activate a student at Keijō University, Shin Hyŏn-jung; and via Shin, a Communist group including three Japanese students was formed on the campus. Contacts were also established with students at the Dental College and at the Second Higher Common School. Shin also directed a Red Friends Society, Chŏk-u-hoe, formed in August 1931 and involving various young men employed as office boys in government institutions, banks, and hospitals.

93. While Yi Chŏng-rim and Yi P'yŏng-san were directing student activities, other colleagues were engaged in separate organizational efforts. Despite some arrests in July 1931, a top-level meeting of Communists was held in the southern city of Taegu on July 25, 1931. The injunction against the establishment of a formal party was maintained, but, beginning in August, the group managed to issue two mimeo-

stantial publication activities were conducted, with some leaflets being printed in quantities up to 5,000. Branches of the Anti-Imperialist League were also planted in major urban centers. One Communist leader, Yi Mun-hong, had considerable success in developing Red peasant unions, especially in South Hamgyŏng Province.[94] Many of North Korea's first Communist leaders were to be Hamgyŏng men.

These achievements were not scored without heavy costs. Successive arrests finally sapped the strength of the Ko Kyŏng-hŭm group, and by the end of 1933 almost all of the key leaders had been removed from the scene. Several thousand students, workers, and farmers, however, had been reached effectively with the Communist message, and a network of organizations remained, at least in skeleton form, after the group's demise. There is little doubt that such success as was attained was a tribute in considerable part to the continued vitality of the old M-L Group, and the ties that it had retained within the country.

Yet another group sought to penetrate Korea from the outside during this period, namely, the men sent from Peking by Kim Won-bong and An Kwang-ch'ŏn. It was this group that was generally regarded as nationalist-Communist because of the unorthodox character of Kim. An, it will be recalled, had been the head of the January Society in Tokyo, and later the secretary of the third Korean Communist Party. In exile in China, he had first met Kim Won-bong in Shanghai. Later, they had moved to Peking, where they established their own League for the Reconstruction of the Korean Communist Party with An as head. Kim, of course, had long been the leader of the Uiyŏldan and, as will be remembered, had established his training school first in Peking, then in Nanking.

From August 1930 onward Kim's graduates started returning to Korea. In the fall of 1932, a few of them started meeting regularly, together with a handful of new recruits. Some division of labor was attempted: Yi Chin-il accepted responsibility for Seoul intellectuals, Yi Kang-myŏng for the urban workers of that area, and Chŏng Tong-won for the farmers of North Chŏlla Province. The government reported in 1934 that the Peking group had also established contacts among workers and students in Sinŭiju, Wonsan, and Taegu. In the end, some 130 individuals were arrested who had supposedly been indoctrinated by Kim's men. This was certainly a modest result for the labors of three years.

In addition to the infiltrators from these diverse exile posts, a number

---

graphed journals, *The Communist* and *The Beacon*, in quantities of 100 to 200 copies. Two labor journals were also published, and in Taegu itself a Taegu Conference for the Establishment of a Red Labor Union was formed. Activities, mainly in the union field, were extended to Kwangju and Pusan. Thus, by the end of 1931, Communist activities existed in most of the major urban centers of Korea, but on an extremely small scale, cell memberships rarely being more than ten to fifteen.

94. See *Shisō ihō, op. cit.,* No. 4, pp. 32–54.

of agents were being dispatched directly to Korea from the Soviet Union. Since they carried instructions and credentials from either the Comintern or the Profintern, another element was added to an already complicated and confused picture. The Comintern-Profintern authorities not only made no effort most of the time to coordinate their agents with those coming from Chinese or Japanese bases, but often failed to give their own agents information about each other. No doubt, this was done primarily for security reasons, but it made the situation hopelessly confused. In some respects, however, agents from the Soviet Union were more successful than those from elsewhere. Their activities, therefore, deserve at least brief notice.

Japanese sources report that the Comintern and Profintern sent eighteen agents into Korea between 1930 and 1935.[95] It is quite possible that the actual number was larger. Almost all of the men sent directly from the Soviet Union were graduates of the Communist University of the Toilers of the East in Moscow. Korea thus had its "returned students era" during this period, just as did China and Japan. Most of these young men, moreover, had had earlier careers as activists either in Korea or in Manchuria before going to Russia.[96]

For the most part, these were Profintern men, and their efforts were directed chiefly toward urban workers, particularly in the northern centers of Hŭngnam, Hamhŭng, and P'yŏngyang. Once again, as a result of Japanese prosecutions, we have extensive records on some of the agents. One incident may be related briefly here, both for its own sake and because it illustrates certain common factors relating to the activities of Soviet-based agents.[97] This case, known as the Pan-Pacific Trade Union case, involved

95. The breakdown for such agents, based upon Japanese intelligence reports, was annually as follows:

	1930	1931	1932	1933	1934	1935	Total
Comintern	—	2	—	2	1	2	7
Profintern	1	—	7	1	1	1	11

96. For the training program and other conditions at the Communist University in Moscow, see a report filed by the Chief of the Police Affairs Bureau, Korean Government-General, "Concerning the Return of Graduates of the International Communist University to Korea," Dec. 28, 1928. This report is based upon the interrogation of two graduates of the University, Chŏng Il-u (Chŏng Sŏk-haeng) and Kim Sŏk-yŏn (Kim To-yŏp), *AJMFA,* R S722.

97. For details, see "The Judicial Decision Concerning the Korean Nitrogen Fertilizer Plant Red Labor Union Incident," *Shisō geppō, op. cit.,* Vol. 3, No. 1, April 1933, pp. 11–29, *AJMFA,* R S358.

The Pan-Pacific Labor Union Secretariat was established in Hankow, China, in May 1927. Through it, the Communists hoped to direct the labor movement in East Asia. After the split between the Kuomintang and the CCP, the secretariat was moved to Shanghai. It was initially headed by Earl Browder, who was also Profintern representative in China. See Ministry of Foreign Affairs, Consulate General in Shanghai,

three Koreans as central participants: Kim Ho-ban, Han Pyŏng-ryu, and Chang Hoe-gŏn. Kim, the key figure, was a Russianized Korean. Since childhood, he had lived in Vladivostok and had received his primary education there. He had come to Communism as a member of a Soviet labor union. This in turn had led him to the Communist University of the Toilers of the East in Moscow. But after one year, he had been expelled on the charge that he had participated in factional struggles. This was in 1925. In June 1928, however, he had joined the Soviet Communist Party in Vladivostok, and in the fall of that year he had been readmitted to the University. After graduating in March 1930, Kim had been dispatched for service to the Vladivostok branch of the Pan-Pacific Trade Union.

As one of his activities, he sent Yi Ri-gyu to Korea to choose two delegates who could represent Korea at the Fifth Profintern Congress to be held in Moscow between August 15 and 30, 1930. Han Pyŏng-ryu and Chang Hoe-gŏn were chosen. Han had been chairman of the Hamhŭng Labor Federation and very active in the labor movement generally. Chang had studied in Tokyo for four years; he subsequently worked as a newspaper reporter and served as an official in the Hamhŭng branch of Shinganhoe. Together with Kim Ho-ban, these two men attended the Profintern Congress, took part in formulating the theses of September 1930, and then returned to Vladivostok in October. There the three held lengthy strategy meetings with Profintern officials, and finally the three, together with Yi Ri-gyu, reentered Korea.

In their subsequent operations, this group showed a high level of sophistication. They aimed at the capture of existing urban and prefectural labor organizations by working on key individuals and by planting cells within the union structure. The first objective was to capture the Hamhŭng Labor Federation. After attracting an important recruit, Yi Chu-ha, the group also penetrated various unions in the P'yŏngyang Labor Federation.[98] Substantial progress was being made when the first arrests took place, in May and June 1931. Chang escaped detection, and continued to supervise

---

Chūnanshi chihō kyōsantō oyobi kyōsanhi kōdō jōkyō ni kansuru chōsa hōkokusho (*Investigation Report on the Activities of the Communist Party and Communist Bandits in South-Central China*), Dec. 1930, p. 145, *AJMFA*, R S55.

98. Initially, activities centered upon the Hŭngnam fertilizer plant, where a "study committee" was organized among the workers. On Jan. 25, 1931, this committee was reorganized into a "Preparatory Society for the Formation of a Left-Wing Labor Union," with one of the plant workers, Kim In-dŏk, selected as chairman. This group in turn was absorbed into the larger Hamhŭng Committee. Meanwhile, Yi Chu-ha, who was to become very prominent in North Korea after World War II, was assigned by Kim Ho-ban the task of surveying prospects for Red union activities in the major cities. Through Chŏng Tal-hŏn in P'yŏngyang, he got in touch with Han Chŏng-yu, an officer of the P'yŏngyang Labor Federation and the P'yŏngyang Transport Workers' Union. They then organized a committee of a type similar to those in Hamhŭng and Hŭngman. See *Shisō geppō, op. cit.*, pp. 22–25.

work in Hŭngnam and P'yŏngyang until his arrest in mid-1932. He, in turn, was succeeded by another returned student, Pak Se-yŏng, who continued operations until his arrest in late 1933.[99]

No more than two hundred individuals were considered sufficiently tainted by these operations to be arrested. But it would be wrong to dismiss the Kim-Han-Chang apparatus as worthless to the Communists. A nucleus of militant workers had been created upon whom, in many cases, the movement could call later. Yi Chu-ha, as we shall note, was but one example. Moreover, the fact that the major contacts were made mainly in the industrial centers of north Korea carried a significance beyond the actual numbers involved. Similarly, the fact that these contacts bore the direct imprint of Soviet guidance, and, in the case of agents like Kim Ho-ban, involved more or less Russianized individuals, also had vital implications for the future.

Agents from the Soviet Union, while they stressed the labor movement, did not neglect the students and intellectuals. Indeed, the Communist cause célèbre of this period in Korea was the discovery that a Japanese professor at Keijō Imperial University, Miyake Shikanosuke, had become involved in sheltering a young Profintern agent. In Korean intellectual and official circles, the Miyake Incident created a major sensation, scarcely less than the case of Kawakami Hajime in Japan.[100]

However, whether the targets were industrial workers or the student-intellectual group, the Communist attempt to mobilize urban forces in Korea during this period was fraught with difficulty. In addition to the extraordinary effectiveness of a Japanese-style police-state, the tightly knit structure of Korean society itself presented the Communists with a major

99. Pak was a man of "pure proletariat" origins, albeit from the proletarian elite. He had been a printer in Seoul since the age of 18, and had been a member of various printers' unions. In 1928, he joined the Communist movement, receiving guidance from the veteran Communist Chŏng Chae-dal. In September 1929, on Chŏng's recommendation, he went to the Soviet Union, took a "short-term course" at the University of the Toilers of the East, and graduated in June 1931. He then received his instructions about Korea from one Grigorii Pak in the Vladivostok office of the Profintern. See *Shisō ihō, op. cit.*, No. 1, pp. 54–55.

100. For the Miyake case and its various ramifications, see *ibid.*, No. 4, pp. 59–68.

In a roundtable discussion published in *Chōsen Kenkyū (Korean Studies)* in August 1966 (a pro-DPRK journal emanating from Tokyo), Miyake claimed that at the time of his arrest he was not involved in the Korean Communist movement. But he admitted that while he had been a student in Berlin previously, he had observed the activities of the German Communist Party and collected Marxist and Leninist books. Miyake also claimed that Yi Chae-yu was a total stranger to him— and merely ran to his house asking for a hiding place, saying that he was being pursued by the police. (Presumably Yi regarded Miyake as sympathetic toward the Left.) Miyake and his wife hid Yi under the floor and then arranged for one of Miyake's students to bring clothing for his disguise. After a trial, Miyake was sentenced to two years in prison (p. 7).

problem they could never solve. It was a problem with many facets. Political recruitment rarely occurred on an individual basis, because each individual functioned only through his reference groups. Commitment, therefore, could be obtained only in terms of family, school, regional, and occupational ties. To be sure, this was often a source of considerable strength for the movement. At the same time, however, it frequently made detection easier, and could lead to group desertions as well as group conversions. The movement was, after all, illegal. More importantly, political commitment of any type other than that involving a purely cultural-ethnic reaction implicitly involved a basic challenge to the entire complex of behavioral patterns, and hence could be made firm only as these patterns were altered or dissolved.

Was this also true of the peasant? One of the most intriguing and least explored issues of modern Asian politics lies precisely here. At first glance, it might be assumed that the high quotient of traditionalism—usually denoted as conservatism—involved in Asian peasant culture provides the answer, and that further inquiry is unnecessary. On closer examination, however, it will be discovered that rural traditionalism was not conservative in all of its manifestations, especially the political ones. Moreover, rural traditionalism encompassed forms of organization that quite possibly had a greater potential for mobilization than existed in the urban, modernized sectors of the society where much was new, fragmented, and lacking in social cohesion. In short, the peasant culture had a political heritage that had not only remained largely intact but was capable of interacting with certain forms of modernity. From time immemorial, the Asian peasant had petitioned for tax reduction in times of distress, rioted—in large groups—when problems of usury or landlordism got out of hand, and developed techniques of self-defense, even offense on occasion, against marauders. In many respects, moreover, the peasants—collectively—had always been at war with the state, seeking to avoid its exactions and escape its impressments. In all of this there was a revolutionary potential, and it is somewhat startling that social scientists have largely ignored this fact. Certainly, the Communists ignored it until circumstances gave them little alternative.

In considerable measure, events during this period in Korea, as in China, bear out this view of peasant culture. Both in numbers, and in qualitative terms the Red peasant movement of this period was more significant than Communist penetrations elsewhere. In the decade beginning 1926, nearly 18,000 Koreans were arrested in connection with subversive activities, and over 5,000 of those were prosecuted, with the high point for both arrests and prosecutions being reached in 1932 (see table 19). A small number of these cases involved conservative and moderate nationalists, but the great bulk of them referred to the Communist efforts that we have discussed. Unfortunately, our Japanese sources do not provide convenient occupational breakdowns of those arrested and prosecuted. It is

TABLE 19
Persons Arrested and Prosecuted in Korea
for Violations of the Security Maintenance Law

Year	Arrested		Prosecuted	
	Cases	Persons	Cases	Persons
1926	45	356	27	157
1927	48	279	32	135
1928	168	1,415	98	494
1929	206	1,271	106	443
1930	252	2,661	140	690
1931	180	1,708	99	651
1932	254	4,381	159	1,011
1933	205	2,007	115	539
1934	145	2,065	84	518
1935	135	1,478	76	437
TOTAL	1,638	17,621	936	5,075
Japanese not included above	21	89	18	33
Chinese	—	3	—	—

SOURCE: *Shisō ihō*, No. 8, pp. 58–60.

possible, however, to compile partial data on this, and the evidence indicates that, despite the intensive Communist efforts to organize urban workers and students, peasants accounted for a significant number of those involved.

In the period between March 1931 and July 1932 alone, some 950 individuals were arrested in connection with the Red peasant movement. Of equal significance, perhaps, is the fact that 819, or 86 percent, of these were from North and South Hamgyŏng provinces in northern Korea. North Hamgyŏng Province bordered both the Soviet Union and Chientao Province in Manchuria; South Hamgyŏng also bordered Manchuria, and in its border areas contained some wild, mountainous country. These were areas that, historically, had often created problems for governments. The Japanese complained that the people of this region were "violent and unruly" in character, fiercely nationalistic, and resistant to authority. In truth, these areas, where living was hard and dangerous and the central government only a distant rumor, had undoubtedly bred a militant political subculture.

Trouble erupted again on an even larger scale in the 1935–36 period. Once more, "outside agitators" were involved—returned students like Hyŏn Ch'un-bong, another Profintern agent and Communist University graduate.[101] What alarmed authorities, however, was the ease with which the Red peasant movement could be generated, and its capacity to maintain itself even when some or most of its leadership was removed. The authorities, indeed, found themselves confronted with a formidable and sophisticated

101. For details on Hyŏn's life and activities, see *ibid.*, No. 7, pp. 246–278.

organizational structure. Youngsters of no more than eleven years of age spied on police stations. Informers were planted within government "self-defense" units. Massive underground hideouts and caves were used to store provisions. In short, all of the peasants' traditional cunning and lore were being harnessed to a new political cause.

In only six months during the 1935–36 period, 1,043 persons were arrested in connection with the Red peasant problem in the Hamgyŏng provinces, and an additional 228 were arrested in 1937. So seriously did Japanese authorities view the situation that in late 1936 they began a crash program in the region aimed at stemming the tide. A special committee was established in charge of "thought purification." Amnesty was promised to Communists surrendering voluntarily, and special programs were developed for the guidance of ex-Communists. In addition, large numbers of young men were put in "self-defense" units that also served as indoctrination programs. Some six hundred lecture meetings were held between December 1936 and March 1937; they were attended by nearly 50,000 Koreans in the area. This general program had earlier been pursued with some success in Manchuria, where a similar problem had been faced.

In general, the Japanese were satisfied with the results. By 1937, when the second China Incident began, the Communist movement within Korea was again at a low ebb. Almost all prominent Communists were imprisoned, in exile, or totally silent. Indeed, Korea was one of the few countries in the world where the major changes signaled by the Seventh Comintern Congress had virtually no impact. The new call for an anti-Fascist united front with bourgeois nationalist forces had little meaning in the Korean context. A small band of surviving Korean Communists, notably Yi Kang-guk and Yi Chu-ha, appear to have distributed the Comintern's theses of 1935; at any rate, a translation was prepared in 1937.[102] Yi Chu-ha was currently seeking to revitalize Red unions in the Wŏnsan area. One other development warrants notice. Yi Kwan-sol, a friend of Yi Chae-yu, who was the central figure in the Miyake episode, started a Communist group in 1937 with the cooperation of his sister. Some of the participants, such as Kim Sam-yong, who was enlisted as principal organizer, and Pak Hŏn-yŏng, who was made the leader upon his release from prison, were to figure prominently in later events. The group ultimately recruited elements from most of the old factions, including the Tuesday Society, M-L, and Shanghai groups.[103] Eventually, however, this movement too fell under the

102. For details, see *ibid.*, No. 14, pp. 48–49.
103. The number of those arrested for subversive activities in Korea in 1937 was 228.

For details, see *Kongsan chu-ui yiron kwa hyŏnsil pip'an chŏnsŏ*, Vol. 5, *Hanguk ui kongsan chu-ui wa Puk-Han ui yŏksa* (*A Critique of Communist Theory and Reality*, Vol. 5, *Communism in Korea and the History of North Korea*), Seoul, 1955, pp. 79–81 (this volume was written by Han Chae-dŏk). See also Hong T'ae-sik, *Hanguk kongsan chu-ui undong yŏngu wa pip'an* (*A Study and Criticism of the Communist Movement in Korea*), Seoul, 1969, pp. 446–447.

ɔws of the Japanese police. Certain arrests occurred in Seoul in December 1940. Other leaders were picked up in the Hamgyŏng provinces in June 1941 and, by October–December of that year, the entire operation had been eliminated.

As World War II approached, however, the only "subversive" activities of any basic concern to Japanese authorities were the attacks by armed "Red bandits" from Manchuria upon Korean border towns. Thus, the Hesanjin Incident of 1937—where Kim Il-sŏng figures prominently in Japanese annals for the first time—was described by a Japanese prosecutor as having "shocked" the entire Korean peninsula. It remains, therefore, to look more closely at these so-called Red bandits, and in particular at one of the young men among them who was destined to rise to power.

The Emergence of Kim Il-sŏng

For North Korea, the 1960s and early 1970s were a Stalinist era during which the cult of personality was advanced to extraordinary heights. Thus, if we rely upon North Korean sources, it is extremely difficult to separate fact from fantasy with respect to Kim Il-sŏng's past. Fortunately, prewar Japanese sources are of assistance at several crucial points, although these sources, voluminous as they are, contain very few direct references to Kim, especially for the period before 1937. The first skimpy (and inaccurate) biography of Kim in Japanese files appears to be the following: "Kim Il-sŏng: Age—30. Origin—Korea. Family whereabouts—unknown. Background—farmer. Has engaged in farming before turning to banditry as a result of Communist propaganda." [104]

This report, dated 1938, is of little help, especially since the entries on Kim's age and occupation are both incorrect. The Japanese were to acquire more information on Kim after this period, but never the details they accumulated on all "important" Communists, and many unimportant ones as well. Why? First, Kim was never captured and therefore not subjected to the type of intensive grilling that generally yielded data in abundance. Many of his close associates were arrested, however, and at least some of them told the Japanese what they knew.

Initially, the Japanese did not regard Kim as significant, and that affected his dossier. After 1937, however, he began to receive considerable publicity, with the Korean-Japanese press ascribing a number of raids or incidents on the Manchurian border to the "Kim Il-sŏng bandits." Since Kim was a shadowy figure to Japanese authorities, his exploits tended to

---

104. Prosecutor Okamoto Goichi, "Manshū ni okeru Chūgoku kyōsantō to kyōsanhi" ("The Chinese Communist Party and the Communist Bandits in Manchuria"), *Shisō jōsei shisatsu hōkokushū* (*Reports of Inspections on the Ideological Situation*), No. 4, Japanese Ministry of Justice, Bureau of Criminal Affairs, Special Series No. 41, 1938.

be exaggerated with a number of crimes assigned to him. After the death of Yang Ching-yü in February 1940, indeed, Kim may have been considered the most significant guerrilla in the Manchurian hinterland. Very soon, however, with Kim's retreat into Siberia, the Japanese considered this problem eliminated. It is doubtful, moreover, whether Japanese authorities ever considered Kim as comparable in significance to such "dangerous radicals" as Kim Won-bong, An Kwang-ch'on, Kim Tan-ya, Kim Sang-sŏn, or Yi Sang-mok on the political front, or Mu Chŏng and Chu Chin on the China-Manchuria military front. To be sure, by 1937 a number of these men, though by no means all of them, were dead, in prison, or had recanted. Kim, along with a handful of competitors, real or potential, *survived,* and in the annals of any turbulent, revolutionary era that single fact is of supreme importance. In the meantime, however, what was the real role of this young man before 1945?

We now know much about Kim's earlier years.[105] He was born Kim Sŏng-ju on April 15, 1912, at the home of his mother's parents near P'yŏngyang, in what is now Ch'ilgol-dong, Mankyŏngdae District. Officially, Kim is described as having come from a "poor peasant background." It would probably be more accurate to describe his immediate family as "lower middle class," although they appear to have had serious economic problems at various times. His father, Kim Hyŏng-jik, was himself from a large peasant family. His mother, born Kang Pan-sŏk, was the second

105. In the years since 1945, various officially sponsored biographies of Kim Il-sŏng have appeared in North Korea. One of the earliest was prepared by the Propaganda and Agitation Department, Central Committee, Korean Workers' Party, entitled *Kim Il-sŏng changgun ui yakjŏn* (*A Short Biography of General Kim Il-sŏng*), P'yŏngyang, 1952 (Hak-u Sŏbang reprint edition, Tokyo, 1954). In the period immediately following the Liberation, eulogistic stories about Kim were written by Han Chae-dŏk. Kim's first official biographer, however, is generally considered to have been Han Sŏl-ya; an English translation of one of Han's works was published on the occasion of Kim's fiftieth birthday: Han Sul Ya, *Hero General Kim Il Sung,* Tokyo, 1962. Han's being purged, therefore, presented a particular embarrassment to Kim and the regime. Undoubtedly, this speeded the preparation of the most detailed biography to date: Paek Pong, *Minjok ui t'aeyang Kim Il-sŏng changgun* (*General Kim Il-sŏng the Sun of the Nation*), P'yŏngyang, 1968. A three-volume English edition of this work has now been published with great fanfare, including a full-page advertisement in the *New York Times* and other major world newspapers: Baik Bong, *Kim Il Sung: Biography,* Tokyo, 1969–70.

Extensive materials on Kim's career are to be found also in more general works published in North Korea. Among the more significant that should be listed: Chosŏn Yoksa P'yŏnch'an Wiwon-hoe (Korean History Editorial Committee), ed., *Chōsen minzoku kaihō tōsō shi* (*A History of the Korean People's Struggle for Emancipation*), Kyoto, 1952 (Japanese translation of a P'yŏngyang original); Yi Na-yŏng, *Chosŏn minjok haebang t'ujaengsa* (*A History of the Korean People's Struggle for Emancipation*), P'yŏngyang, 1958 (Hak-u Sŏbang reprint edition, Tokyo, 1960); and the Center for Historical Studies, Academy of Science, *Chosŏn t'ongsa* (*An Outline History of Korea*), P'yŏngyang, 1958, 3 vols. (Hak-u Sŏbang reprint edition, Tokyo, 1959, 3 vols.).

daughter of a village schoolmaster, a man who had established the Ch'angdŏk School in his home village of Ch'ilgol.

The precise economic status of the Kim Hyŏng-jik family is unclear. According to Yi Ki-gŏn, Kim's father, earlier a primary school teacher, at one point operated a small Chinese medicine shop in Pataokou, on the Manchurian side of the Yalu River.[106] There can be little doubt, however, that the antecedents of Kim's activism lay more in political than in economic concerns. His family definitely had strong nationalist, anti-Japanese proclivities. Like thousands of others, his father participated in the nationalist activities of the 1917–19 period, and as a result was jailed briefly. The family went to Manchuria for the first time in 1919, after Kim Hyŏng-jik had been released from jail; and young Kim attended primary school in Pataokou. He later returned to Korea alone and studied at the school founded by his grandfather. In 1924 his father, having come back to Korea, got into trouble again over political activities and, with his family, he then moved to Manchuria permanently. Both parents died at a relatively early age.[107]

106. Chong-Sik Lee interview with Yi Ki-gŏn, Oct. 7, 1969, Seoul.

107. Kim's father died on June 5, 1926, at the age of 32. Official Communist sources later stated that death resulted from the combination of an injury received in prison and fatigue suffered from lengthy involvement in the nationalist struggle. His mother died in 1932 at the age of 40. Thus, by the time he was 20 Kim had lost both of his parents.

Despite current Party eulogies, it is not clear precisely how involved Kim's parents were in the nationalist cause. Relatively little attention was paid to them until the late 1960s, when suddenly KWP publications began to feature both his father and mother as heroes of the anti-Japanese nationalist movement.

Typical is a *P'yŏngyang Times* article of June 13, 1968, entitled "Mr. Kim Hyŏng-jik Is Indomitable Anti-Japanese Revolutionary Fighter." The article states that Kim's father attended Sungsil Middle School in P'yŏngyang, a missionary school. There, he allegedly led a general strike against "the villainous US missionary who exploited the labor of the students under the signboard of 'charity,' in league with Japanese imperialism." Because of the perfidious actions of the Americans, *and*—it is admitted—because of lack of funds also, he left middle school at the halfway point and became "a professional revolutionary," meanwhile teaching at the Sunhwa primary school and the Myŏngshin school.

Reportedly, on March 23, 1917, the elder Kim organized the Korean National Association, and in the autumn of 1917, together with over a hundred other patriots, he was arrested. After his release, he supposedly shifted the theater of his activities to the border areas along the Yalu River, "rallying the Korean people for anti-Japanese, patriotic pursuits." In this account, there is no mention of Kim Hyŏng-jik having ever been a farmer, or of any other occupation other than primary-school teacher and herb doctor. Thus, he would fit our category of petty intellectual, a category so prominent in the annals of the Korean and other Communist movements.

Naturally, it must be assumed that Kim Hyŏng-jik's political role is now being grossly exaggerated, although it would appear that he was indeed a Korean nationalist who paid the price of brief imprisonment on one occasion for his activities.

The current claims on behalf of Kim Il-sŏng's mother also border on the sensational. It is even asserted that she transported guns for her son at one point. We

Kim attended Yuwen Middle School in Kirin between 1927 and 1929, dropping out of school before graduation. He reportedly began to read socialist literature even before he enrolled in middle school and is supposed to have "organized" the Kirin Communist Youth League in 1927, when he was fifteen. Two years later he was arrested by the Chinese authorities and served a brief prison term, being released in 1930.[108] Incidentally, this

---

do know that a maternal uncle, Kang Chin-sŏk, was deeply involved in anti-Japanese activities and died in prison after thirteen years' incarceration. It appears that politically he was the most involved of Kim's relatives. Even Kim's grandfather, however, is now given credit for being "an ardent patriot who fought for the independence of the fatherland, a pioneer who reared his children into fine anti-Japanese fighters and an energetic educationalist."

For the official North Korean accounts of Kim's family, see Nam Hyo-jae, *Chosŏn ui ŏmŏni* (*Mother of Korea*), P'yŏngyang, 1968; Korean Workers' Party, Central Committee, Party History Study Center, *Pulgul ui pan-Il hyŏngmyŏng t'usa Kim Hyŏng-jik sŏnsaeng* (*Mister Kim Hyŏng-jik, the Indomitable Anti-Japanese Revolutionary Fighter*), Tokyo, 1969; Song Sŭng-ch'il, *Chosŏn inmin ui widaehan suryŏng Kim Il-sŏng tongji ui hyŏngmyŏngjŏk kajŏng* (*The Revolutionary Family of Comrade Kim Il-sŏng, the Great Leader of the Korean People*), P'yŏngyang, 1969; and Baik Bong, *op. cit.*, Vol. I, pp. 19–39.

108. According to Kim's latest official biography, "The General" first discovered books on socialism in the home of a friend of his father, at Hwatien. Imbued with new knowledge, he formed an illegal organization, the Down with Imperialism Union. However, since he could not obtain the facilities for further study and organizational activities in Hwatien *hsien,* he moved to Kirin. He was then 15 years of age. (In point of fact, he appears to have gone to Kirin to enter middle school.)

An intriguing account of Kim's earliest political activities is contained in a rare work published in Seoul in December 1945. According to the author, in 1926 Kim, imbued with strong nationalist sentiments, was a leader of the "boys' movement" in Kirin at a time when such men as Kim Ch'an of the Tuesday faction, Shin Il-yong of the Seoul faction, and Ku Cha-yŏng of the Shanghai faction were seeking to create a socialist united front. Influenced by these efforts, Kim reportedly quit middle school and commenced political activities, making contact with other young men interested in the construction of a new society. "Rejecting both left-wing infantilism and right-wing opportunism," he "organized the T.D.," a Korean branch of the Anti-Imperialism League and also participated in the formation of the Kŏnsŏl Tongjisa, Comrades' Society for Construction.

According to this account, however, Kim continued to have a strong interest in achieving an education despite his political activities. Consequently, he "entrusted his duties to other comrades" and made preparations to go to Moscow to attend the Communist University of the Toilers of the East. However, while he was in Harbin busily acquiring funds for the trip and undertaking the necessary paper work, "problems developed due to the misdeeds of some of his friends." He was thus forced to abandon his plans and return to Fusung with a Chinese friend, Chang Ya-ch'ing.

The above account is contained in the booklet by Ch'oe Hyŏng-u, *Chosŏn hyŏngmyŏng undong sosa* (*A Short History of the Korean Revolutionary Movement*), Seoul, 1945. Pages 28–31 deal with Kim Il-sŏng. The author is strongly laudatory of Kim, but he is equally laudatory of various "rightist" nationalists. We are unable to judge the accuracy of the report on Kim, but the author's general knowledge of pre-1945 nationalist activities is substantial. It is interesting, moreover, to note that

appears to be the only time in his career when he was imprisoned; he was one of the few Korean Communist leaders never captured by the Japanese. After his release, Kim moved to a rural area about forty kilometers from Ch'angch'un and established residence in Kuchiat'un (Kut'un), a small Korean community that had had a history of Communist activities. There, he and others sought to strengthen Communist front organizations among youth, women, and peasants. Reportedly, Kim and his comrades published a magazine, *Bolshevik,* and established a training school that held both political and military courses. From this center, a small armed band was sent to a hamlet in Pongsan Prefecture, South Hamgyŏng Province, in August 1930, where they attacked a police substation. The venture accomplished nothing, and the leader was captured and sentenced to fifteen years' imprisonment.

Early in 1931, Kim headed for Tunhwa hsien with a tiny band of guerrillas. According to Han Sŏl-ya's account, at this point he also assumed the post of secretary of the Special Committee of the East Manchurian Young Communist League. Han also says that he joined the Communist Party in October of the same year.[109] Ordinarily, a young Korean of nineteen would not have been made secretary of the Communist Youth League for the very important East Manchurian region, and indeed Paek Pong, Kim's later biographer, does not mention Kim as having held this position. Nor does he mention Kim's admission to Party membership in October 1931.

pages 83 and 121 of Baik Bong's *Kim Il Sung* (Vol. I) have a photo of this booklet, and the booklet is quoted on pages 82 and 122.

His current biographer indicates that the "progressive" teachers at the Yuwen Middle School, and the reading material available, had a substantial impact in advancing Kim's knowledge of Marxism-Leninism, and that he even read *Das Kapital* during this period. (Surely an international record, reading *Das Kapital* at the age of 15!)

Reportedly, Kim organized the Saenal (New Day) Juvenile Union in Fusung in the winter of 1926. Shortly after his arrival in Kirin, in the spring of 1927, he organized the Association of Korean Juveniles there, and in the summer of 1927, he assumed leadership of the Korean Ryugil Association of Korean Students, a nationalist group that he allegedly turned toward Communism. Meanwhile, he also had gotten together with his old associates from Hwatien, and they had renamed the Down with Imperialism Union the "Anti-Imperialist Youth League." This "secret organization" supposedly spread anti-Japanese, patriotic thought, primarily through various Korean schools.

In line with united front policies, the above organizations were brought under the control of the Young Communist League of Korea which Kim supposedly formed in Kirin in the summer of 1927. No clue is given as to young Kim's associates, political mentors, and superiors during this period. For details, see Baik Bong, *op. cit.,* Vol. I, pp. 69–86 and So Gum I, "Historic Turn in Development of Communist Youth Movement in Our Country," *The Pyongyang Times,* reprinted in *TPK,* Febr. 2, 1972, p. 2.

109. Han Sul Ya, *op. cit.,* p. 4.

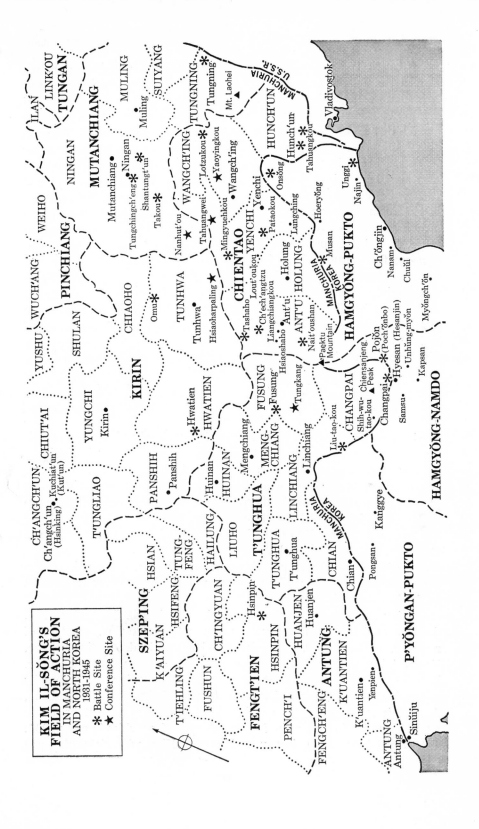

KIM IL-SŎNG'S
FIELD OF ACTION
IN MANCHURIA
AND NORTH KOREA
1931–1945
* Battle Site
★ Conference Site

Here, it is wise to recall the general situation with respect to the Korean Communist movement in Manchuria during this era. In 1926, when Kim first became affiliated with the Communist movement, Korean Communism in Manchuria was largely under the control of the Tuesday Society faction. By mid-1930, however, all Korean Communist organizations in this area had more or less voluntarily disbanded, and the Chinese Communist Party had been given complete control over the movement. Thus, young Kim must have joined the Chinese Communist Party, and worked under Chinese Communist direction. To omit Kim's advance to Party membership in 1931, therefore, can only be interpreted as an attempt to expurgate all mention of Kim's early ties with the Chinese Communist Party; the purpose is clearly to build up Kim as a genuine, all-Korean hero, rather than as someone first nurtured by a foreign Party. One can read the entire first volume of the 1968 biography, a volume that deals extensively with the Communist movement in Manchuria, and not find in it a single direct reference to the Chinese Communist Party. The effort is to convey the impression that Kim organized and led an entirely independent group. Never is there a mention of Kim's superiors, or of the chain of command under which he operated. As we shall see, however, there are oblique, highly critical references to all other Communist elements, with charges of left-wing errors (Li Li-sanism), sectarianism, and "great-power chauvinism" sprinkled throughout the text.

Whether Kim actually held the top secretarial post in the East Manchurian Youth Communist League in 1931 is doubtful. It is true, of course, that the great preponderance of Communists in east Manchuria continued to be Koreans, and also that this was a period when the movement was in a state of complete chaos, with thousands of veteran Communists being arrested, purged from within the ranks, or frightened into silence or recantation. It is possible, therefore, that key positions, especially in the Youth League, were given to individuals of Kim's age and experience at this point. The fact that Paek Pong does not mention it, however, suggests that the Han account was probably inaccurate unless, once again, it was deemed unwise to connect Kim so closely with the Manchurian Communist establishment at this time.

After the outbreak of the Manchurian Incident in September 1931, the Communists were under great pressure to undertake some type of response. In November, a ten-day meeting was held at Mingyuehkou, Yenchi hsien, to discuss the problem of organizing armed partisan units. Kim, then 19 and a Party member of one month's standing, was reportedly assigned the task of organizing such units in Tashaho and Hsiaoshaho, Ant'u hsien. Following this meeting, Kim left the movement briefly to attend to family matters, returning to underground activities in early 1932. The official biographies, however, claim that Kim, with eighteen young fighters, proclaimed the formation of the Anti-Japanese Guerrilla Army in Ant'u on April 25, 1932.[110]

Whatever one may term the young band of guerrillas, mainly students, who gathered around Kim at this point, it is probably appropriate to mark the beginning of Kim's guerrilla career from the spring of 1932 in the hinterland of Ant'u. It will be recalled that although the Li Li-san era was over at this point, the Chinese Communist line continued to be "left," with an emphasis upon the establishment of soviet districts, land confiscation and distribution to "the poor peasants," and ruthless measures against all "imperialists" and their "running dogs." It will also be remembered that, in the fall of 1932, the Korean Communists of East Manchuria had organized five soviet districts in Yenchi, Wangch'ing, and Hunch'un hsien in accordance with these instructions.

These soviet districts were northeast of Ant'u hsien, where Kim had begun his activities. In Ant'u, meanwhile, one of Kim's first efforts was to win the support, or at least the tolerance, of the Chinese National Salvation Army, an army composed of Chinese Nationalist units that fought the Japanese from time to time (they had also fought the Communists). In addition, it tended to be anti-Korean because of the large number of Koreans who worked closely with the Japanese in Manchuria. Kim reportedly began his mission by calling upon one Commander Wei in Ant'u with three or four of his comrades. Supposedly, the twenty-year-old Kim "profoundly moved" Wei in the course of a series of discussions, and the young guerrillas were given permission to operate freely in areas controlled by Wei's units. Kim also sought unsuccessfully during this period to link his minuscule band with Yang Sŏ-bong's Korean Revolutionary Army units, currently active in south Manchuria.

In September 1932, at a meeting in Liangchiangkou (east Manchuria), various Korean guerrilla leaders discussed the issue of a joint struggle with the National Salvation Army versus going it alone. Reportedly, Kim attended this meeting and strongly urged joint action—understandably, since

110. For an earlier account of this period, see *Hang-Il mujang t'ujaeng chŏn-jŏkchi rŭl ch'ajasŏ* (*Visiting the Vestigial Remains of the Anti-Japanese Armed Struggle Area*), a report of an exploration team, P'yŏngyang, 1960, p. 43. In this account, the Ant'u armed force is called "the first revolutionary armed unit of the Korean people in the Ant'u district."

Paek Pong in the 1968 biography greatly inflates the event. "This Anti-Japanese Guerrilla Army," he writes, "organized by General Kim Il Sung was indeed the first Marxist-Leninist revolutionary army made up of progressive workers and peasants and patriotic youths, in the history of the Korean people." Baik Bong, *op. cit.,* Vol. I, pp. 140–141.

Setting aside the other implications of the quotation, it is somewhat difficult to conceive of nineteen young men constituting an army. Before this biography appeared, as we shall see, emphasis had been placed upon Kim's founding of the "Korean People's Revolutionary Army" in March 1934, some two years later.

the Chinese forces were far superior in numbers and fire power to the small bands of Koreans. Meanwhile, Japanese pressure greatly increased. In December 1932, Kim's band was forced to retreat to the inaccessible Mount Laohei in Tungning hsien. When the guerrillas arrived there, in the dead of winter, they had been reduced in numbers to the original eighteen men with whom Kim had begun. In January 1933, the band left Mount Laohei and marched to Yaoyingkou (Wangch'ing hsien), supposedly carrying a banner that read "Anti-Japanese Guerrilla Army." [111]

In Yaoyingkou, Kim's group linked up with another Korean partisan force. The total armed strength of the combined force was ninety, with a few additional unarmed personnel. The Wangch'ing partisans were now organized as a battalion, with Yang Sŏng-yong, the original leader of the group, as battalion commander and Kim as political commissar. (This fact is conspicuously omitted from Paek Pong's account, in line with his effort to portray Kim as the sole innovator and leader.)

It is significant that Kim's career, while closely associated at all points with military operations, was, from the outset, decidedly political. His posts with the Youth League and his subsequent role as political commissar are significant. Like Stalin and Mao, Kim represents a blend of the political and military, petty intellectual and activist, well adapted to the era when the Communist Party had ceased being a study society and was grasping for the reins of power.[112]

In the spring of 1933, the Japanese launched their first large-scale attacks upon the partisan units entrenched in the mountainous areas of east Manchuria. At the same time, they undertook extensive political operations designed to isolate anti-Japanese forces—Communist and non-Communist—from the villages and hamlets of this region. Official North Korean histories have seized upon one episode during this period to magnify Kim's military and political capacities, namely, the partisan attack upon Tungning, an old castle town near the Soviet border, in September 1933.

According to official North Korean accounts, this was the first time that the Korean anti-Japanese partisans had engaged in large-scale joint operations with the Chinese National Salvation Army. Comrade Kim was in charge. At the age of 21, he supposedly commanded three companies of the Wangch'ing Third Regiment and three companies of the Hunch'un Fourth Regiment in coordination with approximately 1,000 Chinese soldiers led by Wu I-ch'êng. North Korean accounts, indeed, imply that the campaign against Tungning was essentially conducted by Kim, with the Chinese playing a subordinate role. Several official versions also state that the Korean partisans saved the seriously wounded Chinese brigade com-

111. *Ibid.*, p. 155.
112. For a more detailed evaluation of the first-generation Korean Communist elite, see Chapter IX.

mander, Shih Chung-heng, after which he and all of his men "joined'
General Kim Il-sŏng's units." [113]

Kim's role in this episode has almost certainly been grossly inflated.
There are, of course, good official reasons for stressing the Tungning en-
gagement. It not only constitutes "proof" of the sterling military and leadership qualities of Kim at a very young age, it also "demonstrates" his ability
to thwart Japanese attempts to drive a wedge between Chinese and Koreans,
thus providing "evidence" of Kim's truly Communist, anti-ethnic roots.
Throughout the saga of Kim's career, North Korean Communist writers
play in contrapuntal fashion upon two basic themes: the leader's complete
grasp of Marxism-Leninism and his consequent sagacity in military and
political matters; and his deep patriotism and devotion to the fatherland,
as evidenced by his unswerving commitment to national liberation and
other nationalist objectives. In the telling of the Kim saga, internationalism
and nationalism are carefully balanced. The Tungning episode serves the
internationalist cause, just as the Tahuangwei and Yaoyingkou meetings of
1935 serve nationalism. But all this remains to be discussed.

As will be recalled, Japanese pressures, both military and political,
greatly increased upon the Communists in 1934–35. In early 1935, the
Korean Communists abandoned the soviet districts in east Manchuria.
Korean partisan units were now amalgamated to form the nucleus of the
Second Army of the Northeastern People's Revolutionary Army. After the
abandonment of the soviet districts, the Second Army moved into the in-

---

113. Among others, Ch'oe Hyŏn presents this thesis in his "Ijŭlssu ŏmnun
ch'ŏtsangbong" ("Unforgettable First Meeting"), KWP CC Center for the Study of
Party History, *Hang-Il ppalchisan ch'amgaja dŭl ui hoesanggi* (*Recollections of the
Participants of the Anti-Japanese Partisan Movement*), reprint edition, Tokyo, 1961,
Vol. I, pp. 1–18. See also Han Sul Ya, *op. cit.,* pp. 12–13.

Once again, however, we turn to Paek Pong to obtain the most recent official
version of the Tungning battle and the events leading up to it. Paek admits that the
combined Japanese military-political campaign had serious consequences, among
them renewed strife between the National Salvation Army and the guerrillas. "Only
General Kim Il Sung had the ability, the igrenuity, the political and ideological preparedness" necessary to solve the problem. The task of wooing the Nationalists,
moreover, was complicated by "leftist errors" within Communist ranks. However,
Kim accompanied by his men (then numbering 100) visited Wu I-ch'êng in June
1933. Once again, Kim reportedly won the respect of "the arrogant Chinese General," and an agreement was made to conduct joint operations against the Japanese.
According to Paek, "the General [Kim] decided to attack Tungning . . ." to
demonstrate the might of the anti-Japanese united front and to instill the conviction
of victory in the troops of the National Salvation Army by showing them the courage
and boldness of the anti-Japanese guerrillas. The battle involved 1,600 troops "under
the General's supreme command"; and while elements of the National Salvation
Army became demoralized and "began retreating," Kim's guerrillas saved the day.
The condescending tone taken toward the Chinese in general, and the Nationalist
forces in particular, is even more pronounced in the Paek biography than in the
earlier works.

terior regions of west Manchuria, near the First Army. In the fall and winter of 1935, however, the pursuing Japanese mounted a series of major attacks. As a result, the Second Army was badly mauled and broke into two parts. One element, the Second Division, moved north to the Ningan region and joined Chou Pao-chung's Fifth Army. The First Division joined the First Army.

The facts given above can be documented from a number of reliable sources. How do the official Korean Communist accounts of this period correspond to reality? "In March 1934," says one typical account, "the General succeeded at last in founding the Korean People's Revolutionary Army, with the anti-Japanese partisan units stationed in various prefectures of east Manchuria as its core. The Korean People's Revolutionary Army was a mighty, large combined army, which had several independent divisions." [114]

At first, it is curious to discover that the standard Japanese and Chinese sources say nothing about this Korean People's Revolutionary Army in connection with this period, not to mention Kim Il-sŏng. The problem is easily solved, however. Yim Ch'un-ch'u, one of Kim's followers, tells us that that Army was in fact the Second Army, a unit composed "entirely of Koreans." When the Army operated in Korea, according to Yim, it was known as the Korean People's Revolutionary Army, but otherwise it was known by its Chinese designation. We know, however, that Kim Il-sŏng neither organized the Second Army of the Northeastern People's Revolutionary Army nor did he lead it. Nor, indeed, was it composed entirely of Koreans.

The head of the Second Army at this point was Wang Tê-t'ai, and his chief of staff was Liu Han-ch'ên, both Chinese. From several Japanese sources, we have some additional information on the Second Army during this period.[115] Reportedly, two "independent divisions" of the Second Army were created in the spring of 1934. The First Independent Division was established following a meeting in March of some fifteen Korean and Chinese Communist leaders at Shantaowai, Yenchi hsien (Kim may have been present). A Korean, Chu Chin, was elected commander; Wang Tê-t'ai became political commissar, finally succeeding Chu as commander. It will be remembered that Chu Chin, falling under suspicion as an enemy agent, later fled and surrendered to the Japanese.[116] The Second Independent Division of the Second Army, according to this same source, was established on May 30, 1934, and was originally made up of forces already operating in Wangch'ing prefecture. A certain Kim Il-sŏn was made politi-

114. Yi Na-yŏng, *op. cit.,* p. 354; and Academy of Science, *Chosŏn t'ongsa, op. cit.,* Vol. II, p. 320.

115. See *Shisō ihō, op. cit.,* No. 3, June 1935, pp. 135–136, and also *Manshū kyōsanhi no kenkyū, op. cit.*

116. *Ibid.,* pp. 166–168.

cal commissar of the Second Regiment of the Second Division. There is good reason to believe that Kim Il-sŏn was Kim Il-sŏng, and that the Chinese, Hou Kuo-chung, listed as commander of the Third Regiment of the Division, was the Hou whose name later appears in Japanese reports coupled with that of Kim.[117]

There is a very considerable difference between the myth that young Kim Il-sŏng at the age of 22 founded the Korean People's Revolutionary Army and the fact that his initial appointment was probably that of regimental political commissar in the Second Army of the Northeastern People's Revolutionary Army, a post similar to the one he had previously held with the Wangch'ing partisans.[118] Moreover, his command assignments for the next several years appear to have been at the company level, involving no more than a hundred men.[119]

However, Yim Ch'un-ch'u insists that, in March 1936, Kim became commander of the Sixth Division of the Second Army, having Chinese as well as Koreans under him as regimental leaders. This statement appears

117. The way the names Kim Il-sŏn and Kim Il-sŏng appear several times in the Japanese records of this period suggest that the same individual is involved.

For example, in *Manshū kyōsanhi no kenkyū, op. cit.,* it is stated that on May 30, 1934, Kim Il-sŏn was political commissar of the 2nd Regiment, 2nd Independent Division of the 2nd Army (p. 167).

In another source, the reports of the Chientao Japanese Consul-General, in the period May–July 1935, Kim Il-sŏng is reported as the commander of the 3rd Company, 1st Regiment, 2nd Division, 2nd Army, operating with about 100 men, in the Wangch'ing area as "a Communist bandit" (pp. 9390, 9396, 9402).

But another branch of the consulate reports Kim Il-sŏn holding the same position, and these two names are also given in the fall of 1935 as commander, 3rd Company, 2nd Division, reported variously in Yenchi, Hunch'un, and Wangch'ing hsien.

All references from *AJMFA*, SP205–5, R SP105, "Summary of Security Conditions in Chientao and Adjacent Areas During 1935" (and 1936).

It is still possible that two men were involved, but it seems far more likely that Kim Il-sŏn and Kim Il-sŏng were the same.

118. Contrast the above facts with the assertion of Kim's biographer Han Sul Ya: "Taking into consideration the situation and conditions at that time, the General tried to organize partisan units in the East Manchurian areas into a large, united army, for the purpose of dealing a still greater blow at the Japanese aggressors.

"In March, 1934, the General succeeded at last in founding the Korean People's Revolutionary Army, with the anti-Japanese partisan units stationed in various prefectures of East Manchuria as its core. The Korean People's Revolutionary Army was a mighty, large combined army, which had several independent divisions": *op. cit.,* pp. 14–15.

119. See the report of the Chientao Consul-General cited in note 117 *supra.* Then, in July, he is recorded as being head of the 3rd Company (1st Regiment, 2nd Division, 2nd Army), having 40 subordinates in T'angsuihotzu, Wangch'ing hsien; and in August, there is a reference to him as the head of the 2nd Company with 100 subordinates based in Yenchi hsien: *ibid.,* p. 9402.

Paek Pong, incidentally, conspicuously omits any detailed discussion of Kim's military and political posts during this period.

to be correct. Thus, Kim's fortunes had advanced by 1936 despite the fact that he was still a very young man. Why? We know, of course, about the demise of Chu Chin—and many others—in the purges that took place in this period. When the ranks were being rapidly depleted both by the Japanese and by the internecine warfare of Communists themselves, those who survived had a chance for rapid advancement. But there may have been an additional factor. Yim Ch'un-ch'u flatly asserts that Kim's influence among Manchurian Koreans began to grow in 1935 because of his "courageous criticism" of the "left extremists" involved in the anti-Minsaengdan movement, to which we earlier referred in some detail.[120]

It will be recalled that the purges, and even executions, of Communists by Communists in these years left deep scars, both among Koreans and between Chinese and Koreans. Yim accuses such Korean functionaries in the CCP as Sim Song-do, head of the East Manchurian Special Committee, and Song Il, head of the Wangch'ing prefecture committee, of having falsely charged some Korean Communists with Minsaengdan membership or acts of treason to the Party. Yim also says that Kim publicly denounced "the sectarian elements' policies that had led the movement into the enemy's trap." This took place at two extremely significant meetings held in the spring of 1935 in Wangch'ing prefecture.[121]

A first meeting was held in the early spring at Tahuangwei, and another conference was convened in March (some sources say May). Reportedly, Kim took a leading role in both of these meetings and delivered major speeches. In these, he "defended the integrity of Korean Communists and nationalists" against the "unjust attacks" leveled upon them earlier. Moreover, he is supposed to have accused local Party leaders, even including Wei Chêng-min, a Moscow returned student serving as top CCP representative in the area, of "leftist deviation," and an "unscientific analysis" of the situation.[122] In the course of these meetings, we are told, Kim also championed a new program for Manchurian Communists. He is supposed to have urged the abolition of permanent partisan bases in favor of large-scale, mobile partisan warfare. Further, he argued that political activities should be stepped up, with new efforts being made to create a broad anti-imperialist front among the workers and peasants.

There can be no doubt that the North Korean line of the 1950s and 1960s was to regard the Yaoyingkou Conference as a meeting of critical importance. Yim asserts that "the revolutionary masses enthusiastically supported Comrade Kim Il-sŏng's speech . . . and as a result, the center

---

120. For detailed treatment of the Minsaengdan incident, see Yim Ch'un-ch'u, *op. cit.,* pp. 91–107; *Manshū kyōsanhi no kenkyū, op. cit.,* pp. 109–126; Baik Bong, *op. cit.,* Vol. I, pp. 221–26.

121. Yim, *op. cit.,* pp. 99–100; Baik Bong, *op. cit.,* Vol. I, pp. 226–232.

122. Yim, *op. cit.,* pp. 100–104.

of leadership for the Korean revolutionary movement was completely concentrated in him." [123] Another Communist source describes the Yaoyingkou meeting as "of epochal significance in tiding over a crisis and bringing about a great upsurge in the revolution."

Certainly a crisis had existed. Communists had been accusing each other of treason and seeking to purge each other for several years. Military adventurism had been consistently rewarded with defeat. Thousands had deserted the ranks, and morale was at an all-time low. Perhaps, in retrospect at least, Kim's ascendancy can be dated from this period, although many obstacles for him lay ahead. But can he be credited with the primary initiative in developing the themes set forth above? The answer is clearly in the negative. The assault upon "left extremism," as noted earlier, had been proceeding for some time, and it was to be climaxed, of course, by the theses of the Seventh Comintern Congress, which were probably being written at this very time. All of the Chinese Communist leaders currently in key positions, including Mao Tse-tung, had gone on record against "left extremism" by this point, admitting that serious errors had been committed.

The evidence, moreover, strongly indicates that the specific decision to abandon the permanent partisan bases was actually made in January 1935. The orders were transmitted in the name of Wei Chêng-min, but, in view of the events occurring at this point in the south, it is probable that they came originally from top Communist quarters. We are told from non-Communist sources that later, on June 3, Wang Ming and K'ang Shêng, Chinese Cominform representatives, sent the CCP representative in Chi-tung (presumably Wei) a letter ordering the Second Army to avoid frontal engagements with the Japanese-Manchukuo forces.[124] It is also reported that this decision was accepted at a meeting of Communist military leaders at Yaoyingkou in *July* 1935.

Whatever the correct date of the Yaoyingkou meeting and other key events of this period, one can be certain that the broad policies now ascribed to Kim Il-sŏng were in truth policies that the Manchurian Communists had already been ordered to follow by top Comintern and Chinese Communist Party officials. It is, of course, quite possible that Kim not only made a speech at Yaoyingkou raising the points mentioned above, but also that he took advantage of the shift in the international and Chinese lines to attack those—both Korean and Chinese—who had previously been in power on the local scene. (That he openly attacked Wei Chêng-min at this point, however, is very doubtful.) In leveling those attacks, moreover, he may well have acquired a significant following. As we have noted earlier, at the climax of the swing to the "left," racial prejudice against Koreans on the

123. *Ibid.,* p. 104.
124. For a Japanese translation of this letter, see *Manshū kyōsanhi no kenkyū, op. cit.,* Appendix, pp. 47–57.

part of the Chinese was a very real factor. If Kim, even by implication, played a nationalist role by defending Koreans *as Koreans,* he might easily have gained politically, and destroyed the old Korean leadership in the process. In sum, the fact that Kim neither formulated nor first advanced the policies at Yaoyingkou with which he is now credited does not negate the possibility that he scored important personal gains by using these policies, and playing the role of Korean nationalist. Moreover, in a period of deep internal division, *he* had an armed force at his disposal, albeit a minuscule one.

We do know that it was only at this point that Kim Il-sŏng began to figure occasionally in the Japanese documentary records of the "Red bandit" problem. In July 1935, when Second Army elements abandoned their original sites and moved north to join the Fifth and First Armies, Kim started from Lotzukou, Wangch'ing Prefecture, with approximately three hundred troops. He reached Fifth Army headquarters at Shantungt'un, Ningan Prefecture, the same month. Some North Korean sources now refer to this rather modest trek as Kim's Long March.

According to Japanese sources, the Manchuria Special Committee of the Chinese Communist Party ordered a military reorganization of its north Manchuria forces in late 1935, and the new structure was finally worked out in April 1936 by the military and political leaders of the two armies, meeting at Takou, Ningan Prefecture.[125] Three area commands were created, an eastern, a central, and a western front, with fourteen military units divided among these fronts. The total military force, if the Japanese order-of-battle information is correct, did not number more than 2,000 men. General Chou Pao-chung, a Chinese, was in overall command; the headquarters political commissar was Hu Jen. Kim Il-sŏng reportedly had command of a mobile unit numbering only 100 men; it was stationed at Omu. However, if Japanese reports are correct, he was also named political commissar to the central front, of which Ch'ai Shih-ying was commander and Chuan Hsien-ming deputy commander. The central front had three other units, totaling some 500 men, in addition to Kim's. But Kim was the only Korean to occupy a leading post at the front level, although two other Koreans commanded small units—Kim Hwa with 28 men at Muling, and Pak Sun-il with 30 men at some unknown location.[126]

North Korean sources present a different story of Kim's activities after February 1936, and in this case their account seems basically accurate. They acknowledge that Kim indeed went north and joined forces with the Fifth Army; nothing is said about his precise position. In February 1936, however, Korean Communist accounts speak of "one of the most important conferences for the Korean Revolution" being held at Nanhut'ou, Ningan hsien. There, Kim and other Korean leaders supposedly conferred with Wei

125. *Ibid.,* pp. 175–178.
126. *Ibid., loc. cit.*

Chêng-min, at this point political commissar of the Second Army, who had just returned from the Seventh Comintern Congress.[127]

Wei reportedly gave a complete account of the basic theses adopted at the Seventh Congress, and also transmitted a Comintern order that the Korean Communist Party be reestablished. In response, Kim supposedly pledged himself to an acceptance of the new Comintern line and announced that he would immediately undertake Party reconstruction, moving his forces to the Manchuria-Korea border so that personnel could be infiltrated into the homeland. All Korean sources assert that Kim and his men left for the Changpai area shortly after the Nanhut'ou conference. By March, the partisan band had reached Mihunchen on the Chientao border. It was at this time, according to Yim, that Kim was officially made commander of the Sixth Division of the Second Army, this presumably being the designation given the units under him at the time. Continuing south, Kim had reached Fusung hsien by May 1936.

At that point, according to North Korean sources, another important conference took place. The place was Tungkang, where the partisan leaders assembled for fifteen days and established the Choguk Kwangbok-hoe (Fatherland Restoration Association). The Association, officially inaugurated on May 5, clearly represented a response to the Comintern demands for an anti-Fascist united front, as can be seen from the ten-point program that it proceeded to adopt.

1. A broad united anti-Japanese front shall be formed with the participation of the whole Korean nation to overthrow the rule of the piratical Japanese imperialists and establish a genuine people's government of the Korean people.

2. In close alliance, the Korean and Chinese nations shall overthrow Japan and its puppet, "Manchukuo"; then the Chinese people shall establish a revolutionary government through elections, and the Korean residents in Chinese territory shall enjoy genuine autonomy.

3. The Japanese army, gendarmerie and police as well as their lackeys shall be disarmed and a revolutionary army which will truly fight for the independence of Korea be formed.

4. All the enterprises, railways, banks, ships, farms, and irrigation facilities owned by the Japanese government and Japanese individuals as well as the traitorous pro-Japanese elements' properties and land shall be confiscated to pay the expenses of the independence movement and a portion of it shall be used for relieving the poor.

5. All bonds, taxes, and the monopoly system of the Japanese and their lackeys shall be abolished; the life of the masses shall be improved; and the national industry, agriculture, and trade be duly developed.

127. See *Hang-Il mujang t'ujaeng chŏnjŏkchi rŭl ch'ajasŏ, op. cit.,* pp. 254–258; Yim Ch'un-ch'u, *op. cit.,* pp. 130 ff.; *Chosŏn t'ongsa, op. cit.,* Vol. 2, pp. 352–355; and Baik Bong, *op. cit.,* pp. 269–271. Once again, Paek omits any mention of the presence of Chinese, and portrays the Nanhut'ou Meeting as conceived and led solely by Kim.

6. Freedom of speech, the press, assembly, and association shall be achieved; the practice of Japanese terrorism and encouragement of feudalistic ideas be opposed; and all political offenders be released.

7. Differences between the nobility and commoners and other inequalities shall be abolished; equality irrespective of sex, nationality, and religion be ensured; the social status of women be enhanced and their personality be respected.

8. Slave labor and enslavement education shall be abolished; forced military service and enforcement of military education for the youth be opposed; education be carried on in our mother tongue and compulsory free education be enforced.

9. An eight-hour day shall be put into effect; labor conditions be improved; wages be raised; labor laws be enforced; the various laws on insurance for workers be enacted by the state organ; and the unemployed working masses be relieved.

10. Those nations and states which approach the Korean nation on an equal basis shall be closely allied with; and comradely friendship shall be maintained with those states and nations which are sympathetically disposed while maintaining neutrality toward our national liberation movement.[128]

It will be noted that the emphasis of these ten points is almost exclusively upon nationalism and democracy. There is virtually no mention of a "socialist" program, no discussion of the "correct" ideology, no demand for proletarian leadership—and no identification of Communist sponsorship. This, of course, was completely in keeping with the new Comintern strategy.

It is very likely that Korean Communist sources once again exaggerate the role of Kim in the so-called Nanhut'ou and Tungkang conferences. Japanese sources of the period mention a high-level Communist conference held much earlier to discuss the revitalization of Communism in Korea, and they do not mention Kim's presence at all.[129] Moreover, Japanese records list the signers of the Restoration Association's program as O Sŏng-rin, Ŏm Su-myŏng, and Yi Sang-jun. Once more, Kim is not mentioned.[130]

128. For a Japanese translation of the text, see *Shisō ihō, op. cit.,* No. 14, p. 64; for another English translation, see Baik Bong, *op. cit.,* pp. 282–283.

129. *Manshū kyōsanhi no kenkyū, op. cit.,* pp. 242–279.

130. According to Yim Ch'un-ch'u, despite his protestations that an older, more experienced man was desirable, Kim Il-sŏng (age 24) was chosen to be the head of the Fatherland Restoration Association, but he decided to issue the Declaration of the Association under a pseudonym, Kim Tong-myŏng (pp. 138–139). Kim Tong-myŏng was a curious pseudonym for Kim Il-sŏng to use, since a Kim Tong-myŏng existed; indeed, he was one of the main leaders of the Manchurian General Bureau of the Korean Communist Party.

Shisō ihō, as noted above, lists other names, but not that of Kim Il-sŏng. *op. cit.,* No. 14, pp. 60–63.

Paek Pong, as might be expected, describing the Nanhut'ou and Tungkang

All sources, however, agree that Kim and his partisans were in the Changpai mountains of Chientao Prefecture, Manchuria, by the fall of 1936. Japanese sources, moreover, confirm the fact that Kim's title was now "commander of the Sixth Division of the Second Army, Northeastern People's Revolutionary Army." As might be expected, however, there is a discrepancy between present-day Korean Communist accounts of Kim's role then and Japanese accounts of the same period. The former highlight only Kim's authority, conferring upon him a solo role of major importance; the latter suggest that Kim shared authority with such individuals as Wei Min-sêng (Wei Chêng-min?), a Chinese who had been dispatched by the CCP Manchuria Special Committee to serve as political commissar of the Sixth Division, and, at a higher level, Kim Kwang, who was currently serving as political commissar of the Second Army. Because of what we know about the general circumstances of this period, we are inclined to accept the Japanese version as the more accurate.

In any case, shortly after the Sixth Division partisans established themselves in the Changpai area, some thirty agents were dispatched throughout the region, beginning in October 1936. Changpai, of course, had a large Korean population. A prefectural committee of the Fatherland Restoration Association was soon established, with such young men as Yi Che-sun actively involved. It was through Yi that, in the winter of 1936, Kim came into contact with Pak Tal and Pak Kŭm-ch'ŏl.[131] By

meetings as "historic conferences that defined the programmatic line and policy of the Korean revolution," asserts flatly that it was Kim who first proposed the establishment of the Fatherland Restoration Association and laid down its guidelines (p. 276). Paek is vague about the authorship of the ten-point program but implies that all aspects of the Tungkang Meeting were under the aegis of Kim: "The guidelines presented by the General at the Tungkang Meeting were a programmatic line which brought about an epochal turn in the development of the Korean revolutionary movement, being the only guide to the course of struggle for the Communists and revolutionaries at home. Those who attended the meeting were greatly impressed anew by the distinguished Marxist-Leninist views of General Kim Il-sŏng and his scientific insight, and enthusiastically supported the General's new policies." (pp. 276–277).

Moreover, Paek states flatly that the Tungkang Meeting elected Kim chairman of the Association and decided to publish a monthly organ: p. 280.

131. Yim Ch'un-ch'u, *op. cit.,* p. 162. Pak Tal relates in his memoirs that he was first approached by Kim Il-sŏng through Pak Kŭm-ch'ŏl in November 1936. After meeting Kim's representative, Kwon Yŏng-byŏk, at Pak's home in Unhŭng-myŏn, Kapsan-gun, Pak Tal crossed the Yalu in early December to meet Yi Che-sun. On his second trip to the Changpai area in late December, Yi led Pak to Kim Il-sŏng's hideout. There, they discussed revolutionary tactics and strategy for two days. Because the man was so young, Pak Tal relates, he did not know until after the session was concluded that the man he had been talking to was Kim Il-sŏng.

At the end of the discussion, Kim supposedly instructed Pak Tal, "in the name of the Commander and the Political Commissar of the 6th Division," to carry out organizational activities for Korean national liberation by concentrating upon establishing local units of the Fatherland Restoration Association: Pak Tal, *Choguk*

January 1937, organizational efforts were under way inside Korea. We have an account of a meeting of the Kapsan Activities Committee held at the home of Pak Kŭm-ch'ŏl in that month.[132] It was agreed that the Committee should be reorganized into the Korean National Liberation League, and that all Koreans opposing Japanese imperialism should be consolidated into this group, making it a true united front. Factionalism was to be rigorously opposed, and all enemy organizations—self-defense units, schools, district and village offices—were to be infiltrated. The ten-point program of the Fatherland Restoration Association was adopted as that of the

ŭn saengmyŏng boda to kwijung hada (*The Fatherland Is More Precious than Life*), P'yŏngyang, 1960, pp. 22–28.

One of the very rare references to Kim Il-sŏng in a source of this period is contained in the November 1938 issue of *Samch'ŏlli* (Vol. 10, No. 11), pp. 136–139 (*Samch'ŏlli*, which means 3,000 ri, refers to Korea, the length of which is about 3,000 ri or 800 miles). In the story, a reporter tells of two young women who had surrendered after being "subordinates" of Kim for five years, and of a 73-year-old man who had been kidnapped by Kim's group and imprisoned for seven months. These events took place in 1936. The girls, both in their late teens, had been born in Chientao. They described Kim as a robust young man of 27, with a wealth of experience in guerrilla warfare. His basic unit, they asserted, contained only sixty individuals, but there were in addition, several hundred others who could be counted as supporters. Among these several hundred, eleven were women and about one-half were Chinese. Describing Kim as a man of few words, they asserted that he took action only after serious consideration, and that he maintained tight discipline over his forces.

The old man, who claimed to have talked to Kim in December 1936 while he was being held in "the bandits' prison" in the Changpai mountains with thirteen others, stated that he complained that the prisoners would die of starvation since they were getting only two dishes of barley gruel a day, upon which Kim promised that he would be given special treatment, with whole barley being prepared, and excused conditions on the basis that "at present, we are not very affluent."

Kim is reported to have said that his family were living in Chientao and that conditions there were not so bad when it came to earning a livelihood, but that he was enduring serious hardships in the mountains for the cause. When the old man asked why he had been kidnapped, Kim allegedly said that his group needed money and that the old man had refused to contribute. But when the old man asked Kim questions about his tactics and purposes, Kim merely told him that he was too old to be able to understand and declined to talk about the movement. Then, when the old man asked if the band intended to attack Changpai, Kim retorted that they could hit the town easily, but under current circumstances they could only hold it for three days and nothing would be gained in imposing such hardships upon the people there. "Some of my naive subordinates argue for it," young Kim reportedly said, "but I am absolutely opposed to it." However, he added, "we have entered most of the small towns along the Yalu. Our main unit is to the north, with sizable force. We are here to survey the situation along the Yalu River," he concluded.

It is interesting that the Japanese should allow the publication of these interviews—which sound genuine and reasonably accurate—in November 1938. It also reveals the surprising liberality of publication rules, long after stringent regulations concerning political *activities* were in existence throughout the Japanese empire. The distinction between what one could *say* and what one could *do* is once again revealed.

132. *Ibid.,* Pak Tal, *op. cit.,* pp. 34–58.

League. Full support was also pledged to the Manchurian partisans. Liaison points were to be established; information, food, clothing, and other supplies for the partisans were to be collected; and "patriotic young men" were to be recruited for service in the "people's army."

Once again, Japanese official records, based upon interrogations, supplement what we know from the recollections of Pak Tal and other Korean Communists. According to the Japanese sources, the primary purpose of the Communist penetration of Korea at this point was to strengthen and unify a so-called Anti-Japanese People's Front by establishing units of the Fatherland Restoration Association, National Liberation League, and similar organizations, and then recruiting the most "advanced" elements within such organizations for membership in the Communist Party. All activities, incidentally, were still under the supervision of the Chinese Communist Party, as the Korean Communists themselves admit.

Communist agents were rapidly seeking to broaden their contacts. For example, special attention was being given to Ch'ŏndogyo members, and some local Ch'ŏndogyo officials in the border area had been recruited. This, too, was a foretaste of things to come; after 1945, Ch'ŏndogyo leaders were to be rigorously wooed by the Communists, partly as a counterbalance to the Christians. Agents were also going "in considerable numbers" to Hŭngnam, Hamhŭng, and Wŏnsan. Plans were being developed for the use of arson and other means of destruction against military factories, railroads, communications facilities, and police stations. One prime objective was to seize weapons and ammunition for partisan operations. Another was to acquire money or negotiable items through robberies.[133]

Primary Communist operations, of course, were in Changpai prefec-

133. *Shisō ihō, op. cit.,* No. 14, March 1938, pp. 53–54; contains a fairly detailed account of the activities of the 6th Division (of which Kim Il-sŏng was the commander) in Changpai Prefecture. The area of operation of the 6th Division included Changpai, Linchiang, Fusung, and Ant'u prefectures. Wei Min-sêng was dispatched by the Manchurian Committee to the 6th Division as political commissar. Under the guidance of the political chief of the 2nd Army, Kim Kwang, Wei sent political agents to various prefectures and strove to organize an anti-Japanese people's front. Kwon Ch'ang-uk and several other agents engaged in political movements from October 1936 to June 1937. Missions assigned to these agents were (1) to organize the Fatherland Restoration Association in Manchuria, (2) to indoctrinate the members of the Association in Communism and select the most able members to organize cells, and (3) to select physically strong persons to participate in the guerrilla movement.

These agents, after consulting with Kim Il-sŏng, commander of the 6th Division, organized the Changpai Prefecture Political Activities Committee in the deep forest, preparatory to the creation of a Changpai Prefecture Party Committee: pp. 55–57.

The Japanese account of Pak Tal's activities is very similar to that of Pak himself: *ibid.,* No. 18, pp. 20–22. It is interesting to note that in May 1937, one month before Kim's foray, Ch'oe Hyŏn of the 4th Division (in 1971 minister of defense of the DPRK) led approximately 200 guerrillas into Musan, attacking a Japanese lumber mill.

ture, Chientao, Manchukuo, and in the border areas of South Hamgyŏng Province, Korea. As we have noted earlier, the historical background of this region, its economic difficulties, and the security problems that stemmed from rugged terrain and primitive communications combined to make it a promising region for revolutionary exploits. Activities mounted during the spring of 1937. Pak Tal and Pak Kŭm-ch'ŏl visited Kim in Manchuria, reporting on progress and receiving additional instructions from Sixth Division personnel. It was decided, for instance, to organize "production partisans," namely, individuals who would alternate their farm work with service as partisans.

As a result of the liaison now established with Korea proper, the Manchurian partisans decided to conduct a raid into Korea in June. The result was the so-called Hesanjin Incident, an event now hailed by Korean Communists as a great milestone in the history of the Korean Revolution. On June 4, 1937, Kim Il-sŏng led a small force of partisans (80 according to the Japanese, 150 according to Korean Communists) in an attack upon the village of Pojŏn (renamed Poch'onbo after 1945), some twenty-four kilometers from Hesanjin, a barren, isolated town on the Yalu River. Crossing the Yalu on rafts provided by sympathizers, Kim's band struck at about ten in the evening, destroying the police station, town office, forestry branch office, agricultural experiment station, post office, and other government buildings. Seven policemen were killed, and seven others wounded. Propaganda leaflets were distributed and supplies collected. The village residents were then assembled to hear Kim deliver an impassioned speech, after which the guerrillas retreated across the river and back into their mountain hideout in Manchuria.

No doubt this raid bolstered partisan morale. The costs involved in such bravado were high, however. Naturally, the Japanese conducted a most painstaking investigation. The result was to expose Communist informers and sympathizers, making it possible to identify underground agents and uncover the local apparatus. Indeed, so many arrests followed the Pojŏn raid that local Communist activities practically ceased. Despite the praise that the North Korean Communists now lavish upon this operation, it was undoubtedly harmful to the movement in general. In fact, it was another example of "blind adventurism." [134]

Somewhat more significant may have been a few direct military clashes between partisans and Japanese military forces during this period. For example, Korean Communists claim to have fought a major battle on

134. See *Shisō ihō, op. cit.,* No. 14, pp. 59–60.
    After the Pojŏn attack, Japanese efforts to uncover all underground activities redoubled. Consequently, for the rest of 1937 and in 1938, almost all of those associated with Kim Il-sŏng were arrested. At this point, incidentally, some of the Communists took to robbery in an effort to replenish Association coffers.
    As we shall note, Kim Il-sŏng himself seems to have viewed some of these escapades with a critical eye a few years later, referring to this type of enterprise as "blind adventurism."

June 30, 1937, with some 600 partisans engaging a vastly superior number of Japanese. Known by Koreans as the battle of Chiensanfêng Peak (in Changpai Prefecture, Manchukuo), this struggle is said to have resulted in the partisans killing, wounding, or taking prisoner 1,500 enemy troops.[135]

Inevitably, the Japanese decided to mount a major campaign to eliminate "Red bandits" from the Manchukuo-Korean border. At the same time they undertook the pacification program noted earlier. From this point on, the partisans and their supporters were almost constantly on the defensive. On the political front, Japanese authorities managed to uncover most aspects of Communist operations, both in Korea and in Changpai. In October 1937, large-scale arrests were made; the total finally reached 221, of whom 59 were from Changpai and the remaining 162 from Korea. Those arrested included Pak Kŭm-ch'ŏl and a number of other key figures.[136] Communist political operations in the border region thereafter were minimal.

On the military front, Communist problems also mounted. Although North Korean Party historians now claim "successive victories" over the Japanese forces during this period, the evidence is strongly to the contrary. Japanese pressures steadily increased and took a heavy toll. The problem of food was particularly acute. The Japanese were now employing a strategic hamlet system, providing key villages with armed self-defense units and rationing the food supplied to inhabitants of isolated villages, so that they could not share provisions with guerrilla forces. On the whole, this system effectively deprived the partisans of necessary supplies, forcing them to spend an increasing amount of time simply trying to survive. It certainly made it impossible for them to launch any meaningful political or military action.

Thus we find that the partisans were forced to abandon their Changpai quarters in 1937. Our accounts place Kim Il-sŏng in Linchiang Prefecture in August of that year, in Mêngchiang Prefecture in the winter, and constantly on the move throughout 1938 and 1939.[137] The Japanese were well pleased by developments. In a 1939 report dealing with T'unghua

135. For details, see Kwahakwon Yŏksa Yŏnguso, *Chosŏn kŭndae hyŏngmyŏng undongsa* (*History of the Modern Korean Revolutionary Movement*), P'yŏngyang, 1961, p. 378.

136. In September 1938, after escaping the first roundup, Pak Tal was also arrested and sentenced to life imprisonment.

137. Kim reportedly was in Linchiang hsien in April 1938. Communist sources later claimed that he then had 400 guerrillas under him. He was again in Mêngchiang in October, and in April 1939 he was located in Changpai hsien.

According to Communist sources, the "arduous march" from Mêngchiang to Changpai was undertaken "to frustrate the enemy's winter punitive campaign, to restore the wrecked revolutionary organization, and to encourage the people." It was conducted during a hundred-day period in which the temperature at times fell to 40 degrees below zero.

During the summer and fall of 1939, Kim was in T'unghua and Ant'u hsien again.

Province, they asserted that security conditions had greatly improved since 1937 as a result of combined military-political efforts.[138] "Red bandits" still existed in T'unghua Province, but they had been forced to retreat into the most remote mountainous and forested areas. The Yang Ching-yü "bandits," some 200 in number, were in the vicinity of Mêngchiang. The Kim Il-sŏng "bandits," also numbering approximately 200, were in the Fusung-Changpai-Linchiang border area, and there were about 100 Ch'oe Hyŏn "bandits" nearby. Approximately 500 of the 900 "bandits" in the province, according to this report, were Korean, and "although they are said to be Communist bandits, they seem to be the same group that was formerly with the old Korean Revolutionary Army under Yang Sŏ-bong." [139] Significantly, Kim was reported to be under Yang Ching-yü, and his group was described as less active than that of Yang.

The combined military-pacification program was continuing. Some fifty surrendered "bandits," for example, were used in an effort to secure defections within Kim's group. Approximately 600 villages in the region had received 16,000 rifles for protection. Nearly 1,000 kilometers of new road had been opened to improve security conditions, and the old roads had been repaired. Telegraphic communication lines had been improved, and additional measures had been taken to cut off the partisans' food supplies. After September 1938, every resident had had to carry a residence certificate with photograph attached. Between September 1938 and February 1939, the Japanese reported that in T'unghua Province, where the

138. See Tsūkashō kōsho (T'unghua Provincial Government), "Kōtoku gonendo fukkō kōsaku jisseki hōkokusho" ("Report on the Result of Rehabilitation Activities During 1938"), General Secretariat, Council of State, Manchukuo, *Senbu geppō* (*Monthly Report on Pacification*), Vol. 4, No. 4, April 1939, pp. 174–193.

139. This Japanese intelligence was essentially correct. From North Korean sources, we now know that in March 1938 the elements of the Korean Revolutionary Army under Ch'oe Yong-gŏn had agreed to join Kim's People's Revolutionary Army. This was the culmination of some years of sporadic efforts on the part of Kim to form a united front with the old Korean Revolutionary Army under Yang Sŏ-bong. As we noted earlier, previous negotiations had failed, since Yang and his group wanted no alliance with the Communists. Once again, after the creation of the Fatherland Restoration Association, Kim sought to reopen negotiations with Yang; meetings took place, but without positive results.

In early 1938, however, Ch'oe and his men joined the Kim band, possibly because of the enormous Japanese pressure upon all guerrilla elements at this point, and the desperate need to survive. It is admitted that Ch'oe and his men were not Communists, although Paek Pong reports that they "grew to be Communists under the paternal solicitude and correct leadership of General Kim Il-sŏng": Vol. I, p. 324. Some would dispute this statement, as we shall see, at least if it is meant to imply that Ch'oe ever became well versed in Marxism-Leninism. There can be no doubt, however, that he became a Kim loyalist and that served to advance him to the second highest position in North Korea.

Thus, the Kim-Ch'oe relationship began as the military union of two leaders of small guerrilla bands, men faced with the threat of extinction in the face of massive Japanese pressure.

partisans were now concentrated, 340 "bandits" had been killed, 106 had been captured, and 608 had surrendered—a total of 1,054.

The 200 troops who remained with Kim—and most of the other partisans in the area—whether "good Communists" or not, were battle-tested veterans. They were also men deeply indoctrinated in the cause of socialism and independence. But training and indoctrination were insufficient to sustain them under the conditions that now prevailed. Korean Communist sources tell us that a partisan conference was finally held in Hsiaoharpaling, Tunhwa Prefecture, Kirin Province, on August 10, 1940.[140] Kim is supposed to have reviewed both the international and local situations before advancing new policies. On the world front, conditions were all growing increasingly favorable: the "glorious victories" of the Eighth Route Army, the New Fourth Army, and the Chinese people; the marvelous growth of the USSR; and the utter failure of American and British imperialist designs.[141] At home, the Japanese had been driven to desperation, especially in Manchuria. They were now gambling everything in an effort to annihilate the partisans and disrupt their food supplies.

The situation, Kim reportedly said, demanded that the partisans preserve their armed strength at this point. The stage of decisive battle had not yet come. To continue attacking the enemy would cost a great number of comrades. "Blind and adventuristic actions had to be abandoned." Rather, "our precious revolutionary strength" must be preserved and nurtured; only then would they be prepared to take advantage of the great events that lay ahead, the global victory of the democratic forces over fascism and reaction. Thus, partisan activities should be reduced to small-scale operations, and much greater attention should be paid to the proper political education of those who would be responsible for the future guidance of the Korean and Chinese masses. Every fighter and every commanding officer had the obligation to increase his political consciousness, making his daily life and struggle a school for the nurturing of dedicated leadership. Every Communist had to become an organizer, propagandist, and agitator. And the Anti-Japanese People's Front had to be based upon the universal truths of Marxism-Leninism. In sum, the international situation was strongly favorable to the liberation struggle, but in Manchuria immediate conditions required a change in tactics.

140. See Yim Ch'un-ch'u, *op. cit.,* pp. 277–281.

North Korean sources claim a series of striking victories over the Japanese by Kim and his partisans in the period between 1938 and 1940. Unquestionably, some ambushes were costly to the Japanese, and total Japanese war losses during this period (as inflicted by *all* Chinese Nationalists and anti-Japanese guerrilla forces) were heavy. When they describe the details of a given battle, however, even North Korean historians are forced to admit that the scale of action was extremely small, and that Kim's "brilliance" consisted largely of using the tactics of "the butterfly against the chicken," namely, flitting over and around the enemy, thereby avoiding encirclement.

141. *Ibid.,* pp. 280–281; Baik Bong, Vol. I, *op. cit.,* pp. 484–487.

Though the current Communist version of Kim's August 1940 remarks is interlaced with a great deal of falsification and the type of ex post facto justification designed to make the Great Leader look omniscient, one can learn much by reading the Communist account carefully. When the nonsense is stripped away, Kim—or others—were saying that it would be suicidal to continue partisan activities in the face of the heavy and unremitting Japanese pressures. Partisan ranks had already been decimated, and many comrades sacrificed, for small purpose. Thus, a retreat to safer ground had to be effected. There, intensive training—both military and political—could be undertaken, while the partisans awaited international events that promised to be favorable. Small-scale organizational and espionage activities in Korea and Manchuria could be continued, but large-scale operations would have to await a better atmosphere.

And where was a privileged sanctuary to be found? Korean Communist sources draw an almost complete curtain of silence over Kim's activities after the spring of 1941. The reasons are not too difficult to understand. Kim and some of his partisans went to the Soviet Union, and there is reason to believe that they were provided with substantial training facilities. Neither the USSR nor Kim has any reason to want the details disclosed. For Russia, it would be one more indication of deep involvement in the Asian Communist movement, and at a time when a nonaggression pact with Japan was supposedly in effect. (A neutrality pact between the USSR and Japan was signed in April 1941.) For Kim, it would promote the thesis that his rise to power was primarily the product of Soviet guidance and support.

Thus, Yim Ch'un-ch'u is very vague about events during the 1941–45 period that relate to Kim and his group. He speaks of the Korean People's Revolutionary Army continuing small-group activities while simultaneously retraining its revolutionary core. The purpose of this retraining, he says, was to develop military and political officers who were both technically and ideologically equipped. His most revealing statement is the following: "According to the wise actions of Comrade Kim Il-sŏng, the People's Army received the unselfish material and spiritual assistance of a brother nation in carrying out military and political studies. This action enabled us to acquire a modern military science and the foundations of Marxism-Leninism." [142]

142. Yim Ch'un-ch'u, *op. cit.,* p. 303. Similarly, Paek Pong is specific only about various small-scale operations in Manchuria and Korea under such men as Kim Il and Kang Kŏn.

In a recent account, Kim is placed at the Chiapikou temporary base in Wangch'ing Prefecture on June 30, 1941, spelling out the correct "line of action" to his followers. No further information concerning his activities during the wartime period is given, although earlier, he is reported to have been in Ant'u and Yenchi prefectures in the spring of 1941. See Li Chang Gyu, "Leader Guided Sacred War of Fatherland Liberation to Victory," *The P'yŏngyang Times* reprinted in *TPK,* Feb. 19, 1972, p. 2.

Although Japanese intelligence reports relating to Kim are very few, one extremely interesting report, dated November 1944, has been uncovered. The following constitutes its essence:

> Kim Il-sŏng holds the posts of political commissar of the North Manchuria Province Committee [of the Chinese Communist Party] and commander of the Tenth Branch Unit of the Third Area Army of the Northeast Anti-Japanese Allied Army. The Chief of the Third Area Army is Chang Shou-hsien. Kim Il-sŏng at present is at the Oganskaya Field School near Vladivostok, busily training insurgent Koreans for activities in Manchuria. According to information recently received, Kim is preparing to dispatch agents to important points along the Korean-Manchurian border area in order to destroy railroads in coordination with the air raids of the United States Air Force in this same area. The destruction of railroads is intended to hamper the transport of military supplies as well as to disturb the people of the area. Air raids are being planned via secret agreements between the United States and the USSR.
>
> Kim Il-sŏng went to Moscow in mid-June 1944; he also went to Chungking and Yenan. He conferred with personnel of the American and Chinese embassies in the Soviet Union, as well as with the Chinese Communists. At that time, he received instructions regarding the above-mentioned operations.[143]

We have no means at present of verifying this Japanese report, particularly the section concerning Kim's travels to Moscow, Chungking, and Yenan. The assertion, however, that Kim was located near Vladivostok and engaged in training Party and military leaders is certainly not inconsistent with Yim's hints, and those of others. Some Korean Communist writers try to give the impression that Kim remained in Manchuria until the end of World War II.[144] The evidence strongly suggests, however, that Kim and his weary, reduced partisan forces retreated into the Soviet Union in the summer of 1941. There they remained (probably near Khabarovsk), except for occasional military forays and political trips, until they were able to reenter Korea with the Soviet army.

As can be seen, the material relating to Kim is far from complete. In time, disclosure or discovery of additional sources will undoubtedly alter some of our statements. But certain old controversies can be resolved at this point. Earlier, a number of Korean writers insisted that Kim is an impostor and a pretender who deliberately tried to masquerade as an older Kim, a nationalist hero who allegedly operated on the Manchuria-Korea border immediately after the annexation in 1910. There is no hard evidence that any such person ever existed. Kim certainly did not claim at any point to be connected with the nationalist movement in which this older Kim was

143. Naimushō, Keihokyoku (Ministry of Home Affairs, Police and Security Bureau), *Tokkō geppō* (*Special Higher Police Monthly Report*), Nov. 1944, p. 76.
144. See for example, Yi Na-yŏng, *op. cit.*, p. 429; and Korean History Editorial Committee, *Chōsen minzoku kaihō tōsō shi, op. cit.*, p. 320.

supposedly involved. It is true that Kim did change his name, since he was born Kim Sŏng-ju. But that was a very common practice among Korean revolutionaries; indeed, nearly all the leaders had one or more aliases. A legend concerning another Kim Il-sŏng is still believed by some Koreans, but, as we shall indicate, there was no other individual of prominence with this name.[145]

The Kim Il-sŏng who governs North Korea today is the same Kim who led small partisan bands in Manchuria between 1932 and 1941. It would have been impossible to fabricate Kim because one would have had to have fabricated the people who have been connected with him since that time. Ch'oe Yong-gŏn, Kim Ch'aek, An Kil, Kang Kŏn, Kim Il, and Ch'oe Hyŏn, all of whom were Kim's comrades during a part of this period, not only have existed; many of them have also followed their leader into positions of eminence. It should be remembered, however, that despite later Communist attempts to build up Kim as a major figure of heroic proportions, he is most accurately described as a relatively minor leader of the period. As we have seen, Kim probably never had direct command of more than 300 partisans, although at several times he may have had a measure of control over groups numbering up to 1,000 and possibly over a somewhat larger force on one or two occasions.

As mentioned earlier, it is easy to find Korean Communists of this period more powerful—and seemingly more promising as future leaders—than Kim Il-sŏng. Two of the most obvious are Kim Won-bong and Mu Chŏng. Kim Won-bong, as the leading nationalist-Communist of the era, came very close to uniting all Korean revolutionaries in the China-Manchuria region into an anti-Japanese front under his command. Mu Chŏng, who had the closest relations with the Yenan Chinese Communists, ultimately won over a significant number of Kim Won-bong's supporters, and after 1940 his star seemed clearly in the ascendancy. There were others, of course, who also seemed more likely to succeed than Kim Il-sŏng. Can we isolate the factors that ultimately brought supreme power to him? Are these to be discerned in the patterns of Korean radicalism in the two decades that preceded Japanese surrender in 1945?

One cannot ignore the factors of skill, luck, and timing. Kim Il-sŏng early demonstrated traits of intellect and character. No young man without ability could have reached the attention of senior Communist colleagues

145. Kim Ch'ang-sun's explanation of the legend is perhaps the most extensive. According to him, during the 1920s when some Korean patriots organized the Chŏnguibu, The Righteous Army, one of the distinguished leaders was said to be a General Kim Il-sŏng. He died of illness in 1931, but a second-generation "Kim Il-sŏng," Kim Yang-nyŏng, succeeded him. He in turn was killed in action in 1937. After this time, many men claimed to be General Kim Il-sŏng, and it is said that, when the Kwangtung Army put a price on the head of General Kim, scores of heads were delivered to army headquarters. Kim Ch'ang-sun, *Puk-Han siponyŏn-sa (Fifteen-Year History of North Korea)*, Seoul, 1961, pp. 55–56.

as quickly as did Kim, and none would have been entrusted with such responsibilities. Moreover, we can assume that Kim was always a man of tremendous drive and commitment. We also know that he possessed the traits of ruthlessness and cruelty that frequently go with such commitment —traits likely to be useful to a Communist leader. As Chinese Communists saw these qualities in Kim in the 1930s, so Russians evidently saw them in the 1940s.

Kim Il-sŏng, however, was by no means alone among Communists in being talented and dedicated. It would be possible to describe in such a fashion at least a hundred Koreans of this period who at one point or another committed themselves to Communism. Most Korean Communist leaders, as we have seen, were petty intellectuals in both training and temperament. In the nature of affairs, moreover, they had to be deeply committed if they were to remain with the movement in the midst of terribly difficult conditions. Administrative capacities and personalities varied greatly, but there is absolutely no evidence that Kim stood in solitary splendor.

Luck, fortune, or fate—however one terms the accidents of life— certainly narrowed the competition. A very substantial number of promising Communists ended their careers in prison, or at least were removed from the possibility of top leadership by this means. Many others were killed in action, or died before the struggle ended. Only a small proportion of the starters survived, and Kim Il-sŏng was one of them.

His survival was undoubtedly connected with the timing of his emergence into the Communist movement, and the special circumstances of his career connected with this timing. In all political movements, there are periods when no one can succeed and when everyone involved is tarred with the brush of failure and disfigured by the nastiness of repeated struggles, internecine as well as against the "enemy." Given the nature of the early Korean Communist movement, any activist coming out of the 1920s had a tremendous handicap in seeking to acquire both the external and the internal support necessary to make the Korean Communist movement unified and powerful. As we shall see, Kim also had major problems. But at least he had the advantage of never having been deeply involved in the old factional struggles, never having been compromised in the course of arrest and imprisonment by the Japanese, *and* never having lost touch with some military organization or other. All of these factors were in some degree the product of the particular period when he entered the movement— in other words, a matter of timing.

Yet none of these elements—ability, luck or timing—really touches on the central reason for Kim's ultimate triumph. That central reason was simply Soviet support. Kim Il-sŏng came into North Korea on the shoulders of Soviet power and anointed by Soviet authority. Of course, the details were complicated. But one must not allow these details to obscure the basic fact that Kim Il-sŏng was the Russian choice, at a time when the Russians had the power to enforce their choice.

Korean Communism Before 1945: Some Observations

Before turning to the post-1945 era, let us enlarge our area of analysis. What are the basic factors concerning the nature of Korean Communism that emerge from a study of the period before World War II? First, that movement was initially characterized by the same general type of leadership that was undertaking both political modernization and nationalist activities —according to whether one adopts a broad or a narrow view—through other political channels. The first Korean Communist leaders came overwhelmingly from the more "Westernized" (in many cases it would be more accurate to say "Japonized") upper educated segment of the society, an elite that certainly represented less than 5 percent of the total Korean population. Their primary and immediate goals were nationalist, developmental, and egalitarian—very radical goals, measured against the values of their society. Their means involved a reliance upon tutelage, the development of a strongly hierarchical organizational structure binding the individual to a rigid group discipline, and an ideological system that rested not only upon reason and faith, but also on the appeal to authority. Given the historic culture of the society, these means were traditional.

With what socioeconomic group within Korean society could this radical intellectual or petty intellectual elite interact most successfully? Not with the urban workers; state authority in the urban centers was too strong, and in any case these workers as a class were in the midst of rapid cultural change and not easily shaped into a disciplined, committed force. The peasant, indeed, was a far more logical target, not so much because of his grievances—these were real, but only a small part of the educated class could really understand or support peasant desires—but rather because the peasant had retained more or less intact a traditional organizational structure, and more than this a capacity for political action, that could be utilized by the Communists. This was particularly so because the Communists were quite prepared to use traditional means to reach radical ends.

It was not accidental that the Korean Communists scored their most significant gains and put down their most meaningful roots in the Manchurian-Korean border areas, among the rural population of Chientao and North and South Hamgyŏng. Not only were these areas under only marginal state control, and hence the natural resort of dissidents, outlaws, and other independent types, but, in addition, it was precisely here that the traditional peasant resistance to government, and the forms of peasant organization so difficult to counteract by any means open to the government, could be brought into play. That issues like nationalism and agrarian reform could be floated on the surface as lures was naturally of great importance. But the grievances actively exploited were often more local and particularistic.

Indeed, one must be extremely careful in ascribing so-called rational motivations to all who joined the Communist movement. The data, including some applying to the period of the late 1930s, suggest that while issues pertaining to nationalism and economic reform were significant factors, of at least equal importance were appeals by friends, relatives, and work associates. In sum, the collectivistic nature of Korean politics showed itself almost as much in commitments to the Communist movement as it did in commitments to other political movements. For every recruit who came to Communism through reading Marxist literature, or because he had become convinced that the Party offered the best hope for national liberation or rapid socioeconomic change, another recruit entered because his schoolmate, closest friend, or brother persuaded him to do so.

If the techniques of operating in the hinterland among the peasants had more success in China than in Korea, it was largely because Japanese authority was more firmly ensconced in Korea, a much smaller country and hence more easily controlled by all the means, both military and political, employed by modern governments. The sophistication of Japanese authority should not be underrated. It is grossly inaccurate to characterize the Japanese approach as purely military. The Japanese experimented with many subtle forms of economic and political programming, from the "strategic hamlet system" to land and credit reforms. They too engaged in ideological training and the promotion of socioeconomic change —albeit not of the type or at the rate that their opponents approved. They could not, of course, meet the nationalist appeals effectively. Nevertheless, acceptance of Japanese authority was greater in Manchuria and Korea in 1940 than it had been at any time in the past, and the Communists were in a state of total despair despite their brave words. Their one hope lay in an external war ending in Japanese defeat. In sum, Japan was able to resist Korean Communism; what she could not resist was the military power of the United States and its Allies.

One other major consideration deserves some further analysis here. Korean Communism, like other aspects of Korean politics in the period before 1945, had had to find its bases and sources of support wherever it could. It therefore lacked organizational cohesion and a unified political perspective. After 1928, Korean Communism was once again forced out of its homeland. From then until 1945, the Communists were compelled to operate primarily from overseas bases, unable to sustain either a Party or a movement in Korea proper. Indeed, all Korean Communists in this era had to join a foreign Party, whether Chinese, Japanese, or Soviet.

Under these conditions, they naturally came under the strong influence of foreign elements. As a result, seeds were planted that grew into the bitter rivalries of the postwar era. To be sure, the prewar situation was mitigated somewhat by the fact that the Comintern had overriding international authority, so that a uniformity of line could everywhere be implanted. Nonetheless, affiliations in Tokyo, Vladivostok, or Yenan, not to mention the underground elements in Korea itself, could influence attitudes, positions on specific issues, and, above all, organizational and personal ties. The shape of Korean Communism could not help being affected powerfully by these facts. If Korea as a whole throughout her history had never been able to maintain her independence except by some type of balance in her relations with Russia, China, and Japan, the Korean Communists would have to face this same problem sooner or later. The moment of truth came after World War II.

CHAPTER IV

KOREAN COMMUNISM UNDER AMERICAN OCCUPATION

At one hour before midnight, August 14, 1945, the top Japanese civil and military authorities in Korea were informed of the Emperor's surrender message. A devastating war had come to an abrupt end. Immediately, Civil Governor Endō Ryūsaku and his chief advisers decided to invite several prominent Korean nationalists in Seoul to assume responsibility for the maintenance of order.[1] The three chosen by Japanese officials were Yŏ Un-hyŏng, An Chae-hong, and Song Chin-u. Each of these men, as will be recognized, had had a lengthy political record. The Japanese were obviously reconciled to the end of their era, and to the drastic changes in the political landscape that would ensue.

Yŏ Un-hyŏng, destined to play a major political role in the days that lay ahead, stood firmly on the left, as we have already noted. He had long worked close to or within the Communist movement. A graduate of Chinlung University in Nanking, Yŏ had first come to prominence politically as the young man primarily responsible for the dispatch of Kim Kyu-sik to the Versailles Peace Conference in 1919. At later points, he had served as delegate to various international conferences, Korean nationalist spokesman in Japan, and ardent worker in Korean radical circles in China.[2] Yŏ's

1. Morita Yoshio, *Chōsen shūsen no kiroku* (*The Record of the End of the War in Korea*), Tokyo, 1964, p. 70. This work is a valuable contribution to the political history of modern Korea. Morita, a former employee of the Japanese government in Korea, is primarily concerned with the story of Japanese repatriation, but he devotes much attention to the general situation in Korea immediately after V-J Day.

2. See pages 38–42 *supra*. As noted earlier, the best source on Yŏ Un-hyŏng remains High Court, Prosecutor's Bureau (Kōtō Hōin Kenjikyoku), "Ro Unkyō jimmon chōsasho" ("Interrogation of Yŏ Un-hyŏng"), *Chōsen shisō undō*

political activities in Shanghai had led to his arrest by Japanese police in 1930, followed by a three-year prison term in Korea. Subsequently, he had become the president of the *Chungang Ilbo* (*Central Daily News*), one of the major daily newspapers of Seoul.

The term *fellow traveler,* imprecise and usually to be avoided, is probably the only political description of Yŏ Un-hyŏng that is both accurate and simple. Unquestionably a strong nationalist, Yŏ had had a lengthy and intimate association with the Korean and Chinese Communist movements. There is conflicting evidence as to when, or even whether, Yŏ became a formal Party member in the era before World War II. He certainly considered himself a Communist at one stage, and he was intimately associated with the movement, as we have seen. After 1945, however, Yŏ was not a KCP member. It is probable, indeed, that if he ever did enjoy formal membership, it ended with his arrest in 1930. Moreover, despite his close association with the Communists in various ventures of the 1945–47 period, Yŏ was never fully trusted by top Communist leaders. At the same time, however, he came to be regarded with deep suspicion by most other elements within the Korean political spectrum, particularly those on the so-called Right, as well as by the top American occupation authorities.

His supporters would assert that this was the inevitable fate of a man staunchly committed to drastic change via the route of democratic socialism, and to the total independence (and unity) of the Korean nation. His opponents (both "left" and "right") would argue that Yŏ was essentially an opportunist, a man whose basic political values changed no less often than his tactical position.[3] Perhaps there is some measure of truth in both of these appraisals. Clearly, Yŏ's basic sympathies lay with the Left, vaguely defined, and after the Japanese surrender he frequently engaged in united front activities with the Communists, including activities initiated and dominated by them. He also established contact with Kim Il-sŏng and the Russians and sought to maintain those ties, even as he retained contacts, sometimes intimate in nature, with American authorities. Above all, Yŏ appears to have been a man deeply torn, pulled in contradictory directions by his political and emotional convictions, and in the final analysis unable to follow any fixed course.

No matter what evaluation of Yŏ is advanced, however, one cannot escape a sense of uneasiness in attempting to establish with precision the motives and position of many of the key political actors in modern Korea.

---

chōsa shiryō (*Research Materials on the Korean Thought Movement*), No. 2, Seoul, 1933. For his younger brother's more recent account, see Yŏ Un-hong, *Mongyang Yŏ Un-hyŏng,* Seoul, 1967. Mongyang is Yŏ Un-hyŏng's pen name.

    3. Kim Nam-sik, for example, asserted flatly that, as a member of the Korean Communist Party, he regarded Yŏ as an opportunist and bourgeois nationalist. Robert A. Scalapino interview with Kim Nam-sik, Seoul, Dec. 7, 1968.

Once again, we must reiterate a familiar theme in this study. The enormously complex character of Korean politics—particularly in the spectrum: radical nationalist-socialist-communist—not only makes it difficult to discern the precise relationship of many individuals to the Communist movement or movements, but also raises the more subtle and intriguing question of what being a "Communist" meant to various persons and groups at various times. For example, when if ever was a man like Kim Tu-bong of the Korean Independence League warranted in considering himself a Communist—or in so appearing to others? Was a tragic figure like Hyŏn Chun-hyŏk "a bona fide Communist," even though he took the lead in establishing the Party organization in P'yŏngyang immediately after the Japanese surrender? Later we will have the opportunity to ponder these matters further. For the moment, we must consider Yŏ Un-hyŏng a dedicated leftist nationalist who did not hesitate to cooperate closely with the Communists and, in so doing, greatly abet their cause, but who could never bring himself to become a central part of their own apparatus.

An Chae-hong had had a less radical political record. A Waseda University graduate, official in the Korean YMCA, one-time superintendent of Chungang High School in Seoul, and later president of two nationalist newspapers, *Chosŏn Ilbo* and *Shidae Ilbo,* An had long supported the nationalist cause ardently. He had served a three-year prison term as a result of his participation in the March First Uprising. Later, he had been active in the Shingan-hoe, serving as one of its principal officers. In 1936, he had sent a young man to Yenan at the request of Kim Tu-bong, head of the Korean Independence League. When this act was uncovered, An was again sentenced to prison for several years.[4]

Song Chin-u, the most moderate of the three men, was a graduate of Meiji University and former principal of Chungang High School, where he had known An well. For many years, moreover, he had been president of *Tong-A Ilbo,* Korea's most prestigious newspaper. (This strikingly similar pattern of most Korean nationalists' careers deserves emphasis: Christian connections, Japanese higher education, and a subsequent career combining political activities with teaching or work in journalism.) Song, too, had served a prison sentence as a result of his involvement in the March First Uprising, and at the time of Japan's defeat he was one of the best known Korean nationalists of moderate political persuasion.

Song, however, refused to honor the Japanese request, making it clear that he did not wish to serve as a guarantor of Japanese personnel and that he questioned the legality of a defeated regime seeking to extend authority to anyone in Korea. Actually, Song wanted the Korean Provisional Government in Chungking to establish itself quickly in Korea as the

4. See "The Secret Activities of An Chae-hong" (A trial statement), High Court, Prosecutor's Bureau, *Shisō ihō,* No. 15, July 1938, pp. 205–208.

legitimate government, and he was prepared to take a leading role in that government.[5]

Thus, the opening political moves among Koreans in Seoul were directed by Yŏ, with the assistance of An who had agreed to work with him. Yŏ had accepted the assignment offered him with the proviso that all political prisoners currently held in police stations and prisons be released at once and, further, that freedom of assembly be guaranteed. To these demands, the Japanese acceded.

The Emergence of the Korean People's Republic

Whatever the Japanese intention in enlisting the aid of the leading Korean nationalists available, Yŏ and An proceeded to make full use of their new positions for their own political purposes. On August 15, only a few hours after they had first been contacted, and following hasty consultations with a number of friends and associates, they set up the Kŏnguk Chunbi Wiwon-hoe (Preparatory Committee for National Construction), with headquarters in Seoul. Yŏ became chairman of the committee, An was named vice-chairman. At 3:00 P.M. on August 16, An delivered the first major speech by any Korean leader after the Japanese surrender, addressing a national audience from the Seoul broadcasting station.[6] He announced formation of the Preparatory Committee, the release of all political prisoners, and the creation of a Korean security force that, he suggested, would be the forerunner to a regular Korean army. Clearly, the Preparatory Committee was seizing the initiative in the political arena— at a time when the Korean Provisional Government and various leaders in exile were still far away.

Japanese officials were startled and dismayed by An's address, despite the appeals for moderation and order that it contained. They had neither intended nor desired any Korean group to undertake formal political activities at this point, and certainly not to assume governmental authority. They had merely summoned a few key Koreans to help them maintain order until Allied authorities arrived. Thus, they immediately attempted to remove the impression that sovereignty had been transferred to the Preparatory Committee by publishing a "correction" on this matter together with the text of An's address on August 17 in *Keijō Nippō*.[7]

They also urged the dissolution of the Preparatory Committee, but without success. On August 20, at the insistence of Japanese military authorities, the civil governor's office ordered all Korean political and "security" organizations to remove their signboards and dissolve. Despite

---

5. Kim Ŭl-han, *Yŏgi ch'am saram i itta* (*Here Are the True People*), Seoul, 1960, p. 99. Kim, a prominent journalist in Korea, had close contacts with most of the political leaders of this period.

6. The text of the speech has been reproduced in Morita, *op. cit.*, pp. 78–80.

7. *Ibid.*, p. 82.

this order, however, Preparatory Committee headquarters were allowed to remain open, on the pledge that the Committee would continue to co-operate in maintaining order.[8]

In spite of serious Japanese misgivings, the influence and power of the Preparatory Committee grew rapidly. Its success was abetted by a number of factors: the dynamism and experience of its two key leaders; its initial access to the mass media which announced its existence and program; and the virtual absence of opposition or of any meaningful alternative. It was through the Preparatory Committee that Korean patriotism, in these first exciting and hectic days, could be most easily expressed. Not until September 7, for example, did certain moderates led by Song Chin-u announce the formation of the Hanguk Minju-dang (Korean Democratic Party), at least potentially a rival organization. Meanwhile, "People's Committees" that were in reality branches of the Preparatory Committee had sprung up throughout the country. By August 31, some 145 such committees had been established in both the south and the north, each of them led by locally prominent individuals.[9] At this point there was every indication that the Preparatory Committee would form the basis for the postwar Korean national government, despite the lengthy existence of a Provisional Government overseas.

It is interesting to note that the Seoul Preparatory Committee quickly came under the control of the Left, whereas the P'yŏngyang branch remained in moderate hands initially. In major part, of course, this was a result of Yŏ's leadership. In any case, most prominent leftists were in the south. In the north, as we shall see, the influence of Cho Man-sik underwrote moderation—until the Russians asserted their authority.

Offices in the original Seoul Preparatory Committee were distributed as follows: chairman, Yŏ Un-hyŏng; vice-chairman, An Chae-hong; General Affairs, Ch'oe Kŭn-u; Organization, Chŏng Paek; Military and Police, Kwŏn T'ae-sik; Finance, Yi Kyu-gap; Propaganda, Cho Tong-ho.[10] A number of these men in addition to Yŏ had strong leftist backgrounds, including those holding some of the primary posts. Chŏng Paek, for example, had been active in Socialist and Communist circles since 1923, when he and Ch'oe Ch'ang-ik had first organized the Minjungsa (The Masses Association), a Socialist study group. Cho Tong-ho, it may be remembered, was one of the founders of the first Korean Communist Party in 1925.

When a new slate of officers was announced on September 2, it became

8. *Ibid.*, pp. 103–104.

9. Hanguk Kunsa Hyŏngmyŏngsa P'yŏnch'an Wiwonhoe (The Editorial Committee for the History of the Korean Military Revolution), *Hanguk kunsa hyŏngmyŏngsa* (*History of the Korean Military Revolution*), Seoul, 1963, Vol. I, p. 7.

10. *Hanguk Ilbo* (*Korea Daily*), Aug. 17, 1955, and *Chosŏn Sinmun* (*Korea News*), June 21, 1959, as cited in Morita, *op. cit.*, p. 76.

evident that the Left had further increased its strength.[11] "Cabinet" posts
were assigned in the following manner: General Affairs, Ch'oe Kŭn-u;
Organization, Yi Kang-guk (a leader of the Communist Wonsan Incident);
Propaganda, Yi Yŏ-sŏng (leader in the old January Society and North Star
Society, later a newspaper reporter); Security, Ch'oe Yong-dal (another
key figure in the Wonsan Incident, a professor); Culture, Ham Pyŏng-gi;
Construction, Yun Kyŏng-sik; Investigation, Ch'oe Ik-han (leader in the
old M-L group) and Ko Kyŏng-hŭm (leader of the M-L reconstruction
movement); Food Administration, Yi Kwang; Welfare, Chŏng Ku-ch'ung;
Finance, Kim Se-yong (leader of the old January Society); Transportation,
Kim Hyŏng-sŏn (leader of the former Masan branch of the KCP); Planning, Pak Mun-gyu (a Marxist agricultural economist); and head of the
secretariat, Ch'oe Sŏng-hwan.

It is to be noted that such key posts as those of Organization, Propaganda, Security, Investigation, Finance, Planning, and Transportation
were given to men directly connected with the prewar Korean Communist
movement, with no evidence that they had altered their political views. It
is significant, moreover, that An Chae-hong, the nationalist vice-chairman
of the Preparatory Committee, resigned his position on September 1 because he was worried about the pronounced leftist trend within the organization. His place was taken by Hŏ Hŏn, a well-known lawyer, formerly
chairman of the Central Committee of the Shingan-hoe and defender of
many Korean Communists during their court trials in the prewar era. Like
Yŏ Un-hyŏng, Hŏ Hŏn was not identified as a Communist Party member
during this period, but his sympathies clearly lay with the Left and he had
a multitude of contacts with Communist leaders.

The rising level of Communist influence within the Preparatory Committee was perhaps most clearly revealed when the Committee held its
so-called All-Nation People's Congress on September 6.[12] The timing of
this Congress was no accident. It took place just two days before the arrival

11. *Hanguk kunsa hyŏngmyŏngsa, op. cit.,* Vol. I, p. 8.

12. For detailed information on the All-Nation People's Congress, see Minjŏn
Samuguk (Secretariat, Democratic National Front), *Chosŏn haebang nyŏnbo (Korean
Liberation Yearbook),* 1946 ed., Seoul, 1946, pp. 85–92. In the backleaf and on the
spine, this volume carries another title, *Chosŏn haebang ilnyŏn-sa (A One-Year History of Korean Liberation).* This is a valuable source for political and socioeconomic
developments of the 1945–46 period from a Communist viewpoint. It was edited by
Yi Kang-guk, Ch'oe Ik-han, Pak Mun-gyu, and Yi Sŏk-t'ae, all important Communist
or Marxist leaders.

Among English-language sources that are useful regarding political activities
during this period, see E. Grant Meade, *American Military Government in Korea,*
New York, 1951, especially pp. 53–73. Meade writes essentially about South Chŏlla
Province. According to him, a preparatory committee was established there as early
as August 17, with moderates in control. A shift to the left took place in the course
of a committee reorganization on August 24, a number of conservatives being voted
out of office. The Left gained further power on September 4, just before the All-
National People's Congress. Meade asserts that, contrary to the belief of some

of American occupation forces in the south, and obviously represented an effort to present the Americans with a fait accompli. The Congress elected a Central Committee of fifty-five members with additional candidate members and advisors. This committee in turn established a government, selecting individuals for key executive and cabinet posts. Thus was the "Korean People's Republic" inaugurated.[13]

On the surface, there had been an accommodation with both the Center and the Right. Syngman Rhee, the long-time symbol of Korean nationalism, was chosen chairman, and Yŏ vice-chairman. Such prominent exiles as Kim Ku, Kim Kyu-sik, and Shin Ik-hi were also included in the government or in the Central Committee, as were a few moderates from within Korea—Kim Sŏng-su, An Chae-hong, and Cho Man-sik, for example. Among the 55 elected Central Committee members, however, 39 were reportedly from the KCP, along with 16 of 20 or so candidate members.[14] Hŏ Hŏn was designated premier of the new government.

It is true that many conservatives and moderates had boycotted the Preparatory Committee and the All-Nation People's Congress because they were fully aware of their political orientation. This had had an impact upon the distribution of offices and also upon policy decisions. Nevertheless, there can be no doubt that the Left, with the Communists most prominently represented, intended to make the Preparatory Committee their vehicle. Indeed, they hoped to manipulate the entire power structure by employing united front tactics in the same fashion as their Chinese and Vietnamese comrades. Clearly, they viewed the situation as ripe for Communist success.

Various internal and external factors tended to support the Communists' optimism. Internally, a sharp turn to the left was natural, especially among students and intellectuals. An old order had been toppled, and with it many old ways of thought. Most of the leading figures of the Korean "establishment," moreover, had been wholly or partly discredited as a result of their past activities and associations. Thus, even if the abrupt

---

American military government officers, the committee had not passed into Communist control at this point. He insists that the province leaders "were neither Party members nor doctrinaire fellow-travelers," and that the Communist Party had only two of thirty-three Executive Council members. Nevertheless, he indicates that the Communists were busily organizing at the county level, and won a smashing victory in the provincial committee elections held late in September. By early October, he says, when the committee officially established itself as a provincial People's Committee of seventy-one elected members, almost all of the leaders were "leftists" (pp. 56–57).

13. O Yŏng-jin, *Hana ui chŭng-ŏn* (*An Eyewitness Report*), no place of publication, 1952, p. 60. O, a prominent writer, was personal secretary to Cho Man-sik during this period. Though deeply involved in the politics of the North, he has maintained a remarkable objectivity in his memoirs.

14. See Pak Il-won, *Nam-No-dang ch'ong pi-p'an* (*General Criticism of the South Korean Workers' Party*), Seoul, 1948, p. 34.

collapse of Japanese rule was wholly the product of external forces, not of internal nationalist efforts, there soon developed a dramatic "liberation" atmosphere drawing most of its political symbolism from the Left. It was natural to equate the colonial era with "privilege, exploitation, and suppression," putting emphasis solely upon its evils.

This was all the easier because of the serious socioeconomic problems afflicting Korean society. Production had, of course, dropped precipitously in the final months of the war. Once controls were removed, inflation became rampant, and a scarcity of goods of all types rapidly ensued. The problem of food became increasingly grave, both in the north and in the south. A serious drought in 1945 further complicated the problem.

There were other factors favoring the Left, particularly within the student-intellectual community. Only a small number of Koreans had received a higher education, and many of the better-known intellectuals were tainted by collaboration with the Japanese. Left-wing revolutionaries, on the other hand, had been romanticized, first sub rosa, then, in the period immediately after Liberation, openly. It was easy to portray them as heroes in the struggle against Japanese oppression, and to bestow upon them all the attributes of Robin Hood. Success, even though it was not due to their efforts, permitted a drastic reinterpretation of the scope and nature of their activities—a common phenomenon under such circumstances. It had once been exceedingly dangerous to be involved in the Communist movement. Now, however, for many of the Korean students, it was not only a harmless act, but one profoundly satisfying at a psychological level. Once again, it should be emphasized that even among the so-called intellectual class, there was little understanding of the meaning of Communism, or of the distinction between Communism, Democratic Socialism, and Liberal Democracy. One must not impose on the Korean politics of this era the views and vantage points of another culture or intelligentsia.[15]

15. One Korean observer has written as follows: "To all appearances, the active offensive of the Left and those who were later called centrists had become natural and in vogue. Most intellectuals and younger people were prepared to reject monopoly capitalism and huge financial cliques. They felt a revulsion against the one-sided accumulation of wealth. During the thirty-six years of Japanese rule, a dividing line had been established between those who cooperated with the Japanese and acquired personal wealth and those who gladly accepted poverty as the price of upholding the Korean national spirit. For those who chose the latter course, wealth in itself became an evil. Thus it was regarded as a duty or an act of conscience for cultured Koreans to denounce monopoly capitalism and one-sided wealth, and to advocate the nationalization or equal distribution of the wealth left behind by the departing Japanese. It was also commonly thought that such policies could only be effected by the Left, and that only such individuals represented sincere, cultured individuals. In this manner, a socialist outlook and socialist policies loomed up as the principal guideposts for the construction of the Fatherland." O Yŏng-jin, *op. cit.*, p. 60. For another discussion of various factors affecting Korean politics at this point, see the fine study of Gregory Henderson, *Korea: The Politics of the Vortex*, Cambridge, Mass., 1968, Chapter V.

The situation was both complex and confused. We have just suggested some of the internal factors abetting the Left at this point, factors not to be minimized. There were also external factors of importance. In the first place, the more sagacious Koreans realized that the Soviet Union would loom large in the future of their nation. Who could forget the recent history of Korea, shaped to such an extraordinary degree by the rivalries of Russia, China, and Japan? Now Japan had been totally removed from the power struggle, China had been bled white by a decade of war, whereas the Soviet Union, despite frightful losses, had emerged from World War II as one of the two great powers. The other major power, the United States, was far away, and its commitments in East Asia were as yet uncertain. The Soviet Union, however, stood on Korea's doorstep, and its interests in the whole of Northeast Asia were clear for all to see. Was a political movement affiliated with Soviet power not likely to prosper?

At first, a number of Koreans (not to mention Japanese) assumed that the Russians would occupy south as well as north Korea. The news of the division at the 38th parallel for purposes of occupation was not immediately known in Korea. Governor Endō reportedly told Yŏ Un-hyŏng that the Russians would be in Seoul by 2:00 P.M. on August 17. On the 16th, a rumor suddenly swept the city that advance Red Army units would arrive at the Seoul railway station at 1:00 P.M. According to Morita, some tens of thousands of people gathered there, Korean and red flags in hand, to welcome Soviet forces.[16] In the days that followed, similar rumors swept Hamhŭng, Taejŏn, Taegu, and Pusan. Everyone expected to see Russians momentarily.

It should be remembered that all Koreans in this period viewed the Russians as part of the Allied forces. Very few, if any, individuals gave serious thought to the possibility of Soviet-American friction. The international political distinctions being made at this point in Korea were as hazy as the ideological ones. This does not negate our earlier thesis that, with the elimination of Japanese power and the massive presence of Russian forces, politically oriented Koreans, especially those on the left, might logically expect Soviet political patterns to be influential.

The Emergence of the Communist Party in South Korea

As the Preparatory Committee was being transformed into a government, the Communists were engaged in independent as well as united front activities. Party reestablishment commenced from the moment of Japanese surrender, with the initial lead apparently taken by elements of the old Seoul and Tuesday factions. Accounts of the opening moves are scanty and conflicting as to detail, but it appears that a preliminary meeting was convened on the very evening of the surrender, August 15. Some accounts would fix the official date for Party reestablishment at August 16; others at

16. Morita, *op. cit.*, p. 68.

August 17. In any case, an opening "declaration" was issued on August 18; on the previous day, a sign, "Seoul District Committee of the Korean Communist Party," had been erected over the Changan Building in downtown Seoul. As a result, this group was subsequently known as the Changan group. Its leaders were Ch'oe Ik-han and Yi Yŏng, prominent figures of the old M-L and Seoul factions respectively. However, members of the old Tuesday faction such as Cho Tong-ho were also active, and the first "Central Committee" of twelve members appears to have had mixed factional representation.[17]

At some point in this period, Pak Hŏn-yŏng, the man destined to be the key leader in the short-lived, stormy Communist movement in South Korea, arrived upon the scene. Pak and a few old comrades issued a statement, dated August 19. The following day, having declined an invitation from the Changan group to take "an important post" at the Party center, Pak established a Preparatory Committee for the Reconstruction of the KCP and demanded the dissolution of the Party that was already in existence.[18]

17. Two near-contemporary Korean accounts of this opening period have been located. The Oct. 4, 1945, issue of *Hyŏngmyŏng Sinmun* (*Revolutionary News*), published by the Changan group, states that on the evening of August 15, various activists of the wartime Communist underground met and established the Korean Communist Party, including a twelve-man Central Committee. The following day, it reported, a Conference of Revolutionaries in Seoul was convened in the auditorium of the Tŏksŏng Industrial High School, with Comrade Hong Nam-p'yo presiding; but upon news that the Soviet army had just entered Seoul, it adjourned with the shout of "Long Live Korean Independence!"

The organ *Chŏnsŏn* (*Battle Front*) of the KCP (Changan) Central Committee, published the following account in its Oct. 31, 1945, issue: On August 16, leading elements of the Revolutionaries' Conference met at Kedong and established the KCP. On the afternoon of the same day, those of the Organization Committee of the Korean Communist Party expressed resentment at the hurried and "sectarian" organization of the Party; but recognizing the historical necessity for speedy action, these elements joined the Party on the same evening. At the same time, the Seoul District Committee was formed.

The American XXIV Corps G-2 Summary, No. 41, dated June 23, 1946, asserts: On the evening of that August Liberation Day (15th) in 1945, two political groups met in Seoul, one to assist Yŏ Un-hyŏng in establishing his preparatory committee and the other to discuss the revival of the KCP. The first group consisted of Yŏ himself, Chŏng Paek, Hong Nam-p'yo, An Ki-sŏng, Hong Chŭng-sik, and Hong Tŏk-yu, the latter two being members of Pak's Tuesday Society faction. The second group consisted of Ch'oe Ik-han, Ha P'il-won, Kim Kwang-su (brother of Kim Ch'ŏl-su), and Yi Yŏng—most of them erstwhile members of the Seoul Young Man's Association. When these two groups became known to each other, they quickly merged, all except Yŏ and Hong Tŏk-yu becoming members of the KCP (Changan faction) on August 17.

18. According to *Chŏnsŏn*, Oct. 31, 1945, Pak arrived in Seoul on August 19 from South Chŏlla Province, where he had been most recently employed as a bricklayer in Kwangju. The XXIV Corps G-2 Summary No. 41 asserts he arrived on the 17th, with "a list of the members of the old 1925 KCP, underground plans for

The August 19 statement of the Pak group sets forth clearly the initial Communist line on several crucial issues.[19] What type of revolution was required in Korea? Pak and his colleagues paid full homage to the necessity for a two-stage revolution. Moreover, they asserted firmly that Korea at this point had to undertake a "bourgeois democratic revolution" —not the old bourgeois revolution but a "special new democratic revolution." This was to result in a new democracy that took account of the colonial and semifeudal conditions imposed upon Korean society, and developed in the midst of an international environment in which socialism was steadily rising and capitalism steadily declining.[20] It is possible that the statement reflected current Chinese Communist writings, especially Mao's, on the so-called New Democracy. However, this need not have been so. The two-stage revolution concept had long been orthodox international Communist policy for Asia, and the Pak group was in all essentials repeating an old line.

And how was the first stage of the revolution to be consummated? A "broad democratic people's front" had to be constructed, with the Communist Party assuming the leadership. This front had to include workers, peasants, the revolutionary intelligentsia, and all petty and national bourgeois elements. Its task was to guide the bourgeois stage to completion as quickly as possible, paving the way for the socialist stage by rendering its chief opponents helpless.

> Of course the current revolutionary stage in Korea is that of capitalistic democracy. We must thoroughly purge Japanese imperialism from Korea and carry out a land reform program under which all of the landlords' holdings will be confiscated and distributed to the tillers. But the present stage requires us to concentrate upon the liquidation of Japanese imperialism from Korea in its entirety. If we thoroughly purge all remaining elements of Japanese imperialism, the big landlords and monopoly capitalists, the primary targets of our struggle, will inevitably fall.[21]

---

reorganizing the Party and latest instructions from Moscow." This last seems highly unlikely, although one may assume that Pak quickly got in touch with the Soviet consulate in Seoul, which had remained in operation despite the sudden Soviet attack upon Japan in early August. Upon Pak's demand, such former associates as Cho Tong-ho, Hong Nam-p'yo, Chŏng Chae-dal, and Ch'oe Won-t'aek withdrew from the Changan Party.

19. Quoted in the "Claims of the Korean Communist Party," dated October 30, 1945, issued in the name of "Pak Hŏn-yŏng, Representative of the Central Committee of the Korean Communist Party." See *Haebang Ilbo (Emancipation,* the organ of the KCP-Pak group), Nov. 5, 1945.

20. Kim Chong-myŏng, *Chōsen shin minshushugi kakumei shi (History of the Korean New Democratic Revolution)*, Tokyo, 1953, p. 96.

21. From the resolution "Concerning the Political Line," adopted by the Enlarged Committee of the South P'yŏngan District of the KCP, Oct. 13, 1945: reprinted in *Haebang Ilbo,* Oct. 31, 1945.

Clearly, this was to be a guided bourgeois revolution during which the foundations of the "capitalist" class (a class that scarcely existed in Korea) would be removed as thoroughly as those of the "feudalists." Like other Communists of the time, the Korean Communists were in reality advocating a continuous revolution, the technique being to seize power before the so-called bourgeois revolution had been completed, and then to proceed to fashion a program that would render the transition to socialism both smooth and inevitable. A Communist-dominated "bourgeois" phase was not likely to retain many of its traditional "bourgeois" characteristics, a fact that the Communists themselves recognized. And the technique of seizing power involved using the tactics of both "united front from below" and "united front from above." Both the masses and the nationalist-oriented elite had to be organized into fronts, with the Party always careful to maintain its separate identity and its manipulative capacities.

For the first time in their troubled history, the Communists were operating openly in Korea. The only serious problem of the moment was an old one: factionalism. From the opening shots marking the onset of the political race, the Communists, as usual, were off and running in different directions. Even the early signs, however, indicated that Pak Hŏn-yŏng and his comrades were likely to constitute the mainstream, at least in the south.

The first issue was that of whether the Changan group's party should be dissolved. According to the Changan organ, *Chŏnsŏn,* the Reconstruction group (Pak's faction) demanded as a condition of participation the right to determine the central headquarters' personnel and to pass upon Party membership. This appears to be correct. After an abortive meeting of August 22, a more important session was held on September 8, at Kedong, Seoul. With some sixty comrades present, Pak presented his views. These in effect included a demand for full authority to reconstruct the Party in whatever manner he saw fit. The Changan group, recognizing that it was in the minority, insisted that the meeting was essentially private and social in nature, and therefore could not pass upon such an important resolution. They further argued that since a Party already existed, Pak was proposing to organize a Party outside the existing one, thereby violating the one country–one party principle. However, a vote was taken. When, as expected, the Reconstruction group carried the day, the Changan group withdrew.[22]

22. We have two versions of the September 8 meeting, one account being that of the Changan group published in *Chŏnsŏn,* Oct. 31, 1945, and the other that of the Reconstruction—KCP-Pak—group, published in *Haebang Ilbo* Sept. 25 and Oct. 12 and 18, 1945. It would appear that the Reconstruction group members attending outnumbered those of the Changan group by about three to one; another faction is also listed, the "Red Flag group," led by Yi Chŏng-yun.

In his speech, Pak declared that the unity of the Party was urgent. In the north, the Red Army had disarmed the Japanese military forces, and declared the freedom

Initial American Policies and the Korean "Left"

This was the situation when the American occupation forces arrived in Korea on September 9. The previous day, while Lieutenant-General J. R. Hodge and his staff were still aboard the AGC *Catoctin,* a group of three Koreans, representing the so-called Provisional Korean Commission, presented themselves. The three were Paek Sang-gyu, Cho Han-yong, and Yŏ Un-hong (Yŏ Un-hyŏng's brother). They talked to Hodge's representatives, naming from memory those Koreans who were "dependable" and those who were "collaborationists." They also sought American views concerning various governments in exile, and asserted their full recognition of the US Military Government. They concluded by offering to render liaison service between that government and the Korean people.[23]

General Hodge invited all political groups to send representatives to

---

and independence of Korea. Soon, the forces of the United States would arrive in the south. Under these conditions, it could be expected that the upper bourgeoisie and landlords would seek to work within as well as outside the Left. A united national front was essential, one of the broadest spectrum, without relation to personal connection or sex. That had been achieved—in the Korean People's Republic; and the election of the Central Committee had been announced.

Reconstruction of the Party had begun under these conditions. Those engaged in the underground movement and those released from prison should form the center of Party reconstruction—combatant elements armed with Marxism, Leninism, and Stalinism—individuals who had had experience in the actual struggle. Regardless of how famous they had been, those who had headed previous factions or who had retired from the movement did not have the qualifications to serve at the center as leaders. (The latter remarks are noteworthy, because many of the Changan group had publicly recanted Communism when incarcerated by the Japanese.)

In the ensuing discussion, Ch'oe Ik-han naturally took a strong position in opposition to Pak's remarks. He denounced the thesis of the Reconstruction group as "reformist, economist, and anarchist." Pak was allowed to summarize after the debate, and he called for a unified Party with many of its leaders drawn from the ranks of workers and farmers. The Party should not be dominated by the revolutionary intelligentsia: "rather it should be a great Bolshevik party combining the revolutionary intelligentsia who have mastered revolutionary theory with the workers who have weathered the experience of the actual movement." In the past, the primary problem of the Party, he asserted, had been its separation from the masses.

The three resolutions proposed by the Reconstruction group—approval of Pak's report, delegation of final authority in the selection of key Party officials to Pak, and the convening of a Party conference to determine the basic platform, strategy, and tactics of the Party—were approved with only a few dissenting votes. The dissidents, however, refused to accept the verdict of this meeting. Yi Yŏng, Chŏng Paek, and Ch'oe Ik-han subsequently spearheaded the group opposed to Pak's dominance, and prepared handbills condemning the meeting as illegal and unrepresentative.

23. According to an Occupation-compiled *History of the US Army Forces in Korea* (Part II), these three men presented themselves as representatives of an organization composed of 135 separate "commissions" throughout Korea, which had as its purpose the establishment of a democratic form of government for the Korean people. It had been decided, however, that General Hodge should not see them himself, both because they were thought to be sponsored by the Japanese and because

the Seoul civic auditorium on September 12. About 1,200 people were present, and the General made it clear that there was no intention of recognizing any single party or group as the government of Korea at that point. Thus began the growing antagonism between the so-called Korean People's Republic and the occupation authorities. Reports by these authorities make it clear that they soon realized the "Republic" was actually a well-organized leftist movement. Indeed, a number of occupation officials regarded it as Communist controlled. As we have seen, this was essentially correct.[24] Thus, in the opening months of the occupation, the United States had to deal with a united front organization, strongly committed to the Left, with the Communists in a dominant position, which claimed to be not a party, but a government—and the only legitimate government of Korea south of the 38th parallel.

How that "government" operated to seize power at the province level is well illustrated by an interview with a former *kun* (prefecture) head in October 1945. On October 9, a rally had been held. It was sponsored by the People's Committee of his *kun,* and attended by some hundred "dele-

---

it was considered unwise to give the slightest possible appearance of favoring any given political group. Thus, if the above statement is accurate, even at this point the United States had formulated a policy of refraining from endorsing any single political group.

According to this same account, the group showed "some concern" over the division of Korea at the 38th parallel, the problems of currency and inflation, and the food situation. They also raised questions about the discipline of American troops when they landed—probably a reflection of the behavior of Soviet troops in the north. For Yŏ Un-hong's account, see his *Mongyang Yŏ Un-hyŏng, op. cit.,* pp. 162–166.

The US Army history cited, as well as the XXIV Corps G-2 summaries, USAFIK (United States Armed Forces in Korea) reports, and documents cited in this chapter, are part of a collection of papers, many of them classified, under Accession No. RG-332, Office of Military History, Department of Defense.

24. USAFIK reports indicated that, by mid-September, the People's Republic had organized many subsidiary groups throughout the provinces: students, farmers, and workers, including a so-called "Student Public Peace Corps," a body reportedly composed of "radical students, thugs, and criminals, armed so far as possible."

Despite Occupation edicts, the People's Republic was assuming government functions in the provinces. When Dr. H. H. Underwood, an American missionary with lengthy experience in Korea, toured the rural areas in December, he reported that the "Republic is the strongest and most active organization throughout the South." Underwood continued by saying that the Democratic Party was poorly organized or unorganized in most places, and seemed to have nothing to offer comparable to the free land and free factories proffered by the People's Republic forces. His evaluation of People's Republic strength was corroborated by military government officers, who added an ominous note: the strength of the "Republic" was growing, they were organizing governments at all levels, and no other party was given a chance of coexisting with them. Without military government intervention in its favor, no other party would be allowed to flourish.

gates" drawn from various villages and towns. The *kun* head, Kim Chung-hi, was caused to return to his office, and to stand before the crowd while the chairman of the People's Committee denounced him as a former agent of the Japanese who was now an agent of the Americans. The chairman then proclaimed that the Korean people would now take over the governance of their own affairs. Someone shouted that the people were now liberating this *kun*. A demand was made that Kim prepare and sign with his official and personal seals a document transferring office to the people, and that the official seal and keys to the office be delivered to the People's Committee. Kim at first refused, stating that General Harris had ordered him to hold office until otherwise notified by military government. The atmosphere, however, was extremely hostile, and various individuals began cursing Kim and making threatening gestures.

Kim finally wrote, at the chairman's dictation, a statement saying that he was therewith transferring all of the administrative work of the *kun* to the chairman of the People's Committee. He was then forced to read this statement to the crowd. The old signboard was removed and that of the People's Committee put up. At the same time, all *kun* department heads were removed and replaced by People's Committee men. The head of the so-called Defense Section of the Committee took over the police station, a move by which the Committee gained control of about fifty rifles and six pistols that had been police property. In such fashion, the People's Committee came into complete control of this particular prefecture. Similar developments were occurring in many parts of South Korea. A showdown between the "Korean People's Republic" and USAFIK (US Armed Forces in Korea) was certain to ensue.

Moreover, as we have already indicated, the Communist role in the People's Republic was extensive and growing. Indeed, Pak's relatively easy victory over the Changan group was due in part to the key role he was playing within this so-called Republic. According to Yi Tong-hwa, a close associate of Yŏ Un-hyŏng during this period, it was none other than Pak Hŏn-yŏng who, with Yŏ's approval, drew up the master plan for the Republic.[25] Pak himself informed his comrades at the time of the September 8 KCP meeting that he was playing a key role in establishing the Republic.[26] And if the Communists were playing a leading role at the top of the Republic's organizational structure, they were also of major importance at secondary levels. Reports from various People's Committees indicated that the Communists held many of the chairmanships and vice-chairmanships at the *kun* and city levels.

25. Chong-Sik Lee interview with Yi Tong-hwa, Seoul, March 29, 1967. Yi added that Yŏ regretted having given his consent to the creation of the Republic.

26. Pak reportedly stated that "the reason that I have not been able to keep in touch with all my comrades in the recent period is because I have been absorbed in the construction of the People's Republic." *Chŏnsŏn*, Oct. 31, 1945.

The Forging of a Communist Program

Meanwhile, on September 11, the Pak group, ignoring the continued protests of the Changan leaders, publicly announced the creation of a united Korean Communist Party. At the same time, *Haebang Ilbo,* the Pak group's organ, carried a four-point program in its inaugural issue.

1. The Korean Communist Party will protect the political, economic, and social interests of the working masses of Korea, including the laborers, farmers, urban indigent, soldiers, and intelligentsia. It will also struggle to bring about a radical improvement in their livelihood.
2. [The Party] will struggle to achieve the complete independence of the Korean people, to eliminate all remnants of feudalism, and to open the route to the advance of freedom.
3. [The Party] will fight for the establishment of a revolutionary democratic people's government that values the interests of the working people.
4. [The Party] has as its ultimate goal the complete liberation of the Korean working class through a proletarian dictatorship and the construction of a Communist society where exploitation, oppression, and class do not exist.[27]

This program provides a clue as to the basic orientation of Pak and his group. Hardened revolutionaries of the pre-1945 era, in this early period they were still committed to the December Theses. The "leftist" thrust of their thinking is suggested even more clearly by a long polemic article published at the same time. Here, a sharp attack was leveled against the landlords and bourgeoisie, who were accused of "joining hands with reactionary fascists to organize the so-called Korean Democratic Party [Hanguk Minju-dang] and other associations to deceive the people." [28] In other words, the Korean People's Republic (with the Communists as its dominant element) represented the only legitimate political government, and all opponents of that government had to be smashed.

It is not clear whether the Soviet Union fully approved of the positions being taken by the new Pak-centered KCP. On September 15, an event took place in P'yǒngyang of direct relevance to the movement in the south: there was an enlarged committee meeting of the South P'yǒngan Province branch of the KCP, headed by Hyǒn Chun-hyǒk. This was certainly the key official Communist group in North Korea at this time, and it was directly under the control of Soviet authorities. Consequently, its pronouncements have the ring of an authentic Soviet view.

27. *Haebang Ilbo,* Sept. 19, 1945.
28. "Support the People's Republic! Destroy All Anti-Government Intrigues": *Ibid.,* p. 1.

The September statement of Hyŏn's group was highly critical of past KCP policy positions. First, the Party had handled the United States and Great Britain in an "ambiguous fashion," suggesting that they were a part of the imperialist camp, rather than a part of the democratic camp. (At this point, the Soviet Union clearly sought to avoid jarring attacks upon the Allies, particularly the United States, since these might disrupt negotiations over the future of Korea.) In addition, the statement stressed the need to form a national united front on the broadest possible basis, excluding only those who represented the remnants of Japanese imperialism. It suggested that only by such a broadly gauged policy could the Party overcome the charge that it was promoting internal dissension, and "stop the onrush of the masses toward the opposition camp, providing them time to comprehend the righteousness and historical inevitability of Communism while at the same time exposing the deceptiveness, reactionary nature, and elitist character of the other side." [29]

Whatever the precise implications of the September statement for the rival southern factions, one fact emerges clearly. The center of the Korean Communist movement was still regarded as being in Seoul, but the center of ultimate authority was in P'yŏngyang—or Moscow—because it was in these two centers of Soviet authority that ultimate decisions on policies were made. Both in the north and in the south, Seoul was considered the location of KCP headquarters, and as of mid-September Pak Hŏn-yŏng was accepted in P'yŏngyang as the Party's national leader. But since the Americans, not the Russians, controlled South Korea, radically different political conditions prevailed there. Both Party growth and Party tactics were inevitably affected. Whereas Soviet control of Korea was limited to the area north of the 38th parallel, its control over the Party, with respect to both policies and leaders, extended north and south. Methods of contact varied. A stream of southern leaders or would-be leaders secretly visited P'yŏngyang. The Soviet consulate of Seoul was readily available, and Party agents from P'yŏngyang were frequently sent south with special instructions. In addition, radio broadcasts and Party publications provided rapid, authoritative means of communication.

29. For the text of the September 15 statement, see *Haebang Ilbo,* Oct. 30, 1945, and *Hyŏngmyŏng Sinmun,* Oct. 16, 1945. Both of these South Korean Communist journals published only excerpts of the northern statement, and there are some interesting differences in the lengthy sections chosen. For example, *Hyŏngmyŏng Sinmun,* the Changan organ, carried the clear orders to stop criticizing the allies and broaden the national united front, ending with the thought that the current situation necessitated a flexible strategy of retreating one step to advance two steps. This section was not included in the Pak group's organ, *Haebang Ilbo.* Also omitted from the latter was a section of the statement calling for the recognition of private property and private landholding, again because of the necessity to isolate the pro-Japanese elements and unite all other forces. It is possible, of course, that the portions printed only in *Hyŏngmyŏng Sinmun* were manufactured by the Changan group.

The Continuing Factional Struggle Within the KCP (South)

As we shall see, the Russians were not loath to apply their authority in making final decisions for the Party. There is no reason to believe, however, that they arrived in Korea with all the answers worked out in advance. Unquestionably, they were often confused about the facts and unable to cut through the welter of conflicting charges. Initially, therefore, factionalism in Seoul was allowed to continue, with the Changan group, despite its earlier setbacks, desperately seeking Soviet approval.

In early October, the Changan leaders began to attack the Reconstruction group for "errors" in connection with the creation of the People's Republic. Their arguments resembled those of the anti-Communists. The sudden convening of an All-Nation People's Representative Congress had been undertaken without proper training or mobilization of the masses. Indeed, "democratic principles were completely trampled upon," since the Congress had been "rounded up" with "childish impetuousness" in a matter of four or five hours. Not surprisingly, therefore, the Provisional Law adopted by the Congress "showed a complete lack of revolutionary character." Thus, with the arrival of the Americans and the occupation government's edict prohibiting the Republic from operating as a government, Republic leaders had been unable to devise any retaliatory tactics.[30]

The Changan spokesmen made it clear that, unlike various bourgeois elements, they did not wish to abolish the People's Republic. Rather, they wanted to see it strengthened. To this end, the People's Committees would have to be reorganized into a tight organizational system for agitation, propaganda, and mobilization. There would also have to be a second All-Nation People's Representative Congress. In point of fact, the People's Republic Central Committee had announced on October 2 that a second congress would be convened on March 1, 1946. But this merely provoked the Changan group to charges of undue haste and left-wing opportunism.

The Pak group tried to brush off all this criticism, but such statements as they made had a defensive ring to them. They did not attempt to deny their key role in the September Congress. They also admitted that, because of the chaotic, changing political situation, representatives had not been elected democratically by a broad segment of the people. (Conspicuously unmentioned was the fact that Pak and his men must have regarded it as essential to organize the People's Republic before American authorities set foot on Korean soil.) However, they argued, the Republic People's Committee should be regarded as a transitional body; its primary duty was to convene a second People's Representative Congress, and establish a permanent People's Government at the earliest possible date. But since

30. For the fullest criticism, see Chu Min, "Proposals Concerning the Convening of a 2nd All-Nation People's Representative Congress," *Hyŏngmyŏng Sinmun*, Oct. 4, 1945, and his "A Revolutionary Regime and the People's Representative Congress," *ibid.*, Oct. 16, 1945.

the working masses had had "little experience in elections or general political action," such actions could not take place immediately.[31] If the Changan attacks seemed to matter little to Pak and his followers, the P'yŏngyang group's statement of September 15 apparently received their closest attention. The next congress, it was asserted, should have the broadest possible representation from all classes, excluding only collaborators with Japanese imperialism and national traitors.

Even as the October assault was being unleashed, the two top leaders of the Changan group, Yi Yŏng and Ch'oe Ik-han, had made a pilgrimage to P'yŏngyang, leaving Seoul on September 30 and returning on October 15. Later, the Pak group were to charge them with scheming against the Party by spreading false reports about it. Of course, this pilgrimage once again symbolized the superiority of the Soviet command and the crucial importance of having Soviet approval. The trip appears to have had two basic objectives: to plead for Soviet anointment, and to learn from top Soviet authorities the correct Party line of the period. Thus, on October 12, the Central Committee of the KCP (Changan faction) met and announced a new "Resolution on the Establishment of the Regime and the National United Front." The resolution was needed, the Committee said, because comrades Yi Yŏng and Ch'oe Ik-han had communicated from P'yŏngyang a firm political line concerning the international situation and the Party would have to amend its strategies accordingly.[32]

The October resolution "boldly recognized" the fact that the Party had committed left-wing extremist deviations, reflective of the petty bourgeois mentality that was deeply implanted in the movement. It also indicated that "the historic contribution" of *both* the USSR and the US had to be correctly evaluated, so that "under their friendship and cooperation, Korean freedom and independence [could] be acquired as quickly as possible." The current revolution in Korea was to be considered a democratic bourgeois revolution that would necessarily move forward. However, the revolutionary pace should not be forced; otherwise, the Party would become alienated from the masses. Because of various weaknesses, the national bourgeoisie could not carry out its historic duties. Thus, the proletariat would, of necessity, lead the revolution in its current phase. But the bourgeoisie must not be pushed into the enemy camp by an open emphasis upon their reactionary character. They would cooperate in some matters, for example in land reform. Consequently, in the establishment of a national front, all elements, including the wealthy, should be involved. Only national traitors should be excluded.

31. "Proposals for the Political Direction of the 2nd All-Nation Representative Congress," editorial, *Haebang Ilbo*, Oct. 18, 1945.

32. *Hyŏngmyŏng Sinmun*, Oct. 31, 1945. Although this account says that the Central Committee met on October 12, the resolution published in *Chŏnsŏn*, Central Committee organ, on October 13, bears the date October 9.

It is clear that this "revised" resolution accurately reflected the current Soviet line on Korean Communism, as acquired by Yi Yŏng and Ch'oe Ik-han in the course of their P'yŏngyang visit, and that the Changan faction did not even wait for their return before hastening to make their own program conform to it.[33] This was not to save Yi Yŏng, Ch'oe Ik-han, and their comrades. On October 13, a Joint Conference of Party Members and Activists from the Five Provinces of North Korea met in P'yŏngyang, and out of this conference came a series of reports and resolutions of major importance to the southern as well as the northern Communists.

Fortunately, the conference minutes are available.[34] At the outset, it is most interesting to note that Pak Hŏn-yŏng was acknowledged by the participants to be the head of the Korean Communist Party, and that Seoul was accepted as the locus of Party headquarters.[35] The speech on the international situation was in all probability presented by a Russian. It suggests a sharp deterioration in USSR-US relations. America and Britain were vigorously attacked for their attitudes on the Polish question and on Eastern Europe in general. The British were accused of seeking to impose an Indian-style colonialism upon Greece. Because much of Europe was currently occupied by US and British forces, the "problem of democracy" had not been solved in France, Greece, Belgium, or the Netherlands. Nevertheless, the speech ended on an optimistic note, suggesting that all these problems would be solved, and urging that world peace be defended, with the USSR, Great Britain, and the United States in cooperation.

A certain Comrade O (probably O Ki-sŏp) presented the report on

33. The complete text of the new resolution can be found in *Chŏnsŏn*, Oct. 13, 1945, and *Hyŏngmyŏng Sinmun*, Oct. 16, 1945. As might have been expected, the resolution castigated the Pak Hŏn-yŏng faction, implying, indeed, that they were the chief culprits in committing Left extremist errors.

34. For the minutes, see Chosŏn Sanŏp Nodong Chosaso (Research Center for Korean Industry and Labor), eds., *Ol-ŭn nosŏn* (*The Correct Line*), Seoul, 1945. The names of the participants have been deleted by the editor and only the family names of the speakers are given.

35. The following telegram was sent to Pak Hŏn-yŏng in Seoul: "We send our gratitude to Marshal Stalin of the Soviet Union, which is the Fatherland of the proletarian class of the entire world, and at the same time express our deep-felt gratitude to Comrade Pak Hŏn-yŏng, who is the leader of the Korean proletariat class, for enabling us to hold the Joint Conference of the Five Provinces in North Korea, following the correct lines established by Comrade Pak Hŏn-yŏng. In Korea, particularly in North Korea, all of the advantageous conditions have been realized because of the heroic struggles of the Red Army led by Marshal Stalin's truly great policies for world peace and liberation. We wish Comrade Pak good health so that our Bolshevik camp may be strengthened and expanded, and all policies may be implemented to solve immediate problems under his correct, Bolshevik guidance.

"Long Live the Korean Communist Party!

"Long Live the Korean People's Republic!

"Long Live Comrade Stalin, the leader of the world's proletariat!

"Long Live Comrade Pak Hŏn-yŏng, head of the Korean Proletariat"

the political tasks of the Party. The order of the day was to establish a unified, independent People's Republic of Korea, acknowledging that during this stage the country would be in a democratic bourgeois phase of development. Once again, the leadership of Pak was asserted and strongly supported, and other elements were as strongly criticized. Korean Communists who had earlier fought "with their mouths only," or had recanted from prison, should be allowed to enter the Party only after serious examination. The Yi Yŏng group in Seoul was specifically singled out for vigorous criticism. Its program was attacked as Trotskyism, which was defined as a form of left extremism that regarded the present stage as one of socialist revolution, that did not recognize the contribution of the Allies in liberating Korea, that used "empty revolutionary phrases," and that had failed to bring the broad masses into the People's Republic. Comrade O concluded that, while the Party also harbored some rightists who were attempting to bring pro-Japanese and reactionary elements into the national front, the main problem was that of left extremism, as exemplified by Yi Yŏng and his faction.

The report on Party organization was presented by "Comrade Kim" (one is tempted to believe that this was Kim Il-sŏng). Pointing out that the Party had been in existence a mere two months and was still very weak, Kim repeated the soft line regarding a national front and a bourgeois democratic stage. Kim praised Pak for repelling all liberal groups within the young Party, and stated that problems would be discussed "under the instructions of Comrade Pak." He urged more attention to workers and peasants in recruiting Party members, and admitted that the Party currently depended mainly on intellectuals, with only 30 percent of its members from the working class (which included both workers and peasants). Like Comrade O, he condemned the group led by Yi Yŏng and Ch'oe Ik-han as left extremists, and denounced them for Trotskyite positions that were, in effect, echoes from the Japanese imperialists. He further charged that they slandered comrades and sold their honor—harsh words indeed.

At this conference, the principle was supposedly established that branches should obey the center. This confirmed the supremacy of Seoul. At the same time, however, because of the "peculiarities" in the Korean situation, it was resolved that a Northern Branch Bureau should be created, and that since it was technically difficult for the Center to print Party membership certificates and then dispatch them to the north, these should be issued in the north under the approval of the Center. There was also a report, to be discussed later, on local and provincial activities in the north. The Conference ended with the appointment of seventeen members to the North Branch Bureau Committee.

As can be seen, these minutes reveal some extremely important developments. Kim Il-sŏng only made his first public appearance in

P'yŏngyang on October 14. He was still unknown in public circles, north or south, at this point. Meanwhile, the northern branches of the Party (presumably under Soviet guidance) had placed their imprimatur upon Pak's leadership and denounced the Changan group in immoderate terms. The demise of the Changan group was now inevitable.

Later, when it became politically essential to do so, Kim Il-sŏng's adherents were to attack the actions of the "Pak Hŏn-yŏng clique" of this period as "right-wing errors" of major proportions.[36] The initial Pak pronunciamento of August 20 was called anti-Soviet and pro-American, a document preaching right-wing defeatism and seeking to paralyze the class consciousness of the masses. This clique, it was now said, even advocated the establishment of a "pro-American bourgeois republic headed by that faithful running dog of American imperialism, Syngman Rhee." But these vicious and false attacks came much later, after Pak had been liquidated. At this point, Pak basked in Soviet approval, and therefore in Kim's, too.

Thus, Yi Yŏng and Ch'oe Ik-han could not have been optimistic about their future when they returned from P'yŏngyang to Seoul on October 15. Probably this is the chief reason why, on October 20, they dispatched a conciliatory letter of the Reconstruction group urging "serious discussions" to overcome factionalism and extreme leftist tendencies within the Party, and to accomplish the creation of a single, unified Party organization.[37] There is no indication that the Reconstruction group bothered to answer this letter. Meanwhile, confronted with the P'yŏngyang line, the Changan group moved sharply to the right of its own accord. On October 24, five Changan representatives signed an agreement with representatives of two conservative parties, Song Chin-u's Korean Democratic Party and An Chae-hong's Nationalist Party (Kungmin-dang), pledging support for the Provisional Government in Chungking and seeking to speed its return to Korea. They also agreed to prepare for the convening of a national conference that would lay the foundations for a "unified, completely democratic, independent and official government of Korea." To achieve these ends, the three participating parties established a five-man Preparatory Committee for a National Conference, consisting of Kim Pyŏng-no, Paek Hong-gyun, Ch'oe Ik-han, Kim Chun-yŏn, and Ch'oe Sŏng-hwan.[38]

36. See, for example, Han Im-hyŏk, *Kim Il-sŏng tongji e ŭihan Chosŏn kong-san-dang ch'ang-gŏn* (*The Construction of the Korean Communist Party by Comrade Kim Il-sŏng*), P'yŏngyang, 1961, pp. 27 ff.

37. This letter was published in *Chŏnsŏn*, Oct. 31, 1945, as part of "A Summary Report on the Acceleration of Party Unification."

38. This agreement and a listing of the steps to implement it were published in a news sheet that asserted that negotiations had commenced on October 17, and that also expressed the hope that these developments would eventually lead to a nationwide united front. Since the announcement is followed by a long statement by the Secretariat of the KCP (Changan), we can assume that the news sheet was published by the Changan group.

On October 25, the day after the conclusion of the three-party alliance, Party representatives, including elements from the Changan group, spent approximately two hours with Syngman Rhee, who had returned to Korea on October 16. Rhee had received a hero's welcome upon his return. He had refused to accept the offer of the presidency of the People's Republic, a body of which the new three-party alliance was also highly critical.

Interestingly enough, the Changan group sought to justify these various political actions by quoting extensively from Mao Tse-tung's *On Coalition Government,* a tract first delivered as a speech at the Seventh National Congress of the CCP on April 24, 1945. Mao had called for the union of all political parties and groups, together with various nonaffiliated elements, and for the establishment of an independent, democratic coalition government. He had proclaimed this the only sound route for the defeat of the Japanese aggressors and the creation of a new China.

Unquestionably, however, it was not Mao but the Soviet leaders in P'yŏngyang who had stimulated the new course of action. But there was a vast difference between the type of coalition that Mao envisaged, "one under the leadership of the proletariat," and the three-party alliance that was now created. The conservative parties were far stronger than the Changan group, a fact that would have made the advantages of this alliance dubious from a Communist standpoint even if the Changan faction had been in favor. The Pak group, in a fiery statement of November 5, naturally excoriated their Communist rivals for joining with "the reactionary portion of the bourgeoisie." [39]

39. "The Council on Immediate Political Measures of the Korean Communist Party," *Haebang Ilbo,* Nov. 5, 1945. This statement began with the charge that "the international Trotskyites" were openly developing reactionary and antipopular schemes in Korea, having earlier misinterpreted the current stage of the Korean revolution by proclaiming the socialist era at hand. It asserted that, despite the fact that the Yi Yŏng–Ch'oe Ik-han group had trampled on the principle of obeying the majority, completely ignored Communist discipline, and "systematically reproduced Trotskyism" in Korea, the Party had ignored their reactionary actions, hoping that they would repent their mistakes. However, the group had persisted, and had even gone to P'yŏngyang, scheming against the Party there, using slander and falsehood. The Five Provinces Conference, however, had correctly indicated their errors and had demanded their dissolution, together with a public admission of error. Although these elements had promised to carry out the conference's directives, they had maneuvered in thir death throes to support the Chungking government and undermine the Korean People's Republic, "the concentrated political expression of the anti-Japanese imperialist struggle." They had surrendered unconditionally to the Korean Democratic Party, and had joined the anticlass, antipeople, antirevolutionary camp.

"Only the most decadent and rotten portion of the bourgeoisie," proclaimed the statement, "would denounce the Central People's Committee under such slanderous and false remarks as 'undemocratic, bureaucratic rigidification, or sectarian closedness.'" The fact also that they had not mentioned a single word about the Righteous Army Movement of Kim Il-sŏng who had continued a heroic struggle against the Japanese army for more than a decade in the wilds of Manchuria and in North

On November 23, the Changan group finally succumbed, after what must have been enormous pressure exercised from both P'yŏngyang and Seoul. It is probable that various emissaries traveled to and from P'yŏngyang, and numerous behind-the-scenes meetings occurred. In any case, the Changan faction publicly announced its dissolution on November 24. The faction's official statement was that it was undertaking this sacrifice on behalf of a unified Party and in order not to impede united front activities. "In the short period of 100 days," the statement proclaimed, "our Party has made many contributions and also committed many errors." [40]

The Strengthening of the Party and Its Fronts

What was the size of the Party in the south in this initial period, and what were the sources of strength upon which it could draw? To the first question, there is no precise answer available. In early September, shortly

---

Korea while speaking of the anti-imperialist forces abroad, "exposes their true color."

So far as can be determined, however, this was the first time that the Pak group had referred publicly to Kim Il-sŏng, and their paucity of information about his activities is apparent when they refer to him erroneously as a part of the Righteous Army Movement (thereby forwarding the myth of an earlier, older Kim).

In this same issue of *Haebang Ilbo*, about one-sixth of the front page was devoted to Kim, with the assertion that "if we are to count the true leaders of our people before August 15, we must count General Kim Il-sŏng first." The article ends with the following slogans: "Long Live the Young Hero General Kim Il-sŏng! Long Live the Absolute Independence of Korea! Long Live the Emancipation of the Working People of Korea!"

In point of fact, the Changan faction had actually hailed Kim a week earlier, in the October 27 issue of *Chŏnsŏn*, publishing an article entitled "Welcome General Kim Il-sŏng." In this article, Kim was called a "comet among the stars," his guerrilla career in Manchuria being briefly noted. He had been compared to Marshal Tito of Yugoslavia as a great general of the guerrilla era. On October 31, moreover, *Hyŏngmyŏng Sinmun* (the Changan organ) published a rather long article hailing the return of two "great leaders of the entire nation," Dr. Syngman Rhee and General Kim Il-sŏng. It asserted that thirty million Koreans had long admired these two heroes and awaited their return.

Kim, as we have indicated, made his public debut in P'yŏngyang on October 14. It is interesting to note the delay in hailing him in Seoul. When the eulogies came, however, they were effusive, suggesting that all Communist leaders of the south had received word that the young, relatively unknown guerrilla fighter had become Russia's chosen political instrument, at least in the north.

40. The Changan group's public statement is carried in *Choyu Sinmun* (*Free News*), Nov. 24, 1945, "Merger and Unity of the Communist Party—The Dissolution of the Changan Group under the Principle of One Country, One Party." (This item was obtained from the private collection of Mr. O Han-gǔn.) The article reported a conference of Changan faction leaders under the chairmanship of Yi Yǒng, and the reasons, summarized above, for the decision to dissolve and join with the Reconstruction Communist party.

after their arrival, American occupation authorities estimated that the KCP had approximately 3,000 members in the area south of the 38th parallel. As of January 1946, the estimated figure had risen to between 20,000 and 30,000, and shortly thereafter, as we shall see, the Communists themselves were to make public claims of massive increases. By the late spring of 1946, KCP leaders were asserting that Party membership had reached 200,000. The figures compiled by American and South Korean authorities were considerably less—generally in the order of 40,000 to 60,000. A year later, in September 1947, after some strenuous events, Party membership was estimated by the Military Government as "probably" between 30,000 and 40,000—and the Party's fortunes were soon to decline.

One problem with all of these figures is that, even if they were accurate, Party membership was at no point a good index of Party power. We have already seen the extraordinary influence the Party was able to wield over the Korean People's Republic and so over the People's Committees throughout the country. By early November, the Party had won virtual control of a number of youth, labor, and peasant front organizations, thus augmenting its power very considerably.

Let us look first at the situation within the labor unions. By early September, the organization of labor had begun under Communist aegis. According to Kim Nam-sik, then a low-level Party cadre, many of the cadres who were given assignments as labor organizers were young men in their twenties, energetic and dynamic, possessed of a middle school education, enthusiastic young revolutionaries who went into the shops and factories in the fashion of the Narodniks. Such young men became the pillars of the Party in such crucial areas as the Yŏngdŭngp'o district of Seoul, one of the most important industrial regions of South Korea.

As early as September 2, *Taejung* (*The Masses*) carried a notice of the creation of a Preparatory Committee for a Transport Workers' Union. Shortly thereafter, the first significant labor disputes occurred, many of them in plants that were Japanese-owned. Since the Japanese were resigned to their departure from Korea as well as to the loss of their plants, concessions were easily obtained. This in turn bolstered the prestige of the labor organizers. Union membership rapidly mushroomed.

Political issues were quickly joined to economic ones, with the young Party cadres calling the signals. Even before the American Military Government had established itself, there were signs that the Communists would monopolize the organized labor movement in South Korea. Social Democrats and others of the moderate Left were preoccupied with party organization. The right-wing leaders could scarcely have been expected to seize the initiative in this field. Rapidly, therefore, the labor movement veered so far to the left under the tutelage of young Party enthusiasts that leaders within the Communist Party itself became critical of certain trends.[41]

On September 26, a Preparatory Committee for an All-Nation Conference of Trade Unions was set up. Throughout October, various unions were organized on a national, industry-wide basis. Finally, on November 5, the National Council of Korean Labor Unions opened its first conference. The conference provides an excellent illustration of the extensive Communist control over South Korean organized labor at this point. Some 505 delegates, coming from all 13 provinces of Korea and purporting to represent 500,000 trade unionists, met in Seoul. After the singing of the Korean national anthem and "The Red Flag," chairman Hŏ Sŏng-t'aek proclaimed the conference officially under way, and four honorary chairmen were selected: Pak Hŏn-yŏng, Kim Il-sŏng, Louis Saillant (secretary-general of the newly formed World Federation of Trade Unions), and Mao Tse-tung. A series of resolutions were then adopted. The first was a message of thanks to "the only leader of the Korean working masses and the great patriot who made this conference possible, Comrade Pak Hŏn-yŏng." There followed a resolution of thanks to the four allied powers for liberation, a resolution to annihilate those "traitors to the working class," Yi Yŏng, Ch'oe Ik-han, and associates, and a resolution to support actively the political line of Comrade Pak Hŏn-yŏng on the establishment of a united front. In the course of the meeting, messages were read from Pak, Yi Chu-sang ("minister of labor of the Korean People's Republic"), Kim Kwang-su of the Seoul People's Committee, Kwon O-jik of the Communist Youth League, and others.[42]

41. See, for example, "The Current Tasks of the Labor Union Movement," *Haebang Ilbo*, Nov. 25, 1945, and Dec. 6, 1945. In this article, the author warned against such acts as the seizure of property, which was bringing about conflicts with American Occupational authorities.

42. For a full report of this meeting, see *Maeil Sinbo* (*The Daily News*), Nov. 6, 1945. It should be added that on the second day of the conference, possibly as an effort to ward off Occupation criticism, three additional honorary chairmen were added: the Labour Minister of Great Britain, the Labor Minister of the USSR, and Mr. Sidney Hillman of the American AFL-CIO.

Chairman Hŏ Sŏng-t'aek and Pak Se-yŏng, who was elected first vice-chairman, were both men of lengthy experience in the pre-1945 communist underground movement.

The following represents a chart of trade union development in both North and South Korea during the first six months after Liberation. It is drawn from composite sources.

We may estimate that about one-half of the reported 574,000 union members as of February 1946 were in North Korea. The 1946 Liberation Yearbook reveals that approximately 75 percent of the union members were male, with about 60 percent of these men being "young men" and the remainder being "men in the prime of life." The average union member's age was probably close to 35. Of the female members, 80 percent were young women, most of them textile workers in their adolescence. See *Chosŏn haebang nyŏnbo, op. cit.*

The conference of November 5 represented the last effort to maintain a united, nationwide trade union movement. The trade unions of the North were soon granted "autonomy," and began to pursue an independent course. In this they were only conforming to developments in the political field. On November 30, a North Korean General Bureau of the All-Nation Council was created. On May 25, 1946, a second and final step was taken when the General Bureau executive committee voted to rename their organization Puk-Chosŏn Chik-ŏp Ch'ong-yŏnmaeng (North Korean General Federation of Professions). This only confirmed the complete separation of actions and officers that was already an administrative fact.

Meanwhile, a major effort to organize farmers had also been completed. On December 8, 1945, the first conference of the National Federation of Farmers' Unions opened in Seoul. A total of 545 delegates from 13 provinces, 22 cities, and 219 prefectures, purporting to represent more than 3,300,000 union members, north and south, met to establish a permanent national organization and work out basic policies. From the figures

The Strength of Labor Unions as of November 1945 and February 1946

Industry	Date Founded[1]	No. of branches Nov. 1945[1]	Of which in No. Korea[1]	No. of branches Feb. 1946[2]	Sub-branches[2]	Membership Feb. 1946[2]
Metal	11-2-45	19	8	20	215	51,364
Chemical	11-3-45	19	9	18	167	49,015
Textile	11-3-45	10	4	16	121	30,268
Publication	?	19	8	16	65	4,368
Transportation	—	—	—	28	140	58,041
Food Processing	11-3-45	23	10	23	108	22,523
Construction	11-3-45	17	7	17	127	59,118
Electric	11-4-45	11	5	14	54	15,742
Lumbering	11-4-45	26	11	11	125	30,722
Fishing	—	—	—	9	50	35,653
Mining	11-1-45	(88)	?	9	123	64,572
Communication	11-3-45	21	10	9	40	10,215
Railroad	11-2-45	20	11	14	117	62,439
General	?	18	10	14	107	17,065
Marine	—	—	—	7	9	4,720
Shipbuilding	11-4-45	13	6	10	38	5,349
United	—	—	—	—	74	53,101
TOTAL		216 (304)	99	235	1,680	574,275

SOURCES: (1) *Chŏnguk Nodongja Sinmun*, Nov. 16, 1945.
(2) Minjŏn Samuguk (Secretariat, Democratic National Front), *Chosŏn haebang nyŏnbo* (*Korean Liberation Yearbook*), 1946 ed., Seoul, 1946, p. 158.

available, we can assume that approximately 2 million of the claimed 3.3 million members lived south of the 38th parallel.[43]

On the second day of the conference, a twenty-eight-point program was adopted. As might have been expected, the key planks related to land reform; they were relatively moderate, reflecting the current Communist position, both north and south. All land belonging to Japanese and to "national traitors" should be confiscated and distributed to poor farmers. On other lands, the tenant fee should be set at 30 percent, and in principle it should be paid in cash, not in kind. All public duties such as taxes should be paid by the landowners, with the costs of seed and fertilizer to be shared equally by landlord and tenant. In case of crop failure, or if land had not been tilled, tenant fees should be waived. Moreover, the state should guarantee a minimum livelihood to all farmers. Debts owed to Japanese or national traitors should be considered null and void, and the interest rate on all other debts should be reduced to 5 percent per annum.[44]

43. The Organized Strength of the All-Nation Federation of the Farmers' Unions
(as of the end of November 1945)

Province	City, prefectural, and island branches	myŏn (township) branches	ri (hamlet) groups	Members
South Chŏlla[a]	14	110	3,019	369,414
North Chŏlla[a]	12	103	2,075	301,645
South Kyŏngsang[a]	15	182	1,877	459,759
North Kyŏngsang[a]	17	127	2,598	275,913
South Ch'ungch'ŏng[a]	12	97	1,890	122,563
North Ch'ungch'ŏng[a]	6	57	1,750	116,978
Kyŏnggi[b]	15	134	3,239	193,549
Kangwŏn[c]	21	179	1,857	175,852
Hwanghae[d]	17	227	981	204,277
South P'yŏngan[d]	14	140	1,640	173,545
North P'yŏngan[d]	19	178	1,600	279,424
South Hamgyŏng[d]	15	135	1,979	450,746
North Hamgyŏng[d]	11	76	783	199,532
TOTAL	188	1,745	25,288	3,323,197

SOURCE: *Chosŏn haebang nyŏnbo, op. cit.*, p. 167.
  [a] South of the 38th parallel
  [b] South of the 38th parallel but small portion in the north
  [c] Divided almost equally at the 38th parallel
  [d] In North Korea

It would appear that the membership figures are based upon varying methods of calculation, some counting heads of households only, others counting all individuals involved.

44. *For details, see Chosŏn haebang nyŏnbo, op. cit.*, p. 168. The KCP resolution on the land problem, which was almost identical, can be found in *Haebang Ilbo*, Oct. 3, 1945.

Like its counterpart in the industrial field, the National Federation of Farmers' Unions was under Communist control from its inception. Union branches, moreover, were usually organized by the same type of young Communist enthusiast as was to be found in the trade union movement. A female Communist cadre who later defected, So Chŏng-ja, has given us a vivid description of the inauguration of a Farmers' Union branch in the Chinju region.[45] After careful preparations by local KCP cadres, who were following standard instructions from Seoul, a meeting date was set. There was maximum advance publicity, and at the appointed time several thousand farmers were gathered to the sound of gongs. The noise was considerable. The police, surprised at the size of the throng, quickly restricted the meeting to five hundred persons. A major argument ensued. After much debate, a compromise was reached; straw ropes were placed around the five hundred people who were declared to be officially involved in the meeting, and several thousand others stood outside the rope-line!

The speeches at the meeting accorded strictly with Communist Party instructions. So's own speech was devoted to an attack upon the US Military Government for its interference with the efforts of the Korean people to organize themselves, both politically and economically. She recalls having shouted: "In North Korea, which was liberated on the same day and hour as us, sovereignty has been transferred to the workers and farmers. Let us, the exploited farmers and workers, unite and become landowners and lords of the nation like our brethren in the north!" (Because of this speech, a warrant for So's arrest was issued. Before it was served, incidentally, she married a young Party official—in a Buddhist temple!)

In appealing to the peasant during this period, the Communists had a number of advantages. But they also had major obstacles to overcome. Their chief advantage was that economic conditions in rural Korea, always extremely bad, had now become even worse as a result of the war. Fertilizer, seed, and other agricultural necessities were in exceedingly short supply, and poor weather further complicated the situation. Thus, from an economic standpoint, there were many appeals to be made. Naturally, the Communists talked of land to the tiller, not collectivization. They emphasized the bitter inequities involved in the yangban (gentry) system, and promised a new, democratic era when all would own their own land, official repression would cease, and taxes would disappear.

Even when this utopia was spread before him, however, the Korean peasant did not always respond in the manner desired. Over the centuries, he had learned how to survive by means of a political culture radically different from that now being offered. Despite much writing to the contrary, this culture was not wholly based upon submissiveness and ignorance. Reciprocities, many of them exceedingly subtle, governed the whole of

45. So Chŏng-ja, *Nae ga panyŏkcha-nya? (Am I a Traitor?)*, Seoul, 1966, pp. 30–31.

Korean rural society, including relations between the rural classes. It was perfectly appropriate to define this system as "conservative." But it *was* a total way of life, and as such it encompassed values, attitudes, and relationships. It was thus political in the most comprehensive sense, although it was a culture in which private government often prevailed over public government.

When the peasant was plunged into the new politics (usually with little understanding of its implications and often as a result of external manipulation), the results could be disastrous. To illustrate how the new politics could affect a village, let us cite a farmer's story drawn from a slightly later period, the time of the Taegu riots of October 1946. Though condensing this account, we have sought to retain the flavor of his words.

> The people of our hamlet live near the city of Taegu. One morning we were awakened early by the sound of our bell. Going outside, I saw some fifty men passing our house, carrying shovels, picks, and clubs. They were farmers from a nearby hamlet. Some were old, some young, and there were even boys who had barely finished elementary school. They were shouting, "Let's go to the myŏn office!"
>
> I joined them, and off we went to the myŏn (township) office, about one kilometer away. There, two young men in Western clothes were making speeches. "Taegu has been occupied by the People's Committee," they said. "The police have been disarmed. Now we must destroy all running dogs of the Japs. We must have a world where there are no more taxes in kind." Later, we found out that these young men were leftist agents who had come to the village during the previous night.
>
> Our life at that time was miserable. Commodity prices were rising daily. "Liberation," moreover, was empty talk. The rascal who had been myŏn office clerk under the Japanese was still there, behaving as arrogantly as ever. If a farmer fell into arrears in paying his taxes, he would make that farmer kneel on the ground, even if it was a rainy day. He himself was a farmer who had gotten rich under the Japanese.
>
> Hence, the farmers marching on the myŏn office were really seeking revenge for the evil tax-in-kind system, and on this arrogant bastard. That was all. But the leadership—and the agitation that provoked us to action—came from those young men who claimed to represent the People's Committee. Of course, at that time, the People's Committees were everywhere. If a person had a sixth grade education, he almost automatically became a member of the local People's Committee.
>
> In any case, the farmers rushed to the myŏn office, destroying everything in it and burning all of the documents. The police fled, as did the clerk. But the farmers followed him, burned his house down, and even built a special fire for the book containing his ancestral records. That night, in celebration, the farmers had a big feast and everyone got drunk. They seemed to think that a world without taxes or clerks had arrived.
>
> The next morning, however, they found that those young men— now totally vanished—were devils, not angels. Taegu had been placed

under martial law, and soon Korean police and American soldiers arrived from the city. Knowing that they were in trouble, all of the villagers fled to the mountains when they heard that the authorities were coming. Shortly, the women and children came back, but the men, fearing arrest, remained in the mountains during the day, coming back only at night. Some were shot to death while trying to avoid capture. The houses of those farmers who had led the riot were burned to the ground and, in some cases, their families were trapped in the fire. The mob in the mountains, moreover, became desperate for food and clothing, and they began to rob the villagers just trying to stay alive. The villagers in turn would then be arrested on the charge that they had provided food to fugitives. Thus, they were beset from all sides and many families became totally destitute. It was a terrible time.[46]

Naturally, things did not go quite as far as this in very many rural hamlets, even those that became politically engaged. This hamlet, it must be remembered, was near the city of Taegu, one of the centers of leftism in South Korea. Nevertheless, this farmer's account has many implications for the broader scene. Unquestionably, legitimate rural grievances existed and went largely unanswered in this period.[47] Indeed, the rural hamlet had

46. Yi Mok-u, "Taegu sip-il p'oktong sakŏn" ("The Taegu October 1st Riot Incident"), *Sedae,* Oct. 1965, pp. 230–231.

47. Peasant grievances and Communist organizational activities are presented from a highly sympathetic point of view by Yi Ŭn-jik (Ri In-choku) in a three-volume novel entitled *Dakuryū (Muddy Stream),* Tokyo, 1967–68. Yi, born in Chŏng-ŭp, Chŏlla Pukto, in 1917, graduated from Japan University, Tokyo, in 1941. In this novel, he deals with the farmers' movement in his home town, and it is possible that the novel contains much that is autobiographical.

The novel opens with the hero, Yi Sang-gŭn, returning to his hamlet from Japan, and finding the peasants all talking about the 7:3 system (70 percent of the produce to the tenant, 30 percent to the landlord). Yi's elder brother had been a tenant farmer under a Japanese landlord, and is asked by the farmers' union to pay 30 percent for the support of the People's Committee—but the US Military Government stops this, causing the money to go to the New Korea Company it has established.

A young man who has come to the hamlet from a nearby town persuades Yi Sang-gŭn to become a farmers' union organizer. In his opening speech to the farmers of his hamlet, Yi tells them that their poverty is the product of yangban and Japanese mistreatment. At first there is reluctance to join the union despite a universal desire for lower tenant fees and interest rates. There is a fear that the landlords, or the government, will create trouble. But finally, after numerous exhortations, all agree to join; Yi is elected head of the union.

When membership blanks are distributed, however, only about 70 percent sign them, mainly the poorer farmers. It is necessary to draw additional recruits from among the more influential elements of the hamlet. When the union has been established, five members, including Yi, visit the local landlord, requesting reduction of rents to 30 percent and reduction of interest rates to 10 percent, with all past debts being annulled. But the delegation is beaten up by the landlord and his men. In retaliation, the union members gather and beat up the landlord. At this point, however, USMG policies begin to oppress the union. The People's Committee is de-no voice in the wider political developments. The American occupation forces rarely operated at the village level, and almost no Americans could communicate with the farmers, since very few spoke Korean. Even at the provincial level, the military government was largely a government by interpreters. In Seoul, at headquarters, a few score Koreans with American or British educational backgrounds, together with a few Americans who had been missionaries in the pre-1945 era, played key roles in this respect. As one went down the ladder toward the local levels of administration, he often found Koreans of questionable qualifications (and morals) acting in the name of occupation personnel of equally questionable qualifications (and morals). Indeed, a number of Koreans at present trace the extensive corruption of the postwar era to the Americans and their interpreters of the 1945–48 period, especially to those who were operating close to the grass roots.

---

nounced, along with all of its peripheral organizations. The landlord's son receives an appointment as *kun* (prefecture) chief, and immediately sends police to arrest Yi and his comrades.

The "organization" (Party) tells Yi to flee to the next *kun*, where he recommences organizational work. Soon, however, comrades in this *kun* urge him to go to the provincial capital, fearing police action. Via a letter of introduction from an old friend, Yi gets a job in the commerce and industry section of the provincial government, and serves as liaison man with an American army captain, the military governor of the province. He sees ignorance, injustice, and arbitrariness in USMG orders, and tries to fight them. (In the novel, it is made to appear that Americans are taking rice from the Korean farmers to ship it to the poor in America, an ironic parody of what the Russians were actually doing in the North.) The "organization," however, tells Yi to keep his emotions in check and not to reveal himself, since he holds a strategic position. Nevertheless, an American missionary turned intelligence agent gets hot on his trail, and Yi is forced to go to Pusan for three months. There he looks after repatriates from Japan.

Ultimately, while trying to convert South Korean police, Yi is betrayed and jailed. He is soon released, however, and has long conversations with two Americans, a military officer and a reporter. In these, some KCP attitudes concerning Americans are clearly revealed. Yi tells Smith, the reporter, that while the United States has studied Japan and is trying there to develop friendly relations, it is treating Korea like a colony, even though it talks about "liberating" the country, thereby revealing a very "insincere attitude." Smith responds by saying that whereas Japanese politicians know how to use Americans skillfully, Koreans—of whatever political hue—don't understand the United States or how to communicate effectively with Americans.

The "organization" then orders Yi to go to Seoul with Smith, to influence him if possible. Yi introduces Smith to a Party economist, and the economist seems to have some rapport with the American. Meanwhile, Yi returns to Pusan to work with the repatriate squatters (who are soon forcefully removed by USMG) and then to make agitational lectures to dock workers and girl textile workers. It becomes more and more difficult, however, to give such lectures without being arrested, and thus the movement loses its momentum.

One can learn much from this novel—in highly romanticized form—about how the South Korean Communists saw themselves, their Korean opponents, and the Americans.

It should not be surprising, therefore, that Communist propagandists found fertile soil in the rural areas. The incident related above, however, illustrates how Communist-inspired acts could lead to tragedy for all concerned—except the agitators. The fact, therefore, that many of the Peasants' Union branches were dominated not by farmers but by young students or so-called intellectuals raised increasing doubts in the minds of many farmers. Was this a genuine farmers' movement, or the here-today–gone-tomorrow game of some city boys? A highly revealing letter was published in the December 14, 1945, issue of *Haebang Ilbo*. Supposedly written by a dirt farmer, it was highly critical of the domination of the National Farmers' Union Conference by intellectuals. One can be certain that this was not a unique response.[48]

The manipulation of workers and farmers by radical petty intellectuals could continue unimpeded in the north, where it had the approval of the authorities, and where the risk accordingly lay not in involvement, but in lack of it. In the south, where the broader political context was drastically different, Communist activities were certain to be challenged, especially as top Party leaders ordered increasingly reckless and violent actions at the local level.

Meanwhile, Party recruitment of youth, especially students, was at the center of Communist organizational efforts in the months immediately following Liberation. We have already suggested why the student was of such crucial importance. He (or she) had the leisure, the daring, and the vigor essential to successful revolutionary activities. He also had the education, the youthfulness, and the self-confidence to become an ardent propagator of Marxist-Leninist doctrines.

The first student organization to emerge was the Chosŏn Haktodae (Korean Student Corps), established only a few days after Japanese surrender, on August 18, 1945. Students at Seoul National University constituted the nucleus of this group, and key figures such as Ch'oe Sang-ho were KCP cadres, although this fact was not revealed at the time.[49] On

48. The writer reported that when he attended the conference, he was confronted with "many fine speeches," but everyone looked like an "interi" (intellectual). Almost all wore Western clothes, had clean-shaven faces, and looked exactly alike. Perhaps, added the writer sarcastically, they had taken the A-frames off their backs, left their carts in storage, and changed into different clothing before coming to the Conference. Then, in a serious vein, he asserted that more bona fide farmers should have attended the meetings. One intellectual among ten delegates would have sufficed. *Haebang Ilbo*, Dec. 14, 1945.

49. Kim Chŏng-gi, who was a college student in 1945 and who joined the KCP in March 1946, has given us many details about activities among the students during this period. Kim states that he himself had not been ideologically oriented before Liberation, but in the fall of 1945 he began to read various pamphlets given to him by fellow students—Kawakami Hajime's *Bimbō monogatari* (*Stories of the Poor*) and other leftist tracts. The next step was to join a "reading circle" promoted by Communist students (although he did not know their political affiliation at the time). He

precisely the same day, an openly Communist unit, the Communist Youth League, was created. In the months that followed, extensive organizational activities were undertaken in every college and middle school. On December 11, 1945, the General League of Korean Youth was established. The League was intended to be a broad front organization, manipulated by the Left, but encompassing moderates as well as radicals. Thus, League platforms tended to be sweeping, vague statements of principle upon which a wide measure of agreement could be obtained. For example, the League's December program pledged the unity of Korean youth on behalf of constructing "a progressive, democratic state" and eliminating "all remnants of Japanese imperialism, feudalism, and reactionarism."

Less than a month after the General League was set up, the trusteeship issue emerged. The youth movement, along with all other political movements, was seriously disrupted, and the Communists were badly hurt. On

---

also began to attend lectures given by leftist professors and became stimulated by "the new knowledge" they dispensed. During this period, he transferred from He-hwa College (later Tongguk University) to Seoul University. The latter school was a center of leftist activities, with such traditions as the Miyake affair a part of its legacy.

By early 1946, according to Kim, most colleges and universities were heavily politicized. Students even chose their classroom neighbors because of their political positions. In the period, the largest KCP student contingent came from Korea University (Koryŏ University) with some thirty student members. Most other colleges had ten to fifteen members. Later, in the South Korea Workers' Party era, the numbers were larger. Student members in the College of Commerce, Seoul University, one of the significant centers of Communist activity, reached two hundred in 1947.

A Party cell was organized if there were more than three members. The organizational structure of student cells was as follows: Cell chairmen received instructions from the Student Section of the Party District Committee. (At the time, there were eight District Committees in Seoul alone, and each district had a Youth Bureau which, in turn, had a Student Section.) All of the Youth Bureaus, in turn, were under the direction of the Youth Bureau of the KCP Central Committee. Student Section heads, and higher officials concerned with student members, were all full-time, professional Party cadres.

According to Kim, student Party members were sufficiently few in the early period so that everyone knew each other—even those from different campuses. Later, however, as student membership expanded, this was no longer the case. Meanwhile, the Party began to concentrate upon middle school students also, establishing "democratic circles" in order to propagandize and recruit. Kim has stated that if there were even five Party members in a class of sixty, classroom opinion could be altered. The Communists, according to him, were enormously effective in manipulating the less politically conscious students. When a campaign was dictated by the Party, cell meetings would be held for several days in advance, with the most minute plans being drawn up. It would be decided who would say what, and in what order. Even the tactic of having someone within the Party challenge an opening speaker so as to provide the appearance of dialogue was often adopted. Inevitably, the unorganized majority was caused to follow the highly organized minority, said Kim, citing the major Communist success in promoting a nationwide student strike in the fall of 1946 against the plan to establish national universities, a strike that spread throughout the south, as we shall see, and lasted until the spring of 1947. Chong-Sik Lee interview with Kim Chŏng-gi, May 26, 1967, Seoul.

April 25, 1946, as a result of internal wrangling, the Communist-led Left formed a new organization, Chosŏn Minju Ch'ŏngnyŏn Tongmaeng (Korean Democratic Youth League).[50] The League supposedly brought together the youth sections of all Communist and Communist front organizations—labor, farmers', women's, and others. It was charged with the tasks of setting up special lectures, reading circles, night schools, musical sessions, and speech contests so as to provide "democratic education" to the youth of South Korea. On occasion, it sponsored sports events, and dispatched workers to help in such tasks as flood relief, street cleaning, and farm labor during the planting and harvesting seasons. The latter efforts, of course, were intended to bring the Party "closer to the masses."

Did the radical South Korean students of this period have any heroes? While Pak Hŏn-yŏng was the most widely accepted leader, there is no evidence that he possessed the charisma necessary to make him a magnetic attraction to youth. Nor did Kim Il-sŏng have great appeal. Indeed, almost nothing was known about him. There is good reason to believe that men like Yŏ Un-hyŏng, Kim Kyu-sik, Kim Ku, and Syngman Rhee—men of widely differing political perspectives—were all capable of drawing more support as individuals than the foremost Communists.

Among the Communists, according to some observers, the Yenan returnees had the greatest initial impact upon the politically conscious youth of this period. Various "student soldiers" who had deserted the Japanese army and made their way to Yenan, joined with the original members of the Korean Independence League and subsequently lived, fought, and studied in the Yenan atmosphere. Together with older nationalist Communists from China, these young revolutionaries now came back to Korea and recounted their adventures. Stories and plays were written to depict life in Yenan. For example, Kim Sa-ryang, a young playwright, wrote *Hojŏp* (*Butterfly*), which portrayed Korean fighters from Yenan in heroic terms. It had a very successful run in Seoul.[51]

The endeavors of the Left to mobilize Korean women had also produced fruit by the end of 1945. December 22 saw the opening of a three-day conference of the newly established Chosŏn Punyŏ Ch'ong-dongmaeng (General League of Korean Women), which claimed a membership of 800,000. Like other front organizations, the League was under firm Com-

---

50. For details, see *Chosŏn haebang nyŏnbo, op. cit.,* pp. 183–185.

51. For observations on the impact of the Yenan returnees, see Pak Sŏng-hwan, *P'ado nŭn naeil do ch'inda* (*The Waves Will Beat Tomorrow Too*), Seoul, 1965, pp. 45–46.

Pak makes the interesting point that the women Communists were particularly effective in the south and constituted a serious problem for the moderates and conservatives during this entire period. He cites, as an example, the impact of Kim Myŏng-shi, one of the Independence League members. When she talked of her life in Yenan at the Seoul YMCA auditorium in the fall of 1945, she was greeted with thunderous applause by the audience, composed largely of young girl students.

munist control. From So Chŏng-ja, whose activities we have already noted, we can learn much about the role of women in the Communist movement during this period. So herself had come to Communism via Marxist literature, which began to reach her shortly after the end of the war. She was one of the first three female members of the Chinju city KCP.[52] One of her early assignments was to contact women textile workers and aid in unionization activities. She also distributed Communist hand-bills at night, placing some of them in the desks of students and teachers at the Chinju Girls' High School, others in the city government office where she worked, and a few in the back yard of the Chinju police station! Initially, she was ordered to keep her Party membership secret so that she could collect information on the city government. Later, however, she "surfaced" as secretary of the Chinju Women's League Executive Department.

Thus, it can be seen that by the end of 1945, the Left, led by the Communists, had done an extraordinary job of organizing fronts, clearly surpassing the forces of the Center and Right. Actual Korean Communist Party membership remained small at this point, as we have seen, but those who could be mobilized for Communist purposes by Communist leaders now numbered in the hundreds of thousands—possibly the millions. Of course, one must be wary of mechanically adding front figures to indicate total Communist strength. Events were to show that, in a crunch, relatively few members of front organizations were willing to sacrifice themselves for Party objectives. Indeed, the rosters of membership were in considerable measure paper rosters, with a handful of activists swimming in a sea of the inactive and the inarticulate. It is against this balance of large numbers and

52. According to So, Communist literature helped her articulate sentiments that had previously been vague in her mind: anti-Japanese feelings and revulsion against a system permitting major discrepancies between rich and poor. The prospect of a society in which there was no oppression, no class distinctions, no poverty, she writes, infatuated her.

From the moment she joined the Party, she discovered that life in the movement was far from ideal. The Party itself, she reports, was a curious mélange of people—idealistic students, rich intellectuals who enjoyed toying with theories, ne'er-do-wells of the Japanese era who saw the Party as a new chance for success, hoodlums who needed a cover for their illegal activities, and assorted workers and peasants (who rarely played key roles).

In this period, however, she was a true believer, prepared to make any sacrifice for the Party. Her accounts of passing out leaflets on bitterly cold nights, taking great personal risks to deliver messages, and later serving as an underground Communist agent indicate the type of dedication the Party is able to command from its loyal fol-lowers. So's own life was a series of adventures and tragedies. Her husband was after-ward captured and executed by South Korean authorities. She went to North Korea, joined the North Korean Army, and participated in the Korean War. Later, she was sent to South Korea as an agent, returned once to the North unharmed, came back a second time, and was captured. She subsequently became a leading anti-Communist propagandist in the South, but died prematurely in 1967. So Chŏng-ja, *op. cit.*

uncertain commitment that one should see trends with respect to Communist Party and front organization membership in South Korea in 1946 and the years that followed.

We must now return to the events of late 1945, because the basic directions of South Korean politics for decades were set in the first six months after Liberation. When the Korean People's Republic was first proclaimed in early September 1945, the Left, as we have seen, was able to take maximum advantage of a frightfully confused situation. In almost every area of the south, "notables," or locally influential individuals, were initially willing to participate in the formation of People's Committees, thus lending them an air of respectability and authority.

Typically, however, members of the local and provincial People's Committees were not truly prominent people. They were young, had not served the Japanese regime in any official capacity, had been educated to a middling level, and did not belong to a landlord family. Many were regarded as intellectuals in their community because they had had middle school training, could read newspapers, and had some friends at the political level directly above. (If the locus was the village, the individual knew someone in the nearest town; if the locus was the province, he knew someone in Seoul.) In sum, the bulk of People's Committee leaders were petty intellectuals.

By no means all of the participants in People's Committees were leftists, especially in the initial period. As the Center and Right leaders in Seoul refused to serve in the "Republic," however, and as US military authorities denied it official recognition, the great bulk of the non-Left dropped out of the Committees. Thus, by November, the People's Republic in all of its various forms was far more clearly an instrument of the Communists, even at local levels, than had been the case in September, although, as we have seen, the Communists had firmly controlled the Center at the outset. In the beginning, American occupation authorities sparred with the Left, seeking to avoid a frontal clash. They were anxious to make the system work on a consensual basis, desirous of avoiding provocations toward the Russians. At the same time, there was certainly no disposition to see the Communists move into political control, and it was not too difficult to discern Communist intentions—or tactics. The first concrete move of military government was to appoint an advisory council to assist General Arnold. It was composed of ten carefully chosen, prominent, moderate to conservative Koreans and the only Leftist appointed, Yŏ Un-hyŏng.

No one liked this system because it was too close to the old Japanese style of governance. The military government had additional problems because it had initially confronted the new republic and the People's Committee structure with Japanese officials and, after these had departed, with many of the same men who had served under the Japanese. These were, of course, the men of experience—and generally the men of moderation, given the alternatives available.

Naturally, relations between the People's Republic and the US Military Government deteriorated. On October 10, General Arnold issued a strong statement.

> There is only one government in Korea south of 38 degrees north latitude. It has exclusive control and authority in every phase of government. Self-appointed "officials," "police" groups, big (or little) conferences "representing all the people," "the (self-styled) government of the People's Republic of Korea," are entirely without any authority, power or reality.
>
> If the men who are arrogating to themselves such high-sounding titles are merely play-acting on a puppet stage with entertainment of questionable amusement value, they must immediately pull down the curtain on the puppet show.
>
> A fraud on the people of Korea has been recently publicized in the free press, namely, the calling of a fictitious election on the 1st of March 1946, at which it is promised "all men and women over the age of eighteen, except for traitors, will have the right to vote." Nothing is more sacred to a free people than the right to vote and to elect their own representatives in government. This right is too sacred to be made the toy of self-appointed statesmen who attempt to lead the people with false hopes.[53]

If there had ever been any doubts about the occupying power's attitude toward the "Korean People's Republic," they should now have been removed once and for all. For their own reasons, however, the Communists in the south also wanted to avoid any frontal clash. Indeed, the Russians were ordering them to avoid such a clash at all costs. Their one hope of achieving power at this point was by the "peaceful" route. Certainly, they could not hope to challenge American military government and win.

What should be their tactic in responding? The answer was revealed in a pamphlet entitled "The Traitors and the Patriots," issued under the imprimatur of the People's Republic and widely distributed in Seoul during the third week of October. In sorrow as much as in anger, the pamphleteers charged that military government had allowed itself to be surrounded by traitorous, reactionary pro-Japanese Koreans, and thereby had become separated from the true voice of the Korean people—a voice clearly reflected in the People's Republic. On October 20 a "Message to USA Citizens" [sic] was distributed bearing a similar theme.

Events were building toward the first great crisis between American military government and the Left, a crisis that reached its climax in late November with the All-Nation Conference of the People's Committee Representatives, called by the People's Republic and held in Seoul between November 20 and 22. The key issue was whether the Conference

53. From General Arnold's October 10 statement as carried in XXIV Corps G-2 Summary, No. 41, June 23, 1946.

would approve military government's demand that the self-proclaimed Korean People's Republic abandon its claim that it was the government of Korea, and accept the status of a political party.

Several events of importance preceded this conference. No political figure was more bitterly fought over during this era than Yŏ Un-hyŏng; each of the major contestants—military government and the Left—strove unceasingly to win his support. On November 12, the Communists suffered a serious political blow when Yŏ, founding father of the People's Republic, suddenly resigned from it and announced the formation of a new People's Party. Yŏ's departure and that of his close comrades left as the key figures of the People's Republic only Hŏ Hŏn and Pak Hŏn-yŏng. There was scarcely a fig leaf now to conceal Communist leadership.

Pak himself maneuvered desperately in this period to avoid a major confrontation. In late October and early November, he granted several press interviews. The burden of his message was that Koreans should cooperate fully with military government. While protests and demands for explanation were legitimate when disagreements arose, there should be no clash with occupation authorities. Pak was extraordinarily generous in his appraisal of the Allies at this point. Until the Korean people realized that their present liberty was due to the Allies and not to the Koreans in exile, he stated, little progress could be made in achieving a united, independent, and democratic Korea.[54]

On November 15, Pak met with Generals Hodge and Arnold. According to information given the press the following day by Pak, the objectives of the US occupation had been explained to him as building a healthy Korean economy and guaranteeing Korean independence. His cooperation had then been requested. Pak told the press that he had expressed his approval of those objectives, and promised full cooperation, reserving, however, the right to criticize military government when it "moved in a wrong direction."

It was against this background that the All-Nation Conference of People's Committee Representatives took place in late November. Some one thousand delegates from both north and south were assembled, and

54. Such a remark, while true, cut in several directions. If it depreciated the role of Syngman Rhee, it did no less for Kim Il-sŏng.

Pak had granted an October 31 interview to the *Korea Free Press*. On the following day, November 1, he gave a widely publicized interview to *Maeil Sinbo*. In the latter interview, he denied earlier reports that he had told an American reporter that he favored the immediate withdrawal of both American and Russian forces from Korea.

Coupled with these interviews were other efforts to make the Communist Party as moderate and "loveable" as possible. For example, an undated handbill distributed by the KCP during this period called the "rumor" that the KCP advocated a proletarian revolution and the establishment of a socialist state "a misconception." It continued: "The Party stands for and always has advocated the foundation of a bourgeois democracy as a necessary step toward full freedom for all classes."

from the opening session, discussions were tense and animated. Several attempts at disruption were made by organized bands of youths, reportedly subsidized by rightist forces. These efforts failed, however, partly because US military police intervened.

The key issue was confronted on the Conference's third and final day. There had been prolonged behind-the-scenes debate and negotiation. Even the senior leadership was apparently divided on the proper course of action. At least, Hŏ Hŏn, so-called premier of the People's Republic, admitted that the Republic Central Committee had not been able to come to an agreement upon the matter. Hŏ, in presenting the issue to the delegates, recited recent developments. Yŏ—before his resignation—had gone to military government on October 29 and argued the position that under international law there could be more than one government in a nation, especially since the People's Republic did not intend to oppose the American military government. Needless to say, this argument did not impress American authorities, and Hŏ acknowledged that three weeks later an impasse still existed. Either the People's Republic would omit the word "state" and substitute the word "party," or it would be ordered dissolved.

Although there is reason to believe that Pak himself wanted an accommodation, the young radicals of the Conference succeeded in preventing the change in designation. Instead a resolution was adopted claiming that the Conference did not have the right to make a decision of this type and postponing the question until another national conference could be held. The resolution further stipulated that while the People's Republic had expressed a desire to cooperate with military government, the latter did not understand the Republic and had rejected its efforts.[55]

The session of November 25 had produced a clear defiance of military government orders. American authorities responded by outlawing the Korean People's Republic. After the Conference had been formally adjourned, Pak and his inner group succeeded in getting the tactic of "developmental dissolution" generally accepted. Developmental dissolution essentially involved allowing the People's Republic to fade away while the Party shifted its energies to constructing a new, broadly based united front, one that would include various elements of the Center and a few select figures of the Right. This tactic was not only in line with Soviet policy; it was the only tactic that might avoid a highly damaging frontal clash with American authorities, a struggle for which the Communists were not prepared at this point. Moreover, it was an approach dictated by several new developments in the domestic political arena. We have already noted the defection of Yŏ Un-hyŏng from the Republic: it would be necessary to bring his People's Party into any meaningful coalition. In addition, at the very time when the All-Nation Conference was meeting, Kim Ku,

55. Minju Chu-ui Minjok Chŏnsŏn Sŏnjŏn-bu (Democratic National Front, Propaganda Department), *Uisarok* (*Minutes of the Conference*), Seoul, 1946.

a celebrated Korean nationalist and head of the Korean Provisional Government in Chungking, had returned to Seoul with a number of his colleagues. Since there was widespread support for the recognition of this government as the Korean people's sole representative (even the Changan group, it will be remembered, had joined a coalition of parties prepared to support the Provisional Government), it was essential to develop tactics that took it into account.

The Competing Drives for Coalition
From the winter of 1945, all forces within the South Korean political arena, including the Americans, concentrated upon the politics of coalition. This situation lasted for nearly a year, with the "Right" and "Left" ultimately moving into two distinct and totally hostile camps. Certain details of this process bear so directly upon the fate of the Communists in the south as to require closer examination. Let us turn, therefore, to the campaigns mounted by each faction, looking first at the efforts of the Left.

With the principles of developmental dissolution now widely accepted, the Communists placed high priority upon the formation of a new national united front that would unify all of the Korean people except "national traitors and reactionaries." In the latter phrase, of course, was contained the problem. From the beginning, for example, the KCP had defined the Korean Democratic Party as such a force and had resolutely refused to participate in any organization harboring KDP members. When Syngman Rhee first returned to Korea on October 16, the Communist Party had made an effort to establish friendly relations with him. For example, when Rhee, on October 25, announced the creation of the Tongnip Ch'oksŏng Chungang Hyŏpui-hoe (Central Conference for the Acceleration of Independence), with some two hundred "political parties" and groups involved, the Communist Party had allowed its name to be listed. Friction rapidly developed, however. At the second session of the Conference, Pak Hŏnyŏng demanded changes in the resolution that Rhee was proposing be addressed to the Allied powers and the American people. Ironically, Pak wanted to tone down Rhee's complaint about partition as well as to eliminate the suggestion that the Provisional Government had been returned to Korea as the recognized government. Pak also wanted to add a firm stricture against the political participation of "pro-Japanese elements," together with a pledge for the quest of national unification.[56]

56. For details concerning this conference, see *Haebang Ilbo, op. cit.*, No. 15, Nov. 25, 1945, and No. 16, Nov. 27, 1945. The latter issue contained a revealing official Party evaluation of the results. First, it reported, through the Conference the true conditions "throughout the nation" had come to be known. In the north, there is no area where People's Committees have not been organized, and even in the south preparations are now under way to complete organizational efforts. Such activities, however, have been obstructed by "pro-Japanese elements and national traitors." They

On November 5, nearly three weeks before the November 22 opening of the All-Nation Conference of People's Committee Representatives, the Communists withdrew from Rhee's Central Conference charging that it showed no desire either to base a national united front upon the masses or to exclude pro-Japanese elements and national traitors. The critical issue was already sharply drawn. The position of the Right, symbolized by Syngman Rhee, was that until full sovereignty had been achieved, *no one* should be excluded from the movement for independence. The entire

are also striving to drive a wedge between the People's Committee and the military government.

Efforts of the allies, both north and south, are praised. In the north, workers are actively carrying out Stakhanovite labor, and farmers are delivering grain to the government, proof against the slanders of the reactionaries. In the south, the military government had arrested the chairman of the South Kyŏngsang Province People's Committee; but when they discovered that the charges raised against him by the reactionaries were false, he was released, and full support for him requested. Thus, "if there is some friction between military government and the People's Committees, it is not as a result of the basic or essential character of military government, but because of the slander and false accusations of national traitors." (Note the extraordinary lengths to which KCP leaders were going to avoid a clash with US authorities and to place the blame for troubles upon "rightists.")

A second accomplishment had been that functional liaison between the center and local People's Committees had been greatly strengthened. Third, "we have also been able to observe the passion with which the Central People's Committee holds the goal of national unity. In each word, the statement issued by the Conference expresses a love toward the nation. It also makes clear that we do not seek to monopolize government in the future but, on the contrary, desire a more completely unified regime based upon democratic principles and a broad, national united front.

"In spite of the fact that the Korean People's Republic is a term ardently desired by the Korean people, our People's Committee has not used this term since military government began negotiations with us concerning the designation 'People's Republic.' Our final statement, moreover, made it clear that as long as American military government exists in Korea south of the 38th parallel, the Republic cannot and will not act as a government. Considering the unanimous outcry for the designation 'state' that was heard at the Conference, this declaration reveals the extent to which we are prepared to go in cooperating with military government." Now, a broader united front must be established.

We have quoted and paraphrased the *Haebang Ilbo* article at length to convey both the substance and the flavor of Communist policies at that time. Pak and his followers were loyally seeking to carry out Soviet instructions to avoid conflict with the United States Military Government and cultivate a position of moderation, including support for Allied authority. Tactically, such a policy made great sense. The best hope for the Communists was to keep their organization intact and protected by a broader united front, in which their role would be extensive if not paramount. From that position, they could hope that Soviet-American negotiations for unification would succeed, counting then upon the system being established in the north to be applicable to the south, with an embryonic structure conducive to that end already in existence.

In view of these facts, it is ironic that Pak and his key supporters, as we shall see, were later to be accused of treasonous activities involving capitulation to American authorities during this period.

spectrum from left to right should be allowed to participate in this struggle, because it was only on the basis of the broadest internal unity that Korean unification and independence could be obtained. After full independence had been attained, the pro-Japanese elements could be handled. The position of the Left, symbolized by Pak Hŏn-yŏng, was that "pro-Japanese elements and national traitors" had to be excluded at the outset. When to this position was appended a solicitude for Allied views, the tactical advantages of the so-called rightist position should be clear. Rhee, with his stubborn insistence upon *total* Korean unity and *immediate* independence (already he had given signs of being willing to defy military government if their position differed from his), was emerging as the purest, most strident nationalist. Even before the traumatic events of December, the Communists —tied to Soviet policy makers—were in danger of being maneuvered into a position whereby it could be said of them that they were delaying unification and independence.

The practical politics of these two opposed stands, of course, was easily understood. If the Communists could exclude "pro-Japanese elements and national traitors," as they would define these, their chances for control of the political arena would be infinitely enhanced. Both they and their opponents knew this elementary fact. At this point, incidentally, the Communists were very reluctant to attack Rhee publicly. He was—by their own admission—a national hero, and indisputably anti-Japanese. Yet without attacking Rhee, they could not maintain their position unequivocally.

Thus, by December, charges and countercharges were becoming more intense. In an editorial of December 4, *Haebang Ilbo,* the KCP organ, charged Rhee with making "the great mistake" of minimizing the revolutionary exploits of the anti-Japanese Korean guerrillas who had fought in Manchuria and China.[57] Rhee, it asserted, had paid no more attention to those elements than to those who had stood aloof from the struggle concentrating upon their own personal safety and material gain. "Dr. Rhee must correctly analyze the role of various groups in the anti-Japanese struggle before Liberation," the editorial concluded. That had become particularly important, it asserted, now that those who constituted the Provisional Government in Chungking were returning to Korea. "We have praised those who persisted in their anti-Japanese attitudes abroad," it continued, but "we must clearly indicate that men connected with that government are only one of the anti-Japanese revolutionary groups abroad, and that

57. In listing these guerrillas, the *Haebang Ilbo* editorial referred to fighters "such as those who had participated in the Anti-Japanese Righteous Army, the May 30th Struggle in Chientao, the northern Korea-southeast Manchurian border struggle led by General Kim Il-sŏng, the anti-Japanese struggle under General Ch'oe Mu-jŏng (Mu Chŏng), and the anti-Japanese efforts of Generals Yi Ch'ŏng-ch'ŏn and Kim Won-bong." *Haebang Ilbo*, No. 21, Dec. 4, 1945.

In the light of subsequent events, it is enormously interesting to note that Kim Il-sŏng was not singled out here for special emphasis.

the major forces abroad were actually in Manchuria and northern China" (italics ours).

While the KCP (South) was unwilling to single out Kim Il-sŏng for special homage at this point, it was quite prepared to place the Communist guerrillas as a group (including the Yenan faction) in a position ahead of the Korean nationalists who had finally operated from Chungking. The factional divisions that had long plagued Korean nationalism in its diverse geographic settings and ideological-political garbs were being rapidly introduced into South Korea. But this time the issue was no less than who should control the future of all Korea. *Haebang Ilbo* put the matter very bluntly in the final sentence of its December 4 editorial. "Various parties and groups must correctly evaluate their role in the history of the Korean revolution, stop taking a self-centered attitude, and recognize the problem of which group should become the central element of the united front." [58]

While the situation within the domestic political arena was thus becoming more complex, a major bombshell burst upon the scene in the form of the decision of the Three Ministers' Conference in Moscow on December 27 to impose a trusteeship upon Korea for a period up to five years.[59] The issue was not totally new. In late October, the press had carried reports that John Carter Vincent, director of the Office of Far Eastern Affairs of the US State Department, had publicly stated that Korea would be placed under a trusteeship.[60] The news had produced an immediate furor in South Korea, with Communist leaders no less exercised than others. Kim Sam-yong, one of the top KCP figures, issued a long statement asserting that while he did not know the Soviet attitude or the nature of the proposed trusteeship, if Vincent's remarks were being accurately quoted, it was "a shocking fact that stems from an erroneous perception of Korean realities and ignores the people's will. . . ." [61]

58. *Ibid.,* p. 1. On December 8, Part III of the editorial was published. It was devoted almost exclusively to an attack upon Syngman Rhee, charging that he was surrounded by a small group of landlords and capitalists and completely isolated from the masses—who were now represented only by the Korean Communist Party.

59. For the official English text of the Moscow Agreement, see *U.S. Department of State Bulletin,* Dec. 30, 1945, p. 1030. The agreement provided for the establishment of "a provisional Korean democratic government," created with the assistance of a Joint Commission, consisting of US and USSR representatives, which would consult with "Korean democratic parties and social organizations." Its recommendations were to be submitted to the governments of the USSR, China, the United Kingdom, and the US prior to a final decision by the two Commission nations. Meanwhile, in similar fashion, an agreement "concerning a four-power trusteeship of Korea for a period up to five years" would also be reached. Representatives of the two occupying powers were to meet within a period of two weeks to commence discussions on coordinated policies for north and south.

60. See *New York Times,* Oct. 21, 1945, p. 22.

61. Kim's statement was carried in *Maeil Sinbo,* Oct. 25, 1945.
On October 21, moreover, *Haebang Ilbo* carried a lengthy article entitled "Trus-

Thus, when news of the Moscow Agreement reached Korea, the initial reaction was almost universally hostile. Syngman Rhee and the entire Right were outraged. Much to the embarrassment of the American Military Government, they promised to fight trusteeship to the bitter end. But the Communists seemed no less angry. On December 29, *Seoul Sinmun* quoted Chŏng T'ae-sik, a prominent KCP leader, as saying: "If it is true that trusteeship is to be imposed upon Korea, we are absolutely opposed. Even if it were for five months, not to mention five years, we would oppose trusteeship." [62] Pak himself, in a personal interview with General Hodge on January 1, indicated that he was totally opposed to trusteeship. In addition, the Communists took the lead in organizing a Citizens' Rally Against Trusteeship and for the Acceleration of National Unification, scheduled for January 3. The Rally was under the immediate leadership of the Seoul City People's Committee and a front group, the Committee on the Joint Struggle Against Fascism.

At some point between January 1 and January 3, however, Communist leaders were "induced" to make a dramatic shift in their position. We have several versions of what happened during these hectic seventy-two hours. According to Pak Il-won, then chief of the Youth Department of the Kyŏnggi Province KCP, immediately after the Moscow decision was announced, Kang Chin, a member of the Party Politburo, had a lengthy conversation with Mr. A. I. Shabshin, Soviet vice-consul in Seoul.[63] Pak further writes that Pak Hŏn-yŏng himself made a hasty, secret trip to P'yŏngyang, returning to Seoul on January 2. Immediately, so his account goes, an enlarged central committee meeting was convened at the home of Ra Tong-uk. Pak made the issue one of Party loyalty, and in spite of substantial opposition a resolution supporting the Moscow decision was rammed through. According to American occupation sources, written instructions issued in the name of the "responsible secretary" of the North

---

teeship Is Outrageous: Concerning the Statement of the Chief of the Far Eastern Section of the US State Department," attacking the trusteeship concept in indignant terms. The author noted that the United States had even promised independence to the Philippines immediately, a nation "several thousand years behind Korea in terms of history or civilization." This theme, with its strong racial-cultural overtones, was scarcely the type of argument that befitted good Marxist-Leninists.

62. *Seoul Sinmun*, Dec. 29, 1945.

63. Pak Il-won, *Nam-No-dang ch'ong pi-p'an, op. cit.*, p. 42.

According to American intelligence information, in this period Shabshin was the one who gave orders to the Korean Communists in the south, transmitting instructions from P'yŏngyang and Moscow. Reportedly, Gerasim Martinovich Balasanov, nominally a member of the Soviet delegation to the US-Soviet Joint Commission and officer-in-charge, Supreme Political Department, 25th Army, P'yŏngyang, had control over KCP operations in the north and, in addition, final responsibility for Korean Communist activities throughout Korea. XXIV Corps G-2 Summary, No. 41, June 23, 1946.

Korea Branch of the KCP to secretaries at all levels and branches enjoined them to support in every possible manner the Moscow Agreement.[64]

Whatever the precise sequence of events, it is clear that the Soviet command in North Korea forced Seoul (and P'yŏngyang) KCP leaders to reverse their initial position on the trusteeship issue despite the massive unhappiness that this caused in Party ranks. Never during this era was Russian authority over the Korean Communist movement to be put to a more crucial test—and never was the power of that authority more strikingly revealed. While the Americans were trying desperately—and unsuccessfully—to line up the non-Communists in support of this extremely unpopular agreement, the Russians illustrated what a truly disciplined political movement could be made to do.

Thus, in an extraordinary about-face, the Citizens' Rally was turned into a demonstration of support for the Moscow Conference! Naturally, the KCP was to pay a heavy price for its new stand. Indeed, some observers, including former Communists, would assert that this event constituted a watershed, and that the Communist Party of the south, forced to oppose Korean nationalist aspirations, was never again able to command the degree of public support that it garnered in the opening months after Liberation. It would be difficult to prove or disprove such a view and, as we shall see, many turning points were yet to be reached. There can be no doubt, however, that the KCP suddenly found itself on the defensive, with almost all tactical advantages shifting to the Center and Right. Even with its own members, the Communist Party had great difficulty. The trusteeship issue, it should be emphasized, took on an intensely emotional quality. Trusteeship was popularly equated in Korea with the League of Nations mandate system, and it was widely charged that Koreans were being treated in the same fashion as "the uncivilized aborigines of the South Seas." Consequently, pride and racial consciousness became inextricably involved in the issue, and an emotional outpouring ensued that threatened to sweep the Communists off the central stage that they had occupied thus far.

To contain the damage, the Communists sought to interpret the Moscow Agreement in such fashion as to put the emphasis upon the pledge to establish a provisional democratic government, not upon trusteeship. They argued that the heart of the decision lay in the provision that stipulated Four Power supervision or support for a *Korean provisional government*. Indeed, the Communists on occasion maintained that they continued to oppose trusteeship while supporting the Agreement. The term *t'ak-ch'i* (trusteeship) was actually banned in the Communist press;

---

64. In raids conducted later, documents dated Jan. 2, 1946, emanating from North Korean Communist Party headquarters, were discovered, prescribing in detail the cheers, slogans, and themes to be used in support of the Moscow decisions. *History of the US Army Forces in Korea,* Part II, *op. cit.,* p. 26.

instead, the term *hu-won* (support) was used whenever there was a need to describe the proposed relation between the foreign overseers and the indigenous leaders. The effort was made, moreover, to accuse the Right of delaying the establishment of a provisional democratic government—and so the process of securing independence—by its refusal to cooperate with the Allies.[65]

The Russians had forced the Korean Communists to accept heavy political costs. But they had brought them into line. The Americans, existing in a very different relation to the non-Communist elements and unprepared to use Soviet tactics, were not able to do the same to the so-called Right, Center, or Moderate Left. General Hodge apparently won the tentative support of Song Chin-u, a KDP leader, by explaining to him that what was really involved was a period of hun-jŏng, or training in government, as a prelude to one of hŏn-jŏng, or constitutional democracy. Song tried to explain this view to Kim Ku, but the latter totally rejected the idea. And on the same day as Song's visit to Kim (December 30, 1945), Song was assassinated by an unknown party, a concurrence that may or may not have been coincidental.[66]

Korean politics, never mild, now took on a deadly quality as emotions mounted. The advocates of trusteeship, whatever their political complexion, had good reason to fear for their lives. But even apart from this specific issue, the political climate rapidly became so charged with hatred, and the political culture so easily accommodated to violence, that terrorism and assassination came to represent major political weapons for all groups.

It was in this atmosphere that the quest for political coalition continued. At first, the Left appeared to be making progress, despite the odds against it. The Communists now concentrated upon the Provisional Government group, many of whose top leaders had recently returned from China. On December 31, four representatives of the People's Republic Central Committee (Hong Nam-p'yo, Chŏng Paek, Hong Chŭng-sik, and Yi Kang-guk) met with three Provisional Government representatives (Ch'oe Tong-o, Sŏng Chu-sik, and Chang Kŏn-sang). The former group proposed

65. For the first public explanation of the new KCP position, see the KCP Central Committee Statement of January 2, 1946, published in *Chosŏn Inminbo,* Jan. 3, 1946.

The statement opened by describing the Three Ministers' Conference as a step forward in the development of democracy in the world. It charged that the anti-trusteeship movement of the Kim Ku group was aimed at misleading the Korean people, equating the Moscow decision with Japanese imperialism. Now, Korea had been promised independence, and if unity could be achieved the period of five years during which its provisional democratic government would be supervised could be shortened. All Koreans should thus concentrate upon the completion of a democratic united front that excluded "pro-Japanese elements, national traitors, and Fascists."

66. Kim Ŭl-han, *Yŏgi ch'am saram i itta, op. cit.,* p. 100.

These facts were also discussed in an interview conducted by Chong-Sik Lee with Hong Chong-in, Berkeley, Calif., Jan. 8, 1966.

the immediate establishment of a united committee. This was rejected by
Provisional Government spokesmen on January 1. On January 7, however,
another effort got under way. The representatives of four political parties
—the Korean People's Party (Yŏ Un-hyŏng), the Korean Nationalist
Party (An Chae-hong), the Korean Democratic Party (now led by Kim
Sŏng-su), and the Korean Communist Party (Pak Hŏn-yŏng)—met and
issued a joint communiqué that proclaimed full support for the "spirit and
intent" of the Moscow Conference on the grounds that it sought to
guarantee "the self-determination and independence of Korea" and offered
support (hu-won) for "Korean democratic development." The communiqué
further stated that the trusteeship question should be resolved by a Korean
government, based upon a spirit of self-determination and independence,
that would be established in the near future. It also denounced all assassinations and terrorist acts.

In the above wording—undoubtedly reached after lengthy and tortuous
negotiations—one can detect a neat evasion of the question of support for
trusteeship. Indeed, it might be more accurately read as a scarcely veiled
statement of opposition to the basic thrust of the Moscow Agreement.
Using this route, could the Left, and particularly the Communists, work
their way back into the main stream?

Despite the tone of the communiqué, the KDP leaders renounced it
almost as soon as it was released. After an emergency session, they issued
a statement asserting that it ignored the spirit of Korean opposition to
trusteeship, and sought to equivocate on the basic issue. Another meeting
of the four-party representatives plus delegates from Yi Kyu-gap's New
Korea National Party was held on January 9, but no agreement was
reached. At still another meeting on January 14, representatives of Yŏ's
Korean People's Party proposed that all parties present support the spirit
of the Moscow Conference but openly oppose trusteeship. The Communists
blocked this proposal, thereby giving a clear indication of the limits to
which they were prepared to go. Right-Center-Left unity could not be obtained on the most crucial issue to confront Korean politicians since Liberation.

On balance, the trusteeship issue proved to be a major asset to the
Right, and a serious debit to the Left. With the failure of the Left and
Center to achieve agreement, the Right proceeded to use the Moscow
decision as a catalytic agent to induce political unity. On February 1, the
Provisional Government leaders convened an emergency political conference that was attended by all moderate and conservative groups. This
conference led on February 8 to the formation of the Taehan Tongnip
Ch'oksŏng Chungang Hyŏpui-hoe (Great Korean Independence Acceleration Council). Syngman Rhee now emerged as undisputed leader of this
movement.

Developments were not precisely in accordance with American hopes.

US Military Government representatives had been feverishly seeking to aid in the construction of a much broader coalition; they wanted the balance of power to rest with those whom they defined as the Center. To this end, the military government sponsored a series of consultations and informal discussions aimed at the establishment of a Korean Representative Democratic Council. Initially, it was hoped that the Left, including the Communists, would participate. Pak Hŏn-yŏng, however, proved uncooperative. He is reported to have asked again and again during the negotiations, "What will the Russians think of this?" [67] Ultimately, he balked at any personal participation, thereby dooming any chance of serious Communist involvement.

The more critical efforts were concentrated upon detaching the non-Communist Left, notably Yŏ Un-hyŏng and his group, from the Communists. Yŏ had three severe conditions: the Council must be advisory, not governmental in character; no decision could be taken by a simple majority vote; and finally, the Council should not take up political matters. The latter condition was manifestly impossible, but it was initially hoped that Yŏ had advanced this for merely tactical reasons. Thus, preparations were made for the opening session of the Council on February 14 with the understanding that Yŏ would attend with a Left delegation, including Ch'oe Ik-han (People's Republic and KCP), Paek Sang-gyu, and Hwang Chin-nam (both of Yŏ's Korean People's Party). Among the 28 council members appointed, the breakdown, in current Korean political parlance, was as follows: rightists, 20; centrists, 4; leftists, 4. On the morning of the fourteenth, however, Yŏ and Ch'oe failed to appear. The previous evening there had been a speech by Ŏm Hang-sŏp, propaganda chief for the Provisional Government, that Yŏ is said to have construed as a violation of his conditions. General Hodge, disappointed in this development, quickly denounced Ŏm's action. Perhaps in response, Yŏ sent Paek and Hwang to the meeting. But they refused to speak, and made no more appearances.

Accordingly, as of mid-February 1946, the intense competition between the conservative-moderates and the Left to create and dominate a strong coalition had ended in a draw. From the beginning, the Democratic Council launched on February 14 was a vehicle of the Right, albeit a Right greatly strengthened by recent events and now wearing proudly—even fiercely—its nationalist colors. On February 15, one day later, the Democratic National Front, instrument of the Left, was formally inaugurated. Abandoning its efforts to win over the moderates, the Left, led by the Communists but with Yŏ and his party cooperating, assembled twenty-nine organizations, most of them Communist fronts. A Central Committee with 305 members supposedly served as the Front's decision-making body.[68]

67. XXIV Corps G-2 Summary, No. 41, June 23, 1946.
68. Details concerning the Democratic National Front can be found in *Chosŏn haebang nyŏnbo, op. cit.,* pp. 12 ff. The formation of the Front got under way on

The timing of these activities was not accidental. On January 14, it had been publicly announced that the US-USSR Joint Commission would meet in Seoul the following month. It was widely believed that at this first session the major decisions leading to a national government would be reached. Naturally, in the shadow of this anticipated event, all political forces in the South worked feverishly to augment their strength.

No crucial decisions, however, were to issue from the Seoul meetings. The Joint Commission quickly became deadlocked over Korean representation, and recriminations between the American and Soviet spokesmen became increasingly bitter. As we shall soon see, this had immediate repercussions upon the South Korean political scene. Meanwhile, both sides continued to work for a coalition, redoubling their efforts after the suspension of commission sessions in May. Once again, American military government authorities concentrated upon the effort to replace the Democratic Council with a more broadly based structure that would include additional elements from the Center and the non-Communist Left. American leaders, from General Hodge down, spent an enormous amount of time wooing Yŏ Un-hyŏng and Kim Kyu-sik in particular.

Once again, however, both the Left and the Right served in different

---

January 19 with a preliminary meeting of the major organizations involved. On January 31, a preparatory committee of 24 members was announced and, the following day, a Declaration of the Front was publicized. In this February 1 Declaration, the leadership made clear its intention to play the role previously undertaken by the Korean People's Republic. After indicating that any "antidemocratic groups" were welcome to join the National Democratic Front provided they first renounced their antidemocratic past, the Declaration stated that, until a People's Representative Conference could be created through general elections, the Front would "play the role of an interim National Assembly, and take the responsibility for organizing a provisional democratic government in Korea under the provisions of the agreement reached at the Three Ministers' Conference. *Ibid.*, p. 96.

Pak Il-won asserts that there were five factors involved in the formation of the Democratic National Front: the trusteeship issue had made a Left-Right union impossible; some dramatic move by the Left was essential to prevent further desertions from its ranks, particularly in the light of the KCP stand on the Moscow Agreement; a body to compete with the New Democratic Council was crucial, given the political stakes of this period; further political expansion in the South could take place only under the rubric of a Front; and only through an organization like the DNF could the KCP expect to control "fraternal parties" such as the People's Party and the New People's Party. Pak, *op. cit.*, pp. 44–45.

An analysis of the seventy-three-member standing committee of the Front reveals that more than three-fourths of the members were connected with the KCP. For a list of the CC and Standing Committee members, see *Chosŏn haebang nyŏnbo, op. cit.*, pp. 129–131. Note the following KCP members and their positions: Chief, Secretariat, Yi Kang-guk; Head, Organization Department, Hong Tŏk-yu (later, Kim Ke-rin); Head, Propaganda Department, Kim O-sŏng (later, Pak Mun-gyu); Head, Cultural Department, Yi T'ae-jun; Head, Finance Department, An Ki-sŏng; Head, Planning Department, Ch'oe Ik-han; Head, Research Department, O Yŏng. *Ibid.*, p. 131.

ways to thwart American hopes. Yŏ himself proved both difficult and increasingly tricky—at least from an American perspective. In the preliminary negotiations, which got under way in late May and early June, he insisted upon involving Hŏ Hŏn at all points, and Hŏ never appeared to deviate from the Communist line. In mid-June, Yŏ indicated that an agreement might be possible. But a few days later, on June 20, Hŏ declared that both he and Yŏ would stand firm in insisting that any conference with a political coalition in view had to begin with a statement of support for the Moscow Agreement. Since the Americans were signatories to the Agreement, this was a position difficult for them to oppose, yet clearly it was one that would block rightist participation. At this point, also, Pak Hŏn-yŏng indicated that many obstacles remained to any major agreement.

However, negotiations continued during the summer, with the Americans doing their best to get results. In July, a formula was reached for preliminary meetings to discuss the idea of a new coalition; it involved a ratio of five rightists to five leftists, with Kim Kyu-sik and Yŏ Un-hyŏng to act as chairmen on alternate weeks. The first such meeting was held on July 22. As might have been expected, leaders like Syngman Rhee took a generally dim view of these developments. More crucial at this point, however, was the fact that the Communists, initially somewhat noncommittal, now put their full efforts into sabotaging the movement.

Behind this new development lay the Soviet hand—more precisely, the decisions reached earlier on these matters in P'yŏngyang. On June 22, P'yŏngyang authorities had announced the formation of the North Korean Democratic National United Front, which was aimed at bringing northern coalition efforts into harmony with those of the southern Left. In making this announcement, Kim Il-sŏng asserted that the Front would enable all Koreans to join in a united struggle against such national traitors as Syngman Rhee and Kim Ku. For a variety of reasons, however, the Communists felt impelled to take another step one month later, namely, the independent unification of the Left into a single, Communist-directed party. Thus, on July 23, the New People's Party (Yenan faction) was caused to send a letter to the North Korean Communist Party proposing a merger. The latter Party acted with extraordinary speed, and a few days later a joint meeting of the two parties' Central Committees got under way. By the end of August a new party, the North Korean Workers' Party, had emerged. In this guise, the Communist Party was to govern North Korea in the decades ahead.

The timing of these events, to be discussed in greater detail later, must be kept in mind when analyzing political developments in the south. Pak and his hard-core Communists had held aloof in the initial stages of the new coalition drive. But they had also indicated a certain ambivalence, which suggested that their policies were not yet firm. In July, however, Pak made a quick, secret trip to P'yŏngyang, returning on the twenty-second. From this point, Pak not only took a strong line against any coalition involving Right and Center elements; he also devoted considerable effort to firming up his own leadership within the Communist movement, and to launching the drive for a merger of Left forces parallel to the one already under way in the north. There could be no doubt now that the Communists' political pattern was the same for north and south, and that they did not intend to brook interference—whether from Americans or indigenous, non-Communist forces.

Yŏ Un-hyŏng now found himself caught in an exceedingly uncomfortable position. Publicly, he had committed himself at this point to going the coalition route with centrists like Kim Kyu-sik. Privately, he appears to have been playing on all sides of the political fence. Korean and American authorities, now suspicious of close ties between Yŏ's party and the Communists, kept both under close surveillance. In early August, a raid conducted against the quarters of certain People's Party staff members turned up a letter dated July 18, 1946, and addressed to Yŏ from Kim Il-sŏng.

> DEAR MR. YŎ UN-HYŎNG: I have received your recent letter and think that what you say is correct and proper. I am very anxious to come down to Seoul to see you, but I am so tied up with civic duties that I cannot very well get away. However, I am looking forward to seeing you within a few days, for I am certain that I shall have a chance to make the visit. Will you please, therefore, make preparations for that occasion. (*signed*) KIM IL-SŎNG[69]

Moreover, when Kim made his final remarks to the NKWP inaugural conference on August 31, he stated that Yŏ had taken the initiative in convening a preliminary meeting of his party and two other leftist parties, the New People's Party and the Communist Party, to discuss a merger. The first meeting had taken place on August 1.[70] The evidence thus suggests that Yŏ continued throughout much of this intensely interesting period to consort secretly with the Communists, both those of the north and those of the south.

On the other hand, Yŏ was holding private conversations with the American authorities. In late July, evidently alarmed at Pak's strong anti-coalition stand after his secret trip to P'yŏngyang, Yŏ hinted to American authorities that unless they dealt with Pak "decisively" and quickly, their joint efforts for coalition would be doomed.[71] Yŏ even suggested that Pak could be implicated in a counterfeiting case that was scheduled for trial on July 29. Privately, General Hodge speculated that recent events had

69. USAFIK, Accession No. RG-332. There is no evidence as to whether Kim actually came south or not.

70. Kim Il-sŏng, "Conclusions on Questions and Discussion," *Kŭlloja* (*The Worker*), No. 1, Oct. 1946, p. 34.

71. XXIV Corps G-2 Summary, Oct. 1946.

suddenly brought to the fore some mortal fear or enmity on the part of Yŏ toward Pak. But it is more likely that Yŏ, having seen himself as the center of a coalition drive that involved the broadest political spectrum possible, realized that, if the Communists sabotaged the drive and concentrated instead upon a merger of the Left, Pak, not he, would constitute the political center in the south. Yŏ may also have felt himself in competition with Pak for northern (that is, Soviet) approval, and have rationalized his general position with the judgment that only he could lead a true unification movement.

Whatever his reasoning, Yŏ kept both Americans and Communists on a string during these complex weeks. However, according to the USAFIK records of the period, his stock fell appreciably with those Americans with whom he had dealings. It was made plain to him that the counterfeiting trial would not be used for political purposes, and that he would have to fight his own battles within the Left, although military government would give the national coalition movement and its leading spirits "all possible support." In actual fact, the American authorities felt that Yŏ, whether from lack of courage or because of secret commitments, was incapable of a showdown with Pak and was looking to them to extricate him from his predicament.[72]

Despite American distrust, Yŏ appeared to move away from the Communists after early August. On August 13, he resigned as chairman of the People's Party, reportedly because he was opposed to any merger with the KCP but no longer strong enough within his own party to block it effectively. Two days later, after the Executive Committee of the People's Party had voted for a merger by 48 to 31, with 53 abstaining, Yŏ resumed leadership of the moderate elements and demanded that the Communists withdraw from the party. Meanwhile, he continued to negotiate with the Center, holding meetings with Kim Kyu-sik and others of similar views. Thus, on August 26, Yŏ and Chŏng No-sik, joined by Chang Kŏn-sang and ten ex-Communists who were hostile to Pak, met with Kim and other Center and Right elements in coalition discussions.

The political complexity of the coalition drive reached new heights in September. Yŏ privately informed American authorities that he was working to overcome Communist-inspired resistance to their hopes of a coalition. However, he continued to stall, and the Left representation at the September meetings of the coalition committee kept changing. On September 20, Yŏ finally presented certain Communist demands to Hodge

72. When Yŏ was asked why he did not undertake an all-out fight against Communist disrupters, he is reported to have replied that the large labor, farmer, and youth groups in South Korea had divided their allegiance between him and Pak and that, if an open break occurred between them, it would harm the movement toward unity. He reiterated that if Pak could be caused to lose face at this moment, he, Yŏ, might be able to win over a considerable portion of these elements to his and hence to our side. *Ibid.*

—clear proof that he had been negotiating with them throughout this period. These demands were: the retraction of the order for the arrest of Pak Hŏn-yŏng and Yi Kang-guk that had been issued in conjunction with a major crackdown on KCP activities; release of the members of the suspended leftist newspapers; and the ending of the suspension of those papers, together with the promise of total press freedom in the future. Yŏ asserted that these demands had been given him by Hong Nam-p'yo and that, if they were not met, the Communists would refuse to participate in any coalition effort. His own position was left somewhat unclear. Ever since September 14, the left-wing camp as a whole had been holding marathon meetings on the issue of the three-party merger as well as the coalition proposal.[73] The schism in the left wing, however, was irreparable. The Communist Party under Pak Hŏn-yŏng had firmly decided on the establishment of the South Korean Workers' Party, and a series of strikes was scheduled to begin on September 24. Evidently sensing the futility of arguing with Pak, Yŏ decided to go to P'yŏngyang.

On his departure, Yŏ left his seal to be used in any agreement that might be reached between his deputies and Kim Kyu-sik. On September 27, agreement in principle on seven basic points was reached, but Yŏ's lieutenants balked at stamping the agreement in the absence of their leader. Yŏ reappeared on October 1 and reported privately to the Americans. He told them that the reason for his trip had been information obtained from a northern source to the effect that southern Communist headquarters was organizing a general strike, and that it would also attempt to launch a "popular revolution" in November, in an effort to wreck coalition talks and discredit the US Military Government. Yŏ claimed it was in order to put a stop to all this that he had decided to go north. Once there, he went on, he had conferred with Kim Il-sŏng, Kim Tu-bong, and others, and had corrected their misapprehensions about American policies. He had also argued with them that Pak's campaign of subversion would lead to widespread violence, clashes with the Americans, and the disadvantage of the Korean people as a whole. The probable result would be that the occupation would be prolonged. (Incidentally, Yŏ also reported that at this point the third member of what he called "the North Korean triumvirate," namely (Kim) Mu Chŏng, was "in disfavor.")[74]

Whatever the full story behind Yŏ's hurried trip to the north, this account, along with other evidence from this period, suggests that Yŏ considered himself in competition with Pak Hŏn-yŏng for the leadership of the South Korean left, and that, to this end, he hoped somehow to get the support of *both* the Americans and the northern Communists. This expectation seems very naive in retrospect, but there can be no doubt that, for their own reasons, both the Americans and the leaders in

73. *Tong-A Ilbo*, Sept. 22, 1946.
74. XXIV Corps G-2 Summary, Oct. 1946.

P'yŏngyang (Russian and Korean) cultivated Yŏ throughout this period.

Whatever the Russian authorities or the North Korean Communists may have promised Yŏ, the Communists in the south proceeded to implement a radical course of action. Railroad workers began a nationwide strike on September 24. Printers' unions followed suit on September 26. On the twenty-ninth, workers of forty factories in Taegu declared a strike. On October 1, all electrical workers in Seoul walked off their jobs. This was followed by the bloody incidents in Taegu known as the October 1 Revolt. Clearly Yŏ no longer wielded any influence over the extreme Left.

On October 4, a few days after his return from P'yŏngyang, Yŏ issued the so-called Seven Principles of Coalition under his name and that of Kim Kyu-sik. The Seven Principles were supposedly a compromise between the Five Principles advanced by the Democratic National Front on July 27 [75] and the Eight Principles advanced by the Right on July 29.[76] But they satisfied neither the Left nor the Right. Whereas the Left had called for complete support of the Moscow Agreement, the coalition committee requested "the establishment of a democratic provisional government by means of a coalition, in accordance with the decision of the Three Ministers' Conference which had guaranteed the democratic independence of Korea." While the Left demanded a program of land reform based simply on confiscation, the coalition called for land reform based on "confiscation, conditional confiscation, and purchase at reduced prices." These compromise measures were too lukewarm for the Communists. The right-wing Korean Democratic Party, on the other hand, issued a strong denunciation of the Seven Principles as leftist-oriented.[77] This denunciation led to the mass resignation of the KDP's more progressive elements, led by Won Se-hun, and to a concentration of intellectuals in the coalition committee. This very development, however, resulted in a political stalemate with no major agreements possible.

Having failed in their original goal of bringing about a coalition, the American occupation authorities began to use the coalition committee as an advisory body on basic problems. Chaos in South Korea had been mounting ever since the October riots. Starting on October 23, the American authorities and the coalition committee held numerous discussion sessions on various pressing matters.[78] The center of stage, however, gradually shifted to Kim Kyu-sik and away from Yŏ Un-hyŏng. Yŏ and Paek Nam-un, the leftists opposed to the South Korean Workers' Party, had launched the Sa-hoe Nodong-dang (Socialist Workers' Party), but they had met with stiff opposition from P'yŏngyang. After visiting P'yŏngyang

75. *Seoul Sinmun,* July 27, 1946.
76. *Tong-A Ilbo,* July 31, 1946.
77. *Ibid.,* Sept. 7, 1946.
78. For details of the Coalition Committee, including its activities, see Chong-Sik Lee, *Usa Kim Kyu-sik,* Seoul, 1972.

and evidently being subjected to extensive pressure, Paek advocated a merger of the SWP with the SKWP. However, the latter balked, calling instead for unconditional dissolution of the SWP.[79] On November 12, Yŏ resigned from the Democratic National Front, and on the thirteenth he advocated the dissolution of the SWP as well as of the moribund coalition committee.[80] Yŏ at this point was a deeply troubled and disillusioned man. A few weeks later, on December 4, he once again declared his retirement from active politics.[81]

The Struggle Within the Communist Party of South Korea

It is appropriate at this point to return to developments within the South Korean Communist Party itself. As noted earlier, Pak Hŏn-yŏng had overcome various challenges to his leadership by the end of 1945 and was exercising his authority with full Soviet support. Once again, however, by the spring of 1946, troubles within the Party were brewing. The embarrassment over the trusteeship issue undoubtedly bruised some feelings and, as we have seen, the Party line on this matter was exceedingly difficult to swallow. However, as long as it seemed possible that the Joint Commission might agree upon a formula for Korean unification, the Party was able to contain its internal problems. It is interesting to note a Communist document of early April that placed Korean politicians into three categories: "Those whom we call our leaders," namely, Pak Hŏn-yŏng, Yŏ Un-hyŏng, Hŏ Hŏn, Kim Tu-bong, Kim Il-sŏng, Yi Chu-ha, (Ch'oi) Mu Chŏng, and Kim Won-bong, in that order; the "neutrals," namely, Kim Kyu-sik, Kim Pyŏng-no, and Hong Myŏng-hui; and the "reactionaries," Syngman Rhee,

---

79. *Tong-A Ilbo*, Nov. 10, 1946, and *Chosŏn Ilbo*, Nov. 12, 1946.

80. See *Tong-A Ilbo*, Nov. 13, 1946, and *Chosŏn Ilbo*, Nov. 16, 1946.

81. Yŏ, of course, did not retire. After he returned from another trip to P'yŏng-yang in late December 1946, his followers began to rally supporters throughout South Korea. On May 24, 1947, Yŏ finally announced the creation of the Kŭllo Inmin-dang (Working People's Party). Before much could be accomplished, however, Yŏ was assassinated on July 19, 1947, near his home. Yŏ Un-hong, *op. cit.*

Even though the intent behind the Kŭllo Inmin-dang was to bring together "like-minded people" excluding the Communists, Yŏ was surrounded by Communists to the end. In March 1947, the USMG offered to send Yŏ to New Delhi to attend an international conference. Yŏ, who yearned to see Nehru, jumped at the opportunity and eagerly accepted the offer while he was in Taegu to deliver a public speech. But when he returned to Seoul, Communist opposition became so strong that Yŏ had to cancel the trip. Chong-Sik Lee interview with Yŏ Un-hong, Feb. 19, 1970.

After Yŏ's death, the Central Committee of the Kŭllo Inmin-dang engaged in a two-day debate, attempting to define Yŏ's ideological views, the Communist elements arguing that Yŏ was a Communist and their opponents denying it. Chong-Sik Lee interview with Yu Pyŏng-muk, Feb. 22, 1970. As we shall note, P'yŏngyang now publicly proclaims Yŏ as a "progressive," suppressing the strong reservations earlier voiced about his role.

Kim Ku, Kim Sŏng-su, Cho Wan-gu, Cho Man-sik, Chang Tŏk-su, and Cho So-ang.[82]

The order in which these "leaders" were placed is of as much interest in connection with this list as the names themselves. All of the key figures, south and north, were to be found. But the southern Party clearly put a higher premium upon its own figures—and on those whom it regarded or hoped to regard as fellow travelers—than it did upon the leaders of North Korea.

At this point, the Joint Commission was still in session in Seoul. Other documents provide interesting evidence on Communist policies and tactics during this period. The critical issue was the exclusion of so-called anti-democratic elements from any Korean government. It was agreed that the commission should be bombarded by a fully mobilized people until the Soviet proposals were accepted. Meanwhile, on the domestic front, the key issues were rice prices, the new law requiring the registration of political parties, and the "vicious" law forcing the closure of certain private schools. On all these matters, a massive campaign by the Party was ordered; de-tailed progress reports were to be submitted by the tenth of each month.[83]

The Communists now displayed considerable sophistication both in their selection of issues and in the manner in which they conducted political

82. Document B dated April 2, 1946, in XXIV Corps, G-2 Report, May 22, 1946.

83. In Document A, also dated in early April and from Pusan, the critical is-sues were set forth: "General Shtikov has shown us clearly the fundamental re-sponsibilities of the Joint Commission, and so we must insist firmly upon the demands of the Soviet representatives." These were "the exclusion of anti-democratic and anti-trusteeship elements from discussions and participation in any government, with the Democratic National Front to constitute the core group; a demand that the Korean people be allowed to establish an anti-Fascist government; and the creation of a demo-cratic Korea that will completely obliterate the old anti-Russian biases."

In this same document, the Party proposed to make the price and scarcity of rice a central issue, and each street was to be organized as a separate unit, so that dis-honest merchants could be exposed, citizens' meetings conducted, and petitions of protest sent to the Military Administration.

To support the Soviet position on unification, the Party ordered a wide range of tactics to reach the maximum number of people: public meetings, pamphlets and leaflets, newspapers, and theatrical performances, among other measures. The Com-mission was to be flooded with petitions, resolutions, and personal letters. In mobiliz-ing people, Party cadres were to put primary emphasis on events, incidents, and de-sires that were immediate and could be easily understood. The words used should be simple, the message brief. "Leaders of the anti-people's front" should be treated "violently," but the common people in the ranks of the opposition should be handled with respect so that they could be won over.

In still another document, dated April 3, it was stated that "although we may send provincial Agitprop leaders to various districts, the campaign should be devel-oped essentially from within the district itself," and the attempts should be made "to avoid anti-American speeches." For these documents, see *ibid.*

campaigns. The issues they advanced were of two basic types: those of intrinsic importance to the Communist Party (and the Soviet Union), such as the rules that would govern unification procedures; and those of immediate concern to the South Korean people, such as the availability and cost of food. Like successful politicians of all kinds, they understood the importance of making appeals on a wide range of issues but focusing upon concerns that were immediate and close to home. Tactically, moreover, the Communists demonstrated that they were prepared to pursue a wide range of mobilization techniques, from letter-writing to street demonstrations and open-air meetings.

To undertake these activities, the Communists had to have substantial funds. Increasingly, American and South Korean authorities interested themselves in the source of those funds. The earliest money, estimated at some 60 million yen, had come principally from the manipulation of Japanese properties and other Japanese sources. In March 1946, evidence emerged that the Soviet occupational forces constituted a new source. Early in their occupation, the Russians had issued Red Army notes in North Korea. Bank of Chosen notes were thereby made available for organizational work in the south. According to several informants, the Russians were now transferring funds to the KCP from the north via the Soviet consulate in Seoul. One report indicated that the Soviet Union had promised to advance some 70 million yen to the Party and that Pak Hŏn-yŏng himself had been given 2 million yen, primarily for use in funding publications. Whatever the facts, many of the KCP leaders seemed to have had no great difficulty in acquiring excellent clothes and automobiles. They were also able to provide lavish entertainment.

As a result of the breakdown of American-Soviet discussions in early May, as well as a number of other factors, relations between the US Military Government and the South Korean Communists were rapidly deteriorating. These same events were inducing the Russians to make some basic policy changes. They now decided to make the Democratic National Front the Soviet coalition effort, north and south, and, beyond this, to reorganize the Communist Party in such fashion as to encompass all leftist elements. These decisions were translated into reality without too much difficulty in the north, where the Russians had firm and total control. But in the south, they created serious problems for Pak Hŏn-yŏng and his comrades.

Even before the thorny problem of Party reorganization was presented to him from the north, Pak had come under attack once again from within the Party. His new critic was Cho Pong-am, a Party leader from the prewar era who was now the key figure in the Inch'ŏn Party branch. Cho had written a lengthy letter to Pak voicing his complaints. In early May, *Tong-A Ilbo* obtained this letter from undisclosed sources and proceeded to publish it. This caused great embarrassment to the Party and revealed a new and substantial fissure within Party ranks. Cho began by criticizing the heavy-handed tactics employed by the Party in establishing the Democratic National Front. "I believe that the Democratic National Front will develop well," he asserted,

> but I also think that the positive involvement of the non-Party masses is automatically constrained because our Party members have infiltrated into it in excessive numbers. As long as the Party has established a large, important front, would it not be sufficient to point the masses down that road? I believe that it is a mistake to issue such directives as the one demanding that Party members hold a membership majority at the branch level.[84]

In addition to charging that everyone knew the National Front was a vehicle of the KCP because of the latter's clumsy tactics, Cho also insisted that the struggle to support the Moscow Agreement had been poorly conducted. The result was that the "unorganized masses" had been lost to the enemy. He cited specifically the abrupt about-face made at the Citizens' Rally of January 3, and asserted that, in the absence of a satisfactory explanation, a "common evaluation" of that event would continue to be held by the masses (presumably an "evaluation" that the Russians had dictated the switch).

Cho then proceeded to attack Pak in highly personal terms, accusing him of lacking principles, pursuing sectarian and "feudalist" policies, and exhibiting favoritism in his appointments. He went on, however, to assert that "we must exercise the greatest vigilance against the heroism of Kim Il-sŏng and Mu Chŏng," thereby indicating his reservations about the northern leaders. In the latter section of his letter, Cho sought to answer the charges that had been raised against him and, in so doing, probably revealed the letter's true raison d'etre. Cho, as we noted earlier, had been a leading figure in the pre-1945 Korean Communist movement, but he was also one of those who had been caused to renounce Communism while in a Japanese prison. Consequently, he had been demoted to the rank of local leader after Liberation, a situation that rankled him greatly.[85]

84. Cho Pong-am, "Chon'gyŏng hanŭn Pak tongmu ege" ("To My Respected Comrade Pak"), *Tong-A Ilbo,* May 9–11, 1946. It seems clear that the letter was not intended for publication outside Party circles. According to a Korean "neutralist," the letter was discovered in the course of a search of Cho's house by American counterintelligence and given to Korea's leading newspaper, *Tong-A Ilbo,* for publication. Yim Yŏng-su, "An Outline of the History of Korean Political Parties," (IV) *Koria Hyŏron* (*Korea Review*), Tokyo, Aug. 1966, p. 43.

85. In his letter, Cho dealt with various charges that had been lodged against him: he denied having misspent MOPR funds in connection with the Pacific Labor Conference; he admitted his "abandonment" of his first wife, a Party member, to marry a non-Party member, confessing that this was a "crime," but, he added, his second wife became a good Party member and played an important role in the Chinese Communist Party. He also admitted administrative responsibility, as senior Party official, for acts of robbery in Shanghai committed by Party members, but denied

As might have been expected, this letter brought about a total rupture between Cho and the Party. In an interview with *Tong-A Ilbo* in early August, Cho admitted as much. He now referred to Pak as "head of the Seoul Com-Group," and accused him of splitting the nation by pursuing "destructive sectarian policies." [86]

The Cho affair, while very embarrassing, was less serious to the Party than the internal crisis that emerged over policies connected with coalition and Party reorganization. Even before the latter issue became a central one, various reports reached the US Military Government that KCP control was passing from Pak's hands. According to these reports, the key roles now rested with Yi Kang-guk, Hong Nam-p'yo, and Yi Chu-ha, with Kim Ch'ŏl-su, a South Chŏlla man of yangban background who was regarded as "an intellectual and a gentleman," scheduled to become the formal leader.[87] However, the reports were exaggerated and, in part, inaccurate; the key figures noted above were a part of the Pak faction. Nevertheless, Pak was having increasing difficulties in the late spring of 1946.

---

any personal involvement in, or knowledge of, such acts at the time. He categorically rejected the charge that he had obtained concessions or lived as a wealthy man after his release from prison, as well as the "rumor" that he was now "an agent of the authorities."

These charges, it should be reiterated, were typical of the accusations leveled by senior Party members against each other in connection with prewar events.

86. This interview was carried in the Aug. 2, 1946, issue of *Tong-A Ilbo*. When Cho was asked whether his use of the term "Seoul Com-Group" indicated that he believed that there were other Communist Parties in Korea than the one led by Pak, he answered that there could be only one Party in one nation but that there were many other Communist groups in Korea apart from the Seoul Com-Group, and only if all groups were united in a single centralized organization would internal Party democracy be established and correct policies be pursued.

Cho's subsequent political career merits brief notice here, since he was destined to continue political activities of significance until his execution in 1959. Having left the Communist Party, Cho entered "rightist" politics, running successfully for the National Assembly of the Republic of Korea in 1948. He was subsequently appointed minister of agriculture by Syngman Rhee. In 1950, he was again elected to the National Assembly and became its speaker. In 1952, he chose to run against Rhee for the presidency, but garnered only 797,504 votes as against Rhee's 5,238,769. In the 1956 presidential election, however, Cho obtained 2,163,808 votes to Rhee's 5,046,437, partly because of the sudden death of the major opposition candidate, Shin Ik-hi, in the final stages of the campaign. Rhee and his followers were, of course, infuriated.

In November of the same year, moreover, Cho organized the Chinbo-dang (Progressive Party), one of its main planks being "the peaceful unification" of Korea. Subsequently, Cho and a number of his associates were charged with conspiracy against the state and collusion with the North Korean Communists. Convicted, Cho was sentenced to death and executed on July 31, 1959. For details, see Yun Ki-jŏng, *Hanguk kongsan chu-ui undong pip'an (A Critique of the Korean Communist Movement)*, Seoul, 1959, pp. 254–489.

87. USAFIK, Accession No. RG-332, *op. cit.*

As internal problems mounted, Pak left in June for the North Korean trip already referred to. He was gone for five weeks. It seems likely that during this time agreements on all matters were reached with Soviet authorities in P'yŏngyang. When Pak returned, he not only took a strong stand against the coalition effort; he struck out against the opposition within the KCP, which had been emboldened by his lengthy absence. His counterattack was launched on several fronts. As a member of the Presidium of the Democratic National Front, he asserted his right to call the Front into special session. He then argued vigorously against any union with Right or Center elements, and in favor of a new, Left-oriented party. Meanwhile, he informed various figures within the KCP that his position as Party secretary had been confirmed in P'yŏngyang, and that those who persisted in questioning his authority would be placing themselves in the most serious jeopardy. According to some reports, Pak also took this occasion to tell a few highly trusted comrades that he had received certain top secret information: the Communists (whether Russian or North Korean was unclear) intended to occupy South Korea within three years, peacefully if possible, but if necessary with force.

At the National Front meeting, Pak specifically demanded that the Left withdraw from the conference being held over the question of a coalition. He moved for a strict prohibition against any collaboration with a purely South Korean legislative body. According to reports that leaked out of the meeting, he was strongly supported by Yi Chu-ha and Hong Namp'yo of the KCP, and by Hŏ Hŏn, who nominally represented the defunct Korean People's Republic. The opposition was led by Yŏ Un-hyŏng, aided by Kim Won-bong; Paek Nam-un straddled the fence during the debate. (It should be remembered that Yŏ's plea to American authorities to deal with Pak "decisively" came during this period.)[88]

Meanwhile, Pak moved against his opponents within the KCP. The Party's internal crisis had spilled over into the public press by early August. The immediate issue was the merger of leftist parties: Pak's opponents insisted that, to be legal, any merger would have to be ratified by a Party congress. On August 4, six central committee members, Kang Chin, Sŏ Chung-sŏk, Kim Ch'ŏl-su, Yi Chŏng-yun, Kim Kŭn, and Mun Kap-song, issued a joint statement charging that those holding Party leadership had displayed bureaucratic and Trotskyist tendencies and were threatening

88. Unable to get the Presidium to go along with him fully, Pak advanced a "compromise," asserting that he would agree to a coalition movement if five positions were accepted: full and unqualified support of the Moscow Agreement; immediate release of all political prisoners; the enactment of a land reform act similar to the one in force in North Korea; the expulsion of "reactionaries" from public life; and the transfer of governmental functions at once from the USMG to the DNF. Given the positions of the Right and the Center, these conditions had not the remotest chance of being accepted.

Party unity. Those named as the chief culprits were Yi Chu-ha, Kim Sam-yong, and Yi Hyŏn-sang. But a separate attack was leveled at Pak.[89]

Kang Chin's repeated references to Trotskyism reveal clearly the need they all had to struggle for Soviet support. In fact, of course, this was a hopeless cause; Pak was the one in closest touch with the Russians. On August 7, Pak announced that Yi Chŏng-yun had been expelled from the Party; Kim Ch'ŏl-su, Sŏ Chung-sŏk, Kang Chin, Kim Kŭn, and Mun Kap-song were suspended indefinitely. Most of these men, it might be noted, were members of the old Seoul faction. The Pak group were often referred to as "the Keijo Imperial University group," because of their association with that institution in the prewar period.

The anti-Pak group did not accept this ouster quietly. They demanded that a Party congress be convened so that the crucial issues could be debated. Using various arguments, including the difficulty of holding an open

89. In this statement and a more lengthy set of charges released later by Kang Chin, a fascinating account of Party operations during this period is presented, one warranting some notice. The account, it must be remembered, is the unconfirmed version of the anti-Pak group. Earlier Party unification (absorption of the Changan group), they charged, had been handled in total secrecy by the Pak group alone. Afterward, some comrades outside the Pak clique were appointed to the Party Central Committee, but they were members in name only, not even being permitted to know the full roster of the CC membership. At some CC meetings, a number of visitors were invited, and no one could be certain of precisely who was an official member. (!!)

More seriously, comrades not belonging to the Pak group were totally excluded from important Party offices and never notified of major decisions. Such matters as finances, personnel assignments, and local or provincial proposals were not reported to the Central Committee. The Secretariat, completely under the control of the Pak clique, exercised even greater power than the Politburo and the Orgburo. For example, the appointment of Kang Mun-sŏk as head of the Propaganda department and Pak Kwang-hui as head of the Youth department, the putting of Kim T'ae-yong in charge of the Inch'ŏn branch and Kim Chŏm-gwon of the Kangwon Province branch were all carried out by the Secretariat without reference to the Orgburo. With the departments at both national and provincial levels under their full control, the Pak group could avoid meetings of such central Party organs as the Political or Organizational Bureaus.

Kang Chin's statement implies that Yi Chu-ha exercised even greater power than Pak Hŏn-yŏng. Yi had returned to his home town of Wonsan after Liberation, gathered relatives, friends, and others—including "fallen elements"—and reconstructed the Communist movement under his leadership. In doing so, he excluded those who had actually been leading the illegal underground movement during the time he was noninvolved. Those who disagreed with him were ousted or suppressed. But because he was a member of the Pak clique, he became second secretary, making him virtually dictator of the Politburo, Orgburo, and Secretariat.

Similar criticism was issued against Kim Sam-yong and Yi Hyŏn-sang. The former was accused of being responsible for the split within the strategic Yŏngdŭngp'o district of Seoul, and also of having been the first person to attack the Moscow Agreement. The latter was accused of rationalizing his actions by mouthing the "international line" but, in reality, being a leader of sectarian Trotskyism. See *Chosŏn Ilbo*, Aug. 25, 29, 30, 1946.

Party congress under prevailing political conditions, Pak and the other leaders resisted this demand. In early September, as we shall shortly see, a number of key Communists were arrested or forced to go underground. Nevertheless, a few weeks later, on September 29, some 250 anti-Pak KCP representatives from various parts of Korea met in Seoul to "reconstruct" the Party. Under the chairmanship of Yun Il, the meeting unanimously passed a vote of no confidence in the current leadership, and selected twenty-seven new central committee members, with Kim Ch'ŏl-su at their head. However, while the conference delegates were listening to regional and local reports, the chairman and several others were arrested by the US military authorities. Although they were released the following day, and the meeting continued, this incident was in keeping with the times. As a result of a turn to the left in Party policies which we shall explore shortly, many key Communists had disappeared from sight, and the Party, quarrelsome and divided although it was, now enjoyed only semilegal status.

Meanwhile, Pak pushed doggedly ahead with plans for a merger of the Left, despite inside opposition from all the Left parties. The creation of the South Korean Workers' Party was announced on September 3, although the formal inauguration of the Party did not take place until November 13. In the interim, the spiraling dance between extremism and repression continued. In the fall of 1946, a wave of bloody riots, strikes, and demonstrations swept the south. Some 1,500 individuals were arrested in connection with these events, many of them prominent Communist leaders.

Thus, by the end of 1946, the Communist movement in South Korea faced very serious problems, although it still had ample strength. Its primary leaders were under sustained assault from all sides, and many of them were underground, in prison, or in the privileged sanctuary of the north. Pak Hŏn-yŏng himself had fled to Haeju, a town just north of the 38th parallel, in October 1946, shortly after a warrant for his arrest had been issued. There, in close coordination with the Political Department of the Soviet Occupation Command, he continued to issue orders and directives to the Party in the south. There can be no doubt that, throughout this entire period, he was firmly in command of all its operations.[90]

The Organizational Structure of the SKWP

To survive in the midst of an increasingly hostile environment placed an even greater premium upon organization. We should therefore examine the organizational structure of the SKWP, if only briefly, in a period when circumstances seemed to dictate both legal and illegal activities, both a formal Party-front structure and an underground apparatus.

---

90. Serving in the temporary Party headquarters under Pak at Haeju were Kwon O-jik, Pak Ch'i-u, Chŏng Chae-dal, Yi Won-jo, and Yi Ta'e-jun. Most of these men were southern intellectuals, and all were subsequently to meet a disastrous end, either being killed during the war or being purged by Kim Il-sŏng. For details, see Pak Il-won, *Nam-No-dang ch'ong pi-p'an, op. cit.*, pp. 88–89.

Theoretically, a National Party Congress was supposed to be held annually to serve as the supreme decision-making body. But it was never possible to convene such a congress. Even the "congress" that launched the SKWP on November 22–23 was largely pro forma, since it was not possible for most members to attend it. The Central Committee, supposedly selected by the Party Congress, numbered between forty-one and forty-five during this period. It should have met at least once every three months, but again, because of the repressive measures being taken against the Party, it never met at all. Instead, a Presidium operated—in its name.[91] In point of fact, however, it was the Political Committee, composed of seven men, who issued all basic political lines, orders, and directives. The members were Hŏ Hŏn, Yi Sŭng-yŏp, Yi Chu-ha (acting for Pak Hŏn-yŏng), Yi Ki-sŏk, Kim Sam-yong, Ku Chae-su, and Kim Yong-am. Hŏ Hŏn and Yi Ki-sŏk can be considered as figureheads. The two central figures were Yi Chu-ha and Yi Sŭng-yŏp, but Pak Hŏn-yŏng was the unchallenged leader at this point, albeit a leader in exile.

The SKWP organizational structure was one typical of all Communist parties. A Central Standing Committee, or Presidium, of eleven to thirteen persons served to carry out the decisions of the Political Committee. Under it, some thirteen departments were scheduled to operate, covering all aspects of Party work, from Organization and Propaganda to such functional groups as Workers, Farmers, Youth, and Women.[92] A Central Inspection Committee also existed, at least on paper; it was charged with the implementation of Party decisions and prosecution of those guilty of "anti-Party" acts.

Under this national structure, a series of regional and local committees were created, beginning with those at the provincial and metropolitan level. SKWP cells, the lowest organizational unit, were divided into subgroups of three to five members in an effort to preserve the security of the Party in a difficult period. In addition to those cells which made up the Party nucleus, the SKWP encouraged the creation of "special cells" in non-Party organizations, especially in organizations that the Party used as fronts. In these cases, Party members did not reveal their identity.

91. Though an official list of CC members was never published, being considered secret information, various lists did reach the press. Of the 45 individuals mentioned by Pak as CC members, 28 were from the old Korean Communist Party, 9 from the People's Party, and 8 from the New People's Party; *ibid.*, pp. 87–88.

92. The thirteen departments were divided into three classes according to their importance. The 1st class departments were three: Organization (Kim Sam-yong), Cadres (Ku Chae-su), and Propaganda and Agitation (Kang Mun-sŏk). The 2nd class departments: Workers (Yi Hyŏn-sang), Farmers (Song Ŭl-su), Youth (Ko Ch'ang-bo), Women (Kim Sang-hyŏk). 3rd class departments: Relief and Assistance (Kim Yong-am), Finance (Yi Ch'ŏn-jin or Sŏng Yu-gyŏng), Cooperatives (Chŏng No-sik or Pak Kyŏng-su), Culture (Kim T'ae-jun), Research (or Investigation) (Chŏng T'ae-sik), and General Affairs (Kim Kwang-su): *ibid.*, pp. 90–91, 148.

The basic front organization for the 1946–47 period was the Democratic National Front, as we have noted. It had a collegiate presidency, shared among six individuals, and a Central Committee of 385 members.[93] The DNF claimed some 7 million adherents in the south in this period, but there was actually no way in which to confirm affiliation or support. At both the national and the provincial level, the SKWP had a firm control over the DNF, with its personnel inserted into the necessary positions. The primary function of the DNF, of course, was to advance the claim that a huge number of citizens supported the Left.

The principal fronts other than the DNF were the national federations of industrial workers, farmers, women, and youth that had been organized, many of them by Communists, shortly after Liberation. The National Council of Labor Unions was totally under Communist control and, at one point, claimed a membership of over 2 million. However, because it was a political union, bound to Party directives, it was repeatedly plunged into disastrous strikes and work stoppages having little or no connection with the workers' immediate economic concerns. As a result, it rapidly lost its appeal to the average worker, especially after 1946, and in many cases only Communist Party members remained active in it at the lower levels.

Despite a claimed membership of 2,015,673 in this period, the All-Nation Farmers' Federation was another Communist front run essentially from Party headquarters. Regional and local branches were weak, with Party cadres filling almost all of the local offices. Consequently, the Farmers' Federation, like its labor counterpart, weakened as its identification with the Communist movement became clear.

The South Korean Democratic Women's League was another Party front that was operated in a highly centralized fashion, with very limited grass-roots support—except from local Party branches. The League claimed a membership of 700,000, but this figure was hotly disputed by non-Communists, and probably, as in most cases, was badly inflated. The Korean Democratic Patriotic Youth League was the Communist youth front after the earlier Korean Democratic Youth League had been outlawed. Almost all of its leaders and members were SKWP adherents. Indeed, this group more than any other served as the militant vanguard of the Party, and was active in guerrilla warfare when the signal for such activities was given.

Until about 1948, a very sizable percentage of the intellectuals in South Korea belonged to the Left. A significant number of writers, artists, musicians, scientists, lawyers, educators, and newspapermen joined the General Federation of Korean Cultural Organizations, yet another organization available to, if not completely dominated by, the Communists. From

93. The first six presidents were Hŏ Hŏn, Pak Hŏn-yŏng, Kim Won-bong, Yŏ Un-hyŏng, Kim Ch'ang-jun, and Kim Ki-jŏn. In addition, ten were listed as vice-presidents.

a political point of view, the General Federation was probably the most diverse unit within the Democratic National Front; not all of its members were Communists by any means, or even affiliated with the SKWP. Nevertheless, the Communists found this group very useful, especially since it contained a number of the most prestigious individuals in South Korea.

Finally, there was the Central Federation of Korean Cooperative Unions, which had grown out of the very active consumers' union movement that flourished in the south immediately after Liberation. Gradually, this organization had come under Communist control, and abandoned most of its original activities. The Central Federation apparently engaged in smuggling goods from North Korea, and so provided considerable funds for the Party.[94] Its claimed membership of over 500,000 was also considered grossly exaggerated.

Even if the various membership figures for these organizations were inflated, and even if, in many cases, the organizations themselves were largely run by a small Communist clique at headquarters, the South Korean Communists initially displayed a remarkable capacity to make these organizations work on their behalf. It was only after the Party had been dispersed and forced to go underground that the fragility of some of these organizational efforts became apparent.

The Mounting Clash Between the Communists and the U.S. Military Government

The Communist line in the opening months of the occupation was one of staunch support for the Allies, and repeated promises were made to live within the rules established by American military authorities. Pak and other Communist leaders of the south had proclaimed that, while they reserved the right to criticize occupation policies when "the wrong direction was taken," they were prepared to acknowledge the debt that all Koreans owed to their liberators, as well as the sincerity of the American commitment to Korean independence and democracy. The problem, as they phrased it, was the character of the Koreans who had surrounded the US Military Government—"reactionaries" and "national traitors" who had maneuvered themselves into positions of influence. Thus, the initial Communist tactic was to make a sharp distinction between military government and the Korean moderate-conservative politicians.

As we have seen, this tactic was challenged by the events of the spring of 1946. After the Joint Commission negotiations had started, the Communists directed much of their energy toward forcing an acceptance of the Soviet position on unification. Gradually, this led to an ever-increasing attack upon American policies in general. This trend was barely under

94. According to the Reverend Kang Won-yong, large-scale smuggling between North and South Korea took place in this period, with the South Korean police either intimidated or bribed by the Communists. Chong-Sik Lee interview with Rev. Kang Won-yong, Seoul, Dec. 12, 1969.

way, moreover, when a bizarre event took place that was destined to do great damage to the KCP, and drive an even deeper wedge between it and the American authorities. On May 6, 1946, American investigators entered the Chikazawa Building in downtown Seoul. The building housed the presses for one of the Communist newspapers as well as the KCP headquarters. All of the paraphernalia of a major counterfeiting operation were discovered, including paper, ink, plates, and bogus money amounting to some 12 million yen (about $120,000 based upon the exchange rate of that period).

A number of Communist Party members, including two Party officials, were involved. General Hodge personally directed that the defendants be tried as individuals, not as KCP members, but the Party was implicated by the very nature of the case. Moreover, at the close of the trial, the defendants rose as a group and sang "The Red Flag." On one occasion during the trial, a mob had tried to free the defendants; as a result, one man was killed and some fifty jailed. All of the defendants were convicted, and in the sensational press coverage of the case it was made clear throughout South Korea that the KCP was involved.[95]

The counterfeiting incident led investigating authorities into uncovering a great many documents pointing to collusion between the South Korean Communists and Soviet authorities. Some of them involved espionage. The first hard evidence of this had come slightly earlier. On March 5, 1946, two Koreans serving as Soviet agents were apprehended in Seoul. Signed confessions were obtained indicating that these two had been sent south to join the Coast Guard school sponsored by the US armed forces. If that proved impossible, they were to visit the principal cities of South Korea and obtain information on US army strength and local economic conditions. Inch'ŏn was a special target, since it provided opportunities to investigate the nature of shipping and trade, and the number of warships in the harbor.

On May 18, agents of the American Counterintelligence Corps seized secret documents at KCP headquarters in Seoul; on June 25, additional documents were obtained from KCP headquarters in Wŏnju, Kangwon Prefecture. The documents proved that subordinate Communist units had been ordered to gather information and report upon US army troop strength, movement, and activities in their area. On June 27, General Hodge reported that the indications were that this information was being pooled via KCP channels and then being given to the Soviet consulate in Seoul.

Communist agents from North Korea were now being intercepted

95. The proceedings of the trial were published by Taegŏn Insoe-so as *Wi-p'e sakŏn kongp'an kirok* (*Record of the Public Trial Involving the Counterfeiting Incident*), Seoul, 1947. Yim Yŏng-su, who is strongly critical of both the USMG and the KCP, insists that the case was unfounded (Yim, *op. cit.*, p. 42) but most sources regard the case as a bona fide one.

regularly. One individual, stopped initially for not being able to produce his cholera vaccination certificate, admitted having attended a secret school in North Korea, run by four Soviet army officers and one Korean lecturer, where he was taught espionage and guerrilla tactics. He claimed that some eight hundred Koreans were enrolled, and that the one key qualification was the ability to speak in a South Korean dialect.

On August 7, a raid was carried out on the home of Kim Se-yong, political affairs chief of the People's Party. Among the materials discovered was information pertaining to US army installations and units, along with detailed data on the Korean police and Coast Guard, and the structure of the US Military Government. These documents revealed that there had been considerable infiltration into Korean units by agents from North Korea.[96]

It can be assumed, of course, that neither espionage nor infiltration were one-way routes. Undoubtedly, American and South Korean agents were seeking to penetrate North Korea during this same period—with what success we do not know. However, the odds clearly favored the Communists. Already the North had become a tightly knit police state with no bona fide opposition parties or organizations. In the south, on the other hand, the Communist Party, and the fronts it controlled, were available as "safe houses" for spies.

It was in this period also that the so-called Communist Master Plan for Korea was first heard of through that murky circuit of informers, agents, and disillusioned ex-Communists that American and South Korean authorities used as primary sources of information. One should emphasize at the outset that there is no positive proof of the existence of such a plan. But reports concerning it came from so many diverse sources and in such similar form that it must have had some basis in fact. In any case, American authorities took it seriously, as did their Korean allies. The plan was outlined as follows: The immediate task of the KCP in the south was to increase its membership as rapidly as possible and also to strengthen all of its front groups. When these latter organizations had been sufficiently strengthened, most or all of them were to disassociate themselves publicly from the KCP. Then the Party would indicate a willingness to compromise with the Right. According to these reports, the Communists counted heavily upon the disassociated front groups being accepted as "neutrals." In this way they hoped to present a picture of relative Communist weakness while in fact laying the foundations for a united front government that would be as far to the left as possible. Since the Communist element in this government would look only minor, the Americans would presumably withdraw once it had been created. Soon afterwards, various incidents and dis-

96. USAFIK, Accession No. RG-332, "Soviet Communist Inspired Espionage in South Korea," a report addressed to the Commanding General, XXIV Corps, undated.

orders would erupt throughout the country. These would have been in-stigated by the Communists. At this point, with the Communists deeply infiltrated into the police and military establishments as well as secretly powerful in the government, they would move to "restore order," and via this route seize command.

It was an ingenious tactic and, in view of the situation in South Korea, not an illogical one. Naturally, however, its disclosure did little to improve relations between Communist and non-Communist forces in South Korea. There followed the wearisome, futile negotiations over a coalition, and the concrete evidence that new Soviet policies for the Korean Communist movement were being transmitted in their pure form by the KCP via Pak Hŏn-yŏng. From Yŏ Un-hyŏng and others, moreover, information was garnered to the effect that the Communists planned to move from non-violent to violent protest.

This information proved to be correct. The second half of 1946 wit-nessed a sharp Communist turn to the left. In July, as we have seen, prompted by the Russians, Pak Hŏn-yŏng had adopted a "new strategy" that placed the primary emphasis upon an attack against American poli-cies and US Military Government. This militancy led in the fall to the September wave of strikes, which were clearly an effort to undermine the South Korean government economically as well as politically. It was no accident that the strikes and sabotage were aimed primarily at the trans-port and electric industries. The railroads were practically the only major form of transportation available in Korea at this point. To stop their operations and cut off or reduce the supply of electricity significantly would have had a devastating effect upon an already seriously weakened economy. It would also have been a dramatic illustration to the South Korean people of Communist power.

The Communist turn to the left, as might have been anticipated, was matched by a tightening of USMG policies. Using the occasion of increas-ingly shrill Communist attacks upon military government and the various Right and Center groups, American authorities on September 6 ordered the suspension of three leftist newspapers, including the *Chosŏn Inminbo* (Korean People's Daily).[97] On the following day, warrants were issued for

97. In the documents seized in late August in a raid on Pusan Communist head-quarters, instructions to Party members contained the following orders: blame for various problems was to be shifted from a primary emphasis upon right-wing parties to focus upon the United States, attacking Military Government as "an organ es-tablished by the United States to make slaves of the Korean People." In the future, therefore, the adjournment of the US-Soviet Joint Commission was not to be blamed solely upon the rightists but also upon "the international reactionary strategy of the American representatives": USAFIK, Accession No. RG-332. By early September, the Communist press was calling for the immediate withdrawal of all American forces and the transfer of supreme power to the People's Committees "as the true representative of the Korean people."

the arrest of Pak Hŏn-yŏng, Yi Kang-guk, and Yi Chu-ha. Of these three key figures, only Yi Chu-ha was actually imprisoned; the other two went underground before they could be apprehended. However, a number of others were arrested at this time. These included Hong Nam-p'yo, Sŏ Chung-sŏk, and Kim Kŭn. Most of them were quickly released, but the signals were clear: the Communists could no longer operate freely in South Korea.

The South Korean Workers' Party finally received its official launching in November, after its beginnings had been delayed both by serious internal wrangling among the leftists and by the general political atmosphere in which it was forced to operate. On September 7, precisely the same day upon which the warrant for Pak's arrest was issued, the acting chairman of Yŏ Un-hyŏng's People's Party had denounced the KCP for "betraying" the other two left parties, and "using coercive methods" to obtain acquiescence in the establishment of the new South Korean Workers' Party. Trouble also erupted during this period within the ranks of the New People's Party. Paek Nam-un, its chairman, recommended on September 19 that his executive committee vote for participation in unity talks, but this was rejected and he resigned. Five days later, a meeting of the party rank and file was convened; Paek Nam-un's resignation was refused and a new committee favorable to participation was selected. In spite of this, the party was split by the issue of merging with the Communists.

As we have seen, the Communists refused to take any part in the new South Korean Interim Legislative Assembly, and urged a boycott of the fall elections. Naturally, when General Hodge appointed some twenty leftist representatives in an effort to provide some balance to the election results, he did not appoint any members of the SKWP. Thus, at the end of 1946, relations between American authorities and the South Korean Communists were characterized by mutual hostility.[98]

On balance, the turn to the left had not served the Communists well. After the reverses of the fall they returned to less militant tactics. A period of greater moderation ensued, with the SKWP seeking to recoup its strength after the heavy blows dealt the movement through the mass arrests and the forced flight of so many key leaders.

98. Evidence from USAFIK reports of this period suggest that General Hodge and his staff finally adopted a hard-line approach to the Communists in August, with the mounting evidence of espionage activities being the conclusive determinant. For political reasons, primarily connected with American-Soviet negotiations, the State Department seems to have hoped that a softer line, more like that of the early occupation period, could continue. Hodge prevailed, however. For example, despite some favorable sentiment in Washington, a proposed mission of the World Federation of Trade Unions to Korea was disapproved by USAFIK, with Hodge pointing out that the All-Korean Federation of Labor had joined WFTU on July 28, 1946, via North Korean channels, and that it was a union completely organized and dominated by the Communists.

In retrospect, it is clear that 1946 was the year in which the Communist Party of South Korea reached the zenith of its strength. Already, by the time the SKWP was inaugurated, that zenith had passed. The problem with extreme militancy—unless it pays off quickly and in the form of total victory—is that it inevitably separates the activists from the masses because it requires a higher price than the latter are willing to pay. Thus, having approached the status of mass party toward the beginning of 1946, the SKWP at the end of that year had been turned into a vanguard party. Even its front organizations were becoming mere extensions of the Party rather than true conduits to the masses. Moreover, by turning sharply to the left, the Communists had finally provoked the US Military Government to work in closer liaison with the Korean Right, and to take an uncompromising stand against leftist activities.

In the months following its inauguration, the SKWP managed to preserve its legality, and the various Communist front organizations were also able to hold their congresses without being suppressed. The Party took the position in its organs that "the people's forces" were too strong to be subjugated either by military government or "reactionaries." However, American authorities during this period were still waiting to see whether any American-Soviet agreement was possible on the Korean problem. Accordingly, they were content not to challenge the Communists frontally as long as they did not resort to illegal actions.

Thus, the Democratic National Front remained officially in existence, with the quartet of Kim Tu-bong, Pak Hŏn-yŏng, Hŏ Hŏn, and Yŏ Un-hyŏng reelected to top leadership in January 29, 1947. Political instability, much of it instigated by the Communists, continued to plague South Korea throughout 1947. The spring was marked by large-scale clashes, climaxed by the riots of March 1. Three weeks later, the Communists sought to paralyze the entire south by means of a general strike, which failed. In so doing, it indicated an ebb in support for the Left. Nevertheless, it succeeded in contributing to the generally troubled atmosphere.[99]

A month earlier, in February, the Central Committee of the SKWP had ordered its various school cells to carry out strikes against the proposal to establish a national university system. Quickly, students in a number of middle schools and colleges in Seoul went out on strike, and the strike soon spread throughout the country. Initially, there was no police intervention. But because the strikers committed a large number of illegal acts, such as beating students who chose not to cooperate and kidnapping opponents, the police finally had to intervene.

99. Yi Sŭng-yŏp, one of the key Communist leaders still in the south, reportedly stated that the general strike was being called to test the solidarity of the Party organization and its auxiliary units, to demonstrate the strength of the Party to the Korean people, and to lend support to the demand for renewed Joint Commission meetings. See Pak Il-won, *op. cit.*, pp. 60–61.

Once again, government authorities, both American and South Korean, met the new challenges with massive, decisive counteraction. Over two thousand individuals, many of them important Party cadres, were arrested in connection with the general strike.

When the Joint Commission reconvened in April, the Party claimed a victory. Simultaneously, it undertook a major recruiting effort; its goal was to increase membership fivefold or more. (Later, Kim Il-sŏng was to charge Pak Hŏn-yŏng with seeking to swell the ranks of the SKWP so that it could overwhelm the NKWP.) The indications are, however, that this campaign was not notably successful. The Communists were soon to concentrate upon the convening of an All-Nation People's Conference, a meeting of representatives from both south and north so that issues pertaining to unification could be discussed by the Korean people themselves. Concerning this conference, we shall have more to say in the next chapter.

Meanwhile, the Communist position on the major issues of this period was clearly set forth in several important documents published in the SKWP organ, *Noryŏk Inmin* (*Working People*). One was a report of the secretariat of the Democratic National Front, adopted June 17, 1947.[100] This report gave full support to the Moscow Decision, denounced Syngman Rhee's call for general elections, and demanded that the new Korean state be known as the Korean Democratic People's Republic, with the legislature called the People's Congress. The report continued by calling for the establishment of People's Committees everywhere and, through these committees, the creation of a "democratic provisional government" that would at first undertake both legislative and administrative functions, drafting a constitution, electing a legislative body, and supervising both domestic and foreign policies. Such a proposal, of course, was completely in line with procedures that had been followed in the North.

The report also contained a vigorous attack upon the South Korean police, denouncing them as "holdovers from the Japanese era." Interestingly, on the subject of leadership for the new state, the report conspicuously avoided naming names. On the contrary, it asserted that power should not be concentrated in the hands of a single individual, on the grounds that there was as yet no "great leader to whom all rights [could] be entrusted." Instead, it called for "collective and democratic leadership" to be established. In the economic arena, as might have been expected, the report issued the familiar call for land reform, the nationalization of basic industries, and other socioeconomic reforms.

At the same time, the Communists continued to attack the Korean Democratic Party, and demand that it be excluded from any participation in Joint Commission activities. In an article by Yi Sŭng-yŏp, the KDP was

100. "The form of political authority should be the People's Committee and the national designation should be the Korean Democratic People's Republic," *Noryŏk Inmin* (*Working People*), June 19, 1947, p. 1.

accused once again of being led by men guilty of pro-Japanese activities and of violent hostility to the Moscow Agreement—despite the willingness of the KDP to subscribe to a Joint Commission statement in order to establish their eligibility for participation.[101] There was absolutely no sign of any rapprochement between the Communists and the Right during this period.

On July 15, the Joint Commission became hopelessly deadlocked. Less than a month later, South Korean authorities began a major roundup of known and suspected leftists. In Seoul, the police chief, Chang T'aek-sang, asserted that the arrests were being undertaken because the Communists intended to take over South Korea by force and overturn the military government. In response to General Shtikov's protests, General Hodge made a similar statement.

By mid-1947, relations between the American occupation authorities and the South Korean Communists were both infrequent and hostile. In considerable measure, of course, this merely paralleled the deterioration of American-Soviet relations; the Cold War had begun in earnest, and its manifestations were to be seen everywhere. But it was particularly evident in Korea. Beyond this, however, the South Korean Communists, by virtue of the circumstances in which they found themselves, now had to opt increasingly for illegal activities. These activities, as we have seen, included large-scale violence, and repression continued to mount.

Though events during late 1947 further weakened the southern Communists, they were still prepared to attempt another offensive. Once again, in February 1948, a general strike was called in the name of the Democratic National Front and other leftist organizations, including the National Council of Trade Unions. The issues were largely political: to oppose separate elections in South Korea and demand the immediate withdrawal of all foreign troops; to insist upon "the right of the Korean people to establish their own government without foreign interference," including interference from the UN; and to fight for the "unification, freedom and democratic independence of the Fatherland."

The strike of February 1948 was accompanied by a great deal of violence. Transport facilities were sabotaged, and numerous police stations attacked. Between the seventh and tenth of February, for example, 6 police were reported killed, and 24 wounded or kidnapped; and 5 government officials or conservative party leaders were killed and 13 wounded or kidnapped. Sixty-eight attacks against electric lines were reported; 39

101. Yi Sŭng-yŏp, "I criticize the statement of the Korean Democratic Party—let us exclude (it) from the Joint Commission by the power of the people." *Ibid.*

In a statement of June 4, 1947, incidentally, the DNF had suggested that it was entitled to 50 percent of the total representation of South Korean political and social organizations, with the Center and Right entitled to the other 50 percent. *Chosŏn Ilbo,* June 5, 1947, p. 1,

locomotives were damaged, with sabotage against bridges and roads also being widely undertaken. On the other side of the ledger, 28 "rioters" were reported killed, 10 wounded, and 1,489 arrested.

Violence continued between February and May, as preparations for the May elections got under way. In early June, *Chosŏn Ilbo* reported that some 388 cases of arson had occurred during the period between February 7 and May 24, no fewer than 308 of them upon the homes of prominent figures. Acts of destruction had been committed against government offices on 22 occasions; against roads and bridges, on 50 occasions; and against election facilities, on 41 occasions. Transport and communications facilities had been particularly hard hit, with 71 locomotive engines destroyed and damaged, and telephone lines cut on 563 occasions. Some 145 government officials, 150 civilians, and 330 "rioters" had been killed, with additional numbers wounded.

Communist Uprisings and Military Revolts

If these figures indicate a struggle still relatively small in proportion to the total population and facilities involved, there can be no doubt that, by early 1948, the Communists were gradually moving into forms of guerrilla warfare, both urban and rural. Indeed, the final chapter in South Korean Communist activities prior to the Korean War revolves largely around efforts to promote revolt within the military and police organization of the Republic of Korea, and to establish guerrilla operations. As was understandable, the Communists had long sought to penetrate the South Korean Constabulary (later transformed into the Republic of Korea Army, better known as ROKA) and the regular police forces. These efforts, moreover, had been crowned with considerable success by 1948, although, as we shall see, it is impossible to estimate with any accuracy the extent of Communist infiltration into the total military-police establishment.

The first major Communist effort to set up a southern People's Liberation Army involving elements of the ROK police force was uncovered in late 1947. On January 3, 1948, the director of the South Korean police announced that some 400 individuals in and around Pusan had been arrested, and that 157 of them were scheduled for trial or had already been tried on charges of involvement with a so-called People's Liberation Army. A number of those implicated were from the police force. A total of 45 military men were court-martialed. According to authorities, captured documents revealed the creation of a fairly impressive nucleus for broader organization activities. The operation had centered around South Kyŏngsang Province, where Han Rin-sik had organized a provincial Military Committee in March 1947, serving as its "chief of staff." Han had appointed Kim Kap-su as "division commander," and regiments had been secretly established in such cities and counties as Pusan, Tongnae, Ulsan, Chinju, and Namhae. By August 1947, a core group of 830 "military" and 763 "political" members had been recruited, and the People's Liberation Army was claiming that it had as many as 36,000 "sympathizers" and potential supporters. Each so-called regiment had special units dealing with military operations, the collection of intelligence, small arms production, and political operations. Activities centered upon efforts to subvert the South Korean armed forces and police, and the collection of information concerning US military forces.[102]

Some effort had been made to provide basic military training for Liberation Army members, with an emphasis upon both house-to-house fighting and mountainous guerrilla warfare. In October 1947, for example, in the mountains near the famed Pŏm-ŏ-sa temple, some fifty men from various prefectures had been given a special training course under the supervision of the head of the Military Training Department. Extensive attention was also given to training for attacks upon police stations and policemen, and a number of such raids were actually carried out, with heavy casualties on both sides.

It was as a result of an investigation of a man suspected of having killed a police detective that a cache of documents pertaining to the People's Liberation Army was uncovered on November 6, 1947. Arrests of a large number of those involved followed one week later.[103] This was not to be the last episode of its kind. More arrests took place in early February 1948, when it was revealed that Communist agents connected with the Liberation Army had penetrated the police establishment at high levels and succeeded in obtaining key posts in the intelligence and communications divisions. More than a hundred classified police documents pertaining to secret codes, security techniques, and confidential suspect lists had been copied or stolen by Communist inside agents.[104] There is good reason to believe, moreover, that the South Korean authorities were able to detect only a fraction of the infiltration and espionage activities going on.

The truly major military challenge to the South Korean government during this period, however, came from Communist-led revolts within South Korean military units. The most serious of these was undoubtedly the Cheju Island uprising which broke out on April 3, 1948. This revolt, Communist-planned and -led, involved the entire military force on the island. It was to last for more than a year, and it spread to other military units.

In certain respects, Cheju was an ideal setting for a Communist military-political effort. Toward the end of World War II, the Japanese

102. The indoctrinational materials used included such booklets as *The History of the Struggle of Kim Il-sŏng, On Chinese Guerrilla Warfare,* and *Survey of the Soviet Red Army.*

103. For details, see *Tong-A Ilbo,* Jan. 4 and 6, 1948.

104. See *Py'ŏnghwa Ilbo (Peace Daily),* Feb. 10, 1948, and *Chosŏn Ilbo,* Feb. 10, 1948.

had turned Cheju into a military fortress, maintaining some 60,000 soldiers there. A large quantity of weapons and ammunition had been stored in mountainous caves, and much of it had been left behind when the Japanese evacuated the island. The population, approximately 150,000 civilians under Japanese rule, had doubled after Liberation. Moreover, many of those returning had come from China or Japan, and had a background of leftist political ties. The Communists, operating through youth, labor, peasant, and women's organizations, had established very strong organizational roots in the period immediately after Japanese surrender.

At 2:00 A.M. on April 3, 1948, military units under the direction of Lieutenant Mun Sang-gil proclaimed a revolt against the U.S. administration and commenced military operations.[105] The top leader of the revolt, however, was Kim Tal-sam, the Party secretary-general on the island. Kim had secretly organized a People's Liberation Army, with Yi Tŏk-ku as commanding officer. The Army, numbering some 500 men with an additional 1,000 auxiliaries, had been trained by returnees from China, some of whom had Yenan connections. The revolt was timed as a protest against the scheduled national elections in South Korea. Government offices and police stations were attacked by a force composed of Communist Youth League members, defecting self-defense unit men, and Communist sympathizers within the regular military forces. Defections snowballed and, for a time, the entire island was under Communist control.

The South Korean Army ordered the 14th Regiment, which was stationed immediately across the channel in Yŏsu, to quell the rebellion. On October 19, however, this regiment itself revolted. In turn, the 15th Regiment stationed in nearby Masan was directed to put down the 14th Regiment. But instead, it joined the 14th Regiment in its struggle against the government. Thus, for weeks, the Rhee administration, in the process of establishing itself as an independent state, was faced with an extremely serious situation in its southernmost region. Both units were finally subjugated after great bloodshed, with some remnants fleeing into the mountains to continue as guerrillas. Meanwhile, the rebels on Cheju fought on stubbornly, gradually retreating into the inaccessible mountains of the interior. The struggle there continued for more than a year.[106]

105. A detailed official account of the Cheju revolt is contained in *Hanguk Chŏnjaeng-sa (History of the Korean War)*, published by the Editorial Committee on War History, Seoul, Vol. 1, 1967. See also a Communist source, Kim Pong-hyŏn, *Chejudo inmindŭl ui 4.3 mujang t'ujaengsa charyojip (Materials on the April 3 Armed Uprising of the Cheju Island People)*, Ōsaka, 1963.

106. As the government was having great problems in getting the army or the police to wage an effective struggle on Cheju, it turned to the Northwest Youth Corps, a strongly anti-Communist organization composed of young refugees from the North. This group subsequently served as the spearhead in fighting the Communists and reestablishing order. According to some accounts, it did not always discriminate in selecting those whom it attacked, and this—together with the fact that

The military rebellions at Yŏsu and Sunch'ŏn were not the last. On December 30, 1948, an uprising was staged by elements within the 6th Regiment stationed in the strategic city of Taegu. It was quickly subdued, however. A few months later, in May 1949, two battalions of the 8th Regiment (6th Division) stationed in Hongch'ŏn and Ch'un-ch'ŏn on the east coast, close to the 38th parallel, defected en masse and crossed into North Korea.

These various events indicated clearly that the Communists had scored some significant successes in their efforts to subvert the South Korean armed forces. While the major portion of the military remained loyal, these events were sufficiently serious to worry the Rhee government deeply and to prompt countermeasures. A purge of "leftists" within the military thus got under way, with Kim Ch'ang-yong placed in charge.[107] In the course of the 1948–49 period, some 5,000 officers and men were dismissed, imprisoned, or executed. The charges ranged from treason or rebellion to "Communist connections." Lists of "national liberation activists" were uncovered, and suspects were ruthlessly interrogated, often under torture. Without a doubt, a number of innocent men were prosecuted, and many of them were killed. It seems clear, however, that this purge also trapped a sizable number of key Communists, and some argue that it

---

its members spoke a dialect radically different from that of the local people—engendered great enmity. Almost every family on the island reportedly suffered some casualties, and many of the young men took to the hills and joined the rebels.

107. Kim Ch'ang-yong had served as a low-level intelligence operator in the Japanese Kwantung Army, stationed at Manchouli on the Soviet border. Reportedly, he had had some success in undermining Chinese and Soviet Communist operations against the Japanese army. However, when he returned to (north) Korea in 1945, an informer told Soviet authorities of his past role, and he suffered extremely harsh treatment, including being twice sentenced to death by the Russians. Naturally, he became bitterly anti-Communist, and escaping to the south he entered the constabulary. He was initially appointed a second lieutenant in army intelligence and, reportedly, he began collecting information on everyone, including high-ranking officers.

Kim eventually reached the rank of major general after the Korean War. At one point, he was regarded as the second most powerful man in the Republic, exceeded in power only by Syngman Rhee. Rhee had complete faith in Kim and gave him virtually a free hand in his intelligence activities. Kim did succeed in clearing the Communists out of the army, but his methods were ruthless and a number of innocent men were among those killed. On occasion officers were executed on the slightest suspicion. In January 1956, Kim himself was killed, on the orders of a ROK army colonel.

It is impossible to ascertain the extent of Communist infiltration into the ROK army during the 1948–49 period. In many cases, undoubtedly, affiliations were blurred. As we have indicated, however, Communist penetration was sufficient to warrant deep concern. Incidentally, Pak Chŏng-hi, the present president of the Republic, was himself under a deep cloud during this period, accused of involvement with the Communists and disloyalty to the government. He barely escaped serious punishment.

saved ROKA from certain destruction at the hands of the Communists when the Korean War broke out a year later.[108]

Meanwhile, the north was taking its own steps to help the southern Communists to establish a military base. At some point between late 1947 and early 1948, the Party established the Kangdong Political Institute in Kangdong, a suburb of P'yŏngyang. The Institute's purpose was to provide military training for those of South Korean origin, after which they were to be sent south as guerrilla fighters. The training generally lasted for a period of from three to six months. Between November 1948 and March 1950, some 2,400 guerrillas were reportedly dispatched to the south, most of them using the route through the eastern coastal mountains. These individuals joined with much larger indigenous elements now in the hills and gave them the latest instructions from the Party. In a number of cases they also assumed positions of leadership. The precise number of Communist guerrillas operating in South Korea at the outbreak of the Korean War cannot be known, but one estimate places it at about 27,000.[109] In any case, after 1948, the Communist movement in South Korea had become largely an insurrectionary one, actively involved in military operations and other forms of violence. That this created serious problems for the South Korean government cannot be doubted. There was another side to this coin, however. As of 1948, the Communist Party in the south had ceased being a mass party and had reverted to a party of the vanguard type, com-

---

108. *Hanguk Chŏnjaeng-sa, op. cit.,* Vol. 1, p. 495. This work, incidentally, blames the USMG for the heavy Communist infiltration of the South Korean police and military forces. It asserts that American authorities were indifferent to screening procedures, allowing anyone to join police and military units, without proper scrutiny of individual backgrounds. The writers of this official work continue by asserting: "If the Yŏsu-Sunch'ŏn Incident had not taken place (which caused the army to take action against Communists in the armed services), the Republic of Korea would have been Communized": *ibid.*

For another source on the problem of Communist infiltration of police-military ranks, see Pak Sŏng-hwan, *op. cit.* Written during Pak Chŏng-hi's presidency, the book states that none of the sources the author has examined implicate Pak with the Communist Party. Pak Sŏng-hwan does allege that many important military men were Communists during this period. He asserts that these included Major Yi Pyŏng-ju, the commanding officer of the Military Police; Major O Il-gyun, the commanding officer of the cadets in the Military Academy; Major Cho Pyŏng-gon, head of the Instruction Department, and a number of others. (At this period, the ranks of major and lieutenant colonel were about the highest ranks in the South Korean constabulary forces.) Pak also says that the third class of the Military Academy, which graduated in 1947, had been heavily infiltrated, that some 80 percent of its members were Communists or Communist sympathizers. These figures seem very high and may be exaggerations, but it is known that Communist influence was strong. The two lieutenants who led the Yŏsu-Sunch'ŏn uprising in 1948, incidentally, were from that class.

109. *Hanguk Chŏnjaeng-sa, op. cit.,* Vol. 1, pp. 499–500.

posed at its core of enormously dedicated and hardened true believers, many of them young, and most quite prepared to die for the cause. But for all this they lacked both the emotional rapport and the organization to bring the masses into the streets or onto the barricades.

An Evaluation

The outside observer, viewing the Korean peninsula on the eve of Japanese surrender, would have been most unlikely to have predicted that the Communist movement could assume formidable proportions in any part of Korean society. Conservative, poor, deeply steeped in Confucian teachings, possessed of a very sparse intelligentsia and a minute industrial working class, Korea was almost totally bereft of the necessary requirements for socialism as sketched by the classic Marxists. Indeed, it did not even fit the Leninist prescription of a society ripe for revolution.

Let us assume, however, that our observer had been told that one part of Korea would shortly develop as a Communist state. Assuming that he were asked to predict which part, purely on the basis of indigenous conditions, he would surely have selected the south. Seoul had always harbored the main forces, such as they were, of nationalism and radicalism. Indeed, Seoul had been the center for all Korean politics. The south, moreover, contained the great majority not only of Korean intellectuals and students, but also of politically articulate Koreans in general. It was also in the south that the denser concentrations of population existed, and hence the more serious urban and rural problems.

Such a prediction would not have been wholly incorrect. The post-Liberation Communist movement did start with its center in Seoul, and with Pak Hŏn-yŏng as its more or less acknowledged national leader. One obvious, crucial, and massive factor, however, intervened. It was the Americans who occupied the south. And it was almost inevitable that whatever efforts toward accommodation were made initially by both sides, sooner or later the American occupation authorities and the Communists would come into conflict. The fundamental objectives of these two groups, as well as the means they were prepared to use in reaching those objectives, differed too radically to permit any meaningful compromise. The Americans, to be sure, were not the only force in South Korea opposed to a Communist power seizure. Indeed, despite the initial organizational successes of the Communists through the Korean People's Republic and many lesser agencies, it must be remembered that the Communists were always camouflaged by skillfully developed fronts in those situations where they were strongest. There is no evidence that the inhabitants of South Korea were prepared to espouse the Korean Communist Party at any point, and in the elections—admittedly a less than perfect measurement of public sentiment—the Communists always did poorly, even at the local level.

Especially after December 1945 the so-called right wing was able to seize the nationalist issue, using it as a political club with which to beat both Americans and Communists.

Nevertheless, it was American power, especially in the first crucial months, that contained the Communists. Otherwise, a little organization and a little power—encased in such a front as the Korean People's Republic —would have gone a long way. It must not be forgotten that while so-called right-wing leaders such as Syngman Rhee and Kim Ku were still thousands of miles away, the Left was mustering all its available strength under the leadership of men like Yŏ Un-hyŏng and Pak Hŏn-yŏng.

Moreover, if it was American power that initially contained the Communists, it was a combination of American and Korean power, or perhaps more accurately, non-Communist South Korean power operating under the American aegis, that smashed the Communist movement a little later. As we have seen, the Communists contributed to their own demise mightily by a series of mistakes, both tactical and strategic. Many, perhaps most, of these mistakes were forced upon them by the Russians, who made all basic decisions for the Communist movement, north and south, during this period. But some mistakes were the products of internal Party factionalism, poor liaison, and similar defects.

It certainly cannot be said that the Communists were totally vanquished in South Korea by 1947–48. A considerable portion of the student-intellectual community continued to have some degree of sympathy for the movement. The various labor, farmer, youth, and women's fronts, moreover, while under severe attack and greatly reduced in strength, harbored additional Communist supporters. Even within the South Korean police and military units, the Communists retained enclaves. And there were the guerrillas in the hills. Nevertheless, as events were to show, the South Korean Communist movement had passed its peak, mainly because it was being forced to operate in an intensely hostile official environment. This very fact pushed it to poorly timed extremist measures that progressively estranged it from the people. By the time of the Korean War, it was largely the true believers who remained.

CHAPTER V

KOREAN COMMUNISM UNDER SOVIET TUTELAGE

Ironically, postwar politics in the northern sector of Korea began on a more moderate note than in the south. Moreover, there is little doubt that, other things being equal, that trend would have continued. North Korea had never been the center of Korean political activity; Seoul consistently had, whether the direction taken by such activity was radical, moderate, or conservative. Beyond this, however, North Korea had no more of the requisites generally considered necessary for a successful Communist revolution than the Outer Mongolia of 1920. Yet these two small Asian societies were to share one countervailing and decisive factor: Soviet presence.

To appreciate the setting in which Korean Communism emerged, a few salient geopolitical facts about the Communist state of North Korea should be noted at the outset. The total land area of Korea is about 85,000 square miles, approximately the size of the state of Kansas and one-half the size of Japan. North Korea constitutes the larger half in land area, some 46,768 square miles to South Korea's 38,031. In population, however, the situation has been different. In May 1944, according to Japanese census statistics, the area south of the 38th parallel contained 15,944,000 people, with a population density of 430 per square mile, whereas the north had 9,170,000 people with a density of only 190 per square mile. Moreover, by September 1946, the southern population had risen to 19,369,270, an increase of some 22 percent. Much of this increase came from the northern exodus. But there was some flow back into both North and South Korea from Manchuria and points overseas.

Whereas South Korea had the bulk of the paddy fields and the light industries, North Korea had a significant amount of dry farm land, most of the country's heavy industry, substantial timber and mineral resources, and plenty of hydroelectric power.[1] Korea as a whole was overwhelmingly agrarian; there were extremely few large cities, and the urban population equaled only 11.6 percent of the total population in 1940. This was a backward, agrarian society, with most of its population living in rural hamlets, under conditions of great poverty.

The Entry of Communists to Power in the North

If the opening political developments in South Korea were strongly influenced by Yŏ Un-hyŏng, those in the north were equally colored by Cho Man-sik, undoubtedly the most respected Korean leader in northern Korea and sometimes referred to as the Korean Gandhi because of his strong commitment to nationalism and nonviolence. The initial involvement of Yŏ and Cho, moreover, occurred under similar circumstances. The Japanese governor of South P'yŏngan Province (in which P'yŏngyang, later capital of North Korea, was located) reportedly listened to a shortwave radio broadcast from San Francisco on the evening of August 12, 1945, recounting events and indicating that Japanese surrender might be imminent. He immediately summoned Cho Man-sik with a request for aid in maintaining order in that eventuality.[2] Cho, a graduate of Meiji University and a Christian elder, had long been an ardent nationalist of moderate political persuasion.

Thus, when the Japanese surrender was announced on August 15, a Security Maintenance Committee for South P'yŏngan Province with Cho as its head was immediately proclaimed. One of the first activities of the Committee was the distribution of handbills urging Koreans to protect the lives of Japanese. On August 16, some 3,000 prisoners, most of them political prisoners, were released from P'yŏngyang's jails and prisons. The following day, the Security Maintenance Committee was reorganized as the South P'yŏngan branch of the Preparatory Committee for National Construction, indicating that liaison with Seoul had been swift and effective. Cho became chairman of the branch and O Yun-sŏn, another Christian elder, vice-chairman. Among the more than twenty initial committee members, only two were Communists, a ratio that probably reflected faith-

1. Note the following statistics on Korean farm land (in acres):

	Paddy land	Dry fields	Total
Southern zone	3,072,300	2,695,000	5,767,300
Northern zone	1,097,600	5,343,450	6,441,050

Cited in George M. McCune with the collaboration of Arthur L. Grey, Jr., *Korea Today*, Cambridge, 1950, p. 53, adapted from A. Grajdanzev, "Korea Divided," *Far Eastern Survey*, Oct. 10, 1945, p. 282.

2. Morita, Yoshio, *Chōsen shūsen no kiroku* (*The Record of the End of the War in Korea*), Tokyo, 1964, pp. 182–183.

fully the true balance of strength between Communists and non-Communist nationalists throughout Korea.[3]

With the arrival of the Russians, however, changes took place rapidly. Soviet forces, despite recurrent rumors of an earlier arrival, did not reach P'yŏngyang until August 24, after an orgy of rape and pillage that did them no credit.[4] Their opening political act was similar to that of the Americans later. On August 25, the Soviet Military Command announced that Japanese authorities would carry out necessary administrative functions as in the past, and that order would be maintained jointly by Soviet and Japanese authorities. Those persecuting Japanese, moreover, would be severely punished.[5] On the very next day, however, this first Russian order was rescinded. The Japanese army and police were disarmed, and authority was transferred to the South P'yŏngan Province Preparatory Committee.

The Russians also took a hand behind the scenes in reorganizing the Committee. According to Han Chae-dŏk, the Soviet Command specifically ordered the dissolution of the old Committee, and the formation of a new one containing an equal number of Communists and non-Communists. Thus the new People's Political Committee was composed of sixteen Communists and sixteen non-Communists. Some stormy scenes followed. According to O Yŏng-jin, personal secretary to Cho Man-sik during this period, Colonel General Ivan Chistiakov, head of the Soviet 25th Army

3. The two Communists were Han Chae-dŏk and Yi Chu-yŏn, both veterans of the movement. In the prewar era, Yi had been a central executive member of the Korean Farmers' Federation, a group under the control of the Tuesday faction, and an officer at Shingan-hoe headquarters between 1927 and 1931. He had been imprisoned for six years for his involvement in radical agrarian activities in Tanch'ŏn in 1931. As we shall note, he was later to rise to significance in the North Korean regime. Han, who later defected, has provided us with a most interesting account of this period: Han Chae-dŏk, *Kim Il-sŏng ŭl kobal handa* (*I Indict Kim Il-sŏng*), Seoul, 1965. Both authors are greatly indebted to him, moreover, for a number of interviews and for other kinds of assistance. Regarding his own career, we shall have more to say below. His death in 1970 was a great loss to scholars concerned with North Korea.

Han, incidentally, asserts that the release of political prisoners in P'yŏngyang added to the strength of the Communists, but he also holds that the ratio of Communists to non-Communists on the Preparatory Committee was an accurate reflection of real strengths. *Ibid.*, p. 50.

4. All accounts, including those of a number of Korean Communists, testify to the bad behavior of the Soviet forces—many of them Soviet Asians—upon their entry into Korea. Conditions were so bad in some areas that women had to disguise themselves as men to avoid rape, and wholesale looting of both Japanese and Korean property occurred. Naturally, this situation did not aid the Korean Communists. It contrasted sharply, moreover, with the general behavior of American forces in the south, and the later behavior of the Chinese Communists.

For a pamphlet very sympathetic to the Communists which admits Soviet misbehavior and urges "understanding," see Ch'oe Pŏm-so, *Puk-Han ui chŏngch'i sangse* (*Political Conditions in North Korea*), Seoul, 1945.

5. Morita, *op. cit.*, p. 184.

and supreme Russian commander in Korea, ordered Cho and his colleagues at their first meeting in P'yŏngyang on August 29 to take directions from the Communist Party on matters relating to provincial government. Angered by the arrogant attitude of the Soviet commander, Cho and other non-Communists present refused to accept the Russian edict and threatened to resign. The Korean Communists in attendance sought to placate the nationalists, and eventually Chistiakov altered the order, directing the nationalists "to cooperate with the Communist Party." [6] This episode, however, was but one of many indicating that the Soviet Military Command intended to make the Communist Party of Korea the dominant political force as soon as possible. The problem, both for them and their Korean comrades, was that the Communist Party was so weak. No Communist, moreover, could compare in popularity with Cho and several other nationalists currently on the scene. Hence, the opening stages of the political drama had to be played carefully by the Communists, particularly since their most prominent leaders were in the south.

The People's Committee now included such Communists as Hyŏn Chun-hyŏk, Kim Yong-bŏm, Pak Chŏng-ae (Mrs. Kim Yong-bŏm), and Chang Si-u, in addition to Yi Chu-yŏn and Han Chae-dŏk, who had been the two Communists on the Security Maintenance Committee.[7] The posts of Internal Affairs (Yi Chu-yŏn), Minerals and Industry (Kim Kwang-jin), and police chief of P'yŏngyang (Song Ch'ang-ryŏm) went to Communists.[8] However, according to O Yŏng-jin, the Soviet Military Command actually ruled North Korea from the day of its arrival, and the People's Committee was little more than its messenger boy.

People's committees like the one in the P'yŏngyang area were soon set up elsewhere. For example, at nearby Chinnamp'o, where a major steel mill was located, a Soviet army detachment arrived on August 25, followed by the main Russian forces on September 2. On the following day, the Chinnamp'o People's Political Committee was established. It was composed of eight persons selected from the local Preparatory Committee branch, eight from the Communist Party, and five from the local Communist-controlled labor union.[9]

6. O Yŏng-jin, *Hana ui chŭng-ŏn* (*An Eyewitness Report*), Pusan, 1952, pp. 111–114. According to O, the Communists were well aware of the popularity of the nationalists, and the thinness of their own support. They knew that without the cooperation of men like Cho, management of the situation would be extremely difficult at this point.

7. Han Chae-dŏk, *op. cit.*, p. 52.

8. According to Han, Kim Kwang-jin, formerly a professor at Posŏng College (now Korea University) and operator of a factory in 1945, was thought to be a non-Communist, but in fact he was the head of the Finance Bureau of the P'yŏng-yang Communist Party; hence, there were actually seventeen Communists and fifteen nationalists on the Committee. *Ibid.*, p. 52.

9. Morita, *op. cit.*, p. 187.

In Hwanghae Province, near the 38th parallel, a more complex, deadly struggle ensued. Its implications for the non-Communists were ominous. At the outset, non-Communists strongly predominated in the quickly established Preparatory Committee branch. When, in late August, this branch was reorganized into the Hwanghae Province People's Political Committee, non-Communists and Communists were given representation in approximately equal proportions, but a non-Communist, Kim Ung-sun, remained chairman. Serious internal friction developed in the Committee. Nevertheless, on September 2, the Soviet Command ordered the Japanese provincial governor to transfer power to the Committee. On that same day, however, two nationalists, one of them Kim Kwang-yŏp, head of the Minerals and Industry Department, were attacked by leftists and seriously injured. The Committee thereupon tendered its resignation on September 4, informing Soviet authorities that it could not undertake governmental functions.

On September 13, however, a newly constituted Hwanghae People's Committee, headed by a Communist leader, Kim Tŏk-yŏng, took over authority from the Japanese governor. Furious at this development, certain non-Communists assaulted the People's Committee headquarters on the sixteenth, killing four Communist leaders. A street battle in Haeju ensued, with the leftists driving the Security Unit, which was the current police-security unit established to enforce law and order and, in this area, under non-Communist control, out of the city and into exile in Seoul. The Communists were now in physical control of the province.[10]

It is clear from these and other events that the Soviet occupation authorities were playing a major role behind the scenes in undermining the position of the non-Communists. Their technique was to reorganize the various northern branches of the Seoul-based Preparatory Committee for National Construction into so-called People's Committees, and in the process to give the Communists greatly enhanced representation, usually membership at least equal to that of the non-Communists. Such Communist representation, of course, bore no relation to the true strength or popular support of the Party. Given this organizational power, however, it was possible for the Communists to apply ever-increasing pressure upon the non-Communists, especially since the latter were not subject to any common discipline and varied considerably in political outlook. Above all, Soviet authority was always in the background, available when needed.

In this fashion, united front politics was developing in North Korea as it was intended to operate—from a Communist point of view. One supremely important variable, however, was the Communist Party itself. Could it be unified? Who would lead it? What relations could and should be established with the Party in the south?

There is no evidence that the Russians had fixed ideas on all of these matters when they first arrived as an occupying force in mid-August. We

10. *Ibid.,* pp. 179–181.

have no firm knowledge as to what type of commitment, if any, had been made to Kim Il-sŏng, whether Kim had rivals for Soviet affections, or what the Russians may have thought about a man like Pak Hŏn-yŏng. As suggested earlier, Pak himself seems to have enjoyed Soviet support. However, the Soviet leaders would certainly have had reason to take a dim view of most "old" Communists, given the dismal history of the Korean Communist movement, the ceaseless factional wrangling, and the inability of the leaders to establish a meaningful Party in Korea after 1928.

At least in the first stage, the Russians clearly intended to depend heavily upon Russianized Koreans, a large number of whom came with the Soviet troops. As we have seen, these were individuals who in most cases had been born in Soviet territory, held Soviet citizenship, and had adopted Russian ways either partially or wholly.[11] They represented the true "Russian faction," and should be distinguished from Kim Il-sŏng and his Manchurian comrades, who had merely spent the wartime period in the Soviet Union. The latter came to be known as the Kapsan faction, after the Kapsan Mountains in which some of their exploits took place.

The combination of Russianized Koreans and the young Kapsan group operating under Soviet direction represented a formidable force, particularly since the Russians themselves were making all the basic political decisions. The key Soviet group making policy for North Korea, commanded by Major General Romanenko, was located in downtown P'yŏngyang, in a building that had formerly been the Japanese Internal Revenue Office. Unlike the Americans in Seoul, the Russians operated with a maximum of discretion and secrecy. They were rarely to be seen in Korean administrative quarters. But the Koreans visited them. Han Chae-dŏk has stated that Kim Il-sŏng himself often went to Romanenko's office three or four times in a single day.[12] The Soviet general and his staff operated primarily through a so-called forty-three-man team. This "team" was composed of the key Russianized Koreans and Kapsan members. It was often assembled in Romanenko's office, where political issues would be discussed, briefings be given, and "suggestions" and orders set forth. This was the nerve center of Soviet authority, the ultimate source of political power in North Korea.[13]

11. Some Russianized Koreans were equivalent to American Nisei, except that they were caused to play major roles in the initial occupation period. Examples of top-ranking Soviet Koreans are Kim Yŏl, Nam Il, Pak Ui-wan, Pak Ch'ang-ok, Pak Ch'ang-sik, Pak Mu, Pak Yŏng-bin, Pang Hak-se, Yu Ki-ch'ŏn, Yi Tal-chin, Yim Hae, Chin Pan-su, Han Il-mu, Hŏ Ik, Hŏ Ka-i, and Hŏ Pin. We shall note that many of these were subsequently purged by Kim and his dominant Kapsan faction, and not a few of them returned to the Soviet Union.

See Chong-Sik Lee and Ki-Wan O, "The Russian Faction in North Korea," *Asian Survey*, April 1968, pp. 270–288.

12. Han Chae-dŏk, *op. cit.*, p. 53.

13. For a graphic description of the Romanenko office and the forty-three-man team, see Kim Ch'ang-sun, *Puk-Han sip-o nyŏnsa (Fifteen-Year History of North*

What did the Russians and their Korean comrades in arms find when they arrived in Korea in mid-August with respect to Party organizational activities? If they had conducted a detailed investigation, they would have discovered that organizational activities were under way throughout most of the northern provinces, and that nearly all of these activities were local or at most regional in character, and led by prewar Communists recently released from prison or emerging from the underground. While contact beyond provincial boundaries was still meager, some ties with Seoul were established early. For many local leaders in the north, Pak Hŏn-yŏng and his Korean Communist Party represented a logical and acceptable national leadership.

Let us turn briefly to some of the regional developments. Quite naturally, the most vigorous activities were taking place in South Hamgyŏng Province, particularly in the cities of Hamhŭng and Hŭngnam. This region had been one of the very few points of sustained urban Communist activity inside northern Korea before 1945. As early as August 16, a number of Communists who had just been released from prison met in Hamhŭng and set up a preliminary organization.[14] Several days later, a Conference of Communists in South Hamgyŏng Province was organized, with about one hundred participants; at that time, it was agreed to push the development of mass organizations, particularly labor unions and farmers' committees, and the Hŭngnam Chemical Workers' Union was established. Meanwhile, a Communist, To Yong-ho, had become head of the Preparatory Committee branch in this region.

The key Communist figure in South Hamgyŏng Province was O Ki-sŏp, and his influence extended into North Hamgyŏng as well. O, an "old" Communist of the Japanese era, was a supporter of Pak Hŏn-yŏng, as were the other key leaders of this province, Chŏng Tal-hŏn, Yi Pong-su, and Chu Nyŏng-ha. By late September at least, liaison had been established between the South Hamgyŏng group and Pak's Seoul Party headquarters.[15] The northern group had declined to issue a separate program, asserting that it would await official policies to be issued in Seoul. Meanwhile, it tailored its own position, including support for the Korean People's Republic, to match the pronouncements of Pak and his group.

Liaison with the south was not uniform throughout the northern provinces, nor were organizational activities as advanced in most other regions as in South Hamgyŏng. Nevertheless, some Communist stirrings could be discovered almost everywhere in the north. In Kangwŏn Province, Party

---

Korea), Seoul, 1961, p. 54. This study is of great value and had been used extensively by us. According to Kim, *all* authority with respect to personnel and administration was in Romanenko's hands until the Russians withdrew from North Korea on Dec. 26, 1948 (p. 81).

14. For more details on provincial activities in South Hamgyŏng and elsewhere, see Ch'oe Pŏm-so, *op. cit.*, and Morita, *op. cit.*, pp. 164–173.

15. Ch'oe Pŏm-so, *op. cit.*, pp. 3–5.

operations centered around the Wŏnsan area, where Yi Chu-ha had organized a local Party. He too was a "domestic" Communist and adherent of Pak Hŏn-yŏng, and he was soon to journey to the south and be picked up by South Korean officials. In North Hamgyŏng Province, Party activities centered around the city of Ch'ŏngjin, with Kim Ch'ae-yong, another indigenous Communist, taking the lead. The situation was complex in North P'yŏngan Province, on the Yalu, with its chief city Sinŭiju. Pak Kyun, another Pak Hŏn-yŏng supporter, had begun Party organizational activities, while certain other "old" Communists—Paek Yong-gu, Kim Chae-gap, and Kim In-jik—were organizing a separate party, the Min-u-hoe (People's Friendship Association). Later, in mid-October, Russian pressure forced these two parties to merge.[16] In Hwanghae Province, activities centered around the city of Haeju. Once again, Pak Hŏn-yŏng supporters were initially dominant, with Kim Tŏk-yŏng and Song Pong-uk, both "old" Communists, taking the lead.

Thus, in the first weeks following Liberation, Pak Hŏn-yŏng, with his headquarters in Seoul, was making significant progress in unifying the Communist movement throughout Korea under his command. He had begun to contact friends and followers, in both north and south, immediately after the war ended. His position had consistently been that Korea had to have only one Communist Party, irrespective of the de facto military division of the country. Based upon this principle, he had gotten his followers to organize branches both north and south of the 38th parallel. Communist billboards in both areas proclaimed, "Long live Pak Hŏn-Yŏng!" And in Hamhŭng, Wŏnsan, Ch'ŏngjin, Sinŭiju, and Haeju (P'yŏngyang was the only exception among the major centers), local Communists acknowledging Pak's leadership had ensconced themselves in power. To take over this organization from the outside would almost certainly precipitate a struggle.

P'yŏngyang, chief city in South P'yŏngan Province, and subsequently to become the capital of North Korea, was naturally of supreme importance in terms of Communist organizational activities. The initial organizing effort of the Party here was led by Hyŏn Chun-hyŏk, another veteran of the radical movement, but a man who appears to have had less commitment to Pak Hŏn-yŏng than many other domestic Communists. Hyŏn, a native of the province, had come to P'yŏngyang from Seoul a few days after his release from prison. His prewar history was a typical one: graduation from Keijō Imperial University; a position teaching at Taegu Normal School; organizer of a Marxist study society, followed by a three-year suspended prison sentence and the loss of his teaching position; return to the north, participation in cooperative organizational activities, and rearrest followed by a prison term.

Hyŏn belonged to that class of men whom Han Chae-dŏk has called

16. Kim Ch'ang-sun, *op. cit.,* p. 91.

"the alumni of Yamato-juku," meaning those who had "graduated" from a special Japanese training course aimed at reforming individuals found guilty of subversive acts or thoughts. Naturally, this included most of the "old" Communists—those who came to be known variously as the "domestic" or "indigenous" faction. Whether Hyŏn was ever a "good Communist" is debatable; at least one close associate considered him essentially a social democrat or "radical liberal" at heart.[17]

In any case, Hyŏn had an appeal to the intelligentsia of P'yŏngyang of the type that the Yenan faction was to have later, and a number joined under his leadership. In addition to being secretary in charge, Hyŏn assumed the post of head of the Political Section. Kim Yong-bŏm, a North Star and North Wind Society man, who, along with his wife Pak Chŏng-ae, had been dispatched by the Comintern to Korea in the 1930s and had subsequently served a prison term, was made the head of Organization (the other two sections were Propaganda and Culture, and Finance). Pak Chŏng-ae reportedly served as an interpreter for the leaders of the P'yŏngyang group with the Soviet command. Yi Chu-yŏn, known as a "domestic faction man," was listed as a member of the Political Section.[18] Thus, the key Party organization in the north—that of P'yŏngyang, where the Soviet high command operated—was led by a somewhat independent figure who gave early evidence of being able to work closely with such distinguished nationalists as Cho Man-sik, and who may have had ambitions that sepa-

17. Stated by Yi Hong-gŭn, interviewed by Chong-Sik Lee, Seoul, Sept. 18, 1966. Yi knew Hyŏn Chun-hyŏk intimately, and we are indebted to him for valuable information on both Hyŏn and this period in North Korea.

Another informant, Yang Ho-min, who had a chance meeting with Hyŏn soon after he arrived in P'yŏngyang from Seoul, recalls their extended discussion well. Hyŏn, according to Professor Yang, was a small man with his hair clipped close to his scalp like a prisoner, and he acknowledged having been released from prison very recently. Hyŏn, he asserts, gave the impression of being an academic or literary type, a reflection of his earlier background as high school teacher. "He fitted the image of a reading-society leader," Yang stated.

At first, Hyŏn identified himself to Yang merely as a member of the Left, but when this subject was pursued further he admitted Communist Party membership. Anxious to know the situation in Seoul, Yang asked Hyŏn about the leadership of the Communist Party there, whereupon Hyŏn identified Chŏng Paek (head of the Changan group) as KCP leader. Hyŏn's own views were disappointingly simple as far as Yang was concerned. He indicated that he believed strongly in nationalism (minjok) and in a socialist economic system as best suited for rapid development with justice and equality in a poor country like Korea. But Hyŏn avoided questions about dialectic materialism and other theoretical issues, asserting that these matters would gradually be explored, with the "wrong education" obtained under the Japanese corrected. In this, we probably have an accurate portrait of the theoretical experience and sophistication of most of the Korean Communists of this era. Chong-Sik Lee interview with Yang Ho-min, Philadelphia, Aug. 29, 1968.

18. *Taejung (The Masses)*, Sept. 8, 1945. A list of the officers of the "South P'yŏngan Branch of the KCP" is provided here. *Taejung* was the official organ of the "Seoul District Committee of the KCP" (Changan faction).

rated him from both Pak Hŏn-yŏng and the Russians. Unquestionably, in September 1945, the two key northern figures in the embryonic Communist Party now being formed were Hyŏn and O Ki-sŏp, with Pak Hŏn-yŏng the most promising national Party spokesman.

The Soviet command in P'yŏngyang, however, did not approve of either Hyŏn or his program. On September 15, an Enlarged Committee of the South P'yŏngan District of the Korean Communist Party was convened. It put forth a trenchant attack on Hyŏn's previous policies. A statement issued under the title "Concerning the Political Line" alleged that the South P'yŏngang District Committee had committed errors in its political line "because of an inaccurate understanding of the international situation." The statement accused the old leadership of not clearly defining the "progressive historical role" played by the United States and Great Britain, with whom "friendly relations" had to be maintained. This theme was followed by an argument for bringing together all anti-Japanese groups, parties, organizations, and classes, both at home and abroad, into a single united front, and for demanding the recognition of private properties and private land holdings.[19] In sum, Hyŏn was accused of having committed left-wing errors in formulating initial Communist policies.

Kim Il-sŏng and the Soviet command were to reverse their stands on these issues very shortly, but the issuing of an open criticism against Hyŏn Chun-hyŏk left no doubt about his status. Clearly, he was a marked man. On September 28, within two weeks after the resolution was adopted, Hyŏn was assassinated in broad daylight in front of the P'yŏngyang city hall, while riding in a truck with Cho Man-sik.[20] A man boarded the truck, thrust a pistol at Hyŏn, and fired a single shot; Hyŏn, sitting in the front seat between Cho and the driver, was killed instantly. Some observers believe that this event had a profound influence upon subsequent developments in North Korea. Hyŏn was exceedingly popular with radical intellectuals and militant nationalists alike. He would have been a stiff competitor for any of the "old" Communists except possibly Pak Hŏn-yŏng (who, however, was a southerner) and certainly could have been expected to outshine a young unknown guerrilla leader like Kim Il-sŏng, had the Russians elected to remain neutral.

The true story of Hyŏn's assassination cannot be established at present with certainty, although much of the evidence suggests that he was killed

19. For the text of this document, see *Haebang Ilbo* (*Emancipation Daily*), Oct. 30, 1945, and *Hyŏngmyŏng Sinmun* (*Revolution News*), Oct. 16, 1945. Along with the resolution on the new political line, the enlarged committee also adopted a twenty-three-point platform. The most noteworthy aspect of the platform was the call for a people's representatives' conference to establish a people's republic. One may interpret the inclusion of this point as an indirect criticism of the People's Republic established by the Pak Hŏn-yŏng group in Seoul.

20. For a detailed account of the Hyŏn assassination, see Kim Ch'ang-sun, *op. cit.*, pp. 66–68.

by elements from within the Communist camp. One writer, Kim Ch'ang-sun, asserts that Kim Il-sŏng had already arrived in P'yŏngyang in early September, and that organizational activities on his behalf, with full Soviet support, had begun within Communist circles. He further argues that General Romanenko had begun to devote his efforts toward weaning away from Hyŏn's influence such P'yŏngyang Communist leaders as Kim Yong-bŏm, Pak Chŏng-ae, Chang Si-u, Ch'oe Kyŏng-dŏk, Yi Chu-yŏn, and Chang Chong-sik—in short, all the key figures in the provincial Party. Hyŏn, learning that the Russians had selected Kim Il-sŏng as Party head, became furious and began counteractivities, according to Kim Ch'ang-sun. Shortly thereafter he was assassinated.[21] Another source, Mun Bong-jae, then head of the Security Maintenance Committee of Hyŏn's home town, Kaech'ŏn, and a non-Communist acquaintance of Hyŏn, states that Hyŏn was killed by fellow Communists vying for power, and that Chang Si-u and Kim Yong-bŏm were involved.[22]

Whatever the truth, the Communists naturally blamed the incident upon "White terrorism," citing the fact that Cho Man-sik had not been harmed as evidence that the plot came from the Right. Hyŏn was given a huge funeral at Kaech'ŏn, with top Soviet and Communist dignitaries present, and the honorary title of "patriot" was bestowed upon him. The assassin, however, was never captured or publicly identified. The Russians, moreover, permitted only the scantiest publicity to be given to the assassination. Hyŏn quickly sank into obscurity. No one visited his grave, and later Kim Il-sŏng publicly attacked him as "a deteriorating nationalist who pretended to be a Communist." [23] There is absolutely no indication, in short, that the Russians—or Kim Il-sŏng—were troubled by Hyŏn's demise.

The Emergence of Kim Il-sŏng

This, then, was the situation when Kim Il-sŏng first appeared upon the public scene. The "domestic" Communists, most of them aligned with Pak Hŏn-yŏng, had worked hard establishing local Party branches throughout the north. Following Hyŏn's death, the P'yŏngyang Party itself was in confusion, available for the man with Russian backing. Kim Ch'ang-sun asserts that Kim Il-sŏng had entered P'yŏngyang in early September, but we have no corroboration of this. The first hard evidence of Kim's presence in the city is the account by Han Chae-dŏk of a meeting between Kim and various local leaders that took place in early October in a Japanese restaurant in P'yŏngyang, with Major General Romanenko present.[24]

21. *Ibid.,* p. 68.
22. Chong-Sik Lee interview with Mun Bong-jae, Seoul, Aug. 1, 1966.
23. Kim Ch'ang-sun, *op. cit.,* p. 68.
24. Han Chae-dŏk, *op. cit.,* p. 90. Han incidentally, claims to have written the first propagandistic eulogies of Kim: "General Kim Il-sŏng's Triumphant Return,"

According to Han, General Romanenko introduced Kim to the gathering of nationalist and Communist leaders, praising his record as a great patriot who had fought against Japanese imperialism. Afterward, Cho Man-sik delivered a brief speech welcoming Kim and urging that all Koreans should work together for the welfare of the nation. Kim then made a few remarks, stressing the need to pool the total strength of the nation for the tasks ahead. Han asserts that all of those present at the meeting were shocked by the fact that Kim—clearly a protégé of the Russians—was so young (33 at that point) and so obviously without polish. Moreover, he had made his appearance with a Russian-style haircut that marked him as an outsider.[25]

These sentiments may have been more broadly shared a few days later when Kim Il-sŏng was introduced to the citizens of P'yŏngyang on October 14 at a mass rally held on the P'yŏngyang athletic field.[26] O Yŏng-jin recounts the deep sense of disappointment and anger that developed among the crowd when they saw and heard Kim. In many minds, the name Kim Il-sŏng had been associated with a legendary hero, a great Korean patriot who had roamed at will over Manchuria, repeatedly defeating vast numbers of Japanese and playing the role of Robin Hood on behalf of the Koreans. This hero in the popular mind was of the generation of Kim Chwa-jin, Yi Tong-hwi, and Syngman Rhee.

Actually, as we have indicated, neither Japanese nor Korean records reveal the existence of any such person, and it may well be that, since Kim Il-sŏng's name had last appeared in Korean newspapers around 1936 in connection with the small-scale guerrilla raids he had led into Korea, everything associated with him had grown out of all proportion to reality. In any case, Kim's debut scarcely seems to have been an overwhelming success.

[The people had anticipated a gray-haired veteran patriot] but they saw a young man of about 30 with a manuscript approaching the microphone. He was about 166 or 167 centimeters in height, of medium weight, and wore a blue suit that was a bit too small for him. His complexion was slightly dark and he had a haircut like a Chinese waiter. His hair

---

"A Brief History of the Kim Il-sŏng Guerrilla Unit," "The Life and Struggles of the Kim Il-sŏng Guerrilla Unit," and "General Kim Il-sŏng and His Soldiers." According to Han, it was he who first attached the title "General" to Kim, "because I did not know what to call him." Some sources indicate that when Kim first arrived in North Korea with Soviet forces, he was wearing a Russian major's insignia and uniform.

Dae-Sook Suh, citing an article in *Shin-Ch'ŏnji* (I, No. 2, March 1946, pp. 230–237), states that Kim's first appearance in Korea appears to have been in Haeju, Hwanghae Province, midway between Seoul and P'yŏngyang, on September 16. Suh, *The Korean Communist Movement, 1918–1948,* Princeton, 1967, p. 318.

25. Han Chae-dŏk, *op. cit.,* p. 58.

26. For details of the P'yŏngyang athletic field rally, see O Yŏng-jin, *op. cit.,* pp. 141–143.

at the forehead was about an inch long, reminding one of a lightweight boxing champion. "He is a fake!" All of the people gathered upon the athletic field felt an electrifying sense of distrust, disappointment, discontent, and anger.

Oblivious to the sudden change in mass psychology, Kim Il-sŏng continued in his monotonous, plain, and ducklike voice to praise the heroic struggle of the Red Army, those allies who had liberated the 30 million Korean people who had suffered such agonies under the oppressive forces of Japanese imperialism. He particularly praised and offered the most extravagant words of gratitude and glory to the Soviet Union and Marshal Stalin, that close friend of the oppressed peoples of the world. The people at this point had completely lost their respect and hope for General Kim Il-sŏng. There was the problem of age, but there was also the content of the speech, which was so much like that of the other Communists whose monotonous repetitions had worn the people out.[27]

Thus did the future leader of North Korea begin his public career! Both O Yŏng-jin and Han Chae-dŏk agree that the weak performance of Kim at the rally served to enhance the stature of Cho Man-sik, who delivered a speech on the same occasion.

What did the Russians think? We have no way of knowing, but subsequent events indicate that Kim continued to receive full Soviet support. The Russian command stood unwaveringly behind Kim Il-sŏng as their man in Korea, and this was all that Kim (or anyone) needed. Why? The complete answer to this question may never be known, but we can advance some hypotheses.

First, however, a story told by O Yŏng-jin is worth recounting. According to O, the Soviets quickly saw that Kim, having had limited political experience despite his military exploits in the small-scale guerrilla battles of Manchuria, could greatly profit by serving an apprenticeship under the veteran Cho Man-sik. Hence General Romanenko implored Cho to support the Moscow Agreement of December 1945, asserting that, if he did so, he would be made the first president of Korea, with Kim Il-sŏng being placed in charge of the Korean army. Had Cho accepted this offer, writes O, the political situation in North Korea would have been very different.[28]

One may doubt the last statement, at least as a long-range prognosis. But it is entirely possible that the Russians did wish Cho Man-sik to serve in a position of titular leadership until Kim could acquire more seasoning. With the Russians themselves making all critical political decisions, it was perfectly possible—perhaps desirable—to have a non-Communist like Cho continue to serve as the nominal head of the united front structure, especially for the impact of such an arrangement upon South Korea. Far more

27. *Ibid.,* p. 143.
28. *Ibid.,* p. 185.

important were questions relating to the structure, policies, and leadership of the Korean Communist Party. Again, we must seek some answer to the question as to why the Russians had chosen Kim as their prime candidate for Party leadership. It was certainly not because there were no alternatives. While no Communist could have matched Cho Man-sik in popularity, such veterans as Pak Hŏn-yŏng and Kim Tu-bong might have been expected to have much greater appeal than Kim Il-sŏng.

One basic factor involving the choice of Kim, as we have already suggested, might well have been a Russian decision to avoid all of the "old" Communists because of their experience with these men during the two decades that preceded World War II. We have seen how discouraged and disgusted Soviet and Comintern authorities were with Korean factional strife during that period. Certainly it must have occurred to those Russians responsible for current Korean policies that to select any of the old factional figures was to court a repetition of the disastrous past.

Kim Il-sŏng, as we have seen, was too young to have been involved in the factional feuds of the past. He, too, had failed, of course, in the face of superior Japanese power. But that failure had driven him into the Soviet Union, where for four years he had been available for indoctrination —and for sizing up. As we have noted earlier, the information on Kim's wartime activities is scanty indeed. We may assume, however, that he received special attention, including advanced training of both a political and military nature. According to O Yŏng-jin, whom Kim befriended until O's escape to South Korea in 1947, Kim said that while he was in the Soviet Union, the Russians took him to Moscow for a few months, "probably because they thought I was fatigued." [29] While there, among other activities, Kim was shown a movie of Vasily Chapayev, a worker of peasant background who had fought brilliantly for the Communists during the Bolshevik Revolution. "In the Soviet Union, they referred to me as the Chapayev of Korea," Kim reportedly said.[30] He also mentioned that while he himself did not participate in any battles against the Germans in the West, some of his subordinates did, "as a type of training program." [31]

After four years of supervision and training for this young man and his comrades, the Russians must have felt that Kim was as well equipped for leadership as others—and far more trustworthy from their standpoint. Indeed, if he was treated like Chapayev, Kim was regarded as an untutored son of the people, a "blank slate" upon whom the Russians could write at will. There is certainly little reason why they would have wished to support

29. *Ibid.,* pp. 172–173.
30. *Ibid.,* p. 173. *Chapayev* is, of course, the motion picture Kim saw. This film, first released in 1934, tells of the exploits of Vasily Ivanovich Chapayev (1887–1919), commander of the 25th Division on the Eastern Front and several times victor over Kolchak's forces, in the Ural region. The movie was based on a novel (1923) by Dmitri Furmanov, who actually was Chapayev's commissar.
31. *Ibid.,* pp. 176–177

any of the leading figures of the Yenan faction. These were men with whom they had had scant contact and who might be expected to forward a Chinese line in a territory most important to Soviet national interest. It is conceivable that the Russians during the early months of the occupation entertained the possibility that Pak Hŏn-yŏng would lead a national Communist movement if Korean unification occurred rapidly as a result of Soviet-American agreement. Certainly, Pak's authority in the south was upheld by Soviet authorities at critical junctures, and he, in turn, gave his loyal support to the Russians on all matters. Did the Russians keep their options open with respect to this, at least until the spring of 1946? We cannot be certain. In any case, after the breakdown of the Joint Commission negotiations it became increasingly clear that the locus of Communist power would be in the north, not the south.

Whatever the reasons, the Soviet commitment to Kim was the crucial factor in his success. Of this there cannot be the slightest doubt. Nevertheless, in the opening months of the Soviet occupation, Kim and his supporters were to face serious challenges from two sources: first, the domestic faction led by Pak Hŏn-yŏng; and second, the Yenan faction led by Kim Tu-bong, Mu Chŏng, Ch'oe Ch'ang-ik, Kim Ch'ang-man, and Yun Kong-hŭm. The manner in which these challenges were handled constitutes a fascinating and vitally important aspect of Kim's rise to power. Let us turn first to the struggle with the domestic faction.

It is impossible to date with precision the opening of the struggle between the Kimists and the Pak group. As we noted earlier, at the highly important Five Northern Provinces Conference in mid-October, Pak had been acknowledged as the "leader of the Korean proletariat," and thanked for allowing the conference to be held. It was at this conference, however, that a Northern Bureau was established, always the first step in setting up a separate Party organization. At a much later point, moreover, spokesmen for Kim were prepared to describe the issues of this period in harsh, antagonistic terms, which suggests that a deadly competition had already begun. The following account is paraphrased from an official history that appeared in 1961.

> Comrade Kim Il-sŏng recognized that the Party should be unified despite the fact that Korea had been divided into two sections as a result of the policies of the American imperialists. With various local and regional Party organizations developing in a scattered, uncoordinated fashion, he saw the need for a centralized, comprehensive Party structure capable of directing national activities in a uniform manner. It was to avoid a split and to practice the principles of democratic centralism that caused him to urge the convening of a national Party conference, with representatives from all parts of the country attending.
>
> At the time, there was clearly no other location for the central headquarters of the Party than in North Korea, where the Soviet Army was

stationed and could provide protection. But the Pak Hŏn-yŏng group, who served as hired spies of American imperialism, were blinded by their desire to take over leadership of the Party. Pak and his stooges in the north insisted upon the legitimacy of the Party headquarters in Seoul, an organization created by sectarian methods. Thus, they obstructed Comrade Kim's efforts in every possible manner. And since the masses had not yet perceived the fact that Pak and his group were anti-Party, anti-revolutionary elements, the task of creating a unified Party required that we cooperate with this group. Otherwise, there would have been the grave danger of a split, and the task of establishing the Party would have been delayed. Therefore, Comrade Kim finally proposed the creation of a Korean Communist Party North Korean Bureau. The Pak clique, realizing that the Bureau would be a deadly blow to them, did their utmost to block this idea. And they also fought vigorously against the proposal to locate Party headquarters in the north, despite the fact that the concentration of international and domestic reactionaries in Seoul made it impossible for the Party to function effectively there.[32]

Since this account was written long after Pak had been purged, and during a period when every effort was being made to equate his name with total evil, we cannot be certain as to whether these issues really emerged at this point or later. Contemporary evidence, as we shall shortly indicate, certainly proves that in public Kim was paying homage at this point to the primacy of both Pak Hŏn-yŏng and the Seoul Party headquarters. Nor can we discern precisely when the sense of Pak as a rival became acute in the minds of Kim and his followers. It would not be surprising, however, if such feelings lurked within Kim from the very beginning, given the backgrounds of the two men and the very different sources of their support.

In any case, the issues of separate northern and southern organizational structures for the Party and the location of headquarters were certain to emerge at some point in view of the radically different political circumstances of the two Koreas. The latter point, moreover, constituted the Achilles' heel of Pak Hŏn-yŏng and his supporters.

Naturally, the Pak group was incensed whenever there was any suspicion of a challenge to the legitimacy of their Party, or any suggestion of the removal of its primary locus of power from Seoul. The central argument, however, was difficult to meet: Could the Party operate effectively under an American occupation, and in a situation where the Left as a whole was engaged in an increasingly acrimonious quarrel with occupation

32. Han Im-hyŏk, *Kim Il-sŏng tongji e ŭihan Chosŏn kongsandang ch'ang-gŏn* (*The Founding of the Korean Communist Party by Comrade Kim Il-sŏng*), P'yŏngyang, 1961, pp. 30–32. Kim-Il-sŏng himself made similar charges against "some of our comrades" in his speech at the second plenum of the North Korean Workers' Party, March 1948, although Pak Hŏn-yŏng was of course not mentioned in the 1948 speech. See Chong-Sik Lee, "Politics in North Korea: Pre-Korean War Stage," in Robert A. Scalapino (ed.), *North Korea Today*, New York, 1963, p. 7.

authorities over the legitimacy of the Korean People's Republic and its successor organizations?

It is idle to speculate as to what might have happened had Pak met this challenge frontally, moved his organization to P'yŏngyang in the early months of the occupation, collected his supporters, and waged an all-out struggle for Party control. Even under these circumstances, the odds would probably have been against him. At some point, Soviet support would have been the decisive factor, and there is no reason to believe that the Russians would have deserted Kim (their Chapayev!) for Pak. Nevertheless, such a course of action might have been a gamble worth taking for the Pak group. In any case, Pak elected to remain in the south and, as we have noted, he did not come north until Kim had already consolidated his power.

The Five Province Conference, it will be recalled, opened on October 10 and continued for four days. On October 14, the day after it ended, Kim made his first public appearance at the mass rally on the P'yŏngyang athletic field.[33] Official North Korean sources, incidentally, often cite October 10, 1945, as the date upon which the Korean Communist Party was launched. Moreover, as we shall see, the Russians made a number of public pronouncements on October 12 in an effort to gain public favor and provide official support for Communist policies.

Clearly, these events represented a major bid for power, albeit with full Russian backing, by Kim Il-sŏng and his faction. Advance preparations had been extensive. For some weeks before to October 10, the Kim faction, no doubt with Soviet support and guidance, had been dispatching its agents throughout North Korea. The idea was to make contact with local and provincial Party branches, and either wrest power from Pak adherents or win them over. Such stalwarts as Kim Ch'aek, An Kil, Kim Il, and many others visited every important center of Party activity in the north.[34] In order to bolster his position, moreover, Kim and his Manchurian comrades had naturally made contact with those few individuals who had cooperated with them from within Korea during the guerrilla days. For example, Pak Kŭm-ch'ŏl who had been associated with the Fatherland Restoration Association effort and only recently released from prison, was enlisted (he was later to attain a high position in the North Korean power structure). Pak Tal, another comrade of that era, was also reached. Ill health prohibited him from playing an active role in postwar

---

33. A preparatory meeting of local Communist representatives on October 5 preceded the main conference of October 10–13. According to Han Im-hyŏk, more than seventy persons participated in the main conference, including both "true revolutionaries" and "sectarians and localists."

34. Han Im-hyŏk, *op. cit.,* p. 36, provides a fairly detailed account of the provincial activities undertaken by the Kim Il-sŏng faction during this period, totally biased in their favor. See *ibid.,* pp. 33–35.

politics, but he was accorded a hero's position in all subsequent Kimist literature.

As noted earlier, Kim addressed the Five Province Conference on its final day. One version of his remarks appear in the 1963 edition of his *Selected Works,* but as indicated previously a near-contemporary version has been located. It is from this latter source that we paraphrase Kim's speech. As his first recorded postwar expression on a wide range of matters, his remarks are of more than ordinary interest.

The first task, according to Kim, was to consolidate the anti-Fascist front. Korea had been liberated by a socialist country, the Soviet Union, and a capitalist country, the United States. Due to White terrorism (presumably in the south), the Party had not been able to unify the working class under it. However, it had only been two months since Party establishment, so naturally it was still weak. Nevertheless, construction of a national, unified government—purged of reactionary bourgeoisie, but with nationalist-capitalists participating alongside the working classes—was the critical task. Initially, this meant the creation of bourgeois democracy, with the Party serving as model and vanguard.

After reviewing the background of the Korean nationalist and revolutionary movements, Kim blamed past failures on the lack of "an advantageous international situation," and the emergence of "liberalistic tendencies" within the old Korean Communist movement. However, with Liberation, various heroes had emerged. Kim then specifically singled out Pak Hŏn-yŏng for praise, asserting that Comrade Pak was "demonstrating the accomplishments of the Korean Communist movement by repelling all liberalistic groups." He continued: "Because our young Party in Korea is not well armed with theory, and because it possesses little experience in struggle, we will face many obstacles. All immediate problems must be discussed under the instructions of Comrade Pak." [Naturally, this section was omitted from the 1963 edition.]

Kim was also critical of the anti-Pak elements within the Party, and outlined the supreme importance of protecting Party discipline and policies. The Party had to enlist the workers and farmers, and beware of those running dogs of the Japanese who shouted "Communism!" but who were false Communists. Kim admitted that the foundations of the Party rested upon the intellectual class, and that only a minority of Party members were workers. He called for a drive to ensure ideological unity by striking out against the left extremist theories of Yi Yŏng and Ch'oe Ik-han, who thought that the Korean situation was one already ripe for socialism. No less dangerous were the "right-wingers" who were "prepared to sell out the Korean people in the opportunistic fashion." [35]

35. Chosŏn Sanŏp Nodong Chosaso (Research Center for Korean Industry and Labor), eds., *Ol-ŭn nosŏn* (*The Correct Line*), Seoul, 1945. (Reprinted by Minjung Shimunsa, Tokyo, 1946.) For the later publication see *Kim Il-sŏng sŏnjip* (*Selected Works of Kim Il-sŏng*), P'yŏngyang, 1963 ed., Vol. I, pp. 3–10.

According to the same version of the speeches delivered at the Five Province Conference, Kim introduced a number of resolutions after his talk, including ones providing for the establishment of a North Korean Bureau of the KCP, the drafting of Party rules, the issuing of Party membership certificates in the north (with the approval of the Seoul Center), and the convening of an All-Nation Representative Conference.[36]

On substantive issues, there were no discernible differences between Kim's views as expressed in this speech and those put forth by Pak's Seoul group in their pronouncements of August 19 and October 30. As might have been expected, moreover, Soviet policies in North Korea had already given effect to the main tactics and policies being espoused. On September 27, the Soviet command in P'yŏngyang had issued a seven-point statement encompassing the following items: All agencies of Japanese rule were to be considered abolished; the Soviet system of government, being unsuitable for Korea, would not be imposed upon that nation; a "capitalist democratic revolution" was to be permitted; the Soviet Union possessed no territorial ambitions with respect to Korea; freedom of religion and speech were to be permitted; land belonging to Japanese or to pro-Japanese individuals was to be confiscated; and tenant fees would be fixed at 30 percent of the crop.

The Russians had launched the "bourgeois democratic revolution" in North Korea on their own. There followed, on October 12, three official statements from Soviet military headquarters, each significant in content and timing. The first, a proclamation of General Chistiakov, announced that the Japanese who had "despised the Korean people, and defiled their customs and culture," had been removed. Henceforth, the freedom and independence of the nation rested in Korean hands. Factory and workshop owners were urged to repair their old plants or to reopen new ones. "The Red Army headquarters will guarantee the protection of your property, and will assist you in every manner possible to maintain the regular activities of your enterprise. Only those who contribute to the progress of the Korean economy and culture through honest enterprise can become patriots and true Koreans." [37] No one could have wished more support for the bourgeois revolution!

36. According to the 1945 version, as we noted earlier, Kim stated (contrary to later Kimist spokesmen) that "it is correct to have the Party Center in Seoul which is the geographic and political center of Korea" and the North requires "close guidance and liaison from and with the Party Center." Moreover, "whenever the Center sees the need to reform or correct Bureau policies, the Bureau has the duty to obey." Nevertheless, such a Bureau was needed, according to Kim, because of the unique conditions affecting North and South Korea. *Ibid.*

It might be noted that the 1963 version of Kim's speech was longer and more elaborate, with certain omissions to which we have referred, but not varying in its basic substantive themes.

See *Kim Il-sŏng sŏnjip, op. cit.,* Vol. I, pp. 3–10.

37. Kim Ch'ang-sun, *op. cit.,* pp. 44–45. He includes a detailed account of initial Russian policies.

A second Soviet statement was entitled "For What Purpose Did the Red Army Come to Korea?" It was a eulogy to Soviet power and intentions, possibly an attempt to offset the odium in which Soviet troops were currently held as a result of their incredibly bad behavior during the opening weeks of the occupation. Koreans were now assured that the Red Army only liberated people, and never conquered them. Specifically, the Russians had no intention of establishing a Soviet political system in the country or acquiring Korean territory.

The third and most important proclamation of October 12 was an "Order of the Commander of the 25th Soviet Army in North Korea." Among other provisions, this order contained a requirement for the registration of all "anti-Japanese parties and democratic organizations" with Russian authorities. A roster of officers and members was required. Moreover, it was necessary to fill out a detailed vita giving the family background of each member for two generations, together with a chronological biography of the individual from the age of 8. This enabled Soviet authorities to acquire a storehouse of information on "activists" and to control organizations deemed subversive. Parties suspected of being anti-Communist or having sympathies with the United States were banned, and a number of individuals in these categories disappeared without a trace.

In addition, the order of October 12 provided that all armed units in North Korea were to be dissolved, and their weapons, ammunition, and other military supplies submitted to the police commander of the Soviet army. However, those People's committees recognized by the Soviet military command would be permitted to establish security units with a set number of personnel, "to maintain public order in cooperation with the Soviet army." As noted earlier, the initial security units attached to the Preparatory Committee branches had generally been composed of non-Communists, and in some cases had fought vigorously against Communist efforts to take over the committee. Hence, many such units were regarded by Communist authorities as unreliable, even dangerous.

Thus, by mid-October, Soviet policies were taking shape. The political tactics of the Russians were simple and generally effective. On the one hand, non-Communist organizations and leaders would be placed under the closest surveillance, and eliminated if necessary. On the other hand, the development of a Communist-dominated united front—both at the local levels and on a "national" (that is, northern) level—would be vigorously supported. Already, the tide of events was impelling the Soviets to give increasing support to Kim Il-sŏng and to the idea of a unified, northern-based Korean Communist Party under his leadership.

Pursuing these policies, the Russians caused a Five Province Administrative Bureau to be established at the close of October. In effect, the embryonic government of North Korea, the Bureau was supposedly controlled by a People's Committee composed of some thirty members, equally

PLATES

Kim Il-sŏng at his first public appearance in
P'yŏngyang, at the Athletic Field, October 14, 1945.
Note the Soviet officers behind Kim.

(Opposite) Two official photographs of the same
event (Kim's first public appearance in
P'yŏngyang, October 14, 1945). The upper
photograph is one frequently published. Note
the absence of Soviet officers.

Pak Hŏn-yŏng (left) with Yŏ Un-hyŏng (probably 1946).

Kim Tu-bong (1947?).

O Ki-sŏp (1947?).

Pak Chŏng-ae (1947?).

Kim Ch'aek.

Chu Nyŭng-ha (1946?).

Hŏ Hŏn (1947?).

Kim Il-Sŏng with
writers—1946–1947(?).
Back row, second
from left,
Han Sŏl-ya;
third from left,
Han Ch'ae-dŏk;
extreme left,
Yi Sŭng-gŭn.
Front row, right,
Kim Il-sŏng.

North Korea People's
Committee—Spring
1947. Rear Row
(From the left):
Kim Chŏng-ju,
Ch'oe Ch'ang-ik,
Chang Chong-sik,
Yi Sun-gŭn,
Han Sŏl-ya,
Ch'oe Yong-dal,
Yi Pong-su.
Center Row
(From the left):
Pak Il-u,
O Ki-sŏp,
Yi Tong-yŏng,
Chang Si-u,
Chŏng Chun-t'aek,
Yi Mun-hwan,
Song Pong-uk?
Front Row (From the
left): Han Pyŏng-ok,
Kang Ryang-uk,
Kim Ch'aek,
Kim Il-sŏng,
Hong Ki-ju,
Hŏ Chŏng-suk,
Yi Kang-guk.

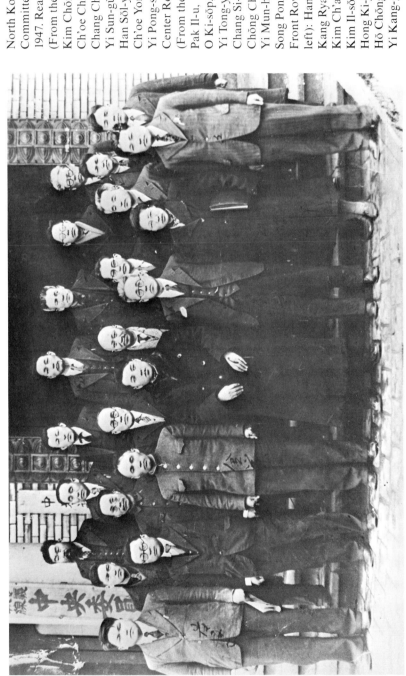

Presumably a vote to confirm Kim Il-sŏng in some office—circa 1949. To the right of Kim, Pak Hŏn-yŏng; to the left, Hŏ Ka-i.

divided between Communists and non-Communists, with Cho Man-sik serving as chairman.[38] It represented the first step toward the establishment of a separate state of North Korea.

Meanwhile, a fascinating new issue had injected itself into North Korean politics, namely, the arrival of Korean forces from China.[39] Some sources claim that certain top political figures of the Korean Independence League arrived in Antung, on the Manchurian side of the Yalu River, as early as mid-September, and that one group proceeded to P'yŏngyang while others remained in Antung to serve as liaison forces. As will be recalled, the League had had its wartime headquarters in Yenan. Under Mao's protection and Mu Chŏng's leadership, it had trained a substantial number of military and political cadres, sending them throughout Manchuria and into certain parts of north China.

It would appear that the advance units of the League involved few if any troops, being mainly the political leaders. In late October, however, some 2,000 Korean Volunteer Army soldiers arrived in Antung. They were led by officers who had served in the Chinese 8th Route Army. The commanding officer of the Yalu detachment was Kim Kang, only 26 years of age; an orphan, he had literally grown up with the 8th Route Army. His political commissar was Kim Ho, a thirty-six-year-old graduate of Whampoa Military Academy. Most of the troops were veterans, but there were also a number of new recruits. Some 70,000 Koreans currently lived in Antung Province alone, economic conditions were extremely bad, and a number of young men had joined the Volunteer Army primarily to obtain food. Thus the total size of the Army had grown to some 4,000 by the fall of 1945.

The two young officers of the Yalu detachment visited the Russian Security Command in North P'yŏngan Province seeking permission to cross the Yalu with their 2,000 men. A delay ensued, and it was not until mid-November that permission was granted. The chief of staff of the 25th Army, Lieutenant General Bankowsky, flew to Sinŭiju and announced that the troops could cross the Yalu after three days. At the same time, however, he reportedly instructed the Soviet colonel at the Security Command in the same city to allow the troops of the Volunteer Army to go no farther than Sinŭiju, and to disarm them immediately.

Thus, the Korean Volunteers received permission to parade through the streets of Sinŭiju, after which they were quartered in the Sinŭiju Higher School. On the first evening, however, their arms were collected, and the bulk of the army was sent back to Manchuria on the following day. No

38. *Ibid.,* p. 190. O's account is slightly different. He states that Cho refused to serve as chairman, therefore the Bureau had no head. O Yŏng-jin, *op. cit.,* pp. 133–139.

39. The following account is drawn mainly from Kim Ch'ang-sun, *op. cit.,* pp. 61–65.

doubt there were ample reasons for this decision other than ones of a strictly political nature. Many of the Volunteers at this point were primarily "rice soldiers," that is, soldiers whose reason for joining the army was to get food, with limited roots in Korea. Nevertheless, the decision had major political implications. Potentially, men like Mu Chŏng, Kim Tubong, Ch'oe Ch'ang-ik, and Han Pin were some of the most powerful figures on the Korean political scene. None of their Communist competitors had had such lengthy practical experience in higher level organizational work. From every indication, moreover, the Yenan group had the strong support of their Chinese comrades, even though the Maoists had little time for involvement in Korean matters at this point. If Mu Chŏng and his colleagues could bring into Korea a sizable number of troops and political cadres, would they not constitute the most formidable political force in the north?

In spite of the restrictions placed upon the Volunteer Army, the Yenan faction developed a number of local strongholds, particularly in North P'yŏngan and Hwanghae provinces. Its leaders, continuing to use the name "Korean Independence League," organized local branches in both North and South Korea. By the fall of 1945, therefore, a complex three-cornered struggle within the Korean Communist movement had unfolded, with the Soviet-Kapsan, domestic, and Yenan factions all engaged in intricate maneuvering.

In the aftermath of the Five Province Conference in P'yŏngyang, a shaky coalition of factions developed. The North Korean Bureau of the Korean Communist Party, formally established at the Conference, had a seventeen-man Executive Committee upon which sat representatives of all major factions. According to Kim Ch'ang-sun, Kim Il-sŏng was selected as first secretary, with Mu Chŏng and O Ki-sŏp jointly holding the post of second secretary.[40] Han Im-hyŏk, on the other hand, asserts that Kim was not elected first secretary until the third Executive Committee meeting in December.[41] In any case, Party offices were carefully balanced during this period, and though the Soviet-Kapsan faction appears to have had substantial advantages, it was far from holding absolute power. For example, the Party organ, *Chŏngno* (*Correct Path*) had as its editor, T'ae Sŏng-su, of the Soviet faction. The chief administrator of the newspaper, however, was Yu Mun-hwa, a Yenan faction representative, and the head of the editorial department was Pak P'al-yang, of the domestic faction.[42]

Kim Il-sŏng and his staunch adherents mark his first major victory in the ascent to total power as coming at the time of the December 17–18 meeting of the Enlarged Executive Committee. Han Im-hyŏk, an official Kimist spokesman, has written that the struggle and subsequent purge of

40. *Ibid.,* p. 95.
41. Han Im-hyŏk, *op. cit.,* p. 55.
42. Kim Ch'ang-sun, *op. cit.,* pp. 95–96.

the factionalists, as well as the removal of errors that had earlier seeped into the Party, began at this point.[43] Kim Il-sŏng himself was later to state, "After the third Executive Committee sessions, our Party's work was placed on its proper course . . . and we succeeded in making our Party a party of the masses." [44]

Why do the Kimists herald the December meeting as a major event, a memorable victory that did much to insure the unchallenged leadership of Kim Il-sŏng? The evidence suggests that the Kim faction maneuvered in such a fashion as to weaken or destroy the strong grip of the domestic faction upon many local and regional Party branches in the north. This was accomplished by securing the passage of measures ostensibly aimed at a Party reorganization that would strengthen the proletarian quotient and remove the "impure elements." Those who carried out these measures would, of course, be in a position to shape the Party in their image.

Naturally, Kim could point to a number of serious defects within the Party.[45] According to him, in the first three months after Liberation, the Communist Party in the north had attained a membership of 4,530 and possessed five news organs. Given the extensive organizational efforts, this was certainly not a spectacular record. Moreover, according to Kim, the Party had serious organizational defects at every level: statistics pertaining to Party membership were inaccurate and members did not even possess standard Party membership cards; many of the local Party committees were poorly constructed; and in a number of factories, enterprises, and farming villages, no Party branch had been established.

More serious was the fact that a number of pro-Japanese elements and other enemies had wormed their way into Party ranks, even at the leadership levels in some cases.[46] In broad terms, moreover, only 30 percent of current Party membership could be classified as coming from the working class; farmer members comprised 34 percent of the total, and the bourgeoisie—the intellectuals, merchants, and others—made up 36 percent.[47] Thus, asserted Kim, the Party was composed mainly of farmers and intellectuals; it was not a true party of the working class, and hence could not carry out their will.[48] Factionalism was also cited as a serious problem, with the Party organizations in Hwanghae, North P'yŏngan, and South Hamgyŏng provinces as prime examples. Some of the local Party committees had either ignored or neglected the instructions of the North

43. Han Im-hyŏk, *op. cit.*, p. 55.
44. *Kim Il-sŏng sŏnjip, op. cit.*, Vol. II, 1954 ed., p. 74, as cited in Han Im-hyŏk, *op. cit.*, pp. 55–56.
45. The entire speech of Kim Il-sŏng before the December 17–18 Enlarged Executive Committee is presented in *Kim Il-sŏng sŏnjip, op. cit.*, Vol. I, 1963 ed., pp. 15–28.
46. *Ibid.*, p. 16.
47. *Ibid.*, p. 17.
48. *Ibid.*

Korean Branch Organization Committee, thereby violating the principle of democratic centralism and weakening Party discipline. He was particularly harsh in his comments upon the South Hamgyŏng Province Committee (a stronghold of the domestic faction).

The local and provincial leaders of the Party, Kim insisted, had faults both numerous and grave. Few of them had visited the factories, enterprises, and farms of their areas. As a result, they knew little about actual conditions. Hence, an event like the Sinŭiju student riot could occur.[49] More important, it was because the Party had weak ties with the masses that its worker membership was low. Certain leaders had practiced nepotism. Others were guilty of corruption. Most were young, with inadequate training and education.

What was to be done? First, Kim signaled what was to be the long-range Communist policy with respect to the unification of Korea: by uniting with "all democratic parties and social organizations," the Communist Party should alter North Korea, making it into "a strong democratic base" by rapidly "democratizing" political, economic, and cultural life there, while at the same time strengthening the united front with the democratic forces of South Korea, preparatory to a unified People's Democratic Republic. Later, this formula was slightly altered: the north was now supposed to serve as the *socialist* base, with the north aiding the south's "liberation struggle against imperialist and reactionary control." However, basic Communist policy had been established on this matter as early as December 1945.

The bulk of Kim's prescriptions related not to unification but to internal Party affairs, especially organizational matters. The Central Organization Committee should be empowered to undertake a thorough scrutiny of current Party members, and issue new, standard membership cards after all undesirable elements had been ejected from the Party. Every effort should be made, moreover, to change the social composition of the Party; the main thing was to add true proletarian elements. Cells should be established in all factories immediately. Meanwhile, Party records re-

49. On Nov. 23, 1945, a serious student revolt against the Communists occurred in Sinŭiju, a city on the south bank of the Yalu. Because of an earlier incident of violence against students by Communists at the nearby town of Yongamp'o on Nov. 18, students of six secondary schools in Sinŭiju conducted a protest march and unarmed "assault" against the provincial police headquarters, the People's Committee, and the provincial Party headquarters calling for the removal of Communist and Soviet military rule. The police and Soviet troops opened fire, killing 23 students and wounding some 700. Kim Il-sŏng was sent the following day to pacify the people. The police chief and some of the Communist leaders were disciplined for "overreaction," but the incident also produced a large-scale roundup of adults unfriendly to the Communists. For details, see Sinŭiju Pan-kong Haksaeng Uigŏ Kinyŏm-hoe (Society to Commemorate the Anti-Communist Student Uprising in Sinŭiju), *Amnokkang byŏn ui hoetpul* (*Torch Light on the Bank of the Yalu*), Seoul, 1964, and Han Chae-dŏk, *op. cit.*, pp. 179–221.

lating to membership and other matters should be improved. More effective training should be given Party officials, and local Party branches should meet regularly to discuss Party tasks.

Kim's proposals were approved, although domestic faction representatives must have been deeply suspicious. Most of the local and provincial Party branches had been launched under their auspices. Any sweeping reorganization would therefore affect them directly. Unfortunately for them, however, it was hard to deny many of Kim's charges. A number of opportunists had entered the Party, and organizational policies had been lax in many cases. Kim had found a vulnerable point, and he was determined to exploit it. Obviously, the capacity to manipulate Party membership and officeholders, and to require the subordination of local units to central headquarters (now effectively limited to the north) was to bring the Party under control. It is not without reason, therefore, that Kim and his historians view December 17–18, 1945, as a major turning point in their struggle for control of the Communist Party of North Korea.

Smashing the Nationalists

Almost immediately, the Communists were plunged into the battle with the non-Communist nationalists over the trusteeship plan. This was of course the issue that effectively separated the two forces. The overwhelming majority of non-Communist nationalists active in Korean politics bitterly opposed the trusteeship concept, and major demonstrations against it were mounted in Seoul and other cities below the 38th parallel. Indeed, it was the adamant position of moderates and rightists on this issue that ultimately became the pretext for the breakup of the Joint Commission meetings, and so ended any chance for Korean unity. The Soviet delegation, as we have noted, insisted upon excluding all opponents of trusteeship from the list of parties and organizations to be consulted. This, in effect, precluded the possibility of establishing any representative political body or coalition government in Korea.

These developments, of course, cannot be separated from the broader context in which they unfolded. The Soviet Union and the United States were rapidly moving from cooperation toward confrontation, and Korea was only one of many issues between them. It is doubtful, however, whether any of the Allied powers anticipated the strenuous objections that the Koreans were to voice concerning trusteeship. There had been warnings, as we have noted. But the United States chose to ignore them. Then, suddenly, it discovered that it could neither control nor greatly influence many of the individuals and groups that were of crucial importance to any balanced, democratic Korean government. The period was therefore one of mounting frustration and anxiety for the American authorities.

The problems of the Russians north of the 38th parallel were scarcely less than those plaguing the Americans in the south. We have already suggested that the Soviet command probably did not arrive in Korea with any fully worked-out political plan or precise timetable. It is more likely that the Russians, like the Americans, came to Korea with nothing more specific in mind than such basic principles as the importance of seeing a "friendly regime" established there. No doubt this position alone created a steeply graded table of probability with respect to ultimate policies. It is possible to argue that the basic policies the Russians and Americans finally pursued were in both cases the most logical, given their respective ideological views and political objectives—or, at least, that they were far more probable than any alternative set of policies. Even if one subscribes to this position, however, events were significant in determining the timing of given policies and the enthusiasm with which they were implemented. This was particularly true of the trusteeship crisis.

We must assume that the Soviet authorities in P'yŏngyang did not intend beforehand to use the trusteeship issue as the weapon to smash the non-Communist nationalists, end all pretenses of a true united front, and thereby accelerate the movement toward a monolithic Communist regime in the north. However, events after December 27, 1945, caused them to operate precisely in this fashion. The key appears to have been Cho Man-sik. Like many of his counterparts in the south, Cho was violently opposed to the idea of a trusteeship and refused, despite all types of pressure, to change his position. According to O Yŏng-jin, Cho was contacted repeatedly by the top Russian authorities in the days that followed the announcement of the Moscow Agreement.[50] There were lengthy conversations. Supposedly, as we have noted, General Romanenko himself promised Cho that, if he would accept trusteeship, he would be made the first president of Korea, with Kim Il-sŏng placed under him as minister of defense. Many other promises and assurances were reportedly advanced. Such leading Communists as Kim and Ch'oe Yong-gŏn also visited Cho repeatedly, imploring him to alter his position.

When these efforts failed, the Russians were confronted with a basic tactical decision. Should they acknowledge the fact that Cho and some others like him spoke for the vast majority of politically articulate Koreans on this issue, and further, that only such men as Cho could effectively represent non-Communist nationalists? Such acknowledgments could conceivably have led to the type of retreat that the American authorities undertook so painfully in South Korea. Or should the Russians push the hard line at all costs, removing from political life all those who continued to resist? Such a decision, they must have seen, would reduce non-Communist representation to a handful of puppets and thrust the Communists into immediate and overwhelming power.

The Russians soon made it clear that they intended to take the hard line. Cho Man-sik clashed publicly with the Soviet command at an Enlarged Conference of the South P'yŏngan Province People's Political Com-

50. O Yŏng-jin, *op. cit.*, pp. 181–182, 185.

mittee, and was immediately put under protective custody. There is some confusion on the precise date; O Yŏng-jin states that it was February 5, 1946, but Han Chae-dŏk, who provides a detailed account of the meeting, recollects it as January 5.[51] According to him, its main purpose was to have the Committee formally support the Moscow Agreement. By this time, a number of non-Communist Committee members had already fled south, and it was obvious from the outset that the vote would be favorable. Therefore, according to Han, Cho Man-sik and his few followers opposed the idea of taking a vote. When the Communists insisted, they submitted their resignations. After much wrangling, General Romanenko supposedly accepted the resignations, and the moderates left the meeting.

Han asserts that Kim Il-sŏng was not present at this meeting since he was not a member of the Committee. In the 1963 edition of Kim's selected works, however, there is a speech allegedly delivered at the Enlarged Conference by Kim. But the date given is January 23.[52] Whether this speech was in truth prepared and delivered by Kim—and at this time— we have no way of determining. It is useful, nonetheless, to note its basic themes briefly, because it illustrates the official Communist position on Cho after the beginning of 1946.

According to Kim, the Cho Man-sik group had now fallen into the category of reactionaries. Despite the correct advice given them by Yi Chu-yŏn and others, they had persisted in opposing the Moscow Agreement in concert with "the reactionary strata of the United States" and other antidemocratic elements. Kim then attacked the past performance of the People's Political Committee itself, alleging that "many rotten bureaucratic and reactionary elements" had crept into the Committee and "played a number of dirty tricks." As a result, the Committee had failed in its tasks, both as these related to the people's livelihood and to the development of democracy.[53]

Cho Man-sik had shown incredible courage and tenacity. He was now to disappear. According to one source, he was kept in the Koryŏ Hotel in P'yŏngyang under strict guard after this time.[54] No one willing to speak

51. See *ibid.*, pp. 182–183, and Han Chae-dŏk, *op. cit.*, pp. 254–257.
52. *Kim Il-sŏng sŏnjip, op. cit.*, Vol. I, 1963 ed., pp. 37–39.
53. *Ibid.*, p. 39.
54. Kim Ch'ang-sun, *op. cit.*, pp. 70–73. Kim's version of the Cho Man-sik incident is as follows: On Jan. 1, 1946, General Romanenko invited Cho to his office and told him, "If you will support the trusteeship plan, you will become the Stalin of Korea; if you continue to oppose it, it will be difficult to guarantee your safety." On Jan. 4, a committee of the Five Province Administrative Bureau was convened to take up the trusteeship issue. Sixteen Communists, and only six nationalists, attended; after lengthy debate the proposal was approved and Cho announced his decision to resign. He was then vehemently denounced by the Communists, who asserted that such an action was an attempt to bring confusion into the movement and violated the principles of the entire Communist International. Cho stood firm. The next day, Jan. 5, he was surrounded by Russian security police as he was about to step out of his office.

knows what ultimately happened to him. There have been rumors that he was killed by Communist authorities just before or during the Korean War, but there is no hard evidence at present on this matter. His own private secretary was not permitted to know Cho's fate.

The Communists now moved quickly to end the role of all men like Cho Man-sik. Cho had been the leader of the Chosŏn Minju-dang (Korean Democratic Party), established in the north on November 3, 1945, as well as serving as chief of the Five Provinces Administrative Bureau. After Cho's purge, Ch'oe Yong-gŏn, who had been second in command, became Democratic Party head. But Ch'oe was a Communist—and an intimate friend of Kim Il-sŏng.[55] Moreover, the new vice-chairman of the party, Chŏng Sŏng-ŏn, was also a Communist, as was Yi Kwang-guk, head of Organization.

Aside from the Ch'ŏndogyo Young Friends' Party, the KDP was the only recognized non-Communist party of this period. Yet its leaders were now being selected by the Communists, from Communist ranks. Party policies or actions, moreover, had to be approved in advance by Communist authorities. Under these circumstances, it scarcely mattered that one or two cabinet posts were filled from the ranks of these puppet parties. United front policies and coalition government had now reached the point of complete fraudulence.

The Structure and Policies of the New Communist State

Having reduced the non-Communist nationalist forces to impotence, the Soviet command now took the first concrete steps toward establishing a separate North Korean state. Presumably, like their American counterparts, the Russian occupation authorities were now moving toward the view that Korean unification was an exceedingly remote possibility. Hence, on February 8, 1946, an Enlarged Conference of the North Korean Democratic Parties, Social Organizations, the Five Provinces Administrative Bureau, and the People's Political Committees was convened in P'yŏngyang. This was clearly a major effort on the part of the Russians. All the political agencies that they had so assiduously cultivated during the previous five months were now brought into play. Moreover, only "democratic" and "progressive" individuals were now involved in these institutions; "reactionaries" either had fled south or had been purged.

Kim's address to the Enlarged Conference of February 8 is available in a 1949 edition of his collected speeches.[56] After an extensive eulogy of

55. As we shall note, Ch'oe was to remain one of Kim's closest associates, being later entrusted with such key positions as those of minister of national defense, vice-premier, and vice-chairman of the Workers' Party.

56. As noted earlier, Kim addressed the conference on the final day. One version of this speech appears in the 1963 edition of his *Selected Works* but, as indicated above, a near-contemporary version has been located, and it is from that version that we take the following remarks. It should be borne in mind that these are the first substantive positions enunciated by Kim in the postwar period.

the Soviet army and the usual condemnation of Japanese imperialism, Kim asserted that the absence of a central political institution constituted a major obstacle to the planned, unified development of North Korean politics, economics, and culture. Therefore, it was essential at this point to organize the North Korean Provisional People's Committee until Korean unification had been accomplished. Such a step had the approval of both Korean democratic leaders and Soviet authorities.

What tasks lay before this Committee? Kim insisted that, first, all "pro-Japanese and anti-democratic elements" had to be thoroughly purged from local and provincial governmental bodies. "This is the most important task confronting the North Korean Provisional People's Committee," he asserted. "We cannot construct a democratic new Korea while we have traitors and renegades in positions of sovereign power." (All nationalists supporting men like Cho Man-sik were thereby put on notice, if they had not already fled.) Second, a thorough land-reform program had to be instituted, with the land of "the Japanese imperialists, national traitors, and big Korean landlords" confiscated and distributed freely to the tillers. Forests also had to be nationalized.

Kim went on to explain that "in our country" the rural villages constituted the foundation of the national economy. The feudalist tenant system then being practiced provided the economic foundation for the power of the reactionary forces. Hence, while the landlords would oppose all democratic reforms, without such reforms a democratic, independent nation could not be created.

Naturally, Kim championed the rapid reconstruction and development of all productive enterprises, together with the systems of transportation, finance, and credit. The free activity of the entrepreneurs and merchants, he insisted, had to be maintained, and the middle-sized and small enterprises encouraged so that consumer necessities could be supplied. At the same time, the labor movement had to be supported, and factory committees organized on an extensive basis. Intensive attention also had to be given to education, with the masses indoctrinated in "democratic thoughts." Finally, "the true intent" of the decision reached at Moscow had to be explained in detail to the people, so that the reactionary efforts to mislead the people and erode the democratic united front could be thwarted.

Taken in its entirety, Kim's speech provided little solace to anyone other than the hard-core Communists or those who had reconciled themselves at this point to being devoted fellow travelers. Gone were the numerous mentions of the importance of working with "patriotic capitalists" or "petty bourgeois nationalists." The cutting edge had become complete: total acceptance of the Moscow Agreement; all nonadherents were "national traitors" and "renegades."

The transition toward a Communist monopoly of power can best be appreciated by examining briefly the key personnel of the Provisional People's Committee. Kim Il-sŏng, of course, served as chairman. Kim Tu-bong became vice-chairman, and Kang Ryang-uk was appointed chief secretary. Kang, a Methodist minister, happened to be Kim's relative on his mother's side; he was registered as a Democratic Party member. Among the fourteen bureau chiefs, who were in fact cabinet officers of the new government, only the heads of Commerce and Public Health were non-Communists. The former was a dentist and the latter a medical doctor. Ch'oe Yong-gŏn, who, as we have noted, was both the new chairman of the Democratic Party and an old Communist comrade-in-arms of Kim Il-sŏng, was made chief of Public Security. This was not the type of government likely to cause Kim or the Soviet command any major difficulties.

With power now securely in Communist hands, "democratic reforms" could follow. Between March and August 1946, a series of basic pieces of legislation affecting every aspect of life in North Korea was promulgated. In Communist theory, these were laws intended to complete the "bourgeois democratic revolution." In reality, they were in line with the "new democracy" of Mao Tse-tung—democracy managed by the Communists in such a fashion as to blur completely the distinction between the much vaunted two stages, "bourgeois" and "socialist." Under Communist tutelage, the revolution could in fact become continuous, with a smooth transition into socialism. Indeed, "socialism in one country" had now been united with "permanent revolution." Stalin and Trotsky had become reconciled in East Asia. Both in theory and in practice, the older, simple concept of a two-stage revolution for colonial societies had been drastically modified, if not completely supplanted.

The first major law promulgated was the Land Reform Act of March 5, 1946. To appreciate the signal importance of this act, from both an economic and a political standpoint, some brief summary of agrarian conditions in Korea must be given. Before Japanese surrender, Korea had been overwhelmingly an agrarian society. Of the entire Korean population, 68.3 percent had been engaged primarily in agriculture, although agrarian output constituted only 46.4 percent of the gross national product. Tenancy, moreover, was a serious problem. Land ownership had been heavily concentrated in Japanese hands and among a small number of Koreans who had made up the rural gentry. At the close of World War II, almost 75 percent of all arable land in Korea was cultivated by tenants.[57] Among

57. For a brief summary of data on the agrarian situation in Korea at the close of the Japanese era, see Andrew J. Grajdanzev, *Modern Korea,* New York, 1944, pp. 84–122.

In Japanese, see Kobayakawa Kurō, *Chōsen nōgyō hattatsu shi: Seisaku-hen (History of the Development of Agriculture in Korea: On Policies)*, Seoul, 1944. For Korean works with a Marxist viewpoint, see two works by In Chŏng-sik, *Chosŏn ui t'oji munje (The Land Problem in Korea)*, Seoul, 1946, and *Chosŏn nongŏp kyŏngje ron (On the Agricultural Economy of Korea)*, Seoul, 1949.

According to a Communist source, in North Korea prior to land reform, 6.8 percent of the farmers (landlords) owned 58.8 percent of the cultivated land, and 70 percent were either tenants or small owner-cultivators, with the latter category

the total number of farm families, approximately one-half owned no land, and an additional one-third rented some portion of the land they tilled.

Asian Communists were quick to realize that any profound change in the structure of agrarian ownership and control would have massive social and political implications. The Chinese Communists, of course, were pioneers in this field after 1927, and most Korean Communists had studied Maoist actions and writings. In many respects, Korean rural society, like its Chinese counterpart, had played the dominant role in shaping the Korean political culture. A very strong family system rooted in Confucian ethics commanded the prior loyalty of each individual, and demanded much of his time, energy, and resources. Political-social units branched out from the family to the clan and village. Regional loyalties tended to remain high. The landed rural gentry constituted a very powerful influence over the mass of peasants. Korea was a society without a sizable middle class or an enlightened upper class. Politics was essentially the business of the rural gentry, many of whose sons did obtain a higher education and, on occasion, became at least minor officials in the Japanese bureaucracy. For most Koreans, the affairs of state were far above and beyond them, willingly left in the hands of their "superiors." Their own energies were expended in seeking to establish the type of client relationship that would safeguard their basic economic interests. This involved a highly intricate politico-social relationship, resting upon hierarchy, with various obligations and rights. However, political communication of any other kind between gentry and peasant was extremely limited.

To remove the rural gentry was thus to remove a major political force within rural Korea. Perhaps more importantly, it was to "liberate" the peasant from the psychological as well as the economic and political restraints of the previous order, rendering him susceptible to, and perhaps needful of, new tutors, mentors, and rulers.

Article I of the Land Reform Act provided that the agricultural system of North Korea was to be characterized by the individual ownership of the land by the tillers.[58] Article II proclaimed that land falling into

---

constituting only 20 percent. Center for Historical Studies, Academy of Science, Democratic People's Republic of Korea, *Chosŏn t'ongsa* (*An Outline History of Korea*), Tokyo, 1959, Vol. III, pp. 30–31. This work, hereafter cited as *Chosŏn t'ongsa*, was originally published in three volumes in P'yŏngyang as the standard history textbook to be used in North Korea. The above work represents the second part of the second volume, covering the period 1945–1956, and reprinted in Korean in Tokyo as Volume III. According to the preface, publication was delayed because of the fierce struggle against "the antiparty and antirevolutionary Ch'oe Ch'ang-ik and his conspirators." Ch'oe, as we shall note, was charged with attempting in August 1956, to overthrow Kim Il-sŏng.

58. The full text of the Land Reform Act as well as the detailed rules concerning its implementation can be found in Minjŏn Samuguk (Democratic National Front, Secretariat), *Chosŏn haebang nyŏnbo* (*Korean Liberation Yearbook*), Seoul, 1946, pp. 429–435.

certain categories would be confiscated and transferred to those who would till it. These categories were: land previously owned by the Japanese, either as state property or by individuals; land owned by "national traitors," including those who had actively participated in the Japanese administration and those who had fled from their districts at the time of Liberation; land owned by individuals who did not till it themselves but rented it solely for tenancy; land, regardless of acreage, that had been continuously in tenancy; land owned by any religious body or group if it had been used in an exploitative fashion and/or exceeded 5 chŏngbo (a total of about 12.25 acres); and all land individually owned in excess of 5 chŏngbo, unless the excess land had been tilled by the farmer himself.

Even if it had been under continuous tenancy, land belonging to schools, hospitals, or scientific institutions was not to be confiscated. But future tenancy in connection with such land was prohibited, and schools were directed to cultivate it with student labor. Forests and orchards were not to be divided, but rather "entrusted" to the state, with appropriate People's Committees taking charge. Irrigation facilities also were to be permanently entrusted to the district People's Committees.

An elite was exempt from the provisions regarding confiscation. This included those who had been "outstandingly active" in the struggle for independence or who occupied positions of importance in the building of a "new, democratic Korea," including certain writers, artists, and scientists.

No compensation was to be paid for land confiscated, and it was to be transferred on the basis of "permanent ownership." Land distributed was to be exempt from debts or other liabilities, and it could not be bought, sold, rented, or mortgaged. The amount of land to be distributed to each farmer depended upon the size of his family and the labor power available in it.

According to a subsequent official report, 981,390 chŏngbo (2,404,-405.5 acres), or some 50 percent of the land under cultivation, was distributed among 725,000 farm families. It is probable that at least one-fourth of the entire northern population was affected directly by this program, which in scope was equivalent to that being undertaken in Japan under the American aegis, or to come later under the Communists in China.[59] Certainly no single piece of legislation could strike more deeply

59. See *Chosŏn t'ongsa, op. cit.,* Vol. III, pp. 31–37. According to the Communists, some 12,000 peasant village committees, consisting of "poor peasants and hired hands," were organized, and these committees administered the land distribution directly. It was admitted, however, that "the Party also sent its able members and progressive workers into villages to guide and aid" the work.

According to the Communists, "The result was a fundamental change in the class structure. The landlords as a class disappeared. The better-off farmers did not lose land but, to the extent they manifested the characteristics of a landlord class, they too suffered. On the other hand, the poor peasants, who constituted a majority in

at the old social order or benefit so many people economically—and hence woo them politically. It is therefore not surprising that land reform was highest on the Communist agenda in North Korea as elsewhere, and that it began scarcely a month after the Communists had obtained firm political control at the national level.[60]

---

traditional Korea, were elevated to the status of middle-class farmers. The land reform of 1946 in North Korea was a bourgeois-democratic revolution carried out under the leadership of the working class and by the people's government. This revolution put an end to feudalism in Korean agriculture. It was not, however, to pave the way to a free bourgeois development in agriculture; rather, it made it possible for the revolution to move forward to the higher goal of socialistic collective management." *Ibid.*, p. 36.

On June 27, 1946, the produce-tax system was put into effect. The regime proclaimed that "all forms of taxes" had been ended for the peasant. Instead, he paid 25 percent of his produce to the state, and was free to dispose of the remainder "according to his free will." The insistence upon not calling this 25 percent levy a tax could not alter its real character, of course. Nevertheless, that amount was significantly less than previous tenant rentals in almost all cases, since they had ranged up to 50 percent of the crop (with seed and equipment furnished in most cases, however). It will be recalled that initial Communist-sponsored agrarian reforms were based upon a maximum 30 percent tenant rental fee. As we shall have occasion to discuss later, the new system's burden depended upon crop assessment.

60. For a lengthy report by Kim Il-sŏng on the land reform program very revealing of Korean Communist ideology, propaganda, and organizational techniques, see "A Summary of Conclusions Concerning the Comprehensive Report on Land Reform," a speech delivered by Kim Il-sŏng before the First Enlarged Executive Committee meeting of the North Korean Provisional People's Committee, April 13, 1946, in *Kin Nichisei senshū* (*The Selected Works of Kim Il-sŏng*), Japanese ed., Kyōto, 1952, Vol. I, pp. 16–25; and Kim Il-sŏng, *Choguk ui t'ongil tongnip kwa minjuhwa rŭl wihayŏ* (*For the United Independence and Democratization of the Fatherland*), P'yŏngyang, 1949, Vol. I, pp. 25–34.

The following passages should suffice to paraphrase Kim's major points. After Japanese imperialism was destroyed by the victory of the Allies, *headed by the Soviet Army* (italics ours), the Korean feudal system was destroyed and the construction of a true democracy begun. The land reform program executed in North Korea will aid in the rapid democratic unification of the presently divided state because it has thrilled the farmers and all of the people of the entire nation. It is a program intended to smash the reactionary landlords who block democracy and to enable the swift establishment of a unified democratic regime throughout Korea.

We have been able to execute this reform smoothly and successfully for several reasons. First, the presence of the Soviet Army, which is most beloved by our people and which reveres people's democracy and freedom, provided the conditions for our democratic development. Another factor was the firm establishment of a democratic united front in North Korea. A third factor was that the workers and farmers were closely united; urban workers dispatched their representatives to farm villages to assist the farmers, thereby enabling the farmers to gain much courage. By destroying the rural feudal system, we have caused the farmers to realize the necessity of union with the more progressive, democratic vanguard, the urban workers. Finally, this was a program long desired by our farmers.

Certain problems did develop. In the course of the reform, we discovered some passive, shaky, or reactionary elements in the people's committees. Some reactionary

Approximately two weeks later, on March 23, Kim Il-sŏng outlined a comprehensive program that his government expected to enact, a twenty-point proposal issued in the name of the North Korean Provisional People's Committee.[61] Kim began with the familiar delineation between "the people" and "the enemies." The latter—"the reactionaries, Fascists, and anti-democratic forces"—had to be mercilessly destroyed. To "the people," all freedoms would be advanced, including freedom of speech, publication, assembly, and religion. "Democratic parties" would be allowed to operate freely, as well as labor and farmer unions and other "democratic social organizations." All Koreans, moreover, would have the right and duty to form people's committees, henceforth to be the local administrative bodies, by general, direct, and secret ballot. The property and privacy of each citizen was to be guaranteed by law. If one happened to belong to "the people" and was able to remain in that category, the future seemed promising indeed. The fact that Stalinist Russia had had similar guarantees for its citizens was unknown to most Koreans, nor could they be expected to guess that a Stalinist era lay ahead for North Korea.

Within his twenty-point program, Kim included a pledge that individual handicrafts and commerce would be preserved as free enterprises. He thereby underwrote the "bourgeois" character of the revolution at this stage. However, he also asserted that large enterprises, transport facilities, and banks were to be nationalized, along with all mines and forests. Prices of necessities were to be regulated, moreover, and a continual struggle conducted against speculators and usurers.

A general compulsory educational system was to be instituted, with state-operated primary and middle schools, colleges, and universities being greatly expanded. It was also essential to enlarge the national culture by developing more theaters, libraries, and radio stations. A rigorous training program for the new bureaucracy had to be established, along with increased support for those professionally engaged in the sciences and arts. The number of state hospitals had to be increased, and all indigent persons were henceforth to be treated without fees.

---

landlord elements retained their influence. On occasion the reforms were intentionally delayed. Sometimes there were plots to destroy the spring tilling plan. Some subversives erroneously labeled progressives national traitors, thereby damaging the integrity of the program. We must swiftly eliminate these reactionary elements from our people's committees.

The propaganda work of most people's committees was also much too meager. At this point, what are our duties? First, to increase production. We must also conserve food. And we must purge incompetent, corrupt officials, bureaucrats, commandists, and reactionaries who are still on people's committees.

61. These twenty program proposals, incidentally, were issued three days after the opening of the American-Soviet Joint Commission meetings in Seoul, meetings to seek agreement on Korean unification. For the full text of the March 23 statement, see *Kim Il-sŏng sŏnjip, op. cit.,* 1963 ed., Vol. I, pp. 54–57, and *Choguk ŭi t'ongil tongnip,* Vol. I, pp. 21–24.

Both the timing and the substance of the reform program and proposals launched in March, together with the propaganda surrounding them,
make it clear that the Communists had launched a major political offensive directed at *both* South and North Korea. These measures were to become the program for a unified "people's democratic dictatorship," the
first phase of a progression that was intended to lead ultimately to "a genuinely socialist Korea." It is also true, however, that the program was
enunciated by a government that could not possibly have won a free election at this point. On the contrary, among those North Koreans with any
political consciousness, the attitude toward the new government was probably a mixture of hostility and fear. This was even more likely to be true
in the south. Kim and his supporters had placed themselves in the position
of openly challenging Korean nationalism on the trusteeship issue. In the
course of this action, moreover, they had treacherously removed the one
man who commanded widespread northern support, Cho Man-sik. In addition, Kim Il-sŏng, whose youth did not help him in this respect, had openly
cultivated the impression, by his lengthy and obsequious eulogies of the
Russians, that he was a mere puppet of a foreign power. And the Russians
were none too popular with any segment of the Korean populace. Finally,
Korean Communists were deeply, albeit secretly, divided among themselves, and there were many who were not prepared to swear allegiance to
a Soviet-sponsored "youth" whom they scarcely knew.

To recite these facts, however, is not to say that the March 23 Program lacked political value. More than 90 percent of all Korean industry
had been owned by the Japanese. Nationalization, therefore, affected almost no Koreans directly. Similarly, there were few large Korean land-
owners. Thus, land reform affected few Koreans adversely in comparison
with the number who stood to benefit. The promise of free education and
extensive cultural improvements, together with pledges of protection to
small and medium businessmen, were well attuned to the hopes and fears
of a large number of citizens.

A second edict, one dealing with labor, was promulgated on June 20.
In introducing it, Kim once again insisted that North Korea was in the
stage of "democratic reform and construction," not socialism.[62] The Korean

---

62. "Announcing the Draft of a Labor Ordinance," June 20, 1946, *ibid.*, Vol.
I, pp. 75–88.

Once again, Kim's speech was oriented almost entirely toward broader political
objectives. There are those, he said, who think that an ordinance protecting the interests of the working class will destroy the democratic united front. On the contrary,
this ordinance rests upon the firm theoretical foundation of the united front. It must
be remembered, said Kim, that the class that fought most bravely against the Kim
Ku–Syngman Rhee fascist remnants at the time of the land reform campaign was the
working class [*sic*]. Although land reform programs have been executed in a number
of emancipated nations, none has adopted a democratic labor ordinance, asserted
Kim. And of course, it would be impossible for the American military government in

economy, he asserted, was at present casting off the remnants of feudalism and colonialism, with private capitalism being allowed to develop. North Korean economic development was thus neither that of a socialist system (hence the labor program did not provide for compensation in accordance with one's need), nor that of American-style democracy (hence the program did not permit "imperialist exploitation").

Kim's statement contained a lengthy and vitrolic attack upon American policy that was to set the tone for the years that lay ahead. American "imperialist exploitation" in South Korea, charged Kim, had reduced the people to utter misery. The workers were wandering about in hunger and rags, just as in the Japanese era. Such traitors as the Kim Ku and Syngman Rhee groups, moreover, were collaborating with the Americans to reduce the people to slavery. Communist propaganda against their American and Korean opponents from this point on became even more extreme than previously. Prior to the Korean War, the results were not spectacular. Many northerners simply did not believe their government. The evidence from interviews, however, indicates much greater success in recent years.[63] The Communists, of course, have had total control of the northern mass media, although they cannot block out all radio transmissions from the south. By interspersing scraps of truth and hard data with massive amounts of sheer fantasy and gross exaggeration, and by making skillful use of defectors and foreign leftist visitors, the North Korean regime over time has effectively indoctrinated most of its people to believe that no matter how miserable conditions were in the north, conditions in South Korea were much worse.

The main provisions of the labor law included an equal wage system, an eight-hour day, regulations concerning child labor, and provisions for a labor organization. All workers and office employees were to be enrolled in the North Korean General Federation of Trade Unions, which would determine such matters as special wages, extra working hours, and workers' compensation.[64]

A law guaranteeing equal rights for women was announced on July 30. Less than two weeks later, on August 10, another law nationalized

---

South Korea—which is manipulating Kim Ku and Syngman Rhee—to issue such an ordinance. In the South, the workers continue to be in desperate conditions, and the traitors Kim Ku and Syngman Rhee are continuing the imperialist Japanese system.

As can be seen, the basic thrust of Kim's speech was the call for revolution in the South, and unification of the nation under Communist control.

63. Our interviews without exception sustain the thesis that continuous, intensive propaganda did have a major effect upon beliefs—and patterns of thought—both at mass and elitist levels. We shall devote considerable attention to this subject in Chapters XI and XII.

64. For the full text of the Labor Ordinance, see Democratic National Front, Secretariat, Chosŏn haebang nyŏnbo, op. cit., pp. 424–428. This and other laws and ordinances of North Korea have been reprinted in Ch'a Rak-hun and Chŏng Kyŏng-mo, eds., Puk-Han pŏmryŏng yŏnhyŏk-jip (Collection of Ordinances in North Korea), Seoul, 1969.

industries, railroads, other transport facilities, and banks. Some 1,043 "major enterprises" were transferred to state control.[65] On October 4, however, the regime announced its intention to continue protection of small-scale private enterprise by promulgating the "Decision Concerning the Protection of Private Ownership in Industrial and Commercial Activity and Procedures for Encouraging the Development of Private Initiative."

Thus, the seven months from March to October 1946 were months of major legislative activity, a period during which the Communist leaders of North Korea, carefully guided and supervised by their Russian mentors, developed the main economic and political structure for the new state. Communist sources insist that their "reform measures" met with fierce class resistance, with pro-Japanese, landlords, "reactionaries," and religious leaders fighting to uphold the old order. There is no doubt that the new government met with opposition, and not merely from spokesmen for "the old order." Unrest in certain rural areas, student riots, and deep nationalist resentment were reported from various sources. As we have noted, the Kim government was the product of Soviet power, not of public popularity. And as we shall see, when given any kind of political choice, many educated North Koreans opted for a "progressive party" other than Kim's Communist Party.

Nevertheless, there was no opportunity for massive resistance in North Korea at this point. Not only had Communist power asserted itself firmly throughout the land; those who might have rallied major resistance had either been removed or, seeing the futility of opposition, had fled.[66] It was

65. According to Communist sources, in 1944, at the end of the Japanese era, only 5 percent of all industrial capital was owned by Koreans; the remainder was in Japanese hands. Moreover, all railroads and other forms of transportation, communications, banks, and major commercial facilities were in Japanese hands. Thus, "nationalization" had an extremely limited impact upon individual Koreans. Also, since the Japanese had fled in the weeks following surrender, these facilities had been operated by People's Committees—with only very minor opposition from "bourgeois" elements, as the Communists themselves admitted. Nationalization in the form underwritten by the August Ordinance was far more simple than the land reform program.

The Communist position in this period was that the measure to nationalize industries was aimed not at removing capitalism but at destroying the vestiges of imperialism. Of total industrial output in 1946, 72.4 percent was from nationalized industries, 27.6 percent from private capitalism. Thus, the measure was defended as a part of the "bourgeois democratic revolution"; but whereas in the case of land reform conditions had merely been created whereby the development of a socialist agrarian economy could take place at a later point, in this case a basic socialist mode of production had already been introduced, albeit in incomplete form. A great leap forward in the people's economy had been achieved. *Chosŏn t'ongsa, op. cit.*, Vol. III, pp. 37–41.

66. It was noted earlier that the population of South Korea increased by a phenomenal 22 percent between 1945 and 1947, and certainly a major factor in that increase was migration from north to south. While accurate figures cannot be obtained, a conservative estimate would be that probably 800,000 persons fled to the South during this period.

generally not necessary, therefore, to engage in the massive, bloody liquidation of the rural gentry that was to characterize the opening phases of Communist land reform in China a few years later. In miniature, however, the North Korean program was a forecast of things to come in China. The peasants were activated through the village land committees, and when one of these committees appeared less resolute in ousting landlords than was deemed desirable, Party members and "progressive" workers were sent to "assist" it. A far-reaching social revolution had been launched throughout rural North Korea.

The United Front Movement in the North

Meanwhile, the Communists were equally active on the political front. They began with a serious effort to formalize a united front structure, so that the economic reforms characterizing this phase of "people's democracy" would have their political counterpart. On June 22, 1946, they announced the formation of the Puk-Chosŏn Minju Chuui Minjok T'ongil Chŏnsŏn (North Korean Democratic National United Front). In explaining its purpose, Kim Il-sŏng stated: "In order for us to construct a new and democratic Korea, we must become one family. We must unite the entire North Korean people and the entire Korean people around the Democratic National United Front." [67] He went on to assert that the Front would lead all Koreans in a united struggle against such national traitors as Kim Ku and Rhee.

One purpose of the Front was thus to serve as a weapon of intervention in the politics of the south. As we have seen, the KCP in the south was engaged in a similar effort. The Front's primary function, however, was fully to mobilize potential Communist strength by providing a vehicle for Communist control of all political and social organizations. Kim, of course, was extremely careful to emphasize the equality of treatment that each unit within the Front would receive. "The democratic tasks of the new Korea," he asserted, "cannot be accomplished by a single political party. Only through the common efforts and united struggle of the democratic parties and social organizations can this be attained." [68] The front would serve as "a common consultative organization," with each party having equal rights and an equal position. Thus, the chairmanship of the group would be rotated among its members, and other democratic procedures would be followed.

We have already seen, however, that the "democratic parties" now permitted to exist had already been brought under Communist control. Whatever threat existed to the Kim faction at this point came from *within*

67. For the speech of Kim Il-sŏng on the occasion of the establishment of the United Front, see *Choguk ui t'ongil tongnip, op. cit.,* Vol. I, pp. 89–98, and *Kin Nichisei senshū, op. cit.,* Vol. I, pp. 68–71.

68. *Ibid.,* pp. 70–71.

the Communist movement. An examination of the "social organizations" fostered during this period makes this fact even clearer. A number of mass organizations had been created in late 1945 and early 1946 as a part of Communist mobilization politics. The most important of these were the Puk-Chosŏn Chikŏp Tongmaeng (North Korean General Federation of Trade Unions), organized in November 1945, and claiming some 350,000 members; the Puk-Chosŏn Minju Ch'ŏngnyŏn Tongmaeng (North Korean Democratic Youth League), founded on January 17, 1946, with some 500,-000 members and redesignated at Soviet request, having earlier been the Communist Youth League; the Puk-Chosŏn Yŏsŏng Tongmaeng (North Korean Women's League), created in November 1945, with 350,000 members; the Puk-Chosŏn Nongmin Tongmaeng (North Korean Farmers' League), established on January 31, 1946, claiming 800,000 members; and the Cho-Sso Munhwa Hyŏp-hoe (Korea-Soviet Cultural Association), founded in November 1945.[69]

Each of these organizations was itself firmly under Communist control. Their combined membership, even if one makes some allowance for exaggeration and duplication, was nearly 2,000,000, dwarfing the Communist Party alone. With these front groups headed by trusted Party personnel, and coordinated through the National United Front (which had local and provincial branches as well as a central headquarters unit), the Party could manipulate all organizations within the state. It was of crucial importance, of course, to make certain that the non-Communist parties continued to be puppets of the Communists. In the case of the Democratic Party, Communist control was overt after February 1946, as we have noted.[70] Control over the Ch'ŏndogyo Young Friends' Party, the member-

69. For details concerning these organizations, their leadership, and their subsequent development, see Kim Ch'ang-sun, *op. cit.,* pp. 166 ff. Democratic National Front, Secretariat, *Chosŏn haebang nyŏnbo, op. cit.,* pp. 423–429, provides details on the North Korean General Federation of Trade Unions.

70. In theory, all those who by virtue of their class were not eligible for Communist Party membership, yet wished to be members of a party aspiring to "progressive" policies, could join the Democratic Party. It is to be noted that this concept is identical with the attitude of the Chinese Communists toward legitimate united front parties: they were to be instrumentalities whereby the petty bourgeois and bourgeois classes were represented *and* educated to accept class elimination. In practice, of course, it was essential to have a combination of pliant, opportunistic elements and bona fide Communists in key leadership positions.

However, in its origins and during the Cho Man-sik era, the Democratic Party no doubt harbored strong nationalist, anti-Communist elements. Even after the liquidation of Cho and the flight of most non-Communist Democratic Party leaders to the South, some of this sentiment remained. On Oct. 11, 1946, a major riot between elements of the Democratic Party and the Worker Party took place in North P'yŏngan Province; and during the Korean War, there were a number of incidents of defeated North Korean soldiers being attacked by members of the North Korean Democratic Party, as we shall see. Nevertheless, after the removal of Cho, the party leadership was completely in Communist hands.

ship of which was about 95 percent peasant, was effected more subtly. The Communists assiduously wooed party leader Kim Tal-hyŏn, and induced him to accept their guidance, meanwhile keeping "suspicious elements" within the party under close surveillance.[71]

By the spring of 1946, another party had made its appearance upon the North Korean political scene. On February 16, the Yenan group announced the formation of the Sinmin-dang   (New People's Party).[72] As will be recalled, the Yenan faction had previously undertaken organizational activities under their old label, the Korean Independence League. Moreover, a number of their leaders had participated in Party and governmental agencies. Basically, however, the Yenan group continued to maintain itself separately from the Soviet-Kapsan group, as the inauguration of the New People's Party clearly indicated.

The new party immediately attracted to itself a number of middle-class types, including a significant proportion of the better educated elements of North Korea, the so-called intelligentsia. Indeed, during the spring of 1946, a curious political trend developed. The Communist Party of North Korea, now securely under Soviet-Kapsan faction control, was rapidly expanding. As it did so, it claimed to be shifting its social foundations toward the worker-peasant alliance that would qualify it as a true party of the proletariat. The New People's Party, meanwhile, was making smaller gains, but these were among precisely the elements of North Korean society whose cooperation was so essential if unity and modernization

---

71. The Ch'ŏndogyo Ch'ŏng'u-dang, or Heavenly Way Young Friends' Party, was officially founded on Feb. 8, 1946, and because it was based upon a national religion opposed to Christianity (Christians were heavily represented in the original Democratic Party movement), it received less harassment from Communists. Christianity to the Communists meant the likelihood of pro-American sentiment, especially since American missionaries had been instrumental in the Korean Christian movement.

Moreover, since that movement had been one of the pillars of the anti-Japanese nationalist movement, the Christians could not be accused effectively of being pro-Japanese or "national" traitors." One route of attack was to encourage a countermovement based upon an indigenous religion—and that was certainly one reason why the Communists viewed the Ch'ŏndogyo group with tolerance. Thus, Christianity became "a tool of American imperialist aggression" and the Heavenly Way Young Friends' Party a group deserving of "benevolent guidance."

After the Communists had finished remolding the Democratic Party, however, they began to become much more strict with the Ch'ŏndogyo group. Kim Tal-hyŏn, the long-time leader of the movement, according to Kim Ch'ang-sun, was made to spy upon his own party members and report to the Communist Party (p. 165). In the spring of 1948, moreover, a mass arrest of Ch'ŏndogyo followers took place, after evidence appeared that they had been in contact with fellow religionists in the South. Again, as we shall note, during the Korean War, Ch'ŏndogyo supporters took advantage of the situation in many cases to attack Communist Party and military personnel.

72. For details, see Kim Ch'ang-sun, *op. cit.,* pp. 97 ff., and Democratic National Front, Secretariat, *Chosŏn haebang nyŏnbo, op. cit.,* pp. 146–149.

were to be attained: the academicians, writers, scientists, and persons with administrative experience.

Thus, on April 20, Kim Il-sŏng announced that some 1,400 "impure elements" had been screened out of the Party, but that as a result of an intensified recruitment campaign, Party membership had increased from 4,530 in December to a current figure of 26,000.[73] He also remarked that there had been a signal improvement in the social composition of Party members, with the Party having firmly rooted itself now among the workers and farmers. If we can rely upon Communist figures, the first six months of 1946 must have represented a period of feverish organizational activities for both the Yenan group and the Soviet-Kapsan faction. According to official Party records, the New People's Party had 90,000 members in August 1946, while the Korean Communist Party had a membership of 276,000.[74] (It will be recalled that a similar campaign to increase Party membership was taking place in the south at this time.)

The success of the Yenan group, of course, was based partly upon the tolerance of Kim Il-sŏng and his supporters. The Soviet-Kapsan faction wanted to avoid a confrontation with the Yenan faction during this period because it was much more concerned about Pak Hŏn-yŏng and his domestic faction. Consequently, the Yenan group enjoyed considerable freedom in its organizational activities, both before and after the emergence of the New People's Party. (The Yenan group's bargaining power in the north was undoubtedly increased because it had certain roots in the south as well, and the Soviet-Kapsan faction did not want it aligned with Pak.)

In spite of all this, those working within the northern Communist movement were well aware of the jealousies and suspicions of the two overseas factions. For example, Han Chae-dŏk states that he decided to write a story about the Yenan group's revolutionary exploits, to parallel an earlier story about "General" Kim Il-sŏng. He interviewed Kim Tu-bong, but obtained rather meager information; Kim was constantly being interrupted by his son-in-law, who evidently feared that if Kim talked too much he might get into trouble. When Han finally published the story, he entitled it "Three Great Returned Leaders," and featured Kim Il-sŏng, Kim Tu-bong, and Ch'oe Yong-gŏn. Even though he put Kim Il-sŏng first and lavished praise upon him, Han was called to Party headquarters and severely scolded by Kim Yong-bŏm for having placed Kim Tu-bong and Ch'oe Yong-gŏn on the same level with Kim Il-sŏng. Had he featured Mu

73. Kim Il-sŏng, "Concerning Our Party's Past and Its Immediate Tasks," delivered at the Enlarged Executive Committee of the South Hamgyŏng Province Party, April 20, 1946, and reproduced in *Kim Il-sŏng sŏnjip, op. cit.,* Vol. I, 1963 ed., pp. 80–88. (The speech, however, is not included in the 1952 Japanese edition of Kim's works, *Kin Nichisei senshū,* raising some question as to its authenticity.)

74. Center for the Study of Party History, Korean Workers' Party Central Committee, *Chosŏn nodong-dang yŏksa kyojae (Teaching Materials on the History of the Korean Workers' Party),* P'yŏngyang, 1964, p. 185.

Chŏng, Han asserts, he would have been even more strongly reprimanded, since the Kim Il-sŏng faction regarded Mu as a more potent rival because of his extensive military background.[75]

It still remains to explore the reasons why the Yenan group was attracting the better educated elements within North Korea, a fact that could not help but concern the Soviet-Kapsan faction deeply. One major factor was possibly the relatively moderate program espoused by the Yenan group. Just prior to the establishment of their new party, the Yenan group set forth their political platform in detail under their old title, the Korean Independence League.[76] While their proposals did not differ greatly from those of the Communist Party, they tended to be couched in somewhat more moderate language, and to stress nationalist over Marxist terminology. For example, the League platform only called for the outright confiscation of properties belonging to the Japanese and to "national traitors," so as to destroy "the economic foundation of the Japanese imperialist forces." Throughout the program, moreover, the emphasis was upon the unity and cooperation of all classes in the building of a democratic republic marked by complete independence, social justice, and full political democracy.

These differences did not escape comment. Paek Nam-un, the leader of the New People's Party in South Korea (where the party was also established), was sharply attacked by the southern Communist Party for his "social democratic" views. Paek, a Japanese-trained Marxian economist, came under assault in early 1946, shortly after the formation of the new party, with the charge that his theories were "unscientific and antirevolutionary." [77] In a pamphlet entitled "The Road for the Korean Nation," Paek had argued that the nationalist and Communist forces within Korea, in spite of certain other differences, shared such basic goals as those of national liberation, democracy, and a democratic economy. Therefore, they should cooperate as equals at this stage, forming a genuine bourgeois-proletariat coalition, a "united new democracy." [78] The Seoul Communists

75. Han Chae-dŏk, op. cit., pp. 225–227.

76. For the full text, see "The Political Platform of the Korean Independence League," Sanŏp Nodong Shibo (Industrial Labor News), No. 1, January 1946, p. 80, and Democratic National Front, Secretariat, Chosŏn haebang nyŏnbo, op. cit., pp. 148–149. On this occasion, the full slate of officers and Executive Committee members were given as follows: President, Kim Tu-bong; Vice Presidents, Ch'oe Ch'ang-ik and Han Pin; Head, Organization Department, Yi Yu-min; Head, Propaganda Department, Kim Min-san; Head, Secretariat, Pyŏn Tong-yun; Head, General Affairs Office, Chang Ch'ŏl. Ibid., p. 149.

77. See Yi Ki-su, "I Renounce Mr. Paek Nam-un's United New Democracy," in Shin Ch'ŏnji (New Universe), June 1946, pp. 44–53, 117. The author was identified as a member of the Kwahakja Tongmaeng (The Scientists' League), a Communist social-science organization in Seoul.

78. For a full exposé of his views, see Paek Nam-un's pamphlet, Chosŏn minjok ui chinro (The Road for the Korean Nation), Seoul, 1946.

regarded Paek as prepared to risk true equality with non-Communist organizations rather than insisting upon Communist dominance. This, of course, was not a new issue among Communists, whether in Korea or elsewhere. It had been a point of debate within the Chinese Communist movement, for instance, for more than two decades.

However, the differences between the published programs of the New People's Party and the Communist Party were subtle at best. Probably the appeal of the Yenan group to the North Korean intelligentsia was more a result of less tangible but more significant differences in the general outlook and social composition of the two overseas factions. The Soviet-Kapsan faction in this period represented a group composed mainly of young former guerrilla fighters with limited education, heavy dependence upon Russian power, and scant regard for Korean nationalism. Indeed, the charge was frequently made that the Communists had collected a significantly large number of bullies, ne'er-do-wells, and urban toughs. Although the Yenan group had been nurtured by the Chinese Communist Party, it contained many individuals who were not doctrinaire Communists. This reflected on the earlier period when a number of well-educated Koreans became involved with the leftist movement as a means of promoting aspirations that were essentially no more than nationalist.[79] Such individuals would have a much greater appeal to those whom the Communists called "petty bourgeois" than would men of Kim Il-sŏng's type.

However, there is another factor that cannot be ignored. It is entirely possible that a number of people who were non-Communist or even anti-Communist joined the New People's Party in an effort to give themselves political protection. Presumably, if one did not wish to join the Communist Party and realized that no benefit would be derived from Democratic Party membership, NPP membership did afford some protective coloration in an era increasingly controlled by the Communists.

The Establishment of the North Korean Workers Party

The New People's Party was to remain an independent entity for only a few months. By the end of August 1946, it had merged with the North Korean Communist Party to form the Puk-Chosŏn Nodong-dang (North Korean Workers' Party).[80] In the south, after great trouble, a similar merger was finally effected in November. Thus, by the end of 1946, there was a single leftist Party in both North and South Korea. In both cases, moreover, the Communists were the dominant force within the Party; in the north, indeed, they were in effect the sole force. Finally,

79. See Chapter III of this study.
80. Kim Il-sŏng used the term "North Korean Communist Party organization" at the December 1945 meeting, but we do not know the exact date when the "North Korean Bureau" was renamed the North Korean Communist Party.

within the Communist movement itself, authority and power were steadily gravitating to North Korea, and in North Korea to the Soviet-Kapsan faction. Some of these events will now be examined in more detail.

According to official Communist accounts, the creation of the North Korean Workers' Party was undertaken on the initiative of the New People's Party.[81] On July 23, 1946, that party sent a letter to the North Korean Communist Party proposing the union. On the following day, the Central Committee having discussed the matter and having "agreed in principle," notified the New People's Party that its proposal had been accepted. On July 28, a three-day conference of the two parties' Enlarged Central Committee opened. Kim Yong-bŏm presided, and Kim Il-sŏng and Kim Tu-bong delivered the two key speeches. A leadership group of seven was chosen: Kim Il-sŏng, Kim Tu-bong, Kim Yong-bŏm, Ch'oe Ch'ang-ik, Hŏ Ka-i, Yi Tong-hwa, and Myŏng Hui-jo. The conference concluded by recommending "unanimously" that unification be speedily effected; both party organizations should be alerted to the decision through local and provincial meetings, and the other necessary preparations should be made.[82]

One month later, on August 29, a three-day Conference to Initiate the North Korean Workers' Party opened in P'yŏngyang with 801 out of a possible 818 chosen delegates present, together with 200 observers. One of its first acts was to elect Marshal Stalin honorary president. The reading of congratulatory messages and telegrams followed, including those from other "democratic" parties. Thirty-one individuals were selected as the conference leaders.[83]

Pak Il-u opened the second day by reporting on the credentials of the delegates.[84] Kim Il-sŏng and Kim Tu-bong then delivered major addresses endorsing the merger, which was immediately approved. The draft platform was presented by Ch'oe Ch'ang-ik and ratified. On the third day, with Chu Nyŏng-ha presiding, T'ae Sŏng-su outlined the proposed organization of the new Party and Kim Yong-bŏm presented the Party regulations, both being approved. One of the last acts was the affirmation of a

81. For one contemporary official account, see Kim Chu-hyŏn, "The Birth of the North Korean Workers' Party," *Kŭlloja* (*The Worker*), No. 1, Oct. 1946, pp. 35–48. The basic factual data contained in our account are drawn from this source.

82. *Ibid.,* pp. 41–42.

83. The thirty-one leaders composing the "Leaders' Group," in the order presented in *Kŭlloja,* were as follows: Kim Il-sŏng, Kim Tu-bong, Kim Yong-bŏm, Ch'oe Ch'ang-ik, Hŏ Ka-i, Kim Ch'aek, Pak Ch'ang-sik, Kim Ch'ang-man, Kim Kyo-yŏng, Pak Il-u, Yi Tong-hwa, Pak Chŏng-ae, Mu Chŏng, Myŏng Hui-jo, Yim Hae, Kim Won-sŏng, T'ae Sŏng-su, Han Sŏl-ya, Chang Sun-myŏng, Kim Chae-uk, O Ki-sŏp, Chu Nyŏng-ha, Chŏng Tu-hyŏn, Hong Sŏng-ik, O Kyŏng-ch'ŏn, Ch'oe Chong-hwan, Kim Il, Kim Ch'an, Kwak Kun-il, Yun Kong-hŭm, and Kim Yong-t'ae.

84. Pak reported that 64 percent of the delegates present had been either confined or imprisoned, 263 of them having spent six months or more in prison. The total period of imprisonment, he announced, came to 1,087 years, *Ibid.,* p. 43.

Central Committee of 43 members, 29 from the North Korean Communist Party, 14 from the New People's Party. An Organization Committee of 13 members and an Inspection Committee of 11 members were also appointed. The meeting ended with a speech by Kim Il-sŏng, followed by five final (and revealing) cheers: Long life to the democracy and complete independence of Korea! Long life to the Democratic National United Front! Long life to the Korean Democratic Republic! Long life to our leader, General Kim Il-sŏng! Long life to the benefactor and friend of the Korean nation, the great Marshal Stalin! [85]

At the first meeting of the Central Committee, held on August 31 before the conclusion of the Initiation Conference, an interesting development occurred. Kim Tu-bong was elected chairman, with Kim Il-sŏng and Chu Nyŏng-ha being elected vice-chairmen.[86] Five members of the Political Bureau were chosen: Kim Tu-bong, Kim Il-sŏng, Chu Nyŏng-ha, Hŏ Ka-i, and Ch'oe Ch'ang-ik. It is to be noted that two of these men were from the Soviet-Kapsan faction, two from the Yenan faction, and the fifth, Chu, was an old domestic faction man who had moved close to Kim Il-sŏng. The 13-man Presidium included the above five together with Kim Ch'aek, T'ae Sŏng-su, Kim Kyo-yŏng, Pak Chŏng-ae, Pak Il-u, Kim Ch'ang-man, Pak Hyo-sam, and O Ki-sŏp. Once again, a careful balance was maintained, with a slight edge given to the Kimists. T'ae Sŏng-su was selected as editor of the new Party organ, *Kŭlloja* (The Worker) and orders were given for a daily newspaper, *Nodong Sinmun* (The Workers' News), to be established as a Party organ, with each provincial branch publishing

---

85. *Ibid.,* p. 47.

86. *Ibid.,* p. 48.

According to Kim Ch'ang-sun, the inside story of Kim Tu-bong's selection as chairman was as follows: At the meeting, Pak Pyŏng-sŏ, a Kim Il-sŏng man in charge of agitprop in the North P'yŏngan Province Party, asserted that Comrade Kim Il-sŏng clearly and rightfully should be chairman of the Workers' Party. His strong remarks provoked dismay among Sinmin-dang members. A Russian colonel, Ignatiev, who apparently was a Romanenko office representative, scribbled a message which was sent to the speaker's rostrum, and the meeting was temporarily adjourned. In the interim, Russian authorities advised the Kim faction that the Sinmin-dang delegates should not be intimidated and frightened at the start of the union, and that there was no necessity for pushing Kim Il-sŏng to the fore at this time.

It was then decided that someone whom the Yenan faction trusted should be chosen to announce that there was no absolute necessity for Kim Il-sŏng being chairman of the Party. O Ki-sŏp, relatively well known and liked by the Yenan group, was chosen and delivered his speech on the 29th, to great applause from the Yenan people. According to Kim Ch'ang-sun, the Russians were really worried that in the balloting Kim Il-sŏng would poll less than 100 percent of the votes while Kim Tu-bong would receive a unanimous vote, since all Communist Party members had been instructed to vote for him, whereas some Sinmin-dang members might refuse to vote for Kim Il-sŏng. Thus, it was decided that Kim Il-sŏng himself would nominate Kim Tu-bong as chairman, and then Kim Il-sŏng would receive a unanimous vote as one of the two vice-chairmen. See Kim Ch'ang-sun, *op. cit.,* pp. 98–101.

an edition (the provincial name was added to the title in each instance). Kim Yong-bŏm was elected chairman of the Inspection Committee, and Chin Pan-su vice-chairman.

Thus was established the Party that was to guide North Korea for the decades ahead. Thus, too, was established the supremacy of Kim Il-sŏng, the real leader of the Party despite the tactical compromise on the chairmanship. But the above account, taken mainly from official sources, is probably false in one major respect. Despite the Communist assertion that the merger was undertaken at the initiative of the New People's Party, the likelihood is overwhelming that it was in fact planned and executed by the Soviet-Kapsan faction, using maximum pressure upon any who resisted.

Why, indeed, should the New People's Party have wished to merge with Kim's faction in the north—or with Pak's group in the south? Its membership, to be sure, was much smaller than that claimed by the Communist Party, but in the north at least it was also of much higher quality. There can be no doubt, moreover, that many People's Party members hated, feared, or had contempt for the North Korean Communist Party. Indeed, Kim Tu-bong alluded to this fact when he chided some of his supporters for committing "right-wing errors" in connection with the merger. The following passage is from his report to the August conference:

> Specifically, there are those [NPP members] who have said: "The reason behind the merger is that the Communist Party has made mistakes in the past whereas the policies of the New People's Party have been correct"; or, "There is a merger because many ignorant people have been gathered in the Communist Party while the more educated people have come into the New People's Party, and hence the merger permits learning [from the New People's Party]"; or, "Since the Communist Party is strong and the New People's Party is relatively weak, there is a danger that all of the official party positions will be taken over by the Communist Party when the merger takes place"; or, "Although the members of the New People's Party are being admitted [to the Workers' Party] at present, there will be a scrutiny of Party members in the not too distant future and a large-scale purge will follow." [87]

Kim Tu-bong cited these "errors" in order to refute them (an action he must have bitterly regretted a decade later), but in so doing he revealed the unrest that evidentally permeated the ranks of his comrades and followers. In an earlier speech, at the Enlarged Committee meetings in July, he had indicated some of the concrete reasons for the merger. The

87. See the full text of Kim Tu-bong's Report at the Initiation Conference of the North Korean Workers' Party, *Kŭlloja* (*The Worker*), No. 1, Oct. 1946, p. 28. Incidentally, despite the fact that Kim Tu-bong was elected chairman of the Central Executive Committee of the Party, his speech *followed* that of Kim Il-sŏng in the first issue of *Kŭlloja*, the Party organ.

New People's Party, he asserted, had developed very rapidly, despite its short history. But this was not merely because of its own strength; it was also due to "the great assistance of the Red Army and the ceaseless aid of the Korean Communist Party." The program of the NPP, Kim argued, closely approached the minimal program of the Communist Party, which was the program for that particular stage of the revolution. Even though this fell far short of the maximal Communist program, it had permitted extensive cooperation with the Communists through the Democratic National United Front. However, some friction between the two parties had developed, especially at the lower levels. Both parties had defects at the organizational level. The Communist Party, for instance, had not been able to mobilize the intelligentsia in any comprehensive manner. Thus, at the present "bourgeois democratic" stage of the revolution, especially when they had the Democratic National United Front, to have two separate parties with nearly identical current platforms not only produced friction but also dissipated democratic strength and produced a shortage of party officials.[88]

Kim Il-sŏng, on the same occasion, set forth similar themes on a broader canvas. The basic task, he asserted, was to establish a unified, democratic, independent Korea as quickly as possible. That required the purging of all "pro-Japanese, fascist, and reactionary forces" and the application of "fundamental democratic reforms *throughout the nation*"; for these purposes, North Korea would be *"the base and the main force."* (Italics ours.) This required the creation of a mass party, uniting workers, farmers, and the intelligentsia. Whoever won over the masses would become the victor. Under these conditions, the merger of the North Korean Communist Party and the New People's Party was a necessary and essential measure.[89]

In his two speeches at the Initiation Conference, Kim Il-sŏng amplified these basic themes, adding some further details.[90] He began by insisting passionately that "today's Korea" was not "the Korea of any other nation," but a country being constructed by the Korean people themselves and ruled by them. If this was logical oratory, it was also a response to those who charged the Communists with being Soviet puppets. And Kim sought mightily to throw that charge back at his opponents. There was a new national enemy, he asserted, and a new group of running dogs, national traitors who wanted to sell Korea out as a colony of monopoly capitalism. This reactionary force, he charged, nesting in South Korea

88. From the July 28–30 Enlarged Committee meeting of the two parties, as reported by Kim Chu-hyŏn, *op. cit.*, p. 40.

89. *Ibid.*, p. 39.

90. Kim Il-sŏng, "All for the Preparation of our Democratic Strength," complete text in *Kŭlloja* (*The Worker*), No. 1, Oct. 1946, pp. 7–18; and Kim Il-sŏng, "Conclusions on Questions and Discussion," *ibid.*, pp. 30–34.

under American military rule, had joined up with Americans to seize sovereignty from the Korean people.

Kim then proceeded to paint a most gruesome picture of the American occupation and life in South Korea. Once again, grasping some actual event, he would distort it beyond all recognition in most cases. Thus, thousands of Korean patriots were rotting in jails; democratic parties and social organizations were being destroyed by terrorists and reactionaries; patriotic scholars and students were being expelled from schools and the schools themselves gradually closed down; all lands belonging to the Japanese had become American property [sic]; workers were being slaughtered by airplanes, tanks, and machine guns just because they had participated in demonstrations; and for merely advocating a labor movement, one worker had received a prison sentence of eight years!

The technique had its merits. Even if exaggeration were suspected, or some element of disbelief were initially present, constant repetition ultimately produced considerable acceptance of these horrendous charges. At that point, one's own lot might not seem quite so bad.

Kim reiterated the importance of working through a strong united front. But to make this technique effective, a unified, firmly disciplined party of the masses had to exist. The Workers' Party therefore had to be developed as "a combat unit of the working masses and their vanguard." Its tasks were formidable. "Only if we completely liberate South Korea," Kim said flatly in his concluding remarks before the Initiation Conference, "can there be any full independence for Korea." [91] Thus, the Party had to strengthen the North Korean Provisional People's Committee, the symbol of a true people's government, and struggle to establish the sovereignty of the people throughout Korea through the local people's committees. Similarly, the reforms begun in North Korea had to be consolidated and extended throughout the nation.

Such assignments, Kim insisted, demanded not only a mass party but one capable of enforcing iron discipline. To read these speeches carefully, particularly as they refer to party organization and discipline, is to understand quickly why many of those not of Kim's faction had deep qualms about the merger. The words were those of a determined, ruthless man, and one who found the harsh language of military command a natural mode of expression. "To achieve party unity and a lofty discipline," proclaimed Kim, there had to be "a merciless struggle against all with opposing inclinations." Spies and other subversives would certainly seek to infiltrate the Party. To prevent this, and to exterminate all sectarian struggles, everything had to be sacrificed for the great cause of "democratic independence." To turn the Party into a powerful combat unit, it would be necessary to struggle constantly to maintain Party purity, unity, and iron discipline. That did not mean that it was correct to advocate any massive purge at

91. *Ibid.*, p. 30.

this time. But neither was it possible to abandon the fight to maintain the Party free from "impure elements."

Were these reassuring words to those of the NPP who feared Kim and his faction?

Kim was also extremely frank in discussing the relationship between the Communists and the Workers' Party. Some "left deviationists" did not understand the requirements of the times, he asserted. It was incumbent upon all Communists to aid in establishing a mass party that took in a broad range of people, a party going beyond any narrow class lines. Only by taking this road would democracy succeed and Korean independence be attained—and only with the complete independence of Korea could there be a victory of Marxism-Leninism in the country.

As to whether Marxism-Leninism should become the guiding ideology of the Workers' Party, Kim stated, it simply was not a problem to be discussed at the Conference. However, he did concede that just because a Communist became a member of the Workers' Party, it did not mean that he had abandoned Marxism-Leninism. On the contrary, such a Communist was acting in accordance with the needs of the present stage of the Korean Revolution, and hence becoming a better Marxist-Leninist. To oppose the establishment of the Workers' Party on the grounds that it implied a surrender to the New People's Party was left-wing deviation. It was right-wing deviation, however, to abandon Marxism-Leninism, weaken inner-Party discipline, and "bring all sorts of elements into the party" under the pretext that the Workers' Party itself was a national united front.

At first glance, this is all very curious. Was the Workers' Party intended to be a Communist Party or not? Did Kim Il-sŏng regard the New People's Party as a non-Communist party and, if so, was Kim Tu-bong himself prepared to accept that designation? To appreciate the true, complex situation, one must draw upon contemporary developments in Eastern Europe, and subsequent events in North Vietnam, with the latter being especially relevant. Kim and his supporters most certainly intended that the Workers' Party be the supreme vehicle of their movement, and they fully intended to guide, shape, and control it at all times. They regarded the New People's Party as primarily bourgeois or, more accurately, petty bourgeois in character. Even its leaders they viewed for the most part as inferior Communists, if Communists at all. These problems, however, could be handled in time. Those who could not be reformed could be removed.

Meanwhile, it was essential for those who considered themselves identified with the Communist movement in some measure, whether on the domestic or the international front, to be united into a single organization. This was particularly important in view of the factional troubles that had plagued the Korean Communist movement since its inception. A single organization could develop a coherent command structure, hammer out a uniform line of policy, and reduce duplication and waste of scarce human and material resources. To accomplish such tasks, however, this organization had to be, or become, a Communist Party in all but name. It would be fatal if the Workers' Party were confused with the Democratic National United Front. Both were necessary, but the former had to have the centralized authority, iron discipline, and "correct line" that would preserve its status as a vanguard party. On the one hand, this required an initial liberality, for both tactical and strategic reasons. The petty bourgeois elements in the New People's Party were indeed being subverted, as they had to be. They should not be frightened too badly in the bargain. Some of them, indeed, would be salvageable. And a mass party had to take in the masses, even if they knew little about Marxism-Leninism.

Liberality in these matters, however, had to be coupled with a very hard line regarding Party organization and the requirements of the future. At all costs, the *ultimate purity* of the Party had to be safeguarded. In essence, this meant that the role and power of "the critical elite"—be it only the supreme leader—had to be protected. From this context, concepts like "democratic centralism" and "iron discipline" drew their inner meaning. A rigorous training program for large numbers of new cadres, under the supervision of Party leadership, was also of supreme importance. The next generation, properly trained, could perform tasks impossible for those scarred by the colonial era. Meanwhile, periodic inspections of an intensive nature would take place within the Party, at both mass and elite levels. Those whose initial weaknesses had not been corrected, those who had betrayed the Party and its principles, those who had failed in the role assigned them would be purged. (More accurately, these would constitute the justifications for all purges.)

If these were the real motives of Kim Il-sŏng and his Soviet mentors, those of Kim Tu-bong are still more difficult to fathom. As we have noted earlier, this man had had a long career as a radical nationalist and proto-Communist, in a pattern not dissimilar to that of Yi Tong-hwi earlier. In his quest for material and political aid, he had gravitated from the Kuomintang to the Chinese Communist Party. One strongly suspects that Kim Tu-bong was less ideologue than activist, that he yearned for top power, felt himself entitled to it and resented having to pay homage to a man over twenty years his junior. But Kim Il-sŏng had an army behind him, and Kim Tu-bong did not. Did the latter believe that his personal prestige, the experience of his key followers, and the general caliber of his supporters would preserve his bargaining power at a high level, and even give him coequal power? It is not clear.

Certainly, Kim Tu-bong's public speeches at this point were those of a man who seemed to have committed himself wholeheartedly to the Communist cause—as defined by Stalin and Kim Il-sŏng. In explaining the role of the New People's Party, for example, he was to assert that while the party had emphasized various policies aiming at Korean independence and democracy, such an emphasis accorded with its proper historical role, and there was nothing in its platform that represented "the interests of the bourgeois or petty bourgeois class." [92] Marshal Stalin, he proclaimed, has said that, at the appropriate time, one must grasp the special link in the chain of a total process whereby one can get hold of the entire chain. Such was the thrust of their present strategy. Opportunist or patriot, "good" or "bad" Communist (and probably all elements were present), Kim Tu-bong had enlisted for the duration.

The establishment of the South Korean Workers' Party was far more painful. In the absence of the Soviet army, the leftists of the south were much less coordinated and disciplined; still less were they capable of swift, monolithic action. In this sense, of course, the southern Left was much less restricted than its northern counterpart. No higher authority was promoting Pak Hŏn-yŏng in the manner in which the Russians were now promoting Kim Il-sŏng, and while their orders could and did have a major effect upon the Communist Party of South Korea (witness the trusteeship issue), the Russians could not provide the constant surveillance and supervision over Party organization, or deal decisively with the whole political spectrum. It was probably for this reason that they came to feel the southern Communist movement had to be subordinate to that of the north.

Basic Trends After One Year of Liberation

By the fall of 1946, three broad trends directly involving the Korean Communist movement had been clearly established. First, deepening American-Russian disagreement, in Korea and elsewhere, made the prospects for Korean unification look dim. Despite the complexities of the quarrel over Korea, the issue boiled down to a single, simple question: Which forces, Communist or non-Communist, would control a unified state? Since there was no easy way to compromise that issue, the impasse remained and the lines grew more and more rigid.

Second, the main outlines of Communist policy for North Korea had already been drawn, and an embryonic North Korean state already existed. Under the rubric of a "managed bourgeois democratic revolution," the Communists had cultivated three separate but closely related instrumentalities of power. At the governmental level, the technique of "people's committees" had been widely applied. From the hamlet or ward, through the city, prefecture, and province, to the "national" level, a hierarchical structure of People's Committees operated or supervised the administration. Through this system popular participation could take place on a wide scale and be adequately controlled at the same time. Applying the standard Communist principle of democratic centralism, and distinguishing between "people" and "enemies of the people," the Communist leaders could

92. Kim Tu-bong's Report at the Initiation Conference, *Kŭlloja, op. cit.,* p. 26.

regulate those who participated in the "new democracy," guide their subsequent actions, and, if necessary, replace them efficiently. At the very top of this political pyramid stood the Soviet command, constantly counseling its protégés behind the silk screen.

To underwrite this administrative structure, the Communists sought to mobilize the masses by means of a wide range of political and social organizations—unions, youth groups, women's organizations, and "democratic" parties. The technique was to make certain that each of these groups was led and guided by Communists under the discipline of the Party, and unified through the Democratic National United Front. In these techniques lay the essence of united front politics, Communist style.

The final and chief instrumentality of power was, of course, the Communist Party itself. The current task was to unify the Party while at the same time advancing it qualitatively and quantitatively. Some unification had been achieved, but at the cost of accepting some balance of power among the factions. "Unfit" and "impure" elements were therefore being weeded out. At the same time, vast numbers of new members were being admitted. Thus, by October 1946 a Party that had claimed only 26,000 members in December 1945, and 165,000 immediately after the merger, now listed its membership at 400,000.

The third trend much in evidence by late 1946 was the increasing dominance of North over South Korea insofar as the Communist movement was concerned; and within North Korea, the continued ascendancy of the Soviet-Kapsan faction led by Kim Il-sŏng. The south still had a formidable Communist force and a resourceful leader. By 1947, the South Korean Workers' Party claimed some 375,000 members, and Pak Hŏn-yŏng would probably have won a popular vote among Korean Communists, could such a vote have been held. But Pak was divorced from any protector, and his organization had begun to face serious problems. Key leaders were being forced to move north, where they were of course entirely dependent upon the existing power structure.[93] That structure still

93. Kim Ch'ang-sun (*op. cit.,* pp. 116–117) puts the problem facing Pak and his faction as follows: As the Communists in South Korea got into trouble with authorities or were defeated in the political arena, they fled to the north. But Pak Hŏn-yŏng barely managed to find jobs for his followers there—all of them, including Pak, were hangers-on, dependent upon Kim Il-sŏng's "natives." The North Korean Workers' Party accorded them treatment which was at best "rough and ready," if not downright rude and coarse. Naturally, the South Korean Workers' Party members were dissatisfied, noting the shabby treatment given their leader. But if they complained to the North Koreans, they were advised in private to change their membership from the southern to the northern party.

Kim continues: It was no secret that Kim Il-sŏng and Pak Hŏn-yŏng did not get along well with each other, and if there were those among the South Korean Workers' Party members who angrily shouted their praise of Pak, letting off steam—usually when they were drunk—they were then accused of engaging in a factional struggle. In this situation, of course, there were "opportunists" and "turncoats" among the

rested upon a carefully prepared equilibrium in which the Soviet-Kapsan and Yenan factions shared key posts, with the domestic faction, currently downgraded, securing fewer top offices, and those for its more "trustworthy" members only. Despite this equilibrium, however, it was now "General" Kim Il-sŏng who received the accolades usually reserved for a supreme leader, and it was his faction that held the preponderance of power at the crucial levels, both within the Party and within the governmental structure.

The Creation of the Democratic People's Republic of Korea

It is in the light of these trends that we must examine closely the political events leading up to the establishment, on September 9, 1948, of the so-called Democratic People's Republic of Korea. During this period, the Communists were actively engaged in three major political tasks: institution building, mass mobilization, and Party consolidation. Each of these activities must now be explored in a somewhat larger context.

Nearly four months before the North Korean Workers' Party was established, the Joint American-Soviet Commission had adjourned on May 8, 1946, completely unable to reach any agreement on procedures for Korean unification. The chasm between the Americans and the Russians had been signaled by an exchange of statements in March, on the eve of the Commission meetings. On March 11, General Hodge outlined the aims of the United States delegation. In so doing, he also set forth the American concept of democracy.

First and foremost, it has been the object of the American Forces to establish and perpetuate the freedoms of speech, assembly, religion and press in Korea. These freedoms are not mere words to be used to gain political favor. They represent principles on which any genuine democracy must be based and are as old as democracy itself. Furthermore, they are absolute and not relative or subject to exceptions. They apply to all democratic persons, all democratic schools of thought, all democratic parties, no matter how small their following or whether or not their programs correspond to the ideas of the existing authorities. Thus in South Korea it has been the American policy to permit all democratic groups, whether moderates or extremists, capitalists or communists, to establish their own parties, hold their own meetings, broadcast their own speeches, propagate their own ideas and philosophies and publish their own newspapers without censorship, restriction, or special privilege. These freedoms are basic in the American idea of democracy. They are also what we believe the vast majority of the Korean people want, and it is what

---

South Korean Party members—those who decided to join the winning side. Thus, Pak was losing men rapidly, and his future began to look dim. While this description probably had even more validity for the period from 1948 to 1950, the trends were in evidence at this time.

the American delegation of the Joint Commission wants to help the Koreans to attain throughout their entire country.[94]

Hodge went on to assert that while it was not the purpose of the American delegation to bring a specific party to power, and while the programs of the various South Korean parties differed considerably from those of the leading American parties, nevertheless the American delegation did most seriously intend to prevent "the domination of Korea by small minorities, no matter how vocal and well organized they are or how energetic they may be in their political activities." [95]

This statement represented a basic challenge to the Russians, both in terms of their application of "democracy" to the north and with respect to their current intentions. Setting aside the niceties of diplomatic exchange, there was a certain irony in Hodge's concluding paragraph, given the thrust of the statement. Hodge noted that Russia was another great nation that had fought for Korean liberation, a signatory to the Moscow Agreement, and a country "greatly interested in making Korea an independent democratic nation." "Therefore," he continued, "it is safe to assume that the two delegations will work together harmoniously and in a truly cooperative effort to accomplish the aims expressed in that agreement."

Almost nothing in the realm of international relations at the moment was less safe to assume. Colonel General T. F. Shtikov, head of the Soviet delegation to the Commission, responded with a statement on March 20, the opening day of the meetings. Naturally, he saw no problems in the Soviet position: "The Soviet people warmly support this right [independence and a free way of life] of the Korean people. The Soviet Union has always championed and will always champion their self-determination and the free existence of any nation, without exception." [96] Indeed, continued Shtikov, the Korean people had already formed their own democratic parties, public organizations, and people's committees as organs of democratic self-government. However, certain serious difficulties stood in the way of spreading democratization to the whole of the Korean people, namely, "the furious resistance of reactionary and anti-democratic groups and certain elements whose object it is to undermine the work of creating and firmly establishing a democratic system in Korea." The future provisional democratic government of Korea, asserted Shtikov, had to be created on the basis of a wide unification of all the democratic parties and organizations, in accordance with the Moscow Agreement. He added an

94. "Aims of the United States Delegation: Statement by Lt. Gen. John R. Hodge, Head of the U. S. Delegation, Joint American-Soviet Commission, March 11, 1946," as reproduced in McCune and Grey, *op. cit.*, pp. 276–278 (at pp. 276–277).
95. *Ibid.*, p. 278.
96. "Aims of the Soviet Delegation: Statement by Col. Gen. T. F. Shtikov, Head of the Soviet Delegation, Joint American-Soviet Commission, March 20, 1946," reproduced in *ibid.*, pp. 279–281 (at p. 279).

interesting final note: "The Soviet Union has a keen interest in Korea being a true democratic and independent country, friendly to the Soviet Union, so that in the future it will not become a base for an attack on the Soviet Union." [97]

Seven weeks later, the Joint Commission adjourned sine die, never having gotten beyond an acrimonious debate over which parties and social organizations should be considered "democratic" and therefore eligible for consultation on future Korean institutions. With the Commission deadlocked, the United States decided to create the South Korean Interim Legislative Assembly to replace the appointive Democratic Council that had been established in February. In August, the rules governing the new Assembly were promulgated; in October and November, the elections were held; and the opening sessions of the full Assembly got under way in December. It is against this background that events in North Korea have to be viewed.

By the beginning of September 1946, the northern Communists had created a unified Party, at least formally, by establishing the NKWP. United front politics could be pursued by means of the DNUF. Thus, in technical terms at least, they were prepared to match any efforts at institution-building in the south.

On September 5, 1946, scarcely a week after the NKWP had been officially inaugurated, and only two weeks after the announcement from the south about the forthcoming Legislative Assembly, a decree was issued in the name of the Provisional People's Committee of North Korea calling for elections on November 3 of representatives to municipal, prefectural, and provincial People's Committees. These elections, it should be noted, were timed to coincide with the establishment of the Assembly in the south —surely no accident. The Communists were launching a two-pronged offensive. On the one hand, existing Communist institutions of government were to be legitimized by "democratic" elections. On the other, similar legitimization efforts in the south were to be met by every possible form of disruption, including violence.

It is interesting to compare American and Soviet institution-building efforts. There were some similarities, but a great many more differences. In one sense, the Americans had decided to begin the fashioning of representative institutions by starting at the top, with the creation of a Legislative Assembly drawn from throughout the south, whereas the Russians had decreed that the first elections would apply to local institutions. To be sure, the Assembly elections as structured by American authorities involved a series of indirect elections, and thus bore some resemblance to the Soviet pattern. In the two situations, however, there were some profound differences. The Soviet institutional pattern had already been imposed upon North Korea, at least in skeleton form, and no one could doubt that it was

97. *Ibid.*, p. 280.

a pattern easier to impose than that of Western-style democracy. In the north, the power structure at the top was now comparatively well established, and the lines of authority, both foreign and indigenous, were clear. The task was therefore the relatively simple one of legitimizing the existing system, using the familiar techniques of Soviet-style elections and so-called democratic centralism. Meanwhile, personnel could be shifted within the system as the situation required. In the south, however, no institutional pattern had yet been imposed and the political situation was relatively fluid, with the power structure at the top, except for the American military command itself, still unformed, and deep fissures both within the indigenous leadership and between that leadership and the Americans. Under the circumstances, legitimization was undoubtedly more necessary in the south —and also much harder to achieve.

As might have been expected, the Communists of the north took their first election very seriously. The electoral provisions were closely modeled after those current in the Soviet Union, as was to be expected. The right to nominate candidates was given to all "democratic" parties, public organizations, and societies registered by the provincial People's Committees. The number of representatives to be chosen was proportional to the density of population within specified territorial units. Factory, school, or union electoral units, such as existed in the Soviet Union, were not created. Workers' Party leaders announced that all of their candidates would be "jointly nominated" with and through the United Front. Thus, the voters were confronted with an official Front candidate for each office, often the only candidate. Meanwhile, the Party had launched a national movement for "ideological enlightenment" via the Front. Propaganda workers, usually headed by Communist cadres, were sent throughout the countryside, and in each district so-called Election Propaganda Rooms were set up (later, they became Democratic Propaganda Rooms).[98]

The November 3 election results were widely hailed by Communist leaders. According to official statistics, 99.6 percent of the registered voters participated, and the United Front elected 97 percent of its nominees for provincial committees, 96.9 percent for county committees, and 95.4 percent for municipal committees. A total of 3,459 representatives were elected, and of these, 1,102 were Workers' Party members, 351 were members of the Democratic Party, 253 were Ch'ŏndogyo members, and 1,753 were members of no party.[99]

A socioeconomic breakdown of the elected representatives is interesting, especially when compared with the situation before the election.[100]

98. See Chosŏn t'ongsa, op. cit., Vol. III, p. 67.
99. Ibid., p. 68.
100. Ibid., pp. 68–69. See also Philip Rudolph, North Korea's Political and Economic Structure, New York, 1959, p. 15.

TABLE 20
Elections of Nov. 3, 1946, Socioeconomic Categories
(in percent)

Category	1946 Elections	Pre-1946 Election Period
Worker	14.5	5.7
Peasant	36.3	71.8
Office Worker	30.6	15.8
Intellectual	9.1	—
Merchant	4.3	4.6
Entrepreneur	2.1	2.1
Clergyman	2.7	—
Former Landowner	0.4	—
TOTAL	100.0	100.0
(Women	13.1)	

SOURCE: *Chosŏn t'ongsa, op. cit.*, Vol. III, pp. 30-31.

These categories, which are from Communist sources, are not sufficiently precise to allow a detailed analysis. But some features are worthy
of note. Slightly over 50 percent of those elected were peasants and
workers—a sign of progress for the much heralded worker-peasant alliance.
Peasants, to be sure, outnumbered workers nearly three to one. However,
this was a much smaller peasant margin than before the election, and gave
these "workers" representation at least proportional to their numerical
strength. Presumably, the "office worker" category included those holding
public and party office—those whose occupation was that of functionary,
official, or politician. This category was significantly high. Only the farmers
were underrepresented on the basis of their actual numbers in the society—
that is, if the sex ratio is not considered.

It is interesting to compare and contrast the results of the Communist elections with those in South Korea. Unquestionably, the northern
elections replicated the actual socioeconomic composition of Korean society
more accurately. Indeed, such replication was an objective, and one can
be certain that the Communist leaders worked diligently to fashion a
"scientific" slate of nominees. To be sure, that slate was somewhat weighted
against the peasant majority and in favor of the Party elite who had to
manipulate the system. The Communists, however, could operate satisfactorily at this level with a minority. They could also afford to allot a
sizable number of posts to the uninitiated. This was possible because the
Communist political structure was designed to be controlled from the top,
by means of a cadre system extending downward into all echelons of the
organization. Moreover, the Party treated the lower-echelon People's Committees as instrumentalities for the execution of policy, not as policy-
making bodies in any basic sense. Similarly, the Congress was a ratifying,

not a decision-making body. Hence, it was essential only that the command structure be zealously guarded, not that talent and expertise be widely tapped. Of course, in some cases the uninitiated might be amenable to instruction. But mostly they were just camouflage.

In contrast, the Western parliamentary model, as applied to South Korea by the Americans, put a much higher premium upon attracting the educated elite into the political process. The Legislative Assembly was considered the apex of legitimization—and of power. Its role was one of decision-making; the very fact that its establishment had been given precedence over an indigenous executive serves as an indication of this. No secret command structure existed to manipulate the elective component, at least in institutional terms. Leadership manifested itself through parties, but these were competitive, combative, and only quasi-legitimate in the public mind. And as South Korean institutionalization progressed, it became clear that the American military government was not itself an acceptable ultimate authority. Indeed, military government was soon fighting for its life against the Assembly it had so formidably endowed with legitimacy and power. Under these circumstances, it would have been ridiculous to have guaranteed a majority of seats to peasants and workers, whatever their numerical claims. However, given the philosophy that prevailed in the American command, the Assembly, by a combination of election and appointment, could claim with justice to represent the political spectrum, if not the socioeconomic composition, of the south far more adequately than any North Korean institution represented that of the north.

In North Korea, the November elections were followed by similar elections for hamlet and ward (ri and tong) People's Committees on February 24 and 25, 1947, and for township (myŏn) Committees on March 5. In the February elections, 99.80 percent of the eligible electorate were reported to have participated, with 86.63 percent of them casting affirmative votes for the Front slate. In the March elections, 99.98 percent of the electorate voted, according to the official account, and 96.80 percent voted affirmatively.[101]

Just before these elections, the Communists took a significant new step in institution-building. On February 17, 1947, they convened a four-day General Congress of People's Committees. The Congress had 1,186 delegates. The newly elected municipal, county, and provincial People's Committees had "selected" one-third of their respective numbers to attend, and an additional thirty-five delegates had been chosen to represent the seven parties and the major social organizations.[102]

The General Congress was clearly a ratifying body, not a deliberative or legislative one. Indeed, its size, method of selection, and functions were all entirely reflective of the National People's Congress of the USSR, from

101. *Chosŏn t'ongsa, op. cit.,* Vol. III, p. 69.
102. *Ibid.,* p. 70.

which model it had been drawn. In less than four days, it proceeded to approve "unanimously" all legislation previously enacted by the Provisional People's Committee of North Korea, accept the economic program for 1947 proposed by Kim Il-sŏng, and make provision for a permanent People's Assembly of North Korea.

The People's Assembly met immediately, on February 21 and 22. One-fifth of the total—237 members—had been selected from the General Congress, according to the same ratio among the various committees that had prevailed earlier. Once again, we have a breakdown of the socio-economic categories represented.[103]

	Percent
Peasant	26
Office Worker	24
Worker	22
Intellectual	15
Merchant	4
Clergyman	4
Entrepreneur	3
Artisan	2

As might have been assumed, the Assembly drew somewhat more heavily than the Congress from elitist elements within the People's Committee structure, with substantial representation given to the bourgeois and petty bourgeois classes. When representation by parties is scanned, however, a clearer profile emerges. This first national People's Assembly included 88 Workers' Party members, 30 members from the Democratic Party and the Ch'ŏndogyo Young Friends' Party, and 89 "unaffiliated" members. When it is remembered that both of the minor parties were under the secure control of the Communists at this point, it can be seen that the Assembly was not likely to cause the regime any trouble, especially since most of the so-called unaffiliated elements were completely tame. In truth, of course, all active, open opponents of the Communists had either gone south or been liquidated. At least on the surface, only "people" now lived in the north, no "enemies."

In its two-day meeting the People's Assembly officially elected an eleven-man Presidium, headed by Kim Tu-bong, to serve as its administrative organ. It also approved a judicial system for North Korea. Finally, it replaced the old Provisional People's Committee of North Korea with a "permanent" People's Committee, thereby signaling a final commitment to the Soviet-style institutional structure now in operation. This Committee, of course, was the ostensible government of North Korea, since its members held the top executive and ministerial posts. Of its 22 members, 16 were Workers' Party leaders, with 2 each from the other two parties

103. *Ibid.*, p. 70.

and 2 "unaffiliated." [104] Naturally, it was headed by Kim Il-sŏng. At this level, the Communists were not interested in concealing—or sharing—their power.

At this point, the south and north were running in tandem. The Legislative Assembly in Seoul, as we noted earlier, had held its first session in December, approximately two months before the first meeting of the North Korean People's Assembly, and from the beginning it had given every evidence of being boisterous, even unmanageable, in stark contrast to the decorum prevailing in the north. Both north and south of the 38th parallel, however, political institutions were being constructed that, if necessary, could become "permanent," although there was ample reason to wonder whether those being built in the south could survive the end of the American occupation.

We have already recounted how, throughout 1947, the Americans and Russians tried to settle their differences over Korea, and how all their efforts came to nothing. There followed the United Nations action of November 1947, and the complex political events within South Korea, culminating in the All-Nation People's Conference held in P'yŏngyang in April 1948, one month before the South Korean elections. Thus, the launching of the Republic of Korea on August 15, 1948, climaxed a process long under way in the south.

Three weeks later, on September 10, 1948, the Democratic People's Republic of Korea was established, with Kim Il-sŏng as premier. Once again, while seeking at each step to sabotage developments in the south, the Communists of the north had continued to match southern institution-building with their own. As early as November 1947, they had created a committee to draft a constitution. The draft was duly presented to the fourth session of the People's Assembly. Moreover, as in the case of the so-called Stalin Constitution of 1936, "public discussions" of the draft were conducted and over 2,000 suggestions supposedly received prior to the preparation of the final version.

Meanwhile, at its fifth session in July 1948, the People's Assembly was caused to decree that general elections would be held *throughout Korea* on August 25 for a new Supreme People's Assembly, so that this new legal body could officially enact the Constitution and inaugurate a formal government. This was the Communist answer to the United States, the United Nations, and the May 10 elections. To implement the "nation-wide" character of the elections, the NKWP Central Committee, in its July 13 session, determined that a "unified command" should be set up with the SKWP. On August 2, a joint Central Committee was created, with almost all of the South Korean Communist leaders coming to the north at this point. Broader united front efforts were also made, including

104. For a list of the committee members, see Kim Ch'ang-sun, *op. cit.,* pp. 204–205.

another appeal to those who had participated in the All-Nation People's Conference of April. On this occasion, however, the southern non-Communists for the most part refused to respond, recognizing the totality of Communist control over this operation.

The Communists, nevertheless, pursued the fiction that they were engaged in nationwide elections. A total of 572 delegates were "elected" to the Supreme People's Assembly, of whom 212 represented the north and 360 held seats in the name of the south. The official claim was that 99.97 percent of the eligible voters of the north had participated in the balloting, with Front nominees receiving 98.49 percent of the vote. The Communists also maintained that 77.80 percent of the eligible electorate of the south had taken part in the underground elections held there.[105] They added that these elections were admittedly "indirect," with "delegates" being selected to represent all of the people of the south, since candidates could not present themselves. This particular claim was sufficiently ridiculous to undermine Communist credibility with respect to other aspects of these elections. Even if leaders of the various front organizations in the south had cast ballots on behalf of their entire membership, as probably was the case in most instances, only a small minority of the South Korean people would have been involved at this point, since the Left had suffered heavy losses in recent months in the south.

It will be recalled that over 1,000 southern "delegates," purportedly elected in South Korea to represent all of its people, met in Haeju, just north of the 38th parallel, from August 22 to 24, and elected 360 of their number to sit in the Supreme People's Assembly. It is abundantly clear from the individuals primarily involved that this entire maneuver was managed by the SKWP and its front organizations in liaison with and under the supervision of the Russians and the North Korean Communist leaders.

On September 2, 1948, the Supreme People's Assembly opened its first session in P'yŏngyang. For ten days it continued in session, performing as a ratification agency in the same manner as had its predecessor, the People's Assembly. Its major actions were to approve the Constitution and to authorize Kim Il-sŏng to form a government. The Constitution in essence underwrote the existing political institutions, which, as we have seen, were modeled after the Soviet system. Legally, the highest organ of government was the Supreme People's Assembly, the equivalent of the Russian National People's Congress (later versions of this model were the Chinese National People's Congress and the North Vietnamese National Assembly). When this body was not in session, the Presidium operated on its behalf. The chief executive organ was the Cabinet of Ministers, with provision for seventeen ministries, headed by a premier. The intermediate

---

105. See the report of Ku Chae-su concerning the qualifications of the delegates in North Korean Workers' Party, *Chosŏn inmin hoe-ui che-il-ch'a munhŏnjip* (*Collection of Documents of the First Korean People's Congress*), P'yŏngyang, 1948.

and local organs of government were the People's Committees, corresponding to the Russian soviets. Each level of government was subordinated to the level immediately above it, preserving the principle of democratic centralism.[106]

The new state also had an army. We shall examine the North Korean People's Army in greater detail at a later point, but it should be noted here that the beginnings of that army can be traced back to the first part of 1946. In July 1946, Ch'oe Yong-gŏn, acting in his capacity as director of the Public Security Bureau, had organized the first *poandae* (security troops), and proceeded to serve as commander of these forces himself. By the spring of 1947, American authorities estimated that the North Korean military force numbered between 120,000 and 150,000 men, all of them supplied with excellent Soviet equipment. When these figures are contrasted with the South Korean force of only 26,000 before the establishment of the Republic, Communist eagerness for a withdrawal of foreign forces from the Korean peninsula can be easily understood.

In the area of mass mobilization, also, the Communists could claim major successes as the new era was launched. By the end of 1947, almost every adult in North Korea had been caused to affiliate—and participate, at least nominally—in one or more political or social organizations. At this point, there were probably around 4.5 million adults in the north. The Workers' Party itself claimed a membership of nearly 700,000 by the end of 1947, making it a Party that had succeeded in involving a far higher percentage of its citizens than any other Communist Party in the world.

The North Korean Farmers' Federation, founded on January 31, 1946, was asserted to have 800,000 members by the same period. It will be recalled that about 724,000 farm families were reported to have received some land in the course of land redistribution. The total number of farm families in North Korea at this time was probably in the neighborhood of 900,000.

The General Federation of Trade Unions of North Korea, set up first in November 1945, now claimed 350,000 members out of a total of 430,000 workers. The four largest unions involved office and clerical workers, miners, chemical workers, and transport workers. The Federation had also penetrated the south via the SKWP, and at one point had had very substantial influence there. Many of the large-scale strikes and labor demonstrations in the south were Communist-inspired, as we have seen. By the end of 1947, however, Communist influence over South Korean workers had receded, as it had in other sectors, since the leadership and most militant cadres had moved north or been imprisoned for illegal activities.

The North Korean Democratic Youth League had been established on January 17, 1946, when the old Communist Youth League changed

106. For the Constitution, see Appendix A.

its name at the "suggestion" of Soviet and Korean Communist authorities in order to widen its appeal. By the close of 1947, it listed 500,000 members. The North Korean Women's Federation, founded in November 1945, claimed 350,000 members. And there were large numbers of other organizations with smaller memberships, many of them in the cultural field. For example, the General Federation of North Korean Writers and Artists and the Korea-Soviet Cultural Association served as vehicles for the mobilization of intellectuals. Some seventeen organizations were coordinated under the Liaison Conference of Central Representatives of the Major Social and Political Organizations, a body set up in February 1946.

While we shall deal analytically with North Korean organizational techniques at a later point, it must be noted here that these efforts represented a milestone for the Communist world of this period. No modern party, Communist or otherwise, had ever placed so much emphasis upon the politics of mass mobilization. The Korean Communists, to be sure, enjoyed certain unique advantages: a small, homogeneous, and relatively concentrated population; a lengthy tradition of organization, albeit private rather than public, and one sustained by recent Japanese rule; and finally, the experience and training received by the Korean Communists, both in the Soviet Union and in China.

In overwhelming measure, these organizations, like the subordinate People's Committees, were ratifying or ceremonial rather than decision-making bodies. Later we shall seek to explore the extent to which they satisfied—or oversatisfied—the ordinary person's desire for participation and affiliation, and the psychological impact they produced. We shall also probe the problem of "quality" under conditions of mobilization as extensive as these. At present, it is sufficient to emphasize the extraordinarily high priority given mobilization politics by the Korean Communists, and their rapid accomplishments in this field, at least if measured in quantitative terms.

Communication was a major element in mobilization, and the Communists placed great emphasis upon it. Kim Il-sŏng was later to state that, by the time of the Korean War, there were eighty national and local newspapers and about half that number of other periodicals published in North Korea, as well as "tens of millions" of books and pamphlets.[107] Indeed, the populace was literally saturated with propaganda, the printed word being supplemented by the radio, theater, and lecture hall. Kim and others were quite frank in admitting that much of the "political" and "cultural" output merely consisted of Soviet materials in translation, along with translations of the Marxist-Leninist classics. In cultural as well as in political terms, this was the Soviet era, with Russian literature, Russian movies, and the Russian language featured everywhere. According to Kim, some

107. Kim Il Sung, *Selected Works,* P'yŏngyang, 1965 ed., Vol. I, "On Communist Education," p. 429.

299 North Korean students were sent to the Soviet Union for study in this period, with 36 Soviet technicians coming to North Korea specifically to teach and aid in the compilation of textbooks and technical manuals.[108]

An effort was also made by the Communists to expand educational facilities, both to meet the need for skilled manpower and to spread the political communication network. The new government claimed to have established 8,061 adult schools in its first years, thus enabling 413,000 illiterates to acquire basic literacy. It also established several colleges and universities, as well as libraries and research institutes. The new premium upon science and technical training, and the consequent downgrading of humanistic education, was much in evidence, a product both of Soviet guidance and of basic Communist objectives. Thus, even by the time of the establishment of the Korean People's Democratic Republic, the expansion of communications and education was among the more significant achievements of the regime, combining political primitivism with technological sophistication in more or less the proportions necessary for political stabilization and economic growth.

Curbing the "Domestic" Faction

Finally, what were the trends within the Communist Party itself? As we have already noted, by the time of creation of the North Korean Workers' Party in August 1946, the old Korean Communist Party had come securely under the control of the Soviet-Kapsan faction. The first major thrust had been in 1945, at the time of the December 17–18 meeting of the Enlarged Executive Committee, when Kim had pushed successfully for an independent party in the north over the opposition of the domestic faction leaders, O Ki-sŏp and Chŏng Tal-hŏn. From this point on, the leadership of the North Korean Communist Party included ever fewer members of the domestic faction. The newly organized Central Committee, dominated by the Soviet-Kapsan group, quickly moved into local and provincial branches throughout the north, ousting domestic faction men as "factionalists" or "sectists." At the end of January 1946, O Ki-sŏp, unquestionably the key "domestic" rival of Kim Il-sŏng in the north, was removed from the position of second secretary. Almost immediately, in the Provisional People's Committee organized on February 8 by the Kimists, he was appointed to head the Agitprop Department. But this was a less significant position. One other feared rival, Mu Chŏng of the Yenan faction, was also reduced during this period; in July, just prior to Party reorganization, he was appointed chief of artillery in the Officer Training School.

If Kim Il-sŏng and his supporters regarded the domestic faction as their chief target during this period, they were still aware of the importance of using at least some domestic-faction men, if they could be won over by means of offices and other emoluments. Thus, Chu Nyŏng-ha, a relatively

108. *Ibid.,* p. 430.

unimportant figure earlier, became vice-chairman of the Workers' Party Central Committee along with Kim Il-sŏng at the time of Party formation.[109] By absorbing certain of the domestic-faction lieutenants, however, Kim was aiming at the generals.

By August 1946, when the Workers' Party was established, none of the key domestic-faction leaders of the north figured prominently in the top Party hierarchy, except those considered loyal to Kim Il-sŏng. The Party, as we have noted, initially represented a balance between the Soviet-Kapsan and Yenan factions, a decided edge being given the former group.

At the important Second Party Congress of March 1948, Kim Il-sŏng struck hard and openly against his political enemies within the Party, concentrating upon domestic-faction leaders. Kim accused O Ki-sŏp "and others" of "engaging in faction-creating activities . . . while they themselves, having no real involvement in the life of the Party, continue to live like frogs in a well." [110] Kim was aiming this gibe not only at O, but also at Chŏng Tal-hŏn, Ch'oe Yong-dal, Yi Pong-su, and Yi Sun-gŭn, all domestic-faction leaders. It was also known that he regarded Mu Chŏng and Yun Kong-hŭm of the Yenan faction with grave suspicion. The open attack, however, was wisely concentrated upon O. After Kim's assault, in accordance with prearranged plans, a procession of speakers opened up on O. These included his former subordinate, Chu Nyŏng-ha, now Party vice-chairman, Hŏ Ka-i, head of Organization, Kim Yŏl, chairman of the Hamgyŏng Namdo Party branch, and Han Il-mu, chairman of the Kangwŏn-do Party branch.

Since O's purge was not untypical of many that were to follow, some of its details should perhaps be noted. Before the Second Party Congress, O had already been demoted, not once but twice. After a brief period as head of propaganda activities for the Provisional People's Committee (in which post he was accused of publicizing himself rather than the Party, that is, rather than Kim Il-sŏng), he was made head of the Labor Affairs Department, an even less important position. In that capacity, he had written an article for the September 1946 issue of *Nodong Sinmun* entitled "The State and Trade Unions." In the article, he had emphasized the importance of unions, asserting that if nationalized industries neglected the workers' interests, it was the duty of the unions to fight for those interests. This gave the Kimists an opportunity for an initial attack. At the November 1946 meeting of the Party Central Committee, the subject of the "leftist and rightist errors of Comrade O Ki-sŏp" was introduced into the second day's agenda. It was Chu Nyŏng-ha who led the attack, stating that O had attempted to apply labor union principles under capitalism to the socialist setting of North Korea, thereby deliberately inciting unthinking workers.

109. For Chu's subsequent career, see Kim Ch'ang-sun, *op. cit.*, pp. 102–103.
110. *Ibid.*, p. 106.

Most of the Central Committee members had not been appraised of the attack beforehand, nor had they read the article. The meeting was adjourned briefly so that O could prepare his response. When it resumed, he took the platform, armed with a Japanese edition of Lenin's *Selected Works*. If Kim Ch'ang-sun's account is accurate, he struck back hard, quoting passages from Lenin precisely like those in the article, and then asserting that if he were really being attacked not because he was guilty of theoretical errors but because he was "a pain in the neck," then why not just pin the label of Trotskyite on him? At this point, Pak Il-u supposedly arose and stated that, since he had not read the essay in question, he would like to see a study committee report on it later. But at this point, according to Kim Ch'ang-sun, Kim Il-sŏng arose without even seeking recognition from Kim Tu-bong, the chairman, and stated that no such committee was necessary since O had made many mistakes apart from the essay—for example, his failure to follow Party orders faithfully when he was sent to North P'yŏngan Province to supervise the land reform program there. On this note, the meeting ended.[111]

Long before the Second Party Congress, therefore, the downfall of O Ki-sŏp had been prepared. His followers either had been induced to desert him or were shunted aside. A careful dossier on his "errors" had been kept. He himself had been reduced in Party position, step by step, and humiliated before the Party elite. It is extraordinarily interesting, however, that in this case, as in a number of others, the victim was neither liquidated physically nor completely removed from Party ranks. Indeed, O remained on the Central Committee after the Congress. However, he was shifted from the Labor Affairs Department to a post as executive in the Russo-Korean Marine Transport Company, a somewhat limited vantage point from which to do battle for Party control. Moreover, most of his key supporters—Chŏng Tal-hŏn, Ch'oe Yong-dal, and Yi Pong-su, among others—lost their positions on the Committee. And shortly, O was removed from the Committee himself.

A potential rival had been whittled down to size, and his faction scattered. The timing was significant: the crucial moves were made as increasing numbers of SKWP members were moving north. Pak Hŏn-yŏng himself was to arrive a few months later. A powerful O Ki-sŏp in alliance with Pak—and with both on the scene—would scarcely aid the fortunes of the Kapsan group. Thus by the time of the People's Republic, O's eclipse was almost complete—although, as we shall see, he was to make a brief comeback eight years later.

The Second Party Congress ratified a Central Committee of 67 mem-

---

111. For details of O's purge, see *ibid.,* pp. 106–111. Pang In-hu, citing the minutes of the Second Congress, probes the details of the purge: see Pang In-hu, *Puk-Han "Chosŏn Nodong-dang" ui hyŏngsŏng kwa palchŏn (The Formation and Development of the North Korean "Korean Workers' Party"),* Seoul, 1967, pp. 112–115.

bers. Their backgrounds indicate that the effort to weld together Kapsan, Soviet, and Yenan elements was continuing, with such domestic Communists included as had not been too closely connected with Kim Il-sŏng's chief rivals. Thus, the Second Central Committee was a broadly based coalition representing several generations. Kim, however, was clearly intent upon containing the domestic faction, especially the portion of it that had been based in the north.

This was the situation within the North Korean Communist movement at the time of the establishment of the People's Republic. Developments between April and September 1948 necessitated a considerable readjustment, especially within governmental posts. Not only did the SKWP leaders have to be accommodated (maximum efforts to indicate a truly *national* government were necessary), but provision also had to be made for other leftist elements who had come north at the time of the Haeju conference or afterward, and remained. The government, in sum, had to have the appearance of a united front.

Thus, the chairman of the Supreme People's Assembly was Hŏ Hŏn, from the south, and the vice-chairmen Kim Tal-hyŏn, head of the Ch'ŏngdogyo Young Friends' Party, and Yi Yŏng, now leader of the South Korean so-called Working People's Party, a minor and relatively insignificant group. Kim Tu-bong, in addition to his Party post, was made chairman of the Presidium, with Hong Nam-p'yo of the domestic faction and Hong Ki-hwang of the Democratic Party as vice-chairmen, and Kang Ryang-uk, Kim's relative and a Democratic Party member, as secretary.

Under Premier Kim Il-sŏng were three vice-premiers: Pak Hŏn-yŏng, Hong Myŏng-hui of the southern Democratic Independence Party, and Kim Ch'aek, a close associate of Kim Il-sŏng and a Kapsan man. In the cabinet, the balance—on paper—seemed remarkably even. Counting the premier, the Soviet-Kapsan group held six posts, and five of these were occupied by men who were actually members of the Kapsan circle, true intimates of Kim Il-sŏng. The domestic faction also held six posts, but one of these was occupied by Chu Nyŏng-ha, who had recently sided with Kim against the domestic faction. Not all of the other domestic-faction men, moreover, were any longer prepared to stand totally with Pak. The Yenan group had four posts, and four others were divided between men from allegedly non-Communist parties, most of them from the south.

Examined more closely, however, the balance was not as equal as it appeared. Soviet-Kapsan men held the key positions of premier, one vice-premier, and minister of Industry (Kim Ch'aek), as well as the minister of Defense (Ch'oe Yong-gŏn). In addition, a Soviet-trained man, Kim Ik-sŏn, was named the first chief justice of the Supreme Court. Other important positions within the cabinet were divided among the Yenan, domestic, and other Party elements. The post of Foreign Affairs held by Pak Hŏn-yŏng was perhaps not as important as it might appear, since

Soviet-North Korean relations were generally conducted through Kim Il-sŏng himself, and these were the only foreign relations of significance at this time. Moreover, from that post, Pak could not be involved so intimately in internal affairs. The Yenan group held more significant positions: Interior (Pak Il-u), Finance (Ch'oe Ch'ang-ik), and Culture and Propaganda (Hŏ Chŏng-suk). In several cases, however, Kim Il-sŏng and his faction felt that they could trust these men; relations between Kim and Pak Il-u, for example, were reportedly close at this point. In some measure, the alliance between the Soviet-Kapsan and Yenan factions continued, with a shield being thrown up against any gains on the part of Pak and his group.

In one way, this strategy was made easier by virtue of the fact that the SKWP and the NKWP did not immediately merge. For nearly three years after the arrival of Pak in North Korea, separate party identities were maintained. This enabled the Kim faction to continue to dominate the NKWP, meanwhile slowly draining Pak's strength by enticing his members one by one to join their group.

Soviet Versus American Tutelage

By 1948 the Soviet occupation was coming to a close, although Russian influence would continue to be dominant for a number of years. Through Soviet power, a Communist regime had been implanted in one of the most conservative societies in Asia. North Korea came to Communism not via an indigenous revolution, not through a union of Communism and nationalism, but on the backs of the Red Army. The result was an extensive use of coercion, even more than might have been necessary had there been a sizable domestic base for the Communist movement. North Korea, especially after the beginning of 1946, became a police state. Some 800,000 individuals fled south between August 1945 and September 1948, when the Communist state was officially inaugurated—and not all of them by any means were "reactionaries," even as defined by the Communists. How many went from south to north is less clear, but it was probably under 25,000. In one sense, of course, this cross-migration was of considerable benefit to the Communists; it eliminated many of their most dangerous enemies.

They proceeded to eliminate others themselves. Cho Man-sik, and probably Hyŏn Chun-hyŏk earlier, were only the most famous of those who disappeared. As we have noted, purges came in many forms. Less dangerous types could be relegated to menial tasks, humiliated before their followers, or sent to some Korean Siberia. Often this was tactically wiser, since it enabled a gradual takeover of the fallen man's organization.

None of this is to assert that violence and coercion were absent from South Korean politics. We have given sufficient indication of the situation there to indicate that assassination and bloodshed were prominent aspects of a chaotic, insecure political scene. The Communists of the south, to be sure, brought much of their woe upon themselves by inciting riots, engaging in violent attacks upon all opponents, and accepting illegality and violence as a way of political life. Under the impact of these developments, even the American military government gradually shifted from a policy of tolerance to one of severity.

The most intriguing aspect of the years 1945 to 1948, however, is the contrast between the application of American and Soviet methods and institutional systems. On most counts, as we have seen, the Soviets had the edge. An authoritarian system, based upon tight elitist controls, permitting a minimum of competition, stressing mass mobilization to ratify the decisions of an elite, could be applied to Korea much more easily than Western-style democracy. Indeed, the very conservatism and political backwardness of that society were positive advantages, on balance, for the Communists. There can be no doubt that, as of the fall of 1948, North Korea was infinitely stronger—both militarily and politically—than South Korea, mainly because it was organized and unified to a far greater degree.

And Kim Il-sŏng? This obscure young man could not possibly have come to power without consistent Soviet support and backing. From this point of view, Kim was a puppet of a foreign power to an extent unmatched by any other individual's relationship to a foreign power during this period. Contrast, for example, the ambivalence the US Military Government felt toward Syngman Rhee—and the almost constant pitched battles fought with him and with most other Korean leaders in the south —with the tight working relations established between General Romanenko's office and Kim. If there were differences, and there probably were, these were carefully concealed, patched over, and compromised, with the bulk of the compromise probably made by Kim. At least, given both the institutions and the timing, it is hard to avoid the suspicion that Russian plans prevailed at all major points.

Sheer survival, however, breeds acceptance. By 1948, Kim had begun to eliminate most of his key opponents or subordinate them to him. He had turned the presses and radio stations of the country into his personal instruments. The institutional structure now worked powerfully for him, because it concentrated real power at the top, and Kim had a secure hold over the Party and key state institutions. And North Korea, while still a poor society, had been fully mobilized at a political level. To the economic developments we shall turn later. But it should be noted here that these were years of great hardship and economic scarcity, alleviated only by some improvement in the 1947–48 period. The political superstructure, however, had been thoroughly laid. The managed bourgeois democratic revolution was on the way to being completed, and the chances for a coup d'etat, not to mention a mass uprising, seemed vastly more remote in the north than they did in the south.

CHAPTER VI

THE WAR YEARS

In the fall of 1948, Kim Il-sŏng and his closest supporters had reason to be generally pleased with developments and confident about the future. Kim himself had survived the first crucial years of the new era, and his primacy in North Korean politics had never seemed more definitely established. Powerful rivals, the foremost of whom was Pak Hŏn-yŏng, were now fixed in secondary posts. The capacity to survive and to remain at the apex of the decision-making structure during the initial, relatively fluid stage of party- or nation-building generally proves to be the most serious test a supreme leader has to face. Once political roles have been clearly allocated among the elite, and the organizational structure has been firmly implanted, effective challenges against the leader are vastly more difficult to mount. This is especially true of the Stalinist model of communism, which allocates public prestige and private power to the key political figure in such a fashion as to make his overthrow extraordinarily difficult, barring some major catastrophe.

To be sure, Kim and his faction had had to pay a price for the gains achieved. Russian power and influence were still omnipresent. When the so-called Democratic People's Republic of Korea was established in September 1948, the Soviet occupation nominally ended. It is true that, shortly thereafter, Soviet military forces were withdrawn. In fact, however, the Soviet role in North Korea was not thereby affected to any appreciable degree, or not at first. The headquarters of the Soviet command was merely transferred to the Soviet Embassy in P'yŏngyang, where Soviet political advisers continued to work with each of the North Korean ministries, reviewing basic policy decisions.[1] At lower levels, Russian technicians and military specialists played a crucial role in the industrial and military development currently under way. Thus, the system, established during the Soviet occupation, of close interaction with and complete loyalty to Soviet authorities on the part of Korean Communist leaders, continued with appropriate adjustments in the post-occupation era.

One prominent aspect of Soviet influence in North Korea had been the presence of Russianized Koreans in positions of major influence. This, too, continued; it has been estimated that they occupied as many as two hundred key posts during this period. Most of these Russianized Koreans, or Soviet-Koreans as they are often called, held dual citizenship.[2] Extensive use had been made of them from the beginning of the Russian occupation. In virtually every major government agency, they had held key positions—often as second in command—which enabled them to exercise great power

1. For certain details, see U.S. Department of State, *North Korea: A Case Study in the Techniques of Takeover.* This report, originally published in May 1951 as a classified document, was declassified in 1961. It was the product of a research team having access to classified materials and commissioned to survey the North Korean political system as it operated before the Korean War.

Note the following passage: "According to informants, several Soviet political advisers worked with the North Korean Cabinet, one of their functions being to review basic policy decisions. Assigned to each Ministry was at least one politically responsible Russian, who generally possessed some competence in the special field of the Ministry. The adviser to the Ministry of Internal Affairs, for example, was Colonel Bodyagin, head of the Soviet secret police during the Soviet occupation. A specialist in Marxist philosophy aided the Minister of Education, and several Red Army generals assisted the Minister of National Defense. One Soviet official advised and prodded the National Planning Commission and still another supervised education at Kim Ilsong University and at technical and military schools" (pp. 100–101).

2. *Ibid.,* p. 101. "A Soviet-Korean held the most powerful post within the inner Labor Party, that of first secretary and liaison to the Soviet Embassy. Another was head of the organization department of Party Central Headquarters. For a long time the provincial branches of the Labor Party were headed by Soviet-Koreans. Every ministry and staff agency counted at least one Soviet-Korean vice-minister, and some particularly essential bureaus (the Political Defense Bureau of the Ministry of Internal Affairs being the outstanding case) had one or more Soviet-Korean vice-chiefs. The vice-president of Kim Ilsong University was a Soviet-Korean, and a number of his fellow repatriates from Soviet Central Asia headed and taught at the Labor Party Central School, the military schools, and the staff school of the Ministry of Internal Affairs. The organ of the Labor Party, *The Workers' News* (*Nodong Sinmun*), was edited by a Soviet-Korean; a Soviet-Korean was one of the chief North Korean representatives on Mortrans (the Soviet-North Korean shipping company), a Soviet-Korean woman headed the Democratic Women's League, and the army was permeated with Soviet-Koreans. Although some of these Koreans from Uzbekistan were on short-term assignments, to all intents and purposes the majority had become repatriated residents of North Korea" (p. 101). For other details, see Chong-Sik Lee and Ki-Wan O, "The Russian Faction in North Korea," *Asian Survey,* April 1968, pp. 270–288.

in a rather more unobtrusive manner than they could have from the top. Some Soviet-Koreans were on short-term assignment, and returned home to the Soviet Union after the completion of a certain period of service. Others, whether freely or as a result of Soviet directives, were prepared to remain indefinitely. Although these individuals, unlike Russians of Caucasian ethnic extraction, generally lived within the Korean community, they were subject to Soviet orders and surveillance. In the most direct and basic sense, they represented a projection of Soviet authority.

On the economic front, the picture was a mixed one at the beginning of the DPRK era. The leadership was preparing to launch its first full-scale economic plan, a Two-Year Plan for the years 1949–1950. As might have been expected, the emphasis during this period was upon heavy industry. State expenditures for industrial development had risen rapidly, and production in certain sectors of the economy was showing a substantial increase. Gains were uneven, however, and North Korean leaders openly admitted serious problems.[3] The difficulties were at least equally severe in agriculture. According to Korean Communist accounts, 1948 grain production was 140.6 percent of 1946 production. But it was also admitted that the 1948 figures were only 10.4 percent above those for 1939, which had been the highest during Japanese rule.[4] This was certainly not a spectacular accomplishment. For the average North Korean, living standards remained extremely low, having changed little if at all from the Japanese era.

In education and health, the Communist leaders could point to significant gains—an emphasis that, like so much else, derived from the Soviet model. In early 1949, Nam Il, then vice-minister of Education, wrote that whereas under Japanese rule a total of 910,000 Korean students were studying in 1,496 elementary and higher schools, there were currently 1,737,358 students "receiving a democratic education" in 4,255 schools, with an additional one million studying in correspondence, adult education,

3. For example, see Kim Il-sŏng's address to the managerial and labor leaders in industry, "Sanŏp pumun kyŏngje mit chikmaeng yŏlsŏngja taehoe esŏ chinsul hasin Kim Il-sŏng susang ui ch'onggyŏl yŏnsŏl" (Concluding Speech of Premier Kim Il-sŏng at the Conference of the Enthusiasts of the Industrial and Economic Sectors and the Professional league," *San-ŏp* (*Industry*), Dec. 1949, pp. 13–31. While claiming that industrial production in 1947 had increased 89 percent over 1946 totals, and 44 percent in 1948 over 1947 totals, Kim admitted "we have to recognize many serious weaknesses in our industries grievously hindering industrial development." He proceeded to indicate that 1949 production plans had encountered major difficulties, and cited some of the reasons: the inability of certain plants to adapt to new conditions, labor shortages, critical shortages of technicians, distribution problems, and the hostility of "antistate elements."

4. See Kim Chong-il, "The Task of Our Party Members During the Spring Sowing Season," *Kŭlloja* (*The Worker*), Feb. 28, 1949, p. 28.

and factory schools.[5] In the three years since 1945, claimed Nam Il, a total of 2,377,734 illiterates had learned to read and write in the hangul (Korean syllabary) schools established for this purpose.[6]

Nam Il also made it clear that the emphasis was upon the socialization of new socioeconomic classes. Before Liberation, he asserted, among the 971 Korean students at P'yŏngyang High School, none were children of workers or poor farmers. "Forty-seven percent were children of merchants, and the rest were children of landlords, moneylenders, or Korean officials serving under the Japanese." Similar statistics were cited for other Korean higher schools. Now, said Nam Il, 90.2 percent of the parents sending children to various schools in North Korea are laborers, poor and middle-class farmers, and white-collar workers.

Communist Political Unification and Reorganization

Naturally, the new educational program was constructed with political as well as economic purposes in mind. In early 1949, Hŏ Ka-i, vice-chairman of the NKWP, could announce that, after nine months of intensive efforts, the Party had some 800,000 members, most of them young people.[7] There were virtually no factories, farming and fishing villages, state agencies, or schools, he asserted, where Party cells could not be found. In most cases, he continued, Party members were playing an active role in economic and political developments. For example, in a recent conference of Party cells in South P'yŏngan Province, some 50 percent of the Party members had participated in the discussions, and 30 percent had "involved themselves in constructive criticism." [8]

Nevertheless, Hŏ pointed to a number of deficiencies, product of "the new, young, and inexperienced Party membership." Some Party cadres concentrated only upon quantitative results, failing to create political enthusiasm on the part of the masses. Bureaucratism and commandism were frequent problems. Another weakness was that instruction within the Party had been carried out on the basis of the social background of the member instead of his educational level. "Often, we have had college graduates and illiterates in the same class." [9]

Speaking broadly, two types of mistakes had been made in connection with Party growth, Hŏ announced. In some cases, a "closed-door" policy had been pursued, that is, a policy of prohibiting some from passing

5. Nam Il, "On the Development of People's Education and the Enforcement of Overall Compulsory Education," *Kŭlloja* (*The Worker*), Jan. 31, 1949, pp. 13–14.
6. *Ibid.*, p. 13.
7. Hŏ Ka-i, "On the Results of the Activities of Local Party Organs During the Past Nine Months and on the Strengthening of Party Guidance Activities," *Kŭlloja* (*The Worker*), March 15, 1949, p. 4.
8. *Ibid.*
9. *Ibid.*, pp. 7–10.

through the Party door because they were adjudged "ignorant," and thereby eliminating many working-class people. In other instances, a "collective" policy had prevailed. People had been admitted to the Party as a group, without their individual eligibility for membership being tested.[10]

Hŏ's report appeared on the eve of the merger between the South and North Korean Workers' parties that was effected between June and August 1949. In retrospect, it is probably correct to assert, as does Kim Ch'ang-sun, that this event signaled the absorption of the southern Party into its northern counterpart, and so paved the way for the later eclipse of Pak Hŏn-yŏng and his supporters.[11]

Pak had resisted this move as long as possible. But by early 1949, he and his group had little choice. Their party, which had claimed some 370,000 members in 1947, had now been reduced to a skeleton as a result of massive desertions, multiple arrests, and cumulative pressures from the Rhee government. As we have noted, almost all the southern leaders had moved north by August 1948, with the so-called Congress of People's Representatives at Haeju serving as their final excuse for leaving. Despite some infiltration from the north, the activities of underground agents and guerrilla fighters in the south were greatly reduced after 1947.[12] Kim Sam-yong and

10. It will be noted shortly that Hŏ himself was subsequently to be charged with applying the "closed door policy" particularly against peasants, thereby erroneously restricting party growth.

11. Kim Ch'ang-sun, *Puk-Han sip-o nyŏnsa* (*Fifteen-Year History of North Korea*), Seoul, 1961, pp. 116–117. The first official mention of the merger of the two parties was made by Kim Il-sŏng on Dec. 21, 1950, at the third plenum of the Central Committee. He said on that occasion: "It has been more than a year since the United Central Committee meeting was held to bring about the merger of the Southern and Northern Korean Workers' Parties. [Over] a year ago, in order to strengthen the power of our Party, and in order to unite the strength of the entire Party under the complicated environment to forcefully carry out democratic construction, consolidate all democratic strength, consolidate all working masses of Korea, around our Party under a united central leadership, a historical Central Committee [meeting] was held, representing the will of the entire Party membership of the Southern and Northern Korean Workers' Parties. As a result, we have established a united central headquarters of the Party, and under a united Party central leadership, and in conjunction with democratic parties and social organizations, we have carried out continuous and forceful struggles toward peaceful unification of the fatherland." *Kim Il-sŏng sŏnjip* (*Selected Works of Kim Il-sŏng*), 1953 edition, Vol. III, pp. 122–123: quoted from Pang In-hu, *Puk-Han "Chosŏn Nodong-dang" ui hyŏngsŏng kwa palchŏn* (*The Formation and Development of the North Korean "Korean Workers' Party"*), Seoul, 1967, p. 138.

12. According to the South Korean Defense Department's official history, some 2,400 guerrillas were dispatched to the south from the north between November 1948 and March 1950.

Between 1948 and 1949, about 800 guerrillas were reported to be in the Odaesan region, 360 in the T'aebaek mountainous area, 350 in the Chi-i mountainous area, and 200 on Cheju Island. However, just before the Korean War, most of these had apparently been regrouped in the North so as to participate in a coordinated invasion,

Yi Chu-ha, incidentally, were among the last important southern leaders to escape arrest (they were finally rounded up on March 27, 1950). Considerably before this time, however, Communist underground operations in South Korea had become sporadic and small-scale.

Thus, the argument that a separate Party was necessary to direct operations in the south lost its validity, particularly since most programs were being fashioned and operators trained in the north. Indeed, Kim Il-sŏng now shrewdly put the emphasis upon a *unified* Party that could take supreme command of the campaign to "liberate" the south from a northern stronghold. Nor could Pak and his followers expect to be treated as true equals by a northern Party that claimed 800,000 members, dominated a state apparatus, and controlled sizable military and police forces.[13] When the merger came, it was Kim Il-sŏng who assumed the chairmanship of the Party Central Committee; Pak Hŏn-yŏng and Hŏ Ka-i were named vice-chairmen. (Within a few years, both vice-chairmen would be dead and discredited.)

Under the reorganization, the post of Party secretary, abolished in August 1946, was reestablished. Three secretaries were named: Hŏ Ka-i, first secretary; Yi Sŭng-yop, second secretary; and Kim Sam-yong, third secretary. Kim Il-sŏng, in addition to holding the premiership of the government and the chairmanship of the Party Central Committee, was also

---

or had been rounded up. Less than 500 were identified by South Korean authorities in the south immediately before the June 1950 attack, although this figure is probably too low. See Republic of Korea, Department of Defense, *Kukpangbusa* (*A History of the Department of Defense*), Seoul, 1954, Vol. I, pp. 40–45.

13. It should also be pointed out, however, that on paper the DPRK had been established on the basis of elections throughout Korea and, thus, *theoretically,* the south was a part of the republic, with the Supreme People's Assembly having a sizable southern delegation. On this basis, the SKWP and Pak could claim major representation in any amalgamated Party, especially if the wooing of the south were to continue. Nevertheless, the true balance of power in the north, not the fictitious, legal one would ultimately be the determining factor.

Already in the early spring of 1948, at the Second Congress of the North Korean Workers' Party, Kim Il-sŏng was making derogatory remarks about those from the south. He said: "Another thing I must mention is the comrades from South Korea. They must win the confidence of the North Korean Workers' Party, but because they also hold a share in the South Korean Workers' Party, they must also pretend to be faithful to it. They take actions that estrange the Southern and Northern Workers' Parties. Their attitude is that since his close friends are in South Korea and since he had been a member of the 'Com group' [Communist group under Pak Hŏn-yŏng], he will have a position there. But this is a childish thought. The South Korean Workers' Party is no longer a party of any sectarian element but it stands on firm ground of the broad masses consisting of laborers, farmers, and working intelligentsia. Although there are two parties because of the 38th parallel, our Party is a single Party. Those driven out of the North Korean Workers' Party can never be accepted in South Korea." *Kim Il-sŏng sŏnjip,* 1954 edition, Vol. II, p. 133: quoted from Pang In-hu, *op. cit.,* p. 136. Unfortunately, we do not know whether the text of this speech was doctored after Pak Hŏn-yŏng et al. were purged.

chairman of the all-important Political Committee, with Pak Hŏn-yŏng (SKWP) as vice-chairman. The remaining seven members, with their affiliations, were Kim Ch'aek (Manchuria guerrilla), Pak Il-u (Yenan), Hŏ Ka-i (CPSU), Yi Sŭng-yŏp (SKWP), Kim Sam-yong (SKWP), Kim Tu-bong (Yenan), and Hŏ Hŏn (SKWP). These same men constituted the Organization Committee, the other crucial headquarters committee, with two additional members, Ch'oe Ch'ang-ik (Yenan), and Kim Yŏl (CPSU). On the surface, Party and government offices under Kim Il-sŏng appeared to have been distributed with considerable care as to factional balance. In fact, however, Kim Il-sŏng was now surrounding himself increasingly with men like Kim Ch'aek upon whose personal loyalty he could depend.[14]

Another political action of significance took place during this period. On June 25, 1949, the old Democratic National United Front (first established on July 22, 1946) was renamed the Democratic Front for the Unification of the Fatherland. In terms of internal North Korean politics, the Front now had a limited meaning. Its leading party component other than the Workers' Party was the Korean Democratic Party. At this point, however, that party was completely under the control of the Communists. Not only was its head, Ch'oe Yong-gŏn, a dedicated Communist, but from late 1947 to early 1948 the party had conducted a searching examination of the social background and ideological views of its members, purging many anti-Communists from its ranks. No new members had been accepted during this period, and any staff personnel who would not follow the Workers' Party line had been replaced. By the fall of 1949, Democratic Party membership had declined to 100,000.[15] The Ch'ŏndŏgyŏ Young Friends' Party had undergone a similar evolution. If the Front had little purpose at this point in North Korea except to provide compliant bourgeois or religious elements with an opportunity to support the Communist cause and present a democratic facade to the gullible, in South Korea it had far greater significance. On the basis of the Front's Declaration of June 1949, for example, the South Korean underground Party launched its so-called July Offen-

14. Kim Ch'aek had a typical "Kapsan" faction background, and epitomized the type now coming to the fore under Kim Il-sŏng. Born in North Hamgyŏng Province, he had participated in the anti-Japanese movement in eastern Manchuria in the 1930s, been pushed (with Kim Il-sŏng and others) into Siberia by the Japanese in 1941, was trained there by the Russians, and reportedly reached the rank of colonel in the Soviet army before returning to Korea with the Soviet army in 1945. We are, however, dubious about the accuracy of assigning Soviet army rank to Kim Ch'aek, Kim Il-sŏng, or any other Korean guerrillas. A long article on Kim Ch'aek, "Uri choguk i naŭn yŏllyŏl han hyŏngmyŏng t'usa Kim Ch'aek tongji" ("Passionate Fighter Comrade Kim Ch'aek Given Birth by Our Fatherland"), can be found in *Minju Chosŏn* (*Democratic Korea*, organ of the DPRK), Jan. 31, 1956.

15. This information, and additional data to be presented later on the Korean Democratic Party, comes from a captured North Korean agent who was formerly a member of that party. The information he provided was checked out against other sources and appears to be reliable.

sive, a series of assaults and acts of sabotage that lasted until September 20.[16] The atmosphere in the south, as we have noted earlier, grew increasingly tense with the anticipation of large-scale northern "aid." The southern leaders who had gone north, having abandoned all hope for the peaceful unification of Korea under their aegis, and forced to conclude that guerrilla efforts in South Korea were doomed to failure without massive external assistance, commenced preparations for the forceful "liberation" of the area below the 38th parallel.

Against this background, many of the Communist speeches of the

16. Chong-Sik Lee interview with Kim Nam-sik, June 16–18, 1970. The Democratic Front for the Unification of the Fatherland opened its first organizational meeting on June 25, 1949, at the Moranbong Theatre in P'yŏngyang, with 700 delegates purporting to represent seventy-one "patriotic parties and social organizations" from both North and South Korea. Its purposes were proclaimed as "achieving the restoration of national territory, completing Korean unification and independence by forcing the withdrawal of American forces, and the destruction of Syngman Rhee's puppet government."

As was to be expected, this organization was totally dominated by the key leaders of the Workers' Party. Forty-one persons were named to the leadership committee: this group was headed by Kim Il-sŏng, Kim Tu-bong, Hŏ Hŏn, Pak Hŏn-yŏng, Kim Ch'aek, Hong Myŏng-hui, Ch'oe Yong-gŏn, and Kim Tal-hyŏn, who were officially listed in that order. These men will be recognized as the Communist and fellow-traveler elite.

A thirty-nine-member platform committee led by Kim Tu-bong and Hŏ Hŏn presented its declaration on the third day, and that declaration was unanimously adopted. Its most revealing sections included statements that acceptance of the Soviet proposals of 1948 for the withdrawal of all foreign forces would have made it possible for the Korean people to have resolved their internal problems without external involvement, and US rejection of this proposal symbolized the fact that the US government was attempting to turn Korea into its colony or one of its Far Eastern military bases; that the government of the Democratic People's Republic of Korea, having been duly constituted and elected, received the support of the great majority of the Korean people; that American imperialists and reactionary Korean elements had established a puppet government in the south, consisting of Korean reactionaries and national traitors, to pursue the policy of dividing Korea, a government isolated from the people and fearful of facing them without American support; and that a further continuation of this division would produce enormous danger for the Korean people.

Hence, proclaimed the DFUF program, we will struggle to achieve the following objectives: withdrawal of American forces and the so-called UN Commission from South Korea, and complete unification of the fatherland; conflict with the Korean traitors preventing unification, and the mobilization of the full capacities of the people for the fight to achieve quick unification; striving to further consolidate and develop the democratic reforms already accomplished in the northern half of Korea; support for the DPRK government, which was established as a result of the general elections of Aug. 25, 1948, and cooperation with that government in promoting the welfare of the Korean people.

This material comes from a manuscript containing the minutes of the June 25–27, 1949 organizational meeting.

It is interesting to compare this program with that of the North Vietnamese Fatherland Front; the similarities are striking.

period have an ominous ring. In a 1949 speech commemorating Korean Liberation, Pak Hŏn-yŏng first eulogized Stalin as "the savior of our nation and of all other liberated peoples of the world," and excoriated American policies in Asia.[17] The achievements of the North Korean government and people were lauded, especially the general effort to reach the goals of the Two-Year Plan under General Kim Il-sŏng, "who is the hero of the Korean nation." In contrast, conditions in the south were described in the most dire terms: South Korea had become America's slave, with factories being destroyed, inflation rampant, and the economy totally exploited for American gain; patriots were being massacred, with no respect for civil rights; the United States, and its instrument the United Nations, was inciting civil war on the Korean peninsula. Pak went on to insist that only the proposals of the Democratic Front for the Unification of the Fatherland represented a proper method of unification because they alone had the support of the Korean people. He ended by stressing that the longer the unification of Korea was delayed, the more lives would be lost in the south. Thus, unification was the most important and most immediate task of the Party and the people.[18]

Military Preparations and the Onset of War

Military growth kept pace with political exhortation during this period. The Korean People's Army (KPA) was not officially created until February 8, 1948, but Korean Communist military preparations had gotten under way as early as 1945. Initially, such preparations had been conducted under the auspices of the Provisional People's Committee Security Bureau, formally established on February 8, 1946. Its first chief was Ch'oe Yong-gŏn, who was to take the position of commander of the Security Cadres Training Center in July 1946.[19]

17. Pak Hŏn-yŏng, "Report on the Occasion of the Fourth Anniversary of the Liberation of August 15," *Kŭlloja* (*The Worker*), Aug. 31, 1949, pp. 3–30. In this lengthy article, Pak demonstrates a broader conversance with the world scene and a variety of literature, including Marxist-Leninist materials, than was to be seen in any other leader's writings, including those of Kim Il-sŏng.

18. *Ibid.*, p. 30. Kim Il-sŏng also sounded this theme in his 1950 New Year's message, which emphasized the need for vigilance against the enemy, a strengthening of the Korean People's Army and police forces, the completion of the two-year plan, a consolidation of Communist "democratic reforms," and the strengthening of guerrilla forces fighting in the South. In the year 1950, Kim declared, "let us strive for the consolidation of the national territory and the achievement of the unification of the Fatherland!" "General Kim Il-sŏng's New Year's Message," *Kŭlloja* (*The Worker*), Jan. 15, 1950, pp. 3–7.

19. An account of the early stages of the formation of the North Korean army has been given by a prominently placed defector who was involved. According to him, in December 1945 a small group of trainees known as officer candidates were enrolled in a program under the control of the South P'yŏngan Province People's Com-

Before 1949, the military organization was based primarily upon "volunteers" from the 18–22 age group, recruited at the rate of approximately 20,000 men per year.[20] The ministry of Defense had fixed quotas that it passed along to various town and village draft boards via the local People's Committees. Using this method, the ministry raised the armed forces to some 60,000 by the end of 1948 (these figures did not include railway and border guards). In 1949, however, the military demand for men rapidly increased, and the existing system was converted into a device for more open conscription. The draft age was gradually raised until, following total mobilization in July 1950, all males between the ages of 31 and 50 were liable for industrial work or auxiliary military duty. To supplement the Democratic Front for the Unification of the Fatherland, the Fatherland Defense Support Association had been created in the summer of 1948. The association played a very important role in Communist war preparations; under its aegis, part-time military training was made compulsory for all between the ages of 17 and 40.[21]

Meanwhile, trained officers and technicians were becoming available in greater quantities, through both internal and Soviet training programs. From late 1945 onward, North Korean youths were taken to Russia for military and technical training, and some of them stayed as long as three years. It has been estimated that at least 10,000 military men were given such training prior to the Korean War. When they returned, they were put in charge of the advanced Soviet equipment that was now flowing into North Korea. Some of them were also put in charge of training programs

mittee Security Bureau. He graduated from this program in February 1946 and was made commanding officer of a special security unit. In October 1946 he became a student in the first class of the North Korean People's Committee Central Higher Staff School in P'yŏngyang. His course ended three months later, on Jan. 25, 1947, and his new assignment was as commanding officer for all "Peace Preservation Corps personnel in South P'yŏngan Province," a post he held until his defection in the fall of 1947. Such "peace preservation corps" and "security corps," including railway security forces, were the basis for the Korean People's Army when it was formally created.

20. Kim Hyŏk, former head of the Military Mobilization Department in North Hamgyŏng Province, related that the preliminary work on military mobilization was handled by the Fatherland Defense Support Society (Choguk Powi Huwon-hoe), created in 1948. At the provincial level, deputy chairmen of the provincial party would lay out the military mobilization plan. Military officers in active duty were dispatched to various factories, enterprises, and institutions to provide military training. Ostensibly, the training was provided under the auspices of the Support Society. The police system was used to register all men of draft age. Then, in March 1949, the Military Mobilization Department was created under the Bureau of Organization-Mobilization of the Ministry of Defense, having the power to conscript men and properties. The head of the provincial Military Mobilization Department was a full colonel of the army. Chong-Sik Lee interview with Kim Hyŏk, Jan. 15, 1970.

21. U.S. Department of State, *North Korea: A Case Study in the Techniques of Takeover, op. cit.,* p. 69.

so that their newly acquired knowledge and skill could be transmitted to others.[22]

Top military leadership continued to be in the hands of veteran guerrilla fighters, many of them old partisan comrades of Kim Il-sŏng. Thus, Ch'oe Yong-gŏn served as minister of Defense; Kim Il held the post of political commissar; other associates like Ch'oe Hyŏn and Kim Kwang-hyŏp held additional important positions.[23] Chief of staff of the North Korean Army on the eve of the invasion was Kang Kŏn, a returnee from the Soviet Union, while Mu Chŏng, formerly the highest ranking Korean officer with the Chinese Communist forces, had the post of commander of the 2nd Army Corps.[24]

22. *Ibid.*, pp. 85–86. During 1949, the military force doubled in strength with the addition of 40,000 conscripts, 20–22,000 Koreans formerly attached to the Chinese Communist Army, and several thousand men returning from the USSR after the completion of their training. In the early months of 1950, the Korean People's Army expanded rapidly to some 150,000 men. During April and May also, large shipments of arms were received from the Soviet Union, including heavy artillery, trucks, tanks, automatic weapons, and new propeller-driven aircraft.

23. Since each of these men was to have a prominent role in the subsequent evolution of the DPRK, it is important to note briefly the similar patterns of their careers up to this point. Ch'oe Yong-gŏn, destined to be No. 2 in the North Korean hierarchy, was born about 1900 in North P'yŏngan Province; had military training in China; fought with the CCP 8th Route Army for a time, and later served as a guerrilla fighter against the Japanese in Manchuria as a part of the Northeastern Anti-Japanese Allied Army; fled to the Soviet Union in 1940 or 1941; was given special military training there and possibly an officer's commission in the Soviet army; and returned with that army to Korea in 1945.

Kim Il, ultimately No. 3 in the hierarchy, was born about 1910 in North Hamgyŏng Province; served as an anti-Japanese guerrilla fighter in Manchuria in the 1930s; proceeded to Siberia in the 1940–41 period; received military training and possibly an officer's commission in the Red Army; and returned to Korea in 1945.

Ch'oe Hyŏn, later No. 5, was born in 1907 in North Hamgyŏng Province; reportedly had some military training in China; commanded an anti-Japanese guerrilla unit operating in China and Manchuria in the 1930s; went to the Soviet Union in 1940–41; reportedly held the rank of captain in the Soviet army; and returned with that army in 1945.

Kim Kwang-hyŏp, No. 6 at a later point, was born in 1913 in North Hamgyŏng Province; raised and educated in the Soviet Union; participated as an anti-Japanese guerrilla fighter in Manchuria; remained in Manchuria until his return to Korea after March 1947; subsequently went to the Soviet Union for advanced training; returned in 1948 to assume command of the new KPA 3rd Division.

It is to be noted that each of these men—like Kim Il-sŏng—was born in the northern part of Korea, served early as a guerrilla fighter against the Japanese in China or Manchuria, proceeded (in most cases) to the Soviet Union after 1940, received advanced political and military training there and, according to some accounts, an officer's commission in the Soviet army, and returned to Korea with the Russians. Such is the background of the small cluster of men who were to constitute Kim's inner group for more than twenty years.

24. The first chief of staff of the Korean military forces appears to have been An Kil, who died in December 1947. He was succeeded by Kang Kŏn, reportedly a

The Russians continued to serve as divisional advisers. In 1949, some twenty Russians were assigned to each division; this was reduced in 1950 to from three to eight Russians per division. By the time of the Korean War, the North Korean armed forces numbered between 150,000 and 200,000 troops, organized into ten infantry divisions, one tank division, and one air force division. Their numbers had grown significantly in the 1949–50 period, not only because of sharp increases in the draft quotas but also because some Korean divisions had been transferred from Manchuria. In 1949, two divisions of the former Korean Volunteer Corps (subsequently designated the 164th and 166th Divisions of the Chinese People's Liberation Army) returned from China to Korea, where they exchanged their Communist Chinese officers and American equipment for an all-Korean command structure, Soviet advisers, and Russian equipment. In April 1950, additional Korean troops arrived from Manchuria. These two transfers added an estimated 40,000 veterans to the North Korean Army and accounted, if American estimates were correct, for at least one-third of its spearhead divisions.[25] Soviet equipment, including automatic weapons of various types, T-34 tanks, and Yak fighter planes, had also been pouring into North Korea throughout the months immediately preceding the Communist invasion of the south.

What of the anti-Communist opposition? Some 500 American military advisers had been working for two years to train the Republic of Korea Army (ROKA). The Army now numbered some 100,000, and the national police force, which was a completely separate entity, some 50,000. These units had been sufficient to wipe out or silence all major Communist guerrilla bands operating in the south. However, the South Korean forces generally lacked heavy equipment. Partly as a result of deliberate American policy (to contain the militancy of Syngman Rhee), ROKA had not been given any significant number of tanks, heavy artillery, or combat airplanes. Indeed, it did not even have a large supply of ammunition. Moreover,

---

Soviet citizen who had been living in Kazakhstan and was formerly a captain in the Soviet army. Kang first organized and commanded the East Kirin (Manchuria) Peace Preservation Army in September 1945 after the Japanese surrender, a unit subsequently coming under the Northeast Democratic Allied Army (Lin Piao, commander). In 1946 Kang became commander of the Korean People's Army 2nd Division in Nanam.

Concerning Mu Chŏng, we have already related some of the most salient facts. In the opening months of the Liberation era, it will be recalled, Kim Il-sŏng evidently regarded Mu Chŏng as a potentially dangerous rival—and not without reason. As a senior officer with the Chinese Communist 8th Route Army and head of the Korean operations in Yenan, Mu Chŏng had more military prestige than any other "guerrilla," and potentially, at least, this could be translated into political prestige. Thus, as we noted earlier, Mu Chŏng, having at first been given certain key posts, quickly "fell into disfavor" and was demoted, even before the Korean War. We will turn shortly to further details.

25. See *Korea—1950,* Washington, 1952, pp. 13–14.

American occupation forces in Japan were represented by units that were below strength, poorly equipped, and poorly trained for combat purposes. They were not combat-ready in any sense, partly because it was stated American policy at this point not to fight on the Korean peninsula. The Defense Department did not even have a contingency plan for American intervention in Korea in the event of a Communist invasion.[26] It is reasonable to assume that all of these facts were known to Communist intelligence, Soviet if not North Korean.

Many aspects of the decision to invade are still shrouded in mystery. Clearly, only a very few of the key North Korean leaders were involved, men at the uppermost rungs of the hierarchy.

> The degree of secrecy is illustrated by two facts. Top secret work plans of the standing committee of Labor [Workers'] Party headquarters dated January to June 1950, make absolutely no reference to the forthcoming invasion, although covering in some detail all other aspects of government policy. Second, a number of fairly high-placed North Korean officers that were interviewed, including the chiefs of staff of two divisions, stated that they had only the barest presentiment of the coming of hostilities, and that they were given no concrete indication of their onset until approximately one week before the invasion took place.[27]

One of the divisional chiefs of staff mentioned above was Yi Hak-kyu. After capture, he testified that Kang Kŏn, North Korean Army chief of staff, issued an order at an emergency meeting of all divisional commanders and chiefs of staff on June 10, 1950, for all units to be combat-ready. According to Yi, this was followed on June 18 by an order from Commander-in-Chief Ch'oe Yong-gŏn for a final precombat inspection, and on June 23 the operational order was issued to attack South Korea on June 25. Yi asserted that this order was known only to Kim Il-sŏng and the highest military officers, and was kept secret from nonmilitary personnel, even cabinet members.[28]

In considerable measure, this account matches with that of Pawel Monat, former Polish military attaché in North Korea.[29] Monat—whose

26. See Glenn D. Paige, *The Korean Decision, June 24–30, 1950,* New York, 1968, p. 128. On the condition of the South Korean forces, see Maj. Robert K. Sawyer, *Military Advisors in Korea: KMAG in Peace and War,* Washington, 1962.

27. U.S. Department of State, *North Korea: A Case Study in the Techniques of Takeover, op. cit.,* p. 113.

28. Yi Hak-kyu was interrogated by allied personnel shortly after his capture.

29. Pawel Monat, "Russians in Korea: The Hidden Bosses," *Life,* June 27, 1960, pp. 76–102 *passim.* Monat is described by the editors of *Life* as having served for three years as Polish military attaché to both China and North Korea, coming to the latter country after the death of his predecessor in an air attack in September 1951. He was reportedly an intelligence specialist, with the rank of colonel. In 1959, he defected with his wife and son: at the time of the writing of this article, he was living in the United States under an assumed name.

report, we must warn, cannot be substantiated in certain respects due to the paucity of sources—asserts flatly that Stalin personally ordered [authorized?] the attack, and that the key Chinese leaders were shown the plans and gave their approval during Mao Tse-tung's visit to Moscow in early 1950. In the following passage, Monat indicates how the fiction of a South Korean attack was maintained:

> Another illusion that was maintained to the end was that Syngman Rhee and the South Koreans, abetted by the American "imperialists," had attacked first; the North Korean army had been forced to counterattack to save its country. Amazingly, even the troops who did the attacking believed this story. Each unit had been told that the South Koreans had attacked in *another* sector and that they must now fight all along the front. Only high-ranking North Korean officers—and of course all the Russians—knew the truth.
>
> One day, talking with the chief of staff of a North Korean army corps, a Major-General, Choy In [Ch'oe In], I learned the facts. I had asked Choy, as one Communist to another, why his troops had so much trouble fighting the Americans. The general must have forgotten the rules against ever mentioning this subject, for he told me everything. I think he wanted me to know that his people had at least done their part.
>
> "We had planned the attack very carefully," Choy said. "We rehearsed every detail over and over. We had ten infantry divisions and one division of armor. A few weeks before we were ready, we moved all the civilians back from the boundary on the 38th Parallel—about seven to ten miles, depending on the terrain. We told them this was for their own safety, since we expected an attack from South Korea. Then we moved our troops in, along six different roads, and awaited the order to attack. We had a timetable worked out showing exactly how far south we should move each day and where we would stop to rest.
>
> "My corps was ordered to capture the ground east of Seoul. We were given exactly forty-eight hours to do this. At first everything went well, but we soon ran into trouble. The roads were very bad, and we hit some opposition from the South Korean army that was far more severe than we had expected. It was clearly easier to plan an attack than to carry it out. But my superiors back at headquarters were heedless of this. They kept looking at their watches and calling me up every hour or so to find out why we weren't on schedule. Later on the Americans got their troops into Korea in large numbers, and American planes began to attack us every time we moved. By this time my superiors had stopped bothering me. They realized that they had overlooked quite a bit when they made the original plans." [30]

30. *Ibid.*, p. 76, 86. We have another account of the invasion decision, equally fascinating but also unfortunately not susceptible to documentary proof. A North Korean who subsequently defected to Japan has asserted that some time in March 1950 a secret conference was held in P'yŏngyang, the most important in the history of the Party. He says it was attended by the top members of the Political Committee, including Kim Il-sŏng, Pak Hŏn-yŏng, Hŏ Ka-i, Kim Tu-bong, Yi Sŭng-yŏp, and Ch'oe

In preparing a cover for their actions, the North Korean leaders were able to take advantage of certain developments in the south. They had, of course, observed the second general elections for the South Korean National Assembly, which had taken place in May, the month before the invasion. In those elections, in which a very heavy vote was cast, the tide went against the Rhee government and toward independent candidates. Economic conditions in the south were, as usual, shaky, and this was certainly one reason for the anti-Rhee vote. Moreover, the Rhee forces' usual tactic of labeling their opponents Communists or pro-Communists had not worked this time. Thus, when the new National Assembly convened in Seoul on June 19— just six days before the invasion—130 of its 210 members were independents. From the northern Communist standpoint, the political situation in the south looked reasonably good.

Earlier, on June 3, to counter the news of the South Korean elections and lay the political background for events to come, Radio P'yŏngyang had announced that 5,300,000 North Koreans had signed petitions demanding the peaceful unification of the country. At the same time, the DPRK presented a proposal: the two national assemblies should be merged on an

---

Yong-gŏn. Kim Il-sŏng is said to have opened for discussion the possibility of military action against the south. It was supposedly agreed that the north could win in three weeks, assuming that the United States did not intervene—and American intervention was regarded as highly unlikely. Even if the United States decided to enter the war, it would take American forces at least fifty days to become effective, it was argued, and this would be too late. Pak Hŏn-yŏng reportedly bolstered the militant course strongly by asserting that if the People's Army invaded the south, 200,000 underground South Korean Communists would emerge to join forces with the northern army. According to this defector's report, only Ch'oe Yong-gŏn registered some doubts, asking whether adequate countermeasures had been prepared in case the Americans did enter the war.

The accounts of Monat and the defector differ in the emphasis given the Russians as the key decision-makers, the latter account suggesting that the key decision lay in Korean hands. The accounts, however, are not necessarily inconsistent. It would have been perfectly logical for Kim, armed with prior Russian approval, or even their urging, to have sought ratification from his top aides. From other sources, we do know that Pak Hŏn-yŏng was strongly in support of a militant course of action (his only hope of regaining his southern base) and did promise massive support from underground southern elements. Indeed, as we shall see, this was one of the charges made against him at the time of his arrest and trial.

Kim Nam-sik also believes that detailed plans were laid around March 1950. He bases his conclusion on the fact that, in this period, certain South Korean guerrilla units were moved north and positioned near the 38th parallel. He cites units under Nam To-bu, for example, which were recalled in this period and subsequently landed on the east coast in Chumunjin. Chong-Sik Lee interview with Kim Nam-sik, Yusŏng, June 16–18, 1970.

The timing of the war, of course, had to take the farming season into consideration. The transplanting of rice plants must be finished, otherwise the year's crop would be ruined. This transplanting takes place in June throughout most of South Korea, being completed by the end of the month.

equal basis (despite the fact that the north had less than one-half the population of the south); nationwide elections should be held in August 1950, with preliminary consultative meetings in the period June 15–17, and with members of the UN Commission on Korea and the principal officials of the Rhee administration, including President Rhee and Prime Minister Yi Pŏm-sŏk, to be banned from participating.[31] The Communists could never have expected the Seoul government to take this proposal seriously and, indeed, P'yŏngyang was feverishly preparing for military action at this very time. Nevertheless, a representative of the UN Commission went to the north to receive a text of the proposal, and three North Korean representatives came south with copies of the plan.

The official Communist version of events was given by Kim Il-sŏng himself only a few hours after the North Korean attack had been launched. According to Kim, the Seoul government, headed by "that bandit-traitor," Syngman Rhee, had rejected Kim's proposals for peaceful unification, and followed that rejection with an invasion of North Korean soil at many points. (It was possible, of course, to point to Rhee's oft-proclaimed intention of marching North.) Now, the lackeys of the Americans would take the consequences of their actions. The south would be liberated by the People's Army; traitors like Rhee would be arrested and executed.[32]

31. For details, see transcript, "Front Discusses Plan for Unification," P'yŏng-yang Radio, June 7, 1950. Those to be excluded from any participation included nine major conservative leaders and the two principal conservative parties of the south, the Hanmin-dang (Korean Democratic Party) and the Kukmin-dang (Nationalist Party). During this period, also, the North Koreans proposed an exchange of Cho Man-sik for Yi Chu-ha and Kim Sam-yong, who were now in South Korean custody —an indication that Cho was still alive. Such an act also served to reduce apprehension in the south about any imminent northern attack.

32. See the transcript of Kim's broadcast, dated June 25, 1950, 2300 GMT, from his P'yŏngyang Radio broadcast. Kim already claimed that the KPA had "liberated" many towns and cities in the south despite his insistence that the "puppet government of country-selling traitor Syngman Rhee" had launched the invasion. His outline of conditions in the south and the failure of the "sincere efforts" of the Communists to achieve unification peacefully provide a rationale of sorts for the purported Southern invasion. Thus, describing the "wreckage of the national economy" by the "American imperialists" in "the southern half of the Republic," Kim claimed: "They are taking away at cheap prices our natural resources, including rice, tungsten, and graphite which are essential for our country. Pressured by American capital, our small and medium-sized industrialists and merchants have been forced into bankruptcy. In the southern half of our fatherland, production is at a standstill, with most of the factories closed down, several millions of the people unemployed, the farmers unable to possess land to this date, and the people suffering from hunger."

What were the objectives to be pursued at this point? "The Korean people must —in this war against the Syngman Rhee country-selling traitor gang—[defend] the Democratic People's Republic of Korea and its constitution; mop up the antipopular, fascist Syngman Rhee puppet regime which has been formed in the southern half; liberate the southern half of our fatherland from the rule of the Syngman Rhee traitor gang and restore in the southern half the People's Committees which are true people's

In subsequent broadcasts, it was repeatedly charged that the United States had really triggered this alleged assault upon the DPRK, with the ROK leaders acting as their puppets. The Communists asserted that John Foster Dulles, then Republican Party adviser to the US Department of State, had given the order to attack when he visited South Korean border forces on June 18. Dulles ridiculed this charge, stating that in point of fact he had been impressed mainly by the South Korean forces' lack of preparation in the face of possible invasion, and had planned to recommend more US military aid.

No responsible non-Communist sources took P'yŏngyang's charges seriously.[33] The evidence against the Communists was overwhelming, most

governments and, under the banner of the Democratic People's Republic of Korea, attain unification for the fatherland and found a powerful, democratic, independent Korea.

"This war—which we are carrying out in opposition to the internecine civil war which the Syngman Rhee country-selling gang has touched off—is a war of righteousness for the cause of the unification, independence, freedom, and democracy of the fatherland."

A slightly different translation of this broadcast is to be found under the title "Every Effort for Victory in the War," in Kim Il Sung, *Selected Works* (English edition, P'yŏngyang, 1965), Vol. I, pp. 123–129.

See also "Let us Resolutely Repulse the U.S. Imperialists' Armed Invasion," a radio broadcast of July 8, 1950, in *ibid.*, pp. 130–139.

For the Korean text, see Kim Il-sŏng, *Chayu wa tongnip ŭl wihan Chosŏn inmin ui chŏngui ui choguk haebang chŏnjaeng* (*The Korean People's Just Fatherland Liberation War for Freedom and Independence*), P'yŏngyang, 1954.

33. For a classic case of muckraking gone awry, see I. F. Stone, *The Hidden History of the Korean War*, New York, 1952. While Stone does not claim that the war was started by the South Koreans, he is very careful not to accuse the North Koreans of guilt, insisting that who started the war and how remains a mystery. The main thrust of the book, however, is to treat the war as a plot, ideal for the purpose of men like MacArthur and Dulles who, according to Stone, were intent upon preventive war against Communism and had "an almost hysterical fear of peace" (the latter phrase, to be found on p. 346, was aimed specifically at President Truman).

The passage of time and events has produced no evidence to sustain the Communist case. On the contrary, a careful perusal of data from all available sources confirms the guilt of the Communists. For an excellent recent treatment of the initial American reaction which also advances the field of decision-making studies, see the work by Glenn D. Paige cited above.

Additional evidence is presented in the intriguing Khrushchev memoirs, the authenticity of which is hotly debated. According to Khrushchev, the initiative for the Korean War came from Kim Il-sŏng, *not* from Stalin. Kim reportedly told Stalin that with one poke of a bayonet an internal explosion would be set off in South Korea, and the people would be liberated from Syngman Rhee's rule. Stalin reportedly told Kim to think it over, make his calculations, and return with concrete plans— and this was done. According to Khrushchev, Kim was convinced that success was assured, but Stalin was not so certain, harboring some fears concerning American intervention. Nevertheless, adds Khrushchev, the Russians were inclined to believe that if the war were fought and won swiftly, American intervention could be avoided.

However, he says, Stalin decided to ask Mao Tse-tung's opinion. Reportedly,

particularly in terms of what happened in the hours and days following the opening assault. The North Korean invasion clearly caught both American and South Korean forces by surprise. Moreover, it took place on a scale that had obviously required a lengthy period of preparation. At 4:00 A.M. on the morning of June 25, the Communists launched a massive artillery barrage. One hour later, between 75,000 and 90,000 North Korean infantrymen struck across the 38th parallel in a carefully coordinated offensive. These troops were supplied with an abundance of ammunition, tanks, unarmored military vehicles, combat planes, and automatic weapons. As noted earlier, many of the initial assault forces were veteran combat soldiers. The South Koreans fought back bravely in some instances. But they were not prepared, either in tactics or in weaponry, for this major attack.

Mao gave his approval, and also indicated his doubts about American involvement. Khrushchev says that he recalls a "high spirited dinner" at Stalin's dacha during which Kim recounted the benefits that would accrue after Korean reunification, with all present toasting the North Koreans and their coming victory.

Khrushchev acknowledges extensive Soviet military assistance, and then states, "the designated hour arrived and the war began. The attack was launched successfully. The North Koreans swept south swiftly. But what Kim Il-sŏng had predicted—an internal uprising after the first shots were fired and Syngman Rhee was overthrown—unfortunately failed to materialize" (p. 369).

Khrushchev, who supports Stalin's decision to aid the attack, claiming he would have done likewise and calling it "a war of liberation," a class war, bitterly condemns Stalin for calling back all Soviet advisers prior to the march south, for fear some might be taken prisoner and the USSR's role thereby revealed. Khrushchev, feeling sorry for Kim after the latter's serious defeat following the Inch'ŏn landing, claims to have urged Stalin to send more Soviet advisers, and suggests that, with a Soviet tank corps or two, Kim could have taken Pusan and ended the war.

This part of Khrushchev's account contradicts Monat's flat statements concerning the presence of Soviet advisers and his interaction with them, as we shall soon note. It is also at variance with numerous Korean accounts and is almost certainly in error. It is probably true, however, that Stalin balked at sending Soviet personnel in significant numbers, or in capacities that would risk a frontal clash with American forces.

Khrushchev further recounts a meeting between Stalin and Chou En-lai that preceded Chinese intervention, indicating that at first the decision seemed to be against intervention, but that this position was reversed before the sessions closed, either on instructions from Mao or on Stalin's initiative.

For Khrushchev's full recital, see *Khrushchev Remembers*, Boston, 1970, pp. 367–373.

The official North Korean version of the commencement of the war remains the same as it was before. Note the following passage from Baik Bong:

"Using the Syngman Rhee puppet army in a frontal attack, U.S. imperialism opened up, by deliberate provocation, a piratic aggressive war against the Korean people. It was a war imposed upon the Korean people by surprise attack, and although the Syngman Rhee puppet army was used as the spearhead, the prime mover and puppet master of the war was U.S. imperialism, the war-maniac." Baik Bong, *Kim Il Sung: Biography*, Tokyo, 1969, Vol. II, p. 271. This much publicized three-volume work is an official translation of Paek Pong's *Minjok ui t'aeyang Kim Il-sŏng changgun* (*Marshal Kim Il-sŏng, the Sun of the Nation*), P'yŏngyang, 1968.

In three days, Seoul had fallen. The Communists entered the city on June 28, as hundreds of thousands of refugees streamed south. Meanwhile, American officials in Seoul, Tokyo, and Washington had begun to recover from their initial shock. Intelligence reports had been received before the attack indicating Communist troop movements southward and buildups at certain points along the 38th parallel. But such reports had been received on other occasions, so they were discounted. The American consensus was that the Communists had no intention of conducting an all-out attack upon the south at this time.

Once the attack came, a decision had to be made. In one sense, the issue was simple. Should American forces be committed to the defense of South Korea? All observers agreed that without American men as well as American equipment, the Republic would be overthrown by the Communists. The decision to defend South Korea was made swiftly by President Truman, with the support of the United Nations being sought and obtained.

It is not our purpose here to recount the story of the Korean War. That has been adequately done elsewhere. Instead, we will refer to developments in that war only as they relate directly to developments in North Korea. Brief attention, however, must be given to the role of the Soviet Union and Communist China during this period. As we have indicated earlier, the Chinese Communists were not in a position to play a significant role in North Korea during the opening years of Communist rule there. Indeed, they did not come to full power until the fall of 1949, and this was a period when their primary energies quite naturally had to be devoted to domestic considerations. Moreover, the treatment accorded those Koreans returning from Yenan and other Chinese Communist areas indicated clearly that Kim and his Soviet-sponsored comrades had little desire for Chinese involvement in Korean affairs. Indeed, such evidence as is available strongly suggests that relations between Chinese and Korean Communists were not harmonious, at least up to 1949. A controversy over reconstruction of the Sup'ung Dam led to Chinese Communist obstruction of North Korean activities during the 1948–49 period. The issues were compromised in early 1949, possibly via Soviet mediation. Other border problems, however, seem to have persisted. In any case, it is curious that the Peking authorities did not send an ambassador to P'yŏngyang until mid-August 1950, after the Korean War had begun, although formal recognition had taken place much earlier.[34]

Nevertheless, as we have seen, Korean forces previously stationed in Manchuria were returned to North Korea in 1949 and 1950, and the Chinese permitted heavy shipments of Soviet military equipment to Korea via Chinese rail lines. Care, however, was taken in the exchange of Party

34. For a thorough, insightful treatment of the Chinese Communist role, see Allen S. Whiting, *China Crosses the Yalu: The Decision to Enter the Korean War*, New York, 1960.

memberships. The North Koreans thoroughly screened Korean applicants from China, including members of the Korean Volunteer Corps, probably because they wished to prevent any Maoist enclave from being established within the NKWP. In contrast, those holding membership in the Soviet Communist Party were automatically accepted.[35]

Whatever Mao and his comrades knew or did not know concerning North Korean plans, it is impossible to believe that the Russians were not deeply involved. This is so even if we treat Pawel Monat's testimony with caution. There is no reason to doubt, moreover, that the Chinese would have approved the "liberation" plans—while hoping and expecting to remain aloof from the actual fighting. It must be remembered that, in the fall of 1949, Liu Shao-ch'i, echoing the basic Peking theme of this period, proclaimed that the path taken by the Chinese Communists in defeating "imperialism and its lackeys" was one that could and should be undertaken by the peoples of other colonial and semicolonial countries.[36] Perhaps it was debatable whether the North Korean assault represented good Maoist tactics. Had the political ground been sufficiently prepared? Could the Korean People's Army (KPA) swim in the sea of the Korean peasantry? Were the military tactics appropriate to Communist strength and that of the enemy? Was the KPA prepared for all military exigencies, including the possibility of an American response and a massive, protracted war? If the answer to some of these questions was clearly no, once again, the predominance of Soviet over Chinese influence was underlined.

Meanwhile, in the months following the opening Communist assault, the war took a series of surprising turns. During the first month of the struggle, the North Koreans scored smashing victories. By the end of July they had pushed the opposing forces into the southeastern corner of the Korean peninsula—the so-called Pusan perimeter. With Taegu and Pusan the only major cities still held by the Americans and their South Korean allies, the military situation was desperate; the Naktong River line was ordered held at all costs. Taking heavy casualties, however, the North Koreans continued to press their initiative. Between late August and mid-September, some of the heaviest fighting of the entire war took place. Taegu remained in American hands, but the pressures on the Naktong line were enormous.

Suddenly, with the Inch'ŏn landing, the tide of battle turned abruptly. By that landing, which took place on September 15, United States forces quickly cut off large Communist units to the south. General MacArthur seized the initiative, cutting swiftly inland. In thirteen days, Seoul was again

35. U.S. Department of State, *North Korea: A Case Study in the Techniques of Takeover, op. cit.,* p. 118.

36. Liu Shao-ch'i, "Speech by Liu Shao-ch'i at the Conference on Trade Unions of Asia and Oceania," *For a Lasting Peace, for a People's Democracy!,* Dec. 30, 1949, p. 2.

in South Korean hands, and the North Koreans had suffered huge losses. By the end of September, nearly all territory south of the 38th parallel was under UN control. The North Korean retreat became a rout.

At this point, a critical decision had to be made: Should UN forces cross the 38th parallel and seek the unification of Korea as a non-Communist state by military action? Debate within top American circles and within the United Nations over this issue was heated, with the American decision finally being made in the affirmative. On September 29, after the Joint Chiefs of Staff had approved a northward advance two days earlier, Secretary of Defense George Marshall sent General MacArthur a "for your eyes only" message stating that, with President Truman's approval, he was free to proceed north. On October 1, the 3rd Division of the ROK 1st Corps crossed the 38th parallel on the east coast of North Korea. After delays due to logistical difficulties, the US 8th Army moved north on October 7. The invasion of the north had officially begun.

Kim Il-sŏng's forces were exhausted, defeated, and in no condition to meet the American and ROK armies. Major sections of North Korea were rapidly overrun. The port of Wŏnsan had already fallen to the ROK 3rd Division on October 11; nine days later, the 8th Army entered the battered city of P'yŏngyang, finding it almost undefended. Kim Il-sŏng and the top officials of his government had fled northward and established a temporary capital at Sinŭiju, having first ordered P'yŏngyang defended to the last man. By the end of October, however, the North Korean army had collapsed, many units fleeing into the mountains near Manchuria and the Soviet Union. United Nations forces moved almost at will throughout the north. By the third week of November, American troops had reached the town of Hyesanjin, from which they could look across the Yalu into China.

Even in late October, however, certain allied field commanders had reported the presence of Chinese soldiers. On November 25, a violent Communist counteroffensive got under way, spearheaded by two Chinese Communist field armies. Within a week, the UN line had been forced back some fifty miles, and soon the UN forces were in serious difficulties; indeed, the 8th Army was threatened with being driven into the Yellow Sea. However, a disaster was prevented, and most UN forces were successfully withdrawn, a new defensive line being established north and east of Seoul. By December 5, the 8th Army had abandoned P'yŏngyang, and by mid-December, the Communists were back in control of almost all of North Korea—except that some three million northerners had moved as refugees to the south. The North Korean army had been reconstituted as a force of approximately 150,000, divided into 15 divisions. The Chinese Communists had some 28 divisions in the field; like the North Koreans, they were willing to take massive losses.[37]

37. For a more detailed account of the invasion of the north and the Chinese counterthrust, see Roy E. Appleman, *South to the Naktong, North to the Yalu: June–*

The Third Plenum of the KWP Central Committee

In the midst of these tumultuous events, a meeting of the Korean Workers' Party Central Committee was convened in December 1950, "to discuss the current political situation and the immediate problems confront-

November 1950, in the series United States Army in the Korean War, Washington, 1961. For an annotated bibliography of books on the Korean War, see Thomas T. Hammond, *Soviet Foreign Relations and World Communism,* Princeton, 1965, pp. 787–806.

Let us note Monat's appraisal of the respective roles of the Russians and Chinese, once the war was under way. It is his basic theme that, during the Korean War, the Russians dominated the North Koreans (including Kim Il-sŏng) completely, but that their relations with the Chinese were far from intimate. The following represents the gist of his remarks on these matters (Pawel Monat, "Russians in Korea," *op. cit.*):

"When I came to North Korea in late 1951, I travelled by train from Mukden to the Yalu River Crossing with a group of some 200 men, all of them dressed in Chinese People's Volunteer (CPV) uniforms but all of them were Russian combat troops —MIG pilots, combat engineers and anti-aircraft gunners. . . . When I was there, at least 5,000 Soviet officers and soldiers were on active duty either in Korea or just over the Yalu River on the MIG bases in Manchuria" (p. 76).

Elaborate precautions were taken, according to Monat, to prevent any knowledge of this Russian presence. Soviet pilots could not fly within ten or fifteen miles of the ocean, or farther south than the Chong-chon River. A Russian joke, said Monat, went as follows:

"First Russian: 'We have the best pilots in the world.'
Second Russian: 'How is that?'
First Russian: 'Because they can fly with no hands.'
Second Russian: 'Why do they do that?'
First Russian: 'They use their hands to slant their eyes so the Americans will think they're Koreans' " (p. 77).

Nevertheless, according to Monat, a number of Russians were killed and the Inch'ŏn landings cut off some Soviet military advisers, who escaped north only by disguising themselves as civilian Koreans. Monat asserts that the Soviet ambassador— who during the time Monat was there was Lieutenant General (in civilian clothes) Vladimir N. Razuvayev—was the "real ruler of North Korea." Monat's appraisal of Kim Il-sŏng, moreover, is scarcely flattering: "As a wartime leader, Kim was hardly a standout. He was fat and rather dull, but since he was under the complete control of the Russians, he did not need much personality. Kim was never allowed to make a decision or a public announcement without the Soviet ambassador's express permission. All North Korean military orders were drafted in Russian and had to be initialed by a Russian officer to become effective. The Russians were always very careful to preserve a facade of diplomatic propriety over this crude power arrangement. North Korea was—and is—no more independent than a man sentenced to prison for life, but no Soviet officer ever gave a direct order *in public.* The illusion of independence was touchingly protected" (p. 77).

This account, written in 1960 and essentially for the American public by a Polish defector, may be exaggerated and too harsh. As we have seen, however, this account of the way the Russians operated accords with what is given in most other sources. In the period during which Monat was in North Korea, moveover, Kim's military and political organizations had been totally shattered, rendering him completely dependent on outside forces. It is entirely possible, indeed, that in the story presented above we can discern the true reasons for Kim's demands for *total independence* in later

ing the country." There was certainly no dearth of problems, and this meeting was undoubtedly called to assign blame for the recent disasters as quickly as possible to prevent an internal crisis.[38] With the Chinese now

---

years. Despite Monat's comment, Kim is not dull intellectually, and his total subordination to the Russians must have embittered him greatly, laying the seeds for events to come.

Very recently, confirmation of a portion of Monat's account has come from a Russian source. Two Soviet authors, writing in 1971, flatly assert that not only were "Soviet air advisors, including prominent military commanders" in Korea but that "Soviet airmen took part in the battles with the aggressors." O. B. Borisov and B. T. Koloskov, *Sovetsko-Kitaiski Otnosheniya 1945–1970, kratkii ocherk,* (Soviet-Chinese Relations 1945–1970, A Brief Essay), Moscow, 1971, p. 55 ff.

Borisov and Koloskov, quoting from M. S. Kapitsa also report that at the request of the People's Republic of China, the Soviet Union transferred elite air force divisions to Manchuria thereby shielding the industrial centers of northeast China from air-raids, and in air battles, "shot down tens of American planes."

Finally, they declare that the Soviet Union "worked in close military cooperation" with the Chinese in Korea, "continuously furnishing the Korean People's Army and the Chinese People's Volunteers with arms, military supplies, fuel, food stuffs, and medicine."

Monat asserts that the Russians, in drawing up the timetable for the Korean War, made two critical mistakes: they underestimated the ability of the US to come to the aid of the South Koreans and they overestimated the ability of the North Korean army (p. 86). Its best officers, few in numbers, were too inexperienced, and its total strength was not sufficient to mount heavy counterattacks. In the first month, according to Monat, the North Koreans lost about 40,000 killed and wounded, approximately one-third of their fighting force.

After the Inch'ŏn landing (which none of the Communists expected, according to Monat), both the Chinese and the Russians were agreed that China would have to enter the war. He asserts flatly that the Chinese were much afraid of General MacArthur, thinking that he might attack across the Yalu or bring Nationalist forces from Taiwan, allowing them to attack; hence, "Mao was determined to defend and hold North Korea as a buffer state to guard his Manchurian border" (p. 94).

Once the so-called CPV (Chinese People's Volunteers) entered the war, they dominated the North Korean scene by the sheer weight of their numbers. According to Monat, their leaders were suspicious of everyone, especially the Russians. Thus, Sino-Soviet liaison was poor, and relations were marked with aloofness. On the other hand, the Chinese established good relations with the North Korean civilians. Says Monat: "They were more popular among the North Korean civilians than either the Russians or the Korean soldiers themselves. The Russians had behaved very badly during their 'liberation' of North Korea. Their troops often got drunk and roamed the countryside, raping women and stealing whatever they could find. The North Korean soldiers lived off the country and showed no compassion at all for the civilians who were starving in order to keep them in the war. The Chinese, by contrast, brought all their own food with them. In some areas Chinese troops voluntarily gave up one meal a day and turned the rice over to orphanages, schools or entire villages. Twice a year during the harvest I saw Chinese troops go into the fields to help the farmers collect their crops" (p. 96).

38. According to Kim Ch'ang-sun, Major General Lebedev, who had earlier been chief of the Intelligence and Propaganda Section, in the headquarters of Soviet Military Government in P'yŏngyang, was now living under the same roof as Kim Il-sŏng

deeply involved in Korea, domestic politics were certain to become more complex.

The Central Committee Third Plenum was held from the twenty-first to the twenty-third of December in Kanggye, a city near the Manchurian border in Chagang Province.[39] A number of key military and party leaders were sharply criticized for alleged inefficiencies, errors, and crimes, and were either purged or demoted. The war to date had gone disastrously for the North Koreans, and Kim must have felt very insecure, despite the full commitment of the Russians to him. In the midst of unprecedented failures, the Party as well as the army had been smashed, with acts of incompetence and disloyalty widespread.

The darkest hours of the war had passed, however, thanks to Chinese intervention. Indeed, according to several accounts, Kim was greatly aided because P'yŏngyang had been retaken ahead of schedule, on December 6. But with the Chinese Communists now a major force in North Korea, Kim had a potential rival in Mu Chŏng, commander of the 2nd Corps. The KPA was a broken reed at this point, and primary military responsibilities now rested with such men as P'eng Teh-huai and other Chinese military veterans commanding the so-called Chinese People's Volunteers. Was it reasonable to fear that they might lend an ear to an old comrade-in-arms like Mu Chŏng, and to other elements of the Yenan faction, rather than to Soviet-oriented groups? Given the character of Sino-Soviet relations during this period, moreover, this possibility must have concerned the Russians quite as much as it concerned Kim Il-sŏng. Perhaps it is not surprising, therefore, that Mu Chŏng was a major casualty of the Third Plenum. He was charged with having failed to perceive the general military situation correctly and, specifically, with having disobeyed orders to defend P'yŏng-yang resolutely. In fact, it is clear that P'yŏngyang could not have been

---

and serving as his close adviser. Kim Ch'ang-sun asserts that Lebedev urged that a meeting of the Central Committee be held quickly so that Kim Il-sŏng himself could be exonerated of blame for the military debacle, with responsibility fixed elsewhere. Kim Ch'ang-sun, *op. cit.*, pp. 126–127.

According to Kim Ch'ang-sun, Mu Chŏng had never liked Kim Il-sŏng. Like O Ki-sŏp (and Pak Hŏn-yŏng), Mu Chŏng found it inconceivable that Kim should be his superior, since he had been a chief artillery officer with the Chinese army and taken part in the Long March, playing a role infinitely more significant than that of Kim in the years before 1945. Moreover, he was undoubtedly bitter at the rebuffs suffered at the hands of Kim.

39. There is some dispute about place of the meeting. Kim Ch'ang-sun asserts that it took place in Pyŏrori, a small village three kilometers north of Manp'o, and almost precisely on the Manchurian border. Another source claims that the sessions were actually held in T'ung-hua, Manchuria. However, Kim Nam-sik, who spent nearly ten years in Kanggye later, asserts that he was told by many high-ranking Party officials that the Third Plenum meetings were held there, in a huge tunnel that had been dug by the Japanese in preparation for the Kanggye thermoelectric plant. Chong-Sik Lee interview with Kim Nam-sik, June 16–18, 1970.

defended successfully at the time, and Mu Chŏng may well have been wise when he retreated into Manchuria and used the Shenyang (Mukden) area as a sanctuary to regroup North Korean forces.

Nevertheless, Mu Chŏng was bitterly attacked; among other crimes, he was even charged with the unwarranted killing of his subordinate commander.[40] Having arrived at the meeting as a Central Committee member, Mu Chŏng left as a virtual prisoner. Removed as commander and stripped of all rank, he was placed in charge of a group of prisoners, and later ordered to supervise a construction gang in the building of the Moranbong underground theater in P'yŏngyang. Significantly, at some point, Chinese authorities requested that he be assigned to them. At that point, however, he appears to have been a broken man. Shortly thereafter he died of an unspecified illness.

We cannot know the degree of jeopardy in which Kim Il-sŏng found himself at the time of the Third Plenum. Although he tried to put the best possible face on developments in his report to the Plenum, he could not avoid admitting major shortcomings on both the military and the political fronts. Thus, after asserting that the Party had correctly trained and equipped the Korean People's Army and the Korean people, praising the assistance being rendered by the Soviet Union and especially by the Chinese People's Volunteers, and talking of the "increasing contradictions" within the enemy camp, Kim was forced to turn to a long list of "serious defects." North Korean military reserves were inadequate; the officers were inexperienced; certain troops lacked discipline; the tactics of guerrilla warfare were pursued mechanically, without genuine creativity; the logistical system was weak; and key leaders had panicked at moments of crisis.[41]

Kim then turned to criticize key figures who had committed errors or crimes. In addition to Mu Chŏng, a number of individuals were summoned to judgment. Kim Il, vice-minister of Defense in charge of political affairs in the KPA, was charged with harboring defeatist thoughts. He had supposedly asserted that, unless air support was forthcoming, victory would be

40. Kim's report to the Third Plenum, delivered Dec. 21, 1950, entitled "Present Conditions and the Tasks at Hand," is contained in *Kin Nichisei senshū* (*Selected Works of Kim Il-sŏng*), Japanese ed., Kyōto, 1952, Vol. II, pp. 105–144.

The attack upon Mu Chŏng by Kim included the charge that, "utilizing the confusion prevailing at that time [during his retreat], he resorted to military cliquism similar to the emperors in the feudalistic period, shooting people at will without any legal procedures." Kim added, "He, of course, must be punished via the law."

41. *Ibid.*, pp. 114–118. For the current official account of the Third Plenum, see Baik Bong, *op. cit.*, Vol. II, pp. 331–335. Acknowledging serious internal difficulties at the time, Paek writes that Kim demanded stern revolutionary discipline, advancing the banners of criticism and self-criticism and calling for the Party to act "as one man" under the orders of the leader. Paek says nothing about the actions taken against specific individuals at this time.

impossible.[42] For "acts of cowardice," Ch'oe Kang, Kim Han-jung, and a number of other North Korean military commanders were removed from their posts. Others, including Yim Ch'un-ch'u, chairman of the Kangwŏn Provincial Party, were charged with failing to carry out retreat operations efficiently.[43] Yim was accused of having failed to organize a proper withdrawal in his haste to flee from allied forces, leaving important Party documents behind. The actions of the Third Plenum, in sum, amounted to a major shake-up in both military and Party ranks. Nam Il became chief of the General Staff,[44] with Kim Ch'aek, an old Kim Il-sŏng stalwart, serving as KPA front-line commander.

Kim ended his report with the admission that Party discipline desperately needed to be strengthened. The war had "clearly exposed who was a true Party member and who was an opportunistic Party member." He acknowledged that a substantial number of "impure elements, cowards, and mixed elements" had been turned up, and that a large number of Ch'ŏndogyo Young Friends' and Democratic Party members in particular had aided the enemy or even joined the "reactionary Self-Defense Units" set up by them. Nevertheless, Kim asserted, the Democratic Front must not be destroyed. Rather, it should be consolidated, with Communists continuing to indoctrinate fraternal members of non-Communist parties and detecting the "reactionary" elements that had penetrated these parties.

Once again, Kim Il-sŏng had managed to turn a dangerous corner, largely because of a change in Communist military fortunes. At the very end of 1950, the Communists launched a major offensive involving 500,000

42. Differing with Kim Ch'ang-sun and several others, including (Big) Kim Il's former secretary, Kim Nam-sik insists that the Kim Il purged during the Korean War was not the Kim Il who was an old Kim Il-sŏng comrade and who later held a top Politburo post. He argues that there were two Kim Ils. One, known as "Big Kim Il, is currently first deputy premier. The other was known as "Small Kim Il," and it was he—a Soviet-Korean—who was purged. He insists that "Big Kim Il" did not have sufficient education or experience to head the political propaganda program for the armed forces. Chong-Sik Lee interview with Kim Nam-sik, June 16–18, 1970. In this, he is supported by a Soviet Korean specialist, G. F. Kim, who corroborated Kim Nam-sik's statement in November 1971 while visiting in the United States.

43. Yim, as we shall see, was later reinstated into the Party, and subsequently served in a variety of capacities before being purged again.

44. Kang Kŏn, previously chief of the General Staff, was killed in action: Kim Ch'ang-sun, *op. cit.*, p. 133. The twentieth anniversary of Kang's death was memorialized in P'yŏngyang on Sept. 7, 1970: *Koria Hyŏron* (*Korea Review*), Tokyo, November 1970, p. 63.

Monat's comments on Nam Il, whom he claimed to know well, are interesting. Nam Il, he asserts, was a Korean in appearance only, being a Soviet citizen who had spent most of his life in the USSR, having come from a family that went to Siberia in the Japanese era. As a captain in the Soviet army, he had fought the Germans at Stalingrad, according to Monat, and later, as chief of staff of a division, he had helped liberate Warsaw. Monat, *op. cit.*, p. 93.

troops, with one million men in reserve. On January 4, 1951, United Nations forces were again forced to evacuate Seoul, and the Communist advance was not stopped until late January. Communist losses were very heavy, but replacements continued to flow into Korea from the Manchurian sanctuary. Seoul was not retaken by the allies until mid-March, at which time only 200,000 pathetic civilians remained in a city formerly occupied by two million inhabitants. On April 22, the Communists undertook another major offensive, using approximately one-half of the 700,000 troops available to them. On this occasion, however, they failed. By May 20, a stalemate had been reached, with the Communist forces bloodied and exhausted. One month later, on June 23, 1951, Jacob Malik, deputy foreign commissar for Foreign Affairs of the Soviet Union, signaled Communist willingness to begin peace talks.

The Fourth Plenum and Its Aftermath

As will be recalled, the Communists made no concessions for nearly two years. Meanwhile, the war continued, with heavy casualties on both sides. On November 2, 1951, the Fourth Plenum of the Party Central Committee was convened. In his report, Kim Il-Sŏng sharply attacked the closed-door policy of restricting Party membership to those whose vitae indicated a true proletarian background or thorough ideological preparation. He demanded that the peasantry be admitted in substantial numbers; they could be trained to become good Marxist-Leninists later.[45] Kim's new

45. Kim's arguments for opening up the Party to the peasantry constitute a valuable revelation of the North Korean Communist concept of the role of their Party at this stage, and the proper relation of various classes to it.

Kim asserted that at the time of "liberation", North Korea had no more than 300,000 workers, and that this number had doubled in five years, with all these new workers coming from the peasant class. Nearly 80 percent of the population, however, remained peasants. Thus, "if we accept only the workers and the small number of Communists, how can our Party develop into a mass party and fulfill its leading role among the masses satisfactorily?"

It was because of the "peculiar conditions" characterizing North Korea at this point that we have made our party a Workers' Party, instead of a Communist Party, said Kim. He went on to argue that, even if it absorbed large numbers of peasants, the Party could not become a party of the peasants, because "invariably it will be guided by the ideology of the working class." He insisted, "We will recruit the best elements of the toiling peasantry into the Party, arm them with the ideology of the working class, and continue to strengthen and develop our Party into a mass political party with the working class as its core."

To close the door to the peasants, to insist upon a certain proportion of workers, Kim argued, is counter to the line of our Party. "We should admit without hesitation large numbers of advanced elements from among the peasants and working intellectuals, and thus continuously develop it into a mass political party." This, of course, did not mean admitting everyone who came along, Kim continued. "There must be no place in our Party for landlords, clergymen, profiteers, or urban loafers." The Party also had to guard against those reactionary-minded and impure elements and spies sneaking into the ranks; although if the children of landlords and profiteers

position was not difficult to understand. The severe criticism of Party members at the time of the Third Plenum had resulted in rigorous investigation of all members, and tightening of recruitment procedures. Meanwhile, as a result of the war, Party membership had shrunk to a fraction of its previous size. Now it was essential to rebuild the Party as a mass-based organization.

It was inevitable that such a policy would downgrade the role of southerners in the Party, and place a new premium upon the recruitment of northerners. Thus, from a policy of rigorous scrutiny, the Party moved to a more relaxed, open-door policy. Large numbers of peasants were brought into the Party with minimal concern for their educational or ideological standards. Restrictions were also eased upon intellectuals and even upon certain former landlords and some individuals previously charged with anti-Communist activities. The Party—out of necessity—embarked upon a desperate search for support.

This shift in policy provided a basis for attack upon Hŏ Ka-i, who had been Party secretary during the period when the closed-door policies had been in effect. Hŏ was relieved of his post, and moved to the harmless and relatively powerless position of vice-premier. It has been suggested that the issues separating Kim and Hŏ may not have been entirely related to the substantive issue discussed above. Kim is said to have long doubted whether Hŏ could control Pak Hŏn-yŏng and the former SKWP elements, and to have worried about Hŏ's tendency to regard these elements as both effective and trustworthy.[46]

---

were prepared to condemn their fathers' crimes and fight for their country, "after careful consideration" the Party should admit them.

"On the Improvement of the Party's Organizational Work—Concluding Speech at the Fourth Plenum of the Central Committee of the Workers' Party of Korea, November 2, 1951," in Kim Il Sung, *Selected Works* (1965 ed.), Vol. I. *op. cit.,* pp. 148–151. This same speech is to be found in the 1952 Japanese edition (*Kin Nichisei senshū*) cited previously, Vol. III, pp. 241–269. Interestingly, the title of Kim's speech is given here as "Concerning Some of the Defects in Party Organizational Activities." An examination of the text, however, does not indicate any significant differences from the 1965 English edition.

46. According to Kim Ch'ang-sun, *op. cit.,* while Hŏ and Kim Il-sŏng had been close since 1945, Hŏ had been much more tolerant of Pak Hŏn-yŏng and the old South Korean Workers' Party members than Kim thought wise. For example, Hŏ had admitted all southern Party members into the North Korean Workers' Party after the 1949 merger, with only nominal screening. Thus, when Hŏ and Pak became deputy chairmen of the unified Party, Kim reportedly worried whether Hŏ would be able to control Pak.

As we shall see, Hŏ was later to be purged completely. Consequently, the official evaluation today is not merely that his policies were in error, but also that he was part of "the enemy plot to disrupt the Party from within." Note the following excerpts from Paek Pong's work: "In those days, the anti-Party factional elements, including Hu Ka I, did not understand the character of the Party as the vanguard of the masses of the entire working people, led by the working class, nor did they understand the position, in which factory workers had been reduced in numbers owing to the war,

At this point, it should be noted that during the war the normal institutions of government were drastically altered. After the commencement of hostilities, a Military Affairs Committee was organized, with Commander-in-Chief Kim Il-sŏng as its head. This committee (laced with Soviet advisers) dominated the political as well as the military scene throughout the war. It had supreme authority, not merely over military matters, but over everything that could be construed as involving the operation of the war.[47]

From the outset of the war, military government was automatically instituted in areas where an enemy presence existed or was threatened. Provincial military affairs committees were established; the provincial Party chairman served as head of the committee, with the military commander for the area and the provincial People's Committee chairman as additional members. In areas occupied by the Chinese People's Volunteers, the Chinese commander was also appointed. After the UN forces had launched their counterattack, however, the entire country was placed under military government.[48]

It can scarcely be overemphasized that the 1950–51 period had been

---

nor did they try to understand it. These anti-Party factional elements, who kept to the idea of maintaining the percentage of members of worker origin, refused to admit to the Party membership the broad toiling peasants fighting at the front and in the rear, displaying their patriotic devotion. The factionalists committed the grave mistake of rejecting, by any possible means, applicants for admission to the Party. If such bureaucratic actions, diametrically contrary to the mass character of the Party and the actual situation, had been left unremedied, the Party would have suffered great losses in failing to consolidate unity with the peasants who made up the overwhelming majority of the population. Further, these factional elements put aside educational work, punished Party members and expelled them from the Party in an unprincipled way, merely because of some slight error during the retreat, and increased formalism and bureaucratism. Over the long term, these evil deeds but helped the enemy plot to disrupt the Party from within, and isolate the Party from the masses." Baik Bong, *op. cit.,* Vol. II, pp. 369–370.

The above account is all the more ironic because Hŏ's strict policies had been ordered by Kim at the time of the Third Plenum.

47. On June 26, 1950, the Presidium of the Supreme People's Assembly issued an edict creating a Military Affairs Committee consisting of Kim Il-sŏng, chairman, and Pak Hŏn-yŏng, Hong Myŏng-hui, Kim Ch'aek, Ch'oe Yong-gŏn, Pak Il-u, and Chŏng Chun-t'aek. Other provisions in the edict were: "Entire sovereignty in the nation shall be concentrated in the Military Affairs Committee. All citizens, and all sovereign agencies, political parties, social organizations, and military agencies must absolutely obey the decisions and instructions of the Military Affairs Committee." Chosŏn Chungang T'ongshinsa (Korean Central News Agency), *Chosŏn Chungang nyŏngam* (*Korean Central Yearbook*), 1950–51 ed., p. 82, quoted from Pang-In-hu, *op. cit.,* p. 139.

48. Chong-Sik Lee interview with Kim Nam-sik, June 16–18, 1970. Kim Hyŏk, in his interview with Chong-Sik Lee on Jan. 15, 1970, stated that division and regimental commanders were required to report to the Party chairman and act according to his orders, indicating a continuing degree of Party dominance, at least in the initial stages of the war.

a devastating one for the Communists, not least of all because large numbers of their own people had turned against them. To understand the context of Kim's remarks at the Fourth Plenum about avoiding excessive harshness with those citizens who had transgressed, it should be noted that some northern villages and towns temporarily occupied by UN forces had cooperated fully after their few Communist leaders had fled. As we shall have occasion to note later, this cooperation took various forms. In not a few instances, key Communists were actually killed by the people. Significant numbers of young men also joined the *ch'i-an-dae* (public security units) that were hastily created by UN authorities to keep order (and annihilate Communists). Sometimes, units were formed spontaneously, like bands of vigilantes, and other kinds of anti-Communist organizations sprang up everywhere. Normally, of course, cooperation took a more casual form: information given, food and drink provided, and similar activities.

The Communist Party "establishment" had fled without any warning, leaving the people alone. Naturally, most of those who remained assumed that it was not likely to return. It is impossible to separate those who cooperated with the UN forces eagerly, and those who did so for opportunistic reasons. The hunting-down of Communists, however, was sufficiently widespread to suggest that Kim and the Party had a far weaker popular base than they had assumed.

When the Party returned—almost as abruptly as it had departed—the first big question was how to handle those who had lapsed. As early as February 1951, the DPRK cabinet issued a set of directives on "the treatment of those who surrendered to the enemy." It was admitted that "American imperialist robbers" had led Koreans to massacre large numbers of "progressive people," and caused many of their fellow citizens to distrust the Party. The document then classified as *chasuja,* or self-surrendered, those who had contemplated, prepared, or committed "criminal actions" against the Party and the government, but who had surrendered voluntarily to Communist authorities. Such individuals would not be prosecuted under the following conditions:

1. If they had merely joined the public security units or local police forces, but had not "murdered" any "patriots" or their families; or if they had arrested someone, but he had not been killed or seriously injured
2. If they were deserters from the Korean People's Army, but had not "murdered patriots or committed other crimes" (they would be put back in the army)
3. If they had resisted the government and were hiding in the mountains, but had not murdered "patriots" or committed other crimes, and had surrendered with their arms
4. If they were soldiers of the "so-called National Defense Army of

the Syngman Rhee Puppet Government" who were hiding in the mountains, but had not committed any crimes and had surrendered with their arms (they too would be put in the KPA).

While they would not be held criminally responsible, however, they would have to undergo "mass trials" held under the auspices of local government agencies. In these trials, they should confess their errors, pledge themselves to be good citizens, and accept surveillance for a certain period. And if they again committed "reactionary deeds," they should be turned over to the people's courts.

Meanwhile, those falling into the following categories should be held criminally responsible:

1. All of those who had directly participated in the "murder of patriots and their families," and all of those informing upon "patriots and their families" in such fashion that it led to their deaths
2. All officers of "reactionary and bandit groups"
3. All of those who resisted with arms against various people's agencies when the latter were engaged in pacification activities
4. All of those who surrendered but deceived the people's government agencies by hiding arms or persisting in reactionary deeds.[49]

Regulations were also issued in this period concerning mass trials. These were to be organized at the hamlet, ri (ward), or town and city level. The court was to have one chief judge and two "people's assessors" (the latter roughly equivalent in function to a jury of citizens). The chief judge was to be elected for three months by the ri or other appropriate People's Assembly, with the people's assessors being "recommended" by the social organizations within the unit concerned at the time of the trial, and confirmed by the appropriate People's Committee. The trial was to be conducted at the place where the crime had been committed, with all of the people being assembled as witnesses. Information concerning the crime was to be presented by state, Party, or social organization representatives, with the masses also presenting such evidence as they possessed. The accused was to be allowed to present his own defense. When the interrogation was finished, a mass discussion was to follow on the questions of guilt and punishment. At its conclusion the chief judge and the people's assessors were to retire to a room and make a final decision, a decision then to be ratified by the masses at the trial.

The regulations also determined that those whose actions did not warrant criminal prosecution, but who had committed "bad deeds," should be punished by tumun, or restriction of movement. This was a social punish-

49. We were able to obtain the original document entitled "Attachment No. 1, Rules Concerning the Treatment of Those Surrendering," a printed sheet, bearing the date Feb. 10, 1951.

ment that required the individual or family concerned to display a sign with the term *tumun* on his gate. For a period to be determined by local officials, he or she would not be allowed to have contact with other citizens, or move about, except as was necessary in connection with his work or to respond to the summons of authorities. If such individuals demonstrated loyalty to the government, the imposition of this punishment might be expunged from his records after a period of six months. But such a decision had to be signed by the chief judge and countersigned by the people's assessors who were present at the original mass trial. All mass meeting records were to be kept in the *ri* or other appropriate People's Committee offices.[50]

There is no evidence available to us of how many individuals were executed or given prison sentences under the mass trial system during this period. However, we have numerous accounts to the effect that many villages were full of big red tumun signs on gates or other conspicuous places in front of the house. In some hamlets, according to certain informants, the number approached 100 percent. Naturally, tumun greatly affected morale and the will to work hard for the regime. With this stigma, did one truly have a future—regardless of Party promises that redemption was possible? This problem was to plague the Party and the state for a long time to come.

The Key Wartime Problem

Unquestionably, the 1951–53 period was the most difficult ever faced by the North Korean regime. The destruction was massive and continual. After ground fighting in the north had ceased, heavy aerial bombardment continued until the eve of the armistice in July 1953. Communist leaders were later to report that some 600,000 private dwellings, 8,700 factories, 5,000 schools, and 1,000 hospitals or clinics had been destroyed as a result of the war, the great bulk of them in 1950 or 1951.[51] Facilities for electrical power, transport, and irrigation had also been badly hit. Scorched earth tactics had been applied by both sides on the ground, and from the UN side the bombing had been both intensive and effective. Cities like P'yŏngyang were almost completely in ruins by the end of 1951. To add to the misery in the north, devastating floods had occurred in that year, making cultivation impossible in certain areas. The full costs of the Communist decision to "liberate" the south were now being exacted. Factionalism at top Party levels grew even more bitter than usual.

Because of the magnitude of the problems, this period can serve as an interesting case study of how a particular Communist regime reacted

50. We were able to use a second document, "Attachment No. 2, Rules Concerning Mass Trial Meetings," dated Jan. 10, 1951.

51. "The Three Year Plan," *Kyŏngje Kŏnsŏl* (*Economic Construction*), Sept. 1956, pp. 5–6.

to crisis: its sense of priorities, its range of response, and its relations to both friend and foe. For this purpose, we have attempted a content analysis of all *Nodong Sinmun* editorials during the critical year 1952 to discern the relative weight given various issues, the terminology applied, and such trends as may have occurred. Eighteen issues of the newspaper for the period involved were not available to us, and in twenty-two issues editorials were replaced by some "important" item. Consequently, we were able to examine only 325 editorials from the period January 1 to December 31, 1952. Our procedure was to tabulate the subject or subjects emphasized. We use here the term "emphasized," because if a topic were merely mentioned and treated casually, without being connected to the main thrust of the editorial, it was not tabulated. On the other hand, many editorials were directed at more than one subject, in which case all themes were tabulated. Before discussing the results in detail, let us set them forth in tabular form. The division "Attacks upon the United States," admittedly somewhat arbitrary, is based on the primary emphasis of the editorial, with each editorial tabulated only once with respect to the broad category. For example, if the basic thrust of the editorial was upon the "imperialist and fascist actions" of the United States, it was put in the "General" category even if some mention was made of treatment of prisoners. If, on the other hand, the primary subject was "the massacre of the Kŏje prisoners," it would be classified "On treatment of prisoners."

As is clear from this table, two interrelated issues dominated the domestic scene in this time of grave peril. On the economic front, the cardinal issue was agrarian production, and, closely related to this, the attitude of the North Korean farmer toward the government and the Party. On the political front, Communist leaders were forced to face up to the decimation of the Party as a result of the war, and the very serious deterioration of relations between the Party and the public at large in a period of relatively loose discipline, enormous hardships, and low morale.

Let us turn first to the agrarian crisis. After the major military campaigns of 1950 and early 1951, much of the North Korean countryside was left utterly desolate, sans shelter, work animals, seeds, or food—and in many cases sans people as well. The precise number of North Koreans who were killed during the war or moved south as refugees will never be known, but civilian deaths have been estimated at one million (with an additional one-half million military casualties), and the refugees at nearly three million. Whatever the true figures, there can be little doubt that the dislocation was very great. Among those who remained, moreover, almost all the able-bodied young men were serving in the army. As in active war zones throughout history, women, young children, and old men made up the bulk of the rural population.

At a later point, Korean Communist authorities released some statistics

TABLE 21
Subjects of Editorials in Nodong Sinmun, 1952

Month	J	F	M	A	M	J	J	A	S	O	N	D	Total
The farmer and agricultural production	5	3	6	8	7	4	5	4	7	9	9	3	70
The worker (or trade union) and industrial production	3	0	2	1	2	0	0	0	0	0	0	1	9
Women	0	1	0	0	2	0	3	1	0	0	0	0	7
Youth	1	1	1	0	1	0	0	0	1	0	0	1	6
Intellectuals	0	0	0	0	0	0	0	1	0	0	1	2	4
"Strengthen the Party"—Party-citizen relationships	9	7	8	7	12	6	6	9	14	6	13	7	104
"Campaign against waste, corruption, bureaucratism"—and exhortation for more discipline and work	6	4	7	4	4	2	8	8	2	2	3	3	53
Appeal to patriotism, nationalism	9	4	5	2	3	2	1	6	7	4	4	1	48
Praise of North Korean People's Army	2	3	0	0	1	1	0	0	1	0	1	2	11
Attacks upon the United States	8	5	8	10	11	12	10	8	6	11	8	9	106
On truce talk specifically	0	0	0	0	0	1	1	0	0	3	0	1	6
On treatment of prisoners in particular	0	2	0	0	2	3	1	0	0	2	2	1	13
On atrocities in particular	1	1	3	2	5	3	3	1	2	2	2	1	26
General	7	2	5	8	4	5	5	7	4	4	4	6	61
Praise of Russians	2	5	4	8	8	4	6	9	6	8	4	6	70
Emphasis upon Stalin in particular	0	0	1	3	1	1	1	1	1	2	0	2	13
Praise of Chinese	0	2	0	2	3	2	2	2	3	4	0	2	22
Praise of and quotes from Kim Il-sŏng	4	3	6	3	7	1	0	5	5	3	1	2	40
Citation of general international support	0	2	0	1	3	6	7	3	3	3	1	3	32
Emphasis upon victory	3	0	1	2	4	2	2	5	2	1	1	2	25
Emphasis upon difficulties, protracted war	2	4	0	0	0	0	1	5	4	2	3	2	23
Emphasis upon struggle for peace	1	1	1	0	2	2	2	1	1	0	0	1	12

pertaining to overall production during the war years. Some of these figures do not match with each other, or with other Communist statements, and we have no way of ascertaining the accuracy of any of them. It would be wise, therefore, to use them with considerable caution. (No source notes have been appended to tables 22–28 because they represent a composite from diverse North Korean sources.)

TABLE 22
North Korea: Indexes of Key Economic Variables, 1946–1953
(1946 = 100)

	1946	1949	1953
National Income	100	209	145
Gross value of industrial production	100	337	216
Production of the means of production	100	375	158
Production of consumer goods	100	288	285
Gross value of agricultural production	100	151	115

TABLE 23
North Korea: Indexes of Key Economic Variables, 1949–1953
(1949 = 100)

	1949	1951	1953
National income	100	—	70
Gross value of industrial production	100	47	64
Production of the means of production	100	33	42
Production of consumer goods	100	65	99

TABLE 24
North Korea: Retail Price Index, 1949–1953
(1949 = 100)

	1949	1953
Price index of retail commodities (including rationed commodities of state and cooperative commercial organs)	100	265

TABLE 25
North Korea: Wages, 1946–1953
(1946 = 100)

	1946	1953
Average wage per worker and office employee	100	105

TABLE 26
North Korea: Total Planted Area of Principal Crops, 1944–1953
(1,000 chŏngbo)

	1944	1946	1947	1948	1949	1951	1952	1953
Total area	2,321	1,934	2,242	2,356	2,386	2,101	2,253	2,295
Food grains	1,996	1,670	2,013	2,127	2,112	1,904	2,062	2,103
Paddy rice	400	388	420	444	382	380	406	432
Dry field food								
Grains	1,596	1,282	1,593	1,683	1,730	1,524	1,656	1,671
Industrial crops	129	79	74	73	107	79	56	54
Vegetables	57	72	45	44	46	32	47	—
Tubers	139	113	110	112	120	83	85	—
Potatoes	121	100	96	99	104	77	80	—

NOTE: Figures for 1944 apply to North Korea only.

TABLE 27
North Korea: Total Output of Food Grain Crops, 1944–1953
(1,000 tons)

1944	1946	1947	1948	1949	1951	1952	1953
2,417	1,898	2,069	2,668	2,654	2,260	2,450	2,327

NOTE: Figures for 1944 apply to North Korea only.

TABLE 28
North Korea: Total Livestock
(as of year end)

	1944	1946	1949	1951	1953
Milk cows	1,391	766	959	444	637
Korean oxen	755,100	470,978	786,765	545,504	503,761
Horses	15,799	9,628	8,787	3,367	6,377
Sheep and goats	30,377	6,913	12,696	12,044	25,286
Hogs	385,147	219,847	659,645	308,843	542,725

NOTE: Figures for 1944 apply to North Korea only.

Had the North Koreans used 1939 as base year, the picture would have been even bleaker, since that year saw the peak production figures for the whole Japanese era. The year 1946, on the other hand, was a bad one due to the postwar upheaval, which included the transition to the Communist regime. American authorities estimated that up to January 1947, the North Korean economy was in chaos, with industrial production operating at no more than 25 percent of capacity (measured against the end of the Japanese era) even after progress was under way, in mid-1947. The North Koreans themselves announced that production in August 1947 was double that of the previous year. In using these statistics, it should be remembered that, under the Japanese, North Korea had always been a region with a very low living standard. In any case, the evidence—even from these incomplete figures—points to a society in the depths of poverty at the close of the Korean War. National income, measured against that of 1949, had been reduced by nearly one-third (table 23). Inflation was rampant, but wages had increased hardly at all (tables 24–25). The agricultural picture is less clear. No 1950 figures were given for agricultural production, and the figures for 1947 and earlier probably include some rather arbitrary adjustments. Nevertheless, it can easily be seen that the figures for 1951 show a decline of some 15 percent since 1949 (table 27). The drop in the number of livestock during the same period is even more marked (table 28).

On occasion, the North Korean government made no effort to hide the gravity of the situation. For example, the year 1951 was openly described by *Nodong Sinmun* as "a year of unbearable trials" for the Korean farmer. "The ferocious violence of our enemies, the shortage of manpower, and the scarcity of cattle, fertilizers, seeds, food, and farming tools, together with the unprecedented natural calamity [the floods], combined to bring extreme difficulties and hardships upon our farmers." [52] In many villages, not a single cow or pig could be found. With the oxen remaining, it was estimated that one ox had to plow between one and one-half times and twice as much land as before the war.[53] Communist sources admitted, moreover, that by the spring of 1951 the three provinces of Hwanghae, South P'yŏngan, and Kangwŏn alone had a shortage of seed grain amounting to some 10,600 tons.

52. "Let Us Respond to the Thoughtful Considerations of the Party and Government by Increasing Production," editorial, *Nodong Sinmun,* March 16, 1952, p. 1 (hereafter cited as *NS*).

This editorial was echoed in many others. For example, the editorial of Jan. 24, 1952, had contained the reminder that Comrade Kim Il-sŏng had stated that "the struggle for food is the struggle for the fatherland and for a guarantee of victory in the war," followed by the exhortation, "Farmers! The war is likely to be protracted. We will face all kinds of hardships and obstacles. Do not succumb, but overcome these courageously. That is the only way to guarantee victory." *Ibid.,* p. 1.

Both farmers and officials came in for criticism. On March 25, a *Nodong Sinmun* editorial sharply criticized some farmers for idleness, claiming that a number had not even attended to spring planting. In late April, however, an editorial was published, entitled "Carry Out the State Grain Loan Tasks More Promptly and Correctly," in which it was asserted that despite Cabinet Order No. 40, which provided for the loan of state grains to those farmers who were without food because of the flood, some officials were not distributing the food promptly, having no concern for the needs of "the starving farmer." *Ibid.,* April 30, 1952, p. 1.

53. Robert A. Scalapino interview with O Ki-wan, Seoul, Dec. 3, 1968.

In seeking to meet this crisis, the battered North Korean government resorted to a variety of appeals and actions. Sometimes, the tone was one of pleading. "Without food, we cannot win the war. We cannot carry out the essential work behind the battle lines. We cannot maintain the life of our people." [54] Most frequently, the appeal was to the "burning patriotism" of the farmer. The following exhortation was typical: "To defend our honorable and precious fatherland, the eternal happiness of later generations, and our bread and freedom [note the Leninist theme], unite around the Party and government more solidly, protect your Party and government, and march forward toward the struggle for the food production increase requested by General Kim Il-sŏng, our beloved leader!" [55] Repeatedly, editorials hailed "those patriotic model farmers" who had "overcome all hardships" to exceed their previous production, while criticizing those "backward elements" guilty of laziness or "antistate" practices. [56]

Despite the effort to portray the overwhelming majority of farmers as aflame with patriotism, and prepared to make any sacrifice for the fatherland, the government in fact faced a sea of weariness and despondency. Hoarding and tax evasion were widespread. Acknowledging the lack of sufficient work animals and fertilizer, the regime urged the substitution of manpower and natural fertilizer, railing against those who used "the excuse of a manpower shortage" to cover up their shortcomings. The collection of taxes in kind in a period of enormous privation presented a particularly difficult problem. The government openly admitted that food collections in 1951 had been "by and large, too high," and, in many cases, "involuntary." [57] Some individuals had become obsessed with that mistake, however, according to government spokesmen. The 1952 harvest was better than that of the previous year, primarily because of excellent climatic conditions (compare table 27, which does indicate modest gains). Throughout the fall of 1952, the regime called upon local units to remedy "the grave defects" existing in the tax program and meet the urgent national needs in a truly patriotic fashion.

"It is not bureaucratism to collect taxes in kind that damage neither

54. "The Task of the Party Organization in Saving Food Under War Conditions," editorial, *NS*, Jan. 25, 1952, p. 1. Many editorials of this period, however, played upon an identical theme.

55. "Guarantee Increases in Food Production by Thoroughgoing Antidrought Measures," editorial, *ibid.*, May 19, 1952, p. 1. Once again, many editorials carried similar messages. See, for example, those of Jan. 24, March 15, and March 16, 1952.

56. See "Develop Broadly an All-People's Movement to Struggle for Savings!" editorial, *ibid.*, Jan. 30, 1953, p. 1.

57. For example, see Kim Il-sŏng's speech before the Conference of City, County, and Provincial People's Committee Chairmen and Party Workers, "The Tasks and Roles of Local Government at the Present Stage," in *ibid.*, Feb. 19, 1952, pp. 1–3. See also "The Task of Assessing the Early Season Crop Harvests," editorial, *ibid.*, May 28, 1952, p. 1.

the state nor the farmers," proclaimed one *Nodong Sinmun* editorial.[58] "On the contrary, we call it bureaucratism when supervision of tax collection is neglected, and the task is merely entrusted to a lower level organization." Many misfits had gotten into tax assessment committees. In some cases, they were the personal appointees of the district People's Committee chairman, rather than having been properly elected. In other localities, committee members had been elected who were either "ignorant of farming" or "backward types" who lacked sympathy with Party policy. Thus, the state was frequently cheated. In some areas, for example, people were assessed taxes on the basis of only one-half their actual harvests.[59]

Communist leaders naturally blamed these problems upon the low political and cultural level of the farmers, and embarked upon a strenuous campaign to make the Party a central force at the all-important village level. To this end, some 5,000 democratic propaganda offices were established throughout North Korea in the 1951–52 period to engage in "adult education work." [60] These offices, indeed, were a mainstay of the government's effort to communicate with the rural masses at a time when regional Party machinery was often in disarray. Posters, wall newspapers, graphs, and cartoons were all to be used to reach the peasant, instructing him with respect to state policy, stimulating his patriotism, and inspiring him with confidence in victory. With millions dead or deserting, the battle

58. "Struggle Strongly Against a Certain Tendency to Pay Smaller Taxes-in-kind!" editorial, *ibid.*, Sept. 25, 1952, p. 1.

59. *Ibid.*, p. 1.
Many other abuses were cited by Party organs, some favorable to the peasants, others unfavorable. Some of the irregularities had to do with the appointment of assessors, who were either friends of the farmers and "conspired" with them to keep assessments low, or were amenable to bribery.

60. For an evaluation of the Democratic Propaganda Offices, see "For the Enhancement of the Work Level of the Rural Village Democratic Propaganda Office Chiefs," editorial, *ibid.*, Sept. 7, 1952, p. 1. According to this editorial, among the major tasks of the village office were "to explain about the nature and objectives of the Fatherland Liberation War, to report and comment upon the national situation promptly in order to raise mass confidence and conviction in our ultimate victory, to teach the people of the correctness of Party and governmental policies by explaining these in detail, to arouse hostility and hatred of the enemy by displaying their atrocities and vicious schemes, and to prevent the activities of spies and subversive elements."

In an earlier editorial, however, the Party organ signaled the difficulties confronting this operation. After suggesting that the propaganda offices had overcome such problems as labor and oxen shortages, it admitted that in many areas, the effort had evidently failed, given the production figures, and in typical fashion it blamed "mechanical distribution" of propaganda, the inability to relate Party policies to the actual life of the farmers, and the tendency to interrupt field work by summoning farmers to meetings.

The real reasons for the weaknesses of the local propaganda offices, of course, lie in the fact that it is monumentally difficult to propagandize starving, demoralized people.

to hold the farmer to the Communist regime took on a desperate quality throughout this period, and the Party, without ever being able to admit all of the facts publicly, used carrot-and-stick policies in an effort to meet the deadly threat.

Propaganda without concrete help would not suffice. One crucial need, particularly in 1951, was to get seed to the farmers and to help them with the spring planting. In the spring of 1951, some 3,100,000 laborers, office workers, students, and soldiers were mobilized as "labor assistance brigades" to assist in sowing seed and transplanting rice seedlings. In some cases, they were aided by members of the Chinese People's Volunteers.[61] The state publicized these and other forms of assistance widely. The poorest farmers and those who had suffered from the 1951 floods were given an exemption from grain taxes, and were also excused from having to return the supplies of grain borrowed earlier from the state.

These measures may have staved off total disaster, but food problems and general agrarian distress remained acute through and beyond the armistice of July 1953. Life had always been harsh in Communist Korea, but in this era it was almost unbearable. As noted earlier, the regime was aided by good weather in 1952. It claimed that the 1952 grain output exceeded that of 1951 by 7.7 percent. Despite this fact, however, widespread famine was prevented only by emergency food shipments from the Soviet Union, the People's Republic of China, and other "fraternal socialist" countries. On April 14, 1952, Stalin offered North Korea 50,000 tons of wheat flour, "knowing," said *Nodong Sinmun*, "that our people are suffering from a severe food shortage due to the enemy's brutal violence and various natural calamities." [62] When the gift was distributed in mid-May, one letter published in *Nodong Sinmun* revealed how much it was needed.

> Our family is seven in number, and we received almost one whole sack [63 kilograms] sent by the great Marshal Stalin. We have never had such beautiful flour in our village. Last year, the flood damaged 3,000 p'yŏng of our land, and we have been receiving food from the state this spring. I was so grateful to get this. Since our food ran out in March, we have received state supplies twice each month, and we have worked very hard on the farm, even with empty stomachs.[63]

61. Mention of CPV aid in the fields appeared in several issues of *Nodong Sinmun* during March 1952 (as well as in Monat's 1960 article cited earlier). Gratitude was also expressed by North Korean officials for the Chinese sharing their food with the people. In a July 1, 1952, editorial entitled "The Eternal and Imperishable Friendship Between the Korean and Chinese Peoples," the following statement appears: "The Chinese people have sent enormous amounts of materials, including grain, textiles, cultural necessities, medicine, food, and entertainers to the Korean people."

62. For public notice of Stalin's offer, see "The Considerations Given by Our Party and Government to Laborers and Clerical Workers," editorial, *ibid.*, April 27, 1952, p. 1.

63. *Ibid.*, May 15, 1952, p. 3.

In 1953, according to the government's own admission, agricultural production declined again. As a result, the agrarian problem continued to dominate the scene. The year got under way with a National Conference of Enthusiastic Farmers, convened in early January in an effort to bolster sagging morale and increase production. An appeal was issued to all farmers. It acknowledged that the constant bombing and machine-gunning by enemy planes made work difficult, but pointed out the desperate need for food, calling upon the farmers to display their patriotic solidarity with the Party and the state. As seedtime approached, full attention was given to getting all available labor into the fields. "The struggle for food is the struggle for the fatherland. Let us all go onto the spring seeding front without any loss of time." [64]

A careful survey of North Korean domestic propaganda would indicate that, at the time of the 1953 armistice, the morale of the North Korean people was dangerously close to the breaking point. It must have constituted an enormous pressure upon the regime to reach some agreement with the UN forces. Editorials and news columns were filled with what amounted to pleas to "hold on," retain the ties of solidarity with the Party, and obey the government's orders. An almost equal number of stories and comments, however, dealt with problems of corruption, poor work habits, and low production.

To combat these problems, the P'yŏngyang authorities as early as the spring of 1952 had announced an antibureaucratism, anticorruption, and antiwaste campaign. In the months that followed, the drive against these evils was repeatedly stressed. This campaign, it should be noted, was virtually a duplicate of the Three-Anti Campaign in China, begun in Manchuria at the end of August 1951. Directives had been issued to all Chinese provincial and municipal organs, as well as to Party branches, to fight against corruption, waste, and bureaucracy, and to concentrate upon economy and increasing output.[65] The evidence suggests that, for the first time, Chinese Communist policies had a direct influence upon North Korean leaders.

In North Korea, a substantial breakdown of discipline throughout this period was frankly admitted. State property was being stolen, waste was taking place on a large scale, and in general there was far too little concern

64. "The Timely Transplantation of Rice Seedlings Is an Important Key to the Guarantee of a Good Rice Harvest," editorial, *ibid.*, May 15, 1952, p. 1.

65. For details of the Three-Anti and Five-Anti campaigns in China, see A. Doak Barnett, *Communist China: The Early Years, 1949–1955*, New York, 1964, pp. 135–171. An editorial entitled "For the Further Strengthening of the Struggle Against Old Ideological Remnants," *NS*, July 24, 1952, p. 1, presents an excellent outline of the Korean campaign, and reveals how strong the influence of Chinese action had become. The emphasis upon "criticism and self-criticism" as "the most important weapon against the old ideology" is a fitting companion to contemporary *Jen-min Jih-pao* editorials.

for the effective utilization of scarce materials. The majority of the people, to be sure, were "sacrificing themselves willingly for the nation," but "anti-state and antipeople" behavior was serious, and had to be challenged.

The main injunction to the Korean people during this period came from a much-quoted speech that Kim Il-sŏng had delivered on February 19, 1952.[66] This speech—which served as a chief reference point for Party spokesmen during the remainder of the war—is worthy of some attention, particularly since it provides an insight into political as well as economic developments. Kim began by quoting Mao Tse-tung to the effect that a "people's regime" enforces dictatorship toward the enemy while practicing democracy toward the people. Our regime, proclaimed Kim, is such a people's democracy, based upon the workers, farmers, intellectuals, and the small propertied class. Our basic task, he asserted, is to rally the entire people around the Korean Workers' Party and develop a national struggle under the aegis of the Fatherland Front against national traitors, pro-Japanese and pro-American compradors, and foreign aggressors.[67]

Comrade Stalin had already indicated the primary tasks of a proletarian regime, Kim stated: first, the resistance of all reactionaries, including landlords and capitalists, must be crushed; second, the workers must be mobilized around the Party for socialist construction; third, the revolutionary army must be organized against foreign enemies and imperialism. The Korean people, he proclaimed, accepted these principles as their historic task.

The specific references in this speech and in many other Communist pronouncements of this period to "traitors" and pro-Japanese or pro-American compradors reflect in part the use of a political weapon to keep grumblers in line. But there was also a very real anxiety about subversives, an anxiety justified by the scale of desertion to the south. In one sense, the opportunity to desert afforded by the war was of major service to the regime, since it drained off the most dissident elements. A decade later, Fidel Castro was to allow voluntary departures from Cuba for this very reason—until the losses in high-level manpower became too costly.

There can be little doubt, however, that the Kim government faced a crisis of confidence in its relations with the North Korean people during this period, and that this situation contributed to the mounting factionalism within the Party and helped to bring about a desperate search for new approaches that might build public support. In his speech of February 19, Kim once again recited his government's accomplishments: land reform, labor legislation, equality between the sexes, industrial nationalization, and numerous other "reforms." A formidable democratic base had been built

66. The full text of Kim's speech, entitled "The Tasks and Roles of Local Government at the Present Stage," is presented in the Feb. 19, 1952, issue of *NS*, pp. 1–3.
67. *Ibid.*, p. 1.

in North Korea, he asserted, and a people's army had been founded. However, the division of the nation and the war had prevented the consolidation of that democratic base and the thorough modernization of the military forces. The first task now was to combat defeatism. Some Koreans, both north and south, doubted that a Korea defeated even by Japan would be able to win against the United States. Yet they could win, Kim insisted. Why? "Because we are not fighting alone. The Chinese people are fighting with us. The peoples of the peoples' democracies, headed by the Soviet Union, the strongest nation in the world, and the freedom-loving people throughout the globe are on our side. Therefore, our strength is greater than that of the enemy." [68]

Moreover, Kim continued, the people of North Korea were fighting on their own territory, whereas the enemy were fighting thousands of miles away from theirs. Thus, the morale of the American soldiers was deteriorating daily. They were fighting for money, whereas the North Koreans were fighting for independence, freedom, and revolution. Their technical level might be the inferior one, but it was improving. Time was on their side, and they had to be prepared to fight a protracted war. The key to victory was endurance, together with full mobilization and effective organization of their resources. First, the people's government had to be strengthened. Second, there had to be closer relation with the masses. Third, the political consciousness of the people had to be aroused so that they would provide the Party and government with more enthusiastic and creative support.

What was preventing these goals from being achieved? Kim placed the primary blame upon Party and government officials. In many of them, he asserted, the ideological remnants of Japanese feudalism were still active. It was the same old bureaucratic style: they were arrogant to people in lower positions while flattering those above them. Refusing to listen to the voice of the people, they merely gave orders. Moreover, they were guilty of falsifying production reports. Various local Party cadres had reported 100 percent fulfillment of their villages' autumn harvest quota to myŏn officials. Such reports were then passed on from the myŏn to the prefecture, and from the prefecture to the province, although the officials at each level knew the reports to be false and the quotas unfulfilled. [69]

Similar problems, asserted Kim, existed with respect to the collection of taxes-in-kind. One locality had appealed against the heavy imposition of taxes. Then it was discovered that a false report had been filed from that village concerning the amount of land under cultivation. Higher authorities had calculated the tax on the basis of this report without bothering to check its validity. In some areas, however, the measures taken by cadres had been too severe. Grain had been collected prematurely, and some People's

68. *Ibid.,* p. 2.
69. *Ibid.,* p. 3.

Committees had forced farmers suffering from flood damage to pay a tax-in-kind even though they had had to buy rice in order to do so.

All of these practices, Kim remarked, constituted forms of commandism. If they continued, the people would become alienated from the government. Some cadres were unconcerned; they were prepared to ignore the discontent of the farmers, calling them backward and insisting that their views did not matter. This was the road to ruin. Even if the cadres had adopted the correct decision, forcing it upon the people against their will, with no role allowed for their creativity in its implementation, would secure only minimal cooperation. Thus, farmers might report that they had finished the autumn cultivation when in fact they had only scratched the surface of the earth.

Kim ended this section of his speech, however, by dwelling upon a contrapuntal theme. If commandism was an evil to be liquidated, that did not mean that government and Party cadres should do as the people wanted them to do. An indiscriminate following of the people constituted tailism, a deficiency as grave as commandism. Among the farmers, there were both progressive and backward elements. This distinction should be clearly understood, and backward elements should never be allowed to influence policy, even if they were in a majority.

Many of the problems of mobilization politics that faced Communist governments were signaled in the passages of Kim's speech summarized above. While we cannot be certain of the extent of popular apathy, weariness, and alienation, it was clearly sufficient to worry the top Communist leadership. A people pushed to the limits of endurance under conditions of unspeakable misery were evidently making known their resentment in a myriad of ways. Kim's response was to blame subordinate government and party cadres, a tactic that was also currently being pursued by the top Chinese Communist leaders and that would be repeated in the aftermath of the Great Leap Forward. No doubt commandism was prevalent; it was both a part of Korean political culture and implicit in the existing North Korean political system. To attack commandism and to dismiss some cadres was also a skillful tactic, since it placed the top political leadership "on the side of the masses" while allowing subordinates to serve as symbols of misplaced trust. Dismissals could serve the dual purpose of keeping cadres on their mettle and alleviating public anger.

Thus, Kim's indignation was ostensibly directed at the officiousness and corruption existing within the cadre class. By his own admission, a number of cadres were overbearing, ignorant, and unconcerned about local conditions; they even tried to deceive their own government. It would be wise, however, to look at the problem from the cadre's point of view. If he falsified reports, it was because failure was an unforgivable sin, no matter what the causes or mitigating circumstances. Quotas had to be fulfilled. Otherwise, the chances of retaining one's position were slim. Knowing this, officials at every level connived at concealing the facts when they were dismal.[70] Once again, a strikingly parallel situation has been indicated in China, particularly during the era of the Great Leap Forward.[71]

With success so crucial to one's future, moreover, it is not surprising that many cadres bore down hard upon the peasant. The Japanese doctrine, *kanson mimpi* ("officials honored, people despised"), continued to have a vitality. Indeed, when the cadre turned to his supreme leader for guidance, he received stern injunctions against both tailism and commandism. If he was not to impose his authority upon the masses without explaining what needed to be done, without soliciting their support and listening to their voices, he was also not to allow himself to be led into error by the masses. How did the cadre steer a path between this Scylla and this Charybdis? Kim and all other mentors offered only subjective guidance: one had to distinguish between "progressive" and "backward" elements. But in the final analysis, of course, this would be determined by shifts of policy and personnel at levels beyond the reach of the average cadre. He was at the mercy of the system.

In the final section of his speech, Kim turned from political to economic questions, concentrating upon the crucial problem of production. He began by admitting serious setbacks: construction had ceased, production had dropped, and corruption was rampant. Some individuals were collaborating with profiteers, stealing state property, or misusing public funds. Within the government itself, corruption was a serious problem and financial controls were lax.

What was the answer? Kim called for a revitalization of the village People's Committees which, according to him, had been allowed to become very weak. The masses, he argued, were not to be found in the offices of the district, prefectural, or city People's Committee chairmen. They were in the villages and factories. It was at this level that they had to be reached. It was therefore necessary for the higher committees to "go down to the level of the village People's Committees," showing them how to organize their tasks, how to relate to the masses, and how to induce mass support. Leadership from above must be both cautious and firm. Inspiration must flow from the masses, but village chiefs and other officials were appointed because they were supposed to know more and work harder. If this was not the case, changes should be made.

Thus, in a time of peril, the struggle was for the peasant. Kim was seeking to rebuild primary-level Party and governmental organization after the unparalleled destruction and defection produced by the war. We have

70. For further discussion of this problem, see Chapters X and XI below.
71. For a detailed discussion of economic and political management that evaluates the alternatives available to the Communists in China, see Franz Schurmann, *Ideology and Organization in Communist China,* Berkeley, 1966, especially Chapters IV and V.

already noted the democratic propaganda offices established throughout the rural areas in 1951–52. And we have seen that the "closed-door" policies of Hŏ Ka-i were sharply criticized at the time of the Fourth Plenum in November 1951, with tens of thousands of new members admitted to the Party thereafter in an effort to bolster its depleted ranks. Thus, in many instances, both the Party and the government were being run by new, inexperienced individuals, especially at the local levels. Thousands of veteran Party members, including a substantial number of local and provincial cadres, were at the front or had been killed. Others had deserted to the south or simply disappeared. The exhortations for more intensive cadre training and the revitalization of village-level organizations must be read in this context.

Structural problems were not limited to the government or the Korean Workers' Party. Communist leaders also lamented the fact that the Democratic Front for the Unification of the Fatherland had fallen into disrepair, along with the non-Communist parties so essential to the strategy of united front politics.[72] Indeed, grave concern was voiced about the loyalty of non-Communists in this period of hardship, especially since substantial numbers of them had already defected to the south. Moreover, as noted previously, the members of these "fraternal parties" had been the first to join the anti-Communist public security units. Consequently, in early 1951, orders were given to reconstruct the Korean Democratic Party. Between February and October, strenuous efforts to reorganize the party were undertaken. From the third general meeting of the party in November 1948 to the Korean War, no new members had been admitted, and a number of "anti-Communists" had been purged. When party reorganization was completed, a membership totaling between 200,000 and 300,000 was claimed, with recruits drawn mainly from small merchants, handicraftsmen, middle-class farmers, and such religious groups as the Christians and Buddhists. After October 1951, however, new members were limited largely to individuals with a religious affiliation. Merchants and handicraftsmen were encouraged to devote their energies to organizing cooperatives.[73]

In the midst of the drive to rebuild the Korean Communist movement

72. See "For the Strengthening of the Fatherland Front," editorial, *NS*, Jan. 14, 1952, p. 1. This editorial admits serious problems with respect to the "friendly parties" aligned with the KWP, but warns against "misjudging" such parties because of the "reactionary actions of those who have infiltrated these parties," stressing that, during a period when "the enemy is not yet completely defeated and the Fatherland is in critical condition," there must be a consolidated struggle of all the people. Hence, the leaders of the "friendly parties" must be allowed to purge their own ranks of impure, reactionary elements "without outside interference." See also the editorial of Jan. 6, 1952, for similar comments.

73. "The Political and Economic Significance of Cooperative Organizations," editorial, *ibid.*, Feb. 10, 1952, p. 1.

and its necessary political accoutrements, the cult of personality centering around Kim Il-sŏng was advanced to new heights. Kim was now being featured by official Party and state organs in a manner roughly parallel to the homage being paid Stalin in the Soviet Union. Pictures of him, accounts of his various public appearances, and detailed reproductions of his major speeches occupied the center of the stage in the mass media. Although this was not exactly novel, the focus on Kim became ever more conspicuous during this period as a desperate effort was made to build loyalty to the Party and state. Typical of the language being used to describe Kim and his role was that set forth in a *Nodong Sinmun* editorial of April 1, 1952, published just before Kim's fortieth birthday.[74] Here, history was reconstructed to present Kim as the key leader in modern Korea. The following sentences convey the tone accurately:

> General Kim Il-sŏng, in his revolutionary activities and entire career, has totally devoted his creative energies and genius to the cause of the freedom, independence, happiness, democracy, and peace of the fatherland. He has become the torchlight for all the pioneers of our country, and his achievements have coincided with the demands for social development and other aspirations of the Korean people, as well as the interests of the Korean working class.[75]

On April 10, 1952, *Nodong Sinmun* published a four-page supplement containing a strongly idealized "life history" of Kim, and during the next few days three prominent Party leaders—Pak Ch'ang-ok, Pak Hŏn-yŏng, and Pak Chŏng-ae—wrote separate articles about him. To compare these articles is interesting, particularly in view of the fate about to befall Pak Ch'ang-ok and Pak Hŏn-yŏng. Pak Ch'ang-ok's lengthy article repeated the stereotyped adulation of Kim, but also stressed the role of the Soviet Army in the "liberation" of Korea.[76] For example, Pak asserted that "if the great Soviet Army had not liberated Korea, the Democratic People's Republic of Korea could not have been founded and the national liberation movement of the Korean people would not have made the victorious advances that we see today." [77] Moreover, Pak devoted a considerable portion of his article to the problems of Party organization and the other requirements for military victory, treating these subjects in an impersonal manner.

Pak Hŏn-yŏng's article was much shorter than Pak Ch'ang-ok's, and more factual, at least in comparative terms. He too stressed the role of the Soviet army and the high level of cooperation that had existed between the Korean and Chinese guerrilla forces in the anti-Japanese struggle.

74. "The People's Love and Respect for the Leader," *ibid.*, April 1, 1952, p. 1.
75. *Ibid.*, p. 1.
76. Pak Ch'ang-ok, "Comrade Kim Il-sŏng Is the Founder and Organizer of the Korean Workers' Party," *ibid.*, April 12, 1952, pp. 3–5.
77. *Ibid.*, p. 3.

Significantly, he also wrote that "Comrade Kim Il-sŏng was *one of the organizers* of the Democratic Front for the Unification of the Fatherland. . . ." (italics ours). Thus he made Kim share the honors with others.[78] At the end of his article, Pak Hŏn-yŏng asserted:

> Today, on the occasion of the fortieth anniversary of our national leader's birthday, the Korean people send enthusiastic congratulations and express our respect to Marshal Stalin who has brought liberation to us, stimulated us to heroic tasks, and inspired our confidence in victory on behalf of peace and liberty—that sagacious leader and teacher of the working people throughout the world.[79]

All Korean leaders during this period, including Kim Il-sŏng himself, were lavish in acknowledging their debt to the "great Soviet Union." As we shall shortly see, the praise of Stalin on all sides was to take the most extreme forms. Nevertheless, one can detect, in the two articles just quoted, a conscious effort to balance the worship of Kim Il-sŏng by mentioning not only the Russians but the problems actually confronting Korea. Pak Ch'ang-ok's primary concern was directed toward the strengthening of Party discipline and morale, and all his praise of Kim was oriented toward that purpose. And it was possible to read into Pak Hŏn-yŏng's article the thesis that the foremost leader for Korean Communists was Josef Stalin, not Kim Il-sŏng.

Pak Chŏng-ae's article, on the other hand, was a work of pure adulation, a perfect "cult of personality" piece. The true Communist Party movement had emerged only with the appearance of "the hero of the Korean people, Kim Il-sŏng." [80] She went on to assert that Kim had all the qualities of an outstanding leader: a correct understanding of the principles of development and the necessary tasks confronting the Korean proletariat; an insightful analysis of Korean revolutionary conditions; revolutionary courage, and a sensitivity to new developments; the infinite love and confidence of the people; an inseparable relationship with the masses; a burning hatred of the enemy; and broad perspectives upon the future. In short, he was a Korean leader cast in the same mold as Lenin and Stalin. Perhaps it is not surprising that, for a long time, Pak Chŏng-ae was to weather the political storms that lay ahead.

The cult of personality now beginning to be focused upon Kim did not stop at mere words alone. On April 12, the Party Presidium ordered the establishment of two Kim Il-sŏng Memorial Halls, one in Kim's birth-

78. Pak Hŏn-yŏng, "On the 40th Anniversary of Comrade Kim Il-sŏng's Birth," *ibid.,* April 15, 1952, p. 2.

79. *Ibid.* When one recalls the adulation given Pak Hŏn-yŏng by the North Korean Branch Bureau in September 1945, the words written by him at this point seem ironic indeed. The task of writing this eulogy must have been bitter for him.

80. Pak Chŏng-ae, "Comrade Kim Il-sŏng Is the Leader of the Korean People," *ibid.,* April 15, 1952, p. 3.

place and the other at the scene of his "major battle within Korea against the Japanese." A Kim Il-sŏng High School was also established at the latter site.

Surveying the press and other public sources of information during this period, one notes that only one other individual received any substantial amount of attention, namely, Pak Hŏn-yŏng. Pak, who held numerous posts including that of minister of Foreign Affairs, and on occasion served as acting premier, had his activities reported more or less completely. It would appear, from the evidence of the time and subsequent interviews, that he was reasonably popular in comparison with other Communist leaders, and that despite his clearly subordinate position to Kim he retained a large personal following and thus a potentially independent base of power. We have noted, moreover, that in his relations with Kim he abjured sycophancy. Understandably, Kim and the Kapsan faction regarded Pak and his domestic faction as dangerous rivals, and a group to be watched constantly.

To cultivate loyalty and combat defeatism, North Korean Communists did not rely solely on revitalizing the Party-state organizational structure, nor yet on personalizing government through the cult of Kim Il-sŏng. Like the Soviet and Chinese Communist leaders before them, they also cast the war in staunchly patriotic terms. The preservation—and unification—of the fatherland were constantly recurrent themes. Classical Korean heroes who had warded off earlier "aggressors" were frequently invoked. And intermingled with these efforts were attempts to play up the ruthlessness and barbarism of the foe. The sustained campaign to picture the Americans as totally villainous reached a high point with the charges of germ warfare, which came to a climax in the spring of 1952.

Indeed, the germ warfare campaign constitutes an excellent case study of Communist propaganda operating for high stakes and over a sustained period of time. The charges that the "bloodthirsty rulers of America" were forcing American science into the mire of degeneracy, causing them to develop nuclear weapons for large-scale slaughter, and using bacilli and beetles to produce both human and plant diseases, had actually been made as early as the fall of 1950 by Chinese sources, at the time when the Chinese People's Volunteers entered the struggle. Moreover, at the time of their last great offensive, from April to May 1951, the Communists made a series of charges relating to poison gas and bacteriological warfare. These included the assertions that the Americans were testing bacteriological weapons on Chinese prisoners and were using poison gas on the Han River front.[81]

81. These charges were renewed in March 1952 in North Korean press and radio broadcasts. For example, on March 14, *Nodong Sinmun* charged that from January 28 to February 17, the US had dropped "bubonic plague, cholera, and other vicious germs" in Kangwŏn, Hwanghae and P'yŏngan provinces, but that with epi-

On May 8, an American prisoner was caused to testify that he had actually used poison gas, and on the following day—the stage having been carefully prepared—it was announced that an International Women's Commission to Investigate US Atrocities in Korea was departing from Prague to examine the evidence. As might have been expected, this group, upon completion of its tour, pronounced itself convinced that the Americans were guilty as charged. The secretary of the commission, a Mrs. Svatosova of Czechoslovakia, announced that the American actions had exceeded the atrocities of the Nazis during World War II. Immediately, the Communists sought worldwide publicity outlets for the commission's report and the supposedly independent views of its members. Peking announced that all of the "fact-finding" commission members were going to report "on the bestiality of the American atrocities in Korea" to their respective countries. Typical of such reports was a news conference held in Prague by the Argentinian delegate at which it was announced that members of the commission had decided to demand the creation of an international tribunal, in the fashion of the Nuremberg trials, at which American crimes could be properly condemned.[82]

There has never been any reliable evidence that any of the charges made against the United States and the UN command with respect to germ warfare or poison gas were true. Indeed, some of the charges, such as the one that Communist prisoners of war had been used as unwilling subjects for medical experiments, were so patently false as to cast a huge shadow of doubt over the entire campaign (nor was this particular charge ever corroborated, even from the Communist side). Nevertheless, the Communists had good reason to be pleased with the results of their campaign. Massive publicity had been given the charges, and it was not usually possible to identify the political affiliations of the various foreigners attesting to their validity. Naturally, the "confessions" of American prisoners were also useful, and the requisite number of "progressive" Americans, Britons, and other Western residents chimed in with vigorous denunciations of the "crimes." It should not be surprising that, at a minimum, confusion and doubt were created in the minds of many non-Communists, especially in the non-Western world.

With the onset of negotiations, the Communists temporarily reduced their war crimes propaganda campaign. But in the spring of 1952, with negotiations lagging and the Americans taking a heavy military toll, the campaign was revitalized. Two groups—the so-called International Democratic Lawyers' Association, a Communist front, and the Chinese Investigation Committee on Germ Warfare—made extensively publicized trips to

demic prevention measures quickly applied, these "inhuman activities" would be met (p. 1). From then and through the rest of the spring, the emphasis on American germ warfare was constant.

82. *Ibid.*, May 27, 1952, p. 1.

North Korea. Their reports also got major publicity, both in Korean Communist organs and in sympathetic journals throughout the world.[83]

At this point, the UN command, through UN Secretary-General Trygve Lie, offered to make available the facilities of the World Health Organization to fight epidemics in North Korea and China, and at the same time proposed a joint investigation concerning the various charges against the UN forces, to be conducted under the auspices of the International Red Cross.

These offers were quickly rejected. On April 21, 1952, Foreign Minister Pak Hŏn-yŏng sent a telegram to Lie asserting that North Korea had no need for such assistance since it was controlling epidemics satisfactorily as a result of aid from "the democratic countries." [84] "As is well known," Pak went on, "the World Health Organization does not have the international prestige that such an organization should have, and thus the Korean people cannot expect any aid from it." The offer of an investigation by the International Red Cross was flatly rejected with the statement that the UN had only one course: to condemn the United States for its use of bacteriological weapons in violation of international law and human morality. *Nodong Sinmun* had earlier argued, in an editorial of March 29, that the offer was merely to divert world attention from the facts. The "investigators" would only seek to cover up American crimes; their real purpose was to get an accurate picture of the results of the germ warfare program and to uncover military secrets in North Korea.[85] With a variety of Communist groups and sympathizers supplying "trustworthy reports" and enabling maximum propaganda, the Communists would have been foolish to have allowed an impartial group of any type to examine the evidence.

The rebuff of UN—and American—offers may have damaged Communist credibility in some circles. But on the whole, the Communists seem to have gone on regarding their germ warfare propaganda campaign as a striking success. Under conditions of near-starvation, inadequate water and sanitation, and poor housing, communicable diseases were a serious problem. Why not blame these on the deliberate policies of the enemy? [86] To

83. See the editorial, "The Indictment of the Peoples of the Whole World Against the Germ Violence of American Imperialists," *ibid.,* Sept. 17, 1952, p. 1. For reports on the activities of the Chinese committee, see *ibid.,* April 11, 1952, p. 1, and for the statement of the International Democratic Lawyers' Association, see *ibid.,* April 18, pp. 2–3, and April 19, p. 2.

84. Pak's telegram to Lie, dated April 21, 1952, is carried in the April 22 issue of *NS,* p. 1.

85. "The US Imperialists Cannot Conceal Criminal Germ Warfare by Any Deceptive Means," *ibid.,* March 29, 1952, p. 1.

86. An editorial, "Further Strengthening Sanitation and Epidemic Prevention Work," of May 12, 1952, in *NS,* (p. 1) is especially interesting. After noting that "the bloodthirsty US imperialist aggressors" have not ceased their germ-warfare campaign, the editorial comments: "Unless we crush the enemy's germ violence, we cannot prevent epidemics and harm to our agricultural production. Thus, the struggle

raise popular hatred of the Americans, and build up an image of their total bestiality, might even induce a terribly weary people to hold on, fearful of the consequences of defeat or defection. Whatever the role of fear and hatred in inducing the people to resist defeatism, however, the only unambiguous morale boosters were the massive presence of Chinese "volunteers" and the substantial aid coming from all parts of the Communist bloc. Every North Korean must have known that without this aid, and particularly without the direct involvement of the Chinese, the Korean Communists would have been totally defeated. In view of this fact, it is all the more interesting that all the official North Korean pronouncements of this period, while expressing appropriate gratitude for Chinese aid, consistently treated the Chinese as equals, while rendering deepest homage to the Russians as superiors. During this period, the attitude of the North Korean Communist leaders toward the Soviet Union, and toward Stalin as an individual, revealed a satellite complex as pure as any that could be found in Eastern Europe.

Emulation of the Soviet experience was definitely the order of the day. For example, on the occasion of the fortieth anniversary of the founding of *Pravda, Nodong Sinmun* could assert: "The newspapers of the people's democracies are successfully constructing a new life, and they together with the progressive press everywhere are absorbing the noble experience of the Bolshevik press and its militant traditions." [87] The Soviet Union was their guide and inspiration:

> The people of the world have sensed the possibility of entering the sublime road leading to peace, democracy, and socialism by following the great Soviet people. This is why all freedom-loving peoples who aspire to peace congratulate the Soviet people [on their victory over the Germans] as if it were their own victory. The Korean people meet today in the glare of the Fatherland Liberation War to send fervent congratulations to the Soviet Union, and with all progressive mankind, bow low with respect and gratitude before her.[88]

All Korean sources invariably listed the Soviet Union first in any ordering of Communist allies. Frequent use was made of the phrase, "the socialist bloc, headed by the great Soviet Union," and on such occasions as the Nineteenth CPSU Congress, pages were devoted to the coverage of

---

against germ warfare is a vital struggle for the defense of our Fatherland and the people. . . . Specifically, we must strive to eliminate all rats, fleas, lice, flies, mosquitoes, and we must prohibit the drinking of unboiled water, or the eating of uncooked meat. Water reservoirs, wells, and similar receptacles must be sterilized, and we must wear clean clothes. . . . In this fashion, we can strengthen our vigilance against the enemy's germ warfare."

Thus was a sanitation campaign—unquestionably needed in the most desperate sense—forwarded, with American "germ warfare" serving as a primary stimulus.

87. "The Bolshevik Press Festival," editorial, *ibid.*, May 5, 1952.

88. "The Victory Over Germany Festival of the Great Soviet Union," editorial, *ibid.*, May 9, 1952, p. 1.

even minute details, despite the scarcity of newsprint and scanty treatment of many events taking place in North Korea. Soviet forces, incidentally, were given credit for the "liberation" of China as well as of Korea. "Thanks to the decisive role of the Soviet Army, the Asian peoples were liberated from their old fetters. . . . Thus, the Chinese people have achieved the victory of their people's revolution, expelling the enemy both within and without." [89]

Adulation of the Soviet Union probably reached its zenith when attention was focused upon Stalin himself. "The Korean people look up to Marshal Stalin as to the sun—the savior of mankind, the benefactor of the Korean people's liberation, our father. We praise him with joy and song, and call on his name as the symbol of happiness and peace." [90]

When Stalin's death was announced in early March 1953, Kim Il-sŏng immediately proclaimed that the nation would observe a period of national mourning until after the funeral, with all flags lowered, memorial meetings at all work places, and funeral salutes being fired in every major city.[91] The press devoted almost all of its space to Stalin's life and events in the Soviet Union during his life. Kim Il-sŏng himself wrote an article "Stalin Is the Inspiration for the Peoples Struggling for Their Freedom and Independence" published on the front page of *Nodong Sinmun*, March 10. Its opening sentences will stand very well for the remainder:

> Stalin has passed away. The ardent heart of the great leader of progressive mankind has ceased to beat. This sad news has spread over Korean territory like lightning, inflicting a bitter blow to the hearts of millions of people. Korean People's Army soldiers, workers, farmers, and students, as well as all residents of both South and North Korea, have heard the sad news with profound grief. The very being of Korea has seemed to bow down, and mothers who had apparently exhausted their tears in weeping for the children they had lost in the bombing of the air bandits sobbed again. . . .[92]

To read passages such as this is to appreciate the profound shock that must have been felt by Kim and other key Korean Communists when they learned of Khrushchev's denunciation of Stalin during the Twentieth CPSU Congress a scant three years later. Indeed, all the publications and speeches of North Koreans during the late Stalinist period reveal how fixed was the hierarchy of nations within the Communist world, how secure, seemingly, was the authority of the Soviet Union, and how readily both P'yŏngyang and Peking paid homage to the supremacy of Russia as

89. *Ibid.*

90. "The Boundless Gratitude of the Korean People Toward Marshal Stalin," editorial, *ibid.*, May 22, 1952, p. 1. For similar extravagant praise, see the editorials of April 4, April 24, and Dec. 21, 1952.

91. For details, see *ibid.*, March 6–10, 1952.

92. *Ibid.*, March 10, 1952, p. 1.

a nation and Stalin as an individual. Insofar as the North Korean leaders were concerned, the relation with Moscow was that of father and son. With Peking, however, it was that of peer to peer, or rather of larger to smaller sibling.

What role, if any, the death of Stalin had in bringing the Korean War to a close remains unclear. Certainly, there was a new uncertainty with respect to Soviet authority. The North Korean press followed events in the Soviet Union very closely in the months after Stalin's death. For example, substantial portions of Malenkov's speech to the Fourth Session of the Supreme Soviet were carried in lieu of an editorial in the *Nodong Sinmun* of March 18. Three days later, the resolutions of the Supreme Soviet Congress were published, and in the weeks that followed, Soviet news was often carried as extensively as news from Korea. Nevertheless, whatever the impact of the changes in Russia, it is also clear that the North Korean leaders were being forced to recognize the omnipresent signs of low morale among their own people. Even by reading the official Communist journals, one can discern ample evidence of food shortages, the heavy toll of Allied bombing, and a growing war weariness.

The basic issue blocking any further progress in the negotiations remained that of prisoner exchange. The Communist side was demanding a total prisoner exchange, while the UN side was standing firm for voluntary repatriation. The issue was no mere formality. It was clear to the Communists that a very large number of the prisoners, both Chinese and North Korean, that were held by the UN forces would elect to go to Taiwan or remain in South Korea if voluntary repatriation were permitted. This would, of course, represent a serious political defeat for the Communist side, and one with potential economic and military repercussions. Nevertheless, American resolve on this matter, bolstered by the adamant position of Syngman Rhee, seemed firm.

Suddenly, on June 18, 1953, Syngman Rhee, without American knowledge or consent, arranged for the release of a large number of North Korean and Chinese prisoners. At last, the Communists had a legitimate reason for protest, and in his letter to Lieutenant General Nam Il, the chief Communist delegate at the negotiations, General William Harrison, the chief UN delegate, apologized, asserting that this release of prisoners was not part of the American intent. In the end, however, the incident proved to be very revealing. While the Communists bitterly condemned the act, they had now decided that a conclusion of the fighting was in their interest. Accordingly, they did not allow the incident to interfere with the reaching of an agreement, even though that agreement involved accepting the principle of voluntary repatriation. When the Communists decided that it was in their interests—indeed, nearly a necessity—to bring the war to a close, they did not stand on face despite the most serious provocation from the UN side during the entire course of negotiations.

The Truce and the Purge of the Pak Group

On July 25, 1953, it was announced that "complete agreement" had been reached in the truce negotiations. On the twenty-eighth, an armistice was jointly proclaimed throughout North Korea by Kim Il-sŏng and Marshal P'eng Teh-huai, the Chinese commanding general for the Korean front. The most disastrous war in Korean history, perpetrated by the Communists in an effort to "liberate" the south, had come to a close. Having long proclaimed that they would achieve total victory, the North Korean leaders now devoted themselves to interpreting the settlement in these terms. Thus, a *Nodong Sinmun* editorial on armistice day heralded the truce as "a glorious victory" that marked the death knell of "imperialist aggression." [93] In the same issue, a long speech by Kim Il-sŏng announced that the successful defense of Korean freedom and independence against "the running dogs of US imperialism, the clique of Syngman Rhee" constituted a great historic victory, although there should be no slackening of revolutionary vigilance in the face of new moves by the imperialists. The war was thus interpreted as a defensive one, in which the Communists had succeeded in blocking the efforts of the South Korean government to unify Korea by force—a total reversal of the facts, but one essential to Communist purposes.

A number of citations and medals were distributed among top Communist leaders, with Kim Tu-bong, Pak Chŏng-ae, and Pak Ch'ang-ok all receiving the Order of the National Flag, Class I. It was also announced that Ch'oe Yong-gŏn had been appointed vice-premier, but there was no mention of Pak Hŏn-yŏng—an ominous sign. Pak, indeed, had not been mentioned since early February, nor had he appeared in public. In all probability, Pak had been placed under arrest shortly after his last appearance, on February 7, when the fifth anniversary of the Korean People's Army had been commemorated in P'yŏngyang with all top Communist leaders in attendance. We can date Pak's removal with reasonable accuracy because, on February 15, *Nodong Sinmun* announced that, in accordance with Kim Il-sŏng's instructions at the Fifth Plenum to root out the remnants of factionalism within the Party, certain factionalists had been discovered and had become a "target of our hatred." [94] Those mentioned were Chu Nyŏng-ha, Yim Hwa, Kim Nam-ch'ŏn, Cho Il-hae, "and others." The attack upon them was fierce. They were charged with not trusting the Party, and with slandering Party policy and Party leadership. Being wise in their own conceit, they conspired to obtain higher positions,

---

93. "The Korean Truce Negotiations Have Reached a Complete Agreement," *ibid*. Despite the effort of this editorial and all other writings of this period to convey the idea of a massive victory, the message that actually comes through is that of enormous relief that the war has ended.

94. "There Is No Room in Our Party Ranks for Those Who Are Not Candid," editorial, *ibid*., Feb. 15, 1953, p. 1.

amassing "localists" and those "whose revolutionary past was unclean," as well as elements not content with their Party rank or position, thereby weakening Party solidarity.[95]

The editorial went on to state that the Party had been tolerant of those who had behaved badly provided that they confessed their past mistakes and then proceeded to serve the Party with loyalty. The present culprits, however, seemed intent upon continuing their anti-Party and anti-state activities. When Yim Hwa and others had made their self-criticism before the P'yŏngyang Municipal Party Plenum, they had failed to demonstrate honesty and candor. Thus Yim Hwa, instead of confessing his unclean life before Liberation, and his anti-Party and anti-state activities after Liberation, and then begging the forgiveness of the Party, had merely admitted vaguely that he had committed rightist errors. Chu Nyŏng-ha, former ambassador to Moscow and vice-minister of Foreign Affairs, refused to admit his mistakes to the very end, and openly criticized the Party leadership.

This, the editorial concluded, was typical of all factionalists. Contrary to what they themselves insisted, the ideological background of their behavior was not the fact that they had originated in North or South Korea. It was simply that they did not support the Party line or Party policies, and did not trust the Party leadership. In short, "north" and "south" were the pretexts by which the factionalists sought to cover their anti-Party and anti-state activities.

At no point was the name of Pak Hŏn-yŏng mentioned, but most of those involved were in fact from the south and had enjoyed close and long standing personal connections with Pak. Actually, the *Nodong Sinmun* editorial provides a clue, corroborated by other sources, to the fact that after the Fourth Plenum, in November 1951, factional intrigues got under way within the highest Party circles. Some of those close to Pak Hŏn-yŏng —Yi Sŭng-yŏp, Cho Il-myŏng, Kim Ŭng-bin, and Pak Sŭng-won—held frequent meetings at Pak's official residence to prepare for a struggle against the Kim Il-sŏng line. Reportedly, they were seeking an understanding with Hŏ Ka-i and his group. It will be recalled that Hŏ had been demoted at

---

95. *Ibid.* Clearly, this editorial signaled a full assault upon the South Korean Workers' Party group clustered around Pak Hŏn-yŏng. It was followed, moreover, on the following day by another editorial, "The Strengthening of Intra-Party Democracy," in which the basic theme was that democracy did not mean anarchism. The minority had to obey the majority, and lower level Party organizations had to obey higher Party organizations. Most important, *all* elements within the Party had to obey the leadership. If intra-Party democracy were used by "slanderers, liberalists, factionalists, and other hostile elements," it would destroy Party organization and weaken the combat strength of the Party. "Such democracy has nothing to do with the genuine democracy of our Party based upon centralized leadership": p. 1. For the attack on Chu Nyŏng-ha, see "Limitless Hatred and Anger Against Impure Elements," conclusions of the KWP Ministry of Foreign Affairs Cell Assembly, *NS,* March 5, 1953.

the time of the Fourth Plenum, after being criticized for his closed-door policy on Party membership. Kim Il-sŏng, getting some wind of these developments, met with his most trusted followers, Kim Il, Pak Chŏng-ae, and Han Sŏl-ya, and reportedly worked out a plan to place the blame for defeat upon Pak Hŏn-yŏng. When arrangements had been completed, he summoned the Central Committee of the Party for a Fifth Plenary Session.

The Fifth Plenum was held between December 15 and 18, 1952. There is evidence that the Kim Il-sŏng forces had made extensive preparations to begin a major purge of the Pak Hŏn-yŏng group. Reportedly, Kim Il-sŏng began his move with the arrest of Yim Hwa. Yim was a poet who had come from the south, and who was connected with the Pak faction. In the autumn of 1952 he had written a war poem that contained the lines: "Forests were put to the fire; houses were burned. If Stalin comes to Korea, there is not a house to put him up for the night." Kim Il-sŏng immediately had Yim arrested for "anti-Communist thoughts." According to one source, Yim, under torture, confessed that he had conspired with Yi Sŭng-yŏp and Cho Il-myŏng against the Kim government. Yim's arrest occurred in the fall of 1952, along with that of such other former SKWP members as Kim Nam-ch'ŏn, Kim Ki-rim, Kim O-sŏng, and Kwon O-jik. Through the months of October, November, and December 1952, various individuals were secretly arrested. There was no publicity for the purge as it spread.

In Kim's speech at the opening of the Fifth Plenum, a substantial amount of attention was devoted to defects within the Party. Some of this was clearly directed against the so-called domestic faction.[96] Without revealing names, Kim charged that substantial elements within the Party lacked "Party character." Once appointed to responsible state or Party positions, they blindly sought special privileges, worked only for their own profit, foresook the masses, forgot the Party and the revolution, and committed state crimes. Instead of performing the duties assigned them, they complained against the Party constantly, and in some instances, while refusing to speak in open Party meetings or raise their criticisms before the appropriate bodies, they met clandestinely, uttering all sorts of libels behind the Party's back.

Kim then warmed to his subject. Certain elements, he stated, were obedient neither to the resolutions of the Party nor to the requirements of the revolution. They enjoyed the glories of office, but they ignored its responsibilities. Inflating their own egos, they claimed to have had a great revolutionary history. But in reality they were accomplishing nothing. Some

96. For an account of the Fifth Plenum and the text of Kim Il-sŏng's speech, "The Organizational and Ideological Consolidation of the Korean Workers' Party Is the Foundation of Our Victory," see *NS,* Dec. 22, 1952, pp. 1–6. Also in *Kim Il-sŏng sŏnjip (Selected Works of Kim Il-sŏng)*, 1953 ed., Vol. IV, pp. 264–337.

It should be noted that, at the same time as the Fifth Plenum, on Dec. 24, 1952, Kim also convened a "Conference of High-Ranking Officers of the People's Army," in part no doubt to assure himself of their support of his new purge.

of these elements, moreover, sought to draw individuals to them on the basis of kinship, friendship, connections with the same school, or common regional origins. Such efforts were symbolic of petty bourgeois liberalism, Kim announced, and had to be crushed. There were no factions within the Korean Workers' Party, but there were still "the remnants of factionalism." Certain unprincipled individuals were seeking to continue the factional struggles of the past by uniting "localist elements" (those inclined to act on the basis of regional identity), those dissatisfied with their position within the Party, those who had been disciplined by the Party, and those with "impure social backgrounds," into a dissident group. Sometimes the appeal to these types was made on the basis that at present "you are not trusted by the Party." The "factionalists," charged Kim, betrayed themselves by the emphasis they placed upon securing posts for *their* group, regardless of the ability, social background, and trustworthiness of the individuals concerned.

Kim ended this section of his report on an ominous note. The factionalists, he observed, were prepared on the one hand to hide the "revolutionary impurities" of their coterie, and on the other to use various means to drive wedges between the Party officers in an effort to divide and conquer. If such actions were ignored, they could turn into "small group activities." Thus, the factionalists had to be challenged frontally and forced to confess their errors frankly before the Party. Their anti-Party activities had to cease. "If we leave these remnants of factionalism undisturbed," Kim said, "the final result, as the experiences of other fraternal parties and people's democracies have shown us, will be to change them into *spies for the enemy*" (italics ours).

Kim's Fifth Plenum report served as the basic document in the purge of the Pak Hŏn-yŏng group. The Party did not rest with the Plenum sessions alone. For many months, all Party units down to the cell level were made to hold discussion meetings, with Kim's report as the basis for criticisms and self-criticisms. Additional reference materials relating to the "crimes" of the Pak group were prepared, and former South Koreans in particular were required to examine their past relations with Pak in detail, reporting upon events that "substantiated" the charges being made.[97]

97. Interesting details have been provided by Kim Chŏng-gi in his interview with Chong-Sik Lee, May 28, 1967, in Seoul. He cited events at the ministry-wide conference of some 400 members of the State Planning Commission as an example. The conference met for a full week. He was instructed by the Party to speak on the second night and was given a small pamphlet containing detailed accusations against Pak Hŏn-yŏng to study in advance. It raised all the points brought out later in the trial and posed a number of questions: Why did the SKWP fail after the October riots? Why did Party membership decline? etc. Kim Chŏng-gi's task was to add details and, in doing so, to implicate Pak and his group in the failures. For several days, he prepared his talk. At its conclusion, he ended in the approved manner: "I had respected Pak Hŏn-yŏng and could not believe the Party's charges initially," he told the as-

It was against this background that the events of February 1953, noted above, took place. Pak Hŏn-yŏng himself was not tried and sentenced to death until mid-December 1955. Thus, for reasons that are not completely clear, the purge of the Pak group was spread over a period of three years. After February 1953, however, Pak was held incommunicado. The first major trial of his associates opened on August 3, 1953, scarcely one week after the Korean War armistice had been promulgated.

At this point, Hŏ Ka-i had already committed suicide. There are two somewhat different versions of the events leading up to this act. According to one account, in the midst of the purge of Pak and his friends, Hŏ was ordered to take charge of repairing the Kyŏngyŏng Reservoir, located about 40 kilometers north of P'yŏngyang, which had been bombed and destroyed so that the neighboring areas were flooded. Hŏ reportedly felt that this assignment was an insult to his status, as well as part of a conspiracy to link him with the Pak group. He therefore remained in P'yŏngyang, preparing countermeasures, whereupon Kim decided to detain him for "insubordination." In early April 1953, when he was ordered to appear before a court of inquiry, he committed suicide. According to Kim Ch'ang-sun, Kim Il-sŏng, worried because Hŏ had failed to check Pak's influence within the Party, and concerned about the possibility of collaboration between the Pak group and Hŏ, accused the latter of having made grave mistakes in Party organization once again. Hŏ reportedly asked for three days in which to reflect upon the charges, returned to his home, and promptly shot himself. Thereupon, the Politburo is said to have condemned Hŏ for committing "an extremely cowardly act," besides having sinned in not revealing his crimes before the Party.[98] Whichever version is correct, another major Communist leader had been removed at Kim Il-sŏng's instigation.

The trials of August 1953 involved twelve defendants, all high-ranking North Korean officials. The list was headed by Yi Sŭng-yŏp, formerly minister of Justice and secretary of the Central Committee of the Korean Workers' Party; Cho Il-myŏng, formerly head of the Editorial Bureau of *Haebang Ilbo* and later vice-minister of the ministry of Culture and Propaganda; Yim Hwa, poet and formerly vice-chairman of the Central Committee of the Korean-Soviet Cultural Association; Pak Sŭng-won, formerly deputy chief of the Liaison Department, Central Committee, Korean Workers' Party; Yi Kang-guk, formerly director of the Bureau of Foreign Affairs of the North Korean People's Committee (a post equivalent to foreign minister); Pae Ch'ŏl, formerly chief of the Liaison Department,

---

sembled audience. "But now I realize that it is true. I was mistaken. The analysis of the Party is correct." According to Kim, some people, such as Yi Ki-sŏk, then minister of Light Industry, were purged because they persisted in doubting the charges. (Yi had been vice-chairman of the SKWP.) Pak Chŏng-ae attacked him, saying: "Do you then argue that we have manufactured the charges?" There was no easy answer to that. At last report, Yi was in charge of a library in Sinŭiju.

98. Kim Ch'ang-sun, *op. cit.*, pp. 134–135

Central Committee, Korean Workers' Party; Yun Sun-dal, formerly deputy chief, Liaison Department, Central Committee, Korean Workers' Party; Yi Won-jo, formerly vice-chief of the Department of Propaganda and Agitation, Central Committee, Korean Workers' Party; Cho Yong-bok, formerly senior member, People's Inspection Committee; Maeng Chong-ho, formerly commander, 10th Independent Branch Unit of the Korean People's Guerrilla Corps; and Sŏl Chŏng-sik, formerly head of the Bureau of Public Opinion, Public Information Office, US Military Government, and later member of Section 7, General Political Bureau, Supreme Command of the Korean People's Army.

The trial, held between August 3 and 6, was public; it was conducted by the Military Tribunal Department of the Supreme Court. The primary charges, which the court declared as having been confirmed by the facts developed in the preliminary examinations and in the present trial, were startling indeed.[99] According to the official verdict, Yi Sŭng-yŏp and his clique had been employed as spies by American authorities, and had infiltrated into high positions within the Korean Workers' Party and the Democratic People's Republic of Korea in order to supply secret information for American intelligence organizations pertaining to military, political, and cultural affairs. This had been done for the purpose of dividing and destroying the capacity of the Korean people to fight for the unification of their fatherland; obstructing the politics of the Party and the government; isolating the government and Party from the masses; and organizing and inciting an armed uprising against the People's Republic "in order to establish a colonial and capitalist regime under the control of the American imperialists."

Thus, it was not sufficient to accuse members of the Pak faction of activities against Kim Il-sŏng and his group. They had to be charged with high treason, in the form of service as spies directly linked with American intelligence. Moreover, this service was not of recent origin, according to the court. Yi Sŭng-yŏp and Cho Il-myŏng had been spies since March 1946, at which time they had been enlisted by an American army lieutenant in charge of political studies in the Bureau of Public Opinion of the Public Information Office, US Military Government in Korea. At this time, both men had furnished the Americans with all information concerning the local and central organization of the Korean Communist Party in South Korea. Yi, moreover, had allegedly acted as a civilian attaché of the US State Department ever since May 1947, operating under the control and direction of Dr. Harold Noble, then the highest political adviser for the commander of USAFIK, Lieutenant General John R. Hodge. Yi allegedly received de-

99. *Nodong Sinmun*, in its issues of August 5, 6, and 7, carried lengthy accounts of the trial. The August 5 issue presented the full indictment (pp. 2–4), and the August 7 issue carried the text of the trial itself, including the "confessions" of those accused (pp. 1, 3–4). The data in the text is drawn from these official reports.

tailed instructions from Noble in July 1948, before entering North Korea. Upon arriving in North Korea, moreover, Yi supposedly met secretly with Cho Il-myŏng, who had come north earlier, in December 1947, so as to coordinate their espionage activities.

In August 1948, the charges continued, they were able to recruit Pak Sŭng-won, former head of the political department of *Haebang Ilbo,* who was then the vice-chief of the First Publishing Company at Haeju, Hwanghae Province. With the addition of Yim Hwa, who had been serving as an American spy since December 1945, under the direction of an American officer, Colonel John N. Robinson, an espionage line was now completed that ran to Noble in Seoul. Still another recruit, Sŏl Chŏng-sik, was supposedly added to the spy ring at this time.

In September 1948, Noble reportedly sent An Yŏng-dal to Yi Sŭng-yŏp with instructions that, if Yi could not come back to South Korea, he should remain in the north and continue to carry out his espionage activities. Yi duly relayed information to Noble via An about Party and government organization and personnel. At this point, Yi and his clique supposedly began to gather military information, especially information pertaining to the size, equipment, and location of Communist forces along the 38th parallel, to aid the "northern expedition plans" of the "American imperialists." This information was reportedly relayed to Noble in Seoul. In the summer of 1949, Yi dispatched Cho to military maneuvers at Wunp'a-san (Mount Wunp'a) to gather information; Cho in turn sent defendant Pak Sŭng-won, and the information obtained by Pak was conveyed to Noble.

After February 1950, Yi had allegedly been in touch with defendant Paek Hyŏng-bok, who had been operating under another American, an Air Force intelligence officer called Nichols, of the Far East Command, and also with An Yŏng-dal and codefendant Cho Yong-bok. Three times, he supplied secret information about the Korean Workers' Party. In May, Noble reportedly instructed him through An, Cho, and Paek that "when American troops invaded North Korea," Yi should create and supply false materials that would make it appear as if the Korean People's Army had started the war. Upon receiving these instructions, Yi advised Noble (again, An was the go-between) that as soon as the American attack began, he should begin radio broadcasts claiming that the KPA had invaded South Korea, have some of the South Korean troops disguised in KPA uniforms, and see that they treated the people harshly in order to arouse hostile feelings against the KPA and the DPRK. Supposedly, Yi also instructed An to infiltrate into the remaining party organization (SKWP) in Seoul, and even gave him a radio transmitter. Later, Paek was placed in the Security Branch of the People's Republic with a view to protecting various spies of the Rhee regime.

Following the outbreak of the war, in July 1950, Yi became chairman of the People's Committee of Seoul city. He then instructed Yim Hwa to take charge of such social and cultural organizations as the General League of Writers and Artists. A study of the situation within the Party, government, and army was made, with the purpose of making this available to the Americans. In 1951, Yi allegedly sought to reestablish his espionage network with its linkage to Noble. Noble sent a Korean agent (a certain Chin) to Yi in July, and the network was then reestablished by bringing in Yi Kang-guk, who "had already promised in 1935 that he would act as a running dog of American intelligence organizations." Yi Kang-guk had supposedly fulfilled this pledge later by offering his mistress to an American colonel who was commander of the 24th Army Corps Military Police. In September 1946, Yi came north "after a fake arrest order by the American Military Government," supposedly to give him the proper credentials as a patriot. Before he left the south, he was allegedly given instructions by the colonel who had shared his mistress to infiltrate the DPRK government structure and collect secret information in the military, political, and cultural fields. From January 1947, Yi Kang-guk was able to utilize his position as director of the Bureau of Foreign Affairs of the North Korean People's Committee "to carry out the orders of his American master."

Following the outbreak of the "War for the Liberation of the Fatherland," Yi Kang-guk met two American military spies in his P'yŏngyang home in July 1950, and discussed his military espionage activities with them. Yi Kang-guk also participated in the Yi Sŭng-yŏp network, supplying secret information via Yim Hwa on four occasions.

According to the court, the Yi Sŭng-yŏp clique not only carried out espionage activities but also helped the Rhee regime and the Americans to destroy the South Korean Workers' Party and kill "numerous democratic patriots, thus destroying and weakening the democratic capacity of the Republic as a whole." Under the direction of an American intelligence officer, the same Nichols, An Yŏng-dal (who had been operating under Yi Sŭng-yŏp's direction), collaborated with Paek Hyŏng-bok, then chief of the central branch office of the Counterintelligence Section of the Internal Security Bureau of the Rhee regime, by infiltrating defendant Cho Yong-bok into the South Korean Workers' Party. With information supplied by An and Cho, Paek was able to arrest Kim Sam-yong, member of the Political Committee of the SKWP, and Yi Chu-ha, on March 27, 1950.

To conceal their own crimes, asserted the court, the defendants did not hesitate to kill those who might expose them. In 1949, Yi Sŭng-yŏp gave orders for the execution of three patriots on false charges of espionage, and between May and August 1948, a total of forty-two patriots were killed as spies by An Yŏng-dal, acting under Yi Sŭng-yŏp's instructions. An also sought to get rid of Kim Chae-ch'an, chairman of the Kaesŏng

Municipal Korean Workers' Party, and So Ku-don, chairman of the Chang-dan Prefectural Party Committee. But this was prevented by the guard unit on the 38th parallel.

Nevertheless, after the outbreak of war, the terrorist activities of the Yi Sŭng-yŏp clique supposedly increased. When he became chairman of the People's Committee of Seoul City on June 28, 1950, Yi Sŭng-yŏp set up "a terrorist murder organization" headed by "his faithful servant," Yi Chung-ŏp. This committee killed seven patriots; later, in July, a so-called Land Investigation Committee, headed by An Yŏng-dal, was created to get rid of a large number of patriots who threatened to get in the way of the clique.

It is at this point in the court record that the name of Pak Hŏn-yŏng enters for the first time. Supposedly, at the end of July 1950, when the fact was revealed that An Yŏng-dal helped in the arrest of comrade Kim Sam-yong, Yi Sŭng-yŏp conferred with Pak Hŏn-yŏng and "in an attempt to conceal their crimes, they caused An Yŏng-dal to be sent to the front lines under Yim Chong-hwan, to whom Yi had sent instructions to execute An."

Pak Hŏn-yŏng was also named in connection with a third charge, that of conspiring to overthrow the government of the People's Republic. According to the court, he defended and encouraged the efforts of the Yi Sŭng-yŏp clique in this direction, using his position as vice-chairman of the Korean Workers' Party and deputy premier of the government for the purpose. This effort supposedly extended back to the very beginning of the post-Liberation era. "Taking advantage of Pak Hŏn-yŏng's ambition to assume supreme power in the People's Republic," the Yi Sŭng-yŏp clique conspired to set up "a puppet government of landlords and capitalists under the control of American imperialists." As evidence, the first item introduced was the fact that Cho Il-myŏng and Pak Sŭng-won, "in response to the propaganda plot of the American imperialists," wrote articles in *Haebang Ilbo,* opposing the trusteeship plan agreed upon at the Moscow Conference of December 1945, while Yi Won-jo and Yim Hwa lectured against it. Moreover, during the period of the Soviet-American Joint Conference, between 1946 and May 1947, the Yi Sŭng-yŏp clique conspired openly to perpetuate the division of the nation at the 38th parallel. Yi had enlisted the services of Yi Kang-guk, Pak Sŭng-won, and Yi Won-jo; after September 1946, they used the First Publishing Company of Haeju as their headquarters.

The court then returned to 1950, asserting that the Yi clique's activities became more open after Yi became chairman of the People's Committee in Seoul. Once again, Noble and An Yŏng-dal supposedly figure in the plot. Before retreating from Seoul, on June 26, 1950, Noble allegedly ordered An to remain in the city. His orders were to contact Yi Sŭng-yŏp and instruct him to organize an armed popular uprising that could be coordinated with an American counterattack. Yi was directed to "protect middle-of-the-road and rightist elements until the return of American troops, using the guise of a so-called benevolent policy." Yi supposedly obeyed; he collected various "turncoats and national traitors," and proceeded to strengthen his power base in Seoul and Kyŏnggi Province.

When the American counterattack came, the court asserted, the Yi clique decided to take advantage of it by organizing a separate command, with the objective of eventually overthrowing the Kim Il-sŏng government and taking power. In a series of secret meetings, it was decided that Yi Sŭng-yŏp would be the general commander, Cho Il-myŏng and Yim Hwa would be in charge of organizing political, propaganda, and agitation activities, Pak Sŭng-won would be chief of staff, Pae Ch'ŏl would be in charge of military organization, and Kim Ŭng-bin would be in charge of armed militia. In order to facilitate swift mobilization, it was planned to move various units to the vicinity of P'yŏngyang, and to increase both personnel and armaments. Headquarters were located at a point near P'yŏngyang. Pae Ch'ŏl and Pak Sŭng-won were given the additional responsibility of strengthening liaison points, and an effort was made to draw elements with an impure past into the Central Liaison Office of the Korean Workers' Party, so that the office could be transformed into the headquarters of the armed units. An effort was also made at this time to organize a Kyŏnggi Province People's Committee under the Yi clique's control, in the hope that the province might become their base.

By November 1952, Yi and his associates had assembled guerrilla forces numbering some 3,900, organized under the 10th Branch Unit of the Guerrilla Corps. Yi sent Maeng Chong-ho to be commander of this force, and appointed Yu Won-sik political commissar, "to imbue the troops with anti-Party and anti-state ideas." Yi reportedly inspected the 10th Branch Unit in person four times between March 1952 and January 1953. Also, to bolster their military strength, in March 1952 he moved an additional unit under Hong Hyŏn-gi to Chung-hwa near P'yŏngyang. Meanwhile, the Yi clique also allegedly strengthened their armament and personnel in various liaison points, and attempted to infiltrate and strengthen their position in various social, state, and Party organizations. With Cho Il-myŏng, Yim Hwa, and Yi Won-jo taking the lead, the clique had entrenched themselves in the ministry of Culture and Propaganda, the General League of Writers and Artists, the Korean-Soviet Cultural Association, and the General Federation of Trade Unions.

Against this background, the Yi clique is supposed to have held a secret meeting early in September 1952 in Pak Hŏn-yŏng's living room. Among those present, reportedly, were Yi Sŭng-yŏp, Pae Ch'ŏl, Cho Il-myŏng, Yim Hwa, Pak Sŭng-won, and Yun Sun-dal. At that time, the discussion centered on a "new Party" and a "new government." It was decided that Pak Hŏn-yŏng should be premier of this government; Chu Nyŏng-ha and Chang Si-u, vice-premiers; Pak Sŭng-won, minister of Internal Affairs; Yi Kang-guk, minister of Foreign Affairs; Kim Ŭng-bin, minister of Defense; Cho Il-myŏng, minister of Propaganda; Yim Hwa, minister of Education; Pae Ch'ŏl, minister of Labor; and Yun Sun-dal, minister of Commerce. Yi Sŭng-yŏp would become the first secretary of the new Party.

Here the court verdict ended, after asserting, "The present court confirms their [the defendants'] crimes committed against the Party, the state, and the people at a time when the Korean people were shedding precious blood in order to repel the armed aggression of the American imperialists." [100] The sentence imposed upon all of the defendants except Yun Sundal and Yi Won-jo was death and the confiscation of all property. Yun was sentenced to imprisonment for 60 years and the confiscation of all property; Yi Won-jo for 33 years and the confiscation of all property.

It is impossible to separate truth and half-truth from total falsity in the myriad of charges made against Pak Hŏn-yŏng and his group. Almost certainly, the charge of being conscious agents of the United States was totally false. It is likely, however, that some of the contacts mentioned did exist, particularly during the period when the South Korean Workers' Party was operating more or less legally. For example, Yi Kang-guk's mistress, Kim Su-in, did live with a senior American officer in the intelligence line of work. The South Korean authorities arrested her for collecting and transmitting military secrets, and for facilitating the escape of a major Communist leader, Yi Chung-ŏp.[101] Both the Communists and the Americans would have been remiss in their respective duties if they had not sought contact—and information—from the other side. And at least some of the American names mentioned in the court verdict are those of individuals serving in the American Military Government during the period mentioned. However, there is not a single shred of evidence available to us that suggests any of the accused were actually paid or volunteer American agents. Indeed, given the many blatant distortions in the court's account, particularly those pertaining to American actions and objectives just before and during the Korean War, there is every reason to believe that these charges were wholly false.

Why, then, were such charges made—and given such prominence? The most logical explanation is also the most simple: those who opposed Kim Il-sŏng and his government, particularly when they were as influential as Pak Hŏn-yŏng, especially among former southern residents, had to be "proven" not merely mistaken, not merely factionalists, but traitors as well. Thus, no one would dare to defend them, and any further association with them would be impossible. This, in fact, was the *true* lesson learned from the experiences of the "other fraternal parties"—notably the CPSU—to

100. *Ibid.*, Aug. 7, 1952, p. 4.
101. See O Che-do, *P'yŏnghwa ui chŏk un nugunya* (*Who Are the Enemies of Peace?*), Pusan, 1952, pp. 9–23.

which Kim Il-sŏng had referred in his report to the Fifth Plenum. Who could forget the lessons of the Great Purge of 1937? Further, the failures of the disastrous war just concluded could now be attributed in part to treason at the highest level.

Some of the charges concerning the unjustifiable killing of "democratic patriots" may have been true, or true as far as the killing was concerned. As we have frequently indicated, internecine warfare among various Communist factions had had a lengthy history, particularly within the South Korean Workers' Party. It would not be surprising if the Pak Hŏn-yŏng faction did get rid of certain rivals, taking advantage of the wartime chaos.[102] That, of course, was precisely what the Kim Il-sŏng group was doing at this point—and had done earlier, in the case of Mu Chŏng.

The real charge, however, was the one made at the end of the verdict, namely, that the Pak Hŏn-yŏng faction had plotted to overthrow the Kim Il-sŏng regime, and had begun to gather both military and political forces for this purpose. The precise extent to which this charge was true is difficult to ascertain. Kim Il-sŏng represented northern domination, and we know that the Pak group had long resented the subordinate role that this implied for them. It is quite possible, as some informants have asserted, that the Pak group did discuss the possibility of effecting a political change by one means or another, and positions in a possible Pak Hŏn-yŏng government may have been tentatively allotted. Such talk would have been particularly likely after a few drinks. It is less clear, however, to what extent concrete plans had been drawn up, or a definite step-by-step program set in motion.

In any case, by mid-1953 Kim Il-sŏng had smashed the Pak Hŏn-yŏng faction. In addition to those involved in the trial of August 1953, a number of other prominent Party and government leaders were purged, most of them former SKWP members. These included Kim Chŏm-gwŏn, Kim Kwang-su, Yi Wi-sang, An Ki-sŏng, Kwon O-jik, Kim O-sŏng, Kim Ki-rim, U Chin-hwan, Yi Chong-gap, Ch'oe Yong-dal, and Ku Chae-su, all former SKWP men; and Chang Si-u, Chu Nyŏng-ha, Chang Sun-myŏng, Kim Chŏn-ju, and Paek Kŭm-nak, from other factions. Kim Ŭng-bin, another associate of Pak Hŏn-yŏng, on getting advance word of the impending purge, supposedly fled; his subsequent fate is unclear, since he disappeared completely.

As noted earlier, Pak Hŏn-yŏng himself was not tried and executed until December 1955. Presumably he was kept in prison for some two and one-half years. The reasons for this delay are not clear. However, since the

---

102. There is evidence that Pak Hŏn-yŏng's chauffeur was bribed or induced to talk by the Kim forces, and that he provided damaging testimony against Pak. From defectors and others, accounts have come of drinking parties at which "slanderous remarks" against Kim's leadership were made by Pak adherents; it would be surprising if this were not the case, given the disastrous nature of events in the 1950–53 period.

Pak trial represented the culmination of the Pak faction purges, it would be appropriate to mention it at this point. He was tried on December 15, 1955, by a special session of the Supreme Court, with the presiding judges having been "determined" by a decision of the presidium of the Supreme People's Assembly on the previous day. The "trial," which was open to the public, lasted only one day. Pak himself wrote a letter stating that "he did not intend to defend himself against the charges, and therefore did not need an advocate." After examination, the court "approved his request," and therefore his advocate did not attend the court trial. The judges were Ch'oe Yong-gŏn, vice-premier and Pak's successor, who presided; Kim Ik-sŏn, minister of State Inspection; Yim Hae, chairman of the Control Commission, Central Committee, Korean Workers' Party; Pang Hak-se, minister of the Interior; and Cho Sŏng-mo, chief justice of the Supreme Court. The chief prosecutor was Prosecutor-General Yi Song-un. Witnesses who appeared were Han Ch'ŏl, Kim So-mok, and Kwon O-jik.[103]

The charges were similar to those leveled against the Yi Sŭng-yŏp group. First, Pak was accused of having been the "boss" of the clique dedicated to "spying, destruction, murder, and treachery" on behalf of "the American imperialists." As with the Chinese Communists accused of anti-Party, anti-state activities during the Cultural Revolution, Pak's "criminal activities" were discovered to have started at a very early point. Allegedly, when he was working as editor of *Yŏja Siron* (Women's Contemporary Magazine) in 1919, he had had close contact with an American missionary, Horace H. Underwood, who served as a professor (later president) of Yonhui University—and as a "US espionage agent." From then on, Pak "cherished an admiration for the United States," according to the indictment. Moreover, on two occasions—in 1925 and in 1939—Pak, when arrested, played the role of renegade, divulging secrets to the Japanese that enabled them to extinguish the existing Korean revolutionary organizations, and being released by the police for his contributions.

In the fall of 1939, Pak had "turned into a traitor of the revolution." In September, he informed Japanese authorities that he had abandoned Communism. The very next month he met with the "US spy" Underwood and, at Underwood's request, signed a pledge signifying that he would "faithfully serve the American imperialists as their espionage agent." Pak fulfilled this promise immediately, according to the indictment. In December 1939, Underwood supposedly instructed Pak "to infiltrate deeply into the Korean revolutionary movement, obtain a high position in the organization, and utilize it to collect secret information for the American imperi-

103. A "full account" of the trial of Pak Hŏn-yŏng is carried in *Nodong Sinmun*, Dec. 18, 1955, p. 2. Pak's trial was given much less attention than the earlier trials of Yi Sŭng-yŏp et al., although a full range of charges against Pak was published in connection with the trial report. The account that follows is taken from this official statement.

alists." In order to carry out his assignment, Pak "intensified his sectarian activities, disguised himself as a patriot, and continued to commit every kind of crime in order to contribute to the American scheme of aggression against Korea." (Note that these "crimes" were presumably being committed against the Japanese!)

Pak was then charged with committing "anti-people" activities on an even larger scale and in a more ingenious manner after 1945. Once again "disguising himself as a patriot," Pak gathered around him "other traitors and sectarian elements," all of them determined to carry out the instructions of American intelligence agencies. Thus, early in September 1945, Pak held "a secret meeting" with General Hodge, "pledging his loyalty to American imperialism." In November, Pak was allegedly "instructed" by Hodge and Underwood to consolidate his position in the South Korean Communist Party, and *also* to plant his influence more extensively in the north.

At this meeting, Pak was supposedly ordered "to provide basic information concerning Party activities and organization, foster division and rivalry within the Party, and induce it to give up the struggle and become a compromising 'pro-American' Party." The secret meetings allegedly continued. For example, at a March 1946 meeting at the Bando Hotel with Hodge, Pak was supposedly instructed to place Yi Sŭng-yŏp, Cho Il-myŏng, and others in important Party posts, and ensure their safety while they were carrying out espionage activities. On six occasions between March 1946 and September 1947, according to the indictment, Pak had Yi and Cho supply the American intelligence agencies with vital information.

It was further charged that on September 5, 1946, at another secret meeting, Hodge instructed Pak "to enter North Korea and take power." To provide a cover, Pak and Yi Kang-guk were caused to denounce the American Military Government, and then a fake arrest order was issued enabling Pak to deceive his comrades when he entered North Korea in early October 1946. By channeling secret information to Yi Sŭng-yŏp, who remained in Seoul, and making Yi Kang-guk chief of the Bureau of Foreign Affairs of the People's Committee, Pak was able to relay vital information concerning the North Korean armed forces, governmental structure, and Communist policies to the Americans.

Under American instructions, Pak allegedly infiltrated a large number of spies into important positions in North Korea. Two of these spies, Alice Hyŏn and William Yi, came to North Korea from the United States using the cover story that they were political exiles. When the Americans began their "northern expedition" in 1950, Pak reportedly increased the scale of his "treacherous crimes," protecting espionage agents Paek Hyŏng-bok, Cho Yong-bok, and An Yŏng-dal in cooperation with Yi Sŭng-yŏp. The charge was repeated that Pak, Yi, and others within the group did not hesitate to liquidate loyal Party members as "traitors, informers, and spies" if they suspected these unfortunate individuals of gaining knowledge of their

crimes or standing in their way. Thus, in March 1950, Kim Sam-yong, chief
of the Seoul Guidance Department of the South Korean Workers' Party,
was arrested and executed with the aid of An, Cho, and Paek—all of whom
were protected by Pak. In June 1950, moreover, after the "liberation" of
Seoul, Pak and Yi, through their secret murder organizations, tortured some
seventy innocent people whom they suspected of knowing about their "antirevolutionary crimes," and executed some of them.

Under Pak's guidance, his supporters infiltrated into key Party and
government positions. As their conspiratorial strength increased, the Pak
clique sought to establish a territorial base for "anti-revolutionary criminal
activities," using the Kaesŏng area. Day by day, their conspiracy intensified,
until "they even planned and prepared an armed uprising to overthrow the
Party and the government." Such plans, first set forth in September 1951
in a secret meeting at Yi Sŭng-yŏp's office, were made concrete one year
later at a meeting held at Pak's home.

To achieve power, Pak allegedly surrounded himself with "impure
elements," concealing their crimes as best he could, and threatening those
who would expose them. He also bought off Party workers, and himself
lived a corrupt life, as was indicated by the fact that at the time of his
arrest he was hiding 879,000 wŏn in cash and 1,600 grams of pure gold.

According to the official public account of the trial, Pak "completely
admitted his crimes." Another source indicates that Pak asserted it was
difficult for him to be held responsible for the attempts to organize a new
government or Party, or engage in a conspiracy for armed rebellion, since
he had neither participated in nor directed such crimes—but that he would
feel responsible to the extent that his subordinates were involved. In any
case, the verdict had long been determined. After a recess, the court sentenced Pak to death and to the confiscation of all property. Presumably,
the sentence was promptly carried out.

As can be seen, the charges against Pak Hŏn-yŏng were precisely the
same as those against his followers—high treason, unjust or criminal treatment of "loyal Communists," and conspiracy to overthrow the Kim Il-sŏng
regime. Once again, the first charge was almost certainly false in every respect, a grotesque travesty on actual events. The evidence is overwhelming
that all responsible Americans regarded Pak as a dedicated Communist and
treated him as such. Nor is there the slightest evidence that Pak ceased at
any point to regard the American government as "the leader of world imperialism" and the Soviet government as "the fatherland of the international
proletariat." The charge that Pak was a conscious agent of United States
intelligence forces is preposterous, completely at variance with the considerable data available to us, and refuted even by the "evidence" presented
in the trial if that "evidence" is examined carefully. The charge of criminal
behavior against rivals within the Communist movement—as in the case of
Yi Sŭng-yŏp and associates—could be true, for reasons set forth earlier.

The final charge of conspiring against the Kim forces, whether it was true or false, was the only reason for the indictment and for Pak's execution.

In the three years between late 1952 and late 1955, Kim Il-sŏng had finally succeeded in liquidating his most dangerous opponent after first destroying that opponent's personal following and organizational bases. The process had begun as early as 1946; by 1948, Kim's authority, as a result of firm, consistent Soviet support, seemed nearly unchallengeable. Pak's fate, however, was sealed by the Communist failure to win the Korean War. Without a physical base from which to exercise power, Pak and his southern group either had to reconcile themselves to a minority position, or risk extinction. Even had the Communists won the war and unified Korea under their control, the probability of a bloody factional struggle for power would have been extremely high. In the brief period during which the Communists occupied portions of the south, the political structure was in most instances dominated by northerners, and north-south rivalries broke out despite the precarious situation. With the Communists pushed back to the north, however, the rapid demise of the "domestic faction" became an even more logical development than before.

The purge of the Pak faction served another purpose: it supplied an answer to the question, "Who was responsible for the loss of the war, and why?" Thus, Pak and his followers became scapegoats in a number of convenient ways. First, the trials served as a forum in which to reiterate the false thesis that the war itself was a result of American and South Korean aggression, not the responsibility of Kim and his cohorts. More importantly, however, the trials provided the supreme rationalization for defeat: the sad state of affairs was due not to the mistakes of the Kim group, but because traitors from within had given overt assistance to the enemy.

The conspiracy theory is a natural, almost essential element in the struggle for power within a political system of the Stalinist type. In such a system, political competition has minimal legitimacy even when it follows the institutional channels provided. To any "opposition" that can be suspected of seeking to supplant the top power holders, legitimacy must be completely denied regardless of the ideological and policy identities involved. Thus, a series of increasingly grave charges, commencing with "error," moving to "crime," and ending with "treason," is mounted against this "opposition." No more convenient means can be devised of removing all vestiges of legitimacy from one's political rivals, and the technique also isolates those rivals from potential supporters, since none dare champion traitors.

In these matters, the Kim Il-sŏng regime was merely following the basic patterns established by Stalin in the 1930s and pursued after 1945 by various Eastern European Communist elites. Those who lost the battle for power in the Communist states of this era generally found their national as well as their class loyalty impugned. In the case of key figures, moreover, their multifarious "crimes" were often dated so as to make it clear that they had *always* been "traitors" to their class and state. Their entire political careers were made synonymous with treachery, and thereby the possibility of redemption was eliminated. Erstwhile heroes stood revealed as generic enemies of the people.[104]

North Korea at the End of the War

Where did Korean Communism stand at the close of the Korean War? The reports of the Fifth (December 1952) and Sixth (August 1953) plenums, together with the data provided by official organs and interviews with ex-Communists who were active during this period, make it possible to set forth the salient trends. Let us begin with an exploration of the economic situation.

As has been noted earlier, the Korean War turned a poor country into a stricken one. From one source who lived in North Korea at this point, we learn that the north was utterly devastated when the truce was signed. People were without food, clothing, and housing, with thousands living in crude air raid shelters or hastily constructed shanties and lean-tos. Indeed, according to this source, many intellectuals believed that Pak Hŏn-yŏng had revealed military secrets to the United States so as to minimize the enormous human sacrifices by ending the war quickly. While such a rumor was false, it reveals the depth of misery existing.

There is ample testimony as to the chaotic state of North Korean production statistics during this period, and to the reason for this state of affairs. Since failure was impermissible, cadres at every level cooperated with each other in providing inflated figures. Even Kim Il-sŏng was forced to recognize the seriousness of the problem, although he, too, used "official

104. It is interesting to see the 1968 Party version of the Pak affair, as recounted in Paek Pong's work.

"As this programme [the program presented at the Fifth Plenum] was unfolded, an extremely astonishing fact came to light. All the crimes were brought to light, the crimes of the Pak Hun Yung and Li Seung Yup clique. As old-time spies in the pay of U.S. imperialism, these had crept into the organs of the Party and the State, and there they had hatched their anti-state intrigues, including espionage, murder and destruction. . . . Since their entry into the northern part, this clique had continued their anti-Party factional intrigues as the faithful running dogs of U.S. imperialism, and during the trying days of the war, had systematically offered Party, state and military secrets to the U.S. CIA. At the time of the 'summer and autumn offensives' of the enemy which were smashed in 1951, the clique had tried to raise armed revolt, timing to the enemy offensive. And when Eisenhower was plotting his 'new offensive,' in line with this, they schemed to topple the Party and the State by means of armed revolt and sell the Korean people as colonial slaves to U.S. imperialism.

"To have successfully fought U.S. imperialism, the strongest enemy, while such wicked spy cliques were entrenched in the Party and carrying out their intrigues! How great is Comrade Kim Il Sung!" Baik Bong, *op. cit.,* Vol. II, pp. 392–393.

statistics" to boost morale. Thus, in his address to the Fifth Plenum of the Central Committee on December 15, 1952, he asserted that overall industrial production for the year was 119 percent of that for 1951. Grain production in 1952, he reported, was 113 percent of that for 1951, an increase of 340,000 metric tons, and the highest yet achieved in North Korea. Production in 1952, he stated, was 130,000 tons higher than the previous high point, achieved in 1948.

These figures would mean a grain production of 2,458,000 metric tons in 1951, and 2,798,000 tons in 1952—figures too high to be believable. As we noted earlier, the government itself later put out different figures, claiming a production of 2,260,000 tons for 1951 and 2,450,000 tons for 1952. Even these figures are probably inflated. Food production *was* increased in 1952, as a result of relatively favorable weather conditions, but these were years when production was probably much lower than the official figures indicate, and food shortages were widespread. In 1953, moreover, production dropped again, despite the almost constant exhortations of the government. Both Kim and subsequent government figures revealed that some 70,000 chŏngbo (171,500 acres) *less* land was being cultivated at this time than in the pre-1945 period. As many as a million farmers, moreover, had fled south during the course of the war, with effects upon production that can be imagined.

Perhaps it was possible to be more frank after the truce had been signed, and the Pak Hŏn-yŏng faction had been liquidated. In his speech before the Sixth Plenum on August 5, 1953, Kim painted a very dark picture of economic conditions.[105] "Comrades, our agriculture suffered enormous damage during the three years of severe war," he reported. He then proceeded to enumerate some of the problems: an acute shortage of farm labor; a drastic decline in the number of domestic animals; and the destruction of many reservoirs and irrigation facilities. He also admitted that many peasant families were short of food and seed grain.

Kim asserted that during the war, when nearly all industrial facilities had been destroyed, the Party and the state had directed all of their attention to rural work. Huge difficulties, however, remained to be overcome. The "impoverished peasants," including those engaged in slash-and-burn cultivation, accounted for 30–40 percent of all farm households, Kim reported. Moreover, they continued to live in dire poverty. Food and seed grain had been loaned to them. They had been exempted from the tax-in-kind. But the land they possessed was poor in quality and, in many cases, insufficient in amount.

What should be done? Certain remedial measures could be undertaken

105. For the text of this speech, see *NS,* Aug. 30, 1953, pp. 1–3. Under the title "Everything for the Postwar Rehabilitation and Development of the National Economy," it is also to be found in Kim Il-Sung, *Selected Works,* P'yŏngyang, 1965, Vol. I, pp. 161–209, and *Kim Il-sŏng sŏnjip,* 1960 ed., Vol. IV, pp. 1–56.

at once. Some farmers could be moved to more fertile land, now lying vacant. Sideline cooperatives to provide extra income, should be encouraged. A few farmers could be moved to state stock farms. But the fundamental answer, Kim asserted, was the development of industry. Ultimately, many peasants had to be removed from the land and brought into industrial work. Kim was careful to emphasize that private peasant farming would continue "for some time to come." The first step, he proclaimed, was to introduce agricultural cooperatives into the private farming system. Such cooperatives, he announced, should be organized on an experimental basis at the beginning of 1954. However, private ownership of land and farm implements should be preserved.

For the time being, then, the Korean Communists, no doubt deeply concerned about the loyalty and the productive commitment of those farmers who had remained in the north, had determined upon a relatively moderate agrarian policy. The private system was not to be fundamentally altered, although agricultural cooperatives were to be encouraged, and some state farms established. Meanwhile, there was to be an emphasis upon agrarian modernization. The state would supply the peasants with new farm implements, sufficient irrigation water, more fertilizer, and good strains of seed. Promises were also made of land reclamation and the development of more irrigated areas.

The livestock situation was particularly bad, as Kim readily admitted. Fortunately, "the fraternal Mongolian people" had provided the government with "hundreds of thousands of head of cattle and sheep" that would serve as the foundation for state stock farms. The postwar development of animal husbandry, Kim announced, would be based upon three principles: the development of a modern, state-owned sector; the establishment of combined agricultural and stockbreeding cooperatives, with special attention being given the poor farmers and backward areas; and finally, a nationwide campaign to encourage stockbreeding, with the aim of bringing the livestock holdings of individual peasants up to the pre-1945 level by 1956. Once again, to stimulate peasant initiative, Kim announced that the state would supply breeding animals and allow the peasants to sell their livestock "freely."

Thus, in general, the immediate postwar agrarian policies of the North Korean Communists were relatively "soft," reflecting a deep anxiety about relations with a battered peasantry (a significant portion of whom had already deserted) and a sense of urgency approaching desperation concerning production.

When Kim admitted that nearly all industrial facilities had been destroyed by the war, he was merely reporting a fact. According to official figures, as we noted earlier, the gross value of industrial production in 1953 was only 64 percent of what it had been in 1949. This figure is misleading, however, because it largely reflects the fact that small units, many involved in military production, had continued to function in some way or other, but the large-scale, modern sector of the North Korean industrial economy had been rendered almost completely inoperative.

In a certain sense, this made possible changes that might otherwise not have been made. Kim himself suggested that some plants and factories should be rebuilt in more convenient locations, closer to sources of raw material or transport and communication facilities. The critical issue, of course, was the establishment of basic priorities and developmental models. Once again, as might have been expected, the Soviet model of economic development was accepted with few, if any, modifications. The emphasis, Kim made clear, would be placed upon heavy industry and production related to defense. Consumer industries and agriculture would not be ignored, he insisted, but in the allocation of capital and resources they would receive secondary attention.

At the Sixth Plenum, a three-phase development program was outlined and approved. The first phase was to be one of preparation and planning, with a period of six months to one year spent in determining priorities and allocations. In the second phase, a Three-Year Plan would be launched, with its basic objective the return of the national economy to prewar levels. In the third phase, the first Five-Year Plan would be drawn up and put into effect, with the aim being the construction of a socialist industrial society. Thus, by 1956, the impact of the war was to have been erased, and by 1961 a socialist economy was to have taken shape.

Even with extensive foreign aid, such a program called for major sacrifices on the part of the North Korean people. The program's basic priorities made this inevitable. And Kim made those priorities explicit in his report of August 1953. First, he said, it was necessary to reconstruct the Hwanghae and Kimch'aek Iron Works, the Sŏngjin and Kangsŏn Steel Works, and the machine-tool industry, "the basic foundation for the industrialization of our country" and "of great importance for national defense." The shipbuilding industry would also be high on the priority list, as well as the power industry. The other industries to be given special attention were chemicals, building materials, and communications.

The problem of manpower and labor efficiency weighed heavily at this point. Hundreds of thousands of males in the prime of their working lives had fled to the south, had been killed, or in some other way had been rendered unavailable or ineffective. Kim admitted, for example, that in heavy industry, only 4 percent of the workers had had as much as ten years' experience, and that more than one-half of all industrial workers had had less than one year's experience at this point. He also complained bitterly about the misuse of such labor as was available. During the war, he noted, urban dwellers in many instances had been evacuated, with jobs being given them in factories or farms located in safe, remote areas. This labor had to be reallocated quickly because it was now being wasted. For instance, some stock farms had more workers than animals, Kim charged, and labor waste was omnipresent, with far too many functionaries, office hands, and other nonproductive elements. Women, who had constituted between one-third and one-half of the labor force during the war, would continue to be employed extensively. In the aftermath of the war, the female-male ratio in the country was 53 to 47.

Despite the priorities it established, the North Korean regime recognized that building an efficient labor force was closely related to meeting at least minimal needs for food, clothing, and housing. Thus, rationing was to be continued, and the 70,000 chŏngbo of cultivable land currently lying idle were, if at all possible, to be returned to production. Inefficiency, waste, and embezzlement clearly still constituted major problems. So did theft, as Kim Il-sŏng admitted in his report of December 1952. He also admitted that the quality of consumer goods was often very bad; that many essential commodities could not be found in state-owned stores or co-operatives; and that due to mismanagement, medicines received as gifts from abroad were rotting in warehouses—and unavailable in local hospitals. The crisis in housing, meanwhile, could scarcely be exaggerated: merely to return to the prewar situation, it would be necessary to rebuild some 300,000 square feet of housing, or approximately 35 percent of all the housing previously existing.

The economic situation was a grim one. The great bulk of the North Korean people were living in total misery, without adequate food, clothing, or housing, and with only the prospect of heavy sacrifices in the immediate future. The promises of extensive foreign aid were the only bright prospects on the immediate horizon. All of these difficulties had complicated the political scene. Success helps to unite an elite, failure serves to divide it. As we have seen, deep internal quarrels had rent the Workers' Party, with the Fifth Plenum heralding the beginning of a major purge directed against the domestic faction.

As the Korean War came to a close, indeed, the old southern Communists were largely liquidated, with the Kapsan-Soviet and Yenan factions playing the major roles, under the increasing dominance of the Soviet-supported Kim Il-sŏng.

Moreover, the Party itself had undergone significant changes. During the early part of the war, Hŏ Ka-i's hard-line policy, together with the war losses and defections, produced a major reduction in Party strength. Alarmed by this trend, Kim repudiated the hard-line policy at the Fourth Plenum of November 1951, and ordered a so-called open-door policy instituted. In his report of December 1952, he reviewed the results. Our Party, he asserted, has grown into a mass political organization with more than one million members and 48,933 basic organizational units. There is no farm village, work place, or military squad in the nation without a Party organization, he stated.[106]

A portion of this membership came from individuals reinstated in the Party. Kim alleged that many Party members had previously been subjected to unjust punishments. Up to October 1952, therefore, 29.8 percent of those who had been expelled from the Party had been readmitted, and 62.1 percent of those demoted from member status to candidate member status had been restored to their original positions. Moreover, 69.2 percent of those subjected to punishment had been released from those punishments. Despite the reinstatement of many old members, some 40 percent of the Party at the close of the Korean War consisted of new members. During the war, Kim claimed, nearly 450,000 new members had joined Party ranks. The social composition of the Party, Kim continued, was now as follows: poor farmers, 57.9 percent; middle farmers, 3.5 percent; workers, 21 percent; office workers, 16.6 percent; others, 1 percent. From these figures, it will be noted that over three-fifths of Korean Communist Party members came from the agrarian strata of society; and the urban "proletariat" constituted no more than one-fifth. Indeed, it is probable that Kim included a number of "intellectuals" in the "workers" category, since he usually referred to the former group as "working intellectuals" and there are no separate categories for such groups as intellectuals, military personnel, or professional Party leaders. Some of these elements may have been placed under "office workers" or "others," but certainly the bulk must have been classed as either the "workers" or "farmers."

It is not difficult to imagine what a tremendous upheaval these changes must have represented, particularly at local, district, and provincial levels. In many respects, the postwar Party was a new Party. Having first expelled thousands of members in an effort to produce a highly committed, efficient, hard-core organization, the top leadership, which had not changed, suddenly found it essential to admit almost anyone in their desperate effort to effect rapport with the ordinary citizen and especially the peasant.

Kim Il-sŏng himself admitted that the new Party recruit was rarely the type of individual glorified in Marxist-Leninist literature as the ideal Party member. Not only was he typically a peasant rather than a worker; in many cases, he was also illiterate or, at best, semiliterate. The great majority of new members were young in both age and experience, and approximately one-half of them could barely understand Korean phonetic script. Some Party organizations, Kim acknowledged, had admitted members to the Party without applying any standards whatsoever. The result was that a number were not politically trustworthy, and almost all needed extensive theoretical and political education.

Under these circumstances, the problems of local leadership were certain to be acute. Some 79 cell chairmen, Kim reported, had been ex-

106. *NS*, Dec. 22, 1952, p. 5.

pelled from the Party during the first half of 1952 because they lacked either ability or political reliability. Some were "spies." Indeed, according to Kim, the enemy had penetrated some ri-level Party organizations, "bribing" the cadres to serve "anti-people" purposes. In the city of P'yŏngyang itself, 37.3 percent of all cell chairmen had been replaced during the first six months of 1952.

To meet these serious problems, Kim outlined a three-pronged offensive aimed at improving Party organization and increasing Party authority. First, the Party should pursue the mass line: It should *learn from the masses,* discerning their views, discovering their problems, and avoiding commandism, bureaucratism, and formalism. But it should also *teach the masses,* making them understand the policies of the Party, causing them to participate "enthusiastically" in executing those policies, and avoiding tailism, lethargy, and corruption. These themes, of course, had long been emphasized and were scarcely original, being central Leninist themes. Kim claimed that "remarkable improvement" had been achieved in strengthening Party-mass relations, and proceeded to quote Comrade Stalin: "As long as the Bolsheviks maintain close relations with the broad masses, they will be invincible."

Second on Kim's agenda for the Party was renewed activity in the thought training and propaganda fields. Since the Korean economy was based upon the predominance of small-scale production, bourgeois thought was likely to emerge over and over again. To guard against this was a primary Party responsibility. The enemy, moreover, would continue to mobilize every available propaganda method in an effort to manipulate the "shaky and unhealthy elements" spawned by the society's various temporary difficulties. Communist propaganda, Kim complained, had been woefully inadequate. In the area of thought training, operations had been superficial and formalistic; so far from reaching the masses, they had not reached Party members or even Party cadres. Frequently, propaganda and agitational activities had been separated from the actual problems of the nation, without focus and without relation to the particular phase or stage of development characteristic of the Korean scene.

Kim also sharply criticized the Party political schools as having inadequate programs and low standards. Even top Party and state leaders had neglected their studies, he maintained, and so failed to improve their ideological understanding. Moreover, far too little literature based upon Marx, Engels, Lenin, and Stalin had been published. The Party had paid little attention to the activities of writers, playwrights, poets, composers, artists, and actors. During the war, almost no good artistic works conveying Marxist-Leninist themes had been produced. Within the creative world, he asserted, a decisive struggle against ideological errors and liberalistic tendencies must be pursued. Once again, Comrade Stalin's words should serve as guideposts. "When Marxist-Leninist educational activities toward Party and state personnel go limp, then the entire activities of the state also go limp."

How should these shortcomings be corrected? It was essential to rebuild the war-ravaged cultural and propaganda agencies of the Party, and improve their work. The Democratic Propaganda Rooms must be refurbished in factories, farms, and fishing villages, and provided with the necessary materials and equipment. Also, motion pictures should be widely used as a means of mass propaganda, with mobile movie teams working regularly in the countryside. In addition, Party schools should be revamped, with improved courses and instructors. In the cultural field, moreover, it was imperative that works in all fields be written "with a view to Korean problems from a Marxist standpoint."

In connection with this latter point, Kim Il-sŏng gave voice to a note of nationalism that was later to play an increasing role in his regime. We have suffered, he proclaimed, the "unforgivable and serious defect of ignoring the noble inheritance of our forefathers who have written histories, geographies, and works in a wide range of other fields, rather than analyzing them from a Marxist-Leninist standpoint, absorbing and developing them." In extreme cases, Kim continued, "all the tales and songs of other countries are admired but our own are despised. We must reconstruct our noble heritage in science and culture, understanding that only on the basis of absorbing and developing our own great scientific and cultural heritage can we correctly adapt the advanced science and culture of other countries."

Kim had found the appeal to racial, cultural, and national sentiments infinitely more effective during the darkest hours of the war than any exhortation to be good Marxist-Leninists. He now appeared ready to advance this appeal more forcefully than in the past, both in order to induce heavy sacrifices in the course of reconstruction, and to continue the war—at least on the verbal level—against the United States and the Republic of Korea.

The third prong in Kim's offensive to regenerate the Party involved an administrative restructuring to strengthen the local political units, reduce and readjust the intermediate units, and thereby enhance the authority of the national unit. At the Sixth Plenum, Kim announced that the myŏn would be abolished and certain changes made in provincial boundaries. At the same time, he asserted, Party and administrative units at the ri level would be greatly strengthened. Henceforth, there were to be intimate ties between cell-level and national-level Party and state operations, with less scope given to intermediate units. Maximum socialization was to be encouraged through small-unit education and political involvement, with "democratic centralism" insuring firm control by Central Party and government institutions. To make this system work, Kim emphasized, it was essential to begin an intensive, stepped-up training program for cadres at the ri level, with all provincial Party and People's Committee schools being activated for this purpose.

The interpretation of the international situation by Kim and other North Korean leaders at the close of the Korean War was naturally attuned to the domestic themes set forth above. Their broadest interpretation was a familiar one: the 'democratic and peaceful camp headed by the great Soviet Union" was rapidly consolidating and increasing its global power and influence, while the capitalist world was sinking into graver and graver crisis. Kim amplified the latter theme in his Sixth Plenum report, arguing that the current crisis within the capitalist world was a result of decolonization: because fewer raw materials and outlets for manufactured goods were available to them, the capitalist states were engaged in a struggle that served only to intensify their inner contradictions. It was to resolve those contradictions that they were resorting to war and destruction with the aim of reducing the global population and bringing great profits to the billionaires. The unity of the socialist world, on the other hand, had never been more brilliantly illustrated than by the assistance being given to North Korea.

Such was the tone and the level of international analysis expounded by Kim and his followers during this period. Clearly, this was a time when the leadership of the Soviet Union was proudly acknowledged on every occasion, and when that leadership was equated with the omniscience of Comrade Stalin. Stalin's words were repeatedly used to fortify Kim's proposals with respect to both domestic and foreign policy, and the adulation that accompanied every mention of his name could not have been surpassed. The Soviet Union, moreover, was credited not only with the broad leadership of the socialist world, but specifically with liberating Korea and preserving it against the onslaughts of the imperialist camp. Despite the enormous sacrifices of the new Chinese People's Republic through its "volunteers," Communist China was treated essentially as a peer: there was no shortage of thanks, but the terms used were not extravagant ones. Nor was specific reference made to Mao Tse-tung, or to Chinese guidance in ideology or policy. Such influence as the Chinese Communist model was having (and we have noted evidence that there *was* increasing influence) was not given public recognition.

With respect to specific foreign policy issues, the Korean issue, with the interrelated question of relations with the United States, understandably dominated the scene. In the light of later events on the Korean peninsula (and in Vietnam) it is both interesting and vitally important to discern how the Communists tended to interpret this period. First, Kim insisted that the Communists had won the Korean War, and rejected even the idea of a stalemate or draw. "The enemy was compelled to sign the armistice agreement," he asserted, "as a result of his irretrievable military, political, and moral defeat in the Korean war, the tenacious and patient efforts of the Korean and Chinese peoples to restore peace in Korea, and the pressure from the public opinion of the peace-loving peoples all over the world.

Thus, the Korean people won a glorious victory in their Patriotic War of Liberation."

What was to be done with this "victory"? Kim made it clear that the Communists intended to pursue their objectives by every possible means. And those objectives could be said to center on the goal of forcing the United States to withdraw from South Korea and thus securing the unification of Korea on Communist terms. At various times during this period, Kim and others spelled out these positions very clearly: "The Korean nation is one and Korea belongs to the Koreans. The Korean question must naturally be settled by the Korean people themselves." In the projected political conference that was to follow the armistice agreement, the Communists would force all United States and "satellite country" forces out of South Korea, "to enable the Korean people to settle the Korean issue by themselves, thus preventing foreigners from interfering in our domestic affairs."

And how did the North Korean leaders view their non-Communist rivals, those with whom they presumably wished to settle the unification issue? The attacks upon Syngman Rhee and all officials of the Republic of Korea were vicious and unmeasured. Rhee and his "clique" were traitors, men totally repudiated by the Korean people, and they could not be recognized in any form. Kim and his followers made it clear that they intended to "settle" the unification issue by dealing with "true spokesmen" for the South Korean people, not with "traitors and lackeys."

The current leaders, Kim insisted, had no public support; without American guns, they would be overthrown overnight. But the "notorious warmonger" Dulles had committed the United States to defend this bunch of criminals, with a mutual defense treaty that permitted "US imperialism to obstruct the peaceful unification of our country and interfere in our domestic affairs." It was, Kim asserted, "a flagrant territorial giveaway under which the Syngman Rhee clique could sell South Korea to the Yankees." However, Kim insisted, the situation in South Korea would work to the benefit of the Communists. The south had now been plunged into hopeless chaos, with the life of the people totally wretched and hatred of both the United States and the Rhee clique growing daily. The people of the south yearned for unity with the north under the guidance of the Workers' Party and the Democratic People's Republic. The task of the Party was to rally all southerners around it, paving the way for a settlement of the Korean question by the Koreans themselves, repudiating the colonial occupation policy, and compelling all American forces to withdraw.

It is impossible to believe that Kim Il-sŏng and the other top northern Communists were unaware of the sharp reaction against Communism in South Korea that had resulted from the war and the temporary Communist occupation of much of the south. That misery prevailed in both south and north, no one can deny. However, the refugee statistics showed that the great flow was to the south, and that it included a huge number of workers and peasants, the very social classes heralded as rulers of the new society. Many of these refugees were fiercely anti-Communist as a result of their experiences. But that sentiment was not merely a refugee sentiment. Under unique circumstances, most of South Korea had experienced Communist rule for a brief period, and then been liberated from that rule. Such sympathy for the Communists as had existed was largely dissipated—indeed, replaced by a strong antagonism, in most cases—as a result of Communist actions in the south. And, in addition, active southern Communist sympathizers or collaborators had for the most part either been killed or had fled to the north as their mentors retreated.

For all these and other reasons, South Korea, in complete contrast to Kim Il-sŏng's remarks, was at this point one of the most staunchly anti-Communist societies in the world. On the other hand, every speech and action of the North Korean officials reflected their deep anxiety regarding the loyalty of their own people, and the deplorable conditions prevailing throughout their country.

Despite the threatening words of Kim regarding the Republic of Korea, his regime was certainly not in any position at this point to back its threats with force. The economy of North Korea lay in ruins, and the task of rebuilding it would be formidable. The Workers' Party had been riven by deaths, purges, and defections to a point where it had to be considered a new Party seeking to reestablish control over the North Korean people. Even at the leadership level, massive and bloody purges had taken place, as the battle between Kim and the Pak Hŏn-yŏng faction reached a climax. Kim, backed by his own and the Yenan faction—and evidently with no interference from foreign Communist sources—won that battle and raised his personal power to a new height. But the bitter political battles within the Korean Communist movement were far from over.

Viewed from any standpoint, the Korean War was a disaster for the Korean Communists despite the fact that they had succeeded in exacting a heavy toll from their enemies and—after massive infusions of Chinese manpower—prevented the establishment of a unified non-Communist Korea. Kim and his followers had probably miscalculated the American response when they began the invasion. In any case, they were not likely soon again to engage in this particular form of struggle. A "people's war" of the Maoist type might involve more intricate forms of preparation and a much longer time span, but its risks were also likely to be much less.

CHAPTER VII

THE FORCED MARCH

The five years that followed the end of the Korean War witnessed major political and economic changes in North Korea. By the end of 1958, another group of top Communist leaders had been removed, and Kim Il-sŏng had reached at last a seemingly unchallengeable position of power and authority. Having already liquidated Pak Hŏn-yŏng and his group, Kim now proceeded to oust certain key figures of both the Soviet and Yenan factions. The climactic struggle came in August 1956, and the finale was reached in 1958 with the removal of Kim Tu-bong. In many respects, as we shall note, the crisis of 1956 was the most serious challenge that Kim Il-sŏng had yet faced, particularly since it produced intervention from both the Soviet Union and the People's Republic of China. Kim weathered the storm without too much difficulty, however, and emerged with every potential rival vanquished. It is from this period, therefore, that the absolute supremacy of Kim Il-sŏng should be dated.

That supremacy was naturally reflected in the military as well as in the Party arena. Kim Il-sŏng, like Mao Tse-tung, was always acutely aware of the ultimate source of power. He had no intention of relinquishing any part of his control over military affairs. Old guerrillas rarely underestimate the importance of holding onto their guns. Thus, in the major upheaval that took place between 1956 and 1958, dubious elements of the Soviet and Yenan factions were removed simultaneously from both army and Party, and replaced by men whom Kim considered totally loyal. Meanwhile, changes were also taking place at the grass roots. The old veterans of the Korean War were mustered out, some 80,000 being discharged in 1959 alone. In their place, a new kind of soldier appeared—a soldier of the Kim Il-sŏng generation who had been recruited by universal conscription. Kim hoped that this "new socialist man," weapon in one hand and Party literature in the other, would aid in "liberating" the south, that major unfinished task.

These were also extremely important years on a second front. Emulating, in some measure, his Chinese comrades, Kim exhorted his people to embark upon a forced march toward reconstruction and development. By the end of 1958, with a Stakhanovite campaign fully under way, the Communist leaders could proudly proclaim that most prewar production figures had been surpassed, and that the nation had been turned into "a socialist industrial-agrarian state with a self-sufficient economic base." As we shall discover, official statistics for this period, particularly with respect to agrarian production, cannot be accepted as reliable. Nor did the Communists present the seamy side of the economic picture, including the great human sacrifices involved. Nevertheless, at a time when South Korea generally continued to flounder economically, the north was making major gains, a fact with political as well as economic significance.

International developments, especially those pertaining to the Communist world, also had a decided impact upon North Korea. Political uncertainty inside the Soviet Union, various new tendencies in Soviet foreign policy, and the substantial influence of Communist China confronted North Korean leaders with both opportunities and risks. Nationalism and independence were given new emphasis. Gradually, Kim steered his state away from its previous satellite status vis-à-vis the Soviet Union. Meanwhile, the fissures in Sino-Soviet relations immediately began to affect internal North Korean politics, exacerbating the factionalism already deeply rooted in the Korean soil.

Rebuilding the Party

It is essential to explore each of the above developments in some detail, at least as they pertain to North Korea. Let us turn first to the political events that led up to Kim's ultimate triumph over his rivals within the Democratic People's Republic of Korea. As we have noted, the attack upon the domestic faction had rendered impotent a group that, despite its basic political weaknesses, possessed a regional identity threatening to Soviet, Kapsan, and Yenan factions alike.[1]

1. As one piece of additional evidence, note the interesting statement of Ch'oe Kwang-sŏk, who went north during the Korean War and was captured in the South as an enemy agent in 1963. "Those most shocked by the purge of Pak Hŏn-yŏng were from South Korea. Regardless of whether one went to North Korea voluntarily or otherwise, Pak's existence meant a great deal to southerners since they received much help from him. Pak was vice-chairman of the Korean Workers' Party and Foreign Minister. Yi Sŭng-yŏp was Party secretary as well as minister of Justice. Thus, if a man from South Korea got involved in a dispute with someone from the north, or if he had some problems involving Party rules, he could expect support from Pak and Yi.

We can only speculate as to why the trial and execution of Pak Hŏn-yŏng was postponed until December 1955. Did either the Russians or the Chinese use their influence on behalf of Pak? We have no evidence of this. Did the delay relate to internal political considerations? As long as Pak lived, the political situation remained in suspense. Anyone even remotely connected with Pak and his group would realize that the affair was not closed, and that extreme caution was required. Other groups would recognize this, too. Moreover, Pak alive could serve as both bait and example. As we shall note, the actual timing of his trial and execution was clearly related to the next purge, which followed immediately.

Meanwhile, in the months after the Sixth Plenum of the Central Committee in August 1953, the political emphasis was upon establishing and maintaining a "steel-like" unity within the Party so that economic goals could be successfully achieved. Official editorials tended to play upon two contrapuntal themes: the Party would reward those who served it loyally, forgiving most mistakes providing they were admitted honestly and candidly, *but* all liberalistic tendencies, bureaucratism, individual heroism, and political discontent had to be relentlessly rooted out.[2] Implicit in Party pronouncements was the fact that the Korean Workers' Party, like every other institution in North Korea, had been shattered by the war and the subsequent brutal assault upon the Pak group. In facing up to the formidable tasks that lay ahead, it lacked personnel with administrative experience or technical training. The ranks of Party veterans had been badly depleted, not merely by purges and war deaths at the top, but by purges, deaths, and desertions at the middle and lower levels as well. New groups of cadres had to be recruited and trained, and relations between Party and public had to be watched constantly. Party leaders were cognizant of the very heavy sacrifices being demanded of the people, and of the meager experience of most Party and government cadres. Consequently, crash training programs for cadres were inaugurated, the campaign against bureaucratism and formalism was speeded up, and public complaints against offenders were solicited.

These activities were closely interrelated with the drive for economic

---

Those from the south also received aid from Pak and Yi in obtaining important positions. Overnight, this source of support was wiped out." Interview with Chong-Sik Lee, Seoul, Nov. 24, 1966. This statement, as we have seen, was confirmed in effect by Kim Il-sŏng himself.

2. See the *Nodong Sinmun* editorials, "Party Members Must Be Honest and Candid Before the Party," Nov. 30, 1953, p. 1, and "Our Party Has Been United and Solidified in Organization and Ideology Like Steel," Dec. 18, 1953, p. 1. In the former, dishonesty is linked with both political and economic activities: to conduct separate organizational activities is to betray the Party, and, likewise, to steal state property, violate labor regulations, produce defective goods, or fail in carrying out assignments —and then to hide one's errors, refusing to be candid—is also to undermine the Party.

rehabilitation. Through a widely publicized speech before the Plenum of the Central Committee in March 1954, Kim Il-sŏng lashed out at various factory managers and ministry officials, citing the offending units—and one individual—by name.[3] He complained that "bureaucratism" was rampant within Party and governmental circles. It displayed a variety of symptoms: preferring the armchair to being out in the field; becoming enamored of "reports," statistics, and other types of paper work; being ignorant of actual conditions, and unwilling to learn new techniques; and indulging in routine, procrastinating actions, the result being waste, inefficiency, and low production.

Kim admitted that a serious deficiency of cadres existed, particularly economic and technical workers. In selecting and allocating such individuals, both a political and a practical criterion should be used: Was the person politically reliable, and was he qualified for the work? In sum, the good cadre had to be both Red and expert. However, this principle was being violated in many cases, Kim asserted. In the Bureau of Electricity, for example, there had been flagrant nepotism. Persons from the same province and intimate friends were being hired without regard to their past experience. The vice-chief of the Bureau, indeed, had hired one Yun to be his drinking companion, despite the fact that this man's father and three brothers had been "reactionaries" and that the man himself had been discharged from the post of deputy manager in the electricity distribution department of P'yŏngyang city.

Other branches of government and factory managers were equally guilty, announced the premier, citing a number of specific cases. Cronyism had even led to the employment of some enemy agents. We must never forget, said Kim, that our enemies are always attempting to smuggle in spies, wreckers, and saboteurs. In addition, there were many qualified individuals who were not being properly used. Of the scarce technical experts, for instance, only 28 percent were directly engaged in enterprises and construction projects as of the beginning of 1954, while some 72 percent were in ministries, bureaus, and other nonproductive agencies.

Kim reserved some of his most severe criticism for provincial, city, and prefectural Party committees. They were not only ill-informed about the situation under their jurisdiction, he proclaimed, but they lacked the knowledge or even the interest to rectify mistakes.

> Thus Party organizations in the enterprises have failed to raise their work to the required political level and Party organizers are not playing their role as Party workers as they should. In most enterprises, Party political work and the struggle for reinforcing discipline in production are perfunctorily conducted; the mass-cultural work is left to take its own course;

3. This important speech of March 21, 1954, can be read in English in Kim Il Sung, *For Socialist Economic Construction in Our Country*, P'yŏngyang, 1958, pp. 79–123; for a Korean version, see *Nodong Sinmun* (hereafter *NS*), March 25, 1954, pp. 1–5.

trade union and democratic youth organizations are wellnigh inactive. No longer can such a state of affairs be tolerated.[4]

The need was for nothing less than a total revolution in methods of thought and work—in short, *the creation of a production culture.* To this end, Kim sternly dedicated every Party organization and member. His closing words were: "March powerfully onwards for the implementation of the Three Year Plan for post-war rehabilitation and development of the national economy without relaxing in the least the tense, mobilized attitude of the war-time!" [5]

What was the impact of such exhortations upon Party cadres? As we shall note in more detail later, a work ethic, reinforced by an inexorable system of punishments and rewards, really did permeate the Party cadre's thought and life. Party cadres, from the highest to the lowest, were expected to set an example; and if captured agents and defectors have reported accurately, the average Party cadre did indeed work terribly hard, with little regard for the hours involved or even for his health. If his work met with Party approval, he could expect rewards in the form of rapid promotions, commendations from the Party, and additional training. If he made mistakes or the production unit under his jurisdiction fell behind, he could expect even more rapid demotion. The obvious flaw in this system was the degree to which it inhibited initiative, and the premium it placed upon covering up failures and deficiencies. As in the Soviet system on which it was modeled, the fear of making a mistake, the reluctance to assume responsibility, and the impossibility of reporting failure represented the underside of the new Communist morality—a morality that centered upon total commitment to "the revolution."

The selection and training of cadres was naturally of major concern to Party leaders. Truly revolutionary cadres, according to Kim Il-sŏng, were distinguished by their "boundless loyalty, a high level of sophistication and dedication to the revolution for which they [had] struggled with full devotion for a long time." For the sake of the revolution and the people, he continued, "they conquer all types of hardships and have the moral character of modest, simple, revolutionary workers." [6] If this type of cadre were placed in leading positions, stated the author of the article from which this quotation is taken, Party-mass relations would be greatly strengthened. Unfortunately, the Party did not have many "seasoned and mature revolutionary cadres"; most candidates were products of the war and the postwar period. Some, however, were war heroes and others were model workers or "labor heroes." It was from this group, the article concluded, that local and provincial cadres should be selected.

4. English version cited above, p. 119.
5. *Ibid.,* p. 123.
6. Quoted in "What Type of Party Member Should Be Elected to the Party Committee?" *NS,* Nov. 17, 1955, p. 2.

The need for cadres was obviously great. By the end of 1955, the Korean Workers' Party had expanded its membership to one million. This was a continuance of the "open-door" policies established during the war; internal purposes were uppermost, but the Party leaders also had the goal of Korean unification in mind. Factories, farms, and schools all had Party units with significant percentages of new recruits. How were they to be indoctrinated and supervised?

During this period, the training of Party cadres was gradually systematized. At the lowest level, city and district Party schools were set up; they often operated at night and on irregular schedules. When a local Party member was selected for initial cadre training, he was sent to one of these schools, frequently continuing his normal pursuits at the same time. The length of training depended upon the subject matter. For instance, one might take a six-week course on local Party organization, or a two-month course on new agricultural methods.

Above this level, provincial Party schools existed, later renamed Communist colleges. The provincial Party school had a three-year program, the sole activity of the student being study. Courses included Party history, Marxist-Leninist ideology, and a variety of administrative and technical subjects. Graduates could expect positions of some importance at the city, district, or provincial level, or subordinate posts in the central government or Party headquarters. At a still higher level, a Central Party School was established. The Central Party School had two programs. The first was a six-month or one-year "refresher program" for Party officials currently in office. The second was the regular three-year course. This latter program was intended for vice-chiefs of departments in city or prefectural Party offices, to prepare them for higher posts. If an individual had graduated from a regular college or university, he did not have to attend the lower-level cadre training schools. But he might go to the Central Party School and, according to some informants, graduates of the latter institution were often able to rise more rapidly than graduates from Kim Il-sŏng University.[7]

Once the cadre took up his new position, he could expect multiple pressures, as the publications of this period make clear. "Leadership at the local levels" was under almost constant criticism. The primary charges were those leveled by Kim: waste, corruption, bureaucratism, and formal-

7. The following figures appeared in *NS,* April 24, 1956: Between 1948 and 1955, the Central Party School produced 9,400 Party cadres, 3,900 being trained in 1948–50, 4,500 in 1950–53, and 1,000 in 1953–55. Provincial Party schools trained a total of 19,135 cadres, 6,100 in 1948–50, 11,800 in 1950–53, and 1,235 in 1953–54. City Party schools trained an additional 4,780 cadres in 1948–53, a total of 33,315 cadres for the period 1948–55.

On June 1, 1956, *Nodong Sinmun* (p. 2) reported that the current student enrollment of the Central Party School was 1,267, of whom 309 were taking the three-year course.

ism. At the same time, however, constantly heavier burdens were thrust in his direction. Local and district Party cadres were exhorted to take a more forceful and direct role in production as well as in political affairs. In the fall of 1954, moreover, a significant constitutional amendment aimed at increasing the authority of local government organs and raising mass participation at the local levels was approved by the Supreme People's Assembly and promulgated forthwith.[8]

As noted above, Party membership was reported as over one million by Kim Il-sŏng at the close of 1955. With the population of North Korea only ten million, this was an extraordinarily high figure, but Kim remarked that when compared with the total population of Korea, thirty million, it was "by no means large." [9] Now, as in the past, the Korean Workers' Party claimed leadership over the whole of Korea.

More specific figures were given at the time of the Third All-Party Congress.[10] As of January 1, 1956, the Korean Workers' Party had 58,259 cells and 1,164,945 members, it was announced. More than one-half (51.7 percent) of these members had joined the Party after the Korean War. Once again, we must accept the categories provided by Communist officials in assessing the socioeconomic composition of the Party at this point. According to them, 56.8 percent of all Party members were "poor farmers," 22.6 percent were "workers," 13 percent were "clerical workers," 3.7 percent were "middle farmers," and 3.9 percent were "others." If we accept these figures, it is clear that more than 60 percent of KWP members were peasants and less than one-fourth workers. Since the Second All-Party Congress, the worker category had increased by 2.4 percent and the poor farmer category by 3.7 percent. The Korean Communist Party at its grass roots thus continued to be predominantly rural, although the ultimate political controls, as we shall note later, rested with professional politicians, many of them with extensive experience in military affairs.

What kinds of appeals were to be directed to the great mass of new Party members, and to their non-Party brethren? The regime certainly knew how much hardship was involved in the decision to concentrate upon heavy industry, and how dissatisfied many people were with economic conditions in the initial postwar period. Much of the blame continued to be assigned to local cadres: they were damaging Party-mass relations by commandism, arrogant behavior, and so on. Undoubtedly, the average citizen derived some therapeutic value from being able to read and hear news of the constant attacks upon "bureaucratism." Moreover, the regime now

8. For details, see *NS*, Nov. 1, 1954, p. 1.

9. Kim Il-sŏng, "On Eliminating Dogmatism and Formalism and Establishing *Chuch'e* in Ideological Work," speech to Party propagandists and agitators, Dec. 28, 1955, in Kim Il Sung, *Selected Works*, P'yŏngyang, 1965, Vol. I, p. 331. Hereafter cited as "On Eliminating Dogmatism."

10. A full report of the Third All-Party Congress is carried in *NS*, April 24, 1956, including all of the figures given here.

began the process of involving all individuals in the process of criticism and self-criticism. In this they were, of course, borrowing from both the Soviet and Chinese repertoire of techniques.

Early in the postwar era, a system was inaugurated of publishing complaints, supposedly written by ordinary citizens, against those in authority. This was an obvious imitation of Soviet practice. Many of these "letters to the editor" were quite severe, although one can be certain that the selection of letters to be published was closely regulated (and possibly certain letters were composed by the Party's own writers). After a time, new types of letters, complimentary in character or exhorting others to match some particular production feat, came into prominence. But critical letters were still occasionally published.[11]

Complaints about the quality of products were very numerous, a clear indication of the consumer's frustrations. One writer, for example, complained of wastage through inferior packaging: cement was sacked so badly that 20 percent was lost in transportation, 50 percent of all cigarettes were unusable because the wrappers were no good, and in one instance 90 percent of a shipment of apples was smashed because they had been poorly crated. Another writer claimed that nearly one-half of a book published by the Democratic People's Republic Press was unreadable because of poor print and typographical errors. Still another wrote in a satirical vein about clothing sizes. No matter what size was given on the label, he stated, the actual size was certain to be irregular and unpredictable. Thus, the coat of a suit might be big enough to serve as a raincoat while the trousers were for a small child. Winter underdrawers were made for men six feet tall, with the tops too small for anyone. Winter clothes were being produced by the ministry of Light Industry for a world of malformed people.[12]

11. For two examples of strong critical letters, note:
"Our farm received a directive of the Agricultural Management Bureau to pick up thirty calves from Annak Farm, but when we sent five workers to get them, we discovered that that same Bureau had already sold them to another farm. The trip was in vain. Then we received a directive to pick up some imported horses at the Sariwon railway station. We sent thirty workers at the designated time, and they waited for ten days, but the horses never arrived. Because of these two futile trips, we wasted 320 working days and 53,000 wŏn at the most busy time of the year."
"Some railway station workers are insincere in their work and discourteous to passengers. On March 26, I bought a ticket to P'yŏngyang and wanted to send my luggage, but I could not find the luggage department man. Therefore, I went to the railway station master to inquire. He said that the man had gone to his quarters for a short time and that I could go there and find him. I found him in his residence and requested his aid, but he said that he did not have time to take care of it and to bring it tomorrow. That was impossible since I had already purchased my ticket for that day. The station master then told me that it would be sent on the next day, but the luggage, which contained my clothing and bedding, has not yet arrived. I demand some attention from the department concerned." (The two letters are from *NS*, Sept. 20, 1954, p. 2.)
12. *NS*, Nov. 15, 1954, p. 3.

Korean Communist leaders now advanced the tactics of criticism and self-criticism as a major weapon of psychopolitical control. By 1955 the North Korean mass media were filled with appeals for all citizens to engage sincerely in "the confession movement." [13] People were urged to scrutinize the attitudes and actions of peers and superiors alike. The practice was supposedly extended into the family itself. The press reported instances of wives "assisting" their husbands by "encouraging" them to admit their corrupt conduct, or to engage in self-criticism concerning such practices as drinking and loafing.

In practice, the individual had to be extremely careful about whom he criticized, and how.[14] There was a narrow line to be walked between refusal to take part, which was totally impermissible, and criticism directed against the wrong people or in the wrong manner.

The "confession movement" was only part of the intensive effort during this period to carry out a mass mobilization that would encompass every person living in North Korea. The basic issue was how to commit each citizen as fully as possible to the Party and the state in a time of great privation when top authorities were seeking to induce that citizen to postpone material gratifications (one might even say material necessities) while expending enormous energy on a Soviet-style program of economic development. As has already been suggested, there was an added complication of which the Communist leaders never lost sight. The unification of Korea on Communist terms remained a supreme objective, and Party-mass relations bore directly upon this goal.

The theories and practices of the Korean Workers' Party with respect to socialization, participation, and the class struggle were fashioned and refashioned with these considerations in mind. In the aftermath of the Korean War, to be sure, there was one major asset: almost all anti-Communists had either been eliminated or had had the opportunity to escape south. Those who had remained in North Korea either supported the regime or had compelling personal reasons for staying. In this respect, it would have been difficult to create a better environment for the Communists. Moreover, the boundary between North and South Korea was now

13. For an authoritative article, see Yi Hyo-sun, "Let Us Carry Out the Confession Movement Thoroughly," *NS,* Dec. 11, 1955, p. 2. Said Yi, some are still trying to hide their errors for the sake of their careers. But the Confession Movement is a severe struggle to reform one's thought, not merely for the purpose of confessing to individual crimes. It is the means whereby the Party must strenuously indoctrinate and reach Party members and others so that they will not deviate into criminal activities. Certain parties did not understand the meaning of this movement and punished those who honestly confessed. Such actions will prevent the success of the movement. The anticorruption and antiwaste struggle connected with this movement is a part of the serious political struggle to reform the old ideology of our people, which must be pursued ceaselessly.

Note the substantial influence of Chinese Communist "thought reform" concepts.

14. See Chapter IX.

so tightly guarded that escape was virtually impossible and communications of all sorts were either prohibited or (such as listening to non-Communist radio stations) made extremely dangerous. Thus, North Korean authorities could report on conditions in South Korea in such fashion as to make even the most lowly North Korean worker feel fortunate. Conditions in South Korea during this period were scarcely good, but the Communist mass media regaled readers and listeners with tales of massive famine, the deaths of hundreds at the hands of American "butchers," and the "Fascist" brutality of the Rhee regime.[15] Exaggeration and falsehood were carried to extraordinary lengths.

The fundamental problem of *class* greatly concerned Korean Communist Party leaders throughout this period and influenced policies toward masses and elites alike. It also illustrated the grave difficulties involved in harnessing Marxist theory to Korean realities. The official doctrine was simple and in basic conformity with contemporary international Communist theory. After Liberation, the working class in the north, under the leadership of the Party, had formed a broad national front with all sections of the population opposing imperialism and feudalism. The basis of this front was a solid alliance with the toiling peasants. Thus, a "people's power" had been set up, and the people themselves had determined its basic policies and organizational structure. It was from the people's action that the regime derived its legitimacy.

The motive force of the revolution was therefore the working class, "the most advanced class in Korea," and the peasantry, "its most reliable ally," together with "broad strata of the petty bourgeois who were opposed to the forces of imperialism and feudalism." [16] We are presented here with a completely orthodox—and totally fictitious—analysis of how power was distributed in the North Korean Communist Party and state. However, in his report of April 1955, Kim acknowledged the serious problem of converting the peasants into good Communists. Somehow, they had to be weaned from their "petty bourgeois" outlook and their strong proclivity

15. Ch'oe Kwang-sŏk has recounted the following story, which illustrates the potential importance to the Communist regime of doctored reports concerning the south: "I was sitting in the yard of my wife's parents' home during the season for transplanting rice shoots. Two farmers were returning to their homes, having worked all day in the field. One of them said, 'From what I heard on this morning's radio, the farmers in the south have to transplant their rice without having any food. They must work all day without having eaten anything. At least we can eat three times a day.' " In fact, reported Ch'oe, food conditions in the north were extremely bad at this point, and these farmers probably had a totally inadequate diet; but accepting the radio report as true, they felt comparatively better off than their southern brethren. Interview with Chong-Sik Lee, Seoul, Nov. 24, 1966.

16. For a lengthy, authoritative exposition of KWP class theory, see Kim Il-sŏng's report to the Central Committee of the Party, April 1, 1955, entitled "On Improving the Class Education of Party Members," in Kim Il Sung, *Selected Works* (1965 ed.), *op. cit.,* Vol. I, pp. 251–272.

for the independent farmer's "small commodity economy." Had he been
more candid, Kim would have admitted that the Party was using every
possible economic and social pressure at this point to induce farmers to
join the cooperative movement "voluntarily." [17] Instead, he was content to
remark merely that the peasants too often forgot the miseries of the past
and sought to place their own interests above those of the state. Even the
Party "vanguard," the working class, was young and inexperienced, with
no great history of struggle; its peasant background, for the most part, was
still recent. The intellectuals, too, were not fully awakened in terms of
class consciousness; many retained liberal tendencies and refused to adjust
to the new era.[18]

Thus, each of the main class elements comprising the Korean Workers' Party had grave deficiencies from the Communist standpoint—hence
the constant exhortation for more and better class education, Marxist-
Leninist study, and attention to Party history. Within Korean Communist
doctrine, itself, however, there ran a deep and consistent paradox. On the
one hand, the united front tactic was heralded both as the appropriate
system of politics for the People's Republic and as the logical means of
attaining Korean unification. And such a tactic put a premium upon the
acceptance of as many elements within the society as possible. On the
other hand, each individual was constantly reminded that the class struggle
had to be fierce and unrelenting.

In the years immediately following the Korean War, this paradox was
evident at many levels. Those with "bad family backgrounds" had no
chance to hold top positions of responsibility or, in most cases, to receive
a higher education. For the sake of one's career, and sometimes one's well-
being, it was crucial to be categorized as of poor farmer, proletarian, or
revolutionary family background.[19] Naturally, the new caste system alien-

17. See pages 1057–1061, Chapter XIII.
18. Kim Il Sung, *Selected Works* (1965 ed.), *op. cit.,* Vol. I, pp. 258–259.
19. Ch'oe Kwang-sŏk, in connection with a story about the ouster of a friend
in the Ministry of Education and Culture, mentioned the case of Dr. Ch'oe Sam-yŏl,
a chemist and chairman of the chemistry department at Kim Il-sŏng University. Ch'oe
Sam-yŏl made a small mistake in his capacity as vice-chairman of the Korean Committee of the World Peace Conference and came under investigation. It was then discovered that he was a graduate of Tokyo Imperial University and of landlord origin,
though his official record had him as of poor farmer origin. The chief of the Cadre
Office was therefore dismissed, charged with having not performed his duty properly,
since any person being sent abroad must be thoroughly investigated.

A more tragic case involved Yi Su-han, a fairly wealthy landlord, and his family.
After liberation, all of Yi's properties were confiscated and he was given a job in the
Hungnam fertilizer plant as a plain laborer. In January 1960—after the period
under discussion here—Yi was expelled from the factory in accordance with a new
cabinet order directing governmental agencies to dismiss everyone with an unfavorable
background. Yi was then sent to a cooperative farm to work as a farm laborer. He
complained that the work was too heavy and the food inadequate, whereupon he was
detained as an antirevolutionary element. Fifteen days later, his family was informed

ated many who might otherwise have served the regime loyally. After the Korean War, moreover, a new problem emerged, namely, how to treat those who had had members of the family flee to the south. Until 1959, there was a policy of general discrimination practiced against the remaining members of all such families. This discrimination extended to rations, education, and employment.[20]

In 1959, a more differentiated approach was adopted, with such families divided into several categories. Those whose family members had fled south after "acting maliciously against the Party" continued to be victims of persecution. To them was applied the slogan, "Let them wear caps!"—meaning they had to be made readily identifiable from the masses. Those belonging to the second category were those whose family members had been "dragged" to the south during the war, either because of clever enemy propaganda or for some other reason not really their fault. These were now considered potentially revolutionary elements in the south, and it was ordered that their families be relieved of discrimination. Care, however, was to be taken before they could be allowed to travel abroad or assigned to positions involving access to secret materials. Those in the third category were individuals with family members who went south before the Korean War without committing any hostile actions against the Party. Since Communism was not firmly established in the north in that era, the Party should show leniency toward them and cease discriminating against their families, except to exercise care in regard to foreign travel.

In many respects, however, the intellectual class constituted the most complex problem that faced the Party during this period. Writing in the fall of 1957, Ha Ang-ch'ŏn, a prominent North Korean intellectual closely identified with the Party, spelled out some of the Communist leadership's concerns in the aftermath of the great purges of 1956–57.[21] The Party had been deeply concerned about the problem of the intellectual and had consistently sought to solve this problem correctly. In numbers, those classified as intellectuals had increased from 39,000 at the time of Liberation to 114,000 in 1956. Eighteen colleges and universities had been established,

---

that he had died. They tried to obtain his body but failed. In late 1965, his twenty-four-year-old daughter was married to another "antirevolutionary" whose father had been executed by the North Korean government during the Korean War and whose mother had been in prison since 1951. Only members of the two families who were immediately at hand attended the wedding, because Party officials were watching to see who would associate with antirevolutionary elements.

20. In instances where rations were inadequate, such families would be left off the list, according to Ch'oe Kwang-sŏk. Also, they were discriminated against when they sought to go beyond middle school, i.e. beyond ninth grade, and they could not hold many positions, not even that of chief of a subteam in an agricultural cooperative. Interview with Chong-Sik Lee, Seoul, Nov. 24, 1966.

21. Ha Ang-ch'ŏn, "Party Policy Indoctrination Among Intellectuals," NS, Sept. 28, 1957, p. 2.

whereas none had existed prior to 1945. A number of new journals and newspapers had been created, together with various scientific and literary societies. "Intellectuals or clerical workers" comprised 27.9 percent of the delegates to the current Supreme People's Assembly.

Did not all of these developments, Ha argued, signify the regard and respect with which the Party treated the intellectual class? It had sought to reform intellectuals educated under the old order, raise up new intellectuals from among the working people, and emphasize the need for solidarity and cooperation between the two groups so that both could serve the fatherland and people loyally under Marxist-Leninist banners. In general, these efforts had been successful; basically, the intellectual class was healthy.

Nevertheless, some "unhealthy elements" did exist, Ha admitted. For example, certain instructors at Kim Il-sŏng University had denounced Party policies in the lecture room. Such "anti-Marxist and anti-Party attitudes" could not be permitted in the fields of education, science, and culture. Some intellectuals failed to appreciate developments within the country, finding valuable contributions only in the policies of foreign parties. They were content to imitate foreign models mechanically, without any sense of independence. To eliminate such unhealthy tendencies, intellectuals had to rally around the Party organizations and the Party cadres. The Party organizations constituted the command units for Party policy. When the command post was weakened, distortion and errors could not be removed by Party authority.[22]

The Top Political Elite of the Initial Postwar Era

Party attitudes toward the intellectuals at this point were closely interwoven with the tumultuous political developments taking place at home and abroad. At the close of the Korean War, as we noted earlier, a major purge of the so-called domestic faction got under way. It centered upon Pak Hŏn-yŏng and his group. After years of intrigue during which, if we may believe the accounts of defectors, both sides inserted spies into the camp of the other and engaged in an endless round of propaganda and counterpropaganda, the dominant Kim forces, in combination with Yenan and domestic "turncoat" elements, succeeded in dealing a lethal blow to the Pak faction. In the aftermath of this purge, the order of priority among the political elite was automatically altered, as can be seen from the composition of the Plenum in August 1953 and succeeding months. Kim Il-sŏng once again seemed without challengers, although a coalition of Soviet and Yenan elements was essential to the unity of the Korean Workers' Party, and behind this coalition—in a somewhat vague and undefined relationship—stood the Russians and the Chinese. As we have seen, the influence of the Chinese Communists had risen substantially as a result of the war and the continued massive presence of Chinese forces on Korean

22. *Ibid.*, p. 2.

soil. In practice, however, homage was still directed first toward the Soviet Union.

The men directly under Kim in the aftermath of the 1953 purge reflected the situation noted above. Officially, the second ranking leader was Kim Tu-bong, doyen of the Yenan group, a radical nationalist who lacked both ideological sophistication and power but was useful as a revolutionary figurehead of an essentially noncompetitive type. Such people are often essential and almost always useful in a political hierarchy. Within the Asian Communist world, Kim Tu-bong had his counterpart in Ton Duc Thang of the Democratic Republic of Vietnam and, in a somewhat different sense, in Sung Ch'ing-ling of the People's Republic of China.

The top five Party members beneath Kim Tu-bong in formal terms were now Pak Chŏng-ae, Ch'oe Yong-gŏn, Pak Ch'ang-ok, Kim Il, and Ch'oe Ch'ang-ik. Each of them is worthy of brief attention at this point. Pak Chŏng-ae, wife of a lesser Communist figure, Kim Yong-bŏm, was the senior female representative of the Korean Communist movement, educated and trained partially in the Soviet Union, a veteran revolutionary who had been imprisoned by the Japanese in the 1930s. While Pak Chŏng-ae had considerable ability, her ascendancy, as we have already suggested, was due primarily to the fact that she was an unquestioning supporter of Kim Il-sŏng, one capable of writing and speaking in lyrical terms about "the Leader." She had no independent power base. Hence, her position would always be dependent upon Kim Il-sŏng's fortunes—and whims.[23]

Ch'oe Yong-gŏn played a different role. For a number of years, as we have noted, Ch'oe headed the Korean Democratic Party, although he was certainly a committed Communist at all times. He did not become a "public" member of the Korean Workers' Party, however, until the mid-1950s. But when the shift was made, he emerged at the top, ranking third after Kim Il-sŏng and Kim Tu-bong, among the seventy-one full members of the Third KWP Central Committee elected in April 1956. He also stood third among the members of the Standing Committee of the Politburo, once more after Kim Il-sŏng and Kim Tu-bong. In both cases, he stood just before Pak Chŏng-ae—although in the 1953–55 period Pak Chŏng-ae was generally listed third at official gatherings.

23. For personal evaluations of some of those people discussed here, we are indebted to O Ki-wan, who served as a special assistant to Kim Il between 1955 and 1957, a period of three years, and subsequently served under Han Chŏn-jong, minister of Agriculture, for one and one-half years. O had the opportunity to observe many North Korean leaders at close hand, and he was naturally aware of the assessment made of each of them by more junior officials.

According to O, Pak Chŏng-ae is an able woman who comes to conclusions quickly and firmly. Listening to a discussion of policy, she often speaks out with a tone of positiveness, "I think . . ." and sums up her position rapidly and succinctly, although not necessarily with great depth. She was trusted by Kim Il-sŏng, in this period at least, but carried little weight. Interview with Chong-Sik Lee, Jan. 15, 1967.

In point of fact, Ch'oe's "pre-Liberation" career was more distinguished than that of Kim Il-sŏng in many respects. Ch'oe had had lengthy relations with both the Chinese revolutionaries and the Soviets. His education had been almost wholly military, first at the Yünnan Military Academy and then at the celebrated Whampoa Military Academy, where he reportedly taught for a brief period. Undoubtedly, it was at this point that he formed a close liaison with the Chinese Communists. Subsequently, he served as an officer with the 8th Route Army, and afterward became a member of the newly organized Korean Volunteer Corps. When Kim Il-sŏng was operating in east Manchuria, Ch'oe Yong-gŏn was conducting guerrilla operations against the Japanese with small-scale forces in north Manchuria, as we have noted. Kim Ch'aek, killed during the Korean War while serving as commander of Korean Communist forces, had been similarly engaged in south Manchuria.

Thus, as anti-Japanese guerrilla fighters, these three men were on a more or less equal footing. Like Kim Il-sŏng and others, Ch'oe was forced by the Japanese to retreat into Soviet Siberia around 1941, was given training near Khabarovsk by the Russians, and by the close of World War II reportedly held an assimilated military rank. In the initial period after 1945, Ch'oe played two roles: first, as head of a "non-Communist" Party he helped to ensure the success of Communist united front policies; second, he did much to develop both the North Korean police and military forces.

Despite rumors of trouble between Ch'oe and Kim Il-sŏng at the outset of the Korean War, there is no evidence that Kim ever regarded Ch'oe as a threatening rival. Although he had had lengthy contact with the Chinese Communists, Ch'oe was never considered a member of the Yenan faction; indeed, he tended to keep aloof from factional intrigue. This, in effect, made him a valuable member of the Kapsan group, and his loyalty to Kim Il-sŏng appears always to have been firm. In addition, Ch'oe was not regarded as intellectually gifted. Without overt political ambitions and without great brains, he survived and moved upward in the hierarchy.[24]

Pak Ch'ang-ok, on the contrary, was one of the few top leaders within the North Korean hierarchy to have considerable intellectual qualities. Pak was a Soviet Korean, born and educated in the Soviet Union—one of the many second-generation Koreans who played such an important part in

24. O says that in comparison with individuals like Kim Il-sŏng, Kim Il, and Pak Kŭm-ch'ŏl, Ch'oe Yong-gŏn is not terribly bright. He has limited ability to analyze complex phenomena or project future developments. On the other hand, he carries out his duties faithfully, always works at a steady pace, and does not engage in political scheming. His relation with Kim Il-sŏng is essentially not personal, but based on policies. Interview, Jan. 15, 1967.

It will be recognized, of course, that O's comments regarding various leaders carry a strong subjective element, but in general they tend to be confirmed by other information and reports.

the establishment of Communism during the Soviet occupation and afterward. By 1950, he had become director of the Propaganda and Agitation Department of the Party Central Committee, and at the Plenum of August 1953 he became one of the Party vice-chairmen. Pak, regarded as a leading theoretician of the Soviet faction, frequently wrote articles setting forth Marxism-Leninism for Korea. He also had close contact with a number of academic and literary figures, including some of those belonging to the "liberal Left" who remained on the periphery of the Party.

Kim Il was also an intelligent man, but with a very different background from that of Pak Ch'ang-ok. Kim, born in North Hamgyŏng Province, had left home to go to Manchuria, and had become involved in Communist activities there at the age of 18. By the time he was 27, he was a part of Kim Il-sŏng's anti-Japanese guerrilla unit, serving in a variety of capacities including that of political commissar. Thus he had served under Kim Il-sŏng at an early point, and could be regarded as one of his true confidants. When the Korean guerrilla forces were pushed into Siberia, Kim Il enrolled in a Russian language institute. But, according to his former assistant, O Ki-wan, after about two months Kim Il was ordered by Kim Il-sŏng to return to Manchuria and engage in underground activities. O states that Kim Il remained there, disguised as a farmer, until the Japanese defeat. He then rejoined the Kim Il-sŏng unit and entered North Korea with it.[25]

After the Korean War, Kim Il moved up quickly. He first became chairman of the Party in South P'yŏngan Province. By 1953 he was a Party vice-chairman. At the beginning of 1954 he was given the crucial post of minister of Agriculture, a position he held until the fall of 1957, when he became vice-premier. Already, by the close of this period, Kim Il was regarded by many as the man most likely to be Kim Il-sŏng's personal choice as his successor should he die or become incapacitated. Kim Il's loyalty and ability sufficed to keep him in the top rungs of the political elite.[26]

Ch'oe Ch'ang-ik, generally considered the true leader of the Yenan faction, had held important positions in the Korean Workers' Party and in the government from the beginning of the Communist era. Long associated with the Chinese Communists, he had returned to North Korea shortly after the beginning of the Soviet occupation. He became a member of the Political Committee of the Workers' Party when it was established, served as minister of Finance from August 1946 to October 1952, when he became

25. Most sources indicate that Kim Il remained in the USSR throughout the later war period, as did a number of other Koreans, but we are inclined to accept O's account, since he knew Kim Il intimately. In any case, it is possible that Kim Il reentered North Korea with the assimilated rank of a Soviet junior officer, as several sources have stated.

26. According to O, Kim Il has a remarkable memory and is often able to embarrass subordinates by asserting, "Three years ago you gave me production figures of . . . Now you give me different figures. Why?"

vice-premier. Ch'oe, like Pak Ch'ang-ok, was regarded as an able theorist, and had a wide range of contacts, both within and outside the Party.

By the fall of 1953, these were the top five North Korean Communists under Kim Il-sŏng and Kim Tu-bong. There was, however, a second group, immediately behind the first ranking leaders, that is worthy of mention. In the official ranking of North Korean dignitaries, the next person listed during this period was Hong Myŏng-hui, titular leader of the unimportant Democratic Independence Party. Hong, as we have noted, was a key figure in leftist united front activities in the south up to mid-1948. According to some reports, his daughter helped Kim run his household in 1949, after the death of Kim's first wife in childbirth. Hong, who held such distinguished posts as that of vice-premier (from September 1948 to September 1961) and vice-president of the Presidium of the Supreme People's Assembly (from September 1961 until his death in 1968), was without a vestige of real power—a figurehead who provided some substance to Communist united front theories, but even more to the importance of being personally bound to Kim Il-sŏng.

Next in the official listings of the 1954–55 period came Chŏng Il-yong, Pak Ui-wan, Pak Kŭm-ch'ŏl, and Pak Yŏng-bin. Chŏng, one of the few technicians to emerge at this level, had been educated in Japan, and he had had both technical and administrative experience in industry when he was pointed out to the Leader. Quickly, he rose to the position of vice-premier and minister of Heavy Industry. Apolitical in the past, he was considered absolutely loyal to Kim Il-sŏng. Pak Ui-wan (Ivan Pak), a Korean born and educated in the Soviet Union, had served in a variety of cabinet and Party posts, including minister of Railroads. By 1954, he was vice-premier and minister of Light Industry. Pak Kŭm-ch'ŏl, another old associate of Kim Il-sŏng, had served as liaison man in the Kapsan area until he was arrested by the Japanese. In August 1953, he was made chief of the Party cadre department, and by 1954 he was serving in the Party's highest echelons. Pak Yŏng-bin also belonged to the Soviet group. In October 1953 he was appointed director of the Organization and Guidance Department of the Party Central Committee, an exceedingly important post.

To place too much emphasis upon factional affiliation is probably a mistake, especially with respect to the so-called Soviet and Yenan factions. Defectors have often stated that the factional divisions were neither as clear-cut nor as meaningful in all cases as non-Communist sources alleged. More-over, as a careful survey of this period reveals, increasingly the only mean-ingful faction was coming to be Kim Il-sŏng's, and the crucial factor, one's personal relationship to Kim, irrespective of one's background. Neverthe-less, there were differences in background, educational experience, and even culture that stemmed from the heterogeneous nature of the Korean revolu-tionary movement. And this did constitute a political problem, as the Ko-rean Communists themselves readily admitted. While factionalism may not have been as important as some South Korean writers have indicated, and undoubtedly involved many more ambivalent and poorly defined factors, it remained a crucial issue in this period.

Of the eleven Communist leaders noted above, five (if we count Kim himself) can be classified as members of Kim Il-sŏng's personal circle. These individuals—Kim, Pak Chŏng-ae, Ch'oe Yong-gŏn, Kim Il, and Pak Kŭm-ch'ŏl—collectively held many of the key levers of Party and governmental power. But the position of the so-called Soviet faction was not negligible. Of its three representatives—Pak Ch'ang-ok, Pak Ui-wan, and Pak Yŏng-bin—only one, Pak Ch'ang-ok, was in the first echelon of leadership. But the group displayed a combination of ideological and technical strength that reflected their Soviet experience and training. In essence, the Kim faction represented the old guerrilla fighters while the Soviet faction represented the ideological and technical primacy—an awkward situation, and potentially dangerous. The Yenan faction was represented in top Party circles at this point by two men, Kim Tu-bong and Ch'oe Ch'ang-ik, but as we have noticed only one of these, Ch'oe, had power. He, too, was a theoretician and a man who supposedly had the confidence of North Korea's Chinese comrades. Significantly, not a single domestic faction representative now remained in the topmost ranks of the Party, since Chŏng Il-yong came from a nonpolitical background.

In functional terms, of course, the key governmental positions of this period were those dealing with economic development on the one hand, and Party reconstruction on the other. As premier and Party chairman, Kim Il-sŏng assumed the leadership on both of these fronts, exercising power with increasing self-confidence. Of the top people discussed briefly above, almost all played important roles in one or both of these tasks. Turnover at the ministerial level was high in the years immediately after the Korean War. Many factors contributed: policy failures for which someone had to be held responsible; errors of judgment, poor administration, and malfeasance that reflected the paucity of capable, trained individuals; and recurrent factional struggles within the Party. While a number of the changes in the 1953–56 period involved key Party leaders, true purges were very few. Of course, the shadow of the Pak Hŏn-yŏng purge loomed menacingly over the entire scene. But the immediate postwar era remained one of coalition politics with only the old SKWP leaders removed from the scene.

Reestablishing Party Foundations

Meanwhile, the task of rebuilding the Party and government structure at the local, district, and provincial levels was a major challenge, as we have noted. Local organization had been shattered by the war, and the drives for political mobilization and economic reconstruction were suffering correspondingly. Party leaders recognized that only if local units were reactivated could the process of translating central Party directives into action be accomplished. Local initiatives were crucial if the myriad tasks of cleaning up the war debris and rebuilding the towns and villages were to be achieved in a minimum of time. Thus, two slogans were prominently displayed during this period: "Cultivate local leadership!" and "Enhance local autonomy!" As we have seen, a tremendous premium was placed on the recruitment and training of cadres to fill the many vacancies at the local levels, and numerous articles were written describing the ideal cadre. Various Party officials also emphasized the importance of greater mass participation in local affairs.

This campaign culminated in the constitutional amendment already referred to. On October 31, 1954, a new local government law was promulgated. The aim was to increase the authority—and responsibility—of government units at the local level. Elections for lower-level Party and government officials took place at various intervals throughout this period. The first local elections for Party officials after the Korean War were held between January and April 1954. Additional Party elections were held between January and March 1955, and in the fall of that year. However, criticism published in various Party organs suggests that in many cases the elections elicited little enthusiasm and were generally conducted in a perfunctory manner.[27]

In the fall of 1956, there were nationwide elections for local, prefectural, and province council and legislative representatives. In mid-November, the Party published a list of recommended candidates, and in so doing revealed the socioeconomic categories to which they allegedly belonged.[28]

27. See, for example, Kim Su, "Let Us Correct the Defects Shown in the Processes of Achievement—Reports and Elections in the Leading Organs of the Party," *NS,* Dec. 14, 1955, p. 1. According to Kim, in many cases, higher Party units provided "insufficient guidance and supervision" for elections. Often they were postponed, and interest in them seemed slight. Moreover, various localist, factional, and generational prejudices interfered with local Party effectiveness. Some people in authority, said Kim, were unduly biased in favor of younger Party members, for instance, and would not give older members a chance.

28. *NS,* Nov. 16, 1956, p. 1. On Nov. 22, the Party organ reported that elections at the hamlet and village level had been completed on Nov. 20, with 99.9 percent of those eligible voting, and 99.73 percent of the votes going to recommended candidates. It was stated that 54,279 persons had been elected, 11,199 of them women.

On Nov. 26, a socioeconomic breakdown of those elected was published, which it is interesting to compare with the recommended list:

Workers	2,115	Independent professionals	2,004
"Clerical workers"	12,143	Individual farmers	4,371
Members of agricultural cooperatives	32,498	Businessmen and merchants	204
Marine cooperative members	285	Others	355
Religious and professional representatives	244		

The above numbers total only 54,219, 60 less than the number reported as elected. Moreover, these figures would appear to challenge Party assertions that 99.73

At the province and special city level, the 1,009 recommended candidates were:

Workers	273	Religious and professional	
"Clerical workers"	253	representatives	36
Members of agricultural		Independent professionals	60
cooperatives	286	Individual farmers	31
Marine cooperative members	15	Businessmen and merchants	28
		Others	27

At the city and prefecture levels, the 9,346 recommended candidates were:

Workers	2,140	Religious and professional	
"Clerical workers"	2,449	representatives	133
Members of agricultural		Independent professionals	505
cooperatives	3,362	Individual farmers	354
Marine cooperative mem-		Businessmen and merchants	197
bers	68	Others	38

At the hamlet and village level, the 54,284 recommended candidates were:

Workers	2,119	Religious and professional	
"Clerical workers"	12,788	representatives	183
Members of agricultural		Independent professionals	1,606
cooperatives	32,316	Individual farmers	4,396
Marine cooperative mem-		Businessmen and merchants	200
bers	278	Others	398

By early 1957, the Party claimed that, although there were still many cadres at the local level who were neglecting their duties, local organizations had improved remarkably. The improvements, it asserted, were primarily the result of increased supervision from higher levels. Previously, central, provincial, and prefectural Party officials had been content with periodic tours of rural villages; now, they were dispatching representatives for varying lengths of time to provide concrete on-the-spot leadership and guidance, themselves attending all of the local meetings and making specific sugges-

---

percent of the votes went to recommended candidates, although quite clearly an overwhelming percentage of votes went to officially approved individuals. The greatest deviations, it will be noted, were in "Clerical workers," with 645 fewer being elected than were recommended (this category clearly included full-time Party and government administrators as well as other types of office workers, and may have included some intellectuals) and Independent professionals, with 398 more being elected than were recommended. There were also 61 more Religious and professional representatives elected than were recommended.

To the extent that these differences are meaningful (the total number of candidates appearing on the ballot was not published by the government), the electorate would appear to have cast votes for a number of "bourgeois" and "petty bourgeois" candidates whom the Party had not approved.

tions. This had not only improved local organizations greatly but had also provided the insights into local conditions essential for higher-level policy-makers.[29]

At this point, KWP leaders, consciously borrowing from Chinese experience, were stressing the holding of local meetings under the aegis of the Party to study and discuss national policies. The general idea was to involve the masses more directly and develop creative ideas concerning policy implementation. Thus, meetings at factories and cooperatives were arranged, while at the national level arrangements were made for a series of so-called conferences of enthusiasts (that is, enthusiasts for production in agriculture, the chemical industry, and so forth). These sessions—both local and national—were to involve criticism and self-criticism. But it appears from the evidence that, at least in this period, the North Korean leaders could not achieve the rigor or level of efficiency claimed by the Chinese. Their mobilization programs appear somewhat less ambitious and considerably more simple. The growing influence of the Chinese experience was nonetheless clear.

The Party used another method of indoctrinating and controlling its members, namely, the periodic redistribution of Party identification cards. At various intervals after the Korean War, and often in conjunction with a purge at top levels, the Party would order the preparation of new identification cards. For example, such an action was ordered in late 1956 following the August 1956 Incident (which we shall shortly discuss), and it was carried out during the first three months of 1957. Party officials made it clear that a thorough deliberation and examination of each Party member should precede the issuance of new cards, with the unfit being weeded out. It was made plain that Party membership—so important to one's status and career—could never be considered permanent; in theory at least, each member was always on probation. Having elected for a mass party, the Com-

---

29. Hwang Hak-song, "Let Us Get Party Leadership Close to the Scene," *NS*, Jan. 4, 1957, p. 1.

However, an article by Pak Chong-sun, "Some Problems Concerning Achievement—Reports and Elections of the Lower Party Organizations' Leading Organs," *NS*, Feb. 17, 1957, indicated continuing problems. Pak, though asserting that the "militancy and efficiency levels" of lower Party organs had improved since the Third Party Conference (April 1956), complained that local organizations still did not have sufficient rapport with the masses, did not listen enough to the voice of the people or the opinions of ordinary Party members. Bureaucratism, formalism, irresponsibility, and liberalism were all problems at the local level, according to Pak. And report-making was generally left up to the arbitrary whims of those few who had a good style, rather than involving collective deliberation and collective wisdom. Too little freedom of criticism existed.

This article—and others of this period—were influenced both by the campaign for collective leadership stemming from events of the Twentieth CPSU Congress in Moscow and the Hundred Flowers campaign then under way in China; about the impact of these events, we shall have more to say later.

munists sought to maintain as constant a surveillance as possible over their members who, as we have seen, were overwhelmingly first- and second-generation peasants with minimal education.

Party leaders were naturally aware of the low level of ideological understanding among Party members—indeed, of the low level of literacy, particularly among the peasants. For both political and economic reasons, therefore, the campaign for adult education and compulsory primary schooling was pushed with vigor throughout this period. In 1958, Han Sŏl-ya, then minister of Education, asserted that North Korean students numbered 2.2 million. All eligible youth, he added, now attended primary schools, and 92.2 percent of primary school graduates were continuing their education.[30] During the first Five-Year Plan, moreover, there would be an attempt to enforce compulsory education through the seventh grade, which would result in doubling the number of middle school students between 1957 and 1961.

Unquestionably, major gains were being made in improving the literacy of North Korean citizens. It would be unwise, however, to accept the official statistics on education without question, or to assume that primary school graduates, particularly in the rural areas, had more than the most basic literacy. The creation of high-level manpower, for both political and economic purposes, remained a formidable problem at the close of this period. When the Central Party School held its graduation ceremony for 291 students on August 18, 1958, *Nodong Sinmun* noted that the school had produced more than 10,000 Party cadres since its foundation in 1946. But it did not disclose how many of these had survived the war and remained in active service.[31]

There can be no doubt, however, that by the close of 1958 North Korean leaders were redoubling their efforts to produce major changes in the political culture of their people. Constantly, they talked of the need for a transformation of the old morality and the creation of a new socialist man.[32] The new morality should involve a deep commitment to labor, a fervent love of the fatherland and a sense of obligation toward it, a basic loyalty to the Party and to concepts of proletarian internationalism, a strong humanistic concern about the public welfare, and a willingness to guard and protect socialist properties.

With these themes, and the policies undertaken to implement them, the Korean Communist leaders were seeking to cultivate a work ethic, a nationalism, a will to sacrifice for the state, and an unshakable commitment to Communism that, in combination, would underwrite the extraordinarily

30. Han Sŏl-ya, "The Tasks Imposed Upon the Field of Education in the Fulfillment of the Cultural Revolution in Our Country," *NS,* March 29, 1958, p. 2.

31. *NS,* Aug. 19, 1958, p. 1.

32. See, for example, the major article, "For the Establishment of Socialist Morality," *NS,* June 1 and June 3, 1958, as well as the editorial of June 4.

ambitious national programs that had been drafted. In the spring of 1955, Party organs had begun to carry illustrations of "the new morality" and "the old morality," managing to spread the series over months.[33]

Indeed, after reading the literature of this period, one cannot escape the strong feeling that, whatever the results, the Party was putting almost unbearable pressures upon the citizens at large, and particularly upon Party cadres. As 1958 ended, Party organs were continuing to raise all of the old criticisms, while proclaiming that significant improvements had occurred. Party and government workers were still making "a number of serious errors," the most grave of which was their formalistic and passive attitude toward Party directives.[34] Instead of seizing the initiative and seeking concrete methods of implementing Party policies with enthusiasm, they were waiting for solutions from above. The only direction to which they looked for progress was government investment. Every local resource, material and human, must be utilized. The key to production, particularly in such fields as light industry, was not to seek assistance from the government, but to mobilize and exploit to the fullest the talent and creativity of the people and hitherto untapped local resources.

If this exhortation sounds surprisingly like an appeal to "free enterprise," it may be because the Party was discovering the serious limits of central authority during this period. The state, not having the resources at the national level to realize its programs, was compelled to place the responsibility upon the local units. This was the true meaning of "local autonomy," North Korean style. Naturally, most local units could not meet those responsibilities to the satisfaction of the central authorities. Under these circumstances, cadres were put under intense pressure to perform miracles, and they in turn were strongly tempted to engage in massive deception of the state, proclaiming quotas attained when in fact they had

33. See the column, "The Moral Outlook of Koreans," *NS,* April 11, 1955, p. 3 (and succeeding issues). Themes introduced included kindness, love of public property, patriotism, mutual assistance, self-reliance, and candor. Frequently, another column entitled "Remnants of the Old Ideology" appeared beside this column, criticizing various "weaknesses."

See also Ku Wu-rin, "The New Mental Features of the Korean People," *Kŭlloja (The Worker),* Sept. 1955. According to Ku, the attitude of the Korean people had changed enormously in the ten years since the advent of Communist rule. Individual heroism, egoism, laziness, and irresponsibility were all manifestations of "old ideologies" that were under sustained attack. A collectivist and socialist mentality was replacing the traditional feudal outlook of the peasant. Together with the new social consciousness was emerging a new type of patriotism, which not only underwrote the defense of the Fatherland against attack, but also pledged "self-sacrificing labor" for the rapid improvement of the material and cultural conditions of the people, for the unification and independence of the Fatherland, for the strengthening of the democratic base in the north, and for "the fulfillment and overfulfillment of economic programs."

34. "What Are the Keys [to the Fulfillment of the June Plenum]?" editorial, *NS,* Sept. 6, 1958, p. 1.

not been, and putting equally heavy pressure upon their subordinates. The result of this system was a combination of progress, resentment, and fear.

Minor Parties and United Front Politics

A second broad concern of top officials during this period was bolstering united front activities. As we noted in the last chapter, the non-Communist parties and groups existing in North Korea had been strongly affected by the Korean War. Large numbers of their members had fled to South Korea after having rendered aid to the United Nations and ROK forces. Others had been killed, by either the Communists or their opponents. Complete reorganization was required. By the mid-1950s, only two parties outside the Korean Workers' Party had any formal structure or membership, namely, the Korean Democratic Party and the Ch'ŏndogyo Young Friends' Party.

These parties were kept alive for obvious reasons. First, as we suggested earlier, they provided a political home for those "bourgeois" elements who could not be admitted into the Workers' Party. After the Korean War, however, this factor became increasingly less important to the regime. "Bourgeois" elements now presented little threat—except as that term was used as an epithet to label one's internal opponents. More significantly, to continue the existence of the non-Communist parties helped to preserve the fiction of a united front government, thereby keeping open a number of Communist options with respect to Korean unification. At some point, these allegedly independent parties might be useful in attracting supporters in the south. In the event of a unification election, they might attract votes.

Thus, throughout this period, both "parties" had representation in various government and front organs. For example, when the Central Committee for the Election of the Second Supreme People's Assembly was organized in June 1957, Pak Chŏng-ae was named chairman, with Chŏng Chun-t'aek of the KDP and Kim Pyŏng-je of the Ch'ŏndogyo Young Friends' Party as two of the four vice-chairmen. Commonly, these third- and fourth-party representatives would be given vice-chairmanships, but rarely after the war did they hold any significant post. Earlier, Cabinet posts had been given to minor party representatives, at a time when every effort was being made to appeal to the South Koreans. That ended with the Korean War. In addition to the two parties that were kept in being, certain individuals who had formerly headed other parties were given minor offices —although as we shall see, their ultimate fate was generally unpleasant.

Let us look briefly at the units and individuals who survived. The KDP, as will be recalled, had lost any basic meaning when its first leader, Cho Man-sik, was imprisoned by the Russians and those who had founded the party fled to the south. For many years, it was headed by Ch'oe Yong-gŏn, and when he openly moved into the Workers' Party, Hong Ki-hwang took his place. At the end of 1958, however, Hong was purged, and Kang

Ryang-uk became chairman of the party's Central Committee. Kang, a Methodist minister, was a maternal relative of Kim Il-sŏng and not likely to cause any trouble. Throughout this period, Kim Tal-hyŏn continued to serve as head of the Ch'ŏndogyo Young Friends' Party (in January 1959 he was replaced by Pak Sin-dŏk). Up to 1950, the Communists had discriminated more against the Christians, regarding them as "tools of American aggression." Hence, they had been careful to maintain direct control over the KDP, the appointed vehicle for Christian elements, while treating the Ch'ŏndogyo Young Friends' Party with some leniency. The war changed this policy. During the conflict, elements from both parties had attacked retreating Communists and welcomed the UN/ROK forces. When the struggle ended, therefore, the Communists were extremely suspicious of all non-Communist groupings, even those that had theoretically been domesticated. Strict supervision became the rule.

To appreciate the role of the two parties after the Korean War, one need only note the top item on the agenda of the Central Committee of each party when they met (separately) in December 1957. That item read: "The current task of the Korean Democratic Party/Ch'ŏndogyo Young Friends' Party related to the speech of Premier Kim Il-sŏng made at the Plenary Session of the Central Committee of the Korean Workers' Party." As can be imagined, the "task" in question was to render wholehearted support to Kim's programs and to rally around "the great leader of the Korean people." As in the People's Republic of China, minor parties no longer sought to maintain any image of independence or difference from the Communist Party. In China, the last effort to do so—during the Hundred Flowers era of 1956—had resulted in severe criticism of those responsible. In North Korea, the final dividing line was the Korean War, although the purge of Cho Man-sik in early 1946 was the truly decisive event.

It will be remembered that a number of leftist politicians in addition to the leaders of the South Korean Workers' Party had come north before the Korean War, most of them arriving in April 1948, in the course of the so-called North-South negotiations conducted under Communist aegis. With them came their parties—sans members except for the handful of those who made the pilgrimage north. What was the fate of these men?

One small group, headed by Paek Nam-un, the noted south Korean Marxist economist, represented the remnants of the Working People's Party, originally founded in Seoul under the leadership of Yŏ Un-hyŏng in May 1947. Paek was one of the few minor party figures to make the transition successfully. At one point he served as minister of Education, and during this period he was president of the Academy of Science. This did not help the WPP. Separated from its membership (which was never large, since this was primarily a party of leaders not followers), it vanished. Moreover, not all of its representatives were as fortunate as Paek. Yi Yŏng, for example, a leader first of the Seoul and later of the Changan faction, who had also come north, was purged in October 1958, and disappeared from public view.

Greater disaster befell those associated with the People's Republican Party. This party, led by Kim Won-bong, had also been established first in Seoul, in July 1946, and had made the move north in 1948. At one point, its principal leaders seemed to have been incorporated into the Communist hierarchy, albeit at generally lower levels. Kim Won-bong himself served for a time as minister of Inspection in the cabinet. His star declined after the Korean War, however, and in December 1958 he and two long-time associates, Sŏng Chu-sik and Han Chi-sŏng, were charged with being "international spies." Kim and Sŏng were imprisoned, and Han was executed, in March 1959. This ended the People's Republican Party in a conclusive fashion.

The Democratic Independence Party, established in Seoul in October 1947, had also gone north in April 1948. Its leader, Hong Myŏng-hui, as we have noted, occupied high but politically insignificant positions. Naturally, his party ceased to exist except as an appendage to his name. Two other minor parties organized in the south and removed to the north in April 1948 were the Popular Alliance and the Korean Healthy People's Association. Na Sŭng-gyu, head of the Popular Alliance, was purged as a reactionary in January 1959. Yi Kŭng-no, leader of the Korean Healthy People's Association, remained in favor, and became one of the figureheads of the unification movement.[35]

Thus, on the whole, those leftists who came to North Korea from the south fared badly. By the end of the 1950s, not only had the old South Korean Workers' Party elements been almost completely eliminated, but a substantial number of minor party leaders had also been removed from office, and some of them imprisoned or executed. Unable to return to the south after having crossed the Rubicon, they were now totally dependent upon the changing currents of Communist politics. Many got too close to Pak Hŏn-yŏng and his group, as was only natural since they shared a common regional base. Others probably became greatly disillusioned, although, once again, we have no evidence that the charges of spying had any foundation in fact. Most importantly, such groups had limited utility for the Communists at this point.

Much more significant for Communist purposes than the minor parties were certain united front organizations. The major organization of this type was the Choguk T'ong'il Minjujuŭi Chŏnsŏn (Democratic Front for

35. Yi, born into a poor family, ultimately graduated from the philosophy faculty of Berlin University, and then went to London where he received his doctorate. He subsequently devoted himself to the Korean Linguistic Association, and although he was not known as a leftist he was imprisoned in 1942 by Japanese authorities in the so-called Korean Linguistic Association incident. Yi went to P'yŏngyang in 1948 to attend the South-North Conference, and decided to stay.

the Unification of the Fatherland), which we earlier discussed briefly. The Front, organized on July 25, 1949, was the result of a union between the North Korea Democratic National Unification United Front (which the Communists had created on July 22, 1946) and such southern elements as had gone north prior to 1949. The new organization theoretically encompassed *all* political groups, and therefore served as an association that attempted to legitimize the Democratic People's Republic of Korea as the spokesman and governing authority for all of the Korean people. Its periodic meetings were devoted to passing resolutions on a wide range of domestic subjects and making appeals to the people of South Korea, with unification and "people's democracy" being the principal themes.

Not satisfied with this instrumentality alone, on July 2, 1956, the Party created a new organization, the Chaebuk P'yŏnghwa T'ong'il Ch'okjjin Hyŏpui-hoe (Council in North Korea for the Peaceful Unification of the Fatherland). At the time of the Korean War, a number of South Korean politicians were either kidnapped and forced to go north, or—in some cases—went there voluntarily. The Council was supposedly founded on the "initiative" of such men. Leading roles were taken by An Chae-hong, noted nationalist leader and publisher; Cho So-ang, "foreign minister" of the Provisional Government in China: Ŏm Hang-sŏp, close associate of Kim Ku and also a member of the Provisional Government; and Yun Ki-sŏp, a veteran Korean nationalist from the 1919 era. The Council periodically issued appeals to its southern brethren to accept the Communist formula for unification, and in general served as a prime propaganda agency for the Communist cause. In late 1958 and 1959, however, a major purge swept through the Council's ranks. Some Council leaders, including Cho So-ang and Yun Ki-sŏp, were charged with being spies and were promptly imprisoned, as was Ŏm Hang-sŏp. Others were purged on less specific charges, and in many cases sent to farms and factories as common laborers. Altogether, more than thirty prominent southerners were treated in this fashion in December 1958 and January 1959, although no publicity was given the purge at this time.[36]

36. During this period, Party leaders continued to refer to "subversive elements" and "imperialist spies" at the same time as they were talking about the importance of intraparty and intraagrarian cooperative democracy via pursuit of the mass line. For example, see *NS*'s report on Kim Il-sŏng's speech to the National Conference of Agricultural Cooperatives, published Jan. 7, 1959, p. 2.

If one scanned the newspapers closely, moreover, one would have noticed that certain names were missing from the official lists of dignitaries present at various functions. At Kim Il-sŏng's New Year's party, for example, one found Kang Ryang-uk and Pak Sin-dŏk listed as guests and chairmen of their respective parties' Central Committees, with no mention of Hong Ki-hwang or Kim Tal-hyŏn. And when the Welcome Committee to Receive Repatriated Korean Residents from Japan was organized Feb. 16, 1959, some names that should have been included were absent.

It is not until many months later that we get some hint of why the extensive purges of ex-South Koreans may have taken place, and then there is no reference to

In any case, by the beginning of 1959, the North Korean front apparatus had been badly damaged by successive purges, starting with the massive purge of former SKWP leaders in 1953–55. The remnants of that group, incidentally, continued to be under the closest surveillance, and in the 1956–59 period at least fifteen additional former SKWP members dropped from sight, having been relieved of their positions for one reason or another. The Democratic Front continued to be the primary vehicle for united front politics, Communist-style—but it was a thin reed indeed. In April 1956, chairmanship of the Front was assumed by Kim Ch'ŏn-hae, a long-time resident of Japan who had been a member of the Japanese Communist Party before returning to North Korea. Yi Kŭng-no, who had entered North Korea in 1948, was made cochairman. Neither of these men was especially important, and increasingly the Front represented an orthodox Communist organization, with a few aging fellow travelers who had long since ceased to have any political appeal.

Party Policies Toward Functional Groups

In approaching functional groups, the Communists, as might be expected, placed their primary emphasis upon five elements: youth, women, industrial workers, peasants, and intellectuals. (The soldier, an all-important sixth element, will be treated separately.) Organizations were maintained for religious groups, such as the Korean Buddhists' League, the All-Korea Confucianists' Association, and the Korean Christian Union. But these were of scant significance. Youth, on the other hand, was of supreme importance, both in view of the need for manpower and of the quest for a new socialist man. Like their comrades elsewhere, the Korean Communist leaders recognized the difficulties in reindoctrinating an older generation, and placed their primary faith upon the "post-Liberation" group. By 1960, the Communists claimed that the Chosŏn Minju Ch'ŏngnyŏn Tongmaeng (Korean Democratic Youth League) had 1,500,000 members, both Party and non-Party. This organization, indeed, was often the crucial arm of the Workers' Party at the local level, with cells in nearly every military unit, factory, agricultural or fishing village.

In the years following the Korean War, the Communist leaders periodically organized gigantic rallies in P'yŏngyang, gathering between

---

them by name. Kim Ch'ang-man, increasingly a key spokesman for the government, in an article to which we shall give detailed attention later, suggested that "many factionalists and anti-revolutionaries" had been contacting the enemy directly and indirectly at an earlier point, cooperating with the international revisionists and plotting to accept neutrality for Korea in exchange for unification: Kim Ch'ang-man, "To Become the Type of Person Needed in the Era of the Flying Horse," *Kŭlloja* (*The Worker*), September 1959 (a speech made before the Third Conference of Korean Students Studying Abroad). While Kim made these remarks about Pak Ch'ang-ok, Ch'oe Ch'ang-ik, and Kim Tu-bong, they may very well have been directed toward the CPUF leaders as well.

100,000 and 200,000 youth from every district of North Korea, with the top Communist leaders in attendance. Amid massed flags, banners, and pictures, the young people would listen to exhortations concerning patriotism, loyalty to the Leader and the Party, and the new socialist morality. Some of the key leaders of the Youth League subsequently rose to positions of prominence in the Workers' Party, as we shall see. Others succumbed to the punishment befalling those judged inadequate.

As we have noted earlier, the women of North Korea took on a special significance during the Korean War, when the need for manpower behind the front lines became extremely acute. The Chosŏn Minju Yosŏng Tongmaeng (Korean Democratic Women's League) was first organized on November 18, 1946, and subsequently merged with its southern counterpart under the SKWP on April 20, 1951. Throughout this period, the chairman of the Women's League Central Committee was the veteran Communist, Pak Chŏng-ae. Under her guidance, the League brought every adult woman at least formally into the organization by setting up branches in each village, workshop, and town. Its first call was "destroy the feudal atmosphere that has surrounded women in traditional Korean society." The League became responsible to a degree not only for indoctrinating North Korean women, but also for recruiting them into economic and political life. Kim Ch'ang-sun has remarked, perhaps unkindly: "It cannot be doubted that the position of women in North Korean society is now a prominent one. They serve as delegates at various levels; they are judges, inspectors, and officials. They surpass men in one important quality: obedience." [37]

The Chosŏn Chikŏp Ch'ongdongmaeng (Korean Trade Union Federation) claimed a membership at the end of 1960 of 1,470,000. The Federation was established in January 1951. It was the product of merger between the North Korean Trade Union Federation, organized in November 1945, and the National Congress of Korean Labor Unions, organized in South Korea at approximately the same time. Both units were Communist-dominated from the beginning; naturally, that continued to be the case. Key figures of the Workers' Party not only occupied the central leadership positions, but also played principal roles in the individual national unions—usually all the way down to the elementary unit level.[38] Thus in reaching the workers, the Party had two channels of more or less equal importance: the Trade Union Federation and the Party itself.

The Chosŏn Nongmin Tongmaeng (Korean Farmers' Union) originated on January 31, 1946, as an auxiliary organization of the North Korean Workers' Party designed to aid in carrying out the Communist land reform program. Like other organizations of its type, it had a southern

37. Kim Ch'ang-sun, *Puk-Han sip-o-nyŏnsa* (*Fifteen-Year History of North Korea*), Seoul, 1961, p. 173.

38. See *ibid.*, pp. 166–167. See also pp. 259–262, supra.

counterpart, the South Korean Farmers' Union, with which it merged on February 11, 1951. Once again, both organizations had been created under Communist aegis. Over the decade following the merger, the League provided an alternate to the Party and the government as a channel for propaganda, political instructions, and technical advice. Its head, Kim Chin-gŏn, who was a member of the Central Committee of the Korean Workers' Party and a long-time associate of Kim Il-sŏng, retained his post until his death in 1963. However, the vice-chairman of this period, Hyŏn Ch'il-jong, was a former member of the SKWP, and in early 1958 he was purged for factionalism.

The North Korean Communists have always conceived of these functional organizations as both alternatives to and extensions of the Party. This is a point that will be developed later. Meanwhile, it should be noted that, by seizing the leadership of each of the above groups, the Party was playing the "vanguard" role and making certain that its policies were translated into mass consciousness and action. Ideally, it also discovered and recruited potential talent in the process. At the same time, through these units, individual members of the community were grouped by status and function in such fashion as to enable a concentration of energies upon precisely the range of social and economic tasks most crucial to the state. And if these groups, or at least some of them, were what we would call interest groups (albeit in an embryonic state), they were so structured as to preclude any true autonomy, and hence any genuine articulation of interests. The Party conceived of these units as organismic parts of a corporate body. Accordingly, on the rare occasions when any league or union leader voiced an anti-Party view, he was quickly challenged. At the same time, however, some of the psychological attributes of pluralism could be replicated under this system. When one marched with one's Youth League unit, or met with one's work team, it was possible to feel an identity separate from that of either the Party or the undifferentiated, monolithic mass of the Communist state.

The Intellectuals as a "Special Problem"

The Party was the first to admit that its problems in this era, insofar as functional groups were concerned, were primarily with the intellectuals. We have already noted Ha Ang-ch'ŏn's earlier remarks on this point, and they were echoed by many other governmental spokesmen at the time. In the intellectual field also, the Communists had attempted a major organizational effort. A Korean Writers' League, Korean Composers' League, and Korean Artists' League had been established on a national scale, in addition to the various "friendship" and "cultural" associations. Both the teachers and the journalists had their unions as well. Certainly, there was no lack of organization.

One problem lay in the fact that a number of intellectuals had come from the south, traditionally the intellectual center of Korea, and that, whether they were to be classified as Communists or as a less easily defined type of liberal-leftist, they tended to be closer to the Pak Hŏn-yŏng group and to the intellectually inclined elements of the Yenan and Soviet factions, than to Kim Il-sŏng and his old guerrilla fighters. Thus, developments pertaining to the intellectuals during this period were inextricably connected with the broader political drama that began to unfold in 1955.

When certain North Korean writers attended the Second All-Soviet Writers' Congress in early 1955, they detected the beginnings of a movement away from dogmatism and formalism. These were the first signs of a shift from Stalinism, although they were certainly not labeled as such at this point. The mood caught on in P'yŏngyang among a small handful of men, and by the spring of 1955 a literary controversy had begun to blossom. Like other disputes of this era, the issues quickly became translated into a factional quarrel. Indeed, the factional crisis of this period may have been the genesis of the debate. Kim Il-sŏng appears to have encouraged certain North Korean writers to take the offensive against the Soviet faction, who were then active in the cultural field, and who were currently aligned with a number of intellectuals from the south.[39]

However this may be, the Party now made a special effort to push the thesis that art and politics were inextricable. Thus, *Nodong Sinmun* carried the injunction that the "militant masses" wanted "militant poems," not the "sentimental world of pure beauty." [40] Juvenile literature was also to be written with indoctrination in mind. Rural life, and exemplary conduct on the part of Korean youth, had not been sufficiently depicted, nor had the nation's historical development been adequately traced, asserted one Party spokesman.[41] The struggle against "the reactionary thought" of Yim Hwa and Yi T'ae-jun after the Fifth Central Committee Plenum had proceeded with determination, but some relics of the past remained—escapist

39. According to Yi Chu-ch'ŏl, who served as chief of the Cultural and Arts Department of *Youth Life,* the Democratic Youth League organ, and later as the associate editor of the organ of the Ministry of Culture and Propaganda until his defection to South Korea in 1957, the root of the problem lay in the factional struggle between the Soviet group and Kim Il-sŏng. He reports that the battle commenced when Ŏm Ho-sŏk attacked Kim Nam-ch'ŏn, a prominent writer of South Korean origin, for departing from socialist realism. Ŏm at the time was a cadre in the literature and arts inspection section of the Publications Bureau, an agency directly under the cabinet. Yi's thesis is that this attack was inspired by Han Sŏl-ya, and possibly by the premier himself. Ki Sŏk-pok, vice-minister of Culture and Propaganda (under Pak Ch'ang-ok) defended Kim Nam-ch'ŏn, but Ŏm refused to retreat, and the attack was gradually broadened to include other writers of South Korean background, proving that Ŏm had the support of the highest Party circles. See Yi Ch'ŏl-ju, *Puk ui yesulin* (*Artists in the North*), Seoul, 1966, pp. 90–96.

40. *NS,* May 25, 1955, p. 1. Songs also were to be militant, with a clear ideological content. See Yi Hi-sŏp, "The Ideological Orientation of Popular Songs," *ibid.,* p. 3.

41. *Ibid.,* June 21, 1955, p. 3.

works and writings that overlooked the serious character of the class struggle.[42]

Since education was regarded as of supreme importance, teachers were being included in the close scrutiny now placed upon intellectuals. Thus, at the National Teachers' Conference of July 1955, resolutions were passed calling for the total elimination of all old-fashioned methods, including that of rote memorization and other forms of stereotyped instruction. In this respect, the instructions of the Fifth Plenum were to be pursued. The new objectives of primary and secondary education included increasing the "scientific" element in learning, heightening its political content, and making education more practical. In short, students were to be turned out both Red and expert. Their indoctrination was to encompass both proletarian internationalism and patriotism, with a special premium upon the sacred quality of labor on behalf of state, Party, and people.[43]

As indicated above, the Party line had been laid down at the Plenum of the KWP Central Committee in April 1955, the most important session since that of August 1953. No less than four separate speeches are attributed to Kim Il-sŏng during this period, three of them in conjunction with the Plenum.[44] We have already outlined the basic themes relating to class, united front politics, and "people's power" put forth by Kim

42. Shin Ko-song, "For the Enhancement of Ideology in Our Literature," *Kŭlloja* (*The Worker*), Sept. 25, 1955.

With respect to rural life, writers' tasks were graphically set forth by Kim Myŏng-su: The Party has as its fundamental goal in our rural areas the mobilization of all farm workers to overfulfill the huge tasks of the Three Year Plan. It seeks to induce them to display more self-dedication in their struggles, to raise their revolutionary alertness, and to cultivate their love of the Fatherland as well as their commitment to internationalism, so that their historic mission can be achieved successfully. Our literature must find its basic themes in these goals. We must contribute to the achievement of the peaceful unification of the Fatherland as well as to the construction of a socialist base in the north. "The Development of Agricultural Management and Some Problems of Literary Creativity," *NS,* Oct. 3, 1955, p. 3.

The role of newsmen was outlined in similar, explicit terms. They are directors of social opinion, and their writings as well as their personal lives should reflect that fact. Either they are models to be followed, or objects of criticism to be corrected. "Reporters Are the Directors of Social Opinion," *ibid.,* June 27, 1955, p. 3.

43. *Ibid.,* July 14, 1955, p. 1.

44. Full texts appear in Kim Il Sung, *Selected Works* (1965 ed.), *op. cit.,* Vol. I. Their titles are "Let Us Exert All Our Strength for the Country's Unification and Independence and for Socialist Construction in the Northern Part of the Country—Theses on the Character and Tasks of Our Revolution, April 1955," pp. 234–250; "On Improving the Class Education of Party Members, Report at a Plenum of the Central Committee of the Workers' Party of Korea, April 1, 1955," pp. 251–272; "On Eliminating Bureaucracy—Report at a Plenum of the Central Committee of the Workers' Party of Korea, April 1, 1955," pp. 273–287; and "On Some Questions Concerning Party and State Work in the Present Stage of the Socialist Revolution—Concluding Speech at a Plenum of the Central Committee of the Workers' Party of Korea, April 4, 1955," pp. 288–314.

Il-sŏng in those speeches.[45] It is now important to observe with care his comments on party loyalty and the problems of subversion and factionalism. Scattered throughout the speeches were assertions that reactionary, anti-Party elements—elements even capable of subversion in the manner of "the Pak Hŏn-yŏng–Yi Sŭng-yŏp gang"—continued to hide within the Party, constituting a major threat. "In his subversive activities, our enemy attempts to utilize the wavering elements who are not steadfast ideologically and those with a murky past," proclaimed Kim.[46] "Under the conditions in which all the reactionary elements in the northern part of Korea have not yet been eliminated," he continued, "the enemy's influence may penetrate into some backward elements in our ranks." Such dangers could be reduced and removed only by improving class education within the Party and among the people at large. However, Party organizations had thus far failed to get rid of formalistic methods of political education. They had merely sought to cram materials into the heads of Party members, taking no account of their level of training and knowledge. Moreover, stated Kim, "some of our propagandists in charge of Party education fail to give their explanations in plain and simple words understandable to the masses, but are fond of reeling off difficult terms and theses which they themselves do not completely understand." [47]

Kim used these criticisms to make his basic point: Many Party organizations and leading functionaries still did not understand that intensive ideological and political work was necessary if the masses were to be inspired, organized, and mobilized to insure the fulfillment of the economic tasks that confronted the nation. Between the lines, one can sense that Kim, aware of widespread popular dissatisfaction with living conditions and the high quotient of inefficiency in economic enterprise, had determined to blame these problems upon the inadequacies of the Party's educational and propaganda activities.

Such criticisms pointed directly at men like Pak Ch'ang-ok, currently chief of Propaganda and Agitation, and some of the "intellectuals" serving with him. Implicit in Kim's remarks at the time of the April Plenum, moreover, was a general skepticism regarding the entire intellectual class. Not only was it going to be "extremely difficult" for them to overcome their past bourgeois training, but many of them retained a superiority complex, a tendency toward egocentricity that made them contemptuous of the masses and prone to liberalism. Later, we shall amplify upon this point, but it is appropriate to signal here the fact that men like Mao Tse-tung and Kim Il-sŏng—old guerrilla fighters lacking extensive formal education and schooled chiefly by practical experience, with a strongly rural flavor—harbored deep suspicions against the urban, Westernized

45. See pp. 472–473.
46. Kim Il-sŏng, "On Improving the Class Education . . . ," *op. cit.,* p. 256.
47. *Ibid.,* p. 270.

intelligentsia, suspicions that in both cases erupted in spectacular fashion onto the political arena.

This is not to imply that no basis in fact existed for such suspicions. The traditional intellectual of Confucian Asia had come from the gentry class, his education had been classical in character, and his basic values were profoundly conservative, especially with regard to such things as physical labor. Nor did "modernization," including the impact of Western education, necessarily alter the character of the Asian intellectual profoundly. The "new education" itself partook of some of the traditional qualities, and it was being extended to students who generally continued to come from the gentry class, especially in such societies as China and Korea. It was a "general" education, whether humanistic or legal, with limited immediate, technical applicability. It usually separated the intellectual further, not merely from the worker-peasant classes, but from his total culture. Nor did it help him to relate his newly acquired culture to the basic political processes at work in his own society. The intellectual became separated from his cultural roots, progressively dissatisfied and hence available to a revolutionary movement like Communism. In the end, however, he was likely to become as alienated from a Communist system as from the old order. Instinctively, men like Kim Il-sŏng and Mao Tse-tung realized this.

Politics and the Army

The Korean People's Army, despite the massive losses it suffered during the Korean War, was the only meaningful national organization outside of Party when that war ended. Now led by battle-tested veterans, the key figures among whom were drawn from the old guerrilla fighters of the 1930s, and with its rank and file recruited from the peasant youth, the army was of critical importance to those holding supreme power. Since a separate chapter is devoted to the military structure, we need only note here the more basic political trends bearing upon the military during this period.

The main task facing the Party in the years immediately after the Korean War was to implant an absolute loyalty to the Leader in every member of the armed forces, and to establish firmly a myth concerning the traditions of the People's Army that would accord with this loyalty. Love, respect, and loyalty to the Party, it was assumed, derived from the bestowal of these precious commodities upon Kim Il-sŏng personally. His words, his picture, his symbols, were now placed in every barracks, on every piece of military literature. And the "heroic accomplishments" of Kim's small guerrilla band were now magnified out of all proportion to reality so that they could serve as the pattern and exemplar for both the People's Army and the militia. Thus, "Learn from the anti-Japanese guerrilla movement" became the slogan for indoctrinating the soldier in all matters—from hygiene, conservation of scarce materials, and relations with civilians, to correct political thoughts, patriotism, and the will to sacrifice.

This intense politicization, and the equation of Kim with all that pertained to the Party and state, did not mean that every reference to fraternal allies was excised. Extensive praise continued to be rendered to the "great Soviet Army," and stories of the heroism of the individual Soviet soldier vied with stories of his North Korean counterpart. Nor did military and political leaders make any attempt to hide the part played by the Soviet Union in training and equipping the armed forces of North Korea. The Chinese contribution was also recognized, albeit less effusively. When pictures were displayed in North Korean journals of KPA personnel mobilized for work in the fields or on irrigation projects, they were frequently wearing Chinese clothing, and sometimes carried Chinese weapons.

Meanwhile, the government continued its effort to bring the army closer to the people. For example, in February 1958, the government authorized a one-month celebration of the tenth anniversary of the founding of the Korean People's Army. Scores of top military men received the DPRK's highest award, the Order of the National Flag, at this time. There were holidays for the workers, giant parades, and innumerable speeches. From every quarter, the People's Army was praised for its role in defending the Fatherland and assisting in production. A nationwide campaign was launched to "support a soldier's family."

The indications are strong that Kim Il-sŏng's drive to cement the loyalty of the army to himself and the Party was successful, and that, as the decade of the 1950s came to a close, he could count upon a powerful, unified, and loyal military force. Only two incidents have been reported during this period that cast doubt upon political loyalty within the military, and in both cases the crucial details are in dispute. Both incidents occurred during the crisis of 1956–58. In March 1958, General Chang P'yŏng-san, a KPA divisional commander, was purged on charges that he had plotted a coup d'etat on behalf of the Pak Ch'ang-ok–Ch'oe Ch'ang-ik group (the story was that he had been preparing to turn his guns on P'yŏngyang and so force the removal of Kim Il-sŏng). There is no question that Chang was removed and that these charges emanated from KWP sources, including Kim Il-sŏng himself. Moreover, Chang was one of the Yenan group and may therefore have sympathized with those currently under attack, including Kim Tu-bong. There is no hard evidence, however, that a coup d'etat was planned, and certainly none appears to have been attempted.[48]

48. Kim Nam-sik, who made some inquiries on this matter, insists that Chang's alleged involvement in a coup was purely a KWP-manufactured story. He asserts that another alleged leader was the chief of the cabinet secretariat, and that he had a relative in that office. When he inquired about the coup, his relative told him that he knew nothing whatsoever about it and believed it to be a hoax.

Kim Nam-sik, while admitting that there were many factions within the army,

The second incident involved relations between certain War College instructors and the Party. According to several sources, a debate took place within military circles in the 1957–58 period as to whether the KPA belonged to the Party or to the people. Some War College officers, including Generals Kim Il-ch'ŏng and Kim Il-gyu, reportedly told their students that the KPA was the army of the Democratic Front for the Unification of the Fatherland, not of any one party or group. Such statements directly challenged the thesis that the KPA was an army of the Party, one that had inherited Kim Il-sŏng's glorious partisan tradition. Reportedly, both generals were arrested and banished, with their families, to the mountains. Certain other War College instructors were sent to the mines. According to some, the whole affair brought about a general shake-up in top military circles.[49]

That Generals Kim Il-ch'ŏng and Kim Il-gyu were consciously defying Marshal Kim and the Party is quite unlikely. The major political fact of this era is that the military did not represent a real threat to Kim and his faction, even in the critical days of August and September 1956. Shrewdly, Kim had much earlier taken care of men like Mu Chŏng. Hence, when a serious crisis involving foreign intervention did emerge, indigenous power was securely in his hands. This fact, and this fact alone, enabled his survival—as it was to enable the survival of Mao under more complex circumstances a decade later.

claims that at this point the Party apparatus was so firmly imbedded in the military and so much of that apparatus was loyal to Kim Il-sŏng that no order given by Chang could possibly have been obeyed by his subordinates, as he himself would have known. Kim further argues that this was but one of many false stories propagated during the course of the "antisectarian" drive of this period. Chong-Sik Lee interview, Seoul, March 5, 1967.

49. During this period, there were a number of major changes at the top of the military structure, although few appear to have been connected with this incident. minister of Defense Ch'oe Yong-gŏn was transferred, as was vice-minister Ch'oe Hyŏn, who became minister of Communications. Both of these men remained close. trusted allies of Kim. The commandant of the War College, General Pang Ho-sang was removed, as was another vice minister of Defense, General Kim Ung. Here, the factors involved are unclear and may have related to the War College incident.

General Kim Kwang-hyŏp became minister of Defense, his star steadily on the rise from this point. Under him, Generals Ch'oe Chong-hak, Yi Kŏn-mu, and Kim T'ae-gun were appointed. Some observers have noted that the latter three men had earlier served with the Chinese Communists, and were generally regarded as belonging to the old Yenan faction. Once again, men from within a given faction were presumably rewarded for forsaking their erstwhile comrades and being prepared to swear loyalty to Kim Il-sŏng. As we shall see, two of the chief gainers as a result of the August 1956 incident and its aftermath were Kim Ch'ang-man and Kim Kwang-hyŏp, the former being another man with an extensive Chinese background. To what extent the advance of such individuals was also a result of the desirability of appointing men compatible with the Chinese is unclear, but this motive cannot be dismissed.

By the end of this period, the KPA numbered four hundred thousand men. In proportion to the size of the North Korean population, it was one of the largest armies in the world. It is thus not surprising that Kim and the Party regarded military indoctrination—and political loyalty—as top priorities. We can also see why they took special care of the soldiers in material terms as well—a factor to be examined more closely later.

The Emergence of Nationalism as an Intra-Party Weapon

In his concluding speech before the April Plenum, Kim launched the most vigorous and specific attack upon factionalism yet uttered before a Party gathering. He began by noting that the total defeat of the Korean Communist movement in the 1920s had been due largely to factional strife, and that some of those involved were still in the Party. While there was no intention of removing them, he asserted, they should get rid of their bad habits and become good Party members. Kim then compared them to rats, who hide when shouted at but run about when one is asleep. But factionalism, Kim made clear, was not merely connected with the domestic Korean Communist movement. The Party was composed of individuals from the Soviet Union and China, as well as those whose political base had been south or north Korea. Factionalists took advantage of this. Some individuals professed to be "representatives" of the region from which they came. Thus, men like Yi Sŭng-yŏp pretended that they alone had found jobs for the people from south Korea and had the authority to decide their destinies, thereby building up a private coterie. Among people from the Soviet Union, Hŏ Ka-i was a similar example, behaving as if he represented all of those who came from the USSR. Pak Il-u sought to play this role for those from China.[50]

Such individuals were constantly supporting policies based upon their own limited view of things and complaining about the unfair allocation of positions.[51] But whether one came from the Soviet Union, China, or from the southern part of the country, he should bear in mind that he was a member of the Workers' Party of Korea. The selection and allocation of cadres should be conducted not from the subjective view of any individual, but always according to Party principles. "Those who lack Party spirit," Kim concluded, "have no real desire to work for the Party and the revolution, and think themselves outstanding figures, are of no use to our Party whether they are from the Soviet Union, China, or even from Heaven. You should understand this clearly." [52]

50. Kim Il-sŏng, "On Some Questions Concerning Party and State Work . . . ," *op. cit.*, pp. 298–299.

51. Speaking of Pak Il-u, Kim said, "Alleging that 'Comrades from China are not promoted to leading posts' or that 'People from the Soviet Union have different manners and customs than those who are from China,' he stealthily schemes to gather around him comrades whose level of class consciousness is low." *Ibid.*, p. 298.

52. *Ibid.*, pp. 299–300.

A more specific warning to the Yenan and Soviet groups could scarcely have been uttered. And it is interesting to observe that in this and other speeches of the same period, for the first time, Kim sounded a cautious note of independence from the big Communist nations surrounding North Korea. He had survived the war and its aftermath; he had overcome key rivals within the Party. He could now begin to assert his own authority.

The next dramatic development came at the end of 1955. In mid-December, as will be recalled, Party authorities finally brought Pak Hŏn-yŏng to trial and executed him. Thus, the issues of factionalism and treason were once more brought before the public. As we have remarked earlier, it is difficult to understand the timing of this trial unless it was connected with intra-Party developments. Nothing on the international scene would seem to have affected it. On the domestic front, however, another crisis was brewing, and the Kim faction may well have considered it wise to have Pak Hŏn-yŏng eliminated before any new purges of top Party leaders got under way.

In any case, on December 28, precisely thirteen days after Pak had been condemned to death, Kim Il-sŏng delivered an extraordinarily important speech to Party propagandists and agitators—a speech that, so far as we can discover, was not made public at the time.[53] Kim began by stressing the critical importance of chuch'e, or the principle of making indigenous need and experience the essential criteria, of implanting *self-sufficiency* as the central theme of the Korean Revolution. Ideological work, aserted Kim, suffered from excessive formalism and dogmatism, with Party propagandists borrowing foreign concepts and practices mechanically. "We are not engaged in the revolution of another country, but in our Korean Revolution," he proclaimed. Thus all work had to be subordinated to the interests of that revolution.[54]

He then proceeded to launch an attack upon Pak Ch'ang-ok directly and by name. Pak and his kind had made serious errors by downgrading the study of Korean history, thereby failing to awake the Korean people to their own glorious traditions. They had closed their eyes, for example, to the Korean literary movement, and in particular to the struggle of the Korean Proletarian Art Federation (KPAF) in the pre-Liberation period. They had ignored the anti-Japanese struggle of the Korean people as exemplified in such events as the Kwangju Student Incident.

---

53. The version of this speech we have used is in Kim Il Sung, *Selected Works,* Vol. I, cited earlier (Kim Il-sŏng, "On Eliminating Dogmatism," pp. 315–340). It is possible that the original has undergone certain changes, additions, and omissions, although the differences between the earlier Korean and Japanese and the later English versions are not significant. For a Korean version, see *Kim Il-sŏng sŏnjip,* Vol. 4 (1960 ed.), pp. 325–354.

54. *Ibid.,* pp. 315–316.

When I asked Pak Ch'ang-ok and his followers why they rejected the KPAF, they answered that they did so because some renegades were involved in it. Did they really mean to say that the KPAF, in which Comrade Yi Ki-yŏng and other prominent writers of our country were the nucleus, was an organization of no importance? We must highly appreciate the feats of those comrades in the revolutionary struggle, and allow them to play the central role in the development of our literature today.[55]

The significance of these remarks can be further appreciated if it is recalled that Yi Ki-yŏng, together with Han Sŏl-ya, was one of those literati high in Party circles who had come under criticism as dogmatists and formalists from the more liberal-minded elements in the aftermath of the Second All-Soviet Writers Congress. The widening cleavage within intellectual circles in North Korea was now making itself felt in top political circles, with Kim Il-sŏng coming down strongly on the side of the "old guard." He coupled this position, however, with a firm nationalist stance aimed particularly at key figures in the Soviet faction, including Pak Ch'ang-ok. Not only was Korean history largely ignored, Kim continued. "Once I visited a People's Army vacation hostel, where I saw a picture of the Siberian steppe on the wall. That landscape of the steppe probably pleases the Russians. But the Korean people prefer the beautiful scenes of their own country." [56] At a local Democratic Propaganda Room, moreover, he had seen diagrams of the Soviet Union's Five-Year Plan, but no diagrams illustrating the Korean Three-Year Plan. At a primary school, there were portraits of such foreigners as Mayakovsky and Pushkin on the wall, but none of Koreans.

Worse, those veteran comrades who had participated in the early *Korean* revolutionary movement (as opposed to those with foreign revolutionary experience) had been left on the shelf by the Party for many years, or relegated to minor positions. "Today our functionaries have become so insolent that they have no respect for their seniors." This error had not occurred within the Korean People's Army. There, old revolutionary cadres had made up the core, and as a result the Army had performed brilliantly, despite the prediction of "some foreigners" that when our military units were trapped by enemy encirclement, they would not be able to get back. Kim then became even more specific:

Comrade Pak Yŏng-bin, upon returning from the Soviet Union, said that since the Soviet Union was following the line of easing international tension we, too, had to drop our slogans against US imperialism. His assertion has nothing in common with revolutionary initiative; it will dull the revolutionary vigilance of our people. The US imperialists scorched our land, slaughtered our innocent people en masse, and are still occupying

55. *Ibid.*, pp. 318–319.
56. *Ibid.*, p. 319.

the southern part of our country. They are our sworn enemy, are they not? [57]

Some comrades, asserted Kim, had sought to copy the Soviet Union mechanically in their work in the Propaganda and Agitation Department of the Party. Their failure to study Korean history had sometimes led them into ideological error. Thus, Pak Ch'ang-ok had been in league with the reactionary bourgeois writer, Yi T'ae-jun, because he did not know Korean history and had the conceited idea that he knew everything. "The harm he did to our ideological work is very serious." [58]

Kim went on in an impersonal vein to insist that internationalism and patriotism were inseparably linked together. "To love Korea is to love the Soviet Union and the socialist camp and, likewise, to love the Soviet Union and the socialist camp means loving Korea." He added: "He who does not love his own country cannot be loyal to internationalism, and he who is unfaithful to internationalism cannot be faithful to his own country and people. A true patriot is an internationalist and vice versa." [59]

None of this was particularly unorthodox when viewed against current trends in the international Communist movement. Chinese Communist doctrine was emphasizing much the same themes, and the Soviet Union itself would have found the passages just quoted entirely acceptable. What was striking, however, was the fact that Kim Il-sŏng, who owed his own position entirely to Soviet power and Soviet support in the early stages of his career, and who had formerly insisted upon an almost slavish adherence to Soviet patterns, was now seeking to use nationalist weapons against elements within his Party, weapons that on occasion seemed to presage a new position of independence from the Soviet Union. It should also be remembered that the events recounted here were taking place *before* the Twentieth Congress of the CPSU. This does not mean that they had no connection with developments abroad. The political instability evidenced in Moscow, and the signs there of an interest in some accommodation with the United States, were producing reverberations in P'yŏngyang, as Kim indicated in his remarks about Pak Yŏng-bin. The influence of the Chinese, moreover, was on the rise. Essentially, however, Kim's new nationalism was the product at this point of internal, not international, considerations,

57. *Ibid.*, p. 322. Kim did go on to insist that it was "utterly ridiculous" to believe that the struggle against the US conflicted with the efforts of the Soviet people to ease international tension; on the contrary, the Korean struggle against aggressive American policies aided the struggle of the world's people to lessen international tension and defend peace.

58. *Ibid.*, pp. 322–323. Kim also charged Pak with having wanted to support Yi Kwang-su, a writer who had once "leveled insults at revolutionaries discharged from prison" and who had claimed that the Korean and Japanese people were descended from the same ancestors. "I refused to allow Pak and his followers to give prominence to such a fellow," asserted Kim.

59. *Ibid.*, p. 326.

namely, his growing concern about the power and the policies of the Soviet and Yenan factions.

The new nationalist tone was rapidly communicated to Party organs. On January 1, 1956, *Nodong Sinmun* published a picture of Ch'ŏnji, the famed Paektu Mountain lake, a place traditionally regarded as sacred by the Korean people, and fraught with nationalist symbolism. Accompanying the picture was a poem by Hong Sun-ch'ŏl entitled "A New Year Greeting," which carried the cult of Kim Il-sŏng to new heights. A rough translation of the first two stanzas might read as follows:

> "As the sun shines upon the earth
> As far as one's eyes can reach
> Our prospects are bright by virtue of
> The light that shines from our Leader.

> "Being nearby with us, you are
> Our Sublime Conscience and Wisdom.
> Ten million support you therefore as one.
> Oh, your love, warm as a mother's embraces!" [60]

It might have been thought that Kim's blast against Pak Ch'ang-ok would have signaled his immediate demise, but such was not the case. However, attacks continued, with men like Han Sŏl-ya taking the lead, upon the "remnants of reactionary bourgeois ideology" as represented by those writers in the "Pak Hŏn-yŏng entourage"—Yim Hwa, Kim Nam-ch'ŏn, and Yi T'ae-jun. At the Conference of Enthusiasts in Literature, Art, and Press Propaganda, which took place on January 23 and 24, Han delivered a lengthy speech in which renewed excoriation of Yim and the others was coupled with a philippic against Pak Ch'ang-ok and several associates. Han's speech was not published until February 15, which—possibly by coincidence—was the opening day of the Twentieth Party Congress of the CPSU.[61] On the next day, moreover, a lengthy article by Pak Kŭm-ch'ŏl was published that sharply attacked factionalism in all its forms and warned that the Party would not allow itself to be split by "spies and factionalists," however craftily they might operate and whatever measures might have to be taken to oust them.[62] Pak Kŭm-ch'ŏl's article mentioned only the names

60. *NS*, Jan. 1, 1956, p. 2. Hong Sun-ch'ŏl, it should be noted, was a prominent Party worker, member of the Central Committee of the Korean Writers' Union, and active in other Party-sponsored cultural groups.

61. For the full text, see *NS*, Feb. 15, 1956, pp. 2–3. Han cited various poems and writings of Yim, Kim, and Yi to "prove" their past collaboration with Japanese authorities and their general bourgeois philosophy. He then accused literary critics and writers like Kim Sŏk-bok, Ch'ŏn Tong-hyŏk, and Chŏng Ryuk of befriending and admiring them, under the benevolent protection and approval of Pak Ch'ang-ok.

62. Pak Kŭm-ch'ŏl, "The Strengthening of Party Loyalty on the Part of Party Members in the Struggle for the Strengthening of Party Organization," *NS*, Feb. 16, 1956, pp. 1–2.

of those already purged, notably Pak Hŏn-yŏng and his group, but no great imagination was now required to realize that another major crisis was erupting within top Communist circles, and that a major purge was about to take place.

De-Stalinization and the Third Congress of the KWP

Meanwhile, extensive and favorable coverage was given to the Twentieth Party Congress of the CPSU. Lengthy excerpts from the speeches of Shepilov, Suslov, and Khrushchev were published in *Nodong Sinmun*. But there was absolutely no mention at this point of Khrushchev's off-the-record attack upon Stalin. Praise of the Twentieth Party Congress, indeed, continued on an almost daily basis into March, together with periodic attacks upon the remnants of bourgeois ideology in the field of Korean literature and art.[63] Significantly, however, Ch'oe Yong-gŏn, head of the KWP delegation to the Twentieth Congress, made no public report, although excerpts from the reports of certain foreign Communist leaders, including Togliatti and Rakosi, gradually began to be published.

Only on April 2, some six weeks after the Congress had concluded, did *Nodong Sinmun* finally publish a *Pravda* editorial entitled "Why Personal Worship Has Nothing to Do with Marxism-Leninism," revealing to North Koreans for the first time that Stalin had been criticized by CPSU leaders for various shortcomings, including that of fostering a cult of personality. Six days later, on April 8, the same source reprinted a major Chinese Communist pronouncement, "On Historical Experience Concerning the Dictatorship of the Proletariat," which had first appeared in *Jen-min Jih-pao* on April 5.

Kim Il-sŏng and his group were obviously deeply troubled by the attack led by Khrushchev upon Stalin, an attack that served to accentuate certain other signs of relaxation now being signaled from Soviet quarters. These events could scarcely have come at a more inopportune time for Kim. Not only was the Workers' Party involved in a serious internal crisis but, since 1953, a cult of personality had developed around Kim to an extraordinary degree. Hong Sun-ch'ŏl's poem of January 1, 1956, cited earlier, was but one small example of a process of glorification that had been accelerating through the years. At this point, monuments to Kim abounded, his partisan days had been depicted in superlative terms, and all that was good, true, and pure was attributed to his genius. When to this was added the fact that Kim himself had repeatedly eulogized Stalin in the extravagant terms already noted, had recently erected monuments to him, had named a major thoroughfare in P'yŏngyang after him, and had

63. Ŏm Ho-sŏk was finally caused to swing into line, striking out at "the anti-revolutionary literature" of Yi T'ae-jun in an article for *NS*, March 7, 1956, which criticized other "liberals" such as Yim Hwa, Kim Nam-ch'ŏn, Sŏl Chŏng-sik, Cho Il-myŏng, and Yi Won-jo.

appeared under his gigantic picture on countless occasions, the profoundly embarrassing nature of the abrupt de-Stalinization campaign emanating from Moscow can be appreciated.

It was under these circumstances that the Third All-Party Congress of the Korean Workers' Party opened on April 23. This Congress, the first to be held in eight years, came at a crucial moment.[64] In his very lengthy report, Kim Il-sŏng showed himself capable of rolling with the punch in a shrewd fashion. Retreating from any open attack upon the Soviet faction, Kim concentrated upon the iniquities of the Pak Hŏn-yŏng clique, and asserted that the struggle against factionalism had been gravely hampered by an ideology of personal worship that had permeated certain Party circles. If the cadres of the South Korean Workers' Party had not idealized Pak Hŏn-yŏng and other factionalists, their crimes could have been discovered in time and serious damage prevented.[65] In this fashion, the cult of personality was turned against the factionalists!

Kim (together with all the other speakers) emphasized the importance of collective leadership, and much of the paraphernalia of hero-worship present at recent Party meetings was absent or muted on this occasion. However, he did not retreat from many of the themes that he had stressed in April and December 1955. Outstanding Party cadres had to be produced in the fields of politics, economics, and culture, he asserted, adding that many defects still existed in the work of political indoctrination. Once again, the importance of chuch'e was emphasized, and the essential task was defined as adapting all techniques to the Korean Revolution. Moreover, criticism of certain elements within the intelligentsia remained a central theme. The development of science and culture, proclaimed Kim, was lagging behind the development of the economy. The political level of teachers had to be improved. Some "scientists" were studying with old-fashioned methodologies. Some writers and artists had failed to overcome their bourgeois liberalism. The struggle to acquire correct Marxist-Leninist vision, and to reach the masses, had to continue.

The Character of the 1956 Party

To what type of audience was Kim addressing himself? The socio-economic composition of the Third All-Party Congress, with its 914 members, is of considerable interest. The data are from official Party sources.[66]

64. The Third KWP Congress was the first meeting since its formation in June 1949. In one sense, therefore, this was the First Party Congress. The previous congresses were those of July 28, 1946, at the time of the NKCP merger with the New People's Party, and March 29, 1948.

65. Kim Il-sŏng's report to the Third All-Party Congress, *NS,* April 24, 1956, pp. 1–8.

66. *NS,* April 26, 1956, p. 3.

TABLE 29
Third All-Party Congress, KWP, 1956, Socioeconomic Data

Occupation	Number	Percent
Party workers	316	34.6
Government workers	120	13.1
Social organization workers	27	3.0
Industrial and transportation managers	142	15.5
(Administrators, 61; technicians, 19; workers, 62)		
Forestry and marine	19	2.0
Production workers	19	2.0
Agricultural managers and workers	107	11.7
(State farm workers, 27; Agricultural cooperative		
workers, 75; Individual farmers, 5)		
Producers' cooperative and marine	5	0.5
cooperative representatives		
Financial and commercial workers	12	1.3
Educational and culture workers	46	5.0

NOTE: Only 813 members, or 88.7 percent of the total, are recorded here.

Age	Number	Percent
Below 26	16	1.8
26–30	57	6.2
31–40	470	51.4
41–50	301	32.9
51 and over	70	7.7

Length of Revolutionary Experience	Number	Percent
Participants in the revolutionary movement before 1945	90	9.8
Participants after liberation at the time of Party formation	471	51.5
Participants after liberation and before the Korean War	300	32.8
Participants during the Korean War	52	5.7
Participants after the Korean War	1	0.1

Educational Level	Number	Percent
College or university graduate	72	7.9
High school or technical school graduate	146	16.0
Middle school graduate	55	6.0
Primary school graduate	641	70.1

NOTE: 512 or 56.0% had attended Party schools.

TABLE 29 (*continued*)

Type of Revolutionary Experience	Number	Percent
Participants in anti-Japanese movement	221[a]	24.2
Fought in Korean War	270	29.5
Imprisoned in course of revolutionary experience	221	24.2
Imprisoned less than 5 years	154	69.7[b]
Imprisoned less than 10 years	44	19.9[b]
Imprisoned 10 years or more	23	10.4[b]

[a] There would appear to be some discrepancy between this figure and that relating to participants in the revolutionary movement before 1945 (90). Possibly the former figure includes those merely involved in some form of non-Communist nationalist activity.

[b] These represent percentages of those imprisoned.

Honors Received	
771	84.4%

NOTE: Including 10 Heroes and 37 Labor Heroes.

Perhaps the most important aspects of this profile are those pertaining to age, education, and occupation. Nearly 60 percent of the delegates to the Third Congress were 40 years of age or younger (one should remember that Kim Il-sŏng himself was barely 44 at this point). Their formal education had been very limited: 70 percent had completed only primary school, and no more than 8 percent had graduated from a college or university. Once again, the majority were close in profile to their leader. Most —over 80 percent—had come into the revolutionary movement for the first time between 1945 and 1950. Veterans whose experience extended into the pre-1945 period represented a mere 8 percent of the total. As for occupation, the delegates were overwhelmingly professional Party or government workers (bureaucrats, to use a term considered an epithet in North Korea) or industrial and agrarian managers and workers. Intellectual, commercial, and professional representatives were remarkably few. In sum, these delegates mirrored a party of young workers and peasants, limited in revolutionary experience—a party rapidly developing into a bureaucratic elite (with a heavier military representation than these figures show), but lacking the intellectual roots associated with previous bureaucracies.

These circumstances were of immeasurable benefit to Kim Il-sŏng in his confrontation with other factions, as can readily be appreciated. The southerners had a limited base from which to draw support, and one that grew more limited every year. Similarly, without external support, the Soviet and Yenan factions could have only slight appeal to a young, postwar generation of North Koreans. For this latter group, the revolutionary days in China or the Soviet experience had little meaning. Kim Il-sŏng, building upon his own myth—and there were few to disprove it—represented to the postwar generation the only leader, the only revolutionary experience that their lives encompassed. Out of survival, legitimacy is built —and Kim at this point had survived the storms and stresses of more than a decade. That decade, moreover, represented the total political experience of some 90 percent of the Party cadres. In this lay an advantage not to be underestimated.

When the seventy-one members of the new Central Committee (the third) were elected by the congress, on April 29, the changes appeared to be less significant than one might have expected. The top ten members, in order of their listing, were Kim Il-sŏng, Kim Tu-bong, Ch'oe Yong-gŏn, Pak Chŏng-ae, Kim Il, Pak Kŭm-ch'ŏl, Pak Ch'ang-ok, Ch'oe Ch'ang-ik, Pak Ui-wan, and Chŏng Il-yong.[67] The Standing Committee, or Politburo, of the Central Committee consisted of Kim Il-sŏng, Kim Tu-bong, Ch'oe Yong-gŏn, Pak Chŏng-ae, Kim Il, Pak Kŭm-ch'ŏl, Yim Hae, Ch'oe Ch'ang-ik, Chŏng Il-yong, Kim Kwang-hyŏp, and Nam Il, with the candidate or alternate members being Kim Ch'ang-man, Yi Chong-ok, Yi Hyo-sun, and Pak Ui-wan. Pak Ch'ang-ok had been dropped from fifth to seventh position on the Central Committee and removed from the Standing Committee. Ch'oe Ch'ang-ik had been dropped from sixth to eighth position, but remained on the Standing Committee. Pak Yŏng-bin, however, had been completely removed from the Central Committee.

Among the group at the very top, those who had improved their positions were Ch'oe Yong-gŏn (from fourth to third at the expense of Pak Chŏng-ae), Kim Il (from sixth to fifth at the expense of Pak Ch'ang-ok), and Pak Kŭm-ch'ŏl (from tenth to sixth at the expense of Pak Ch'ang-ok, Ch'oe Ch'ang-ik, Chŏng Il-yong, and Pak Ui-wan). Each of these three individuals, it will be recalled, could be considered as belonging to Kim Il-sŏng's personal circle. Now only Kim Tu-bong among the top six members of the Central Committee lay outside that circle.

If one looked closely at the rest of the Central Committee, as well as at the all-important Standing Committee and Organization Committee,[68] one could discern a few other individuals who were moving upward, notably Yim Hae, Kim Kwang-hyŏp, Nam Il, Kim Ch'ang-man, Yi Chong-ok, Yi Hyo-sun, Han Sang-du, Ha Ang-ch'ŏn, Kim Hwang-il, Pak Hun-il, Pak Il-yŏng, Yi Il-gyŏng, Han Sŏl-ya, and Sŏ Hwi. Six of these were members of Kim's personal circle, and with one exception their star continued to rise during the next decade. Yi Chong-ok currently held the post of chairman of the State Planning Commission. Yi Hyo-sun was head of the Cadre De-

67. For the listings, see *NS,* April 30, 1956, p. 1. The next ten CC members in order were Han Sang-du, Ha Ang-ch'ŏn, Kim Hwang-il, Pak Hun-il, Yi Hyo-sun, Pak Il-yŏng, Yi Il-gyŏng, Han Sŏl-ya, Sŏ Hwi, and Yim Hae.

68. The Organization Committee, in order, consisted of Kim Il-sŏng, Ch'oe Yong-gŏn, Pak Chŏng-ae, Pak Kŭm-ch'ŏl, Chŏng Il-yong, and Han Sang-du. The chairman of the Central Committee was Kim Il-sŏng. The five vice-chairmen were Ch'oe Yong-gŏn, Pak Chŏng-ae, Pak Kŭm-ch'ŏl, Chŏng Il-yong, and Kim Ch'ang-man.

partment of the Party. Han Sang-du was director of the Party Organization Department. Pak Il-yŏng was shortly to be sent as ambassador to various posts in Eastern Europe. Yi Il-gyŏng had been named director of the Party Propaganda and Agitation Department in February 1956. Han Sŏl-ya, Kim's biographer and a well-known Party novelist, was to become minister of Education in May 1956. Among this group, only Han was to fall from grace during the next ten years (he was purged in 1962). It is to be noted, moreover, that by this time Kim Il-sŏng had individuals whom he trusted implicitly in almost all of the key Party and government posts.

Four of the upwardly mobile group listed above had Yenan antecedents, a fact that reflected the considerable strength displayed by the old Yenan element at the Third KWP Congress. Indeed, some sources have argued that this Congress was a great "victory" for the members of the Yenan faction, and relate their success to the strong Chinese influence now affecting the Korean Communist movement.[69] Such a theory should not be pushed too far, as can be seen from a close analysis of the leading person-

69. A source who wishes to remain anonymous takes this position, asserting that among the 71 Central Committee members, 22 can be accounted of "Yenan" origin, 11 of Soviet background, 11 belonging to the Kim Il-sŏng circle, 11 formerly SKWP members, 7 indigenous Communists of the old NKWP group, 1 from the JCP originally, and 12 unknowns. (Such a listing totals 75, not 71.) This same source asserts that among the 45 candidate members, the Yenan group had 7, the Soviet group 4, the Kim group 7, the ex-SKWP group 4, the ex-NKWP group 2, and nearly one-half—21—were unknown, most of them young army officers from Korean units that had entered North Korea from China during the Korean War and therefore had Chinese backgrounds.

Whereas the Yenan group made major gains, this source asserts, the Soviet and domestic factions lost heavily as a result of the demise of Hŏ Ka-i and Pak Hŏn-yŏng, the assault upon Pak Ch'ang-ok and his followers, and the general unhappiness with Khrushchev's de-Stalinization venture.

Our own reconstruction of the factional origins of the Third Central Committee suggests the following divisions: Kim's "Kapsan" group, 12; new recruits, 7 (younger elements brought into the Party after 1945 and raised to the Central Committee after the Korean War); ex-NKWP elements, 15; ex-SKWP elements, 7; Yenan faction, 15; Soviet faction, 12; Japanese Communist Party background, 1; unknown, 2—total, 71. (Sources: Han Chae-dŏk, *Hanguk ui kongsan chu-ui wa Puk-Han ui yŏksa* (*Communism in Korea and the History of North Korea*), Seoul, 1955, pp. 306–313; Chong-Sik Lee interview with O Ki-wan, Jan. 15, 1967; Kasumigaseki-kai (Foreign Ministry), *Gendai Chōsen jimmei jiten* (*Biographical Dictionary of Contemporary Korea*), Tokyo, 1962.)

One problem with such breakdowns as these is that they imply that all individuals stayed with the group in which they "originated." But as we have seen, Kim used those elements within a faction who would cooperate to liquidate other elements, rewarding them in the process. Those who survived had to be in Kim's faction—irrespective of their background—although Kim called this "Party unity" and the absence of factionalism.

In very general terms, however, the so-called domestic faction had been reduced to a mere shadow at this point, and the Soviet-Koreans were also under suspicion, as Kim's December 1955 address makes clear. In relative terms, and for the moment, the Yenan group was better off.

alities involved, together with a study of subsequent events. Of the Yenan men, Ha Ang-ch'ŏn was one of the loyal intellectuals, dutifully attacking "reactionary" intellectuals in his capacity as director of Science and School Education. He was not destined to rise much higher, however, and in a few years he fell into some difficulty.[70] Pak Hun-il, a second Yenan man and currently director of the Agricultural Department of the Party, was shortly to be purged, as was Sŏ Hwi, vice-chairman and, in May, chairman of the Central Committee of the Trade Union Federation. Kim Ch'ang-man, however, as we have already mentioned, was to continue his rise to power in the tense months ahead by siding with Kim Il-sŏng against former colleagues.

Only one of those listed above was truly a Soviet Korean. Nam Il, at this point minister of Foreign Affairs, was the single Soviet Korean to grow in prominence in the years that lay ahead. A second, Yim Hae, has occasionally been listed as a Soviet Korean, but in fact he appears to have been a member of Ch'oe Yong-gŏn's guerrilla group in Manchuria before he went to the Soviet Union. Reportedly, he attended a Communist university there, and later returned to Korea with the others. After serving in a variety of capacities, including ambassador to the Soviet Union, head of the Party liaison department, and minister of Agriculture, he was purged and sent down to a farm as a worker. Kim Hwang-il, the only long-time domestic Communist in the group, was to be purged in 1957.

In sum, the old factional groupings were gradually being reduced to impotence, with only a few individuals from each group's original list successfully making the transition to Kim Il-sŏng's banners. To have started out in Kim's faction, of course, was of huge advantage.

The Era of Political Crisis

Having amended the Party constitution and approved the Five-Year Plan, the Third Party Congress adjourned. Shortly thereafter, Kim Il-sŏng, in an interview with an Indian newsman, made his first public comment on the issue of Stalin. "I fully approve of the critical attitude shown at the Twentieth Congress of the CPSU," he asserted.

> We Communists criticize [Stalin] for his violation of Leninist collective leadership and Marxist-Leninist ideology. This does not mean that we deny the role of the individual in history. Marxism-Leninism recognizes the important role of leaders in history.
>
> Stalin was a strong Marxist-Leninist who made a significant contribution to the international proletarian movement and played a historic role in the construction of socialism in the Soviet Union, the victory of the socialist revolution and the defeat of Fascism, thereby achieving great fame.

70. Ha became president of Kim Il-sŏng University in December 1960; he was relieved of the post in 1965. In 1966, he was a candidate member of the Central Committee, a considerable demotion from his earlier rank.

Nevertheless, he became excessively conceited during the last stage of his life and consequently inflicted considerable damage upon the Party as well as the government by violating Leninist principles of collective leadership. It is entirely proper, therefore, for the CPSU to expose and criticize his errors vigorously while recognizing his great contributions.[71]

Kim's remarks were identical to those already made in Peking and by Asian Communist leaders elsewhere, indicating a mutuality of interest on this matter.

On June 1, Kim left P'yŏngyang at the head of a delegation that made an extended trip to the Soviet Union and Eastern Europe.[72] Precisely what occurred behind closed doors during the two months of Kim's absence will perhaps never be known. Some sources indicate that Pak Ch'ang-ok took the lead in an active effort to fashion an anti-Kim coalition, taking his stand on three issues: first, relying upon the decisions of the Twentieth CPSU Congress, he attacked one-man dictatorship, and insisted that both the People's Committee and the Trade Union Federation should play more important roles, separate from that of the Party; second, he demanded an alteration in the government's economic development program, so that more attention would be given to the ordinary person's standard of living, and less to the development of heavy industry, which mainly benefited the state; and finally, that in the selection of Party officials, cronyism and factional balance be rejected as criteria in favor of merit.

Substantial evidence, including later statements by the Kim Il-sŏng coterie, indicates that these were indeed the basic issues, especially the first two. The precise role of Pak—and others—is by no means clear, although he above all would have had ample reasons for dissidence, as we have seen. In any case, both Pak and Ch'oe Ch'ang-ik did use the channels provided by the mass media to attack the cult of personality and give strong support to collective leadership. They were careful, of course, to avoid any overt criticism of Kim Il-sŏng.[73] In this connection, it is also interesting to note that on June 17 *Nodong Sinmun* published a summary of a May 26 address of Lu Ting-i to a conference of scientists, writers, and artists in Peking. In

71. Kim Il-sŏng's press interview with V. V. Prasad, *NS*, May 31, 1956, p. 1.

72. The delegation included Pak Chŏng-ae, Nam Il, Yi Chong-ok, Ko Chun-t'aek (vice-chairman of the KDP), Kim Pyŏng-je (vice-chairman of the Chŏndogyo Young Friends' Party), Ch'oe Hyŏn, and Cho Kŭm-song (dean of the Kim Ch'aek Technical College).

73. According to Kim Ch'ang-sun, Ch'oe Yong-gŏn reported to the KWP Central Committee upon the events of the Twentieth CPSU Congress very frankly, and both Pak and Ch'oe, as leading theorists, began to harbor hopes that, under the impetus provided by the Soviet Union, collective leadership could actually be established in North Korea. Their first move, according to Kim, was to work hard to elect members of their factions to the new Central Committee—although the results of that election, in Kim Ch'ang-sun's view, were to confirm Kim Il-sŏng's hegemony over the Party. At the same time, they began the publication of the articles noted above. Kim Ch'ang-sun, *op. cit.,* pp. 151–156.

comparison with the line of Ha Ang-ch'ŏn, Han Sŏl-ya, and other spokesmen for the Kim regime, Lu's address had an amazingly liberal ring, reflective of the thaw that was developing at this point in China. For example,
Lu asserted that natural and medical science could not be either "feudalistic"
or "socialistic," and that while socialist realism was the best literary style,
artists and writers had to be free to choose their own approach. The important thing was to eliminate sectarianism and doctrinaire tendencies.
Writers, artists, and scientists should learn from the people, from the Soviet
Union and other fraternal nations, and "even from our enemies." [74]

The more sensational accounts of the events leading up to the Plenum
of August 1956 depict the emergence of a rather broadly gauged anti-Kim
coalition that made contact with both Soviet and Chinese authorities, and
carried out extensive preparations for a showdown, dogged of course by
informers who relayed highly secret information to the Kim group.[75] It is

74. *NS,* June 17, 1956, p. 4.
75. According to the same anonymous source quoted earlier, Pak Ch'ang-ok,
advancing the themes outlined above, gradually gathered together an inner group led
by himself and Ch'oe, Ko Pong-gi (chairman of the North Hwanghae Province
Party; Yenan faction), Yun Kong-hŭm (minister of Commerce; Yenan faction), Kim
Sŭng-hwa (minister of Construction; Soviet faction), and Yi Sang-jo (ambassador to
the USSR; Soviet faction).
With the support of Kim Tu-bong, chairman of the Standing Committee of the
Supreme People's Assembly (Yenan faction), they undertook contacts with members
of the P'yŏngyang Municipal Party Committee and other local committees, the
Academy of Science, instructors at Kim Il-sŏng University, and the Central Com-
mittee itself. Supposedly, they won considerable support in the course of this venture,
including that of eleven CC members—Pak Ui-wan (vice-premier; Soviet faction),
Hŏ Pin (North Hwanghae Party leader; Soviet faction), Pak Hun-il (director of the
Agriculture Department of the Party; Yenan faction), Sŏ Hwi (chairman of the
Trade Union Federation; Yenan faction), and Cho Yŏng (chairman of the Yanggang
and Chagang Province Party; Yenan faction), in addition to those already mentioned.
According to this account, Pak Ui-wan, Yi Sang-jo, and Sŏ Hwi approached the
Soviet Embassy in P'yŏngyang, the Soviet government in Moscow, and the Chinese
Embassy in P'yŏngyang respectively, obtaining a tacit understanding with them. However, supposedly, two Yenan faction men—Kim Ch'ang-man and General Kim Ch'ang-
dŏk—served as informers, notifying Acting Premier Ch'oe Yong-gŏn and Pak Kŭm-
ch'ŏl of the plot. Kim Il-sŏng thereupon is said to have hastened home and begun a
thorough investigation. He discovered that the anti-Kim group had not yet penetrated
the KPA or the secret police (Ministry of Internal Affairs), whereupon he decided
to meet the group for a showdown at the August Plenum.
To what extent this account is correct, we cannot say. It has the principal actors
correctly identified and placed, but we have no further corroboration of the details
outlined here. Kim Nam-sik presents a somewhat more "relaxed" picture of the
August Plenum, without downgrading its seriousness. According to him, the Plenum
was originally convened to deal not with factional problems but with the problem
of public health. However, when certain criticisms of policy were made that appeared subversive to the leadership, purges were undertaken.
Kim Nam-sik acknowledges that the substantive issues were those set forth above,

difficult to reconstruct the details of events leading up to the August Plenum with any certainty, since they involved Party intrigue at the highest levels; we can only verify the primary issues and the principal actors on both sides. In the weeks immediately preceding the Plenum, incidentally, a series of articles and editorials were published on the problem of the intellectuals, indicating that Party leaders continued to view this matter as one of the utmost seriousness. Otherwise, no unusual signs appeared on the horizon. And if one were to have relied merely upon the account of the August Plenum initially published in *Nodong Sinmun,* one would have assumed it was a very routine meeting. In its brief announcement, the Party organ stated that the Plenum had been devoted to two agenda items, the Premier's report on the Korean delegation's foreign trip and the issue of strengthening public health measures. Discussion followed both reports, and appropriate measures were taken. "The problem of Party organization was also discussed in the Plenary Session." [76]

From other sources, additional details are available. Probably by prearrangement, Yun Kong-hŭm, minister of Commerce, took the floor and raised some of the basic issues festering within "anti-Kim" circles. The Party was accused of having ignored the issue of the "people's livelihood" by continuing to give too great a priority to heavy industry, with the result that the people were miserable and discontented. Light industry should be developed immediately so that more clothing, food, and housing were available. Secondly, the Premier had engaged in no self-criticism concerning the problem of hero-worship, and in this respect the Party was running counter to the spirit and actions of the Twentieth CPSU Congress. Indeed, in connection with the attempt to glorify one man, a number of fictional elements had been introduced into modern Korean history.[77]

Evidently, confusion reigned at certain points during this speech, with

especially the question of collective leadership. He points out that many publications from East Europe were reaching North Korea during this period, some of them being translated and published in a monthly journal established for the purpose of such publication. Thus, scholars and Party officials were being subjected to a series of new ideas in the aftermath of the Twentieth CPSU Congress, ideas that disturbed the precariously balanced internal Party milieu. Economic issues—the question of overemphasis upon heavy industry as against consumer needs—were also important. And, according to Kim, there was discontent over certain new appointments, particularly the sudden elevation of Ch'oe Yong-gŏn, previously chairman of the KDP, to the post of vice-chairman of the KWP, and the advance of Yi Chong-ok, a man "who had donated considerable sums of money to the Japanese government during the war to purchase airplanes and was an arch-collaborator." Chong-Sik Lee interview with Kim Nam-sik, March 5, 1967.

76. *NS,* Sept. 5, 1956, p. 1.

77. For one account of Yun's speech, see Kim Ch'ang-sun, *op. cit.,* pp. 156–157. According to Kim, among other things Yun asserted that wages for the farmers were too low and those for army officers too high. We have obtained other accounts of the Plenum from Kim Nam-sik and our anonymous source.

Kim supporters—in the majority—shouting accusations at Yun, calling him an anti-Party reactionary and seeking to silence him. One account relates that, when the meeting went into recess at noon on the first day, a complete state of disorder prevailed. At some point, certain anti-Kim leaders recognized that they were in personal danger, and four of them, including Yun Kong-hŭm, decided to flee to Communist China. When this was discovered —too late to prevent it—the Kim forces moved against the major leaders on the second day. Pak Ch'ang-ok and Ch'oe Ch'ang-ik were immediately divested of their government posts and Central Committee positions, and Yun Kong-hŭm, Sŏ Hwi, Yi P'il-gyu, and Kim Kang—those who had fled —were expelled from the Party.[78]

The issue, however, was not settled. Whatever their previous knowledge of the issues and individuals involved, the Russians and the Chinese now stepped into the scene. Those who had fled to Peking immediately contacted no less a person than P'eng Teh-huai, minister of Defense, and presented their case. Earlier, in Moscow, Yi Sang-jo, who had leaned toward the anti-Kim group, had supposedly been keeping the Soviet leaders informed of Kim Il-sŏng's "errors." [79] It happened that Mikoyan was currently in Peking. Together with P'eng Teh-huai, he made a hurried, highly secret trip to P'yŏngyang in early September, just before the opening of the Eighth Party Congress of the CCP, which began in Peking on September 15. On September 23, the Central Committee met again and "decided" to restore Ch'oe Ch'ang-ik and Pak Ch'ang-ok to their Central Committee positions, and to reinstate Yun Kong-hŭm, Sŏ Hwi, and Yi P'il-gyu as Party members. The errors committed by these comrades were undoubtedly serious, the Central Committee resolution stated, but the Party had decided to treat these comrades generously, giving them the opportunity to reconsider their errors by indoctrinating them thoroughly in the correct line. The pres-

78. Once again, our anonymous source provides interesting but unverifiable details. According to him, when the anti-Kim group returned to their homes after the first day's noon recess, they found that their telephone lines had been cut and their automobiles confiscated by the police. Yun Kong-hŭm, Sŏ Hwi, and Yi P'il-gyu then gathered at the home of Kim Kang, whose automobile remained in his possession since the Kim regime had not yet fingered him. Using this car, the four left P'yŏngyang immediately without notifying their colleagues, traveling by way of Sinŭiju, the Yalu River, and Antung.

When the four did not appear in the afternoon, the Kim faction reportedly assumed that they had fled to South Korea, and immediately established cordons in an attempt to stop them. On the second day, an intensive questioning of the remaining anti-Kim elements is said to have occurred, with the ousters from office following.

79. According to our anonymous source, Pak Ch'ang-ok had been informing the Soviet government in writing of Premier Kim's "misdeeds" via Yi Sang-jo, ambassador to the USSR. However, in forwarding the second report, the group supposedly entrusted the communication to "an unreliable individual" who turned it over to the Kim Il-sŏng group, thereby producing another leak. Yi Sang-jo reportedly resigned his post and remained in the Soviet Union after the events of August.

ent need was to strengthen the ideological unity of the Party, and move forward in undertaking the revolutionary tasks confronting the nation.[80]

Precisely what Mikoyan and P'eng Teh-huai told Kim Il-sŏng and others is not known. It would appear, in any case, that this Sino-Soviet intervention in the internal affairs of the Korean Workers' Party infuriated Kim, and he was not to forget it.[81] Years later, with this incident clearly in mind, he would remark that he had had some experience with the interference of foreign parties in Korea's internal affairs.

Kim Il-sŏng had no alternative at this point except to accept the Sino-Soviet "advice." But he had no intention of allowing men like Pak and Ch'oe to regain their old influence. Thwarted at the top, the Kim forces launched an "antisectarian struggle" from below. By the beginning of 1957, under the Central Party's "concentrated guidance" campaign, provincial-level Party and government officials were mobilized to conduct attacks upon sectarianism. This campaign gradually grew in intensity throughout 1957 and early 1958, being climaxed by the First Conference of Party Representatives held in March 1958.[82]

80. For the full text of the CC resolution, see *NS,* Sept. 29, 1956, p. 1.

81. Kim Nam-sik asserts that he heard about Kim Il-sŏng's anger from those who had returned from a meeting of provincial Party chairmen. Incidentally, according to some sources, Mao Tse-tung later expressed the view to Kim that this intervention was wrong, at a time when the Chinese were wooing the North Koreans. There is also the suggestion that when Kim and his delegation arrived in Moscow in early June, before the August incident, Khrushchev did not meet with them, although he did confer with them after the East European tour, when they were en route home. The accuracy of these reports is uncertain, but they are a part of the "evidence" used on occasion to explain Kim's growing unhappiness with Khrushchev and his increasing orientation toward Peking's policies. Impersonal factors, however, would have been sufficient to account for these trends.

82. Kim Nam-sik has given us a detailed account of the "concentrated guidance" campaign, in which he participated. Beginning in early 1957, vice-chairmen of provincial governments and vice-chiefs of departments of the provincial Party were brought to P'yŏngyang for intensive indoctrination so that lower echelon personnel who were factionalists could be identified.

The methods employed can be illustrated by the campaign directed toward the National Library, whose head was then Han Pin. Kim To-man, later to be head of the Party's Propaganda and Agitation Department, was put in charge of the campaign. For some six months, meetings were held every night. At first, discussions centered on Party organizational principles and the dangers of factionalism. Then, criticisms became specific. Books at the library were placed so that Marxist-Leninist books were less prominently displayed than other books. On occasion, books about Kim Il-sŏng were put in back—and this obviously had a relation to his sectarian opponents. Ultimately, with such points being manufactured, the finger was pointed at Han Pin as the chief instigator of sectarian evils.

Kim Nam-sik recalls that, as a member of a provincial Party Propaganda Department, after his training he had the task of publicizing the "crimes" committed by so-called sectarian elements; but nothing came from central headquarters in the form of materials or guidance. Finally, following the March 1958 Representatives Conference, a headquarters official in charge of speeches came to the province and com-

By this means, Kim Il-sŏng and his followers gradually isolated their opponents, removing all local sources of support and rendering them impotent. Sometimes, in a fashion both clever and cruel, individuals marked for purging were caused to participate actively in the programs designed to undermine them. A leader like Pak Ui-wan, for example, would be sent to a conference or provincial Party meeting to make a speech condemning sectarianism. Meanwhile, instructions had been sent from Party headquarters to the local officials to discuss Pak and his speech after he had departed. Moreover, general directions for the criticism of Pak would accompany such instructions.[83] Incidentally, because it included many of the national leaders, the P'yŏngyang Municipal Party played a leading role in Kim's campaign to oust his rivals by attacks from below.

"Settling" the Problem of Factionalism

The climax came in early 1958, when the Kim Il-sŏng group decided that the time was ripe to "settle" the problem of factionalism permanently. A number of preliminary steps had been taken during 1957. On August 29, an election was conducted to select members for the Second Supreme People's Assembly. It was nine years almost to the day after the first election, which had been held on August 25, 1948. In that year, it will be recalled, the Communists claimed to have conducted not only a regular election in North Korea, but an "underground election" in the south as well. On this, indeed, they based the claim of the Democratic People's Republic of Korea to represent all of Korea. According to the DPRK constitution, a general election was to be held every four years. The regime attributed the delay to the war and the problems of postwar reconstruction. In the aftermath of the Third Party Congress and the August Incident, however, the Kim group saw significant advantages in electing a new Supreme People's Assembly.

In the election of August 1957, no attempt was made to hold "underground elections" in the south. Thus, the number of seats in the Assembly was cut from 600 to 210, and the composition of the new members was radically altered. One survey of the first Assembly has indicated that of the 600 seats, 360, or 60 percent, were held by individuals from South Korea. In the 1957 election, however, southerners obtained only 34 seats, or 16 percent of the total, while northerners took 176 seats, or 84 percent. Naturally, the regime used the elections as an occasion not only to create a northern majority, but also to rid the Assembly of "factionalists." It also presented an opportunity for leading figures of the regime to defend govern-

---

plained to Kim Nam-sik that it took innumerable drafts before Party leaders would approve a speech. This situation reflected some uncertainty about how to handle the "factionalists" as well as being the result of the fact that new "evidence" was steadily being manufactured, lesser Party officials being forced to await the production of charges substantial enough to warrant an exposé.

83. Chong-Sik Lee interview with Kim Nam-sik, March 5, 1967.

ment policies. The mass media carried pictures and stories of Kim Il-sŏng, Ch'oe Yong-gŏn, Hong Myŏng-hui, and others canvassing in their respective districts. As in other Communist states, elections represented a legitimization process that the leadership took very seriously. In an effort to induce public participation, the government sought to create a festival-like atmosphere, organizing musical contests, artists' competitions, and recreational outings (with food). The published results were highly satisfactory: 99.99 percent of the eligible electorate participated, according to government officials, and 99.92 percent voted for government-recommended candidates. In Kim Il-sŏng's district, 100 percent of the electorate voted. Naturally, they cast 100 percent of their votes for Kim.[84]

The Supreme People's Assembly was, of course, the primary government outlet for non-Party representatives. Although the real powers of the Assembly were negligible, the allocation of positions in the second Assembly reflected the status of various individuals and organizations outside the formal framework of the Korean Workers' Party, as well as the positioning of individuals inside the Party. Ch'oe Yong-gŏn was made chairman of the Assembly's Presidium, with Yi Kŭng-no (South Korean, SKWP, and Democratic Front leader), Hyŏn Ch'il-jong (an indigenous North Korean Communist and president of the Farmers' League), and Kim Won-bong (People's Republican Party) as vice-chairmen, and Kang Ryang-uk (Korean Democratic Party) as secretary. The sixteen ordinary members of the Presidium represented both Communist and officially non-Communist groups, with some care being given to symbolic representation.[85]

On September 20, Kim Il-sŏng presented his new cabinet to the

84. *NS*, Aug. 30, 1957, pp. 1–2. According to this account, 215 SPA delegates were elected on a single-member district basis. Earlier, in a detailed discussion of the criteria for a government-recommended candidate, an *NS* writer said that priorities had been given to those who had performed outstanding service in Party, government, or social organizations; had been notable administrators or workers in industrial or agricultural production; or had made creative contributions in the intellectual sphere. (See *ibid.*, July 15 and 16, 1957, pp. 1–2.)

85. The members were Pak Chŏng-ae, Kang Chin-gŏn (chairman, Korean Farmers' Union), Sŏng Chu-sik (vice-chairman of the Peoples' Republican Party), Kim Pyŏng-je (director of the Korean Literature Research Center of the Academy of Sciences), Won Hong-gu (biologist and member of the Academy of Sciences), Yi Man-gyu (Working People's Party), Yi Song-un (chairman, P'yŏngyang City KWP Central Committee), Han Sang-du (Chairman, Trade Union Federation), Kim Ch'ang-dŏk (lieutenant general and KWP leader), Chŏng No-sik (member of the Central Inspection Committee of the KWP), Kim Ch'ŏn-hae (chairman, DFUF; member of KWP Central Committee), Ha Ang-ch'ŏn (KWP Central Committee and director of the Science and School Education Bureau of the Party), Chang Hae-u (ex-SKWP member and chairman of the Fatherland Defense Supportive Association CC), Kye Ŭng-sang (from South Korea, member of the Agricultural Science Commission, Ministry of Agriculture), Yi Myŏn-sang (composer and chairman of the CC of the Korean Composers' League), and Song Yŏng (writer and member of General League of Literature and Arts).

People's Assembly for its approval. Vice-premierships were assigned to Kim Il, Hong Myŏng-hui, Chŏng Il-yong, Nam Il, Pak Ui-wan, and Chŏng Chun-t'aek. The crucial ministerial posts of Defense and Interior were assigned to Kim Kwang-hyŏp and Pang Hak-se.[86] Nam Il remained minister of Foreign Affairs, with Hŏ Chŏng-suk minister of Justice.[87] Other posts went mostly to familiar faces, but Pak Ch'ang-ok and Ch'oe Ch'ang-ik were noticeably absent from the roster, as were the great majority of their followers.[88]

It is interesting to analyze the political affiliations of these top People's Assembly and ministry officials, and then correlate that affiliation with the subsequent fate of each individual. It is helpful to divide the group into five categories: members of Kim Il-sŏng's personal circle; KWP members with other factional affiliations or backgrounds; minor Party representatives; Party intellectuals; and technicians (individuals who were Party members, but had been selected essentially for their technical skills).

Among the twenty-one Presidium members, five (Ch'oe Yong-gŏn, Pak Chŏng-ae, Yi Sŏng-ŏn, Han Sang-du and Kang Chin-gŏn) could be considered part of Kim's coterie. Each of them—except for Kang Chin-gŏn, who died in 1963—would continue to have a successful career, at least for the next decade.

Of the eight generally considered to have other factional affiliations or backgrounds, four (Yi Kŭng-no, Chŏng No-sik, Chang Hae-u, and Kye Ŭng-sang) were former members of the SKWP. One of this group (Chang)

86. Pang was a Soviet-Korean who reportedly returned to the Soviet Union shortly after being relieved of his post in November 1960. It is revealing that a Soviet-Korean would be in charge of the most sensitive security matters and of the police during this period.

87. Hŏ Chŏng-suk, whose background was Yenan, was the daughter of Hŏ Hŏn and the former wife of Ch'oe Ch'ang-ik. She had served as minister of Culture and Propaganda for nearly ten years, from September 1948 to August 1957, and was later made chief justice of the Supreme Court (October 1959 to November 1960); but in early 1961, she was purged.

88. The cabinet at this point consisted of the premier, six vice-premiers, and 25 ministers, including two without portfolio. Those named by Kim in the new cabinet in addition to the ministers listed above were Pak Mun-gyu, minister of State Supervision; Yi Chong-ok, chairman of the State Planning Commission; Pak Ui-wan, chairman of the State Construction Commission; Chŏng Il-yong, minister of the Metal Industry; Hŏ Sŏng-t'aek, minister of the Coal Industry; Yi Ch'ŏn-ho, minister of the Chemical Industry; Han Chŏn-jong, minister of Agriculture; Kim Tu-sam, minister of Electricity; Mun Man-uk, minister of Light Industry; Chu Kwang-sŏp, minister of Marine Production; Kim Hoe-il, minister of Transportation; Ch'oe Chae-u, minister of Construction and Construction Materials; Yi Chu-yŏn, minister of Finance; Chin Pan-su, minister of Internal and External Commerce; Ko Chun-t'aek, minister of Communications; Han Sŏl-ya, minister of Education; Yi Pyŏng-nam, minister of Public Health; Kim Ŭng-gi, minister of Labor; Chŏng Sŏng-ŏn, minister of Local Management; Kim Tal-hyŏn, minister without portfolio; and Hong Ku-hwang, minister without portfolio.

was purged subsequently, in 1959. Two others in this category (Kim Ch'ang-dŏk and Ha An-ch'ŏn) had Yenan backgrounds, and Ha, as we mentioned earlier, was demoted in 1965. One of the group (Kim Ch'ŏn-hae), who had come out of the Japanese Communist movement, continued to do well. Hyŏn Ch'il-jong, the last member, had a domestic Communist background in North Korea, and was purged for factionalism in early 1958. Thus, two of the eight in this category were shortly to be purged, and a third was later reduced in rank.

Four of the twenty-one (Kim Won-bong, Kang Ryang-uk, Sŏng Chu-sik, and Yi Man-gyu) were representatives of minor parties. Kim and Sŏng, from the People's Republican Party, were both purged as "international spies" in December 1958. Kang, representing the KDP, was related to Kim Il-sŏng, and naturally continued to thrive, as did Yi, formerly with the Working People's Party. Thus, casualties in this group were 50 percent.

The remaining four members of the group (Kim Pyŏng-je, Won Hong-gu, Yi Myŏn-sang, and Song Yŏng) were Party intellectuals. Each of them was to continue without mishap. There were no technicians—as we have defined the term here—among the top twenty-one members of the Assembly.

At the Cabinet level, as we have seen, there were thirty-two in all: the premier, six vice-premiers, and twenty-five cabinet ministers. Of these, only three (Kim Il, Yi Chong-ok, and Mun Man-uk) could be counted as members of Kim's personal circle. Each was to enjoy continued favor, although Mun suffered a demotion at one point.

Some twelve had other factional affiliations or backgrounds. Four of this group (Yi Pyŏng-nam, Pak Mun-gyu, Kim Ŭng-gi, and Hŏ Sŏng-t'aek) were from South Korea and had had ties with the old SKWP. Of these four, Hŏ was purged in 1959, and Yi was also relieved of his post in that year. The other two made the transition to Kim Il-sŏng's banner without further travail. Two other members of the thirteen (Yi Chu-yŏn and Han Chŏn-jong) were Communists with a domestic North Korean background, and each continued to do well. Four of the thirteen (Pak Ui-wan, Nam Il, Pang Hak-se, and Chin Pan-su) had extensive Soviet backgrounds, and most, if not all of them, had been born and raised in the Soviet Union. Pak was purged in 1958, Chin was purged in 1959, and Pang was relieved of his post late in 1960. Only Nam Il was to survive at the top of the North Korean hierarchy. Some of the others, incidentally, returned to the USSR. Finally, only one of the thirteen (Hŏ Chŏng-suk) had a Yenan background. As we have noted, Hŏ fell by the wayside in 1961.

Only six among the thirty-two could be counted as representatives of minor parties, two from the Ch'ŏndogyo Young Friends' Party (Kim Tal-hyŏn and Chu Kwang-sŏp), three from the Korean Democratic Party (Ko

Chun-t'aek, Chŏng Sŏng-ŏn, and Hong Ku-hwang), and one from the Democratic Independence Party. Both of the Ch'ŏndogyo men were shortly to run into serious trouble: Chu was relieved of his post in September 1958, and Kim was attacked as an antirevolutionary element at the end of that year. Two of the three KDP men were also to fall: Hong Ku-hwang (purged in 1958) and Chŏng (relieved of his post in 1960). Only Ko and Hong Myŏng-hui were able to move into the next decade unscathed.

One individual could be defined as a Party intellectual, namely, Han Sŏl-ya. As we have mentioned, he was to be purged as a traditionalist and liberalist in 1962, despite his monumental efforts for Kim and the Party. However, he was later permitted to return to the Central Committee before disappearing from view again. Five men (Chŏng Il-yong, Chŏng Chun-t'aek, Kim Tu-sam, Kim Hoe-il, and Ch'oe Chae-u) could be classified as technicians, and all except Chŏng Il-yong survived. We are unable to categorize Yi Ch'ŏn-ho, but he was to be relieved of his post in August 1959.

When one studies these data, several facts stand out clearly. The so-called "domestic faction," particularly those people from South Korea who had once been associated with Pak Hŏn-yŏng, had been reduced to impotence, and even for the few remaining survival was difficult. The Soviet and Yenan elements had also felt the brunt of Kim's doubt concerning their loyalty in the 1958–59 period. It was in this period, incidentally, that the Kim Il-sŏng group insisted upon ending dual citizenship for Soviet-Koreans, forcing them to choose between North Korea and the USSR. By the end of 1960, as one can see, there were extremely few Soviet and Yenan elements remaining in the top echelons of the Party and government. In fact, only those remained who had been adjudged innocent of factionalism, that is, loyal to Kim Il-sŏng.

This was also an extremely difficult period for representatives of minor parties. Their utility was low. Hence, they were easily expendable, particularly if they showed any signs of deviation from the Party line. The events in China during and immediately after the Hundred Flowers Campaign had certainly not escaped the notice of KWP leaders. There, when permitted, certain spokesmen of minor parties had publicly protested their satellite status, then been forced to make humble recantations when the antirightist campaign got under way.

At this point, the intellectuals, in the main, had been sorted out, with the ones guilty of "factionalism" or "subversive thoughts" eliminated, and the loyal ones (who in some cases were primarily apolitical) rewarded. One begins to see in this period the emergence of the technicians—men trained in the Soviet Union or elsewhere as engineers, scientists, or managers. Naturally, they were of great utility to a state so sorely lacking in high-level manpower. It should be emphasized, however, that this latter group generally occupied secondary or tertiary levels of power, and rarely penetrated the top echelon. In any case, the only relatively secure individuals were those who could count themselves among Kim's old personal friends or who were proven supporters of his policies.

With the so-called Concentrated Guidance campaign effectively blanketing local Party units, a Supreme People's Assembly that had been elected in accordance with Party instructions, and a new cabinet already inaugurated, the Kim forces were ready to deliver the coup de grace to their opponents within the Party. To be sure, the attacks upon the Pak Ch'ang-ok–Ch'oe Ch'ang-ik group had never really ceased. By the beginning of 1957, moreover, these men were once more being criticized in Party organs by name. One *Kŭlloja* writer, for example, asserted in the February 1957 issue that, contrary to the arguments of "anti-Party factionalists" such as Ch'oe, Pak, Yun Kong-hŭm, Sŏ Hwi, Yi P'il-gyu, and others—men who "were crushed in the August and September plenums of last year"—the economic policies of the government had been "consistently correct," both in the past and in the present.[89] In the July issue, an anonymous author in the important lead article, citing the same culprits, with the addition of Kim Sŭng-hwa, asserted that they had attempted to subvert the unity of the Party by "babbling about so-called freedom and the expansion of democracy, just as was done in bourgeois propaganda." The real purpose of their slogans "freedom" and "democracy" was to turn the Party into "a factionalist clique of pedagogues."[90]

By November 1957, Kim Il-sŏng was calling Ch'oe Ch'ang-ik and his group "traitors of the revolution and extremely corrupt elements" whose "conspiracy was so extremely sinister that had it not been uncovered and crushed in time, it might have brought grave consequences to our Party and our revolution."[91] Moreover, while this group had no mass base, its influence had not been wiped out completely. And as long as that "evil influence" continued, "it could be utilized by external enemies who always [sought] to subvert the Party from within." Consequently, all Party members and organizations had to be mobilized to destroy completely "the false ideology" of the factionalists. The August Plenum had done an excellent job, Kim asserted, and many Party members had recognized their errors and confessed them frankly before the Party. Such individuals had taken

89. Pak Yŏn-baek, "The Historical Significance of the Second Party Congress," *Kŭlloja (The Worker)*, Feb. 1957, pp. 23–34.

90. "The Leninist Unity of the CPSU Is Invulnerable," *Kŭlloja (The Worker)*, July 25, 1957. The author ended with the assertion that some comrades rejected Party assignments on the score that the work was not suited to their personality or tastes. But this was incorrect. The need was to combine individuality and Party loyalty, eliminating the substantial elements of individualistic psychology and liberalism that still remained, even among Party members. Only strenuous ideological study and self-criticism, as well as the assistance of other comrades, would correct these defects.

91. Kim Il-sŏng, "The Friendship and Solidarity of Socialist Countries," *Kŭlloja (The Worker)*, Nov. 25, 1957, pp. 8–15.

the first step in being restored to the Party's confidence and trust. Others, however, had refused to confess, slipping back into factional, anti-Party, antirevolutionary activities. In this vein, Kim signaled his determination to destroy the Ch'oe-Pak groups completely.

The occasion used was the First Conference of Representatives of the Korean Workers' Party, which met from the third to the sixth of March 1958, in P'yŏngyang, to discuss the first Five-Year Plan, "problems of Party unity and solidarity," and organizational issues.[92] On the second day of the Conference, Pak Kŭm-ch'ŏl launched the final assault. In a lengthy speech, he charged that some people had taken advantage of "generous Party policies" to continue their factional mischief, "raising their heads at a time of grave national and Party crisis." Recently disclosed information, moreover, revealed that Ch'oe Ch'ang-ik and Pak Ch'ang-ok's factionalism had gone beyond the usual anti-Party factionalism. "It was antirevolutionary activity which they had been plotting for a long time." As was the case with other factionalists, they lacked specific programs— except for their ambition to acquire hegemony over the Party and the government. But they had chosen a time when the international reactionaries had strengthened their anti-Communist, anti-Soviet campaign, when the Rhee clique had renewed its clamor for a march to the north, and when the nation was engaged in the difficult tasks of postwar economic reconstruction.

They had attacked the Party and government, Pak Kŭm-ch'ŏl continued, with revisionist slogans and theories, seeking to deny the Party's leading role in the settlement of problems involved in the socialist revolution, and even seeking to place the trade unions above the Party. They had opposed the principles of democratic centralism that constituted the basis of Marxism-Leninism, demanding "unprincipled intraparty democracy and freedom for factional activities." They had even gone so far as to advocate a theory that factionalism had advantages. All of this indicated their sinister attempts to introduce anarchistic confusion into the Party, not to mention the "nasty and shameless slanders" they had aimed at Party leaders. While pretending to uphold legal procedures and defend human rights, the Ch'oe faction had violated the most basic precepts of people's democracy, turning instead to rightist surrender and bourgeois freedom.

Pak Kŭm-ch'ŏl then turned to the international scene. The Ch'oe faction had sought to undermine the traditional friendship of the KWP with the Parties of other countries, and had plotted to make the DPRK a neutral country by separating it from the socialist camp headed by the Soviet Union. Thus, they had attacked the KWP leadership aggressively at Central Committee Plenum sessions, while at the same time privately organizing demonstrations and rebellions against both the Party and the government. None of this was unprecedented. Ch'oe Ch'ang-ik, after all,

92. For detailed reports, see *NS*, March 4–7, 1958, pp. 1–4.

had been a leader of the M-L Group in the 1920s, and had inflicted serious damage upon the Korean labor movement at that time by waging factional struggles under the pretext of eliminating factionalism.

All of this, asserted Pak Kŭm-ch'ŏl, proved that the August Plenum decision was a correct one. The Party would continue its policy of reforming followers by means of reindoctrination while severely punishing their leaders, as had been done at the time of the struggle against the Pak Hŏn-yŏng–Yi Sŭng-yŏp group.

Kim Il-sŏng, in the concluding address before the Conference, reiterated the basic themes set forth by Pak, and revealed that Kim Tu-bong was among those leaders scheduled for "severe punishment."

> We worked with Kim Tu-bong for ten years. But during those years he nurtured an evil dream. While remaining uncommunicative with us, he opened up his heart only to Han Pin and Ch'oe Ch'ang-ik.
> Despite the fact that the Party hated Han Pin as an element subversive of our Party, Kim Tu-bong found in him his closest friend. If Kim Tu-bong had ever been a Communist, if he had ever been a man who worked for the sake of the Party, how are we to interpret his having been on the most intimate terms with a man hated by the Party? . . . Kim Tu-bong used to bring forth some new proposal each time he had been to Han Pin's house and spent a night there. His proposals were all aimed at undermining our Party.[93]

Finally, Kim Il-sŏng came to the point. "The crime of Kim Tu-bong is really serious. He spoiled no small number of young people. The Party and the government gave assignments to simple and honest people to work at the Presidium of the Supreme People's Assembly. However, many of them were ruined there." [94]

Kim Il-sŏng's speech reveals further charges against various individuals being purged. His main attack was leveled at Ch'oe Ch'ang-ik, whom he now equated with Pak Hŏn-yŏng, although no specific charges of treason were raised. Other "factionalists" condemned by Kim for this "distrust of the Party" and suspicion of others included Yu Ch'uk-un and General Kim Ung, formerly chief of the General Staff. O Ki-sŏp once again was purged; he was accused by Kim of "individualist heroism," a fault characterized by "disloyalty to the Party, careerism, and a thirst for fame." Sŏ Hwi was charged with wanting to free the Trade Union Federation from Party control. As noted earlier, General Kim Ŭl-gyu was accused of having talked about the KPA not being an army of the Party, but an army of the Democratic Front.

93. "For the Successful Fulfillment of the First Five-Year Plan," Concluding Speech at the First Conference of the Workers' Party of Korea, March 6, 1958, in Kim Il Sung, *Selected Works* (1965 ed.), Vol. I, *op. cit.,* pp. 341–372 (at 364–366).
94. *Ibid.,* p. 367.

"All these are ideological viewpoints that reject Party leadership," stated Kim Il-sŏng. What, then, should be done to people like Kim Tu-bong, Pak Ui-wan, and O Ki-sŏp? So far, he asserted, there was no evidence that they had taken part in any conspiracy to stage a counterrevolutionary revolt (in distinction from Ch'oe and Pak Ch'ang-ok). However, Kim Tu-bong and Pak Ui-wan had been seeking to oust the Party leadership, and O, while not openly carrying out such factional activities, "was caught doing it stealthily like some stray cat." While these individuals now admitted their wrongdoings, they had done so only when confronted with the evidence. "They are still two-faced, and do not open their hearts to the Party."

As for Kim Tu-bong, Pak Ui-wan, and O Ki-sŏp, said Kim Il-sŏng, they should be given as much as they had "earned." (In short, let the punishment fit the crime!)

Interestingly, Kim Il-sŏng did not mention Pak Ch'ang-ok, one of his leading opponents. According to some sources, Pak Ch'ang-ok had reached a safe haven, having fled to the Soviet Union. Other sources claim that Pak was assigned to a brick or cement factory as an assistant manager or ordinary laborer. Kim Sŭng-hwa definitely did return to the USSR, where he became a researcher.[95] A number of Soviet-Koreans reportedly did likewise during this period. Ch'oe Ch'ang-ik's fate is not known. Kim Tu-bong reportedly was put to work as a laborer in an agricultural and livestock farm.

At least ninety prominent persons in North Korea were purged or removed from office in the 1958–59 period. Some thirty of these, as we noted earlier, were non-Party figures, mostly from South Korea, who were members of the Communist-sponsored Council in North Korea for the Peaceful Unification of the Fatherland. Others were leaders of minor parties. Once the crisis within the Party was settled decisively, the Kim group professed to find similar "dangers" outside the Party. Another small group of Party intellectuals were also brought under attack and expelled.[96] But the main brunt of the attack fell upon the so-called Soviet and Yenan factions.

95. We have had occasion earlier to cite his study of the Korean revolutionary movement, published in Russian after his return to the Soviet Union. See Chapter I.
96. As noted above, the search for "bourgeois remnants" within North Korean literary and artistic circles continued feverishly after the August 1956 incident. In January 1957, for example, a Standing Committee meeting of the CC, KWP, adopted a resolution to liquidate bourgeois ideology completely and support socialist realism in the arts. An Mak, a well-known literary critic educated in the prewar era at Waseda University and a man who had reached the position of vice-minister of Culture and Propaganda, Ch'oe Sŭng-hui, a famous dancer and director of the State Dance Theatre as well as An Mak's wife, and several others were brought under criticism, together with their followers. Later, in 1959, as we shall see, An Mak was purged as a "traditionalist" and "reactionary," and his wife also got into deep trouble.

The Supremacy of Kim Il-sŏng

In sum, what were the most significant political developments of this period? First in importance was the consolidation of the Korean Workers' Party and the Korean People's Army—the two essential instruments of power—under the tight control of Kim Il-sŏng and those whom he considered loyal to him personally. Most of them were old comrades from the days of anti-Japanese partisan guerrilla struggles in Manchuria. There was some truth in the assertion of Kim and his group that factionalism had finally been liquidated during this period, especially after 1958. At least, those factions born in the pre-1945 era appeared to have been totally crushed. Only one significant faction survived—that of Kim Il-sŏng.

To insure the supremacy of the Kim faction, the cult of personality was raised to new heights during this period. Kim's early exploits as a guerrilla fighter were magnified out of all proportion to their significance; indeed, the truth was left far behind. Kim's statements were now all ex cathedra pronouncements, and complete obedience to them became the criterion for being considered a good Communist. Kim himself was deified, in song, verse, and story. All of this was perhaps the more remarkable because it occurred at the very time when de-Stalinization broke upon the Communist world like a clap of thunder, the cult of personality being one of the primary issues. Kim and his followers, to be sure, paid lip service to collective leadership and, as we have seen, even sought to pin the error of "excessive personal heroism" upon the tattered Pak Hŏn-yŏng forces. Such efforts, however, were both crude and short-lived. The central trend of the period was the enhancement of Kim, the Leader, to a point beyond the reach of mortal man. The cult of Stalin in its most excessive phases was now equaled—or surpassed.

Apart from this effort to personalize loyalty, supplementing institutions with a charismatic leader, the Kimists also introduced a new weapon to insure victory over their internal opponents: nationalism. It was in this period, as we have seen, that the concept of chuch'e was first emphasized and various nationalist symbols reintroduced. After years as a perfect satellite, North Korea in this era showed the first timid signs of making independent decisions. As we have noted, the new trend was intimately connected with internal factional strife, notably the struggle between the Kimists and the Soviet- or Chinese-oriented groups led by Pak Ch'ang-ok, Ch'oe Ch'ang-ik, and Kim Tu-bong. It also related, however, to developments in post-Stalinist Russia and to the general increase in Chinese influence over North Korea. As we shall note, homage to the Soviet Union by no means disappeared. For the first time, however, Korean Communist spokesmen, led by Kim Il-sŏng himself, placed some emphasis upon the Korean way, and began to talk of the Korean Revolution.

In broader terms, this period witnessed the first beginnings of a change in the character of the political elite. At the top, as we have observed, there was a progressive narrowing of the authority structure. The old factional coalitions were irreparably broken. Kim Il-sŏng emerged as the sole leader, and around him were grouped a coterie of faithful followers, most of them "old guerrillas." These were men who had been with him since the 1930s, although the coterie included a few who had demonstrated loyalty in the post-Liberation era. Most of these men were poorly educated in formal terms. They had had to pick up what they knew along the way, mainly through military experience and education. They varied considerably, moreover, in native ability. Only in their loyalty to Kim did they share a common denominator.

Beneath them, however, was emerging a new, postwar generation. As we have noted, the Communists during this period scored considerable successes in rebuilding the Party and other mass organizations. Indeed, on paper at least, no people was as thoroughly organized as the North Koreans. Out of a population of scarcely ten million, the Party alone claimed more than a million members. Youth, women, farmers, workers, each had special organizations; as we have seen, they were large in scale and designed to reinforce the Party. Under these circumstances, the typical Party cadre now making his way upward was a northerner, under 40, somewhat better educated than his seniors, who had had no experience with the old factions. With the purge of the Pak Hŏn-yŏng faction and the election of the Second Supreme People's Assembly, the influence of southerners in the DPRK became negligible.[97] Very few of the middle-echelon Party and government leaders, moreover, had had any pre-1945 "revolutionary" experience. The great bulk of them, as we have noted, had entered the Party between 1945 and 1950, and came from peasant or worker backgrounds. Indeed, the Korean Workers' Party was to a great extent a peasant party at the grass roots. Even now, it had comparatively few industrial workers, and most of these were first-generation peasants. The old guerrillas at the top distrusted intellectuals profoundly, and no group, with the exception of the rural gentry, had had a more serious problem of survival. A new elite, however, was emerging—a technical-managerial elite possessed of those skills so essential to the one-generation industrial revolution to which the Party was so thoroughly committed. This group was still very small and politically inconsequential. But its star could be glimpsed on the distant horizon, or so it seemed. If "old intellectuals" were disappearing, "new intellectuals" were emerging.

Finally, some changes in institutional structure and function were attempted during this period. As Party unity was imposed at the top,

97. After the purges in 1957–1958 of Hŏ Sŏng-t'aek, Yu Ch'uk-un, Yi In-ju, Song Ŭl-su, and Kim Sang-hyŏk, the old South Korean Workers' Party element was almost completely excluded from Party or governmental positions of true importance. Only Ch'oe Wŏn-t'aek and Pak Mun-gyu remained, and they had become Kim Il-sŏng men.

"local autonomy" was encouraged for the bottom. This "autonomy" had nothing to do with the right to make decisions concerning basic policy, and still less with any element of independence at the ideological level. "Bourgeois liberalism" in all its forms remained anathema. Rather, it signified a determination on the part of the central government to place heavier responsibilities upon local units for mobilizing resources—human and material—and executing programs already carefully defined at higher levels. The capacities of national institutions were still limited, especially in the light of the economic priorities that had been established. Moreover, the historic operative unit of Korean society had been a local one. Could that unit, now encased in a new national structure, be utilized for the purposes at hand? Precisely what the formidable organizational efforts of the Communists meant to the average citizen, we shall explore in chapter IX. Here it is sufficient to indicate that the Korean Communists, like their Chinese counterparts, sought—in part unconsciously—to utilize traditional as well as modern modes of organization, indigenous as well as foreign-derived administrative units.

Economic Development on the Soviet Model

Accompanying all these political trends and interacting with them were economic developments of major significance. Let us now explore the more important of these, leaving many of the details to the special chapters on agriculture and industry.

On August 5, 1953, less than a fortnight after the signing of the armistice that ended the Korean War, Kim Il-sŏng, in a report before the KWP Central Committee, had outlined the basic principles that would govern postwar reconstruction.[98] Henceforth, industrialization would receive top priority. It was entirely proper, stated Kim, that their first concern during the war had been with agrarian production. But now Korea must be developed as a modern society, with the creation of an industrial base that eliminated "the colonial one-sidedness" produced in the Japanese era. Moreover, the first industries that should be constructed or reconstructed were those "basic industrial establishments" that could "accelerate the general rehabilitation and development of the national economy," namely, iron and steel, machine tools, shipbuilding, mining, electric power, chemicals, and building materials, in that order.[99] Kim and his regime, like their Chinese comrades, had clearly opted for a Soviet-style development model, with the primary emphasis upon heavy industry.

98. "The Struggle for Post-War Rehabilitation and Development of National Economy and Party's Future Tasks in Connection with Signing of Armistice Agreement," Report Delivered at the Sixth Plenum of the Central Committee of the Korean Workers' Party, August 5, 1953, in Kim Il Sung, *For Socialist Economic Construction in Our Country, op. cit.,* pp. 1–41.

99. *Ibid.,* pp. 2–7.

Reconstruction, Kim asserted, should proceed in terms of three stages: first, a preparatory period of six months to one year during which the basic plans should be drafted and preparations made for their execution; second, a three-year program with the fundamental object of restoring the economy to the pre-1950 level; third, the Three-Year Plan, to be followed by a Five-Year Plan for the general industrialization of the country.

Naturally, Kim did not omit other aspects of the economy from his report. Second priority would go to light industry; textile production in particular had to be increased. Transport, especially railroads, had to be rehabilitated as quickly as possible. With respect to agriculture, Kim sounded a cautious note, suggesting that major changes were not likely to occur soon. An individual peasant economy would continue to exist. The first task was to increase the peasants' productivity by expanding the acreage under irrigation, popularizing new farming methods, and making available high-yield seeds and more fertilizer. Starting from 1954, agricultural cooperatives would be organized on an experimental basis in certain areas, but they would be subject to "the principle of preserving private ownership of land and farm implements." State-owned farms would also be established.[100] However, the primary emphasis at this point would be upon increasing production.

The cities and towns of North Korea also had to be rebuilt. Kim announced that the ministry of City Construction was to be reorganized as the ministry of City Management. He outlined an elaborate, phased program of urban reconstruction, with both temporary and permanent buildings envisaged.

Where would the funds for this program come from? On August 8, in a closing speech before the Plenum, Kim announced that the Soviet Union and the People's Republic of China had both promised to render as much aid as possible in meeting the needs for the rapid reconstruction of the country.[101] The USSR would provide a gift of one billion rubles. Other Communist states would also assist, demonstrating a true fraternal spirit.

Nevertheless, Kim's program was certain to require massive sacrifices on the part of every North Korean citizen, and particularly the farmers and workers. Kim himself recognized this from the outset, and constantly exhorted the Party to prepare the people for the hardships they would have to endure. He admitted, moreover, that inexperience, waste, and weariness

100. *Ibid.,* p. 11. Kim seemed particularly interested in the creation of state stock farms, noting that, despite the gift of "hundreds of thousands of cows and sheep from the Mongolian comrades," the livestock problem was acute. In addition to state stock farms, he urged the creation of agro-stock cooperatives.

101. "All for the Post-War Rehabilitation and Development of the National Economy," Conclusion Made at the Sixth Plenum of the CC of the Korean Workers' Party, August 8, 1953, in Kim Il Sung, *For Socialist Economic Construction in Our Country, op. cit.,* pp. 41–65.

were serious problems in both the industrial and agrarian sectors. The industrial labor force, for example, was such that less than 4 percent had worked in industry for more than ten years. Agrarian productivity was abysmally low. Above all, the people were bone-tired after the long struggle to survive. The call, nevertheless, was for a maximum expenditure of energy —for an indefinite period.

Even before the Sixth Plenum met, and before the armistice was signed, a ten-man North Korean delegation, headed by minister of Commerce Yi Chu-yŏn, had been visiting various Communist capitals. They did not return until the end of November, having spent five months discussing North Korea's reconstruction needs with officials of various Eastern European nations, as well as those of Mongolia and North Vietnam. Meanwhile, Kim Il-sŏng himself made two separate trips during the fall of 1953 to the big Communist states, the USSR and the CPR. On September 1, he left P'yŏngyang for Moscow via railway, accompanied by Pak Chŏng-ae, Chŏng Il-yong, Nam Il, Chŏng Chun-t'aek, Kim Hoe-il, Hŏ Chŏng-suk, Kim Hyŏng-guk, and Shin Chun-t'aek, a delegation that included most of those responsible for economic development at the top level. Discussions were held with almost all key Soviet officials during the two weeks the delegation remained in Moscow.

In his report to the Supreme People's Assembly on December 20, Kim stated that discussions had centered upon how to use the one billion ruble aid, and that it was agreed that these funds would be used to reconstruct major factories and institutions, with industry and transport at the head of a long list of needs that included communications, agriculture, and education.[102] It was to be a crash program. Three-quarters of the aid would be given in 1954, the remainder coming in 1955. The Soviet government, Kim stated, had also agreed to cancel more than one-half of the wartime debt contracted by North Korea, and to postpone the time of repayment for the remainder.

Kim's report did not conclude merely with this good news. During November, he and another cabinet-level delegation had visited Peking. The discussions, conducted between November 14 and 22, had "greatly strengthened economic and cultural cooperation" between the DPRK and the CPR, Kim announced. China had canceled the entire debt contracted between June 25, 1950, and December 31, 1953, and had agreed to give North Korea aid totaling 800 million yuan between 1954 and 1957, with 300 million yuan to be furnished during the first year. These funds would be used primarily for supplies of food, textiles, cotton, and coal, as well as construction materials and machinery. During 1954, Kim stated, the

102. For the full text of Kim's report, see *NS,* Dec. 22, 1953, pp. 1–4. Specifically, Russian funds would be used to reconstruct the Kim Ch'aek Iron and Steel Plant, the Hungnam Fertilizer Plant, the Namp'o Refinery, the Sup'ung Power Station, and a number of other plants and facilities.

Chinese would provide North Korea with 100,000 tons of grain, several tens of millions of meters of cloth, fishing boats, coal, and other equipment. Moreover, China would assist in the rehabilitation of North Korea's railway system.

Thus, while the Soviet Union was to play the major role in the construction of the basic industrial complex, China was to provide the North Koreans with sufficient necessities of life, and also play a role in such areas as transport to the extent her capacities allowed. Each of the Eastern European Communist countries, moreover, had agreed to undertake some rehabilitation projects as their contribution. The Czech government, for example, would rehabilitate the cement factories and power stations in the Hŏch'ŏn River, Mojin River, and Pujŏn River areas; the Polish government had agreed to refurbish three coal mines and to construct a locomotive factory and repair shop; the Hungarians would build a chemical factory and a dye works among other things; the East Germans had agreed to construct a diesel engine factory, an electric bulb factory, and a printing machine factory; other commitments had been made by the Romanians, Bulgarians, and Albanians. In essence, foreign Communist aid to North Korea was to proceed on a package basis, with each of the assisting states, large and small, assuming responsibility for the complete rehabilitation of some plant, industry, facility, or town.

The preparatory period to which Kim referred in his report of August 1953 was considered to be over at the beginning of 1954, which was therefore proclaimed the first year of the Three-Year Plan. It is instructive to peruse Party organs during the first months of this year. A combination of articles and pictures sought to tell a story of rapid development and new hope. Beneath the surface, however, one could discern ample evidence of incredible hardship and serious morale problems. The mass media carried innumerable stories about the arrival of construction materials, necessities of life, and technicians from "our fraternal allies." There can be no question but that the Communist world moved quickly to avert the collapse of North Korea. Railcar loads of food arrived from China, sometimes pulled by the same locomotive that brought steel and other construction materials from Russia. Science students could be seen in P'yŏngyang laboratories wearing Chinese winter clothing.

Both North Korean and Chinese soldiers were also thrown into the breach. As early as 1953, they had jointly begun to rebuild the major railway bridge leading into P'yŏngyang. News pictures showed them working with the peasants at seeding and harvest times. *Nodong Sinmun* also ran pictures of P'yŏngyang "rising from the ashes," as reconstruction of the city commenced after military and civilian personnel had cleaned at least some of the debris away. New buildings, most of them of Soviet design and from Soviet materials, began to appear.[103]

103. According to Ch'oe Kwang-sŏk, a heated argument among Party leaders developed somewhat later in connection with the reconstruction of P'yŏngyang and

Kim Il-sŏng outlined some of the problems in a speech of March 21, 1954, before the Central Committee.[104] Everything had to be done at once, he admitted. Temporary dwellings had to be erected for hundreds of thousands of displaced people, and food provided for them. At the same time, there had to be enough work animals and tools to get the peasants started again. Mills and factories had to be rehabilitated speedily, but rehabilitation of transport facilities was an immediate necessity. Everything had a high priority. Unfortunately, Korean administrative and managerial capacities were still extremely limited. Once again, Kim vigorously attacked "formalism" and "bureaucratism" as major obstacles to progress. At the same time he sketched the goals of the Three-Year Plan. Using 1949 as a base, heavy industry was to reach 120 percent, light industry 137 percent, and chemical and building materials industries 90 percent. In short, said Kim, almost all branches of the national economy would reach or far exceed the pre-Korean War level of production by the end of 1956.[105]

On August 14, 1956, some two years and eight months after the Plan was officially launched, it was announced that each industrial field had overfulfilled its Plan quota. A major success was claimed. The date was chosen, of course, to coincide with the August 15 celebrations of liberation from Japanese rule. At the end of the year, the government provided a huge array of statistics to demonstrate the gains made in industrial development during the previous three years.[106]

The major gains were in heavy industry, particularly metallurgy, machine tools, electric power, chemicals, and mining—industries receiving priorities in terms of investment and trained personnel.[107] Some 80 percent of the state capital investment for industrial construction had been allocated

---

other cities. One group, led by Kim Sŭng-hwa, then minister of Construction, were against the use of prefabricated processes, holding that buildings so constructed would have to be rebuilt within a few years at great cost; hence, while it would take somewhat longer, "more solid structures" should be built. Chong-Sik Lee interview with Ch'oe Kwang-sŏk, Seoul, Nov. 24, 1966.

In his speech before the October Plenum of the Central Committee, Oct. 19, 1957, Kim Il-sŏng referred to this controversy, castigating Kim Sŭng-hwa and other "anti-Party" elements for delaying construction. See "Concluding Speech Made at the October Plenum, Central Committee, Workers' Party of Korea," Oct. 19, 1957, in Kim Il Sung, *For Socialist Economic Construction in Our Country, op. cit.*, pp. 343–344.

104. "Defects in Industry and Transport and the Immediate Task Confronting the Party, State and Economic Organs and Their Personnel for Removing the Defects," Report Made at the Plenary Meeting of the CC, Workers' Party of Korea, March 21, 1954, in *ibid.*, pp. 79–123.

105. *Ibid.*, p. 81.

106. For the report of the Central Statistical Bureau, State Planning Commission, on the Conclusion of the Three-Year Plan, see *NS*, Feb. 24, 1957, pp. 1–2. For additional data, see Chapter XIV of this study.

107. The Bureau claimed that the following percentages of Three-Year Plan goals had been reached, based upon ministry-wide figures: ministry of Metal Industry, 135 percent; ministry of Coal Industry, 110 percent; ministry of Machine Industry,

to the heavy industrial sector, and that sum represented nearly 40 percent of the total state investment for the period of the Plan. Soviet assistance, moreover, had been heavily concentrated in this area. The statistics released by the government appear more spectacular than the actual development warranted, because the base lines used were those of 1949 and 1953. As we remarked earlier, 1949, while representing a significant improvement over the earliest postwar years, was far from the peak production of the Japanese era, and 1953 was an extremely bad year, as can be imagined. For instance, the government admitted that during that year not a ton of chemical fertilizer was produced.

Nevertheless, the data confirm the basic economic trends outlined earlier. North Korea had been committed to Soviet-model development. The crucial priorities, both in terms of domestic and foreign input, had gone to heavy industry. As a result, very substantial progress was recorded during the course of the Three-Year Plan. A considerable gap, however, was developing between gross national product and living standards. With a few exceptions, consumer-goods industries were growing very slowly. Wages remained low and, as we shall see shortly, agrarian development constituted the regime's major economic problem. This gap had political repercussions. By 1956, the Kim group was under severe attack from factional opponents for ignoring the miserable plight of the average citizen in its "over-emphasis" upon heavy industry.

Transport and communication had also received considerable attention. Alert to the military as well as the economic importance of these aspects of the infrastructure, the DPRK government had invested more in them than in the agrarian sector, and a large portion of the destroyed facilities had been rebuilt. Foreign trade, almost all of it with the Communist bloc, was also increasing at a reasonably satisfactory rate. Agriculture, however, constituted a major bottleneck, as the Communists themselves, in moments of candor, admitted. Indeed, in the midst of the Three-Year Plan, Kim Il, minister of Agriculture, was forced to acknowledge that agricultural goals were unrealistic and had to be scaled down, and also that state investment in this sector of the economy was too low and had to be increased by 26.7 percent more than had originally been planned.

Even so, production fell below official hopes. In an effort to provide the basis for more rapid modernization, the regime decided to accelerate the agricultural cooperative program. Thus, by the end of the Three-Year Plan, it was announced that four-fifths of all farm households had been incorporated into cooperatives. With agriculture being collectivized at a rapid rate, the government could assert that whereas the "socialist form of production" had involved only 45 percent of the economy in 1949, by the

---

158 percent; ministry of Electricity, 125 percent; ministry of Chemical Industry, 122 percent. *NS*, Feb. 24, 1957, p. 1.

end of 1956 it extended to 82 percent, the agrarian sector having gone from 3.2 percent to 73.9 percent.[108]

Agricultural Policies Under the Three-Year Plan

The cooperative movement was not just a product of ideological commitment; it grew directly out of the economic ravages of the Korean War. The campaign for cooperativization was first signaled by Kim Il-sŏng himself in a speech of February 16, 1954, when he indicated that rural conditions could not be improved under the "individual economy system," and called for the "voluntary cooperation" of all farmers in pooling land and labor power.[109] A few months later, in November 1954, Kim acknowledged that agriculture was lagging behind industry in growth. In the near future, he asserted, annual grain output was to be boosted to 2.9 or 3 million tons (the official 1954 figure was 2,230,000 tons), annual meat output to between 100,000 and 200,000 tons, and the annual output of textiles to between 150 and 200 million meters.[110]

Kim's report in the fall of 1954 became the blueprint for North Korean agriculture over the remainder of the Three-Year Plan and beyond. The government, however, continued to receive some rude shocks. Kim, in his November speech, had assumed an optimistic air, even asking that the grain target be raised for 1955 from 3.2 to 3.6 million metric tons. By the time of the April Plenum, however, the government had been forced to scale down its agrarian production goals drastically, and increase its investment in this sector, although it did not fully admit as much until the end of the year. Serious food shortages continued through 1954 and 1955, a fact not admitted by the government until the end of 1956.[111]

Official government statistics on grain production (in 1,000 tons) were as follows:[112]

1953	1954	1955	1956	1957	1958
2,327	2,230	2,340	2,873	3,201	3,700

108. Central Statistical Bureau report, *ibid.*, p. 2.

109. "Grain—An Important Key to the Solution of All Problems in the Post-War Reconstruction," Speech Made at the National Conference of Active Bumper Crop Raisers [*sic*], Feb. 16, 1954, in Kim Il Sung, *For Socialist Economic Construction in Our Country, op. cit.*, pp. 66–78 (at 72).

110. "On the Policy of Our Party for Further Developing Agriculture," Concluding Speech Made at the Plenum of the CC of the Workers' Party of Korea, November 3, 1954, in *ibid.*, pp. 143–165 (at 145–146).

111. Natural calamities, together with wartime destruction, were blamed for the shortages.

112. Chosŏn Chungang T'ongshinsa (Korean Central News Agency), *Chosŏn chungang nyŏngam (Korean Central Yearbook)*, P'yŏngyang, 1958 ed., p. 27. As we shall indicate later, the figures for 1957 and 1958 at least are grossly inflated. More reliable production estimates for those two years are 2,995 and 2,878 thousand metric tons. What element of inflation is involved in earlier figures, it is difficult to say. 1944 production in North Korea, it may be recalled, was 2,417 metric tons.

Meanwhile, the cooperatives program proceeded at full speed. At the end of 1956, with the Three-Year Plan completed, the government announced that whereas only 1.2 percent of all farm households had been in cooperatives in 1953, there were now over 15,000 agricultural cooperatives comprising 80.9 percent of all farm households and 77.9 percent of all cultivated land.[113]

In the agricultural section of the final report on the Three-Year Plan, the government emphasized the increased investment it had allotted to the agrarian sector, the expansion of irrigation facilities, the increase in available supplies of chemical fertilizer, the success of the cooperatives program, and, finally, the significant increase in grain production in 1956. The claim of 2,873,000 tons, or a production 24 percent greater than that of 1953, is probably inflated. It is possible, however, that in 1956, for the first time, grain production in North Korea reached or came close to reaching the 1949 level (2,654,000 tons). Interestingly, the report indicated that state farms and cooperatives (supposedly cultivating 77.9 percent of the land) had accounted for 72 percent of the total grain production. Obviously, collectivization was not yet an outstanding success.

The Three-Year Plan Assessed

In addition to its economic consequences, the Three-Year Plan had an almost immediate impact upon the Korean social structure. Industrialization was rapidly increasing the number of urban blue- and white-collar workers. By the end of the Plan, some 40 percent of the working population fell into these two categories, as against somewhat over 56 percent in the "farmer" category. Compared to earlier ratios, this was a major change. Moreover, "bourgeois" elements at this point had been reduced to insignificance. According to official statistics, national income had doubled between 1953 and 1956, but the major gains were in the production of the means of production (to use North Korean terms), with decidedly smaller gains in consumer goods and foods. Unquestionably, however, the so-called socialist sector of the economy greatly increased during this period, largely as a result of developments in agriculture.

Along with a substantial increase in the urban labor force, significant increases in labor productivity were claimed. The improvements were attributed partly to the fact that, during the Three-Year Plan, some 800 foreign trainees and 11,000 graduates of indigenous colleges and technical institutes had been channeled into productive enterprises. In addition, 32,000 graduates of workers' technical training courses had taken up productive labor.[114]

Measured in terms of the regime's objectives, the Three-Year Plan was a striking success. Supplied with massive amounts of foreign aid, focusing

113. Central Statistical Bureau report, *op. cit.*, p. 2. For details, see Chap. XIII.
114. *Ibid.*

attention largely upon certain specific economic goals, and mobilizing almost every citizen through a political system that maintained a rigorous control, the Korean Communist leaders had made some crucial gains in the terribly difficult first years after the Korean War. In contrast to the fumblings that were taking place in South Korea, heavy industrial production had moved ahead rapidly. To service it, a new managerial-technical class was being created, albeit more slowly than was required for true efficiency and high quality production. On the other side of the ledger, however, agricultural production, together with production in most consumer industries, remained a serious and unresolved problem. All defectors, as well as the few independent sources having extensive contact with North Korea during this period, testify to the fact that, for the average citizen, living conditions were extremely bad; there were serious food shortages, while most other necessities were inadequate in amount and very poor in quality. Nor did living conditions improve greatly during this period, government statistics notwithstanding. Thus, the charges of Yun Kong-hŭm at the fateful meeting of August 30, 1956, must have stung the Kim Il-sŏng faction to the quick.

Political exhortations to sacrifice willingly for state, Party, Leader, and people were powerful, as we have seen. Once again, the North Korean citizen was committed—whether he liked it or not—to a war. It was not a war against the "bourgeoisie" or the UN forces, but against backwardness. The terminology used, however, was frequently the same as had been applied to the earlier wars. It appeared that Kim Il-sŏng and his old guerrilla fighters—like the Maoists—were incapable of thinking in any but martial terms. Thus, every citizen was to engage in a "militant struggle." There was to be no relaxation, and no compromise with the forces of evil—waste, corruption, and bureaucratism. It was necessary to "charge" production quotas, climbing over them with the cry of victory on one's lips. In this fashion, Marshal Kim sought to summon the troops to another series of battles.

The Five-Year Plan

In 1957, the Five-Year Plan was launched. Shortly thereafter, North Koreans were told that development had to move at an even faster rate. Unquestionably influenced by Mao's Great Leap Forward, Kim Il-sŏng unveiled his own Ch'ŏllima (Flying Horse) Campaign.[115] By late 1958, it was in full swing. During the same period, it was announced that agricultural cooperatives now encompassed every farm household, and that the traditional family farm had been totally eliminated. Thus, in economic terms, the years that lay immediately ahead after 1956 were of considerable sig-

---

115. According to Kim Nam-sik, the Ch'ŏllima Movement was actually launched shortly after the December 1956 Plenum, but the term was not applied until somewhat later. Chong-Sik Lee interview with Kim Nam-sik, Seoul, March 6, 1967.

nificance. After the crisis of August 1956, North Korea attained an even higher degree of internal political stability. The harshest years of the postwar period were presumably over. Rudimentary needs could now be met in more adequate fashion. A fund of administrative experience had been acquired, and a new labor force at least partially trained. To what extent could these developments result in greater production, and—more importantly for the average North Korean—in raising the standard of living?

In an effort to suggest answers to these basic questions, let us look at the key developments under the Five-Year Plan. In an important speech before the second Supreme People's Assembly on September 20, 1957, Kim Il-sŏng summarized the purposes of the Plan.

> The basic tasks provided for in the Five-Year Plan lie in further consolidating the economic foundation of socialism in the northern part of the Republic and in solving in the main the food, clothing, and housing questions facing the people.
>
> By further developing the industrial productive forces, we must lay the groundwork for socialist industrialization which will make it possible to equip all the branches of the national economy with modern techniques and launch capital construction on a wider scale.
>
> During the Five-Year Plan period, agricultural collectivization will have to be completed, and the socialist economic pattern be further consolidated in all the domains of the national economy.[116]

The main objective of the Three-Year Plan had been to recover from the Korean War. Thus, the primary effort had been reconstruction rather than growth, although various leaders had pointed out the advantages of replacing antiquated machinery and outmoded plants with new equipment. As Kim indicated in his remarks, the purpose of the new plan was to construct a socialist, industrial society, with the collectivization of agriculture scheduled for rapid completion.

Kim Il-sŏng himself asserted firmly in the fall of 1957 that "the experience of agricultural cooperativization in the Soviet Union served as a guide to our Party's policy on agricultural cooperativization." [117] There seems little doubt that this was true up to that point. As we have seen, however, Kim became profoundly disturbed with Soviet actions and attitudes during this period, and in a variety of ways began to reassess North Korea's position vis-à-vis the Soviet Union. His new emphasis upon chuch'e and his increasing sympathy with the foreign policy of Peking undoubtedly had some influence upon trends in domestic policy. Certainly, both the new cooperative system and the Ch'ŏllima Campaign bore the unmistakable imprint of Chinese influence.

116. "Speech Delivered at the First Session of the Second Supreme People's Assembly," Sept. 20, 1957, in Kim Il Sung, *For Socialist Economic Construction in Our Country, op. cit.*, pp. 319–339.

117. "The Idea of October Is Triumphant," Oct. 22, 1957, in *ibid.*, p. 359.

The purposes of the new rural system were clear. It was hoped that the larger administrative units would make possible a more efficient use of available resources, stimulate the "local autonomy" that the central government was promoting so strongly, and eliminate some of the duplication and waste that had characterized the old socioeconomic structure, with its dual economy and small basic units.

In a major policy speech of January 1959, Kim Il-sŏng assessed the results of government policies toward agriculture to date, presenting the official version of successes and requirements.[118] The speech sounded a highly optimistic note, reflecting the regime's new confidence. Factional opponents had been smashed, and a new degree of internal unity had been attained at the highest political levels. Industrial accomplishments under the first Five-Year Plan continued to be impressive. Moreover, as will soon be apparent, Kim was borrowing extensively both from the Great Leap Forward techniques of his Chinese comrades and from the buoyant optimism that went with those techniques. Miracles could be achieved. A new socialist man was possible. The doubters, the pessimists, the cynics, had been proven completely wrong.

What had been accomplished thus far? Kim outlined the main achievements of the past. First, the private peasant economy had been totally eliminated. This was essential for both political and economic reasons. The contradictions between socialist industry and a private peasant economy were dangerous ones, and only with the end of the old rural economy could exploitation and class distinctions be wiped out in the countryside. Moreover, an "advanced" industrial sector and a "backward" rural one accentuated the rural-urban gap, providing a general drag upon socialist development.

The first step, asserted Kim, was to return land to the tiller, thereby eliminating the landlord class and further reducing the rich peasants, always a weak force in Korean society. The next step was to popularize various cooperative forms of labor, a necessity upon which they had concentrated during the Korean War when agricultural production was the primary con-

118. "Victory of the Socialist Co-operation of Agriculture and the Future Development of Agriculture in Our Country," Report to the National Congress of Agricultural Co-operatives, Jan. 5, 1959, in Kim Il Sung, *Selected Works* (1965 ed.), *op. cit.,* Vol. I, pp. 431–486.

This speech was given before some 4,692 representatives of the 3,800 new agricultural cooperatives on the opening day of a five-day conference designed to launch the new agrarian system with maximum fanfare, indoctrination, and official support.

According to a *Nodong Sinmun* report, the delegates included 2,144 agricultural cooperative managers and workers, 1,883 Party workers in the cooperatives, 148 state farm managers and workers, 54 individuals from industrial plants supporting the coops, and 463 local and provincial government leaders; there were as well a number of foreign guests representing agrarian cooperative managers and specialists from the Soviet Union, China, Bulgaria, North Vietnam, Romania, and Mongolia. *NS,* Jan. 6, 1959, p. 4.

cern. From mutual cooperation, the peasant had learned to appreciate the agricultural cooperative. Relying initially upon the poor peasant, they had begun the cooperative movement in an experimental fashion. As a result of "the tireless organizational and political work" carried out by the Party among "broad sections of the peasants," not only the poor peasants but also the middle peasants had been drawn into the cooperative movement, which thus entered the "stage of development on a mass scale." [119]

They had proceeded slowly at first, Kim insisted, by different levels or stages of cooperativization. But as "the enthusiasm of the peasants ran higher and higher, the Party vigorously stepped up the cooperative movement," providing at the same time a greater measure of political and economic guidance. From early 1955, concentrated or intensive guidance was provided to each unit once or twice a year, when thousands of central and local functionaries were mobilized.[120]

The culmination of the agrarian revolution, according to Kim, had come in the summer and fall of 1958. First, agricultural cooperatives had encompassed all farm households by August, signifying a "great revolution" in the countryside and a "brilliant victory" for the Party's agricultural policy. "Class enemies" had attempted to sabotage the cooperatives in various ways. But all to no avail. Firm reliance on the poor peasants, strengthening the alliance with the middle peasants, and restricting and remolding the rich peasants—this was the keynote of the Party's policy. Moreover, as productive and technical forces developed, the relatively small scale of the agricultural cooperatives began to constitute a hindrance to further progress. Hence the changes of October, when all farmers were "voluntarily" integrated into larger cooperatives and the ri had become the basic unit. Thus 13,309 "old" cooperatives were thereby integrated into 3,843 "new" ones, with the chairman of the ri People's Committee also serving as chairman of the ri cooperative. At the same time, the number of households per cooperative rose from an average of 80 to 300, and the land under cultivation from 130 to 500 chŏngbo.

Meanwhile, Kim stated, the government had invested some 1,200 million wŏn (equal to 120 million wŏn after the conversion of February 1959) in agriculture since the Korean War; loaned over 300,000 tons of grain for food and seed, as well as 24,300 million wŏn of farming funds; and written off 160,000 tons of tax-in-kind and loaned grain, together with over 1,400 million wŏn in loans. Taxes, he claimed, had been reduced in 1956 substantially.

Most state investment, Kim continued, had gone into irrigation projects. As a result, paddy fields under irrigation had increased from 227,000

119. "Victory of the Socialist Co-operation of Agriculture," op. cit., p. 440.
120. It will be recalled that this intensive guidance was closely connected with the campaign of attacking sectarians from below that followed the Sino-Soviet intervention of September 1956.

to 463,000 chŏngbo, some 91 percent of the total. Stocks of chemical fertilizer and farm implements had also increased, and more advanced rice-growing procedures were being pushed. The area devoted to corn had increased more than threefold, from 236,000 chŏngbo in 1954 to 826,000 chŏngbo in 1958. In the same period, total land utilization had risen from 125 percent to 161 percent of the 1953 figure. Given these developments, total grain production had reached 2,870,000 tons in 1956, 3,200,000 tons in 1957, and 3,700,000 tons in 1958.[121]

In the course of this optimistic account, Kim outlined the priorities of the future, priorities that could be summarized in three words: irrigation, mechanization, and electrification. Within one to two years, he announced, they had to expand the area under irrigation to 1 million chŏngbo. Mechanization was equally important: for example, at least 30,000–35,000 tractors and 25,000–30,000 trucks were needed, with 5,000 tractors and 2,500 trucks to be delivered during 1959. Finally, further electrification was essential. Some 67 percent of all rural ri and 49 percent of all peasant households now had electricity, but the target in both cases was 100 percent, as it was for radio rediffusion receivers.

From these broad priorities, Kim turned to more specific means whereby production could be increased: deep ploughing, close planting, and liberal fertilization. All this indicated that he had closely followed the themes then emanating from the Chinese People's Republic; identical proposals were getting extensive publicity there in conjunction with the fantastic production gains being claimed as a part of the Great Leap Forward. But Kim also set some very ambitious goals of his own. Yields per chŏngbo were to be raised within the next four or five years to levels whereby a total production of seven million tons of grains could be "easily fulfilled." [122] Within six to seven years, the annual output of fabrics was to be increased to 500 million meters. Meat yields were to reach 400,000 tons within the next four to five years. Other statistics cited were in the same vein. The prospects of a reasonably affluent society were spread before an eager audience.

As 1958 came to a close, the enthusiasm manifested concerning the prospects for agriculture, with more reason, was equally apparent with respect to industrial growth. Officials, including Kim Il-sŏng himself, were now predicting that the Five-Year Plan launched at the beginning of 1957 could be completed by at least mid-1960, one and one-half years ahead of schedule.

At the outset of the new Plan, beginning with the Plenum of the KWP Central Committee in December 1956, when the onset of the program was officially authorized, one central issue was posed, namely, how to maintain

121. As we have remarked earlier, official grain production figures for this period are in all probability substantially inflated. We will go further into this matter later.
122. *Ibid.,* p. 468.

and advance production increases with less capital investment. Thus, production increases *and* savings was the slogan during 1957. Numerous spokesmen pointed out that, from this point on, development would be largely the product of self-help; the era of large-scale foreign assistance was coming to a close. The DPRK was still behind the advanced countries, admitted a *Nodong Sinmun* writer, in making effective use of its resources. Hence, a rigid economy program must be imposed upon the whole of North Korean life, particularly with respect to fuel, electricity, metal, wood, and foreign exchange.[123]

Austerity was thus to continue. However, for political as well as economic reasons, the government did begin to place somewhat greater emphasis on both consumer-goods production and more efficient marketing. An effort was made to enlarge commercial outlets in urban centers so that food and other necessities would be more consistently available. But the strict rationing of all necessities continued. In March 1957 the government announced that it planned greater increases in the production of consumer goods than in the production of "means of production." One Party spokesman acknowledged that the most urgent requirements currently were to meet the "increasing demands" of the growing urban, industrial population while transforming the market into a socialist one.[124]

Consumer-goods production did increase in the course of the next two years, although the major gains continued to be scored in heavy industry. At the end of 1957, the Central Statistical Bureau reported, total industrial output had overfulfilled the Plan for the year by 17 percent, with products such as iron ore, pig iron, steel, and chemical fertilizer among the leading gainers. The pace was accelerated in 1958. At the third session of the second Supreme People's Assembly, on June 11, 1958, Kim Il-sŏng, in the course of a lengthy speech, mentioned for the first time the word *ch'ŏllima.*[125]

> Today, our country is taking rapid strides forward and the entire outlook of society is also changing rapidly, progressing on the road to socialism. The prestige of the Party has been further heightened among the masses, and they are consolidated around the Party. All of the workers are, upon the call of the Party, riding a flying horse [ch'ŏllima] running forward to socialism [loud applause]. . . . Our task is to organize and lead the revolutionary spirit of the masses onto the highest tides [*sic:* via an amphibious horse?] in order to overfulfill the Five-Year Plan and accelerate the construction of socialism in the northern half of our country. . . . We

123. See An Kwang-jŭp, "The Execution of the First Five-Year Plan and the Problem of Capital Funds," *NS,* April 5, 1958, p. 2, for one of many discussions of the problem of funding the Plan.

124. Nam Chun-hwa, "The Rise of the People's Economy and the Task of Commercial Activities," *NS,* March 4, 1957, pp. 2–3.

125. The full text of Kim's speech appears in *NS,* June 12, 1958, pp. 1–2.

must not follow upon the tail of the people. We must stand in front of them to lead them to greater victories.[126]

In this fashion was the Flying Horse Campaign publicly launched, approximately one year after the Chinese had commenced the Great Leap Forward. From June 13, under the heading "Let Us Ride the Flying Horse for the Successful Execution of the Great Program," *Nodong Sinmun* carried daily charts to indicate the progress of the Plan. During the last three months of 1958, the Flying Horse Campaign was being given maximum publicity. The first steam shovel to be produced in North Korea was named the Ch'ŏllima steam shovel, and various other products were given the same name. Billboards, magazines, and newspapers all carried the picture of a winged horse. Pegasus had become the symbol for North Korea's Great Leap Forward.

In certain other ways, the tempo—and the temper—of the Great Leap Forward appeared to have had its influence upon Kim and his supporters. Thus, in the fall of 1958, he began to talk about catching up with Japan in industrial production in the same fashion that Chinese comrades were talking about catching up with Great Britain.[127] The highly optimistic North Korean predictions about agrarian production cited earlier must be fitted into the mood of this era, no less than the miraculous claims emanating from Peking.

In connection with a major address at the meeting in the fall of 1958 celebrating the tenth anniversary of the founding of the DPRK, Kim Il-sŏng gave full voice to the pride and optimism that the Party was now seeking to convey at home and abroad. "Our heroic working class," Kim proclaimed, "topped the 1957 plan for industrial production by 17 percent, and are triumphantly overfulfilling the 1958 plan, too. In 1957, industrial output increased by 44 percent compared with the preceding year, and in the first half of 1958 by 34 percent as against the corresponding period of last year." [128]

126. *Ibid.,* p. 1.
127. See "On Communist Education," Speech at a Short Course for the Agitators of the City and Prefecture Party Committees of the Country, November 20, 1958, in Kim Il Sung, *Selected Works* (1965 ed.), *op. cit.,* Vol. I, pp. 404–430 (at pp. 406–408).

Kim's specific references were to per capita production, as he made clear, but toward the end of this particular section of his speech, he seemed to get carried away, claiming that the DPRK would soon catch up with Japan in the machine-building industry, and ending with the assertion: "It is really a splendid thing that today we are catching up with and outstripping Japan, which once dreamed of conquering the whole of Asia and extending her claws of aggression even to the Soviet Union." *Ibid.,* 408).

128. "Report at the Celebration Meeting of the 10th Anniversary of the Founding of the D.P.R.K.," Sept. 8, 1958, in Kim Il Sung, *For Socialist Economic Construction in Our Country, op. cit.,* pp. 495–534 (at 501).

Kim went on to announce that the Five-Year Plan would be completed by the fifteenth anniversary of the liberation of Korea from Japanese rule, namely, August 15, 1960, with the Party making a "leaping advance along the road of socialism." Once again the accomplishments of the past and the requirements of the future were painstakingly recited, with the pledge that the targets now set would be reached or exceeded.

What generalizations can legitimately be drawn about the economic developments of this period? First, North Korea, it should be reiterated, had many of the indigenous requirements for industrial development. Natural resources in most fields were adequate, and in some fields abundant. The commitment of the political elite to industrial modernization, as has been made emphatically clear, was extremely high, and their capacity to exercise control was equal to their commitment. The internecine warfare in top Party circles never seriously affected lower Party ranks, nor the average worker and peasant. With most of the dissidents gone, North Korea remained a very controlled society, operating under a system of rewards and punishments that we shall subsequently examine in greater detail. Finally, the Japanese had left a small but meaningful pool of skilled and semiskilled industrial manpower.

Progress in light industry and agriculture, however, did not come close to equaling that in heavy industry during this period. Consequently, living standards remained extremely low, despite the substantial gains in gross national product. In this, one sees a familiar picture of Communism in its early stages, exacerbated by certain problems unique to North Korea, or at least to societies at a similar stage of development. Korean living standards had always been very low. The Korean War, moreover, had wreaked havoc with both agriculture and the consumer economy. The decision to emphasize heavy industry governed the crucial allocations of capital, manpower, and resources in the first postwar years. Thus, from a low initial base, pushed further downward by the war, North Korea moved only slowly upward in the years between 1953 and 1958. Despite all the government's efforts—or, quite possibly, because of them—agricultural productivity remained a problem. Light industry, especially in certain fields, did show signs of making satisfactory gains as the period came to a close. But quality remained extremely low, and demand far exceeded supply.

To draw a balance sheet on the North Korean economy between 1954 and 1959 is thus not a simple matter, especially since the available data must be used with caution. One should not underestimate the accomplishments. Even if official estimates are reduced to take account of statistical overestimates and other factors, growth during the reconstruction period (1954–56) was extremely high. Moreover, this high rate of growth continued through the Five-Year Plan period, with original targets being attained by mid-1959. Official growth claimed during this latter period (1956–59) was an unprecedented 45 percent per annum; even if this is reduced to 36 percent per annum, as one recent study suggests is appropriate, that would still be an extraordinary record.[129] On the other hand, the average North Korean worker and peasant remained desperately poor, a reflection of the type of growth that was being encouraged as well as the low base from which it was proceeding. Later, we will attempt more precise estimates of living standards. Here, we would suggest that the North Korean in 1958 lived close to a marginal subsistence level. He spent more than 85 percent of his income on food and clothing, and had a daily food intake of 2,000 calories or less. Thus, while the government had good reason to be optimistic from its standpoint, Marshal Kim was wise to place the primary emphasis upon the future when talking to the average citizen. The common man's best hope lay in Kim's dreams coming true.

Unification and Foreign Policy in an Era of Change

It remains to explore briefly the basic trends in North Korean foreign policy during this period. The months immediately after the 1953 armistice, as we have seen, witnessed a thorough canvass of the Communist world by North Korean leaders for aid in rehabilitation and reconstruction; Kim himself had led delegations to the two big Communist states. Even the two latter trips, incidentally, revealed much about Korean Communist priorities. The first pilgrimage was to the Soviet Union, and the delegation making that journey was larger and more prestigious than the one that went to Peking. A myriad of other signs during this period pointed to the fact that North Korea still treated China as a brother, while Russia continued to project a father image. When aid was acknowledged, the formula was "brotherly support from the great Soviet Union, the People's Republic of China, and other fraternal countries." The Communist world was invariably "headed by" the Soviet Union, and all Koreans were exhorted to learn from that nation. At times of celebration, Malenkov's picture preceded that of Mao Tse-tung. Despite the seemingly disproportionate sacrifices of Russia and China during the Korean War and the presence on Korean soil of a large Chinese military force, Korean Communist leaders gave every public indication of continuing their traditional homage to Moscow.

The first significant international parley in which North Korea participated after the 1953 armistice was the Geneva Conference of 1954. Nam Il headed the North Korean delegation as foreign minister. Both at Geneva and upon his return home, Nam Il took a very hard line with respect to all issues concerning the Korean problem. He advanced what had become the standard North Korean formula for unification:

1. An All-Korea Commission, composed of an equal number of North and South Koreans, should be established, with the power to agree

---

129. Pong S. Lee, "An Index of North Korean Industrial Output—1946–1963," to appear in *Asian Survey*, June 1972.

upon the conditions leading to unification, meanwhile promoting economic and cultural exchange between the north and south.

2. All foreign troops should be withdrawn from both South and North Korea, allowing the future of Korea to be decided by the Korean people themselves.

3. Once foreign troops were withdrawn, provisions for general elections to establish a National Assembly should be undertaken by the All-Korea Commission.

4. The peaceful development of Korea should be guaranteed by all nations concerned with the Far East.

Nam Il complained that while the Soviet Union and China had supported this basic formula, the United States and South Korea had insisted that any general election be supervised by the United Nations, a position totally unacceptable to the DPRK. Both the Soviet Union and China had proposed alternatives such as "neutralist" supervision. Moreover, on June 15, the DPRK delegation had made certain proposals to guarantee peaceful conditions in Korea during the interim: all foreign troops should be reduced on a proportionate basis, with the participants to the Geneva Conference reaching a general agreement upon a date of evacuation; within one year, the governments of North and South Korea should reduce their armies to 100,000 men each; an ad hoc committee composed of representatives of both North and South Korea should be created to discuss this matter; neither North nor South Korea should have a military alliance with an outside force; an All-Korea Commission should be created to promote economic and cultural relations; all Geneva participants should recognize the necessity of creating conditions for the peaceful unification of the country. The Communist participants, asserted Nam Il, had supported this six-point proposal, and Chou En-lai had proposed a seven-nation conference to implement it, consisting of the People's Republic of China, the USSR, the US, Great Britain, France, the DPRK, and the ROK. This, too, had been rejected.

None of these proposals was new, and the UN allies had repeatedly made it clear that the Communist formula was unacceptable, as it applied both to troop withdrawal and to unification. An earlier withdrawal of American forces had led to Communist aggression, and there was no desire among either non-Communist Koreans or Americans to test this matter again. The Western position that the United Nations was the proper instrumentality for supervising elections extended back to the 1940s, as we have seen. Upon it rested the legitimacy of the Republic of Korea, and the challenge to the legitimacy of the Democratic People's Republic of Korea, particularly its right to claim jurisdiction over the whole of Korea. Faith, moreover, was very limited in the capacity of any "neutral" or mixed commission of Communists and non-Communists to perform effectively in this situation, or, indeed, to perform at all. The record elsewhere with respect to such groups was not promising.

Naturally, the North Korean leaders continued to press their position with vigor, with one eye always upon political and economic conditions south of the 38th parallel. In the fall of 1954, the Supreme People's Assembly adopted an "Appeal to the South Korean People." This proposed a joint North-South Conference involving the bringing together of the South Korean National Assembly and the North Korean Supreme People's Assembly, to meet in either P'yŏngyang or Seoul during the year 1955. To establish the agenda for such a meeting, and to open preliminary economic and cultural contacts, designated representatives from North and South Korea should meet at P'anmunjŏm or Kaesŏng during the month of February 1955.[130]

Under the circumstances, no one in North Korea could have regarded this as more than a propaganda gesture. But they may have hoped that, repeated over months and years, it would reap political dividends. In any case, a few days later, on November 3, 1954, Kim Il-sŏng made some extremely revealing remarks on the subject of "peaceful unification." [131] Some people, he stated, regarded peaceful unification as impossible and viewed the Assembly's proposal as a mere formality. Moreover, certain comrades, having noted prevailing theories about the possibility of the coexistence of socialist and capitalist systems, believed that they could apply to North and South Korea.

The general theory of coexistence was correct, Kim asserted, but the idea of coexistence "between the two parts of our divided country, North and South Korea," was very dangerous. "People who have such an idea," Kim continued, "seem to think that the responsibility for the revolution in South Korea rests entirely upon the South Korean people and that we, the people in North Korea, are not responsible for liberating the south. This is nothing but an attempt to justify the division of the country and perpetuate it. Such a tendency must be thoroughly done away with." [132]

It would have been difficult to state more baldly the Communist position on involvement in the internal affairs of the Republic of Korea than Kim did in this speech. His broad tactics were simply phrased: "We must tirelessly endeavor to exert our Party's influence upon the South Korean people and arouse them to a struggle against the US imperialists and the traitorous Syngman Rhee clique, and we must further fortify the democratic base in the northern part of the country into an impregnable bastion." [133]

To Kim, "fortifying the democratic base" meant "further consolidating

130. For the full text of the SPA resolution, see *NS,* Oct. 30, 1954, p. 1.
131. "On Our Party's Policy for the Further Development of Agriculture," in Kim Il Sung, *Selected Works* (1965 ed.), *op. cit.,* Vol. I, pp. 210–233.
132. *Ibid.,* p. 228.
133. *Ibid.,* p. 230.

our Party and the organs of state power." It meant, in other words, a steel-like ideological unity coupled with rapid economic growth, both for the sake of state power and to gain popular support. It also meant strengthening the Korean People's Army in every way. The only element missing from this frank program of bringing the south under Communist control was the openly subversive element: agents and guerrilla forces. To launch the latter was obviously premature, but as early as 1954 the former were being trained, taking up the tasks interrupted by the war. Naturally, it would have been indelicate to have discussed this aspect of policy publicly.

Having made Communist tactics clear, Kim proceeded to define them as the route to "peaceful unification." The Korean people did not want war, Kim proclaimed, particularly fratricidal war. Yet Syngman Rhee was raving about a "march north to unify the country." However, to abandon our quest for peaceful unification, Kim warned, would cause the Korean people to turn elsewhere—so great was their desire for a unified nation.

Thus, as early as 1954, Kim and his colleagues had determined upon the basic strategy that was to govern Communist attitudes and policies toward Korean unification in the years that lay ahead. The slogan was "peaceful unification," meaning that the Communists did not intend to re-peat the disaster of 1950–53. "Peaceful unification" involved instead a sustained political campaign that, in all probability, would culminate in a revolution, with "progressives" both north and south combining to over-throw the "enemies of the people." How could such a revolution be com-patible with *peaceful* unification? That issue was never clarified, except by the implication that the "Fascist Rhee lackeys" were so isolated from the people of the south that little blood would be shed upon their overthrow. Moreover, the Communists always kept open the possibility that South Korea would at some time accept their proposals for unification, allowing them to compete in southern elections.[134]

The Communist strategy for unification was not lacking in sophistica-tion, particularly when compared with that of the southern leaders. Rhee was once again issuing occasional calls for a march to the north, but it is extremely doubtful whether anyone, including the Communist leaders, took them seriously. Communist intelligence was undoubtedly good enough to disclose the absence of any concrete preparations for this alleged march, as well as the adamant opposition of the United States to any such form

134. Ch'oe Kwang-sŏk has told us that agents being trained to go to the south were told that their first task was to build Communist cells and reestablish the "pro-gressive" forces, because if the Communists could win the support of one-third of the people in the south they could win any election.

According to Ch'oe, interest in southern political activities even influenced poli-cies within the north. In 1959, for example, a more lenient policy was inaugurated toward the families of those who had fled south, primarily so that they and their separated kin could be used in the political struggle. Chong-Sik Lee interview with Ch'oe Kwang-sŏk, Nov. 24, 1966.

of adventurism. Rhee's speeches had to be read as propaganda. Otherwise, South Korea was doing little about the unification issue except reacting negatively to North Korean schemes. Some agents, to be sure, were being sent north, but these were for the purpose of collecting information—not for creating guerrilla bases.

The Communist unification strategy, on the other hand, consisted in an intricate series of policies that added up to involvement in the politics of the south at many levels, overt and covert. The hope was that political instability and economic stagnation below the 38th parallel, actively stimulated by North Korea and ultimately given northern leadership, would end in Korean unification on Communist terms. It was in this sense that the North was to serve as the "broad democratic base"; it would serve as example, stimulant, *and* source of guidance and leadership—political and, if necessary, military.

Up to a point, the Communists were prepared to use democratic procedures. Knowing that they represented a distinct minority, and that the north had scarcely one-half the population of the south, Workers' Party leaders talked about the importance of having the full support of all northerners *plus* the sympathy of enough southerners to make possible the winning of some possible future national election. And to win southern support, a steady stream of propaganda was beamed to the south, describing conditions in the north as akin to paradise in comparison with the "misery, barbarism, and hopelessness" characteristic of the "Fascist Rhee lackeys" and their "American imperialist overlords." Initially, the attack was primarily upon the southern leadership; later, it shifted to the Americans, in the hope of appealing to southern nationalist sentiments.

To forward such propaganda and to advance concrete unification proposals, the Communists, as we have noted, maintained a variety of organizations. The Democratic Front for the Unification of the Fatherland continued to be the ultimate vehicle for united front politics. The immediate instrument of Communist unification politics was the Committee for the Peaceful Unification of the Fatherland, and its figurehead leaders represented a fair range of ex-southern politicians—until, as we have seen, most of them were purged in the winter of 1958–59.

But if the Communists were prepared to use the democratic route to the extent that it served their purposes, at no point did they feel bound by it. In this period, as we have already pointed out, facilities were expanded for the training of agents to undertake southern operations of a covert nature. Military actions were by no means ruled out. Indeed, Kim and his associates assumed that unification could only be achieved on Communist terms after the south had undergone a violent "revolution." In any such struggle, North Korea intended to play an active role, as Kim made clear. At this point, however, guerrilla activities were regarded as decidedly premature.

On balance, North Korea had clearly seized the strategic initiative with respect to relations with South Korea and the unification issue. Once again, the situation reflected the relatively refined Communist tactics of combined political-military assault, as well as the absence of an effective non-Communist counterpart. Indeed, North Korea had little reason to fear South Korea as a revolutionary force. The Republic of Korea was simply not equipped to use the Communist strategy of subversion, nor did conditions in North Korea—one of the tightest police states in the world—permit it. From a defensive standpoint, therefore, the Communists were in generally excellent shape. Their assets lay not only in the internal political unity enforced by the Communist system, but also in the substantial economic progress being made, particularly in the highly visible field of heavy industry. At the end of this period, economic comparisons were very painful for the Republic of Korea, despite the fact that if one measured only standards of living, the north probably had no edge on the south. Finally, control of information was infinitely more effective in the north and, when combined with intensive indoctrination, tended to produce a citizen whose belief patterns probably mirrored those of the regime in at least some crucial areas.

On the other hand, it would be very unwise to overlook Communist debits. In truth, South Korea at this point was one of the most thoroughly and deeply anti-Communist communities in the non-Western world. There were essentially two reasons for this. First, Communist behavior toward the southern populace during the war had, on balance, been bad. Those who had lived under Communist occupation were usually very alienated from the Communists. Second, the entire southern Communist apparatus had surfaced during the conflict. Naturally, Party members and sympathizers had been forced to flee as UN forces returned to occupied areas. The Korean War had provided an almost unparalleled opportunity for "natural selection," with anti-Communists going south and pro-Communists going north. The south, of course, had won this competition in overwhelming measure. And for the Communists, the task of rebuilding their organization below the 38th parallel was a formidable one, particularly since there were now millions—both northerners and southerners—who had lived under Communism and wanted no more of it.

Understandably, the Communists aimed at the youth. Promises of handsome scholarships and support for study abroad were offered to students who would come north. Guarantees of the "personal security and freedom" of those who came were coupled with exhortations to students to fight for the evacuation of foreign troops and the peaceful unification of Korea.[135] Using ad hoc groups such as the so-called National Conference of College Student Enthusiasts, the P'yŏngyang authorities directed "open

135. See Cabinet Ordinance No. 40, signed by Kim Il-sŏng, entitled, "On the Protection of the Youth and Students of South Korea Who Are Fighting Against US Imperialism and Syngman Rhee's Regime," in *NS*, April 17, 1955, p. 1.

letters" to the youth of South Korea on behalf of Communist proposals.

Meanwhile, maximum use was also made of former South Korean politicians, particularly in the period between 1954 and 1957. Individuals such as Kim Won-bong wrote articles comparing North and South Korea to the advantage of the former, and urging that the initial steps toward unification be taken.[136] In mid-1955, a new unification offensive was launched when a group of former South Korean politicians associated with the Committee for the Peaceful Unification of the Fatherland issued a common statement in full support of the Communist unification proposals.[137]

This period also witnessed substantial efforts to mobilize the Koreans resident in Japan on behalf of the Communist unification program. These efforts scored impressive successes. Some 600,000 Koreans remained in Japan, largely ignored by the Republic of Korea and increasingly the object of attention from the People's Republic. The General Federation of Koreans Resident in Japan, by all odds the most significant Korean organization in Japan, was openly proclaimed an auxiliary of the DPRK by the Communists, and used as such. On issues such as unification, it conducted demonstrations and educational campaigns upon request.[138]

Despite these various efforts, however, no progress toward unification was made during this period, and Communist goals seemed as distant at the beginning of 1959 as they had in August 1953. The prospects for a political conference centering upon the Korean problem and involving Korean War or Geneva (1954) participants faded away; the distance between the rival

136. In an article entitled "Economic and Cultural Exchanges Between South and North Korea Are the First Step to the Peaceful Unification of the Fatherland" (*NS,* Jan. 10, 1955, p. 3), Kim Won-bong praised "the brilliant achievements of the DPRK during the past year in the fields of politics, economics and culture." He asserted, "Whereas the people of North Korea are enjoying meaningful lives filled with happiness and hope, the people in South Korea are panting under the despotic, terroristic rule of Syngman Rhee and the US imperialists, suffering severe economic wreckage, starvation, and cultural debasement. Our national culture is being effaced and, in its place, American culture, which imbues people with a spirit of hostility toward human beings, a pursuit of animalistic pleasures, and a nihilistic decadence, is prevailing. How can any conscientious and patriotic individual stand in such a state of misery?"

Four years later, as we have noted, Kim Won-bong would stand condemned by the Kim Il-sŏng group as an "international spy" and disappear from sight.

137. For the statement, see *NS,* Nov. 13, 1955, p. 1. It was signed by O Ha-yŏng, former ROK minister of Interior, Yun Ki-sŏp, former vice-president of the South Korean Interim Legislative Assembly, Cho So-ang, well-known southern politician, Song Ho-sŏng, former ROK general, An Chae-hong, former chief of the Civil Administration under the US occupation in South Korea, and Ŏm Hang-sŏp, former minister of Public Information in the Shanghai Provisional Government. Most of these people dropped from sight at the time of the 1958–59 purges.

138. Thus, Communist organs in Japan and North Korea were flooded with letters from Koreans urging acceptance of DPRK unification proposals.

groups appeared too vast to warrant such an exercise. Largely for the reasons set forth above, Communist subversive activities in South Korea made little headway, despite the country's multiple problems. Only among the Koreans in Japan did the Communists continue to score major political successes.

Meanwhile, a grave new problem confronted P'yŏngyang, namely, the increasing vibrations within the Communist world as a result of the Twentieth CPSU Congress and the train of events that followed. As a result, the unification campaign that had been mounted with increasing vigor between 1954 and 1956 dropped off precipitously after this time. Propaganda and the training of agents, of course, continued. Nor did the official DPRK position shift.[139] The Communists were frank to admit, however, that disunity within the international socialist community jeopardized their efforts for Korean unification, among other things. Indeed, as this period came to a close, they suggested that a number of former southern politicians currently in the north and even some KWP members had been sufficiently tainted with revisionist currents to support the idea of unification on the basis of true neutrality and some form of meaningful power-sharing. For this heresy to the cause of Marxism-Leninism, heads were to fall. Meanwhile, the unification campaign fell into the doldrums. At most, the KWP leaders could claim to have inoculated their own people successfully against any appeals the south might have had for them. By a steady drumfire of

139. For a reiteration of the North Korean position, see the interview between Nam Il and a British reporter carried in *NS*, Jan. 22, 1956, p. 1. When asked whether he envisaged a new war in Korea, Nam Il responded by saying that an armistice was not a stable peace and, while the Four Power Geneva Conference of June 1955 had reduced international tension, the United States continued to violate the armistice terms "constantly."

The only way to maintain the peace, Nam Il asserted, was for a "strict observance" of the armistice agreement, the evacuation of all foreign troops from Korean soil, and a peaceful settlement of the Korean problem by the Koreans themselves, with such preliminary moves as the establishment of cultural and economic contacts, the guarantee of free political activities, and the mutual reduction of military forces.

Kim Il-sŏng, in an interview of May 31, 1956, made the same points. But it is instructive to contrast these interviews with an article entitled "On Various Forms of Socialist Transition," by Kim Si-ch'ŏn, published in the August 1956 issue of *Kŭlloja*. In the course of explaining that every country had its own peculiarities that would affect its particular form of socialism, Kim asserted that "our peculiarities" are these: Our political power is limited to the northern part of Korea only, whereas our government reflects the general will of the entire Korean people. We are the only legitimate government. The whole of Korean sovereignty is possessed by the DPRK, which includes among its institutions the DFUF, the legitimate representative of all democratic parties and social organizations of South Korea as well as North Korea. Thus, concluded Kim, ours is the only suitable regime for constructing socialism in the northern part of the country while simultaneously carrying out the anti-imperialist, anti-feudal democratic revolution throughout the country and the unification of the Fatherland.

propaganda about the south that combined truth and fiction to produce a highly exaggerated picture, the Communists undoubtedly succeeded in impressing the average northern resident.[140]

However, as we have noted, there was no diminution of the Hate America campaign during this entire period. When Kim Il-sŏng castigated Pak Yŏng-bin in December 1955 for suggesting that North Korea might alter its approach to the United States in line with current Soviet efforts to reduce international tension, he voiced the position that was to remain Korean Communist policy throughout this period. Three recurrent themes can be discerned in connection with the anti-American drive. The first, a familiar one in international Communist circles, was that the socialist world was rising and the capitalist world declining. Korean Communist organs periodically produced figures to indicate that the Soviet Union was sweeping ahead of the United States in terms of economic development, that the United States was entering a deep economic depression, and that both foreign aid and military policies were the result of a desperate effort to extricate the American people from the economic crisis.

The second theme, also familiar, was closely related to the first: the United States was the leader of the capitalist world and, as such, the leader of the forces of imperialism and aggression. Specifically, the United States was promoting war in both Europe and Asia. For these purposes, it was constructing regional military alliances such as CENTO, SEATO, and—if it could—NEATO. All peace-loving peoples opposed this, including all Asians.

From time to time, the North Korean leaders sought to make the fear of an American-inspired war upon North Korean soil real to their people. For example, in mid-December 1956, shortly after the Hungarian revolt, the North Korean authorities conducted a highly publicized trial of several persons alleged to be United States spies who had been sent to develop a Hungarian-type revolt to be coupled with an American invasion.[141] Undoubtedly, this trial and other propaganda of the times had both long- and short-range purposes. The DPRK leaders were anxious that *their* version of Hungary be accepted by the people. It was also important to justify the extremely heavy military expenditures and, for these purposes, the American threat was as useful as the ROK threat.

Attitudes toward the United States influenced North Korean policies toward Japan and the neutrals. Ironically, the Communists, despite the violently anti-Japanese tone of their internal propaganda, showed remarkable flexibility in dealing with Japan during this period, in strident contrast

---

140. Every defector and captured agent appears to agree on this point. In later years, such people professed themselves amazed by the difference between what they saw with their own eyes in the south, and the picture of conditions portrayed to them.

141. For details, see *NS*, Dec. 16, 1956, p. 1.

to the policies of the ROK government. In part, this was an effort to culti-vate a cleavage between the US and Japan. More importantly, it related to Communist desires to maintain as wide a channel of access as possible to the Koreans in Japan.

Thus, as early as 1954, Nam Il announced that his government wel-comed trade proposals currently being made by Japanese businessmen, and looked forward to both cultural and economic exchange with Japan. At the end of 1955, preliminary negotiations with the Japanese government had resulted in the designation of the Red Cross organizations of both countries as agencies for settlement of the repatriation issue. On February 27, 1956, an agreement was reached whereby those Koreans in Japan wishing to come to North Korea would be allowed to do so, and DPRK authorities promised to provide each repatriate with an initial sum of 60,000 yen (approximately US $140) for living expenses.[142] A trade agreement was also concluded at this time, and soon after, the first Japanese cultural delegation, a group from the National Railway Workers' Union, came to P'yŏngyang. Mean-while, relations between the Republic of Korea and Japan remained in a glacial state.

The Japanese government, it should be noted, remained completely aware of the character and purposes of the DPRK. It established no diplo-matic relations with P'yŏngyang, and in 1955 refused to grant visas to a DPRK delegation seeking to attend the Hiroshima Peace Conference (the Communists then proceeding to use leaders of the General Federation of Korean Residents in Japan as their delegation). It also continued to keep illegal Korean entrants (including a number of North Korean agents) in the Omura detention camp. Trade, moreover, was very small. Thus, relations between P'yŏngyang and Tokyo remained more or less minimal and in any case decidedly cool. The main Communist objective of the period, however, had been secured: continued control over, and the right to speak for, the bulk of Koreans in Japan.[143]

While Kim Il-sŏng and his followers, like Mao Tse-tung, believed that there could be no neutrality for good Marxist-Leninists; they saw major advantages in wooing the Asian and African "neutrals" during this period. Understandably, the North Koreans were anxious to obtain the maximum amount of international recognition and, like their Chinese comrades, they

142. For the agreement and North Korean commentary, see *NS,* Feb. 29, 1956, p. 1.

143. Attacks upon the Japanese government by North Korean authorities be-came sharper as this period came to a close. On Sept. 16, 1958, Nam Il issued a state-ment blaming the Japanese government for throwing obstacles in front of repatriation and the release of Koreans from Ōmura. The DPRK was also making increasing use of leftist Japanese to support their position. For example, a Japanese delegation visit-ing North Korea issued a communiqué in mid-September jointly with five Korean organizations, endorsing DPRK foreign policy and scheduled to coincide with Nam Il's statement.

saw the best opportunities in the Afro-Asian world. Moreover, they regarded such moves as contributing to the isolation of the United States from the world community. As a result, such leaders as Nehru, Sukarno, and Nasser received exceedingly favorable publicity. For example, on October 28, 1955, Kim Il-sŏng expressed his "deep respect" for Nehru, calling him an outstanding leader and praising the Indian government for its "peace-loving foreign policy."

Moreover, whenever invited, North Korean leaders appeared eager to attend international conferences. The opportunities were limited, being primarily confined to Communist-line meetings under the aegis of such veteran organizations as the World Peace Council and the World Federation of Trade Unions. However, Pak Chŏng-ae did attend the Afro-Asian Conference in New Delhi in early April 1955, a conference that preceded Bandung. The Bandung Conference itself, to which neither North nor South Korea was invited, was hailed by the Communists, who sought to highlight its anti-American aspects.

At the close of 1958, the North Koreans had some reason to feel satisfied with the progress made in expanding diplomatic contacts. Ties with the UAR, India, Indonesia, Burma, and Cambodia had been established. Nevertheless, the regime remained basically foreign to the non-Communist world. Its political and economic ties continued to be overwhelmingly with the Communists, and at least one non-Communist diplomat who had occasion to be stationed in the country found most North Korean officials "ill at ease" when dealing with non-Communists, even those from "friendly" governments.

The great challenge to North Korean foreign policy during this period, however, related to developments in the international Communist movement. In the years immediately after the Korean War, the North Korean government had displayed all of the manifestations of a true Soviet satellite, an Asian Bulgaria, despite the omnipresent Chinese forces. News concerning the Soviet Union was given almost the same prominence as that accorded to domestic events. A regular column devoted to the Soviet Union ran in *Nodong Sinmun,* with such features as "A Day in the Life of a Party Secretary," "Soviet Party Management," and "The Development of Plant Pathology in the Soviet Union."

This was but a small part of the process of "learning from the rich experiences of the Soviet Union." On the occasion of the second anniversary of Stalin's death, memorial services were held throughout the nation. Meanwhile, his *Collected Works* continued to be published in Korean translation (the twelfth volume, covering only the period between April 1929 and June 1930, came off the press in July 1955). On May Day 1955, gigantic pictures of Lenin and Stalin towered above the streets of P'yŏngyang, with those of Bulganin, Kim Il-sŏng, and Mao Tse-tung beneath them.

Initially, moreover, the new trends in Soviet foreign policy did not seem too hard to follow. When Foreign Minister Molotov signaled a shift away from the Cold War policies of the Stalinist era in his speech of February 1955 before the Supreme Soviet, *Nodong Sinmun* carried the speech in its entirety, and thereafter dutifully took up the theme of the importance of relaxing the international atmosphere.[144] The Four-Power Summit Conference held in Geneva in July 1955 received a favorable assessment in P'yŏngyang, and not even the speeches of Eisenhower and Eden were attacked. The rise of Khrushchev received scant notice at first, but the Bulganin-Khrushchev visit to India, Burma, and Afghanistan in the winter of 1955 was given extensive and favorable treatment. Indeed, a *Nodong Sinmun* commentator entitled his end-of-year appraisal "A Victorious Year for the Ideas of Peace and Cooperation." [145]

These facts reinforce our earlier thesis that Kim Il-sŏng's speech on the importance of chuch'e in the Korean Revolution—a speech delivered at precisely this time (December 28, 1955)—was primarily related to internal events, notably Kim's struggle against Pak Ch'ang-ok, Ch'oe Ch'ang-ik, and the factions led by them. What had been true up to this point, however, did not continue to be true over the next twelve months. Up to the Twentieth CPSU Congress, North Korean leaders and the North Korean mass media continued to speak of "the brilliant victory of Soviet peace-loving foreign policy" and "the undeniable correctness of the principles of peaceful coexistence." As we have already noted, however, that Congress, and specifically Khrushchev's attack upon Stalin, shocked Kim Il-sŏng and his followers profoundly, particularly since these events quickly became part of the most serious internal political crisis yet faced by the Kim faction. Favorable comments on the Congress poured forth daily from P'yŏngyang organs, but not until April 2, while a vitally significant plenum of the KWP Central Committee was under way, did the Kim group publicly reveal the de-Stalinization move in Moscow—and then only by publishing a *Pravda* editorial.

Six days later, on April 8, without any interim comment, Peking's position was published in extenso, as we have noted, via a *Jen-min Jih-pao* editorial. And Peking's position became that of P'yŏngyang, as Kim Il-sŏng made clear in his May interview, already quoted, with the Indian correspondent.[146]

Moreover, when Kim Il-sŏng returned from his extended trip to Russia

144. As an example, see Kim Hyŏng, "On the Conditions of Mutual Trust in International Relations," *NS,* June 23, 1955, p. 4. This piece amounted to a eulogy of the Soviet Union for its efforts to improve the international situation, and hailed the coming Geneva Conference as the fruit of those efforts.

145. Ch'ŏn In-ch'ŏl, in *NS,* Dec. 31, 1955. Said Ch'ŏn: the Geneva spirit is the antithesis of the cold war, and it is receiving support from all of the peace-loving people of the world. The statement that came from the Supreme Soviet this year has cast up new hope for the people of the world.

146. For the complete interview, see *NS,* May 31, 1956, p. 1.

and Eastern Europe on July 19, the beginnings of a profound shift made their appearance. Again, domestic considerations were crucial. Kim returned to find what he considered a full-fledged plot against him. Elements affiliated with both Moscow and Peking were seeking to challenge him, or at least certain crucial policies of his administration. And they were using the Twentieth Congress documents as major weapons.

Two days after Kim's return, on July 21, 1956, *Nodong Sinmun* published a most important article by Kim Chin-t'aek, entitled "For a Correct Understanding of the Word 'Autonomy.' " [147] While this article contained no basic themes that had not previously been introduced by Kim Il-sŏng, at least privately, it could easily be read as a public declaration of independence from Moscow, given its timing and the circumstances surrounding it.

According to Kim Chin-t'aek, Lenin had proved the possibility of conducting a proletarian revolution successfully in one country. This meant that the working class of each individual country could take the initiative for decisive revolutionary actions on its own. Both the great October Revolution in the Soviet Union and the Chinese Revolution proved the correctness of Leninist doctrine. Comrade Kim Il-sŏng's championing of autonomy stemmed from these facts. By carrying out the peaceful unification of the fatherland and constructing socialism in the northern part of the country, Kim was supporting the international revolutionary movement. In this fashion, internationalist and nationalist duties were being combined. "The establishment of autonomy means subordinating *everything* to the success of the revolution in *our* country so that we can carry our maximum load on behalf of the international revolutionary movement." If one ignored the need for unifying international and national duties, one was liable to fall into the errors of nationalism and chauvinism. But to neglect indigenous conditions and insist upon following the pattern of foreign countries mechanically was to abandon the revolution. Rightly, the article concluded, persons committing these errors had become the objects of mass scorn.

Whatever the precise status of relations between Kim Il-sŏng and the Russians in July, those relations certainly worsened during the course of events in August and September. We have ample evidence that Kim was furious over the Soviet-Chinese intervention. Another story is relayed by O Ki-wan.[148] According to him, in the course of the crisis, the Soviet ambassador to North Korea, having been contacted by the dissidents, called upon Kim without appointment and informed him that he had been "too severe," and would have to reconsider the situation. Kim reportedly became very angry, raising the question of interference in the internal politics of Korea, and challenging the ambassador by saying: "You are a foreign

147. Kim Chin-t'aek, "For a Correct Understanding of the Word 'Autonomy,' " *NS,* July 21, 1956, p. 1.
148. O Ki-wan interview with Chong-Sik Lee, Jan. 15, 1967.

ambassador. How can you walk into my office in this manner? If I had wanted you, I would have called for you, or you could have come via the foreign minister." Supposedly, Kim then gave him twenty-four hours to leave the country, threatening otherwise to issue an order for his expulsion. He then reportedly telephoned Khrushchev in Moscow, repeating the demand and the threat. Khrushchev supposedly asked for a few days' delay, a request that Kim denied.

This story may be apocryphal. But Ivanov, the Soviet ambassador, *was* recalled during this period, so it may have some elements of truth. In any case, a dramatic shift in attitude toward the Soviet Union could be detected in official North Korean circles in the early fall of 1956. It was evidenced by a host of signs, including the drastic reduction in press coverage of Soviet news. Then came Hungary. There can be no doubt that the Hungarian revolt disturbed Peking and P'yŏngyang almost as much as it did certain hard-line Eastern European Communists.

The new DPRK position was set forth in an extremely interesting article by Pak Kŭm-ch'ŏl in mid-February 1957.[149] Pak first made clear his deep concern over the repercussions of Communist disunity. Events like Hungary and the Suez crisis, he asserted, were the direct products of cracks in socialist solidarity—deviations from the truth of Marxism-Leninism and proletarian internationalism that had spawned revisionism, opportunism, exclusivism, and bourgeois nationalism. All of this helped the imperialists. To counter this danger, "an absolute support for the Soviet Union is our sacred duty."

At the same time, socialist unity could only be achieved and maintained if there existed "a correct understanding of the particular conditions of a given country" that governed the manner in which it applied Marxism-Leninism. (Russians, take notice!) *However,* the enemy was utilizing problems in this respect to divide socialists. Under no circumstances, could the special conditions of a given country be allowed *to justify a denial of the general truth of Marxism-Leninism* (italics ours). Had Imre Nagy, for example, been left in power he would have destroyed the Party and subverted the revolution. Yet Tito, in an act profoundly antagonistic to the international socialist movement, had supported Nagy and had criticized the Soviet Union and others for their correct stand.[150]

149. Pak Kŭm-ch'ŏl, "It Is Our Sublime Duty to Be Loyal to Proletarian Internationalism," *NS,* Feb. 14, 1957, p. 1.

150. Attitudes toward Tito up to the time of the Hungarian outbreak, incidentally, had been cautiously favorable, no doubt reflecting post-Stalinist Soviet hopes for a rapprochement. For example, *Nodong Sinmun,* commenting on a speech given by Tito to the Yugoslav parliament, asserted on March 15, 1955, that we should look forward, not backward. Though Tito continues to oppose certain aspects of Soviet policy, hostility between the USSR and Yugoslavia benefits only the enemies of world peace.

The Tito–U Nu Joint Communiqué issued following the Yugoslav leader's visit to Burma was reported favorably in P'yŏngyang on June 21, 1955.

Pak's article set the tone for others to follow. Throughout 1957 and much of 1958, the new line was championed by such KWP stalwarts as Kim Il-sŏng, Kim Ch'ang-man, Yi Hyo-sun, and many others. A careful reading of these articles indicates certain significant changes from the pre-1956 era. The acceptance by the Soviet Union of the "full equality and autonomy" of each Communist Party was repeatedly hailed. On occasion, moreover, as in the case of Kim Ch'ang-man's article, the emphasis was placed upon eternal solidarity with *the people* of the Soviet Union.[151] Nevertheless, in the aftermath of the Hungarian crisis, and out of concern for its own future, P'yŏngyang rallied loyally to the defense of the Soviet Union in an effort to firm up Soviet foreign policy and discourage the forces of "appeasement" in Moscow. Thus, Kim Ch'ang-man vigorously denounced the "national communism" and "neutralism" of Yugoslavia as defiling the purity of Marxism-Leninism. Yi Hyo-sun proclaimed that there was "no struggle for Communism without protecting the Soviet Union," since the power of the USSR was the decisive element in guaranteeing the common future.[152] And when the ouster of Malenkov, Kaganovich, and Molotov was announced in July 1957, the official KWP organs hailed this event as an action overcoming factional activities within the CPSU, strengthening the unity of the Party, and identical in meaning to the ouster of the Pak Ch'ang-ok and Ch'oe Ch'ang-ik factions from the KWP! (Such a twist must have produced some grim humor in Kim Il-sŏng's circle.)

Staunch North Korean support for Soviet leadership and policies continued through the Taiwan Straits crisis of 1958. But, as 1958 came to a close, there were signs of a new deterioration, connected with Sino-Soviet difficulties. North Korean sources presented the Joint Communiqué signed by Khrushchev and Mao with an accent upon the positive, asserting that it underlined the unity and solidarity within the socialist camp, and should therefore serve as a severe warning to the imperialists. However, an abrupt shift occurred in the tenor of North Korean statements in the winter of 1958, one apparently connected with Peking's increasing disenchantment with Nikita Khrushchev and his policies. To pursue joint consultations, Kim Il-sŏng and a high-level DPRK delegation made a lengthy trip to Peking and Hanoi, returning to Peking in the November–December period. This trip marked an important turning point in North Korean foreign policy, with a decided shift away from support of Khrushchevian policies.

Thus, as this period ended, the North Korean leaders were engaged in another agonizing reappraisal of the international Communist scene. There

151. Kim Ch'ang-man, "We Shall Be Eternally with the People of the Soviet Union," *NS,* March 17, 1957, p. 3.

152. Yi Hyo-sun, "The Great Banner of October Is Inspiring the Struggle of the Korean People," *Kŭlloja (The Worker)*, Aug. 25, 1957. Yi asserts quite bluntly that the strength and unity of the socialist camp "centering around the Soviet Union" is the "essential guarantee" for ultimate socialist victory throughout Korea.

can be no doubt that this reappraisal was powerfully stimulated by Peking. From the time of the Twentieth Party Congress, Kim Il-sŏng and his government had looked increasingly to Peking for guidance in threading their way through the extraordinary complications that had ensued. It had been a Peking editorial that set the line on Stalin. Peking's policies regarding Hungary, and her analysis of the Hungarian situation, had been incorporated into North Korean policy by the end of 1956. Support for the Soviet Union in the difficult months of 1957 and early 1958, and during the recurrent crises in the fall of 1958, were also reflective of Chinese patterns.[153] It would be erroneous, however, to assume that Kim Il-sŏng intended to establish a relationship with the CPR similar to that which had once prevailed with the USSR. As a result of the recent deep internal struggles that had racked the KWP, Kim undoubtedly was motivated more strongly than ever before toward the reduction of *both* Chinese and Soviet influence *within* North Korea. In this sense, the evacuation of all Chinese People's Volunteers during 1958 probably relieved Kim's mind and possibly improved the overall position of Peking, too. It may or may not be true, as alleged, that Mao personally apologized to Kim for Chinese intervention at the time of the 1956 Plenum's aftermath. Certainly, the Chinese appear to have been careful in this period not to pursue policies of "big-nation chauvinism" toward P'yŏngyang.

The decisive factor in shifting Kim Il-sŏng toward the Chinese line, however, was an estimate of his own interests. Though the Korean Communists had praised Khrushchevian policies at the outset—perhaps out of habit, perhaps because they regarded them as only tactical—Kim and his supporters found Khrushchevism as it unfolded basically incompatible with their own desires and needs. They wanted a policy that challenged the United States, placed it on the defensive, and rolled it back. Their primary concern in foreign policy at this point, like that of their Chinese comrades, was the unification of their country—on *their* terms—and the removal of the United States from Asia. These primary desires were interrelated, and neither was served by an American-Soviet rapprochement. The basic reason for disenchantment with Soviet leadership and policies lay in this elemental fact.

153. For the broad details of this period, see Donald S. Zagoria, *The Sino-Soviet Conflict: 1956–1961,* Princeton, 1962, especially Chapters 6 and 7, pp. 172–221.

CHAPTER VIII

THE FORGING OF A MONOLITHIC SYSTEM

When Kim Il-sŏng stood before the faithful on November 2, 1970, delivering his report to the Fifth Korean Workers' Party Congress, he probably harbored mixed private emotions despite the generally optimistic tone of his public remarks. From his standpoint, the positive side of the ledger was a substantial one. He had been the supreme leader of a tightly knit, highly disciplined Party for more than a decade, with no serious challenges to his power. Truly, this had been a Stalinist era for North Korea.

Meanwhile, a new generation of North Koreans had been reared. All the external signs indicated that it was a generation totally committed to the Leader, steeled by "socialist patriotism," and prepared for lengthy sacrifices on behalf of the state. The triumph of militant nationalism, underwritten by a fierce allegiance to the Leader, had been most conspicuous among the youth. And the significance of this fact extended to the military as well as the political arena. Kim had every reason to expect his military forces to perform well, responding to any command, and enduring any hardship.

In the international arena, moreover, Kim's small state, sandwiched between two quarreling Communist giants, had managed to survive without capitulating to either. Indeed, by a process of weaving and feinting, first to one side, then to the other, Kim and his Party had established a certain independence and "neutrality." To be sure, this status was precarious. Despite the constant exhortations for all citizens to be guided by chuch'e, elements of military, political, and economic dependence persisted because of the very nature of North Korea. Yet the state and the Leader had come a considerable distance since the era of the Soviet occupation.

Kim could also take considerable pride in the indices of economic growth, particularly those relating to industrial production. Admittedly, the costs had been very high, and the results less spectacular than the published statistics indicated. Nevertheless, as of 1970, the economic development of North Korea had been rapid, especially in the heavy industrial sector. In addition, a moderately well-trained class of managers and technicians had emerged as a significant class—the "new intellectuals" of the DPRK's industrial age.

Today, North Korea is no longer a primitive agrarian society. But neither is it the "progressive" or "advanced" industrial-agrarian state that the Communists sometimes claim it to be. It can probably be characterized most accurately as an industrial-agrarian state with a high but dramatically uneven rate of growth and level of technical development, still "backward" and poor in many respects, but now largely acculturated to rapid economic modernization.

Already, however, we have glimpsed some of the "negative" items on the KWP's balance sheet. In many respects, the decade of the 1960s, as we shall see, was one of frustration and anxiety for the North Korean leaders in both the economic and political spheres. At the outset of this decade, Kim had promised his people that they would eat an abundance of rice, wear silk, and live in fine, new houses in the foreseeable future. Yet as the 1960s came to an end, the average North Korean remained poor, with a livelihood that was sufficient to meet his minimal needs, but that contained few elements of true comfort, not to mention luxury. And to obtain this livelihood, that average citizen had to work extraordinarily hard while enduring levels of tension that were far too high for his psychological well-being. The "good life" has remained a dream, scarcely nearer for most "new socialist men" in 1970 than in 1960.

Even in terms of GNP increases, economic performance in the 1960s, while substantial, fell below the expectations of the North Korean leaders. Later, we shall explore the primary reasons for these economic setbacks. Here, let it suffice to say that the North Korean Communists in this decade experienced difficulties in connection with economic growth similar to those faced earlier in the Soviet Union. These difficulties related to the drawbacks of "self-sufficiency"; the dilemma of priorities, especially the continued drain of military commitments; the problems implicit in long-term use of Stakhanovite methods; and, most serious of all, the very nature of the Communist administrative-managerial system. Thus, if the Fifth Party Congress was timed to coincide with the "successful completion" of the Seven-Year Plan, there was also evidence, in the remarks of Kim and others, of concern over economic problems, a concern made more conspicuous by the signs of significant growth in South Korea.

In the political arena also, Kim was confronted with major disappointments. The campaign to "liberate" South Korea, which had been given very high priority, had gone badly from the Communist standpoint. Indeed, it had gone so badly that Kim assigned responsibility for the failures by removing from office some of those who had earlier been given the key "liberation" assignments. Thus, one of the great goals of this era remained unachieved, and seemed even more distant as the new decade began.

Nor was the international scene as favorable as had been anticipated at the time of the Fourth KWP Congress in 1961. Then, it appeared as if a combination of Communist and united front movements might dominate the non-Western world, providing an alternative international order to the one that had based itself so precariously on the United Nations, and establishing the context for the "continuous revolution" to which all late-twentieth-century Asian Communist leaders, including Kim, have been dedicated. As the Fifth KWP Congress opened, however, the Communist world itself remained seriously divided. On balance, the Communist position in the Afro-Asian-Latin American world was probably less promising than it had been a decade earlier, although any general assessment was fraught with difficulties. Certainly, North Korea's own position in the world had changed very slightly. She remained largely isolated, involved primarily with those societies and movements that were either firmly committed at the ideological level or desperately in search of allies.

Thus, despite the extravagant words with which the Fifth Congress began and ended, the balance sheet pertaining to North Korea was exceedingly mixed, *even* if interpreted according to Communist values. Let us now turn to the most prominent details of the interesting period after 1959 in an effort to analyze the major trends, and provide a basis for later theoretical hypotheses.

Politics in a Monolithic Setting

The most conspicuous feature of North Korean politics in the past decade has been monocracy, government by a single man. It is, however, a modern not a traditional monocracy, since it employs mass organizational tactics in order to implement mobilization-style politics. The Leader and the Party remain conceptually unintegrated, despite the elaborate institutional structure that has been created around them. But that is of long-range not short-range significance. Today, Kim Il-sŏng *is* the Party—and the Party is currently the state in every meaningful sense.

By early 1959, Kim had almost completely eliminated the leaders of the old factions. The era that had begun for Korean Communism in the early 1920s was finally over. Gone were the principal spokesmen for the domestic, Yenan, and Soviet factions—executed, behind prison walls, or toiling as laborers on state livestock farms. Seemingly, only one faction now existed: that of Kim Il-sŏng. After the Twentieth CPSU Congress, the Kim faction did hastily drum up support for the principle of collective leadership. Nevertheless, the cult of Kim moved inexorably forward.

In spite of the general trend toward monocracy, the period after 1958, involving as it did substantial reorganization of the rural cooperative system, also saw renewed attention being paid to the local Party structure. The stage was thus set for the new guidelines of February 1960. Using a political technique that was to become standard, Kim Il-sŏng himself launched the new line by first taking over "on-the-spot guidance" in the *ri* of Ch'ŏngsan, Kangsŏ Prefecture, a few miles west of P'yŏngyang. With a group of high-level cadres from P'yŏngyang, including the Central Party's deputy chiefs of Organization and Propaganda, Kim Il-sŏng descended on the villages. There he found that the leadership of the cooperative was deficient in knowledge of agriculture and management; planning was totally inadequate, resulting in waste of manpower, materials, and funds; and there were too many work teams, most of which were doing nonessential tasks, thus reducing total productivity. He also found Party organization at the *ri* level totally ineffective in providing leadership and guidance to the cooperative.[1]

Obviously, these weaknesses resulted from the sudden changes in the administrative and production system. What was unforgivable from the Leader's point of view, however, was that the prefecture cadres, who possessed superior knowledge and skills, were sitting at their desks issuing written orders and demanding statistics. How could those without any knowledge of planning draw up plans? How could the cooperatives without technicians successfully carry out tasks requiring special skills? The obvious conclusion was that the cadres in the prefectures had to go down to the lower levels and talk to the farmers. After collecting the opinions of the lower cadres, they could then draw up plans for them. The prefectural Party unit had to become the key link in the system connecting the Central Party to the village. In a speech at the Kangsŏ Prefectural Party Plenum (February 18), and again at the Enlarged Meeting of the Presidium of the Central Committee (February 23), Kim Il-sŏng ordered the prefectural Party organization to provide "direct guidance" to organizations below it. The prefectural Party, as Kim phrased it, was to be the terminal leadership organ for local economic and political operations.[2]

At this point, there were 173 prefectures in North Korea. The Party

1. For Kim's speech before the Ch'ŏngsan-ri Party Assembly on Feb. 8, 1960, "For the Correct Management of the Socialist Agrarian Economy," see *Kim Il-sŏng chŏjak sŏnjip (Selected Writings of Kim Il-sŏng)*, P'yŏngyang, 1968, Vol. II, pp. 446–479.

2. For Kim's speech before the Kangsŏ Prefectural Party Plenum, "On Improving Work Methods of the Prefectural Party Organizations to Keep Pace with New Conditions," see *ibid.*, pp. 480–504. For the speech before the Enlarged Conference of the Presidium of the Central Committee, "On Lessons Obtained from Guiding the Activities of the Kangsŏ Prefectural Party," see *ibid.*, pp. 505–542.

had clearly decided that, given the size of these units and the number of trained cadres available, the prefectural Party was the logical unit to transmit and supervise central Party policies at the grass-roots level. It is significant that these administrative decisions were being made only a short time after the establishment of the commune system in China, although there is scant mention of the Chinese experiment in the North Korean literature of this period.

The so-called Ch'ŏngsan-ri Method basically involved the equipping of local-level cadres with both political-ideological and technical skills. The *primacy* of politics continued to be stoutly maintained as the only means whereby Party directives could be faithfully observed and the masses induced to participate "enthusiastically" in the implementation of all policies, economic and political. First and foremost, Party cadres were to be Red. At the same time, however, if they were to be successful, they had to improve their technical knowledge so that they could truly guide the enterprises for which they were responsible. Thus, the goal was to be both Red and expert. Once again, the themes of contemporary Chinese Communism were much in evidence.

In his remarks before the Kangsŏ Plenum and throughout the decade that followed, Kim Il-sŏng railed against "bureaucratism, formalism, and commandism," those historic proclivities of the functionary. The Ch'ŏngsan-ri Method, he insisted, involved moving out of one's office, going into the field to observe actual conditions, and then drawing up a comprehensive plan for tackling whatever problems existed. Planning is fundamental, asserted Kim, and rule-of-thumb management, whether political or economic, must be eliminated. Local Party organizations must analyze existing conditions correctly, put first things first, and focus energy at the right place and the right time.

If the Party leadership was to be successful, moreover, it was essential to follow the mass line. The mass line involved wedding the masses to Party policies by causing them to participate in the processes whereby those policies were elucidated, enforced, and expanded. When Party leaders like Kim sought to emphasize the "democratic" aspects of the mass line, they stressed the importance of learning from the masses, listening to the voice of the masses, and heeding the needs of the masses. When they wanted to underline the utility of the mass line for the Party, they put the emphasis upon making the masses "clearly understand" the intention of the Party and the Leader, causing them to examine the reasons for such failures in performance as occurred, and binding them psychologically to the decision-making process, and so to its responsibilities. Once again, the close relationship to Chinese trends is to be seen.

Several months after the Kangsŏ Plenum, a startling event, pregnant with possibilities for the Communists, occurred in the south. Challenged by a massive student revolt, the regime of Syngman Rhee finally collapsed in April 1960. A bitterly hated enemy of the Communists had been ousted from power. Communist organs naturally gave enormous coverage to the events surrounding Rhee's overthrow, providing their own inimitable interpretations. As soon as the dust had begun to settle, moreover, they redoubled their efforts to initiate a new joint conference and other movements toward unification.[3] Quickly, however, the interim Hŏ Chŏng government came under Communist attack as "another puppet regime to support American imperialism," as did the government of Chang Myŏn that succeeded it.

In his speech of August 14, 1960, commemorating Korean Liberation, Kim Il-sŏng asserted that the newly born Chang Myŏn government was no different from that of Rhee. The Americans, he asserted, continued to dominate the south, and only the Communists could end the crisis, unifying the nation and solving its problems. However, Kim went on to propose a federal system for Korea so as to "alleviate fears" on the part of the South Korean government that the entire country would be brought under Communist control.[4]

Developments during this period indicate that the Communists were caught off guard by the April student revolt and its aftermath, and were generally unable to take advantage of the political chaos that had erupted in the south. There is absolutely no evidence, for example, that any of the actions taking place there were Communist-inspired, nor did any Communist cells or front organizations emerge in the immediate aftermath of Rhee's downfall. All of this was eloquent testimony to the current weakness of the Communists in South Korea, a situation intimately related to the Korean War. Kim Il-sŏng was soon to reflect upon this missed opportunity and order a drastic shift in policy.

Meanwhile, attention in P'yŏngyang was focused upon economic concerns. Constant references were made to the new Ch'ŏngsan-ri Method as a means of improving both political organization and economic productivity. And by the fifteenth anniversary of Liberation, the symbol of the Flying Horse was omnipresent, together with production figures and goals. Placed on huge billboards, they vied with the gigantic portraits of Kim and Khrushchev standing side by side that graced the central section of the city.

In connection with the celebration of August 15, incidentally, it was announced that all political prisoners whose sentences were for ten years or less would receive an amnesty and be set free. Those serving longer sentences would have their sentences reduced by one-third. All criminals receiving amnesty, moreover, would have their full civil rights restored. No

3. For details on DPRK appeals to the South Korean people and to the new government, see *Nodong Sinmun* (hereafter *NS*), April 22 and April 28, 1960, p. 1.
4. For full text of Kim's speech of Aug. 14, 1960, see *Kŭlloja* (*The Worker*), August 1960, pp. 3–28.

indication was given, however, of the number of individuals affected by this order.[5]

At this point, the regime seemed more self-confident than at any time since its establishment. Faced with no internal political crisis, it was now capable of demonstrating leniency, at least to the minor figures caught up in the stormy political crises of earlier years. It was also in this period, however, that a massive rewriting of Korean Communist history got under way.[6] From this point on, Kim became the source of all wisdom and all

5. The order, dated August 9, 1960, was reported in the August 10 issue of *Nodong Sinmun*. On the occasion of the twentieth anniversary of liberation, in 1965, a similar amnesty was decreed.

6. Two illustrations of the new effort are the report of Pak Kŭm-ch'ŏl at the fifteenth anniversary of the founding of the Korean Workers' Party (October 1960) and an article by Yim Ch'un-ch'u which appeared in *Kŭlloja* in April 1961. Pak's analysis of the past can be presented succinctly as follows: The Korean Communist Party was founded in 1925 as a reflection of the demands of the growing working class and peasant masses. Because petty-bourgeois intellectuals occupied the leading positions in the Party, however, and engaged in continuous factional strife, the Party was unable to root itself in the masses, became prey to the rigorous oppression of the Japanese, and had to be disbanded in 1928.

At this point, the opportunists deserted the movement, but a new group of Communists under the leadership of Comrade Kim Il-sŏng emerged. For the first time, a correct revolutionary line was established, with the principles of Marxism-Leninism being creatively applied to the concrete practices and needs of the Korean revolution. Under Kim, the national liberation struggle against the Japanese was developed to a higher stage: the stage of armed struggle. Despite most difficult circumstances and a powerful foe, the guerrillas did not yield; carrying out their struggle for over fifteen years, they ultimately overcame all odds. Thus, at the conclusion of World War II, a refined, trained Communist core under the leadership of Comrade Kim had been forged in the crucible of revolutionary experience. The brilliant revolutionary traditions of the Korean Communist movement had been established.

All had not been smooth after Liberation. Various factionalists had sought to worm their way back into control of the Party. However, under the leadership of Comrade Kim, the Party had remained loyal to Marxism-Leninism, applying it creatively to the realities of Korea and regarding the ties with the masses as the most important element. (Pak Kŭm-ch'ŏl, "A Report Made at the 15th Anniversary Commemorating the Founding of the Korean Workers' Party," *Kŭlloja* (*The Worker*), Oct. 15, 1960, pp. 2–16.)

In his article, Yim, recalling April 1940 "with profound emotion," wrote that between the fall of 1938 and March 1940, Korean revolutionary forces under Kim Il-sŏng had inflicted heavy casualties upon the Japanese, but at that point the imperialists mobilized huge army units "to exterminate us." Thousand of elite Japanese troops were brought into the Tumen River area, with airplanes, reconnaissance units, and other special aids. Our hardships, asserted Yim, were indescribable. We had to march and fight every day to break out of the enemy's encirclement—across snow-covered mountains and through dense jungles. Rations ran out. Many comrades became ill. Nevertheless, because of our outstanding leader, Marshal Kim Il-sŏng, we marched forward to victory through every difficult circumstance, inspired by his teachings.

Kim, according to Yim, not only showed great bravery and marvelous compassion, but extraordinary political sagacity as well. In mid-April, arriving in a jungle area, our forces took a ten-day rest, wrote Yim. During this time, Kim convened

truth—indeed, the sole reference point of significance with relation to the Korean Communist movement, past, present, and future. However, assiduous cultivation of the cult of Kim did not interfere with demands that, at all other levels within the Party, collective leadership be instituted. Kim was caused to stand above Party and state, in the tradition of the absolute monarch. The reintegration of Leader with Party, Leader with state, and Leader with society, became a task for the future.

The Fourth Congress of the Korean Workers' Party

Both political and economic conditions now warranted the convening of a Party Congress. Kim and his supporters had gained firm control over the state and all Party organs. The Five-Year Plan had been successfully completed, ahead of schedule, and a new Seven-Year Plan had been prepared. Thus, on September 11, 1961, the Fourth Congress of the Korean Workers' Party opened. Voting delegates present numbered 1,157; no fewer than thirty-two foreign countries sent representatives, among them Frol Kozlov, Teng Hsiao-p'ing, and K'ang Sheng. According to the Credentials Committee report, 57 percent of the delegates were "workers," 4.1 percent were "revolutionaries and military men," 27.3 percent were "farmers," and 11.6 percent were "officials (including students)."

Kim Il-sŏng's major report to the Congress reflected the newly found confidence of a man who had completely smashed internal dissension and succeeded in pushing his people through years of bitter sacrifice on behalf of state development with a substantial degree of success. His initial and primary emphasis was upon economic progress.

> The historic revolutionary tasks of completing socialist transformation in town and country and building the foundation of socialism have been triumphantly carried out. Under the leadership of the Party, our people, surmounting all difficulties, have continued the grand Ch'ŏllima march, conquered the first summit of socialist construction, and built up an impregnable revolutionary democratic base in the northern half of the Republic.[7]

---

the cadres and presented them with "a brilliant, detailed analysis of the situation—local, regional and international." (Yim Ch'un-ch'u, "The 200,000 ri Long March—A Recollection of April 1940," ibid., April 15, 1961.) A ri is 0.4 kilometers; hence 200,000 ri would be approximately 80,000 kilometers! We rechecked the figures because they are unbelievable—but presumably the Korean Long March had to surpass that of the Chinese. In any case, the parallel is too obvious to be missed and is but one of many indications of the types of stimuli that could serve in the building of those Communist traditions suitable to the age of Kim Il-sŏng.

7. Kim Il Sung, Report of the Central Committee of the Workers' Party of Korea to the Fourth Congress, Sept. 11, 1961, in Documents of the Fourth Congress of the Workers' Party of Korea, P'yŏngyang, 1961, p. 1. For the Korean text, see Kim Il-sŏng chŏjak sŏnjip, op. cit., Vol. III, pp. 66–203.

We shall have occasion to explore the purely economic aspects of Kim's report later. Here, it suffices to note that, after dismissing the critics of his economic program with a few contemptuous remarks, Kim stressed three basic accomplishments: far-reaching increases in industrial productivity; the creation of a small and medium factory complex, widely dispersed geographically and geared to consumer goods production; and substantial increases in agricultural production, resulting from major advances in irrigation, electrification, and mechanization—the three central tasks confronting the agrarian sector.

The keynote to the economic section of Kim's report was a strident optimism. "It can now be said that we have basically solved the food problem," he announced. And he followed this assertion with the statement that, with the foundations of a "self-reliant, modern industry" having already been laid, mass living standards would rise dramatically in the years immediately ahead. Agriculture, moreover, was also being modernized at an extraordinary pace. Hence, the many problems of the rural-urban gap were on the way to being solved. The worker and the peasant would shortly arrive at roughly the same level of technological development.

Even in the economic portions of his report, however, Kim's attention was firmly fixed upon "politics first." Material incentives, he admitted, had to bolster political and moral incentives to labor. Distribution according to the quality and quantity of work performed was indeed an objective law in any socialist society. Moreover, expertise was crucial. The role of the scientist and technician was of supreme importance to the success or failure of any economic program. Nevertheless, the primary task was to cultivate the political and ideological consciousness of the masses, to inculcate in them the spirit of faithfully serving the Party and the revolution with a spirit of unselfish devotion to country and people. Armed with the monolithic ideology of the Party, spurred onward by "socialist patriotism," and equipped with advanced technical training, the new socialist man (as Kim imagined him) should combine faith and science— faith in the Party, and science for greater productivity.

Although both doctrine and experience taught that it was more important to be Red than expert, Kim made it clear that he did not regard the two qualities as separable. The issue of the expert's class origins, however, was not overlooked. "We have completely smashed the wrong view that a definite category of people alone can develop science and technology," he asserted. In the past, there had been a tendency to underestimate the creativity and initiative of the workers and peasants. Now, the scientist, technician, worker, and peasant must work together, and become as one.

In this fashion, Kim struck out obliquely at the "old intellectuals," almost all of whom had come from a gentry background, and called for the creation of a new, technologically oriented intellectual class, stemming from worker-peasant roots. This led him into a general survey of class trends in the DPRK. North Korea, he proclaimed, had become a state in which industry and the working class now predominated—a socialist industrial-agricultural state, with 52 percent of the total population composed of factory and office workers. Meanwhile, the peasants, "embraced in the socialist collective farming system," had been liberated, and had consequently become a reliable ally of the working class. The intellectuals, too, had been radically changed. "Thanks to the persevering education by our Party and through the struggle for revolution and construction, old intellectuals have been remolded into socialist intellectuals. At the same time, a large army of new intellectuals are faithfully serving the Party and the cause of the working class, playing a great role in socialist construction."

These changes in the class structure of Korean society, together with increases in productivity, required alterations in the economic and political administrative structure. As industry expanded rapidly, it was necessary to relieve the ministries and bureaus of their burdens by strengthening the local industrial management apparatus. It was for this reason that the Ch'ŏngsan-ri Method had been introduced, and a new premium placed upon the prefectural Party. Kim voiced the familiar complaints about bureaucratism and the other deficiencies of the cadres, but asserted that, in the main, these problems had been remedied. Party functionaries were now "establishing a genuinely popular style of work," going to the masses, bringing the Party line and policy home to them while working with them, discussing and "solving all matters directly with the masses by giving play to their zeal and initiative."

Thus was the mass line repeatedly stressed in Kim's report. In the five years since the Third Party Congress, he proclaimed at another point in his report, an epochal change had been brought about in the struggle to improve the Party's style of guidance and method of work. The Party had sought to marshal the inexhaustible strength of the masses, tap their creative energies, and mobilize their great enthusiasm so that Party policies could be implemented while the Party at the same time positively served mass needs.[8]

Kim's confidence with respect to economic matters was matched by his glowing report on political developments. Never in its history, he proclaimed, had the Party been so completely unified. Membership now totaled 1,311,563, including 1,166,359 full members and 145,204 candidate members—a total of 146,618 more than at the time of Third Party Congress in 1956.

The central task confronting the Party, he asserted, had been to improve the qualitative composition of the cadres. To this end, old revolutionary cadres had been used as the firm core, along with cadres of working-class origin. Meanwhile, "large numbers of new intellectuals from among

8. *Ibid.,* p. 161. *Documents* (English), p. 88.

the workers and peasants" had been raised up, while at the same time old intellectuals were being "reeducated." Thus, cadres of working-class origin were being "correctly combined" with those from intellectual sources. The number of working-class cadres in Party and state organs, Kim asserted, had increased from 24 percent in 1956 to 31 percent at present, with "old revolutionary cadres" and cadres of labor origin playing a crucial role.

The major speakers at the Fourth Congress in addition to Kim Il-sŏng were Kim Il, who presented a lengthy report on the Seven-Year Plan, Pak Kŭm-ch'ŏl, Kim Ch'ang-man, and Yi Hyo-sun. In these reports there was no deviation from Kim Il-sŏng's basic themes, which were often reproduced in his exact words. Kim Il reiterated the basic purposes and the two-stage character of the Seven-Year Plan, providing elaborate details on priorities and goals.[9] Pak Kŭm-ch'ŏl worked to fortify the anti-Japanese partisan myth; he recited past travails and accomplishments, and provided his own interpretation of the mass line.

> The Party and government leaders went down to work places, brought home to the masses the hard situation facing the country, discussed with them ways of fulfilling the plan, mapped out the plan together with them, worked out measures for tapping more reserves, and thus called forth the entire working people to the devoted struggle for the maximum production and economization.[10]

Pak also reiterated the purposes of Party reorganization. Central Party guidance was to be brought closer to the lower Party organs, with the individual member regarded as the first and most essential target of all guidance work. To relate the prefectural Party to the *ri* for these purposes was essential, just as the central Party had to give the provincial Party effective guidance, and the provincial Party in turn had to provide the prefectural Party with such aid.

Kim Ch'ang-man, in a manner that reflected earlier Chinese Communist comparisons with Great Britain, gave a detailed statistical analysis of the areas in which North Korean per capita production of certain major industrial products exceeded that of Japan. Naturally, he concluded that North Korea's "Great Leap"—the Ch'ŏllima Movement—had been a massive success. He also connected it with the establishment of chuch'e as the governing principle of Party life and work.

Yi Hyo-sun's speech was, like the others, a paean of praise for Kim Il-sŏng in the classic "cult of personality" tradition.[11] It was also Yi's

---

9. Kim Il, "Report on the Seven-Year Plan for the Development of the National Economy of the DPRK," Sept. 16, 1961, in *Documents of the Fourth Congress of the Workers' Party of Korea,* P'yŏngyang, 1961, pp. 159–260.

10. "Speech by Comrade Pak Keum Chul," vice-chairman of the CC, KWP, Sept. 12, 1961, in *ibid.,* pp. 216–285 (at p. 269).

11. "Creatively applying the general principles and propositions of Marxism-Leninism to the specific conditions of our country, Comrade Kim Il-sŏng has not

task to recite at length the crimes, failures, and general impotence of the South Korean government, and to call for a Communist-led uprising in the south. He left no doubt of the role that Communism was expected to play in Korea's future: "No one can think of the future of Korea and raise the question of the unification of the country apart from the Korean Communists and the firm material foundation established by them in the northern part." [12]

At the close of the Fourth Congress, 85 full and 50 candidate Central Committee members were elected. Some measure of the upheaval within the Party after 1956 can be gathered from the fact that, of the 85 full Central Committee members, only 28 had been reelected from the Third Central Committee of 1956, with an additional 12 having been promoted from the status of candidate members of the Third Central Committee. A total of 45, however, or more than one-half, were new members. Thus, of the 71 Central Committee members elected by the Third Party Congress in April 1956, 43 failed to reappear on the rosters. There could be no better indication of how savage the factional struggle had been. Moreover, among the 50 candidate Central Committee members, only one (not counting the 12 elevated to full membership) had been reelected from the Third Congress. Thus of the 45 candidate members chosen in April 1956, 32 had disappeared from the roster.

The eleven key figures of the Korean Workers' Party, listed in order of their ranking on the Political Committee, were now Kim Il-sŏng, Ch'oe Yong-gŏn, Kim Il, Pak Kŭm-ch'ŏl, Kim Ch'ang-man, Yi Hyo-sun, Pak Chŏng-ae, Kim Kwang-hyŏp, Chŏng Il-yong, Nam Il, and Yi Chong-ok. These were followed by the five candidate members of the Political Committee: Kim Ik-sŏn, Yi Chu-yŏn, Ha Ang-ch'ŏn, Han Sang-du, and Hyŏn Mu-gwang.[13] At the top, as will be noted, the changes were not major ones when measured against the positions held after 1958, but they obviously represented a dramatic shift from 1956. At the lower levels, however, significant developments were still occurring. Important Party posts were being assigned to a large number of younger individuals in their thirties and forties, individuals who had emerged in the period after the Korean War and were generally unconnected with the factional divisions of the past. They could be expected to be personally loyal to Kim Il-sŏng, for they were of the "post-Kim" generation.

---

only correctly laid down the general line of socialist revolution and socialist construction in our country but also clearly indicated with an outstanding insight and scientific foresight the direction of activities and policy of our Party in conformity with each period and stage in the complicated development of the revolution and brilliantly materialized them with a staunch fighting spirit and revolutionary sweep." "Speech by Comrade Li Hyo Soon, Vice Chairman of the CC, Workers' Party of Korea, September 15, 1961," in *ibid.*, pp. 315–339 (at p. 317).

12. *Ibid.*, p. 336.

13. Chosŏn Chungang T'ongshinsa (Korean Central News Agency), *Chosŏn chungang nyŏngam (Korean Central Yearbook)*, P'yŏngyang, 1962, p. 217.

Meanwhile, certain changes were made in Party organization. The most important was the assignment of the five Party vice-chairmen to be in charge of various departments. Thus, Ch'oe Yong-gŏn was placed in charge of the Legislative Department; Kim Il of the Administrative Department; Pak Kŭm-ch'ŏl of the Organization Department; Kim Ch'ang-man of the Propaganda and Agitation Department; and Yi Hyo-sun of the International Department. At the same time, the Party Standing Committee was redesignated the Political Committee, and the Organization and Cadre departments were combined into one Organization and Guidance Department. This new department was headed by Kim Yŏng-ju, the younger brother of Kim Il-sŏng and now a rising star on the political horizon.[14] At the local level, the lowest unit of Party organization was redesignated a cell, and large plants, with three hundred or more Party members, were granted permission to organize their own Party committees, equal in rights to those of the district and prefectural Party committees.

In surveying the internal political scene at the time of the Fourth Party Congress, one cannot avoid placing the emphasis upon two inter-related developments that dominated all else: political stability and a new era of independence. As we have emphasized, a supreme confidence on the part of Kim and his associates was made manifest in each of the major reports delivered before the Congress. For the first time since its emergence upon the political scene, the Kim group was able to regard itself as immune from internal or external threat. In the aftermath of the massive purges of 1956–58, intra-Party squabbles had disappeared. Intervention by either of the major Communist powers, moreover, seemed most improbable in view of their failure in the 1956 intervention and the rising Sino-Soviet cleavage. Indeed, North Korea was now being ardently wooed by both Moscow and Peking. Finally, events in South Korea augured well for the Communists' dream of unification under their banner. Thus, Kim's chuch'e had set the tone for the new era. The old cry, "Learn from the Soviet Union!" had now been replaced by a new and longer one, "Learn from the glorious revolutionary tradition founded by Kim Il-sŏng and his anti-Japanese partisans!"

Economic Advances and Goals

Although a detailed discussion of the North Korean economy is contained in chapters XIII and XIV below, a basic outline of economic developments must be presented here, so that political and social trends can be seen in a broader context.

The Fourth Party Congress of September 1961 was held as the new Seven-Year Plan got under way, and almost all the major reports to that

14. Kasumigaseki-kai, *Gendai Chōsen jimmei jiten* (*Biographical Dictionary of Contemporary Korea*), Tokyo, 1962, appendix p. 23.

Congress, including Kim Il-sŏng's, dealt extensively with economic accomplishments and goals. The regime, as we have seen, was greatly encouraged by developments on the economic front during the 1958–61 period. A mood of strident optimism permeated the Congress, and while this was customary—indeed mandatory—in official Communist proceedings of this type, there is reason to believe that in this case it was genuine.

The Central Statistical Bureau had announced in mid-January 1960 that the Five-Year Plan had been completed the previous June, in a record time of two and one-half years.[15] At that point it was indicated that an interim buffer period would ensue, with a new plan being launched in 1961 after proper preparations had been completed. In his report to the Fourth Party Congress, Kim Il-sŏng gave a lengthy recital of achievements during the Five-Year Plan period. He asserted that in the four years between 1957 and 1960, total industrial output had increased 3.5 times, and that the average annual increase in industrial production had been 36.6 percent. In agriculture, the three major tasks—irrigation, electrification, and mechanization—had been significantly advanced. Some 800,000 chŏngbo, seven times the acreage of the pre-Liberation era, were now under irrigation, including all paddy fields. Rural electrification had proceeded to the point where 92.1 percent of all villages and 62 percent of all peasant households had electricity. Mechanization, while proceeding more slowly, was making progress; some 13,000 tractors were now in use, he announced, together with a large number of other farm machines.

These gains, together with increases in cultivated acreage and use of fertilizer, had resulted in substantial production increases. In 1960, Kim claimed, grain production had totalled 3,803,000 metric tons. Villages were now being encouraged to place less emphasis upon grain production and more upon producing commercial products essential to light industry. For 1961, nevertheless, the Party had set a target of a one-million-ton increase in grain production. Livestock, fruit growing, and sericulture were also making satisfactory progress, according to Kim. Representative of his report as a whole was the flat assertion, "It can be said that we have now basically solved the food problem." [16]

Even before the Fourth Party Congress, the government had sought to publicize the measures being taken to raise the deplorably low living standards of the North Korean people. During 1959, the prices of rationed goods had been reduced, the agricultural tax-in-kind lowered, and wages and salaries raised until the average wage was 43 percent above the 1948 figure. Housing facilities had also been expanded. With the criticisms of the 1956–58 period still clearly in mind, Kim and his key administrators were undoubtedly anxious to reduce one of the chief potential causes of

15. For the Central Statistical Bureau report of January 16, 1960, see NS, Jan. 17, 1960, pp. 1–2.

16. Kim Il Sung, Report, op. cit., p. 21.

political unrest. There were equally good economic reasons for seeking to raise living standards, however, since the level of sacrifice being demanded required more than political-ideological incentives, whatever the regime might assert. Increased productivity—and particularly improved quality—hinged to a considerable extent upon meeting the elemental needs of the primary producers.

As we shall see later, living standards during this period remained extremely low, despite the government's assertions. At best, progress for the average North Korean was from marginal-subsistence livelihood to guaranteed poverty-subsistence livelihood, with the peasant in particular merely existing.

Kim Il-sŏng himself indirectly admitted these facts in outlining the basic purposes of the Seven-Year Plan before the Fourth Party Congress. Its fundamental task, he proclaimed, was "to carry out an overall technical reconstruction and a cultural revolution, and to radically improve the livelihood of the people, resting on the triumphant socialist system." [17] The new plan was based upon the concept of a two-stage progression. During the first three years (1961–63), the aim would be to improve living standards by increasing the proportion of state investment going into light industry, agriculture, and marine production. Investments in heavy industry would be confined primarily to the expansion of existing facilities. In the final four years of the plan (1964–67), emphasis would be placed upon the creation of new facilities for heavy industry—notably in mining, fuels, electric power, chemicals, machine tools, iron and steel, and transportation. At the end of this period, Kim promised, "all of the people [will] be well off in every aspect of their life."

The Seven-Year Plan was extraordinarily ambitious, reflecting the soaring optimism of the North Korean leaders. Under the Plan, total industrial output was scheduled to increase annually by an average of 18 percent, with machine tools, chemicals, fuel and power, and iron and steel the primary targets.[18] Marine products were to be boosted to an annual yield of 1 to 1.2 million tons by the end of the Plan. And, in the most ambitious goal of all, total grain production was to reach 6 to 7 million metric tons by the same date.

How much improvement in living standards was promised? The Plan envisaged a 2.7-fold increase in national income, with the real incomes of factory and office workers scheduled to rise 1.7-fold and those of all workers (including peasants) 1.5-fold. In the course of the Plan, the living standard of the average farmer was to be raised to that of "well-to-do middle peasants." Taxes were to be "abolished"; state income would be totally derived from state enterprises. Refusing to acknowledge that totally controlled prices (and wages) represented one of the more rigorous forms

17. *Ibid.*, p. 42.
18. *Ibid.*, p. 45.

of taxation, Kim asserted: "By abolishing the income tax levied on the peasants, we will do away once and for all with the tax system, the legacy of the old society, and completely free the working people from the burden of all taxes, and, accordingly, their real incomes will increase." [19]

It was acknowledged that the basic gains projected both in industry and agriculture would require major increases in the quantity and quality of scientific and technical personnel. In August 1960, at the Plenum of the Central Committee, Kim Il had indicated that North Korea currently had 32,214 technicians and "experts," 4.3 times as many as had existed in 1953. In addition, some 66,998 "lower-level technicians" were working as of the end of 1959. Given the needs of the new era, he proclaimed, these numbers were woefully inadequate. In the course of the new Seven-Year Plan, therefore, some 180,000 "engineers and high-level specialists" and 460,000 "technicians and secondary specialists" were to be trained.

Such a program would require the rapid expansion of technical higher schools and colleges, agricultural institutes, and similar vocational training centers. It was from this point that Kim Il-sŏng and other leaders began to place great emphasis upon work-study programming, or combining further education with full-time work. Every Korean worker should be enrolled in a factory college or in some training program that would further his technical (and political) education. The true cultural revolution would be achieved when the entire laboring class had been given sufficient education to be considered working intellectuals. Meanwhile, leaders like Kim Ch'ang-man continued to complain that while most old Korean intellectuals had been "reeducated," the relevance of higher education to the actual production processes was still insufficient. Here, one sees the beginnings not merely of the changes that were already in the works for the North Korean educational system, but of those that loomed ahead for China.[20]

19. *Ibid.*, p. 63.

20. One *Kŭlloja* writer asserted that the supply of technicians in the major industrial fields was only 35.4 percent of the demand, and in the machine-manufacturing field, it was barely 20.1 percent. He stressed the need to attach as much importance to on-the-job training as to formal, full-time classroom work, and urged the creation of classes in each factory, corporation, and cooperative. Old-fashioned educational techniques, he asserted, had to be rooted out of the schools, and the tie between production, actual life, and the classroom made much closer. Only in this fashion could maximal training efficiency be attained with minimal expenditure of time and funds. At the same time, care had to be taken to give first attention to ideological training, so as to instill in this new scientific-technocratic class the central political-moral values of the anti-Japanese partisans. See Chŏng Ki-nyŏn, "Our Party's Policy to Train More and Better Technical Personnel Faster," *Kŭlloja* (*The Worker*), Aug. 15, 1960, pp. 40–43.

In the light of the subsequent Chinese Cultural Revolution, which revolved in part around similar issues, these developments of 1960–61 in North Korea are most interesting.

Given these ambitious new goals, it was natural that the government should continue to accelerate the Ch'öllima Campaign. On every factory wall, cooperative bulletin board, and urban billboard, the 1,000-ri Flying Horse was to be seen, symbol of North Korea's Stakhanovite program. Exhortations to overfulfill production quotas, the publicity given "labor heroes," and the selection of individual factories or cooperatives that had reached levels of production qualifying them for the title of Ch'öllima work teams occupied the major attention of the media. By the end of August 1961, on the eve of the Fourth Party Congress, Kim Il-söng asserted, some 2 million workers had become a part of the Ch'öllima work-team movement, with 4,958 workshops involving 125,028 individuals having received the title of Ch'öllima workshops, and 55 work teams involving 1,459 individuals qualifying as "double Ch'öllima." In this manner, the pressures to increase production were steadily maintained.

Meanwhile, as we have suggested earlier, new administrative and managerial techniques were introduced that affected both industry and agriculture. For the next decade and beyond, the Ch'öngsan-ri Method was to serve as a guideline for proper administrative-managerial operations. With the Prefectural Party Committee made centrally responsible for production at this level and below, the concepts of "politics first" and the mass line were injected into the economic as well as the political realm. Moreover, the union of political and economic skills that the cadres were supposed to exemplify was to be conferred on each worker and peasant through on-the-spot guidance and listening to, as well as teaching, the masses. Shortly, another principle—the Taean Method—was to be set forth. This method was aimed at replacing the single-manager system of decision-making with a system of collective decision-making involving the entire work force of the factory or cooperative, with the local Party committee playing the key role.

By means of the Ch'öngsan-ri and Taean methods, the Party hoped to enhance administrative efficiency at the local levels, extend a feeling of responsibility for production to the whole work force, and wed psychological and political stimuli firmly to economic ones. Borrowing from earlier Soviet and later Chinese ideas, the North Koreans in this period set up the basic political-administrative framework for economic development that was still governing their society as they sought to scale "new socialist heights" in the 1970s.

Despite the constant emphasis upon chuch'e in all economic as well as political matters, it is abundantly clear that Soviet aid and trade were crucial elements in the future economic plans of North Korea at this point. For example, the ninth session of the Korean-Soviet Scientific and Technical Cooperation Committee, meeting on December 8, 1960, produced a Soviet pledge to send technical materials relating to mining, metal manufacturing, and electrical equipment to Korea, to train additional Korean technicians in the chemical field, and to send some Soviet technicians to aid in both the chemical and metal products industries.[21] On December 24, moreover, a major trade and economic cooperation agreement was concluded between the Soviet Union and the DPRK in Moscow for the years 1961–67— the period of the Seven-Year Plan. For the first five years, trade was scheduled to increase 80 percent in comparison with the previous five years, with Korea agreeing to supply certain metals, machine tools, cement, tobacco, and foodstuffs in exchange for Soviet machine parts, metals, chemicals, oil, and cotton. The Soviet Union also agreed to furnish technical assistance on a number of industrial projects, one of the most important of which was the expansion of the Kim Ch'aek Iron and Steel Plant in Ch'ŏngjin. Moreover, while there was naturally no public announcement, we know from defectors and captured agents that the USSR remained vital to Kim's military expansion program—indeed, to almost every aspect of the North Korean military establishment. Accordingly, if relations between P'yŏngyang and Moscow began to deteriorate in the same way as relations between Moscow and Peking, the repercussions upon the North Korean economy would probably be immediate and serious.

Instability in the Communist World

Thus, trends within the international Communist movement were of great concern to the P'yŏngyang leaders.

We may now turn to developments in the period immediately prior to the Fourth Party Congress. We know that in 1959 relations between Moscow and Peking became much more tense. In June of that year, some six months before their agreements with the North Koreans, the Russians had reneged (as the Chinese viewed it) on the military agreement of October 1957 by refusing to furnish certain types of atomic information or materials to China. In September, moreover, when open clashes between China and India occurred over the Himalayan border controversy, an official Soviet statement was interpreted by Peking as showing sympathy toward the Indian position. Even more upsetting were the signs of American-Soviet rapprochement and the fact that Khrushchev, returning home from Washington by way of Peking, saw fit to lecture the Chinese leaders on such topics as the importance of conducting a revolution "peacefully," the dubious worth of communes, and the reasons for avoiding war with the United States.

What were the repercussions of these developments in P'yŏngyang? In the broadest terms, it can be said that the unfolding of the Sino-Soviet quarrel caused North Korea initially to draw closer to certain Asian Communist parties, particularly those of Japan, Vietnam, and Indonesia, in an effort to establish a joint position of nonalignment between the two Communist giants. Such a position, however, was exceedingly difficult to

21. *NS,* Dec. 8, 1960, p. 2.

maintain and P'yŏngyang gradually began to shift toward the Peking line, mainly because on the critical substantive issues the North Korean leaders found themselves largely in agreement with the Chinese and strongly opposed to the current Khrushchevian policies.

The events of early 1959 illustrate the beginning of these trends. On February 26, the Japanese Communist Party leaders who had attended the Twenty-first CPSU Congress stopped in P'yŏngyang on their way home. These included Miyamoto Kenji, Kasuga Shōichi, and Nishizawa Tomio— all key figures in the JCP Politburo.[22] Kamiyama Shigeo, himself a high ranking JCP functionary at this time, was later to remark that, from this point on, "peace" disappeared as the featured theme in Party circles, and "independence" took its place. He attributed this to the power of the Chinese line that each Communist Party should be free, independent, and sovereign, and should not submit to the "baton" of the Soviet Party.[23]

Unquestionably, Khrushchev at this point was seeking to woo Kim and his supporters. On April 3, Ch'oe Yong-gŏn, president of the Presidium of the Supreme People's Assembly, and the second-ranking Communist of the realm, left for Moscow at the invitation of the Russians. With him were two united front spokesmen, Hong Myŏng-hui and Kang Ryang-uk, and the vice-minister of Foreign Affairs, Yi Tong-gŏn. The group was given a grand tour of the Soviet Union, visiting factories, rural collective farms, and various major cities. Accompanied by Mikoyan, among others, they met with Khrushchev in Yalta. After the Soviet trip, the group continued to Eastern Europe, not returning to P'yŏngyang until June 19.

In Albania, incidentally, Ch'oe expressed the same themes as elsewhere. "The international reactionaries and their lackeys," he asserted, had "resorted to every conceivable trick to split the unity of the socialist family and alienate people oriented toward peace and socialism from the banners of Marxism-Leninism." These maneuvers had failed, however, with the result that the solidarity of the socialist camp was growing ever stronger. "The Korean people," he concluded, "will uphold the purity of Marxism-Leninism at all times and make every effort to strengthen the unity and solidarity of the Socialist camp headed by the Soviet Union, further struggling with the Albanian people for a happy future."[24]

22. The importance of this event to the KWP is signaled by the fact that the JCP delegation was met at the airport by such important KWP members as Pak Chŏng-ae, Pak Kŭm-ch'ŏl, Kim Ch'ang-man, Yi Hyo-sun, Yi Chong-ok, Ha Ang-ch'ŏn, Kim Ik-sŏn, and Yi Song-un. See NS, Feb. 27, 1959, p. 1.

23. Robert A. Scalapino, The Japanese Communist Movement, 1920–1966, Berkeley, 1967, p. 108, note 18.

24. For Ch'oe's speech, see NS, June 7, 1959, p. 1. (The Soviet-Albania Joint Communiqué, issued June 1, 1959, was reported extensively in the June 2 issue of Nodong Sinmun.)

When Ch'oe returned and presented a public report on his trip, he stressed two themes: first, the remnants of bourgeois ideology were being eliminated in all Com-

Already the two basic themes of the future were being formed: unity at all costs within the international movement—*and* no retreat from revolutionary Marxism-Leninism. In these slogans, one can discern a certain concern among Asian Communist leaders, including those of North Korea, over trends in the Soviet Union. As yet, however, there was not the slightest hint of public criticism in regard to the Khrushchevian policies; on the contrary, the Twenty-first CPSU Congress was warmly extolled in the North Korean media. Kim Il-sŏng himself had headed the Korean delegation to the congress, and he had delivered a speech fulsome in its praise of Soviet accomplishments. Moreover, when the fact that Khrushchev would visit the United States was announced in August 1959, *Nodong Sinmun* hailed the visit in an editorial as "a great international event" that could "moderate international tension and promote peace." It cited this act as further evidence of "the consistent, peace-loving policy of the Soviet Union." It was of more than passing interest, however, that the editorial interpreted the meeting as proof that the United States had been compelled to the conference route because it had backed itself into a corner.[25] One implication of these and similar remarks was that the Soviet Union now commanded a superior or at least equal power position and should act accordingly.

The following month, the North Koreans were confronted with a new international crisis, the Sino-Indian border conflict. The P'yŏngyang media did present the basic facts, but they also featured the Soviet position, which was that the two governments concerned should settle the "misunderstanding" on the basis of their mutual interests and traditional friendship, and not allow the cold warriors to instigate trouble. Only this type of outcome would strengthen those struggling for peace and international cooperation.[26]

Then came the successful Soviet moon shot, followed closely by the Camp David talks between Khrushchev and Eisenhower. Regarding the latter event, the North Koreans held to a consistent theme: the trip was the result of the outstanding success of the Soviet Union's peace policies. Thanks to Russian efforts, the Cold War atmosphere had begun to melt away despite the continued efforts of American imperialists to threaten the socialist camp. Now, however, the balance of power between East and West had clearly changed in favor of the East. Consequently, the historic

munist states, with the masses being rearmed with the revolutionary ideology of Marxism-Leninism; second, this ideology was being "creatively" applied and developed in each country in accordance with its particular proletarian revolutionary traditions—just as in Korea. At the conclusion of his report, Ch'oe shouted, "Long live the unshakable unity and solidarity of the socialist camp headed by the Soviet Union! Long live the banners of Marxism-Leninism and proletarian internationalism!" *NS,* June 27, 1959, pp. 2–3.

25. *NS,* Aug. 4, 1959, p. 1.

26. For a full report of official Soviet statements, see *NS,* Sept. 11, 1969, p. 4.

imperialist policy of playing from a position of power had collapsed.[27] For the North Korean leaders, as for their Chinese comrades, the wish was father to the thought. But both wish and thought were being translated into not-so-subtle pressures upon Soviet policy-makers to maintain a hard line.

At this very time, another major Korean delegation headed by Kim Il-sŏng, and including such figures as Kim Ch'ang-man and Kim Kwang-hyŏp, was setting out for Peking to attend the celebrations commemorating the tenth anniversary of the founding of the CPR. They left P'yŏngyang by train on September 25. Two days later, a major article under Kim Il-sŏng's by-line appeared in the North Korean press. Kim, after referring to Korea and China as "two brothers in the great family of the Socialist camp headed by the Soviet Union," praised the People's Republic unstintingly for its accomplishments and its fraternal assistance to the DPRK in war and peace. "They took more than 20,000 of our war orphans," he announced, "to rear them as their own children." Moreover, since the war, the Chinese people had given Korea some 800 million yuan of free aid to help in the difficult tasks of reconstruction, and trade between the two nations had increased seventeenfold.

Only through continued close cooperation, friendship, and solidarity, asserted Kim, could the imperialist forces of aggression be driven from the Far East permanently and a victory for socialism in Asia be secured. The presence of the United States in South Korea and Taiwan, he continued, made it essential that the Korean and Chinese people pit themselves against this "common, vicious enemy" directly, and resolutely carry forward the tense struggle.[28] Kim's words suggest that if the Soviet Union were to falter in confronting the United States, P'yŏngyang and Peking, banded together, should nevertheless carry on.

The Korean delegation was met at the Peking railway station by Chou En-lai, P'eng Chen, Ch'en Yi, Ho Lung, and a large Chinese contingent. Presumably, Kim and his group were briefed at some point by the Chinese Communist leaders on their problems with the Soviet leadership. Ho Lung, incidentally, had contributed a major article to the September 29 issue of *Nodong Sinmun*. After reciting all the Chinese accomplishments, the old soldier paid full tribute to Soviet assistance and gave no direct evidence of displeasure with Khrushchevian policies. However, like all other Chinese and North Korean leaders during this period, he

27. Khrushchev's American trip was given extensive coverage in the North Korean press, with almost every public remark and speech reprinted in full or in the form of lengthy excerpts. For example, see the Sept. 29, 1959, issue of *Nodong Sinmun,* including the editorial, "The Victory of the Peace-Loving Foreign Policy of the Soviet Union."

28. Kim Il-sŏng, "The Militant Friendship of the Korean and Chinese Peoples —Congratuations Upon the 10th Anniversary of the Founding of the People's Republic of China," *NS,* Sept. 27, 1959, p. 1.

attacked the "forces of modern revisionism and imperialism who are seeking to destroy the unity of the socialist camp." [29]

Thus, as 1959 drew to a close, Kim and other North Korean leaders had given signs that they were worried about the emergence of "modern revisionism" (source unnamed) within the socialist camp, and prepared to join with other Asian Communist allies in fighting it—especially if it threatened such goals as ousting the United States from Asia and carrying out the unification of Korea. In this connection, we may refer again to a speech of Kim Ch'ang-man delivered in mid-1959, at the third Conference of Korean Students Studying Abroad.[30] Kim admitted that the years 1956–57 had constituted the most difficult period since the truce. "International reactionaries" had combined with "antirevolutionary, anti-Party factionalists" to attack the Party and the revolution in desperate fashion. "The U.S. imperialists and the Rhee clique" had infiltrated spies into the north in an effort to instigate a rebellion in collaboration with such anti-revolutionary elements as Ch'oe Ch'ang-ik and Pak Ch'ang-ok. At that time, Kim remarked, (Ambassador) Yi Sang-jo had "opened his big mouth in Moscow, saying 'Why do you attack Syngman Rhee? Our country should be a neutral state.' " Such nonsense was no accident, Kim observed. "These unhealthy elements were merely propagating international revisionism. If we had vacillated at that time, the situation could have become very serious."

If this were necessary, Kim's speech put all listeners (including the

29. Ho Lung, "Ten Glorious Years for the Chinese People," *NS,* Sept. 29, 1959, p. 2. (Marshal Ho Lung, purged during the Cultural Revolution, at this point was a member of the CCP Politburo, vice-premier, and vice-chairman of the National Defense Council.)

30. Kim Ch'ang-man, "To Become the Type of Person Needed in the Era of the Flying Horse," *Kŭlloja (The Worker),* Sept. 1959, pp. 19–26.

Kim's further comments to his student audience on Russia and America are of interest. Admitting Korean poverty and the extraordinary pressure being put upon every citizen, Kim announced that, despite the grumbling of those who wanted to go slower, there would be no slackening. Moreover, the Korean people would do more and more for themselves. They could not continue to rely exclusively upon the economic aid of others. It should be remembered, noted Kim, that the Soviet people did not achieve their present happiness with ease. They too were poor in the past and lived under circumstances of capitalist encirclement. Thus, our posterity will be talking about our current hardships as we talk about the earlier hardships of the Soviet people.

Some students, he remarked, forgetting that their fathers could not even go to primary school, had become conceited and, having learned something abroad, they came home critical of certain Party policies. One student who was placed in a truck factory quit, saying he disliked so many conferences and the rigid discipline that prevailed in that factory. "Yet there is rigid discipline *everywhere* in Korea," Kim warned. How else could we face American imperialism? Some individuals even seek to find freedom by copying the American way of life—"their filthy music, dances, etc. This is to become enslaved by bourgeois ideology."

Russians) on notice that the events of 1956–57 had not been forgotten. One sees the strong suggestion in his remarks that Moscow might even have been amenable to a neutral Korea, for it is difficult to believe that Yi Sang-jo, a Soviet-Korean, would have spoken as Kim reported (if, indeed, he did so speak) without Russian approval. At least, that thought must have been in the minds of Kim's audience, as he presumably desired. Beyond this, however, Kim Ch'ang-man, like every other North Korean spokesman of this period, was making it emphatically clear that, insofar as P'yŏngyang was concerned, under present conditions there could be no reduction in international tension, and above all no rapprochement with the United States.

An agreement, however, was reached with one of the foremost American allies in Asia: Japan. After long and wearisome negotiations through their respective Red Cross agencies, Japan and North Korea finally reached an agreement upon the conditions governing the repatriation of those among the 600,000 Koreans living in Japan who desired to go to North Korea. On December 16, 1959, the first group of repatriates, 975 in number, arrived at the port of Ch'ŏngjin; a second group of 978 arrived one week later. Naturally, the North Korean government made a major effort to score a propaganda coup. Repatriates were photographed and interviewed as they viewed various industrial plants and model farms. A mass rally was held to welcome them. They were furnished with newly built apartments, and Kim Il-sŏng himself visited them in their new quarters "to show his concern for their welfare." Whatever future problems they might represent, at this point the repatriates were a propaganda boon for the Communists, both in Korea and in Japan.[31]

The fuse to an explosion was lit in the spring of 1960, when the CPSU, on the eve of the Bucharest meeting of Communist and Workers' Parties (held in conjunction with a Congress of the Rumanian Communist Party), distributed a "Letter of Information," dated June 21, to all participating parties. It should be noted that, two months earlier, the Chinese had prepared and widely disseminated a pamphlet called "Long Live Leninism!" in connection with the ninetieth anniversary of Lenin's

31. A Korean resident in Japan has asserted that certain repatriates arranged a code system so that in their letters to friends and relatives remaining in Japan they could indicate their true feelings and provide guidance as to whether others should join them. According to him, a number of complaints were quickly voiced. One repatriate wrote a friend in Tokyo: "Life here is wonderful. I urge you to come, and be sure to bring your son and his wife." The recipient's son was two years old. Robert A. Scalapino interview with Chŏn Chun, Tokyo, Oct. 26, 1968.

As we shall later note, Koreans who had come from Japan, young and old, came to be regarded as ideologically suspect, and close surveillance was maintained over them. Nevertheless, by 1970, some 65,000 had migrated from such crowded Korean ghettos as those of Ōsaka and Tokyo.

birth. This tract was a thinly veiled criticism of Khrushchevism, although
only the Yugoslav "revisionists" were mentioned by name. The Soviet
letter, ostensibly sent to the Chinese Communist Party, was a response,
and it contained a biting criticism of CCP policies and actions. At the
meeting itself, Khrushchev charged the Chinese Communists with de-
siring to unleash World War III, operating as bourgeois nationalists with
respect to the Indian border issue, and behaving like "Trotskyites" in
their assaults upon the Soviet Union.

So far as can be determined, Kim Ch'ang-man and Pak Yong-guk,
the chief KWP representatives at the Bucharest Conference, took no
part in the quarrel. Kim's speech, delivered on June 22, was published
in P'yŏngyang on June 25. After praising the achievements of the Ro-
manian people under Communism and heralding "the brilliant results"
that had been achieved in Korea, he paid homage to "the great Soviet
Union," which was "solidly located in the center of the international
Communist and labor movements."

Kim, Pak, and other members of the delegation were witnesses to
events in Bucharest, and they must have given a complete report of the
trouble upon their return. They were not the only North Koreans to
learn of the Sino-Soviet breach through first-hand experience. Han Sŏl-ya,
for example, represented the Party at the July meeting of the World
Peace Council in Stockholm, where a new round of Sino-Soviet sparring
was to be seen. Others were traveling to the Soviet Union, Eastern
Europe, and Cuba. Thus, information must have been garnered on the
growing crisis from a number of sources. What may have been highly
privileged knowledge prior to June 1960, confined to Kim Il-sŏng and a
small group of his closest advisers, now became a topic of common
information and concern among the top KWP hierarchy.

Evidently, Kim Ch'ang-man provided some details to the KWP
Central Committee at their enlarged Plenum, which opened on August 8,
1960. It is interesting to note that while other reports were presented in
extenso in *Nodong Sinmun,* Kim's report was given only in a brief,
innocuous form. The Committee did pass a resolution pledging continued
support to the Moscow Declaration of 1957. That resolution noted once
again that "imperialism" was declining, whereas the socialist camp headed
by the Soviet Union was "daily gaining strength." The Korean people,
moreover, would "enhance their alertness to the aggressive conspiracy of
the imperialists by defending the eastern outpost of socialism against
American imperialism." They would maintain "the great banner of Marxism-Leninism against the imperialist aggressors and their lackeys, the
revisionists, thereby further strengthening the unity and solidarity of the
Socialist camp." [32]

32. For the resolution, see *NS,* Aug. 12, 1960, p. 1.

In the report of Pak Kŭm-ch'ŏl, delivered about two months later on the occasion of the fifteenth anniversary of the founding of the Korean Workers' Party, one could note a certain increase in Korean Communist impatience with "revisionists, including the Tito clique," who had tried to "infuse the Socialist camp with bourgeois ideas and to 'beautify imperialism' [a term now commonly used by the Chinese]." American imperialism, Pak went on, was the "boss of the international reactionaries, the ferocious enemy of mankind, and the implacable foe of the Korean people." However, all enemies and all difficulties could be overcome if the Party continued its course of the past fifteen years, and if "the solidarity of the Socialist camp headed by the great Soviet Union was maintained." [33] The anxieties were becoming clearer, the warnings sharper, the terminology more in conformity with the messages emanating from Peking.

The KWP delegation to the Moscow meetings of November 1960 was headed by Kim Il and included Kim Ch'ang-man, Yi Hyo-sun, and Kim Yong-guk. Surprisingly little coverage was given these meetings by the North Korean media.[34] As we noted earlier, however, 1960 ended with important scientific, technical, and economic agreements being reached between Moscow and P'yŏngyang, notwithstanding the recent breakdown in Sino-Soviet cooperation.

In the months immediately preceding the Fourth Party Congress of September 1961, it appeared that Kim Il-sŏng and his Party might be able to retain close ties with both Moscow and Peking despite their rift. Indeed, the importance of North Korea, both to the Communist giants and to other Asian Communist Parties, now seemed to grow. On May 30, five Soviet delegates headed by Aleksei Kosygin arrived in P'yŏngyang. The primary purpose of this trip was presumably to finalize arrangements for a new defense agreement paralleling the one that existed between the United States and both South Korea and Japan. We may assume, however, that the Russian visitors engaged in an earnest defense

33. Pak Kŭm-ch'ŏl, "A Report Made at the 15th Anniversary," *op. cit., Kŭlloja* (*The Worker*), Oct. 15, 1960.

34. A report on the Moscow Party Conference was given at the December 28–30 Plenum of the KWP, but the published account of this report in *NS*, Dec. 24, 1960, pp. 1–2, gave no hint of the fact that vigorous arguments had taken place among the participants, particularly the Russians and the Chinese. It stressed only that the KWP had striven "successfully" to stand by the principles of Marxism-Leninism and proletarian internationalism, "demonstrating the correct line and policy of the Party." It also repeated the thesis that the unity of the socialist camp was unshakable.

For accounts of developments at the Moscow Conference from Japanese sources, see Scalapino, *The Japanese Communist Movement, op. cit.*, pp. 107–109. See also Donald S. Zagoria, *The Sino-Soviet Conflict: 1956–1961*, Princeton, 1962, pp. 343–369.

of Soviet policies and solicited support for them. No major Russian concessions appear to have been made on ideological or policy matters. Kosygin's remarks, as published in North Korea, stressed the theme of peaceful coexistence and expressed hope for the success of the forthcoming Khrushchev-Kennedy meetings. He also praised Khrushchev extensively as a "dauntless fighter for peace" and a "loyal Leninist."

One month later, the stage was set for Kim's trip to Moscow. He arrived there on June 29, at the head of a delegation that included Kim Ch'ang-man, Kim Kwang-hyŏp, Yi Chong-ok, Pak Sŏng-ch'ŏl, and Yi Song-un (DPRK ambassador to the USSR). On this occasion, in contrast to certain previous ones, Khrushchev himself was at the airport to welcome the guests. Kim immediately went into a lengthy conference with Khrushchev and Brezhnev, then president of the Supreme Soviet Presidium. On July 6, the Korean-Soviet Treaty of Friendship, Cooperation, and Mutual Assistance was signed. This treaty, which was scheduled to be in effect for ten years, with an additional five-year tenure unless one party indicated an intention to abrogate it a year in advance, pledged each state to come to the defense of the other in case of attack, to refrain from making a hostile alliance against one of the parties, and to strengthen and develop economic and cultural relations "based on the principles of equality, mutual respect for national sovereignty, territorial integrity and noninterference in each other's domestic affairs." Both parties also agreed to support "the peaceful unification of Korea." [35]

At the ratification ceremony, both Khrushchev and Kim spoke at length. Khrushchev praised the rapid development of North Korea, and attacked US policy in South Korea, stressing the defensive character of the military alliance, and proclaiming that it was inevitable under the circumstances. (He may have been referring to the military coup that had taken place in South Korea in May.) He also promised further "material" and "spiritual" assistance to the DPRK. Kim adopted a more emotional tone, appealing to the historic relation between the two states. He called the ratification "of great historical significance," and asserted that the Korean people regarded it as "their sacred obligation to support and protect the Soviet Union and to strengthen friendship and solidarity with the Soviet people, doing everything possible to build socialist unity."

Naturally, we cannot know the nature of the private talks that took place between the Soviet and Korean leaders, nor the contents of a discussion held on the morning of July 6 between the Koreans and Chinese Foreign Minister Ch'en Yi, who was also in Moscow at this time. We can be certain that Sino-Soviet relations were dealt with exhaustively, and it is quite possible that Kim sought to provide his services as mediator. No major issues, however, had been resolved when the

35. For the full text, see *NS,* July 7, 1961, p. 1.

Korean delegation left the Soviet Union on July 10, although the echo of Russian sweet talk may have lingered in Korean ears.[36]

In accordance with North Korea's new foreign policy, the next step for the delegation was Peking, where a similar treaty was signed and similar ceremonies performed. The Chinese, too, were at the airport in strength. All of the top Chinese dignitaries except Mao were present, and some 500,000 citizens had been mobilized to greet the visiting Koreans. On the following day, July 11, after a lengthy conference, the DPRK-CPR Treaty of Friendship, Cooperation, and Mutual Assistance was signed. Its major provisions were almost identical with those of the Korean-Soviet Treaty, but the Chinese treaty omitted to prescribe a termination date and contained such ringing phrases as "continuously consolidate and develop economic, cultural, and scientific-technical cooperation," and "militant friendship and solidarity sealed in blood"—a contrast with the more formal language approved by the Russians. Apparently, the Chinese were anxious to stress the personal and historic bonds between two near neighbors who were also Asian peoples, and Kim was prepared to respond in kind. In his public remarks, he emphasized the intense struggle against imperialism and colonialism shared by the two countries, a struggle that continued, with the United States the great common enemy.

When Kim and his group returned to P'yŏngyang on July 15, 1961, some 300,000 citizens had been assembled in welcome. This time— unlike that fateful August in 1956—no political crisis awaited him.

In this period Kim continued to draw closer to the Asian Communist Parties, notably those of Japan, Indonesia, and North Vietnam. On June 17, for example, Pham Van Dong, premier of the Democratic Republic of Vietnam, had led a North Vietnamese delegation to P'yŏngyang. Kim Il-sŏng, Ch'oe Yong-gŏn, Kim Il, and all other important DPRK leaders were at the airport to greet the Vietnamese. Pham Van Dong made a long, emotional speech in which he asserted that the ocean might become dry and the mountains flat, but the Vietnamese—and Korean—national aspiration for unification would never cease. His attack upon "US imperialism" was harsh and in precisely the same vein so often enunciated by the Korean Communists.

Thus, by the time of the Fourth Party Congress, Kim and his followers had taken advantage of the widening Sino-Soviet breach to push

36. For example, at a breakfast meeting on June 30, Khrushchev heaped lavish praise upon Kim, referring to his "brilliant leadership" and predicting that the "just struggle" for the unification of Korea would eventually succeed. Kim in turn expressed his admiration for the Soviet people and his gratitude for Russian aid, and pledged himself to the threefold objective of strengthening solidarity within the socialist camp, accelerating socialist development in the north, and achieving peaceful unification. Or at least so the breakfast (attended by all Soviet cabinet ministers) was reported in P'yŏngyang. See *ibid.*

chuch'e forward in the field of foreign policy as well as on the domestic front. In the concluding section of his report to the congress, Kim dealt with the international scene.[37] Familiar themes were reiterated. The socialist forces were advancing, those of imperialism disintegrating. A strong defense of the Soviet Union was voiced: "The Soviet Union is the hope of progressive mankind and the powerful bulwark of peace, national independence, and socialism." But it was followed by strongly laudatory if somewhat less sweeping remarks regarding Communist China: "In People's China, the socialist revolution has already won a victory and socialist construction is making successful headway. The political and economic might of the Chinese People's Republic is further growing, and this constitutes an important factor in strengthening the might of the socialist camp and consolidating peace in the Far East and the world."

Kim spent much time heralding the "fierce flames" of the national liberation struggle, particularly the victories in Africa and in Cuba. His interpretation of American Far Eastern policy was as might have been expected: the United States was seeking to provoke a new war on the Korean peninsula, occupying Taiwan and persisting in hostile acts against the Chinese People's Republic, bent on aggression in Southeast Asia, seeking to revive Japanese militarism, and trying to create a NEATO. Thus, the United States constituted "the main force of aggression and war," and "the most vicious enemy of mankind." In this setting, peace could only be won by struggle. Only when "the peace-loving forces" were strong and united, waging a resolute fight against the imperialists, would peace be achieved. "Should the imperialist maniacs make a reckless venture," Kim thundered, "people will sweep away capitalism and bury it once and for all." In this Kim, though using Khrushchev's words, appeared to support Mao's thought.

What of the rift in the socialist camp? On this point, Kim trod with extreme caution. He began with a patent falsehood: "Today, the socialist countries are firmly united in a big family under the banner of Marxism-Leninism and proletarian internationalism and are supporting and closely cooperating with each other." Then he proceeded to emphasize the importance of unity and pay homage to the assistance given North Korea by the two big Communist states, carefully measuring his words so as to praise each in approximately equal terms, although the Soviet Union naturally came first in the eulogy.

Perhaps the main point in this exercise was to be found in two sentences. At the end of the eulogy to the Soviet Union, Kim asserted: "Unshakable and everlasting are the friendship and solidarity between the peoples of Korea and the Soviet Union which have been firmly

37. Kim Il-sŏng, "Report of the CC of the Workers' Party of Korea to the Fourth Congress," *Kim Il-sŏng chŏjak sŏnjip, op. cit.,* Vol. III, pp. 198–201.

established through the flames of the struggle for liberation and which have been developed and consolidated on the road indicated by the great Lenin." And at the end of the section praising China: "The militant friendship and solidarity firmly established between the Korean and Chinese peoples through their joint struggle against the common enemy are being further consolidated with each passing day and there is no force that can break them."

The message should have been clear to both the Khrushchevites and the Maoists. Korea did not intend to side with one or the other of the major contestants but, in its own interests, to maintain cordial relations with both, hoping meanwhile to help end the cleavage. Despite the bold words he had uttered at the outset, Kim could not completely hide his anxiety about the trouble now existing within the Communist world. "The imperialists and their cat's-paws, the revisionists, are maliciously plotting to undermine the unity of socialist camp and to split the international communist movement," he admitted. Moreover, revisionism, a reflection of bourgeois ideology, remained the chief danger to the international communist movement. "The contemporary revisionists represented by the Yugoslav revisionists are scheming to emasculate the revolutionary spirit of Marxism-Leninism, to paralyze the fighting spirit of the working class, and to undermine the socialist camp and the international communist movement from within, coming out in defense of imperialism and its reactionary policies." (Only the Yugoslavs?)

Dogmatism, Kim added, was also harmful to revolutionary work, and could become "the chief danger at particular stages in the development of individual Parties." (Which Parties?) The Korean Workers' Party, he proclaimed, would intensify its struggle against both revisionism and dogmatism, fully supporting the principles laid down in the Moscow Statement of 1960.

Now wooed by both Moscow and Peking, North Korea had adopted a policy of "equal cordiality plus equal independence" toward each big neighbor, a type of nonalignment that extended into the ideological as well as the politicoeconomic arena. Seeking a balance that was manifest in their carefully chosen words and phrases, North Korean leaders coupled praise with admonitions. Already, the signals were clear: "Russians, avoid revisionism! Chinese, cast off dogmatism!" Could the policy of "equal cordiality plus equal independence" be maintained in the midst of these stormy international seas? It would require both skill and luck. For the moment, however, this policy seemed to provide the maximum advantage to a small state irrevocably squeezed in between two huge and mutually hostile nations. The foreign policies of North Korea and Outer Mongolia represented the two broad alternatives available to small Communist states in such a position.

The Issue of Unification

Meanwhile, the DPRK's efforts at unification appeared to have reached an impasse. In reviewing the question before the Supreme People's Assembly in October 1959, Nam Il made the following basic points: first, the US-ROK Mutual Defense Pact of 1954, together with the Protocol on Military and Economic Aid, represented a US policy "for turning South Korea into an atomic base" that would threaten the peace of Asia. Despite the DPRK's proposals, made on February 5, 1958, for the withdrawal of all foreign troops from Korean soil, and the subsequent complete withdrawal of the Chinese People's Volunteers, "the U.S. imperialist aggressive army" had not yet left South Korea.[38]

This, according to Nam Il, constituted "the decisive obstacle" to restoring peace in Korea and accomplishing the peaceful unification of the nation. He reviewed previous proposals for a joint North-South meeting, and charged that the Syngman Rhee government feared free elections, negotiations, the opening of any trade, the establishment of communications, postal exchange, or the free travel of inhabitants between North and South Korea. The US and South Korean authorities were even "barring the helping hand of compatriotic love of the Government of our Republic from reaching the unemployed, foodless peasants, typhoon and flood victims and orphans in South Korea . . ." [39]

Nam Il then proceeded to outline once again the three basic Communist proposals on unification: first, the numerical strength of the North and South Korean armies should be reduced to 100,000 men each, or less; second, both sides should solemnly declare that they would not resort to arms against each other;[40] third, after *all* foreign troops had been withdrawn from South Korea, national elections should be held as an expression of the free will of the Korean people.[41] To move in this direction, a permanent commission comprising the representatives of the parliaments, governments, or various political parties and social organizations of North and South Korea should be formed to serve as a discussion-negotiation group. "We are ready to negotiate at any time with anyone, irrespective of po-

38. "Report on the Peaceful Unification of the Fatherland Delivered by Vice-Premier Nam Il at the Sixth Session of the Second Supreme People's Assembly," Oct. 26, 1959, in *For the Peaceful Unification of the Country,* P'yŏngyang, 1959, pp. 1–53.

39. *Ibid.,* p. 29. Despite the drastic shortages in the north, on the occasion of serious floods in the south in the fall of 1959, the North Korean cabinet voted in September to offer relief supplies—including food, textiles, cement, lumber, and shoes (!)—to flood victims, knowing that such an offer would be declined.

40. Said Nam Il in this connection, "Such a step is of realistic significance, the more so in the light of world trends at the present juncture when, thanks to the initiative of the Soviet Union, tensions are being considerably relaxed in the international arena and the question of universal and complete disarmament is on the agenda of the day." *Ibid.,* p. 33.

41. *Ibid.,* p. 33.

litical views, knowledge, and religious beliefs, so long as he genuinely desires the peaceful unification of the fatherland," proclaimed Nam Il.

Did this represent a significant change in the Communist position from the period when they were not prepared to recognize men like Syngman Rhee in any form? The answer is unclear, but in all probability (and to judge from later events), Rhee would *not* have been defined by Nam Il as one of those who "genuinely desires the peaceful unification of the fatherland." In any case, proposals of the type set forth by Nam Il could be advanced without great concern for their consequences, since the Communists knew that the South Korean leaders were adamantly opposed to giving the northern regime any recognition whatsoever. Thus, Nam Il was free to recommend that mutual visits and postal exchange between North and South Korea begin immediately, and relations in the fields of the economy, science, arts, and sports as soon as possible. Identical points were made in a letter, dispatched in late October, from the Supreme People's Assembly to the National Assembly of the Republic of Korea and "the people of South Korea." In one succinct sentence, the so-called letter made clear the primary purpose of the unification movement at this point: "People of all walks of life and every stratum in South Korea, firmly unite as one man and form a broad anti-American, country-saving united front!" [42]

These efforts, however, were of scant importance, essentially because, as we have noted, the reputation of the Communists in South Korea was extraordinarily bad. The KWP was still dealing with people who had lived through the Korean War and were not likely to forget Communist actions. It will also be remembered that most of the prominent South Korean politicians who had been taken north or gone there during the war had been purged only a few months before this latest campaign was undertaken. All articulate Koreans in the south, therefore, realized the meaning of unification, Communist style.

As we have indicated, however, events in South Korea during 1960–61 —the April student revolt, the overthrow of the Rhee regime, the new opportunities afforded by the weak Chang Myŏn government, and the military coup of May 1961—caught the North Koreans off guard and unprepared. Immediately after news of the coup reached P'yŏngyang, the authorities scheduled a giant rally involving some 200,000 people.[43]

Kim Il served as the major speaker, and a call to revolt was broad-

42. "Letter of the Supreme People's Assembly of the Democratic People's Republic of Korea to the House of Representatives of the Republic of Korea and to the South Korean People," in *ibid.,* pp. 44, dated Oct. 27, 1959.

43. For details, see *NS,* May 21, 1961, p. 1. See also the *NS* editorial of May 20, entitled "The US Imperialists Are Forcing South Korea into the Crucible of Military Fascism," in which the United States is accused of having instigated the military coup as an act of desperation, after all else had failed.

cast widely in the south. A new organization had been formed just a few months previously, on January 13, 1961, to take advantage of the freedom allowed under Chang Myŏn. It had taken the title Commission for the Peaceful Unification of the Fatherland, and all seven of the men at the helm bore familiar faces: Hong Myŏng-hui was elected chairman, and the vice-chairmen were Pak Kŭm-ch'ŏl, Yi Hyo-sun, Kang Ryang-uk, Pak Sin-dŏk, Paek Nam-un, and Yi Kŭng-no. Since, like its predecessors, the new organization was consciously fashioned as a united front group, four of the seven were not officially KWP members.

This was the situation when the Fourth Party Congress convened. In his major report, Kim Il-sŏng dwelt at length on the unification question and other aspects of the North-South issue. He began by calling the uprising of April 1960 "a new turning point in the anti-American, national salvation struggle of the South Korean people." The last days of the Chang Myŏn regime, he declared, had been marked by "extremely acute" political and economic crises. South Korean youth, he noted, had come out openly with proposals for North-South negotiations and intercourse, with a "broad section" of the populace supporting them. All the trends were moving in this direction, and to counter them "the U.S. imperialists and South Korean reactionaries" had set up a "Fascist military dictatorship." But this act, Kim contended, would only hasten the end of American colonial rule over South Korea.[44]

How should the Party respond to current developments? To carry on the anti-imperialist, anti-feudal struggle and emerge victorious from it, Kim proclaimed, it was necessary for the South Korean people to have a revolutionary party that took Marxism-Leninism as its guide and represented "the interests of workers, peasants, and all other sections of the broad popular masses." Thus, the first step was the reconstruction of a Communist Party in the south. The absence of such a Party, according to Kim, had caused the April uprising to be abortive and had permitted the coup led by Pak Chŏng-hi. At the same time, he urged the South Korean people to engage in all types of resistance to the United States and its policies: youth should refuse to serve in the armed forces; workers should engage in sabotage in their factories and use strikes as a political weapon; and all people should struggle against the US military bases. The South Korean people must not give the Americans "even a single grain of rice or a drop of water." And when all the "patriotic forces" of South Korea had united and arisen, the "American imperialists" would be driven out at last. Thus, nationalism or, more accurately, an appeal to anti-American sentiments provided the major thrust of Kim's call for a revolution in the south. He coupled this, however, with a comparison between the northern "paradise" and the southern "hell," implying that the south would now

44. Kim Il Sung, *Report of the CC of the Workers' Party of Korea to the Fourth Congress, op. cit.* (English ed.), p. 68.

have to fight for the same political and economic reforms that had turned the northern section of the country into a "people's democracy."

The main themes enunciated by Kim at the September congress were identical with those set forth by various Communist spokesmen earlier. Freedom and liberation could be won only through struggle. The "US imperialists" had to be forced to withdraw from Korea, the Pak government had to be overthrown, and only then could the country be "peacefully unified." To accomplish this revolution, a true Marxist-Leninist Party was necessary. Later, unification could be accomplished by the Korean people themselves, without outside interference. Free elections could take place, with all political parties, public organizations, and individual personages in both North and South Korea enabled to announce their platforms and views "openly and freely before the people, and engage in free activities in any part of the country." [45]

In the light of the true political situation in North Korea, these promises had an almost garish quality, and it was not to be expected that many southerners would take them seriously. But Kim's call for a new Communist Party in the south, and his further appeal for the establishment of a united anti-US National Salvation Front, paralleling the one recently established in the north, deserve careful attention. As indicated earlier, Kim bitterly regretted not having been prepared to take advantage of the political turmoil in South Korea following Rhee's overthrow and, according to some sources, actually toyed with the idea of some type of intervention notwithstanding the absence of preparations. He was determined not to allow such an opportunity to be missed again. It is from this period, therefore, that we can date his renewed interest in taking concrete steps to abet southern "liberation"—steps that, as we shall see, were soon to lead to far-reaching policy alterations.

Toward a Monolithic Party and a Unitary Ideology

In the aftermath of the Fourth Party Congress, the attention of Kim Il-sŏng and other Party leaders was focused upon strengthening the Party organizationally and administratively so that it could cope with its new responsibilities in the field of economics. The Central Party distributed reams of material on the improvement of cadre training, the elimination of bureaucratism, and the tightening of the organizational structure, particularly at the provincial and prefectural levels. Exhortations to pursue the mass line were almost as numerous as references to the Ch'ŏllima Movement, with the Ch'ŏngsan-ri Method and the Taean System held up as ideal forms of political-administrative operations.

In addition, a "new" method of applying the mass line was now being disseminated throughout the country. This was the so-called Five-Family System. First introduced, supposedly by Kim Il-sŏng, in Ch'angsŏng

45. *Ibid.*, p. 77.

Prefecture in July 1958 during one of his "on-the-spot guidance" exercises, this system in reality was identical with the tonarigumi system widely employed by the Japanese to secure allegiance during the militarist era. But its roots lay deep in traditional northeast Asia; indeed, they could be traced back to the pao-chia system of ancient China. The primary unit was five households, with a "leading Party worker" being made responsible for the guidance and indoctrination of these families on a permanent basis. Silent upon its past usage, Party spokesmen now proclaimed it as a method superior to that of assembling people for general speeches, since only limited interaction was possible among large audiences. Asserted one writer, "The five-family system calls for commentary-dialogue leaders to take charge of a small number of families (more or less five). In this way, they can accurately grasp and understand, through their everyday contacts with each family and person, that person's level of knowledge, talents, tastes, hopes, and ideological trends." [46]

Thus, to previous methods and systems was now added the Ch'angsŏng-kun Approach as yet another weapon in the arsenal of organizational-indoctrinational techniques to bind the citizen to the purposes of Party and state. And those purposes were for the moment primarily economic. With the internal political struggle that had racked the Party earlier now a thing of the past, attention at the highest level could be concentrated upon meeting the ambitious goals of the Seven-Year Plan. The top leadership needed to devote less attention to political maneuvers at the summit, and could thus spend more time seeking to devise a workable administrative-technical system that would underwrite the extraordinarily rapid industrial-agrarian revolution that they hoped to accomplish.

In this special sense, despite the emphasis upon "politics first," politics in the grand style became of less concern. The battle for power was over, at least for this period. The Party was now under the complete control of a single man—to the extent that any single man can control a vast, complex system. Party documents now proclaimed not only the supremacy of Kim Il-sŏng, but the attainment of "a unitary ideology," a single system of thought derived from his "genius." Thus, politics could be directed outward from a monolithic Central Party toward the lesser cadres and the masses. This was politics as faith rather than politics as struggle and, as in China, it focused upon an increasingly simplistic catechism, "the thought of Kim Il-sŏng."

With the passage of time, moreover, new blood would inevitably enter both the Party and the state organs. The elections of October 8, 1962, for the Third Supreme People's Assembly were one indication of that fact. Actually, those elections should have been held in 1961, since

46. See Ch'oe Song-gŭn, "The Five Family System in Mass Political Indoctrination," *Kŭlloja* (*The Worker*), Nov. 20, 1962, pp. 30–34.

the Second Supreme People's Assembly had been elected on August 27, 1957, and the DPRK Constitution provided that Supreme People's Assembly elections should be conducted at intervals of four years, barring an emergency. This was not necessarily just a Communist transgression, since Asian tradition directs that the law be treated as an ideal, not a precise requirement. In any case, the government proudly announced that, in the 1962 elections, 100 percent of the eligible voters had cast their ballots, and that they had voted *unanimously* for the endorsed candidates. It added without any visible humor that this was "an epochal victory unprecedented in the entire history of elections." [47]

A Japanese analyst has provided a breakdown of the elected members of the Third Supreme People's Assembly. According to his calculations, in terms of age, 12 were 18–29; 99 were 30–39; 181 were 40–49; 71 were 50–59; and 20 were 60 and over. Among the members, there were 215 "workers," 101 "clerical workers, intellectuals, and others" (presumably including military men), and 62 farmers. The newly elected Supreme People's Assembly contained 34 "anti-Japanese partisan fighters," in addition to more than 80 individuals who had taken some role in the struggle against Japanese imperialism. Thirty-five of those elected were women; and a total of 112 members were reelected.[48]

Thus, the top legislative body of the state retained its comparative youthfulness. Some 27 percent of the total People's Assembly membership were under 40, and 75 percent were under 50. If we accept the socioeconomic data provided by the Communists, moreover, "workers" now provided nearly 57 percent of the total representation, with a mixed group of functionaries, intellectuals, and military personnel contributing at least 27 percent, leaving the farmers with only 16 percent—far below their percentage within the society.

In the Standing Committee of the Third People's Assembly, Ch'oe Yong-gŏn was reelected chairman, and the number of vice-chairmen was increased from three to five, with Pak Kŭm-ch'ŏl, Pak Chŏng-ae, and Hong Myŏng-hui being added, and Han Sŏl-ya being removed. In terms of events involving an individual, the purge of Han was the most significant development of this period, and one that we shall have occasion to explore in detail later because of its importance in defining the relationship between the regime and the intellectual class.[49] As will be recalled, Han, a long-time leftist writer and the official biographer of Kim Il-sŏng, had risen

47. The system of "certifying" candidates was the same as that employed in the past, namely, the DFUF and similar organizations (as directed by the KWP) endorsed certain individuals who were then registered as official candidates by the election committee of each electoral district. These were "elected unanimously" by the voters. See "The Unity of the Party and the People," *ibid.,* Oct. 1962, pp. 2–5.

48. Matsuda Tomohiro, "On the Shift of Political Power in North Korea," *Tairiku mondai (Continental Problems),* Sept. 1963.

49. See Chapter XI.

to the top of North Korean literary and art circles, at least insofar as the top was definable in political terms. His trenchant attacks upon "bourgeois" tendencies in literature, coupled with his own strict adherence to "socialist realism" (and his eulogistic treatment of the Leader), had raised him to a position of seeming impregnability following the purges of the Pak Ch'ang-ok group. He became minister of Education, chairman of the Korean Writers' League, chairman of the Korean National Committee for the Protection of World Peace, and a member of the Party Central Committee.

Han's purge therefore had strong repercussions within intellectual circles, and led to lengthy, searching political sessions. The charges, as we shall see, were both personal and political, with the former probably central. When Han fell, a number of his protégés were affected, as was customary in this political culture. Thus, Sin Pul-ch'ul, the comedian, together with the actors Sim Yŏng and Pae Yŏng, and the famous dancer Ch'oe Sŭng-hui, together with her husband, An Mak, were all brought under attack.

The Emphasis Upon Military Preparedness

At the end of 1962, however, a policy decision was signaled that dwarfed in significance the purge of Han and his followers. At the Fifth Plenum of the Fourth Central Committee, held from the tenth to the fourteenth of December, Kim Il-sŏng led the Party into a commitment to place "equal emphasis" upon military preparation on the one hand, and economic development on the other.[50] This decision, it was admitted, "might affect to a certain degree the development of the national economy." However, given the increasingly grave situation in the international arena, and the "acute crisis" in South Korea, the defences of the DPRK had to be strengthened, no matter what the sacrifices involved—or so the leadership reported.

Kim and other spokesmen at the Fifth Plenum naturally placed the blame upon "American imperialism," citing the danger of an American attack upon North Korea. They advanced the familiar Communist thesis that while the general situation was developing favorably for the socialist forces, and hundreds of millions of Asian, African, and Latin American people were "casting off the yoke of imperialism and colonialism," imperialism "never leaves the historical arena of its own free will." It followed that the United States was now expanding its armaments and preparing for open warfare. As prima facie evidence, the speakers cited the actions of the Kennedy government in the recently concluded Cuban missile crisis, together with the "undeclared war" in South Vietnam, the in-

50. For the communiqué on the Fifth Plenum, see *The People's Korea* (hereafter *TPK*), No. 96, Tokyo, Jan. 1, 1963, pp. 1–2, or the *Supplement to Korea Today*, No. 80, Jan. 1963 (7 pp.).

tensifying "anti-China campaign" centered on the occupation of Taiwan, and American instigation of the "reactionary ruling circles of India" in connection with the Sino-Indian border dispute. Major emphasis, moreover, was devoted to South Korea, which was portrayed as an American "atomic and rocket base." The United States was reportedly seeking to provoke another war on the Korean peninsula, hoping to use Japanese militarists as their "shock brigade."

We shall have occasion soon to explore more thoroughly the true attitude of the North Koreans toward these various developments. Suffice it to say here that events in Cuba and the Himalayan area and America's policy toward Japan *were* of deep concern, primarily because the P'yŏng-yang leaders were now acutely conscious of the indecision and divisions within the Communist camp, with Khrushchevian policies being increasingly challenged. The ever stronger emphasis upon chuch'e in all matters —independence in politics, self-sufficiency in the economy, and self-defense—undoubtedly reflected a growing distrust of Soviet attitudes and policies.

In addition, however, the North Korean analysis of developments pertaining to South Korea suggests another basic consideration underlying the policy shift. It was patently false to assert that war preparations were going on in South Korea, or that the United States had the remotest interest in provoking a new conflict on the Korean peninsula. Further, it is extremely doubtful whether the North Korean leaders really believed such a line themselves, at this point or any time later. An elementary intelligence service would have indicated otherwise—and the North Korean intelligence, together with that of the Soviets and Chinese, was more than elementary. However, it was natural enough for the North Koreans to describe the crisis in these terms even if their concerns were very different.

As indicated earlier, there is very good reason to believe that Kim Il-sŏng was deeply disturbed by the fact that North Korea was not able to take advantage of the opportunities afforded by the political turmoil in the south during the 1960–61 period. He also had occasion during this period to ponder the policies that had been worked out by Hanoi in 1959–60, namely, the commencement of the strategy to "liberate" South Vietnam. Such a policy might warrant adaptation to the Korean peninsula—and, as we have noted, ties with North Vietnam were now close. In addition, it is quite likely that Kim was concerned about the timing as well as the style of the next "liberation" effort. Judging from the experience of others, a Vietnam-type effort would require substantial preparations. A southern branch of the Party and a substantial guerrilla force would have to be built, and the north would have to be guarded against retaliation when the military pressures upon the south mounted. In short, South Korea was not South Vietnam at this point. Kim and his generation were determined to "liberate" the south on their terms, and a full decade might be required. By that time, he would be approaching 60. Moreover, any delay might indeed produce a new opponent, whether alone or allied with the old ones. Unquestionably, Kim and his advisers regarded the substitution of Japanese for American power in northeast Asia as likely within the foreseeable future. To wait too long would be to face a rearmed, committed Japan— in addition to whatever forces the South Koreans and Americans possessed in the area.

There is reason to believe that these were the primary considerations prompting the substantial policy shift to equal emphasis upon "defense" and growth, a policy first enunciated publicly in the course of the Fifth Plenum at the end of 1962. It is also possible that one additional factor was involved. By the end of 1962, North Korea may have been threatened or in some other way begun to feel the effect of its criticism of "modern revisionism." In any case, at some point the deterioration of relations with Moscow led to a reduction in Soviet assistance. Consequently, P'yŏngyang was forced to mobilize more of its already strained resources for military purposes. We cannot be certain of the timing of this development, but the threat or fear of Soviet retaliation probably preceded the reality in any case. Whatever the precise reasons, however, the new policy was to have a profound effect both upon the economy and upon the North Korean people in the decade ahead.

From this point, the North Korean military forces were much more prominently featured in the Party's propaganda. An effort was made to bring army and people "closer together in mutual love," and to emphasize the new military line. That line, as enunciated at the time of the Fifth Plenum, was "to strengthen the Korean People's Army to the utmost." It included such provisions as training each military man to assume the function of the rank above his in case of need; "to arm the entire people," meaning in practice to enlist almost all able-bodied males and females into the People's Militia; and "to turn the whole country into an impregnable fortress," by providing huge underground facilities, thousands of tunnels, and major defense works in depth, especially in the forward areas.[51]

It should be noted, incidentally, that beginning in the summer of 1963 small-scale assaults were launched by the North Koreans across the truce line against American and South Korean troops. As time passed, these attacks were intensified. Kim Il-sŏng apparently intended to keep the level of

51. See, for example, the article by Hŏ Pong-hak, "The Korean People's Army Is an Invincible Armed Force Which Has Inherited the Revolutionary Tradition of the Anti-Japanese Partisan Struggle," *NS*, Jan. 29, 1963, p. 1.

Another article of interest published during this period is Pak Tong-nyŏl, "Comrade Kim Il-sŏng's Policy on the Armament of the Entire Populace and Its Realization in the Guerrilla Base of Eastern Manchuria," *Kŭlloja (The Worker)*, No. 9, May 1963, pp. 20–25. According to Pak, Kim first adopted in 1932 the correct line of arming the entire populace and building an impregnable fortress, making it into standard Communist policy, and enabling the Korean guerrillas to continue the struggle against the Japanese until final victory.

tension high in order to justify the new sacrifices for which he was now calling.

Meanwhile, the process continued of building an ever tighter internal political structure. On December 3, 1963, local elections were held for deputies to the provincial, municipal, city, district, prefectural, and ri People's Committees. Once again, officials claimed that 100 percent of the electorate voted, with 100 percent voting for the recommended candidates. In his report to the Supreme People's Assembly in mid-December, Pak Kŭm-ch'ŏl provided an analysis of current local officeholders. Of the 2,517 deputies elected to the provincial (metropolitan) People's Committees, 673 were workers, 464 peasants, 1,002 functionaries of Party, state, and economic organs, and 378 "scientists, technicians, and men of culture and the arts," with 571 of those elected being women. The city and prefectural People's Committees consisted of 14,303 deputies, of whom 4,062 were workers, 3,708 peasants, 5,419 functionaries, and 1,114 scientists, technicians, and intellectuals, with 3,820 being women. At the lowest level, the ri and urban ward People's Committees, 70,250 deputies were elected, of whom 6,644 were workers, 45,429 peasants, 13,980 functionaries, and 4,197 scientists, technicians, and intellectuals, with 21,062 being women. According to Pak, among those elected there were a total of 24,167 who had been the recipients of various awards and medals. These included 32 Heroes of the Republic, 138 Labor Heroes, 100 Miners of Merit, 28 Lumbermen of Merit, 9 Stockbreeders of Merit, 10 Teachers of Merit, 1 People's Artist and 2 Artists of Merit, 3 Athletes of Merit, and 732 Ch'ŏllima work-team leaders.[52]

It will be noted that full-time functionaries of the Party and state played a substantial role in these local bodies; indeed, they constituted some 40 percent of the representation at the provincial and metropolitan level, and nearly the same percentage at the city and prefectural level, substantially outnumbering "workers" at both levels. At the local level, as might have been expected, the great majority were peasants, since the bulk of these Committees were in rural areas. But even here, the percentage of functionaries was comparatively high, equaling approximately 20 percent. It is also interesting to observe that, in proportion to their total numbers in the society, scientists, technicians, and "men of culture" were strongly represented. In broad terms, one might assert that workers and peasants, comprising about 90 percent of the society, received 40–50 percent of the representation at the provincial, city, and prefectural levels, with 50–60 percent going to the official and intellectual classes. At the local level, worker-peasant representation reached nearly 75 percent. However, slightly more than one-quarter of the representatives at this level came from the sociopolitical elite. Women, who constituted approximately 51 percent of

52. Pak Kŭm-ch'ŏl, "The Local Administrative Elections Summed Up," NS, Jan. 1, 1964, p. 1.

the society, received 25–30 percent of the representation at each of the levels.

Under these circumstances, it is not difficult to see how the Party had firm control of the People's Committees, with its own professional, full-time workers providing the backbone of the whole structure. And even though the details on representatives provided by Pak are relatively meager, they add up to a pattern familiar to those acquainted with either Soviet or Chinese elected state bodies.

In this period (1963–64), the Korean Workers' Party membership was officially listed at 1.3 million. This meant that a large number of members had been recruited in recent years (particularly since, at the time of the 1956–58 purge, and the subsequent "concentrated guidance" campaign, many Party members had been dropped). A sizable number of these new members, moreover, were workers and peasants of very limited education, and Party leaders were naturally concerned about the level of their political understanding. Even with respect to Party cadres, many of them hastily recruited and from the same social backgrounds, the problems were serious. A great deal of attention in Party journals, therefore, was given to "raising the standard" of Party members and workers. In his public utterances, Kim Il-sŏng and other Party leaders talked at length about the importance of a "cultural revolution" as the indispensable precursor of the technical and political revolutions that had been planned, and also as a necessary forerunner to the successful unification of the nation.

"In the future," wrote one Party spokesman, "we must carry out the difficult task of reeducating and reforming the workers, farmers, and intellectuals of South Korea so that they will come to the support of our Party." [53] If that task were to be successfully accomplished, the general level of KWP members and workers would have to be significantly raised so that their superior ideological, theoretical, and cultural knowledge would dominate both North and South Korea. Ordinary educational programs, and the classroom technique, would not work. Most Party members were occupied with full-time work schedules. Hence, the old methods of studying should be dispensed with in favor of the revolutionary study methods of the old anti-Japanese guerrillas. Study and work had to be combined, and a concrete study plan developed for every Party member, with specific times, places, and methods allotted.[54]

53. Pak Ki-son, "Let Us Strengthen the Struggle to Raise the General Standard of Party Members and Workers to a New Plateau," *Kŭlloja* (*The Worker*), April 5, 1964, pp. 2–10 (at p. 3).

54. Pak cited the experiences of the Party committee of a certain *ri* in South Hamgyŏng Province as a model to be followed. Individual study plans had been drafted for 1,300 farmers, with the goal of having 41 farmers attain an education equivalent to that of a graduate of a Communist college, 50 to reach the level of a graduate of the prefectural Party school, 160 to have an education equivalent to a workers' school graduate, 200 to reach the level of some workers' school education, another 200 to have the education of a technical school graduate, 35 to attain the status of engineer,

As can be seen, if there was a tremendous need for more trained technicians, there was also an ardent desire to improve the political consciousness of Party members. Both elements were now to be found in the Party's
plans for a broad adult education program, supplementary to the formal
training from primary school through the university. Every Party member
and many non-Party members were to undergo lifelong education, with an
equal emphasis upon political and technical training. In the process of advancing this program, moreover, Party leaders directed substantial criticism
at the formal educational system that had prevailed to date, questioning its
relevance, doubting its political contributions, and evidencing suspicion of
the "old intellectuals" who still commanded a few of its ramparts. In this
can be seen the essence of the "cultural revolution" concerning which Kim
and others spoke at length, and which was shortly to foster such a traumatic
struggle in the People's Republic of China.

In this period also, efforts were made to tie mass organizations more
closely to Party goals. The Democratic Youth League, reorganized at its
Fifth Congress in May 1964 as the Socialist Working Youth League,
claimed a membership at this point of 2.6 million, and a number of its
leaders were reportedly serving in Party and government posts. According
to one Party writer, 1,668,000 League members were participating in the
Ch'ŏllima Movement by early 1964, and more than 761,000 had received
Ch'ŏllima awards.[55] At a lower age level, the Korean Young Pioneers,
numbering some 1.6 million youth under 14 years of age, were also involved in the Stakhanovite movement, "busy trying to earn the title of
Model Young Pioneers Organization for their units."

Similar activities were being promoted within labor, farmer, and
women's organizations. On March 27, 1965, the Korean Farmers' Union
changed its name to Korean Agricultural Workers' League to symbolize
the growing "proletarianization" of the peasant. Its basic mission was defined as that of carrying out Kim Il-sŏng's 1964 theses on agriculture (discussed below), and mobilizing all farm workers for a unified ideological,
technical, and cultural revolution.[56] Identical types of orders were being

---

and 150 to obtain technical training of various sorts. The remainder presumably
would aim at acquiring basic literacy and an elementary education.

Various technical, political, and general education courses were established under
the jurisdiction of the Party, some of them by correspondence. Each farmer involved
was required to submit a study schedule; study was to be undertaken "while he is at
work, resting, at home, or even walking." All Party cadres and members, moreover,
were ordered not to leave the teaching merely to the appointed instructors, but to
become a part of the teaching staff themselves, with older, more experienced members
paying particular attention to younger members.

55. Hong Sung-won, "The Reorganization of the Youth League," NS, April 24,
1964, pp. 2–3.

56. "The Founding of the Korean Agricultural Workers' League—An Epochal
Event in the Solution of the Farm Problem," Kŭlloja (The Worker), April 5, 1965,
pp. 2–8.

given the Korean Trade Union Federation, described as "the transmission belt linking the Party with the working class," and the Korean Democratic Women's League, an organization nominally encompassing some 2.5 million women.

On two occasions during 1965, Kim Il-sŏng addressed the nation: at Wŏnsan on August 15, on the occasion of the twentieth anniversary of Liberation, and again on October 10 in P'yŏngyang, in celebration of the twentieth birthday of the Korean Workers' Party.[57] The first speech was a perfunctory, brief address. The October speech, however, was interesting for the light that it shed upon both past events and future goals. Kim clearly regarded internal politics as having passed a major watershed, with the 1958–59 period constituting the dividing line. The past decade, he asserted, had been "a decade of brilliant victories in the struggle for the organizational and ideological consolidation of the Party." [58] According to Kim, because of the complex conditions surrounding the emergence of the DPRK and the low level of "Marxist-Leninist education" among Party cadres, dogmatism had exercised considerable influence upon the Party in the earlier period. This had gradually been overcome, "but some obstinate dogmatists infected with flunkeyism towards the great powers continued to obstruct the implementation of the Party's correct line and policies, doing harm to our work." [59]

A decisive step, according to Kim, was taken by Party leadership in 1955, with the determination to establish chuch'e as the governing doctrine in all spheres. From this point, all Party cadres, as well as all citizens, were caused to study their own history and traditions, and to cultivate a spirit of solving all problems in accordance with the actual conditions in Korea. Everyone learned to accept the Party's line and policies as the sole direction of their activities. In this fashion, Marxism-Leninism was creatively applied to national realities.

57. English translations of these two speeches are carried in *TPK,* Aug. 18, p. 1, and Oct. 20, 1965, pp. 1–8.

58. *Ibid.,* p. 4. Kim went on to say, "The struggle against factionalism and for strengthening the Party's unity, the struggle against dogmatism and for establishing *chuch'e,* and the struggle against modern revisionism and for safeguarding the purity of Marxism-Leninism, have been the main struggles in the postwar years on the ideological front within the Party."

59. *Ibid.* "All the factionalists who appeared in our Party," Kim proclaimed, "were, without exception, dogmatists and the worshipers of the great powers. After the war such elements manifested dogmatism most flagrantly. They not only disregarded the actual conditions of their country but also they even ignored their country's history, cultural and revolutionary traditions and they degenerated into national-nihilists who disparage all that is their own and admire all foreign things. While refusing to be guided by the line and policies of their own Party in their work, they would only turn to others, ready to follow them blindly. They did not have any faith in the strength of their own country, only willing to rely on others. Thus, the harm of dogmatism and flunkeyism toward the great powers became intolerable."

However, no sooner had one danger, that of dogmatism, been vanquished, said Kim, when modern revisionism reared its head, first in the international movement, then in Korea, where "the factionalists" had smuggled it in. The attacks of "these opportunists" had reached their climax in 1956–57. "At that time, a handful of anti-Party factionalists and die-hard dogmatists hiding within the Party challenged our Party, in conspiracy with each other on the basis of revisionism and with the backing of outside forces. They not only castigated the line and policies of our Party, but they also plotted together to subvert the leadership of our Party." [60]

The Party triumphed, of course, over both the "anti-Party elements" that had burrowed into it and those "outside forces" that had attempted intervention. "Our Party," Kim went on, "made clean riddance of the factionalism which had done such tremendous harm to the Communist movement throughout history, and attained a firm unity of ideology and will within its ranks." True Marxism-Leninism had thus prevailed over modern revisionism, dogmatism was defeated, and chuch'e was everywhere ascendant.

Kim declared that the Party, now 1.6 million strong, had achieved unprecedented unity by practicing the mass line, as exemplified by the Ch'ŏngsan-ri Method. For the first time in its history, the Party had one ideology and one set of policies (he might have added, one leader). Nothing could separate the Party from the people, Kim concluded. It now remained for the Party to increase the political consciousness of all members, particularly the cadres; to guard against those familiar evils, bureaucratism and commandism, and to advance the mass line; and finally, armed with a unitary ideology, to assault the twin fortresses of total military defense and rapid socialist construction.

The October 1965 speech can be seen as an expression of mixed bitterness and confidence—bitterness concerning the "wrongs" perpetrated

60. *Ibid.* For the first time, Kim was very explicit in outlining the issues involved in the 1956 crisis as *he* interpreted them: "The modern revisionists, by creating illusions about U.S. imperialism in particular, tried to divert our Party and people from a resolute fight against American imperialism. They also opposed the socialist revolution in our country, prattling that it was as yet premature; they opposed our Party's line of socialist industrialization, the line of the construction of an independent national economy in particular; and they even brought economic pressure to bear upon us, inflicting tremendous losses upon our socialist construction. The aim of the modern revisionists was to make our Party betray Marxism-Leninism and revolution, give up the anti-U.S. struggle and take the road of right capitulationism, following in their footsteps."

A more explicit attack upon Khrushchevian policies—and their presumed manifestation at a very early point within Korean politics—could scarcely have been made. In the charges concerning "economic pressure," moreover, Kim was in reality talking about contemporary problems, for even as he spoke North Korea was suffering substantial economic difficulties, as we shall see, partly because of the very strained relations with Russia which had recently prevailed.

against the Party (and Kim) in the past and confidence that, with the successful counterattack that had culminated in the major purges of 1957–59, a new era of internal political tranquility, enforced by Kim's strong grip over all aspects of the domestic scene, had been attained. This analysis was essentially correct. In the years that followed, however, a more or less continuous series of purges was to take place involving men at the very top of the Party and, in some cases, the military structure. For the most part, the victims were Party veterans, and their personal loyalty to Kim had seemingly been impeccable.

Purges of Top Cadres

The years between 1966 and 1970 provided ample evidence that security was an elusive commodity for those who had reached the top rungs of Party and military power. It is startling to realize that of the eighteen members of the Political Committee (twelve full and six alternate members) who were in office in the fall of 1964, only five were reappointed to the Political Committee at the Fifth Party Congress in November 1970 (four being full members and one an alternate member). One of the eighteen (Yi Chu-yŏn) is known to have died of natural causes. At least three evidently remained in the Party's (that is, Kim's) reasonably good graces, because, at the Fifth Congress, they were listed among the thirty-nine members of the Presidium, even though they were not reelected to the Political Committee. (The three were Nam Il, listed ninth in the Presidium list, Pak Chŏng-ae, listed eleventh, and Kim Ik-sŏn, listed twelfth.) But nine of the original eighteen—or 50 percent—have disappeared from sight, and it is clear that most if not all of them have been purged, ending their careers in disgrace and obscurity. They include such major political and military figures as Kim Ch'ang-man, Pak Kŭm-ch'ŏl, Yi Hyo-sun, Chŏng Il-yong, Kim Kwang-hyŏp, Han Sang-du, Yi Chong-ok, Ha Ang-ch'ŏn, and Kim Ch'angbong.

Life at the top of the North Korean Party and military ladder thus remains precarious, if the evidence of recent years is carefully weighed. The top three men of the regime—Kim Il-sŏng, Ch'oe Yong-gŏn, and Kim Il—have remained in their original positions and Party order. But every member of the next echelon—the seven who constituted the remaining full members of the Political Committee in 1964—have been either demoted or dismissed. Moreover, only two of the six alternate members have survived, although one, Pak Sŏng-ch'ŏl, has been advanced to fourth rank on the Fifth Congress Political Committee, immediately after the veteran triumvirate.

What has caused this continued upheaval? Is it the paranoia of an aging dictator, as ex-Communists like Han Chae-dŏk have claimed? Is it the product of significant policy differences, differences born out of setbacks and failures, as much of the scanty evidence would suggest? Is it a by-product of shifts in the relation between Korea and the international Communist world, affecting "pro-Chinese" and "pro-Soviet" remnants within the Korean Workers' Party? Is it connected with a recurrent factionalism and power struggle involving both Party and military forces? Before seeking to weigh the degree to which these and other factors have been involved, let us examine such evidence as is currently available, drawing heavily upon a combination of published materials furnished by the North Koreans themselves and the testimony of defectors.

The first key figure to be ousted in this period was Kim Ch'ang-man, who seems to have been removed from office at the very beginning of 1966. Kim, it will be recalled, although he had spent much of his early life in China and was connected at one point with the Korean Independence League, had long been considered a member of Kim's personal circle and had stood by Kim during the 1956–58 crisis. The reasons for Kim Ch'ang-man's ouster remain unclear. One story is that Kim Il-sŏng discovered that, contrary to orders, he had given a lavish New Year's party on January 1, 1966. This angered the Leader, who was currently demanding austerity from key Party officials.[61] Others believe that despite Kim Ch'ang-man's earlier support of Kim Il-sŏng, his ideological-political views, and those of his group, were too close to Peking, and that Kim Il-sŏng, now trying to reestablish a "neutral" position between Moscow and Peking after a period of decided coolness toward the Russians, found it expedient to remove him. The causes of Kim's downfall, however, still lie shrouded in mystery. His ouster has never been mentioned publicly, nor has his name appeared since October 1965, when he gave an interview to *Jen-min Jih-pao*.

The Second Party Conference

The next political changes, far more significant, were to take place in the course of the following year. They were revealed at the Second Korean Workers' Party Conference, which opened on October 5, 1966, with 1,275 voting and 48 nonvoting delegates in attendance. The decision to hold a conference and not a congress is noteworthy. A first Party Conference had been held from the third to the sixth of March 1958, two years after the Third Party Congress, in the aftermath of the major purges. As suggested earlier, it had been concerned primarily with internal matters, among them restructuring the Party. We can guess the reasons for not calling a Fifth Congress in 1966. Traditionally, the congress had been the occasion for announcing the successful completion of one economic program and the launching of a new one, as well as for "pointing with pride" to accomplishments in the political arena, both foreign and domestic. The year 1966 offered no such opportunities. Yet there were "many urgent problems," as Ch'oe Yong-gŏn phrased it in the opening speech, and this made a general Party meeting desirable.

61. Robert A. Scalapino interview with Han Chae-dŏk, Seoul, Nov. 8, 1968.

The October Conference, lasting a full week, dealt with a wide range of issues: the complex, dangerous international situation; the disappointing economic picture (although, as we shall see, the full extent of the problem was carefully veiled); and domestic political issues. We shall deal only with the latter issues at this point, reserving comment on the first two until later. Ch'oe Yong-gŏn, in his opening remarks, repeated what had now become a standard line: the Korean Workers' Party, he asserted, had grown into an invincible Party, steel-like and monolithic, united by a single ideology, a single set of policies, and a single Great Leader.

The Great Leader in question delivered a lengthy speech on October 5, divided into three major sections.[62] The first dealt wholly with international problems, and was devoted primarily to the tense situation within the Communist world. The third was devoted to the issue of North-South unification. In the second, Kim addressed himself to domestic questions. Here his main concern was to give a vigorous defense of the basic line enunciated in late 1962, the line of equal emphasis upon "socialist construction" and "the strengthening of the revolutionary base." His defense hinged upon the thesis that there remained an imminent threat of war as a result of the type of aggression that "US imperialism" had already undertaken against Cuba and was now planning to undertake against North Korea. In his speech, Kim made no direct reference to the serious economic problems that had recently emerged as a result of the new policy. Nor did he mention the problems being caused by the estrangement from the Soviet Union. He did, however, acknowledge that substantial sacrifices were called for, and urged a tense, mobilized attitude on the part of all citizens.

The second major theme that ran through this section of Kim's address was a strident defense of chuch'e. "We should continue to strictly abide by the principle of establishing chuch'e in ideology, independence in politics, self-reliance in the economy, and self-defense in national defense." Kim then spoke of the very important place which "socialist patriotism" should occupy in the education of the working people.[63] Socialist patriotism, of course, was to be distinguished from bourgeois nationalism, and closely linked with proletarian internationalism—an old Communist theme. "Only one who is boundlessly faithful to the revolution of one's own country can remain loyal to the revolutionary cause of the international working class, and only a true internationalist can become a true patriot. The national

62. For the full text of Kim's speech in English, "The Present Situation and the Task Confronting Our Party," see Supplement (1) to *The P'yŏngyang Times,* No. 41, Oct. 13, 1966, pp. 1–16.

63. *Ibid.,* p. 12. Kim's definition of socialist patriotism is a familiar one: "Socialist patriotism is the patriotism of the working class and the working people aspiring to socialism and Communism; it combines class consciousness with the spirit of national independence, the love for their class and system with that for their nation and country."

and international duties of the working class are united with each other." [64]

Kim's arguments notwithstanding, the distinctions between "socialist patriotism" and "bourgeois nationalism" are extremely hard to detect. Indeed, North Korea in this period displayed many if not all of the signs of traditional Western nationalism in its most extreme forms: a demand for uniform, unquestioning allegiance to country and leader; the construction of a *national* culture, and repeated insistence upon its superiority; the creation of myths that would undergird the new nation-state, and the inculcation of these myths at the primary and secondary school levels, as well as in the media; substantial signs of chauvinism and xenophobia, drawn from the past in some respects, but now revitalized; and a new emphasis upon a martial spirit, including an effort to raise the military to a

---

64. *Ibid.,* p. 13. Yet another passage or two will indicate the thrust of Kim's remarks, and his efforts to summon up all the nationalist appeals without appearing to abandon "proletarian internationalism." "One who does not love one's own country and nation," he asserted, "cannot cherish a warm passion for the revolution of one's country and cannot devote oneself to its victory. This is why we Communists love our Fatherland and nation more ardently than anyone else, determinedly fight for national independence and prosperity, treasure national culture and all the fine heritages and traditions of the nation and endeavor to carry forward and develop them. Communists oppose all forms of national oppression and inequality, and reject national nihilism" (p. 12).

"What is of great importance here is to educate the working people to take a correct attitude towards the legacies of national culture and national traditions which have been formed historically. We must neither get into the nihilist deviation of negating and obliterating all past things, nor into the deviation of restoring the past without criticism. These deviations pose big obstacles both to creating a new socialist culture and way of life, and to imbuing the working people with the ideas of socialist patriotism. Only if backward and reactionary elements are sifted out of national legacies and all progressive and popular elements among them are taken over and developed critically, is it possible to create a new socialist culture and way of life and develop these further" (p. 12).

And finally, "We must arm the entire working people more firmly with the ideas of proletarian internationalism, with the spirit of internationalist solidarity among the revolutionary peoples. . . . We should educate the working people to fight for the victory of the revolution of their own country and, at the same time, fight for the advancement of the world revolutionary movement and always resolutely support and encourage the liberation struggle of the oppressed nations and the exploited people" (p. 13). This passage concludes with an additional appeal to learn from the successes and experiences of others.

As can be seen from the above quotations, Kim, in the fashion of many other leaders of emerging societies, was seeking to draw *selectively* from Korean tradition to underwrite modernization efforts, and to utilize a combination of emotional and rational appeals to serve Party and state ends. In the mammoth demonstrations mounted by the regime on ceremonial occasions, with military and militia units featured, huge parades with a sea of North Korean flags being borne, mass calisthenics in open-air stadiums, and the marching of hundreds of thousands of people, one recalls the techniques of the Fascists, Nazis, and Soviet Communists—the visual impression being closest to the former two, and especially to Hitler's public pageantry.

high peak of prestige, a call for sacrifice on behalf of the fatherland, and a straightforward defense of the use of force on behalf of "just" causes.

With the nationalist appeal went the demand for perfecting the new socialist culture, a culture that had to be both Spartan and collective. "We must categorically reject the reactionary bourgeois ideology and the corrupt bourgeois morality and way of life," proclaimed Kim, "oppose egoism, liberalism, and other remnants of outworn ideas and backward conventions, and tirelessly strive for the triumph of Communist ideas and morality, for the establishment of a Communist atmosphere of life. We should see that all working people oppose degradation and indolence, lead a frugal life, display voluntary zeal in labor, love the collective and organization, and endeavor to bring prosperity to all, helping and leading each other forward." [65]

Kim also devoted considerable attention to the class and mass lines underlining the Party's operational techniques, providing once again an exposition of the Party leadership's current attitudes toward North Korean society. Here, his remarks were entirely orthodox and traditional. Revolutionary leadership had been seized and was being executed by the working class, and that class was performing its historic mission: transforming the society into a truly socialist one. The peasantry, the workers' "most reliable ally," had been close to the center of the regime's concern. At this point, the socialist revolution had not only changed the peasantry's socioeconomic position, but also their ideological consciousness, with distinctions between town and country, working class and peasantry, gradually being obliterated. The great task of the Party was to consolidate and continue that process.

There were, finally, the intellectuals, and from the first days of its founding the Party had valued their important role. It had made persistent efforts to educate and remold the old-line intellectuals, while rearing a large number of new intellectuals from among the working class. This policy, proclaimed Kim, had been a brilliant success. Hundreds of thousands of new intellectuals had emerged, forming a reliable contingent within the intellectual class. It was true, he admitted, that the intellectual community as a whole was still influenced by the remnants of bourgeois and petty bourgeois thought, but it was "fundamentally wrong to distrust, for this reason, the revolutionary spirit of the intellectuals." (Was this a reference to current developments in China?) Indeed, argued Kim, "to

---

65. *Ibid.,* p. 12. And a special call was issued in connection with military needs: "We should also see to it that the army men and the people are not immersed in a peaceful mood but sharpen their vigilance and maintain a strained posture at all times against the aggressive maneuvers and possible war provocation of the enemy. Communists do not want war, but they never fear it. To be afraid of war is a manifestation of bourgeois pacifism and a revisionist ideological trend. We must strictly prevent such an ideological virus from appearing within our ranks or infiltrating from without" (p. 9).

suspect and reject the intellectuals is a factionalist tendency. To underestimate their role is a trend toward ignoring science and technology. These tendencies have nothing to do with our Party policy towards the intelligentsia." [66]

Kim also called for more lenient treatment of people "with complicated social and political backgrounds," urging that more faith be shown in the possibility of converting them to the proper path, so that they could work "without any worries" for the Party and state. "This line of our Party," he continued, "can shatter all the estrangement maneuvers of the enemy, win over the masses of the people of all circles and strata to the side of the Party and the revolution, isolate hostile elements still further and give them no room to set foot." [67]

This 90/10 strategy, wooing and uniting with 90 percent of the people to isolate and oppose the remaining 10 percent, was of course not new, nor was it original with Kim Il-sŏng. It had long been a premise of Maoism and of other "united front" strategies. Close examination of Kim's October speech, as published, discloses no reference to any economic crisis, nor any concern about Party unity. Kim did warn in one section that even though factionalism within the Party had been overcome, and Party unity was currently unprecedented, there was no room for self-complacency. Referring to the past, he remarked that as long as there were "opportunist trends and great-nation chauvinist tendencies within the world Communist movement," it was impossible to write off the possibility of further outside interference like that of 1956. "Under the present complicated situation, waverers may appear within our ranks too, particularly under sectarian and other opportunist influences from without. We must, therefore, always sharpen our vigilance against factionalism."

In point of fact, however, significant changes were made in the Political Committee at this time. They appear to have been connected primarily with the recent economic setbacks, although other factors may have been involved. On October 12, the final day of the Party Conference, the Fourteenth Plenum of the Fourth Central Committee was held. At its conclusion, certain changes in the Party organizational structure were announced, together with new personnel. The posts of chairman and vice-chairman were abolished, in favor of a general secretary with a panel of ten secretaries, the whole group forming a Secretariat. This was a system akin to that of the Soviet Union. It was stipulated that the Secretariat would

66. *Ibid.*, p. 11. Almost certainly Kim wanted these remarks and the ones that followed to be interpreted as a rebuke to the Maoists, who were currently engaged in a major assault upon key elements within the Chinese intelligentsia, with Red Guards being used as a vanguard.

67. *Ibid.* Kim continued, "We have to carry on the Party's class and mass lines fully so that we may further expand and reinforce our revolutionary ranks and turn the whole society into a great family, closely united and harmonious, cheerful and vivacious" (p. 11).

take primary responsibility for implementing the lines, policies, and resolutions of the Party, as well as supervising routine Party work. It was to be a supreme coordinating body of an administrative nature, with the Political Committee continuing as the Party's highest policy-making body. It was further announced that the Political Committee would have a six-member Presidium, presumably as a day-to-day operating body at the supreme level.

The members of the Presidium appointed at this time were Kim Il-sŏng, Ch'oe Yong-gŏn, Kim Il, Pak Kŭm-ch'ŏl, Yi Hyo-sun, and Kim Kwang-hyŏp, in that order. The additional full members of the Political Committee appointed were Kim Ik-sŏn, Kim Ch'ang-bong, Pak Sŏng-ch'ŏl, Ch'oe Hyŏn, and Yi Yŏng-ho. Alternate members elected were Sŏk San, Hŏ Pong-hak, Ch'oe Kwang, O Chin-u, Yim Ch'un-ch'u, Kim Tong-gyu, Kim Yŏng-ju, Pak Yong-guk, and Chŏng Kyŏng-bok.

Members of the Political Committee dropped in addition to Kim Ch'ang-man were Chŏng Il-yong, Nam Il, Yi Chong-ok, Pak Chŏng-ae, and Yi Chu-yŏn, the last five of the full-member roster elected in 1961, and Ha Ang-ch'ŏn, Han Sang-du, and Hyŏn Mu-gwang, the second, third, and fourth alternate members. Kim Ch'ang-bong and Pak Sŏng-ch'ŏl had been advanced to full membership from their previous alternate status.

As could have been anticipated, Kim Il-sŏng was elected general secretary of the Party, and the ten secretaries under him were all full or alternate members of the revised Political Committee.[68]

No explanation was given either at this point or later for the structural and personnel changes. With respect to the latter, however, we can advance certain hypotheses. First, it should be noted that these changes did not constitute a full-scale purge of the type inaugurated in the 1956–58 period. With a few exceptions, the individuals adversely affected continued to hold Party and state offices and to function as members of the political elite. Some of them, moreover, were to return to the Political Committee at a later point, or at least to be promoted again. So far as we can determine, in addition to Kim Ch'ang-man only Ha Ang-ch'ŏn was really purged. Ha, president of Kim Il-sŏng University, was not to be featured publicly again. Was he held responsible for certain signs of intellectual unrest there to which we shall later refer?

The most important indicator of the reasons behind the change was the fact that six of the individuals demoted had previously held key posts in the economic production field. Chŏng Il-yong had been responsible for the electric and coal industries, Nam Il had been head of the State Planning Commission, Yi Chong-ok had been minister of Mining and Chemicals, Yi Chu-yŏn had been Trade minister, Hyŏn Mu-gwang had been a Machine Industry minister, and Han Sang-du had been minister of Finance. The

68. The ten secretaries initially appointed were Ch'oe Yong-gŏn, Kim Il, Pak Kŭm-ch'ŏl, Yi Hyo-sun, Kim Kwang-hyŏp, Sŏk San, Hŏ Pong-hak, Kim Yŏng-ju, Pak Yong-guk, and Chŏng Kyŏng-bok.

rate of economic growth had declined drastically in this period, and evidently Kim Il-sŏng was determined that the key ministers take the responsibility. The reasons for Pak Chŏng-ae being removed from the Political Committee are not clear. She continued to occupy a prominent role in the Party.

Similarly, we can conjecture about the reasons for the rise at this point of such individuals as Kim Ch'ang-bong, Ch'oe Hyŏn, Hŏ Pong-hak, Ch'oe Kwang, and O Chin-u. These were all professional military men, and central to the current policy of emphasizing the creation of a totally militarized state. Sŏk San was the new chief of Internal Security, an equally important position. The remaining new alternate members of the Politburo came from a different source, and were of equal interest and importance. Kim Yŏng-ju was the younger brother of Kim Il-sŏng, now for the first time moved into top Party ranks, and clearly a man to watch. Pak Yong-guk, of Kim Yŏng-ju's generation (he was about 46), represented one of the young, rising Party functionaries, and this was also true of Kim Tong-gyu, Chŏng Kyŏng-bok, and Yim Ch'un-ch'u.

Thus, in the fall of 1966, many of those centrally connected with economic policies were demoted, whereas a number of key military figures were promoted, so that the Party acquired a decidedly heavier representation of professional military men in its top ranks. At the same time, however, a second generation of functionaries, in their late forties and early fifties, were now raised to the level of alternate Political Committee membership. Of these, the truly powerful figure was Kim Yŏng-ju—a man with a prestigious relative in government.

Within the next year, there were to be more purges. The major victims were Pak Kŭm-ch'ŏl and Yi Hyo-sun, who had ranked respectively fourth and fifth in the Party. The ouster of Pak and Yi was probably consummated at the Plenum of the Central Committee in April 1967, or shortly thereafter. Both men were listed as being on the platform at the opening of the seventh session of the Third Supreme People's Assembly on April 24, but apparently neither was on the reviewing stand a week later, at the time of the May 1 parade. It is also possible that the purge took place somewhat later. Seoul Radio, presumably based upon intelligence reports, announced on November 7 that there had been a new purge, aimed at consolidating the position of Kim Il-sŏng. It listed Pak and Yi as the key figures involved, but stated that others had also been swept out, including Ko Hyŏk, who had been appointed one of ten vice-premiers in December 1966, and Yim Ch'un-ch'u, new Political Committee member and secretary-general of the Presidium of the Supreme People's Assembly.

In any case, none of these men were reappointed to their previous posts when the newly elected Supreme People's Assembly approved a new cabinet on December 16, 1967; and they disappeared from the Party roster as well. Also absent from the December sessions were two other top

Party members, Pak Yong-guk and Kim To-man (the latter having been listed by Seoul Radio as also purged).

Yi Hyo-sun, it may be recalled, had been a Kapsan Communist, having assisted his brother, Yi Che-sun, in his underground work in the Kapsan region (it was this work that had made Kim's Pojŏn sortie possible). After Liberation, his role had been that of Party official, starting at the provincial level. At the time of his removal, Yi was not only a member of the Presidium of the Political Committee and of the Secretariat, but also head of the Party's vital South Korea bureau.

Pak Kŭm-ch'ŏl had also been one of Kim's prime agents in Kapsan, working closely with Pak Tal and Yi Che-sun. He was released from prison only after Liberation, and was long considered one of the intimate circle around the Leader. He currently ranked number four, immediately behind the Kim Il-sŏng–Ch'oe Yong-gŏn–Kim Il triumvirate, and held a number of top Party and state posts. The demise of these two men indicated once again that historic intimacy with Kim Il-sŏng did not prevent repeated testings or an eventual toppling.

Ko Hyŏk, in addition to his post as deputy premier, had also been head of the Culture Department of the Party. Yim Ch'un-ch'u, as noted, had been a "company commander" under Kim before 1945, and was secretary-general of the People's Assembly and an alternate member of the Political Committee. Kim To-man was head of the Propaganda and Agitation Department of the Party, and Pak Yong-guk reportedly was the head of the International Department. Kim To-man and Pak Yong-guk had been considered by some observers as two of the rising trio of the younger generation, the third being Kim Yŏng-ju, the Leader's younger brother.

What caused this new series of purges? At the time of their occurrences, Party organs were completely silent. Various rumors circulated that they involved a conflict between military and civilian leaders. Clearly, they seemed to relate in part to policies with respect to South Korea, since both Yi and Pak Yong-guk were key figures from the Party side responsible for policies in this regard. The Party's "intellectual" and "propaganda" outlets were also centrally involved, as the demise of Ko and Kim To-man indicated. Only at the time of the Central Committee Plenum in April 1968, did Kim Il give some hint of one central issue. In his report, speaking of the attempt to execute the new line of "equal emphasis" on military preparedness and economic construction, he noted that "like the carrying through of any and every new line, this great revolutionary upsurge was effected through a severe struggle against all that was old and stale." [69]

69. "On the People's Economic Development Plan for 1968 for Carrying on More Successfully Economic Construction and Defense Building in the Face of the Obtaining Situation," a report delivered by Kim Il, secretary of the KWP Central Committee and first vice-premier, at the April 22, 1968, CC Plenum, published in *Foreign Broadcast Information Service* Supplement, May 3, 1968, as transmitted over P'yŏngyang Domestic Service in Korean, April 23, 1968, pp. 1–43 (at p. 4).

The major obstacle, he continued, was posed by those exhibiting "passivism and conservatism." These traits "stemmed from a lack of confidence in the might of our heroic worker class." Kim continued:

> The passive elements and conservatives clung to the outdated notions of an official capacity and norm, mythicized science and technology, restricted the initiatives of the masses, stopped working people from working more, kneeled before difficulties, feared mass innovation, and attempted to block the grand onward movement. Without destroying passiveness and conservatism, wavering and false cleverness, it was impossible to effect a new upsurge on all fronts of socialist economic construction and defense building.[70]

We can read the above passages to indicate that Pak, Yi, and certain subordinates stood accused of questioning the economic feasibility of current policies and urging a somewhat reduced tempo. Confronted with the sharp setbacks of 1966 in the economic field, they presumably argued that both men and machinery were being driven too hard; that greater attention should be paid to providing a truly modern scientific base so that the quality of production could be improved, with less focus upon sheer quantity; and that priorities should be readjusted, with some possibility of reducing the mushrooming military expenditures and stretching out the military preparedness program. We emphasize that to formulate their position in this precise manner is conjectural, since no records are yet available which would make their views explicit. It is clear, however, that they stood accused of being doubting Thomases concerning the new plan. Later, Kim Il-sŏng himself was to assert that those harboring passivism and conservatism had advanced the line that after a nation reached a certain level of economic growth, it could not expect to continue the same high percentage of annual growth. He condemned this as an evidence of lack of faith in the proletariat—another "crime" of the ousted group.

To what extent this conflict had the ingredients of a civilian-military struggle cannot be clarified at this point. As we noted earlier, the professional military had recently made significant gains in Political Committee membership. Undoubtedly, they would view with a jaundiced eye any reduction in military expenditures or shifting of basic priorities. Yet the evidence is too scanty to permit us to draw the battle lines of 1967

70. *Ibid.* At a slightly later point in his speech, Kim Il revealed that during 1967 the Party had struggled against "revisionism, left-wing opportunism, toadyism, bourgeois thoughts, feudalistic Confucian thoughts, sectarianism, localism, and familyism."

"In the course of this struggle, there was established among the entire Party membership and all people a revolutionary trait which accepts no other ideas but Comrade Kim Il-sŏng's revolutionary ideas, our Party's ideas of *chuch'e,* a trait which makes thinking and action conform to our Party's policy, and which accepts the policy and carries it through unconditionally, without the slightest swerving in any winds and waves."

Certainly no further evidence would be needed to warn Party leaders against differing with The Leader on policy matters.

clearly.[71] Whatever the precise causes of this upheaval, and whoever the combatants may have been, two veterans of the movement were removed from office, as were a number of men presumably associated with them. The ouster or demotion of Ko Hyŏk and Kim To-man, as well as of Yim Ch'un-ch'u, may or may not have been connected with the same issue. Having zigged in 1966 by holding those in charge of an unrealistic economic program responsible for its shortcomings, Kim Il-sŏng zagged in 1967 by sacking the critics of that program—for which he, after all, was primarily responsible.

At the close of 1967, Kim Il-sŏng announced a new ten-point political program for the nation at the first session of the newly elected Fourth Supreme People's Assembly.[72] The decision to advance ten points, no more and no less, related to the fact that Kim had supposedly established a ten-point program for the Fatherland Front in 1935. Thus the new program was given a link with Communist history. The ten points can be summarized as follows:

1. The establishment of chuch'e in all fields.
2. The liberation of South Korea.
3. The "revolutionization" and "proletarianization" of all members

71. For additional analysis of civil-military relations during this period, see Chapter XII.

72. The elections for 457 SPA delegates were held on November 25, and once again it was announced that 100 percent of the electorate had voted, and had cast 100 percent of their ballots for the officially approved candidates. See *TPK,* Nov. 29, 1967, pp. 1–2.

Kim Il-sŏng ran in the Songnim constituency. The following account (*ibid.*) of his meeting with his constituents warrants reproduction to illustrate the status of the cult of personality at this point.

"The entire voters and citizens of Songrim [Songnim] were once again overwhelmed with boundless emotion and joy at having nominated as their candidate for deputy to the Supreme People's Assembly the great leader of our people, Comrade Kim Il-sŏng, peerless patriot, national hero, ever-victorious, iron-willed commander, and an outstanding leader of the international working-class movement, who always leads our people to victory and glory, to happiness and prosperity, shouldering the destiny of the country and the nation upon himself, and triumphantly exploring the path of Korean revolution.

"From early in the morning, the heroic steel fighters of the Hwanghae Iron Works, workers, office workers, youths and students, housewives and cooperative farmers in the vicinity came out to the street in their holiday best, with pennants and flowers in their hands, to meet their respected and beloved leader, Comrade Kim Il-sŏng.

"The city of Songrim was decorated like a festive day. Waiting for the arrival of the respected and beloved leader, Comrade Kim Il-sŏng, 50,000 welcoming people extending four kilometers lined the street, exuberantly singing and dancing. At 10, the car carrying Comrade Premier arrived at the rotary at the entrance of the city. The shouts of 'Long live Comrade Kim Il-sŏng!' and 'Long live the Korean Workers' Party!' broke out from the enthusiastic crowds and echoed throughout the city."

On November 30, elections for the local assemblies were held, with similar results.

of the society, including the peasants and intellectuals, under the leadership of the KWP and the working class.

4. The elimination of bureaucratism, and the application of the mass line so as to organize and mobilize the entire people for revolution and construction.

5. The "consolidation" of an independent national economy so as to improve the general standard of living.

6. The advancement of science and technology, and the building of a socialist culture.

7. The increase of national defense capacities, and the raising of the military posture of the entire people.

8. The establishment of economic relations and the development of foreign trade with other countries, within the framework of an independent economy.

9. The struggle on behalf of the national interests and rights of all Korean compatriots abroad.

10. The promotion of friendly relations with all nations that oppose imperialist aggression, respect the independence of Korea, and desire to establish state relations with Korea on a basis of equality.[73]

For the most part, the ordering of these points appears to indicate the priorities attached to them. The exception is item 7, which should have occupied second or third position. None of these policies was new, as can be observed, but in the months ahead all Party meetings were devoted to discussions of the Ten-Point Program and how to achieve the stipulated goals most effectively and most quickly.

Throughout 1968, the citizenry were driven at an unremitting pace in an effort to move forward with the Seven-Year Plan, now extended for an additional three years, and scheduled for fulfillment in 1970. Military expenditures continued to account for approximately one-third of all budgetary allocations, indicating clearly the tremendous importance that the regime was giving its military program.

The major public event of the year took place on September 7 and 8, when the twentieth anniversary of the founding of the Democratic People's Republic of Korea was celebrated. The pageantry of this occasion, and the major actors in it, symbolized the degree to which Kim Il-sŏng now dominated all political activity in the nation. Behind the main platform that accommodated all of the current political elite stood a huge portrait

73. For the full English language text of Kim's speech, see "Let Us Embody More Thoroughly the Revolutionary Spirit of Independence, Self-Sustenance and Self-Defense, in All Fields of State Activity, the Historic Political Program of the DPRK Government Announced by Premier Kim Il-sŏng, At the First Session of the Fourth Supreme People's Assembly on December 16, 1967," *TPK,* Dec. 20, 1967, pp. 2–12.

of the Leader, wreathed in flowers and set off by a gigantic North Korean flag that stretched across the entire rear of the stage. In his opening remarks, Ch'oe Yong-gŏn, the durable, noncompetitive president of the Supreme People's Assembly, eulogized Kim in the extravagant terms now so frequently and so precisely repeated as to have become ritualistic. A scrutiny of the list of those on the platform indicates that no prominent figures had been removed from the scene since the 1967 purges. Among those present was "a delegate of the South Korean revolutionary organizations," as well as a group representing the Koreans living in Japan.

Kim Il-sŏng's address contained no new themes pertaining to the domestic scene.[74] He urged an implementation of the Ten-Point Program set forth the previous year, and devoted considerable attention to the drive to capture the "remaining heights" of the Seven-Year Plan. There was no hint in Kim's speech that a major purge was in the offing. Yet scarcely three months later, at the very end of 1968, a new storm shook the topmost political and military circles. Three veteran military men, Kim Ch'ang-bong, Hŏ Pong-hak, and Ch'oe Kwang, were suddenly ousted, amid rumors of a fiery denunciation of these men by Kim Il-sŏng himself. All three were old comrades-in-arms of Kim and trusted members of the Kapsan group. Moreover, each of them had long held top posts in the military establishment. Kim Ch'ang-bong was currently serving as vice-premier and minister of Defense, and had earlier been head of the People's Militia. As noted previously, he had been elevated to full membership on the Party Political Committee as recently as 1966. Hŏ Pong-hak, another senior general, was reportedly in charge of operations in South Korea; he was a former head of the KPA Political Department. Ch'oe Kwang held the position of chief of the KPA General Staff. These men ranked respectively sixth, fourteenth, and sixteenth in the Party listings; the latter were both alternate members of the Political Committee. Thus, their purge, which struck the North Korean political and military elite like a thunderclap, sharply reduced the number of professional military men at the top of the Party structure, and reversed the trend that seemed so apparent in October 1966.

What were the causes of this major upheaval? In chapter XII, which is devoted specifically to the military, we shall examine in some detail what purport to be notes from the KPA Party Committee meeting of January 1969, at which Kim leveled his charges against the three.[75] Suffice it to say here that these charges ranged from a failure to carry out the type

74. For the full English language text, see "The Democratic People's Republic of Korea Is the Banner of Freedom and Independence for Our People and the Powerful Weapon of Building Socialism and Communism," a report of Kim Il-sŏng, *The P'yŏngyang Times,* Sept. 12, 1968, pp. 3–16.
75. See Chapter XII, pp. 969–973.

of military program that had been ordered, to emasculating the Party within the armed forces, to accusations that these men spent funds lavishly and engaged in cliquism, threatening Party unity. Behind the spoken charges, moreover, there was probably an unspoken one: the failure of the southern "liberation" campaign.

At a time when Mao Tse-tung, having smashed his own Party, was forced to turn to the People's Liberation Army to maintain order and administer much of the nation, Kim Il-sŏng was giving evidence of having his army as firmly under his personal control as the Party. Kim Ch'ang-bong was succeeded as minister of Defense by Ch'oe Hyŏn, reportedly a man more trusted by Kim Il-sŏng than any other individual (presumably with the exception of his brother, Kim Yŏng-ju). The new army chief of staff became General O Chin-u. In the months immediately after the purge, Ch'oe, O, and other military men repeatedly averred their absolute loyalty to the Leader and obedience to Party directives.[76] Kim Il-sŏng could face the Fifth Party Congress with even greater confidence in his total political control over Party and state than had been the case at the triumphal Fourth Party Congress of 1961—despite the fact that some of the optimism of yesteryear had been tarnished by the economic troubles of the mid-1960s.

Walking on Three Legs: The Economic Efforts of the 1960s

Before turning to the events of the Fifth Congress, it is necessary to examine not only the general trend of economic developments but events on the international scene. Once again, the reader should keep in mind the fact that later chapters are devoted exclusively to the economy of the DPRK. Accordingly, only an outline will be attempted here.

The targets set in the new Seven-Year Plan were extraordinarily ambitious. The Plan envisaged an annual increase in industrial production of 18 percent. By the end of the Plan, grain production was to reach 6 to 7 million metric tons. With this level attained, Kim asserted, the food problem would at last be solved. Major increases in subsidiary foods and in industrial crops were also planned, as well as in livestock production. Kim acknowledged the need for a rapid improvement in living standards, asserting that the Plan envisaged a 2.7-fold increase in national income, with factory and office workers' real incomes scheduled to rise 1.7-fold. Peasant income would also bound upward, so that the living standard of the average peasant would reach that of "well-to-do middle peasants" in the course of the Plan.

Kim and other leaders who spoke at the Fourth Congress laid heavy emphasis upon the technical and scientific revolution that loomed ahead. Kim himself called for the training of 460,000 technicians and secondary

76. See, for example, the Feb. 7, 1969, speech of O Chin-u, commemorating the twenty-first birthday of the KPA, and the *Nodong Sinmun* editorial of Feb. 8.

specialists in the course of the Seven-Year Plan, as well as of some 180,000 engineers and high-level specialists.

The 1961–62 period was to represent the high point of economic hope and expectation for some years. Approximately fifteen months later, at the end of 1962, a radical departure from earlier priorities was signaled with the announcement of a new strategy: the equal emphasis upon military preparedness and "socialist construction" that we have already discussed.

There was still great optimism in top Party circles concerning the economic picture. Speaking at the first session of the Third People's Assembly in the fall of 1962, Kim Il-sŏng described the period of the Five-Year Plan as the time when a big tree had put its roots deep into the soil to allow the trunk to grow strong. The era of the Seven-Year Plan, he continued, was the time during which the tree would have flowers and bear fruit. The new organizational methods being applied to both agriculture and industry at this point, as exemplified by the Ch'ŏngsan-ri Method and the Taean System, were being heralded as the Party's primary weapons in the struggle to attain such new goals as a grain production of 5 million metric tons and 800,000 metric tons of marine products.

Some sources went so far as to proclaim that prosperity for the average citizen was just around the corner. When the 1963 targets were reached, one Party organ announced, all the working people in North Korea would be able to "lead a rich life, living in tile-roofed houses, having rice and meat, and wearing fine clothes." In short, the "long-cherished desire of the working people" would be realized "in our generation." [77]

In its report on 1962 grain production, the Central Statistical Board claimed that the target of 5 million tons had been successfully reached. As we shall soon indicate, later evidence suggests that, in reality, grain production for that year was probably around 4 million tons. By 1963, the regime was forced to recognize that the new policy of undertaking a massive military buildup was causing economic dislocations. At the Seventh Plenum of the Fourth Central Committee, held in early September, it was announced that gross industrial output would probably grow by some 8 percent over the previous year—substantially behind the goals established earlier. In admitting that some slippage had occurred, Party spokesmen blamed the need to increase military expenditures. They were careful, moreover, to cite recent incidents involving "American brutality and aggressiveness" as ample justification for the new course despite the sacrifices it entailed.

For the next several years, it is possible only to estimate economic production, since after 1963 North Korean authorities stopped releasing Central Statistical Board figures. This alone was sufficient evidence of

77. *TPK*, Jan. 1, 1963, p. 1.

problems. However, by utilizing clues provided by the DPRK government itself, and also figures developed by South Korean specialists, we can advance some probable production figures for the 1964–66 period, both in industry and in agriculture. We shall have occasion later to discuss economic trends during this period in some detail.[78] Here, we need merely note the basic figures at which we have arrived: in 1963, total industrial production rose 8 percent over that of 1962; the figure for 1964 was up by a significant 17 percent; in 1965, it increased by 14 percent; but in 1966, it actually declined by 3 percent, compared to 1965. Meanwhile, actual grain production in 1961—as opposed to the official figures—was probably around 3,378,000 metric tons. No figures are available for 1962, but in 1963 it is estimated that total grain production reached 4,850,000 metric tons, declining in 1964 to 4,450,000 metric tons, and then rising slightly in 1965 to 4,526,000 metric tons. By 1966, it had reached close to 5 million metric tons—a level finally attained in 1967.

In sum, if these estimates are correct, industrial growth between 1961 and 1967 averaged 12 percent per annum. However, with growth in all other areas, including agriculture, increasing at an average rate of only 3.5 percent per annum, the average annual increase in gross national product for this period was probably in the neighborhood of 8.6 percent. Certainly, this was far from a disgraceful performance. But it also fell far short of stated goals. Despite gains, moreover, agricultural production presented a special problem, particularly in light of the inflated official statistics—and public claims—of earlier years. The spotty performance of the economy was all the more serious because of the voracious demands of the military establishment during this period.

It is against this background that the political events of 1966 take on additional meaning. One earlier clue to the increasing concern with which the regime viewed developments on the agrarian front lies in the fact that, in 1964, Kim Il-sŏng felt it necessary to engage in on-the-spot guidance and then issue his "Theses on the Socialist Agrarian Question in Our Country." These policies, which we shall examine later, were to form the major new guidelines for agriculture in what was clearly an effort to stimulate production.

The Party Conference of October 1966 was thus held in the midst of a serious economic crisis. The causes for this crisis will be explored in chapter XIV; they related to both immediate and longer-range factors. Among the former, the adverse impact of the heavy allocations of man-power and resources to military buildup and operations was obviously the cardinal element. But other factors were present, including the impact of very strained relations with the Soviet Union in the final months of the Khruschevian era. Kim Il, in his major economic report before the con-

78. See Chapters XIII and XIV

ference, admitted that the requirements for military preparations made it necessary to postpone completion of the Seven-Year Plan for three years.[79] He claimed that the annual rate of growth in industrial production for the previous five years had been 14.3 percent, but he said nothing about 1966 industrial production alone.

His comments on agricultural production were as follows: "Though in recent years, agricultural production has suffered to a certain degree from severe natural calamities such as drought, floods, storm, frost damage, and damage by blight and noxious insects which visited our country in succession, the grain yield in 1965 was 10 per cent larger than in 1960." This was scarcely the record the North Korean leaders had set for themselves, and it revealed the degree to which an agricultural bottleneck was developing—another factor that must surely have figured in the 1966 crisis.

Kim Il and others tried to make the best of a difficult situation. They claimed that national income had grown 1.6-fold in the 1960–65 period. They further argued that such policies as the abolition of the agricultural tax-in-kind, together with other social benefits, had produced substantial improvements in living standards. This is almost universally denied by people who lived in North Korea during this period. They testify that no improvements in living conditions occurred until after 1966, and that the period between 1961 and 1966 was one of great austerity and hardship. Once again, circumstantial evidence can be provided to back up their assertions. The types of challenges posed to Party policies in this period were indeed similar to the ones posed in 1956, when similar hardships were being endured in the cause of heavy industry. This time, however, the goal was rapid militarization.

Fortunately, for Kim and his supporters, economic conditions improved in the next several years. We are dependent largely upon official statistics but, as we shall suggest later, they appear to be relatively accurate for this period. According to the government, total industrial production in 1967 increased 17 percent over the previous year and, more importantly, total grain production increased 16 percent. Begining in early 1968, the tone of official economic reports was definitely more optimistic, as is well exemplified by Kim Il's report to the Plenum of the Central Committee on April 22, 1968.[80]

After outlining the progress made during the previous year, Kim Il set forth the tasks of the immediate future. First, precedence had to be given the power industry, particularly the electric industry, and the fuel extraction industry. The growing demand for raw materials and fuels, Kim

79. "On the Immediate Tasks of Socialist Economic Construction," a summary of the report delivered by Kim Il, Oct. 10, 1966, in Supplement (2) to The P'yŏngyang Times, Oct. 13, 1966, pp. 1–2.

80. Kim Il, "On the People's Economic Development Plan for 1968 . . . ," op. cit.

indicated, was the chief bottleneck to the further development of such industries as metallurgy, machine tools, and chemicals. Second, major increases were of critical importance in the iron and steel industry. Here, Kim set a target for 1968 of increasing granulated and pig iron output by 36 percent and steel and structural steel by 33 percent over the previous year. Another area requiring special attention, according to Kim Il, was that of precision machine production and the chemical industry. Finally, the primary needs in the field of agriculture were to increase chemicalization and mechanization.

In his report to those gathered to celebrate the twentieth anniversary of the founding of the DPRK, on September 7, 1968, Kim Il-sŏng maintained the generally optimistic tone set by Kim Il, albeit with some caveats.[81] He admitted that the Seven-Year Plan had been delayed because of the need to strengthen the north's military forces. Nevertheless, he proclaimed himself confident that they would equal or surpass the goals of the Seven-Year Plan that very year "in a number of industrial branches such as the production of coal, chemical fertilizer, major nonferrous metals and timber." [82] He further stated that local industry now accounted for one-half of the total output of consumer goods, and was playing a major role in the development of the national economy as a whole.

In referring to agricultural production, Kim produced a rather esoteric comparison. Although there had been an unprecedented flood last year, he said, the grain output was 2.7 times that immediately after Liberation, and the production of industrial crops, vegetables, fruit, and animal products also rose sharply. "We are not only self-sufficient in food grain, but have come to have a considerable reserve of it and have built the firm foundations for developing all branches of agriculture onto a higher level." [83]

In 1969, *Nodong Sinmun,* in a New Year's Day editorial, asserted that once again total industrial production had increased by approximately 17 percent. It did not specify agricultural gains.[84] However, in January 1970, one year later, North Korean authorities announced that gross industrial production had increased 15 percent over the preceding year, with total grain output up by 11 percent. They also stated that the "main heights of the Seven-Year Plan" had finally been scaled. Anticipating the final fulfillment of the Plan, they announced that the Fifth Party Congress would be held in October. Thus, after a decade of struggle, hardship, and uneven development, the people of North Korea were promised a new era by the

81. Kim Il-sŏng, "The Democratic People's Republic of Korea Is the Banner . . . ," *op. cit.*

82. *Ibid.,* p. 8.

83. As shown in Chapter IX, grain production in 1946, according to official reports, was 1,898,000 metric tons. This would bring the figure for 1967 to 5.1 million tons.

84. "Let Us Adorn the New Year, 1969, with a New, Greater Victory," *NS,* Jan. 1, 1969, p. 1.

Party. As a first installment, the government announced a 31.5 percent average wage increase for all industrial and office workers on the eve of the new Congress, testimony in itself to the nature of the sacrifices that the working class had endured on behalf of the militarization program.[85]

Applying Chuch'e to the International Front

Before looking at the economic goals set forth in late 1970, let us turn again to the international scene. As we have already suggested, developments abroad, both in the Communist camp and outside it, had had a major impact upon the domestic scene.

Just one month after the close of the Fourth KWP Congress, the Twenty-Second CPSU Congress opened in Moscow. Present at this historic meeting was a North Korean delegation headed by Kim Il-sŏng, and including Pak Kŭm-ch'ŏl and Hŏ Pong-hak. They were met at the airport by Kosygin and other Soviet dignitaries. Interestingly, for the first time, the North Korean mass media treated a CPSU Congress in a fairly subdued fashion. Most of the major Soviet addresses, including Khrushchev's, were presented in the form of summaries, and coverage of the Congress itself was comparatively brief. *Nodong Sinmun* did not even print Khrushchev's picture. Compared with the treatment accorded major events in the Soviet Union a few years earlier, this was indeed a striking and significant change.

Only Kim Il-sŏng's speech before the Congress got prominent attention. That speech, however, merely reechoed familiar themes: the Korean Workers' Party would give its complete support to the Soviet leaders in their efforts to preserve world peace, including the emphasis upon peaceful coexistence. In his remarks, Kim quite explicitly acknowledged the CPSU as "the vanguard of the international Communist movement." He did not, however, pay special homage to Khrushchev, and it is noteworthy that his delegation had earlier placed wreaths on the tombs of *both* Lenin and Stalin.

The dramatic highpoints of the Congress, as is well known, were Khrushchev's open criticism of Albania, which prompted the Chinese delegation to walk out, and his further bitter attack upon Stalin. An open break between the two Communist giants had finally occurred. The Sino-Soviet quarrel was now public property.

Unlike the Chinese, Kim and the rest of the North Korean delegation remained in Moscow throughout the Congress. But they too came home earlier than might have been expected, arriving back in P'yŏngyang on November 2, only two days after the Congress adjourned, without waiting to celebrate the forty-fourth anniversary of the Soviet Army. No mass welcome for the returning delegation was arranged at the P'yŏngyang air-

85. *NS,* Sept. 1, 1970, p. 1.

port, nor was any immediate public report issued to the Korean people.[86]

Only on November 27, in his report to a Central Committee Plenum, did Kim Il-sŏng set forth certain views on the burning international issues of the day. In this rather brief statement, Kim first pledged that the KWP would continue to strengthen its solidarity with the CPSU, "the vanguard of the international Communist movement," and then praised the Soviet Union for having "contributed much" to that movement. Regarding Stalin, Kim asserted that as an *international* Communist (italics ours) he had played a role of some importance, but that the personality cult issue, as well as that of anti-Party factionalism within the CPSU, were internal problems, not suitable for discussion by outside Parties. They had always held, said Kim, that no Communist Party had the right to interfere in the internal life of a fraternal Party. This was a principle that all fraternal Parties had to observe if mutual relations were to be properly preserved. Hence, the issue of Stalin and the anti-Party group within the CPSU could not become objects of discussion within the KWP.[87]

Once again, it must have given Kim enormous pleasure, despite his anxieties, to use this veiled allusion to the 1956 incident in order to escape from the dilemma of how to handle the thorny issue of de-Stalinization and the Khrushchevian attack upon Molotov and the rest. Albania, however, was another matter, not to be avoided so easily. Clearly, this was *not* merely an internal matter. Kim handled the subject cautiously. Admitting that relations between the CPSU and the Albanian Workers' Party were "abnormal" and not improving, Kim asserted that if that situation continued it would prove a serious detriment to the entire Communist world. He expressed the "urgent hope" that the issue would be solved—but offered no solution. Kim rested his case by adopting a neutral stance. All fraternal Parties were equal and independent, he emphasized, and all started from Marxist-Leninist theory, together with those concrete experiences and realities within their own societies that required adaptation of that theory. Further, all fraternal Parties should abide by the principle of mutual assistance, and absorb the experiences of other Parties in accordance with their own actualities and needs. Finally, fraternal Parties should always consult each other "on common problems." Equality, noninterference, and mutual consultation—this was the appropriate formula, Kim implied, whereby to solve the Soviet-Albanian quarrel.

86. At the conclusion of the Congress, a *Nodong Sinmun* editorial paid extravagant praise to the Soviet Union in traditional manner. It hailed the Soviet people as standing at the head of the struggle for world peace, and called "the mighty power of the Soviet Union" a decisive factor in preventing war and maintaining the peace. The editorial concluded with the theme that the Korean Workers' Party would continue to struggle for unity within the socialist camp—without specific reference to the events that had just occurred. *NS,* Nov. 2, 1961, p. 1.

87. For Kim's November 27th report, see *NS,* Nov. 28, 1961, p. 1.

Earlier, on November 7, the Korean leaders had made it clear that they did not intend to follow the CPSU in boycotting the Albanians. On that date, Party leaders sent a message of "earnest congratulations" to the Albanian Workers' Party and the Albanian people on the occasion of the twentieth anniversary of the founding of the Party. While slightly less courteous and reverent language was used than in messages sent to the Soviet Union on such occasions, the dispatch struck an entirely favorable and friendly note, and certainly must have served as a signal to the Russians of the North Korean position on this matter, if one were needed at this point.[88]

On the previous day, November 6, the KWP, in the name of Kim Il-sŏng and Ch'oe Yong-gŏn, had sent a message to Khrushchev and Brezhnev on the occasion of the forty-fourth anniversary of the Russian Revolution. This message, too, was entirely favorable, even eulogistic at points.

> Today, as a country with the highest development in science, technology and culture, the Soviet Union is marching vigorously forward on the path toward the building of communism. The building of communism in the Soviet Union constitutes the most powerful and important cause of the following effects: the strengthened power of the socialist camp; control over imperialist aggression and war policies; and a solid world peace. The new principles of the CPSU adopted only a short while ago at the Twenty-Second Party Congress of the CPSU constitute an admirable Marxist-Leninist document that not only shows clearly the great plans for the building of communism in the Soviet Union and the concrete means for so doing, but also indicates to all humanity the bright future for communism.
>
> The Soviet people are solidly behind the Central Committee of the

88. So revealing is this message of the tightrope the North Koreans were seeking to walk that it deserves to be quoted at some length. "The Albanian Workers' Party, founded in the struggle against Fascist aggressors, has fought heroically for its country's freedom and independence, and is confidently leading the Albanian people to the creation of a new life—after the liberation, the Albanian people have, under the leadership of the Albanian Workers' Party, won victories in socialist reconstruction and have changed a backward agricultural state into a socialist agrarian-industrial state. The Albanian Workers' Party is defending the achievements of the Revolution and is fighting for the victory of socialism, peace in Europe, and peace in the world. The Korean people rejoice in the achievements of the Albanian people in their socialist construction as if they were their own achievements.

"The unity and solidarity of the socialist camp today constitutes a dependable guarantee for victory for all socialist states in their common struggle for peace and socialism. We firmly believe that the friendship and solidarity between the peoples of Albania and Korea will continue to develop and become stronger in the future under the principles of Marxism-Leninism and proletarian internationalism—within the great family of the socialist camp headed by the USSR. The CC of the Korean Workers' Party send you wishes for your Party's success in its work for the country's socialist construction and for world peace. With fraternal greetings." NS, Nov. 8, 1961, p. 1.

CPSU headed by Comrade Khrushchev and have risen united to attain the goals pointed out by the Twenty-Second Party Congress.

The unceasing growth of the might of the USSR gives unlimited encouragement to the Korean people who are engaged in the struggle to build socialism and peacefully unify their fatherland. The brotherly Soviet people have in the past and are now helping the Korean people in their struggle for freedom, unification, and independence, and a new life. No might can destroy the friendship and solidarity [between our two peoples] which have been forged throughout history and in the struggle for socialism and communism; the Korean people treasure and cherish the undefeatable alliance with the Soviet people who are their true liberators and helpers. The Korean people will continue in the future to hold the banner of invincible, certain-to-win Marxism-Leninism and proletarian internationalism, will defend as their own eyeballs [sic] the unity and solidarity of the socialist camp, and will do everything in their power to further strengthen the powers of that camp.

Dear Comrades! We send you our sincere wishes for your new successes in your noble efforts dedicated to the building of communism, strengthening the unity of the socialist camp, and maintaining as well as strengthening world peace.[89]

The position of the KWP was made further manifest on November 28, when the two top KWP leaders sent Enver Hoxha, Haxhi Lleshi, and Mehmet Shehu a congratulatory message on the occasion of the seventeenth anniversary of the liberation of Albania. The message included the statement, "The Albanian people, the country's master for seventeen years since the liberation, have *under the correct leadership of the Albanian Workers' Party* [italics ours] overcome difficulties bravely. . . ." [90] Certainly Khrushchev and the other Soviet leaders could not have been pleased when this message was called to their attention, even though the note once again referred to "the great family of the socialist camp headed by the USSR."

By studying these and other North Korean communiqués during this period, we can discern the basic position of Kim Il-sŏng and his followers as the era after the Fourth Party Congress commenced. That position can be summarized under three heads. First, the fact that the CPSU holds the vanguard position in the international Communist movement is a historical fact and cannot be denied (or canceled by a somewhat wayward figure like Nikita Khrushchev). The Soviet people created the first Communist state under Lenin's aegis, giving an impetus to revolutionary people everywhere, and Soviet power constitutes the umbrella protecting the entire socialist cause. It is imperative that this power be maintained and used.

Second, Stalin must be treated in two ways. He is an international figure, and each Party has a right to pass judgment upon him. We in North

89. *NS*, Nov. 7, 1961, p. 1.
90. *NS*, Nov. 29, 1961, p. 1.

Korea regard Stalin as an individual whose influence was great upon the international Communist movement (and generally beneficial). But as the leader of a fraternal Party, Stalin must be judged by that Party, because that is an internal matter, and neither the KWP nor any other external force has a right to pass judgment on it.

Third, the rancorous quarrel between the CPSU and the Albanian Workers' Party is deeply to be regretted, and must be healed if the socialist camp is not to suffer serious damage. Meanwhile, the KWP refuses to "take sides," and will not abandon its fraternal relations with either Party, treating both as equals, and urging that the principles commonly agreed upon in the Moscow Statement of 1960 be applied.

There is very good reason to believe that these principles were not created in isolation. North Korean leaders had had substantive conversations during this period with Vietnamese, Indonesian, Japanese, and Chinese comrades, among others. Slowly, a type of alliance centering upon the small Communists of Asia—with some liaison with Peking—was emerging. Common tactics and strategies were being devised. The basic purposes behind this alliance were first, to create pressure on the rest of the Communist world, particularly Moscow, to reach some suitable compromise on current differences, a compromise that would in no way weaken the stand against "world imperialism" and especially the United States; and second, to insist collectively upon the independence of small Communist states and Parties in a period when Communist international relations were increasingly beginning to resemble those of European countries with each other in the late nineteenth century.

Throughout much of 1962, an uneasy truce was in effect between the Soviet Union and China. For instance, at the Eighth Gensuikyo (Japanese Council Against Atomic and Hydrogen Bombs) Conference at Hiroshima in August, the Russians and Chinese managed to stand together despite important shadings of difference in their positions. Consequently, the North Korean leaders remained relatively quiet, refraining from public comment on most developments and hewing to previously established policy lines. Suddenly, in the fall of the year, a series of events occurred in rapid succession that shook the entire Communist community: attempts at Soviet-Yugoslav rapprochement, an upsurge of the troubles over the Indian border, and, above all, the Cuban crisis. All the Asian Communist Parties, including the Korean Workers' Party, were put under enormous strain.

Kim Il-sŏng and his followers were almost certainly opposed to every major action taken by Khrushchev in the international arena during this period. They wanted a hard line against Yugoslavia, not rapprochement. Soviet assistance to India in any form at this point they regarded as a scandalous affront to Peking. And above all, they wanted a firm stand against the United States on an issue like Cuba, whatever the risks. However, only the most veiled comments on these matters issued from P'yŏngyang at this time. Then, in the fall of 1962, came the congresses of certain East European Parties, at which more or less open attacks were launched by the pro-Moscow forces not only upon China and Albania, but also upon North Korea. Finally, in a major editorial of January 30, 1963, *Nodong Sinmun* struck back in unmistakable tones.[91]

The editorial began with a customary theme: the unity of the socialist camp was crucial to any victory for socialism or peace. It was especially vital to Korean Communists because they were "defending the eastern outpost of socialism, fighting against all kinds of aggressive machinations on the part of the enemy, standing face to face with the US imperialist aggressors, the chieftain of world reaction."

The editorial went on to assert that the "abnormal relations" between various fraternal Parties were a matter of great regret. Equally tragic were the attempts to attack and isolate the Chinese Communist Party; indeed, they were clearly in violation of the 1960 Moscow Statement. In the final analysis, continued the editorial, such actions were tantamount to joining in the anti-China chorus of the enemy. "It is clear to everyone that today one cannot talk about the unity of the socialist camp or about the increase of its might apart from the existence of the powerful Chinese People's Republic and solidarity with it, whose population accounts for two-thirds of that of the socialist camp, no more than apart from the great Soviet Union, the first socialist state in the world." It was for this reason, reported the editorial, that the KWP opposed the unilateral attacks upon the CCP, and had felt forced to express itself on this matter at the Czech and East German Party Congresses, when such attacks were again launched. Certain people had then asked, "On whose side are you standing?" Such people were themselves dividing the Communist movement, the editorial suggested. "Our Party is standing on this very Marxist-Leninist position [of defending the common interests of the Communist world] and on the side of the interests of revolution and solidarity." If things continued in the recent pattern, first one Party and then another would be isolated and ostracized.

Then, in a reproachful tone, the editorial recalled that, at the East German Congress, the Korean delegate had not even been allowed to deliver his speech of congratulations, although a delegate of "the revisionist Tito group" had been given the floor. There followed a bitter attack upon Tito. No Party, the editorial continued, had the right to contravene unilaterally either the Moscow Declaration or the Moscow Statement. It then quoted from the latter: the socialist countries were to "base their relations on principles of complete equality, respect for territorial integrity, national independence and sovereignty and noninterference in one another's affairs." Thus open polemics should cease. But some comrades, while talking in

91. For an English translation, see "Let Us Safeguard the Unity of the Socialist Camp and Strengthen the Solidarity of the International Communist Movement," *TPK*, Feb. 6, 1963, pp. 1–2.

support of such action, continued to criticize others openly, and unilaterally attack the stand of fraternal Parties. "This can in no way be regarded as a sincere attitude."

The editorial ended on a conciliatory note: "It is ridiculous indeed for the enemy hopefully to watch for any rift in relations between our Workers' Party of Korea and the fraternal Soviet and Chinese Communist Parties. However serious the differences of views among fraternal Parties may be, the socialist camp and the international Communist movement will always march in close unity when it comes to the struggle against imperialism. . . . We Korean Communists deem it our lofty internationalist duty to unite with the great Communist Party of the Soviet Union, unite with the Chinese Communist Party, unite with other Communist and Workers' Parties, and struggle to consolidate the unity of the socialist camp and the international Communist movement." [92]

Thus, the end of 1962 marked the beginnings of a major shift in North Korea's position within the Communist world and her policies toward it. Neutralism had seemingly failed. Now came alignment. In another major article published in March, only one month after the editorial quoted at length above, *Nodong Sinmun* launched a frontal assault on revisionism. The center of the attack dealt with Tito's efforts to achieve peaceful coexistence with the United States, but the real target was clearly Khrushchev. In early June, moreover, a delegation consisting of Yi Hyo-sun, Pak Sŏng-ch'ŏl, and Kang Hi-won, with Ch'oe Yong-gŏn at their head, went to Peking. They were greeted at the railway station by Liu Shao-ch'i, Chou En-lai, Chu Teh, and Tung Pi-wu, among others, and some 300,000 Peking citizens lined the streets to cheer them.

In his speech at the banquet of June 6 in honor of his delegation, Ch'oe stated: "Today, the Parties and peoples of our two countries, holding high the banner of Marxism-Leninism, are closely united in waging a resolute struggle against imperialism and revisionism, making contributions to the cause of world peace and world revolution. Through this common struggle, the friendship and unity of our two peoples have been further strengthened and developed. . . ." [93]

In the joint communiqué issued on the final day of the Korean delegates' visit to Peking, the full range of differences separating the Chinese

92. *Ibid.*, p. 2. Yi Hyo-sun's speech to the GDR Congress, which he was not allowed to deliver, was published in various North Korean sources. For an English version, see *TPK*, Jan. 30, 1963, pp. 1–2.

93. *TPK*, June 12, 1963, p. 1. Ch'oe continued, "The friendship and unity of our two Parties and peoples, which were sealed with blood in our protracted struggles against our common enemies and firmly pledged under the banner of revolution and Marxism-Leninism, are indestructible by any force. No matter what storms may rise, our people will forever fight together with the Chinese people and forever remain their loyal comrades-in-arms."

and North Koreans from the Russians was skillfully set forth in a final section:

1. The Korean and Chinese Parties and the two countries have always adhered to Marxism-Leninism and the revolutionary principles of the 1957 Declaration and the 1960 Statement. Revisionism is the main danger in the current international Communist movement. The modern revisionists emasculate the revolutionary essence of Marxism-Leninism, paralyze the revolutionary will of the working class and working people, meet the needs of imperialism and the reactionaries of various countries, and undermine the unity of the socialist camp and the revolutionary struggles of all peoples. They do not themselves oppose imperialism, and forbid others to make revolution. . . .

2. Both sides were of the agreed view that the Tito clique of Yugoslavia is typical of modern revisionism. It has openly betrayed the socialist camp and, serving as a special detachment of US imperialism, is engaged in sabotage against the socialist camp, the national revolutionary movement, and the people of the world.

3. While combating modern revisionism, it is also necessary to combat dogmatism. Dogmatists run diametrically counter to the principle of integrating the universal truth of Marxism-Lenism with the concrete practice of revolution at home and internationally. . . .

4. Both sides emphasized that it is in the fundamental interests of the people of the world to strengthen the unity of the socialist camp and the international Communist movement on the basis of Marxism-Leninism and proletarian internationalism and of the 1957 Declaration and the 1960 Statement. . . . Socialist countries must base their mutual relations on the principles of complete equality, respect for each other's territorial integrity, independence, and sovereignty, and on noninterference in each other's internal affairs. It is absolutely impermissible to go against the principle of consultation on an equal footing and force the will of one party or one country on another. . . .

5. Both sides held that the differences now existing in the socialist camp and the international Communist movement must be settled through inter-Party consultations on an equal footing. In order to eliminate the differences and strengthen unity, it is necessary to hold a meeting of representatives of the Communist and Workers' Parties of the world. Both sides expressed the sincere hope that the talks between the Chinese and Soviet Parties would yield positive results and prepare the necessary conditions for the convocation of the international meeting of fraternal Parties.[94]

Understandably, the theme now dominating all aspects of North Korean life was chuch'e, or self-reliance. As we have seen, it paralleled expressions then being spread throughout China. Meanwhile, at such meet-

94. "Joint Statement of President Ch'oe Yong-gŏn and Chairman Liu Shao-ch'i," *TPK,* July 3, 1963, pp. 2–3.

ings as the World Congress of Women, North Korean representatives took an exceedingly hard line. For instance, Kim Ok-sun remarked, "The noisy talk of the US imperialists about 'peace' is nothing but a ruse for blunting the vigilance of the international proletariat and progressive women and diverting them from the anti-imperialist, national liberation struggle." Also during this period, there was a revival of atrocity tales concerning American actions during and after the Korean War, the whole gamut being run from bacteriological warfare to the wanton murder of women and children by American soldiers stationed in South Korea.

By the fall of 1963, North Korean attacks upon Soviet policies had dropped their heavy camouflage. In a remarkable article "Let Us Defend the Socialist Camp," published by *Nodong Sinmun* on October 28, the KWP pointed its arrows directly at the CPSU, omitting only the actual title of the Party. Instead, it borrowed the Chinese technique of referring to the object of its attack as "some people" or "some Parties." We shall now paraphrase this extraordinary article and also quote from it at length, because it tells us so much not merely about current Soviet–North Korean relations, but about the past as well. The North Koreans were never to publish a more revealing document.

The article began with a stark charge: "Some people are deviating farther from the principles of Marxism-Leninism and proletarian internationalism and being bogged deep in the mire of revisionism. Modern revisionism has created a great obstacle to the people's cause of revolution and peace."

A bill of particulars was then presented: "Today, certain people are actively vindicating the Titoites and increasing confusion in the socialist camp, thereby going ahead on the dangerous road of splitting it. This means that they are aligning themselves with the imperialists and Titoites in their machinations to wreck the socialist camp."

While it was the touchstone of proletarian internationalism in the past, the article continued, to support and defend the Soviet Union as the one and only socialist state in the world, now the situation was altogether different. New shock brigades had emerged in the form of people's democracies, from China and Korea to Czechoslovakia and Hungary. Hence, it had become "easier for our Party to fight," and its work, too, had become "more delightful." The base of world revolution was "not a certain country but the entire socialist camp." Therefore, it was a genuine internationalist act to support and defend *both* the Soviet Union and all other socialist states, that is, the socialist camp as a whole.

According to the article, a big country that had achieved revolution ahead of others could make a greater contribution by strengthening the might of the socialist camp and supporting the liberation struggles of all oppressed peoples. It could also play a bigger role in defending world peace. But this did not mean that any one country could represent or act on behalf of the entire socialist camp. The might of one country, no matter how big and advanced, could not take the place of the might of the entire socialist camp, and one country could not play the role of the entire socialist camp.

> If leaders of this or that Party only boast that their country is large, is a great power with huge economic might, and underrate fraternal Parties and states, it will weaken the might and undermine the unity of the whole socialist camp and do great harm to the international Communist movement. Recently, some people have been behaving as if they would not mind cutting some countries loose from the socialist camp. This is a concrete expression of the error that a certain country can do anything it likes from its privileged position and that other countries do not play any important role.

The article then confronted the Chinese question. Of late, a worldwide crusade had been launched against the Chinese People's Republic. The imperialists and international reactionary forces, deeply resenting the victory of the Chinese revolution, were dead set on impairing the prestige of China and isolating her.

> Certain people who call themselves Communists have joined hands with the imperialists in hurling groundless slanders and diatribes at the Chinese Communist Party and the Chinese People's Republic and fiercely attacking them. This is a shameful and extremely dangerous act. To isolate China means, in fact, to split the socialist camp. To be frank, how can one talk about the socialist camp if China, which comprises two-thirds of the population of the socialist camp, is excluded? . . . The socialist camp cannot be made a plaything of any individual. The socialist camp can fulfill its historic mission only when it is firmly united in a monolithic contingent to oppose imperialism and revisionism resolutely, and forges ahead holding aloft the banner of revolution.

At this point the article reviewed the Moscow Declaration and Statement, and concluded that, in recent years, the standards set forth in those documents had been "grossly contravened." Democratic centralism, it asserted, could not be allowed to govern relations among fraternal Parties, or the arrogance of great-power chauvinism and bureaucratic despotism would prevail, and mutual distrust be created. In short, exclusive leadership from one "center" has become both impossible and unnecessary. Fraternal Parties of all countries had to achieve unanimity through collective consultations on questions of common concern, thus working out a unified strategy and tactics for the international Communist movement. Having done so, they should unanimously hold to their joint assessment and conclusions. If differences of views arose between fraternal Parties, they should be solved through "comradely consultations on the basis of facts and principles." There followed the most stinging—and revealing—denunciation of Soviet practices that had yet emanated from P'yŏngyang. It is worth quoting at length.

But today, some people have discarded at will the principles agreed on by the fraternal Parties. Instead, they are using various coercive methods in an effort to dispose of differences and the problems they cause. Thus they arbitrarily apply the labels of "dogmatism," "sectarianism," "nationalism," "adventurism," and "warlike elements" to those fraternal Parties that do not obey their will. . . . They have unilaterally repealed their agreements with fraternal countries and have virtually cut off relations of economic and technical cooperation. They frequently expel ambassadors and other diplomats, as well as correspondents. They do not hesitate to sever even state relations with fraternal countries. . . .

Some people allege that the Parties in Asia are not capable of acting independently because of their "lack of experience." And still others look down on the class brothers of other countries, boasting of the "superiority" and distinguished role of a certain nation or a certain race.

All such statements evince an arrogant attitude, insulting the fraternal Parties and undermining class solidarity by their chauvinism. . . . The idea of "backward Asia" or "superior nation" and "inferior nation" are old survivals that were repudiated and buried long ago. . . .

The practice of one side interfering in the other's internal affairs and demanding unilateral respect on the latter's part is the main obstacle preventing normal relations among fraternal Parties and countries.

Some meddle in the domestic affairs of fraternal Parties and enforce their unilateral will under the name of aid. It is the acknowledged internationalist duty of the Communist and Workers' Parties and socialist countries to support and cooperate with each other in the struggle for their common cause. And such mutual assistance and cooperation is needed by all the fraternal Parties and countries alike, not by any one of them alone. Accordingly, giving aid is neither doing a favor nor adding one more item to the credit account, as merchants do. . . .

"Aid" with strings attached or "aid" given as a precondition for interference in others' internal affairs, as practiced among capitalist countries, cannot exist and must not exist among socialist countries. The aid of socialist countries should serve to promote the consolidation of sovereignty and independence of each recipient and the strengthening and development of the socialist camp. . . .

It is still more impermissible to try to force the "antipersonality cult" campaign on other parties, and behind this smoke screen interfere in the internal affairs of brother Parties and countries and even scheme to overthrow their Party leadership. Is it not true that precisely because of the "antipersonality cult" clamors, many fraternal Parties suffered from unnecessary "fever" and the international Communist movement sustained serious losses?

In the past period, some comrades also failed to express due understanding or support for our Party's policy for socialist construction.

Without any clear notion of our actual conditions, they took issue with us, saying: "The Five-Year Plan is an illusion"; "You needn't build a machine-tool industry"; "How can you cooperativize the rural economy without farm machines?"—and so on. . . . Of course, we did not suffer big losses on account of these counsels, because we acted independently, as we had already decided to do. . . .

However, some people who are accustomed to dipping their fingers in others' internal affairs are not interested in the actual achievements of the fraternal Parties in the revolutionary struggle and construction, nor do they rejoice in them. Instead, they always harbor doubts about fraternal Parties, and are interested only in keeping a close watch as to whether the fraternal Parties act as they are "instructed" and whether they follow the foreign practices being pressed upon them dogmatically, without any changes whatsoever.

Thus, they unilaterally insist that fraternal countries are obliged to report the decisions and documents of a certain Party in their press and radio, and even try to supervise how the fraternal countries shall study the history of a certain Party, and how they shall learn the language of a certain country, and go so far as to demand to know whether they like or dislike the films of a certain country, and interfere in this matter. The spirit of equality and mutual respect can no longer be seen here. These are nothing but expressions of great-power chauvinism.

The historic experiences accumulated in the past by the Soviet people in their socialist revolution and socialist construction under the leadership of the Communist Party of the Soviet Union, which was headed by Lenin and afterwards by his successor Stalin, constitute precious assets of universal significance.

To negate this historical experience and describe the past period of the Soviet people as a "dark period" is to depart from the road of universal truth of Marxism-Leninism and the road of the October Revolution. The so-called Yugoslav road proposed by the Tito clique is a case in point.

Communists must believe in their own strength before anything else. To mobilize under the guidance of the Party the inexhaustible strength of the people and their own countries' inner resources to the maximum—this is the basic requirement for successful socialist construction. . . . Only when economic independence is secured can one consolidate the political independence of one's country and build up a modern, developed state. . . .

Yet certain persons doggedly oppose and obstruct the line of self-reliance and of building an independent economy in the socialist countries. They brand the construction of an independent national economy as a "nationalistic tendency" or "closed economy," and accuse it of being a "politically dangerous and economically harmful" line. Distorting the facts, they paint a false picture, making out that independent economic development runs counter to cooperation and assistance among the socialist countries. . . .

The socialist camp is the champion of world peace and security for all nations. The socialist countries do not want war. But as long as imperialism exists, the danger of war cannot be removed. . . . Therefore, the slightest weakening of the armed forces of the socialist camp under whatever pretext is absolutely impermissible.

However, certain persons propagandize as though a certain individual country's armed forces alone were safeguarding the entire socialist camp, as though the latest military technique of a certain individual country alone were maintaining the security of the socialist camp and world peace. They make light of the role of the other fraternal countries in the defense of the socialist camp, and neglect the cooperation necessary to the strengthening of the defenses of these countries. . . . This does not mean that the defense of the socialist camp can be left entirely with the military power of any one country . . . it should not rest solely on a certain weapon of the latest type, but should rest first and foremost on the strength of the people. . . .

All this shows that the class struggle should not be weakened in the socialist countries. The Parties in the socialist countries should strengthen the dictatorship of the proletariat, a powerful weapon in the hands of the working class, and further upgrade its role.

At present, some people, while speaking about "freedom," "democracy," "law-abiding spirit," and "humanism," try to create ideological chaos, paralyzing the class consciousness of the working people. What they really want is to give up the class struggle.

They allege that the dictatorship of the proletariat has completed its mission. "Hostile classes have been liquidated," they say, and "There are no more political criminals." They even claim that "objects of repression no longer exist." This is an attitude that runs a serious risk of weakening the socialist position.

As our experience shows, if education is not given in a correct way to the people of socialist countries, and if the dictatorship of the proletariat is weakened, bourgeois ideologies will stage a comeback. The people will come to seek degenerate pleasures, and relax their vigilance. . . .

The Party in each socialist country must make continued and unremitting efforts to increase the class consciousness of the masses and imbue them with a sense of responsibility for the historic mission of the proletariat and the will to carry through the revolution.

The national and international tasks of the revolution are inseparably linked with each other. . . . But some people now want to limit the superiority of the socialist system to economic competition. All will go well, they say, if people in socialist countries lead a life of plenty and are able to indulge their every whim . . . they are trying to subordinate the revolutionary struggle of the oppressed peoples to economic competition. . . . They say that if the socialist countries win an economic competition, the world's peoples will automatically be liberated, and so there is no need to launch a revolutionary struggle or make sacrifices for it.

As a matter of fact, such allegations are nothing but attempts to persuade people that they should go on accepting the despotic rule of imperialism and colonialism. They are intended to block support and assistance to the people's revolutionary struggle and to the development of the world revolutionary movement. . . .

It is the international duty of the socialist countries and Communists to support and assist the world revolution.

To refuse to support the revolutionary struggles of the working class and the national liberation struggles of the peoples of Asia, Africa, and Latin America in order to be on good terms with the imperialists and not to offend them, to oppose the armed struggle of these peoples on the grounds that it is fraught with the danger of war—all this is a betrayal of their revolutionary cause and a capitulation to the imperialists.

Today, we have to ask ourselves whether we should adhere to Marxism-Leninism or not, whether we should fight against imperialism or not, whether we should carry the revolution forward to the end or not. . . .

Under the pretext that the "situation has changed," the modern revisionists emasculate the revolutionary essence of Marxism-Leninism and are openly violating the revolutionary principles of the Declaration and Statement of the Meetings of Representatives of the Communist and Workers' Parties. . . . There cannot be any compromise between Marxism-Leninism and revisionism; the revolutionary line is incompatible with the opportunist line. . . . We must exert pressure on the revisionists, isolate them, and prevent revisionism from being infiltrated into the masses.

The differences that have emerged in the international Communist movement today are in the final analysis both ideological and political. As such, they concern the basic stand of all Parties and all Communists. Such a question cannot be solved by coercion or by glossing over the state of affairs. It can be settled only through criticism and self-criticism, through a serious ideological struggle by all Communists.

The article concluded with the ringing words, "The defeat of revisionism and the victory of Marxism-Leninism are inevitable." [95]

Through this extraordinary document, so closely paralleling every basic position of Peking, Kim Il-sŏng had crossed the Rubicon in his relations with Khrushchev. He had now laid bare every critical issue, past and present, between the USSR and North Korea. Moreover, he had strongly hinted at a degree of past subservience that not even his regime's

95. All of the above quotations are taken from "Let Us Defend the Socialist Camp," *TPK*, Oct. 28, 1963, pp. 1–2.

A second article, "Hold High the Revolutionary Banner of National Liberation," published in *NS*, repeated many of the same basic themes. Its central line, however, was that "the modern revisionists" were not supporting the fighting peoples of Africa, Asia, and Latin America; rather, they were undermining their unity and will to struggle. The article also took a strongly militant stand on how freedom and independence were to be won, quoting Stalin to the effect that "the liberation of colonial and dependent countries from imperialism cannot be achieved without a revolution; no one will be given his independence gratis." *NS*, Jan. 27, 1964, p. 1.

"The revisionists," continued the author, "claim that, today, the very nature of war has changed totally with the advent of nuclear weapons. They declare that there is no longer any distinction between just and unjust wars in the age of nuclear weapons. . . .

"This is a crude falsification of Marxism-Leninism. . . . This assertion is tantamount to urging the fighting people to give up revolution and endure oppression and exploitation by the imperialists . . . This is nothing but a trick of theirs to blackmail and threaten the oppressed people . . ." *Ibid.*, p. 2.

staunchest critics had imagined. To analyze this article closely is to understand much concerning the character of this entire dispute within the Communist world, including the reasons for the intense bitterness that accompanied it.

Relations with the Soviet Union continued to deteriorate throughout 1964. The KWP strongly supported the Japanese Communist Party in its serious quarrel with the Russians, and opposed any international meeting that might produce a split (the CPSU was, of course, urging such a meeting). "Some people" were duly denounced for supporting the revisionist line "completely." Occasionally, all pretenses were dropped. For example, *Pravda* was attacked by name for depreciating the results of the second Asian Economic Seminar held in P'yŏngyang in mid-1964. Ties with China, on the other hand, became ever closer. Increasingly, the official pronouncements of the two countries on international issues contained similar phrasing as well as near-identical basic themes.

At this point, however, the North Koreans were reaching out beyond China. Contacts with the small Asian Communist states and Parties (with the pointed exception of the Mongolian People's Republic) continued to grow. Relations with the Parties of Japan, North Vietnam, and Indonesia were especially intimate, with many visitations, exchanges of messages, and discussions of common problems. A working alliance had been forged. It also became clear that, for the North Korean leaders, Cuba had a special symbolic meaning.

Here was a *small* state (smallness had now become a virtue in itself) confronting successfully the American Goliath and surviving in spite of Soviet policies (or so P'yŏngyang viewed it). Thus, Cuban visitors were among the most feted guests in North Korea during this era, and various Koreans also traveled the long distance to Havana. It was during this period too that the Romanians took the opportunity to visit P'yŏngyang, suggesting the possibility of a breach in Russia's East European armor.

In addition to these contacts with certain "special" Parties and states, the North Koreans, with their Chinese comrades, now undertook a far more active diplomacy aimed at the creation of an anti-Western, anti-Soviet "Third World" force. The imagery of the world's "peasants" and "progressive bourgeoisie"—particularly those from the nonwhite world—joining together under "proletarian" banners captivated P'yŏngyang's leaders. With Mali, Tanzania, Iraq, the UAR, Cuba, and Indonesia as allies, who need either love or fear the Soviet Union, the United States, or, for that matter, the United Nations? Thus, the North Koreans opened their doors to divers Africans, Latin Americans, and Asians. During 1964, for example, Modibo Keita, president of Mali, paid a state visit, closely followed by President Sukarno. Prince Sihanouk, too, was ardently wooed. Parliamentary delegations arrived from such unlikely areas as the Congo (Brazzaville), and diplomatic relations were established with Mauritania, a state the location of which was probably a mystery even to most of the North Korean elite. In November and December 1964, Ch'oe Yong-gŏn actually led a North Korean delegation on a goodwill tour of the UAR, Algeria, Guinea, and (on the way home) Cambodia. These were only a few of the wide range of contacts being established.

In October 1964, it will be recalled, Khrushchev was deposed as Soviet premier and first secretary of the CPSU and replaced by Kosygin in the former post and Brezhnev in the latter. A few months later, in February 1965, Kosygin made a visit to P'yŏngyang, signaling that, with Khrushchev gone, relations between Moscow and P'yŏngyang might improve. From both sides, there were ample reasons to explore a more friendly relationship. The North Korean need for Soviet technical and economic assistance, both in the military and in the industrial fields, was extensive. Indeed, the inability to get spare parts and replacements during this period, even for North Korea's small navy, had some dramatic consequences, and revealed to the leaders in P'yŏngyang the risks as well as the sacrifices involved in total chuch'e. Thus the reestablishment of "normal" relations with the Soviet Union came close to being a military necessity, especially if the "liberation" of the south were to be envisaged as a realistic possibility.

From the Soviet standpoint, of course, the need to win friends and neutralize enemies, especially in Asia, was all the greater because relations with China were not likely to undergo any rapid improvement. Unquestionably, the new Soviet leaders viewed Khrushchev's foreign policies in Asia and elsewhere as unnecessarily impetuous and crude. On the most fundamental issues, however, they were not prepared to make the type of changes demanded by Peking—and P'yŏngyang. Therein lay the heart of the dilemma. How far could civility, with a little reciprocity based upon immediate interests and needs, go in improving relations between Parties and states that, on the truly crucial, long-range issues, continued to have very different basic positions?

In the case of the USSR and North Korea, the diplomatic testing that got under way in early 1965 offered enough promise to be continued for the rest of the year. Kosygin's public remarks while he was in P'yŏngyang were entirely conciliatory, with a strong emphasis upon the great need for unity within the socialist camp. Subsequent events, however, were to reveal that the road to that "complete socialist solidarity" of which all Parties talked was destined to be tortuous and unending. Whatever the nature of private discussions at this point and later between Russians and North Koreans, there was to be no return to the old relationship that the Koreans had recently condemned so strongly as of a colonial type. Yet the new relationship, based as it was upon the "complete independence" of both parties, upon the more dubious premise of their "equality," upon certain mutual interests, but even more prominently upon an agreement to disagree on a wide range of fundamental questions, seemed precariously fragile.

International developments, however, were now occurring that made it even more imperative to normalize relations with the Soviet Union. On the whole, trends in Asia and in the world during the 1965–66 period were not in accordance with P'yŏngyang's expectations or desires. In Northeast Asia, Japan had finally established close formal ties with the Republic of Korea, ties carrying very significant economic as well as political implications for the future. No issue occupied the attention of the North Korean leaders during 1965 more than this development, but they were powerless to prevent it. In vain, they called upon the Koreans in the south to "throw their bodies in front of the frenzied drive of the American imperialists, the Pak Chŏng-hi puppets and the Japanese reactionaries." The treaty between Japan and South Korea was ratified. Japanese investment began to flow into Korea, and this development, along with others, stimulated the first sustained high-level economic growth in the south.

From this point on, North Korean spokesmen were to regard "the menace of Japanese militarism" as second only to "the threat of American imperialism." The Communist analysis of the future was set forth clearly in these respects by Kim Il-sŏng in the major address to the Party Conference of October 1966 that we have already cited.

> The U.S. imperialists have revived Japanese militarism to make use of it as their "shock-brigade" of aggression in Asia. They have aligned the forces of Japanese militarism with the South Korean puppets and are scheming to rig up a "Northeast Asian Military Alliance" with the former as its core. . . . We should harbor no illusion whatsoever as to the Japanese ruling circles and should not pin any hopes on them. If we overlook the danger of Japanese militarism and become intimate with the Sato Government, it is, in fact, tantamount to encouraging the foreign expansion of the Japanese ruling circles and to consolidating the position of U.S. imperialism in Asia.[96]

96. Kim Il-sŏng, "The Present Situation and the Task Confronting Our Party," *op. cit.,* p. 2.

Kim's fuller remarks on Japan warrant some attention because they indicate the line also being taken by China, and the arguments being advanced in 1966 were to grow in intensity in the years ahead. "We must be aware of the danger of Japanese militarism in Asia along with that of West German militarism in Europe. As all the socialist countries struggle against West German militarism along with U.S. imperialism in Europe, so they should fight against Japanese militarism along with U.S. imperialism in Asia.

"Japanese militarism has made its appearance in Asia as a dangerous force of aggression today. The Japanese military forces harbor an illusion of realizing that old dream of the 'Greater East Asia Co-prosperity Sphere' with U.S. backing. Japan's Sato Government, with the active support of U.S. imperialism, has not only mapped out the plans of war to invade Korea and other Asian nations but has already started stretching its tentacles of aggression to South Korea. . . .

"At U.S. instigation, the Sato Government pursues a hostile policy towards our

Kim and other Communist spokesmen wildly exaggerated Japan's military strength and commitments. But they were quite right to fear that the emergence of a new great power in Asia, fabulously successful in its economic development, and capable of providing stimulus—both as model and as source of economic interaction—to many non-Communist states, including the Republic of Korea, would be a serious new problem from their standpoint.

In Southeast Asia, of course, the paramount issue was now Vietnam. And contrary to the expectations of many, the escalation of the Vietnam War, including the extensive American commitment, did not bring the international Communist community closer together. On the contrary, Vietnam became another major bone of contention between the Soviet Union and China, triggering events that greatly complicated North Korean relations with both.[97] A Communist victory in Vietnam had seemed within sight in early 1965. Then came the American decision to attempt to prevent this, a decision that involved the dispatch of hundreds of thousands of American troops to South Vietnam and the bombing of North Vietnam. By 1966, it was clear that the war would be long and costly for all parties concerned. The North Koreans, of course, were embarrassed by the fact that, whereas South Korea had dispatched some 50,000 troops to fight in South Vietnam, their own aid to North Vietnam was negligible. However, from time to time they did offer to send volunteers if these should be desired.

The truly important question for the Communists, however, was whether the Sino-Soviet quarrel could be settled or set aside in such a manner as to let Hanoi have the type of Communist support—military, political, and economic—that it now needed so badly. The issue was put to the test in the spring of 1966, when a Japanese Communist mission traveled for several months between China, North Vietnam, and North Korea seeking a formula for unified Communist aid to the North Vietnamese.[98] The Japanese mission failed, and the Japanese Communists placed the blame on the Chinese, particularly Mao Tse-tung. Miyamoto Kenji and

---

country and the other socialist countries in Asia. It also intensifies its economic and cultural infiltration into a number of Asian, African and Latin-American countries under the special name of 'aid,' 'joint development' and 'economic and technical cooperation.'

"The struggle against Japanese militarism is a struggle to defend peace in Asia and the world and is an important part of the struggle against U.S. imperialism. All the socialist countries should attach importance to the struggle against Japanese militarism and frustrate its aggressive designs by concerted actions. Especially, they should thoroughly lay bare and baffle the schemes of the Sato Government to disorganize the anti-imperialist front under the guise of being a 'friend' of the Afro-Asian and Latin-American peoples." *Ibid.*, p. 2.

97. See Donald S. Zagoria, *Vietnam Triangle: Moscow/Peking/Hanoi*, New York, 1967.

98. For details, see Scalapino, *The Japanese Communist Movement, op. cit.*, pp. 266–272.

others were unable to persuade "the old man" that the attack on "modern revisionism" had to be balanced against the desperate need for a united front against "American imperialism." Mao, with his Cultural Revolution under way and the threat of an American attack upon China of less concern than at an earlier point, was not prepared to normalize relations with the Soviet Union even for the sake of North Vietnam.

This position cost Mao and the Chinese Party heavily in their relations with other Asian Communists. From this point on, criticism of China mounted within Asian Communist circles, with North Korean and Japanese Party spokesmen taking the lead. Nor did the excesses accompanying the Cultural Revolution improve the Chinese image in P'yŏngyang. By the fall of 1966, Kim Il-Sŏng was dispensing criticism against *both* major Communist states in almost equal amounts, and in neither case was the criticism trivial. The attitude that one took toward "US imperialist aggression in Vietnam," proclaimed Kim, showed whether or not one was resolutely opposed to imperialism, and whether or not one actively supported the people's liberation struggle. *"The attitude towards the Vietnam question is a touchstone that distinguishes between the revolutionary stand and the opportunist stand, between proletarian internationalism and national egoism."* [99] (Italics ours.)

These remarks, like those that followed, were directed at least as much at the People's Republic of China as at the Soviet Union. The fact that the socialist countries were "not keeping step with each other" in opposing the US and aiding the Vietnamese, Kim added, affected the fighting people of Vietnam and really saddened "us Communists." At one time, Kim argued, the Soviet Union stood as the sole revolutionary state. It was thus forced to solve all the socialist world's problems, including those involving military support. But that situation no longer prevailed. Now, *all* countries within the powerful socialist camp were duty bound to offer aid to the Democratic Republic of Vietnam and the Vietnamese people.[100]

99. Kim Il-sŏng, "The Present Situation," *op. cit.,* p. 3.
100. In his remarks, Kim issued an open demand that the Communist bloc dispatch volunteers to Vietnam to match the allied forces fighting there, and implied that one of the major Communist states (China?) was blocking this necessary move. His words were: "In the light of the situation where the U.S. imperialists are expanding aggression to the Democratic Republic of Vietnam by bringing in troops of their subordinate countries and puppets, every socialist country must dispatch volunteers to Vietnam to defend the southeastern outpost of the socialist camp and preserve peace in Asia and the world. This is its internationalist duty to the brotherly Vietnamese people. *No one, whoever one may be, is allowed to oppose the socialist countries dispatching volunteers to Vietnam."* (Italics ours.) *Ibid.*
The importance Kim attached to the Vietnamese issue is manifest in the prominence given that issue in his speech, the urgent tone used in discussing it, and such passages as this: "If all the socialist countries assist the Vienamese people in shattering U.S. aggression, U.S. imperialism will be doomed like the sun setting in the west

This scarcely veiled criticism of Chinese policies extended beyond the issue of Vietnam. The overthrow of Sukarno and the virtual obliteration of the Indonesian Communist Party (PKI) had been a tremendous blow to the North Koreans and their hopes for a powerful Third World bloc. Kim Il-sŏng himself had made his first trip to a non-Communist state when he went to Indonesia in April 1965—six months before the abortive coup and Sukarno's fall from power.[101] Reflecting upon these events from the perspective of late 1966, Kim commented:

> Developments in Indonesia offer a serious lesson to all Communists. It shows that the more the Communist Parties and revolutionary forces grow, the more desperately foreign imperialism and local reactionary forces maneuver to stifle them. Communists should maintain the sharpest vigilance over this and always be prepared to counter the possible savage suppression of the enemy organizationally and ideologically, strategically and tactically. Revolution is complicated and requires a scientific art of leadership. It can be won only when the line of struggle is set forth scientifically and scrupulously and the most appropriate time is chosen to unfold a decisive fight on the basis of a correct judgment on the revolutionary situation and an exact calculation of the balance of forces between the two opposing sides. We should deeply bear in mind such experience and lessons of the international revolutionary movement and make good use of them in our own revolutionary struggle.[102]

It is not necessary, of course, to read into these specific remarks a criticism of the Chinese. But it *is* significant that Kim here was blaming "Communists" in general for badly misjudging the situation in Indonesia at a time when Soviet organs were openly charging the Chinese with prime responsibility for the Indonesian debacle, on the grounds that they had prodded Aidit and the PKI into premature action. Kim was certainly aware of these Soviet charges when he uttered the remarks quoted above.

On a broader front, moreover, the North Koreans now gave nearly equal prominence to the dangers of modern revisionism *and* dogmatism. Once again, Kim's speech of October 1966 provides ample evidence. After

---

and the revolutionary movements in all countries in Asia and the rest of the world will surge forward greatly." *Ibid.*

Moreover, he ended this section by asserting flatly that the KWP regarded the Vietnam struggle as its own, and was preparing to send volunteers if so requested by the DRV government.

101. In his welcoming speech at the Djakarta airport, President Sukarno said, "Premier Kim Il-sŏng will see that the Indonesian people, firmly united in one mind and one will, are fighting unyieldingly against imperialism and old and new colonialism and realize how anxious our people are to strengthen the friendship with the Korean people. . . . The Indonesian people are well aware that victory can be won only by waging this struggle shoulder to shoulder with the new emerging forces of the world. . . ." *TPK,* April 14, 1965, p. 1.

102. *Ibid.,* p. 4.

referring to the "harsh trials" experienced by the socialist camp in recent years, he condemned "modern revisionism and dogmatism" as both having created the gravest obstacles to the development of the international revolutionary movement. To achieve unity, it would be necessary to overcome both Right *and* Left opportunism while defending the purity of Marxism-Leninism. Right opportunism revised Marxism-Leninism and emasculated its revolutionary essence, using as pretexts the so-called changing situation and something called "creative development." Such opportunism was on the decline, asserted Kim, but it was still a major threat, and one that found expression above all in a weak attitude toward imperialism and a passive approach to the revolutionary struggles of other peoples. Left opportunism, on the other hand, could be as much of a threat as Right opportunism. It took no account of changed realities, clinging instead to dogmatic interpretations of Marxist-Leninist propositions torn out of context. Thus it led people to extremist actions under superrevolutionary slogans. Furthermore, it divorced the Party from the masses, splitting the revolutionary forces and thereby preventing any concentrated attack on the main enemy.[103]

With respect to the general situation in the international Communist camp, incidentally, Kim was grimly pessimistic. He admitted that the differences among fraternal Parties had become so serious that there was no hope for any settlement at this point. He also acknowledged that this situation was of great advantage to the "enemy." He pleaded, however, for the avoidance of an organizational split. Meanwhile, the ultimate solution lay in unity through ideological struggle, a sincere and honest criticism of "mistaken comrades" undertaken in a friendly spirit. At all times, a distinction between "socialist countries" and those in the "imperialist camp" had to be maintained. There were *thirteen* of the former, and *no one* could admit or expel any state unilaterally. Thus, the effort to smuggle the Titoites of Yugoslavia into the socialist camp had to be firmly resisted, as well as any effort to oust members like Albania.

Thus, despite the coolness that had developed toward Peking, Kim was prepared to make no concessions to the Russians on the old issues that had separated P'yŏngyang and Moscow. In his concluding remarks on the international situation, while urging a tolerant and restrained attitude on the part of all Parties toward "fraternal comrades" with whom differences existed, Kim made a spirited defense of the new chuch'e foreign policy.

> There are certain persons at present who attach the labels of middle-roadism," "eclecticism," "opportunism," and the like to our Party and other Marxist-Leninist parties. They say we are taking the "road of unprincipled compromise" and "sitting straddling two chairs." This is nonsense. We have our own chair. Why should we give up our own chair and sit uncomfortably straddling two others' chairs? We will always sit on our upright Marxist-Leninist chair. Those who accuse us, who are sitting on

103. *Ibid.*

our upright chair, of sitting straddling two chairs, are no doubt sitting on a chair crooked to the left or to the right.[104]

The strident tones of independence now being voiced by Kim Il-sŏng seemed on occasion to involve a balancing of hostility rather than of friendship toward Moscow and Peking. And for its part, Peking at least was now prepared to reciprocate. While the Russians sent Aleksandr N. Shelepin, a prominent Politburo member, to the celebrations in August 1965 commemorating the twentieth anniversary of Korean Liberation, the Chinese delegation was composed of minor officials, led by Wu Hsin-yu, Party chairman of Liaoning Province. By February 1967, moreover, Red Guard posters were appearing in Peking covered with derogatory remarks about Kim Il-sŏng. Kim was called a "fat revisionist" and a "disciple of Khrushchev." In August, other posters accused the Kim government of living in luxury while the people suffered, and of creating economic chaos through its policies.

Dramatic charges against Kim personally continued to be made in Red Guard publications at least until the spring of 1968. Note the following:

> Kim Il-sŏng is an out-and-out counterrevolutionary revisionist of the Korean revisionist clique, as well as a millionaire, an aristocrat, and a leading bourgeois element in Korea. His house commands a full view of the Moranbong, the Taedong River, and the Pot'ong River. . . . The estate covers an area of several ten thousand square meters and is surrounded on all sides by high walls. All sides of the estate are dotted with sentry posts. One has to pass through five or six doors before one comes to the courtyard. This really makes one think of the great palaces of emperors in the past.[105]

Ignoring Kim's 1966 defense of North Korean foreign policy, Feng Piao, director of information for *Jen-min Jih-pao,* strongly criticized the DPRK in January 1968 for "sitting on the fence" in the Sino-Soviet dispute.

104. *Ibid.,* p. 7.
105. This attack was published in a Cultural Revolution bulletin, the Canton *Wen-ko T'ung-hsün,* on Feb. 15, 1968.
    The attack continued: "Kim Il-sŏng has his own palaces everywhere in North Korea. The first villa lies in the pine zone of the Sanmien District in the suburbs of P'yŏngyang. The second villa is located at the scenic spot of the Chin Mountains. The third villa is situated at Chuyueh (Chuwol) Hot Springs. The fourth villa lies in Sinŭiju. The fifth villa is located along the coast in the vicinity of Ch'ŏngjin Wharf. . . . All of these villas are on a grand scale. Although Kim Il-sŏng stays in these villas for only a few days every year, such stays usually require the services of large numbers of military and security personnel."
    The article went on to attack Kim for building a special cemetery to show piety for his parents and ancestors, and then charged that Pak (presumably Pak Yŏng-sun), minister of Posts and Telecommunications, on the occasion of his sixtieth birthday celebration in 1965, had received more than 200 tables as gifts, and many other presents from government "big-shots," with the implication that extensive gift-giving and lavish parties were the rule among governmental officials in North Korea.

"Korea is opposed to Mao Tse-tung's thought and to China, day-by-day. It advocates the road of neutrality, opposition to imperialism but not to revisionism, and sits all the time on its own bench. This is impossible. It can be perceived that it has serious problems in the political field as well as in the economic field." [106]

Despite these attacks, however, the North Koreans did not answer in kind. Indeed, by 1968, DPRK spokesmen were generally refraining from comment on their problems with major Communist allies. This suggests an attempt to put into practice Kim's injunction on treating wayward comrades with care and understanding. Such "struggle" as was now taking place toward the international Communist community was taking place in private. P'yŏngyang's caution in criticizing either Moscow or Peking publicly during this period may have been induced partly by the stepped-up "liberation" campaign directed toward South Korea, and the fixation with "the American menace" that accompanied it.

Throughout this period, the most extreme language available was used to describe the United States and its policies. A typical example is contained in the "report" of Ch'ae Yun-byŏng, vice-chairman of the Central Commit-

---

106. The animosity between the Chinese and the North Koreans at this time may have reached a point of open hostilities. The *New York Times* reported on Nov. 23, 1970, that Chinese and North Korean troops had had "shooting incidents" in 1968 over border disputes. A 100-square-mile strip in the Mount Paektu (or Changpai) area had been contested for several decades between the Chinese and Korean governments. According to the *New York Times,* the Chinese Communists initially pressed the claim in 1965 when "North Korea shifted to the Moscow camp," and revived it in 1968. The Chinese, however, agreed to abandon the claim "during an exchange of goodwill delegations between Peking and P'yŏngyang on the occasion of the 20th anniversary of the entry of Chinese forces into the Korean War in October 1970."

More direct evidence concerning the gravity of relations is available from no less a person than K'ang Sheng, long head of Chinese Communist intelligence operations and a key "Maoist" during the Great Proletarian Cultural Revolution. In a speech of Feb. 8, 1968, to certain mass-organization and military representatives of Kirin Province, after castigating various traitors K'ang remarked that the comrades of the northeast must be especially alert to enemy intelligence activities:

"Think about what you are facing. You have experienced Japanese imperialism, then the Kuomintang and U.S. imperialism. You are still facing the activities of the Soviet and Korean revisionists' special agents. The enemy agent activities of the Korean revisionists have a long-term foundation in your area. Recently we know that the Korean revisionists were organizing traitorous activities through their embassy, and I believe that that must have taken place in your area. . . . You must pay attention and definitely search out the Soviet and Korean revisionist enemy agents and the traitors. Learn from Heilungkiang and Liaoning. They have already done much work, have come to understand some circumstances, have acquired some ability." Excerpts from a speech by Comrade K'ang Sheng on Special Case Work, pp. 135–140, in *Ch'ang-li chieh-chi tui-wu (The Purification of Class Ranks)*, compiled by the Paoshan (Yunnan) Revolutionary Committee Political Work Section, January 1969, and translated in U.S. Joint Publications Research Service, *Translations on Communist China,* No. 140, March 18, 1971, JPRS S2658, pp. 34–38 (p. 36).

tee of the Korean Journalists' Union, to a session of the so-called International Organization of Journalists held in P'yŏngyang in September 1969. "US imperialism," asserted Ch'ae, "is the main force of aggression and war, international gendarme, bulwark of modern colonialism, and the most heinous common enemy of the peoples of the whole world." [107]

Kim Il-sŏng was equally harsh in his speech at the twentieth anniversary celebration of the founding of the DPRK. "US imperialism is the most barbarous and most shameless aggressor of modern times and the chieftain of world imperialism. . . . No place on earth is safe from the tentacles of aggression stretched out by US imperialism and no country is free from the menace of US imperialist aggression." [108] Kim then repeated the oft-proclaimed thesis that, while the Korean people did not want war, they were never afraid of it. If the enemy were to force a new war upon them, he stated, they would rise as one in a heroic struggle to defend the socialist fatherland and unify the country.

Throughout this period, Kim Il-sŏng and all other North Korean spokesmen talked incessantly of the probability of a second Korean War, a war that would result in Communist victory and the unification of Korea under their aegis. To be sure, they claimed that the war would be instigated by "the American imperialists." But, as we have seen, in point of fact, the North Korean leaders had been engaged in a militarization program almost without parallel for a nation of this size, and were now infiltrating sizable units into South Korea.

It was also in this period that the North Koreans took their most significant gamble, namely, the seizure of the USS *Pueblo* and its crew of eighty-two Americans on January 23, 1968. The *Pueblo,* engaged in electronic surveillance along the North Korean coast, was seized, according to P'yŏngyang authorities, because it had intruded into the territorial waters of North Korea (the charge was subsequently denied by all of the Americans involved).[109] According to later statements by Kim Il-sŏng and others,

107. For a full English-language text of Ch'ae's report, see "Tasks of Journalists of Whole World Fighting Against Aggression of U.S. Imperialism," *TPK,* Oct. 16, 1969, pp. 1–8.

108. Kim Il-sŏng, "The Democratic People's Republic of Korea Is the Banner . . ." *op. cit.,* p. 14. Kim continued: "The U.S. imperialists have brutally suppressed the national-liberation movements of the Asian, African and Latin American peoples and turned up as the heinous strangler of national independence. The U.S. imperialists are stepping up armed intervention in Laos and trampling upon the territorial integrity of Cambodia, while persisting in provocative acts against the Cambodian people. The U.S. imperialists instigated the Israeli expansionists to an aggressive war against the Arab peoples and are making a malicious attempt to stifle their struggle for national independence and a new life." *Ibid.*

109. For a detailed account of this case from the perspective of the captain of the *Pueblo,* see Lloyd M. Bucher with Mark Rascovich, *Bucher: My Story,* New York, 1970. Bucher presents a graphic account of the inhumane treatment suffered by the crew at the hands of the North Koreans, including savage beatings and innumerable

a real fear that the United States might retaliate swept through North Korea immediately after the ship's capture, and full-scale alerts were established. There was no American response, however, and the *Pueblo* case became a major propaganda victory for the Communists. Staged confessions—later revealed to be fraudulent—were publicized throughout the world. And the victory was sealed by an American "letter of apology" which was finally signed in order to obtain the release of the captured men.[110]

On the eve of the Fifth Party Congress, changing events in Asia again introduced new elements into North Korean foreign policy without altering any of its basic elements. In the spring and early summer of 1970, P'yŏng-yang was to greet two important visitors: Chou En-lai and Norodom Sihanouk. Some improvement in relations with China had been signaled earlier, when the North Korean delegation to the celebration of the twenti-eth anniversary of the founding of the CPR on October 1, 1969, was headed by Ch'oe Yong-gŏn. The speeches made during Chou's visit, and the joint communiqué issued on April 7, suggested that the primary catalytic agent in bringing Peking and P'yŏngyang closer together was once again the desire and need to form a common front against their enemies in Asia.

The number one enemy, at least publicly, remained the United States. In every speech by Chou and Kim, "American imperialism" was singled

---

humiliations. He also recounts the way in which "confessions" were obtained, indicat-ing how the men drafting these statements sought to signal to Americans their fraudu-lence. Bucher denies vigorously that his ship was at any time in North Korean ter-ritorial waters, and offers what appears to be incontrovertible evidence on this matter, although it is conceivable that the ship's instruments were not working properly.

It is his opinion that the *Pueblo* (captured one day after the unsuccessful North Korean attempt to assassinate President Pak) was seized on the mistaken assumption that it was a South Korean Navy ship bent on a retaliation mission; and that when they finally became aware of the fact that the ship and crew were entirely Americans, the North Koreans had no alternative except to bluff their way through by claiming an intrusion into their territorial waters (pp. 405–406).

Some senior American officials are dubious of this interpretation, pointing out that there was ample opportunity to contact key North Korean authorities after the presence of Americans on the ship had been verified, and that, given the nature of the regime, this must have been done.

For two other accounts, see Ed Brandt, *The Last Voyage of USS Pueblo,* New York, 1969, and Edward R. Murphy, Jr., *Second in Command,* New York, 1971.

110. The signing of this "letter" was surely one of the more bizarre episodes in modern American diplomacy. American authorities announced beforehand that the "letter" contained false statements, that no crimes had been committed, and that it was being signed only to secure the release of eighty-one Americans (one having died).

However, for the North Koreans, this was the equivalent of having "American imperialism" kowtow before the leaders of P'yŏngyang, and they were subsequently to boast repeatedly that, because of the impregnable defenses that had been created in the north, the enemy did not dare to take military action and was forced to admit his crimes before the world.

out for vitriolic attack. Now, however, "Japanese militarism" was receiving almost equal attention, and we must also assume that in view of the events of 1969 on the Sino-Soviet border, the problem of the USSR loomed very large, especially from Peking's perspective. It may have been the Soviet threat, indeed, that produced the reversal of Chinese policy toward P'yŏng-yang—as it was later to do with respect to Washington.

In North Korea, however, the enemy publicly attacked was the United States. Perhaps Chou En-lai's brief remarks upon his arrival at the P'yŏngyang airport on April 5 best summarize the theme that prevailed throughout the week.

> China and Korea are neighbors as closely related as lips and teeth, and our two peoples are intimate brothers. Both in the long struggle against Japanese imperialism and in the war of resistance against U.S. imperialist aggression, our two peoples stood together and fought shoulder to shoulder. Common struggles have bound our two peoples in a profound militant friendship. Our friendship is cemented with blood; it has been long tested and will stand up to future tests.
>
> At present, U.S. imperialism is advocating in Asia a policy of war expansion of making "Asians fight Asians." Fostered energetically by U.S. imperialism, the Japanese reactionaries are stepping up the revival of militarism, willingly serving as the former's shock troops. Colluding with each other, the U.S. and Japanese reactionaries are directing the spearhead of their aggression squarely against the peoples of China, Korea, the three countries of Indo-China, and other Asian countries. Under such circumstances, the further strengthening of the militant unity between the Chinese and Korean peoples is of great significance. The Chinese people will forever stand by the fraternal Korean people in their struggle to defend the security of their Fatherland.[111]

Sihanouk arrived in mid-June, some two months after Chou's visit. His trip was a short one, since he was now a resident of Peking. On June 25, while he was still in North Korea, a mass rally of 200,000 citizens was held in P'yŏngyang on what was proclaimed a Day of Struggle Against US Imperialism. In addition to the Cambodian delegation, foreign visitors present on the rostrum included Huang Yung-sheng, chief of staff of the Chinese People's Liberation Army, and Li Tso-peng, Politburo member and political commissar of the Chinese navy, together with various Vietnamese and Laotian Communist or front representatives. All of the prominent Korean leaders participated in this event; Kim Il delivered the main speech on be-

111. The Foreign Languages Press of Peking has published an English-language pamphlet which contains all the official speeches and the joint communiqué. It is entitled *Premier Chou En-lai Visits the Democratic People's Republic of Korea,* Peking, 1970.

half of the DPRK.[112] This occasion symbolized the great significance that Kim Il-sŏng and his government now placed upon building an All-Asian united front—a sort of anti-American–anti-Japanese alliance. The Russians, who had earlier called for some type of collective Asian defense (a remark widely interpreted as being directed against China, not the United States), were conspicuous by their absence. So, of course, were some old figureheads of the Communist-led Asian united front, notably Sukarno. However, the effort continued to make Indochina a testing ground in the struggle between Communists and non-Communists. The overthrow of Sihanouk, and his new dependence upon Asian rather than Soviet Communists, made the effort in many respects even more significant.[113]

The Faltering "Liberation" Campaign

One of the prime reasons for Kim Il-sŏng's great interest in normalizing relations with the Soviet Union, reconstructing "fraternal ties" with China, and seeking once again to build a Communist-led Asian united front lay in his continued commitment to "liberate" South Korea. As a crucial aspect of North Korean foreign policy, therefore, we must briefly examine policies toward the Republic of Korea after the Fourth Congress in 1961.

---

112. For a summary of the key speeches, see *TPK*, July 1, 1970, pp. 1–2. Sihanouk reportedly said, "Nineteen fifty was the year of the great Korean War forced by the U.S.A. Nineteen seventy is a year of the great Indochinese war forced by the same United States.

"Following the brilliant and admirable example of the heroic, fraternal Korean people, the three Indochinese peoples united in one front of struggle are fighting without the spirit of retreat against the common enemy to completely and definitely clear him out of Indochina.

"The inevitable defeat of U.S. imperialism in Indochina as well as its involuntary 'success' in the formation in Asia of the immense, indivisible united front of the Korean, Chinese, Vietnamese, Cambodian, and Laotian peoples will, I am convinced, bring about disastrous consequences for the future of the American imperialists in Asia, Africa and Latin America and, consequently, bring a favorable future for all the peoples of the third world."

Huang, a rising star at that point on the Chinese political as well as military horizon, is reported to have declared that the Korean victory in 1950–53 had foiled the American plan to invade Asia and dominate the world, and had safeguarded the security of China. He then attacked the Japanese-American joint statement of November 1969, and the US-Japan military alliance, promising full Chinese support should "the U.S. imperialists and the Japanese militarists dare to force a war of aggression upon the Chinese and Korean peoples." *Ibid.*, p. 2.

Vietnamese and Laotian representatives, including Tran Huu Duc (DVR), Nguyen Van Hieu (Provisional Revolutionary Government of the Republic of South Vietnam), and Sanan Soutthichia (head of the Laotian Patriotic Front delegation), spoke in a similar vein.

113. Unverified rumors of North Korean volunteers in Cambodia came from Phnom Penh by the early fall of 1970. At this writing, there is no proof of the truth or falsity of these rumors.

The basic Communist strategy with respect to South Korea did not change in the decade before the Fifth Party Congress in 1970, but there were various tactical changes. As we have earlier indicated, there is some reason to believe that the major shift in priorities undertaken in December 1962, and the new emphasis upon large-scale militarization, were directly connected with a decision that South Korea had to be "liberated" in the early 1970s at the latest. The frustration of being unable either to take advantage of Rhee's overthrow or to prevent the subsequent military takeover undoubtedly contributed to this decision. But there was also rising concern over Japan's potential role in Northeast Asia. Later, the increasing signs of economic growth in South Korea were to have the same effect.

With respect to their public, political formula for unification, the Communists stood by their proposals at the Fourth KWP Congress. However, it was also in that Congress that Kim had called openly for the establishment of "a true Marxist-Leninist Party" in the south, and asserted emphatically that Korea would be "peacefully unified" only when the Americans had been driven out of South Korea and the Pak government overthrown. This, Kim certainly implied, would require a revolution, and a violent one.

Thus, the renewed "liberation" drive was to be conducted on the pattern of Vietnam, not the Korean War. The north would serve as a training and infiltration base while a revolutionary movement was constructed in the south. Only when that movement had become strong would further steps be taken, combinations of legal and illegal action, as well as guerrilla warfare. At this later stage, North Korea could determine its role in accordance with the circumstances, supposedly secure in the knowledge that its internal defenses were impregnable. As we have noted, an analogy was drawn with the supposed strategy of Kim during the days of his Manchurian guerrilla exploits: build an impregnable inner fortress from which forays can be undertaken in the secure knowledge that one's own core territory is inviolable. Finally, in the event of large-scale North-South conflict, North Korean involvement must be made to appear a defensive response to aggression from South Korea. In this one respect, the strategy of the 1950 era was to be repeated.

When did efforts to implement Kim Il-sŏng's call for the establishment of a South Korean Communist Party get under way? We are dependent primarily upon Communist accounts and trial testimony as published in South Korea. According to official KWP sources, the RPU, the Revolutionary Party for Unification (T'ongil Hyŏngmyŏng-dang), was founded as an underground revolutionary organization in South Korea on March 15, 1964, nearly two and one-half years after the 1961 Congress. The "Party" was organized by Kim Chong-t'ae, a graduate of Tongguk University (then 38 years of age). The other central figures were Yi Mun-gyu (then 28) and Kim Chin-nak (then 30), both graduates of Seoul National University's

College of Liberal Arts and Sciences (Kim later operated a tavern for college graduates).[114]

However, some of those involved in the RPU case appear to have made secret trips to P'yŏngyang as early as December 1961, soon after the Fourth Party Congress in October. There, they received espionage training for six months, after which they returned to the south armed with cipher codes, and with nearly 2 million wŏn (approximately US$6,000) for operational funds and clandestine programs. The basic purpose of the RPU was to establish itself as a Communist movement under the leadership of Kim Il-sŏng and the Korean Workers' Party, building various front organizations in the south, with a special effort made to win over disaffected intellectuals.

Kim Chong-t'ae admitted in court that he had made some thirteen trips to P'yŏngyang aboard speedboats and had received his initial instructions to form the RPU from Kim Il-sŏng himself. The key figures had all joined the Korean Workers' Party while in P'yŏngyang, and had been liberally supplied with money. Kim Chong-t'ae reportedly had been given operational funds totaling some 23.5 million wŏn (about US$70,000). Yi Mungyu had been given 1 million wŏn to operate the tavern (which served as a cover for political activities), and to form a National Liberation Front designed to attract intellectuals and college students. Yi also served as editor of the monthly magazine *Ch'ŏng-maek* (Blue Vein), which first appeared in August 1964 and according to the Communists had 44,000 copies in print by June 1967 (it was a legal publication). Another defendant in the 1968 trial, Yun Sang-su, admitted obtaining 500,000 wŏn from North Korean authorities in P'yŏngyang in December 1965; he operated a barber shop as a front for political activities in Mokp'o, South Chŏlla Province, working under Kim Chong-t'ae's direction.

The RPU represented the first Communist underground movement in South Korea since the old Party had been smashed in the course of the Korean War. (Some student groups in the Chang Myŏn era had engaged in activities later considered "subversive," such as advocating direct North-South discussions at P'anmunjŏm, but, as noted earlier, there is no evidence that these activities were guided by the KWP.) In the period between 1965 and 1967, this new Party reportedly set up various front organizations— groups with familiar names such as the National Liberation Front (Yi Mun-gyu, chief secretary) and the Fatherland Liberation Front (Kim Chin-nak, chief secretary). More specialized groups included the Society for the Study of the New Culture, the Young Literary Men's Association,

114. "The Indomitable Revolutionary Struggle by Members of the Unification-Revolution Party Armed with the Revolutionary Ideas of Marshal Kim Il-sŏng, *TPK*, Feb. 5, 1969, pp. 4–5. In his 1968 trial, however, Kim Chong-t'ae indicated that the Party had been founded in November 1965.

the Buddhist Youth Society, the Tonghak Research Institute, the Ch'ŏng-maek-hoe (Blue Vein Society), the Society for the Study of Comparative Nationalism, the Christian Youth Economic Welfare Society, the Kyŏng-wu Society, and the Tavern for College Graduates. According to Communist sources, these nine front organizations were intended to embrace "the masses of all strata," forming a united anti-US national salvation front under the aegis of the Party.[115]

As can be imagined, all of these groups had minuscule memberships. Ultimately, 158 persons were accused of some involvement in the RPU or its fronts in the course of the 1968 trials, but initially there were only twenty-seven defendants. Of course, if Communist sources were to be believed, the underground activities of this group were rapidly expanding.[116] The evidence, however, is to the contrary. Whatever the dissatisfaction of the intellectuals and young students in South Korea during this period—and it was not insubstantial—the Communists were not an attraction.

By greatly inflating the actual size and accomplishments of the RPU, Kim Il-sŏng and his regime could not only impress their own people with the supposed strength of the revolutionary movement in the south, but also provide a camouflage for northern infiltration. Thus, according to Communist sources, "Along with the lawful mass struggles [of the type noted above], this party vigorously pushed ahead with preparations for organizing and waging an active armed guerrilla struggle, and exerted efforts for building a solid base for it." [117] In point of fact, none of the RPU members had engaged in guerrilla activities for the simple reason that they lacked the strength as yet to move to such a stage. They had stored some food and supplies in caves in preparation for the future.

Nevertheless, organizational activities continued. According to the Communists, the party formed a Central Committee in August 1969, and adopted a program and manifesto, both published in its underground organ, *Hyŏngmyŏng Chŏnsŏn* (Revolutionary Front). These documents, reproduced in various Communist and radical sources abroad, unabashedly support Kim Il-sŏng and the Korean Workers' Party, making no effort to hide

115. *Ibid.,* p. 4.

116. According to the Communist version, "the members of the Unification-Revolution Party themselves went down among the masses of the people and widely propagandized among them the history of the great revolutionary struggle of Marshal Kim Il-sŏng, the respected and beloved leader, and the judiciousness of his leadership, and his lofty virtues, and explained and propagandized the superiority of the socialist system established in the northern half of the Republic under his leadership, leaving a deep impress upon the people." *Ibid.* The article continues by asserting that Kim Chong-t'ae and his URP comrades not only proselyted among "the masses" but also among the soldiers, securing some converts. The URP is further credited with organizing and guiding demonstrations against both the National Assembly elections of June 1967 and the visit of Vice-President Humphrey.

117. *Ibid.,* pp. 4–5.

the identification.[118] The manifesto, for example, contains the following paragraphs:

> The Revolutionary Party for Unification is a new-type Marxist-Leninist Party, qualitatively distinct in its class basis, in its guiding principle and in its aim of struggle from all the existing political parties and groups. Our Party represents and defends the interests of the working class and peasants, the main-stays of our society, and the rest of the toiling masses. The Party is organized with the advanced elements of the workers, peasants and working intellectuals. . . .
>
> The guiding principle of the Revolutionary Party for Unification is Comrade Kim Il-sŏng's great idea of *chuch'e* which is the original embodiment of Marxism-Leninism in the present era and in the actual conditions of our country. The idea of *chuch'e* represents the Marxism-Leninism of our times, the perfect merit of which has been saliently proved throughout the 40 years and more of severe revolutionary storms. Its vitality is permanent and inexhaustible not only for the past and present but also for all time to come. It brightly illumines the course to follow for our people as well as for millions of peoples the world over.[119]

Among the Party's twelve principles was one that pledged a reduction of the armed forces of South Korea to 200,000 or less; another that called for an independent foreign policy, with the abolition not only of ROK ties with the United States but of the ROK-Japanese treaty as well; and "the peaceful reunification of the country . . . relying on the independent democratic will of the people in the North and South and on the nation's own efforts without any foreign interference." [120]

118. According to Communist sources, the Revolutionary Party for Unification documents were published in three US newspapers, including *The Black Panther,* the British newspaper *Guardian,* and the Algerian publication *Revolution Africaine,* among others. For an English version, see *TPK,* June 24, 1970, pp. 4–5.

119. *Ibid.,* p. 4. It should be noted that Communist sources published in English frequently refer to the RPU as the Revolutionary Party for Reunification (RPR).

120. According to Point 12, " 'Anti-communist reunification' or 'U.N.-supervised reunification' shall be rejected." In its place, talks shall be opened between the North and the South, with mutual contacts, interviews, personal visits, free movement, encouraged. Then, "when the revolution triumphs and the independent people's government is established, North-South negotiations shall be opened without delay, and by agreement between both sides a peace declaration on the termination of the state of war and on the abolition of the truce line shall be made.

"A nation-wide general election shall be held under the joint administration of the governments of both sides, on the basis of ensuring the freedom of political activities both in the North and South, to set up a unified central government. Thus shall be achieved the great cause of reunification of the country, the supreme task of the nation." *Ibid.,* p. 6. By a not-so-strange coincidence, this is precisely the position of the Korean Workers' Party.

The other planks in the RPU program could be rather easily guessed. They include (1) "To overthrow the colonial rule of U.S. imperialism and establish independent democratic government. (2) To liquidate fascist dictatorship and realize democracy in socio-political life. (3) To carry out democratic land reform and to

The RPU was smashed in August 1968 when the Republic of Korea Central Intelligence Agency intercepted a North Korean speedboat that was attempting to establish liaison with its key figures. The plan had been to take Kim Chong-t'ae north to attend the twentieth anniversary celebration of the DPRK as the representative of South Korean revolutionaries. After a widely publicized trial, the three top leaders, Kim Chong-t'ae, Yi Mun-gyu, and Kim Chin-nak, were executed on January 25, 1969, along with two others. Some twenty-five additional RPU members, including Yim Yun-suk, the wife of Kim Chong-t'ae, received lengthy prison sentences.[121]

Although the minuscule Communist underground group was smashed in its infancy, the authorities in P'yŏngyang decided to keep alive the myth that a large movement was afoot in the south. In addition to continuous publicity allocated to the RPU in North Korean organs, the Communists also resumed publication of *Hyŏngmyŏng Chŏnsŏn,* the party organ. A new series bearing that title and the serial number "Resumption No. 1, Cumulative No. 206" was issued under the dateline June 1, 1970. The first four issues of the weekly tabloid, featuring either pictures of Kim Il-sŏng or his speeches on the front page, were clearly printed outside South Korea (probably in P'yŏngyang), but Seoul was given as the place of publication. However, recipients of the paper in the United States were surprised to find that this "Seoul underground paper" bore the following return address: Apartado 4132, Zona Postal Habana-4, Habana, Cuba!

Brief mention should also be made of the so-called East Berlin Incident, primarily because it reflected still another facet of Communist policies toward the south. This case broke in the spring of 1967, when several hundred persons, mainly students and intellectuals who had traveled in the West, especially Germany and France, were questioned concerning their contacts abroad. The South Korean government had come into possession of data indicating that the North Koreans, operating out of East Berlin, were making contact with various South Koreans living abroad.

Eventually some thirty-four people were brought to trial in Seoul in December 1967. Some of them had been brought back to Korea under

---

eradicate poverty in farming and fishing villages. (4) To nationalize major industries and build an independent national economy. (5) To enforce democratic labor laws and improve the socioeconomic status of workers. (6) To ensure the rights and interests of women and enhance their social status. (7) To bring about the efflorescence and development of a democratic national culture and to ensure the livelihood of intellectuals. (8) To renovate education and enforce a system of education free from fees and providing scholarships for the sons and daughters of working people. (9) To establish an advanced public health service system and enforce a system of extensive free medical care." *Ibid.,* p. 6.

121. Members of the Party included students, a chief clerk in the Science and Technology ministry, a demographer, a literary critic, and a young businessman. Once again, the absence of true workers or peasants is noteworthy. Predominantly, the nucleus of the Party's tiny membership lay with young intellectuals, with Seoul National University's Commerce and Liberal Arts schools once again involved.

extraordinary circumstances. Indeed, for a time, a rupture in relations between West Germany and South Korea was threatened because of indications that certain people had literally been kidnapped from their residences in West Germany by South Korean intelligence agents. During the trial, it developed that some of the defendants, many of whom had resided outside South Korea since the Rhee era, had been induced to visit North Korea secretly, with all expenses paid by the DPRK.[122] Others had cooperated in some degree with the North Koreans. For example, one young man studying in the United States had furnished them with a list of Koreans studying there.

Only a few of these people appear to have been fully committed, ideologically and politically, to North Korea. However, it was established that P'yŏngyang agents had given funds to one of the defendants to set up a restaurant in Bonn where South Korean students could meet North Korean agents, and other evidence brought out during the trials indicated a fairly extensive North Korean operation abroad to attract South Korean students and intellectuals and, if possible, obtain information from them.

An equally bizarre case was that of Yi Su-gun, formerly deputy director of the North Korean News Agency, who had supposedly defected to the south in a dramatic fashion at P'anmunjŏm. Yi, signaling to Americans that he wished to escape, jumped into the back seat of an automobile and made his exit to the south amid a hail of North Korean bullets. Feted by South Korean authorities, Yi was given substantial financial support, remarried, and was used throughout South Korea as an anti-Communist lecturer. In early 1969, however, Yi was captured in Saigon while attempting to flee the country, and it developed that he had been sent south by Kim Il-sŏng personally, to serve as an agent.

The infiltration of agents from the North has continued. The people sent, moreover, have represented a curious melange. Some have been exsouthern intellectuals. Others have been skilled workers or people whose backgrounds would scarcely seem to qualify them for the work of agents. Some have also been hoodlums or petty criminals with records as pickpockets in the north. More serious, of course, has been the infiltration of military elements. In January 1968, thirty-one DPRK soldiers got inside the city limits of Seoul in an expedition to assassinate President Pak Chŏng-hi (there had already been other such attempts, as we shall see). In late 1968, military infiltration reached a peak with the landing of 120 guerrillas on the northeast coast of South Korea in late October and early November. These men had been trained in a special unit, the 124th Army Unit; their mission

122. Some of the defendants took North Korean funds because they were in desperate financial straits. Others were induced to visit North Korea by being told that they could see relatives from whom they had long been separated, or—in the case of the famous composer, Yun I-sang—that he could examine musical developments in North Korea. About one-half were more involved ideologically, and at least two or three joined the Korean Workers' Party when they were in North Korea.

seems to have been to survey the area for possible sites for guerrilla activity, and to make contact with the peasants to determine whether they could be utilized. The mission was a failure: almost the entire infiltrator band was wiped out, except for two who surrendered. The purge of General Hŏ Pong-hak, director of the General Bureau for Activities in South Korea, the following month suggests that Kim Il-sŏng was not happy.

Reportedly, the key agency for South Korean activities was then transferred to the KWP Secretariat, and one secretary—Kim Chung-rin—placed in charge. At the same time, military activities directed toward the south continued. Two special companies, the 198th and 907th, devoted to "special maneuvers," were formally placed under the Reconnaissance Bureau of the National Defense Ministry, while actually under the control of the Party Secretariat. It is believed that some 10,400 soldiers were committed to military training for southern operations as of 1970, and that the Bureau had under its jurisdiction about one hundred small vessels, capable of transporting from 1,300 to 2,000 at one time. (This was in addition to some 60 helicopters that could transport from 700 to 2,000 men in an airborne operation.)

Thus, the military component available for northern guerrilla operations in the south has probably not been reduced since 1969. However, after the failures of late 1968, military infiltration decreased, at least until the time of the Fifth Party Congress, and some observers believe that new tactics had been signaled. Supposedly, these involved heavy concentration upon the political front, with strenuous efforts to rebuild the shattered Revolutionary Party for Unification and its front organizations. For these purposes, and as a source of intelligence, increasing numbers of fishermen were to be picked up, indoctrinated for varying lengths of time, and returned to South Korea. Meanwhile, an effort was to be made to assassinate prominent southern political figures, and to undertake other spectacular political moves of this nature, possibly involving sabotage. Armed guerrilla forays, however, would not be emphasized at this point, although tension would be increased along the demilitarized zone from time to time in order to keep open the possibility of "defensive" action.

Such a strategy once again underlined the probability that Kim Il-sŏng was contemplating a Vietnam-type liberation effort. Certainly the Twelve-Point Program of the RPU was remarkably similar to that of the South Vietnamese National Liberation Front and its controlling Communist unit, the People's Revolutionary Party.

The Fifth Congress

We have seen that the issue that in many respects dominated the decade of the 1960s for North Korea—the driving insistence of Kim Il-sŏng that South Korea be "liberated" under his aegis—remained no closer to resolution in 1970 than it had been in 1960. Indeed, it could be argued that in the light of the Republic of Korea's improving economic development, and the new concern of Japan with the security of this state, as well as the mixed economic picture of the DPRK during the 1960s, the chances of Communist success had been considerably better at an earlier stage. At the Fifth Party Congress, however, Kim Il-sŏng again made it abundantly clear that the goal of Korean unification under Communist control was to be pursued.

The Fifth KWP Congress opened in P'yŏngyang on November 2, 1970, some nine years after the Fourth Congress. The Mansudae Assembly Hall was filled with 1,734 voting and 137 nonvoting delegates when Kim stepped onto the stage at 9:00 A.M. Interestingly, there were no foreign guests present, because the KWP had sent out word that it wanted only messages, not delegations (presumably, the idea was to avoid facing the embarrassment of further entanglement in the Sino-Soviet dispute). The description of Kim carried by the North Korean media conveys the extremities to which the cult of personality had been carried at this point: "Comrade Kim Il-sŏng, the great leader of the 40 million Korean people [a figure used consistently in recent years], peerless patriot, national hero, ever-victorious, iron-willed brilliant commander, one of the outstanding leaders of the international Communist movement and working-class movement, and general secretary of the Central Committee of our Party." [123]

Kim's major address was delivered on the opening day of the Congress.[124] He began with an admission of problems. The nine years since the Fourth Congress, he confessed, had been "a period of severe trials with very complicated and difficult circumstances prevailing in our revolution and construction." Nevertheless, he added, great victories had been scored on all fronts. First, the Seven-Year Plan had at last been fulfilled. Gross industrial output would be 11.6 times the value of output in 1956, "production of the means of production" 13.3 times as great, and that of consumer goods 9.3 times as great. Industrial production, he continued, had increased on an average of 19.1 percent for the period 1957 to 1970, the

---

123. As reported in the *Foreign Broadcast Information Service Daily Report* (hereafter *FBIS Daily Report*), Nov. 2, 1970, from P'yŏngyang KCNA International Service (in English).

Periodically, during the congress, announcements were made of messages of greeting received from such groups as "the members of the 'Group for the Study of the Works and Revolutionary Activities of Comrade Kim Il-sŏng' of the Asian, African, and Latin American students studying in Czechoslovakia, the members of the 'Group for the Study of the Works of Comrade Kim Il-sŏng' of the Tawai Branch, Aden, and William Aniche and Mchan Tampi, authorized by the 'Group for the Study of the Works of Comrade Kim Il-sŏng' in Berlin." Clearly Kim and the KWP did not intend to be eclipsed by Mao Tse-tung!

124. We have used the English-language text of Kim Il-sŏng's report as carried by P'yŏngyang Domestic Service (in Korean), Nov. 2, 1970, and translated in *FBIS Daily Report*, Nov. 16, 1970, No. 222, Supplement 21, 70 pp. In Korean, see *NS*, Nov. 3, 1970, pp. 1–7.

entire period during which the Five- and Seven-Year Plans were in effect.[125]

A few days later, Kim Il, in his report to the congress, presented some figures for a different time span. The value of industrial output for 1970 would be 3.3 times as great as in 1960, he asserted, with a 3.7-fold increase in "production of the means of production" and a 2.8-fold increase in production of consumer goods. Total industrial production had grown at a rate of 12.8 percent annually over the ten-year period from 1961 to 1970.[126]

While both leaders claimed that the Seven-Year Plan had finally been achieved, there was a noticeable reluctance to provide all of the critical details. Kim Il-sŏng stated that heavy industry had made particularly rapid strides, with the greatest achievement being the creation of a self-sufficient machine-tool industry. Kim presented detailed 1970 statistics relating to electric power (16.5 billion kilowatt hours); coal (27.5 million metric tons); steel (2.2 million metric tons); chemical fertilizer (1.5 million metric tons), and cement (4 million metric tons). If these figures are accurate, they would suggest that the Seven-Year Plan target had been slightly exceeded with respect to coal, but that electric power, steel, chemical fertilizer, and cement production had fallen below the goals set. (Kim Il, however, quoted cement production as 5 million tons, the target figure.)

Moreover, neither leader mentioned a specific figure with respect to grain production, suggesting that performance here fell below the pledges of 6 to 7 million metric tons. Kim Il-sŏng made the following comments:

> Despite certain fluctuations in agricultural production caused by the unusually severe natural calamities which continually hit our country over the past few years, we repeated a good harvest every year, and this year too, we have gathered in a bumper harvest. In our country, the food problem has now been solved completely and the firm basis of grain production has been laid which will make it possible to develop all other domains of the rural economy more speedily.

However, the claim that the food problem had been solved had been made at the time of the 1961 Congress, as was noted earlier, and the only specific figures cited by Kim related to eggs, and to rates of increase in rural electrification, chemicalization, and mechanization.

The only statistic advanced in the field of light industry was Kim Il's assertion that North Korea would produce "400 million meters of various high-quality fabrics" in 1970 (against a target of 500 million meters of textiles in the Seven-Year Plan). Kim Il did claim that major improvements had been made in the general standard of living, citing the recent 31.5 percent wage increase for workers, and the fact that the per-peasant-house-

125. *Ibid.*, p. 2.
126. Kim Il's report, "On the Six Year (1971–1976) Plan for the Development of the National Economy of the DPR," delivered at the Nov. 9 session of the congress, is carried in *NS*, Nov. 5, 1970. See *FBIS Daily Report*, Nov. 10, 1970, reported from P'yŏngyang KCNA International Service (in English), Nov. 10, 1970.

hold distribution of grain had increased 1.8 times between 1961 and 1968, and that of money had doubled in the same period. Meanwhile, according to Kim Il, the prices of daily necessities had been lowered, and reductions made in various service charges. Moreover, benefits amounting to approximately 50 percent of their monetary earnings were granted to peasants, according to Kim, and such benefits to the peasant householder together with food allotments were nearly equal to a worker's wages. He added that substantial gains in health care had contributed to making the average life expectancy over twenty-six years longer than it had been before Liberation.

These figures would indeed seem to represent a substantial improvement in livelihood for the average North Korean. The wage increases, however, were put into effect only in September 1970, and the new goal was only an average monthly wage of 70 wŏn for all workers, technicians, and office employees—certainly not a level approaching prosperity. Kim Il-sŏng moreover, despite earlier propaganda, admitted that the peasants' standard of living was not yet equal to that of the urban workers. As already noted, defectors have generally insisted that living standards did not improve until after 1966, when some improvements did take place. The average North Korean, however, continues to live at an extremely modest level, in part because of the continuing heavy military expenditures.

On the educational front, the claim was made that 3.2 million students were enrolled in the compulsory nine-year technical education program as of 1970, with an additional 200,000 students studying in 129 colleges and universities and nearly 500 higher technical schools. Nearly 400,000 technicians and specialists, he claimed, had been newly trained during the period of the Seven-Year Plan.[127]

When the total economic scene, as described by Kim Il-sŏng and Kim Il, is examined carefully, it can be seen why the tone of their reports, particularly that of the premier, was somewhat restrained, and not as exuberant as in 1961. Despite the purge of the "passivists and conservatives" who suggested that the growth rates of more developed societies naturally declined, North Korean industrial growth had declined during the period of the Seven-Year Plan, averaging 12–13 percent. We may guess that non-industrial productivity did not increase at an average annual rate of more than 3 to 4 percent for the same period at most (one Soviet source, as we shall note, places agricultural gains much lower). Thus, total

127. These figures are from Kim Il's report. According to Kim Il-sŏng, there were currently more than 497,000 engineers, assistant engineers, and specialists in the national economy, or 4.3 times more than in 1960. There are some problems in matching the two sets of figures.

Kim Il-sŏng added that each prefecture (kun) now had more than one higher technical school or higher school, with the major industrial districts all having factory technical schools and factory colleges. Each province (do), moreover, reportedly had an agricultural and medical college, teachers' college, a Communist Party college, and other educational facilities.

economic growth in this period was probably no greater than that taking place in the Republic of Korea. With military expenditures accounting for more than 30 percent of the budget, moreover, the standard of living had to remain low.

The goals of the future were unveiled in the form of the new Six-Year Plan. The term chosen—six years—is highly unusual, and we know that the plan was initially drafted as a Five-Year Plan, with the decision then being made that it could not be achieved in that period of time. The new plan, as outlined by the two men, looked toward an average annual industrial growth of 14 percent, with a priority upon the power and fuel industries, where a bottleneck has clearly existed. In agriculture, the pledge was to increase grain production significantly, so that, by 1976, a production of 7 to 7.5 million metric tons would be reached, 3.5 million of which would be rice. Increased vegetable production was also promised, so that the workers could have vegetables throughout the year, and a rise of marine products to between 1.6 and 1.8 million metric tons, of which 1.3 million would be fish. Similarly, substantial increases in consumer goods were called for, including 500 to 600 million meters of textiles, 10 million pairs of leather shoes, and major increases in processed foods.

Kim Il admitted that one of the reasons why the consumer demands of the working people were not currently being satisfied was the low quality of goods produced, and he promised major improvements over the next six years. National income, he pledged, would expand by 80 percent during the period of the Six-Year Plan. The average monthly wage of factory and office workers would reach 90 wŏn. The monetary income of the average peasant household would top 1,800 wŏn yearly. Prices for consumer goods would be cut by an average of 30 percent, with a better distribution system put into effect. Meanwhile, social and cultural services would increase 1.5 times, and all people would enjoy free education, free medical service, and ample leaves for rest and recuperation. New housing for more than 1 million families would be provided, with the houses being made "more attractive, modern, and useful." In P'yŏngyang, central heating would be introduced, and in the countryside every village and farm would have its own water supply. The production of bicycles would be increased, so that personal transportation would become easier. Finally, efforts would be made to eliminate the seasonal imbalance in the supply of nonstaple foods.

In these very promises, one can sense the low living standards that currently prevail. The promises, moreover, would probably be more exciting if many of them had not been advanced much earlier. It was in the early 1960s, it will be recalled, that the Korean people were promised that after the hard labor involved in meeting the Seven-Year Plan had been completed—by 1967—they would eat rice, wear silk, and live a carefree life. The pledges for 1976 are clearly more modest.

There has been no reduction, however, in the demand that every citizen fulfill his socialist duty. The Ch'ŏllima Movement will continue, and high work quotas will continue to be set. Kim Il acknowledged that strengthening work administration posed "a very urgent problem," and he set forth its dimensions in a straightforward manner:

> There are many cadres who come from peasant and worker families and have very little education among the leading functionaries in state economic organizations and enterprises. They strive to do a good job and are loyal to the Party, but they lack a knowledge of the socialist economy and cannot perform economic guidance and business management properly.
>
> Those who have good educations, on the other hand, lack the ability to analyze the economics of the productive activities in their enterprises, although they are well versed in their particular fields.[128]

One aspect of the problem of "Red versus expert" has rarely been put more succinctly.

Kim Il also called for extensive improvement of industrial techniques, great economies in the use of labor and raw materials, more use of female labor, an end to the waste and misuse of machinery and supplies, and a system of making certain that enough spare parts were on hand in every productive unit to last for more than three months. In these remarks, he signaled some of the problems that had recently beset the industrial sector of the economy.

In the educational field also, wide-scale expansion was pledged. During the period of the Six-Year Plan, more than 600,000 technicians and specialists were to be trained, with the number then working in the national economy to exceed 1 million. Existing institutions of higher schooling and technical training were to be expanded, and new "colleges"—including those devoted to automation, shipbuilding, pomiculture and economics —were to be established. Kim Il also pledged a major increase in factory colleges and higher technical schools, as well as night schools and correspondence courses. The quality of education at all levels, he admitted, needed great improvement. Every student, moreover, should be taught some basic skill. One goal would be to teach all students the basic principles governing the operation of automobiles and tractors so that they could drive when they finished school.

When one looks at the decade of the 1960's from the perspective of economic growth in North Korea, the results appear mixed. We can assume that the figures provided at the Fifth Party Congress are basically accurate, although, as we shall note later, they probably obscure certain deficiencies relating to type of commodity within a given sector, and— on a broader scale—to the quality of production. Thus, we can assume that the overall annual growth rate averaged 8 to 9 percent for the period of the Seven-Year Plan, with industrial growth running at 12 to 13 percent,

128. Kim Il report, *op. cit.*

and other growth, including agriculture, at 3 to 4 percent. While this is high measured against performance elsewhere, during the mid-sixties the regime faced a serious economic crisis. We have already indicated certain problems confronting the government with long-range implications. The attempt to place equal priority on militarization and economic growth produced dislocations of manpower and resources. Further complications were added when the Soviet Union ceased cooperating fully, complications that were felt particularly in the military and heavy industrial fields. In any case, the insistence upon a largely self-reliant economic system was bound to create problems and demand greater sacrifices. Intense economic nationalism exacts its price.

In addition, with more than 30 percent of the national budget going to the military sector, improvements in living standards could only be limited. Promises long held out to the ordinary North Korean citizen had therefore to be reduced or postponed. Now, the schedule of promises has been adjusted and reestablished, with the next target date being 1976. Meanwhile, even in the words of Kim Il-sŏng, one senses that the atmosphere of euphoria associated with the Fourth Party Congress was not present at the Fifth Congress. On the economic front, problems were acknowledged in near-proportion to progress.

The ordinary North Korean certainly lives better today than he did before 1966, and he is guaranteed a minimal livelihood. In this latter respect, indeed, the North Korean is currently better off than the lowest group of his South Korean counterparts. But he is very poor, despite the extraordinary work schedule he performs, and to a considerable extent this is the product of the heavy allocation of human and material resources to the cause of state power.[129]

What factors connected with domestic politics were revealed at the Fifth Congress? Here, Kim Il-sŏng and his followers evidenced greater confidence. "Now we can say," Kim asserted, "that flunkeyism, national nihilism and dogmatism as ideological trends have been eliminated in the main from among our Party members and people. The establishment of *chuch'e* in ideology is a great victory in the realm of the ideological revo-

---

129. Twice during this lengthy speech, Kim Il-sŏng confirmed this fact in essence when he said: "The national defense capabilities we have now have been achieved at a very big cost. Frankly speaking, our national defense expenditures, as compared with the small size of the country and its population, have proven to be too great a burden. If even a single, small portion of it had been allocated to economic construction, our people's economy would have developed even faster and our people's living standards would have improved to a much higher level.

"However, the situation did not permit us to do so. We could not afford to give up the basic interests of the revolution for the sake of brief comfort, and we did not want to become country-ruining traitors." Kim Il-sŏng report, *op. cit.*, p. 15. For a similar statement, see *ibid.*, p. 37. Here, Kim calls upon his people to shun "luxury and extravagance," to lead "a frugal life befitting a people in the era of revolution."

lution that has freed our people from the shackles of obsolete ideas detrimental to their consciousness of national independence." [130]

Kim's primary concern, reflecting the purge of late 1968, seemed to be with the army. The Party, he said, had tirelessly conducted political-ideological education among the officers and men of the People's Army, guarding against the tendency in the army to neglect such work and cling only to military-technical affairs. Moreover, the entire people had been armed, and the whole country fortified. "In our country, everyone knows how to fire a gun and carries a gun with him."

On other political issues, Kim's words had an old, familiar ring. The ideological revolution had to take precedence over all other work, since this was the struggle to eliminate capitalism from the domain even of man's consciousness. All people, and especially the younger generation who would grasp the mantle of the revolution in the future, had to be taught to despise individualism and egotism and to love collectivism and organization. They had to be indoctrinated in socialist patriotism and love of the socialist fatherland, and in hatred of the enemy, so that they would "battle staunchly at any time to force the US imperialists out of South Korea and carry the revolutionary cause of national unification through to the end." To accomplish these goals, "revolutionary organizational life" had to be strengthened.

> Organizational life is a furnace for ideological training and a school for revolutionary education. . . . All people should be brought to take an active part in organizational life, observe organizational discipline of their own accord, faithfully carry out what is entrusted and assigned to them by their organizations, live under the guidance and control of their organizations and constantly receive revolutionary education.[131]

Perhaps, however, it was less in the words of Kim Il-sŏng and more in the actions at the close of the Fifth Party Congress that one can discern basic political trends. Eleven people emerged as full members of the new Political Committee, and four men were elected as alternate members.[132]

130. *Ibid.,* p. 56. What is Kim's latest definition of *chuch'e?* "In a nutshell," *chuch'e* means "having the attitude of master toward revolution and construction in one's own country. This means holding fast to an independent position, refraining from dependence upon others and using your own brains, believing your own strength and displaying the revolutionary spirit of self-reliance, and thus solving your own problems for yourself on your own responsibility under all circumstances. It means adhering to the creative position of opposing dogmatism and applying the universal principles of Marxism-Leninism and the experiences of other countries to suit the historical conditions and national peculiarities of your own country" (p. 55).

131. *Ibid.,* p. 33.

132. The members of the Political Committee selected on Nov. 13, 1970, at the conclusion of the Fifth Congress were Kim Il-sŏng, Ch'oe Yong-gŏn, Kim Il, Pak Sŏng-ch'ŏl, Ch'oe Hyŏn, Kim Yŏng-ju, O Chin-u, Kim Tong-gyu, Sŏ Ch'ŏl, Kim Chung-rin, and Han Ik-su—full members; Hyŏn Mu-gwang, Chŏng Chun-t'aek, Yang Hyŏng-sŏp, and Kim Man-gŭm—alternate members, in the order given.

The basic functions of these men (excluding Kim Il-sŏng) are as follows: Ch'oe,

Who were the top fifteen as the new era began? Three basic factors can be noted in connection with the new Political Committee. First, it has become a supreme reflection of Kim Il-sŏng's absolute authority. Of the eleven full members, *all* have long been considered in Kim Il-sŏng's personal circle, and ten (all except Kim Chung-rin) appear to have fought in Manchuria in the 1930s as guerrilla fighters against the Japanese, most of them in Kim's band. This is also true of two of the four alternate Political Committee members. Second, the military component of the new Political Committee is sharply reduced from the 1966–68 period. Perhaps Kim Il-sŏng observed events in China closely. The key military figures are now Ch'oe Hyŏn and O Chin-u, both of them old guerrilla fighters under Kim, and as trusted as any individuals with whom he has had contact over the past thirty years. And they, together with Han Ik-su, another member of Kim's old guerrilla unit, are now the *only* professional military men still in active service to sit on the Political Committee. (Sŏ Ch'ŏl holds the rank of general but, like others of a similar category, he has long been separated from a military command post.) Kim Kwang-hyŏp, who was previously number four on that committee, has been removed from the roster, and his fate is currently unknown. Has he joined Kim Ch'ang-bong, Hŏ Pong-hak, and Ch'oe Kwang in oblivion? If the top of the Party roster is any indication, the current political situation in North Korea is significantly different from that in China, at least prior to the purge of Lin Piao. One should be cautious, however, in generalizing too broadly from data pertaining only to the topmost echelon of the Party, as we shall indicate at a later point.

In addition, some figures centrally concerned with internal security and with policies directed toward South Korea are also missing from the new Political Committee. As noted earlier, Yi Hyo-sun and Pak Yong-guk fell in 1967 (they had been connected with the External Liaison Department of the Party). It now appears that Chŏng Kyŏng-bok, made vice-

---

ceremonial figure; Kim Il, chief administrative official and economic overseer; Pak Sŏng-ch'ŏl, foreign affairs; Ch'oe Hyŏn, top military man; Kim Yŏng-ju, Party functionary; O Chin-u, second ranking military man; Kim Tong-gyu, Party functionary (secretary, P'yŏngyang Party Committee); Sŏ Ch'ŏl, foreign affairs; Kim Chung-rin, South Korean affairs (?); and Han Ik-su, military man. It will thus be noted that among the full members of the Political Committee, two can be accounted general administrators, with three more second-line Party functionaries; three, professional military men; two, foreign affairs; and one (Ch'oe Yong-gŏn) the chief ceremonial figure of the regime at present.

Among the alternate members, three can be considered economic administrators, one a specialist in education and ideology (Yang Hyŏng-sŏp).

The average age of the nine (of eleven) full members of the Political Committee for whom data is available is 59.8 years; there appears to be little, if any, difference here insofar as the alternate members are concerned, although we have firm data on only one of them. The top political elite of North Korea, thus, are no longer young, although they are not as old as their counterparts in China at present. For other data, see Chapter IX,

director of the Party's South Korea bureau in April 1967, suffered the same fate at some point prior to the Fifth Congress. (Kim Chung-rin is now the Political Committee member most closely connected with South Korean affairs, having been director of the South Korea Bureau since April 1967, when Chŏng Kyŏng-bok was appointed). Kim Ik-sŏn, Yi Yŏng-ho, and Sŏk San—in addition to various other assignments—had each been deeply involved at one point or another in internal security matters. Thus, it would appear that Kim Il-sŏng wants neither a Zhukov (read Lin Piao) nor a Beria (read K'ang Sheng) at his right hand at this point—unless Ch'oe Hyŏn is another Lin Piao, a dubious equation.

On the other hand, Kim is keeping certain economic administrators at the second echelon of Party power. Three of the four alternate members of the Political Committee fit this category, with one (Hyŏn Mu-gwang) associated with heavy industry, a second (Chŏng Chun-t'aek) with light industry, and a third (Kim Man-gŭm) with agriculture. Hyŏn, moreover, was once demoted, suggesting that a few individuals can be rewarded after being punished. Yang Hyŏng-sŏp, formerly head of the Central Party School and minister of Higher Education, is the only "ideologue" presently in the upper echelons except for Kim Il-sŏng.

Finally, Kim Il-sŏng's younger brother, Kim Yŏng-ju, has progressively advanced, now ranking sixth although he is believed to be only 48–50 years of age. Quite possibly, he is now the most powerful man in North Korea next to Kim Il-sŏng himself.

As one looks at the top roster, the predominance of the old guerrillas from Manchuria, the men of Kim's most intimate circle, stands out. Most of them have long ceased to be active military men. They are administrators and generalists. Meanwhile, a second echelon of Party functionaries has begun to emerge, with Kim's younger brother clearly at their head. The professional military, at least for the moment, are decidedly subordinate within the top two Party echelons, which are full and alternate membership of the Political Committee.

Nine secretaries were chosen under Secretary-General Kim Il-sŏng to form the Secretariat. These were Ch'oe Yong-gŏn, Kim Il, Kim Yŏng-ju, O Chin-u, Kim Tong-gyu, Kim Chung-rin, Han Ik-su, Hyŏn Mu-gwang, and Yang Hyŏng-sŏp. As will be noted, each of these men was a full or alternate member of the Political Committee. The new Central Committee of the Fifth Congress consisted of 117 full and 55 alternate members. This total of 172 members represented a considerable expansion over the 135 members of the previous Central Committee.

Equally significant, an extraordinarily high turnover continued to take place among the top Party elite, despite the fact that Kim Il-sŏng himself had faced no serious challenges for more than a decade. Fifty-four (65 percent) of the 85 Fourth Central Committee members are not among the

117 members of the Fifth Central Committee, and among these are 18 from the ranking 30 leaders of 1961. In addition to those already mentioned as having been purged or having disappeared from view, Pak Chŏng-ae, Chŏng Il-yong, Yi Chong-ok, and Kim Ik-sŏn are missing. The full members of the Fifth Central Committee consist of 31 full Fourth Central Committee members, 15 alternate Fourth Central Committee members, and 71 new members. Of the 55 alternate Fifth Central Committee members, 48 (94 percent) are totally new, with only 7 having been on the Fourth Central Committee. This is truly a remarkable turnover.

It would appear that only 4 of the 117 full Fifth Central Committee members are female, with an additional 5 female members among the 55 alternates. With Pak Chŏng-ae gone, there is not a single woman of real political significance in her own right. The top ranking female is Hwang Sun-hui, an associate of Kim's since Manchuria guerrilla days, who now serves as director of the Korean Revolutionary Museum. Next comes Kim Sŏng-ae, Kim Il-sŏng's wife, vice chairman, Democratic Women's League (Elected chairman in October 1971); the wives of both Kim Il and Ch'oe Yong-gŏn are among the alternate members.

Nepotism does not stop with wives. In addition to his wife and younger brother, Kim Il-sŏng has also made his cousin's husband (Hŏ Tam) minister of Foreign Affairs, with twenty-ninth rank on the Fifth Central Committee. Ch'oe Yong-gŏn's cousin, Ch'oe Chong-gŏn, is director of the General Political Bureau of the Air Force, and holds an alternate membership.

The prominence of the old Manchuria guerrilla group in the Fifth Central Committee is pronounced. Between 35 and 40 of the full Fifth Central Committee members have such a background, and almost all of them occupy ranks in the fiftieth centile or above. Indeed, at least 34 (65 percent) of the top 53 members come from such a background. Of equal importance is the fact that at least 27 members of this same group are either generals on active duty or currently fulfill such important military functions as serving on the Military Affairs Committee of the Party, and hold the rank of general or marshal. (The latter group would consist of men like Kim Il-sŏng, Ch'oe Yong-gŏn, Kim Il, and Pak Sŏng-ch'ŏl.) Those who could be considered professional military men comprise close to 50 percent of the upper echelon of the Fifth Central Committee membership. Thus, if this group has slipped at the topmost (Political Committee) level, it remains supremely important at the level just below.

Other notable features of the Fifth Central Committee include the fact that at least 20 (17.1 percent) have had higher education in the Soviet Union or Eastern Europe since 1945 (this reflects an earlier era when training was still sought from the Soviet bloc). A small but important number of members also come from a background of foreign service or international liaison work, including Pak Sŏng-ch'ŏl, Kim Tong-gyu, Sŏ Ch'ŏl, Han Ik-su, and Hŏ Tam. Further analysis is provided in chapter IX.

Meanwhile, the following generalizations are in order here. First, in a relatively tranquil decade, the turnover within the top political elite of North Korea has nevertheless been amazingly high. Over two-thirds of the Party elite have been purged, died, or faded from the scene in the years between 1961 and 1970. Second, the ironlike control of Kim Il-sŏng over the Party has never been more clearly demonstrated than in the Fifth Central Committee, with at least one-third of its members old cronies whose personal acquaintanceship extends back thirty-five years, and with new signs of nepotism, including at least three relatives serving as full Central Committee members. The Party is totally dominated by one man —and through that one man, by a combination of old guerrillas and at least one key family member, Kim Yŏng-ju.

A third point, however, should be quickly added. Fuller data will probably reveal that younger people—men and women whose total political experience has occurred during the Kim era and who are not always personally known to Kim—are now beginning to come into the Central Committee in larger numbers, especially at the lower end of the rankings. Many younger (40–50), relatively unknown men are to be found on the new roster, men who have come up either through provincial Party experience or from professional military life. Fourth, the professional military remain a very important element within the Party, at least as important as any other single occupational or socioeconomic group.

Other points of significance can be advanced. The Party high command remains almost exclusively a male preserve. Incomplete data would suggest that the average age of the more senior, upper-ranking members of the Fifth Central Committee is about 60, and that of the younger members about 50. The latter, in most cases, have had more formal education, and a career pattern that commenced with local or regional service prior to movement to the Central Party or, in the case of the military men, encompassed gradual promotions from lower ranks rather than immediate appointment as general. In these respects, and in others, a changing of the guard is at hand, despite the continued and formidable presence of the Leader.

It remains to note briefly the assessment made by Kim Il-sŏng and others at the Fifth Congress of the international situation and its implications for DPRK foreign policy. All speakers continued to emphasize the immediate threat of war as a result of "American imperialist aggression" and the need for continuing the militarization program. Said Kim Il-sŏng: "Comrades, the situation in our country still remains tense and strained. The US imperialists continue to step up their aggressive maneuvers, and their schemes to touch off a new war are becoming more and more undisguised. . . . In our country, the threat of war is growing bigger with every passing day." And how was this threat to be met?

> To cope with the situation thus created, we must further strengthen our national defense capabilities while simultaneously accelerating socialist construction to the maximum. We should continue to hold fast to the line already put forth by the Party, the line of arming the entire people, turning the whole country into a fortress, converting the whole army into a cadre army, and modernizing the whole army, and we should implement more thoroughly the principle of self-defense in national defense.[133]

As might have been expected, Kim linked "the American problem" directly with the unification issue, thereby revealing the true nature of his concern. How was the south to be "liberated" under Communist aegis? The earlier formula was explicitly repeated. South Korean "revolutionaries" should actively advance the liberation movement by combining all forms of struggle—legal, semilegal, and illegal, violent and nonviolent, small and large. The important task was to mount mass struggles to oppose "the colonial rule" of the United States and the "Fascist tyranny" of the Pak government.

It was essential that the Pak government be overthrown, according to Kim. "We have made it clear time and again that if democratic personages with a national conscience come to power in South Korea and demand the withdrawal of U.S. troops, release of political prisoners and guarantee of democratic freedom, then we are ready to hold negotiations with them on the question of the peaceful unification of the Fatherland at any time and at any place." [134] The basic formula remained: Overthrow the Pak regime, drive the Americans out, establish a "peace-loving, neutralist" regime, reduce the two armies to 100,000 men or less, conclude a nonaggression pact, establish economic and cultural intercourse, and then build a "unified democratic government" through "free North-South elections," or establish a confederation as a transitional step.

The proposals of President Pak Chŏng-hi for peaceful unification were rejected out of hand. "The South Korean puppets," exclaimed Kim, "prattle about 'unification by prevailing over Communism.' " These were "wild day-dreams." Communist ideas had "firmly gripped the hearts of the

---

133. Kim Il-sŏng report, *op. cit.,* p. 34. Kim continued: "In order to reinforce the defense power of the nation, the whole Party and the entire people also should buckle down to a further acceleration of war preparations. All the Party members and working people should combat indolence and slackness and always maintain a sharp revolutionary vigilance, keeping themselves alert and ready so that they can fight to repulse the enemy without the slightest flurry, no matter when he may launch a surprise attack. We must never be captivated by a pacifist mood and, in particular, must strictly guard against the revisionist ideological trend of war phobia, to prevent it from infiltrating into our ranks," *Ibid.,* p. 36.

134. *Ibid.,* p. 46.

people," and the concept of a non-Communist Korea was "the jargon of a stupid person." Thus, the DPRK's position on unification remained essentially that of the DRV's Vietnam formula: a Marxist-Leninist Party, proclaimed to be growing in strength daily, would blaze the trail in the south by toppling the present government, with the north serving as an "impregnable rear base." Kim Il-sŏng, according to the Party line, was already "the Leader of the 40 million Korean people, the sun in their hearts." It remained only to translate popular desires into political and legal fact.

In the broader global arena, Kim admitted that the situation remained "very complicated." Only by resolutely maintaining chuch'e in Korean foreign policy could "imperialist machinations" and "revisionist ideological trends" be resisted. And Kim made it clear that revisionism continued to be the central problem for the international Communist movement. In a lengthy passage, he set forth the evils of revisionism and, in so doing, emphasized the distance between North Korea and the Soviet Union on critical issues of ideology and foreign policy.[135] On the other hand, the absence of any attack upon "dogmatism" signaled the fact that, once again, North Korea had veered in the direction of Peking. The main reasons, no doubt, were her immediate interest in undermining the American and Japanese positions in Asia and in obtaining unstinting support for her unification campaign.

Thus, other Parties were warned against having "any illusions" concerning "Japanese reactionary ruling circles." To get on intimate terms with the present Japanese government, asserted Kim, was tantamount to increasing the risks of war in Asia and encouraging Japanese expansion overseas. (Russians, take note!) Asia, Kim argued, was the central battle-

135. The following passage from Kim's report is worthy of quotation at some length: "Revisionism is a trend of the counter-revolutionary, opportunist ideology aimed at emasculating the revolutionary quintessence of Marxism-Leninism. The greatest harm of revisionism lies in denying the leadership of the Marxist-Leninist Party and the dictatorship of the proletariat, opposing the class struggle, obscuring the line of demarcation between friend and foe, yielding to U.S. imperialism, scared by its policy of nuclear blackmail, casting sheep's eyes at the imperialists while paying lip-service to an anti-imperialist position, giving up the struggle against imperialism and compromising with it, disarming people ideologically by spreading war phobia, bourgeois pacifistic ideas and illusions about imperialism and reaction, and in abhorring and hindering the revolution of the oppressed peoples.

"The cancer of revisionism lies also in objecting to revolutionary organizational discipline and advocating bourgeoise liberalism, in encouraging selfishness and making people indolent, dissolute and afraid of work. Revisionism is, in the final analysis, a dangerous idea that undermines socialism and revives capitalism. Therefore, we can never neglect the struggle against revisionism among Party members and working people. If a Marxist-Leninist Party does not stage a struggle against revisionism but tolerates the revisionist ideological trend in itself even to the slightest degree, such a Party cannot become a fighting Party, a militant revolutionary Party, and will be reduced to an impotent petty-bourgeois Party in the long run." *Ibid.,* p. 66.

front against imperialism today, and the United States the central foe. It was thus essential to support both the Japanese and American "progressives" in their struggle for revolution at home.[136] Through union with all revolutionaries, it would be possible to "tear the arms and legs off U.S. imperialism and behead it in all parts of the world." [137] In a final section, Kim Il-sŏng summarized the Party's chief mission as follows:

> The basic task for our Party at the present stage is to step up socialist construction energetically in the northern half of the Republic and support the South Korean people to accomplish the South Korea revolution and

136. This policy has led to a conspicuous wooing of the Black Panther party and assorted white "radicals" in addition to the American Communist Party. Eldridge Cleaver has now made several trips to North Korea, the most recent in the fall of 1970, and his wife traveled there to have her second child. Panther publications have carried Korean Communist materials, as noted earlier, and generally substituted P'yŏngyang for an earlier infatuation with Havana—with Cuba now regarded as "racist." A tiny but vocal group of white American "radicals" has also taken up the cause of North Korea, dutifully proclaiming Kim's virtues and lauding the "pure revolutionary qualities" of the DPRK. Some of them have also visited North Korea as state guests.

Kim has directed special attention recently to the Japanese Socialist Party as well as the JCP, and with great success. The Japanese Socialists, who cannot be considered "neutral" in foreign policy matters at present, sent a top-level delegation to P'yŏngyang in August 1970, and signed a joint communiqué at the conclusion of their visit. Among other matters, the communique spoke of reaching "a unanimity of views" on all questions discussed, including the struggle against "the U.S. imperialists" and against "the revival of Japanese militarism." (P'yŏngyang, Sept. 3, 1970, KCNA dispatch.)

137. *Ibid.,* p. 53. Recent evidence suggests that the DPRK may have aspired to succeed, or supplement, the Chinese People's Republic as a leading training center for global revolutionaries. Arrests in Mexico provided the first concrete evidence. According to the Mexican government, some fifty young Mexicans visited P'yŏngyang, where they were given training, literature, and substantial funds for the purpose of recruitment of members in preparation for guerrilla activities.

Shortly thereafter, the government of Ceylon ordered the North Korean Embassy in Colombo closed and its personnel ousted from the country, accusing the North Koreans of complicity in the insurgent activities in Ceylon which exploded in the spring of 1971. The DPRK representatives were charged with having provided funds, advice on the making of bombs, training in guerrilla warfare, and quantities of literature to the young terrorists.

Other sources claim that some 1,500–2,000 young foreign revolutionaries, from over twenty countries, have been "trained" in North Korea in recent years. These developments make a remark attributed to Eldridge Cleaver more understandable. He is reported to have said, "The Democratic People's Republic of Korea has the most revolutionary Party in the world today."

More recently, however, the events beginning with the invitation to the American ping-pong players by Peking, and including the DPRK acceptance of the ROK invitation for a meeting of Red Cross representatives, shocked Cleaver. In tones of sorrow mixed with anger, he publicly lamented the lapse of revolutionary ardor on the part of such Parties as the CCP and the KWP, suggesting that true revolutionaries might now be on their own.

attain the unification of the Fatherland. Our efforts to strengthen the
Party organizationally and ideologically are, after all, aimed at increasing
the fighting power of the Party and successfully carrying out this revolutionary task lying before us.[138]

In the Aftermath of the 5th Congress

In the year following the Fifth Party Congress, domestic issues took
a secondary position to certain dramatic developments on the international
arena, and with respect to North-South relations. A new and potentially
far-reaching series of events began to unfold in the spring of 1971, centering upon Sino-American relations. First, Peking extended an invitation to
visit China to an American ping-pong team while it was in Japan, and
that visit took place in April, amid clear indications that it was a thoroughly considered, carefully planned move on the part of the Chinese
Communist leaders. Three months later, on July 15, President Nixon
announced to a startled world that in the course of a secret series of meetings between Dr. Henry Kissinger and Premier Chou En-lai in the Chinese
capital, an invitation had been extended to him to visit Peking and that he
was accepting with pleasure.

Subsequent events suggested that a wide range of considerations
motivated the leaders of the Chinese People's Republic in their favorable
response to the public and private overtures of the Nixon administration.
A deep Chinese concern over Soviet attitudes and policies was a central
factor. Sino-Soviet relations had reached an all-time low point in 1969,
the threat of war being openly voiced. Chou En-lai continued to refer to
the military danger "from the northwest" two years later, and the construction of air-raid shelters and other defense preparations in China's
major cities added credence to the premier's words. In 1971, the cleavage
between the Chinese People's Republic and the USSR seemed as deep and
difficult to bridge as ever. It was not illogical, therefore, for Peking to
end its international isolation and to seek greater flexibility vis-à-vis the
West, including that more distant superpower, the United States.

Other factors, however, also contributed to the shift in Chinese foreign policy. Peking evidenced a great fear of the reestablishment of "Japanese militarism" and a determination to prevent Japan from playing "the
American role" in Asia, after the United States itself had assumed a lower
posture. Indeed, in mid-1971, Chou En-lai told a Yugoslav correspondent
that American imperialism was now "in the greatest danger," both from
within and from without, and hence it was precisely the appropriate time
to "compel the United States to accept the demands of the Asian people."
Chou continued by asserting that it would take time for Japanese militarism
to be revitalized, or for the various anti-Communist elements in Southeast

138. *Ibid.*, p. 67.

Asia to be equipped for military operations on their own, and that these dangers could be nipped in the bud by prompt action.[139]

In making these latter statements, the Chinese premier was undoubtedly speaking to "leftist" elements within China as well as to Peking's allies—those assorted Parties and revolutionary movements that might regard the new Chinese policies as a betrayal of the international revolutionary cause. Was P'yŏngyang deeply disturbed by Peking's moves, or did she regard them as essentially tactical, signifying no basic changes in earlier "hard-line" policies? At this point, no certain answer can be given to this crucial question. For several weeks after the Nixon announcement, no public statements whatsoever were forthcoming from Kim Il-sŏng or others. Not until August was an official interpretation finally provided: the Nixon trip to Peking was "not the march of a victor but the trip of a defeated." [140] The lengthy effort to isolate and blockade the People's Republic of China had ended in total failure, as even "the chieftain of American imperialism" now had to admit. With its ventures into Indochina, South Korea, and Taiwan also bankrupt, the US had no choice except to recognize the power of the great Chinese People's Republic. No force, however, could destroy the friendship and solidarity "sealed in blood" between the peoples of Korea and China.[141]

Was P'yŏngyang confident that it would not be sold out by yet another round of superpower diplomacy? Certainly Peking went to major lengths to reassure the North Koreans that its attitude on crucial issues involving them and other Asian Communists had not changed and would remain constant. In the month of August, no less than three substantial North Korean delegations visited Peking. An economic delegation headed by Vice-

139. The interview between Chou En-lai and Dara Janekovic, editor of *Vjesnik* of Zagreb, was carried by Belgrade Tanjug International Service in English on Aug. 26, 1971, as reported by *FBIS,* Aug. 30, 1971, No. 168, No. 1, pp. A1–2.

140. See the *NS* editorial of August 9, 1971. This editorial, incidentally, was immediately published in China without comment, the first commentary to be published by the Chinese on the projected Nixon trip either from foreign or domestic sources after a brief announcement about the visit published on July 16 in the Peking *Jen-min Jih-pao.* It might signify either Chinese approval of the editorial or solicitude for P'yŏngyang's feelings and views—or both.

It should be noted that a high-level DPRK delegation was visiting China at the time of the first announcement of Nixon's visit. The public purpose of the delegation's visit was to commemorate the tenth anniversary of the signing of the Sino-Korean Treaty of Friendship, Cooperation, and Mutual Assistance. The delegation, headed by Kim Chung-rin, KWP Politburo member and reportedly the man in charge of South Korean "liaison" activities on behalf of the Party, included Kim Man-gŭm, vice-premier and alternate Politburo member, as well as a number of other high-ranking Party and military officials. Li Hsien-nien, vice-premier of the CPR and a CCP Politburo member, headed a comparable Chinese delegation visiting North Korea for the same stated purpose.

141. *Ibid.*

Premier Chŏng Chun-t'aek came first, and took home with it a new agreement on economic cooperation between the CPR and the DPRK. A delegation of Korean journalists followed, led by the director of the Korean Central News Agency, Kim Sŏng-gŏl. The month was climaxed by the visit of a high-level North Korean military delegation headed by KPA Chief of Staff and Politburo member O Chin-u, and including Lieutenant-General O Kŭk-ryŏl, commander of the North Korean air force.

At a banquet given by Huang Yung-sheng, PLA chief of staff and then one of the most prominent leaders of the CPR, the host reiterated certain basic pledges that Peking had earlier given the North Koreans.[142] First, the Korean People's Army was praised for dealing "telling blows" to the "US-puppet reactionaries," with the assurance that every achievement of the KPA was viewed by the PLA as akin to an achievement of its own. Huang then admitted that "great division and great reorganization prevailed throughout the world," but he interpreted the situation—as usual —as developing favorably for all revolutionaries and unfavorably for "US imperialism and its lackeys." The US was still "hanging on" in Indochina, "forcibly occupying" South Korea, and also "China's territory, Taiwan Province," and "Japanese militarism" had "stretched its claws to South Korea" and was "wildly attempting to lay its hands on Taiwan Province." But Huang indicated that none of these ventures would succeed, and he praised the Korean people for their "principled stand" on all of these issues. He asserted China's complete support for the DPRK position on unification and on other matters.

O Chin-u's response was equally effusive. He praised the PLA for its active role in the Great Proletarian Cultural Revolution, and noted that the "international status and prestige" of the CPR was rapidly rising. Even "the allies and vassal countries" of the US had gradually raised the banners of opposition to the American policy of hostility toward China. Indeed, quoting Kim Il-sŏng, O asserted that recent developments proved that "the US imperialists have at last succumbed to the pressure of the mighty anti-imperialist revolutionary forces of the world," leading to a "tremendous victory" for both the Chinese and all revolutionaries.

At the same time, however, O cautioned that the US threat should not be underestimated. Applying the technique of "using Asians to fight Asians," the US was "directing the spearhead of its aggression against Asia." The Japanese, moreover, were willing accomplices, "itching for action." O ended with the assertion that while the US and Japanese "aggressors" would "inevitably meet with ignominious doom," the situation demanded that the revolutionary people of Korea, China, and the rest of Asia "further consolidate their militant unity." So long as a united front

142. The full text of Huang Yung-sheng's speech was carried by Peking NCNA International Service in English, Aug. 18, 1971, as reported by *FBIS*, Aug. 19, 1971, No. 161, Vol. I, pp. A3–A6.

were built and joint action against "US imperialism" were taken, victory for the common cause was ensured.[143]

Undoubtedly, hours of private discussions took place during this period between Chinese and North Korean representatives, with Peking seeking to reassure the Koreans of their fidelity and determination, and almost certainly, to persuade P'yŏngyang to pursue similar tactics.

There was a familiar ring to the North Korean public pronouncements at this point. One recalls similar statements directed toward Premier Khrushchev in the 1961–62 period: praise mixed with a strong admonition to treat "US imperialism" with the utmost seriousness and severity.[144] At the same time, whatever the course of future international relations, P'yŏngyang must regard the present era with uncertainty and some trepidation, given the recent history of her relations with both Moscow and Peking. "Big power diplomacy," Communist or non-Communist, evokes unpleasant images. This was one reason why Washington and Peking publicly announced that they would restrict discussions during President Nixon's visit to matters concerned with their bilateral relations.[145]

143. The full text of O Chin-u's speech was also carried by NCNA International Service, and appears in *ibid.*, A6–A10.

144. In an interview with Gotō Motoo, managing editor of *Asahi Shimbun,* on Sept. 25, 1971, Kim Il-sŏng reiterated and elaborated upon earlier official views of Washington-Peking moves. The United States, he asserted, had come to its new China policy from necessity and weakness. Yet there was a hint of disapproval in Kim's words when he suggested that the US should not be let off the hook.

The premier indicated that he had little faith in a long-term detente between Communists and non-Communists, but he implied that a change in tactics at this point might have merit. In excoriating terms, he compared American policies with those of Hitler—signing treaties with opponents before reaching out in an effort to smash them. However, Kim firmly asserted that China was not abandoning her position "as a socialist nation," and he indicated that the DPRK had no intention of running counter to the prevailing trend, that of "easing tensions." *Asahi Evening News* (in English), Sept. 28, 1971, p. 4.

145. Under the sympathetic questioning of Mr. Gotō, Kim expanded upon his views of the international scene (*ibid.*). North Korea's policy toward the United States would be determined by the American attitude toward the Korean issue, not by Sino-American agreements, he insisted, thereby strongly asserting the thesis that the DPRK had an independent foreign policy. The most important requirement, Kim stated, was total US withdrawal from South Korea. He indicated that he might favor an international meeting on the Korean question; and by asserting firmly that the DPRK was respecting the UN Charter, he left the suggestion that North Korea might now be aiming at UN membership, especially since changes were occurring in that body and it would no longer be "dominated" by the United States.

On matters within the Communist world, Kim spoke circumspectly, keeping that part of the interview short. He stated that he could say "with conviction" that war between the USSR and the CPR would not ensue. But in discussing the importance of ideology, Kim admitted that, even among socialist nations, there were countries that had "deteriorated ideologically," yet another indication of the fact that Kim and the Russians continued to be on different wave-lengths. The premier went on to state that the Party was considering the construction of a new socialist culture "suited to

Nevertheless, the most recent diplomatic moves of North Korea clearly mirror the latest patterns of Chinese diplomacy. The new tactics emanating from Peking appear to have impressed Kim Il-sŏng. It is likely that during the lengthy discussions between key Chinese and North Korean officials commencing in mid-1971, mutually agreed on, coordinated approaches were effected. Indeed, signals indicating that the time was ripe for tackling the Korean problem anew were given Americans by no less a man than Chou En-lai shortly thereafter.

In the international arena, P'yŏngyang's most recent emphasis has been on united front policies and people-to-people diplomacy in an effort to outflank hostile governments and end DPRK isolation. Nowhere is this new policy more dramatically revealed than with respect to Japan. Since the beginning of 1972, an intensified North Korean campaign has been launched to use a direct approach to various Japanese as individuals and as representatives of important interest groups, coupled with an intensive public relations campaign. The aim is to break down past Japanese official policies and expand Japan-DPRK relations without sacrificing any basic North Korean positions.

Thus, P'yŏngyang hailed the creation of a Dietmen's League for the Promotion of Japan-Korea Friendship, a group claiming to have a roster of 234 upper and lower house members, with Kuno Chuji, a Liberal Democratic Party man, as provisional chairman. In late January 1972, a delegation from this group headed by Kuno visited North Korea, and on January 23, a trade agreement was signed by this group and a North Korean Committee for the Promotion of International Trade. An economic link similar in type to that existing between the Chinese People's Republic and Japan had been fashioned. A month later, moreover, it was announced that a Korea-Japan Export and Import Corporation would soon be established to facilitate trade and economic intercourse.

The visit of the Dietmen who were accompanied by a large retinue

---

young people," in order to prevent "the decayed culture of Western Europe" from invading the nation. The suggestion was that despite policies of intense isolation and continuous indoctrination combined with major cultural differences, Kim was apprehensive lest modern Western culture (possibly via South Korea) contaminate North Korean youth.

On Japan, Kim signaled once again the possibility of a North Korean diplomatic offensive in the Chinese mold, with emphasis upon people-to-people diplomacy. Proclaiming that future official relations between the DPRK and Japan depended not just on a change of cabinet but also on a change in governmental attitudes and policies, he noted a major difference between the people of Japan and the "reactionary elements" in power. Because the people were now different than they had been in the pre-1945 era, he continued, Japanese militarism was not necessarily going to develop. Even if it did, the people could prevent the emergence of a "war policy." Kim held out the prospect of trade once political differences were resolved, and asserted that meanwhile, North Korea would welcome visits from conservatives, including Liberal Democratic Party members as well as others.

of newspaper, radio and television reporters, clearly carried with it the imagery of the forthcoming Nixon trip to China. In addition, in February the North Koreans had their Olympic team visit with such sympathetic politicians as Governor Minobe Ryōkichi of Tokyo, various top figures of the media, and other prominent Japanese. This was ping-pong diplomacy, North Korean style.

Having given one important interview to Gotō of *Asahi Shimbun,* Kim Il-sŏng utilized the Japanese media again in late January to reiterate and amplify his earlier remarks. On this occasion, he provided a written response to a series of questions submitted by the staff of *Yomiuri Shimbun.*[146] The poor relations between Japan and (North) Korea, Kim asserted, represented "a very abnormal situation," one entirely the responsibility of the Japanese government. We have always wanted close ties, he stated. What was required? The Japanese government should abandon its hostile policies toward the Democratic People's Republic of Korea; abrogate the South Korea-Japan treaty; stop "reinvading" South Korea; and "renounce the foolish act of trying to make Koreans fight Koreans by instigating the South Korean puppets."

Fortunately, in Kim's view, "an extensive campaign" had gotten underway among the Japanese people and progressive circles for the establishment of good-neighbor relations. "If the Korean and Japanese people jointly struggle," he asserted, "diplomatic relations between our two countries will be possible. Meanwhile, we are ready to have more visits of personages as far as possible and to undertake wide-scale trade and intercourse in the economic and cultural fields."

At the same time, Kim made it clear that North Korea intended to abandon none of her basic positions on current issues. The struggle, for example, to enable Koreans living in Japan to have a "national education" taught in the Korean language, by (Communist) Koreans, funded from P'yŏngyang, and separate from Japanese training would continue. Also, P'yŏngyang would vigorously oppose "the immoral policy" of forcing Korean residents in Japan to apply for "permanent residence" status and accept Republic of Korea nationality. "But," added Kim, "even if they accept ROK nationality, they will give active support to the DPRK just as the South Korean people unanimously support us today."

Because of these policies and others, the Sato government continued to come under Kim's savage attack. Only a few Asians like Sato were "stupid" enough to support the Nixon Doctrine, he proclaimed. And in a broader vein, he alleged, "Under US aegis, the Japanese militarists have turned into dangerous forces of aggression in Asia with the backing of

146. For the full text of the Yomiuri "interview," see "On Immediate Political and Economic Policies of the DPRK and Some International Problems—Answer to Questions Raised by Newsmen of Japanese Newspaper 'Yomiuri Shimbun'," in *The People's Korea,* January 26, 1972, pp. 1–6. The quotations and paraphrasing that follows are all taken from this official English-language source.

US imperialism. This is a hard fact." Japanese "militarists" were "invading other countries, subordinating them economically, and through intensified ideological and cultural infiltration."

Once again, however, Kim counted upon a united front of progressives to stop these machinations: "the Japanese people are now resolutely struggling against the militarist forces of aggression and for democracy, neutrality and peace. This struggle brings great pressure to bear upon the reactionary ruling circles of Japan, Kim announced, and even within these ruling circles, opinion was now divided upon the question of whether to launch a war of aggression.

The central objective was to establish an economic and cultural beach-head in Japan, penetrating Japanese domestic politics, building a united front against the "reactionaries," and at the same time, creating tensions between Japan and the South Korean government. It was a diplomatic offensive showing some definite parallels with the new Chinese foreign policy, and causing a mixture of interest, uncertainty and apprehension in Japanese official circles.

Notwithstanding the violent rhetoric that continued to mark Kim's assaults upon President Nixon and official US foreign policy, there were indications that the North Korean government intended to approach the American "problem" in a fashion similar to that now being employed on the Japan front. There would be no retreat from the all-out assault upon "American imperialism," Kim assured his listeners. Indeed, that campaign had almost been won: starting with her "ignominious defeat" in the Korean War, the US had been successively "pounded and mauled" in all parts of the world. She faced the gravest crises, at home and abroad, with the anti-war movement sweeping over America with great force; increasing antagonisms erupting within the ruling circles of America; the domestic economy confronted with chronic stagnation; the international monetary system within the capitalist world chaotic; and the United States increasingly isolated from its "satellites" and "imperialistic colleagues" alike.

The Nixon China trip continued to be interpreted as an acknowledgment of failure and bankruptcy. The pilgrimage to Peking was heralded as a Chinese triumph: "The might of the People's Republic of China is growing while the U.S. imperialists are floundering in acute crisis." The concessions rendered by Nixon had thrown American "puppets and satellites" into great confusion, whereas the Chinese side in the communique had "maintained its consistent revolutionary principle and expressed it with clarity."

Unlike Hanoi, P'yŏngyang did not permit itself the slightest open criticism of the new Maoist diplomacy. Earlier hints of apprehension, however, continued to find their way into official statements such as the Yomiuri interview. Thus Kim warned that the "various catastrophies" that had befallen it did not mean that "US imperialism" was completely ruined, or had changed its true colors. "Whenever the imperialists get into hot water, they usually perpetrate crafty acts of aggression and war under the signboard of peace." Consequently, all nations must heighten their vigilance against the new aggressive and war machinations of the US imperialists.

This was as clear a warning to Peking as was voiced. In commenting upon the joint communique that concluded the Nixon trip, Kim remarked that while the United States had used "honeyed words," it remained for Washington to prove their validity by concrete deeds, and thus far, "the US was continuing its war of aggression everywhere." [147]

While the DPRK would vigorously fight on against US policies, however, it was prepared and eager to unite with the revolutionary people of the world, including progressive Americans, for the new era.[148] Moreover,

147. For a more recent assault, note the following: "U.S. State Secretary Rogers, the notorious war-maniac, submitted on March 7 the so-called 'annual foreign policy report' to the Congress.

"The 'report' of Rogers the rascal, filled from beginning to end with all sorts of sophistry and deception and an aggressive ambition, is a swindler's deceptive document, for whitewashing the disgraceful bankruptcy of the 'Nixon Doctrine' and a heinous war document of a brigand which outlined a plan of adventurous aggression the U.S. imperialists are going to further intensify in Asia and other parts of the world in the future behind the smokescreen of 'peace'." As reported from P'yŏngyang KCNA International Service in English, March 10, 1972 in *FBIS, Daily Report, Asia and Pacific,* March 13, 1972, p. D1.

Earlier, Rogers had held out a cautious olive branch to P'yŏngyang, ignoring this type of savage attack. In a press conference of February 1972, he cited "indications" that North Korea wanted to improve its relations with the United States, and asserted that the Nixon administration held a "general willingness to improve relations with all countries," and added that that naturally included North Korea. He also noted the fact that certain spokesmen for the P'yŏngyang regime had suggested that an initial step would be to call their nation by its rightful name, the Democratic People's Republic of Korea. The new era between the US and China, it will be remembered, began in a similar fashion, when Nixon in an October 1970 toast to President Nicolae Ceausescu of Romania, for the first time, used the term "People's Republic of China."

148. See the interesting interview of Kim Pyong-sik by Selig S. Harrison of the *Washington Post,* conducted in Tokyo on March 6, 1972. Kim Pyŏng-sik, first vice-chairman of the General Federation of Korean Residents in Japan, is probably the leading spokesman for North Korea in Japan, and a member of the DPRK Supreme People's Assembly. He told Harrison, "The time has come for further relations with the peace-loving people of the United States and for seeking the normalization of our relations," and asserted that a withdrawal of American forces from Korea need not precede "expanded relations and an end to our confrontation with the United States."

Kim, however, continued the hard line against the Nixon administration, asserting that while the President's visit to Peking was related to the Presidential election and the desire of the American people for peace, he did not think that the Shanghai communiqué would be enough "to deceive public opinion in the United States." Nixon he asserted, would be forced to end the war in Vietnam before the election and "compelled" to clarify his attitude toward the Korean question.

Once they understand it, argued Kim, a "broad section of the American people,

Kim indicated that P'yŏngyang might be receptive to entering the United Nations, and engaging in economic and cultural relations with all peoples. There would be no abandonment of principle, however: the US should get out of Korea totally, including the removal of its war equipment; the United Nations should repeal its hostile resolution falsely condemning the Communists as aggressors in the Korean War. (It should be emphasized, however, that neither of these proposals was made a firm condition for a new turn outward).

Meanwhile, two important missions were sent to the Communist world, presumably to test the impact of China's new foreign policy upon other Communist states, to ascertain attitudes concerning the further erosion of Sino-Soviet relations, and to explore the advantages and disadvantages of an altered foreign policy for North Korea. On March 2, 1972, a delegation headed by Foreign Minister Hŏ Tam returned to P'yŏngyang after having visited Romania, Czechoslovakia, East Germany, the USSR and Yugoslavia. The Moscow talks were described as taking place in an atmosphere of "mutual understanding and cordial friendship." [149] There were strong indications, however, that Moscow and P'yŏngyang continued to operate on different wavelengths, and that the Soviet campaign to woo the North Koreans away from Peking's policies was less than totally successful. The promise that efforts would be made "unceasingly" to "further expand and strengthen the fraternal friendship and all-around cooperation between the DPRK and the Soviet Union" was itself a hint that a considerable distance remained to be bridged. Moreover, the Hŏ Tam delegation symbolically went directly from Moscow to Belgrade. On the same day as the return of this delegation to North Korea, a second delegation headed by Pak Sŏng-ch'ŏl, fourth ranking Politburo member, also returned home, having visited Cuba, Poland and Hungary. A thorough canvass of the Communist world had been undertaken.

---

including the conservative elements, will support our stand on reunification," including the idea of a peace agreement between North and South. He further "expressed the hope" that US political leaders, businessmen, scholars and journalists would "gradually be able to visit our country as the atmosphere improves." This would expose the "ridiculous" effort of Pak Chŏng-hi to depict P'yŏngyang as bent on military aggression. See "North Korea Hints Shift on U.S. Ties," by Selig S. Harrison, *The Washington Post,* March 7, 1972, p. 1. (Such visits were inaugurated with the trip of Harrison Salisbury and John Lee to North Korea in the early summer of 1972.)

The Communists also broadcast a revealing statement over their "underground" South Korean radio station, the Voice of the Revolutionary Party for Unification, which purports to operate in South Korea but undoubtedly transmits from the North: "Our people will not fail to drive the U.S. aggressors out of our land through our own struggle, overthrow the traitorous Pak Chŏng-hi clique, and fulfill the cause of national unification jointly with the brothers in the north." As reported in *ibid.,* March 3, 1972, p. E3.

149. A report on the Moscow visit, including the joint communique issued at its conclusion was carried by P'yŏngyang KCNA International Service, Feb. 26, 1972 in *FBIS, Daily Report, Asia and Pacific,* Feb. 28, 1972, p. D3.

Whatever the difficulties, North Korea under Kim Il-sŏng seemed determined to pursue *chuch'e* in foreign policy, as in domestic affairs. Indeed, it hoped to elevate the nationalist issue into the central theme in its campaign for South Korean "liberation." The North Koreans, however, could not escape from their heavy dependence upon the big Communist states, and particularly the USSR, for modern military weapons. Yet in this era, it was Chinese foreign policy that continued to exert major influence upon P'yŏngyang, as events after mid-1971 underlined.

Meanwhile, a dramatic new era was inaugurated in North-South relations, albeit with limited changes in basic positions. On August 12, 1971, the South Korean Red Cross, obviously acting on the initiative of the Pak government, suggested that a meeting with the North Korean Red Cross take place to discuss the problem of Korea's divided families: how to locate missing relatives, inform them of each other's condition, and arrange for reunions. A preliminary meeting to be held in Geneva before the end of October was suggested. To millions of Koreans, this is an issue of direct, personal concern. Two days later, via P'yŏngyang Radio, the North Korean Red Cross, officially responding, proposed that preliminary talks take place in September at P'anmunjŏm, and indicated that on August 20, its representatives would deliver an official letter at that site to South Korean Red Cross representatives. On that date, a four-minute meeting ensued, the first bilateral contacts carried out solely by North and South Koreans in the troubled history of a divided Korea.[150] On June 16, 1972, after ten months of negotiations, both sides agreed on the agenda for future discussions, a first step. It was clear that substantive agreements would come slowly and painfully.[151] Nevertheless, a historic turn in the road had been taken, and a retreat back to total noncommunication seemed unlikely.

Whence came the initiative, and what were the implications of this

150. Earlier, face-to-face meetings between representatives of North and South Korea had occurred twice, on both occasions under the aegis of the International Olympic Committee. The first of these meetings took place in Lausanne, Switzerland, in January 1963, with an IOC representative presiding. The IOC had approved North Korea's membership in the Olympic association, and had recommended the organization of a combined North-South team for the 1964 Tokyo Olympic Games. While agreement was reached in Lausanne that the folk-song *Arirang* would be used instead of a national anthem, other issues, such as the question of a national flag, remained unresolved, and it was agreed to solicit IOC advice.

North Korea then proposed a second meeting, which took place in Hong Kong in May 1963. It proved impossible to reach any agreements on a wide range of issues, however, and negotiations were broken off.

151. The first agreement was that the formal conference, once under way, should convene alternately in Seoul and P'yŏngyang. However, when the preliminary discussions were turned toward such basic issues as the scope of the visitation program and the rules that should govern it, agreement proved to be extremely difficult. The tactic of the North was to argue for the widest latitude, whereas the South initially adopted a cautious approach, insisting upon clear-cut regulations and a more restricted program.

new era? The first overture was clearly made by the Republic of Korea, possibly under the assumption that it would be rejected. Increasingly, the issue of unification has projected itself into South Korean politics, and gradually the Pak administration has sought to accommodate itself to that issue, permitting scholarly conferences and public discussion of the question to take place. Unquestionably, the startling developments in US-CPR relations, together with the signs of a lowered American profile in Asia, accelerated the trend. A proposal based upon humanitarian grounds was a logical first step.

The DPRK could assert that it had long advocated North-South discussions at P'anmunjŏm, and on several occasions had sought to engineer meetings with students and other groups in this manner. At the same time, however, up to the very eve of the ROK overture, P'yŏngyang had maintained its hard line against the south, calling for the overthrow of the Pak regime.[152] Did Peking play any role in Kim Il-sŏng's decision to enter into negotiations with the South Korean government? As we have already suggested, it is entirely possible that Peking's explanation to the North Koreans of the reasons for its own change of policies had an influence. Presumably, individuals like Chou En-lai argued that this was an appropriate period for the Asian Communist states to conduct a diplomatic and political offensive, seeking international recognition and moving to thwart such "imperialist schemes" as perpetuating divided states at a time when the United States was in retreat and Japan had not yet determined upon a coherent foreign policy. Under such conditions, a coordination of Chinese and North Korean foreign policies—underwritten by pledges of full Chinese support—would have considerable appeal, both in Peking and in P'yŏngyang.

Despite the surprising developments of recent months, current North Korean policy does not represent an abandonment of past pledges to "liberate" the South. In intent, at least, the shift is a tactical one, with greater emphasis to be placed in the immediate future upon a political-diplomatic offensive designed to put the Pak government on the defensive with its own people by making a strenuous bid for the "peace, unification and national independence" vote in the South. Thus, the Communists advance a liberal

152. For example, see the article by Kim Yang-je, "Strategy and Tactics for the South Korean Revolution," *Nodong Chŏngnyŏn*, July 18, 1971, pp. 3–4, translated in *JPRS* Translations on North Korea, No. 222, Sept. 20, 1971, pp. 1–12. The author, quoting extensively from Kim Il-sŏng, asserts that "the Party must uphold violent revolution, place primacy on violent struggle, and correctly combine this with all forms of struggle such as the political struggle, the economic struggle, the legal struggle, the anti-legal struggle, and the illegal struggle so as to have all forms of struggle serve the violent struggle for the seizing of political power, and to move on to the decisive struggle to smash reactionary rule . . ." (p. 8).

He goes on to assert that the strategic and tactical policies of Kim call for the close coordination of the revolutions in North and South, with a merger of the two revolutionary forces "at the decisive moment" (p. 11).

exchange program, advocate substantial military reductions, emphasize peaceful unification, and focus attention upon getting rid of the American presence in South Korea.

All available evidence suggests that Kim Il-sŏng hopes to utilize the new era to penetrate the south more deeply politically, setting aside military efforts at this point. If this accords with the present international environment, it also accords, as we have seen, with the current needs of the North —where intensive militarization and extreme tension had reached a point of greatly diminished returns. Secure in the control of their own society, with a complete monopoly of organization and media in the North, the Communists hope to cultivate "people to people" relations so as to exploit the looser, more open political system of the South. Already, they have caused a considerable tightening of the latter system in response. To put maximum pressure upon Pak, Kim Il-sŏng has now shown a willingness to negotiate with all political groups, including Pak Chŏng-hi and the ruling Democratic Republican Party.

Let us turn to the specific events relating to these matters. On April 13, 1971, Foreign Minister Hŏ Tam presented an Eight-Point Program in proposing that unification discussions be held either in P'anmunjŏm or a third country. Essentially this program was a reiteration of the points advanced by Kim Il-sŏng in his Fifth Party Congress report. Later, Kim was to insist that point eight was an innovation, since the Communists agreed to the participation of *all* South Korean political parties, not restricting negotiations only to those dedicated to "peace and democracy." This proposal was repeated in Kim's speech of August 6, 1971, in his New Year's message of 1972, and in the Yomiuri interview.

In the latter interview, Kim sought to place the military shoe on the South Korean foot. Times have changed, he asserted. In the South, the drive for peaceful unification was rapidly growing, together with the struggle against "fascist rule" and for the democratization of the society. It was becoming an irresistible force.

The days are gone, insisted Kim, when the "US imperialists" can perpetuate the division of our nation into North and South, abusing the name of the United Nations in the process. At present, "the US imperialists and the Japanese militarists" can barely attend to their own affairs. "We think the time has come when the South Korean rulers should give up the antinational stand they have held, seeking a way out by clinging to the sleeves of the US imperialist aggressors and ushering in the Japanese aggressors, turning their back on their compatriots." [153]

153. The Eight-Point Ho Tam proposal was: (1) All US forces should withdraw from South Korea. (2) The armed forces of both the North and the South should be reduced to 100,000 men each, or less. (3) All treaties and agreements between the two Korean governments and foreign countries should be abolished. (4) A unified central government should be established to conduct North-South general elec-

Kim then vigorously denied that the North had ever harbored the thought of invading the South, and asserted that the South should abandon "the absurd notion" of building up its military strength with the backing of outside powers so as to overcome North Korea by force, and attempting to attain reunification by seeking to prevail over Communism. Rather, it should accept the North's generous offer: to remove current tensions, the Korean Armistice Agreement should be replaced by a peace agreement between North and South. Such an agreement should involve "a drastic cut" in the armed forces, under conditions where US troops were withdrawn totally from the South. Then Kim repeated his stand on negotiations: "We always keep our door open to anyone for negotiations and contacts between the North and South. If anyone, though he committed crimes against the country and the people, sincerely repents of his past doings and takes the road of patriotism for the peaceful reunification of the country, we will not ask about his crimes but gladly negotiate with him about the question of the country's reunification." [154]

Meanwhile, infiltration did not cease although it was considerably reduced from the high-tide of 1968. A tragic event underlining that fact occurred on the very day of the first P'anmunjŏm meeting. On August 20, 1971, just one hour after the Red Cross representatives met, a clash occurred between North Korean infiltrators and South Korean security forces on Kanghwa Island in the Han River estuary according to Seoul authorities, resulting in the deaths of two North Koreans and three South Koreans. Four days earlier, five North Korean infiltrators and one South Korean had been killed in the eastern sector of the demilitarized zone. The North also alleged that it continued to capture South Korean spies sent above the 38th parallel. Irrespective of the future, the relation between the two Koreas in 1971–1972 was vastly different from that between the two Germanys.

Moreover, the northern-sponsored Revolutionary Party of Unification continued its efforts to operate as Kim Il-sŏng's underhand. Averring its complete allegiance to "the glorious leader of the forty million Korean people," the RPU sought to establish a base in South Korea, and called for the overthrow of the Pak regime through the armed uprising of "the whole South Korean people"—even as Kim assailed "US imperialists and their South Korean puppets" for attempting to pit Korean against Korean in military strife.

---

tions. (5) Guarantees of total political freedom should be granted to all political parties, public organizations, and individuals. (6) A confederation of North and South Korea should be established as a transitional step toward unification. (7) Trade and economic cooperation and intercourse should be promoted, together with interchanges in various other fields. (8) A political conference between North and South Korea, attended by all political parties and public organizations, to negotiate the above-mentioned problems, should take place.

154. Kim Il Sung, "On Immediate Political and Economic Policies," *op. cit.,* p. 3.

Kim himself, while asserting that the North would never "invade" the South, did not deny earlier emphatic statements that a revolution would be necessary in the course of southern liberation, and that the North intended to serve as the "firm base" for that revolution. Indeed, the activities of the RPU reaffirmed those positions. Through an evolutionary process, such commitments might change, but the South's wariness of dealing with the Communists as if they were just another wing of the parliamentary movement was understandable.

There can be little question, however, that the government of Pak Chŏng-hi found itself on the defensive as the North Korean political-diplomatic thrust got underway, due both to domestic and international developments. In response to the initial Northern moves of April 13 and August 6, 1971, President Pak in a speech of August 15, 1971, on the occasion of the twenty-sixth anniversary of Liberation, restated his position of a year earlier:

"If the North Korean Communists should even now awaken from their illusions, discarding their avowed militant policy and dogmatic attitude, and if they are willing to join in the new international current, it would not only serve as a significant turning point in the building of world peace, but indeed, provide a great hope for the peaceful unification of the country.

"I would also like to offer the assurance that a forum for peaceful unification can be arranged at any time, if and when the North Korean Communists genuinely renounce their policy of force and violence and assume a sincere attitude concerning peaceful unification." [155]

Pressure had steadily mounted upon the South to take a fresh approach to the reunification issue, as we have noted. The question figured prominently in the 1971 Presidential elections there. The new American-Chinese relationship, and the changing character of Asian international relations which it appeared to augur added significantly to the pressures. These and other considerations formed the background to Pak's August 1971 initiative in offering the North discussions via Red Cross representatives on the question of contacts between divided families.

The Southern position on reunification was spelled out in broader terms by Foreign Minister Kim Yong-sik in connection with the Red Cross meetings. He proposed a three-stage program for Korean unification. The first stage would be the solution of "purely humanitarian problems," such as the issue of divided families. The second would be the establishment of "nonpolitical exchanges" in the fields of trade, travel, and culture. The final stage would consist of tackling the political problems of unification. Kim stressed, however, that North Korea would have to renounce the use of violence against the South before the second stage could be entered, and he also asserted that the political problems of unification should be approached in accordance with the long-established United Nations for-

155. See the *New York Times,* Aug. 15, 1971, pp. 1, 4.

mula, namely, free elections throughout the peninsula under UN supervision. He added that he doubted whether the Korean question could be resolved merely by a dialogue between South and North Korea outside the framework of the United Nations.

In a dramatic joint communiqué issued on July 4, 1972, with the DPRK, the government of the Republic of Korea appeared to modify if not reverse its position on some of these points. That communiqué was issued against a cloak-and-dagger series of events. Secret negotiations were apparently launched through the initiation of UN Secretary-General Kurt Waldheim, who had contacts in Vienna with North Korean representatives in March. Waldheim reportedly conveyed North Korean "suggestions" to the South Koreans. Thus, ironically, despite the Communists' insistence on the solution of the Korean problem without outside interference, the UN played a critical role in inaugurating the most recent development.

With great secrecy (and reportedly without notification to any outside power), Yi Hu-rak, trusted confidant of the President and head of the South Korean CIA, went to P'yŏngyang and, between May 2 and 5, conducted discussions with Kim Yong-ju, currently director of the KWP Organization and Guidance Department and, as we have emphasized, the second most important man in the North, being Kim Il-sŏng's younger brother. Pak Sŏng-ch'ŏl, in turn, was sent to Seoul for further discussions between May 29 and June 1. Both emissaries met the two top leaders as well. Clearly, Pak Chŏng-hi and Kim Il-sŏng appear determined to keep developments under their personal control at this stage.

The first agreed on principle was that "unification shall be achieved through independent Korean efforts without being subject to external imposition of interference." This certainly represents a concession to P'yŏngyang, since the wording is an almost exact reproduction of earlier North Korean proposals. Already, however, its meaning to the two parties has been cast in some doubt. Yi Hu-rak, for example, stated at a news conference that South Korea would "welcome" a UN role in unifying Korea through the supervision of all-Korea elections, since the UN could not be considered a "bad foreign force." And as noted, the UN had already played a role, albeit unofficially, with strong indications that Kim Il-sŏng is now aiming for UN membership.

The North Korean emphasis was on using this clause to get the United States out of South Korea. Pak Sŏng-ch'ŏl declared in a P'yŏngyang news conference that a primary objective in working toward unification was "to remove outside influences," adding that "the U.S. imperialists must no longer meddle in the domestic affairs of our country," and that "they must withdraw [their troops from South Korea] at once." The South Koreans, on the other hand, stressed the need for the continued presence of US forces, as a part of the need to negotiate with the Communists from strength.

The second principle underlined in the communiqué was a concession to an oft-repeated ROK demand. It stated that "unification shall be achieved through peaceful means and not through the use of force against each other." And it was coupled by an agreement to install a direct telephone line between Seoul and P'yŏngyang (implemented within hours) "to prevent the outbreak of unexpected military incidents." In addition, the two parties agreed "not to slander or defame each other . . . in order to ease tensions and foster an atmosphere of mutual trust." Would this also apply to the North Korean-sponsored Revolutionary Party for Unification? If so, it would constitute a major victory for the South? If not, the gain would be much more limited.

The third major decision was to establish a South-North coordinating committee, headed by Yi and Kim, to implement the agreements as well as to "solve various existing problems and to settle the unification problems." Both parties pledged to seek national unity, "transcending differences in policies, ideologies, and systems." [156]

The road to Korean unity is likely to be lengthy and tortuous despite this pledge, as even the post-July 4 pronouncements of the parties have indicated. Both sides continue to suspect each other—and with good reason. Suspicion of North Korean motives and intentions is deeply ingrained in the South, and it will take a succession of deeds, not just words, to alter the doubts and fears. It is extremely doubtful, moreover, whether Kim Il-sŏng and his followers truly expect to achieve Korean unification under their aegis (a continuing goal) by relying wholly on the legal, political route. However, as we have seen, the North does have confidence that a rapid expansion of "people-to-people" contacts between North and South will advance its cause, given its much firmer control over all political and social institutions above the 38th parallel and its significant economic growth over the past fifteen years.

The testing of this proposition may be at hand. Despite the evidence that enormous obstacles remain to any normal South-North intercourse—social, economic, or political—a major corner has been turned. It has been turned, moreover, in a period when the political configuration of East Asia appears to be undergoing momentous changes. Thus, for the present at least, P'yŏngyang and Seoul will commence a dialogue that may broaden in time, each action bringing new challenges and new risks to both parties.

Looking Toward the Future

In 1970, at the Fifth Party Congress, Kim Il-sŏng recommitted himself (and his 14 million people) to the twin tasks of "building socialism"

---

156. For an English text of the joint communiqué, see the *New York Times,* July 5, 1972, p. 16. For other accounts, see *ibid.,* July 4, 1972, pp. 1–2; July 5, pp. 1, 16; and UPI and AP reports from Seoul as carried in the *Washington Post,* July 5, 1972, pp. 1 and 16; and the *Philadelphia Inquirer,* July 4 and 5, 1972, p. 1.

and "conducting revolution." Those tasks seem likely to require sacrifices in the decade ahead almost as harsh as those in the decade past. Events since the Fourth Party Congress of 1961 signal four basic trends, all of which appear destined to continue for the near future. First, in approximately fifteen years, Kim and his key followers have been able to construct a tightly organized society, and a Party that appears to come as close to being monolithic as a human institution can. The organizational principles have been essentially Stalinist, and the cult of personality has gradually become the supreme weapon. Hence, the post-Kim era looms ahead as one of great uncertainty. For the present, however, all institutions, including the military, have been firmly subordinated to a "monolithic" Party, a "unitary" ideology, and a "peerless" Leader.

Meanwhile, economic development has also proceeded generally in accordance with the earlier Soviet model, adapted in certain respects in an effort to fit it to the contours of North Korean society, and exhibiting, on occasion, signs of contemporary Chinese influence. Industrial development has been very substantial, as we have noted, and the claim that North Korean society has successfully accomplished a one-generation industrial revolution has considerable validity. The decade of the 1960s, however, has revealed many of the same types of economic problems that accompanied the Soviet revolution—problems that we shall analyze in some detail. The issues of managerial efficiency, labor productivity, efficient use of resources, and the quality of product have by no means been solved. Moreover, looming over the entire economic landscape remains the question of agricultural productivity. Though gains in this sector appear to have been significant, they have fallen short of the hopes and expectations of the regime, and they currently constitute one of the principal obstacles to more rapid growth. An overall growth rate of 8 to 9 percent, with nonindustrial production growing at the rate of 3 to 4 percent, is certainly impressive, particularly if it can be regularized and sustained. Given the present policies of the North Korean regime, however, and particularly the commitment to a high level of militarization, it is not sufficient to raise general living standards dramatically. From all indications, the North Korean people will continue to be poor, and forced to work exceedingly hard for some distant future "after unification," unless basic alterations in policy occur. Very recently, some reduction of military expenditures appears to have been undertaken. Its extent and duration remain unclear and undoubtedly hinge in part on developments in North-South relations. The new emphasis on a political offensive toward the South—and in the world —cannot be separated from P'yŏngyang's internal requirements if economic goals are to be achieved.

Meanwhile, North Korea is an excellent context in which to view the triumph of nationalism over certain traditional Communist values. It is, of course, possible to speak of a merger of these two political forces, but that is to obscure the fact that, under Kim Il-sŏng, chuch'e has become a symbol for "true Marxism-Leninism," when in fact it is a policy strongly contrary to proletarian internationalism as either Marx or Lenin would have understood it. Moreover, North Korea's commitment to "self-sufficiency" in the economy, to total independence in matters of foreign and domestic policy, and to a massive "self-defense" program have all been born out of her historic experience with "proletarian internationalism, Soviet-style." This program is being pursued—at great cost to the Korean people—in lieu of any feasible alternative.

In this, there is much to ponder. Ironically, the Communist world since World War II has shown itself far less adept at flexible international cooperation within its own camp than has the non-Communist world. Internationalism under the Soviet aegis has invariably been conducted with a heavy reliance upon precisely the same techniques that the Soviet government uses on the domestic scene. In short, Soviet political culture, at home and abroad, does not differ greatly. The principles of "democratic centralism," the concept of orthodoxy versus heresy, the insistence upon unquestioning obedience—in sum, the true neocolonialism—has been found in the so-called socialist community. Nor has Peking always proved to be immune from the same practices in its dealings with small Communist states and Parties. Hence, the enormously costly chuch'e policies that Kim Il-sŏng now proclaims as a supreme virtue in fact constitute a virtual necessity if any true Korean autonomy is to be maintained, given the principles of international relations that currently prevail *within* the Communist world.